C#
HOW TO PROGRAM

H. M. Deitel
Deitel & Associates, Inc.

P. J. Deitel
Deitel & Associates, Inc.

J. Listfield

T. R. Nieto
Deitel & Associates, Inc.

C. Yaeger
Deitel & Associates, Inc.

M. Zlatkina

Prentice Hall

PRENTICE HALL, Upper Saddle River, New Jersey 07458

Library of Congress Cataloging-in-Publication Data

On file

Vice President and Editorial Director: *Marcia Horton*
Acquisitions Editor: *Petra J. Recter*
Associate Editor: *Jennifer Cappello*
Assistant Editor: *Sarah Burrows*
Project Manager: *Crissy Statuto*
Vice President and Director of Production and Manufacturing, ESM: *David W. Riccardi*
Executive Managing Editor: *Vince O'Brien*
Assistant Managing Editor: *Camille Trentacoste*
Formatters: *Victoria Johnson, Chirag Thakkar*
Software Production Editor: *Bob Engelhardt*
Software Formatter: *Edward Cadillo*
Director of Creative Services: *Paul Belfanti*
Senior Manager, Artworks: *Patricia Burns*
Managing Editor, Audio-Visual Assets: *Grace Hazeldine*
Audio-Visual Editor: *Xiaohong Zhu*
Creative Director: *Carole Anson*
Design Technical Support: *John Christiana*
Chapter Opener and Cover Designer: *Tamara L. Newnam*
Cover Illustration: *Tamara L. Newnam, Steve Lefkowitz*
Manufacturing Manager: *Trudy Pisciotti*
Manufacturing Buyer: *Lisa McDowell*
Marketing Manager: *Jennie Burger*
Marketing Assistant: *Barrie Rheinhold*

© 2002, by Prentice-Hall, Inc.
Upper Saddle River, New Jersey 07458

Printed in the United States of America

10 9 8 7 6

ISBN 0-13-062221-4

Prentice-Hall International (UK) Limited, *London*
Prentice-Hall of Australia Pty. Limited, *Sydney*
Prentice-Hall Canada Inc., *Toronto*
Prentice-Hall Hispanoamericana, S.A., *Mexico*
Prentice-Hall of India Private Limited, *New Delhi*
Prentice-Hall of Japan, Inc., *Tokyo*
Pearson Education Asia Pte. Ltd., *Singapore*
Editora Prentice-Hall do Brasil, Ltda., *Rio de Janeiro*

C#

HOW TO PROGRAM

Deitel™ Books, Cyber Classrooms, Complete Training Courses and Web-Based Training Courses published by Prentice Hall

How to Program Series

Advanced Java™ 2 Platform How to Program
C How to Program, 3/E
C++ How to Program, 3/E
C# How to Program
e-Business and e-Commerce How to Program
Internet and World Wide Web How to Program, 2/E
Java™ How to Program, 4/E
Perl How to Program
Python How to Program
Visual Basic® 6 How to Program
Visual Basic® .NET How to Program, 2/E
Visual C++® .NET How to Program (2002)
Wireless Internet & Mobile Business How to Program
XML How to Program

Multimedia Cyber Classroom and Web-Based Training Series

(for information regarding Deitel™ Web-based training visit **www.ptgtraining.com**)
Advanced Java™ 2 Platform Multimedia Cyber Classroom
C++ Multimedia Cyber Classroom, 3/E
C# Multimedia Cyber Classroom
e-Business and e-Commerce Multimedia Cyber Classroom
Internet and World Wide Web Multimedia Cyber Classroom, 2/E
Java™ 2 Multimedia Cyber Classroom, 4/E
Perl Multimedia Cyber Classroom
Python Multimedia Cyber Classroom
Visual Basic® 6 Multimedia Cyber Classroom
Visual Basic® .NET Multimedia Cyber Classroom, 2/E
Visual C++® .NET M/M Cyber Classroom (2002)
Wireless Internet & Mobile Business Programming Multimedia Cyber Classroom
XML Multimedia Cyber Classroom

The Complete Training Course Series

The Complete Advanced Java™ 2 Platform Training Course
The Complete C++ Training Course, 3/E
The Complete C# Training Course
The Complete e-Business and e-Commerce Programming Training Course
The Complete Internet and World Wide Web Programming Training Course, 2/E
The Complete Java™ 2 Training Course, 4/E
The Complete Perl Training Course
The Complete Python Training Course
The Complete Visual Basic® 6 Training Course
The Complete Visual Basic® .NET Training Course, 2/E
The Complete Visual C++® .NET Training Course (2002)
The Complete Wireless Internet & Mobile Business Programming Training Course
The Complete XML Training Course

.NET Series

C# How to Program
Visual Basic® .NET How to Program, 2/E
Visual C++® .NET How to Program (2002)

Visual Studio® Series

Getting Started with Microsoft® Visual C++™ 6 with an Introduction to MFC
Visual Basic® 6 How to Program
C# How to Program
Visual Basic® .NET How to Program, 2/E
Visual C++® .NET How to Program (2002)

For Managers Series

e-Business and e-Commerce for Managers

Coming Soon

e-books and e-whitepapers
Course Compass, WebCT and Blackboard Multimedia Cyber Classrooms versions

To communicate with the authors, send e-mail to:

> **deitel@deitel.com**

For information on corporate on-site seminars and public seminars offered by Deitel & Associates, Inc. worldwide and to register for the *Deitel Buzz* e-mail newsletter, visit:

> **www.deitel.com**

For continuing updates on Prentice Hall and Deitel & Associates, Inc. publications visit the Prentice Hall Deitel Web site or the InformIT Deitel kiosk:

> **www.prenhall.com/deitel** or **www.InformIT.com/deitel**

In loving memory of our Uncle and Granduncle David Gewanter:

We are deeply grateful that he shared with us his love, encouragement, knowledge, insight and wisdom.

Harvey and Paul Deitel

To my parents:

You have guided me through the years and made me who I am.

Jeff

In loving memory of Grandpa Corbit.

Tem R. Nieto

To my parents and brother:

For always supporting me through good times and bad. Thank you for everything—I will never forget the tears, hugs and laughter.

Cheryl

To my mom and grandma:

Who have supported me with their endless love, courage and strength. Thank you for always being there for me.

Marina

Trademarks

Adobe® Photoshop® Elements are either registered trademarks or trademarks of Adobe Systems Incorporated in the United States and/or other countries.

Compaq, the Compaq Logo, iPAQ, and the iPAQ Pocket PC product design are trademarks of Compaq Information Technologies Group, L.P. in the United States and other countries.

Java and all Java-based marks are trademarks or registered trademarks of Sun Microsystems, Inc. in the United States and other countries. Prentice Hall is independent of Sun Microsystems, Inc.

Contents

Illustrations

7   Arrays

8   Object-Based Programming

9   Object-Oriented Programming: Inheritance

10   Object-Oriented Programming: Polymorphism

11   Exception Handling

12   Graphical User Interface Concepts: Part 1

13   Graphical User Interface Concepts: Part 2

16 Graphics and Multimedia

17 Files and Streams

18 Extensible Markup Language (XML)

19   Database, SQL and ADO .NET

20 ASP .NET, Web Forms and Web Controls

21 ASP .NET and Web Services

24 Accessibility

Preface

Live in fragments no longer. Only connect.
Edward Morgan Forster

We wove a web in childhood,
A web of sunny air.
Charlotte Brontë

Welcome to C# and the world of Windows, Internet and World-Wide-Web programming with Visual Studio and the .NET platform! This book is the second in our new *.NET How to Program* series, which presents various leading-edge computing technologies in the context of the .NET platform.

C# is the next phase in the evolution of C and C++ and was developed expressly for Microsoft's .NET platform. C# provides the features that are most important to programmers, such as object-oriented programming, strings, graphics, graphical-user-interface (GUI) components, exception handling, multithreading, multimedia (audio, images, animation and video), file processing, prepackaged data structures, database processing, Internet and World-Wide-Web-based client/server networking and distributed computing. The language is appropriate for implementing Internet- and World-Wide-Web-based applications that seamlessly integrate with PC-based applications.

The .NET platform offers powerful capabilities for software development and deployment, including independence from a specific language or platform. Rather than requiring developers to learn a new programming language, programmers can contribute to the same software project, but write code using any (or several) of the .NET languages (such as C#, Visual Basic .NET, Visual C++ .NET and others) with which they are most competent. In addition to providing language independence, .NET extends program portability by enabling .NET applications to reside on, and communicate across, multiple platforms—thus facilitating the delivery of Web services over the Internet. The .NET platform enables Web-based applications to be distributed to consumer-electronic devices, such as cell phones and personal digital assistants, as well as to desktop computers. The capabilities that Microsoft has incorporated into the .NET platform create a new software-development paradigm that will increase programmer productivity and decrease development time.

New Features in *C# How to Program*

This edition contains many new features and enhancements, including:

- *Two-Color Presentation.* This book is in two color. Two color enables readers to see sample outputs similar to how they would appear on a color monitor. Also, we syntax color the C# code similar to the way Visual Studio .NET colors the code in its editor window. Our syntax-coloring conventions are as follows:

```
comments
keywords
literal values
errors and ASP .NET directives
text, class, method and variable names
```

- *"Code Washing."* This is our term for the process we use to format the programs in the book so that they have a carefully commented, open layout. The code appears in full color and is grouped into small, well-documented pieces. This greatly improves code readability—an especially important goal for us, considering that this book contains approximately 23,500 lines of code.

- *Web Services and ASP .NET.* Microsoft's .NET strategy embraces the Internet and Web as integral to the software development and deployment processes. Web services—a key technology in this strategy—enables information sharing, commerce and other interactions using standard Internet protocols and technologies, such as Hypertext Transfer Protocol (HTTP), Simple Object Access Protocol (SOAP) and Extensible Markup Language (XML). Web services enable programmers to package application functionality in a form that turns the Web into a library of reusable software components. In Chapter 21, ASP .NET and Web Services, we present a Web service that allows users to make airline seat reservations. In this example, a user accesses a Web page, chooses a seating option and submits the page to the Web server. The page then calls a Web service that checks seat availability. We also present information related to Web services in Appendix P, Crystal Reports® for Visual Studio® .NET, which discusses popular reporting software for database-intensive applications. Crystal Reports, which is integrated into Visual Studio .NET, provides the ability to expose a report as a Web service. The appendix provides introductory information and directs readers to a walkthrough of this process on the Crystal Decisions Web site (**www.crystalde-cisions.com/net**).

- *Web Forms, Web Controls and ASP .NET.* Application developers must be able to create robust, scalable Web-based applications. The .NET platform architecture supports such applications. Microsoft's .NET server-side technology, Active Server Pages (ASP) .NET, allows programmers to build Web documents that respond to client requests. To enable interactive Web pages, server-side programs process information users input into HTML forms. ASP .NET is a significant departure from previous versions of ASP, allowing developers to program Web-based applications using the powerful object-oriented languages of .NET. ASP .NET also provides enhanced visual programming capabilities, similar to those used in building Windows forms for desktop programs. Programmers can create Web pages visually, by dragging and dropping Web controls onto Web forms. Chapter 20, ASP .NET, Web Forms and Web Controls, introduces these powerful technologies.

- *Object-Oriented Programming.* Object-oriented programming is the most widely employed technique for developing robust, reusable software, and C# offers enhanced object-oriented programming features. This text offers a rich presentation of object-oriented programming. Chapter 8, Object-Based Programming, introduces how to create classes and objects. These concepts are extended in Chapter 9, Object-Oriented Programming: Inheritance, which discusses how programmers can create new classes that "absorb" the capabilities of existing classes. Chapter 10, Object-Oriented Programming: Polymorphism, familiarizes the reader with the crucial concepts of polymorphism, abstract classes, concrete classes and interfaces, which facilitate powerful manipulations among objects belonging to an inheritance hierarchy.

- *XML.* Use of Extensible Markup Language (XML) is exploding in the software-development industry, the e-business and e-commerce communities, and is pervasive throughout the .NET platform. Because XML is a platform-independent technology for describing data and for creating markup languages, XML's data portability integrates well with C#'s portable applications and services. Chapter 18, Extensible Markup Language (XML), introduces XML. In this chapter, we introduce basic XML markup and discuss the technologies such as DTDs and Schema, which are used to validate XML documents' contents. We also explain how to programmatically manipulate XML documents using the Document Object Model (DOM™) and how to transform XML documents into other types of documents via Extensible Stylesheet Language Transformations (XSLT).

- *Multithreading.* Computers enable us to perform many tasks in parallel (or concurrently), such as printing documents, downloading files from a network and surfing the Web. Multithreading is the technology through which programmers can develop applications that perform concurrent tasks. Historically, a computer has contained a single, expensive processor, which its operating system would share among all applications. Today, processors are becoming so inexpensive that it is possible to build affordable computers that contain many processors that work in parallel—such computers are called multiprocessors. Multithreading is effective on both single-processor and multiprocessor systems. C#'s multithreading capabilities make the platform and its related technologies better prepared to deal with today's sophisticated multimedia-intensive, database-intensive, network-based, multiprocessor-based distributed applications. Chapter 14, Multithreading, provides a detailed discussion of multithreading.

- *ADO .NET.* Databases store vast amounts of information that individuals and organizations must access to conduct business. As an evolution of Microsoft's ActiveX Data Objects (ADO), ADO .NET represents a new approach for building applications that interact with databases. ADO .NET uses XML and an enhanced object model to provide developers with the tools they need to access and manipulate databases for large-scale, extensible, mission-critical multi-tier applications. Chapter 19, Database, SQL and ADO .NET, details the capabilities of ADO .NET and the Structured Query Language (SQL) to manipulate databases.

- *Visual Studio .NET Debugger.* Debuggers are programs that help programmers find and correct logic errors in program code. Visual Studio .NET contains a powerful debugging tool that allows programmers to analyze their programs line-by-line as those programs execute. In Appendix D, Visual Studio .NET Debugger, we explain how to use key debugger features, such as setting breakpoints and "watches," stepping into and out of procedures, and examining the procedure call stack.

- *COM (Component Object Model) Integration.* Prior to the introduction of .NET, many organizations spent tremendous amounts of time and money creating reusable software components called COM components, which include ActiveX® controls and ActiveX DLLs (dynamic link libraries) for Windows applications. In Appendix H, COM Integration, we discuss some of the tools available in Visual Studio .NET for integrating these legacy components into .NET applications. This integration allows programmers to use existing sets of COM-based controls with .NET components.

- *XML Documentation.* Documenting program code is crucial for software development, because different programmers often work on an application during the software's lifecycle, which usually includes multiple versions and can span many years. If programmers document software code and methods, other programmers working on the application can learn and understand the logic underlying the code, thus saving time and avoiding misunderstandings. To automate documenting programs, Visual Studio .NET provides an XML tool for C# programmers. Appendix E, XML Documentation, explains how a programmer can insert comments in the code, which produces a separate file providing the code documentation.

- *Career Opportunities.* Appendix C, Career Opportunities, introduces career services available on the Internet. We explore online career services from both the employer's and employee's perspectives. We list many Web sites at which you can submit applications, search for jobs and review applicants (if you are interested in hiring someone). We also review services that build recruiting pages directly into e-businesses. One of our reviewers told us that he had used the Internet as a primary tool in a recent job search, and that this appendix would have helped him expand his search dramatically.

- *Unicode.* As computer systems evolved worldwide, computer vendors developed numeric representations of character sets and special symbols for the local languages spoken in different countries. In some cases, different representations were developed for the same languages. Such disparate character sets hindered communication among computer systems. C# supports the *Unicode Standard* (maintained by a non-profit organization called the *Unicode Consortium*), which maintains a single character set that specifies unique numeric values for characters and special symbols in most of the world's languages. Appendix G, Unicode, discusses the standard, overviews the Unicode Consortium Web site (**www.uni-**

`code.org`) and presents a C# application that displays "Welcome to Unicode!" in several languages.

- **XHTML.** The World Wide Web Consortium (W3C) has declared HTML to be a legacy technology that will undergo no further development. HTML is being replaced by the Extensible Hypertext Markup Language (XHTML)—an XML-based technology that is rapidly becoming the standard for describing Web content. We use XHTML in Chapter 18, Extensible Markup Language (XML), and offer an introduction to the technology in Appendix K, Introduction to XHTML: Part 1, and Appendix L, Introduction to XHTML: Part 2. These appendices overview headers, images, lists, image maps and other features of this emerging markup language. (We also present a treatment of HTML in Appendices I and J, because ASP .NET, used in Chapters 20 and 21, generates HTML content).

- **Accessibility.** Although the World Wide Web has become an important part of many people's lives, the medium currently presents many challenges to people with disabilities. Individuals with hearing and visual impairments, in particular, have difficulty accessing multimedia-rich Web sites. In an attempt to improve this situation, the World Wide Web Consortium (W3C) launched the Web Accessibility Initiative (WAI), which provides guidelines for making Web sites accessible to people with disabilities. Chapter 24, Accessibility, describes these guidelines and highlights various products and services designed to improve the Web-browsing experiences of individuals with disabilities. For example, the chapter introduces VoiceXML and CallXML—two XML-based technologies for increasing the accessibility of Web-based content for people with visual impairments.

- **Bit Manipulation.** Computers work with data in the form of binary digits, or bits, which can assume the values 1 or 0. Computer circuitry performs various simple bit manipulations, such as examining the value of a bit, setting the value of a bit and reversing a bit (from 1 to 0 or from 0 to 1). Operating systems, test-equipment, networking software and many other kinds of software require that programs communicate "directly with the hardware" by using bit manipulation. Appendix O, Bit Manipulation, overviews the bit manipulation capabilities that the .NET Framework provides.

Some Notes to Instructors

Students Enjoy Learning a Leading-Edge Language

Dr. Harvey M. Deitel taught introductory programming courses in universities for 20 years with an emphasis on developing clearly written, well-designed programs. Much of what is taught in such courses represents the basic principles of programming, concentrating on the effective use of data types, control structures, arrays and functions. Our experience has been that students handle the material in this book in about the same way that they handle other introductory and intermediate programming courses. There is one noticeable difference, though: Students are highly motivated by the fact that they are learning a leading-edge language, C#, and a leading-edge programming paradigm (object-oriented programming) that will be immediately useful to them as they enter the business world. This increases their enthusiasm for the material—which is essential when you consider that there is much more to learn in a C# course now that students must master both the base language and substantial class libraries as well. Although C# is a new language that may require programmers to revamp their skills, programmers will be motivated to do so because of the powerful range of capabilities that Microsoft is offering in its .NET initiative.

A World of Object Orientation

In the late 1990s, universities were still emphasizing procedural programming. The leading-edge courses were using object-oriented C++, but these courses generally mixed a substantial amount of procedural programming with object-oriented programming—something that C++ lets programmers do. Many instructors now are emphasizing a pure object-oriented programming approach. This book—the first edition of *C# How to Program* and the second text in our .NET series—takes a predominantly object-oriented approach because of the object orientation provided in C#.

Focus of the Book

Our goal was clear: Produce a C# textbook for introductory university-level courses in computer programming aimed at students with little or no programming experience, yet offer the depth and the rigorous treatment of theory and practice demanded by both professionals and students in traditional, upper-level programming courses. To meet these objectives, we produced a comprehensive book that patiently teaches the principles of computer programming and of the C# language, including control structures, object-oriented programming, C# class libraries, graphical-user-interface concepts, event-driven programming and more. After mastering the material in this book, students will be well-prepared to program in C# and to employ the capabilities of the .NET platform.

Multimedia-Intensive Communications

People want to communicate. Sure, they have been communicating since the dawn of civilization, but the potential for information exchange has increased dramatically with the evolution of various technologies. Until recently, even computer communications were limited mostly to digits, alphabetic characters and special characters. The current wave of communication technology involves the distribution of multimedia—people enjoy using applications that transmit color pictures, animations, voices, audio clips and even full-motion color video over the Internet. At some point, we will insist on three-dimensional, moving-image transmission.

There have been predictions that the Internet will eventually replace radio and television as we know them today. Similarly, it is not hard to imagine newspapers, magazines and books delivered to "the palm of your hand" (or even to special eyeglasses) via wireless communications. Many newspapers and magazines already offer Web-based versions, and some of these services have spread to the wireless world. When cellular phones were first introduced, they were large and cumbersome. Today, they are small devices that fit in our pockets, and many are Internet-enabled. Given the current rate of advancement, wireless technology soon could offer enhanced streaming-video and graphics-packed services, such as video conference calls and high-power, multi-player video games.

Teaching Approach

C# How to Program contains a rich collection of examples, exercises and projects drawn from many fields and designed to provide students with a chance to solve interesting, real-world problems. The code examples in this text have been tested on Windows 2000 and

Windows XP. The book concentrates on the principles of good software engineering, and stresses program clarity. We are educators who teach edge-of-the-practice topics in industry classrooms worldwide. We avoid arcane terminology and syntax specifications in favor of teaching by example. The text emphasizes good pedagogy.[1]

LIVE-CODE™ *Teaching Approach*

C# How to Program is loaded with numerous LIVE-CODE™ examples. This style exemplifies the way we teach and write about programming and is the focus of our multimedia *Cyber Classrooms* and Web-based training courses. Each new concept is presented in the context of a complete, working example that is immediately followed by one or more windows showing the program's input/output dialog. We call this method of teaching and writing the *LIVE-CODE™ Approach. We use programming languages to teach programming languages.* Reading the examples in the text is much like entering and running them on a computer.

World Wide Web Access

All of the examples for *C# How to Program* (and our other publications) are available on the Internet as downloads from the following Web sites:

```
www.deitel.com
www.prenhall.com/deitel
```

Registration is quick and easy and these downloads are free. We suggest downloading all the examples, then running each program as you read the corresponding text. Make changes to the examples and immediately see the effects of those changes—a great way to learn programming. Each set of instructions assumes that the user is running Windows 2000 or Windows XP and is using Microsoft's Internet Information Services (IIS). Additional setup instructions for Web servers and other software can be found at our Web sites along with the examples. [*Note:* This is copyrighted material. Feel free to use it as you study, but you may not republish any portion of it in any form without explicit permission from Prentice Hall and the authors.]

Visual Studio .NET, which includes C#, can be purchased and downloaded from Microsoft. Three different versions of Visual Studio .NET are available—Enterprise, Professional and Academic. Visit **developerstore.com/devstore/** for more details and to order. If you are a member of the Microsoft Developer Network, visit **msdn.microsoft.com/default.asp**.

Objectives

Each chapter begins with objectives that inform students of what to expect and give them an opportunity, after reading the chapter, to determine whether they have met the intended goals. The objectives serve as confidence builders and as a source of positive reinforcement.

Quotations

The chapter objectives are followed by sets of quotations. Some are humorous, some are philosophical and some offer interesting insights. We have found that students enjoy relat-

---

1. We use fonts to distinguish between Visual Studio .NET's Integrated Development Environment (IDE) features (such as menu names and menu items) and other elements that appear in the IDE. Our convention is to emphasize IDE features in a sans-serif bold Helvetica font (e.g., **Project** menu) and to emphasize program text in a serif bold Courier font (e.g., `bool x = true;`).

ing the quotations to the chapter material. Many of the quotations are worth a "second look" *after* you read each chapter.

Outline

The chapter outline enables students to approach the material in top-down fashion. Along with the chapter objectives, the outline helps students anticipate future topics and set a comfortable and effective learning pace.

Approximately 23,500 Lines of Code in 204 Example Programs (with Program Outputs)

We present C# features in the context of complete, working C# programs. The programs range in size from just a few lines of code to substantial examples containing several hundred lines of code. All examples are available on the CD that accompanies the book or as downloads from our Web site, **www.deitel.com**.

607 Illustrations/Figures

An abundance of charts, line drawings and program outputs is included. The discussion of control structures, for example, features carefully drawn flowcharts. [*Note:* We do not teach flowcharting as a program-development tool, but we do use a brief, flowchart-oriented presentation to explain the precise operation of each C# control structure.]

509 Programming Tips

We have included programming tips to help students focus on important aspects of program development. We highlight hundreds of these tips in the form of *Good Programming Practices, Common Programming Errors, Testing and Debugging Tips, Performance Tips, Portability Tips, Software Engineering Observations* and *Look-and-Feel Observations.* These tips and practices represent the best the authors have gleaned from a combined seven decades of programming and teaching experience. One of our students—a mathematics major—told us that she feels this approach is like the highlighting of axioms, theorems and corollaries in mathematics books; it provides a foundation on which to build good software.

91 Good Programming Practices

Good Programming Practices are tips that call attention to techniques that will help students produce better programs. When we teach introductory courses to nonprogrammers, we state that the "buzzword" for each course is "clarity," and we tell the students that we will highlight (in these Good Programming Practices) techniques for writing programs that are clearer, more understandable and more maintainable.

165 Common Programming Errors

Students learning a language—especially in their first programming course—tend to make certain kinds of errors frequently. Pointing out these Common Programming Errors reduces the likelihood that students will make the same mistakes. It also shortens long lines outside instructors' offices during office hours!

44 Testing and Debugging Tips

When we first designed this "tip type," we thought the tips would contain suggestions strictly for exposing bugs and removing them from programs. In fact, many of the tips describe aspects of C# that prevent "bugs" from getting into programs in the first place, thus simplifying the testing and debugging process.

57 Performance Tips

In our experience, teaching students to write clear and understandable programs is by far the most important goal for a first programming course. But students want to write programs that run the fastest, use the least memory, require the smallest number of keystrokes or dazzle in other ways. Students really care about performance and they want to know what they can do to "turbo charge" their programs. We have included 57 Performance Tips *that highlight opportunities for improving program performance—making programs run faster or minimizing the amount of memory that they occupy.*

16 Portability Tips

We include Portability Tips *to help students write portable code and to provide insights on how C# achieves its high degree of portability.*

115 Software Engineering Observations

The object-oriented programming paradigm necessitates a complete rethinking of the way we build software systems. C# is an effective language for achieving good software engineering. The Software Engineering Observations *highlight architectural and design issues that affect the construction of software systems, especially large-scale systems. Much of what the student learns here will be useful in upper-level courses and in industry as the student begins to work with large, complex real-world systems.*

21 Look-and-Feel Observations

We provide Look-and-Feel Observations *to highlight graphical-user-interface conventions. These observations help students design attractive, user-friendly graphical user interfaces that conform to industry norms.*

Summary (1277 Summary bullets)
Each chapter ends with additional pedagogical devices. We present a thorough, bullet-list-style summary of the chapter. On average, there are 39 summary bullets per chapter. This helps the students review and reinforce key concepts.

Terminology (2932 Terms)
We include an alphabetized list of the important terms defined in the chapter in a *Terminology* section. Again, this serves as further reinforcement. On average, there are 89 terms per chapter. Each term also appears in the index, so the student can locate terms and definitions quickly.

693 Self-Review Exercises and Answers (Count Includes Separate Parts)
Extensive self-review exercises and answers are included for self-study. These questions and answers give the student a chance to build confidence with the material and prepare for the regular exercises. Students should be encouraged to attempt all the self-review exercises and check their answers.

367 Exercises (Solutions in Instructor's Manual; Count Includes Separate Parts)
Each chapter concludes with a substantial set of exercises that involve simple recall of important terminology and concepts; writing individual C# statements; writing small portions of C# methods and classes; writing complete C# methods, classes and applications; and writing major projects. These exercises cover a wide variety of topics, enabling instructors to tailor their courses to the unique needs of their audiences and to vary course assignments

each semester. Instructors can use the exercises to form homework assignments, short quizzes and major examinations. The solutions for the exercises are included in the *Instructor's Manual* and on the disks *available only to instructors* through their Prentice-Hall representatives. **[NOTE: Please do not write to us requesting the instructor's manual. Distribution of this publication is strictly limited to college professors teaching from the book. Instructors may obtain the solutions manual from their regular Prentice Hall representatives. We regret that we cannot provide the solutions to professionals.]** Solutions to approximately half the exercises are included on the *C# Multimedia Cyber Classroom* CD-ROM (available in April 2002 at `www.InformIT.com/cyberclassrooms`; also see the last few pages of this book or visit `www.deitel.com` for ordering instructions). Also available in April 2002 is the boxed product, *The Complete C# Training Course*, which includes both our textbook, *C# How to Program* and the *C# Multimedia Cyber Classroom*. All of our *Complete Training Course* products are available at bookstores and online booksellers, including `www.InformIT.com`.

Approximately 5,420 Index Entries (with approximately 6,450 Page References)

We have included an extensive Index at the back of the book. Using this resource, students can search for any term or concept by keyword. The Index is especially useful to practicing programmers who use the book as a reference. Each of the 2932 terms in the Terminology sections appears in the Index (along with many more index items from each chapter). Students can use the index in conjunction with the Terminology sections to ensure that they have covered the key material in each chapter.

"Double Indexing" of All C# LIVE-CODE™ Examples

C# How to Program has 204 LIVE-CODE™ examples, which we have "double indexed." For every C# source-code program in the book, we took the file name with the `.cs` extension, such as `ChessGame.cs`, and indexed it both alphabetically (in this case, under "C") and as a subindex item under "Examples." This makes it easier to find examples using particular features.

C# Multimedia Cyber Classroom and The Complete C# Training Course

We have prepared an interactive, CD-ROM-based, software version of *C# How to Program,* called the *C# Multimedia Cyber Classroom*. This resource is loaded with e-Learning features that are ideal for both learning and reference. The *Cyber Classroom* is packaged with the textbook at a discount in *The Complete C# Training Course*. If you already have the book and would like to purchase the *C# Multimedia Cyber Classroom* separately, please visit `www.InformIT.com/cyberclassrooms`. The ISBN number for the *C# Multimedia Cyber Classroom* is 0-13-064587-7. All Deitel™ *Cyber Classrooms* are available in CD-ROM and Web-based training formats.

The CD provides an introduction in which the authors overview the *Cyber Classroom*'s features. The textbook's 204 LIVE-CODE™ example C# programs truly "come alive" in the *Cyber Classroom*. If you are viewing a program and want to execute it, you simply click the lightning-bolt icon, and the program will run. You immediately will see—and hear, when working with audio-based multimedia programs—the program's outputs. If you want to modify a program and see the effects of your changes, simply click the floppy-disk icon that causes the source code to be "lifted off" the CD and "dropped into" one of your own directories so you can edit the text, recompile the program and try out your new version. Click the audio icon, and one of the authors will discuss the program and "walk you through" the code.

The *Cyber Classroom* also provides navigational aids, including extensive hyper-linking. The *Cyber Classroom* is browser based, so it remembers sections that you have visited recently and allows you to move forward or backward among these sections. The thousands of index entries are hyperlinked to their text occurrences. Furthermore, when you key in a term using the "find" feature, the *Cyber Classroom* will locate occurrences of that term throughout the text. The Table of Contents entries are "hot," so clicking a chapter name takes you immediately to that chapter.

Students like the fact that solutions to approximately half the exercises in the book are included with the *Cyber Classroom*. Studying and running these extra programs is a great way for students to enhance their learning experience.

Students and professional users of our *Cyber Classrooms* tell us that they like the inter-activity and that the *Cyber Classroom* is an effective reference due to its extensive hyper-linking and other navigational features. We received an e-mail from a person who said that he lives "in the boonies" and cannot take a live course at a university, so the *Cyber Classroom* provided an ideal solution to his educational needs.

Professors tell us that their students enjoy using the *Cyber Classroom* and spend more time on the courses and master more of the material than in textbook-only courses. For a complete list of the available and forthcoming *Cyber Classrooms* and *Complete Training Courses*, see the *Deitel™ Series* page at the beginning of this book, the product listing and ordering information at the end of this book or visit **www.deitel.com**, **www.pren-hall.com/deitel** and **www.InformIT.com/deitel**.

Deitel e-Learning Initiatives

e-Books and Support for Wireless Devices

Wireless devices will play an enormous role in the future of the Internet. Given recent band-width enhancements and the emergence of 2.5 and 3G technologies, it is projected that, within two years, more people will access the Internet through wireless devices than through desktop computers. Deitel & Associates, Inc., is committed to wireless accessibil-ity and has recently published *Wireless Internet & Mobile Business How to Program*. To fulfill the needs of a wide range of customers, we currently are developing our content both in traditional print formats and in newly developed electronic formats, such as e-books so that students and professors can access content virtually anytime, anywhere. Visit **www.deitel.com** for periodic updates on this initiative.

e-Matter

Deitel & Associates, Inc., is partnering with Prentice Hall's parent company, Pearson PLC, and its information technology Web site, **InformIT.com**, to launch the Deitel e-Matter series at **www.InformIT.com/deitel**. This series will provide professors, students and professionals with an additional source of information on specific programming topics. e-Matter consists of stand-alone sections taken from published texts, forthcoming texts or pieces written during the Deitel research-and-development process. Developing e-Matter based on pre-publication books allows us to offer significant amounts of the material to early adopters for use in courses. Some possible C# e-Matter titles we are considering include *Object-Based Programming and Object-Oriented Programming in C#*; *Graphical User Interface Programming in C#*; *Multithreading in C#*; *ASP .NET and Web Forms: A C# View;* and *ASP .NET and Web Services: A C# View.*

Course Management Systems: WebCT, Blackboard, and CourseCompass

We are working with Prentice Hall to integrate our *How to Program Series* courseware into three Course Management Systems: WebCT, Blackboard™ and CourseCompass. These Course Management Systems enable instructors to create, manage and use sophisticated Web-based educational programs. Course Management System features include course customization (such as posting contact information, policies, syllabi, announcements, assignments, grades, performance evaluations and progress tracking), class and student management tools, a gradebook, reporting tools, communication tools (such as chat rooms), a whiteboard, document sharing, bulletin boards and more. Instructors can use these products to communicate with their students, create online quizzes and tests from questions directly linked to the text and automatically grade and track test results. For more information about these upcoming products, visit **www.deitel.com/ whatsnew.html**. For demonstrations of existing WebCT, Blackboard and Course-Compass courses, visit **cms.prenhall.com/WebCT**, **cms.prenhall.com/ Blackboard** and **cms.prenhall.com/CourseCompass**, respectively.

Deitel and InformIT Newsletters

Deitel Column in the InformIT Newsletters

Deitel & Associates, Inc., contributes a weekly column to the popular *InformIT* newsletter, currently subscribed to by more than 800,000 IT professionals worldwide. For opt-in registration, visit **www.InformIT.com**.

Deitel Newsletter

Our own free, opt-in newsletter includes commentary on industry trends and developments, links to articles and resources from our published books and upcoming publications, information on future publications, product-release schedules and more. For opt-in registration, visit **www.deitel.com**.

The Deitel .NET Series

Deitel & Associates, Inc., is making a major commitment to .NET programming through the launch of our .NET Series. *C# .NET How to Program* and *Visual Basic .NET How to Program, Second Edition* are the first books in this new series. We intend to follow these books with *Advanced C# How to Program* and *Advanced Visual Basic .NET How to Program*, which will be published in December 2002. We also plan to publish *Visual C++ .NET How to Program* in July 2002, followed by *Advanced Visual C++ .NET How to Program* in July 2003.

Advanced C# How to Program

C# How to Program covers introductory through intermediate-level C# programming topics, as well as core programming fundamentals. By contrast, our upcoming textbook *Ad-*

vanced C# How to Program will be geared toward experienced C# developers. This new book will cover enterprise-level programming topics, including: Creating multi-tier, database intensive ASP .NET applications using ADO .NET and XML; constructing custom Windows controls; developing custom Web controls; and building Windows services. The book also will include more in-depth explanations of object-oriented programming (with the UML), ADO .NET, XML Web services, wireless programming and security. *Advanced C# How to Program* will be published in December 2002.

Acknowledgments

One of the great pleasures of writing a textbook is acknowledging the efforts of many people whose names may not appear on the cover, but whose hard work, cooperation, friendship and understanding were crucial to the production of the book.

Many other people at Deitel & Associates, Inc., devoted long hours to this project.

- Sean E. Santry, a graduate of Boston College with degrees in Computer Science and Philosophy, Director of Software Development at Deitel & Associates, Inc., and co-author of *Advanced Java 2 Platform How to Program*, contributed to Chapters 1–10, 12–13 and 18–23.

- Matthew R. Kowalewski, a graduate of Bentley College with a degree in Accounting Informations Systems, is the Director of Wireless Development at Deitel & Associates, Inc. He contributed to Chapters 19–20, Appendices B, F, I–N, P and edited the Index.

- Jonathan Gadzik, a graduate of the Columbia University School of Engineering and Applied Science with a major in Computer Science, co-authored Chapter 17 and contributed to Chapters 9, 22 and Appendices D and E.

- Kyle Lomelí, a graduate of Oberlin College with a degree in Computer Science and a minor in East Asian Studies, contributed to Chapters 11, 14–15, 19 and 24.

- Lauren Trees, a graduate if Brown University in English, edited the entire manuscript for smoothness, clarity and effectiveness of presentation; she also co-authored the Preface, Chapter 1 and Appendix P.

- Rashmi Jayaprakash, a graduate of Boston University with a major in Computer Science, co-authored Chapter 24 and Appendix G.

- Laura Treibick, a graduate of the University of Colorado at Boulder with a degree in Photography and Multimedia, is Director of Multimedia at Deitel & Associates, Inc. She contributed to Chapter 16 and enhanced many of the graphics throughout the text.

- Betsy DuWaldt, a graduate of Metropolitan State College of Denver with a major in Technical Communications (Writing and Editing emphasis) and a minor in Computer Information Systems, is Editorial Director at Deitel & Associates, Inc. She co-authored the Preface, Chapter 1 and Appendix P and managed the permissions process for the book.

- Barbara Deitel applied the copy edits to the manuscript. She did this in parallel with handling her extensive financial and administrative responsibilities at Deitel

& Associates, Inc., which include serving as Chief Financial Officer. [Everyone at the company works on book content.]

- Abbey Deitel, a graduate of Carnegie Mellon University's Industrial Management Program and President of Deitel & Associates, Inc., recruited 40 additional full-time employees and interns during 2001. She also leased, equipped and furnished our second building to create the work environment from which *C# How to Program* and our other year 2001 publications were produced. She suggested the title for the *How to Program* series, and edited this preface and several of the book's chapters.

We would also like to thank the participants in the Deitel & Associates, Inc., College Internship Program.[2]

- Jeffrey Hamm, a sophomore at Northeastern University in Computer Science, co-authored Chapters 16, 18, 20–21 and Appendices D and H.

- Kalid Azad, a sophomore at Princeton University in Computer Science, contributed to Chapters 1, 2, 12–13, 16 and Appendix D. He created PowerPoint-slide ancillaries for Chapters 1–7 and researched Visual Studio .NET and Microsoft's .NET initiative.

- Christopher Cassa, a junior at MIT in Computer Science, contributed to Chapters 3–7 and 18.

- David Tuttle, a senior at Harvard in Computer Science, contributed to Chapters 8, 18–19 and 24 and coded examples for Chapters 3–6, 7, 11,16–17,19, 23 and 26.

- Ori Schwartz, a sophomore at Boston University in Computer Science, produced solutions for all the chapters and contributed to Chapter 16.

- Thiago Lucas da Silva, a sophomore at Northeastern University in Computer Science, tested all the programming examples through the various beta releases and release candidates of Visual Studio .NET.

- Matthew Rubino, a sophomore at Northeastern University in Computer Science, created ancillary materials for the entire book.

- Elizabeth Rockett, a senior in English at Princeton University, edited 1-3, 7–8, 14, 17 and 19-24.

- Barbara Strauss, a senior in English at Brandeis University, edited Chapters 1–6, 9–13 and 18–24.

- Christina Carney, a senior in Psychology and Business at Framingham State College, helped with the Preface.

---

2. The *Deitel & Associates, Inc. College Internship Program* offers a limited number of salaried positions to Boston-area college students majoring in Computer Science, Information Technology, Marketing, Management and English. Students work at our corporate headquarters in Sudbury, Massachusetts full-time in the summers and (for those attending college in the Boston area) part-time during the academic year. We also offer full-time internship positions for students interested in taking a semester off from school to gain industry experience. Regular full-time positions are available to college graduates. For more information about this competitive program, please contact Abbey Deitel at **deitel@deitel.com** and visit our Web site, **www.deitel.com**.

- Reshma Khilnani, a junior in Computer Science and Mathematics at Massachusetts Institute of Technology, contributed to Chapter 18 and Appendix E.

- Brian Foster, a sophomore at Northeastern University in Computer Science, helped with the Preface and Bibliography.

- Mike Preshman, a sophomore at Northeastern University with a major in Computer Science and minors in Electrical Engineering and Math, helped with the Bibliography.

We are fortunate to have been able to work on this project with the talented and dedicated team of publishing professionals at Prentice Hall. We especially appreciate the extraordinary efforts of our Computer Science editor, Petra Recter and her boss—our mentor in publishing—Marcia Horton, Editorial Director of Prentice-Hall's Engineering and Computer Science Division. Camille Trentacoste and her boss Vince O'Brien did a marvelous job managing the production of the book. Sarah Burrows handled editorial responsibilities on the book's extensive ancillary package.

The *C# Multimedia Cyber Classroom* was developed in parallel with *C# How to Program*. We sincerely appreciate the "new media" insight, savvy and technical expertise of our electronic-media editors, Mark Taub and Karen McLean. They and project manager Mike Ruel did a wonderful job bringing the *C# Multimedia Cyber Classroom* and *The Complete C# Training Course* to publication.

We owe special thanks to the creativity of Tamara Newnam (`smart_art@earthlink.net`), who produced the art work for our programming-tip icons and for the cover. She created the delightful creature who shares with you the book's programming tips. Barbara Deitel and Abbey Deitel contributed the bugs' names for the front cover.

During the development of this manuscript, we were fortunate to have had two universities—the Massachusetts Institute of Technology and Yale University—beta-test the book in the Fall 2001 semester. MIT Professor John Williams used the text to teach the graduate-level class, *Web System Architecting—Part I: Programming Clients and Web Services Using C# and .NET,* for the Off-Campus Advanced Study Program. Chris Cassa, a summer 2001 intern at Deitel & Associates, Inc., was the teaching fellow for the class. Yale Professor Paul Hudak used the manuscript for an *Introduction to Programming* class, which taught object-oriented programming languages. We would like to thank Professor Williams, Professor Hudak and Chris for their contributions. The feedback we received was crucial to fine-tuning this text.

We wish to acknowledge the efforts of our first- and second-round reviewers and to thank Crissy Statuto and Jennifer Cappello of Prentice Hall, who recruited the reviewers and managed the review process. Adhering to a tight time schedule, these reviewers scrutinized the text and the programs, providing countless suggestions for improving the accuracy and completeness of the presentation. It is a privilege to have the guidance of such talented and busy professionals.

C# How to Program reviewers:
Hussein Abuthuraya (Microsoft)
Lars Bergstrom (Microsoft)
Indira Dhingra (Microsoft)
Eric Gunnerson (Microsoft)
Peter Hallam (Microsoft)

Habib Hegdarian (Microsoft)
Anson Horton (Microsoft)
Latha Lakshminarayanan (Microsoft)
Kerry Loynd (Microsoft)
Tom McDade (Microsoft)
Syed Mehdi (Microsoft)
Cosmin Radu (Microsoft)
Ratta Rakshminarayana (Microsoft)
Imtiaz Syed (Microsoft)
Ed Thornburg (Microsoft)
Richard Van Fossen (Microsoft)
Rishabh Agarwal (Delteq Systems Pte. Ltd.)
José Antonio González Seco (Sadiel S.A.)
Paul Bohman (WebAIM)
Alex Bondarev (SureFire Commerce, Inc.)
Ron Braithwaite (Nutriware)
Filip Bulovic (Objectronics PTY Ltd.)
Mark Burhop (University of Cincinnati)
Carl Burnham (Southpoint)
Matt Butler (Oakscape Inc.)
Andrew Chau (Rich Solutions, Inc.)
Dharmesh Chauhan (Microsoft Consultant, Singapore)
Shyam Chebrolu (SAIC Broadway & Seymour Group)
Kunal Cheda (DotNetExtreme.com)
Edmund Chou (MIT Student, www.devhood.com project, Microsoft Intern)
James Chegwidden (Tarrant County College)
Vijay Cinnakonda (University of Toledo)
Michael Colynuck (Sierra Systems)
Jay Cook (Canon Information Systems)
Jeff Cowan (Magenic Technologies)
Robert Dombroski (AccessOnTime)
Shaun Eagan ((Eagan Consulting)
Brian Erwin (Extreme Logic)
Hamilton Fong (Montag & Caldwell, Inc.)
Gnanavel Gnana Arun Ganesh (Arun Microsystems)
Sam Gentile (Consultant)
Sam Gill (San Francisco State University)
John Godel (TJX)
David Haglin (Minnesota State University in Mankato)
Jeff Isom (WebAIM)
Rex Jaeschke (Consultant)
Amit Kalani (MobiCast)
Priti Kalani (Consultant)
Bryan Keller (csharphelp.com)
Patrick Lam (EdgeNet Communications)
Yi-Fung Lin (MIT Student, www.devhood.com project, Microsoft Intern)

Maxim Loukianov (SoloMio Corporation)
Gaurav Mantro (EDS PLM Solutions)
Jaimon Mathew (Osprey Software Technology)
Robert Meagher (Compuware NuMega Lab)
Arun Nair (iSpan Technologies)
Saurabh Nandu (Mastercsharp.com)
Simon North (Synopsys)
Jibin Pan (csharpcorner.com)
Graham Parker (VBUG)
Bryan Plaster (Valtech)
Chris Rausch (Sheridan Press)
Debbie Reid (Santa Fe Community College)
Bryn Rhodes (Softwise, Inc.)
Craig Schofding (C.A.S. Training)
Rahul Sharma (Maxutil Software)
Devan Shepherd (XMaLpha Technologies)
David Talbot (Reallinx, Inc.)
Satish Talim (Pune-Csharp)
Pavel Tsekov (Consultant)
John Varghese (UBS Warburg)
Peter Weng (MIT Student, www.devhood.com project, Microsoft Intern)
Jesse Wilkins (Metalinear Media)
Warren Wiltsie (Fairleigh Dickinson University/Seton Hall University)
Phil Wright (Crownwood Consulting Ltd.)
Norimasa Yoshida (MIT Graduate Student)

We would sincerely appreciate your comments, criticisms, corrections and suggestions for improving the text. Please address all correspondence to:

`deitel@deitel.com`

We will respond promptly.

Well, that's it for now. Welcome to the exciting world of C# programming. We hope you enjoy this look at leading-edge computer applications. Good luck!

Dr. Harvey M. Deitel
Paul J. Deitel
Tem R. Nieto
Cheryl H. Yaeger
Marina Zlatkina
Jeff Listfield

About the Authors

Dr. Harvey M. Deitel, CEO and Chairman of Deitel & Associates, Inc., has 40 years experience in the computing field, including extensive industry and academic experience. Dr. Deitel earned B.S. and M.S. degrees from the Massachusetts Institute of Technology and a Ph.D. from Boston University. He worked on the pioneering virtual-memory operating-systems projects at IBM and MIT that developed techniques now widely implemented in systems such as UNIX, Linux and Windows NT. He has 20 years of college teaching experience, including earning tenure and serving as the Chairman of the Computer Science Department at Boston College before founding Deitel & Associates, Inc., with his son, Paul J. Deitel. He is the author or co-author of several dozen books and multimedia packages and is writing many more. With translations published in Japanese, Russian, Spanish, Traditional Chinese, Simplified Chinese, Korean, French, Polish, Italian and Portuguese, Dr. Deitel's texts have earned international recognition. Dr. Deitel has delivered professional seminars to major corporations and to government organizations and various branches of the military.

Paul J. Deitel, Executive Vice President and Chief Technical Officer of Deitel & Associates, Inc., is a graduate of the Massachusetts Institute of Technology's Sloan School of Management, where he studied Information Technology. Through Deitel & Associates, Inc., he has delivered Java, C, C++, Internet and World Wide Web courses to industry clients including Compaq, Sun Microsystems, White Sands Missile Range, Rogue Wave Software, Boeing, Dell, Stratus, Fidelity, Cambridge Technology Partners, Open Environment Corporation, One Wave, Hyperion Software, Lucent Technologies, Adra Systems, Entergy, CableData Systems, NASA at the Kennedy Space Center, the National Severe Storm Laboratory, IBM and many other organizations. He has lectured on C++ and Java for the Boston Chapter of the Association for Computing Machinery and has taught satellite-based Java courses through a cooperative venture of Deitel & Associates, Inc., Prentice Hall and the Technology Education Network. He and his father, Dr. Harvey M. Deitel, are the world's best-selling Computer Science textbook authors.

Tem R. Nieto, Director of Product Development of Deitel & Associates, Inc., is a graduate of the Massachusetts Institute of Technology, where he studied engineering and computing. Through Deitel & Associates, Inc., he has delivered courses for industry clients including Sun Microsystems, Compaq, EMC, Stratus, Fidelity, NASDAQ, Art Technology, Progress Software, Toys "R" Us, Operational Support Facility of the National Oceanographic and Atmospheric Administration, Jet Propulsion Laboratory, Nynex, Motorola, Federal Reserve Bank of Chicago, Banyan, Schlumberger, University of Notre Dame, NASA, various military installations and many others. He has co-authored numerous books and multimedia packages with the Deitels and has contributed to virtually every Deitel & Associates, Inc., publication.

Cheryl H. Yaeger, Director of Microsoft Software Publications with Deitel & Associates, Inc., graduated from Boston University in 3 years with a bachelor's degree in Computer Science. Other Deitel publications she has contributed to include *Perl How to Program, Wireless Internet & Mobile Business How to Program* and *Internet and World Wide Web How to Program, Second Edition*. Cheryl is increasingly interested in Microsoft's .NET strategy and in learning how Microsoft's .NET initiative will develop in the coming year.

Marina Zlatkina graduated from Brandeis University in three years with degrees in Computer Science and Mathematics and is pursuing a Master's degree in Computer Science at Brandeis. During her Brandeis career, she has conducted research in databases and has been a teaching assistant. She has also contributed to the Deitel & Associates, Inc. publication, *e-Business & e-Commerce for Managers*.

Jeff Listfield is a senior at Harvard College in Computer Science. His coursework includes classes in computer graphics, networks and computational theory and he has programming experience in C, C++, Java, Perl and Lisp. Jeff also contributed to the Deitel & Associates, Inc., publication *Perl How to Program*.

About Deitel & Associates, Inc.

Deitel & Associates, Inc., is an internationally recognized corporate training and content-creation organization specializing in Internet/World Wide Web software technology, e-business/e-commerce software technology, object technology and computer programming languages education. The company provides courses on Internet and World Wide Web/ programming, wireless Internet programming, object technology, and major programming languages and platforms, such as Visual Basic .NET, C#, Java, advanced Java, C, C++, XML, Perl, Python and more. The founders of Deitel & Associates, Inc., are Dr. Harvey M. Deitel and Paul J. Deitel. The company's clients include many of the world's largest computer companies, government agencies, branches of the military and business organizations. Through its 25-year publishing partnership with Prentice Hall, Deitel & Associates, Inc., publishes leading-edge programming textbooks, professional books, interactive CD-ROM-based multimedia *Cyber Classrooms*, *Complete Training Courses*, e-books, e-matter, Web-based training courses and course management systems e-content. Deitel & Associates, Inc., and the authors can be reached via e-mail at:

    deitel@deitel.com

To learn more about Deitel & Associates, Inc., its publications and its worldwide corporate on-site curriculum, see the last few pages of this book or visit:

    www.deitel.com

Individuals wishing to purchase Deitel books, *Cyber Classrooms*, *Complete Training Courses* and Web-based training courses can do so through bookstores, online booksellers and:

    www.deitel.com
    www.prenhall.com/deitel
    www.InformIT.com/deitel
    www.InformIT.com/cyberclassrooms

Bulk orders by corporations and academic institutions should be placed directly with Prentice Hall. See the last few pages of this book for worldwide ordering details.

The World Wide Web Consortium (W3C)

Deitel & Associates, Inc., is a member of the *World Wide Web Consortium (W3C)*. The W3C was founded in 1994 "to develop common protocols for the evolution of the World Wide Web." As a W3C member, Deitel & Associates, Inc., holds a seat on the W3C Advisory Committee (the company's representative is our Chief Technology Officer, Paul Deitel). Advisory Committee members help provide "strategic direction" to the W3C through meetings held around the world. Member organizations also help develop standards recommendations for Web technologies (such as XHTML, XML and many others) through participation in W3C activities and groups. Membership in the W3C is intended for companies and large organizations. To obtain information on becoming a member of the W3C visit **www.w3.org/Consortium/Prospectus/Joining**.

C#

HOW TO PROGRAM

1

Introduction to Computers, the Internet, the Web and C#

Objectives

- To understand basic computer concepts.
- To learn about various programming languages.
- To become familiar with the history of the C# programming language.
- To understand the Microsoft® .NET initiative.
- To preview the remaining chapters of the book.

Things are always at their best in their beginning.
Blaise Pascal

High thoughts must have high language.
Aristophanes

Our life is frittered away by detail…Simplify, simplify.
Henry David Thoreau

Before beginning, plan carefully….
Marcus Tullius Cicero

Look with favor upon a bold beginning.
Virgil

I think I'm beginning to learn something about it.
Auguste Renoir

Outline

1.1 Introduction

Welcome to C#! In creating this book, we have worked hard to provide students with the most accurate and complete information regarding the C# language, and the .NET platform. The book is designed to be appropriate for readers at all levels, from practicing programmers to individuals with little or no programming experience. We hope that working with this text will be an informative, entertaining and challenging learning experience for you.

How can one book appeal to both novices and skilled programmers? The core of this book emphasizes the achievement of program clarity through proven techniques of *structured programming*, *object-based programming*, *object-oriented programming (OOP)* and *event-driven programming*. Nonprogrammers learn basic skills that underlie good programming; experienced developers receive a rigorous explanation of the language and may improve their programming styles. Perhaps most importantly, the book presents hundreds of complete, working C# programs and depicts their outputs. We call this the *LIVE-CODE*™ *approach*. All of the book's examples are available on the CD-ROM that accompanies this book and on our Web site, **www.deitel.com**.

Computer use is increasing in almost every field of endeavor. In an era of steadily rising costs, computing costs have decreased dramatically because of rapid developments in both hardware and software technology. Computers that filled large rooms and cost millions of dollars just two decades ago now can be inscribed on the surfaces of silicon chips smaller than a fingernail, costing perhaps a few dollars each. Silicon is one of the most abundant materials on earth—it is an ingredient in common sand. Silicon-chip technology has made computing so economical that hundreds of millions of general-purpose computers are in use worldwide, helping people in business, industry, government and their personal lives. Given the current rate of technological development, this number could easily double over the next few years.

In beginning to study this text, you are starting on a challenging and rewarding educational path. As you proceed, if you would like to communicate with us, please send an e-mail to **deitel@deitel.com** or browse our World Wide Web sites at **www.deitel.com**, **www.prenhall.com/deitel** and **www.InformIT.com/ deitel**. We hope that you enjoy learning C# through reading *C# How to Program*.

1.2 What Is a Computer?

A *computer* is a device capable of performing computations and making logical decisions at speeds millions and even billions of times faster than those of human beings. For example, many of today's personal computers can perform hundreds of millions—even billions—of additions per second. A person operating a desk calculator might require decades to complete the same number of calculations that a powerful personal computer can perform in one second. (*Points to ponder*: How would you know whether the person had added the numbers correctly? How would you know whether the computer had added the numbers correctly?) Today's fastest *supercomputers* can perform hundreds of billions of additions per second— about as many calculations as hundreds of thousands of people could perform in one year! Trillion-instruction-per-second computers are already functioning in research laboratories!

Computers process *data* under the control of sets of instructions called *computer programs*. These programs guide computers through orderly sets of actions that are specified by individuals known as *computer programmers*.

A computer is composed of various devices (such as the keyboard, screen, mouse, disks, memory, CD-ROM and processing units) known as *hardware*. The programs that run on a computer are referred to as *software*. Hardware costs have been declining dramatically in recent years, to the point that personal computers have become a commodity. Software-development costs, however, have been rising steadily, as programmers develop ever more powerful and complex applications without being able to improve significantly the technology of software development. In this book, you will learn proven software-development methods that can reduce software-development costs—top-down stepwise refinement, functionalization and object-oriented programming. Object-oriented programming is widely believed to be the significant breakthrough that can greatly enhance programmer productivity.

1.3 Computer Organization

Virtually every computer, regardless of differences in physical appearance, can be envisioned as being divided into six *logical units*, or sections:

1. *Input unit.* This "receiving" section of the computer obtains information (data and computer programs) from various *input devices.* The input unit then places this information at the disposal of the other units to facilitate the processing of the information. Today, most users enter information into computers via keyboards and mouse devices. Other input devices include microphones (for speaking to the computer), scanners (for scanning images) and digital cameras (for taking photographs and making videos).

2. *Output unit.* This "shipping" section of the computer takes information that the computer has processed and places it on various *output devices,* making the information available for use outside the computer. Computers can output information in various ways, including displaying the output on screens, playing it on audio/video devices, printing it on paper or using the output to control other devices.

3. *Memory unit.* This is the rapid-access, relatively low-capacity "warehouse" section of the computer, which facilitates the temporary storage of data. The memory unit retains information that has been entered through the input unit, enabling that information to be immediately available for processing. In addition, the unit retains processed information until that information can be transmitted to output devices. Often, the memory unit is called either *memory* or *primary memory—random access memory (RAM)* is an example of primary memory. Primary memory is usually volatile, which means that it is erased when the machine is powered off.

4. *Arithmetic and logic unit (ALU).* The ALU is the "manufacturing" section of the computer. It is responsible for the performance of calculations such as addition, subtraction, multiplication and division. It also contains decision mechanisms, allowing the computer to perform such tasks as determining whether two items stored in memory are equal.

5. *Central processing unit (CPU).* The CPU serves as the "administrative" section of the computer. This is the computer's coordinator, responsible for supervising the operation of the other sections. The CPU alerts the input unit when information should be read into the memory unit, instructs the ALU about when to use information from the memory unit in calculations and tells the output unit when to send information from the memory unit to certain output devices.

6. *Secondary storage unit.* This unit is the long-term, high-capacity "warehousing" section of the computer. Secondary storage devices, such as hard drives and disks, normally hold programs or data that other units are not actively using; the computer then can retrieve this information when it is needed—hours, days, months or even years later. Information in secondary storage takes much longer to access than does information in primary memory. However, the price per unit of secondary storage is much less than the price per unit of primary memory. Secondary storage is usually *nonvolatile*—it retains information even when the computer is off.

1.4 Evolution of Operating Systems

Early computers were capable of performing only one *job* or *task* at a time. In this mode of computer operation, often called single-user *batch processing,* the computer runs one program at a time and processes data in groups called *batches*. Users of these early systems typically submitted their jobs to a computer center on decks of punched cards. Often, hours or even days elapsed before results were returned to the users' desks.

To make computer use more convenient, software systems called *operating systems* were developed. Early operating systems oversaw and managed computers' transitions between jobs. By minimizing the time it took for a computer operator to switch from one job to another, the operating system increased the total amount of work, or *throughput*, computers could process in a given time period.

As computers became more powerful, single-user batch processing became inefficient, because computers spent a great deal of time waiting for slow input/output devices to complete their tasks. Developers then looked to multiprogramming techniques, which enabled many tasks to *share* the resources of the computer to achieve better utilization. *Multiprogramming* involves the "simultaneous" operation of many jobs on a computer that splits its resources among those jobs. However, users of early multiprogramming operating systems still submitted jobs on decks of punched cards and waited hours or days for results.

In the 1960s, several industry and university groups pioneered *timesharing* operating systems. Timesharing is a special type of multiprogramming that allows users to access a computer through *terminals* (devices with keyboards and screens). Dozens or even hundreds of people can use a timesharing computer system at once. It is important to note that the computer does not actually run all the users' requests simultaneously. Rather, it performs a small portion of one user's job and moves on to service the next user. However, because the computer does this so quickly, it can provide service to each user several times per second. This gives users' programs the appearance of running simultaneously. Timesharing offers major advantages over previous computing systems in that users receive prompt responses to requests, instead of waiting long periods to obtain results.

The UNIX operating system, which is now widely used for advanced computing, originated as an experimental timesharing operating system. Dennis Ritchie and Ken Thompson developed UNIX at Bell Laboratories beginning in the late 1960s and developed C as the language in which they wrote it. They freely distributed the source code to other programmers who wanted to use, modify and extend it. A large community of UNIX users quickly developed. The operating system grew as UNIX users contributed their own programs and tools. Through a collaborative effort among numerous researchers and developers, UNIX became a powerful and flexible operating system able to handle almost any type of task that a user required. Many versions of UNIX have evolved, including today's phenomenally popular *open-source* Linux operating system. Typically, the source code for open-source products is freely available over the Internet. This enables developers to learn from, validate and modify the source code. Often, open-source products require that developers publish any enhancements they make so the open-source community can continue to evolve those products.

1.5 Personal Computing, Distributed Computing and Client/Server Computing

In 1977, Apple Computer popularized the phenomenon of *personal computing*. Initially, it was a hobbyist's dream. However, the price of computers soon dropped so far that large numbers of people could buy them for personal or business use. In 1981, IBM, the world's largest computer vendor, introduced the IBM Personal Computer. Personal computing rapidly became legitimate in business, industry and government organizations.

The computers first pioneered by Apple and IBM were "stand-alone" units—people did their work on their own machines and transported disks back and forth to share information. (This process was often called "sneakernet.") Although early personal computers were not powerful enough to timeshare several users, the machines could be linked together into computer networks, either over telephone lines or via *local area networks* (*LANs*) within an organization. These networks led to the *distributed computing* phenomenon, in which an organization's computing is distributed over networks to the sites at which the work of the organization is performed, instead of being performed only at a central computer installation. Personal computers were powerful enough to handle both the computing requirements of individual users and the basic tasks involved in the electronic transfer of information between computers. *N-tier applications* split up an application over numerous distributed computers. For example, a *three-tier application* might have a user interface on one computer, business-logic processing on a second and a database on a third; all interact as the application runs.

Today's most advanced personal computers are as powerful as the million-dollar machines of just two decades ago. High-powered desktop machines—called *workstations*—provide individual users with enormous capabilities. Information is easily shared across computer networks, in which computers called *servers* store programs and data that can be used by *client* computers distributed throughout the network. This type of configuration gave rise to the term *client/server computing*. Today's popular operating systems, such as UNIX, Solaris, MacOS, Windows 2000, Windows XP and Linux, provide the kinds of capabilities discussed in this section.

1.6 Machine Languages, Assembly Languages and High-Level Languages

Programmers write instructions in various programming languages, some directly understandable by computers and others that require intermediate *translation* steps. Although hundreds of computer languages are in use today, the diverse offerings can be divided into three general types:

1. Machine languages
2. Assembly languages
3. High-level languages

Any computer can understand only its own *machine language* directly. As the "natural language" of a particular computer, machine language is defined by the computer's hardware design. Machine languages generally consist of streams of numbers (ultimately reduced to 1s and 0s) that instruct computers how to perform their most elementary operations. Machine languages are *machine-dependent*, which means that a particular machine language can be used on only one type of computer. The following section of a machine-language program, which adds *overtime* pay to *base pay* and stores the result in *gross pay*, demonstrates the incomprehensibility of machine language to the human reader.

```
+1300042774
+1400593419
+1200274027
```

As the popularity of computers increased, machine-language programming proved to be excessively slow, tedious and error prone. Instead of using the strings of numbers that computers could directly understand, programmers began using English-like abbreviations to represent the elementary operations of the computer. These abbreviations formed the basis of *assembly languages. Translator programs* called *assemblers* convert assembly language programs to machine language at computer speeds. The following section of an assembly-language program also adds *overtime pay* to *base pay* and stores the result in *gross pay*, but presents the steps more clearly to human readers than does its machine-language equivalent:

```
LOAD    BASEPAY
ADD     OVERPAY
STORE   GROSSPAY
```

Such code is clearer to humans but incomprehensible to computers until translated into machine language.

Although computer use increased rapidly with the advent of assembly languages, these languages still required many instructions to accomplish even the simplest tasks. To speed up the programming process, *high-level languages*, in which single statements accomplish substantial tasks, were developed. Translation programs called *compilers* convert high-level-language programs into machine language. High-level languages enable programmers to write instructions that look almost like everyday English and contain common mathematical notations. A payroll program written in a high-level language might contain a statement such as

```
grossPay = basePay + overTimePay
```

Obviously, programmers prefer high-level languages to either machine languages or assembly languages.

The compilation of a high-level language program into machine language can require a considerable amount of time. However, this problem was solved by the development of *interpreter* programs that can execute high-level language programs directly, bypassing the compilation step. Although programs that are already compiled execute faster than interpreted programs, interpreters are popular in program-development environments. In these environments, developers change programs frequently as they add new features and correct errors. Once a program is fully developed, a compiled version can be produced so that the program runs at maximum efficiency.

1.7 C, C++, Visual Basic .NET and Java™

As high-level languages develop, new offerings build on aspects of their predecessors. C++ evolved from C, which in turn evolved from two previous languages, BCPL and B. Martin Richards developed BCPL in 1967 as a language for writing operating systems, software and compilers. Ken Thompson modeled his language, B, after BCPL. In 1970, Thompson used B to create early versions of the UNIX operating system. Both BCPL and B were "typeless" languages, meaning that every data item occupied one "word" in memory. Using these languages, programmers assumed responsibility for treating each data item as a whole number or real number, for example.

The C language, which Dennis Ritchie evolved from B at Bell Laboratories, was originally implemented in 1973. Although C employs many of BCPL and B's important concepts, it also offers data typing and other features. C first gained widespread recognition as a development language of the UNIX operating system. However, C is now available for most computers, and many of today's major operating systems are written in C or C++. C is a hardware-independent language, and, with careful design, it is possible to write C programs that are portable to most computers.

C++, an extension of C using elements from Simula 67, a simulation programming language, was developed by Bjarne Stroustrup in the early 1980s at Bell Laboratories. C++ provides a number of features that "spruce up" the C language, but, more importantly, it provides capabilities for *object-oriented programming (OOP)*.

At a time when demand for new and more powerful software is soaring, the ability to build software quickly, correctly and economically remains an elusive goal. However, this problem can be addressed in part through the use of *objects,* or reusable software *components* that model items in the real world (see Section 1.11). Software developers are discovering that a modular, object-oriented approach to design and implementation can make software development groups much more productive than is possible via previous popular programming techniques, such as structured programming. Furthermore, object-oriented programs are often easier to understand, correct and modify.

In addition to C++, many other object-oriented languages have been developed. These include Smalltalk, which was created at Xerox's Palo Alto Research Center (PARC). Smalltalk is a pure object-oriented language, which means that literally everything is an object. C++ is a hybrid language—it is possible to program in a C-like style, an object-oriented style or both. Although some perceive this range of options as a benefit, most programmers today believe that it is best to program in a purely object-oriented manner.

Developing Microsoft Windows-based applications in languages such as C and C++, however, proved to be a difficult and cumbersome process. When Bill Gates founded Microsoft Corporation, he implemented *BASIC* on several early personal computers. BASIC (Beginner's All-Purpose Symbolic Instruction Code) is a programming language developed in the mid-1960s by Professors John Kemeny and Thomas Kurtz of Dartmouth College as a language for writing simple programs. BASIC's primary purpose was to familiarize novices with programming techniques. The natural evolution from BASIC to Visual Basic was introduced in 1991 as a result of the development of the Microsoft Windows graphical user interface (GUI) in the late 1980s and the early 1990s.

Although Visual Basic is derived from the BASIC programming language, it is a distinctly different language that offers such powerful features as graphical user interfaces, event handling, access to the *Windows 32-bit Application Programming Interface (Win32 API)*, object-oriented programming and error handling. Visual Basic is one of the most popular event-driven, visual programming interfaces.

The latest version of Visual Basic, called *Visual Basic .NET*[1], is designed for Microsoft's new programming platform, .NET. Earlier versions of Visual Basic provided object-oriented capabilities, but Visual Basic .NET offers enhanced object orientation and makes use of the powerful library of reusable software components in .NET.

Around the same time that Visual Basic was being developed, many individuals projected that intelligent consumer-electronic devices would be the next major market in which microprocessors would have a profound impact. Recognizing this, Sun Microsystems in 1991 funded an internal corporate research project code-named Green. The project

---

1. The reader interested in Visual Basic .NET may want to consider our book, *Visual Basic .NET How to Program, Second Edition.*

resulted in the development of a language based on C and C++. Although the language's creator, James Gosling, called it Oak (after an oak tree outside his window at Sun), it was later discovered that a computer language called Oak already existed. When a group of Sun employees visited a local coffee place, the name Java was suggested, and it stuck.

Unfortunately, the Green project ran into some difficulties. The marketplace for intelligent consumer-electronic devices was not developing as quickly as Sun had anticipated. Worse yet, a major contract for which Sun competed was awarded to another company. The project was, at this point, in danger of being canceled. By sheer good fortune, the World Wide Web exploded in popularity in 1993, and Sun saw immediate potential for using Java to design *dynamic content* (i.e., animated and interactive content) for Web pages.

Sun formally announced Java at a conference in May 1995. Ordinarily, an event like this would not generate much publicity. However, Java grabbed the immediate attention of the business community because of the new, widespread interest in the World Wide Web. Developers now use Java to create Web pages with dynamic content, to build large-scale enterprise applications, to enhance the functionality of World Wide Web servers (the computers that provide the content distributed to our Web browsers when we browse Web sites), to provide applications for consumer devices (e.g., cell phones, pagers and PDAs) and for many other purposes.

1.8 C#

The advancement of programming tools (e.g., C++ and Java) and consumer-electronic devices (e.g., cell phones) created problems and new requirements. The integration of software components from various languages proved difficult, and installation problems were common because new versions of shared components were incompatible with old software. Developers also discovered they needed Web-based applications that could be accessed and used via the Internet. As a result of mobile electronic device popularity, software developers realized that their clients were no longer restricted to desktop computers. Developers recognized the need for software that was accessible to anyone and available via almost any type of device. To address these needs, Microsoft announced its *.NET* (pronounced "dot-net") *initiative* and the *C#* (pronounced "C-Sharp") programming language.

The *.NET platform* is one over which Web-based applications can be distributed to a great variety of devices (even cell phones) and to desktop computers. The platform offers a new software-development model that allows applications created in disparate programming languages to communicate with each other. The C# programming language, developed at Microsoft by a team led by Anders Hejlsberg and Scott Wiltamuth, was designed specifically for the .NET platform as a language that would enable programmers to migrate easily to .NET. This migration is made easy due to the fact that C# has roots in C, C++ and Java, adapting the best features of each and adding new features of its own. Because C# has been built upon such widely used and well-developed languages, programmers will find learning C# to be easy and enjoyable.

C# is an event-driven, fully object-oriented, visual programming language in which programs are created using an *Integrated Development Environment* (*IDE*). With the IDE, a programmer can create, run, test and debug C# programs conveniently, thereby reducing the time it takes to produce a working program to a fraction of the time it would have taken without using the IDE. The process of rapidly creating an application using an IDE is typically referred to as *Rapid Application Development (RAD)*.

C# also enables a new degree of language interoperability: Software components from different languages can interact as never before. Developers can package even old software to work with new C# programs. In addition, C# applications can interact via the Internet, using industry standards such as the Simple Object Access Protocol (SOAP) and XML, which we discuss in Chapter 18, Extensible Markup Language (XML). The programming advances embodied in .NET and C# will lead to a new style of programming, in which applications are created from building blocks available over the Internet.

1.9 Other High-Level Languages

Although hundreds of high-level languages have been developed, only a few have achieved broad acceptance. This section overviews several languages that, like BASIC, are long-standing and popular high-level languages. IBM Corporation developed Fortran (FORmula TRANslator) between 1954 and 1957 to create scientific and engineering applications that require complex mathematical computations. Fortran is still widely used.

COBOL (COmmon Business Oriented Language) was developed in 1959 by a group of computer manufacturers in conjunction with government and industrial computer users. COBOL is used primarily for commercial applications that require the precise and efficient manipulation of large amounts of data. A considerable portion of today's business software is still programmed in COBOL. Approximately one million programmers are actively writing in COBOL.

Pascal was designed in the late 1960s by Professor Nicklaus Wirth and was intended for academic use. We explore Pascal in the next section.

1.10 Structured Programming

During the 1960s, many large software-development efforts encountered severe difficulties. Development typically ran behind schedule, costs greatly exceeded budgets and the finished products were unreliable. People began to realize that software development was a far more complex activity than they had imagined. Research activity, intended to address these issues, resulted in the evolution of *structured programming*—a disciplined approach to the creation of programs that are clear, demonstrably correct and easy to modify.

One of the more tangible results of this research was the development of the *Pascal* programming language in 1971. Pascal, named after the seventeenth-century mathematician and philosopher Blaise Pascal, was designed for teaching structured programming in academic environments and rapidly became the preferred introductory programming language in most universities. Unfortunately, because the language lacked many features needed to make it useful in commercial, industrial and government applications, it was not widely accepted in these environments. By contrast, C, which also arose from research on structured programming, did not have the limitations of Pascal, and programmers quickly adopted it.

The *Ada* programming language was developed under the sponsorship of the United States Department of Defense (DOD) during the 1970s and early 1980s. Hundreds of programming languages were being used to produce DOD's massive command-and-control software systems. DOD wanted a single language that would meet its needs. Pascal was chosen as a base, but the final Ada language is quite different from Pascal. The language was named after Lady Ada Lovelace, daughter of the poet Lord Byron. Lady Lovelace is generally credited with writing the world's first computer program, in the early 1800s (for the Analytical Engine mechanical computing device designed by Charles Babbage). One important capability of Ada is *multitasking*, which allows programmers to specify that many activities are to occur in parallel. As we will see in Chapter 14, C# offers a similar capability, called *multithreading*.

1.11 Key Software Trend: Object Technology

One of the authors, HMD, remembers the great frustration felt in the 1960s by software-development organizations, especially those developing large-scale projects. During the summers of his undergraduate years, HMD had the privilege of working at a leading computer vendor on the teams developing time-sharing, virtual-memory operating systems. It was a great experience for a college student, but, in the summer of 1967, reality set in. The company "decommitted" from producing as a commercial product the particular system that hundreds of people had been working on for several years. It was difficult to get this software right. Software is "complex stuff."

As the benefits of structured programming (and the related disciplines of *structured systems analysis and design*) were realized in the 1970s, improved software technology did begin to appear. However, it was not until the technology of object-oriented programming became widely used in the 1980s and 1990s that software developers finally felt they had the necessary tools to improve the software-development process dramatically.

Actually, object technology dates back to at least the mid-1960s, but no broad-based programming language incorporated the technology until C++. Although not strictly an object-oriented language, C++ absorbed the capabilities of C and incorporated Simula's ability to create and manipulate objects. C++ was never intended for widespread use beyond the research laboratories at AT&T, but grass-roots support rapidly developed for the hybrid language.

What are objects, and why are they special? Object technology is a packaging scheme that facilitates the creation of meaningful software units. These units are large and focused on particular applications areas. There are date objects, time objects, paycheck objects, invoice objects, audio objects, video objects, file objects, record objects and so on. In fact, almost any noun can be reasonably represented as a software object. Objects have *properties* (i.e., *attributes*, such as color, size and weight) and perform *actions* (i.e., *behaviors*, such as moving, sleeping or drawing). Classes represent groups of related objects. For example, all cars belong to the "car" class, even though individual cars vary in make, model, color and options packages. A class specifies the general format of its objects; the properties and actions available to an object depend on its class.

We live in a world of objects. Just look around you—there are cars, planes, people, animals, buildings, traffic lights, elevators and so on. Before object-oriented languages appeared, *procedural programming languages* (such as Fortran, Pascal, BASIC and C) focused on actions (verbs) rather than things or objects (nouns). We live in a world of objects, but earlier programming languages forced individuals to program primarily with verbs. This paradigm shift made program writing a bit awkward. However, with the advent of popular object-oriented languages, such as C++, Java and C#, programmers can program in an object-oriented manner that reflects the way in which they perceive the world. This process, which seems more natural than procedural programming, has resulted in significant productivity gains.

One of the key problems with procedural programming is that the program units created do not mirror real-world entities effectively and therefore are not particularly reusable. Programmers often write and rewrite similar software for various projects. This wastes precious time and money as people repeatedly "reinvent the wheel." With object technology, properly designed software entities (called objects) can be reused on future projects. Using libraries of reusable componentry can greatly reduce the amount of effort required to implement certain kinds of systems (as compared to the effort that would be required to reinvent these capabilities in new projects). C# programmers use the .NET Framework Class Library (known commonly as the FCL).

Some organizations report that software reusability is not, in fact, the key benefit of object-oriented programming. Rather, they indicate that object-oriented programming tends to produce software that is more understandable because it is better organized and has fewer maintenance requirements. As much as 80 percent of software costs are not associated with the original efforts to develop the software, but instead are related to the continued evolution and maintenance of that software throughout its lifetime. Object orientation allows programmers to abstract the details of software and focus on the "big picture." Rather than worrying about minute details, the programmer can focus on the behaviors and interactions of objects. A roadmap that showed every tree, house and driveway would be difficult, if not impossible, to read. When such details are removed and only the essential information (roads) remains, the map becomes easier to understand. In the same way, a program that is divided into objects is easy to understand, modify and update because it hides much of the detail. It is clear that object-oriented programming will be the key programming methodology for at least the next decade.

Software Engineering Observation 1.1

Use a building-block approach to creating programs. By using existing pieces in new projects, programmers avoid reinventing the wheel. This is called software reuse, *and it is central to object-oriented programming.*

[*Note*: We will include many of these *Software Engineering Observations* throughout the text to explain concepts that affect and improve the overall architecture and quality of a software system and, particularly, of large software systems. We will also highlight *Good Programming Practices* (practices that can help you write programs that are clearer, more understandable, more maintainable and easier to test and debug), *Common Programming Errors* (problems to watch for to ensure that you do not make these same errors in your programs), *Performance Tips* (techniques that will help you write programs that run faster and use less memory), *Portability Tips* (techniques that will help you write programs that can run, with little or no modification, on a variety of computers), *Testing and Debugging Tips* (techniques that will help you remove bugs from your programs and, more importantly, write bug-free programs in the first place) and *Look-and-Feel Observations* (techniques that will help you design the "look and feel" of your graphical user interfaces for appearance and ease of use). Many of these techniques and practices are only guidelines; you will, no doubt, develop your own preferred programming style.]

The advantage of creating your own code is that you will know exactly how it works. The code will be yours to examine, modify and improve. The disadvantage is the time and effort that goes into designing, developing and testing new code.

Performance Tip 1.1

Reusing proven code components instead of writing your own versions can improve program performance, because these components normally are written to perform efficiently.

Software Engineering Observation 1.2

Extensive class libraries of reusable software components are available over the Internet and the World Wide Web; many are offered free of charge.

1.12 Hardware Trends

Every year, people generally expect to pay at least a little more for most products and services. The opposite has been the case in the computer and communications fields, especially with regard to the costs of hardware supporting these technologies. For many decades, and continuing into the foreseeable future, hardware costs have fallen rapidly, if not precipitously. Every year or two, the capacities of computers approximately double.[2] This is especially true in relation to the amount of memory that computers have for programs, the amount of secondary storage (such as disk storage) computers have to hold programs and data over longer periods of time and their processor speeds—the speeds at which computers execute their programs (i.e., do their work). Similar improvements have occurred in the communications field, in which costs have plummeted as enormous demand for communications bandwidth (i.e., information-carrying capacity) has attracted tremendous competition. We know of no other fields in which technology moves so quickly and costs fall so rapidly. Such phenomenal improvement in the computing and communications fields is truly fostering the so-called *Information Revolution*.

When computer use exploded in the 1960s and 1970s, many discussed the dramatic improvements in human productivity that computing and communications would cause. However, these improvements did not materialize. Organizations were spending vast sums of capital on computers and employing them effectively, but without fully realizing the expected productivity gains. The invention of microprocessor chip technology and its wide deployment in the late 1970s and 1980s laid the groundwork for the productivity improvements that individuals and businesses have achieved in recent years.

1.13 History of the Internet and World Wide Web

In the late 1960s, one of the authors (HMD) was a graduate student at MIT. His research at MIT's Project Mac (now the Laboratory for Computer Science—the home of the World Wide Web Consortium) was funded by ARPA—the Advanced Research Projects Agency of the Department of Defense. ARPA sponsored a conference at which several dozen ARPA-funded graduate students were brought together at the University of Illinois at Urbana-Champaign to meet and share ideas. During this conference, ARPA rolled out the blueprints for networking the main computer systems of approximately a dozen ARPA-funded universities and research institutions. The computers were to be connected with communications lines operating at a then-stunning 56 Kbps (1 Kbps is equal to 1,024 bits per second), at a time when most people (of the few who had access to networking technologies) were connecting over telephone lines to computers at a rate of 110 bits per second.

---

2. This often is called *Moore's Law.*

HMD vividly recalls the excitement at that conference. Researchers at Harvard talked about communicating with the Univac 1108 "supercomputer," which was located across the country at the University of Utah, to handle calculations related to their computer graphics research. Many other intriguing possibilities were discussed. Academic research was about to take a giant leap forward. Shortly after this conference, ARPA proceeded to implement what quickly became called the *ARPAnet*, the grandparent of today's *Internet*.

Things worked out differently from the original plan. Although the ARPAnet did enable researchers to network their computers, its chief benefit proved to be the capability for quick and easy communication via what came to be known as *electronic mail (e-mail)*. This is true even on today's Internet, with e-mail, instant messaging and file transfer facilitating communications among hundreds of millions of people worldwide.

The network was designed to operate without centralized control. This meant that, if a portion of the network should fail, the remaining working portions would still be able to route data packets from senders to receivers over alternative paths.

The protocol (i.e., set of rules) for communicating over the ARPAnet became known as the *Transmission Control Protocol (TCP)*. TCP ensured that messages were properly routed from sender to receiver and that those messages arrived intact.

In parallel with the early evolution of the Internet, organizations worldwide were implementing their own networks to facilitate both intra-organization (i.e., within the organization) and inter-organization (i.e., between organizations) communication. A huge variety of networking hardware and software appeared. One challenge was to enable these diverse products to communicate with each other. ARPA accomplished this by developing the *Internet Protocol (IP),* which created a true "network of networks," the current architecture of the Internet. The combined set of protocols is now commonly called *TCP/IP*.

Initially, use of the Internet was limited to universities and research institutions; later, the military adopted the technology. Eventually, the government decided to allow access to the Internet for commercial purposes. When this decision was made, there was resentment among the research and military communities—it was felt that response times would become poor as "the Net" became saturated with so many users.

In fact, the opposite has occurred. Businesses rapidly realized that, by making effective use of the Internet, they could refine their operations and offer new and better services to their clients. Companies started spending vast amounts of money to develop and enhance their Internet presence. This generated fierce competition among communications carriers and hardware and software suppliers to meet the increased infrastructure demand. The result is that *bandwidth* (i.e., the information-carrying capacity of communications lines) on the Internet has increased tremendously, while hardware costs have plummeted. It is widely believed that the Internet played a significant role in the economic growth that many industrialized nations experienced over the last decade.

The *World Wide Web* allows computer users to locate and view multimedia-based documents (i.e., documents with text, graphics, animations, audios and/or videos) on almost any subject. Even though the Internet was developed more than three decades ago, the introduction of the World Wide Web (WWW) was a relatively recent event. In 1989, Tim Berners-Lee of CERN (the European Organization for Nuclear Research) began to develop a technology for sharing information via hyperlinked text documents. Basing the new language on the well-established *Standard Generalized Markup Language (SGML)*—a standard for business data interchange—Berners-Lee called his invention the *HyperText*

Markup Language (HTML). He also wrote communication protocols to form the backbone of his new hypertext information system, which he referred to as the *World Wide Web*.

Historians will surely list the Internet and the World Wide Web among the most important and profound creations of humankind. In the past, most computer applications ran on "stand-alone" computers (computers that were not connected to one another). Today's applications can be written to communicate among the world's hundreds of millions of computers. The Internet and World Wide Web merge computing and communications technologies, expediting and simplifying our work. They make information instantly and conveniently accessible to large numbers of people. They enable individuals and small businesses to achieve worldwide exposure. They are profoundly changing the way we do business and conduct our personal lives.

1.14 World Wide Web Consortium (W3C)

In October 1994, Tim Berners-Lee founded an organization, called the *World Wide Web Consortium (W3C)*, that is devoted to developing nonproprietary, interoperable technologies for the World Wide Web. One of the W3C's primary goals is to make the Web universally accessible—regardless of disabilities, language or culture.

The W3C is also a standardization organization and is comprised of three *hosts*—the Massachusetts Institute of Technology (MIT), France's INRIA (Institut National de Recherche en Informatique et Automatique) and Keio University of Japan—and over 400 members, including Deitel & Associates, Inc. Members provide the primary financing for the W3C and help provide the strategic direction of the Consortium. To learn more about the W3C, visit `www.w3.org`.

Web technologies standardized by the W3C are called *Recommendations*. Current W3C Recommendations include *Extensible HyperText Markup Language (XHTML™)*, *Cascading Style Sheets (CSS™)* and the *Extensible Markup Language (XML)*. Recommendations are not actual software products, but documents that specify the role, syntax and rules of a technology. Before becoming a W3C Recommendation, a document passes through three major phases: *Working Draft*—which, as its name implies, specifies an evolving draft; *Candidate Recommendation*—a stable version of the document that industry can begin to implement; and *Proposed Recommendation*—a Candidate Recommendation that is considered mature (i.e., has been implemented and tested over a period of time) and is ready to be considered for W3C Recommendation status. For detailed information about the W3C Recommendation track, see "6.2 The W3C Recommendation track" at

```
www.w3.org/Consortium/Process/Process-19991111/
process.html#RecsCR
```

1.15 Extensible Markup Language (XML)

As the popularity of the Web exploded, HTML's limitations became apparent. HTML's lack of *extensibility* (the ability to change or add features) frustrated developers, and its ambiguous definition allowed erroneous HTML to proliferate. In response to these problems, the W3C added limited extensibility to HTML. This was, however, only a temporary solution—the need for a standardized, fully extensible and structurally strict language was apparent. As a result, XML was developed by the W3C. XML combines the power and extensibility of its parent language, Standard Generalized Markup Language (SGML), with the simplicity that the Web community demands. At the same time, the W3C began developing XML-based standards for style sheets and advanced hyperlinking. *Extensible Stylesheet Language (XSL)* incorporates elements of both Cascading Style Sheets (CSS), which is used to format HTML documents and *Document Style and Semantics Specification Language (DSSSL)*, which is used to format SGML documents. Similarly, the *Extensible Linking Language (XLink)* combines ideas from *HyTime* and the *Text Encoding Initiative (TEI)*, to provide extensible linking of resources.

Data independence, the separation of content from its presentation, is the essential characteristic of XML. Because an XML document describes data, any application conceivably can process an XML document. Recognizing this, software developers are integrating XML into their applications to improve Web functionality and interoperability. XML's flexibility and power make it perfect for the middle tier of client/server systems, which must interact with a wide variety of clients. Much of the processing that was once limited to server computers now can be performed by client computers, because XML's semantic and structural information enables it to be manipulated by any application that can process text. This reduces server loads and network traffic, resulting in a faster, more efficient Web.

XML is not limited to Web applications. Increasingly, XML is being employed in databases—the structure of an XML document enables it to be integrated easily with database applications. As applications become more Web enabled, it seems likely that XML will become the universal technology for data representation. All applications employing XML would be able to communicate, provided that they could understand each other's XML markup, or *vocabulary*.

Simple Object Access Protocol (SOAP) is a technology for the distribution of objects (marked up as XML) over the Internet. Developed primarily by Microsoft and DevelopMentor, SOAP provides a framework for expressing application semantics, encoding that data and packaging it in modules. SOAP has three parts: The *envelope*, which describes the content and intended recipient of a SOAP message; the SOAP *encoding rules*, which are XML-based; and the SOAP *Remote Procedure Call (RPC) representation* for commanding other computers to perform a task. Microsoft .NET (discussed in the next two sections) uses XML and SOAP to mark up and transfer data over the Internet. XML and SOAP are at the core of .NET—they allow software components to interoperate (i.e., communicate easily with one another). SOAP is supported by many platforms, because of its foundations in XML and HTTP. We discuss XML in Chapter 18, Extensible Markup Language (XML) and SOAP in Chapter 21, ASP .NET and Web Services.

1.16 Introduction to Microsoft .NET

In June 2000, Microsoft announced its *.NET initiative*, a broad new vision for embracing the Internet and the Web in the development, engineering and use of software. One key aspect of the .NET strategy is its independence from a specific language or platform. Rather than forcing developers to use a single programming language, developers can create a .NET application in any .NET-compatible language. Programmers can contribute to the same software project, writing code in the .NET languages (such as C#, Visual C++ .NET, Visual Basic .NET and many others) in which they are most competent. Part of the initiative includes Microsoft's *Active Server Pages (ASP) .NET* technology, which allows programmers to create applications for the Web.

The .NET architecture can exist on multiple platforms, further extending the portability of .NET programs. In addition, the .NET strategy involves a new program-development process that could change the way programs are written and executed, leading to increased productivity.

A key component of the .NET architecture is *Web services*, which are applications that can be used over the Internet. Clients and other applications can use these Web services as reusable building blocks. One example of a Web service is Dollar Rent a Car's reservation system.[3] An airline partner wanted to enable customers to make rental-car reservations from the airline's Web site. To do so, the airline needed to access Dollar's reservation system. In response, Dollar created a Web service that allowed the airline to access Dollar's database and make reservations. Web services enable the two companies to communicate over the Web, even though the airline uses UNIX systems and Dollar uses Microsoft Windows. Dollar could have created a one-time solution for that particular airline, but the company would not have been able to reuse such a customized system. By creating a Web service, Dollar can allow other airlines or hotels to use its reservation system without creating a custom program for each relationship.

The .NET strategy extends the concept of software reuse to the Internet, allowing programmers to concentrate on their specialties without having to implement every component of every application. Instead, companies can buy Web services and devote their time and energy to developing their products. The .NET strategy further extends the concept of software reuse to the Internet by allowing programmers to concentrate on their specialties without having to implement every component. Visual programming (discussed in Chapter 2) has become popular, because it enables programmers to create applications easily, using such prepackaged components as buttons, text boxes and scrollbars. Similarly, programmers may create an application using Web services for databases, security, authentication, data storage and language translation without having to know the internal details of those components.

The .NET strategy incorporates the idea of software reuse. When companies link their products in this way, a new user experience emerges. For example, a single application could manage bill payments, tax refunds, loans and investments, using Web services from various companies. An online merchant could buy Web services for online credit-card payments, user authentication, network security and inventory databases to create an e-commerce Web site.

The keys to this interaction are XML and SOAP, which enable Web services to communicate. XML gives meaning to data, and SOAP is the protocol that allows Web services to communicate easily with one another. XML and SOAP act as the "glue" that combines various Web services to form applications.

Universal data access is another essential concept in the .NET strategy. If two copies of a file exist (such as on a personal and a company computer), the less recent version must constantly be updated—this is called file *synchronization*. If the separate versions of the file are different, they are *unsynchronized*, a situation that could lead to errors. Under .NET, data could reside in one central location rather than on separate systems. Any Internet-connected device could access the data (under tight control, of course), which would then be

---

3. Microsoft Corporation, "Dollar Rent A Car E-Commerce Case Study on Microsoft Business," 1 July 2001 `<www.microsoft.com/BUSINESS/casestudies/b2c/dollarrentac-ar.asp>`.

formatted appropriately for use or display on the accessing device. Thus, the same document could be seen and edited on a desktop PC, a PDA, a cell phone or other device. Users would not need to synchronize the information, because it would be fully up-to-date in a central area.

Microsoft's *HailStorm Web services* facilitate such data organization.[4] HailStorm allows users to store data so that it is accessible from any HailStorm-compatible device (such as a PDA, desktop computer or cell phone). HailStorm offers a suite of services, such as an address book, e-mail, document storage, calendars and a digital wallet. Third-party Web services also can interact with HailStorm—users can be notified when they win online auctions or have their calendars updated if their planes arrive late. Information can be accessed from anywhere and cannot become unsynchronized. Privacy concerns increase, though, because all of a user's data resides in one location. Microsoft has addressed this issue by giving users control over their data. Users must authorize access to their data and specify the duration of that access.

Microsoft plans to create Internet-based client applications. For example, software could be distributed over the Internet on a *subscription basis*, enabling immediate corrections, updates and communication with other applications over the Internet. HailStorm provides basic services at no charge and users can pay via subscription for more advanced features.

The .NET strategy is an immense undertaking. We discuss various aspects of .NET throughout this book. Additional information is available on Microsoft's Web site (**www.microsoft.com/net**).

1.17 .NET Framework and the Common Language Runtime

The Microsoft® *.NET Framework* is at the heart of the .NET strategy. This framework manages and executes applications and Web services, contains a class library (called the *Framework Class Library* or *FCL*), enforces security and provides many other programming capabilities. The details of the .NET Framework are found in the *Common Language Specification* (*CLS*), which contains information about the storage of data types, objects and so on. The CLS has been submitted for standardization to ECMA (the European Computer Manufacturers Association), making it easier to create the .NET Framework for other platforms. This is like publishing the blueprints of the framework—anyone can build it, following the specifications. Currently, the .NET Framework exists only for the Windows platform, although a version is under development for the FreeBSD operating system.[5] The FreeBSD project provides a freely available and open-source UNIX-like operating system that is based on that UC Berkeley's *Berkeley System Distribution* (BSD).

The *Common Language Runtime (CLR)* is another central part of the .NET Framework—it executes C# programs. Programs are compiled into machine-specific instructions in two steps. First, the program is compiled into *Microsoft Intermediate Language (MSIL)*, which defines instructions for the CLR. Code converted into MSIL from other languages and sources can be woven together by the CLR. Then, another compiler in the CLR compiles the MSIL into machine code (for a particular platform), creating a single application.

---

4. Microsoft Corporation, "Building User-Centric Experiences: An Introduction to Microsoft Hail-Storm," 30 July 2001 <**http://www.microsoft.com/net/hailstorm.asp**>.
5. Microsoft Corporation, "The Microsoft Shared Source C# and CLI Specifications," 30 July 2001 <**http://www.microsoft.com/net/sharedsourcewp.asp**>.

Why bother having the extra step of converting from C# to MSIL, instead of compiling directly into machine language? The key reasons are portability between operating systems, interoperability between languages and execution-management features such as memory management and security.

If the .NET Framework exists (and is installed) for a platform, that platform can run any .NET program. The ability of a program to run (without modification) across multiple platforms is known as *platform independence*. Code written once can be used on another machine without modification, saving both time and money. In addition, software can target a wider audience—previously, companies had to decide whether converting their programs to different platforms (sometimes called *porting*) was worth the cost. With .NET, porting is no longer an issue.

The .NET Framework also provides a high level of *language interoperability*. Programs written in different languages are all compiled into MSIL—the different parts can be combined to create a single, unified program. MSIL allows the .NET Framework to be *language independent*, because .NET programs are not tied to a particular programming language. Any language that can be compiled into MSIL is called a *.NET-compliant language*. Figure 1.1 lists many of the current languages that support the .NET platform.[6]

Language interoperability offers many benefits to software companies. C#, Visual Basic .NET and Visual C++ .NET developers, for example, can work side-by-side on the same project without having to learn another programming language—all their code compiles into MSIL and links together to form one program. In addition, the .NET Framework can package old and new components to work together. This allows companies to reuse the code that they have spent years developing and integrate it with the new .NET code that they write. Integration is crucial, because companies cannot migrate easily to .NET unless they can stay productive, using their existing developers and software.

Programming Languages	
APL	Oberon
C#	Oz
COBOL	Pascal
Component Pascal	Perl
Curriculum	Python
Eiffel	RPG
Fortran	Scheme
Haskell	Smalltalk
Java	Standard ML
JScript	Visual Basic .NET
Mercury	Visual C++ .NET

Fig. 1.1   .NET Languages .

---

6. Table information from Microsoft Web site, **www.microsoft.com**.

Another benefit of the .NET Framework is the CLR's execution-management features. The CLR manages memory, security and other features, relieving the programmer of these responsibilities. With languages like C++, programmers must take memory management into their own hands. This leads to problems if programmers request memory and never return it—programs could consume all available memory, which would prevent applications from running. By managing the program's memory, the .NET Framework allows programmers to concentrate on program logic.

The .NET Framework also provides programmers with a huge library of classes. This library, called the Framework Class Library (FCL), can be used by any .NET language. The FCL contains a variety of reusable components, saving programmers the trouble of creating new components. This book explains how to develop .NET software with C#. Steve Ballmer, Microsoft's CEO, stated in May 2001 that Microsoft was "betting the company" on .NET. Such a dramatic commitment surely indicates a bright future for C# and its community of developers.

1.18 Tour of the Book

In this section, we tour the chapters and appendices of *C# How to Program*. In addition to the topics presented in each chapter, several of the chapters contain an Internet and World Wide Web Resources section that lists additional sources from which readers can enhance their knowledge of C# programming.

Chapter 1—Introduction to Computers, Internet, World Wide Web and C#
The first chapter familiarizes the reader with what computers are, how they work and how they are programmed. We explain the evolution of programming languages, from their origins in machine languages to the development of high-level, object-oriented languages. We overview the history of the Internet, World Wide Web and various technologies (such as HTTP, SOAP and XML) that have led to advances in how computers are used. We then discuss the development of the C# programming language and the Microsoft .NET initiative, including Web services. We explore the impact of .NET on software development and conclude by touring the remainder of the book.

Chapter 2—Introduction to the Visual Studio® .NET IDE
Chapter 2 introduces Microsoft Visual Studio .NET, an *integrated development environment* (*IDE*) for the creation of C# programs. Visual Studio .NET enables *visual programming*, in which *controls* (such as buttons or text boxes) are "dragged" and "dropped" into place, rather than added by typing code. Visual programming has led to greatly increased productivity of software developers because it eliminates many of the tedious tasks that programmers face. For example, object properties (information such as height and color) can be modified through Visual Studio .NET windows, allowing changes to be made quickly and causing the results to appear immediately on the screen. Rather than having to guess how the GUI will appear while writing a program, programmers view the GUI exactly as it will appear when the finished program runs. Visual Studio .NET also contains advanced tools for debugging, documenting and writing code. The chapter presents features of Visual Studio .NET, including its key windows, toolbox and help features and overviews the process of compiling and running programs. We provide an example of the capabilities of Visual Studio .NET by using it to create a simple Windows application without typing a single line of code.

Chapter 3—Introduction to C# Programming

This chapter introduces readers to our LIVE-CODE™ approach. Every concept is presented in the context of a complete working C# program and is followed by one or more sample outputs depicting the program's execution. In our first example, we print a line of text and carefully discuss each line of code. We then discuss fundamental tasks, such as how a program inputs data from its users and how to write arithmetic expressions. The chapter's last example demonstrates how to print a variety of character strings in a window called a message box.

Chapter 4—Control Structures: Part 1

This chapter formally introduces the principles of structured programming, a set of techniques that will help the reader develop clear, understandable, maintainable programs throughout the text. The first part of this chapter presents program-development and problem-solving techniques. The chapter demonstrates how to transform a written specification to a program by using such techniques as *pseudocode* and *top-down, stepwise refinement*. We then progress through the entire process, from developing a problem statement into a working C# program. The notion of algorithms is also discussed. We build on information presented in the previous chapter to create programs that are interactive (i.e., they change their behavior to suit user-supplied inputs). The chapter then introduces the use of control structures that affect the sequence in which statements are executed. Control structures produce programs that are easily understood, debugged and maintained. We discuss the three forms of program control—sequence, selection and repetition—focusing on the **if/then** and **while** control structures. Flowcharts (i.e., graphical representations of algorithms) appear throughout the chapter, reinforcing and augmenting the explanations.

Chapter 5—Control Structures: Part 2

Chapter 5 introduces more complex control structures and the logical operators. It uses flowcharts to illustrate the flow of control through each control structure, including the **for**, **do/while** and **switch** structures. We explain the **break** and **continue** statements and the logical operators. Examples include calculating compound interest and printing the distribution of grades on an exam (with some simple error checking). The chapter concludes with a structured programming summary, including each of C#'s control structures. The techniques discussed in Chapters 4 and 5 constitute a large part of what has been taught traditionally under the topic of structured programming.

Chapter 6—Methods

A *method* allows the programmer to create a block of code that can be called upon from various points in a program. Groups of related methods can be separated into functional blocks (classes), using the "divide and conquer" strategy. Programs are divided into simple components that interact in straightforward ways. We discuss how to create our own methods that can take input, perform calculations and return output. We examine the .NET library's **Math** class, which contains methods (i.e., methods in a class) for performing complex calculations (e.g., trigonometric and logarithmic calculations). *Recursive* methods (methods that call themselves) and method overloading, which allows multiple methods to have the same name, are introduced. We demonstrate overloading by creating two **Square** methods that take an integer (i.e., whole number) and a floating-point number (i.e., a number with a decimal point), respectively. To conclude the chapter, we create a graphical simulation of the "craps" dice game, using the random-number generation techniques presented in the chapter.

Chapter 7—Arrays

Chapter 7 discusses arrays, our first data structures. (Chapter 24 discusses the topic of data structures in depth.) Data structures are crucial to storing, sorting, searching and manipulating large amounts of information. *Arrays* are groups of related data items that allow the programmer to access any element directly. Rather than creating 100 separate variables that are all related in some way, the programmer instead can create an array of 100 elements and access these elements by their location in the array. We discuss how to declare and allocate arrays, and we build on the techniques of the previous chapter by passing arrays to methods. In addition, we discuss how to pass a variable number of arguments to methods. Chapters 4 and 5 provide essential background for the discussion of arrays, because repetition structures are used to iterate through elements in the array. The combination of these concepts helps the reader create highly-structured and well-organized programs. We then demonstrate how to sort and search arrays. We discuss multidimensional arrays (both rectangular and jagged), which can be used to store tables of data.

Chapter 8—Object-Based Programming

Chapter 8 serves as our introduction into the powerful concepts of objects and *classes* (classes are programmer-defined types). As mentioned in Chapter 1, object technology has led to considerable improvements in software development, allowing programmers to create reusable components. In addition, objects allow programs to be organized in natural and intuitive ways. In this chapter, we present the fundamentals of object-based programming, such as encapsulation, data abstraction and abstract data types (ADTs). These techniques hide the details of components so that the programmer can concentrate on the "big picture." To demonstrate these concepts, we create a time class, which displays the time in standard and military formats. Other topics examined include abstraction, composition, reusability and inheritance. We overview how to create reusable software components with assemblies, namespaces and Dynamic Link Library (DLL) files. You will learn how to create classes like those in the Framework Class Library. Other C# features discussed include properties and the **readonly** and **const** keywords. This chapter lays the groundwork for the next two chapters, which introduce object-oriented programming.

Chapter 9—Object-Oriented Programming: Inheritance

In this chapter, we discuss inheritance—a form of software reusability in which classes (called *derived classes*) are created by absorbing attributes and methods of existing classes (called *base classes*). The inherited class (i.e., the derived class) can contain additional attributes and methods. We show how finding the commonality between classes of objects can reduce the amount of work it takes to build large software systems. These proven techniques help programmers create and maintain software systems. A detailed case study demonstrates software reuse and good programming techniques by finding the commonality among a three-level inheritance hierarchy: the point, circle and cylinder classes. We discuss the software engineering benefits of object-oriented programming. The reader learns important object-oriented programming fundamentals, such as creating and extending customized classes.

Chapter 10—Object-Oriented Programming: Polymorphism

Chapter 10 continues our formal introduction of object-oriented programming. We discuss polymorphic programming and its advantages. *Polymorphism* permits classes to be treated in a general manner, allowing the same method call to act differently depending on context (e.g., "move" messages sent to a bird and a fish result in dramatically different types of action—a bird flies and a fish swims). In addition to treating existing classes in a general manner, polymorphism allows new classes to be added to a system easily. We identify situations in which polymorphism is useful. A payroll system case study demonstrates polymorphism—the system determines the wages for each employee differently to suit the type of employee (bosses paid fixed salaries, hourly workers paid by the hour, commission workers who receive a base salary plus commission and piece workers who are paid per item produced). These programming techniques and those of the previous chapter allow the programmer to create extensible and reusable software components.

Chapter 11—Exception Handling
Exception handling is one of the most important topics in C# from the standpoint of building mission-critical and business-critical applications. People can enter incorrect data, data can be corrupted and clients can try to access records that do not exist or are restricted. A simple division-by-zero error may cause a calculator program to crash, but what if such an error occurs in the navigation system of a flying airplane? Programmers must deal with these situations, because in some cases, the results of program failure could be disastrous. Programmers need to know how to recognize the errors (*exceptions*) that could occur in software components and handle those exceptions effectively, allowing programs to deal with problems and continue executing instead of "crashing." This chapter overviews the proper use of exception handling and various exception-handling techniques. We cover the details of C# exception handling, the termination model of exception handling, throwing and catching exceptions, and library class **Exception**. Programmers who construct software systems from reusable components built by other programmers often deal with the exceptions that those components may throw.

Chapter 12—Graphical User Interface Concepts: Part 1
Chapter 12 explains how to add graphical user interfaces (GUIs) to our programs, providing a professional look and feel. By using the techniques of rapid application development (RAD), we can create a GUI from reusable components, rather than explicitly programming every detail. The Visual Studio .NET IDE makes developing GUIs even easier by allowing the programmer to position components in a window through so-called visual programming. We discuss how to construct user interfaces with *Windows Forms* GUI components such as labels, buttons, text boxes, scroll bars and picture boxes. We also introduce *events*, which are messages sent by a program to signal to an object or a set of objects that an action has occurred. Events are most commonly used to signal user interactions with GUI components, but also can signal internal actions in a program. We overview event handling and discuss how to handle events specific to controls, the keyboard and the mouse. Tips are included throughout the chapter to help the programmer create visually appealing, well-organized and consistent GUIs.

Chapter 13—Graphical User Interface Concepts: Part 2
Chapter 13 introduces more complex GUI components, including menus, link labels, panels, list boxes, combo boxes and tab controls. In a challenging exercise, readers create an application that displays a disk drive's directory structure in a tree—similar to that created by Windows Explorer. The *Multiple Document Interface* (*MDI*) is presented, which allows

multiple documents (i.e., forms) to be open simultaneously in a single GUI. We conclude with a discussion of how to create custom controls by combining existing controls. The techniques presented in this chapter allow readers to create sophisticated and well-organized GUIs, adding style and usability to their applications.

Chapter 14—Multithreading

We have come to expect much from our applications. We want to download files from the Internet, listen to music, print documents and browse the Web—all at the same time! To do this, we need a technique called *multithreading*, which allows applications to perform multiple activities concurrently. C# includes built-in capabilities to enable multithreaded applications, while shielding programmers from complex details. C# is better equipped to deal with more sophisticated multimedia, network-based and multiprocessor-based applications than other languages that do not have multithreading features. This chapter overviews the built-in threading classes of C# and covers threads, thread life-cycles, time-slicing, scheduling and priorities. We analyze the producer-consumer relationship, thread synchronization and circular buffers. This chapter lays the foundation for creating the impressive multithreaded programs that clients demand.

Chapter 15—Strings, Characters and Regular Expressions

In this chapter, we discuss the processing of words, sentences, characters and groups of characters. In C#, **string**s (groups of characters) are objects. This is yet another benefit of C#'s emphasis on object-oriented programming. Objects of type **string** contain methods that can copy, create hash codes, search, extract substrings and concatenate strings with one another. As an interesting example of strings, we create a card shuffling-and-dealing simulation. We discuss regular expressions, a powerful tool for searching and manipulating text.

Chapter 16—Graphics and Multimedia

In this chapter, we discuss *GDI+* (an extension of the *Graphics Device Interface—GDI*), the Windows service that provides the graphical features used by .NET. The extensive graphical capabilities of GDI+ can make programs more visual and fun to create and use. We discuss C#'s treatment of graphics objects and color control, and we discuss how to draw arcs, polygons and other shapes. We use various pens and brushes to create color effects and include an example demonstrating gradient fills and textures. This chapter introduces techniques for turning text-only applications into exciting, aesthetically pleasing programs that even novice programmers can write with ease. The second half of the chapter focuses on audio, video and speech technology. We discuss adding sound, video and animated characters to programs (primarily using existing audio and video clips). You will see how easy it is to incorporate multimedia into C# applications. This chapter introduces an exciting technology called *Microsoft Agent* for adding *interactive animated characters* to a program. Each character allows users to interact with the application, using more natural human communication techniques, such as speech. The agent characters accept mouse and keyboard interaction, speak and hear (i.e., they support speech synthesis and speech recognition). With these capabilities, your applications can speak to users and actually respond to their voice commands!

Chapter 17—Files and Streams

Imagine a program that could not save data to a file. Once the program is closed, all the work performed in the program is lost forever. For this reason, this chapter is one of the most important for programmers who will be developing commercial applications. We explain how to input and output streams of data from and to files, respectively. We discuss how programs read and write data from and to secondary storage devices (such as disks). A detailed example demonstrates these concepts by allowing the user to read and write bank account information to and from files. We introduce those classes and methods in C# that help perform input and output conveniently—they demonstrate the power of object-oriented programming and reusable classes. We discuss benefits of sequential files, random-access files and buffering. This chapter is crucial for developing C# file-processing applications and networking applications (Chapter 22), which also use the techniques in this chapter to send and receive data.

Chapter 18—Extensible Markup Language (XML)[7]

The Extensible Markup Language (XML) derives from SGML (Standardized General Markup Language), which became an industry standard in 1986. Although SGML is employed in publishing applications worldwide, it has not been incorporated into the mainstream computing and information technology curricula because of its sheer size and complexity. XML is an effort to make SGML-like technology available to a much broader community. It was created by the World Wide Web Consortium (W3C) for describing data in a portable format, is one of most important technologies in industry today and is being integrated into almost every field. XML differs in concept from markup languages such as the HyperText Markup Language (HTML). HTML is a markup language for describing how information is rendered in a browser. XML is a language for creating markup languages for virtually any type of information. Document authors use XML to create entirely new markup languages to describe specific types of data, including mathematical formulas, chemical molecular structures, music and recipes. Markup languages created with XML include WML (Wireless Markup Language), XHTML (Extensible HyperText Markup Language, for Web content), MathML (for mathematics), VoiceXML™ (for speech), SMIL™ (Synchronized Multimedia Integration Language, for multimedia presentations), CML (Chemical Markup Language, for chemistry) and XBRL (Extensible Business Reporting Language, for financial data exchange). Companies and individuals constantly are finding new and exciting uses for XML. In this chapter, we present examples that illustrate the basics of marking up data with XML. We demonstrate several XML-derived markup languages, such as *XML Schema* (for checking an XML document's grammar), *XSLT (Extensible Stylesheet Language Transformations,* for transforming an XML document's data into another text-based format such as XHTML) and Microsoft's *BizTalk*™ (for marking up business transactions). (For readers who are unfamiliar with XHTML, we provide Appendices K and L, which provide a detailed introduction to XHTML.)

Chapter 19—Database, SQL and ADO .NET

Access and storage of data are integral to creating powerful software applications. This chapter discusses .NET support for database manipulation. Today's most popular database systems are relational databases. In this chapter, we introduce the Structured Query Language (SQL) for performing queries on relational databases. We introduce ADO .NET—an extension of Microsoft's ActiveX Data Objects that enables .NET applications to access and

---

7. The reader interested in a deeper treatment of XML may want to consider our book, *XML How to Program.*

manipulate databases. ADO .NET allows data to be exported as XML, which enables applications that use ADO .NET to communicate with a variety of programs that understand XML. The reader will learn how to create database connections, using tools provided in Visual Studio .NET, and will learn how to use the classes in the **System.Data** namespace.

Chapter 20—ASP .NET, Web Forms and Web Controls

Previous chapters demonstrated how to create applications that execute locally on the user's computer. In this chapter and the next, we discuss how to create Web-based applications using *Active Server Pages (ASP) .NET*. This is a crucial aspect of .NET and of Microsoft's vision of how software should be deployed on the Internet. ASP .NET is an integral technology for creating dynamic Web content marked up as HTML. (For readers who are unfamiliar with HTML, we provide a detailed introduction in Appendices I and J.) *Web Forms* provide GUIs for ASP .NET pages and can contain *Web controls*, such as labels, buttons and text boxes with which users interact. Like Windows Forms, Web Forms are designed using visual programming. This chapter presents many interesting examples, which include an online guest book application and a multi-tier, database intensive application that allows users to query a database for a list of publications by a specific author. Debugging Web Forms using the **Trace** property is also discussed.

Chapter 21—ASP .NET and Web Services

Chapter 21 continues our discussion of ASP .NET. In this chapter, we introduce *Web services*, which are programs that "expose" services (i.e., methods) to clients. Using Web services, programmers can create methods that anyone can invoke. This enables applications to invoke methods remotely over a network. Web services offer increased software reusability, making the Internet, in essence, a programming library available to programmers worldwide. Web services use XML and SOAP to mark up and send information, respectively. This chapter presents several interesting examples that include Web services for manipulating huge numbers (up to 100 digits), simulating the card game of blackjack and implementing an airline reservation system. One particularly interesting example is our temperature server, a Web service that gathers weather information for dozens of cities in the United States.

Chapter 22—Networking: Streams-Based Sockets and Datagrams

Chapter 22 introduces the fundamental techniques of C#-based networking—streams and datagrams. We demonstrate how streams-based *sockets* allow us to hide many networking details. With sockets, networking is as simple as if we were reading from and writing to a file. We also introduce *datagrams* in which packets of information are sent between programs. Each packet is addressed to its recipient and sent out to the network, which routes the packet to its destination. The examples in this chapter focus on communication between applications. One example demonstrates using streams-based sockets to communicate between two C# programs. Another similar example, sends datagrams between applications. We also show how to create a multithreaded-server application that can communicate multiple clients in parallel. In this client/server tic-tac-toe game, the server maintains the status of the game and two clients communicate with the server to play the game.

Chapter 23—Data Structures and Collections

This chapter discusses arranging data into aggregations such as linked lists, stacks, queues and trees. Each data structure has properties that are useful in a wide variety of applications, from sorting elements to keeping track of method calls. We discuss how to build each of these data structures. This is also a valuable experience in crafting useful classes. In addition, we cover prebuilt collection classes in the .NET Framework Class Library. These data structures have many useful methods for sorting, inserting, and deleting items, plus methods to enable data structures to resize themselves dynamically. When possible, C# programmers should use the Framework Class Library to find appropriate data structures, rather than implementing these data structures themselves. This chapter reinforces much of the object technology discussed in Chapters 8, 9 and 10, including classes, inheritance and composition.

Chapter 24—Accessibility

The World Wide Web presents a challenge to individuals with disabilities. Multimedia-rich Web sites are difficult for text readers and other programs to interpret; thus, users with hearing and visual impairments may have difficulty browsing such sites. To help rectify this situation, the World Wide Web Consortium (W3C) launched the *Web Accessibility Initiative (WAI)*, which provides guidelines for making Web sites accessible to people with disabilities. This chapter provides a description of these guidelines, such as the use of the **<head-ers>** tag to make tables more accessible to page readers, the **alt** attribute of the **<img>** tag to describe images, and XHTML and CSS to ensure that a page can be viewed on almost any type of display or reader. We illustrate key accessibility features of Visual Studio .NET and of Windows 2000. We also introduce *VoiceXML* and *CallXML*, two technologies for increasing the accessibility of Web-based content. VoiceXML helps people with visual impairments to access Web content via speech synthesis and speech recognition. CallXML allows users with visual impairments to access Web-based content through a telephone. In the chapter exercises, readers create their own voice mail applications, using CallXML.

Appendix A—Operator Precedence Chart

This appendix lists C# operators and their precedence.

Appendix B—Number Systems

This appendix explains the binary, octal, decimal and hexadecimal number systems. It also reviews the conversion of numbers among these bases and illustrates mathematical operations in each base.

Appendix C—Career Opportunities

This appendix provides career resources for C# programmers.

Appendix D—Visual Studio .NET Debugger

This appendix introduces the Visual Studio .NET debugger for locating logic errors in programs. Key features of this appendix include setting breakpoints, stepping through programs line-by-line and "watching" variable values.

Appendix E—Generating Documentation in Visual Studio

Appendix E discusses how to create comments within C# code that can be extracted to create powerful, XML-based documentation.

Appendix F—ASCII Character Set

This appendix contains a table of the 128 ASCII alphanumeric symbols and their corresponding ASCII (American Standard Code for Information Interchange) numbers.

Appendix G—Unicode®
This appendix introduces the Unicode Standard, an encoding scheme that assigns unique numeric values to the characters of most of the world's languages. We include a Windows application that uses Unicode encoding to print welcome messages in several different languages.

Appendix H—COM Integration
Prior to .NET, COM (Component Object Model) was critical for specifying how different Windows programming languages communicate at the binary level. For example, COM components such as ActiveX controls and ActiveX DLLs often were written in Microsoft Visual C++, but used in other programs. The .NET platform does not directly support COM components, but Microsoft provides tools for the integration of COM components with .NET applications. In this appendix, we explore some of these tools by integrating an ActiveX control and an ActiveX DLL into C# applications.

Appendices I and J—Introduction to HyperText Markup Language 4: 1 & 2 (on CD)
These appendices provide an introduction to *HTML*—the *Hypertext Markup Language*. HTML is a *markup language* for describing the elements of an HTML document (Web page) so that a browser, such as Microsoft's Internet Explorer, can render (i.e., display) that page. These appendices are included for our readers who do not know HTML or who would like a review of HTML before studying Chapter 20, ASP .NET, Web Forms and Web Controls. We do not present any C# programming in these appendices. Some key topics covered in Appendix I include: incorporating text and images in an HTML document, linking to other HTML documents on the Web, incorporating special characters (such as copyright and trademark symbols) into an HTML document and separating parts of an HTML document with horizontal lines (called *horizontal rules*). In Appendix J, we discuss more substantial HTML elements and features. We demonstrate how to present information in *lists* and *tables*. We discuss how to collect information from people browsing a site. We explain how to use *internal linking* and *image maps* to make Web pages easier to navigate. We also discuss how to use *frames* to display multiple documents in the browser window.

Appendices K and L—Introduction to XHTML: Parts 1 & 2 (on CD)
In these appendices, we introduce the Extensible Hypertext Markup Language (XHTML). XHTML is an emerging W3C technology designed to replace HTML as the primary means of describing Web content. As an XML-based language, XHTML is more robust and extensible than HTML. XHTML incorporates most of HTML 4's elements and attributes—the focus of these appendices. Appendices K and L are included for our readers who do not know XHTML or who would like a review of XHTML before studying Chapter 18, Extensible Markup Language (XML) and Chapter 24, Accessibility.

Appendix M—HTML/XHTML Special Characters (on CD)
This appendix provides many commonly used HTML/XHTML special characters, called *character entity references*.

Appendix N—HTML/XHTML Colors (on CD)
This appendix lists commonly used HTML/XHTML color names and their corresponding hexadecimal values.

Appendix O—Bit Manipulation
This appendix discusses C#'s powerful bit-manipulation capabilities. This helps programs process bit strings, set individual bits on or off and store information more compactly. Such capabilities—inherited from C—are characteristic of low-level assembly languages and are valued by programmers writing systems software, such as operating system and networking software.

1.19 Internet and World Wide Web Resources

www.deitel.com
This is the official Deitel & Associates, Inc. Web site. Here you will find updates, corrections, downloads and additional resources for all Deitel publications. In addition, this site provides information about Deitel & Associates, Inc. professional, on-site seminars offered worldwide. In the near future, you will be able to register here to receive the *Deitel Buzz* e-mail newsletter.

www.prenhall.com/deitel
This is Prentice Hall's Web site for Deitel publications, which contains information about our products and publications, downloads, Deitel curriculum and author information.

www.InformIT.com/deitel
This is the Deitel & Associates, Inc. page on the InformIT Web site. InformIT is an all-around resource for IT professionals providing articles, electronic publications and other resources for today's hottest technologies. The Deitel kiosk at InformIT.com will have free articles and for-purchase electronic publications. In addition, you can purchase all Deitel products at this site.

www.w3.org
The World Wide Web Consortium (W3C) is an organization that develops and recommends technologies for the Internet and World Wide Web. This site includes links to W3C technologies, news, mission statements and frequently asked questions (FAQs).

www.elsop.com/wrc/h_comput.htm
This site contains presents the history of computing, content about famous innovators, the evolution of languages and the development of operating systems.

www.w3.org/History.html
This site overviews the history of the Internet. After briefly covering developments from 1945–1988, the site details technological advances on a year-by-year basis, from 1989 to the present day.

www.netvalley.com/intval.html
This site presents the history of the Internet and the World Wide Web.

www.microsoft.com
The Microsoft Corporation Web site provides information and technical resources for all Microsoft products, including .NET, enterprise software and the Windows operating system.

SUMMARY

[This chapter is primarily a summary of the rest of the book, so we have not provided a summary section. The remaining chapters include detailed summaries of their contents.]

TERMINOLOGY

action	algorithm
"administrative" section of the computer	Apple Computer
Advanced Research Projects Agency (ARPA)	arithmetic and logic unit (ALU)

assembler
assembly language
bandwidth
batch
batch processing
building-block approach
C programming language
C# programming language
C++ programming language
calculation
Cascading Style Sheets (CSS)
central processing unit (CPU)
clarity
class
class libraries
Common Language Runtime (CLR)
Common Language Specification (CLS)
compiler
component
computation
computer
computer program
computer programmer
data
data independence
decision
disk
distributed computing
ECMA (European Computer
   Manufacturer's Association)
e-mail (electronic mail)
Framework Class Library (FCL)
functionalization
HailStorm Web service
hardware
hardware platform
high-level language
HTML (HyperText Markup Language)
HTTP (HyperText Transfer Protocol)
IBM (International Business Machines)
input device
input unit
Internet
interpreter
intranet
IP (Internet Protocol)
Java programming language
job
keyboard
language independence

language interoperability
live-code™ approach
logical decision
logical unit
machine dependent
machine language
maintenance of software
"manufacturing" section of the computer
memory
memory unit
Microsoft .NET
Microsoft Intermediate Language (MSIL)
mouse
multiprogramming
multitasking
.NET Framework
.NET initiative
.NET language
n-tier application
object
object-based programming
object-oriented language
object-oriented programming (OOP)
operating system
output device
output unit
Pascal programming language
personal computer
platform independence
portability
porting
primary memory
processing unit
program
programmer
property of an object
"receiving" section of the computer
reusable software component
screen
secondary storage
share the resources of a computer
"shipping" section of the computer
silicon chip
SOAP (Simple Object Access Protocol)
software
software component
software reuse
structured programming
subscription-based software
task

TCP (Transmission Control Protocol)
TCP/IP (Transmission Control
    Protocol/Internet Protocol)
terminal
throughput
timesharing
translator program
universal data access
UNIX
virtual-memory operating system
Visual Basic .NET programming language

visual programming
W3C (World Wide Web Consortium)
W3C Recommendation
"warehouse" section of the computer
Web Form
Web service
Web site
Win32 API (Windows 32-bit Application
    Programming Interface)
World Wide Web (WWW)
XML (Extensible Markup Language)

SELF-REVIEW EXERCISES

1.1   Fill in the blanks in each of the following statements:
- a) A computer can directly understand only its native _____ language, which is composed only of 1s and 0s.
- b) Computers process data under the control of sets of instructions called computer _____.
- c) SOAP is an acronym for _____.
- d) _____ is a technology derived from SGML that is used to create mark up languages.
- e) The three types of languages discussed in the chapter are machine languages, _____ and _____.
- f) Programs that translate high-level language programs into machine language are called _____.
- g) Visual Studio .NET is a/an _____ (IDE) in which C# programs are developed.
- h) C is widely known as the development language of the _____ operating system.
- i) The _____ provides a large programming library for .NET languages.
- j) The Department of Defense developed the Ada language with a capability called multitasking, which allows programmers to specify activities that can proceed in parallel. C# offers a similar capability called _____.
- k) Web services use _____ and _____ to mark up and send information over the Internet, respectively.

1.2   State whether each of the following is *true* or *false*. If *false*, explain why.
- a) Universal data access is an essential part of .NET.
- b) W3C standards are called recommendations.
- c) C# is an object-oriented language.
- d) The Common Language Runtime (CLR) requires that programmers manage their own memory.
- e) C# is the only language available for programming .NET applications.
- f) Procedural programming models the world more naturally than object-oriented programming.
- g) Computers can directly understand high-level languages.
- h) MSIL is the common intermediate format to which all .NET programs compile, regardless of their original .NET language.
- i) The .NET Framework is portable to non-Windows platforms.
- j) Compiled programs run faster than their corresponding interpreted programs.
- k) Throughput is the amount of work a computer can process in a given time period.

ANSWERS TO SELF-REVIEW EXERCISES

1.1 a) machine. b) programs. c) Simple Object Access Protocol. d) XML. e) assembly languages, high-level languages. f) compilers. g) integrated development environment (IDE). h) UNIX. i) Framework Class Library (FCL). j) multithreading. k) XML, SOAP.

1.2 a) True. b) True. c) True. d) False. The CLR handles memory management. e) False. C# is one of many .NET languages (others include Visual Basic and Visual C++). f) False. Object-oriented programming is a more natural way to model the world than is procedural programming. g) False. Computers can directly understand only their own machine languages. h) True. i) True. j) True. k) True.

EXERCISES

1.3 Categorize each of the following items as either hardware or software:
   a) CPU.
   b) Compiler.
   c) Input unit.
   d) A word-processor program.
   e) A Visual Basic .NET program.

1.4 Distinguish between the terms HTML, XML and XHTML.

1.5 Translator programs, such as assemblers and compilers, convert programs from one language (referred to as the source language) to another language (referred to as the object language or target language). Determine which of the following statements are *true* and which are *false*:
   a) An assembler translates source language programs into machine language programs.
   b) A compiler converts source-language programs into object-language programs.
   c) High-level languages are generally machine dependent.
   d) A machine-language program requires translation before it can be run on a computer.
   e) The Visual Basic .NET compiler translates a high-level language into SMIL.

1.6 What are the basic requirements of a .NET language? What is needed to run a .NET program on a new type of computer (machine)?

1.7 Expand each of the following acronyms:
   a) W3C.
   b) XML.
   c) SOAP.
   d) TCP/IP.
   e) OOP.
   f) CLR.
   g) CLS.
   h) FCL.
   i) MSIL.

1.8 What are the key benefits of the .NET Framework and the CLR? What are the drawbacks?

Introduction to the Visual Studio .NET IDE

Objectives

- To become familiar with the Visual Studio .NET integrated development environment (IDE).
- To become familiar with the types of commands contained in the IDE's menus and toolbars.
- To identify and understand the use of various kinds of windows in Visual Studio .NET.
- To understand the features provided by the **toolbox**.
- To understand Visual Studio .NET's help features.
- To be able to create, compile and execute a simple C# program.

Seeing is believing.
Proverb

Form ever follows function.
Louis Henri Sullivan

Intelligence… is the faculty of making artificial objects, especially tools to make tools.
Henri-Louis Bergson

Outline

2.1 Introduction

Visual Studio .NET is Microsoft's integrated development environment (IDE) for creating, documenting, running and debugging programs written in a variety of .NET programming languages. Visual Studio .NET also offers editing tools for manipulating several types of files. Visual Studio .NET is a powerful and sophisticated tool for creating business-critical and mission-critical applications. In this chapter, we provide an overview of the Visual Studio .NET features needed to create a simple C# program. We introduce additional IDE features throughout the book.

2.2 Visual Studio .NET Integrated Development Environment (IDE) Overview

When Visual Studio .NET is executed for the first time, the **Start Page** is displayed (Fig. 2.1). This page contains helpful links, which appear on the left side of the **Start Page**. Users can click the name of a section (such as **Get Started**) to browse its contents. We refer to single-clicking with the left mouse button as *selecting* or *clicking* and to clicking twice with the left mouse button as *double-clicking*. [*Note*: The user should be aware that there are slight differences in the way Visual Studio appears based on the version being used.]

The **Get Started** section contains links to recently opened projects. The most recently opened projects appear on this list (such as **WindowsApplication1** in Fig. 2.1), along with their modification dates. Alternately, the user can go to the select **Recent Projects** from the **File** menu. The first time Visual Studio .NET is loaded, this section will be empty. There are two *buttons* on the page: **Open Project** and **New Project**. A button is a raised, rectangular area that performs an action when clicked.

The **What's New** section displays new features and updates for Visual Studio .NET, including downloads for code samples and new programming tools. The **Online Community** section includes ways to contact other software developers, using newsgroups, Web pages and other online resources. The **Headlines** section provides a way to browse news,

Navigation buttons   Location bar

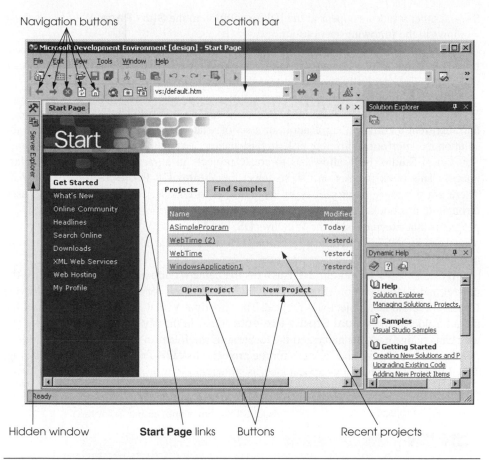

Hidden window   **Start Page** links   Buttons   Recent projects

Fig. 2.1   Start Page in Visual Studio .NET.

---

articles and how-to guides. Use the **Search Online** section to browse through the *MSDN* (*Microsoft Developer Network*) online library. The MSDN site includes numerous articles, downloads and tutorials for a variety of technologies. The **Downloads** section allows the user to obtain updates and code samples. The **XML Web Services** page provides programmers with information about *Web services*, which are reusable pieces of software available on the Internet. We discuss this technology in Chapter 21, ASP .NET and Web Services. **Web Hosting** provides information for developers who wish to post their software (such as Web services) online for public use. The **My Profile** page allows users to customize Visual Studio .NET, such as setting keyboard and window layout preferences. Users also can customize Visual Studio .NET selecting **Options...** or **Customize...** from the **Tools** menu. [*Note*: From this point forward, we use the **>** character to indicate the selection of a menu command. For example, we use the notation **Tools > Options...** and **Tools > Customize...** to indicate the selection of the **Options...** and **Customize...** commands, respectively.] Visual Studio .NET can even browse the Web—Internet Explorer is part of the IDE. To access a Web page, type its address into the location bar (see Fig. 2.1) and press the *Enter* key. [*Note*: The computer must be connected to the Internet.]

Several other windows appear in the IDE in addition to the **Start Page**. We discuss these windows in the following sections.

To create a new C# program, click the **New Project** button in the **Get Started** section. This action displays the *dialog* in Fig. 2.2. Dialogs are windows used to communicate with users. They typically contain buttons that allow the users to make decisions.

Visual Studio .NET organizes programs into *projects* and *solutions*. A project is a group of related files, such as C# code, images and documentation. A solution is a group of projects that represent a complete application, or a set of related applications. Each project in the solution may perform a different task. In this chapter, we create a single-project solution.

Visual Studio .NET allows us to create projects in a variety of programming languages. This book focuses on C#, so select the **Visual C# Projects** folder (Fig. 2.2). There are a variety of project types from which to choose, several of which are used throughout this book. In this case, create a *Windows application*. Windows applications are programs that execute inside the Windows OS, like Microsoft Word, Internet Explorer and Visual Studio .NET. Typically, they contain *controls*—graphical elements, such as buttons and labels—with which the user interacts.

By default, Visual Studio .NET assigns the name `WindowsApplication1` to the project and to the solution (Fig. 2.2). The default location for storing related files is the folder where the last project was created. The first time Visual Studio .NET executes, the default folder is the **Visual Studio Projects** folder in the **My Documents** folder. The user can change both the name and the location of the folder in which to save the project. After selecting a name and location for the project, click **OK** in the **New Project** dialog. The IDE will then change its appearance, as shown in Fig. 2.3.

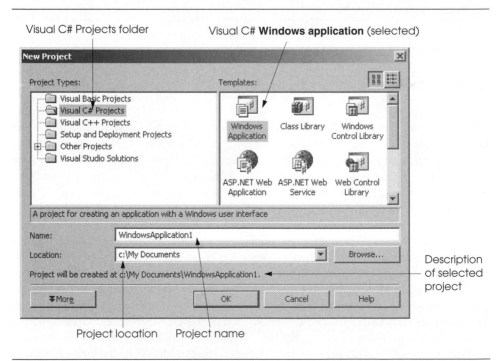

Fig. 2.2   New Project dialog.

Tabs   Menu   Title bar   Menu bar   **Solution Explorer**

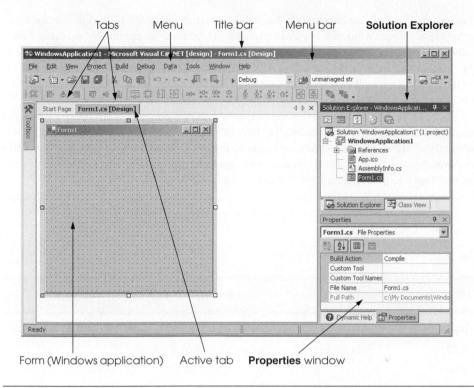

Form (Windows application)   Active tab   **Properties** window

Fig. 2.3   Visual Studio .NET environment after a new project has been created.

The gray rectangle represents the window for our application. This rectangle is called the *form*. We discuss how to add controls to the form later in this chapter. The form and controls are the *graphical user interface* (*GUI*) of the program. They are the graphical components through which the user interacts with the program. Users enter data (*inputs*) into the program by entering information from the keyboard and by clicking the mouse buttons. The program displays instructions and other information (*outputs*) for users to read in the GUI.

The top of the IDE window (the *title bar* in Fig. 2.3) displays **Windows-Application1 - Microsoft Visual C# .NET [design] - Form1.cs [Design]**. This title provides the name of the project (**WindowsApplication1**), the programming language (**Microsoft Visual C# .NET**), the *mode of the IDE* (**design** mode), the file being viewed (**Form1.cs**) and the mode of the file being viewed (**Design** mode). The file name **Form1.cs** is the default for Windows applications. We discuss the various modes in Section 2.6.

Notice how a tab appears for each open document. In our case, the documents are the **Start Page** and **Form1.cs [Design]**. To view a tabbed document, click the tab with the name of the document you wish to view. Tabbing saves space and allows easy access to multiple documents.

2.3 Menu Bar and Toolbar

Commands for managing the IDE and for developing, maintaining and executing programs are contained in the menus. Figure 2.4 shows the menus displayed on the menu bar. Menus contain groups of related commands that, when selected, cause the IDE to perform various actions (e.g., open a window). For example, new projects can be created by selecting **File > New > Project...** from the menu bar. The menus shown in Fig. 2.4 are summarized in Fig. 2.5. Visual Studio .NET provides different modes for the user. One of these modes is the design mode, which will be discussed later. Certain menu items appear only in specific IDE modes.

Rather than having to navigate the menus for certain commonly used commands, the programmer can access the commands from the *toolbar* (Fig. 2.6). The toolbar contains pictures called *icons* that represent commands. To execute a command, click its icon. Click the *down arrow* beside an icon to display other available options. Figure 2.6 shows the standard (default) toolbar and an icon that uses the down arrow.

File   Edit   View   Project   Build   Debug   Data   Format   Tools   Window   Help

Fig. 2.4   Visual Studio .NET menu bar.

Menu	Description
File	Contains commands for opening projects, closing projects, printing projects, etc.
Edit	Contains commands such as cut, paste, find, undo, etc.
View	Contains commands for displaying IDE windows and toolbars.
Project	Contains commands for adding features, such as forms, to the project.
Build	Contains commands for compiling a program.
Debug	Contains commands for debugging and executing a program.
Data	Contains commands for interacting with databases.
Format	Contains commands for arranging a form's controls.
Tools	Contains commands for additional IDE tools and options for customizing the environment.
Windows	Contains commands for arranging and displaying windows.
Help	Contains commands for getting help.

Fig. 2.5   Visual Studio .NET menu summary.

Toolbar icon (indicates a command to open a file)

Toolbar

Down arrow indicates additional commands

Fig. 2.6   Visual Studio .NET toolbar.

Holding the mouse pointer over an icon on the toolbar highlights that icon and displays a description called a *tool tip* (Fig. 2.7). Tool tips help users understand the purposes of unfamiliar icons.

2.4 Visual Studio .NET Windows

Visual Studio .NET provides users with windows for exploring files and customizing controls. In this section, we discuss the windows that are essential for developing C# applications. These windows can be accessed using the toolbar icons below the menu bar and on the right edge of the toolbar (Fig. 2.8), or by selecting the name of the desired window from the **View** menu.

2.4.1 Solution Explorer

The **Solution Explorer** window (Fig. 2.9) lists all the files in the solution. When Visual Studio .NET is first loaded, the **Solution Explorer** is empty—there are no files to display. After a new project has been created or an existing project has been loaded, the **Solution Explorer** displays that project's contents.

The *startup project* of the solution is the project that runs when the solution is executed. It appears in bold text in the **Solution Explorer**. For our single-project solution, the startup project (**WindowsApplication1**) is the only project. The C# file is **Form1.cs**; it contains the program's code. We discuss the other files and folders later in the book.

The plus and minus boxes to the left of the project and solution names expand and collapse the tree, respectively (similar to those in Windows Explorer). Click a plus box to display more options; click a minus box to collapse a tree that already is expanded. Users also can expand or collapse a tree by double-clicking the name of the folder. Many other Visual Studio .NET windows use the plus/minus convention as well.

Fig. 2.7 Tool tip demonstration.

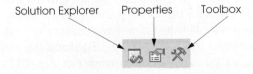

Fig. 2.8 Toolbar icons for various Visual Studio .NET windows.

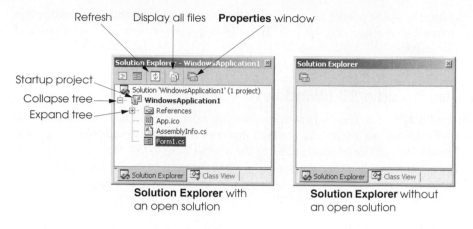

Fig. 2.9   Solution Explorer window.

The **Solution Explorer** contains a toolbar. One icon on the toolbar reloads the files in the solution (refreshes), and another icon displays all files in the solution (including hidden ones). The number of icons in the toolbar changes depending on the type of file selected. We discuss these icons later in the book.

2.4.2 Toolbox

The **Toolbox** (Fig. 2.10) contains reusable software components (or controls) that can be used to customize applications. Using *visual programming*, programmers can "drag and drop" controls onto a form instead of writing code themselves. Just as people do not need to know how to build an engine to drive a car, programmers do not need to build a control to use it. This allows them to concentrate on the big picture, rather than the complex details of every control. The wide variety of tools available to programmers is a powerful feature of C#. We demonstrate the power of the controls in the **Toolbox** when we create our own program later in the chapter.

The **Toolbox** contains groups of related components (e.g., **Data**, **Components**, **Windows Forms**). Expand the members of a group by clicking the name of the group. Users can scroll through the individual items by using the black scroll arrows on the right side of the **Toolbox**. The first item in the group is not a control—it is the mouse pointer. Clicking this icon allows the user to deselect the current control in the **Toolbox**. Note that there are no tool tips, because the **Toolbox** icons already are labeled with the names of the controls. In later chapters, we discuss many of these controls.

Initially, the **Toolbox** may be hidden, with only the name of the window showing on the side of the IDE (Fig. 2.11). Moving the mouse pointer over a window name opens this window. Moving the mouse pointer outside the window causes the window to disappear. This feature is known as *auto hide*. To "pin down" the **Toolbox** (i.e., disable auto hide), click the pin icon in the upper right corner of the window (see Fig. 2.11). To enable auto hide (if it previously has been disabled), click the pin icon again. Notice that when auto hide is enabled, the pin points to the side, as is shown in Fig. 2.11.

Toolbox group

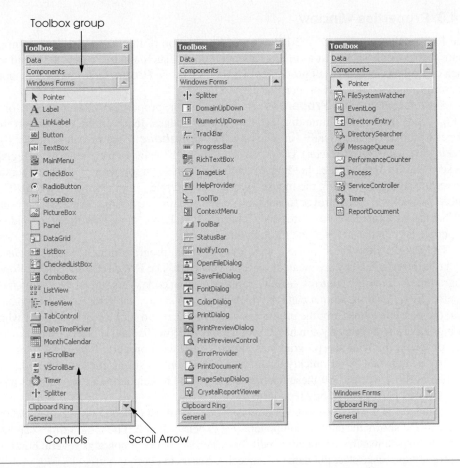

Controls   Scroll Arrow

Fig. 2.10 Toolbox window.

Mouse over window name   Toggle auto hide   Close button

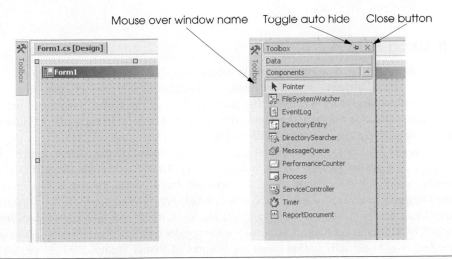

Fig. 2.11 Demonstrating window auto-hide.

2.4.3 Properties Window

The **Properties** window (Fig. 2.12) allows manipulation of the *properties* for a form or control. Properties specify information about a control, such as size, color and position. Each control has its own set of properties. The bottom of the **Properties** window contains a description of the selected property.

The left column of the **Properties** window shows the properties of the control (a form in Fig. 2.12). The right column displays their current values. Icons on the toolbar sort the properties either alphabetically (by clicking the ***Alphabetic*** *icon*) or categorically (by clicking the ***Categorized*** *icon*). Users can scroll through the list of properties by *dragging* the scrollbar up or down (i.e., holding down the left mouse button while the mouse cursor is over the scrollbar, moving the mouse up or down and releasing the mouse button). The ***Event*** *icon* allows the control or form to respond to certain user actions. We discuss events in Chapter 12, Graphical User Interface Concepts: Part 1. We show how to set individual properties later in this chapter and throughout the book.

The **Properties** window also is important to visual programming. Controls are usually customized after they are created from the **Toolbox**. The **Properties** window allows programmers to modify controls visually, without writing code. This setup has a number of benefits. First, the programmer can see which properties are available for modification and what the possible values are; the programmer does not have to look up or remember what settings a particular property can have. Second, the window displays a brief description of each property, allowing the programmer to understand each property's purpose. Third, a property's value can be set quickly using the window; only a single click is required, and no code need be written. All these features are designed to help software developers program without performing many repetitive tasks.

At the top of the **Properties** window is a drop-down list called the *component selection*. This list shows the current component that is being altered. The programmer can use the list to choose which component to edit. For example, if a GUI contains several buttons, the programmer can select the name of a specific button to configure.

2.5 Using Help

Visual Studio .NET has an extensive help mechanism. The ***Help*** *menu* contains a variety of options. The ***Contents*** *menu item* displays a categorized table of contents. Menu item ***Index*** displays an alphabetical index that users can browse. The **Search** feature allows users to find particular help articles based on a few search words. In each case, a filter can narrow the search to articles related only to C#.

Dynamic help (Fig. 2.13) provides a list of articles based on the current content (i.e., the items around the location of the mouse cursor). To open dynamic help (if it is not already open), select the **Help** menu's **Dynamic Help** command. Once you click an object to display in Visual Studio .NET, relevant help articles will appear in the **Dynamic Help** window. The window lists relevant help entries, samples and "Getting Started" information, in addition to providing a toolbar for the regular help features. Dynamic help is an excellent way to get information about the features of Visual Studio .NET. Note that for some users, **Dynamic Help** slows down Visual Studio.

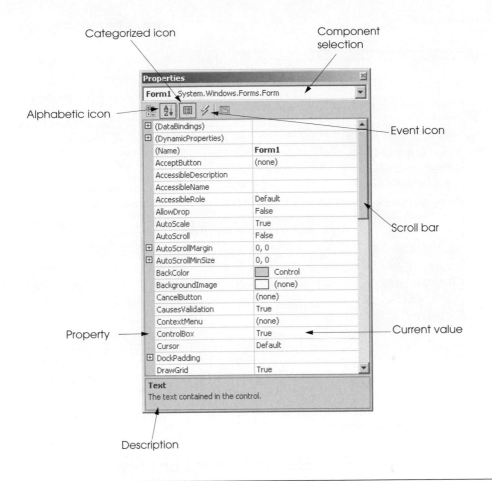

Fig. 2.12   Properties window.

Performance Tip 2.1

If you experience slow response times from Visual Studio, you can disable (i.e., close) **Dynamic Help** *by clicking the* **X** *in the upper-right corner of the window.*

In addition to dynamic help, Visual Studio .NET provides *context-sensitive help*. Context-sensitive help is similar to dynamic help, except that context-sensitive text immediately brings up a relevant help article rather than presenting a list. To use context-sensitive help, select an item and press the *F1* key. Help can appear either *internally* or *externally*. With external help, a relevant article immediately pops up in a separate window, outside the IDE. With internal help, a help article appears as a tabbed window inside Visual Studio .NET. The help options can be set from the **My Profile** section of the **Start Page**. Dynamic help and context-sensitive help are explained in the context of C# code later in the book.

Selected item   **Dynamic Help** window

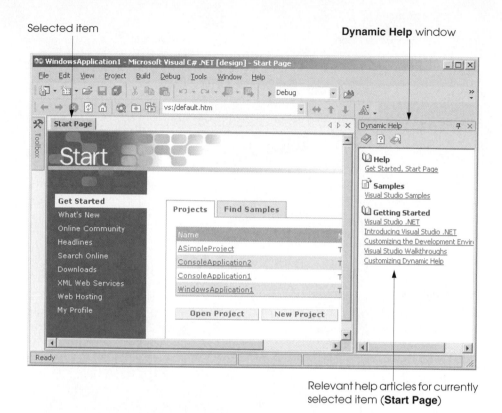

Relevant help articles for currently
selected item (**Start Page**)

Fig. 2.13 **Dynamic Help** window.

2.6 Simple Program: Displaying Text and an Image

In this section, we create a program that displays the text "`Welcome to C#!`" and an image. The program consists of a single form that uses a label to display text and a picture box to display an image. Figure 2.14 shows the program as it executes. The example here (as well as the image file used in the example) is available on our Web Site (`www.deitel.com`) under the **Downloads/Resources** link.

We do not write a single line of program code. Instead, we use the techniques of visual programming. Various programmer *gestures* (such as using the mouse for pointing, clicking, dragging and dropping) provide Visual Studio .NET with sufficient information for it to generate all or a major portion of the program code. In the next chapter, we begin our discussion of writing program code. Throughout the book, we produce increasingly substantial and powerful programs. Visual C# programming usually involves a combination of writing a portion of the program code and having Visual Studio .NET generate the remaining code.

To create, run and terminate this first program, perform the following steps:

1. *Create the new project.* If a project is already open, close it by selecting **File > Close Solution** from the menu. A dialog asking whether to save the current solution may appear in order to keep any unsaved changes, save the solution. Create

Fig. 2.14 Simple program as it executes.

a new Windows application for our program. Open Visual Studio .NET, and select **File > New > Project... > Visual C# Projects > Windows Application** (Fig. 2.15). Name the project **ASimpleProject**, and select a directory in which to save the project. To do this, click the **Browse...** button, which opens a **Project Location** dialog (Fig. 2.16). Navigate through the directories, find one in which to place the project and select **OK**. This selection returns us to the **New Project** dialog; the selected folder appears in the **Location** text field. When you are satisfied with the location of the project, click **OK**. Visual Studio .NET will load the new solution, and a form labeled **Form1** will appear.

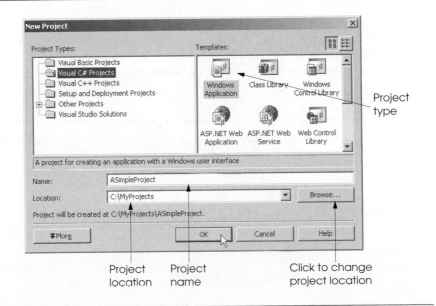

Fig. 2.15 Creating a new Windows application.

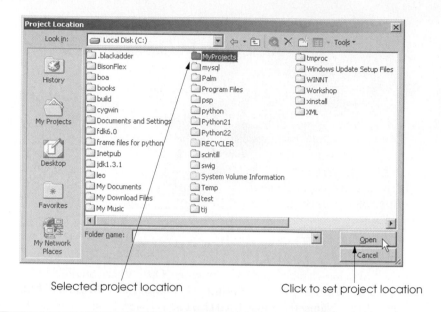

Selected project location   Click to set project location

Fig. 2.16   Setting the project location.

2. *Set the form's title bar.* First, set the text that appears in the title bar. This text is determined by the form's **Text** property (Fig. 2.17). If the form's **Properties** window is not open, click the **Properties** icon in the toolbar or select the **View** menu's **Properties Window** command. Use the mouse to select the form; the **Properties** window shows information about the currently selected item. In the window, click in the box to the right of the **Text** property's box. To set a value for the **Text** property, type the value in the box. In this case, type **A Simple Program**, as in Fig. 2.17. Press the *Enter* key (the *Return* key) when you have finished to update the form's title bar in the design area.

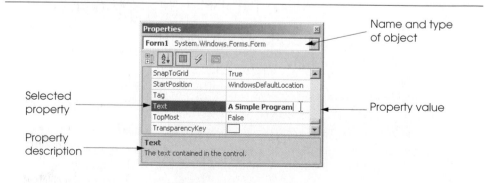

Fig. 2.17   Setting the form's **Text** property.

3. *Resize the form.* Click and drag one of the form's enabled *sizing handles* (the small squares around the form shown in Fig. 2.18) to change the size of the form. Enabled sizing handles are white. The mouse cursor changes appearance when it is over an enabled sizing handle. Disabled sizing handles are gray. The grid on the background of the form is used to align controls and does not appear when the program executes.

4. *Change the form's background color.* The **BackColor** property specifies a form's or control's background color. Clicking **BackColor** in the **Properties** window causes a down-arrow button to appear next to the property value (Fig. 2.19). When clicked, the down arrow drops down to display other options. (The options vary, depending on the property.) In this case, it displays the tabs **System** (the default), **Web** and **Custom**. Click the **Custom** tab to display the *palette* (a selection box of colors). Select the box that represents yellow. The palette will disappear, and the form's background color will change to yellow.

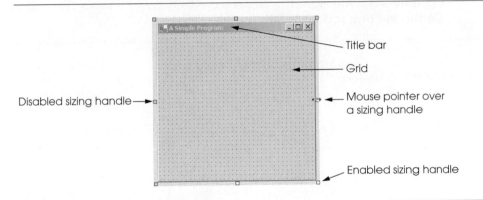

Fig. 2.18 Form with sizing handles.

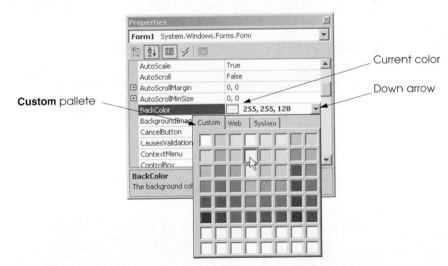

Fig. 2.19 Changing property **BackColor**.

5. *Add a label control to the form.* Double-click the label control in the **Toolbox**. This action creates a label with sizing handles in the upper-left corner of the form (Fig. 2.20). Double-clicking any **Toolbox** control places it on the form. Alternatively, programmers can "drag" controls from the **Toolbox** to the form. Labels display text; our label displays **label1** by default. Notice that our label is the same color as the form's background color. The form's background color is also the default background color of controls added to the form.

6. *Set the label's text.* Select the label so that its properties appear in the **Properties** window. The label's **Text** property determines the text (if any) that the label displays. The form and label each have their own **Text** property. Forms and controls can have the same types of properties without conflict. We will see that many controls have property names in common. Set the **Text** property of the label to **Welcome to C#!** (Fig. 2.21). Resize the label (using the sizing handles) if the text does not fit. Move the label to the top center of the form by dragging it or using the arrow keys. Alternatively, you can move the label by selecting **Format > Center In Form > Horizontally** from the menu bar.

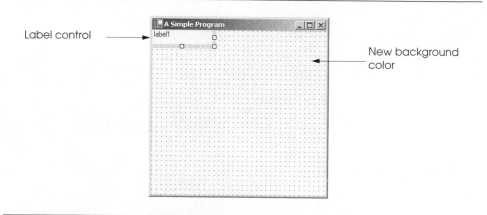

Fig. 2.20   Adding a new label to the form.

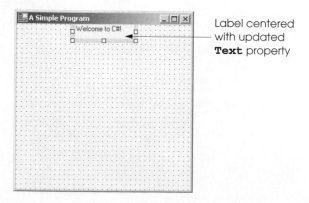

Fig. 2.21   Label in position with its **Text** property set.

7. *Set the label's font size, and align the label's text.* Clicking the **Font** property value causes an *ellipsis* button (...) to appear next to the value, as in Fig. 2.22. The ellipsis button indicates that a dialog will appear when the programmer clicks the button. When the button is clicked, the **Font** *window* shown in Fig. 2.23 is displayed. Users can select the font name (**Microsoft Sans Serif**, **Arial**, etc.), font style (**Regular**, **Bold**, etc.) and font size (**8**, **10**, etc.) in this window. The text in the **Sample** *area* displays the selected font. Under the **Size** category, select **24** and click **OK**. If the text does not fit on a single line, it will wrap to the next line. Resize the label if it is not large enough to hold the text. Next, select the label's **TextAlign** property, which determines how the text is aligned within the label. A three-by-three grid of alignment choices is displayed, corresponding to where the text appears in the label (Fig. 2.24). Select the top-center grid item, so that the text will appear at the top center of the label.

8. *Add a picture box to the form.* The picture-box control displays images. This step is similar to Step 5. Find the picture box in the toolbox, and add it to the form. Move it underneath the label, by either dragging it or using the arrow keys (Fig. 2.25).

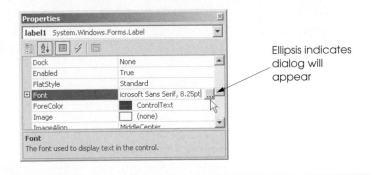

Fig. 2.22   **Properties** window displaying the label's properties.

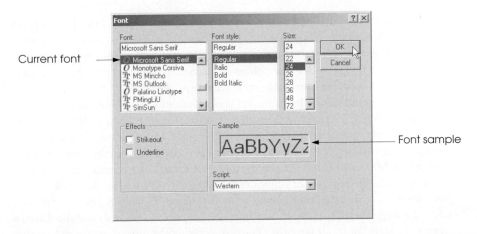

Fig. 2.23   **Font** window for selecting fonts, styles and sizes.

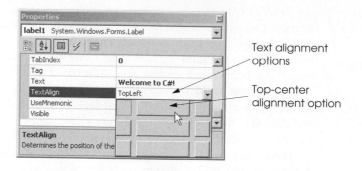

Text alignment options

Top-center alignment option

Fig. 2.24   Centering the text in the label.

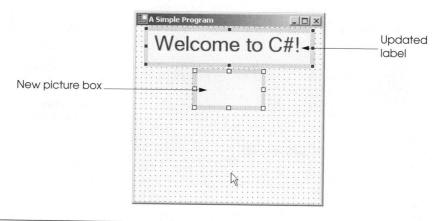

Updated label

New picture box

Fig. 2.25   Inserting and aligning the picture box.

9. *Insert an image.* Click the picture box to load its properties in the **Properties** window, and find the ***Image*** *property*. The **Image** property shows a preview of the current picture. No picture has been assigned, so the **Image** property displays **(none)** (Fig. 2.26). Click the ellipsis button to display an **Open** dialog (Fig. 2.27). Browse for a picture to insert, and press *Enter* key. The proper formats of an image include PNG (Portable Networks Graphic), GIF (Graphic Interchange Format) and JPEG (Joint Photographics Experts Group). Each of these file formats is widely supported on the Internet. To create a new picture, it is necessary to use image-editing software, such as Jasc Paint Shop Pro, Adobe Photoshop Elements or Microsoft Paint. We use the picture **ASimpleProgramImage.png**, which is located with this example on the CD that accompanies the book and on our Web site (**www.deitel.com**). After the image has been inserted, the picture box displays as much of the picture as it can (depending on size) and the **Image** property shows a small preview. To display the entire image, resize the picture box by dragging the picture box's handles (Fig. 2.28).

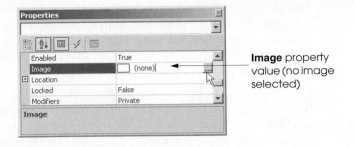

Image property
value (no image
selected)

Fig. 2.26 **Image** property of the picture box.

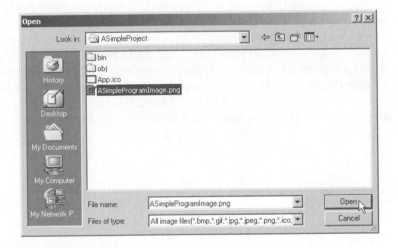

Fig. 2.27 Selecting an image for the picture box.

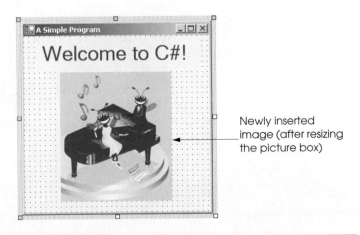

Newly inserted
image (after resizing
the picture box)

Fig. 2.28 Picture box after the image has been inserted.

10. *Save the project.* Select **File > Save All** to save the entire solution. To save an individual file, select it in the **Solution Explorer**, and select **File > Save**. The created program stores the source code in the C# file **Form1.cs**. The project file contains the names and locations of all the files in the project. Choosing **Save All** saves both the project and the C# file.

11. *Run the project.* Prior to this step, we have been working in the IDE *design mode* (i.e., the program being created is not executing). This mode is indicated by the text **Microsoft Visual C# .NET [design]** in the title bar. While in design mode, programmers have access to all the environment windows (i.e., **Toolbox** and **Properties**), menus, toolbars and so forth. While in *run mode*, however, the program is executing, and users can interact with only a few IDE features. Features that are not available are disabled or grayed out. The text **Form1.cs [Design]** in the title bar means that we are designing the form visually, rather than programming it using code. If we had been writing code, the title bar would have contained only the text **Form1.cs**. To execute or run our program, we first need to compile it, which is accomplished by clicking on the ***Build Solution*** option in the ***Build*** menu (or type *<Ctrl> + Shift + B*). The program can then be executed by clicking the ***Start*** button (the blue triangle), selecting the **Debug** menu's **Start** command or pressing the *F5* key. Figure 2.29 shows the IDE in run mode. Note that the IDE title bar displays **[run]** and that many toolbar icons are disabled.

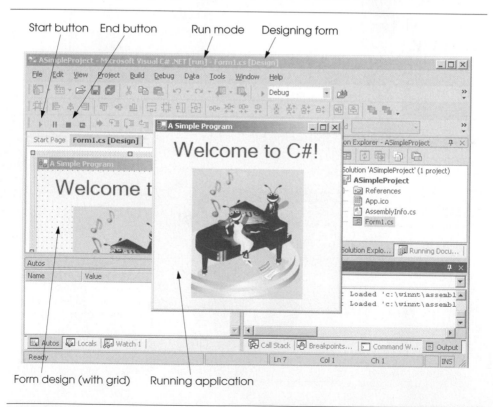

Fig. 2.29 IDE in run mode, with the running application in the foreground.

12. *Terminating execution.* To terminate the program, click the running application's **Close** button (the **x** in the top-right corner). Alternatively, click the **End** button (the blue square) in the toolbar. Either action stops program execution and puts the IDE into design mode.

We have just created a working C# program without writing a single line of code. Visual programming allows us to create controls and set properties using windows, rather than lines of code. In the next chapter, we discuss nonvisual, or conventional, programming—we create a program using only code. C# programming is a mixture of the two styles: Visual programming allows us to develop a GUI and avoid tedious tasks, while conventional programming specifies the behavior of our program. The most important part of an application is its behavior, which we explain how to program in the upcoming chapters.

Software Engineering Observation 2.1

Visual programming can be simpler and faster than writing code.

Software Engineering Observation 2.2

Most programs require more than visual programming. In such programs, some code must be written by hand. Examples include applications that use event handlers (used to respond to the user's actions), databases, security, networking, text editing, graphics and multimedia.

SUMMARY

- Visual Studio .NET is Microsoft's integrated development environment (IDE) for creating, documenting, running and debugging programs.
- When Visual Studio .NET is loaded for the first time, the **Start Page** is displayed. This page contains helpful links, such as recent projects, online newsgroups, downloads and user profile settings.
- The **Get Started** section contains links to recent files.
- The **My Profile** page allows users to customize Visual Studio .NET.
- In the Visual Studio .NET IDE, users can browse the Web via Internet Explorer.
- Dialogs are windows that are used to communicate with users.
- Programs in Visual Studio .NET are organized into projects and solutions. A project is a group of related files. A solution is a group of projects that are combined to solve a developer's problem.
- Windows applications are programs that execute inside the Windows OS, like Microsoft Word, Internet Explorer and Visual Studio .NET. They contain controls—reusable graphical elements, such as buttons and labels—which the user uses to interact with the application.
- The form is what the users interact with and view when programs run.
- The form and its controls constitute the graphical user interface (GUI) of the program. Controls are the graphical components with which the user interacts. Users enter data (inputs) into the program by entering information from the keyboard and clicking the mouse buttons. The program displays instructions and other information (outputs) for users to read in the GUI.
- The title bar displays the name of the project, the programming language, the mode of the IDE, the file being viewed and the mode of the file being viewed.
- To view a tabbed document, click the tab with the name of the document. Tabbing saves space and allows easy access to multiple documents.

- Menus contain groups of related commands that, when selected, cause the IDE to perform some action. Visual Studio .NET provides different modes for the user. Certain menu items appear only in some of these modes.

- The toolbar contains icons that represent menu commands. To execute a command, click the corresponding icon. Click the down arrow beside an icon to display other available options.

- Moving the mouse pointer over an icon highlights the icon and displays a tool tip.

- The **Solution Explorer** window lists all the files in the solution.

- The startup project of the solution is the project that runs when the program is executed.

- The plus and minus boxes to the left of the project and solution names expand and collapse the tree, respectively.

- The **Toolbox** contains controls that customize forms.

- By using visual programming, programmers can "drag and drop" controls onto the form instead of writing the code themselves.

- Moving the mouse pointer over the label of a hidden window opens the window. Moving the mouse pointer outside the window causes the window to disappear. This feature is known as auto hide. To "pin down" the **Toolbox** window (i.e., to disable auto hide), click the pin icon in the upper-right corner.

- The **Properties** window displays the properties for a form or control. Properties are information about a control, such as size, color and position.

- Each type of control has its own set of properties.

- The left column of the **Properties** window shows the properties of the control. The right column displays their current values. The toolbar sorts the properties either alphabetically (by clicking the **Alphabetic** icon) or categorically (by clicking the **Categorized** icon).

- The **Properties** window allows programmers to modify controls visually, without writing code.

- The **Help** menu contains a variety of options. The **Contents** menu item displays a categorized table of contents. Menu item **Index** displays an alphabetical index that can be browsed. The **Search** feature allows users to find particular help articles, based on a few search words.

- For each option of the **Help** menu, a filter can be used to narrow the search to articles relating only to C#.

- Dynamic help provides a list of articles, based on the current content (i.e., the location of the mouse cursor).

- Context-sensitive help is similar to dynamic help, except that context-sensitive help immediately brings up a relevant help article. To use context-sensitive help, select an item and press the *F1* key.

- Visual C# programming usually involves a combination of writing a portion of the program code and having Visual Studio .NET generate the remaining code.

- To create a new Windows Forms project, open Visual Studio .NET and select **File > New > Project...> Visual C# Projects > Windows Application**. Name the project, and select a directory. Then click **OK**. Visual Studio .NET will load the new solution, and a blank form labeled **Form1** will appear.

- The text that appears on the top of the form (the title bar) is determined by the `Text` property of the form. To set a value for the property, simply type it in the space provided. Press the *Enter* key (*Return* key) when you have finished.

- To resize the form, click and drag one of the form's enabled sizing handles (the small squares around the form). Enabled sizing handles are white; disabled sizing handles are gray.

- The grid on the background of the form is used to align controls and does not appear when the program is running.

- The **BackColor** property specifies a form's or control's background color. The form's background color is the default background color for any controls added to the form.
- Double-clicking any **Toolbox** control icon places a control of that type on the form. Alternatively, programmers can "drag" controls from the **Toolbox** to the form.
- The label's **Text** property determines the text (if any) that the label displays. The form and label each have their own **Text** property.
- When clicked, the ellipsis button displays a dialog.
- In the **Font** dialog users can select a font using the font name, font style and font size.
- The **TextAlign** property determines how the text is aligned within the label's boundaries.
- The picture-box control allows us to display an image on the form. The **Image** property shows a preview of the current picture. To select an image, click the ellipsis button, which displays an **Open** dialog. Browse for a picture to insert (of the proper format, such as PNG, GIF or JPEG), and then press the *Enter* key.
- Select **File > Save All** to save the entire solution. To save an individual file, select it in the **Solution Explorer** and select **File > Save**.
- The IDE design mode (i.e., the program is not executing) is indicated by the text **Microsoft Visual C# .NET [Design]** in the title bar.
- While in run mode, the program is executing, and users can interact with only a few IDE features.
- When designing a program visually, the name of the C# file will appear in the title bar, followed by **[Design]**.
- To execute or run a program, click the **Start** button (the blue triangle), or select **Debug> Start**. The IDE title bar displays **[Run]**, and many toolbar icons are disabled.
- Terminate execution by clicking the **Close** button. Alternatively, click the **End** button (a blue square) in the toolbar.

TERMINOLOGY

Alignment property
Alphabetic icon
Appearance category in the
    Properties window
auto hide
BackColor property
background color
Build menu
button
Categorized icon
clicking
close a project
Close button icon
collapse a tree
compile a program
context-sensitive help
control
control layout
customize a form
customize Visual Studio .NET
Data menu

debug a program
Debug menu
design mode
dialog
double-clicking
down arrow
dynamic help
Dynamic Help window
Edit menu
expand a tree
external help
F1 help key
File menu
find
Font property
font size
font style
Font window
form
form's background color
form's title bar

Format menu
GUI (Graphical User Interface)
help filter
Help menu
icon
IDE (integrated development environment)
input
internal help
Internet Explorer
label
menu
menu bar in Visual Studio .NET
mouse pointer
new project in Visual Studio .NET
opening a project
output
palette
paste
picture box
pin a window
print a project
project
Project menu
Properties window
property

property for a form or control
recent project
Run menu
run mode
selecting
single-clicking with the left mouse button
sizing handle
solution
Solution Explorer in Visual Studio .NET
Start button
Start Page
startup project
tabbed window
Text property
title bar
tool tip
toolbar
toolbar icon
Tools menu
undo
View menu
Visual Studio .NET
window layout
Windows application
Windows menu

SELF-REVIEW EXERCISES

2.1   Fill in the blanks in each of the following statements:
   a) The technique of _____ allows us to create a GUI without writing any code.
   b) A _____ is a group of related files, compiled into one application.
   c) The _____ feature saves screen space when the mouse is moved away from a window.
   d) A _____ appears when the mouse cursor hovers over an icon.
   e) The _____ window allows you to browse the files in your solution.
   f) A plus icon indicates that the tree in the **Solution Explorer** can _____.
   g) The **Properties** window can be sorted _____ or _____.
   h) The form's _____ property determines the text that appears in its title bar.
   i) The _____ allows us to add controls to the form visually.
   j) _____ displays relevant help articles, based on the current context.

2.2   State whether each of the following is *true* or *false*. If *false*, explain why.
   a) The title bar displays the mode of the IDE.
   b) The **Start Page** allows the user to customize the IDE.
   c) The **x** button toggles auto hide in most windows.
   d) The toolbar provides a convenient way to execute certain menu commands.
   e) The toolbar contains the control icons.
   f) A form's sizing handles are always enabled when the form is selected.
   g) Both forms and labels have a title bar.
   h) Controls can be modified only by writing code.
   i) Buttons usually perform actions when clicked.
   j) The grid appears when designing a form, but not during execution.

ANSWERS TO SELF-REVIEW EXERCISES

2.1 a) visual programming. b) project. c) auto hide. d) tool tip. e) **Solution Explorer**. f) expand. g) alphabetically, categorically. h) **Text**. i) **Toolbox**. j) Dynamic help.

2.2 a) True. b) True. c) False. The pin icon toggles auto hide. d) True. e) False. The **Toolbox** contains the control icons. f) False. Some of a form's sizing handles are disabled. g) False. Forms have a title bar; labels do not. h) False. Control properties can be set using the **Properties** window. i) True. j) True.

EXERCISES

2.3 Fill in the blanks in each of the following statements:
  a) The _____ button in the **Properties** window indicates that a dialog will appear.
  b) To save every file in a solution, use the menu selection _____.
  c) _____ help immediately brings up a relevant article. It can be accessed pressing the _____ key.
  d) GUI stands for _____.

2.4 State whether each of the following is *true* or *false*. If *false*, explain why.
  a) Certain menu items appear only when designing a form.
  b) The form, label and picture box have identical properties.
  c) A person can browse the Internet from within Visual Studio .NET.
  d) Visual C# programmers often create complex applications without writing any code.
  e) Sizing handles are visible during execution.

2.5 Some features appear throughout Visual Studio .NET, performing similar actions in different contexts. Explain and give examples of how plus/minus icons, ellipsis buttons, down arrows and tool tips act in this manner. Why do you think Visual Studio .NET was designed to be this way?

2.6 Build the GUIs described in each part of the exercise. (You need not provide any functionality.) Execute each program, and determine what happens when a control is clicked with the mouse. Drag controls from the **Toolbox** onto the form, and resize them as necessary.
  a) This GUI consists of a **MainMenu** and a **RichTextBox**. Both controls can be dragged from the **ToolBox** onto the form or double clicked. After inserting the **MainMenu**, add items by clicking in the **Type Here** section, typing in the name of a menu item and pressing the *Enter* key. Resize the **RichTextBox** to fill the form.

b) This GUI consists of two **Label**s (font size 12, yellow background): a **MonthCalendar** and a **RichTextBox**. The calendar is displayed when the **MonthCalendar** is dragged on the form. The **MonthCalendar** and **RichTextBox** controls are similar to the controls we have seen previously. They can be dragged onto the form (or double clicked), then manipulated with the **Properties** window. [*Hint*: Use the **BackColor** property to change the background color of the labels.]

2.7   Fill in the blanks in each of the following statements:
a) The _____ property specifies which image a picture box displays.
b) The _____ has an icon in the **Toolbox**, but is not a control.
c) The _____ menu contains commands for arranging and displaying windows.
d) Property_____ determines a form's or control's background color.

2.8   Briefly describe each of the following IDE features:
a) toolbar
b) menu bar
c) toolbox
d) control
e) form
f) project
g) title bar

Introduction to C#
Programming

Objectives

- To be able to write simple C# programs.
- To be able to use input and output statements.
- To become familiar with primitive data types.
- To understand basic memory concepts.
- To be able to use arithmetic operators.
- To understand the precedence of arithmetic operators.
- To be able to write decision-making statements.
- To be able to use relational and equality operators.

Comment is free, but facts are sacred.
C. P. Scott

The creditor hath a better memory than the debtor.
James Howell

When faced with a decision, I always ask, "What would be the most fun?"
Peggy Walker

Equality, in a social sense, may be divided into that of condition and that of rights.
James Fenimore Cooper

3.1 Introduction

This chapter introduces C# programming and presents examples that illustrate several important features of the language. Examples are analyzed one line at a time. In this chapter, we create *console applications*—applications that contain only text output. There are several types of projects that we can create in C#; the console application is one of the basic types. Text output in a console application is displayed in a *console window* (also called a *console window*). On Microsoft Windows 95/98, the console window is the **MS-DOS prompt**. On Microsoft Windows NT/2000/XP, the console window is called the **command prompt**. With C#, a program can be created with multiple types of output (windows, dialogs and so forth). These programs are called *Windows applications* and provide graphical user interfaces. We showed an example of a Windows application in Chapter 2, when we printed a message on a form. These types of applications will be discussed in greater detail, beginning with Chapter 4, Control Structures: Part 1 and Chapter 5, Control Structures: Part 2. In these chapters, we will also provide a detailed treatment of *program development* and *program control* in C#.

3.2 Simple Program: Printing a Line of Text

C# uses some notations that might appear strange to nonprogrammers. We begin by considering a simple program that displays a line of text. The program and its output are shown in Fig. 3.1. The program is followed by an output window that displays the program's results. When you execute this program, the output will appear in a console window.

```
1   // Fig. 3.1: Welcome1.cs
2   // A first program in C#.
3
4   using System;
5
6   class Welcome1
7   {
8      static void Main( string[] args )
9      {
10         Console.WriteLine( "Welcome to C# Programming!" );
11      }
12   }
```

Fig. 3.1   Our first program in C#. (Part 1 of 2.)

```
Welcome to C# Programming!
```

Fig. 3.1   Our first program in C#. (Part 2 of 2.)

This program illustrates several important features of C#. All programs we present in this book will include line numbers for the reader's convenience; these line numbers are not part of the C# programs. Line 10 in Fig. 3.1 does the "real work" of the program, displaying the phrase **Welcome to C# Programming!** on the screen.

Line 1 begins with **//**, indicating that the remainder of the line is a *comment*. Programmers insert comments to *document* and improve the readability of their code. Comments also help other people read and understand your programs. This comment simply indicates the figure number and file name for this program. We begin each program in this book in this manner. In this case, we have named the file **Welcome1.cs**. A comment that begins with **//** is called a *single-line comment*, because the comment terminates at the end of the line. Single-line comments can be placed almost anywhere in the program.

There is also a syntax for writing *multiple-line comments*. A multiple-line comment, such as

```
/* This is a multiple-line
   comment. It can be
   split over many lines */
```

begins with *delimiter* **/*** and ends with *delimiter* ***/**. All text between these delimiters is treated as a comment and is ignored by the compiler. In the Visual Studio .NET IDE, all comment text appears in green. Comments of the form **//** and **/* ... */** are ignored by the compiler; therefore, they do not cause the computer to perform any action when the program executes.

Common Programming Error 3.1

Forgetting one of the delimiters of a multiple-line comment is a syntax error. A syntax error is caused when the compiler cannot recognize a statement. The compiler normally issues an error message to help the programmer locate and fix the incorrect statement. Syntax errors are violations of the language rules. Syntax errors are also called compile errors, compile-time errors *or* compilation errors *because they are detected during the compilation phase. A program cannot compile or execute until all the syntax errors are corrected.*

Software Engineering Observation 3.1

Visual Studio will often times catch syntax errors as you are creating the program, even before the program is compiled. Look out for red jagged lines that may appear directly below a syntax error.

C# uses the same syntax as the C programming language for multiple-line comments (**/*...*/**) and the same syntax as C++ for single-line comments (**//**). C# programmers generally use C++-style single-line comments, instead of C-style comments. Throughout this book, we use mostly C++-style single-line comments.

Good Programming Practice 3.1

Every program should begin with one or more comments that describe the program's purpose.

Line 4 (known as a ***using*** *directive*) is generated by the Visual Studio IDE and declares that the program uses features in the ***System*** *namespace*. A *namespace* groups various C# features into related categories. One of the great strengths of C# is that C# programmers can use the rich set of namespaces provided by the .NET framework. These namespaces contain code that programmers can reuse, rather than "reinventing the wheel." This makes programming easier and faster. The namespaces that are defined in the .NET Framework contain preexisting code known as the *.NET Framework Class Library*. An example of one of the features in namespace **System** is **Console**, which we discuss momentarily. The various features are organized into namespaces that enable programmers to locate them easily. We discuss many namespaces and their features throughout the book.

Line 5 is a blank line. Programmers often use blank lines and space characters throughout a program to make the program easier to read. Collectively, blank lines, space characters, newline characters and tab characters are known as *whitespace* (space characters and tabs are known specifically as *whitespace characters*). *Newline characters* characters are "special characters" that indicate when to position the output cursor at the beginning of the next line in the console window to continue output. The compiler ignores blank lines, tabs and extra spaces that separate language elements. Several conventions for using whitespace characters are discussed in this and subsequent chapters.

Good Programming Practice 3.2

Use blank lines, space characters and tab characters in a program to enhance program readability.

Lines 6–12 define our first *class* (these lines collectively are called a *class definition*). C# programs consist of pieces called classes, which are logical groupings of members (e.g., *methods*) that simplify program organization. These methods (which are like functions in procedural programming languages) perform tasks and return information when the tasks are completed. A C# program consists of classes and methods created by the programmer and of preexisting classes found in the Framework Class Library. Throughout this book, we will teach the reader how to use both techniques in their programs. Every program in C# consists of at least one class definition that the programmer defines. These classes are known as *programmer-defined classes*. In Chapter 8, Object-Based Programming, we discuss programs that contain multiple programmer-defined classes. The ***class*** *keyword* begins a class definition in C# and is followed immediately by the *class name* (**Welcome1**, in this example). Keywords (or *reserved words*) are reserved for use by C# and always consist of lowercase letters. (A complete table of C# keywords is presented in the next chapter.) By convention, each word in a class name begins with an uppercase first letter and has an uppercase letter for each word in the class name (e.g., **SampleClassName**). The name of the class is known as an *identifier*, which is a series of characters consisting of letters, digits, underscores (_) and "at" symbols (**@**). Identifiers cannot begin with a digit and cannot contain spaces. Examples of valid identifiers are **Welcome1**, **_value**, **m_inputField1** and **button7**. The name **7button** is not a valid identifier because it begins with a digit, and the name **input field** is not a valid identifier because it contains a space. The "at" character (**@**) can be used only as the first character in an identifier. C# is *case sensitive*—uppercase and lowercase letters are considered different letters, so **a1** and **A1** are different identifiers.

Common Programming Error 3.2

*C# is case sensitive. Not using the proper case for an identifier, e.g., writing **Total** when the identifier is **total**, is a compiler error.*

Good Programming Practice 3.3

Always begin a class name with an uppercase first letter. This practice makes class names easier to identify.

The *left brace* (**{**) at line 7 begins the *body of the class definition*. The corresponding *right brace* (**}**) at line 12 ends the class definition. Notice that lines 8–11 in the body of the class are indented. This is one of the spacing conventions mentioned earlier. Indentation improves program readability. We define each spacing convention as a *Good Programming Practice*.

Common Programming Error 3.3

If braces do not occur in matching pairs, a syntax error occurs.

Good Programming Practice 3.4

*When typing an opening left brace (**{**) in a program, immediately type the closing right brace (**}**) then reposition the cursor between the braces to begin typing the body. This practice helps prevent missing braces. Readers may notice that, when they type the closing brace, Visual Studio .NET makes both braces bold (as well as the first line of the class definition). This is helpful in the creation of more complex programs that involve multiple sets of opening and closing braces.*

Good Programming Practice 3.5

*Indent the entire body of each class definition one "level" of indentation between the left brace (**{**) and the right brace (**}**) that delimit the class body. This emphasizes the structure of the class definition and helps make the class definition easier to read. Visual Studio .NET provides indentation in several places as programmers enter code.*

Line 8 is present in all C# console and Windows applications. These applications begin executing at **Main**, which is known as the *entry point* of the program. The parentheses after **Main** indicate that **Main** is a program building block, called a method. C# class definitions normally contain one or more methods and C# applications contain one or more classes. For a C# console or Windows application, exactly one of those methods must be called **Main**, and it must be defined as shown on line 8; otherwise, the program is not executable. Normally, a console applications's **Main** method is defined as shown on line 8. Methods are explained in detail in Chapter 6, Methods. For now, simply mimic **Main**'s first line in each C# application.

The left brace (**{**) on line 9 begins the *body of the method definition* (the code which will be executed as a part of our program). A corresponding right brace (**}**) terminates the method definition's body (line 11). Notice that the line in the body of the method is indented between these braces.

Good Programming Practice 3.6

*Indent the entire body of each method definition one "level" of indentation between the left brace (**{**) and the right brace (**}**) that define the method body. This makes the structure of the method stand out, improving the method definition's readability.*

Line 10 instructs the computer to perform an *action*, namely, to print a series of characters contained between the double quotation marks. Characters delimited in this manner are called *strings*, *character strings* or *string literals*. We refer to characters between double quotation marks generically as strings. Whitespace characters in strings are significant—the compiler does not ignore these characters when they appear in strings.

The **Console** *class* enables programs to output information to the computer's *standard output*. Class **Console** provides methods that allow C# programs to display strings and other types of information in the Windows command prompt.

Method **Console.WriteLine** *displays* (or *prints*) a line of text in the console window. When **Console.WriteLine** completes its task, it positions the *output cursor* (the location where the next character will be displayed) at the beginning of the next line in the console window. (This is similar to pressing the *Enter* key when typing in a text editor—the cursor is repositioned at the beginning of the next line in the file.)

The entire line, including **Console.WriteLine**, its *argument* in the parentheses (**"Welcome to C# Programming!"**) and the *semicolon* (**;**), is called a *statement*. Every statement must end with a semicolon (known as the *statement terminator*). When this statement executes, it displays the message **Welcome to C# Programming!** in the console window (Fig. 3.1).

In C# statements we normally precede each class name with its namespace name and a period. For example, line 10 would normally be

```
System.Console.WriteLine( "Welcome to C# Programming!" );
```

for the program to run correctly. The **using** directive on line 4 eliminates the need to specify explicitly the namespace **System** when using classes in the namespace. This can save time and confusion for programmers.

Common Programming Error 3.4

Omitting the semicolon at the end of a statement is a syntax error.

Testing and Debugging Tip 3.1

When the compiler reports a syntax error, the error might not be on the line indicated by the error message. First, check the line where the error was reported. If that line does not contain syntax errors, check the lines that precede the one reported.

Now that we have presented this program to you, let us explain step-by-step how to create and run it in Visual Studio.

1. *Create the console application.* Go to the **File** menu and choose **New**, then **Project...**. A dialog will appear. In the left pane, choose **Visual C# Projects**; from the right pane, choose **Console Application**. It is possible to specify other information about the project in the bottom portion of this dialog (i.e., the name and location of the project). After entering all the necessary information, click **OK** to create the project. The project is created, and the code window is opened for editing. The new application is shown in Fig. 3.2. Note that this is the same way we created our application in Chapter 2, except that now we have chosen a console application, instead of a Windows application.

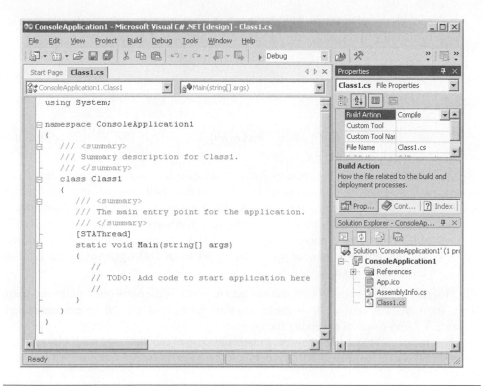

Fig. 3.2 Visual Studio .NET-generated console application.

This application can be built (compiled) and executed, but will not do anything until we add more code (this is done in Step 3). Let us briefly look at the code generated for us by the IDE.

Notice that this code contains features that we have not yet discussed. We have done this for both display and clarity reasons—at this point in the book, this code is neither required nor relevant to the discussion of this program. Much of the extra code that the IDE provides is used either for documentation or to help create graphical user interfaces. One of the things that the reader will no doubt notice is that we do not show the lines directly above and below the class definition. These lines are used to create namespaces, a topic that will be discussed in Chapter 8, Object-Based Programming. [*Note*: Several times early in this text, we ask the reader to mimic certain C# features that we introduce. We do this especially when it is not yet important to know all the details of a feature to use that feature in C#. All programmers initially learn how to program by mimicking what other programmers have done. For each detail, we ask the reader to mimic, we indicate where the full discussion will be presented later in the text.] The code for all examples in the book is included for the reader on our Web site **www.deitel.com** under the **Downloads/Resources** link.

2. *Change the name of the program file.* For the programs in this book, we usually change the name of the code file. By default, the file is named **Class1.cs**. This can be changed by right-clicking the name of the file in the **Solution Explorer**

and selecting **Rename**. The reader can then enter a new name for the file, provided that this file ends in **.cs** (the file extension for C# code files).

3. *Complete the code.* In the text editor, replace the comment

```
//
// TODO: Add code to start application here
//
```

which is located within method **Main** with line 10 from Fig. 3.1 (this comment is no longer necessary, for we are adding code to the program).

4. *Run the program.* We are now ready to compile and execute our program. To do this, we simply follow the same steps that we executed for the example in Chapter 2. To compile the program, go to the **Build** menu and select **Build Solution**. If the program contains no syntax errors, the preceding command creates a new file called **Welcome1.exe**, containing the MSIL code for our application. To execute this program, choose option **Start Without Debugging**[1] in the **Debug** menu.

Program execution begins with method **Main**, which is the entry point to the program. Next, the statement at line 10 of **Main** displays **Welcome to C# Programming!** Figure 3.3 shows result of executing the program.

The message **Welcome to C# Programming!** can be displayed via multiple method calls. Class **Welcome2** of Fig. 3.4 uses two statements to produce the same output shown in Fig. 3.3.

Lines 10–11 of Fig. 3.4 display one line in the console window. The first statement calls **Console** method **Write** to display a string. Unlike **WriteLine**, **Write** does not position the output cursor at the beginning of the next line in the console window after displaying its string. The next character displayed in the console window appears immediately after the last character displayed with **Write**. Thus, when line 11 executes, the first character displayed (**C**) appears immediately after the last character displayed with **Write** (i.e., the space character after the word **"to"** in line 10). Each **Write** or **WriteLine** statement resumes displaying characters from where the last **Write** or **WriteLine** stopped.

Fig. 3.3   Execution of the **Welcome1** program.

---

1. Selecting **Debug > Start Without Debugging** causes the command window to prompt the user to press a key after the program terminates, allowing the user to observe the program's output. In contrast, if we run this program using **Debug > Start**, as we did for the Windows application in Chapter 2, a command window opens, the program displays the message **Welcome to C# Programming!**, then the command window closes immediately.

```
1   // Fig. 3.4: Welcome2.cs
2   // Printing a line with multiple statements.
3
4   using System;
5
6   class Welcome2
7   {
8      static void Main( string[] args )
9      {
10         Console.Write( "Welcome to " );
11         Console.WriteLine( "C# Programming!" );
12      }
13   }
```

```
Welcome to C# Programming!
```

Fig. 3.4   Printing on one line with separate statements.

A single statement can display multiple lines by using newline characters. Recall that these characters indicate when to position the output cursor at the beginning of the next line in the console window to continue output. Figure 3.5 demonstrates using newline characters.

Line 10 produces four separate lines of text in the console window. Normally, the characters in a string are displayed exactly as they appear between the double quotes. However, notice that the two characters "\" and "n" do not appear on the screen. The *backslash* (\) is called an *escape character*. It indicates that a "special" character is to be output. When a backslash is encountered in a string of characters, the next character is combined with the backslash to form an *escape sequence*. This escape sequence \n is the *newline character*. It causes the *cursor* (i.e., the current screen position indicator) to move to the beginning of the next line in the console window. Some common escape sequences are listed in Fig. 3.6.

```
1   // Fig. 3.5: Welcome3.cs
2   // Printing multiple lines with a single statement.
3
4   using System;
5
6   class Welcome3
7   {
8      static void Main( string[] args )
9      {
10         Console.WriteLine( "Welcome\nto\nC#\nProgramming!" );
11      }
12   }
```

```
Welcome
to
C#
Programming!
```

Fig. 3.5   Printing on multiple lines with a single statement.

Escape sequence	Description
\n	Newline. Position the screen cursor to the beginning of the next line.
\t	Horizontal tab. Move the screen cursor to the next tab stop.
\r	Carriage return. Position the screen cursor to the beginning of the current line; do not advance to the next line. Any characters output after the carriage return overwrite the previous characters output on that line.
\\	Backslash. Used to print a backslash character.
\"	Double quote. Used to print a double quote (") character.

Fig. 3.6   Some common escape sequences.

Although the first several programs display output in the command prompt, most C# applications use windows or *dialogs* to display output. As mentioned earlier, dialogs are windows that typically display important messages to the user of an application. The .NET Framework Class Library includes class **MessageBox** for creating dialogs. Class **MessageBox** is defined in namespace **System.Windows.Forms**. The program in Fig. 3.7 displays the same string as Fig. 3.5 in a message dialog using class **MessageBox**.

```
1    // Fig. 3.7: Welcome4.cs
2    // Printing multiple lines in a dialog Box.
3
4    using System;
5    using System.Windows.Forms;
6
7    class Welcome4
8    {
9       static void Main( string[] args )
10      {
11         MessageBox.Show( "Welcome\nto\nC#\nprogramming!" );
12      }
13   }
```

Fig. 3.7   Displaying multiple lines in a dialog.

Many compiled classes in C# (including **MessageBox**) need to be referenced before they can be used in a program. Depending on the type of application we create, classes may be compiled into files with a **.exe** (*executable*) extension, a **.dll** (or *dynamic link library*) extension or one of several other extensions. Such files are called *assemblies* and are the packaging units for code in C#. [Note: Assemblies can be comprised of many files of several different types.] Namespaces group related *classes* together; the assembly is a package containing the Microsoft Intermediate Language (MSIL) code that a project has been compiled into, plus any other information that is needed for these classes. The assembly that we need to reference can be found in the Visual Studio .NET documentation (also called the MSDN Documentation) for the class we wish to use. The easiest way to access this information is to go to the **Help** menu in Visual Studio, and choose **Index**. The reader can then type in the name of the class to access the documentation. Class **MessageBox** is located in assembly **System.Windows.Forms.dll**. As mentioned previously, we must add a reference to this assembly to use class **MessageBox** in our program. Let us discuss an example of adding a reference to **System.Windows.Forms** within the IDE.

Common Programming Error 3.5

*Including a namespace with the **using** directive, but not adding a reference to the proper assembly, results in a compiler error.*

To begin, make sure you have an application open. Select the **Add Reference...** option from the **Project** menu, or right click the **References** folder in the **Solution Explorer** and select **Add Reference...** from the popup menu that appears. This opens the **Add Reference** dialog (Fig. 3.8). Double click **System.Windows.Forms.dll** to add this file to the **Selected Components** list at the bottom of the dialog, then click **OK**. Notice that **System.Windows.Forms** now appears in the **References** folder of the **Solution Explorer** (Fig. 3.8).

After referencing the appropriate assembly and providing a **using** directive for the corresponding namespace (line 5), we can use the classes in that namespace (such as **MessageBox**).

The reader may notice that we did not add any references to our previous programs. Visual Studio adds a few common references when a project is created. Also, by default, some assemblies do not require references. Class **Console**, for instance, is located in the assembly **mscorlib.dll**, but a reference to this assembly is not required to use it.

The **System.Windows.Forms** namespace contains many classes that help C# programmers define graphical user interfaces (GUIs) for their applications. *GUI components* (e.g., buttons) facilitate both data entry by the user and the formatting or presenting of data outputs to the user. For example, Fig. 3.9 is an Internet Explorer window with a bar containing menus (**File**, **Edit**, **View** etc.). Below the menu bar there is a set of buttons, each with a defined task in Internet Explorer. Below the buttons there is a *text field* in which the user can type the location of a World Wide Web site to visit. To the left of the text field is a *label* that indicates the purpose of the text field. The menus, buttons, text fields and labels are part of Internet Explorer's GUI. They enable users to interact with the Internet Explorer program. C# contains classes that create the GUI components described here. Other classes that create GUI components will be described in Chapters 12 and 13, Graphical User Interfaces: Part 1 and Graphical User Interfaces: Part 2.

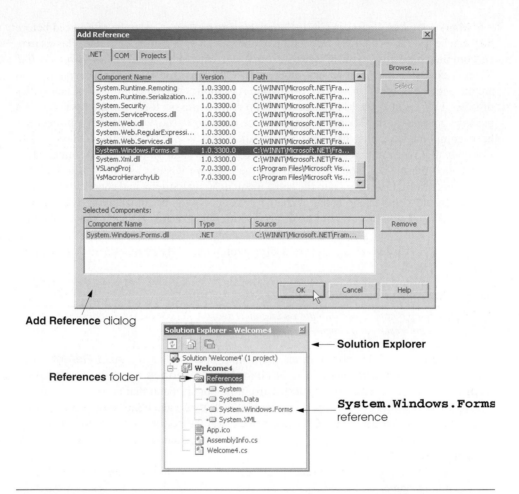

Fig. 3.8   Adding a reference to an assembly in Visual Studio .NET.

In **Main**, line 11 calls method *Show* of class **MessageBox** (Fig. 3.7). This method takes a string as an argument and displays it to the user in a message dialog. Method **Show** is called a *static method*. Such methods are always called by using their class name (in this case, **MessageBox**) followed by a *dot operator* (**.**) and the method name (in this case, **Show**). We discuss static methods in Chapter 8, Object-Based Programming.

Line 11 displays the dialog box shown in Fig. 3.10. The dialog includes an **OK** button that allows the user to *dismiss (close)* the dialog. Positioning the *mouse cursor* (also called the *mouse pointer*) over the **OK** button and clicking the mouse dismisses the dialog.

C# allows large statements to be split over many lines. For example, we could have split the statement on line 11 into the following two lines:

```
MessageBox.Show(
    "Welcome\nto\nC#\nprogramming!" );
```

All statements end with a semicolon (**;**), so the compiler recognizes that these two lines represent only one statement. However, you cannot split a statement in the middle of an identifier (e.g., the class name) or a string.

Label   Button   Menu   Text field   Menu bar

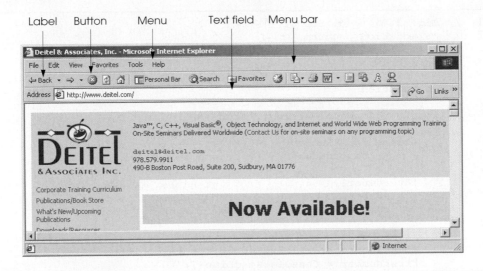

Fig. 3.9   Internet Explorer's GUI.

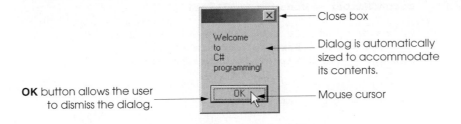

Fig. 3.10   Dialog displayed by calling **MessageBox.Show**.

Common Programming Error 3.6

Splitting a statement in the middle of an identifier or a string is a syntax error.

The user can close the dialog by clicking the **OK** button or the close box. Once this occurs, the program terminates, because the **Main** method terminates.

3.3 Another Simple Program: Adding Integers

Our next application (Fig. 3.11) inputs two integers (whole numbers) typed by a user at the keyboard, computes the sum of these values and displays the result. As the user types each integer and presses the *Enter* key, the integer is read into the program and added to the total. Lines 1–2 are single-line comments stating the figure number, file name and purpose of the program.

As stated previously, every C# program consists of at least one class definition. Line 6 begins the definition of class **Addition**. Lines 7–37 define the body of the class. Recall that all class definitions start with an opening left brace (**{**) and end with a closing right brace (**}**).

```
1   // Fig. 3.11: Addition.cs
2   // An addition program.
3
4   using System;
5
6   class Addition
7   {
8      static void Main( string[] args )
9      {
10         string firstNumber,      // first string entered by user
11                secondNumber;      // second string entered by user
12
13         int number1,             // first number to add
14             number2,             // second number to add
15             sum;                 // sum of number1 and number2
16
17         // prompt for and read first number from user as string
18         Console.Write( "Please enter the first integer: " );
19         firstNumber = Console.ReadLine();
20
21         // read second number from user as string
22         Console.Write( "\nPlease enter the second integer: " );
23         secondNumber = Console.ReadLine();
24
25         // convert numbers from type string to type int
26         number1 = Int32.Parse( firstNumber );
27         number2 = Int32.Parse( secondNumber );
28
29         // add numbers
30         sum = number1 + number2;
31
32         // display results
33         Console.WriteLine( "\nThe sum is {0}.", sum );
34
35      } // end method Main
36
37   } // end class Addition
```

```
Please enter the first integer: 45

Please enter the second integer: 72

The sum is 117.
```

Fig. 3.11 Addition program that adds two values entered by the user.

The program begins execution with method **Main** on line 8. The left brace (line 9) begins **Main**'s body and the corresponding right brace (line 35) terminates **Main**'s body.

Lines 10–11 are a *declaration*. The words **firstNumber** and **secondNumber** are the names of *variables*. A variable is a location in the computer's memory where a value can be stored for use by a program. All variables must be declared with a name and a data type before they can be used in a program. This declaration specifies that the variables **firstNumber** and **secondNumber** are data of type *string*, which means that these variables store strings of characters. There are certain data types already defined in the .NET Framework, known as *built-in data types* or *primitive data types*. Types such as **string**, **int**, **double** and **char** are examples of primitive data types. Primitive type names are keywords. The 15 primitive types are summarized in Chapter 4, Control Structures: Part 1.

A variable name can be any valid identifier. Declarations end with a semicolon (**;**) and can be split over several lines with each variable in the declaration separated by a comma (i.e., a *comma-separated list* of variable names). Several variables of the same type may be declared in one or in multiple declarations. We could have written two declarations, one for each variable, but the preceding declaration is more concise. Notice the single-line comments at the end of each line. This is a common syntax used by programmers to indicate the purpose of each variable in the program.

Good Programming Practice 3.7

Choosing meaningful variable names helps a program to be "self-documenting" (i.e., easier to understand simply by reading it, rather than having to read manuals or use excessive comments).

Good Programming Practice 3.8

*By convention, variable-name identifiers begin with a lowercase letter. As with class names, every word in the name after the first word should begin with a capital letter. For example, identifier **firstNumber** has a capital **N** in its second word, **Number**.*

Good Programming Practice 3.9

Some programmers prefer to declare each variable on a separate line. This format allows for easy insertion of a comment that describes each variable.

Lines 13–15 declare that variables **number1**, **number2** and **sum** are of data type **int**, which means that these variables will hold *integer* values (i.e., whole numbers such as –11, 7, 0 and 31914). In contrast, the data types **float** and **double** specify real numbers (i.e., floating-point numbers with decimal points, such as 3.4, 0.0 and –11.19) and variables of type **char** specify character data. A **char** variable may hold only a single lowercase letter, a single uppercase letter, a single digit or a single character, such as **x**, **$**, **7**, ***** and escape sequences (like as the newline character **\n**). Oftentimes in programs, characters are denoted in single quotes, such as **'x'**, **'$'**, **'7'**, **'*'** and **'\n'**, to differentiate between a value and a variable name. C# is also capable of representing all Unicode characters. *Unicode* is an extensive international *character set* (collection of characters) that enables the programmer to display letters in different languages, mathematical symbols and much more. For more information on this topic, see Appendix G, Unicode.

Lines 18–19 prompt the user to input an integer and read from the user a **string** representing the first of the two integers that the program will add. The message on line 18 is called a *prompt*, because it directs the user to take a specific action. Method **ReadLine** (line 19) causes the program to pause and wait for user input. The user inputs characters from the keyboard, then presses the *Enter* key to return the string to the program. Unfortunately, the .NET Framework does not provide a simple input dialog. For this reason, the examples in these early chapters receive user input through the command prompt.

Technically, the user can send anything to the program as input. For this program, if the user types a noninteger value, a *run-time logic error* (an error that has its effect at execution time) occurs. Chapter 11, Exception Handling, discusses how to make your programs more robust by handling such errors.

When the user enters a number and presses *Enter*, the program assigns the string representation of this number to variable **firstNumber** (line 19) with the *assignment operator =*. The statement is read as, "**firstNumber** *gets* the value returned by method **ReadLine**." The **=** operator is a *binary operator*, because it has two *operands*—**firstNumber**, and the result of the expression **Console.ReadLine**. The entire statement is an *assignment statement*, because it assigns a value to a variable. In an assignment statement, first the right side of the assignment is evaluated, then the result is assigned to the variable on the left side of the assignment. So, line 19 executes method **ReadLine**, then assigns the string value to **firstNumber**.

Good Programming Practice 3.10

Place spaces on either side of a binary operator. This makes the operator stand out and makes the program more readable.

Lines 22–23 prompt the user to enter a second integer and read from the user a string representing the value. Lines 26–27 convert the two strings input by the user to **int** values that can be used in a calculation. Method ***Int32.Parse*** (a static method of class **Int32**) converts its **string** argument to an integer. Class **Int32** is part of the **System** namespace. Line 26 assigns the integer that **Int32.Parse** returns to variable **number1**. Any subsequent references to **number1** in the program use this integer value. Line 27 assigns the integer that **Int32.Parse** returns to variable **number2**. Any subsequent references to **number2** in the program use this integer value. You can eliminate the need for **string** variables **firstNumber** and **secondNumber** by combining the input and conversion operations as follows:

```
int number1;
number1 = Int32.Parse( Console.ReadLine() );
```

In C#, users input data as **string**s. We convert these strings to perform integer arithmetic. Arithmetic operations, as we will discuss in Section 3.5, do not work with **string**s the same way operations work with integers. To add numbers and get the proper sum, we must convert the strings to integers. The preceding statements do not make use of the **string** variable (**firstNumber**). This variable is required only to store the **string** temporarily until the program converts it. Reading the **string** and converting it on one line makes the variable unnecessary.

The assignment statement on line 30 calculates the sum of the variables **number1** and **number2** and assigns the result to variable **sum** by using the assignment operator **=**. The statement is read as, "**sum** *gets* the value of **number1** plus **number2**." Most calculations are performed in assignment statements.

After performing the calculation, line 33 displays the result of the addition. In this example, we want to output the value in a variable using method **WriteLine**. Let us discuss how this is done.

The *comma-separated* arguments to **Console.WriteLine**

```
"\nThe sum is {0}.", sum
```

use **{0}** to indicate a placeholder for a variable's value. If we assume that **sum** contains the value **117**, the expression evaluates as follows: Method **WriteLine** encounters a number in curly braces, **{0}**, known as a *format*. This indicates that the variable found after the string in the list of arguments (in this case, **sum**) will be evaluated and incorporated into our string, in place of the format. The resulting string will be "**The sum is 117**." Similarly, in the statement

```
Console.WriteLine(
    "The numbers entered are {0} and {1}", number1, number2 );
```

the value of **number1** would replace **{0}** (because it is the first variable) and the value of **number2** would replace **{1}** (because it is the second variable). The resulting string would be **"The numbers entered are 45 and 72"**. More formats can be used (**{2}**, **{3}** etc.) if there are more variables to display in the string.

Good Programming Practice 3.11

Place a space after each comma in a method's argument list to make programs more readable.

Some programmers find it difficult, when reading or writing a program, to match the left and right braces (**{** and **}**) that delimit the body of a class or method definition. For this reason, some programmers include a single-line comment after each closing right brace that ends a method or class definition, as we do in lines 35 and 37.

Good Programming Practice 3.12

*Follow the closing right brace (**}**) of the body of a method or class definition with a single-line comment. This comment should indicate the method or class that the right brace terminates.*

3.4 Memory Concepts

Variable names, such as **number1**, **number2** and **sum**, actually correspond to *locations* in the computer's memory. Every variable has a *name,* a *type,* a *size* and a *value.*

In the addition program in Fig. 3.11, the statement (line 26)

```
number1 = Int32.Parse( firstNumber );
```

converts to an **int** the string that the user entered. This **int** is placed into a memory location to which the name **number1** has been assigned by the compiler. Suppose the user enters the string **45** as the value for **firstNumber**. The program converts **firstNumber** to an **int**, and the computer places the integer value **45** into location **number1**, as shown in Fig. 3.12.

When a value is placed in a memory location, this value replaces the previous value in that location. The previous value is lost (or destroyed).

number1   45

Fig. 3.12   Memory location showing name and value of variable **number1**.

When the statement (line 27)

```
number2 = Int32.Parse( secondNumber );
```

executes, suppose the user types **72** as the value for **secondNumber**. The program converts **secondNumber** to an **int**, the computer places the integer value **72** into location **number2** and memory appears as shown in Fig. 3.13.

Once the program has obtained values for **number1** and **number2**, it adds these values and places their total into variable **sum**. The statement

```
sum = number1 + number2;
```

performs the addition and replaces (i.e., destroys) **sum**'s previous value. After calculating the **sum**, memory appears as shown in Fig. 3.14. Note that the values of **number1** and **number2** appear exactly as they did before the calculation of **sum**. These values were used, but not destroyed, as the computer performed the calculation. Thus, when a value is read from a memory location, the process is *nondestructive*.

3.5 Arithmetic

Most programs perform arithmetic calculations. Figure 3.15 summarizes the *arithmetic operators*. Note the use of various special symbols not used in algebra. The *asterisk* (*****) indicates multiplication, and the *percent sign* (**%**) represents the *modulus operator*, which is discussed shortly. The arithmetic operators in Fig. 3.15 are binary operators, because they each require two operands. For example, the expression **sum + value** contains the binary operator **+** and the two operands **sum** and **value**.

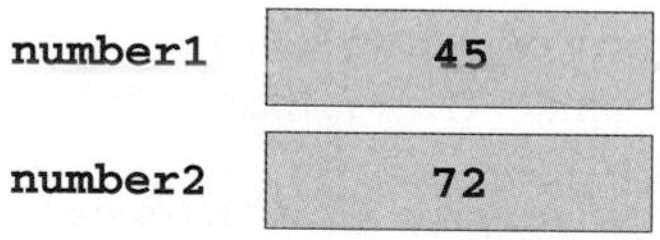

Fig. 3.13   Memory locations after values for variables **number1** and **number2** have been input.

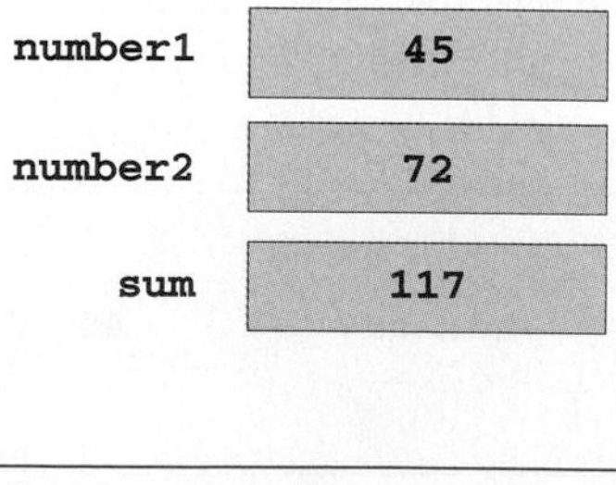

Fig. 3.14   Memory locations after a calculation.

C# operation	Arithmetic operator	Algebraic expression	C# expression
Addition	+	$f + 7$	**f + 7**
Subtraction	–	$p - c$	**p - c**
Multiplication	*	bm	**b * m**
Division	/	$x / y \ or \ \dfrac{x}{y} \ or \ x \div y$	**x / y**
Modulus	%	$r \ mod \ s$	**r % s**

Fig. 3.15 Arithmetic operators.

Integer division contains two **int** operands. The result of this computation is an integer quotient; for example, the expression **7 / 4** evaluates to **1** and the expression **17 / 5** evaluates to **3**. Note that any fractional part in integer division simply is discarded (i.e., truncated)—no rounding occurs. C# provides the modulus operator, **%**, which yields the remainder after integer division. The expression **x % y** yields the remainder after **x** is divided by **y**. Thus, **7 % 4** yields **3** and **17 % 5** yields **2**. This operator is used most commonly with integer operands, but also can be used with other arithmetic types. In later chapters, we consider interesting applications of the modulus operator, such as determining whether one number is a multiple of another. There is no arithmetic operator for exponentiation in C#. (Chapter 6, Methods, discusses how to perform exponentiation in C#.)

Arithmetic expressions in C# must be written in *straight-line form* to facilitate entering programs into a computer. Thus, expressions such as "**a** divided by **b**" must be written as **a / b** so that all constants, variables and operators appear in a straight line. The following algebraic notation generally is not acceptable to compilers:

$$\frac{a}{b}$$

C# expressions can use parentheses in the same manner as in algebraic expressions. For example, to multiply **a** times the quantity **b + c**, we write

    a * (b + c)

C# applies the operators in arithmetic expressions in a precise sequence, determined by the following *rules of operator precedence,* which are generally the same as those followed in algebra:

1. Operators in expressions contained within pairs of parentheses are evaluated first. Thus, *parentheses may be used to force the order of evaluation to occur in any sequence desired by the programmer.* Parentheses are at the highest level of precedence. With *nested* (or *embedded*) parentheses, the operators in the innermost pair of parentheses are applied first.

2. Multiplication, division and modulus operations are applied next. If an expression contains several multiplication, division and modulus operations, operators are

applied from left to right. Multiplication, division and modulus are said to have the same level of precedence.

3. Addition and subtraction operations are applied last. If an expression contains several addition and subtraction operations, operators are applied from left to right. Addition and subtraction have the same level of precedence.

The rules of operator precedence enable C# to apply operators in the correct order. When we say operators are applied from left to right, we are referring to the *associativity* of the operators. If there are multiple operators, each with the same precedence, the associativity determines the order in which the operators are applied. We will see that some operators associate from right to left. Figure 3.16 summarizes the rules of operator precedence. This table will expand as we introduce additional C# operators in subsequent chapters. See Appendix A for a complete operator-precedence chart.

Notice in the chart that we make note of nested parentheses. Not all expressions with several pairs of parentheses contain nested parentheses. For example, the expression

```
a * ( b + c ) + c * ( d + e )
```

has multiple sets of parentheses, but not nested parentheses. Rather, these parentheses are said to be "on the same level."

Let us consider several expressions in light of the rules of operator precedence. Each example lists an algebraic expression and its C# equivalent.

The following is an example of an arithmetic mean (average) of five terms:

$$\text{Algebra: } m = \frac{a+b+c+d+e}{5}$$

```
C#: m = ( a + b + c + d + e ) / 5;
```

The parentheses are required because division has higher precedence than addition. The entire quantity (a + b + c + d + e) is to be divided by 5. If the parentheses are erroneously omitted, we obtain a + b + c + d + e / 5, which evaluates as

Operator(s)	Operation	Order of evaluation (precedence)
( )	Parentheses	Evaluated first. If the parentheses are nested, the expression in the innermost pair is evaluated first. If there are several pairs of parentheses "on the same level" (i.e., not nested), they are evaluated left to right.
*, / or %	Multiplication Division Modulus	Evaluated second. If there are several such operators, they are evaluated left to right.
+ or –	Addition Subtraction	Evaluated last. If there are several such operators, they are evaluated left to right.

Fig. 3.16 Precedence of arithmetic operators.

$$a + b + c + d + \frac{e}{5}$$

The following is the equation of a straight line:

Algebra: $y = mx + b$

C#:   `y = m * x + b;`

No parentheses are required. The multiplication occurs first because multiplication has a higher precedence than addition. The assignment occurs last because it has a lower precedence than multiplication and division.

The following example contains modulus (**%**), multiplication, division, addition and subtraction operations:

Algebra: $z = pr\%q + w/x - y$

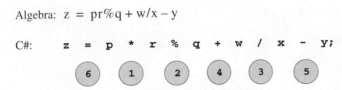

The circled numbers under the statement indicate the order in which C# applies the operators. The multiplication, modulus and division operators evaluate first in left-to-right order (i.e., they associate from left to right). The addition and subtraction evaluate next. These also are applied from left to right.

To develop a better understanding of the rules of operator precedence, consider how a second-degree polynomial ($y = ax^2 + bx + c$) evaluates:

The circled numbers under the statement indicate the order in which C# applies the operators. There is no arithmetic operator for exponentiation in C#; x^2 is represented as **x * x**. The .NET Framework Class Library provides method **Math.Pow** for exponentiation (see Chapter 6, Methods).

Suppose **a**, **b**, **c** and **x** are initialized as follows: **a = 2**, **b = 3**, **c = 7** and **x = 5**. Figure 3.17 illustrates the order of evaluation of the operators.

As in algebra, it is acceptable to place unnecessary parentheses in an expression to make the expression easier to read. Unnecessary parentheses are also called *redundant parentheses*. For example, the preceding assignment statement might be parenthesized as

`y = ( a * x * x ) + ( b * x ) + c;`

 Good Programming Practice 3.13

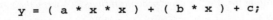

Using parentheses for more complex arithmetic expressions, even when the parentheses are not necessary can make the arithmetic expressions easier to read.

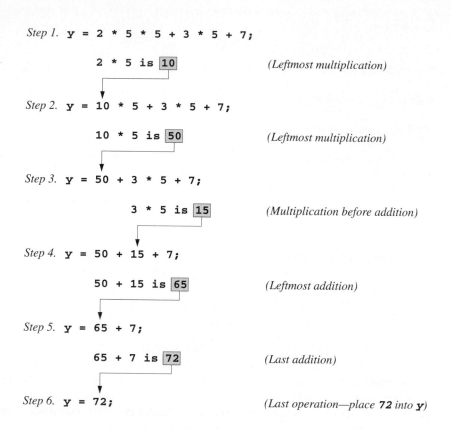

Step 1. `y = 2 * 5 * 5 + 3 * 5 + 7;`

`2 * 5 is 10`   *(Leftmost multiplication)*

Step 2. `y = 10 * 5 + 3 * 5 + 7;`

`10 * 5 is 50`   *(Leftmost multiplication)*

Step 3. `y = 50 + 3 * 5 + 7;`

`3 * 5 is 15`   *(Multiplication before addition)*

Step 4. `y = 50 + 15 + 7;`

`50 + 15 is 65`   *(Leftmost addition)*

Step 5. `y = 65 + 7;`

`65 + 7 is 72`   *(Last addition)*

Step 6. `y = 72;`   *(Last operation—place 72 into y)*

Fig. 3.17   Order in which a second-degree polynomial is evaluated.

3.6 Decision Making: Equality and Relational Operators

This section introduces C#'s *if* structure, which allows a program to make a decision based on the truth or falsity of some *condition*. If the condition is met (i.e., the condition is *true*), the statement in the body of the *if* structure executes. If the condition is not met (i.e., the condition is *false*), the body statement does not execute. Conditions in *if* structures can be formed by using the *equality operators* and *relational operators,* summarized in Fig. 3.18. The relational operators all have the same level of precedence and associate from left to right. The equality operators both have the same level of precedence, which is lower than the precedence of the relational operators. The equality operators also associate from left to right.

Common Programming Error 3.7
It is a syntax error if the operators ==, !=, >= and <= contain spaces between their symbols (as in = =, ! =, > =, < =).

Common Programming Error 3.8
Reversing the operators !=, >= and <= (as in =!, => and =<) is a syntax error.

Standard algebraic equality operator or relational operator	C# equality or relational operator	Example of C# condition	Meaning of C# condition
Equality operators			
=	==	x == y	**x** is equal to **y**
≠	!=	x != y	**x** is not equal to **y**
Relational operators			
>	>	x > y	**x** is greater than **y**
<	<	x < y	**x** is less than **y**
≥	>=	x >= y	**x** is greater than or equal to **y**
≤	<=	x <= y	**x** is less than or equal to **y**

Fig. 3.18 Equality and relational operators.

Common Programming Error 3.9

Confusing the equality operator **==** *with the assignment operator* **=** *is a logic error. The equality operator should be read "is equal to," and the assignment operator should be read "gets" or "gets the value of." Some people prefer to read the equality operator as "double equals" or "equals equals."*

The next example uses six **if** statements to compare two numbers input into a program by the user. If the condition in any of these **if** statements is true, the assignment statement associated with that **if** executes. The user inputs values that the program converts to integers and stores in variables **number1** and **number2**. The program compares the numbers and displays the results of the comparison in the command prompt. The program and sample outputs are shown in Fig. 3.19.

```
1   // Fig. 3.19: Comparison.cs
2   // Using if statements, relational operators and equality
3   // operators.
4
5   using System;
6
7   class Comparison
8   {
9      static void Main( string[] args )
10     {
11        int number1,          // first number to compare
12            number2;          // second number to compare
13
14        // read in first number from user
15        Console.Write( "Please enter first integer: " );
16        number1 = Int32.Parse( Console.ReadLine() );
17
```

Fig. 3.19 Using equality and relational operators. (Part 1 of 2.)

```
18            // read in second number from user
19            Console.Write( "\nPlease enter second integer: " );
20            number2 = Int32.Parse( Console.ReadLine() );
21
22            if ( number1 == number2 )
23               Console.WriteLine( number1 + " == " + number2 );
24
25            if ( number1 != number2 )
26               Console.WriteLine( number1 + " != " + number2 );
27
28            if ( number1 < number2 )
29               Console.WriteLine( number1 + " < " + number2 );
30
31            if ( number1 > number2 )
32               Console.WriteLine( number1 + " > " +  number2 );
33
34            if ( number1 <= number2 )
35               Console.WriteLine( number1 + " <= " + number2 );
36
37            if ( number1 >= number2 )
38               Console.WriteLine( number1 + " >= " + number2 );
39
40        } // end method Main
41
42    } // end class Comparison
```

```
Please enter first integer: 2000

Please enter second integer: 1000
2000 != 1000
2000 > 1000
2000 >= 1000
```

```
Please enter first integer: 1000

Please enter second integer: 2000
1000 != 2000
1000 < 2000
1000 <= 2000
```

```
Please enter first integer: 1000

Please enter second integer: 1000
1000 == 1000
1000 <= 1000
1000 >= 1000
```

Fig. 3.19   Using equality and relational operators. (Part 2 of 2.)

The definition of class **Comparison** begins on line 7, and the **Main** method begins on line 9. Lines 11–12 declare the variables used in method **Main**. Note that there are two variables of type **int**. Remember that variables of the same type may be declared in one declaration or in multiple declarations. Also recall that, if more than one variable is placed in one declaration (lines 11–12), those variables are separated by commas (**,**). The comment at the end of each line indicates the purpose of each variable in the program.

Line 16 reads in the first number from the user. Line 20 reads in the second number from the user. These values are stored in variables **number1** and **number2**, respectively. Recall that arithmetic operators cannot be used with strings. Relational and equality operators also cannot be used with strings. Therefore, the two input strings must be converted to integers.

Lines 16 and 20 both get an input, convert the input to type **int** and assign the values to the appropriate variable in one step. Notice that this step can be combined with the variable declaration and placed on one line with the statement

```
int number1 = Int32.Parse( Console.ReadLine() );
```

which declares the variable, reads a string from the user, converts the string to an integer and stores the integer in the variable.

The **if** structure in lines 22–23 compares the values of the variables **number1** and **number2** for equality. If the values are equal, the program outputs the value of **number1 + " == " + number2**. Notice that this expression uses the operator **+** to "add" (or combine) numbers and strings. C# has a version of the **+** operator used for *string concatenation*. Concatenation is the process that enables a **string** and a value of another data type (including another **string**) to be combined to form a new **string**.

If **number1** contains the value **1000** and **number2** contains the value **1000**, the expression evaluates as follows: C# determines that the operands of the **+** operator are of different types and that one of them is a **string**. Next, **number1** and **number2** are converted to a **string** and concatenated with **" == "**. At this point, the **string**, namely **"1000 == 1000"**, is sent to **Console.WriteLine** to be output. As the program proceeds through the **if** structures, more **string**s will be output by these **Console.WriteLine** statements. For example, given the value **1000** for **number1** and **number2**, the **if** conditions at lines 34 (**<=**) and 37 (**>=**) will also be true. Thus, the output displayed will be

```
1000 == 1000
1000 <= 1000
1000 >= 1000
```

The second of output window of Fig. 3.19 demonstrates this case.

Common Programming Error 3.10

*Confusing the + operator used for string concatenation with the + operator used for addition can lead to strange results. For example, assuming integer variable **y** has the value 5, the expression **"y + 2 = " + y + 2** results in the string **"y + 2 = 52"**, not **"y + 2 = 7"**. First the value of **y** (5) is concatenated with the string **"y + 2 = "**, then the value 2 is concatenated with the new, larger string **"y + 2 = 5"**. The expression **"y + 2 = " + (y + 2)** produces the desired result.*

Common Programming Error 3.11

*Replacing operator == in the condition of an **if** structure, such as **if (x == 1)**, with operator =, as in **if (x = 1)**, is a logic error.*

Notice the indentation in the **if** statements throughout the program. Such indentation enhances program readability.

Good Programming Practice 3.14

*Indent the statement in the body of an **if** structure to make the body of the structure stand out and to enhance program readability.*

Good Programming Practice 3.15

Place only one statement per line in a program. This enhances program readability.

Common Programming Error 3.12

*Forgetting the left and right parentheses for the condition in an **if** structure is a syntax error. The parentheses are required.*

There is no semicolon (**;**) at the end of the first line of each **if** structure. Such a semicolon would result in a logic error at execution time. For example,

```
if ( number1 == number2 );
    Console.WriteLine( number1 + " == " + number2 );
```

would actually be interpreted by C# as

```
if ( number1 == number2 )
    ;

Console.WriteLine( number1 + " == " + number2 );
```

where the semicolon on the line by itself—called the *empty statement*—is the statement to execute if the condition is true. When the empty statement executes, no task is performed. The program continues with the **Console.WriteLine** statement, which executes regardless of whether the condition is true or false.

Common Programming Error 3.13

*Placing a semicolon immediately after the right parenthesis of the condition in an **if** structure is normally a logic error. The semicolon causes the body of the **if** structure to be empty, so the **if** structure performs no action, regardless of whether its condition is true. Worse, the intended body statement of the **if** structure becomes a statement in sequence with the **if** structure and always executes.*

Notice the use of spacing in Fig. 3.19. Remember that the compiler normally ignores whitespace characters, such as tabs, newlines and spaces. Statements may be split over several lines and may be spaced according to the programmer's preferences without affecting the meaning of a program. It is incorrect to split identifiers and string literals. Ideally, statements should be kept small, but it is not always possible to do so.

Good Programming Practice 3.16

A lengthy statement may be spread over several lines. If a single statement must be split across lines, choose breaking points that make sense, such as after a comma in a comma-separated list or after an operator in a lengthy expression. If a statement is split across two or more lines, indent all subsequent lines with one level of indentation.

The chart in Fig. 3.20 shows the precedence of the operators introduced in this chapter. The operators are displayed from top to bottom in decreasing order of precedence. Notice that all these operators, with the exception of the assignment operator **=**, associate from left to right. Addition is left associative, so an expression such as **x + y + z** is evaluated as if it were written **(x + y) + z**. The assignment operator **=** associates from right to left, so an expression such as **x = y = 0** is evaluated as if it were written **x = (y = 0)**. The latter expression, **x = (y = 0)**, first assigns the value **0** to variable **y** and then assigns the result of that assignment, **0**, to **x**.

Good Programming Practice 3.17

Refer to the operator-precedence chart when writing expressions containing many operators. Confirm that the operators in the expression are performed in the expected order. If you are uncertain about the order of evaluation in a complex expression, use parentheses to force the order, as you would do in an algebraic expression. Remember that some operators, such as assignment (=), associate from right to left rather than from left to right.

In this chapter, we introduced important features of C#, including displaying data on the screen, inputting data from the keyboard, performing calculations and making decisions. The next chapter demonstrates many similar techniques, as we reintroduce C# Windows applications (applications that provide a graphical user interface). We also introduce *structured programming* and familiarize the reader further with indentation techniques. We study how to specify and vary the order in which statements execute—this order is called *flow of control*.

SUMMARY

- A console application is an application that, predominantly, displays text output in either a console window (or MS-DOS window). This is also called a command prompt.

- Programmers insert comments to document programs and improve program readability. Every program should begin with a comment describing the purpose of the program.

- A comment that begins with **//** is called a single-line comment, because the comment terminates at the end of the current line. A **//** comment can begin in the middle of a line and continue until that line's end. Multiple-line comments begin with the delimiter **/*** and end with delimiter ***/**. The compiler ignores all text between the delimiters of the comment.

- A namespace groups various C# features into related categories, providing programmers with the ability to locate them quickly.

Operators	Associativity	Type
( )	left to right	parentheses
* / %	left to right	multiplicative
+ –	left to right	additive
< <= > >=	left to right	relational
== !=	left to right	equality
=	right to left	assignment

Fig. 3.20　Precedence and associativity of operators discussed in this chapter.

- The **using** directive declares the use of a namespace.
- Programmers use preexisting code to make programming easier and faster.
- Blank lines, space characters and tab characters are known as whitespace (space characters and tabs are known, specifically, as whitespace characters). Such characters are ignored by the compiler and used to improve program readability.
- Classes consist of pieces (called methods) that perform tasks and return information (or simply control) when they complete their tasks. The programmer can program each piece that is needed to form a C# program.
- Classes defined by the programmer are known as programmer-defined or user-defined classes.
- The **class** keyword introduces a class definition and is followed immediately by the class name.
- Keywords are reserved for use by C# and are always spelled with lowercase letters.
- By convention, all class names in C# begin with an uppercase letter and have an uppercase letter for the beginning of every word in the class name.
- The name of a class is called an identifier. An identifier is a series of characters, consisting of letters, digits, underscores (_) and "at" symbols (**@**), that does not begin with a digit and does not contain any spaces.
- C# is case sensitive—uppercase and lowercase letters are different, thus **a1** and **A1** are distinct identifiers.
- A left brace (**{**) begins the body of every class or method definition. A corresponding right brace (**}**) must end each class or method definition. If braces do not occur in matching pairs, the compiler indicates an error.
- Set a convention for the indent size you prefer and apply that convention uniformly.
- C# applications begin executing at **Main**, which is known as the entry point of the program.
- C# class definitions normally contain one or more methods. C# applications contain one or more classes. For a C# application, one of the classes in the application must contain method **Main**.
- Methods can perform tasks and return information when these tasks complete. Information also can be passed to a method. This information may be necessary for the method to complete its task and is called an argument.
- A string sometimes is called a character string, a message or a string literal.
- Whitespace characters in strings are not ignored by the compiler.
- Every statement must end with a semicolon (the statement terminator). Omitting the semicolon at the end of a statement is a syntax error.
- A syntax error occurs when the compiler cannot recognize a statement. The compiler normally issues an error message to help the programmer locate and fix the incorrect statement. Syntax errors are violations of the language's rules.
- When the compiler reports a syntax error, the error might not be on the line indicated by the error message. First, check the line where the error was reported. If that line does not contain syntax errors, check the preceding several lines in the program.
- Unlike **WriteLine**, method **Write** does not position the output cursor at the beginning of the next line in the console window after displaying its argument.
- A single statement can display multiple lines by using newline characters.
- C# has a version of the **+** operator for string concatenation that enables a string and a value of another data type (including another string) to be concatenated—the result of this operation is a new (and normally longer) string.

- The backslash (****) is called an escape character. It indicates that a "special" character is to be output. When a backslash is encountered in a string of characters, the next character is combined with the backslash to form an escape sequence.
- String contents always must be delimited with double quotes.
- Class **MessageBox** allows you to display a dialog containing information.
- Class **MessageBox** is defined in namespace **System.Windows.Forms**.
- The predefined namespaces in C# contain classes that are collectively referred to as the .NET Framework Class Library.
- GUI components facilitate data entry by the user and the formatting or presenting of data outputs to the user.
- Method **MessageBox.Show** is a special method of class **MessageBox**, called a static method. Such methods are always called with their class name followed by a dot operator (**.**) and the method name.
- Depending on the type of application we create, classes may be compiled into files with a **.exe** (executable) extension, a **.dll** (or dynamic link library) extension or one of several other extensions. This file is called an assembly, which is the packaging unit for code in C#.
- We need to add a reference to an assembly if we wish to use its classes. References to assemblies can be created easily in Visual Studio .NET by selecting the **Add Reference...** option from the **Project** menu and finding the necessary **.dll**.
- The **System.Windows.Forms** namespace contains many classes that help C# programmers define graphical user interfaces (GUIs) for their applications.
- A message dialog by default includes an **OK** button that allows the user to dismiss the dialog.
- A variable is a location in memory where a value can be stored for use by a program.
- All variables must be declared with a name and a data type before they can be used in a program.
- A variable name can be any valid identifier.
- Declarations end with a semicolon (**;**) and can be split over several lines, with each variable in the declaration separated by a comma.
- Several variables of the same type may be declared in either one declaration or separate declarations.
- The keywords **int**, **double** and **char** are primitive types.
- Primitive type names are keywords.
- A prompt is a message that directs the user to take a specific action.
- The = operator is called a binary operator, because it has two operands. A statement containing an = operation is called an assignment statement, because it assigns a value to a variable. The expression to the right side of the assignment operator = is always evaluated before the assignment occurs.
- Method **Int32.Parse** (a static method of class **Int32**) converts its **string** argument to an integer.
- Sometimes, when displaying strings C# encounters a format. A format specifies a placeholder for a value that will be inserted in a string.
- Variable names actually correspond to locations in the computer's memory. Every variable has a name, a type, a size and a value.
- Whenever a value is placed in a memory location, this value replaces the previous value in that location. The previous value is destroyed (lost).
- When a value is read from a memory location, the process is nondestructive.

- Integer division yields an integer quotient. Note that any fractional part in integer division is simply discarded (i.e., truncated)—no rounding occurs.
- The modulus operator (%) yields the remainder after integer division.
- Arithmetic expressions must be written in straight-line form to facilitate entering programs into the computer.
- Parentheses are used in C# expressions in the same manner as in algebraic expressions.
- C# applies the operators in arithmetic expressions in a precise sequence determined by the rules of operator precedence.
- As in algebra, it is acceptable to place unnecessary (redundant) parentheses in an expression to make the expression clearer.
- The **if** structure allows a program to make a decision based on the truth or falsity of some condition. If the condition is met (i.e., the condition is true), the statement in the body of the **if** structure executes. If the condition is not met (i.e., the condition is false), the body statement does not execute.
- Conditions in **if** structures can be formed by using equality operators and relational operators.
- A string containing no characters is known as an empty string.
- Every variable declared in a method must be initialized (given a value) before it can be used in an expression, or a syntax error will occur.
- A semicolon by itself (not preceded by an actual statement) is known as an empty statement. When an empty statement executes, no task is performed.

TERMINOLOGY

!= is-not-equal-to operator
" double quotation
% modulus operator
*/ end a multiline comment
/* start a multiline comment
// single-line comment
; statement terminator
< less-than operator
<= less-than-or-equal-to operator
= assignment operator
== is-equal-to operator
> is-greater-than operator
>= greater-than-or-equal-to operator
\\ escape sequence
\n escape sequence
\r escape sequence
\t escape sequence
_ underscore
{ left brace
} right brace
, comma
Add Reference dialog
algebraic notation
application
argument
arithmetic calculation

arithmetic operators
assembly
assignment statement
associativity of operators
asterisk (*) indicating multiplication
average
backslash (\)
binary operator
blank line
body of a class definition
body of a method definition
built-in data type
button
C# compiler
carriage return
case sensitive
char variable
character set
character string
class
class definition
class keyword
class name
comma (,)
command prompt
comma-separated list of variable names

comment
compile-time error
compiler
concatenation of **string**s
condition
console application
Console class
Console.ReadLine method
console window
Console.Write method
Console.WriteLine method
data type
decision
declaration
dialog
display output
documentation
dot (**.**) operator
double
embedded parentheses
empty statement (**;**)
Enter (or *Return*) key
entry point of a program
error handling
escape sequence
exponentiation
float
flow of control
format
formatting strings
identifier
if structure
indentation in **if** statements
indentation techniques
innermost pair of parentheses
inputting data from the keyboard
Int32.Parse method
integer division
integer quotient
keyboard
keyword
left-to-right evaluation
location in the computer's memory
logic error
Main method
making decisions
matching left and right braces
MessageBox class
method
method definition

MS-DOS prompt
MSIL (Microsoft Intermediate Language)
multiple-line comment (**/***... ***/**)
name of a variable
namespace
nested parentheses
.NET Framework Class Library
nondestructive
object
OK button on a dialog
operand
operator precedence
output
parentheses **()**
parentheses "on the same level"
Parse method
performing a calculation
polynomial
precedence
primitive data type
programmer-defined class
prompt
ReadLine method
real number
redundant parentheses
"reinventing the wheel"
reserved word
reuse
robust
rounding
run-time logic error
self-documenting code
single-line comment
size of a variable
space character
spacing convention
special character
standard output
statement
static method
straight-line form
string
string concatenation
string formatting
string literal
string of characters
string type
structured programming
syntax error
System namespace

System.Windows.Forms namespace
tab character
text editor
truncate
type of a variable
Unicode
unnecessary parentheses
user-defined class
using directive
value of a variable

variable
Visual Studio .NET-generated console application
void keyword
whitespace character
Windows 95/98
Windows application
Windows NT/2000
Write method of class **Console**
WriteLine method of class **Console**

SELF-REVIEW EXERCISES

3.1 Fill in the blanks in each of the following statements:
   a) The _____ and _____ begin and end every method body.
   b) Every statement must end with a _____ statement terminator.
   c) The _____ structure makes decisions.
   d) _____ begins a single-line comment.
   e) _____, _____, _____ and _____ are known as whitespace.
   f) Class _____ displays message dialogs.
   g) _____ are reserved for use by C#.
   h) C# applications begin execution at method _____.
   i) Methods _____ and _____ display information in the console window.
   j) A _____ method is invoked by preceding its name with its class name and a dot (**.**).
   k) A _____ begins the body of a method definition.
   l) A C# program includes _____ directives to indicate that we are incorporating class-es from certain namespaces.
   m) When a value is placed in a memory location, this value _____ the previous value in that location.
   n) Saying that operators are applied from left to right refers to the _____ of the operators.
   o) C#'s **if** structure allows a program to make a decision based on the _____ or _____ of a condition.
   p) Types such as **int**, **float**, **double** and **char** are often called _____ data types.
   q) A variable is a location in the computer's _____ where a value can be stored .
   r) Data types _____ and _____ contain decimal points for storing numbers such as 3.44 or 1.20846.
   s) The expression to the _____ of the assignment operator (**=**) is always evaluated first.
   t) Arithmetic expressions in C# must be written in _____ form to facilitate entering programs into the computer.

3.2 State whether each of the following is *true* or *false*. If *false*, explain why.
   a) Comments cause the computer to print the text after the **//** on the screen when the program is executed.
   b) All variables must be given a type when they are declared.
   c) C# considers the variables **number** and **NuMbEr** to be identical.
   d) The arithmetic operators *****, **/**, **%**, **+** and **–** all have the same level of precedence.
   e) Method **Int32.Parse** converts an integer to a **string**.
   f) A comment that begins with **//** is called a single-line comment.
   g) A string of characters contained between double quotation marks is called a phrase or phrase literal.
   h) Blank lines, space characters, newline characters and tab characters are ignored by the compiler when placed outside strings.

i) Every C# application must contain one **Main** method.
j) Curly braces that define bodies of classes and methods need not occur in matching pairs.
k) C# applications begin executing at **Main**.
l) The compiler uses **class** statements to identify namespaces referenced in a C# program.
m) Integer division yields an integer quotient.
n) Parentheses cannot be used in an arithmetic expression to force the order of evaluation of operators to occur in a sequence determined by the programmer.

ANSWERS TO SELF-REVIEW EXERCISES

3.1　　a)　Left brace (**{**), right brace (**}**). b) Semicolon (**;**). c) **if**. d) **//**. e) Blank lines, space characters, newline characters and tab characters. f) **MessageBox**. g) Keywords. h) **Main**. i) **Console.Write** and **Console.WriteLine**. j) static. k) left brace. l) **using**. m) replaces. n) associativity. o) truth, falsity. p) primitive (or built-in). q) memory. r) **float**, **double**. s) right. t) straight-line.

3.2　　a) False. Comments do not cause any action to be performed when the program is executed. They are used to document programs and improve their readability. b) True. c) False. C# is case sensitive, so these variables are distinct. d) False. The operators *****, **/** and **%** are on the same level of precedence, and the operators **+** and **-** are on a lower level of precedence. e) False. Method **Integer.Parse** converts a **string** to an integer (**int**) value. f) True. g) False. A string of characters is called a string or string literal. h) True. i) True. j) False. Curly braces that do not match cause syntax errors. k) True. l) False. The compiler uses **using** directives to identify and load namespaces. m) True. n) False. Parentheses can be used to force the order of evaluation.

EXERCISES

3.3　　Write C# statements that accomplish each of the following tasks:
a) Display the message **"Enter two numbers"**, using class **MessageBox**.
b) Assign the product of variables **b** and **c** to variable **a**.
c) State that a program performs a sample payroll calculation (i.e., use text that helps to document a program).

3.4　　What displays in the message dialog when each of the following C# statements is performed? Assume the value of **x** is 2 and the value of **y** is 3.
a) **MessageBox.Show("x = " + x);**
b) **MessageBox.Show("The value of x + x is " + (x + x));**
c) **MessageBox.Show("x =");**
d) **MessageBox.Show((x + y) + " = " + (y + x));**

3.5　　Given $y = ax^3 + 7$, which of the following are correct statements for this equation?
a) **y = a * x * x * x + 7;**
b) **y = a * x * x * (x + 7);**
c) **y = (a * x) * x * (x + 7);**
d) **y = (a * x) * x * x + 7;**
e) **y = a * (x * x * x) + 7;**
f) **y = a * x * (x * x + 7);**

3.6　　Indicate the order of evaluation of the operators in each of the following C# statements, and show the value of **x** after each statement is performed.
a) **x = 7 + 3 * 6 / 2 - 1;**
b) **x = 2 % 2 + 2 * 2 - 2 / 2;**
c) **x = (3 * 9 * (3 + (9 * 3 / (3))));**

3.7   Write an application that displays the numbers 1 to 4 on the same line with each pair of adjacent numbers separated by one space. Write the program using the following methods:

a) Use one **Console.Write** statement.
b) Use four **Console.Write** statements.

3.8   Write an application that asks the user to enter two numbers, obtains the two numbers from the user and prints the sum, product, difference and quotient of the two numbers.

3.9   Write an application that inputs from the user the radius of a circle and prints the circle's diameter, circumference and area. Use the following formulas (r is the radius): $diameter = 2r$, $circumference = 2\pi r$, $area = \pi r^2$.

3.10   Write an application that displays in the console window a box, an oval, an arrow and a diamond, using asterisks (*****) as follows:

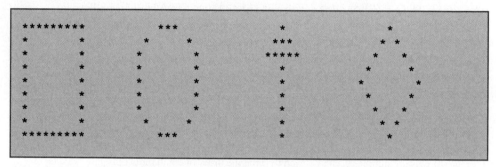

3.11   Modify the program you created in Exercise 3.12 to display the shapes in a **MessageBox** dialog. Does the program display the shapes exactly as in Exercise 3.12?

3.12   What does the following code print?

```
Console.WriteLine( "*\n**\n***\n****\n*****" );
```

3.13   What does the following code print?

```
Console.Write( "*" );
Console.Write( "***" );
Console.WriteLine( "*****" );
Console.Write( "****" );
Console.WriteLine( "**" );
```

3.14   Write an application that reads in two integers and determines and prints whether the first is a multiple of the second. For example, if the user inputs 15 and 3, the first number is a multiple of the second. If the user inputs 2 and 4, the first number is not a multiple of the second. [*Hint*: Use the modulus operator.]

3.15   Here is a peek ahead. In this chapter, you learned about integers and the data type **int**. C# can also represent uppercase letters, lowercase letters and a considerable variety of special symbols. Every character has a corresponding integer representation. The set of characters a computer uses and the corresponding integer representations for those characters is called that computer's character set. You can indicate a character value in a program simply by enclosing that character in single quotes, as with **'A'**.

You can determine the integer equivalent of a character by preceding that character with **(int)**—this is called a cast. (We will say more about casts in Chapter 4.)

```
( int ) 'A'
```

The following statement would output a character and its integer equivalent:

```
Console.WriteLine(
    "The character " + 'A' + " has the value " + (int) 'A' );
```

When the preceding statement executes, it displays the character **A** and the value **65** (from the Unicode character set) as part of the string.

Write an application that displays the integer equivalents of some uppercase letters, lowercase letters, digits and special symbols. As a minimum, display the integer equivalents of the following: **A B C a b c 0 1 2 $ * + /** and the blank character.

3.16 Write an application that inputs one number consisting of five digits from the user, separates the number into its individual digits and prints the digits separated from one another by three spaces each. For example, if the user types in the number **42339**, the program should print

```
4    2    3    3    9
```

[*Hint*: This exercise is possible with the techniques you learned in this chapter. You will need to use both division and modulus operations to "pick off" each digit.]

For the purpose of this exercise, assume that the user enters the correct number of digits. What happens when you execute the program and type a number with more than five digits? What happens when you execute the program and type a number with fewer than five digits?

3.17 Using only the programming techniques you learned in this chapter, write an application that calculates the squares and cubes of the numbers from 0 to 10 and prints the resulting values in table format, as follows:

```
number   square   cube
0        0        0
1        1        1
2        4        8
3        9        27
4        16       64
5        25       125
6        36       216
7        49       343
8        64       512
9        81       729
10       100      1000
```

[*Note*: This program does not require any input from the user.]

3.18 Write a program that reads a first name and a last name from the user as two separate inputs and concatenates the first name and last name, but separated by a space. Display the concatenated name at the command prompt.

Control Structures: Part 1

Objectives

- To understand basic problem-solving techniques of programming.
- To develop algorithms through the process of top-down, stepwise refinement.
- To use the **if** and **if/else** selection structures to choose among alternative actions.
- To use the **while** repetition structure to execute statements in a program repeatedly.
- To understand counter-controlled repetition and sentinel-controlled repetition.
- To use the increment, decrement and assignment operators.

Let's all move one place on.
Lewis Carroll

The wheel is come full circle.
William Shakespeare, *King Lear*

How many apples fell on Newton's head before he took the hint?
Robert Frost, Comment

Outline

4.1 Introduction

Before writing a program to solve a problem, it is essential to have a thorough understanding of the problem and a carefully planned approach. When writing a program, it is equally essential to understand the types of building blocks that are available and to employ proven program construction principles. In this chapter and the next, we present the theory and principles of structured programming. The techniques you will learn are applicable to most high-level languages, including C#. When we study object-based programming in more depth in Chapter 8, we will see that control structures are helpful in building and manipulating objects. The control structures discussed in this chapter will enable you to build these objects in a quick and easy manner.

4.2 Algorithms

Any computing problem can be solved by executing a series of actions in a specific order. A *procedure* for solving a problem in terms of

1. the *actions* to be executed and

2. the *order* in which these actions are to be executed

is called an *algorithm*. The example that follows demonstrates the importance of correctly specifying the order in which the actions are to be executed.

Consider the "rise-and-shine algorithm" followed by one junior executive for getting out of bed and going to work: (1) get out of bed, (2) take off pajamas, (3) take a shower,

(4) get dressed, (5) eat breakfast, (6) carpool to work. This routine gets the executive to work well-prepared to make critical decisions.

Suppose that the same steps are performed in a slightly different order: (1) get out of bed, (2) take off pajamas, (3) get dressed, (4) take a shower, (5) eat breakfast, (6) carpool to work. In this case, our executive shows up for work soaking wet.

The importance of correctly specifying the order in which actions appear applies to computer programs, as well. *Program control* refers to the task of ordering a program's statements correctly. In this chapter, we begin to investigate the program control capabilities of C#.

4.3 Pseudocode

Pseudocode is an artificial and informal language that helps programmers develop algorithms. The pseudocode we present is particularly useful for developing algorithms that will be converted to structured portions of C# programs. Pseudocode is similar to everyday English; it is convenient and user-friendly, and it is not an actual computer programming language.

Pseudocode is not executed on computers. Rather, pseudocode helps the programmer "think out" a program before attempting to write it in a programming language, such as C#. In this chapter, we provide several examples of pseudocode algorithms.

 Software Engineering Observation 4.1

Pseudocode helps the programmer conceptualize a program during the program design process. The pseudocode may then be converted to C#.

The style of pseudocode that we present consists solely of characters, thus programmers may type pseudocode conveniently using an editor program. Programmers can convert carefully prepared pseudocode programs to corresponding C# programs easily. In many cases, this conversion takes place simply by replacing pseudocode statements with their C# equivalents.

Pseudocode normally describes only executable statements—the actions that are performed when the pseudocode is converted to C# and executed. Declarations are not executable statements. For example, the declaration

```
int i;
```

informs the compiler of the type of variable **i** and instructs the compiler to reserve space in memory for this variable. This declaration does not cause any action, such as input, output or a calculation, to occur when the program executes. Some programmers choose to list variables and their purposes at the beginning of a pseudocode program.

4.4 Control Structures

Normally, statements in a program execute one after the other in the order in which they appear in the program. This is called *sequential execution*. Various C# statements enable the programmer to specify that the next statement to execute may not be the next one in sequence. A *transfer of control* occurs when a statement other than the next one in the program executes.

During the 1960s, it became clear that the indiscriminate use of transfers of control was causing difficulty for software development groups. The problem was the **goto** *statement,* which, in some programming languages, allows the programmer to specify a transfer of control to one of a wide range of possible destinations in a program. This caused programs to become quite unstructured and hard to follow. The notion of *structured programming* became almost synonymous with "**goto** elimination."

The research of Bohm and Jacopini[1] demonstrated that all programs with **goto** statements could be written without them. The challenge of the era for programmers was to shift their styles to "**goto**-less programming." It was not until the 1970s that programmers started taking structured programming seriously. The results were impressive, as software development groups reported reduced development times, more frequent on-time delivery of systems and more frequent within-budget completion of software projects. The key to these successes was that structured programs were clearer, easier to debug and modify and more likely to be bug-free in the first place.

Bohm and Jacopini's work demonstrated that all programs could be written in terms of only three *control structures*, namely, the *sequence structure*, the *selection structure* and the *repetition structure*. The sequence structure is built into C#. Unless directed otherwise, the computer executes C# statements one after the other in the order in which they appear in a program. The *flowchart* segment of Fig. 4.1 illustrates a typical sequence structure in which two calculations are performed in order.

A flowchart is a graphical representation of an algorithm or of a portion of an algorithm. Flowcharts contain certain special-purpose symbols, such as rectangles, diamonds, ovals and small circles. These symbols are connected by arrows called *flowlines,* which indicate the order in which the actions of the algorithm execute. This order is known as the flow of control.

Like pseudocode, flowcharts often are useful for developing and representing algorithms, although pseudocode is preferred by many programmers. Flowcharts show clearly how control structures operate; that is all we use them for in this text. The reader should compare carefully the pseudocode and flowchart representations of each control structure.

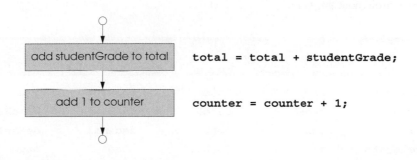

Fig. 4.1   Flowcharting C#'s sequence structure.

1. Bohm, C., and G. Jacopini, "Flow Diagrams, Turing Machines, and Languages with Only Two Formation Rules," *Communications of the ACM*, Vol. 9, No. 5, May 1966, pp. 336–371.

Consider the flowchart segment for the sequence structure in Fig. 4.1. We use the *rect-angle symbol*, also called the *action symbol,* to indicate any type of action, including a calculation or an input/output operation. The flowlines in the figure indicate the order in which the actions are to be performed—first, **studentGrade** is to be added to **total**, then **1** is to be added to **counter**. We can have as many actions as we want in a sequence structure. Anywhere in a sequence that a single action may be placed, several actions may also be placed.

When drawing a flowchart that represents a complete algorithm, an *oval symbol* containing the word "Begin" is the first symbol used; an oval symbol containing the word "End" indicates where the algorithm ends. When drawing only a portion of an algorithm, as in Fig. 4.1, the oval symbols are omitted in favor of using *small circle symbols,* also called *connector symbols*.

Perhaps the most important flowcharting symbol is the *diamond symbol*, also called the *decision symbol,* which indicates that a decision is to be made. We discuss the diamond symbol in Section 4.5.

C# provides three types of selection structures, which we discuss in this chapter and the next. The **if** selection structure performs (selects) an action if a condition is true or skips the action if the condition is false. The **if/else** selection structure performs an action if a condition is true and performs a different action if the condition is false. The **switch** selection structure, discussed in Chapter 5, Control Structures: Part 2, performs one of many actions, depending on the value of an expression.

The **if** structure is called a *single-selection structure* because it selects or ignores a single action (or a single group of actions). The **if/else** structure is called a *double-selection structure* because it selects between two different actions (or groups of actions). The **switch** structure is called a *multiple-selection structure* because it selects among many different actions (or groups of actions).

C# provides four repetition structures—**while**, **do/while**, **for** and **foreach** (**while** is covered in this chapter, **do/while** and **for** are covered in Chapter 5, Control Structures: Part 2, and **foreach** is covered in Chapter 8, Object-Based Programming). Each of the words **if**, **else**, **switch**, **while**, **do**, **for** and **foreach** are C# keywords. Figure 4.2 lists the complete set of C# keywords. We discuss the vast majority of C#'s keywords throughout this book.

C# Keywords				
abstract	as	base	bool	break
byte	case	catch	char	checked
class	const	continue	decimal	default
delegate	do	double	else	enum
event	explicit	extern	false	finally
fixed	float	for	foreach	goto
if	implicit	in	int	interface

Fig. 4.2   C# keywords. (Part 1 of 2.)

C# Keywords				
internal	is	lock	long	namespace
new	null	object	operator	out
override	params	private	protected	public
readonly	ref	return	sbyte	sealed
short	sizeof	stackalloc	static	string
struct	switch	this	throw	true
try	typeof	uint	ulong	unchecked
unsafe	ushort	using	virtual	void
volatile	while			

Fig. 4.2   C# keywords. (Part 2 of 2.)

C# has only eight control structures—sequence, three types of selection and four types of repetition. Each program is formed by combining as many of each type of control structure as is necessary. As with the sequence structure in Fig. 4.1, each control structure is flowcharted with two small circle symbols, one at the entry point to the control structure and one at the exit point.

Single-entry/single-exit control structures make it easy to build programs—the control structures are attached to one another by connecting the exit point of one control structure to the entry point of the next. This is similar to the stacking of building blocks; thus, we call it *control-structure stacking*. There is only one other way control structures may be connected, and that is through *control-structure nesting*, where one control structure can be placed inside another. Thus, algorithms in C# programs are constructed from only eight different types of control structures combined in only two ways.

4.5 `if` Selection Structure

In a program, a selection structure chooses among alternative courses of action. For example, suppose that the passing grade on an examination is 60 (out of 100). Then the pseudocode statement

> *If student's grade is greater than or equal to 60*
> > *Print "Passed"*

determines if the condition "student's grade is greater than or equal to 60" is true or false. If the condition is true, then *Passed* is printed, and the next pseudocode statement in order is "performed." (Remember that pseudocode is not a real programming language.) If the condition is false, the print statement is ignored, and the next pseudocode statement in order is performed. Note that the second line of this selection structure is indented. Such indentation is optional, but it is highly recommended because it emphasizes the inherent structure of structured programs. The preceding pseudocode *If* statement may be written in C# as

```
if ( studentGrade >= 60 )
    Console.WriteLine( "Passed" );
```

Notice that the C# code corresponds closely to the pseudocode, demonstrating how pseudocode can be useful as a program development tool. The statement in the body of the **if** structure outputs the character string **"Passed"** in the console window.

The flowchart in Fig. 4.3 illustrates the single-selection **if** structure. This flowchart contains the most important flowcharting symbol—the decision (or diamond) symbol, which indicates that a decision is to be made. The decision symbol contains a condition, that can be either **true** or **false**. The decision symbol has two flowlines emerging from it. One indicates the direction to be taken when the condition in the symbol is true; the other indicates the direction to be taken when the condition is false. A decision can be made on any expression that evaluates to a value of C#'s **bool** type (i.e., any expression that evaluates to **true** or **false**).

Note that the **if** structure, too, is a single-entry/single-exit structure. The flowcharts for the remaining control structures also contain (aside from small circle symbols and flowlines) only rectangle symbols, to indicate the actions to be performed, and diamond symbols, to indicate decisions to be made. This is the *action/decision model of programming* we have been emphasizing.

We can envision eight bins, each containing control structures for only one of the eight types. The control structures in each bin are empty; nothing is written in the rectangles or diamonds. The programmer's task is to assemble a program using as many control structures as the algorithm demands, combining those control structures in only two possible ways (stacking or nesting), then filling in the actions and decisions in a manner appropriate for the algorithm. We will discuss the variety of ways in which actions and decisions may be written.

4.6 if/else Selection Structure

The **if** selection structure performs an indicated action only when the condition evaluates to true; otherwise, the action is skipped. The **if/else** selection structure allows the programmer to specify different actions to perform when the condition is true and when the condition is false. For example, the pseudocode statement

If student's grade is greater than or equal to 60
     Print "Passed"
Else
     Print "Failed"

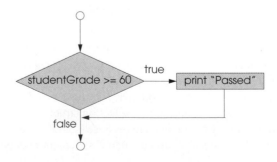

Fig. 4.3   Flowcharting a single-selection **if** structure.

prints *Passed* if the student's grade is greater than or equal to 60, and prints *Failed* if the student's grade is less than 60. In either case, after printing occurs, the next pseudocode statement in sequence is "performed."

The preceding pseudocode *If/Else* structure may be written in C# as

```
if ( studentGrade >= 60 )
    Console.WriteLine( "Passed" );
else
    Console.WriteLine( "Failed" );
```

 Good Programming Practice 4.1

*Indent both body statements of an **if/else** structure.*

Note that the body of the **else** statement also is indented. The indentation convention you choose should be applied carefully throughout your programs. It is difficult to read programs that do not use uniform spacing conventions.

The flowchart in Fig. 4.4 illustrates the flow of control in the **if/else** structure. Note that (besides small circles and arrows) the only symbols in the flowchart are rectangles (for actions) and a diamond (for a decision). We continue to emphasize this action/decision model of computing.

The *conditional operator (?:)* is related closely to the **if/else** structure. The **?:** is C#'s only *ternary operator*—it takes three operands. The operands and the **?:** form a *conditional expression*. The first operand is a *condition* (i.e., an expression that evaluates to a **bool** value), the second is the value for the conditional expression if the condition evaluates to **true** and the third is the value for the conditional expression if the condition evaluates to **false**. For example, the output statement

```
Console.WriteLine( studentGrade >= 60 ? "Passed" : "Failed" );
```

contains a conditional expression that evaluates to the string **"Passed"** if the condition **studentGrade >= 60** is true and evaluates to the string **"Failed"** if the condition is false.

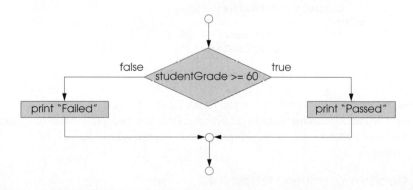

Fig. 4.4   Flowcharting a double-selection **if/else** structure.

The statement with the conditional operator performs in the same manner as the preceding **if/else** statement. The precedence of the conditional operator is low, so the entire conditional expression normally is placed in parentheses. Conditional operators can be used in some situations where **if/else** statements cannot, such as the argument to the **WriteLine** method shown earlier.

*Nested **if/else** structures* can test for multiple cases by placing **if/else** structures inside other **if/else** structures. For example, the following pseudocode statement will print **A** for exam grades greater than or equal to 90, **B** for grades in the range 80–89, **C** for grades in the range 70–79, **D** for grades in the range 60–69 and **F** for all other grades:

> *If student's grade is greater than or equal to 90*
> > *Print "A"*
>
> *Else*
> > *If student's grade is greater than or equal to 80*
> > > *Print "B"*
> >
> > *Else*
> > > *If student's grade is greater than or equal to 70*
> > > > *Print "C"*
> > >
> > > *Else*
> > > > *If student's grade is greater than or equal to 60*
> > > > > *Print "D"*
> > > >
> > > > *Else*
> > > > > *Print "F"*

This pseudocode may be written in C# as

```
if ( studentGrade >= 90 )
   Console.WriteLine( "A" );
else
   if ( studentGrade >= 80 )
      Console.WriteLine( "B" );
   else
      if ( studentGrade >= 70 )
         Console.WriteLine( "C" );
      else
         if ( studentGrade >= 60 )
            Console.WriteLine( "D" );
         else
            Console.WriteLine( "F" );
```

If **studentGrade** is greater than or equal to 90, the first four conditions are true, but only the **Console.WriteLine** statement after the first test executes. After that particular **Console.WriteLine** executes, the program skips the **else** part of the "outer" **if/else** structure.

Good Programming Practice 4.2

If there are several levels of indentation, each level should be indented the same additional amount of space.

Most C# programmers prefer to write the preceding **if** structure as

```
if ( studentGrade >= 90 )
   Console.WriteLine( "A" );
else if ( studentGrade >= 80 )
   Console.WriteLine( "B" );
else if ( studentGrade >= 70 )
   Console.WriteLine( "C" );
else if ( studentGrade >= 60 )
   Console.WriteLine( "D" );
else
   Console.WriteLine( "F" );
```

Both forms are equivalent. The latter form is popular because it avoids the deep indentation of the code. Such indentation often leaves little room on a line, forcing lines to be split and decreasing program readability.

The C# compiler always associates an **else** with the previous **if**, unless told to do otherwise by the placement of braces (**{ }**). This is referred to as the *dangling-else problem*. For example,

```
if ( x > 5 )
   if ( y > 5 )
      Console.WriteLine( "x and y are > 5" );
else
   Console.WriteLine( "x is <= 5" );
```

appears to indicate that if **x** is greater than **5**, the **if** structure in its body determines if **y** is also greater than **5**. If so, the string **"x and y are > 5"** is output. Otherwise, it *appears* that if **x** is not greater than **5**, the **else** part of the **if/else** structure outputs the string **"x is <= 5"**.

Testing and Debugging Tip 4.1

The reader can use Visual Studio to indent code properly. In order to check indentation, the reader should highlight the relevant code and press Ctrl-K *followed immediately by* Ctrl-F.

However, the preceding nested **if** structure does not execute as its indentation implies. The compiler actually interprets the structure as

```
if ( x > 5 )
   if ( y > 5 )
      Console.WriteLine( "x and y are > 5" );
   else
      Console.WriteLine( "x is <= 5" );
```

in which the body of the first **if** structure is an **if/else** structure. This structure tests if **x** is greater than **5**. If so, execution continues by testing if **y** is also greater than **5**. If the second condition is true, the proper string—**"x and y are > 5"**—is displayed. However, if the second condition is false, the string **"x is <= 5"** is displayed, even though we know **x** is greater than **5**.

To force the preceding nested **if** structure to execute as it was originally intended, the structure must be written as follows:

```
if ( x > 5 )
{
   if ( y > 5 )
      Console.WriteLine( "x and y are > 5" );
}
else
   Console.WriteLine( "x is <= 5" );
```

The braces (**{}**) indicate to the compiler that the second **if** structure is in the body of the first **if** structure and that the **else** is matched with the first **if** structure.

The **if** selection structure normally expects only one statement in its body. To include several statements in the body of an **if**, enclose these statements in braces (**{** and **}**). A set of statements contained in a pair of braces is called a *block*.

Software Engineering Observation 4.2

A block can be placed anywhere in a program at which a single statement can be placed.

The following example includes a block in the **else** part of an **if/else** structure:

```
if ( studentGrade >= 60 )
   Console.WriteLine( "Passed" );
else
{
   Console.WriteLine( "Failed" );
   Console.WriteLine( "You must take this course again." );
}
```

In this case, if **studentGrade** is less than 60, the program executes both statements in the body of the **else** and prints

```
Failed
You must take this course again.
```

Notice the braces surrounding the two statements in the **else** clause. These braces are important. Without the braces, the statement

```
Console.WriteLine( "You must take this course again." );
```

would be outside the body of the **else** and would execute regardless of whether the grade is less than 60.

Common Programming Error 4.1

Forgetting one of the braces that delimit a block can lead to syntax errors. Forgetting both of the braces that delimit a block can lead to syntax and/or logic errors.

Syntax errors, such as when one brace in a block is left out of the program, are caught by the compiler. A *logic error*, such as the error caused when both braces in a block are left out of the program, has its effect at execution time. A *fatal logic error* causes a program to fail and terminate prematurely. A *nonfatal logic error* allows a program to continue executing, but the program produces incorrect results.

Software Engineering Observation 4.3

*Just as a block can be placed anywhere a single statement can be placed, it is also possible to have an empty statement, which is represented by placing a semicolon (**;**) where a statement normally would be.*

Common Programming Error 4.2

*Placing a semicolon after the condition in an **if** structure leads to a logic error in single-selection **if** structures and a syntax error in double-selection **if** structures (if the **if** clause contains a nonempty body statement).*

Good Programming Practice 4.3

Some programmers prefer to type the beginning and ending braces of blocks before typing the individual statements within the braces. This practice helps avoid omitting one or both of the braces.

In this section, we introduced the notion of a block. A block may contain declarations. The declarations in a block commonly are placed first in the block before any action statements, but declarations may be intermixed with action statements.

4.7 `while` Repetition Structure

A *repetition structure* allows the programmer to specify that an action is to be repeated while a condition remains true. The pseudocode statement

> *While there are more items on my shopping list*
> *Purchase next item and cross it off my list*

describes the repetition that occurs during a shopping trip. The condition, "there are more items on my shopping list" may be true or false. If it is true, then the action, "Purchase next item and cross it off my list" is performed. This action executes repeatedly while the condition remains true. The statement(s) contained in the *while* repetition structure constitute the body of the *while*. The *while* structure body may be a single statement or a block. Eventually, the condition becomes false (when the last item on the shopping list has been purchased and crossed off the list). At this point, the repetition terminates, and the first statement after the repetition structure executes.

As an example of a **while** structure, consider a program segment designed to find the first power of 2 larger than 1000. Suppose **int** variable **product** contains the value 2. When the following **while** structure finishes executing, **product** contains the result:

```
int product = 2;

while ( product <= 1000 )
    product = 2 * product;
```

The flowchart in Fig. 4.5 illustrates the flow of control of the preceding **while** repetition structure. Once again, note that (besides small circles and arrows) the flowchart contains only a rectangle symbol and a diamond symbol.

Common Programming Error 4.3

*Not providing in the body of a **while** structure an action that eventually causes the condition to become false is a logic error. Normally, such a repetition structure will never terminate, which is an error called an "infinite loop."*

Common Programming Error 4.4

*Beginning the keyword **while** with an uppercase W, as in **While**, is a syntax error. Remember that C# is a case-sensitive language. All of C#'s keywords—**while**, **if**, **else**, etc.—contain only lowercase letters.*

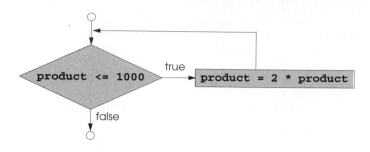

Fig. 4.5   Flowcharting the **while** repetition structure.

 Testing and Debugging Tip 4.2

Visual Studio .NET will not color a keyword properly unless that keyword is spelled correctly and with the correct case.

Imagine, again, a deep bin of empty **while** structures that may be stacked and nested with other control structures to form a structured implementation of an algorithm's flow of control. The empty rectangles and diamonds are filled with appropriate actions and decisions. The flowchart clearly shows the repetition. The flowline emerging from the rectangle indicates that program control continues with the decision, which is tested during each iteration of the loop until the decision eventually becomes false. At this point, the **while** structure terminates, and control passes to the next statement following the **while** structure in the program.

When the **while** structure begins executing, **product** is 2. Variable **product** is repeatedly multiplied by 2, taking on the values 4, 8, 16, 32, 64, 128, 256, 512 and 1024, successively. When **product** becomes 1024, the condition **product <= 1000** in the **while** structure becomes **false**. This terminates the repetition with 1024 as **product**'s final value. Execution continues with the next statement after the **while**. [*Note*: If a **while** structure's condition is initially **false**, the body statement(s) will never be executed.]

4.8 Formulating Algorithms: Case Study 1 (Counter-Controlled Repetition)

To illustrate how algorithms are developed, we solve several variations of a class-averaging problem. Consider the following problem statement:

> *A class of ten students took a quiz. The grades (integers in the range 0 to 100)*
> *for this quiz are available to you. Determine the class average on the quiz.*

The class average is equal to the sum of the grades divided by the number of students. The algorithm for solving this problem on a computer must input each of the grades, perform the averaging calculation and display the result.

Let us use pseudocode to list the actions to execute and to specify the order of execution. We use *counter-controlled repetition* to input the grades one at a time. This technique uses a variable called a *counter* to control the number of times a set of statements will execute. In this example, repetition terminates when the counter exceeds 10. This section presents a pseudocode algorithm (Fig. 4.6) and the corresponding program (Fig. 4.7). In

Section 4.9, we show how to develop a pseudocode algorithm. Counter-controlled repetition is also called *definite repetition* because the number of repetitions is known before the loop begins executing.

Set total to zero
Set grade counter to one

While grade counter is less than or equal to ten
    Input the next grade
    Add the grade into the total
    Add one to the grade counter

Set the class average to the total divided by ten
Print the class average

Fig. 4.6   Pseudocode algorithm that uses counter-controlled repetition to solve the class-average problem.

```
1   // Fig. 4.7: Average1.cs
2   // Class average with counter-controlled repetition.
3
4   using System;
5
6   class Average1
7   {
8      static void Main( string[] args )
9      {
10         int total,          // sum of grades
11             gradeCounter,    // number of grades entered
12             gradeValue,      // grade value
13             average;         // average of all grades
14
15         // initialization phase
16         total = 0;           // clear total
17         gradeCounter = 1;    // prepare to loop
18
19         // processing phase
20         while ( gradeCounter <= 10 )  // loop 10 times
21         {
22            // prompt for input and read grade from user
23            Console.Write( "Enter integer grade: " );
24
25            // read input and convert to integer
26            gradeValue = Int32.Parse( Console.ReadLine() );
27
28            // add gradeValue to total
29            total = total + gradeValue;
30
```

Fig. 4.7   Class average program with counter-controlled repetition. (Part 1 of 2.)

```
31              // add 1 to gradeCounter
32              gradeCounter = gradeCounter + 1;
33          }
34
35          // termination phase
36          average = total / 10;   // integer division
37
38          // display average of exam grades
39          Console.WriteLine( "\nClass average is {0}", average );
40
41      } // end Main
42
43  } // end class Average1
```

```
Enter integer grade: 100
Enter integer grade: 88
Enter integer grade: 93
Enter integer grade: 55
Enter integer grade: 68
Enter integer grade: 77
Enter integer grade: 83
Enter integer grade: 95
Enter integer grade: 73
Enter integer grade: 62

Class average is 79
```

Fig. 4.7   Class average program with counter-controlled repetition. (Part 2 of 2.)

Note the references in the algorithm (Fig. 4.6) to a total and a counter. The pseudocode variable *total* accumulates the sum of a series of values. A counter is a variable that counts—in this case, that counts the number of grades entered. Variables that store totals normally should be initialized to zero before being used in a program; otherwise, the sum would include the previous value stored in the total's memory location.

Testing and Debugging Tip 4.3

Initialize counters and totals.

Line 6 begins the definition of class **Average1**. Remember that an application class definition must contain a **Main** method (lines 8–41) to begin execution of the application.

Lines 10–13 declare variables **total**, **gradeCounter**, **gradeValue** and **average** to be of type **int**. Variable **gradeValue** will store the value the user inputs after the value is converted from a **string** to an **int**.

Good Programming Practice 4.4

Always place a blank line between a declaration and executable statements. This makes the declarations stand out in a program and contributes to program clarity.

Lines 16–17 are assignment statements that initialize **total** to **0** and **grade-Counter** to **1**. Variables **total** and **gradeCounter** are initialized before they are used in a calculation. Recall that using uninitialized variables in calculations results in compilation errors.

Line 20 indicates that the **while** structure should continue as long as the value of **gradeCounter** is less than or equal to 10. Lines 23 and 26 correspond to the pseudocode statement *"Input the next grade."* The statement on line 23 displays the prompt *"**Enter integer grade:**"* on the screen. The statement on line 26 reads the information entered by the user, converts it to an **int** and stores the value in **gradeValue**. Next, line 29 updates the **total** with the new **gradeValue** by adding **gradeValue** to the previous value of **total** and assigning the result to **total**.

The program is now ready to increment the variable **gradeCounter** to indicate that a grade has been processed. Line 32 adds **1** to **gradeCounter**, so the condition in the **while** structure eventually will become false and terminate the loop. Line 36 assigns the results of the average calculation to variable **average**. Line 39 displays a message containing the string **"Class average is "** followed by the value of variable **average**.

The averaging calculation produces an integer result. Actually, the sum of the grade-point values in this example is 794, which, when divided by 10, yields 79.4. Such numbers with a decimal point are called floating-point numbers; we discuss floating-point numbers in the next section.

4.9 Formulating Algorithms with Top-Down, Stepwise Refinement: Case Study 2 (Sentinel-Controlled Repetition)

Let us generalize the class-average problem. Consider the following problem:

> Develop a class-averaging program that processes an arbitrary number of grades each time the program executes.

In the first class-average example, the number of grades (10) was known in advance. In this example, no indication is given of how many grades are to be input. The program must process an arbitrary number of grades. How can the program determine when to stop the input of grades? How will it know when to calculate and print the class average?

One way to solve this problem is to use a special value called a *sentinel value* (also called a *signal value*, a *dummy value* or a *flag value*) to indicate "end of data entry." The user inputs all grades and then types the sentinel value to indicate that the last grade has been entered. Sentinel-controlled repetition often is called *indefinite repetition* because the number of repetitions is not known before the loop begins executing.

The sentinel value cannot be confused with an acceptable input value. Grades on a quiz are normally nonnegative integers, thus -1 is an acceptable sentinel value for this problem. A run of the class-average program might process a stream of inputs such as 95, 96, 75, 74, 89 and -1. The program would then compute and print the class average for the grades 95, 96, 75, 74 and 89. The sentinel value, -1, should not enter into the averaging calculation.

Common Programming Error 4.5

Choosing a sentinel value that is also a legitimate data value results in a logic error and may prevent a sentinel-controlled loop from terminating properly, a problem known as an infinite loop.

We approach the class-average program with *top-down, stepwise refinement*, a technique essential to the development of well-structured algorithms. We begin with a pseudocode representation of the *top:*

Determine the class average for the quiz

The top is a single statement that conveys the overall function of the program. As such, the top is a complete representation of a program. Unfortunately, the top rarely conveys a sufficient amount of detail from which to write the C# algorithm. Therefore, we conduct the refinement process. We divide the top into a series of smaller tasks and list these in the order in which they must be performed. This results in the following *first refinement*:

> *Initialize variables*
> *Input, sum up and count the quiz grades*
> *Calculate and print the class average*

Here, only the sequence structure has been used—the steps listed are to be executed in order, one after the other.

Software Engineering Observation 4.4

Each refinement, including the top, is a complete specification of the algorithm; only the level of detail in each refinement varies.

To proceed to the next level of refinement (i.e., the *second refinement*), we commit to specific variables. We need a running total of the numbers, a count of how many numbers have been processed, a variable to receive the value of each grade and a variable to hold the calculated average. The pseudocode statement

> *Initialize variables*

may be refined as follows:

> *Initialize total to zero*
> *Initialize counter to zero*

Notice that only the variables *total* and *counter* are initialized before they are used; the variables *average* and *grade* (for the calculated average and the user input, respectively) need not be initialized because their values are determined as they are calculated or input.

The pseudocode statement

> *Input, sum up and count the quiz grades*

requires a repetition structure (i.e., a loop) that successively inputs each grade. We do not know how many grades are to be processed, thus we use sentinel-controlled repetition. The user types in legitimate grades one at a time. After the last legitimate grade is typed, the user types the sentinel value. The program tests for the sentinel value after each grade is input and terminates the loop when the user enters the sentinel value. The second refinement of the preceding pseudocode statement is then

> *Input the first grade (possibly the sentinel)*
>
> *While the user has not as yet entered the sentinel*
>   *Add this grade into the running total*
>   *Add one to the grade counter*
>   *Input the next grade (possibly the sentinel)*

We do not use braces around the pseudocode that forms the body of the *while* structure. We simply indent the pseudocode under the *while* to show that it belongs to the *while* structure.

Note that a value is input both before reaching the loop and at the end of the loop's body. As we enter the loop, the value input before the loop is tested to determine whether it is the sentinel. If so, the loop terminates; otherwise, the body of the loop executes. The body processes the grade, then inputs the next grade. Then, the new grade is tested at the top of the loop to determine if that grade is the sentinel.

The pseudocode statement

> *Calculate and print the class average*

may be refined as follows:

> *If the counter is not equal to zero*
> > *Set the average to the total divided by the counter*
> > *Print the average*
>
> *Else*
> > *Print "No grades were entered"*

We test for the possibility of division by zero—a logic error that, if undetected, causes the program to produce invalid output. The complete second refinement of the pseudocode algorithm for the class-average problem is shown in Fig. 4.8.

Testing and Debugging Tip 4.4

When performing division by an expression whose value could be zero, explicitly test for this case and handle it appropriately in your program, possibly printing an error message.

Good Programming Practice 4.5

Include blank lines in pseudocode programs for increased readability. The blank lines separate pseudocode control structures and the program's phases.

Initialize total to zero
Initialize counter to zero

Input the first grade (possibly the sentinel)

While the user has not as yet entered the sentinel
> *Add this grade into the running total*
> *Add one to the grade counter*
> *Input the next grade (possibly the sentinel)*

If the counter is not equal to zero
> *Set the average to the total divided by the counter*
> *Print the average*

Else
> *Print "No grades were entered"*

Fig. 4.8   Pseudocode algorithm that uses sentinel-controlled repetition to solve the class-average problem.

Software Engineering Observation 4.5

Many algorithms can be divided logically into three phases—an initialization phase that initializes the program variables, a processing phase that inputs data values and adjusts program variables accordingly and a termination phase that calculates and prints the results.

The pseudocode algorithm in Fig. 4.8 solves the more general class-averaging problem. This algorithm was developed after only two levels of refinement. Sometimes more levels are necessary.

Software Engineering Observation 4.6

The programmer terminates the top-down, stepwise refinement process when the pseudocode algorithm is specified in sufficient detail for the programmer to convert the pseudocode to a C# program. Implementing the C# program then normally occurs in a straightforward manner.

The C# program for this pseudocode is shown in Fig. 4.9. Notice from the output that each grade entered is an integer, although the averaging calculation is likely to produce a number with a decimal point. The type **int** cannot represent real numbers, so this program uses data type ***double*** to handle floating-point numbers.

The program also introduces the *cast operator* (line 44) to handle the type conversion for the averaging calculation. These features are explained in detail in our discussion of Fig. 4.9.

```
1   // Fig. 4.9: Average2.cs
2   // Class average with sentinel-controlled repetition.
3
4   using System;
5
6   class Average2
7   {
8      static void Main( string[] args )
9      {
10         int total,            // sum of grades
11             gradeCounter,     // number of grades entered
12             gradeValue;       // grade value
13
14         double average;       // average of all grades
15
16         // initialization phase
17         total = 0;            // clear total
18         gradeCounter = 0;     // prepare to loop
19
20         // processing phase
21         // prompt for input and convert to integer
22         Console.Write( "Enter Integer Grade, -1 to Quit: " );
23         gradeValue = Int32.Parse( Console.ReadLine() );
24
25         // loop until a -1 is entered by user
26         while ( gradeValue != -1 )
27         {
28            // add gradeValue to total
29            total = total + gradeValue;
```

Fig. 4.9   Class-average program with sentinel-controlled repetition. (Part 1 of 2.)

```
30
31              // add 1 to gradeCounter
32              gradeCounter = gradeCounter + 1;
33
34              // prompt for input and read grade from user
35              // convert grade from string to integer
36              Console.Write( "Enter Integer Grade, -1 to Quit: " );
37              gradeValue = Int32.Parse( Console.ReadLine() );
38
39           } // end while
40
41           // termination phase
42           if ( gradeCounter != 0 )
43           {
44              average = ( double ) total / gradeCounter;
45
46              // display average of exam grades
47              Console.WriteLine( "\nClass average is {0}", average );
48
49           }
50           else
51           {
52              Console.WriteLine( "No grades were entered." );
53           }
54
55        } // end method Main
56
57  } // end class Average2
```

```
Enter Integer Grade, -1 to Quit: 97
Enter Integer Grade, -1 to Quit: 88
Enter Integer Grade, -1 to Quit: 72
Enter Integer Grade, -1 to Quit: -1

Class average is 85.6666666666667
```

Fig. 4.9   Class-average program with sentinel-controlled repetition. (Part 2 of 2.)

In this example, we examine how control structures may be stacked on top of one another, in sequence. The **while** structure (lines 26–39) is followed immediately by an **if** structure (lines 42–51). Much of the code in this program is identical to the code in Fig. 4.7, so we concentrate on the new features in this example.

Line 14 declares variable **average** to be of type **double**. This change allows us to store the result of the class-average calculation as a floating-point number. Line 18 initializes **gradeCounter** to **0** because no grades have been input yet—recall that this program uses sentinel-controlled repetition. To keep an accurate record of the number of grades entered, variable **gradeCounter** is incremented only when a valid grade value is input.

Notice the differences between sentinel-controlled repetition and the counter-controlled repetition of Fig. 4.7. In counter-controlled repetition, we read a value from the user during each pass of the **while** structure for the specified number of iterations. In sentinel-controlled repetition, we read one value (line 23) before the program reaches the **while** structure. This value is used to determine if the program's flow of control should enter the body of the **while** structure. If the **while** structure condition is false (i.e., the user has entered the sentinel value), the body of the **while** structure does not execute (i.e., no grades were entered). If, on the other hand, the condition is true, the body begins execution, and the value input by the user is processed (added to the **total**). Then, the next value is input from the user before the end of the **while** structure's body. When program control reaches the closing right brace (**}**) of the body (line 39), execution continues with the next test of the **while** structure condition. The new value input by the user determines if the **while** structure's body should execute again. Notice that the next value is input from the user immediately before the **while** structure condition is evaluated (line 37). This allows the program to determine whether the value just input by the user is the sentinel value *before* the program processes that value as a valid grade. If the value is the sentinel value, the **while** structure terminates, and the value is not added to the **total**.

Notice the block that composes the **while** loop in Fig. 4.9. Without the braces, the last three statements in the body of the loop would be outside the loop, causing the computer to interpret the code incorrectly, as follows:

```
while ( gradeValue != -1 )

   // add gradeValue to total
   total = total + gradeValue;

// add 1 to gradeCounter
gradeCounter = gradeCounter + 1;

// prompt for input and read grade from user
Console.Write( "Enter Integer Grade, -1 to Quit: " );
gradeValue = Int32.Parse( Console.ReadLine() );
```

An infinite loop occurs in the program if the user fails to input the sentinel **-1** as the input value at line 23 (before the **while** structure).

Common Programming Error 4.6
Omitting the curly braces that delimit a block in a repetition structure can lead to logic errors, such as infinite loops.

Good Programming Practice 4.6
In a sentinel-controlled loop, the prompts requesting data entry should remind the user of the sentinel value.

Averages do not always evaluate to integer values. Often, an average is a value such as 3.333 or 2.7, that contains a fractional part. These values are floating-point numbers and usually are represented by the data type **double**. We declare the variable **average** as type **double** to capture the fractional result of our calculation. However, the result of the calculation **total / gradeCounter** is an integer because **total** and **grade-Counter** are both integer variables. Dividing two integers results in *integer division*, in which any fractional part of the calculation is *truncated* and the result is a whole number. The calculation is performed first, thus the fractional part is lost before the result is assigned to **average**. To produce a floating-point calculation with integer values, we must create temporary values that are floating-point numbers for the calculation. C# provides the *unary* *cast operator* to create this temporary value. Line 44 uses the cast operator **(double)** to create a temporary floating-point copy of its operand—**total**. Using a cast operator in this manner is called *explicit conversion*. The value stored in **total** is still an integer. The calculation now consists of a floating-point value (the temporary **double** version of **total**) divided by the integer **gradeCounter**. Note that the cast does not modify the value stored in memory for **total**. Rather it creates a temporary value that is used only for this calculation.

Common Programming Error 4.7

Assuming that integer division rounds (rather than truncates) can lead to incorrect results.

C# can evaluate only arithmetic expressions in which the data types of the operands are identical. To ensure that the operands are of the same type, C# performs *implicit conversion* (also called *promotion*) on selected operands. Through implicit conversion, in an expression containing the data types **int** and **double**, **int** operands are *promoted* to **double**. In our example, the temporary **double** version of **total** is divided by the **int** **gradeCounter**. Therefore, a temporary version of **gradeCounter** is promoted to **double**, the calculation is performed and the result of the floating-point division is assigned to **average**.

Cast operators are available for most data types. The cast operator is known as a *unary operator* (i.e., an operator that takes only one operand) and is formed by placing parentheses around a data type name. In Chapter 3, Introduction to C# Programming, we studied the binary arithmetic operators. C# also supports unary versions of the plus (**+**) and minus (**-**) operators, so the programmer can write expressions like **-7** or **+5**. Cast operators associate from right to left and have the same precedence as other unary operators, such as unary **+** and unary **-**. This precedence is one level higher than that of the *multiplicative operators* *****, **/** and **%** and one level lower than that of parentheses. (See the operator precedence chart in Appendix A.) In our precedence charts, we indicate the cast operator with the notation *(type)* to show that any type name can form a cast operator.

Common Programming Error 4.8

Using floating-point numbers in a manner that assumes that they are precisely represented real numbers can lead to incorrect results. Real numbers are represented only approximately by computers.

Good Programming Practice 4.7

Do not compare floating-point values for equality or inequality. Rather, test that the absolute value of the difference between two floating-point numbers is less than a specified small value.

Despite the fact that floating-point numbers are not always "100% precise," they have numerous applications. For example, when we speak of a "normal" body temperature of 98.6, we do not need to be precise to a large number of digits. When we view the temperature on a thermometer and read it as 98.6, it may actually be 98.5999473210643. Calling such a number simply 98.6 is fine for most applications.

Floating-point numbers also develop through division. When we divide 10 by 3, the result is 3.3333333…, with the sequence of 3s repeating infinitely. The computer allocates only a fixed amount of space to hold such a value, so the stored floating-point value can be only an approximation.

Line 47 displays the value of **average**. We specify average as the second argument to **WriteLine**. Method **WriteLine** will convert this argument to a **string** and display its value.

4.10 Formulating Algorithms with Top-Down, Stepwise Refinement: Case Study 3 (Nested Control Structures)

Let us work through another complete problem. We will again formulate the algorithm using pseudocode and top-down, stepwise refinement; we will write a corresponding C# program.

Consider the following problem statement:

A college offers a course that prepares students for the state licensing exam for real estate brokers. Last year, several of the students who completed this course took the licensing examination. The college wants to know how well its students did on the exam. You have been asked to write a program to summarize the results. You have been given a list of the 10 students. Next to each name is written a 1 if the student passed the exam and a 2 if the student failed the exam.

Your program should analyze the results of the exam as follows:

> 1. *Input each test result (i.e., a 1 or a 2). Display the message "Enter result" on the screen each time the program requests another test result.*
> 2. *Count the number of test results of each type.*
> 3. *Display a summary of the test results, indicating the number of students who passed and the number of students who failed the exam.*
> 4. *If more than 8 students passed the exam, print the message "Raise tuition."*

After reading the problem statement carefully, we make the following observations about the problem:

> 1. The program must process test results for 10 students. A counter-controlled loop will be used.
> 2. Each test result is a number—either a 1 or a 2. Each time the program reads a test result, the program must determine if the number is a 1 or a 2. We test for a 1 in our algorithm. If the number is not a 1, we assume that it is a 2. (An exercise at the end of the chapter considers the consequences of this assumption.)
> 3. Two counters keep track of the exam results—one to count the number of students who passed the exam and one to count the number of students who failed.
> 4. After the program processes all the results, it must decide if more than eight students passed the exam.

Let us proceed with top-down, stepwise refinement. We begin with a pseudocode representation of the top:

Analyze exam results and decide if tuition should be raised

Once again, it is important to emphasize that the top is a complete representation of the program, but several refinements are likely to be needed before the pseudocode can be evolved naturally into a C# program. Our first refinement is

Initialize variables
Input the ten exam grades and count passes and failures
Print a summary of the exam results and decide if tuition should be raised

Even though we have a complete representation of the entire program, further refinement is necessary. We must commit to specific variables. Counters are needed to record the passes and failures. A counter controls the looping process and a variable stores the user input. The pseudocode statement

Initialize variables

may be refined as follows:

Initialize passes to zero
Initialize failures to zero
Initialize student to one

Only the counters for the number of passes, number of failures and number of students are initialized. The pseudocode statement

Input the ten quiz grades and count passes and failures

requires a loop that successively inputs the result of each exam. Here, it is known in advance that there are precisely ten exam results, so counter-controlled repetition is appropriate. Inside the loop (i.e., *nested* within the loop) a double-selection structure determines whether each exam result is a pass or a failure, and the structure increments the appropriate counter accordingly. The refinement of the preceding pseudocode statement is

While student counter is less than or equal to ten
    Input the next exam result

    If the student passed
        Add one to passes
    Else
        Add one to failures

    Add one to student counter

Notice the use of blank lines to offset the *If/Else* control structure to improve program readability. The pseudocode statement

Print a summary of the exam results and decide if tuition should be raised

may be refined as follows:

Print the number of passes
Print the number of failures

If more than eight students passed
    Print "Raise tuition"

The complete second refinement appears in Fig. 4.10. Notice that blank lines also set off the *While* structure for program readability.

    The pseudocode now is refined sufficiently for conversion to C#. The C# program and sample executions are shown in Fig. 4.11.

Initialize passes to zero
Initialize failures to zero
Initialize student to one

While student counter is less than or equal to ten
    Input the next exam result

    If the student passed
        Add one to passes
    Else
        Add one to failures

    Add one to student counter

Print the number of passes
Print the number of failures

If more than eight students passed
    Print "Raise tuition"

Fig. 4.10   Pseudocode for examination-results problem.

```
1   // Fig. 4.11: Analysis.cs
2   // Analysis of Examination Results.
3
4   using System;
5
6   class Analysis
7   {
8      static void Main( string[] args )
9      {
10        int passes = 0,          // number of passes
11            failures = 0,        // number of failures
12            student = 1,         // student counter
13            result;              // one exam result
14
15        // process 10 students; counter-controlled loop
16        while ( student <= 10 )
17        {
18           Console.Write( "Enter result (1=pass, 2=fail): " );
19           result = Int32.Parse( Console.ReadLine() );
20
21           if ( result == 1 )
22              passes = passes + 1;
23
24           else
25              failures = failures + 1;
```

Fig. 4.11   C# program for examination-results problem. (Part 1 of 2.)

```
26
27              student = student + 1;
28          }
29
30          // termination phase
31          Console.WriteLine();
32          Console.WriteLine( "Passed: " + passes );
33          Console.WriteLine( "Failed: " + failures );
34
35          if ( passes > 8 )
36              Console.WriteLine( "Raise Tuition\n" );
37
38      } // end of method Main
39
40  } // end of class Analysis
```

```
Enter result (1=pass, 2=fail): 1
Enter result (1=pass, 2=fail): 2
Enter result (1=pass, 2=fail): 1
Enter result (1=pass, 2=fail): 1
Enter result (1=pass, 2=fail): 1
Enter result (1=pass, 2=fail): 1
Enter result (1=pass, 2=fail): 1
Enter result (1=pass, 2=fail): 1
Enter result (1=pass, 2=fail): 1
Enter result (1=pass, 2=fail): 1

Passed: 9
Failed: 1
Raise Tuition
```

```
Enter result (1=pass, 2=fail): 1
Enter result (1=pass, 2=fail): 2
Enter result (1=pass, 2=fail): 2
Enter result (1=pass, 2=fail): 2
Enter result (1=pass, 2=fail): 2
Enter result (1=pass, 2=fail): 2
Enter result (1=pass, 2=fail): 1
Enter result (1=pass, 2=fail): 1
Enter result (1=pass, 2=fail): 1
Enter result (1=pass, 2=fail): 1

Passed: 5
Failed: 5
```

Fig. 4.11 C# program for examination-results problem. (Part 2 of 2.)

Lines 10–13 declare the variables used in **Main** to process the examination results. We have taken advantage of a C# feature that incorporates variable initialization into declarations (**passes** is assigned **0**, **failures** is assigned **0** and **student** is assigned **1**). Programs that contain repetition may require initialization at the beginning of each repetition;

such initialization normally occurs in assignment statements. Notice the use of the nested **if/else** structure (lines 21–25) in the **while** structure's body. Also, notice the new statement at line 31 that uses **Console.WriteLine** to output a blank line.

Software Engineering Observation 4.7

The most difficult part of solving a problem on a computer is developing the algorithm for the solution. Once a correct algorithm has been specified, the process of producing a working C# program from the algorithm is normally straightforward.

Software Engineering Observation 4.8

Many experienced programmers write programs without ever using program development tools like pseudocode. These programmers feel that their ultimate goal is to solve the problem on a computer, and that writing pseudocode merely delays the production of final output. Although this may work for simple and familiar problems, it can lead to serious problems on large, complex projects.

4.11 Assignment Operators

C# provides several assignment operators for abbreviating assignment expressions. For example, the statement

```
c = c + 3;
```

can be abbreviated with the *addition assignment operator* **+=** as

```
c += 3;
```

The **+=** operator adds the value of the expression on the right of the operator to the value of the variable on the left of the operator and stores the result in the variable on the left of the operator. Any statement of the form

>   *variable* **=** *variable   operator   expression***;**

where *operator* is one of the binary operators **+, -, *, /** or **%** (or others we will discuss later in the book), can be written in the form

>   *variable   operator***=** *expression***;**

Figure 4.12 includes the arithmetic assignment operators, sample expressions using these operators and explanations.

Common Programming Error 4.9

Placing a space character between symbols that compose an arithmetic assignment operator is a syntax error.

Assignment operator	Sample expression	Explanation	Assigns
Assume: `int c = 3, d = 5, e = 4, f = 6, g = 12;`			
+=	c += 7	c = c + 7	10 to c

Fig. 4.12   Arithmetic assignment operators. (Part 1 of 2.)

Assignment operator	Sample expression	Explanation	Assigns
-=	d -= 4	d = d - 4	1 to d
*=	e *= 5	e = e * 5	20 to e
/=	f /= 3	f = f / 3	2 to f
%=	g %= 9	g = g % 9	3 to g

Fig. 4.12   Arithmetic assignment operators. (Part 2 of 2.)

4.12 Increment and Decrement Operators

C# provides the unary *increment operator*, **++**, and the unary *decrement operator*, **--**, which are summarized in Fig. 4.13. A program can increment the value of a variable called **c** by 1 using the increment operator, **++**, rather than the expression **c = c + 1** or **c += 1**. If an increment or decrement operator is placed before a variable, it is referred to as the *preincrement* or *predecrement operator*, respectively. If an increment or decrement operator is placed after a variable, it is referred to as the *postincrement* or *postdecrement operator*, respectively.

Preincrementing (or predecrementing) a variable causes the variable to be incremented (or decremented) by 1, and then the new value of the variable is used in the expression in which it appears. Postincrementing (or postdecrementing) the variable causes the current value of the variable to be used in the expression in which it appears, and then the variable value is incremented (or decremented) by 1.

The application in Fig. 4.14 demonstrates the difference between the preincrementing version and the postincrementing version of the **++** increment operator. Postincrementing the variable **c** causes it to be incremented after it is used in the **Console.WriteLine** method call (line 14). Preincrementing the variable **c** causes it to be incremented before it is used in the **Console.WriteLine** method call (line 21).

Operator	Called	Sample expression	Explanation
++	preincrement	++a	Increment **a** by 1, then use the new value of **a** in the expression in which **a** resides.
++	postincrement	a++	Use the current value of **a** in the expression in which **a** resides, then increment **a** by 1.
--	predecrement	--b	Decrement **b** by 1, then use the new value of **b** in the expression in which **b** resides.
--	postdecrement	b--	Use the current value of **b** in the expression in which **b** resides, then decrement **b** by 1.

Fig. 4.13   The increment and decrement operators.

```
1   // Fig. 4.14: Increment.cs
2   // Preincrementing and postincrementing
3
4   using System;
5
6   class Increment
7   {
8      static void Main( string[] args )
9      {
10        int c;
11
12        c = 5;
13        Console.WriteLine( c );    // print 5
14        Console.WriteLine( c++ ); // print 5 then postincrement
15        Console.WriteLine( c );    // print 6
16
17        Console.WriteLine();       // skip a line
18
19        c = 5;
20        Console.WriteLine( c );    // print 5
21        Console.WriteLine( ++c ); // preincrement then print 6
22        Console.WriteLine( c );    // print 6
23
24     } // end of method Main
25
26  } // end of class Increment
```

```
5
5
6

5
6
6
```

Fig. 4.14 The difference between preincrementing and postincrementing.

The program displays the value of **c** before and after the **++** operator is used. The decrement operator (**--**) works similarly.

 Good Programming Practice 4.8

For readability, nary operators should be placed next to their operands, with no intervening spaces.

Line 17,

```
    Console.WriteLine();        // skip a line
```

uses **Console.WriteLine** to output a blank line. If **Console.WriteLine** receives no arguments, it simply outputs a newline character.

The arithmetic assignment operators and the increment and decrement operators can be used to simplify program statements. For example, the three assignment statements in Fig. 4.11 (lines 22, 25 and 27)

```
passes = passes + 1;
failures = failures + 1;
student = student + 1;
```

can be written more concisely with assignment operators as

```
passes += 1;
failures += 1;
student += 1;
```

with preincrement operators as

```
++passes;
++failures;
++student;
```

or with postincrement operators as

```
passes++;
failures++;
student++;
```

It is important to note here that when incrementing or decrementing a variable in an expression or statement by itself, the preincrement and postincrement forms have the same effect, and the predecrement and postdecrement forms have the same effect. It is only when a variable appears in the context of a larger expression that preincrementing and postincrementing the variable have different effects (and similarly for predecrementing and postdecrementing).

Common Programming Error 4.10

Attempting to use the increment or decrement operator on an expression other than a variable reference *is a syntax error. A* variable reference *is a variable or expression that can appear on the left side of an assignment operation. For example, writing ++ (x + 1) is a syntax error, because (x + 1) is not a* variable reference.[2]

The chart in Fig. 4.15 shows the precedence and associativity of the operators introduced to this point. The operators are shown top to bottom in decreasing order of precedence. The second column describes the associativity of the operators at each level of precedence. Notice that the conditional operator (**? :**), the unary operators increment (**++**), decrement (**--**), plus (**+**), minus (**-**), cast and the assignment operators (**=, +=, -=, *=, /= and %=**) associate from right to left. All other operators in the operator precedence chart of Fig. 4.15 associate from left to right. The third column names the groups of operators.

Operators	Associativity	Type
()	left to right	parentheses
++ --	right to left	unary postfix

Fig. 4.15 Precedence and associativity of the operators discussed so far in this book. (Part 1 of 2.)

---

2. The term *variable reference* is equivalent to the term *lvalue* ("left value"), which is popular among C and C++ programmers.

Operators	Associativity	Type
++ -- + - (*type*)	right to left	unary prefix
* / %	left to right	multiplicative
+ -	left to right	additive
< <= > >=	left to right	relational
== !=	left to right	equality
?:	right to left	conditional
= += -= *= /= %=	right to left	assignment

Fig. 4.15 Precedence and associativity of the operators discussed so far in this book. (Part 2 of 2.)

4.13 Introduction to Windows Application Programming

Today, users demand software with rich GUIs that allow them to click buttons, select items from menus and much more. In this chapter and the previous, we created console applications. However, most C# programs used in industry are Windows applications with GUIs. For this reason, we are introducing Windows applications early in the book, although doing so exposes some concepts that we do not explain fully until later chapters.

In Chapter 2, Introduction to the Visual Studio .NET IDE, we introduced the concept of visual programming, which allows programmers to create graphical user interfaces (GUIs) without writing any programming code. In this section, we combine visual programming with the conventional programming techniques introduced in this chapter and Chapter 3, Introduction to C# Programming. Through this combination, we can enhance considerably the Windows application introduced in Chapter 2.

Load the project **ASimpleProject** from Chapter 2 into the IDE. To identify easily the form and its controls in the program code, change the **(Name)** properties of the form, label and picture box to **ASimpleProgram**, **welcomeLabel** and **bugPictureBox**, respectively. To change a GUI component's properties, select (click) the component in the design window, then locate the property in the **Properties** window. Click the box to the right of the property name to input a new value, then press the *Enter* key.

With visual programming, the IDE generates the program code that creates the GUI. This code contains instructions for the creation of the form and every control on it. Unlike a console application, a Windows application's program code is not displayed initially in the editor window. Once the program's project (e.g., **ASimpleProgram**) is opened in the IDE, the program code can be viewed by selecting **View > Code**. Figure 4.16 shows the code editor displaying the program code.

Windows applications use classes. We already have seen examples of classes such as **Console** and **MessageBox**, which are defined within the .NET Framework Class Library. Classes are logical groupings of methods and data that simplify program organization. In-depth coverage of classes is provided in Chapter 8, Object-Based Programming.

Every Windows application consists of at least one class that *inherits* from class **Form** (which represents a form) in the .NET Framework Class Library's **System.Windows.Forms** namespace. The keyword **class** begins a class definition and is followed

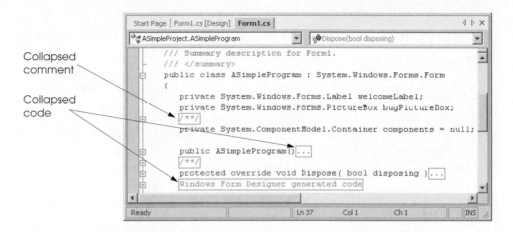

Collapsed comment

Collapsed code

Fig. 4.16   IDE showing program code for Fig. 2.15.

immediately by the class name (**ASimpleProgram**). Recall that the form's name is set using the **(Name)** property. A colon (**:**) indicates that the class **ASimpleProgram** inherits existing pieces from another class. The class from which **ASimpleProgram** inherits—here, **System.Windows.Forms.Form**—appears to the right of the colon. In this inheritance relationship, **Form** is called the *base class* (or *superclass*), and **ASimpleProgram** is called the *derived class* (or *subclass*). With inheritance **ASimpleProgram**'s class definition has the *attributes* (data) and *behaviors* (methods) of class **Form**. We discuss the significance of the keyword **public** in Chapter 6. [*Note*: Changing a control's name in the **Properties** window may not change all occurrences of the control's name in the code. The reader should search the code and replace names that were not changed by the IDE. For example, the original form name (and class name) was **Form1**. Search the code for **Form1** and change any remaining instances to **ASimpleProgram**.]

A key benefit of inheriting from class **Form** is that someone else has previously defined "what it means to be a form." The Windows operating system expects every window (e.g., form) to have certain attributes and behaviors. However, because class **Form** already provides those capabilities, programmers do not need to "reinvent the wheel" by defining all those capabilities themselves. In fact, class **Form** has over 400 methods! In our programs up to this point, we have used only one method (i.e., **Main**), so you can imagine how much work went into creating class **Form**. The use of the colon to extend from class **Form** enables programmers to create forms quickly.

In the editor window (Fig. 4.16), notice the text **Windows Form Designer generated code**, which is colored gray and has a plus box next to it. The plus box indicates that this section of code is *collapsed*. Although collapsed code is not visible, it is still part of the program. Code collapsing allows programmers to hide code in the editor, so that they can focus on smaller (and perhaps more important) code segments. Notice that the entire class definition also can be collapsed by clicking the minus box to the left of **public**. In Fig. 4.16, the description in gray indicates that the collapsed code was created by the *Windows Form Designer* (i.e., the part of the IDE that creates the code for the GUI). This collapsed code contains the code created by the IDE for the form and its controls, as well as code that enables the program to run. Click the plus box to view the code.

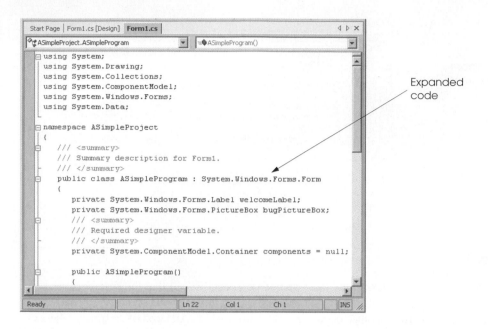

Fig. 4.17 Windows Form Designer generated code when expanded.

Upon initial inspection, the *expanded code* (Fig. 4.17) looks incredibly complex.This code is created by the IDE and normally is not edited by the programmer. We feel it is important for novice programmers to see the amount of code that is generated by the IDE, even though much of the code is not explained until later in the book. This type of code is present in every Windows application. Allowing the IDE to create this code saves the programmer considerable development time. If the IDE did not provide the code, the programmer would have to write it, and this would require a considerable amount of time. The vast majority of the code shown has not been introduced yet, so you are not expected to understand how it works. However, certain programming constructs, such as comments and control structures, should be familiar. Our explanation of this code will enable us to discuss visual programming in greater detail. As you continue to study C#, especially in Chapters 8–13, the purpose of this code will become clearer.

When we created this application in Chapter 2, we used the **Properties** window to set properties for the form, label and picture box. Once a property was set, the form or control was updated immediately. Forms and controls contain a set of *default properties*, which are displayed initially in the **Properties** window when a form or control is selected. These default properties provide the initial characteristics of a form or control when it is created. When a control, such as a label, is placed on the form, the IDE adds code to the class (e.g., **ASimpleProgram**) that creates the control and that sets some of the control's property values, such as the name of the control and its location on the form. Figure 4.18 shows a portion of the code generated by the IDE for setting the label's (i.e., **welcomeLabel**'s) properties. These include the label's **Font**, **Location**, **Name**, **Text** and **TextAlign** properties. Recall from Chapter 2 that we explicitly set values for the label's **Name**, **Text** and **TextAlign** properties. Other properties, such as **Location** are set only when the label is placed on the form.

Property initializations   Click here for   Click here for
for **welcomeLabel**   design view   code view

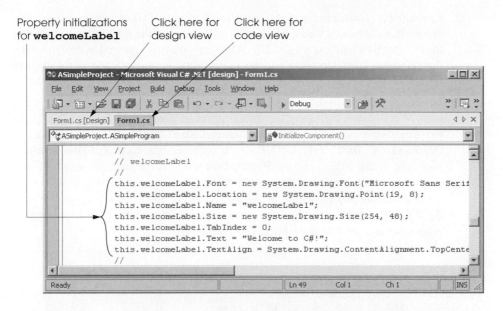

Fig. 4.18 Code generated by the IDE for **welcomeLabel**.

The values assigned to the properties are based on the values in the **Properties** window. We now demonstrate how the IDE updates the Windows Form Designer generated code it generates when a property value in the **Properties** window changes. During this process, we must switch between code view and design view. To switch views, select the corresponding tabs—**Form1.cs*** for code view and **Form1.cs* [Design]** for design view. Alternatively, the programmer can select **View > Code** or **View > Designer**. Perform the following steps:

1. *Modify the label control's* **Text** *property using the* **Properties** *window*. Recall that properties can be changed in design view by clicking a form or control to select it, then modifying the appropriate property in the **Properties** window. Change the **Text** property of the label to "**Deitel**" (Fig. 4.19).

Text
property

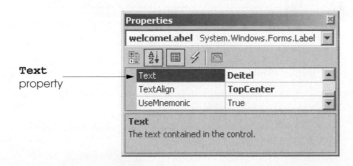

Fig. 4.19 Using the **Properties** window to set a property value.

2. *Examine the changes in the code view*. Switch to code view and examine the code. Notice that the label's **Text** property is now assigned the text that we entered in the **Properties** window (Fig. 4.20). When a property is changed in design mode, the Windows Form Designer updates the appropriate line of code in the class to reflect the new value.

3. *Modifying a property value in code view*. In the code view editor, locate the three lines of comments indicating the initialization for **welcomeLabel** and change the **string** assigned to **this.welcomeLabel.Text** from "**Deitel**" to "**Visual C# .NET**" (Fig. 4.21). Now, switch to design mode. The label now displays the updated text, and the **Properties** window for **welcomeLabel** displays the new **Text** value (Fig. 4.22). [*Note*: Property values should not be set using the techniques presented in this step. Here, we modify the property value in the IDE generated code only as a demonstration of the relationship between program code and the Windows Form Designer.]

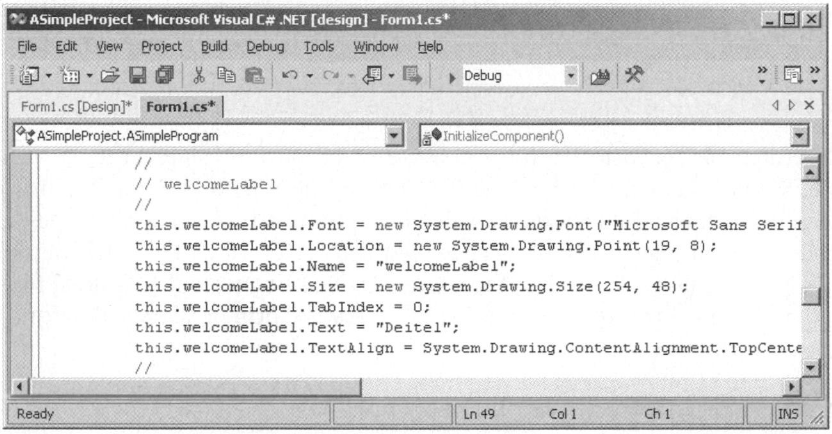

Fig. 4.20 Windows Form Designer generated code reflecting new property values.

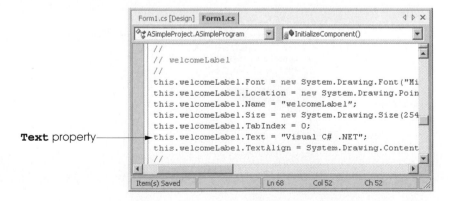

Fig. 4.21 Changing a property in the code view editor.

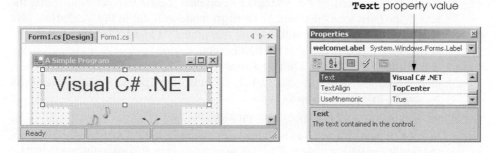

Fig. 4.22 New **Text** property value reflected in design mode.

4. *Change the label's* **Text** *property at runtime.* In the previous steps, we set properties at design time. Often, however, it is necessary to modify a property while a program is running. For example, to display the result of a calculation, a label's text can be assigned a **string** containing the result. In console applications, such code is located in **Main**. In Windows applications, we must create a method that executes when the form is loaded into memory during program execution. Like **Main**, this method is invoked when the program is run. Double-clicking the form in design view adds a method named **ASimpleProgram_Load** to the class (Fig. 4.23). The cursor is placed in the body of the **ASimpleProgram_Load** method definition. Notice that **ASimpleProgram_Load** is not part of the Windows Form Designer generated code. Add the statement **welcomeLabel.Text = "C#";** in the body of the method definition (Fig. 4.23). In C#, properties are accessed by placing the property name (i.e., **Text**) after the object name (i.e., **welcomeLabel**), separated by the dot operator. This syntax is similar to that used when accessing object methods. Notice that the *IntelliSense* feature displays the **Text** property in the member list after the class name and dot operator have been typed (Fig. 4.24). In Chapter 8, Object-Based Programming, we discuss how programmers can create their own properties.

ASimpleProgram_Load method

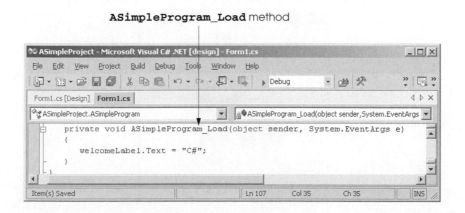

Fig. 4.23 Method **ASimpleProgram_Load**.

5. *Examine the results of the **ASimpleProgram_Load** method.* Notice that the text in the label looks the same in **Design** mode as it did in Fig. 4.22. Note also that the property window still displays the value "**Visual C# .NET**" as the label's **Text** property and that the IDE generated code has not changed either. Select **Build > Build** then **Debug > Start** to run the program. Once the form is displayed, the text in the label reflects the property assignment in **ASimpleProgram_Load** (Fig. 4.25).

6. *Terminate program execution.* Click the close button to terminate program execution. Once again, notice that both the label and the label's **Text** property contain the text **Visual C# .NET**. The IDE generated code also contains the text **Visual C# .NET**, which is assigned to the label's **Text** property.

In this chapter, we introduced program building blocks called control structures. We also discussed aspects of Windows application programming. In Chapter 5, Control Structures: Part 2, we continue our discussion of control structures by presenting additional selection and repetition structures. In addition, we also build upon the Windows application concepts presented in this chapter by creating a richer Windows application.

SUMMARY

- Executing a series of actions in a specific order can solve many computing problems.
- A procedure for solving a problem in terms of the actions to execute and the order in which these actions execute is an algorithm.
- Program control specifies the order in which statements execute in a computer program.
- Pseudocode is an artificial and informal language that helps programmers develop algorithms and "think out" a program during the program design process.
- C# code corresponds closely to pseudocode. This is a property of pseudocode that makes it a useful program development tool.
- Normally, statements in a program execute one after the other in the order in which they appear. This is called sequential execution.

Fig. 4.25   Changing a property value at runtime.

- Various C# statements enable the programmer to specify that the next statement to execute may be other than the next one in sequence. This is called transfer of control.

- Many programming complications in the 1960's were a result of misusing the **goto** statement, which allows the programmer to specify a transfer of control to one of a wide range of possible destinations in a program. The notion of structured programming became almost synonymous with "**goto** elimination."

- Bohm and Jacopini's work demonstrated that all programs could be written in terms of only three control structures—namely, sequence, selection and repetition.

- The sequence structure is built into C#. Unless directed otherwise, the computer executes C# statements one after the other in the order in which they appear.

- A flowchart is a graphical representation of an algorithm or of a portion of an algorithm. Flowcharts are drawn using symbols, such as rectangles, diamonds, ovals and small circles; these symbols are connected by arrows called flowlines, which indicate the order in which the algorithm's actions execute.

- The **if** selection structure performs (selects) an action if a condition is true or skips the action if the condition is false.

- The **if/else** selection structure performs an action if a condition is **true** and performs a different action if the condition is **false**.

- A single-selection structure is one that selects or ignores a single action.

- A double-selection structure is one that selects between two actions.

- A multiple-selection structure is one that selects among many actions.

- Keywords are reserved by the language to implement various features, such as C#'s control structures. Keywords cannot be used as identifiers.

- Each program is formed by combining as many of each type of C#'s eight control structures as is appropriate for the algorithm the program implements.

- Single-entry/single-exit control structures make it easy to build programs. The control structures are attached to one another by connecting the exit point of one control structure to the entry point of the next. This is called control-structure stacking.

- Algorithms in C# programs are constructed from only eight different types of control structures combined in only two ways.

- The decision symbol has two flowlines emerging from it. One indicates the direction to be taken when the expression in the symbol is true; the other indicates the direction to be taken when the expression is false.

- Control structure flowcharts contain (besides small circle symbols and flowlines) only rectangle symbols to indicate the actions to be performed and diamond symbols to indicate decisions to be made. This is the action/decision model of programming.

- The ternary conditional operator (**?:**) is closely related to the **if/else** structure. The operands and the **?:** form a conditional expression. The first operand is a condition that evaluates to a **bool** value, the second is the value for the conditional expression if the condition evaluates to **true** and the third is the value for the conditional expression if the condition evaluates to **false**.

- Nested **if/else** structures test for multiple cases by placing **if/else** structures inside other **if/else** structures.

- A set of statements in a pair of braces is called a block. A block can be placed anywhere in a program that a single statement can be placed.

- A syntax error is caught by the compiler at compile time, while a logic error has its effect during execution.

- A fatal logic error causes a program to fail and terminate prematurely. A nonfatal logic error allows a program to continue executing, but the program produces incorrect results.

- A repetition structure repeats an action (or set of actions) while some condition remains true.

- Eventually, the condition in a **while** structure will become false. At this point, the repetition terminates, and the first statement after the repetition structure executes.

- It is a logic error to fail to provide in the body of a **while** structure an action that eventually causes the condition to become false. Normally, such a repetition structure will never terminate, which is an error called an "infinite loop."

- We use counter-controlled repetition to input data values one at a time, a specified number of times. This technique uses a variable called a *counter* to control the number of times a set of statements will execute.

- Counter-controlled repetition often is called definite repetition because the number of repetitions is known before the loop begins executing.

- Sentinel-controlled repetition is often called indefinite repetition because the number of repetitions is not known before the loop begins executing.

- The sentinel value (also called the signal value, dummy value or flag value) determines when to terminate a repetition structure.

- We approach programming problems with top-down, stepwise refinement—a technique that is essential to the development of well-structured algorithms.

- The top is a single statement that conveys the overall function of the program. As such, the top is a complete representation of a program.

- We divide the top into a series of smaller tasks and list these in the order in which they must be performed. Each refinement, including the top itself, is a complete specification of the algorithm; only the level of detail in each refinement varies.

- Many algorithms can be divided logically into three phases—an initialization phase that initializes the program variables, a processing phase that inputs data values and adjusts program variables accordingly and a termination phase that calculates and prints the results.

- The programmer terminates the top-down, stepwise refinement process when the pseudocode algorithm is specified in sufficient detail for the programmer to convert the pseudocode to a C# program.

- Omitting the curly braces that delineate a block in the body of a repetition structure can lead to logic errors, such as infinite loops.

- Dividing two integers results in integer division, in which any fractional part of the calculation is truncated.

- To ensure that the operands in an expression are of the same type, C# performs implicit conversion on selected operands and promotes them to the same type.

- C# provides the unary increment operator, **++**, and the unary decrement operator, **--**. These operators add 1 to or subtract 1 from their operand, respectively.

- If an increment or decrement operator is placed before a variable, it is referred to as the preincrement or predecrement operator, respectively.

- If an increment or decrement operator is placed after a variable, it is referred to as the postincrement or postdecrement operator, respectively.

- A key benefit of extending classes using inheritance is that all the general capabilities are provided by the original class—programmers do not need to define these capabilities on their own.

- Method **InitializeComponent** contains the code to configure component properties in a GUI.

- The value in parentheses after the type in a **new** operation initializes the new object.

- Visual Studio .NET generates code that builds the GUI for an application.
- The primitive types are the building blocks for more complicated types.

TERMINOLOGY

--, unary decrement operator
%=, modulus assignment operator
(*type*), cast operator
*=, multiplication assignment operator
++, unary increment operator
+=, addition assignment operator
/=, division assignment operator
;, empty statement
=, assignment operator
-=, subtraction assignment operator
?:, ternary conditional operator
{, open brace
}, close brace
abbreviating an assignment expression
action/decision model of programming
action symbol
algorithm
application class definition
assignment operator (=)
associate left to right
associate right to left
associativity of operators
binary arithmetic operator
block
body of the **while**
bool primitive data type
boolean expression
braces that delimit a block
building block
case-sensitive language
cast operator
collapsed code
complete representation of a program
conditional expression
conditional operator (**?:**)
connector symbol
control structure
control-structure nesting
control-structure stacking
counter
counter-controlled repetition
dangling-else problem
decision symbol
declaration
definite repetition
design phase

diamond symbol
Dispose method
division by zero
do/while repetition structure
double primitive data type
double-selection structure
else statement
empty statement (**;**)
end of data entry
#endregion directive
entry point of control structure
examination-results problem
exit point of control structure
expanded code
explicit conversion
false
fatal logic error
first refinement
flag value
floating-point data type
floating-point division
floating-point number
flow of control
flowchart
flowline
for repetition structure
fractional result
goto elimination
"**goto**-less programming"
graphical representation of an algorithm
if selection structure
if/else selection structure
implicit conversion
indefinite repetition
indentation
indentation convention
infinite loop
inheriting from
    System.Windows.Forms.Form class
initialization phase
initialize
InitializeComponent method
input/output operation
integer division
integral data type
IntelliSense

keyword
level of refinement
logic error
loop
main form
multiple-selection structure
multiplicative operators: **, /** and **%**
nonfatal logic error
oval symbol
postdecrement operator
postdecrementing
postincrement operator
postincrementing
precedence of operators
predecrement operator
predecrementing
preincrement operator
preincrementing
preprocessor directives
primitive (or built-in) data type
procedure for solving a problem
processing phase
program control
program development tool
promotion
pseudocode
pseudocode algorithm
real number
rectangle symbol
refinement process
#region directive

repetition structure
second refinement
selection structure
sentinel-controlled repetition
sentinel value
sequence structure
sequential execution
signal value
single-entry/single-exit control structure
single-selection structure
small circle symbol
string primitive data type
strongly typed language
structured programming
switch selection structure
syntax error
System.Windows.Forms.Form class
temporary value
termination phase
ternary operator (**? :**)
top-down, stepwise refinement
transfer of control
true
truncate
unary operator
Unicode
variable reference
vertical spacing
while repetition structure
white-space characters

SELF-REVIEW EXERCISES

4.1   Fill in the blanks in each of the following statements:

a) All programs can be written in terms of three types of control structures: _____, _____ and _____.

b) The _____ selection structure executes one action when a condition is true and another action when a condition is false.

c) Repetition of a set of instructions a specific number of times is called _____ repetition.

d) When it is not known in advance how many times a set of statements will be repeated, a _____ value can be used to terminate the repetition.

e) Specifying the order in which statements are to be executed in a computer program is called _____.

f) _____ is an artificial and informal language that helps programmers develop algorithms.

g) _____ are reserved by C# to implement various features, such as the language's control structures.

h) A(n) _____ statement specifying that no action is to be taken is indicated by placing a semicolon where a statement normally would be.

     i) The increment operator (**++**) and decrement operator (**--**) increment and decrement a variable's value by _____.

     j) Explicit conversion makes use of the _____ operator.

4.2   State whether each of the following is *true* or *false*. If *false*, explain why.

     a) It is difficult to convert pseudocode into a working C# program.

     b) Sequential execution refers to statements in a program that execute one after another.

     c) It is recommended for C# programmers to use **goto** statements.

     d) The **if** structure is called a single-selection structure.

     e) Structured programs are clear, easy to debug and modify and more likely than unstructured programs to be bug-free in the first place.

     f) The sequence structure is not built into C#.

     g) Pseudocode usually resembles actual C# code.

     h) Placing a semicolon after the condition in an **if** structure is a syntax error.

     i) The **while** structure body may be a single or a block.

4.3   Write four different C# statements that each add 1 to integer variable **x** and store the result in **x**.

4.4   Write C# statements to accomplish each of the following:

     a) Assign the sum of **x** and **y** to **z** then increment **x** by 1 after the calculation. Use only one statement.

     b) Test if the value of the variable **count** is greater than 10. If it is, print **"Count is greater than 10"**.

     c) Decrement the variable **x** by 1, then subtract it from the variable **total**. Use only one statement.

     d) Calculate the remainder after **q** is divided by **divisor** and assign the result to **q**. Write this statement two different ways.

4.5   Write a C# statement to accomplish each of the following tasks:

     a) Declare variables **sum** and **x** to be of type **int**.

     b) Assign **1** to variable **x**.

     c) Assign **0** to variable **sum**.

     d) Add variable **x** to variable **sum** and assign the result to variable **sum**.

     e) Print **"The sum is : "** followed by the value of variable **sum**.

4.6   Combine the statements that you wrote in Exercise 4.5 into a C# application that calculates and prints the sum of the integers from 1 to 10. Use the **while** structure to loop through the calculation and increment statements. The loop should terminate when the value of **x** becomes 11.

4.7   Determine the values of each variable after the calculation is performed. Assume that when each statement begins executing, all variables have the integer value 5.

     a) **product *= x++;**

     b) **quotient /= ++x;**

4.8   Identify and correct the errors in each of the following:

     a)
```
while ( c <= 5 )
   {
       product *= c;
       ++c;
```

     b)
```
if ( gender == 1 )
       Console.WriteLine( "Woman" );
   else;
       Console.WriteLine( "Man" );
```

4.9   What is wrong with the following **while** repetition structure?

```
while ( z >= 0 )
   sum += z;
```

ANSWERS TO SELF-REVIEW EXERCISES

4.1   a) sequence, selection, repetition.   b) **if/else**.   c) counter-controlled or definite.   d) sentinel, signal, flag or dummy.   e) program control. f) Pseudocode.   g) Keywords.   h) empty.   i) one.   j) cast.

4.2   a) False. Pseudocode should convert easily into C# code.   b) True.   c) False. Some programmers argue that **goto** statements violate structured programming and cause considerable problems.   d) True.   e) True.   f) False. The sequence structure is built into C#; lines of code execute in the order in which they are written, unless explicitly directed to do otherwise. g) True. h) False. Placing a semicolon after the condition in an **if** structure is usually a logic error.   i) True.

4.3
```
x = x + 1;
x += 1;
++x;
x++;
```

4.4
```
a) z = x++ + y;
b) if ( count > 10 )
       Console.WriteLine( "Count is greater than 10" );
c) total -= --x;
d) q %= divisor;
   q = q % divisor;
```

4.5
```
a) int sum, x;
b) x = 1;
c) sum = 0;
d) sum += x; or sum = sum + x;
e) Console.WriteLine( "The sum is: " + sum ); or
   Console.WriteLine( "The sum is: {0}", sum );
```

4.6

```
1    // Calculate the sum of the integers from 1 to 10
2
3    using System;
4
5    class Calculate
6    {
7       static void Main( string[] args )
8       {
9          int sum, x;
10
11         x = 1;
12         sum = 0;
13
14         while ( x <= 10 )
15         {
16            sum += x++;
17         }
```

```
18
19          Console.WriteLine( "The sum is: " + sum );
20       }
21    }
```

4.7 a) **product = 25, x = 6;**
b) **quotient = 0, x = 6;**

4.8 a) Error: Missing the closing right brace of the **while** body.
Correction: Add closing right brace after the statement **++c;**.
b) Error: Semicolon after **else** results in a logic error. The second output statement will always be executed.
Correction: Remove the semicolon after **else**.

4.9 The value of the variable **z** is never changed in the **while** structure. Therefore, if the loop-continuation condition (**z >= 0**) is true, an infinite loop is created. To prevent the infinite loop, **z** must be decremented so that it eventually becomes less than 0.

EXERCISES

4.10 Drivers are concerned with the mileage obtained by their automobiles. One driver has kept track of several tankfuls of gasoline by recording miles driven and gallons used for each tankful. Develop a C# program that will input the miles driven and gallons used (both as doubles) for each tankful. The program should calculate and display the miles per gallon obtained for each tankful and print the combined miles per gallon obtained for all tankfuls up to this point. All average calculations should produce floating-point results.

4.11 Develop a C# application that will determine if a department store customer has exceeded the credit limit on a charge account. For each customer, the following facts are available:
a) Account number
b) Balance at the beginning of the month
c) Total of all items charged by this customer this month
d) Total of all credits applied to this customer's account this month
e) Allowed credit limit

The program should input as integers each of these facts, calculate the new balance (= *beginning balance + charges – credits*), display the new balance and determine if the new balance exceeds the customer's credit limit. For those customers whose credit limit is exceeded, the program should display the message, "Credit limit exceeded."

4.12 Write a C# application that uses looping to print the following table of values:

N	10*N	100*N	1000*N
1	10	100	1000
2	20	200	2000
3	30	300	3000
4	40	400	4000
5	50	500	5000

4.13 *(Dangling-Else Problem)* Determine the output for each of the following, when **x** is **9** and **y** is **11** and when **x** is **11** and **y** is **9**. Note that the compiler ignores the indentation in a C# program. Also, the C# compiler always associates an **else** with the previous **if** unless told to do otherwise by the placement of braces (**{}**). On first glance, the programmer may not be sure which **if** and **else** match; this is referred to as the "dangling-else" problem. We have eliminated the indentation from the following code to make the problem more challenging. (*Hint*: Apply indentation conventions that you have learned.)

a)
```
if ( x < 10 )
if ( y > 10 )
Console.WriteLine( "*****" );
else
Console.WriteLine( "#####" );
Console.WriteLine( "$$$$$" );
```

b)
```
if ( x < 10 ) {
if ( y > 10 )
Console.WriteLine( "*****" );
}
else {
Console.WriteLine( "#####" );
Console.WriteLine( "$$$$$" );
}
```

4.14   A palindrome is a number or a text phrase that reads the same backwards as forwards. For example, each of the following five-digit integers are palindromes: 12321, 55555, 45554 and 11611. Write an application that reads in a five-digit integer and determines whether it is a palindrome. If the number is not five digits, display an error message dialog indicating the problem to the user. When the user dismisses the error dialog, allow the user to enter a new value.

4.15   A company wants to transmit data over the telephone, but they are concerned that their phones may be tapped. All their data are transmitted as four-digit integers. They have asked you to write a program that will encrypt their data so that it may be transmitted more securely. Your application should read a four-digit integer entered by the user in an input dialog and encrypt it as follows: Replace each digit by *(the sum of that digit plus 7) modulus 10*. Then swap the first digit with the third, and swap the second digit with the fourth. Print the encrypted integer. Write a separate application that inputs an encrypted four-digit integer and decrypts it to form the original number.

4.16   The factorial of a nonnegative integer n is written $n!$ (pronounced "n factorial") and is defined as follows:

$n! = n \cdot (n - 1) \cdot (n - 2) \cdot ... \cdot 1$ (for values of n greater than or equal to 1)

and

$n! = 1$ (for $n = 0$).

For example, $5! = 5 \cdot 4 \cdot 3 \cdot 2 \cdot 1$, which is 120.

a) Write an application that reads a nonnegative integer from an input dialog and computes and prints its factorial.

b) Write an application that estimates the value of the mathematical constant e by using the formula

$$e = 1 + \frac{1}{1!} + \frac{1}{2!} + \frac{1}{3!} + ...$$

c) Write an application that computes the value of e^x by using the formula

$$e^x = 1 + \frac{x}{1!} + \frac{x^2}{2!} + \frac{x^3}{3!} + ...$$

Control Structures: Part 2

Objectives

- To be able to use the **for** and **do/while** repetition structures to execute statements in a program repeatedly.
- To understand multiple selection that uses the **switch** selection structure.
- To be able to use the **break** and **continue** program-control statements.
- To be able to use the logical operators.

Who can control his fate?
William Shakespeare, *Othello*

The used key is always bright.
Benjamin Franklin

Man is a tool-making animal.
Benjamin Franklin

Intelligence … is the faculty of making artificial objects, especially tools to make tools.
Henri Bergson

5.1 Introduction

Chapter 4 began our introduction to the types of building blocks that are available for problem solving and used those building blocks to implement proven program-construction principles. In this chapter, we continue our presentation of the theory and principles of structured programming by introducing C#'s remaining control structures. As in Chapter 4, the C# techniques you learn here are applicable to most high-level languages. When we begin our formal treatment of object-based programming in C# in Chapter 8, we will see that the control structures we study in this chapter and in Chapter 4 are helpful in building and manipulating objects.

5.2 Essentials of Counter-Controlled Repetition

In the last chapter, we introduced the concept of counter-controlled repetition. In this section, we formalize the elements needed in counter-controlled repetition, namely:

1. The *name* of a *control variable* (or loop counter), used to determine whether the loop continues.

2. The *initial value* of the control variable.

3. The *increment* (or *decrement*) by which the control variable is modified each time through the loop (also known as *each iteration of the loop*).

4. The condition that tests for the *final value* of the control variable (i.e., whether looping should continue).

To see the four elements of counter-controlled repetition, consider the simple program in Fig. 5.1, which displays the digits 1–5.

The declaration (line 10)

```
int counter = 1;
```

names the control variable (**counter**), declares it to be an integer, reserves space for it in memory and sets it to an *initial value* of **1**. This statement is a declaration that includes an

```
1    // Fig. 5.1: WhileCounter.cs
2    // Counter-controlled repetition.
3
4    using System;
5
6    class WhileCounter
7    {
8       static void Main( string[] args )
9       {
10         int counter = 1;             // initialization
11
12         while ( counter <= 5 )       // repetition condition
13         {
14            Console.WriteLine( counter );
15            counter++;                // increment
16
17         } // end while
18
19      } // end method Main
20
21   } // end class WhileCounter
```

```
1
2
3
4
5
```

Fig. 5.1   Counter-controlled repetition with **while** structure.

initialization. The declaration and initialization of **counter** could also have been accomplished with the declaration and statement

```
int counter;   // declare counter
counter = 1;   // initialize counter to 1
```

The declaration is not executable, but the assignment statement is. We use both approaches to initialization throughout this book.

Lines 12–17 define the **while** structure. During each iteration of the loop, line 14 displays the current value of **counter**, and line 15 *increments* the control variable by **1** upon each iteration of the loop. The loop-continuation condition in the **while** structure tests whether the value of the control variable is less than or equal to **5** (the *final value* for which the condition is true). The body of this **while** is performed even when the control variable is **5**. The loop terminates when the control variable exceeds **5** (i.e., **counter** becomes **6**).

The program in Fig. 5.1 can be made more concise by initializing **counter** to **0** and replacing the **while** structure with

```
while ( ++counter <= 5 )   // repetition condition
   Console.WriteLine( counter );
```

This code saves a statement and eliminates the need for braces around the loop's bod,y because the incrementing occurs directly in the **while** condition before the condition is tested (remember that the precedence of **++** is higher than **<=**).

Good Programming Practice 5.1

Control counting loops with integer values.

Good Programming Practice 5.2

Place a blank line before and after each major control structure to make it stand out in the program.

Good Programming Practice 5.3

Vertical spacing above and below control structures, and indentation of the bodies of control structures within the control structure headers, gives programs a two-dimensional appearance that enhances readability.

5.3 **for** Repetition Structure

The **for** repetition structure handles the details of counter-controlled repetition. To illustrate the power of **for**, let us rewrite the program in Fig. 5.1. The result is displayed in Fig. 5.2.

The **Main** method (lines 8–14) operates as follows: When the **for** structure (line 12) begins executing, the program initializes the control variable **counter** to **1** (the first two elements of counter-controlled repetition—control variable *name* and *initial value*). Next, the program tests the loop-continuation condition, **counter <= 5**. The initial value of **counter** is **1**, thus the condition is true, so line 13 outputs the **counter**'s value. Then, the program increments variable **counter** in the expression **counter++**, and the loop begins again with the loop-continuation test. The control variable is now equal to **2**. This value does not exceed the final value, so the program performs the body statement again (i.e., performs the next iteration of the loop). This process continues until the control variable **counter** becomes **6**, causing the loop-continuation test to fail and repetition to terminate. The program continues by performing the first statement after the **for** structure. (In this case, method **Main** terminates because the program reaches the end of **Main**'s body.)

```
1   // Fig. 5.2: ForCounter.cs
2   // Counter-controlled repetition with the for structure.
3
4   using System;
5
6   class ForCounter
7   {
8      static void Main( string[] args )
9      {
10        // initialization, repetition condition and incrementing
11        // are all included in the for structure
12        for ( int counter = 1; counter <= 5; counter++ )
13           Console.WriteLine( counter );
14     }
15  }
```

Fig. 5.2   Counter-controlled repetition with the **for** structure. (Part 1 of 2.)

```
1
2
3
4
5
```

Fig. 5.2   Counter-controlled repetition with the **for** structure. (Part 2 of 2.)

Figure 5.3 takes a closer look at the **for** structure in Fig. 5.2. The first line of the **for** structure (including the keyword **for** and everything in parentheses after **for**) sometimes is called the ***for** structure header*. Notice that the **for** structure specifies each of the items needed for counter-controlled repetition with a control variable. If there is more than one statement in the body of the **for**, braces (**{** and **}**) are required to define the loop's body.

Figure 5.2 uses the loop-continuation condition **counter <= 5**. If the programmer incorrectly writes **counter < 5**, the loop executes only four times. This common logic error is called an *off-by-one error*.

Common Programming Error 5.1
*Using an incorrect relational operator or using an incorrect final value for a loop counter in the condition of a **while**, **for** or **do/while** structure (introduced in Section 5.6) can cause an off-by-one error.*

Common Programming Error 5.2
Floating-point values may be approximate, so controlling counting loops with floating-point variables can result in imprecise counter values and inaccurate tests for termination.

Testing and Debugging Tip 5.1
*Using the final value in the condition of a **while** or **for** structure and using the **<=** relational operator will help avoid off-by-one errors. For a loop used to print the values from 1 to 10, for example, the loop-continuation condition should be **counter <= 10**, rather than **counter < 10** (which is an off-by-one error) or **counter < 11** (which also works). This approach is commonly known as* one-based counting. *When we study arrays in Chapter 7, Arrays, we will see when programmers prefer* zero-based counting, *in which to count 10 times through a loop,* **counter** *is initialized to zero and the loop-continuation test is* **counter < 10**.

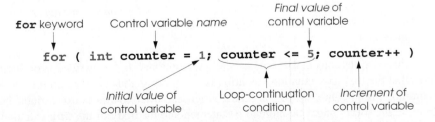

Fig. 5.3   Components of a typical **for** header.

The general format of the **for** structure is

```
for ( expression1; expression2; expression3 )
   statement
```

where *expression1* names the loop's control variable and provides its initial value, *expression2* is the loop-continuation condition (containing the control variable's final value) and *expression3* increments or decrements the control variable. In most cases, the **for** structure can be represented with an equivalent **while** structure, with *expression1*, *expression2* and *expression3* placed as follows:

```
expression1;

while ( expression2 )
{
   statement
   expression3;
}
```

In Section 5.7, we discuss an exception to this rule.

In C#, programmers may declare the control variable in *expression1* of the **for** structure header (i.e., the control variable's type is specified before the variable name), rather than earlier in the code. When this occurs, the control variable can be used only in the body of the **for** structure (i.e., the name of the control variable will be unknown outside the **for** structure). Such a restriction on the use of a control variable name defines the variable's *scope*. The scope of a variable defines where it can be used in a program. Scope is discussed in detail in Chapter 6, Methods.

Common Programming Error 5.3

*When a **for** structure declares its control variable in the initialization section of the **for** structure header, using the control variable after the **for** structure's body is a compiler error.*

Sometimes, *expression1* and *expression3* in a **for** structure are comma-separated lists of expressions that enable the programmer to use multiple initialization expressions and/or multiple increment or decrement expressions. For example, there may be several control variables in a single **for** structure that must be initialized and incremented or decremented.

Good Programming Practice 5.4

*Place only expressions involving control variables in the initialization and increment or decrement sections of a **for** structure. Manipulations of other variables should appear either before the loop (if they execute only once, like initialization statements) or in the loop body (if they execute once per iteration of the loop, like incrementing or decrementing statements).*

The three expressions in the **for** structure are optional. If *expression2* is omitted, C# assumes that the loop-continuation condition is always true, thus creating an infinite loop. A programmer might omit *expression1* if the program initializes the control variable before the loop. *Expression3* might be omitted if statements in the body of the **for** calculate the increment or decrement, or if no increment or decrement is necessary. The increment (or decrement) expression in the **for** structure acts as if it were a standalone statement at the end of the **for** body. Therefore, the expressions

```
counter = counter + 1
counter += 1
++counter
counter++
```

are equivalent when used in *expression3*. Some programmers prefer the form **counter++**, because the control variable increment occurs after the loop body executes. For this reason, the postincrementing (or postdecrementing) form in which the variable is incremented after it is used seems more natural. Because the variable being either incremented or decremented does not appear in a larger expression, preincrementing and postincrementing the variable have the same effect. The two semicolons in the **for** structure are required.

Common Programming Error 5.4

*Using commas in a **for** structure header instead of the two required semicolons is a syntax error.*

Common Programming Error 5.5

*Placing a semicolon immediately to the right of a **for** structure header's right parenthesis makes the body of that **for** structure an empty statement. This is normally a logic error.*

The initialization, loop-continuation condition and increment or decrement portions of a **for** structure can contain arithmetic expressions. For example, assume that **x = 2** and **y = 10**. If **x** and **y** are not modified in the loop body, the statement

```
for ( int j = x; j <= 4 * x * y; j += y / x )
```

is equivalent to the statement

```
for ( int j = 2; j <= 80; j += 5 )
```

The "increment" of a **for** structure may be negative, in which case it is really a decrement and the loop actually counts downward.

If the loop-continuation condition in the **for** structure is initially false, the body of the **for** structure does not execute. Instead, execution proceeds with the statement that follows the **for** structure.

The control variable frequently is printed or used in calculations in the body of a **for** structure, but it does not have to be. Often the control variable simply controls repetition and is not mentioned in the body of the **for** structure.

Testing and Debugging Tip 5.2

*Avoid changing the value of the control variable in the body of a **for** loop, to avoid subtle errors.*

The **for** structure flowchart is similar to that of the **while** structure. For example, the flowchart of the **for** structure in Fig. 5.2 appears in Fig. 5.4. This flowchart clarifies that the initialization occurs only once, and that incrementing occurs each time *after* the body statement is performed. Note that (besides small circles and flowlines) the flowchart contains only rectangle symbols and a diamond symbol. The rectangles and diamonds are filled with actions and decisions appropriate to the algorithm.

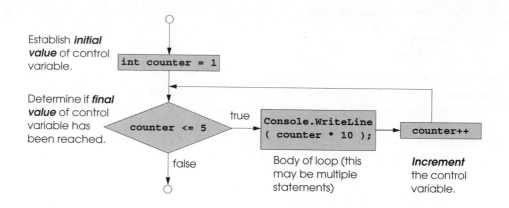

Fig. 5.4   Flowcharting a typical **for** repetition structure.

5.4 Examples Using the `for` Structure

The following examples demonstrate methods of varying the control variable in a **for** structure. In each case, we write the appropriate **for** header. Note the change in the relational operator for loops that decrement the control variable.

a) Vary the control variable from **1** to **100** in increments of **1**.

```
for ( int i = 1; i <= 100; i++ )
```

b) Vary the control variable from **100** to **1** in increments of **–1** (decrements of **1**).

```
for ( int i = 100; i >= 1; i-- )
```

c) Vary the control variable from **7** to **77** in steps of **7**.

```
for ( int i = 7; i <= 77; i += 7 )
```

d) Vary the control variable from **20** to **2** in steps of **–2**.

```
for ( int i = 20; i >= 2; i -= 2 )
```

e) Vary the control variable over the sequence of the following values: **2, 5, 8, 11, 14, 17, 20**.

```
for ( int j = 2; j <= 20; j += 3 )
```

f) Vary the control variable over the sequence of the following values: **99, 88, 77, 66, 55, 44, 33, 22, 11, 0**.

```
for ( int j = 99; j >= 0; j -= 11 )
```

Common Programming Error 5.6

Not using the proper relational operator in the loop-continuation condition of a loop that counts downward (e.g., using **i <= 1** *in a loop counting down to 1) is usually a logic error that will yield incorrect results when the program runs.*

The next two sample programs demonstrate simple applications of the **for** repetition structure. The program in Fig. 5.5 uses the **for** structure to sum all the even integers from **2** to **100**, then displays the result in a **MessageBox**. Remember that to use **MessageBox**, you must add a reference to **System.Windows.Forms.dll** to your project, as explained in Chapter 3 (Section 3.2).

Figure 5.5 uses a version of method **MessageBox.Show** (lines 16–19) that takes four arguments. The dialog in the output of Fig. 5.5 illustrates the four arguments. As with the version that takes one argument, the first argument is the message to display. The second argument is the string to display in the dialog's title bar. The third argument is a value indicating which button(s) to display. The fourth argument indicates which icon to display to the left of the message. The MSDN documentation provided with Visual Studio .NET includes the complete listing of **MessageBoxButtons** and **MessageBoxIcon** choices. Figure 5.6 describes the message-dialog icons and Fig. 5.7 describes the message-dialog buttons.

```
1   // Fig. 5.5: Sum.cs
2   // Summation with the for structure.
3
4   using System;
5   using System.Windows.Forms;
6
7   class Sum
8   {
9      static void Main( string[] args )
10     {
11        int sum = 0;
12
13        for ( int number = 2; number <= 100; number += 2 )
14           sum += number;
15
16        MessageBox.Show( "The sum is " + sum,
17           "Sum Even Integers from 2 to 100",
18           MessageBoxButtons.OK,
19           MessageBoxIcon.Information );
20
21     } // end method Main
22
23  } // end class Sum
```

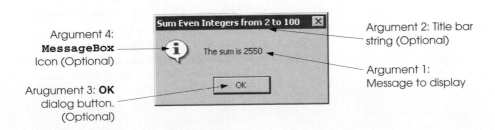

Fig. 5.5   Summation using **for**.

MessageBox Icons	Icon	Description
MessageBoxIcon.Exclamation		Specifies an exclamation point icon. Typically used to caution the user against potential problems.
MessageBoxIcon.Information		Specifies that the dialog contains an informational message for the user.
MessageBoxIcon.Question		Specifies a question mark icon. Typically used in dialogs that ask the user a question.
MessageBoxIcon.Error		Specifies a dialog with an **x** in a red circle. Alerts user of errors or important messages.

Fig. 5.6   Icons for message dialogs.

MessageBox Buttons	Description
MessageBoxButton.OK	Specifies that the dialog should include an **OK** button.
MessageBoxButton.OKCancel	Specifies that the dialog should include **OK** and **Cancel** buttons. Warns the user about some condition and allows the user to either continue or cancel an operation.
MessageBoxButton.YesNo	Specifies that the dialog should contain **Yes** and **No** buttons. Used to ask the user a question.
MessageBoxButton.YesNoCancel	Specifies that the dialog should contain **Yes**, **No** and **Cancel** buttons. Typically used to ask the user a question but still allows the user to cancel the operation.
MessageBoxButton.RetryCancel	Specifies that the dialog should contain **Retry** and **Cancel** buttons. Typically used to inform a user about a failed operation and allow the user to retry or cancel the operation.
MessageBoxButton.AbortRetryIgnore	Specifies that the dialog should contain **Abort**, **Retry** and **Ignore** buttons. Typically used to inform the user that one of a series of operations has failed and allow the user to abort the series of operations, retry the failed operation or ignore the failed operation and continue.

Fig. 5.7   Buttons for message dialogs.

The body of the **for** structure in Fig. 5.5 actually could be merged into the rightmost portion of the **for** header by using a *comma* as follows:

```
for ( int number = 2; number <= 100;
      sum += number, number += 2)
    ; // empty statement
```

Similarly, the initialization **sum = 0** could be merged into the initialization section of the **for** structure. Statements that precede a **for** and statements in the body of a **for** often can be merged into the **for** header. However, such merging could decrease the readability of the program.

Good Programming Practice 5.5

Limit the size of control structure headers to a single line if possible.

The next example uses a **for** structure to compute compound interest. Consider the following problem statement:

A person invests $1000.00 in a savings account yielding 5% interest. Assuming that all interest is left on deposit, calculate and print the amount of money in the account at the end of each year for 10 years. To determine these amounts, use the following formula:

$$a = p(1 + r)^n$$

where

> *p* is the original amount invested (i.e., the principal)
> *r* is the annual interest rate
> *n* is the number of years
> *a* is the amount on deposit at the end of the *n*th year.

This problem involves a loop that performs the indicated calculation for each of the 10 years that the money remains on deposit. A solution is the program shown in Fig. 5.8.

Line 11 in method **Main** declares two *decimal* variables—**amount** and **principal**—and initializes **principal** to **1000.00**. The type **decimal** is a primitive data type used for monetary calculations. C# treats such constants as the **1000.00** in Fig. 5.8 as type **double**. Similarly, C# treats whole number constants, like 7 and -22, as having type **int**. Values of type **double** cannot be converted implicitly to type **decimal**, so we use a cast operator to convert the **double** value 1000.00 to type **decimal**. It also is possible to specify that a constant is of type **decimal** by appending the letter **m** to the constant, as in 1000.0m. Line 12 declares **double** variable **rate**, which we initialize to **.05**.

```
1    // Fig. 5.8: Interest.cs
2    // Calculating compound interest.
3
4    using System;
5    using System.Windows.Forms;
6
7    class Interest
8    {
```

Fig. 5.8   Calculating compound interest with **for**. (Part 1 of 2.)

```
9       static void Main( string[] args )
10      {
11         decimal amount, principal = ( decimal ) 1000.00;
12         double rate = .05;
13         string output;
14
15         output = "Year\tAmount on deposit\n";
16
17         for ( int year = 1; year <= 10; year++ )
18         {
19            amount = principal *
20               ( decimal ) Math.Pow( 1.0 + rate, year );
21
22            output += year + "\t" +
23               String.Format( "{0:C}", amount ) + "\n";
24         }
25
26         MessageBox.Show( output, "Compound Interest",
27            MessageBoxButtons.OK, MessageBoxIcon.Information );
28
29      } // end method Main
30
31   } // end class Interest
```

Fig. 5.8   Calculating compound interest with **for**. (Part 2 of 2.)

The **for** structure executes its body 10 times, varying control variable **year** from **1** to **10** in increments of **1**. Note that **year** represents *n* in the problem statement. C# does not have an exponentiation operator, so we use **static** method **Pow** in class **Math** for this purpose. **Math.Pow(x, y)** calculates the value of **x** raised to the **y**th power. Method **Math.Pow** takes two arguments of type **double** and returns a **double** value. Lines 19–20 perform the calculation from the problem statement

$$a = p (1 + r)^n$$

where *a* is **amount**, *p* is **principal**, *r* is **rate** and *n* is **year**.

Lines 22–23 append additional text to the end of the string **output**. The text includes the current **year** value, a tab character to position to the second column, the result of the method call **String.Format("{0:C}", amount)** and a newline character to position to the next line. The call to method **String.Format** converts **amount** to a **string** and formats this **string** so that it will display with two decimal places. [*Note*: Method **Format** uses the string formatting codes to represent numeric and monetary values in a form that is appropriate to the execution environment. For example, in the US, monetary values are formatted with two digits to the right of the decimal point and the thousands separator is a comma.] The first argument is the format string. We have already seen such strings in the form **{0}**, **{1}** and so on. In those cases, the digit indicated the argument being displayed. In more complicated format strings, such as the one shown in this example (**"{0:C}"**), the first digit (**0**) still represents the argument to display. The information specified after the colon (**:**) specifies the formatting of the argument, and usually is called the *formatting code*. In this case, we are using formatting code **C**, which indicates that our string should be displayed as a monetary amount with two digits after the decimal point. There are several other formatting codes, which can be found in the MSDN documentation. Figure 5.9 shows several formatting codes.

The variables **amount** and **principal** were declared to be of type **decimal** because the program deals with fractional parts of dollars. In such cases, programs need a type that allows decimal points in its values. Variable **rate** is of type **double** because it is used in the calculation **1.0 + rate**, which appears as a **double** argument to the **Pow** method of class **Math**. Note that the calculation **1.0 + rate** appears in the body of the **for** statement. The calculation produces the same result each time through the loop, so repeating the calculation is unnecessary.

Performance Tip 5.1

Avoid placing expressions with values that do not change inside a loop. Such expressions should be evaluated once before the loop. Most good compilers will fix this automatically with a process that compilers perform called optimization.

Format Code	Description
C or **c**	Formats the string as currency. Precedes the number with an appropriate currency symbol (**$** in the US). Separates digits with an appropriate separator character (comma in the US) and sets the number of decimal places to two by default.
D or **d**	Formats the string as a decimal. Displays number as an integer.
N or **n**	Formats the string with commas and two decimal places.
E or **e**	Formats the number using scientific notation with a default of six decimal places.
F or **f**	Formats the string with a fixed number of decimal places (two by default).
G or **g**	General. Either **E** or **F**.
X or **x**	Formats the string as hexadecimal.

Fig. 5.9   **string** formatting codes.

5.5 `switch` Multiple-Selection Structure

The previous chapter discussed the **if** single-selection and the **if/else** double-selection structures. Occasionally, an algorithm contains a series of decisions in which the algorithm tests a variable or expression separately for each *constant integral expression* or *constant string expression* the variable or expression may assume. A constant integral expression is any expression involving character and integer constants that evaluates to an integer value (i.e., values of type **byte**, **sbyte**, **short**, **ushort**, **int**, **uint**, **long**, **ulong** and **char**). A constant string expression is any expression composed of string literals that always results in the same **string**. The algorithm then takes different actions based on those values. C# provides the ***switch*** *multiple-selection structure* to handle such decision making.

In the next example (Fig. 5.10), let us assume that a class of 10 students took an exam and that each student received a letter grade of A, B, C, D or F. The program will input the letter grades and summarize the results by using **switch** to count the number of each different letter grade that students earned on an exam. Line 10 declares variable **grade** as type **char**. Lines 11–15 define counter variables that the program uses to count each letter grade. This variable stores the user's input for each grade. Line 17 begins a **for** structure that loops 10 times. At each iteration, line 19 prompts the user for the next grade, and line 20 invokes **Char** method **Parse** to read the user input as a **char**. Nested in the body of the **for** structure is a **switch** structure (lines 22–56) that processes the letter grades. The **switch** structure consists of a series of ***case*** *labels* and an optional ***default*** *case*.

When the flow of control reaches the **switch** structure, the program evaluates the *controlling expression* (**grade** in this example) in the parentheses following keyword **switch**. The value of this expression is compared with each **case** label until a match occurs. Assume the user entered the letter **B** as the grade. **B** is compared to each **case** in the **switch**, until a match occurs at line 29 (**case 'B':**). When this happens, the statements for that **case** execute. For the letter **B**, lines 31–32 increment the number of **B** grades stored in variable **bCount**, and the **switch** structure exits immediately with the ***break*** *statement*. The **break** statement causes program control to proceed with the first statement after the **switch** structure. In this case, we reach the end of the **for** structure's body, so control flows to the control-variable increment expression in the **for** structure header. Then the counter variable in the **for** structure is incremented, and the loop-continuation condition is evaluated to determine whether another iteration of the loop is necessary.

```
1   // Fig. 5.10: SwitchTest.cs
2   // Counting letter grades.
3
4   using System;
5
6   class SwitchTest
7   {
8      static void Main( string[] args )
9      {
10         char grade;        // one grade
11         int aCount = 0,    // number of As
12             bCount = 0,    // number of Bs
13             cCount = 0,    // number of Cs
```

Fig. 5.10 **switch** multiple-selection structure. (Part 1 of 3.)

```
14                    dCount = 0,   // number of Ds
15                    fCount = 0;   // number of Fs
16
17          for ( int i = 1; i <= 10; i++ )
18          {
19              Console.Write( "Enter a letter grade: " );
20              grade = Char.Parse( Console.ReadLine() );
21
22              switch ( grade )
23              {
24                 case 'A':   // grade is uppercase A
25                 case 'a':   // or lowercase a
26                    ++aCount;
27                    break;
28
29                 case 'B':   // grade is uppercase B
30                 case 'b':   // or lowercase b
31                    ++bCount;
32                    break;
33
34                 case 'C':   // grade is uppercase C
35                 case 'c':   // or lowercase c
36                    ++cCount;
37                    break;
38
39                 case 'D':   // grade is uppercase D
40                 case 'd':   // or lowercase d
41                    ++dCount;
42                    break;
43
44                 case 'F':   // grade is uppercase F
45                 case 'f':   // or lowercase f
46                    ++fCount;
47                    break;
48
49                 default:    // processes all other characters
50                    Console.WriteLine(
51                       "Incorrect letter grade entered." +
52                       "\nGrade not added to totals." );
53                    break;
54
55              } // end switch
56
57          } // end for
58
59          Console.WriteLine(
60             "\nTotals for each letter grade are:\nA: {0}" +
61             "\nB: {1}\nC: {2}\nD: {3}\nF: {4}", aCount, bCount,
62             cCount, dCount, fCount );
63
64       } // end method Main
65
66  } // end class SwitchTest
```

Fig. 5.10 **switch** multiple-selection structure. (Part 2 of 3.)

```
Enter a letter grade: a
Enter a letter grade: A
Enter a letter grade: c
Enter a letter grade: F
Enter a letter grade: z
Incorrect letter grade entered.
Grade not added to totals.
Enter a letter grade: D
Enter a letter grade: d
Enter a letter grade: B
Enter a letter grade: a
Enter a letter grade: C

Totals for each letter grade are:
A: 3
B: 1
C: 2
D: 2
F: 1
```

Fig. 5.10   **switch** multiple-selection structure. (Part 3 of 3.)

Good Programming Practice 5.6

*Indent the body statements of each **case** in a **switch** structure.*

If no match occurs between the controlling expression's value and a **case** label, the **default** case (line 49) executes. Lines 50–52 display an error message. Note that the **default** case is optional in the **switch** structure. If the controlling expression does not match a **case** and there is no **default** case, program control proceeds to the next statement after the **switch** structure. It is also important to understand that, in C#, only the statements for one **case** can be executed in one **switch** statement.

Each **case** can contain multiple actions or no actions at all. A **case** with no statements is considered an *empty case*, and can omit the **break** statement. The **break** statement is required for each **case** (including the **default** case) that contains statements. The last **case** in a **switch** structure must not be an empty **case**. If the **case** label for an empty **case** matches our controlling expression, *fall through* occurs. This means that the **switch** structure executes the statements in the next case. If that **case** is also empty, this process will continue until a nonempty case is found, and then that **case**'s statements will execute. This provides the programmer with a way to specify statements to executed for several labels. Figure 5.10 demonstrates this. Lines 26–27 execute for both cases on lines 24–25 (if the grade entered was either **A** or **a**), lines 31–32 execute for both cases on lines 29–30 (if the grade entered was either **B** or **b**) and so on.

Common Programming Error 5.7

*Not including a **break** statement at the end of each **case** in a **switch** is a syntax error. The exception to this rule is the empty **case**.*

Common Programming Error 5.8

*Be sure to check all possible values when creating **cases** to confirm that no two **cases** in a **switch** statement are for the same integral value. If the values are the same, a compile-time error will occur.*

Finally, it is important to notice that the **switch** structure is different from other structures in that braces are not required around multiple actions in a **case** of a **switch**. The general **switch** structure (using a **break** in each **case**) is flowcharted in Fig. 5.11.

Again, note that (besides small circles and flowlines) the flowchart contains only rectangle and diamond symbols. The programmer fills the rectangles and diamonds with actions and decisions appropriate to the algorithm. Although nested control structures are common, it is rare to find nested **switch** structures in a program.

Good Programming Practice 5.7

*Provide a **default** case in every **switch** structure. Cases not explicitly tested in a **switch** that lacks a **default** case are ignored. Including a **default** case focuses the programmer on processing exceptional conditions. There are situations, however, in which no **default** processing is required.*

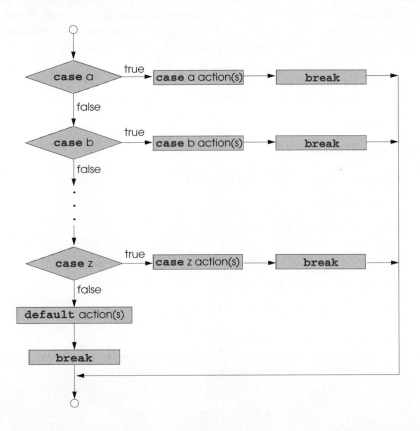

Fig. 5.11 Flowcharting the **switch** multiple-selection structure.

Good Programming Practice 5.8

*Although the **cases** in a **switch** structure can occur in any order, it is considered a good programming practice to place the **default** case last.*

When using the **switch** structure, remember that all cases in a particular switch structure must be either integral values or strings. A *character constant* is represented as a specific character in single quotes (such as **'A'**). An integer constant is simply an integer value. The expression after each **case** can also be a *constant variable*—a variable that contains a value that does not change throughout the entire program. Such a variable is declared with keyword **const** (discussed in Chapter 6, Methods).

Chapter 10, Object-Oriented Programming: Polymorphism, presents a more elegant way of implementing **switch** logic. We use a technique called polymorphism to create programs that are clearer and easier to maintain and extend than programs that use **switch** logic.

5.6 do/while Repetition Structure

The ***do/while*** repetition structure is similar to the **while** structure. In the **while** structure, the test of the loop-continuation condition occurs at the beginning of the loop, before the body of the loop executes. The **do/while** structure tests the loop-continuation condition *after* the loop body executes; therefore, *the loop body always executes at least once*. When a **do/while** structure terminates, execution continues with the statement after the **while** clause. The program in Fig. 5.12 uses a **do/while** structure to output the values 1–5.

```
1   // Fig. 5.12: DoWhileLoop.cs
2   // The do/while repetition structure.
3
4   using System;
5
6   class DoWhileLoop
7   {
8      static void Main( string[] args )
9      {
10         int counter = 1;
11
12         do
13         {
14            Console.WriteLine( counter );
15            counter++;
16         } while ( counter <= 5 );
17
18      } // end method Main
19
20   } // end class DoWhileLoop
```

```
1
2
3
4
5
```

Fig. 5.12   **do/while** repetition structure.

Lines 12–16 demonstrate the **do/while** structure. When program execution reaches the **do/while** structure, the program executes lines 14–15, which display the value of **counter** (at this point, **1**) and increment **counter** by **1**. Then, the program evaluates the condition on line 16. At this point, variable **counter** is 2, which is less than or equal to 5, so the **do/while** structure's body executes again. The fifth time the structure executes, line 14 outputs the value **5** and line 15 increments **counter** to **6**. Then the condition on line 16 evaluates to false and the **do/while** structure exits.

The **do/while** flowchart (Fig. 5.13) makes it clear that the loop-continuation condition does not execute until the body executes at least once. The flowchart contains only a rectangle and a diamond. The programmer fills the rectangle and diamond with actions and decisions appropriate to the algorithm.

Note that it is not necessary to use braces in the **do/while** structure if there is only one statement in the body. However, the braces normally are included to avoid confusion between the **while** and **do/while** structures. For example,

```
while ( condition )
```

typically is the header to a **while** structure. A **do/while** with no braces around the single statement body appears as

```
do
    statement
while ( condition );
```

which can be confusing. The last line—**while(** *condition* **);**—might be misinterpreted by the reader as a **while** structure containing an empty statement (the semicolon by itself). Thus, the **do/while** with one statement often is written as follows to avoid confusion:

```
do
{
    statement
} while ( condition );
```

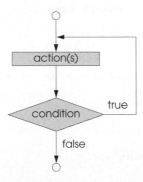

Fig. 5.13   Flowcharting the **do/while** repetition structure.

Good Programming Practice 5.9

*Some programmers always include braces in a **do/while** structure, even when the braces are unnecessary. This helps eliminate ambiguity between a **while** structure and a **do/while** structure that contains only one statement.*

Common Programming Error 5.9

*Infinite loops occur when the loop-continuation condition in a **while**, **for** or **do/while** structure never becomes false. To prevent this, make sure there is no semicolon immediately after the header of a **while** or **for** structure or after the word **do** in a **do/while** statement. In a counter-controlled loop, make sure the control variable is incremented (or decremented) in the body of the loop. In a sentinel-controlled loop, make sure the sentinel value eventually is input.*

5.7 Statements break and continue

The **break** and **continue** statements alter the flow of control. The **break** statement, when executed in a **while**, **for**, **do/while** or **switch** structure, causes immediate exit from that structure. Execution continues with the first statement that follows the structure. Common uses of the **break** statement are to exit prematurely from a loop or to exit a **switch** structure (as in Fig. 5.10). Figure 5.14 demonstrates the **break** statement in a **for** repetition structure.

When the **if** structure in line 16 detects that **count** is **5**, **break** is executed. This terminates the **for** structure and the program proceeds to line 24 (immediately after the **for**). The string-concatenation statement produces the string that is displayed in the message dialog in lines 26–27. The loop executes its body only four times.

```
1   // Fig. 5.14: BreakTest.cs
2   // Using the break statement in a for structure.
3
4   using System;
5   using System.Windows.Forms;
6
7   class BreakTest
8   {
9      static void Main( string[] args )
10     {
11        string output = "";
12        int count;
13
14        for ( count = 1; count <= 10; count++ )
15        {
16           if ( count == 5 )
17              break;              // skip remaining code in loop
18                                  // if count == 5
19
20           output += count + " ";
21
22        } // end for loop
23
```

Fig. 5.14 break statement in a **for** structure. (Part 1 of 2.)

```
24              output += "\nBroke out of loop at count = " + count;
25
26          MessageBox.Show( output, "Demonstrating the break statement",
27              MessageBoxButtons.OK, MessageBoxIcon.Information );
28
29      } // end method Main
30
31  } // end class BreakTest
```

Fig. 5.14 **break** statement in a **for** structure. (Part 2 of 2.)

The **continue** statement, when executed in a **while**, **for** or **do/while** structure, skips the remaining statements in the body of that structure and proceeds with the next iteration of the loop. In **while** and **do/while** structures, the loop-continuation condition evaluates immediately after **continue** executes. In a **for** structure, the increment/decrement expression executes, then the loop-continuation test evaluates.

We have stated that the **while** structure can replace the **for** structure in most cases. One exception occurs when the increment/decrement expression in the **while** structure follows the **continue** statement. In this case, the increment/decrement does not execute before the repetition-continuation condition is tested, and the **while** does not execute in the same manner as the **for**.

Figure 5.15 uses the **continue** statement in a **for** structure to skip the string-concatenation statement on line 19 when the **if** structure (line 15) determines that the value of **count** is **5**. When the **continue** statement executes, program control continues with the increment of the control variable in the **for** structure.

Good Programming Practice 5.10

*Some programmers believe that **break** and **continue** violate structured programming. The effects of these statements can be achieved by structured programming techniques, so these programmers avoid **break** and **continue**.*

```
1   // Fig. 5.15: ContinueTest.cs
2   // Using the continue statement in a for structure.
3
4   using System;
5   using System.Windows.Forms;
6
7   class ContinueTest
8   {
9       static void Main( string[] args )
10      {
11          string output = "";
```

Fig. 5.15 **continue** statement in a **for** structure. (Part 1 of 2.)

```
12
13              for ( int count = 1; count <= 10; count++ )
14              {
15                 if ( count == 5 )
16                    continue;          // skip remaining code in loop
17                                        // only if count == 5
18
19                 output += count + " ";
20              }
21
22              output += "\nUsed continue to skip printing 5";
23
24              MessageBox.Show( output, "Using the continue statement",
25                 MessageBoxButtons.OK, MessageBoxIcon.Information );
26
27           } // end method Main
28
29     } // end class ContinueTest
```

Fig. 5.15   continue statement in a **for** structure. (Part 2 of 2.)

Performance Tip 5.2

*When used properly, the **break** and **continue** statements perform faster than their corresponding structured techniques.*

Software Engineering Observation 5.1

There is a debate between achieving quality software engineering and achieving the best performing software. Often, one of these goals is achieved at the expense of the other. For all but the most performance-intensive situations, apply the following "rule of thumb": First, make your code simple and correct; then make it fast and small, but only if necessary.

5.8 Logical and Conditional Operators

So far, we have studied only *simple conditions,* such as **count <= 10**, **total > 1000** and **number != sentinelValue**. These conditions were expressed in terms of the relational operators **>**, **<**, **>=** and **<=** and the equality operators **==** and **!=**. Each decision tested one condition. To test multiple conditions in the process of making a decision, we performed these tests in separate statements or in nested **if** or **if/else** structures.

C# provides several *logical and conditional operators* that may be used to form complex conditions by combining simple conditions. The operators are **&&** (*conditional AND*), **&** (*logical AND*), **||** (*conditional OR*), **|** (*logical OR*), **^** (*logical exclusive OR or logical XOR*) and **!** (*logical NOT,* also called *logical negation*). We will consider examples using each of these operators.

Common Programming Error 5.10

*Placing a space between the **&&** or **||** operator results in a syntax error.*

Suppose we wish to ensure that two conditions are *both* true in a program before we choose a certain path of execution. In this case, we can use the conditional **&&** operator as follows:

```
if ( gender == 1 && age >= 65 )
    ++seniorFemales;
```

This **if** statement contains two simple conditions. The condition **gender == 1** might be evaluated to determine whether a person is female. The condition **age >= 65** is evaluated to determine whether a person is a senior citizen. The two simple conditions are evaluated first, because the precedences of **==** and **>=** are both higher than the precedence of **&&**. The **if** statement then considers the combined condition

```
gender == 1 && age >= 65
```

This condition is true *if and only if* both the simple conditions are true. Finally, if this combined condition is true, the body statement increments the count of **seniorFemales** by **1**. If either or both of the simple conditions are false, the program skips the incrementing and proceeds to the statement that follows the **if** structure. The preceding combined condition can be made more readable by adding redundant parentheses:

```
( gender == 1 ) && ( age >= 65 )
```

The table in Fig. 5.16 summarizes the **&&** operator. The table shows all four possible combinations of false and true values for *expression1* and *expression2*. Such tables often are called *truth tables*. C# evaluates to true or false expressions that include relational operators, equality operators, logical operators and/or conditional operators.

Now let us consider the **||** (conditional OR) operator. Suppose we wish to ensure that either *or* both of two conditions are true before we choose a certain path of execution. We use the **||** operator in the following program segment:

```
if ( semesterAverage >= 90 || finalExam >= 90 )
    Console.WriteLine( "Student grade is A" );
```

expression1	expression2	expression1 && expression2
false	false	false
false	true	false
true	false	false
true	true	true

Fig. 5.16   Truth table for the **&&** (conditional AND) operator.

which also contains two simple conditions. The condition **semesterAverage >= 90** determines whether the student deserves an "A" in the course because of a solid performance throughout the semester. The condition **finalExam >= 90** determines whether the student deserves an "A" in the course because of an outstanding performance on the final exam. The **if** statement then considers the combined condition

```
semesterAverage >= 90 || finalExam >= 90
```

and awards the student an "A" if either or both of the simple conditions are true. Note that the message "**Student grade is A**" prints unless *both* of the simple conditions are false. Figure 5.17 is a truth table for the conditional OR operator (||).

The **&&** operator has a higher precedence than the || operator. Both operators associate from left to right. An expression containing **&&** or || operators is evaluated only until truth or falsity is known. Thus, evaluation of the expression

```
gender == 1 && age >= 65
```

stops immediately if **gender** is not equal to **1** (i.e., the entire expression is false) and continue if **gender** is equal to **1** (i.e., the entire expression is true, even if the condition **age >= 65** is true). This performance feature for the evaluation of conditional AND and conditional OR expressions is called *short-circuit evaluation.*

Performance Tip 5.3

*In expressions using operator **&&**, if the separate conditions are independent of one another, make the condition most likely to be false the leftmost condition. In expressions using operator ||, make the condition most likely to be true the leftmost condition. This use of short-circuit evaluation can reduce a program's execution time.*

The *logical AND* (**&**) and *logical OR* (|) operators are similar to the conditional AND and conditional OR operators, with one exception—the logical operators always evaluate both of their operands (i.e., there is no short-circuit evaluation). Therefore, the expression

```
gender == 1 & age >= 65
```

evaluates **age >= 65**, regardless of whether **gender** is equal to **1**. This is useful if the right operand of the logical AND or logical OR operator includes a needed *side effect*—a modification of a variable's value. For example, the expression

```
birthday == true | ++age >= 65
```

expression1	expression2	expression1 || expression2
false	false	false
false	true	true
true	false	true
true	true	true

Fig. 5.17 Truth table for the || (conditional OR) operator.

guarantees that the condition **++age >= 65** evaluates and increments the variable **age** in the preceding expression, regardless of whether the overall expression is true or false. Likewise, if we want the condition in the right operand to be the result of a method call, and we want the method to execute in any case, then we can use the | operator.

Common Programming Error 5.11

Avoid expressions with side effects in conditions. The side effects might look clever, but they often cause subtle errors and can be confusing to other people reading or maintaining your code.

A condition containing the *logical exclusive OR* (^) operator is true *if and only if one of its operands results in a true value and one results in a false value*. If both operands are true or both are false, the result of the entire condition is false. Figure 5.18 is a truth table for the logical exclusive OR operator (^). This operator evaluates both of its operands (i.e., there is no short-circuit evaluation).

C# provides the ! (logical negation) operator to enable a programmer to "reverse" the meaning of a condition. Unlike the logical operators **&&, &, ||, |** and ^, which combine two conditions (binary operators), the logical negation operator has only a single condition as an operand (unary operator). The logical negation operator is placed before a condition to choose a path of execution if the original condition (without the logical negation operator) is false. This is demonstrated by the following program segment:

```
if ( ! ( grade == sentinelValue ) )
    Console.WriteLine( "The next grade is " + grade );
```

The parentheses around the condition **grade == sentinelValue** are needed because the logical negation operator has a higher precedence than the equality operator. Figure 5.19 is a truth table for the logical negation operator.

expression1	expression2	expression1 ^ expression2
false	false	false
false	true	true
true	false	true
true	true	false

Fig. 5.18   Truth table for the logical exclusive OR (^) operator.

expression	!expression
false	true
true	false

Fig. 5.19   Truth table for operator ! (logical NOT).

In most cases, the programmer can avoid using logical negation by expressing the condition differently with relational or equality operators. For example, the preceding statement may also be written as follows:

```
if ( grade != sentinelValue )
    Console.WriteLine( "The next grade is " + grade );
```

This flexibility can help a programmer express a condition more naturally.

The console application in Fig. 5.20 demonstrates all the conditional and logical operators by displaying their truth tables in a label.

```
1    // Fig. 5.20: LogicalOperators.cs
2    // Demonstrating the logical operators.
3    using System;
4
5    class LogicalOperators
6    {
7        // main entry point for application
8        static void Main( string[] args )
9        {
10           // testing the conditional AND operator (&&)
11           Console.WriteLine( "Conditional AND (&&)" +
12               "\nfalse && false: " + ( false && false ) +
13               "\nfalse && true:  " + ( false && true ) +
14               "\ntrue && false:  " + ( true && false ) +
15               "\ntrue && true:   " + ( true && true ) );
16
17           // testing the conditional OR operator (||)
18           Console.WriteLine( "\n\nConditional OR (||)" +
19               "\nfalse || false: " + ( false || false ) +
20               "\nfalse || true:  " + ( false || true ) +
21               "\ntrue || false:  " + ( true || false ) +
22               "\ntrue || true:   " + ( true || true ) );
23
24           // testing the logical AND operator (&)
25           Console.WriteLine( "\n\nLogical AND (&)" +
26               "\nfalse & false: " + ( false & false ) +
27               "\nfalse & true:  " + ( false & true ) +
28               "\ntrue & false:  " + ( true & false ) +
29               "\ntrue & true:   " + ( true & true ) );
30
31           // testing the logical OR operator (|)
32           Console.WriteLine( "\n\nLogical OR (|)" +
33               "\nfalse | false: " + ( false | false ) +
34               "\nfalse | true:  " + ( false | true ) +
35               "\ntrue | false:  " + ( true | false ) +
36               "\ntrue | true:   " + ( true | true ) );
37
38           // testing the logical exclusive OR operator (^)
39           Console.WriteLine( "\n\nLogical exclusive OR (^)" +
40               "\nfalse ^ false: " + ( false ^ false ) +
41               "\nfalse ^ true:  " + ( false ^ true ) +
```

Fig. 5.20 Conditional and logical operators. (Part 1 of 2.)

```
42                "\ntrue ^ false:   " + ( true ^ false ) +
43                "\ntrue ^ true:    " + ( true ^ true ) );
44
45           // testing the logical NOT operator (!)
46           Console.WriteLine( "\n\nLogical NOT (!)" +
47                "\n!false: " + ( !false ) +
48                "\n!true:  " + ( !true ) );
49      }
50  }
```

```
Conditional AND (&&)
false && false: False
false && true:  False
true && false:  False
true && true:   True


Conditional OR (||)
false || false: False
false || true:  True
true || false:  True
true || true:   True


Logical AND (&)
false & false: False
false & true:  False
true & false:  False
true & true:   True


Logical OR (|)
false | false: False
false | true:  True
true | false:  True
true | true:   True


Logical exclusive OR (^)
false ^ false: False
false ^ true:  True
true ^ false:  True
true ^ true:   False


Logical NOT (!)
!false: True
!true:  False
```

Fig. 5.20 Conditional and logical operators. (Part 2 of 2.)

On line 11, we begin class **LogicalOperators**. Method **Main** (lines 8–49) contains the code for this program. Lines 11–15 demonstrate the **&&** operator; lines 25–29 demonstrate the **&** operator. Notice that, to display one **&** symbol, two **&**s are required. The remainder of the constructor demonstrates the **| |**, **|**, **^** and **!** operators.

When a **bool** value is concatenated to a **string**, C# adds the string representation of the boolean value, which will be either **"False"** or **"True"**.

Figure 5.21 shows the precedence and associativity of the C# operators introduced to this point. The operators are shown from top to bottom in decreasing order of precedence.

5.9 Structured-Programming Summary

Just as architects design buildings by employing the collective wisdom of their profession, so should programmers design programs. Our field is younger than architecture is, and our collective wisdom is considerably sparser. We have learned that structured programming produces programs that are easier to understand, test, debug, modify and prove correct in a mathematical sense than unstructured programs.

Figure 5.22 summarizes C#'s control structures. Small circles in the figure indicate the single entry point and the single exit point of each structure. Connecting individual flowchart symbols arbitrarily can lead to unstructured programs. Therefore, the programming profession has chosen to combine flowchart symbols to form only a limited set of control structures and to build structured programs by combining control structures in only two simple ways.

For simplicity, only single-entry/single-exit control structures are used—there is only one way to enter and only one way to exit each control structure. To connect control structures in sequence to form structured programs, the exit point of one control structure is connected to the entry point of the next control structure (i.e., the control structures are simply placed one after another in a program). We call this process "control-structure stacking." The rules for forming structured programs also allow control structures to be nested. Figure 5.23 contains the rules for forming properly structured programs. The rules assume that the rectangle flowchart symbol can indicate any action, including input/output.

Operators	Associativity	Type
( )	left to right	parentheses
++ --	right to left	unary postfix
++ -- + - ! (*type*)	right to left	unary prefix
* / %	left to right	multiplicative
+ -	left to right	additive
< <= > >=	left to right	relational
== !=	left to right	equality
&	left to right	logical AND
^	left to right	logical exclusive OR
|	left to right	logical inclusive OR
&&	left to right	conditional AND
||	left to right	conditional OR
? :	right to left	conditional
= += -= *= /= %=	right to left	assignment

Fig. 5.21   Precedence and associativity of the operators discussed so far.

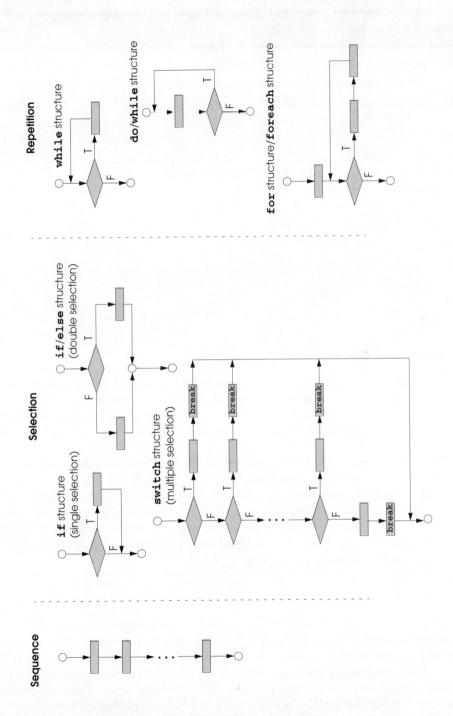

Fig. 5.22 C#'s single-entry/single-exit sequence, selection and repetition
structures.

Rules for Forming Structured Programs

1)   Begin with the "simplest flowchart" (Fig. 5.24).

2)   Any rectangle (action) can be replaced by two rectangles (actions) in sequence.

3)   Any rectangle (action) can be replaced by any control structure (sequence, **if**, **if/else**, **switch**, **while**, **do/while**, **for** or **foreach**, as we will see in Chapter 7, Arrays).

4)   Rules 2 and 3 may be applied as often as you like and in any order.

Fig. 5.23 Rules for forming structured programs.

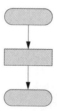

Fig. 5.24 Simplest flowchart.

Applying the rules of Fig. 5.23 always results in a structured flowchart with a neat, building-block appearance. For example, repeatedly applying rule 2 to the simplest flowchart results in a structured flowchart that contains many rectangles in sequence (Fig. 5.25). Notice that rule 2 generates a stack of control structures; therefore, we call rule 2 the *stacking rule*.

Rule 3 is the *nesting rule*. Repeatedly applying rule 3 to the simplest flowchart results in a flowchart with neatly nested control structures. For example, in Fig. 5.26, the rectangle in the simplest flowchart first is replaced with a double-selection (**if/else**) structure. Then rule 3 is applied again to both rectangles in the double-selection structure, replacing each of the rectangles with a double-selection structure. The dashed boxes around each of the double-selection structures represent the rectangles that were replaced with these structures.

 Good Programming Practice 5.11

Too many levels of nesting can make a program difficult to understand. As a general rule, try to avoid using more than three levels of nesting.

Rule 4 generates larger, more involved and deeply-nested structures. The flowcharts that emerge from applying the rules in Fig. 5.23 constitute the set of all possible structured flowcharts and the set of all possible structured programs.The structured approach has the advantage of using only eight simple single-entry/single-exit pieces and allowing us to assemble them in only two simple ways. Figure 5.27 shows the kinds of correctly stacked building blocks that emerge from applying rule 2 and the kinds of correctly nested building blocks that emerge from applying rule 3. The figure also shows the kind of overlapped building blocks that cannot occur in structured flowcharts (as a result of avoiding **goto** statements).

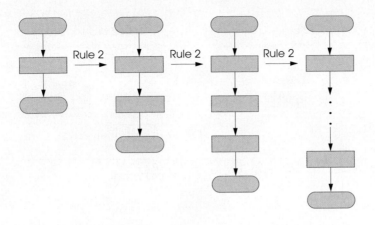

Fig. 5.25   Repeatedly applying rule 2 of Fig. 5.23 to the simplest flowchart.

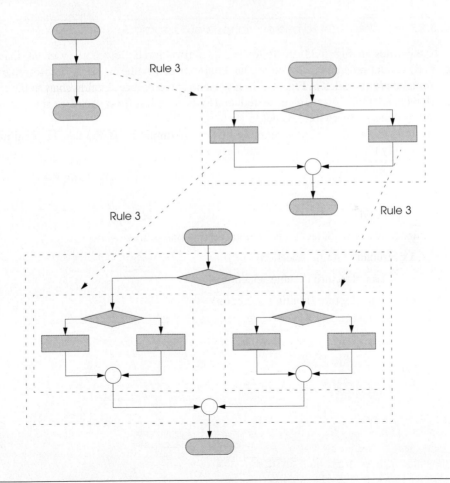

Fig. 5.26   Applying rule 3 of Fig. 5.23 to the simplest flowchart.

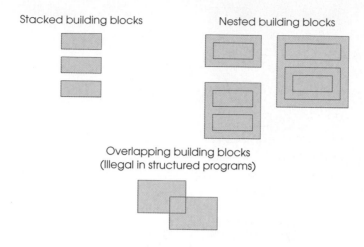

Fig. 5.27 Stacked, nested and overlapped building blocks.

If the rules in Fig. 5.23 are followed, an unstructured flowchart (such as that in Fig. 5.28) cannot be created. If you are uncertain about whether a particular flowchart is structured, apply the rules in Fig. 5.23 in reverse to try to reduce the flowchart to the simplest flowchart. If the flowchart can be reduced to the simplest flowchart, the original flowchart is structured; otherwise, it is not.

In summary, structured programming promotes simplicity. Bohm and Jacopini have found that only three forms of control are necessary:

- Sequence
- Selection
- Repetition

Sequence is trivial. Selection is implemented in one of three ways:

- **if** structure (single selection)
- **if/else** structure (double selection)
- **switch** structure (multiple selection)

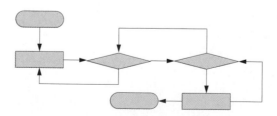

Fig. 5.28 Unstructured flowchart.

In fact, it is straightforward to prove that the **if** structure is sufficient to provide any form of selection. Everything that can be done with the **if/else** and **switch** structures can be implemented by combining **if** structures (although perhaps not as elegantly).

Repetition is implemented in one of four ways:

- **while** structure
- **do/while** structure
- **for** structure
- **foreach** structure (discussed in Chapter 7)

It is straightforward to prove that the **while** structure is sufficient to provide any form of repetition. Everything that can be done with the **do/while**, **for** and **foreach** structures can be done with the **while** structure (although perhaps not as elegantly).

Combining these results illustrates that any form of control ever needed in a C# program can be expressed in terms of:

- sequence
- **if** structure (selection)
- **while** structure (repetition)

These control structures can be combined in only two ways—stacking and nesting. Indeed, structured programming promotes simplicity.

In this chapter, we discussed how to compose programs from control structures that contain actions and decisions. In Chapter 6, Methods, we introduce another program-structuring unit, called the *method*. We will learn to compose large programs by combining methods that are composed of control structures. We also discuss how methods promote software reusability. In Chapter 8, Object-Based Programming, we discuss in more detail another C# program-structuring unit, called the *class*. We then create objects from classes and proceed with our treatment of object-oriented programming—the key focus of this book.

SUMMARY

- Counter-controlled repetition requires the name of a control variable (or loop counter), the initial value of the control variable, the increment (or decrement) by which the control variable is modified each time through the loop and the condition that tests for the final value of the control variable (i.e., whether looping should continue).

- Declarations that include initialization are executable statements.

- Floating-point values may be approximate, so controlling counting loops with floating-point variables may result in imprecise counter values and inaccurate tests for termination.

- If there is more than one statement in the body of the **for**, braces (**{** and **}**) are needed to define the body of the loop.

- Using an incorrect relational operator or an incorrect final value of a loop counter in the condition of a **while**, **for** or **do/while** structure can cause an off-by-one error.

- The general format of the **for** structure is

```
for ( expression1; expression2; expression3 )
   statement
```

where *expression1* names the loop's control variable and provides its initial value, *expression2* is the loop-continuation condition (containing the control variable's final value) and *expression3* increments the control variable.

- In most cases, the **for** structure can be represented with an equivalent **while** structure with *expression1*, *expression2* and *expression3* placed as follows:

```
expression1;

while ( expression2 )
{
    statement
    expression3;
}
```

- If the initialization section in the **for** structure header defines the control variable, the control variable can be used only in the body of the **for** structure.
- The scope of a variable defines where the variable can be used in a program.
- The three expressions in the **for** structure are optional. The two semicolons in the **for** structure are required.
- If the loop-continuation condition is initially false, the body of the **for** structure does not execute.
- Changing the value of the control variable in the body of a **for** loop can lead to subtle errors.
- Do not use variables of type **float** or **double** to perform precise monetary calculations. The imprecision of floating-point numbers can cause errors that will result in incorrect monetary values. Type **decimal** is available for performing monetary calculations properly.
- The **switch** multiple-selection structure consists of a series of **case** labels and an optional **default** case. Each label (**case** or **default**) contains statements to be executed if that label is selected.
- A **break** is required in every **case** of a **switch** structure, except for empty **case**s.
- Listing **case** labels together (such as **case 'C': case 'c':**, with no statements between the cases) causes the same set of actions to be performed for each of the **case**s.
- When using the **switch** structure, remember that the expression after each **case** must be a constant integral expression (i.e., any combination of character and integer constants that evaluates to a constant integer value) or a string.
- The **do/while** structure tests the loop-continuation condition after the loop body executes; therefore, the loop body always executes at least once.
- The **break** statement, when executed in a **while**, **for**, **do/while** or **switch** structure, causes immediate exit from that structure. Execution continues with the first statement after the structure.
- The **continue** statement, when executed in a **while**, **for** or **do/while** structure, skips the remaining statements in the body of that structure and proceeds with the next iteration of the loop.
- C# uses conditional and logical operators to form complex conditions by combining simple ones.
- The conditional and logical operators are **&&** (conditional AND), **&** (logical AND), **||** (conditional OR), **|** (logical inclusive OR), **^** (logical exclusive OR) and **!** (logical NOT, also called logical negation).
- The conditional **&&** operator ensures that two conditions are both **true** before we choose a certain path of execution.
- The logical **||** operator ensures that at least one of two conditions is **true** before we choose a certain path of execution.

- A condition containing the boolean logical exclusive OR (^) operator is true if and only if one of its operands is true and one is false.
- The ! (logical negation) operator "reverses" the meaning of a condition.
- When a **bool** value is concatenated to a **string**, C# adds the string **"False"** or **"True"** based on the **bool** value.
- In flowcharts, small circles indicate the single entry point and exit point of each structure.
- Connecting individual flowchart symbols arbitrarily can lead to unstructured programs. Therefore, the programming profession has chosen to combine flowchart symbols to form a limited set of control structures and to build structured programs by properly combining control structures in two simple ways—stacking and nesting.
- Structured programming promotes simplicity.
- Bohm and Jacopini have given us the result that only three forms of control are needed—sequence, selection and repetition.
- Selection is implemented with one of three control structures—**if**, **if/else** and **switch**.
- Repetition is implemented with one of four control structures—**while**, **do/while**, **for** and **foreach**.
- The **if** structure is sufficient to provide any form of selection.
- The **while** structure is sufficient to provide any form of repetition.

TERMINOLOGY

! logical NOT
!= "is not equal to"
& logical AND
&& conditional AND
^ boolean logical exclusive OR
| boolean logical inclusive OR
|| conditional OR
<= less than or equal
AND operator boolean logical
AND operator logical
binary
binary operator
body of a loop
bool values
braces (**{** and **}**)
break statement
buttons for message dialogs
C formatting code
case
conditional AND operator (**&&**)
conditional OR operator (**||**)
const variable
constant integral expression
constant variable
continue statement
control structure
control variable

controlling expression
control-structure nesting
control-structure stacking
counter variable
counter-controlled repetition
D formatting code
decimal
decrement expression
default statement
delay loop
diamond symbol
do/while structure
double-selection structure
E formatting code
empty **case**
empty statement (semicolon by itself)
entry point of a control structure
Error
F formatting code
flowchart symbol
for structure
for structure header
foreach structure
formatting code
formatting data
G formatting code
goto statement

SELF-REVIEW EXERCISES

5.1 State whether each of the following is *true* or *false*. If *false*, explain why.

a) The **default** case is required in the **switch** selection structure.

b) If there is more than one statement in the body of the **for**, braces (**{** and **}**) are needed to define the body of the loop.

c) The expression (**x > y && a < b**) is true if either **x > y** is true or **a < b** is true.

d) An expression containing the **||** operator is true if either or both of its operands is true.

e) The expression (**x <= y && y > 4**) is true if **x** is less than or equal to **y** or **y** is greater than 4.

f) A **for** loop requires two commas in its header.

g) Infinite loops are caused when the loop-termination condition is always true.

h) The following syntax continues iterating the loop while $10 < x < 100$:

```
while ( x > 10 && x < 100 );
```

     i) The **break** statement, when executed in a repetition structure, causes immediate exit from the repetition structure.

     j) The || operator has a higher precedence than the && operator.

5.2   Fill in the blanks in each of the following statements:

     a) Specifying the order in which statements are to be executed in a computer program is called _____.

     b) Placing a semicolon after a **for** statement typically results in a _____ error.

     c) A **for** loop should count with _____ values.

     d) Using the < relational operator instead of <= in a **while**-repetition condition that should loop 10 times (as shown below) causes an _____ error:

```
int x = 1;
while ( x < 10 ) …
```

     e) A control variable initialized within a **for** loop can be used only in the body of the loop. This is called the _____ of the variable.

     f) In a **for** loop, incrementing occurs _____ the body of the structure is performed each time.

     g) Multiple initializations in the **for** structure header should be separated by _____.

     h) Placing expressions whose values do not change inside _____ can lead to poor performance.

     i) The four types of **MessageBox** icons are exclamation, information, error and _____.

     j) The value in parentheses immediately following the keyword **switch** is called the _____.

5.3   Write a C# statement or a set of C# statements to accomplish each of the following tasks:

     a) Sum the odd integers between 1 and 99, using a **for** structure. Assume that the integer variables **sum** and **count** have been declared.

     b) Calculate the value of **2.5** raised to the power of **3**, using the **Math.Pow** method.

     c) Print the integers from 1 to 20, using a **while** loop and the counter variable **x**. Assume that the variable **x** has been declared, but not initialized. Print only five integers per line. [*Hint*: Use the calculation **x % 5**. When the value of this is 0, print a newline character; otherwise, print a tab character. Use the **Console.WriteLine()** method to output the newline character, and use the **Console.Write('\t')** method to output the tab character.]

     d) Repeat part c, using a **for** structure.

ANSWERS TO SELF-REVIEW EXERCISES

5.1   a) False. The **default** case is optional. If no default action is required, then there is no need for a **default** case. b) True. c) False. Both of the relational expressions must be true for the entire expression to be true. d) True. e) False. The expression (x <= y && y > 4) is true if x is less than or equal to y and y is greater than 4. f) False. A **for** loop requires two semicolons in its header. g) False. Infinite loops are caused when the loop-continuation condition is always true. h) True. i) True. j) False. The && operator has higher precedence than the || operator.

5.2   a) program control. b) logic. c) integral. d) off-by-one. e) scope. f) after. g) comma. h) loops. i) question. j) controlling expression.

5.3   a)
```
sum = 0;
for ( count = 1; count <= 99; count += 2 )
   sum += count;
```

b) `Math.Pow( 2.5, 3 )`

c) `x = 1;`

```
while ( x <= 20 )
{
   Console.Write( x );

   if ( x % 5 == 0 )
      Console.WriteLine();
   else
      Console.Write( '\t' );

   ++x;
}
```

d)
```
for ( x = 1; x <= 20; x++ )
{
   Console.Write( x );

   if ( x % 5 == 0 )
      Console.WriteLine();
   else
      Console.Write( '\t' );
}
```

or

```
for ( x = 1; x <= 20; x++ )

   if ( x % 5 == 0 )
      Console.WriteLine( x );
   else
      Console.Write( x + "\t" );
```

EXERCISES

5.4   The *factorial* method is used frequently in probability problems. The factorial of a positive integer *n* (written *n!* and pronounced "n factorial") is equal to the product of the positive integers from 1 to *n*. Write a program that evaluates the factorials of the integers from 1 to 20 with different integer data types. Display the results in a three-column output table. [*Hint*: create a Windows application, using **Label**s as the columns and the `'\n'` character to line up rows.] The first column should display the *n* values (1-20). The second column should display *n!*, calculated with **int** (**Int32**, a 32-bit integer value). The third column should display *n!*, calculated with **long** (**Int64**, a 64-bit integer value). What happens when **int** (**Int32**) is too small in size to hold the result of a factorial calculation?

5.5   Write two programs that each print a table of the binary, octal, and hexadecimal equivalents of the decimal numbers in the range 1–256. If you are not familiar with these number systems, read Appendix C, Number Systems, first.

  a) For the first program, print the results to the console without using any **string** formats.

  b) For the second program, print the results to the console using both the decimal and hexadecimal **string** formats (there are no formats for binary and octal in C#).

5.6   (*Pythagorean Triples*) A right triangle can have sides that are all integers. A set of three integer values for the sides of a right triangle is called a Pythagorean triple. These three sides must satisfy the relationship that the sum of the squares of the two sides is equal to the square of the hypotenuse. Write a program to find all Pythagorean triples for **side1**, **side2** and **hypotenuse**, none larger than 30. Use a triple-nested **for** loop that tries all possibilities. This is an example of "brute force" computing. You will learn in more advanced computer science courses that there are several problems for which there is no other known algorithmic approach.

5.7   Write a program that displays the following patterns separately, one below the other. Use **for** loops to generate the patterns. All asterisks (*) should be printed by a single statement of the form **Console.Write('*');** (this causes the asterisks to print side by side). A statement of the form **Console.WriteLine();** can be used to position to the next line. A statement of the form **Console.Write(' ');** can be used to display spaces for the last two patterns. There should be no other output statements in the program. [*Hint*: The last two patterns require that each line begin with an appropriate number of blanks.]

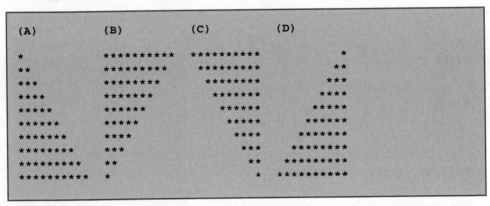

5.8   Modify Exercise 5.7 to combine your code from the four separate triangles of asterisks into a single program that prints all four patterns side by side, making clever use of nested **for** loops.

5.9   Write a program that prints the following diamond shape. You may use output statements that print a single asterisk (*), a single space or a single newline character. Maximize your use of repetition (with nested **for** structures) and minimize the number of output statements.

5.10   Modify the program you wrote in Exercise 5.9 to read an odd number in the range from 1 to 19 to specify the number of rows in the diamond. Your program should then display a diamond of the appropriate size.

6

Methods

Objectives

- To construct programs modularly from small pieces called methods.
- To introduce the common math methods available in the Framework Class Library.
- To be able to create new methods.
- To understand the mechanisms for passing information between methods.
- To introduce simulation techniques that use random number generation.
- To understand how the visibility of identifiers is limited to specific regions of programs.
- To understand how to write and use methods that call themselves.

Form ever follows function.
Louis Henri Sullivan

E pluribus unum.
(One composed of many.)
Virgil

O! call back yesterday, bid time return.
William Shakespeare

Call me Ishmael.
Herman Melville

When you call me that, smile.
Owen Wister

6.1 Introduction

Most computer programs that solve real-world problems are much larger than the programs presented in the first few chapters of this text. Experience has shown that the best way to develop and maintain a large program is to construct it from small, simple pieces, or *modules*. This technique is known as *divide and conquer*. This chapter describes many key features of the C# language that facilitate the design, implementation, operation and maintenance of large programs.

6.2 Program Modules in C#[1]

Modules in C# are called *methods* and *classes*. C# programs are written by combining new methods and classes that the programmer writes with "prepackaged" methods and classes available in the *.NET Framework Class Library* (*FCL*). In this chapter, we concentrate on methods. We discuss classes in detail in Chapter 8, Object-Based Programming.

The FCL provides a rich collection of classes and methods for performing common mathematical calculations, string manipulations, character manipulations, input/output

---

1. It is important to note that we are discussing modules in an abstract sense. In C#, there is another form of code packaging (other than assemblies), called modules. This is not what we are discussing in this chapter, but the reader should know that this term can be used in two ways.

operations, error checking and many other useful operations. This set of modules makes the programmer's job easier, because the modules provide many of the capabilities programmers need. The FCL methods are part of the .NET Framework, which includes FCL classes **Console** and **MessageBox** used in earlier examples.

Software Engineering Observation 6.1

Familiarize yourself with the rich collection of classes and methods in the FCL.

Software Engineering Observation 6.2

When possible, use .NET Framework classes and methods instead of writing new classes and methods. This reduces program development time and avoids the introduction of new errors.

The programmer can write methods to define specific tasks that may be used at many points in a program. Such methods are known as *programmer-defined* (or *user-defined*) *methods*. The actual statements defining the method are written only once and are hidden from other methods.

A method is *invoked* (i.e., made to perform its designated task) by a *method call*. The method call specifies the name of the method and may provide information (as *arguments*) that the called method requires to perform its task. When the method call completes, the method either returns a result to the *calling method* (or *caller*) or simply returns control to the calling method. A common analogy for this is the hierarchical form of management. A boss (the calling method or caller) asks a worker (the *called method*) to perform a task and report back (i.e., *return*) the results after completing the task. The boss method does not know *how* the worker method performs its designated tasks. The worker may also call other worker methods, and the boss will be unaware of these calls. We will see how this "hiding" of implementation details promotes good software engineering. Figure 6.1 shows a **boss** method communicating with worker methods **worker1**, **worker2** and **worker3** in a hierarchical manner. Note that **worker1** acts as a "boss" method to **worker4** and **worker5** in this particular example.

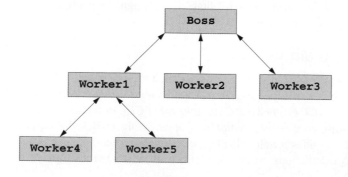

Fig. 6.1   Hierarchical boss method/worker method relationship.

6.3 **Math** Class Methods

Math class methods allow the programmer to perform certain common mathematical calculations. We use various **Math** class methods to introduce the concept of methods in general. Throughout the book, we discuss many other methods from the classes of the Framework Class Library.

Methods are called by writing the name of the method, followed by a left parenthesis, the *argument* (or a comma-separated list of arguments) of the method and a right parenthesis. The parentheses may be empty, if we are calling a method that needs no information to perform its task. For example, a programmer wishing to calculate and print the square root of **900.0** might write

```
Console.WriteLine( Math.Sqrt( 900.0 ) );
```

When this statement executes, the method **Math.Sqrt** calculates the square root of the number in parentheses (**900.0**). The number **900.0** is the argument to the **Math.Sqrt** method. The **Math.Sqrt** method takes an argument of type **double** and returns a result of type **double**. The preceding statement uses the result of method **Math.Sqrt** as the argument to method **Console.WriteLine** and displays **30.0**. Note that all **Math** class methods must be invoked by preceding the method name with the class name **Math** and a dot (**.**) operator (also called the member access operator).

Software Engineering Observation 6.3

*It is not necessary to add an assembly reference to use the **Math** class methods in a program. Class **Math** is located in namespace **System**, which is available to every program.*

Common Programming Error 6.1

*Forgetting to invoke a **Math** class method by preceding the method name with the class name **Math** and a dot operator (**.**) results in a syntax error.*

Method arguments may be constants, variables or expressions. If **c1 = 13.0, d = 3.0** and **f = 4.0**, then the statement

```
Console.WriteLine( Math.Sqrt( c1 + d * f ) );
```

calculates and displays the square root of **13.0 + 3.0 * 4.0 = 25.0**, which is **5.0**.

Figure 6.2 summarizes some **Math** class methods. In this figure, the variables **x** and **y** are of type **double**; however, many of the methods provide versions that take values of other data types as arguments. The **Math** class also defines two commonly used mathematical constants—**Math.PI** (3.14159265358979323846) and **Math.E** (2.7182818284590452354). The constant **Math.PI** of class **Math** is the ratio of a circle's circumference to its diameter. The constant **Math.E** is the base value for natural logarithms (calculated with the **Math.Log** method).

6.4 Methods

Methods allow programmers to modularize programs. Variables declared in method definitions are *local variables*—only the method that defines them knows they exist. Most methods have a list of *parameters* that enable method calls to communicate information between methods. A method's parameters are also variables local to that method and are not visible in any other methods.

Method	Description	Example
Abs(x)	absolute value of x	Abs(23.7) is 23.7 Abs(0) is 0 Abs(-23.7) is 23.7
Ceiling(x)	rounds x to the smallest integer not less than x	Ceiling(9.2) is 10.0 Ceiling(-9.8) is -9.0
Cos(x)	trigonometric cosine of x (x in radians)	Cos(0.0) is 1.0
Exp(x)	exponential method e^x	Exp(1.0) is approximately 2.7182818284590451 Exp(2.0) is approximately 7.3890560989306504
Floor(x)	rounds x to the largest integer not greater than x	Floor(9.2) is 9.0 Floor(-9.8) is -10.0
Log(x)	natural logarithm of x (base e)	Log(2.7182818284590451) is approximately 1.0 Log(7.3890560989306504) is approximately 2.0
Max(x, y)	larger value of x and y (also has versions for **float**, **int** and **long** values)	Max(2.3, 12.7) is 12.7 Max(-2.3, -12.7) is -2.3
Min(x, y)	smaller value of x and y (also has versions for **float**, **int** and **long** values)	Min(2.3, 12.7) is 2.3 Min(-2.3, -12.7) is -12.7
Pow(x, y)	x raised to power y (x^y)	Pow(2.0, 7.0) is 128.0 Pow(9.0, .5) is 3.0
Sin(x)	trigonometric sine of x (x in radians)	Sin(0.0) is 0.0
Sqrt(x)	square root of x	Sqrt(900.0) is 30.0 Sqrt(9.0) is 3.0
Tan(x)	trigonometric tangent of x (x in radians)	Tan(0.0) is 0.0

Fig. 6.2   Commonly used **Math** class methods.

There are several motivations for modularizing a program with methods. The divide-and-conquer approach makes program development more manageable. Another motivation is *software reusability*—using existing methods (and classes) as building blocks to create new programs. With proper method naming and definition, we can create programs from standardized methods, rather than building customized code. For example, we did not have to define how to convert **string**s to integers—The .NET Framework Class Library already defines such methods for us (**Int32.Parse**). A third motivation is to avoid repeating code in a program. Packaging code as a method allows that code to be executed from several locations in a program—we simply have to call that method.

Good Programming Practice 6.1
Make good use of modularity to increase the clarity and organization of your program. This will not only help others understand your program, but it also will aid in program development, testing and debugging.

Software Engineering Observation 6.4
To promote reusability, each method should perform a single, well-defined task, and the name of the method should express that task effectively.

Software Engineering Observation 6.5
If you cannot choose a concise name that expresses what the method does, it is possible that your method is attempting to perform too many diverse tasks. Usually it is best to break such a method into several smaller methods.

6.5 Method Definitions

The programs presented up to this point each contained at least one method definition (such as **Main**) that called FCL methods to accomplish the program's tasks. We now consider how to write customized methods.

Consider the Windows application in Fig. 6.3, which uses a method called **Square** to calculate the squares of the integers from 1 to 10. Notice the comment on line 15

```
// Visual Studio .NET generated code
```

Throughout the book we will use this comment to denote code that we are not displaying in the chapter. In all cases, this represents code created by the IDE. Most of this code initializes properties of GUI components. The examples in all chapters of the book are included in their entirety on the CD that accompanies this book. The examples also can be downloaded from **www.deitel.com** via the **Downloads/Resources** link. Figure 6.4, displays all the code. However, you do not need to understand all the code at this point in the book. Chapter 12, Graphical User Interfaces: Part 1, presents an example in which we discuss all the code in detail.

```csharp
1   // Fig. 6.3: SquareInt.cs
2   // Demonstrates a programmer-defined Square method.
3   using System;
4   using System.Drawing;
5   using System.Collections;
6   using System.ComponentModel;
7   using System.Windows.Forms;
8   using System.Data;
9
10  public class SquareInt : System.Windows.Forms.Form
11  {
12      private System.Windows.Forms.Button calculateButton;
13      private System.Windows.Forms.Label outputLabel;
14
15      // Visual Studio .NET generated code
```

Fig. 6.3   Using programmer-defined method **Square**. (Part 1 of 2.)

```
16
17     [STAThread]
18     static void Main()
19     {
20        Application.Run( new SquareInt() );
21     }
22
23     // Square method definition
24     int Square( int y )
25     {
26        return y * y; // return square of y
27
28     } // end method Square
29
30     private void calculateButton_Click( object sender,
31        System.EventArgs e )
32     {
33        outputLabel.Text = "";
34
35        // loop 10 times
36        for ( int counter = 1; counter <= 10; counter++ )
37        {
38           // calculate square of counter and store in result
39           int result = Square( counter );
40
41           // append result to outputLabel
42           outputLabel.Text += "The square of " + counter +
43              " is " + result + "\n";
44        }
45
46     } // end method calculateButton_Click
47
48  } // end of class SquareInt
```

Fig. 6.3   Using programmer-defined method **Square**. (Part 2 of 2.)

Until now, our programs have used methods of class **Console** to obtain user input from the command prompt. These programs output their results either to the command prompt or in **MessageBox**es. Although these are valid ways to receive input from a user and display output, they are fairly limited in their capabilities—the command prompt can obtain only one value at a time from the user, and a message dialog can display only one message. It is much more common for programs to read multiple inputs simultaneously (e.g., when the user enters name and address information) or to display many pieces of data at once (such as the values of the first ten squares in this example). To introduce more elaborate user interfaces, the program in Fig. 6.3 illustrates two graphical user interface concepts—attaching multiple GUI components to an application and *event handling*.

To build this application, we use the Windows Form Designer to add a **Button** GUI component object to the **Form**. This example also uses a label to display the results of calculating the first ten squares. The program invokes a special method, known as an *event handler*, when the user clicks the **Calculate Squares** button. An event handler is a method that performs some action in response to an *event*. Events occur when certain actions take place in a graphical user interface, such as when the user clicks a button. Using GUI component objects and events together allows programmers to create applications that interact with users in more sophisticated ways than we have seen previously. In Visual Studio .NET's Windows Form Designer, double clicking on a GUI component object causes Visual Studio .NET to generate an empty event handler method. The event handler method's name defaults to the GUI component's name, followed by an underscore and the name of the event. The programmer then can fill in the event handler method with code that performs a particular task.

In Fig. 6.3, method **calculateButton_Click** (lines 30–46) is an event handler method for **calculateButton**'s **Click** event (i.e., the event that occurs when the user clicks the button). When the user clicks the button, line 33 assigns the empty string (**""**) to **outputLabel**'s **Text** property to ensure that the output does not scroll off the form if the user presses the **Calculate Squares** button more than once. Lines 36–44 repeatedly invoke method **Square** to calculate the squares of the integers from 1 to 10. Line 39 invokes the **Square** method and passes the variable **counter** as an argument.

As in some of our previous Windows applications, we create a label called **outputLabel** to display the program's output. Every label contains a **string** property called **Text**, which can be accessed using the dot operator (**.**). We append the results of the square calculations to this label's **Text** property.

Line 39 declares **int** variable **result** to store the result of each square calculation. Lines 36–44 contain a **for** repetition structure in which each iteration of the loop calculates the **Square** of the current value of control variable **counter** and stores the value in **result**. Lines 42–43 concatenate each result to the **Text** property of **outputLabel**. At the end of the loop, the **Label** contains the results of squaring the values from 1 to 10.

The program invokes method **Square** on line 39. The parentheses, **()**, after **Square** represent the *method-call operator*, which has high precedence. At this point, the program makes a copy of the value of **counter** (the argument to the method call), and program control transfers to method **Square** (defined at lines 24–28). Method **Square** receives the copy of the value of **counter** in the *parameter* **y**. Then, **Square** calculates **y * y** (line 26). Method **Square** uses a **return** statement to return (i.e., give back) the result of the calculation to the statement that invoked **Square** (located in line 39). Line 39 then assigns the returned value to variable **result**. Lines 42–43 concatenate **"The square of"**, the value of **counter**, **" is "**, the value of **result** and a newline character to the end of **outputLabel**'s **Text** property. The **for** repetition structure repeats this process 10 times.

The definition of method **Square** (line 24) shows (inside the parentheses) that **Square** expects an integer parameter **y**. Parameter **y** is the name that holds the value passed to **Square** as an argument. The parameter name provides access to the argument value, so that code in the method body can use the value. Keyword **int**, which precedes the method name, indicates that method **Square** returns an integer result. The **return** statement in **Square** (line 26) passes the result of the calculation **y * y** back to the calling statement. Note that the entire method definition appears inside the braces of class **SquareInt**. All methods must be defined inside a class definition.

Good Programming Practice 6.2

Place a blank line between method definitions to separate the methods and enhance program readability.

Common Programming Error 6.2

Defining a method outside the braces of a class definition is a syntax error.

The format of a method definition is

```
return-value-type   method-name ( parameter-list )
{
    declarations and statements
}
```

The first line is sometimes known as the *method header*. The *method-name* is any valid identifier. The *return-value-type* is the data type of the result that the method returns to its caller. The *return-value-type* **void** indicates that a method does not return a value. Methods can return at most one value.

Common Programming Error 6.3

Omitting the return-value-type *in a method definition is a syntax error. If a method does not return a value, the method's* return-value-type *must be* **void***.*

Common Programming Error 6.4

Forgetting to return a value from a method that is supposed to return a value is a syntax error. If a return-value-type *other than* **void** *is specified, the method must contain a* **return** *statement that returns a value.*

Common Programming Error 6.5

Returning a value from a method whose return type has been declared **void** *is a compilation error.*

The *parameter-list* is a comma-separated list in which the method declares each parameter's type and name. The method call must specify one argument for each parameter in the method definition and the arguments must appear in the same order as the parameters in the method definition. The arguments also must be compatible with the parameter's type. For example, a parameter of type **double** could receive values of 7.35, 22 or –.03546, but not **"hello"** because a **double** variable cannot contain a **string**. If a method does not receive any values, the parameter list is empty (i.e., the method name is followed by an empty set of parentheses). Each parameter in a method's parameter list must have a data type; otherwise, a syntax error occurs.

Common Programming Error 6.6

Declaring method parameters of the same type as **float x, y** *instead of* **float x, float y** *is a syntax error, because types are required for each parameter in the parameter list.*

Common Programming Error 6.7

Placing a semicolon after the right parenthesis enclosing the parameter list of a method definition is a syntax error.

Common Programming Error 6.8

Redefining a method parameter in the method's body is a compilation error.

Common Programming Error 6.9

Passing to a method an argument that is not compatible with the corresponding parameter's type is a syntax error.

The declarations and statements within braces form the *method body*. The method body is also referred to as a block. As discussed previously, a block is a set of declarations and statements enclosed in curly braces. Variables can be declared in any block, and blocks can be nested.

Common Programming Error 6.10

Defining a method inside another method is a syntax error (i.e., methods cannot be nested).

Good Programming Practice 6.3

Choosing meaningful method names and parameter names makes programs more readable and helps avoid excessive use of comments.

Software Engineering Observation 6.6

As a rule of thumb, a method should be no longer than one page. Better yet, a method should be no longer than half a page. Regardless of how long a method is, it should perform one task well. Small methods promote software reusability.

Testing and Debugging Tip 6.1

Small methods are easier to test, debug and understand than large methods.

Software Engineering Observation 6.7

A method requiring a large number of parameters may be performing too many tasks. Consider dividing the method into smaller methods that perform separate tasks. As a rule of thumb, the method header should fit on one line (if possible).

Software Engineering Observation 6.8

The number, type and order of arguments in a method call must exactly match those of the parameters in the corresponding method header.

There are three ways to return control to the point at which a method was invoked. If the method does not return a result (i.e., the method has a **void** return type), control returns when the program reaches the method-ending right brace or when the statement

```
return;
```

executes. If the method does return a result, the statement

```
return expression;
```

returns the value of *expression* to the caller. When a **return** statement executes, control returns immediately to the point at which the method was invoked.

Notice the syntax that invokes method **Square** in Fig. 6.3—we use the method name, followed by the arguments to the method in parentheses. Methods in a class definition are allowed to invoke all other methods in the same class definition by using this syntax (an exception to this is discussed in Chapter 8, Object-Based Programming). We now have seen three ways to call a method—a method name by itself (as shown with **Square(x)**), a reference to an object followed by the dot (**.**) operator and the method name (such as **string1.CompareTo(string2)**) and a class name followed by a method name (such as **Math.Sqrt(9.0)**). The last syntax is for calling the ***static*** *methods* of a class (discussed in detail in Chapter 8, Object-Based Programming).

The application in our next example (Fig. 6.4) uses programmer-defined method **Maximum** to determine and return the largest of three floating-point values that the user inputs through the program's graphical user interface. Note that in this example, we show all of the code that the Windows Form Designer generates. Throughout the rest of the book, we omit portions of the generated code that are not relevant to our discussions. In such programs, we place a comment that indicates where the Visual Studio .NET generated code appears in the original source file.

```
1   // Fig. 6.4: MaximumValue.cs
2   // Finding the maximum of three double values.
3   using System;
4   using System.Drawing;
5   using System.Collections;
6   using System.ComponentModel;
7   using System.Windows.Forms;
8   using System.Data;
9
10  namespace MaximumValue
11  {
12      /// <summary>
13      /// Summary description for Form1.
14      /// </summary>
15      public class MaximumValue : System.Windows.Forms.Form
16      {
17          private System.Windows.Forms.Label firstNumberLabel;
18          private System.Windows.Forms.Label secondNumberLabel;
19          private System.Windows.Forms.Label thirdNumberLabel;
20          private System.Windows.Forms.Label maximumLabel;
21          private System.Windows.Forms.TextBox firstNumberTextBox;
22          private System.Windows.Forms.TextBox secondNumberTextBox;
23          private System.Windows.Forms.TextBox thirdNumberTextBox;
24          private System.Windows.Forms.Button calculateButton;
25
26          /// <summary>
27          /// Required designer variable.
28          /// </summary>
29          private System.ComponentModel.Container components = null;
30
```

Fig. 6.4   Programmer-defined **Maximum** method. (Part 1 of 5.)

```
31          public MaximumValue()
32          {
33             //
34             // Required for Windows Form Designer support
35             //
36             InitializeComponent();
37
38             //
39             // TODO: Add any constructor code after
40             //         InitializeComponent call
41             //
42          }
43
44          /// <summary>
45          /// Clean up any resources being used.
46          /// </summary>
47          protected override void Dispose( bool disposing )
48          {
49             if( disposing )
50             {
51                if (components != null)
52                {
53                   components.Dispose();
54                }
55             }
56             base.Dispose( disposing );
57          }
58
59          #region Windows Form Designer generated code
60          /// <summary>
61          /// Required method for Designer support - do not modify
62          /// the contents of this method with the code editor.
63          /// </summary>
64          private void InitializeComponent()
65          {
66             this.calculateButton =
67                new System.Windows.Forms.Button();
68             this.secondNumberTextBox =
69                new System.Windows.Forms.TextBox();
70             this.thirdNumberTextBox =
71                new System.Windows.Forms.TextBox();
72             this.firstNumberLabel =
73                new System.Windows.Forms.Label();
74             this.secondNumberLabel =
75                new System.Windows.Forms.Label();
76             this.thirdNumberLabel =
77                new System.Windows.Forms.Label();
78             this.maximumLabel = new System.Windows.Forms.Label();
79             this.firstNumberTextBox =
80                new System.Windows.Forms.TextBox();
81             this.SuspendLayout();
```

Fig. 6.4   Programmer-defined **Maximum** method. (Part 2 of 5.)

```
82              //
83              // calculateButton
84              //
85              this.calculateButton.Location =
86                 new System.Drawing.Point(24, 120);
87              this.calculateButton.Name = "calculateButton";
88              this.calculateButton.Size =
89                 new System.Drawing.Size(112, 23);
90              this.calculateButton.TabIndex = 0;
91              this.calculateButton.Text = "Calculate Maximum";
92              this.calculateButton.Click +=
93                 new System.EventHandler(this.calculateButton_Click);
94              //
95              // secondNumberTextBox
96              //
97              this.secondNumberTextBox.Location =
98                 new System.Drawing.Point(176, 49);
99              this.secondNumberTextBox.Name = "secondNumberTextBox";
100             this.secondNumberTextBox.TabIndex = 2;
101             this.secondNumberTextBox.Text = "";
102             //
103             // thirdNumberTextBox
104             //
105             this.thirdNumberTextBox.Location =
106                new System.Drawing.Point(176, 81);
107             this.thirdNumberTextBox.Name = "thirdNumberTextBox";
108             this.thirdNumberTextBox.TabIndex = 3;
109             this.thirdNumberTextBox.Text = "";
110             //
111             // firstNumberLabel
112             //
113             this.firstNumberLabel.Location =
114                new System.Drawing.Point(8, 16);
115             this.firstNumberLabel.Name = "firstNumberLabel";
116             this.firstNumberLabel.Size =
117                new System.Drawing.Size(136, 23);
118             this.firstNumberLabel.TabIndex = 4;
119             this.firstNumberLabel.Text =
120                "First Floating-Point Value:";
121             //
122             // secondNumberLabel
123             //
124             this.secondNumberLabel.Location =
125                new System.Drawing.Point(8, 48);
126             this.secondNumberLabel.Name = "secondNumberLabel";
127             this.secondNumberLabel.Size =
128                new System.Drawing.Size(152, 23);
129             this.secondNumberLabel.TabIndex = 5;
130             this.secondNumberLabel.Text =
131                "Second Floating-Point Value:";
132             //
133             // thirdNumberLabel
134             //
```

Fig. 6.4   Programmer-defined **Maximum** method. (Part 3 of 5.)

```
135              this.thirdNumberLabel.Location =
136                  new System.Drawing.Point(8, 80);
137              this.thirdNumberLabel.Name = "thirdNumberLabel";
138              this.thirdNumberLabel.Size =
139                  new System.Drawing.Size(144, 23);
140              this.thirdNumberLabel.TabIndex = 6;
141              this.thirdNumberLabel.Text =
142                  "Third Floating-Point Value:";
143              //
144              // maximumLabel
145              //
146              this.maximumLabel.Location =
147                  new System.Drawing.Point(176, 120);
148              this.maximumLabel.Name = "maximumLabel";
149              this.maximumLabel.Size =
150                  new System.Drawing.Size(100, 80);
151              this.maximumLabel.TabIndex = 7;
152              //
153              // firstNumberTextBox
154              //
155              this.firstNumberTextBox.Location =
156                  new System.Drawing.Point(176, 16);
157              this.firstNumberTextBox.Name = "firstNumberTextBox";
158              this.firstNumberTextBox.TabIndex = 1;
159              this.firstNumberTextBox.Text = "";
160              //
161              // MaximumValue
162              //
163              this.AutoScaleBaseSize = new System.Drawing.Size(5, 13);
164              this.ClientSize = new System.Drawing.Size(292, 205);
165              this.Controls.AddRange(
166                  new System.Windows.Forms.Control[] {
167                      this.firstNumberTextBox,
168                      this.maximumLabel,
169                      this.thirdNumberLabel,
170                      this.secondNumberLabel,
171                      this.firstNumberLabel,
172                      this.thirdNumberTextBox,
173                      this.secondNumberTextBox,
174                      this.calculateButton
175                  }
176              );
177              this.Name = "MaximumValue";
178              this.Text = "MaximumValue";
179              this.ResumeLayout(false);
180
181          }
182      #endregion
183
184          /// <summary>
185          /// The main entry point for the application.
186          /// </summary>
187          [STAThread]
```

Fig. 6.4   Programmer-defined **Maximum** method. (Part 4 of 5.)

```
188        static void Main()
189        {
190            Application.Run(new MaximumValue());
191        }
192
193        // Method Maximum uses method Math.Max to determine the
194        // maximum value among the three double arguments
195        double Maximum( double x, double y, double z )
196        {
197            return Math.Max( x, Math.Max( y, z ) );
198        }
199
200        // get the floating-point values that the user entered and
201        // invoke method Maximum to determine the maximum value
202        private void calculateButton_Click( object sender,
203            System.EventArgs e )
204        {
205            // get inputted values and convert strings to doubles
206            double number1 =
207                Double.Parse( firstNumberTextBox.Text );
208
209            double number2 =
210                Double.Parse( secondNumberTextBox.Text );
211
212            double number3 =
213                Double.Parse( thirdNumberTextBox.Text );
214
215            // invoke method Maximum to determine the largest value
216            double maximum = Maximum( number1, number2, number3 );
217
218            // display maximum value
219            maximumLabel.Text = "maximum is: " + maximum;
220
221        } // end method calculateButton_Click
222
223    } // end class MaximumValue
224
225 } // end namespace MaximumValue
```

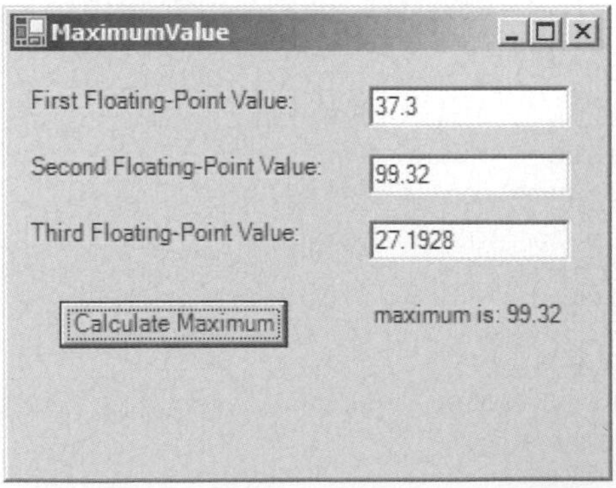

Fig. 6.4   Programmer-defined **Maximum** method. (Part 5 of 5.)

The graphical user interface for this program consists of three **TextBox**es in which the user can enter floating-point numbers, a **Button** for calculating the maximum, **Label**s for each **TextBox** and a **Label** for displaying the maximum value. Lines 31–182 contain the Visual Studio .NET generated code for constructing this graphical user interface. Lines 31–42 define a special type of method called a *constructor*. Programs invoke constructors to create objects. The constructor performs tasks necessary for preparing an object for use in a program. We discuss constructors in detail in Chapter 8. In the case of Windows applications, the constructor invokes method **InitializeComponent** to create the program's graphical user interface (line 36). Method **InitializeComponent** (lines 64–181) configures and arranges the program's graphical user interface component objects, such as its **Label**s, **Button**s and **TextBox**es.

When the user closes a program's window, the system invokes method **Dispose** (lines 47–57) to "clean up" resources used by the Window.

To create the graphical user interface for this program, drag the appropriate components from the **Toolbox** onto the **Form** in the Windows Form Designer. Arrange the components as shown in the screen capture of Fig. 6.4 and set the **Text** properties for the **Label**s and **Button**. Then, double click the **Calculate Maximum** button to add an empty event handler. Fill in this empty event handler with the code shown on lines 202–221. Lines 206–213 invoke **Double** method **Parse** on the **Text** property of each **TextBox** to retrieve the values that the user entered. Line 216 then invokes our **Maximum** method to determine which value is the largest. Method **Maximum** provides the largest number as its return value, which line 216 stores in **double** variable **maximum**. Line 219 appends the **maximum** value to the **maximumLabel**'s **Text** property to display the result to the user.

Now let us examine the implementation of method **Maximum** (lines 195–198). The first line indicates that the method returns a **double** floating-point value, that the method's name is **Maximum** and that the method takes three **double** parameters (**x**, **y** and **z**). The statement in the body of the method (line 197) returns the largest of the three floating-point values using two calls to method **Math.Max**. First, method **Math.Max** is invoked and passed the values of variables **y** and **z** to determine the larger of these two values. Next, the value of variable **x** and the result of the first call to **Math.Max** are passed to method **Math.Max**. Finally, the result of the second call to **Math.Max** is returned to the caller.

6.6 Argument Promotion

Another important feature of method definitions is the *coercion of arguments* (i.e., forcing arguments to the appropriate type to pass to a method). This process commonly is referred to as *implicit conversion*, in that a copy of the variable's value is converted to a different type without an explicit cast. *Explicit conversion* occurs when an explicit cast specifies that conversion is to occur. Such conversions also can be done with class **Convert** in namespace **System**. C# supports both widening and narrowing conversions—*widening conversion* occurs when a type is converted to other types (usually types that can hold more data) without losing data, and a *narrowing conversion* occurs when data may be lost through a conversion (usually to types that hold a smaller amount of data). Figure 6.5 shows allowed implicit conversions.

Type	Can be Converted to Type(s)
`bool`	`object`
`byte`	`decimal`, `double`, `float`, `int`, `uint`, `long`, `ulong`, `object`, `short` or `ushort`
`sbyte`	`decimal`, `double`, `float`, `int`, `long`, `object` or `short`
`char`	`decimal`, `double`, `float`, `int`, `uint`, `long`, `ulong`, `object` or `ushort`
`decimal`	`object`
`double`	`object`
`float`	`double` or `object`
`int`	`decimal`, `double`, `float`, `long` or `object`
`uint`	`decimal`, `double`, `float`, `long`, `ulong`, or `object`
`long`	`decimal`, `double`, `float` or `object`
`ulong`	`decimal`, `double`, `float` or `object`
`short`	`decimal`, `double`, `float`, `int`, `long` or `object`
`ushort`	`decimal`, `double`, `float`, `int`, `uint`, `long`, `ulong` or `object`

Fig. 6.5   Allowed implicit conversions.

For example, the **Math** class method **Sqrt** can be called with an integer argument, even though the method is defined in class **Math** to receive a **double** argument. The statement

```
Console.WriteLine( Math.Sqrt( 4 ) );
```

correctly evaluates **Math.Sqrt(4)** and displays the value **2**. C# implicitly converts the **int** value 4 to the **double** value 4.0 before passing the value to **Math.Sqrt**. In many cases, C# applies implicit conversions to argument values that do not correspond precisely to the parameter types in the method definition. In some cases, attempting these conversions leads to compiler errors because C# uses conversion rules to determine when a widening conversion can occur. In our previous **Math.Sqrt** example, C# converts an **int** to a **double** without changing its value. However, converting a **double** to an **int** truncates the fractional part of the **double** value. Converting large integer types to small integer types (e.g., **long** to **int**) also can result in changed values. Such narrowing conversions can lose data; therefore, C# does not allow narrowing conversions without an explicit cast operation.

The conversion rules apply to expressions containing values of two or more data types (also referred to as *mixed-type expressions*) and to primitive data-type values passed as arguments to methods. C# converts the type of each value in a mixed-type expression to the "highest" type in the expression. C# creates a temporary copy of each value and uses it in the expression—the original values remain unchanged. A method argument's type can be promoted to any "higher" type.

Converting values to lower types can result in data loss. In cases where information could be lost through conversion, the compiler requires the programmer to use a cast to force the conversion to occur. To invoke our **Square** method, which takes an integer parameter (Fig. 6.3) with the **double** variable **y**, the method call would be written as

```
int result = Square( ( int ) y );
```

This statement explicitly casts (converts) a copy of the value of **y** to an integer for use in method **Square**. Thus, if **y**'s value is **4.5**, method **Square** returns **16**, not **20.25**.

Common Programming Error 6.11

When performing a narrowing conversion (e.g., ***double*** *to* ***int***), *converting a primitive-data-type value to another primitive data type may result in loss of data.*

6.7 C# Namespaces

As we have seen, C# contains many predefined classes that are grouped into namespaces. Collectively we refer to this preexisting code as the Framework Class Library. The actual code for the classes is located in **.dll** files called assemblies.

Throughout the text, **using** statements specify the namespaces we use in each program. For example, a program includes the statement

```
using System;
```

to tell the compiler that we are using the **System** namespace. This **using** statement allows us to write **Console.WriteLine** rather than **System.Console.WriteLine** throughout the program. To use a class in a particular namespace, we must add a reference to the appropriate assembly (demonstrated in Section 3.2). Assembly references for namespace **System** are added automatically—other assemblies must be added explicitly.

We exercise a large number of the FCL classes in this book. Figure 6.6 lists a subset of the many namespaces in the FCL and provides a brief description of each. We use classes from these namespaces and others throughout the book. This table introduces readers to the variety of reusable components in the FCL. When learning C#, spend time reading the descriptions of the classes in the documentation.

Namespace	Description
System	Contains essential classes and data types (such as **int**, **double**, **char**, etc.). Implicitly referenced by all C# programs.
System.Data	Contains classes that form ADO .NET, used for database access and manipulation.
System.Drawing	Contains classes used for drawing and graphics.
System.IO	Contains classes for the input and output of data, such as with files.
System.Threading	Contains classes for multithreading, used to run multiple parts of a program simultaneously.
System.Windows.Forms	Contains classes used to create graphical user interfaces.
System.Xml	Contains classes used to process XML data.

Fig. 6.6   Namespaces in the Framework Class Library.

The set of namespaces available in the FCL is quite large. In addition to the namespaces summarized in Fig. 6.6, the FCL includes namespaces for complex graphics, advanced graphical user interfaces, printing, advanced networking, security, multimedia, accessibility (for people with disabilities) and many more. For an overview of the namespaces in the FCL, look up ".NET Framework, class library" in the help documentation.

6.8 Value Types and Reference Types

In the next section, we will discuss passing arguments to methods by value and by reference. To understand this, we first need to make a distinction between types in C#. Data types are either *value types* or *reference types*. A variable of a value type contains data of that type. A variable of a reference type, in contrast, contains the address of the location in memory where the data are stored. Value types normally represent single pieces of data, such as **int** or **bool** values. Reference types, on the other hand, refer to objects, which can contain many individual pieces of data. We discuss objects in detail in Chapters 8, 9 and 10 (Object-Based Programming, and Object-Oriented Programming parts 1 and 2).

C# includes built-in value types and reference types. The built-in value types are the *integral types* (**sbyte**, **byte**, **char**, **short**, **ushort**, **int**, **uint**, **long** and **ulong**), the *floating-point types* (**float** and **double**) and the types **decimal** and **bool**. The built-in reference types are **string** and **object**. Programmers also can create value types and reference types. The reference types that programmers can create are classes (Chapter 8), interfaces (Chapter 8) and delegates (Chapter 9).

The table in Fig. 6.7 lists the primitive data types, which are building blocks for more complicated types. Like its predecessor languages C and C++, C# requires all variables to have a type before they can be used in a program. For this reason, C# is referred to as a *strongly typed language*.

Type	Size in bits	Values	Standard
bool	8	**true** or **false**	
char	16	**'\u0000'** to **'\uFFFF'**	(Unicode character set)
byte	8	0 to 255	(unsigned)
sbyte	8	−128 to +127	
short	16	−32,768 to +32,767	
ushort	16	0 to 65,535	(unsigned)
int	32	−2,147,483,648 to 2,147,483,647	
uint	32	0 to 4,294,967,295	(unsigned)
long	64	−9,223,372,036,854,775,808 to +9,223,372,036,854,775,807	
ulong	64	0 to 18,446,744,073,709,551,615	(unsigned)
decimal	128	1.0×10^{-28} to 7.9×10^{28}	
float	32	$\pm 1.5 \infty 10^{-45}$ to $\pm 3.4 \infty 10^{38}$	(IEEE 754 floating point)

Fig. 6.7   C# built-in data types. (Part 1 of 2.)

Type	Size in bits	Values	Standard
double	64	$\pm5.0 \infty 10^{-324}$ to $\pm1.7 \infty 10^{308}$	(IEEE 754 floating point)
object			
string			(Unicode character set)

Fig. 6.7   C# built-in data types. (Part 2 of 2.)

In C and C++ programs, programmers frequently must write separate program versions to support different computer platforms because the primitive data types are not guaranteed to be identical from computer to computer. For example, an **int** value on one computer might occupy 16 bits (2 bytes) of memory, whereas an **int** value on another computer might occupy 32 bits (4 bytes) of memory. In C#, **int** values are always 32 bits (4 bytes).

Portability Tip 6.1

Primitive data types in C# are portable across all platforms that support C#.

Each data type in the table is listed with its size in bits (there are 8 bits to a byte) and its range of values. The designers of C# wanted code to be portable; therefore, they chose to use internationally recognized standards for both character formats (Unicode) and floating-point numbers (IEEE 754).

6.9 Passing Arguments: Pass-by-Value vs. Pass-by-Reference

Two ways to pass arguments to methods in many programming languages are *pass-by-value* and *pass-by-reference*. When an argument is passed by value, the called method receives a *copy* of the argument's value.

Testing and Debugging Tip 6.2

With pass-by-value, changes to the called method's copy do not affect the original variable's value. This prevents some possible side effects that hinder the development of correct and reliable software systems.

When an argument is passed using pass-by-reference, the caller gives the method the ability to access and modify the caller's original data directly. Pass-by-reference can improve performance because it eliminates the overhead of copying large data items such as objects; however, pass-by-reference can weaken security because the called method can modify the caller's data.

Software Engineering Observation 6.9

*When returning information from a method via a **return** statement, value-type variables always are returned by value (i.e., a copy is returned), and reference-type variables are always returned by reference (i.e., a reference to the object is returned).*

To pass an object reference into a method, simply specify the reference name in the method call. Then, in the method body, reference the object using the parameter name. This refers to the original object in memory, which allows the called method to access the original object directly.

In Section 6.8, we discussed the difference between value types and reference types. At this point, the reader can understand one of the major differences between the two data types—value-type variables are passed to methods by value, whereas reference-type variables are passed to methods by reference. What if the programmer would like to pass a value type by reference? To do this, C# provides the ***ref*** and ***out*** *keywords*. The **ref** keyword specifies that a value-type argument should be passed by reference, which enables the called method to modify the original variable. This keyword is used for variables that already have been initialized. The **out** keyword specifies an output parameter, which is an argument to which the called method will assign a value. Normally, when a method receives an uninitialized value, the compiler generates an error. Preceding the parameter with keyword **out** specifies that the called method will initialize the variable and prevents the compiler from generating an error message for the uninitialized variable. Figure 6.8 demonstrates using the **ref** and **out** keywords to manipulate integer values.[2]

This program contains three methods to calculate the square of an integer. The first method, **SquareRef** (lines 26–29), multiplies its argument **x** by itself and assigns the new value to **x**. **SquareRef** receives its argument as a **ref int**, specifying that **x** is an integer that is passed by reference to the method. As a result, the assignment at line 28 modifies the original argument's value, rather than a copy of that value.

The second method, **SquareOut** (lines 33–37), does the same thing, but initializes **x** to **6** on line 35. **SquareOut** receives its argument as an **out int**, which indicates that **x** is an integer variable that the caller passes to method **SquareOut** by reference and that **SquareOut** can assign a new value to this variable. The final method, **Square** (lines 41–44), simply takes **x** as a value-type integer argument and squares its value.

```
1   // Fig. 6.8: RefOutTest.cs
2   // Demonstrating ref and out parameters.
3   using System;
4   using System.Drawing;
5   using System.Collections;
6   using System.ComponentModel;
7   using System.Windows.Forms;
8   using System.Data;
9
10  public class RefOutTest : System.Windows.Forms.Form
11  {
12     private System.Windows.Forms.Button showOutputButton;
13     private System.Windows.Forms.Label outputLabel;
14
15     // Visual Studio .NET generated code
16
17     // main entry point for application
18     [STAThread]
19     static void Main()
20     {
21        Application.Run( new RefOutTest() );
22     }
```

Fig. 6.8   Demonstrating **ref** and **out** parameters. (Part 1 of 3.)

2. In Chapter 7 we discuss passing reference-type arguments by value and by reference.

```
23
24      // x passed by reference and method modifies
25      // original variable's value
26      void SquareRef( ref int x )
27      {
28         x = x * x;
29      }
30
31      // x passed as out parameter and method initializes
32      // and modifies original variable's value
33      void SquareOut( out int x )
34      {
35         x = 6;
36         x = x * x;
37      }
38
39      // x passed by value and method cannot modify
40      // original variable's value
41      void Square( int x )
42      {
43         x = x * x;
44      }
45
46      private void showOutputButton_Click(
47         object sender, System.EventArgs e )
48      {
49         int y = 5; // create new int and initialize to 5
50         int z;     // declare z, but do not initialize it
51
52         // display original values of y and z
53         outputLabel.Text = "Original value of y: " + y + "\n";
54         outputLabel.Text +=
55            "Original value of z: uninitialized\n\n";
56
57         // pass y and z by reference
58         SquareRef( ref y );
59         SquareOut( out z );
60
61         // display values of y and z after modified by methods
62         // SquareRef and SquareOut
63         outputLabel.Text +=
64            "Value of y after SquareRef: " + y + "\n";
65         outputLabel.Text +=
66            "Value of z after SquareOut: " + z + "\n\n";
67
68         // pass y and z by value
69         Square( y );
70         Square( z );
71
72         // display unchanged values of y and z
73         outputLabel.Text += "Value of y after Square: " + y + "\n";
74         outputLabel.Text += "Value of z after Square: " + z + "\n";
75
```

Fig. 6.8   Demonstrating **ref** and **out** parameters. (Part 2 of 3.)

```
76
77    } // end method showOutputButton_Click
78 }
```

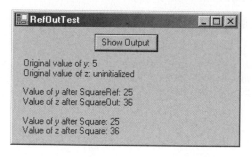

Fig. 6.8   Demonstrating **ref** and **out** parameters. (Part 3 of 3.)

Method **showOutputButton_Click** (lines 46–77) is an event handler that invokes methods **SquareRef**, **SquareOut** and **Square** when the user clicks the **Show Output** button. This method begins by initializing **y** to **5** and declaring (but not initializing) **z**. Lines 58–59 call methods **SquareRef** and **SquareOut**. Notice the syntax used for passing **y** and **z**—in each case, we precede the argument either with **ref** or with **out**. The output displays the values of **y** and **z** after the function calls. Notice that **y** has been changed to **25** and **z** has been set to **36**. Finally, on lines 69–70 we call method **Square**. Arguments **y** and **z** both are passed by value—only copies of their values are passed to the method. As a result, the values of **y** and **z** remain **25** and **36**, respectively.

Common Programming Error 6.12

*The **ref** and **out** arguments in a method call must match those specified in the method definition; otherwise, a syntax error occurs.*

Software Engineering Observation 6.10

By default, C# does not allow the programmer to choose whether to pass each argument by value or by reference. Value-type variables are passed by value. Objects are not passed to methods; rather, references to objects are passed to methods. The references themselves are passed by value. When a method receives a reference to an object, the method can manipulate the object directly, but the reference value cannot be changed (e.g., to refer to a new object).

6.10 Random-Number Generation

We now take a brief and hopefully entertaining diversion into a popular programming application—simulation and game playing. In this section and the next, we develop a nicely structured game-playing program that includes multiple methods. The program uses most of the control structures we have studied to this point and also introduces several new concepts.

There is something in the air of a gambling casino that invigorates every type of person—from the high rollers at the plush mahogany-and-felt craps tables to the quarter poppers at the one-armed bandits. It is the *element of chance,* the possibility that luck will convert a pocketful of money into a mountain of wealth. The element of chance can be introduced into computer applications with the ***Random*** class (located in namespace **System**).

Consider the following statements:

```
Random randomObject = new Random();
int randomNumber = randomObject.Next();
```

The **Next** method generates a positive **int** value between zero and the constant **Int32.MaxValue** (the value 2,147,483,647). If **Next** produces values at random, every value in this range has an equal *chance* (or *probability*) of being chosen when **Next** is called. Note that values returned by **Next** are actually *pseudo-random numbers*—a sequence of values produced by a complex mathematical calculation. A *seed* value is required in this mathematical calculation. When we create our **Random** object, we use the current time of day as the seed. A particular seed value always produces the same series of random numbers. Programmers commonly use the current time of day as a seed value, since it changes each second and, therefore produces different random-number sequences each time the program executes.

The range of values produced directly by **Next** often is different from the range of values required in a particular application. For example, a program that simulates coin-tossing might require only 0 for "heads" and 1 for "tails." A program that simulates rolling a six-sided die would require random integers in the range 1–6. A video-game program that randomly predicts the next type of spaceship (out of four possibilities) that will fly across the horizon might require random integers in the range 1–4.

The one-argument version of method **Next** returns values in the range from 0 up to (but not including) the value of that argument. For example,

```
value = randomObject.Next( 6 );
```

produces values from 0 through 5. This is called *scaling*, because the range of values produced has been scaled down from over two billion to only six. The number 6 is the *scaling factor*. The two-argument version of method **Next** allows us to *shift* and scale the range of numbers. For example, we can use method **Next** as follows

```
value = randomObject.Next( 1, 7 );
```

to produce integers in the range from 1 to 6. In this case, we have shifted the numbers to produce a range from 1 up to (but not including) 7.

The Windows application of Fig. 6.9 simulates 20 rolls of a six-sided die and shows the integer value of each roll. The dice-rolling simulation begins when the user clicks the **Show Ouput** button, which invokes the **showOutputButton_Click** event handler (lines 24–44). The **for** loop on lines 32–43 repeatedly invokes method **Next** of class **Random** to simulate rolling the die. Lines 37–38 append the value rolled to **output-Label**'s **Text** property. After every five rolls, line 42 appends a newline character to make the output more readable.

```
1   // Fig. 6.9: RandomInt.cs
2   // Generating random integer values.
3   using System;
4   using System.Drawing;
```

Fig. 6.9   Random integers in the range 1–6. (Part 1 of 2.)

```
5   using System.Collections;
6   using System.ComponentModel;
7   using System.Windows.Forms;
8   using System.Data;
9
10  public class RandomInt : System.Windows.Forms.Form
11  {
12     private System.Windows.Forms.Button showOutputButton;
13     private System.Windows.Forms.Label outputLabel;
14
15     // Visual Studio .NET generated code
16
17     // the main entry point for the application
18     [STAThread]
19     static void Main()
20     {
21        Application.Run( new RandomInt() );
22     }
23
24     private void showOutputButton_Click( object sender,
25        System.EventArgs e )
26     {
27        Random randomInteger = new Random();
28
29        outputLabel.Text = "";
30
31        // loop 20 times
32        for ( int counter = 1; counter <= 20; counter++ )
33        {
34           // pick random integer between 1 and 6
35           int nextValue = randomInteger.Next( 1, 7 );
36
37           outputLabel.Text +=
38              nextValue + "    "; // append value to output
39
40           // add newline after every 5 values
41           if ( counter % 5 == 0 )
42              outputLabel.Text += "\n";
43        }
44     }
45  }
```

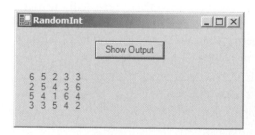

Fig. 6.9   Random integers in the range 1–6. (Part 2 of 2.)

The Windows application of Fig. 6.10 simulates rolls of four dice. The program enables the user to click a button that "rolls" four dice at a time and displays an image of each die in the window. The next example (Fig. 6.11) uses many of this example's features to demonstrate that the numbers generated by **Next** occur with approximately equal likelihood.

```
1   // Fig. 6.10: RollDie.cs
2   // Using random number generation to simulate dice rolling.
3   using System;
4   using System.Drawing;
5   using System.Collections;
6   using System.ComponentModel;
7   using System.Windows.Forms;
8   using System.Data;
9   using System.IO;    // enables reading data from files
10
11  public class RollDie : System.Windows.Forms.Form
12  {
13      private System.Windows.Forms.Button rollButton;
14
15      private System.Windows.Forms.Label dieLabel2;
16      private System.Windows.Forms.Label dieLabel1;
17      private System.Windows.Forms.Label dieLabel3;
18      private System.Windows.Forms.Label dieLabel4;
19
20      private Random randomNumber = new Random();
21
22      // Visual Studio .NET generated code
23
24      // method called when rollButton clicked,
25      // passes labels to another method
26      protected void rollButton_Click(
27          object sender, System.EventArgs e )
28      {
29          // pass the labels to a method that will
30          // randomly assign a face to each die
31          DisplayDie( dieLabel1 );
32          DisplayDie( dieLabel2 );
33          DisplayDie( dieLabel3 );
34          DisplayDie( dieLabel4 );
35
36      } // end rollButton_Click
37
38      // determines image to be displayed by current die
39      public void DisplayDie( Label dieLabel )
40      {
41          int face = randomNumber.Next( 1, 7 );
42
43          // displays image specified by filename
44          dieLabel.Image = Image.FromFile(
45              Directory.GetCurrentDirectory() +
46              "\\images\\die" + face + ".gif" );
47      }
```

Fig. 6.10   Rolling dice in a Windows application (Part 1 of 2.).

```
48
49      // main entry point for application
50      [STAThread]
51      static void Main()
52      {
53          Application.Run( new RollDie() );
54      }
55
56  } // end class RollDie
```

 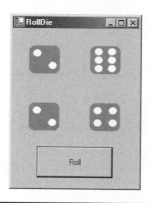 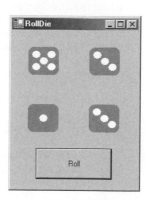

Fig. 6.10   Rolling dice in a Windows application (Part 2 of 2.).

Method **DisplayDie** (lines 39–47) invokes **Random** method **Next** to simulate a roll of a die (line 41) and loads an image that corresponds to the value rolled (lines 44–46). Line 44 uses class **Label**'s **Image** property to display the die. Notice that we specify which image will be displayed by invoking method *FromFile* of class **Image**, which specifies the location of the file on disk that contains the image. Each click of the button displays four images that represent the four new values of the dice. Note that the user must click **rollButton** at least once to display the dice. **Directory** method **GetCurrentDirectory** (line 45) returns the path of the folder in which the program is executing. If you run the program from Visual Studio .NET, this will be the **bin\Debug** directory in the project's directory. The die images must be in this folder for the example to operate properly. These images are placed in the proper folders on the CD that accompanies this book.

To show that class **Random** produces numbers with approximately equal likelihood, let us modify the program in Fig. 6.10 to keep some simple statistics. The Windows application of Fig. 6.11 provides a **Roll** button for rolling the dice and a **TextBox** that displays the frequencies for each value rolled. The program output shows the results of clicking **Roll** 10 times.

When the user clicks the **Roll** button, the program invokes the **rollButton_Click** event handler on lines 38–73. This event handler invokes method **DisplayDie** for each of the 12 dice that the program simulates (lines 43–54). Lines 56–71 then calculate the frequencies for each die and displays the results by appending the information to **displayTextBox**'s **Text** property. Method **displayDie** (lines 76–113) simulates a die roll (line 78), loads the appropriate **Image** and increments the frequency count for the rolled value.

```
1   // Fig. 6.11: RollDie2.cs
2   // Rolling 12 dice with frequency chart.
3   using System;
4   using System.Drawing;
5   using System.Collections;
6   using System.ComponentModel;
7   using System.Windows.Forms;
8   using System.Data;
9   using System.IO;
10
11  public class RollDie2 : System.Windows.Forms.Form
12  {
13      private System.Windows.Forms.Button rollButton;
14
15      private System.Windows.Forms.RichTextBox displayTextBox;
16
17      private System.Windows.Forms.Label dieLabel1;
18      private System.Windows.Forms.Label dieLabel2;
19      private System.Windows.Forms.Label dieLabel3;
20      private System.Windows.Forms.Label dieLabel4;
21      private System.Windows.Forms.Label dieLabel5;
22      private System.Windows.Forms.Label dieLabel6;
23      private System.Windows.Forms.Label dieLabel7;
24      private System.Windows.Forms.Label dieLabel8;
25      private System.Windows.Forms.Label dieLabel9;
26      private System.Windows.Forms.Label dieLabel10;
27      private System.Windows.Forms.Label dieLabel11;
28      private System.Windows.Forms.Label dieLabel12;
29
30      private Random randomNumber = new Random();
31
32      private int ones, twos, threes, fours, fives, sixes;
33
34      // Visual Studio .NET generated code
35
36      // simulates roll by calling DisplayDie for
37      // each label and displaying the results
38      protected void rollButton_Click(
39          object sender, System.EventArgs e )
40      {
41          // pass the labels to a method that will
42          // randomly assign a face to each die
43          DisplayDie( dieLabel1 );
44          DisplayDie( dieLabel2 );
45          DisplayDie( dieLabel3 );
46          DisplayDie( dieLabel4 );
47          DisplayDie( dieLabel5 );
48          DisplayDie( dieLabel6 );
49          DisplayDie( dieLabel7 );
50          DisplayDie( dieLabel8 );
51          DisplayDie( dieLabel9 );
52          DisplayDie( dieLabel10 );
```

Fig. 6.11 Simulating rolling 12 six-sided dice. (Part 1 of 3.)

```
53          DisplayDie( dieLabel11 );
54          DisplayDie( dieLabel12 );
55
56          double total = ones + twos + threes + fours + fives + sixes;
57
58          // display the current frequency values
59          displayTextBox.Text = "Face\t\tFrequency\tPercent\n1\t\t" +
60              ones + "\t\t" +
61              String.Format( "{0:F2}", ones / total * 100 ) +
62              "%\n2\t\t" + twos + "\t\t" +
63              String.Format( "{0:F2}", twos / total * 100 ) +
64              "%\n3\t\t" + threes + "\t\t" +
65              String.Format( "{0:F2}", threes / total * 100 ) +
66              "%\n4\t\t" + fours + "\t\t" +
67              String.Format( "{0:F2}", fours / total * 100 ) +
68              "%\n5\t\t" + fives + "\t\t" +
69              String.Format( "{0:F2}", fives / total * 100 ) +
70              "%\n6\t\t" + sixes + "\t\t" +
71              String.Format( "{0:F2}", sixes / total * 100 ) + "%";
72
73      } // end rollButton_Click
74
75      // display the current die, and modify frequency values
76      public void DisplayDie( Label dieLabel )
77      {
78          int face = randomNumber.Next( 1, 7 );
79
80          dieLabel.Image = Image.FromFile(
81              Directory.GetCurrentDirectory() +
82              "\\images\\die" + face + ".gif" );
83
84          // add one to frequency of current face
85          switch ( face )
86          {
87              case 1:
88                  ones++;
89                  break;
90
91              case 2:
92                  twos++;
93                  break;
94
95              case 3:
96                  threes++;
97                  break;
98
99              case 4:
100                  fours++;
101                  break;
102
103              case 5:
104                  fives++;
105                  break;
```

Fig. 6.11   Simulating rolling 12 six-sided dice. (Part 2 of 3.)

```
106
107                case 6:
108                    sixes++;
109                    break;
110
111           } // end switch
112
113       } // end DisplayDie
114
115       // main entry point for the application
116       [STAThread]
117       static void Main()
118       {
119           Application.Run( new RollDie2() );
120       }
121
122 } // end of class RollDie2
```

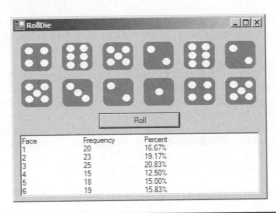

Fig. 6.11   Simulating rolling 12 six-sided dice. (Part 3 of 3.)

As the program output demonstrates, over a large number of dic rolls, each of the possible faces from 1 through 6 appears with approximately equal likelihood (i.e., about one-
sixth of the time). After studying arrays in Chapter 7, Arrays, we will show how to replace
the entire **switch** structure in this program with a single-line statement.

6.11 Example: Game of Chance

One of the most popular games of chance is a dice game known as "craps," played in casi-
nos and back alleys throughout the world. The rules of the game are straightforward:

> *A player rolls two dice. Each die has six faces. Each face contains 1, 2, 3, 4, 5 or 6 spots.
> After the dice have come to rest, the sum of the spots on the two upward faces is calculated.
> If the sum is 7 or 11 on the first throw, the player wins. If the sum is 2, 3 or 12 on the first
> throw (called "craps"), the player loses (i.e., the "house" wins). If the sum is 4, 5, 6, 8, 9 or
> 10 on the first throw, that sum becomes the player's "point." To win, players must continue
> rolling the dice until they "make their point" (i.e., roll their point value). The player loses by
> rolling a 7 before making the point.*

Figure 6.12 simulates the game of craps with a simple graphical user interface.

Notice that the player rolls two dice on each roll. When executing the application, clicking the **Play** button begins the game and makes the first roll. The form displays the results of each roll. The screen captures show the execution of several games.

```csharp
1   // Fig. 6.12: CrapsGame.cs
2   // Simulating the game of Craps.
3   using System;
4   using System.Drawing;
5   using System.Collections;
6   using System.ComponentModel;
7   using System.Windows.Forms;
8   using System.Data;
9   using System.IO;
10
11  public class CrapsGame : System.Windows.Forms.Form
12  {
13      private System.Windows.Forms.Button rollButton;
14      private System.Windows.Forms.Button playButton;
15
16      int myPoint; // player's point value
17      private System.Windows.Forms.PictureBox pointFirstDieImage;
18      private System.Windows.Forms.Label statusLabel;
19      private System.Windows.Forms.PictureBox firstDieImage;
20      private System.Windows.Forms.PictureBox pointSecondDieImage;
21      private System.Windows.Forms.PictureBox secondDieImage;
22      private System.Windows.Forms.GroupBox pointGroupBox;
23      int myDie1; // value of first die
24      int myDie2; // value of second die
25
26      public enum DiceNames
27      {
28          SNAKE_EYES = 2,
29          TREY = 3,
30          YO_LEVEN = 11,
31          BOX_CARS = 12,
32      }
33
34      // Visual Studio .NET generated code
35
36      // simulate next roll and result of that roll
37      protected void rollButton_Click(
38          object sender, System.EventArgs e )
39      {
40          int sum = rollDice();
41
42          if ( sum == myPoint )
43          {
44              statusLabel.Text = "You Win!!!";
45              rollButton.Enabled = false;
46              playButton.Enabled = true;
47          }
```

Fig. 6.12 Program to simulate the game of craps. (Part 1 of 4.)

```
48          else
49             if ( sum == 7 )
50             {
51                 statusLabel.Text = "Sorry. You lose.";
52                 rollButton.Enabled = false;
53                 playButton.Enabled = true;
54             }
55
56      } // end rollButton_Click
57
58      // simulate first roll and result of that roll
59      protected void playButton_Click(
60          object sender, System.EventArgs e )
61      {
62          pointGroupBox.Text = "Point";
63          statusLabel.Text = "";
64          pointFirstDieImage.Image = null;
65          pointSecondDieImage.Image = null;
66
67          myPoint = 0;
68          int sum = rollDice();
69
70          switch ( sum )
71          {
72             case 7:
73             case ( int ) DiceNames.YO_LEVEN:
74                 rollButton.Enabled = false;  // disable Roll button
75                 statusLabel.Text = "You Win!!!";
76                 break;
77
78             case ( int ) DiceNames.SNAKE_EYES:
79             case ( int ) DiceNames.TREY:
80             case ( int ) DiceNames.BOX_CARS:
81                 rollButton.Enabled = false;
82                 statusLabel.Text = "Sorry. You lose.";
83                 break;
84
85             default:
86                 myPoint = sum;
87                 pointGroupBox.Text = "Point is " + sum;
88                 statusLabel.Text = "Roll Again";
89                 displayDie( pointFirstDieImage, myDie1 );
90                 displayDie( pointSecondDieImage, myDie2 );
91                 playButton.Enabled = false;
92                 rollButton.Enabled = true;
93                 break;
94
95          } // end switch
96
97      } // end playButton_Click
98
```

Fig. 6.12   Program to simulate the game of craps. (Part 2 of 4.)

```
99      // display an image for the specified face
100     private void DisplayDie( PictureBox dieImage, int face )
101     {
102        dieImage.Image = Image.FromFile(
103           Directory.GetCurrentDirectory() +
104           "\\images\\die" + face + ".gif" );
105     }
106
107     // simulates rolling two dice
108     private int RollDice()
109     {
110        int die1, die2, dieSum;
111        Random randomNumber = new Random();
112
113        die1 = randomNumber.Next( 1, 7 );
114        die2 = randomNumber.Next( 1, 7 );
115
116        displayDie( firstDieImage, die1 );
117        displayDie( secondDieImage, die2 );
118
119        myDie1 = die1;
120        myDie2 = die2;
121        dieSum = die1 + die2;
122        return dieSum;
123
124     } // end method rollDice
125
126     // main entry point for the application
127     [STAThread]
128     static void Main()
129     {
130        Application.Run( new CrapsGame() );
131     }
132
133  } // end of class CrapsGame
```

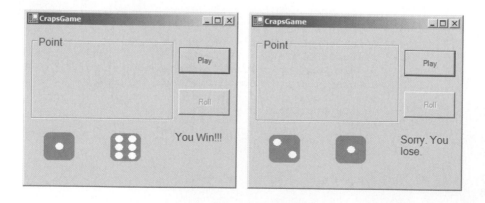

Fig. 6.12   Program to simulate the game of craps. (Part 3 of 4.)

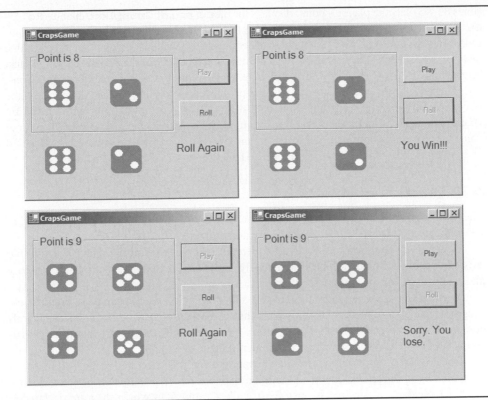

Fig. 6.12 Program to simulate the game of craps. (Part 4 of 4.)

Before its method definitions, the program includes several declarations, including an *enumeration* on lines 26–32. An enumeration is a value type that contains a set of constant values and is created using the keyword **enum**. This enumeration is a convenient way of referring to constant values used throughout the program. We have used the identifiers **SNAKE_EYES**, **TREY**, **YO_LEVEN** and **BOX_CARS**, to represent significant values in craps. Using these identifiers makes the program more readable. Additionally, if we need to change one of these values, we can modify the enumeration instead of changing the values where they are used throughout the program.

This example introduces a few new GUI components. The first, called a *GroupBox*, displays the user's point. A **GroupBox** is a container for other components and helps group components logically. Within the **GroupBox**, we add two *PictureBoxes*—components that display images. These are added, as with other components, by clicking **PictureBox** in the **ToolBox** and dragging this component within the borders of the **GroupBox**.

The **playButton_Click** event handler begins the game. Line 68 invokes method **RollDice** (defined on lines 108–124), which rolls the dice, displays the dice and returns their sum. Lines 70–95 use a **switch** structure to determine whether the player won, lost or established a point value. If the player won by rolling a 7 or 11, line 74 disables **Roll-Button** to prevent the player from rolling the dice again. Line 75 displays a message to indicate that the user won. If the player lost by rolling **SNAKE_EYES**, **TREY** or **BOX_CARS** (i.e., 2, 3 or 12), line 82 displays a message to indicate that the user lost. Otherwise, the default case (lines 85–93) sets the player's point, displays the dice in **pointGroupBox**, enables **Roll-Button** and disables **playButton**. Notice that for many of the **case**s, we cast the enumeration values to type **int**. Although each enumeration value is assigned an integer value on lines 26–32, each value is considered to be of **enum** type **DiceNames**, and therefore must be cast to **int** for use in the **switch** structure, which requires constant integral expressions.

The **rollButton_Click** event handler's task is to roll the dice and determine if the player won by making the point value or lost by rolling 7. Line 40 calls method **Roll-Dice**. Lines 42–54 in method **rollButton_Click** analyze the roll. Depending on the value of the roll, the buttons **rollButton** and **playButton** will become either disabled or enabled. This is done by setting the **Enabled** property to **true** or **false**.

6.12 Duration of Variables

The attributes of variables include name, type, size and value. Each variable in a program has additional attributes, including *duration* and *scope*.

A variable's duration (also called its *lifetime*) is the period during which the variable exists in memory. Some variables exist briefly, some are created and destroyed repeatedly and others exist for the entire execution of a program.

A variable's *scope* is where the variable's identifier (i.e., name) can be referenced in a program. Some variables can be referenced throughout a program, while others can be referenced from limited portions of a program. This section discusses the duration of variables. Section 6.13 discusses the scope of identifiers.

Local variables in a method (i.e., parameters and variables declared in the method body) have *automatic duration*. Automatic duration variables are created when program control reaches their declaration; that is, they exist while the block in which they are declared is active, and they are destroyed when that block is exited. For the remainder of the text, we refer to variables of automatic duration as automatic variables, or local variables.

The instance variables of a class are initialized by the compiler if the programmer does not provide initial values. Variables of most primitive data types are initialized to zero, **bool** variables are initialized to **false** and references are initialized to **null**. Unlike instance variables of a class, automatic variables must be initialized by the programmer before they can be used.

Common Programming Error 6.13

Automatic variables must be initialized before their values are used in a method; otherwise, the compiler issues an error message.

Variables of *static duration* exist from the time at which the class that defines them is loaded into memory. These variables then last until the program terminates. Their storage is allocated and initialized when their classes are loaded into memory. Static-duration variable names exist when their classes are loaded into memory, but this does not mean that these identifiers necessarily can be used throughout the program—their scopes may be limited as we will see in the next section.

6.13 Scope Rules

The *scope* (sometimes called *declaration space*) of an identifier for a variable, reference or method is the portion of the program in which the identifier can be accessed. A local variable or reference declared in a block can be used only in that block or in blocks nested within that block. The possible scopes for an identifier are *class scope* and *block scope*.

Members of a class have class scope and are visible in what is known as the *declaration space of a class*. Class scope begins at the opening left brace (**{**) of the class definition and terminates at the closing right brace (**}**). Class scope enables methods of a class to access all members defined in that class. In Chapter 8, Object-Based Programming, we see that **static** members are an exception to this rule. In a sense, all instance variables and methods of a class are *global* to the methods of the class in which they are defined (i.e., the methods can modify the instance variables directly and invoke other methods of the class).

Identifiers declared inside a block have block scope (*local-variable declaration space*). Block scope begins at the identifier's declaration and ends at the block's terminating right brace (**}**). Local variables of a method have block scope, as do method parameters, which are local variables of the method. Any block may contain variable declarations. When blocks are nested in a method's body, and an identifier declared in an outer block has the same name as an identifier declared in an inner block, an error is generated. On the other hand, if a local variable in a method has the same name as an instance variable, the value in the calling method (main program) is "hidden" until the method terminates execution. In Chapter 8, Object-Based Programming, we discuss how to access such "hidden" instance variables. The reader should note that block scope also applies to methods and **for** structures. With **for** structures, any variable declared in the initialization portion of the **for** header will be in scope only within that **for** structure.

Good Programming Practice 6.4

Avoid local-variable names that hide instance-variable names.

The program in Fig. 6.13 demonstrates scoping issues with instance variables and local variables. Instance variable **x** (line 15) is initialized to 1. This instance variable is hidden in any block (or method) that declares a local variable named **x**. The **showOutputButton_Click** event handler (lines 47–63) declares a local variable **x** and initializes it to 5 (line 50). Lines 52–53 display the value of this local variable to show that instance variable **x** (with value 1) is "hidden" in method **showOutputButton_Click**.

```
1   // Fig. 6.13: Scoping.cs
2   // Demonstrating scope of local and instance variables.
3   using System;
4   using System.Drawing;
5   using System.Collections;
6   using System.ComponentModel;
7   using System.Windows.Forms;
8   using System.Data;
9
10  public class Scoping : System.Windows.Forms.Form
11  {
12      private System.Windows.Forms.Label outputLabel;
13      private System.Windows.Forms.Button showOutputButton;
14
15      public int x = 1; // instance variable
```

Fig. 6.13   Scoping. (Part 1 of 3.)

```
16
17      // Visual Studio .NET generated code
18
19      public void MethodA()
20      {
21         int x = 25;     // initialized each time a is called
22
23         outputLabel.Text = outputLabel.Text +
24            "\n\nlocal x in MethodA is " + x +
25            " after entering MethodA";
26
27         ++x; // increment local variable x
28
29         outputLabel.Text = outputLabel.Text +
30            "\nlocal x in MethodA is " + x +
31            " before exiting MethodA";
32      }
33
34      public void MethodB()
35      {
36         outputLabel.Text = outputLabel.Text +
37            "\n\ninstance variable x is " + x +
38            " on entering MethodB";
39
40         x *= 10;
41
42         outputLabel.Text = outputLabel.Text +
43            "\ninstance varable x is " + x +
44            " on exiting MethodB";
45      }
46
47      private void showOutputButton_Click( object sender,
48         System.EventArgs e )
49      {
50         int x = 5; // local x in method showOutputButton_Click
51
52         outputLabel.Text =
53            "local x in method showOutputButton_Click is " + x;
54
55         MethodA();       // MethodA has automatic local x;
56         MethodB();       // MethodB uses instance variable x
57         MethodA();       // MethodA creates new automatic local x
58         MethodB();       // instance variable x retains its value
59
60         outputLabel.Text = outputLabel.Text + "\n\n" +
61            "local x in method showOutputButton_Click is " + x;
62
63      }   // end method showOutputButton_Click
64
65      // main entry point for the application
66      [STAThread]
67      static void Main()
68      {
```

Fig. 6.13 Scoping. (Part 2 of 3.)

```
69              Application.Run( new Scoping() );
70       }
71
72   } // end of class Scoping
```

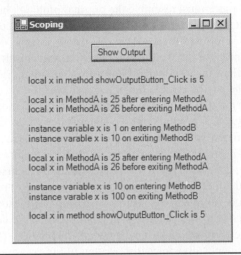

Fig. 6.13 Scoping. (Part 3 of 3.)

The program defines two other methods—**MethodA** and **MethodB**—that take no arguments and return nothing. The program calls each method twice from method **Scoping**. **MethodA** defines local variable **x** (line 21) and initializes it to **25**. Each call to **MethodA** displays the variable's value in **outputLabel**, increments the variable and displays it again before exiting the method. Each call to **MethodA** recreates automatic variable **x** and initializes it to **25**. Method **MethodB** does not declare any variables. Therefore, when it refers to variable **x**, the instance variable **x** is used. Each call to **MethodB** displays the instance variable in **outputLabel**, multiplies it by **10** (line 40) and displays it again before exiting the method. The next time method **MethodB** is called, the instance variable begins with its modified value, **10**. After the calls to **MethodA** and **MethodB**, the program again displays the local variable **x** in method **showOutputButton_Click** to show that none of the method calls modified this specific variable **x**, as the methods all referred to variables in other scopes.

6.14 Recursion

The programs we have discussed generally are structured as methods that call one another in a hierarchical manner. For some problems, it is useful to have a method actually call itself. A *recursive method* is a method that calls itself either directly or indirectly through another method. Recursion is an important topic discussed at length in upper-level computer science courses. In this section and the next, we present two simple examples of recursion. We consider recursion conceptually first, then examine several programs containing recursive methods.

Recursive problem-solving approaches have a number of elements in common. A recursive method is called to solve a problem. The method actually knows how to solve only the simplest case(s), or *base case(s)*. If the method is called with a base case, the method returns a result. If the method is called with a more complex problem, the method divides the problem into two conceptual pieces—a piece that the method knows how to perform (base case) and a piece that the method does not know how to perform. To make recursion feasible, the latter piece must resemble the original problem, but be a slightly simpler or smaller version of it. The method invokes (calls) a fresh copy of itself to work on the smaller problem—this is referred to as a *recursive call*, or a *recursion step*. The recursion step also normally includes the keyword **return**, because its result will be combined with the portion of the problem that the method knew how to solve. Such a combination will form a result that will be passed back to the original caller.

The recursion step executes while the original call to the method is still "open" (i.e., it has not finished executing). The recursion step can result in many more recursive calls, as the method divides each new subproblem into two conceptual pieces. Each time the method calls itself with a slightly simpler version of the original problem, the sequence of smaller and smaller problems must converge on the base case, so the recursion can eventually terminate. At that point, the method recognizes the base case and returns a result to the previous copy of the method. A sequence of returns ensues up the line until the original method call returns the final result to the caller. As an example of these concepts, let us write a recursive program to perform a popular mathematical calculation.

The factorial of a nonnegative integer *n*, written *n!* (and pronounced "*n* factorial"), is the product

$$n \cdot (n - 1) \cdot (n - 2) \cdot \ldots \cdot 1$$

with 1! equal to 1, and 0! defined as 1. For example, 5! is the product $5 \cdot 4 \cdot 3 \cdot 2 \cdot 1$, which is equal to 120.

The factorial of an integer **number** greater than or equal to 0 can be calculated *iteratively* (nonrecursively) using **for** as follows:

```
factorial = 1;

for ( int counter = number; counter >= 1; counter-- )
   factorial *= counter;
```

We arrive at a recursive definition of the factorial method with the following relationship:

$$n! = n \cdot (n - 1)!$$

For example, 5! is clearly equal to 5 * 4!, as shown by the following:

$$5! = 5 \cdot 4 \cdot 3 \cdot 2 \cdot 1$$
$$5! = 5 \cdot (4 \cdot 3 \cdot 2 \cdot 1)$$
$$5! = 5 \cdot (4!)$$

A recursive evaluation of 5! would proceed as in Fig. 6.14. Figure 6.14a shows how the succession of recursive calls proceeds until 1! is evaluated to be 1, which terminates the recursion. Each rectangle represents a method call. Figure 6.14 shows the values returned from each recursive call to its caller until the final value is calculated and returned.

Figure 6.15 uses recursion to calculate and print the factorials of the integers 0–10. The recursive method **Factorial** (lines 17–24) first determines whether its terminating condition is **true** (i.e., **number** is less than or equal to 1). If **number** is less than or equal to 1, **factorial** returns 1, no further recursion is necessary and the method

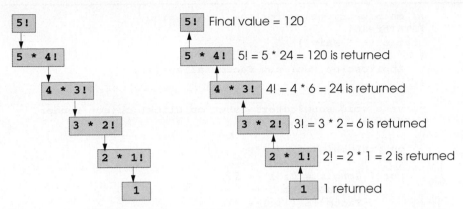

(a) Procession of recursive calls   (b) Values returned from each recursive call

Fig. 6.14   Recursive evaluation of 5!.

returns. If **number** is greater than 1, line 23 expresses the problem as the product of **number** and a recursive call to **Factorial**, evaluating the factorial of **number - 1**. Note that **Factorial(number - 1)** is a slightly simpler problem than the original calculation **Factorial(number)**.

```
1    // Fig. 6.15: FactorialTest.cs
2    // Calculating factorials with recursion.
3    using System;
4    using System.Drawing;
5    using System.Collections;
6    using System.ComponentModel;
7    using System.Windows.Forms;
8    using System.Data;
9
10   public class FactorialTest : System.Windows.Forms.Form
11   {
12      private System.Windows.Forms.Button showFactorialsButton;
13      private System.Windows.Forms.Label outputLabel;
14
15      // Visual Studio .NET generated code
16
17      public long Factorial( long number )
18      {
19         if ( number <= 1 )        // base case
20            return 1;
21
22         else
23            return number * Factorial( number - 1 );
24      }
25
```

Fig. 6.15   Calculating factorials with a recursive method. (Part 1 of 2.)

```
26        // main entry point for the application
27        [STAThread]
28        static void Main()
29        {
30            Application.Run( new FactorialTest());
31        }
32
33        private void showFactorialsButton_Click( object sender,
34            System.EventArgs e )
35        {
36            outputLabel.Text = "";
37
38            for ( long i = 0; i <= 10; i++ )
39                outputLabel.Text += i + "! = " +
40                    Factorial( i ) + "\n";
41        }
42
43  } // end of class FactorialTest
```

Fig. 6.15   Calculating factorials with a recursive method. (Part 2 of 2.)

Method **Factorial** receives a parameter of type **long** and returns a result of type **long**. As seen in Fig. 6.15, factorial values become large quickly. We choose data type **long** so the program can calculate factorials greater than 20!. Unfortunately, the **Factorial** method produces large values so quickly, even **long** does not help us print many more factorial values before the size of even the **long** variable is exceeded.

Factorials of larger numbers require the program to use **float** and **double** variables. This points to a weakness in most programming languages, namely, that the languages are not easily extended to handle the unique requirements of various applications. As we will see in our treatment of object-oriented programming beginning in Chapter 8, C# is an extensible language—programmers with unique requirements can extend the language with new data types (called classes). A programmer could create a **HugeInteger** class, for example, that would enable a program to calculate the factorials of arbitrarily large numbers.

 Common Programming Error 6.14

Forgetting to return a value from a recursive method can result in syntax and/or logic errors.

Common Programming Error 6.15

Omitting the base case or writing the recursion step so that it does not converge on the base case will cause infinite recursion, eventually exhausting memory. Infinite recursion is analogous to the problem of an infinite loop in an iterative (nonrecursive) solution.

6.15 Example Using Recursion: The Fibonacci Series

The Fibonacci series

0, 1, 1, 2, 3, 5, 8, 13, 21, ...

begins with 0 and 1 and has the property that each subsequent Fibonacci number is the sum of the previous two Fibonacci numbers.

The series occurs in nature and, in particular, describes a form of spiral. The ratio of successive Fibonacci numbers converges on a constant value of 1.618.... This number, too, repeatedly occurs in nature and has been called the *golden ratio* or the *golden mean*. Humans tend to find the golden mean aesthetically pleasing. Architects often design windows, rooms and buildings whose length and width are in the ratio of the golden mean. Postcards often are designed with a golden mean width-to-height ratio.

The recursive definition of the Fibonacci series is as follows:

Fibonacci(0) = 0
Fibonacci(1) = 1
Fibonacci(n) = *Fibonacci*(n – 1) + *Fibonacci*(n – 2)

Note that there are two base cases for the Fibonacci calculation—*fibonacci(0)* evaluates to 0, and *fibonacci(1)* evaluates to 1. The application in Fig. 6.16 calculates the ith Fibonacci number recursively using method **Fibonacci**. The user enters an integer in the text box, indicating the ith Fibonacci number to calculate, and clicks the **calculateButton** (which displays the text **Calculate Fibonacci**). Method **calculateButton_Click** (lines 22–29) executes in response to the user interface event and calls recursive method **Fibonacci** to calculate the specified Fibonacci number. In Fig. 6.16, the screen captures show the results of calculating several Fibonacci numbers.

```
1   // Fig. 6.16: FibonacciTest.cs
2   // Recursive fibonacci method.
3   using System;
4   using System.Drawing;
5   using System.Collections;
6   using System.ComponentModel;
7   using System.Windows.Forms;
8   using System.Data;
9
10  public class FibonacciTest : System.Windows.Forms.Form
11  {
12      private System.Windows.Forms.Button calculateButton;
13
14      private System.Windows.Forms.TextBox inputTextBox;
```

Fig. 6.16 Recursively generating Fibonacci numbers. (Part 1 of 2.)

```
15
16        private System.Windows.Forms.Label displayLabel;
17        private System.Windows.Forms.Label promptLabel;
18
19        // Visual Studio .NET generated code
20
21        // call Fibonacci and display results
22        protected void calculateButton_Click(
23            object sender, System.EventArgs e )
24        {
25            int number = Convert.ToInt32( inputTextBox.Text );
26            int fibonacciNumber = Fibonacci( number );
27            displayLabel.Text =
28                "Fibonacci Value is " + fibonacciNumber;
29        }
30
31        // calculates Fibonacci number
32        public int Fibonacci( int number )
33        {
34            if ( number == 0 || number == 1 )
35                return number;
36            else
37                return Fibonacci( number - 1 ) + Fibonacci( number - 2 );
38        }
39
40        // main entry point for the application
41        [STAThread]
42        static void Main()
43        {
44            Application.Run( new FibonacciTest() );
45        }
46
47    } // end of class FibonacciTest
```

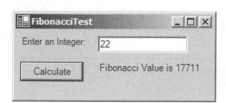

Fig. 6.16   Recursively generating Fibonacci numbers. (Part 2 of 2.)

The call to **Fibonacci** (line 26) from **calculateButton_Click** is not a recursive call, but all subsequent calls to **Fibonacci** from line 37 are recursive. Each time **Fibonacci** is invoked, it immediately tests for the base case—**number** equal to 0 or 1 (line 34). If this is true, **Fibonacci** returns **number** (*fibonacci(0)* is 0 and *fibonacci(1)* is 1). Interestingly, if **number** is greater than 1, the recursion step generates *two* recursive calls (line 37), each of which is for a slightly simpler problem than the original call to **Fibonacci**. Figure 6.17 shows how method **Fibonacci** would evaluate **Fibonacci(3)**.

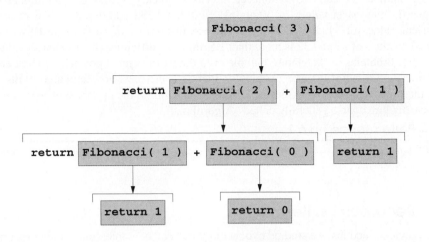

Fig. 6.17   Set of recursive calls to method **Fibonacci**.

This figure raises some issues about the order in which C# compilers will evaluate operands. Figure 6.17 shows that, during the evaluation of **Fibonacci(3)**, two recursive calls will be made—**Fibonacci(2)** and **Fibonacci(1)**. In what order will these calls be made? Most programmers assume the operands will be evaluated from left to right; in C# this is indeed true.

The C and C++ languages (on which many of C#'s features are based) do not specify the order in which the operands of most operators (including **+**) are evaluated. Therefore, in those languages, the programmer can make no assumption about the order in which these calls execute. The calls could, in fact, execute **Fibonacci(2)**, then **Fibonacci(1)**, or they could execute in the reverse order (**Fibonacci(1)**, then **Fibonacci(2)**). In this program and in most other programs, the final result would be the same. However, in some programs, the evaluation of an operand could have *side effects* that would affect the expression's final result. C# specifies that the order of evaluation of the operands is from left to right. Thus, the method calls are first **Fibonacci(2)**, then **Fibonacci(1)**.

Good Programming Practice 6.5

Do not write expressions that depend on the order of evaluation of the operator's operands. Doing so often results in programs that are difficult to read, debug, modify and maintain.

A word of caution about using a recursive program to generate Fibonacci numbers: each invocation of the **Fibonacci** method that does not match one of the base cases (i.e., 0 or 1) results in two recursive calls to the **Fibonacci** method. This quickly results in many method invocations. Calculating the Fibonacci value of 20 using the program in Fig. 6.16 requires 21,891 calls to the **Fibonacci** method; calculating the Fibonacci value of 30 requires 2,692,537 calls to the **Fibonacci** method.

As the programmer tries larger values, each consecutive Fibonacci number that the program is asked to calculate results in a substantial increase in the number of calls to the **Fibonacci** method and hence in calculation time. For example, the Fibonacci value 31 requires 4,356,617 calls, and the Fibonacci value of 32 requires 7,049,155 calls. As you can see, the number of calls to Fibonacci increases quickly—1,664,080 additional calls between the Fibonacci values of 30 and 31, and 2,692,538 additional calls between the Fibonacci values of 31 and 32. This difference in number of calls made between the Fibonacci values of 31 and 32 is more than 1.5 times the difference for Fibonacci values of 30 and 31. Problems of this nature humble even the world's most powerful computers! In the field called *complexity theory*, computer scientists determine how hard algorithms work to do their jobs. Complexity issues are discussed in detail in the upper-level computer science curriculum course generally called "Algorithms."

Performance Tip 6.1

Avoid Fibonacci-style recursive programs, which result in an exponential "explosion" of method calls.

6.16 Recursion vs. Iteration

In the previous sections, we studied two methods that can be implemented either recursively or iteratively. In this section, we compare the two approaches and discuss why the programmer might choose one approach over the other.

Both iteration and recursion are based on a control structure—iteration uses a repetition structure (such as **for**, **while** or **do/while**) and recursion uses a selection structure (such as **if**, **if/else** or **switch**). Both iteration and recursion involve repetition—iteration explicitly uses a repetition structure and recursion achieves repetition through repeated method calls. Iteration and recursion each involve a termination test—iteration terminates when the loop-continuation condition fails and recursion terminates when a base case is recognized. Iteration with counter-controlled repetition and recursion both gradually approach termination—iteration keeps modifying a counter until the counter assumes a value that makes the loop-continuation condition fail and recursion keeps producing simpler versions of the original problem until a base case is reached. Both iteration and recursion can execute infinitely—an infinite loop occurs with iteration if the loop-continuation test never becomes false and infinite recursion occurs if the recursion step does not reduce the problem in a manner that converges on a base case.

Recursion has disadvantages as well. It repeatedly invokes the mechanism, and consequently the overhead, of method calls. This can be costly in both processor time and memory space. Each recursive call creates another copy of the method (actually, only the method's variables); this can consume considerable memory. Iteration normally occurs within a method, so the overhead of repeated method calls and extra memory assignment is omitted. Why then would a programmer choose recursion?

Software Engineering Observation 6.11

Any problem that can be solved recursively also can be solved iteratively (nonrecursively). A recursive approach normally is chosen in preference to an iterative approach when the recursive approach more naturally mirrors the problem and results in a program that is easier to understand and debug. Recursive solutions also are chosen when iterative solutions are not apparent.

Performance Tip 6.2

Avoid using recursion in performance situations. Recursive calls take time and consume additional memory.

Common Programming Error 6.16

Accidentally having a nonrecursive method call itself through another method can cause in-finite recursion.

Most programming textbooks introduce recursion much later than we have done in this book. We feel that recursion is a sufficiently rich and complex topic that it is better to intro-duce it early and spread its examples over the remainder of the text.

6.17 Method Overloading

C# enables several methods of the same name to be defined in the same class, as long as these methods have different sets of parameters (number of parameters, types of parameters or or-der of the parameters). This is called *method overloading*. When an overloaded method is called, the C# compiler selects the proper method by examining the number, types and order of the call's arguments. Method overloading commonly is used to create several methods with the same name that perform similar tasks, but on different data types. Figure 6.18 uses overloaded method **Square** to calculate the square of an **int** and a **double**.

Good Programming Practice 6.6

Overloading methods that perform closely related tasks can make programs more readable and understandable.

```
1   // Fig. 6.18: MethodOverload.cs
2   // Using overloaded methods.
3   using System;
4   using System.Drawing;
5   using System.Collections;
6   using System.ComponentModel;
7   using System.Windows.Forms;
8   using System.Data;
9
10  public class MethodOverload : System.Windows.Forms.Form
11  {
12     private System.Windows.Forms.Button showOutputButton;
13     private System.Windows.Forms.Label outputLabel;
14
15     // Visual Studio .NET generated code
16
17     // first version, takes one integer
18     public int Square ( int x )
19     {
20        return x * x;
21     }
22
23     // second version, takes one double
24     public double Square ( double y )
25     {
26        return y * y;
27     }
28
```

Fig. 6.18 Using overloaded methods. (Part 1 of 2.)

```
29        // main entry point for the application
30        [STAThread]
31        static void Main()
32        {
33            Application.Run( new MethodOverload() );
34        }
35
36        private void showOutputButton_Click( object sender,
37            System.EventArgs e )
38        {
39            // call both versions of Square
40            outputLabel.Text =
41                "The square of integer 7 is " + Square( 7 ) +
42                "\nThe square of double 7.5 is " + Square ( 7.5 );
43        }
44
45    } // end of class MethodOverload
```

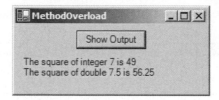

Fig. 6.18 Using overloaded methods. (Part 2 of 2.)

The compiler distinguishes overloaded methods by their *signatures*. A method's signature is a combination of the method's name and parameter types. If the compiler looked only at method names during compilation, the code in Fig. 6.18 would be ambiguous—the compiler would not know how to distinguish the two **Square** methods. The compiler uses *overload resolution* to determine which method to call. This process first searches for all the methods that *can* be used in the context, based on the number and type of arguments that are present. It might seem that only one method would match, but recall that C# can convert variable values to other data types implicitly. Once all matching methods are found, the closest match is chosen. This match is based on a "best-fit" algorithm, which analyzes the implicit conversions that will take place.

Let us look at an example. In Fig. 6.18, the compiler might use the logical name "**Square** of **int**" for the **Square** method that specifies an **int** parameter (line 30) and "**Square** of **double**" for the **Square** method that specifies a **double** parameter (line 36). If a method **Foo**'s definition begins as

```
void Foo( int a, float b )
```

the compiler might use the logical name "**Foo** of **int** and **float**." If the parameters are specified as

```
void Foo( float a, int b )
```

the compiler might use the logical name "**Foo** of **float** and **int**." The order of the parameters is important to the compiler; it considers the preceding two **Foo** methods distinct.

So far, the logical names of methods that have been used by the compiler have not mentioned the methods' return types. This is because method calls cannot be distinguished by return type. The program in Fig. 6.19 illustrates the syntax error that is generated when two methods have the same signature and different return types. Overloaded methods with different parameter lists can have different return types. Overloaded methods need not have the same number of parameters.

Common Programming Error 6.17

Creating overloaded methods with identical parameter lists and different return types is a syntax error.

SUMMARY

- The best way to develop and maintain a large program is to construct it from small pieces, or modules. This technique is called divide and conquer.

- Modules can be created with methods and classes.

- Programs are written by combining new methods and classes that the programmer writes with "prepackaged" methods and classes in the .NET Framework Library, and in various other method and class libraries.

- The .NET Framework Library provides a rich collection of classes and methods for performing common mathematical calculations, string manipulations, character manipulations, input/output, error checking and other useful operations.

```
1   // Fig. 6.19: InvalidMethodOverload.cs
2   // Demonstrating incorrect method overloading.
3
4   public class InvalidMethodOverload
5   {
6      public int Square( double x )
7      {
8         return x * x;
9      }
10
11     // ERROR! Second Square method takes same number, order
12     // and types of arguments.
13     public double Square( double y )
14     {
15        return y * y;
16     }
17  }
```

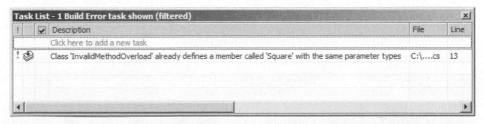

Fig. 6.19 Syntax error generated from overloaded methods with identical parameter lists and different return types.

- The programmer can write methods to define specific tasks that may be used at many points in a program. These methods sometimes are referred to as programmer-defined methods.

- The actual statements defining the method are written only once and are hidden from other methods.

- Methods are called by writing the name of the method (sometimes preceded by the class name and a dot operator), followed by a left parenthesis, the method's argument (or a comma-separated list of arguments) and a right parenthesis.

- All variables declared in method definitions are local variables—they are known only in the method in which they are defined.

- Packaging code as a method allows that code to be executed from several locations in a program when the method is called.

- The **return** statement in a method passes the results of the method back to the calling method.

- The format of a method definition is

  > *return-value-type method-name* **(** *parameter-list* **)**
  > **{**
  >   *declarations and statements*
  > **}**

- The first line of a method definition is sometimes known as the method header. The attributes and modifiers in the method header are used to specify information about the method.

- The method *return-value-type* is the data type of the result that is returned from the method to the caller. Methods can return one value at most.

- The *parameter-list* is a comma-separated list containing the declarations of the parameters received by the called method. There must be one argument in the method call for each parameter in the method definition.

- The declarations and statements within the braces that follow the method header form the method body.

- Variables can be declared in any block, and blocks can be nested.

- A method cannot be defined inside another method.

- In many cases, an argument value that does not correspond precisely to the parameter types in the method definition is converted to the proper type before the method is called.

- When an argument is passed by value, a copy of the argument's value is made and passed to the called method.

- With pass-by-reference, the caller enables the called method to access the caller's data directly and to modify that data if the called method chooses.

- The class **Random** can be used to generate random numbers.

- An event is a signal that is sent to a program when some action takes place, such as when the user clicks a button. The programmer writes the application to perform tasks when these events occur. An event handler is a method that executes when an event occurs (or is "raised").

- An identifier's duration (its lifetime) is the period during which that identifier exists in memory.

- Identifiers that represent local variables in a method (i.e., parameters and variables declared in the method body) have automatic duration. Automatic-duration variables are created when program control reaches the variable's declaration. They exist while the block in which they are declared is active, and they are destroyed when the block in which they are declared is exited.

- The scope (sometimes called a declaration space) of an identifier for a variable, reference or method is the portion of the program in which that identifier can be referenced.

- A local variable or reference declared in a block can be used only in that block or in blocks nested within that block.

- Members of a class have class scope and are visible in what is known as the declaration space of the class.

- Class scope enables a class's methods to access directly all members defined in that class or inherited into that class. (**static** members are an exception to this rule.)

- Any variable declared in the initialization portion of a **for** structure will be visible only within that **for** structure.

- A recursive method is one that calls itself either directly, or indirectly through another method.

- A recursive method knows how to solve only the simplest case(s), or base case(s). If the method is called with a base case, the method returns a result. If the method is called with a more complex problem, the method divides the problem into two conceptual pieces—a piece that the method knows how to solve (base case) and a piece that the method does not know how to solve.

- To make recursion feasible, the portion of the problem that the method does not know how to solve must resemble the original problem, but be a slightly simpler or smaller version.

- Certain recursive methods can lead to an exponential "explosion" of method calls.

- Both iteration and recursion are based on a control structure. Iteration uses a repetition structure (such as **for**, **while** or **do/while**); recursion uses a selection structure (such as **if**, **if/else** or **switch**).

- Both iteration and recursion involve repetition. Iteration explicitly uses a repetition structure; recursion achieves repetition through repeated method calls.

- Iteration and recursion each involve a termination test. Iteration terminates when the loop-continuation condition fails; recursion terminates when a base case is recognized.

- Both iteration and recursion can execute infinitely. An infinite loop occurs with iteration if the loop-continuation test never becomes false; infinite recursion occurs if the recursion step does not reduce the problem in a manner that converges on the base case.

- A recursive approach normally is chosen in preference to an iterative approach when the recursive approach more naturally mirrors the problem and results in a program that is easier to understand and debug.

- Several methods can have the same name, as long as these methods have different sets of parameters, in terms of number of parameters, types of the parameters and order of the parameters. This is called method overloading.

- Method overloading commonly is used to create several methods with the same name that perform similar tasks, but on different data types.

TERMINOLOGY

. (dot operator)
argument to a method call
automatic duration
automatic initialization of a variable
base case
Button class
calling method
cast operator
class
Click event

coercion of arguments
comma-separated list of arguments
complexity theory
constant variable
control structures in iteration
control structures in recursion
divide-and-conquer approach
duration of an identifier
event handling
exhausting memory

exponential "explosion" of calls
factorial method
Fibonacci series defined recursively
golden ratio
hierarchical structure
infinite loop
infinite recursion
instance variables of a class
invoke a method
lifetime of an identifier
local variable
method
method body
method call
method header
method overloading
modularizing a program with methods
monolithic program
named constant
nested block
nested control structure
out parameter
overloaded method
parameter list

pass-by-reference
pass-by-value
principle of least privilege
programmer-defined method
promotions for primitive data types
Random class
recursive evaluation
recursive method
ref parameter
return keyword
return-value type
scaling factor
scope of an identifier
sequence of random numbers
shifting value
side effect
signature
simulation
software reusability
static duration
termination test
user-defined method
user interface event
void return-value type

SELF-REVIEW EXERCISES

6.1   Fill in the blanks in each of the following statements:
   a) Program modules in C# are called _____ and _____.
   b) A method is invoked with a _____.
   c) A variable known only within the method in which it is defined is called a _____.
   d) The _____ statement in a called method can be used to pass the value of an expression back to the calling method.
   e) The keyword _____ is used in a method header to indicate that a method does not return a value.
   f) The _____ of an identifier is the portion of the program in which the identifier can be used.
   g) The three ways to return control from a called method to a caller are _____, _____ and _____.
   h) The _____ method is used to produce random numbers.
   i) Variables declared in a block or in a method's parameter list are of _____ duration.
   j) A method that calls itself either directly or indirectly is a _____ method.
   k) A recursive method typically has two components: one that provides a means for the recursion to terminate by testing for a _____ case, and one that expresses the problem as a recursive call for a slightly simpler problem than the original call.
   l) In C#, it is possible to have various methods with the same name that operate on different types or numbers of arguments. This is called method _____.
   m) Local variables declared at the beginning of a method have _____ scope, as do method parameters, which are considered local variables of the method.
   n) Iteration is based on a control structure. It uses a _____ structure.
   o) Recursion is based on a control structure. It uses a _____ structure.

p) Recursion achieves repetition through repeated _____ calls.

q) The best way to develop and maintain a large program is to divide it into several smaller program _____, each of which is more manageable than the original program.

r) It is possible to define methods with the same _____, but different parameter lists.

s) Recursion terminates when a _____ is reached.

t) Placing a semicolon after the right parenthesis that encloses the parameter list of a method definition is a _____ error.

u) The _____ is a comma-separated list containing the declarations of the parameters received by the called method.

v) The _____ is the data type of the result returned from a called method.

w) A _____ is a signal that is sent when some action takes place, such as a button being clicked or a value being changed.

6.2   State whether each of the following is *true* or *false*. If *false*, explain why.

a) **Math** method **Abs** rounds its parameter to the smallest integer.

b) **Math** method **Exp** is the exponential method, e^x.

c) Variable type **float** can be promoted to type **double**.

d) Variable type **char** cannot be promoted to type **int**.

e) A recursive method is one that calls itself.

f) When a method recursively calls itself, it is known as the base case.

g) 0! is equal to 1.

h) Forgetting to return a value from a recursive method when one is needed results in a syntax error.

i) Infinite recursion occurs when a method converges on the base case.

j) A recursive implementation of the **Fibonacci** method is always efficient.

k) Any problem that can be solved recursively also can be solved iteratively.

6.3   For the following program, state the scope (either class scope or block scope) of each of the following elements:

a) The variable **x**.

b) The variable **y**.

c) The method **cube**.

d) The method **paint**.

e) The variable **yPos**.

```
public class CubeTest {
    int x;

    public void paint()
    {
        int yPos = 25;

        for ( x = 1; x <= 10; x++ ) {
            Console.WriteLine( x );
            yPos += 15;
        }
    }

    public int cube( int y )
    {
        return y * y * y;
    }
}
```

6.4   Write an application that tests whether the examples of the math library method calls shown in Fig. 6.2 actually produce the indicated results.

6.5   Give the method header for each of the following methods:
  a) Method **hypotenuse**, which takes two double-precision, floating-point arguments **side1** and **side2** and returns a double-precision, floating-point result.
  b) Method **smallest**, which takes three integers, **x**, **y**, **z**, and returns an integer.
  c) Method **instructions**, which does not take any arguments and does not return a value. [*Note*: Such methods commonly are used to display instructions to a user.]
  d) Method **intToFloat**, which takes an integer argument, **number**, and returns a floating-point result.

6.6   Find the error in each of the following program segments and explain how the error can be corrected:

a)
```
int g() {
    Console.WriteLine( "Inside method g" );
    int h() {
        Console.WriteLine( "Inside method h" );
    }
}
```

b)
```
int sum( int x, int y ) {
    int result;
    result = x + y;
}
```

c)
```
int sum( int n ) {
    if ( n == 0 )
        return 0;
    else
        n + sum( n - 1 );
}
```

d)
```
void f( float a ); {
    float a;
    Console.WriteLine( a );
}
```

e)
```
void product() {
    int a = 6, b = 5, c = 4, result;
    result = a * b * c;
    Console.WriteLine( "Result is " + result );
    return result;
}
```

ANSWERS TO SELF-REVIEW EXERCISES

6.1   a) methods, classes. b) method call. c) local variable. d) **return**. e) **void**. f) scope. g) **return;, return** *expression;*, encountering the closing right brace of a method. h) **Random.Next**. i) automatic. j) recursive. k) base. l) overloading. m) block. n) repetition. o) selection. p) method. q) modules. r) name. s) base case. t) syntax. u) parameter list. v) return-value-type. w) event.

6.2   a) False. **Math** method **Abs** returns the absolute value of a number. b) True. c) True. d) False. Type **char** can be promoted to **int**, **float**, **long** and **double**. e) True. f) False. When a method recursively calls itself, it is known as the recursive call or recursion step. g) True. h) True. i) False. Infinite recursion will occur when a recursive method does not converge on the base case. j) False. Recursion repeatedly invokes the mechanism, and consequently, the overhead, of method calls. k) True.

6.3   a) Class scope. b) Block scope. c) Class scope. d) Class scope. e) Block scope.

6.4   The following code demonstrates the use of some **Math** library method calls:

```
1   // Exercise 6.4: MathTest.cs
2   // Testing the Math class methods
3   using System;
4
5   public class MathTest {
6       public static void Main( string[] args )
7       {
8           Console.WriteLine( "Math.Abs( 23.7 ) = " +
9                               Math.Abs( 23.7 ) );
10          Console.WriteLine( "Math.Abs( 0.0 ) = " +
11                              Math.Abs( 0.0 ) );
12          Console.WriteLine( "Math.Abs( -23.7 ) = " +
13                              Math.Abs( -23.7 ) );
14          Console.WriteLine( "Math.Ceiling( 9.2 ) = " +
15                              Math.Ceiling( 9.2 ) );
16          Console.WriteLine( "Math.Ceiling( -9.8 ) = " +
17                              Math.Ceiling( -9.8 ) );
18          Console.WriteLine( "Math.Cos( 0.0 ) = " +
19                              Math.Cos( 0.0 ) );
20          Console.WriteLine( "Math.Exp( 1.0 ) = " +
21                              Math.Exp( 1.0 ) );
22          Console.WriteLine( "Math.Exp( 2.0 ) = " +
23                              Math.Exp( 2.0 ) );
24          Console.WriteLine( "Math.Floor( 9.2 ) = " +
25                              Math.Floor( 9.2 ) );
26          Console.WriteLine( "Math.Floor( -9.8 ) = " +
27                              Math.Floor( -9.8 ) );
28          Console.WriteLine( "Math.Log( 2.718282 ) = " +
29                              Math.Log( 2.718282 ) );
30          Console.WriteLine( "Math.Log( 7.389056 ) = " +
31                              Math.Log( 7.389056 ) );
32          Console.WriteLine( "Math.Max( 2.3, 12.7 ) = " +
33                              Math.Max( 2.3, 12.7 ) );
34          Console.WriteLine( "Math.Max( -2.3, -12.7 ) = " +
35                              Math.Max( -2.3, -12.7 ) );
36          Console.WriteLine( "Math.Min( 2.3, 12.7 ) = " +
37                              Math.Min( 2.3, 12.7 ) );
38          Console.WriteLine( "Math.Min( -2.3, -12.7 ) = " +
39                              Math.Min( -2.3, -12.7 ) );
40          Console.WriteLine( "Math.Pow( 2, 7 ) = " +
41                              Math.Pow( 2, 7 ) );
42          Console.WriteLine( "Math.Pow( 9, .5 ) = " +
43                              Math.Pow( 9, .5 ) );
44          Console.WriteLine( "Math.Sin( 0.0 ) = " +
45                              Math.Sin( 0.0 ) );
46          Console.WriteLine( "Math.Sqrt( 25.0 ) = " +
47                              Math.Sqrt( 25.0 ) );
48          Console.WriteLine( "Math.Tan( 0.0 ) = " +
49                              Math.Tan( 0.0 ) );
50      }
51  }
```

```
Math.Abs( 23.7 ) = 23.7
Math.Abs( 0.0 ) = 0
Math.Abs( -23.7 ) = 23.7
Math.Ceiling( 9.2 ) = 10
Math.Ceiling( -9.8 ) = -9
Math.Cos( 0.0 ) = 1
Math.Exp( 1.0 ) = 2.71828
Math.Exp( 2.0 ) = 7.38906
Math.Floor( 9.2 ) = 9
Math.Floor( -9.8 ) = -10
Math.Log( 2.718282 ) = 1
Math.Log( 7.389056 ) = 2
Math.Max( 2.3, 12.7 ) = 12.7
Math.Max( -2.3, -12.7 ) = -2.3
Math.Min( 2.3, 12.7 ) = 2.3
Math.Min( -2.3, -12.7 ) = -12.7
Math.Pow( 2, 7 ) = 128
Math.Pow( 9, .5 ) = 3
Math.Sin( 0.0 ) = 0
Math.Sqrt( 25.0 ) = 5
Math.Tan( 0.0 ) = 0
```

6.5 a) `double hypotenuse( double side1, double side2 )`
b) `int smallest( int x, int y, int z )`
c) `void instructions()`
d) `float intToFloat( int number )`

6.6 a) Error: Method **h** is defined in method **g**.
Correction: Move the definition of **h** out of the definition of **g**.
b) Error: The method is supposed to return an integer, but does not.
Correction: Delete variable **result** and place the following statement in the method:
`return x + y;`
or add the following statement at the end of the method body:
`return result;`
c) Error: The result of **n + sum(n - 1)** is not returned by this recursive method, resulting in a syntax error.
Correction: Rewrite the statement in the **else** clause as
`return n + sum( n - 1 );`
d) Error: The semicolon after the right parenthesis that encloses the parameter list, and the redefining of the parameter **a** in the method definition are both incorrect.
Correction: Delete the semicolon after the right parenthesis of the parameter list and delete the declaration **float a;**.
e) Error: The method returns a value when it is not supposed to.
Correction: Change the return type to **int**.

EXERCISES

6.7 What is the value of **x** after each of the following statements is performed?
a) `x = Math.Abs( 7.5 );`
b) `x = Math.Floor( 7.5 );`
c) `x = Math.Abs( 0.0 );`
d) `x = Math.Ceiling( 0.0 );`

```
e) x = Math.Abs( -6.4 );
f) x = Math.Ceiling( -6.4 );
g) x = Math.Ceiling( -Math.Abs( -8 + Math.Floor( -5.5 ) ) );
```

6.8   A parking garage charges a $2.00 minimum fee to park for up to three hours. The garage charges an additional $0.50 per hour for each hour *or part thereof* in excess of three hours. The maximum charge for any given 24-hour period is $10.00. Assume that no car parks for longer than 24 hours at a time. Write a program that calculates and displays the parking charges for each customer who parked a car in this garage yesterday. You should enter in a **TextBox** the hours parked for each customer. The program should display the charge for the current customer. The program should use the method **CalculateCharges** to determine the charge for each customer. Use the techniques described in the chapter to read the double value from a **TextBox**.

6.9   Write a method **IntegerPower(base, exponent)** that returns the value of

$$base^{\,exponent}$$

For example, **IntegerPower(3, 4) = 3 * 3 * 3 * 3**. Assume that **exponent** is a positive, nonzero integer, and **base** is an integer. Method **IntegerPower** should use **for** or **while** to control the calculation. Do not use any **Math** library methods. Incorporate this method into a Windows application that reads integer values from **TextBox**es for **base** and **exponent** from the user and performs the calculation with the **IntegerPower** method.

6.10   Define a method **Hypotenuse** that calculates the length of the hypotenuse of a right triangle when the other two sides are given. The method should take two arguments of type **double** and return the hypotenuse as a **double**. Incorporate this method into a Windows application that reads integer values for **side1** and **side2** from **TextBox**es and performs the calculation with the **Hypotenuse** method. Determine the length of the hypotenuse for each of the following triangles:

Triangle	Side 1	Side 2
1	3.0	4.0
2	5.0	12.0
3	8.0	15.0

6.11   Write a method **SquareOfAsterisks** that displays a solid square of asterisks whose side is specified in integer parameter **side**. For example, if **side** is **4**, the method displays

```
****
****
****
****
```

Incorporate this method into an application that reads an integer value for **side** from the user and performs the drawing with the **SquareOfAsterisks** method. This method should gather data from **Textbox**es and should print to a **Label**.

6.12   Modify the method created in Exercise 6.11 to form the square out of whatever character is contained in character parameter **fillCharacter**. Thus, if **side** is **5** and **fillCharacter** is "**#**," this method should print

```
#####
#####
#####
#####
#####
```

6.13 Write an application that simulates coin tossing. Let the program toss the coin each time the user presses the "**Toss**" button. Count the number of times each side of the coin appears. Display the results. The program should call a separate method **Flip** that takes no arguments and returns **false** for tails and **true** for heads. [*Note*: If the program realistically simulates the coin tossing, each side of the coin should appear approximately half of the time.]

6.14 Computers are playing an increasing role in education. Write a program that will help an elementary school student learn multiplication. Use the **Next** method from an object of type **Random** to produce two positive one-digit integers. It should display a question in the status bar, such as

    How much is 6 times 7?

The student should then type the answer into a **TextBox**. Your program should check the student's answer. If it is correct, draw the string **"Very good!"** in a read-only **TextBox**, then ask another multiplication question. If the answer is wrong, draw the string **"No. Please try again."** in the same read-only **TextBox**, then let the student try the same question again until the student finally gets it right. A separate method should be used to generate each new question. This method should be called once when the program begins execution and each time the user answers the question correctly.

6.15 (*Towers of Hanoi*) Every budding computer scientist must grapple with certain classic problems and the Towers of Hanoi (Fig. 6.20) is one of the most famous. Legend has it that in a temple in the Far East, priests are attempting to move a stack of disks from one peg to another. The initial stack had 64 disks threaded onto one peg and arranged from bottom to top by decreasing size. The priests are attempting to move the stack from this peg to a second peg under the constraints that exactly one disk is moved at a time, and at no time may a larger disk be placed above a smaller disk. A third peg is available for temporarily holding disks. Supposedly, the world will end when the priests complete their task, so there is little incentive for us to facilitate their efforts.

Let us assume that the priests are attempting to move the disks from peg 1 to peg 3. We wish to develop an algorithm that will print the precise sequence of peg-to-peg disk transfers.

If we were to approach this problem with conventional methods, we would find ourselves hopelessly knotted up in managing the disks. However, if we attack the problem with recursion in mind, it becomes tractable. Moving *n* disks can be viewed in terms of moving only *n* – 1 disks (and hence, the recursion) as follows:

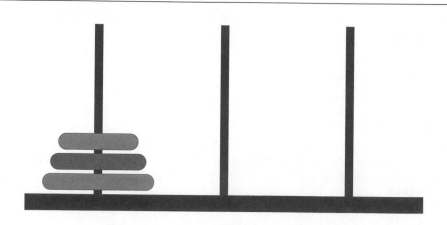

Fig. 6.20 The Towers of Hanoi for the case with four disks.

   a) Move $n-1$ disks from peg 1 to peg 2, using peg 3 as a temporary holding area.

   b) Move the last disk (the largest) from peg 1 to peg 3.

   c) Move the $n-1$ disks from peg 2 to peg 3, using peg 1 as a temporary holding area.

The process ends when the last task involves moving $n = 1$ disk (i.e., the base case). This is accomplished by trivially moving the disk without the need for a temporary holding area.

Write a program to solve the Towers of Hanoi problem. Allow the user to enter the number of disks in a **TextBox**. Use a recursive **Tower** method with four parameters:

   a) The number of disks to be moved

   b) The peg on which these disks are threaded initially

   c) The peg to which this stack of disks is to be moved

   d) The peg to be used as a temporary holding area

Your program should display in a read-only **TextBox** with scrolling functionality the precise instructions for moving the disks from the starting peg to the destination peg. For example, to move a stack of three disks from peg 1 to peg 3, your program should print the following series of moves:

   $1 \rightarrow 3$ (This means move one disk from peg 1 to peg 3.)

   $1 \rightarrow 2$

   $3 \rightarrow 2$

   $1 \rightarrow 3$

   $2 \rightarrow 1$

   $2 \rightarrow 3$

   $1 \rightarrow 3$

6.16   The *greatest common divisor* of integers **x** and **y** is the largest integer that evenly divides both **x** and **y**. Write a recursive method **Gcd** that returns the greatest common divisor of **x** and **y**. The Gcd of **x** and **y** is defined recursively as follows: If **y** is equal to **0**, then **Gcd(x, y)** is **x**; otherwise, **Gcd(x, y)** is **Gcd(y, x % y)**, where **%** is the modulus operator.

6.17   (*"The Twelve Days of Christmas" Song*) Write an application that uses repetition and **if** structures to print the song "The Twelve Days of Christmas." Visit the Web site **www.12days.com/library/carols/12daysofxmas.htm** for the complete lyrics to the song.

7

Arrays

Objectives

- To introduce the array data structure.
- To understand how arrays store, sort and search lists and tables of values.
- To understand how to declare an array, initialize an array and refer to individual elements of an array.
- To be able to pass arrays to methods.
- To understand basic sorting techniques.
- To be able to declare and manipulate multiple-subscripted arrays.

With sobs and tears he sorted out
Those of the largest size ...
Lewis Carroll

Attempt the end, and never stand to doubt;
Nothing's so hard, but search will find it out.
Robert Herrick

Now go, write it before them in a table,
and note it in a book.
Isaiah 30:8

'Tis in my memory lock'd,
And you yourself shall keep the key of it.
William Shakespeare

Outline

7.1 Introduction

This chapter serves as an introduction to data structures. *Arrays* are data structures consisting of data items of the same type. Arrays are "static" entities, in that they remain the same size once they are created. We begin by learning about creating and accessing arrays, then use this knowledge to begin more complex manipulations of arrays, including powerful searching and sorting techniques. We then demonstrate creating more sophisticated arrays that have multiple dimensions. Chapter 24, Data Structures, introduces dynamic data structures such as lists, queues, stacks and trees that can grow and shrink as programs execute. We also introduce C#'s predefined data structures that enable the programmer to use existing data structures for lists, queues, stacks and trees, rather than having to "reinvent the wheel."

7.2 Arrays

An array is a group of contiguous memory locations that all have the same name and type. To refer to a particular location or element in the array, we specify the name of the array and the *position number* (a value that indicates a specific location within the array) of the element to which we refer.

Figure 7.1 shows an integer array called **c**. This array contains 12 *elements*. A program can refer to any element of an array by giving the name of the array followed by the position number of the element in square brackets (**[]**). The first element in every array is the *zeroth element*. Thus, the first element of array **c** is referred to as **c[0]**, the second element of array **c** is referred to as **c[1]**, the seventh element of array **c** is referred to as **c[6]** and so on. The *i*th element of array **c** is referred to as **c[i - 1]**. Array names follow the same conventions as other variable names, as discussed in Chapter 3, Introduction to C# Programming.

The position number in square brackets is more formally called a *subscript* (or an *index*). A subscript must be an integer or an integer expression. If a program uses an expression as a subscript, the program evaluates the expression first to determine the subscript. For example, if variable **a** is equal to **5** and variable **b** is equal to **6**, then the statement

```
c[ a + b ] += 2;
```

adds 2 to array element **c[11]**. Note that a subscripted array name is an *lvalue*—it can be used on the left side of an assignment to place a new value into an array element.

Let us examine array c in Fig. 7.1 more closely. The name of the array is **c**. Every array in C# "knows" its own length. The length of the array is determined by the expression:

```
c.Length
```

The array's 12 elements are referred to as **c[0]**, **c[1]**, **c[2]**, ..., **c[11]**. The *value* of **c[0]** is **-45**, the value of **c[1]** is **6**, the value of **c[2]** is **0**, the value of **c[7]** is **62** and the value of **c[11]** is **78**. To calculate the sum of the values contained in the first three elements of array **c** and to store the result in variable **sum**, we would write

```
sum = c[ 0 ] + c[ 1 ] + c[ 2 ];
```

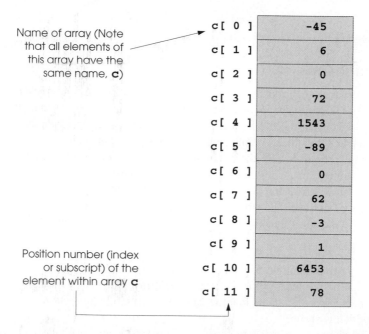

Fig. 7.1   A 12-element array.

To divide the value of the seventh element of array **c** by **2** and assign the result to the variable **x**, we would write

```
x = c[ 6 ] / 2;
```

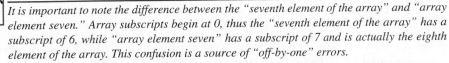

Common Programming Error 7.1

It is important to note the difference between the "seventh element of the array" and "array element seven." Array subscripts begin at 0, thus the "seventh element of the array" has a subscript of 6, while "array element seven" has a subscript of 7 and is actually the eighth element of the array. This confusion is a source of "off-by-one" errors.

The brackets that enclose the subscript of an array are operators. Brackets have the same level of precedence as parentheses. The chart in Fig. 7.2 shows the precedence and associativity of the operators introduced to this point in the text. They are displayed top to bottom in decreasing order of precedence, with their associativity and type. The reader should note that the **++** and **--** operators in the first row represent the postincrement and postdecrement operators, while the **++** and **--** operators in the second row represent the preincrement and predecrement operators. Also, notice that in the first row the associativity is mixed. This is because the associativity of the postincrement and postdecrement operators is right to left, while the associativity for the other operators is left to right.

7.3 Declaring and Allocating Arrays

Arrays occupy space in memory. The programmer specifies the type of the elements and uses operator **new** to allocate dynamically the number of elements required by each array. Arrays are allocated with **new** because arrays are objects and all objects must be created with **new**. We will see an exception to this rule shortly.

Operators	Associativity	Type
( ) [ ] . ++ --	left to right	highest (unary postfix)
++ -- + - ! (*type*)	right to left	unary (unary prefix)
* / %	left to right	multiplicative
+ -	left to right	additive
< <= > >=	left to right	relational
== !=	left to right	equality
&	left to right	logical AND
^	left to right	logical exclusive OR
|	left to right	logical inclusive OR
&&	left to right	conditional AND
||	left to right	conditional OR
? :	right to left	conditional
= += -= *= /= %=	right to left	assignment

Fig. 7.2   Precedence and associativity of the operators discussed so far.

The declaration

```
int[] c = new int[ 12 ];
```

allocates 12 elements for integer array **c**. The preceding statement can also be performed in two steps as follows:

```
int[] c;              // declares array reference
c = new int[ 12 ];    // allocate array and assign to reference
```

When arrays are allocated, the elements are initialized to zero for the numeric primitive-data-type variables, to **false** for **bool** variables and to **null** for reference types.

Common Programming Error 7.2

Unlike in C or C++, in C# the number of elements in the array is never specified in the square brackets after the array name. The declaration ***int c[12];*** *causes a syntax error.*

Memory may be reserved for several arrays with a single declaration. The following declaration reserves 100 elements for **string** array **b** and 27 elements for **string** array **x**:

```
string[] b = new string[ 100 ], x = new string[ 27 ];
```

Similarly, the following declaration reserves 10 elements for **array1** and 20 elements for **array2** (both of type **double**):

```
double[] array1 = new double[ 10 ],
         array2 = new double[ 20 ];
```

Arrays may be declared to contain most data types. In an array of value types, every element of the array contains one value of the declared type. For example, every element of an **int** array is an **int** value.

In an array of reference types, every element of the array is a reference to an object of the data type of the array. For example, every element of a **string** array is a reference to a **string**. Each of these **string** references has the value **null** by default.

7.4 Examples Using Arrays

This section presents several examples using arrays that demonstrate declaring arrays, allocating arrays, initializing arrays and manipulating array elements in various ways. For simplicity, the examples in this section use arrays that contain elements of type **int**. Please remember that a program can declare arrays of most data types.

7.4.1 Allocating an Array and Initializing Its Elements

Figure 7.3 creates three integer arrays of 10 elements and displays those arrays in tabular format. The program demonstrates several techniques for declaring and initializing arrays.

```
1   // Fig 7.3: InitArray.cs
2   // Different ways of initializing arrays.
3
4   using System;
5   using System.Windows.Forms;
```

Fig. 7.3   Initializing element arrays in three different ways. (Part 1 of 2.)

```
 6
 7   class InitArray
 8   {
 9       // main entry point for application
10       static void Main( string[] args )
11       {
12          string output = "";
13
14          int[] x;                // declare reference to an array
15          x = new int[ 10 ];      // dynamically allocate array and set
16                                  // default values
17
18          // initializer list specifies number of elements
19          // and value of each element
20          int[] y = { 32, 27, 64, 18, 95, 14, 90, 70, 60, 37 };
21
22          const int ARRAY_SIZE = 10; // named constant
23          int[] z;                   // reference to int array
24
25          // allocate array of ARRAY_SIZE (i.e., 10) elements
26          z = new int[ ARRAY_SIZE ];
27
28          // set the values in the array
29          for ( int i = 0; i < z.Length; i++ )
30             z[ i ] = 2 + 2 * i;
31
32          output += "Subscript\tArray x\tArray y\tArray z\n";
33
34          // output values for each array
35          for ( int i = 0; i < ARRAY_SIZE; i++ )
36             output += i + "\t" + x[ i ] + "\t" + y[ i ] +
37                "\t" + z[ i ] + "\n";
38
39          MessageBox.Show( output,
40             "Initializing an array of int values",
41             MessageBoxButtons.OK, MessageBoxIcon.Information );
42
43       } // end Main
44
45   } // end class InitArray
```

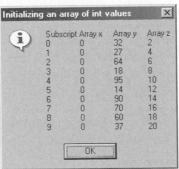

Fig. 7.3   Initializing element arrays in three different ways. (Part 2 of 2.)

Line 14 declares **x** as a reference to an array of integers. Each element in the array is of type **int**. The variable **x** is of type **int[]**, which denotes an array whose elements are of type **int**. Line 15 allocates the 10 elements of the array with **new** and assigns the array to reference **x**. Each element of this array has the default value 0.

Line 20 creates another **int** array and initializes each element using an *initializer list*. In this case, the number of elements in the initializer list determines the array's size. For example, line 20 creates a 10-element array with the indices **0–9** and the values **32, 27, 64**, and so on. Note that this declaration does not require the **new** operator to create the array object—the compiler allocates memory for the object when it encounters an array declaration that includes an initializer list.

On line 22, we create constant integer **ARRAY_SIZE** using keyword **const**. A constant must be initialized in the same statement where it is declared and cannot be modified thereafter. If an attempt is made to modify a **const** variable after it is declared, the compiler issues a syntax error.

Constants also are called *named constants*. They often are used to make a program more readable and are usually denoted with variable names in all capital letters.

Common Programming Error 7.3

Assigning a value to a constant after the variable has been initialized is a compiler error.

On lines 23 and 26, we create integer array **z** of length 10 using the **ARRAY_SIZE** named constant. The **for** structure in lines 29–30 initializes each element in array **z**. The values are generated by multiplying each successive value of the loop counter by **2** and adding **2** to the product. After this initialization, array **z** contains the even integers **2, 4, 6, …, 20**. The **for** structure in lines 35–37 uses the values in arrays **x**, **y** and **z** to build an output string, which will be displayed in a **MessageBox**. Zero-based counting (remember, array subscripts start at 0) allows the loop to access every element of the array. The constant **ARRAY_SIZE** in the **for** structure condition (line 29) specifies the arrays' lengths.

7.4.2 Totaling the Elements of an Array

Often, the elements of an array represent series of values to be used in calculations. For example, if the elements of an array represent the grades for an exam in a class, the professor may wish to total the elements of an array, then calculate the class average for the exam.

The application in Fig. 7.4 sums the values contained in the 10-element integer array **a** (declared, allocated and initialized on line 12). Line 16 in the body of the **for** loop performs the addition using the array element at position **i** during each loop iteration. Note that the values being supplied as initializers for array **a** normally would be read into the program. For example, in a Windows application, the user could enter the values through a **TextBox**, or the values could be read from a file on disk. (See Chapter 17, Files and Streams.)

```
1   // Fig. 7.4: SumArray.cs
2   // Computing the sum of the elements in an array.
3
4   using System;
5   using System.Windows.Forms;
```

Fig. 7.4   Computing the sum of the elements of an array. (Part 1 of 2.)

```
6
7    class SumArray
8    {
9        // main entry point for application
10       static void Main( string[] args )
11       {
12           int[] a = { 1, 2, 3, 4, 5, 6, 7, 8, 9, 10 };
13           int total = 0;
14
15           for ( int i = 0; i < a.Length; i++ )
16               total += a[ i ];
17
18           MessageBox.Show( "Total of array elements: " + total,
19               "Sum the elements of an array",
20               MessageBoxButtons.OK, MessageBoxIcon.Information );
21
22       } // end Main
23
24   } // end class SumArray
```

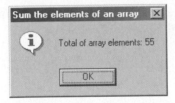

Fig. 7.4   Computing the sum of the elements of an array. (Part 2 of 2.)

7.4.3 Using Histograms to Display Array Data Graphically

Many programs present data to users in a graphical manner. For example, numeric values often are displayed as bars in a bar chart. In such a chart, longer bars represent larger numeric values. One simple way to display numeric data graphically is with a *histogram* that shows each numeric value as a bar of asterisks (*).

Our next application (Fig. 7.5) reads numbers from an array and graphs the information in the form of a bar chart, or histogram. The program displays each number followed by a bar consisting of a corresponding number of asterisks. The nested **for** loops (lines 18–24) append the bars to the **string** that will be displayed in the **MessageBox**. Note the loop continuation condition of the inner **for** structure on line 22 (**j <= n[i]**). Each time the program reaches the inner **for** structure, the loop counts from **1** to **n[i]**, using a value in array **n** to determine the final value of the control variable **j** and the number of asterisks to display.

```
1    // Fig. 7.5: Histogram.cs
2    // Using data to create a histogram.
3
4    using System;
5    using System.Windows.Forms;
```

Fig. 7.5   Program that prints histograms. (Part 1 of 2.)

```
6
7   class Histogram
8   {
9       // main entry point for application
10      static void Main( string[] args )
11      {
12          int[] n = { 19, 3, 15, 7, 11, 9, 13, 5, 17, 1 };
13          string output = "";
14
15          output += "Element\tvalue\tHistogram\n";
16
17          // build output
18          for ( int i = 0; i < n.Length; i++ )
19          {
20              output += "\n" + i + "\t" + n[ i ] + "\t";
21
22              for ( int j = 1; j <= n[ i ]; j++ ) // print a bar
23                  output += "*";
24          }
25
26          MessageBox.Show( output, "Histogram Printing Program",
27              MessageBoxButtons.OK, MessageBoxIcon.Information );
28
29      } // end Main
30
31  } // end class Histogram
```

Fig. 7.5   Program that prints histograms. (Part 2 of 2.)

7.4.4 Using the Elements of an Array as Counters

Sometimes programs use a series of counter variables to summarize data, such as the results of a survey. In Chapter 6, Methods, we used a series of counters in our dice-rolling program to track the number of occurrences of each side on a six-sided die as the program rolled 12 dice at a time. We also indicated that there is a more elegant method than that in Fig. 6.11 for writing the dice-rolling program. An array version of this application is shown in Fig. 7.6.

The program uses the seven-element array frequency to count the occurrences of each side of the die. Line 94, which uses the random **face** value as the subscript for array **fre-**

quency to determine which element should be incremented during each iteration of the loop, replaces lines 85–111 of Fig. 6.11. The random number calculation on line 88 produces numbers 1–6 (the values for a six-sided die); thus, the **frequency** array must be large enough to allow subscript values of 1–6. The smallest number of elements required for an array to have these subscript values is seven elements (subscript values 0–6). In this program, we ignore element 0 of array **frequency**. Lines 75–80 replace lines 59–71 from Fig. 6.11. We can loop through array **frequency**; therefore, we do not have to enumerate each line of text to display in the **Label**, as we did in Fig. 6.11.

```
1   // Fig. 7.6: RollDie.cs
2   // Rolling 12 dice.
3
4   using System;
5   using System.Drawing;
6   using System.Collections;
7   using System.ComponentModel;
8   using System.Windows.Forms;
9   using System.Data;
10  using System.IO;
11
12  public class RollDie : System.Windows.Forms.Form
13  {
14      private System.Windows.Forms.Button rollButton;
15
16      private System.Windows.Forms.RichTextBox displayTextBox;
17
18      private System.Windows.Forms.Label dieLabel1;
19      private System.Windows.Forms.Label dieLabel2;
20      private System.Windows.Forms.Label dieLabel3;
21      private System.Windows.Forms.Label dieLabel4;
22      private System.Windows.Forms.Label dieLabel5;
23      private System.Windows.Forms.Label dieLabel6;
24      private System.Windows.Forms.Label dieLabel7;
25      private System.Windows.Forms.Label dieLabel8;
26      private System.Windows.Forms.Label dieLabel9;
27      private System.Windows.Forms.Label dieLabel10;
28      private System.Windows.Forms.Label dieLabel11;
29      private System.Windows.Forms.Label dieLabel12;
30
31      private System.ComponentModel.Container components = null;
32
33      Random randomNumber = new Random();
34      int[] frequency = new int[ 7 ];
35
36      public RollDie()
37      {
38          InitializeComponent();
39      }
40
41      // Visual Studio .NET generated code
42
```

Fig. 7.6   Using arrays to eliminate a **switch** structure. (Part 1 of 3.)

```
43        [STAThread]
44        static void Main()
45        {
46            Application.Run( new RollDie() );
47        }
48
49        private void rollButton_Click(
50            object sender, System.EventArgs e )
51        {
52            // pass the labels to a method that will
53            // randomly assign a face to each die
54            DisplayDie( dieLabel1 );
55            DisplayDie( dieLabel2 );
56            DisplayDie( dieLabel3 );
57            DisplayDie( dieLabel4 );
58            DisplayDie( dieLabel5 );
59            DisplayDie( dieLabel6 );
60            DisplayDie( dieLabel7 );
61            DisplayDie( dieLabel8 );
62            DisplayDie( dieLabel9 );
63            DisplayDie( dieLabel10 );
64            DisplayDie( dieLabel11 );
65            DisplayDie( dieLabel12 );
66
67            double total = 0;
68
69            for ( int i = 1; i < 7; i++ )
70                total += frequency[ i ];
71
72            displayTextBox.Text = "Face\tFrequency\tPercent\n";
73
74            // output frequency values
75            for ( int x = 1; x < frequency.Length; x++ )
76            {
77                displayTextBox.Text += x + "\t" +
78                    frequency[ x ] + "\t\t" + String.Format( "{0:N}",
79                    frequency[ x ] / total * 100 ) + "%\n";
80            }
81
82        } // end rollButton_Click
83
84        // simulates roll, display proper
85        // image and increment frequency
86        public void DisplayDie( Label dieLabel )
87        {
88            int face = randomNumber.Next( 1, 7 );
89
90            dieLabel.Image = Image.FromFile(
91                Directory.GetCurrentDirectory() +
92                "\\images\\die" + face + ".gif" );
93
94            frequency[ face ]++;
95        }
```

Fig. 7.6   Using arrays to eliminate a **switch** structure. (Part 2 of 3.)

```
96
97   } // end class RollDie
```

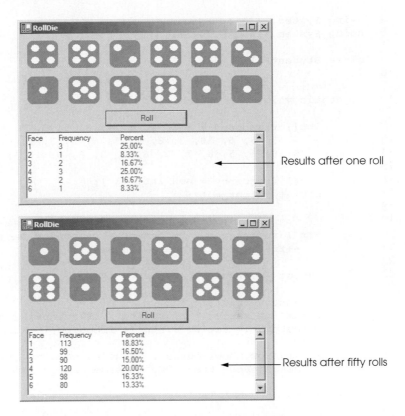

Results after one roll

Results after fifty rolls

Fig. 7.6   Using arrays to eliminate a **switch** structure. (Part 3 of 3.)

7.4.5 Using Arrays to Analyze Survey Results

Our next example uses arrays to summarize the results of data collected in a survey. Consider the following problem statement:

> *Forty students were asked to rate the quality of the food in the student cafeteria on a scale of 1 to 10, with 1 being awful and 10 being excellent. Place the 40 responses in an integer array and summarize the frequency for each rating.*

This is a typical array processing application (Fig. 7.7). We wish to summarize the number of responses of each type (i.e., 1–10). The array **responses** is a 40-element integer array of the students' responses to the survey. We use an 11-element array **frequency** to count the number of occurrences of each response. We ignore the first element, **frequency[0]**, because it is more logical to have a response of **1** increment **frequency[1]** than **frequency[0]**. We can use each response directly as a subscript on the **frequency** array. Each element of the array is used as a counter for one of the survey responses.

```csharp
1   // Fig. 7.7: StudentPoll.cs
2   // A student poll program.
3
4   using System;
5   using System.Windows.Forms;
6
7   class StudentPoll
8   {
9      // main entry point for application
10      static void Main( string[] args )
11      {
12         int[] responses = { 1, 2, 6, 4, 8, 5, 9, 7, 8, 10, 1,
13            6, 3, 8, 6, 10, 3, 8, 2, 7, 6, 5, 7, 6, 8, 6, 7,
14            5, 6, 6, 5, 6, 7, 5, 6, 4, 8, 6, 8, 10 };
15
16         int[] frequency = new int[ 11 ];
17         string output = "";
18
19         // increment the frequency for each response
20         for ( int answer = 0; answer < responses.Length; answer++ )
21            ++frequency[ responses[ answer ] ];
22
23         output += "Rating\tFrequency\n";
24
25         // output results
26         for ( int rating = 1; rating < frequency.Length; rating++ )
27            output += rating + "\t" + frequency[ rating ] + "\n";
28
29         MessageBox.Show( output, "Student poll program",
30            MessageBoxButtons.OK, MessageBoxIcon.Information );
31
32      } // end method Main
33
34   } // end class StudentPoll
```

Fig. 7.7   Simple student-poll analysis program.

Good Programming Practice 7.1

Strive for program clarity. It is sometimes worthwhile to trade off the most efficient use of memory or processor time for writing clearer programs.

The **for** loop (lines 20–21) takes the responses from the array **response** one at a time and increments one of the 10 counters in the **frequency** array (**frequency[1]** to **frequency[10]**). The key statement in the loop is on line 21, which increments the appropriate counter in the **frequency** array, depending on the value of element **responses[answer]**.

Let us consider several iterations of the **for** loop. When counter **answer** is **0**, **responses[answer]** is the value of the first element of array **responses** (i.e., **1**). In this case, the program interprets **++frequency[responses[answer]];** as **++frequency[1];**, which increments array element one. In evaluating the expression, start with the value in the innermost set of square brackets (**answer**). Once you know the value of **answer**, plug that value into the expression and evaluate the next outer set of square brackets (**responses[answer]**). Use that value as the subscript for the **frequency** array to determine which counter to increment.

When **answer** is **1**, **responses[answer]** is the value of the second element of array **responses** (i.e., **2**), so the program interprets

```
++frequency[ responses[ answer ] ];
```

as **++frequency[2];**, which increments array element two (the third element of the array). When **answer** is **2**, **responses[answer]** is the value of the third element of array **responses** (i.e., **6**), so the program interprets

```
++frequency[ responses[ answer ] ];
```

as **++frequency[6];**, which increments array element six (the seventh element of the array) and so on. Note that, regardless of the number of responses processed in the survey, only an 11-element array is required (ignoring element zero) to summarize the results, because all the response values are between 1 and 10, and the subscript values for an 11-element array are 0–10. The results are correct, because the elements of the **frequency** array were initialized to zero when the array was allocated with **new**.

If the data contained invalid values, such as 13, the program would attempt to add **1** to **frequency[13]**. This is outside the bounds of the array. In the C and C++ programming languages, no checks are performed to prevent programs from reading data outside the bounds of arrays. At execution time, the program would "walk" past the end of the array to where element number 13 would be located and add 1 to whatever data are stored at that location in memory. This could potentially modify another variable in the program or even result in premature program termination. The .NET framework provides mechanisms to prevent accessing elements outside the bounds of arrays.

Testing and Debugging Tip 7.1

When a C# program executes, array element subscripts are checked for validity (i.e., all subscripts must be greater than or equal to 0 and less than the length of the array).

Testing and Debugging Tip 7.2

*Exceptions indicate when errors occur in programs. Programmers can write code to recover from exceptions and continue program execution instead of terminating the program abnormally. When an invalid array reference occurs, C# generates an **IndexOutOfRangeException** exception. We discuss exceptions in more detail in Chapter 11, Exception Handling.*

Common Programming Error 7.4

Referring to an element outside the array bounds is a logic error.

Testing and Debugging Tip 7.3

When looping through an array, the array subscript never should go below 0 and should al-ways be less than the total number of elements in the array (one less than the **length** *of the array). The loop-terminating condition should prevent accessing elements outside this range.*

Testing and Debugging Tip 7.4

Programs should validate the correctness of all input values to prevent erroneous infor-mation from affecting a program's calculations.

7.5 Passing Arrays to Methods

To pass an array argument to a method, specify the name of the array without using brack-ets. For example, if array **hourlyTemperatures** declared as

```
int[] hourlyTemperatures = new int[ 24 ];
```

the method call

```
ModifyArray( hourlyTemperatures );
```

passes array **hourlyTemperatures** to method **ModifyArray**. Every array object "knows" its own size (via the **Length** instance variable), so when we pass an array object into a method, we do not pass the size of the array as an argument separately.

Although entire arrays are passed by reference, individual array elements of primitive data types are passed by value, the same way as simple variables are. (The objects referred to by individual elements of a nonprimitive-type array are still passed by reference.) Such simple single pieces of data are sometimes called *scalars* or *scalar quantities.* To pass an array element to a method, use the subscripted name of the array element as an argument in the method call.

For a method to receive an array through a method call, the method's parameter list must specify that an array will be received. For example, the method header for method **ModifyArray** might be written as

```
public void ModifyArray( int[] b )
```

indicating that **ModifyArray** expects to receive an integer array in parameter **b**. Arrays are passed by reference; when the called method uses the array name **b**, it refers to the ac-tual array in the caller (array **hourlyTemperatures**).

The application in Fig. 7.8 demonstrates the difference between passing an entire array and passing an array element.

The **for** loop on lines 32–33 appends the five elements of integer array **a** to the **Text** property of **outputLabel**. Line 33 invokes method **ModifyArray** and passes to it array **a**. Method **ModifyArray** multiplies each element by 2. To illustrate that array **a**'s elements were modified, the **for** loop on lines 41–42 appends the five elements of integer array **a** to the **Text** property of **outputLabel**. As the screen capture indicates, the ele-ments of **a** are modified by **ModifyArray**.

```
1   // Fig. 7.8: PassArray.cs
2   // Passing arrays and individual elements to methods.
3   using System;
4   using System.Drawing;
5   using System.Collections;
6   using System.ComponentModel;
7   using System.Windows.Forms;
8   using System.Data;
9
10  public class PassArray : System.Windows.Forms.Form
11  {
12     private System.Windows.Forms.Button showOutputButton;
13     private System.Windows.Forms.Label outputLabel;
14
15     // Visual Studio .NET generated code
16
17     [STAThread]
18     static void Main()
19     {
20        Application.Run( new PassArray() );
21     }
22
23     private void showOutputButton_Click( object sender,
24        System.EventArgs e )
25     {
26        int[] a = { 1, 2, 3, 4, 5 };
27
28        outputLabel.Text = "Effects of passing entire array " +
29           "call-by-reference:\n\nThe values of the original " +
30           "array are:\n\t";
31
32        for ( int i = 0; i < a.Length; i++ )
33           outputLabel.Text += "   " + a[ i ];
34
35        ModifyArray( a );    // array is passed by reference
36
37        outputLabel.Text +=
38           "\n\nThe values of the modified array are:\n\t";
39
40        // display elements of array a
41        for ( int i = 0; i < a.Length; i++ )
42           outputLabel.Text += "   " + a[ i ];
43
44        outputLabel.Text += "\n\nEffects of passing array " +
45           "element call-by-value:\n\na[ 3 ] before " +
46           "ModifyElement: " + a[ 3 ];
47
48        // array element passed call-by-value
49        ModifyElement( a[ 3 ] );
50
51        outputLabel.Text +=
52           "\na[ 3 ] after ModifyElement: " + a[ 3 ];
53     }
```

Fig. 7.8   Passing arrays and individual array elements to methods. (Part 1 of 2.)

```
54
55      // method modifies the array it receives,
56      // original will be modified
57      public void ModifyArray( int[] b )
58      {
59         for ( int j = 0; j < b.Length; j++ )
60            b[ j ] *= 2;
61      }
62
63      // method modifies the integer passed to it
64      // original will not be modified
65      public void ModifyElement( int e )
66      {
67         outputLabel.Text +=
68            "\nvalue received in ModifyElement: " + e;
69
70         e *= 2;
71
72         outputLabel.Text +=
73            "\nvalue calculated in ModifyElement: " + e;
74      }
75   }
```

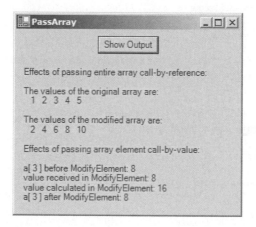

Fig. 7.8   Passing arrays and individual array elements to methods. (Part 2 of 2.)

To show the value of **a[3]** before the call to **ModifyElement**, lines 44–46 append the value of **a[3]** (and other information) to **outputLabel.Text**. Line 44 invokes method **ModifyElement** and passes **a[3]**. Remember that **a[3]** is a single **int** value in the array **a**. Also, remember that values of primitive types always are passed to methods by value. Therefore, a copy of **a[3]** is passed. Method **ModifyElement** multiplies its argument by 2 and stores the result in its parameter **e**. The parameter of **ModifyElement** is a local variable, so when the method terminates, the local variable is destroyed. Thus, when control is returned to **PassArray**, the unmodified value of **a[3]** is appended to the **outputLabel.Text** (line 51–52).

7.6 Passing Arrays by Value and by Reference

In C#, a variable that "stores" an object, such as an array, does not actually store the object itself. Instead, such a variable stores a reference to the object (i.e., the location in the computer's memory where the object itself is stored). The distinction between reference variables and primitive data type variables raises some subtle issues that programmers must understand to create secure, stable programs.

When a program passes an argument to a method, the called method receives a copy of that argument's value. Changes to the local copy do not affect the original variable that the program passed to the method. If the argument is of a reference type, the method makes a local copy of the reference itself, not a copy of the actual object to which the reference refers. The local copy of the reference also refers to the original object in memory. Thus, reference types are always passed by reference, which means that changes to those objects in called methods affect the original objects in memory.

Performance Tip 7.1

Passing arrays and other objects by reference makes sense for performance reasons. If arrays were passed by value, a copy of each element would be passed. For large, frequently passed arrays, this would waste time and would consume considerable storage for the copies of the arrays—both of these problems cause poor performance.

C# also allows methods to pass references with keyword **ref**. This is a subtle capability, which, if misused, can lead to problems. For instance, when a reference-type object like an array is passed with **ref**, the called method actually gains control over the passed reference itself, allowing the called method to replace the original reference in the caller with a different object or even with **null**. Such behavior can lead to unpredictable effects, which can be disastrous in mission-critical applications. The program in Fig. 7.9 demonstrates the subtle difference between passing a reference by value and passing a reference with keyword **ref**.

Lines 26 and 29 declare two integer array variables, **firstArray** and **firstArray-Copy** (we make the copy so we can determine whether reference **firstArray** gets overwritten). Line 26 initializes **firstArray** with the values **1**, **2** and **3**. The assignment statement on line 29 copies reference **firstArray** to variable **firstArrayCopy**, causing these variables to reference the same array object in memory. The **for** structure on lines 38–39 prints the contents of **firstArray** before it is passed to method **First-Double** (line 42) so we can verify that this array is passed by reference (i.e., the called method indeed changes the array's contents).

The **for** structure in method **FirstDouble** (lines 99–100) multiplies the values of all the elements in the array by **2**. Line 103 allocates a new array containing the values **11**, **12** and **13**; the reference for this array then is assigned to parameter **array** (in an attempt to overwrite reference **firstArray**—this, of course, will not happen, because the reference was passed by value). After method **FirstDouble** executes, the **for** structure on lines 48–49 prints the contents of **firstArray**, demonstrating that the values of the elements have been changed by the method (and confirming that in C# arrays are always passed by reference). The **if/else** structure on lines 52–57 uses the **==** operator to compare references **firstArray** (which we just attempted to overwrite) and **firstArrayCopy**. The expression on line 40 evaluates to **true** if the operands to binary operator **==** indeed reference the same object. In this case, the object represented is the array allocated in line 26—not the array allocated in method **FirstDouble** (line 103).

```
1    // Fig. 7.9: ArrayReferenceTest.cs
2    // Testing the effects of passing array references
3    // by value and by reference.
4    using System;
5    using System.Drawing;
6    using System.Collections;
7    using System.ComponentModel;
8    using System.Windows.Forms;
9    using System.Data;
10
11   public class ArrayReferenceTest : System.Windows.Forms.Form
12   {
13      private System.Windows.Forms.Label outputLabel;
14      private System.Windows.Forms.Button showOutputButton;
15
16      [STAThread]
17      static void Main()
18      {
19         Application.Run( new ArrayReferenceTest() );
20      }
21
22      private void showOutputButton_Click( object sender,
23         System.EventArgs e )
24      {
25         // create and initialize firstArray
26         int[] firstArray = { 1, 2, 3 };
27
28         // copy firstArray reference
29         int[] firstArrayCopy = firstArray;
30
31         outputLabel.Text =
32            "Test passing firstArray reference by value";
33
34         outputLabel.Text += "\n\nContents of firstArray " +
35            "before calling FirstDouble:\n\t";
36
37         // print contents of firstArray
38         for ( int i = 0; i < firstArray.Length; i++ )
39            outputLabel.Text += firstArray[ i ] + " ";
40
41         // pass reference firstArray by value to FirstDouble
42         FirstDouble( firstArray );
43
44         outputLabel.Text += "\n\nContents of firstArray after " +
45            "calling FirstDouble\n\t";
46
47         // print contents of firstArray
48         for ( int i = 0; i < firstArray.Length; i++ )
49            outputLabel.Text += firstArray[ i ] + " ";
50
```

Fig. 7.9   Passing an array reference by value and by reference. (Part 1 of 3.)

```
51        // test whether reference was changed by FirstDouble
52        if ( firstArray == firstArrayCopy )
53           outputLabel.Text +=
54              "\n\nThe references refer to the same array\n";
55        else
56           outputLabel.Text +=
57              "\n\nThe references refer to different arrays\n";
58
59        // create and initialize secondArray
60        int[] secondArray = { 1, 2, 3 };
61
62        // copy secondArray reference
63        int[] secondArrayCopy = secondArray;
64
65        outputLabel.Text += "\nTest passing secondArray " +
66           "reference by reference";
67
68        outputLabel.Text += "\n\nContents of secondArray " +
69           "before calling SecondDouble:\n\t";
70
71        // print contents of secondArray before method call
72        for ( int i = 0; i < secondArray.Length; i++ )
73           outputLabel.Text += secondArray[ i ] + " ";
74
75        SecondDouble( ref secondArray );
76
77        outputLabel.Text += "\n\nContents of secondArray " +
78           "after calling SecondDouble:\n\t";
79
80        // print contents of secondArray after method call
81        for ( int i = 0; i < secondArray.Length; i++ )
82           outputLabel.Text += secondArray[ i ] + " ";
83
84        // test whether reference was changed by SecondDouble
85        if ( secondArray == secondArrayCopy )
86           outputLabel.Text +=
87              "\n\nThe references refer to the same array\n";
88        else
89           outputLabel.Text +=
90              "\n\nThe references refer to different arrays\n";
91
92     } // end method showOutputButton_Click
93
94     // modify elements of array and attempt to modify
95     // reference
96     void FirstDouble( int[] array )
97     {
98        // double each element's value
99        for ( int i = 0; i < array.Length; i++ )
100           array[ i ] *= 2;
101
```

Fig. 7.9   Passing an array reference by value and by reference. (Part 2 of 3.)

```
102          // create new reference and assign it to array
103          array = new int[] { 11, 12, 13 };
104       }
105
106       // modify elements of array and change reference array
107       // to refer to a new array
108       void SecondDouble( ref int[] array )
109       {
110          // double each element's value
111          for ( int i = 0; i < array.Length; i++ )
112             array[ i ] *= 2;
113
114          // create new reference and assign it to array
115          array = new int[] { 11, 12, 13 };
116       }
117    }
```

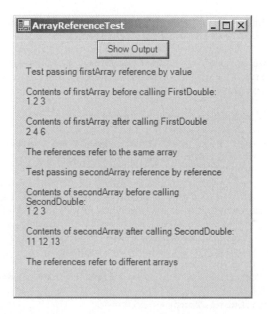

Fig. 7.9   Passing an array reference by value and by reference. (Part 3 of 3.)

Lines 60–90 perform similar tests, using array variables **secondArray** and **secondArrayCopy** and method **SecondDouble** (lines 108–116). Method **SecondDouble** performs the same operations as **FirstDouble**, but receives its array argument using keyword **ref**. In this case, the reference stored in **secondArray** after the method call is a reference to the array allocated on line 115 of **SecondDouble**, demonstrating that a reference passed with keyword **ref** can be modified by the called method so that the reference actually points to a different object, in this case an array allocated in procedure **SecondDouble**. The **if/else** structure in lines 85–90 demonstrates that **secondArray** and **secondArrayCopy** no longer refer to the same array.

Software Engineering Observation 7.1

When a method receives a reference-type object parameter by value, the object is not passed by value—the object still passes by reference. Rather, the object's reference is passed by value. This prevents a method from overwriting references passed to that method. In the vast majority of cases, protecting the caller's reference from modification is the desired behavior. If you encounter a situation where you truly want the called procedure to modify the caller's reference, pass the reference-type using keyword **ref**—*but, again, such situations are rare.*

Software Engineering Observation 7.2

*In C#, objects (including arrays) always pass by reference. So, a called method receiving a reference to an object can modify the caller's object via a non-***const*** reference parameter.*

7.7 Sorting Arrays

Sorting data (i.e., arranging the data into some particular order, such as ascending or descending) is one of the most important computing applications. A bank sorts all checks by account number so that it can prepare individual bank statements at the end of each month. Telephone companies sort their lists of accounts by last name, and within that, by first name to make it easy to find phone numbers. Virtually every organization must sort some data, and in many cases, massive amounts of it. Sorting data is an intriguing problem that has attracted some of the most intense research efforts in the computer science field. In this section, we discuss one of the simplest sorting schemes. In the exercises, we investigate more sophisticated sorting algorithms.

Performance Tip 7.2

Sometimes, the simplest algorithms perform poorly. Their virtue is that they are easy to write, test and debug. Complex algorithms sometimes are needed to realize maximum performance of a program.

Figure 7.10 sorts the values of the 10-element array **a** into ascending order. The technique we use is called the *bubble sort*, because smaller values gradually "bubble" their way to the top of the array (i.e., toward the first element) like air bubbles rising in water. The technique sometimes is called the *sinking sort*, because the larger values sink to the bottom of the array. Bubble sort uses nested loops to make several passes through the array. Each pass compares successive pairs of elements. If a pair is in increasing order (or the values are equal), the values remain in the same order. If a pair is in decreasing order, the bubble sort swaps the values in the array. The program contains methods **Main**, **BubbleSort** and **Swap**. Method **sortButton_Click** (lines 23–41) creates array **a**, invokes **BubbleSort** and displays output. Line 34 of **sortButton_Click** invokes method **BubbleSort** (lines 44–52) to sort array **a**. Line 51 in method **BubbleSort** calls method **Swap** (lines 55–62) to exchange two elements of the array.

```
1   // Fig. 7.10: BubbleSorter.cs
2   // Sorting an array's values into ascending order.
3   using System;
4   using System.Drawing;
5   using System.Collections;
```

Fig. 7.10 Sorting an array with bubble sort. (Part 1 of 3.)

```
 6   using System.ComponentModel;
 7   using System.Windows.Forms;
 8   using System.Data;
 9
10   public class BubbleSorter : System.Windows.Forms.Form
11   {
12      private System.Windows.Forms.Button sortButton;
13      private System.Windows.Forms.Label outputLabel;
14
15      // Visual Studio .NET generated code
16
17      [STAThread]
18      static void Main()
19      {
20         Application.Run( new BubbleSorter() );
21      }
22
23      private void sortButton_Click( object sender,
24            System.EventArgs e )
25      {
26         int[] a = { 2, 6, 4, 8, 10, 12, 89, 68, 45, 37 };
27
28         outputLabel.Text = "Data items in original order\n";
29
30         for ( int i = 0; i < a.Length; i++ )
31            outputLabel.Text += "   " + a[ i ];
32
33         // sort elements in array a
34         BubbleSort( a );
35
36         outputLabel.Text += "\n\nData items in ascending order\n";
37
38         for ( int i = 0; i < a.Length; i++ )
39            outputLabel.Text += "   " + a[ i ];
40
41      } // end method sortButton_Click
42
43      // sort the elements of an array with bubble sort
44      public void BubbleSort( int[] b )
45      {
46         for ( int pass = 1; pass < b.Length; pass++ ) // passes
47
48            for ( int i = 0; i < b.Length - 1; i++ )   // one pass
49
50               if ( b[ i ] > b[ i + 1 ] )        // one comparison
51                  Swap( b, i );                  // one swap
52      }
53
54      // swap two elements of an array
55      public void Swap( int[] c, int first )
56      {
57         int hold;      // temporary holding area for swap
58
```

Fig. 7.10   Sorting an array with bubble sort. (Part 2 of 3.)

```
59              hold = c[ first ];
60              c[ first ] = c[ first + 1 ];
61              c[ first + 1 ] = hold;
62          }
63      }
```

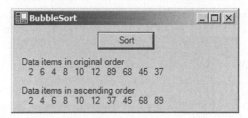

Fig. 7.10   Sorting an array with bubble sort. (Part 3 of 3.)

Method **BubbleSort** receives the array as parameter **b**. The nested **for** loop on lines 46–51 performs the sort. The outer loop controls the number of passes of the array. The inner loop controls the comparisons and necessary swapping of the elements during each pass.

Method **BubbleSort** first compares **b[0]** to **b[1]**, then **b[1]** to **b[2]**, then **b[2]** to **b[3]** and so on, until it completes the pass by comparing **b[8]** to **b[9]**. Although there are 10 elements, the comparison loop performs only nine comparisons. As a result of the way the successive comparisons are made, a large value may move down the array (sink) many positions (and sometimes all the way to the bottom of the array) on a single pass. However, a small value may move up (bubble) only one position. On the first pass, the largest value is guaranteed to sink to the bottom element of the array, **b[9]**. On the second pass, the second largest value is guaranteed to sink to **b[8]**. On the ninth pass, the ninth largest value sinks to **b[1]**. This leaves the smallest value in **b[0]**, so only nine passes are needed to sort a 10-element array.

If a comparison reveals that the two elements appear in descending order, **BubbleSort** calls **Swap** to exchange the two elements so they will be in ascending order in the array. Method **Swap** receives a reference to the array (which it calls **c**) and one integer representing the subscript of the first element of the array to be exchanged. Three assignments on lines 59–61 perform the exchange, where the extra variable **hold** temporarily stores one of the two values being swapped. The swap cannot be performed with only the two assignments

```
c[ first ] = c[ first + 1 ];
c[ first + 1 ] = c[ first ];
```

If **c[first]** is **7** and **c[first + 1]** is **5**, after the first assignment, both elements of the array contain **5** and the value **7** is lost—hence, the need for the extra variable **hold**.

The advantage of the bubble sort is that it is easy to program. However, the bubble sort runs slowly, which becomes apparent when sorting large arrays. More advanced courses (often titled "Data Structures" or "Algorithms" or "Computational Complexity") investigate sorting and searching in greater depth. Note that the .NET framework includes a built-in array-sorting capability that implements a high-speed sort. To sort the array **a** in Fig. 7.10, you can use the statement

```
Array.Sort( a );
```

7.8 Searching Arrays: Linear Search and Binary Search

Often, programmers work with large amounts of data stored in arrays. It might be necessary in this case to determine whether an array contains a value that matches a certain *key value*. The process of locating a particular element value in an array is called *searching*. In this section, we discuss two searching techniques—the simple *linear search* technique and the more efficient *binary search* technique. Exercises 7.8 and 7.9 at the end of this chapter ask you to implement recursive versions of the linear and binary search.

7.8.1 Searching an Array with Linear Search

In the program in Fig. 7.11, method **LinearSearch** (defined on lines 44–54) uses a **for** structure containing an **if** structure to compare each element of an array with a *search key* (line 44). If the search key is found, the method returns the subscript value for the element to indicate the exact position of the search key in the array. If the search key is not found, the method returns **-1**. (The value **-1** is a good choice because it is not a valid subscript number.) If the elements of the array being searched are not in any particular order, it is just as likely that the value will be found in the first element as in the last. On average, the program will have to compare the search key with half the elements of the array. The program contains a 100-element array filled with the even integers from 0–198. The user types the search key in a **TextBox** (called *inputTextBox*) and clicks the **findButton** to start the search. [*Note*: The array is passed to **LinearSearch** even though the array is an instance variable of the class. This is done because an array normally is passed to a method of another class for searching.]

```
1    // Fig. 7.11: LinearSearcher.cs
2    // Demonstrating linear searching of an array.
3    using System;
4    using System.Drawing;
5    using System.Collections;
6    using System.ComponentModel;
7    using System.Windows.Forms;
8    using System.Data;
9
10   public class LinearSearcher : System.Windows.Forms.Form
11   {
12      private System.Windows.Forms.Button searchButton;
13      private System.Windows.Forms.TextBox inputTextBox;
14      private System.Windows.Forms.Label outputLabel;
15
16      int[] a = { 2, 4, 6, 8, 10, 12, 14, 16, 18, 20, 22, 24, 26,
17                  28, 30, 32, 34, 36, 38, 40, 42, 44, 46, 48, 50 };
18
19      // Visual Studio .NET generated code
20
21      [STAThread]
22      static void Main()
23      {
```

Fig. 7.11 Linear search of an array. (Part 1 of 2.)

```
24              Application.Run( new LinearSearcher() );
25           }
26
27           private void searchButton_Click( object sender,
28              System.EventArgs e )
29           {
30              int searchKey = Int32.Parse( inputTextBox.Text );
31
32              int elementIndex = LinearSearch( a, searchKey );
33
34              if ( elementIndex != -1 )
35                 outputLabel.Text =
36                    "Found value in element " + elementIndex;
37
38              else
39                 outputLabel.Text = "Value not found";
40
41           } // end method searchButton_Click
42
43           // search array for the specified key value
44           public int LinearSearch( int[] array, int key )
45           {
46              for ( int n = 0; n < array.Length; n++ )
47              {
48                 if ( array[ n ] == key )
49                    return n;
50              }
51
52              return -1;
53
54           } // end method LinearSearch
55        }
```

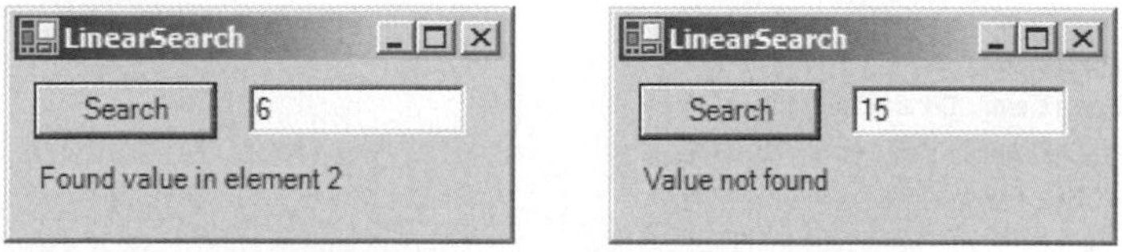

Fig. 7.11 Linear search of an array. (Part 2 of 2.)

7.8.2 Searching a Sorted Array with Binary Search

The linear search method works well for small or unsorted arrays. However, for large arrays, linear searching is inefficient. If the array is sorted, the high-speed *binary search* technique can be used. The binary search algorithm eliminates half of the elements in the array being searched after each comparison. The algorithm locates the middle array element and compares it with the search key. If they are equal, the search key has been found, and the subscript of that element is returned. Otherwise, the problem is reduced to searching half of the array. If the search key is less than the middle array element, the first half of the array is searched; otherwise, the second half of the array is searched. If the search key is not the middle element in the specified subarray (a piece of the original array), the algorithm is repeated in one quarter of the original array. The search continues until the search key is equal to the middle element of a subarray, or until the subarray consists of one element that is not equal to the search key (i.e., the search key is not found).

In a worst-case scenario, searching an array of 1024 elements will take only 10 comparisons by using a binary search. Repeatedly dividing 1024 by 2 (after each comparison we eliminate from consideration half the array) yields the values 512, 256, 128, 64, 32, 16, 8, 4, 2 and 1. The number 1024 (2^{10}) is divided by 2 only ten times to get the value 1. Dividing by 2 is equivalent to one comparison in the binary search algorithm. An array of 1,048,576 (2^{20}) elements takes a maximum of 20 comparisons to find the key. An array of one billion elements takes a maximum of 30 comparisons to find the key. This is a tremendous increase in performance over the linear search, which required comparing the search key with an average of half the elements in the array. For a one-billion-element array, the difference is between an average of 500 million comparisons and a maximum of 30 comparisons! The maximum number of comparisons needed for the binary search of any sorted array is the exponent of the first power of 2 greater than the number of elements in the array.

Figure 7.12 presents the iterative version of method **BinarySearch** (lines 59–85). The method receives two arguments—an integer array called **array** (the array to search) and an integer **key** (the search key). The array is passed to **BinarySearch** even though the array is an instance variable of the class. Once again, this is done because an array normally is passed to a method of another class for searching. Line 67 calculates the middle element of the array being searched by determining the number of elements in the array and dividing this value by 2. Recall that using the **/** operator with integers performs an integer division, which truncates the result. So, when there is an even number of elements in the array there is no "middle" element—the middle of our array is actually between two elements. When this occurs, the calculation on line 67 returns the smaller index of the two middle elements.

```
1   // Fig. 7.12: BinarySearchTest.cs
2   // Demonstrating a binary search of an array.
3
4   using System;
5   using System.Drawing;
6   using System.Collections;
7   using System.ComponentModel;
8   using System.Windows.Forms;
9   using System.Data;
10
11  public class BinarySearchTest : System.Windows.Forms.Form
12  {
13     private System.Windows.Forms.Label promptLabel;
14
15     private System.Windows.Forms.TextBox inputTextBox;
16
17     private System.Windows.Forms.Label resultLabel;
18     private System.Windows.Forms.Label displayLabel;
19     private System.Windows.Forms.Label outputLabel;
20
21     private System.Windows.Forms.Button findButton;
22
```

Fig. 7.12 Binary search of a sorted array. (Part 1 of 4.)

```
23          private System.ComponentModel.Container components = null;
24
25          int[] a = { 0, 2, 4, 6, 8, 10, 12, 14, 16,
26                      18, 20, 22, 24, 26, 28 };
27
28          // Visual Studio .NET generated code
29
30          // main entry point for application
31          [STAThread]
32          static void Main()
33          {
34             Application.Run( new BinarySearchTest() );
35          }
36
37          // searches for an element by calling
38          // BinarySearch and displaying results
39          private void findButton_Click( object sender,
40             System.EventArgs e )
41          {
42             int searchKey = Int32.Parse( inputTextBox.Text );
43
44             // initialize display string for the new search
45             outputLabel.Text = "Portions of array searched\n";
46
47             // perform the binary search
48             int element = BinarySearch( a, searchKey );
49
50             if ( element != -1 )
51                displayLabel.Text = "Found value in element " +
52                   element;
53             else
54                displayLabel.Text = "Value not found";
55
56          } // end findButton_Click
57
58          // searchs array for specified key
59          public int BinarySearch( int[] array, int key )
60          {
61             int low = 0;                        // low subscript
62             int high = array.Length - 1;  // high subscript
63             int middle;                         // middle subscript
64
65             while ( low <= high )
66             {
67                middle = ( low + high ) / 2;
68
69                // the following line displays the portion
70                // of the array currently being manipulated during
71                // each iteration of the binary search loop
72                BuildOutput( a, low, middle, high );
73
74                if ( key == array[ middle ] )   // match
75                   return middle;
```

Fig. 7.12 Binary search of a sorted array. (Part 2 of 4.)

```
76                 else if ( key < array[ middle ] )
77                    high = middle - 1;    // search low end of array
78                 else
79                    low = middle + 1;
80
81          } // end binary search
82
83          return -1;   // search key not found
84
85       } // end method BinarySearch
86
87       public void BuildOutput(
88          int[] array, int low, int mid, int high )
89       {
90          for ( int i = 0; i < array.Length; i++ )
91          {
92             if ( i < low || i > high )
93                outputLabel.Text += "     ";
94
95             // mark middle element in output
96             else if ( i == mid )
97                outputLabel.Text +=
98                   array[ i ].ToString( "00" ) + "* ";
99             else
100               outputLabel.Text +=
101                  array[ i ].ToString( "00" ) + "   ";
102         }
103
104         outputLabel.Text += "\n";
105
106      } // end BuildOutput
107
108 } // end class BinarySearchTest
```

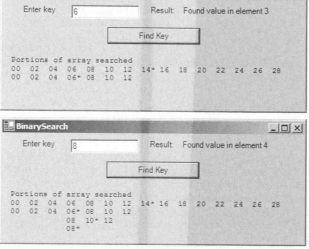

Fig. 7.12   Binary search of a sorted array. (Part 3 of 4.)

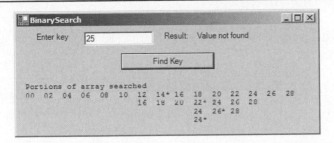

Fig. 7.12   Binary search of a sorted array. (Part 4 of 4.)

If **key** matches the **middle** element of a subarray (line 74), **BinarySearch** returns **middle** (the subscript of the current element), indicating that the value was found and the search is complete. If **key** does not match the **middle** element of a subarray, **Binary-Search** adjusts the **low** subscript or **high** subscript (both declared in the method) so that a smaller subarray can be searched. If **key** is less than the middle element (line 76), the **high** subscript is set to **middle - 1**, and the search continues on the elements from **low** to **middle - 1**. If **key** is greater than the middle element (line 78), the **low** subscript is set to **middle + 1**, and the search continues on the elements from **middle + 1** to **high**. These comparisons occur in the nested **if/else** structure on lines 74–79.

The program uses a 15-element array. The first power of 2 greater than the number of array elements is 16 (2^4)—so at most four comparisons are required to find the **key**. To illustrate this concept, method **BinarySearch** calls method **BuildOutput** (lines 87–106) to output each subarray during the binary search process. **BuildOutput** marks the middle element in each subarray with an asterisk (*****) to indicate the element with which the **key** is compared. Each search in this example results in a maximum of four lines of output—one per comparison. Note that the .NET framework includes a built-in array-searching capability that implements the binary-search algorithm. To search for the key 7 in the sorted array **a** in Fig. 7.12, you can use the statement

```
Array.BinarySearch( a, 7 );
```

7.9 Multiple-Subscripted Arrays

So far we have studied *single-subscripted* (or *one-dimensional*) arrays—i.e., those that contain single lists of values. In this section, we introduce *multiple-subscripted* (often called *multidimensional*) arrays. Such arrays require two or more subscripts to identify particular elements. Arrays that require two subscripts to identify a particular element commonly are called *double-subscripted arrays*. We concentrate on *double-subscripted arrays* (often called *two-dimensional arrays*). There are two types of multiple-subscripted arrays—*rectangular* and *jagged*. Rectangular arrays with two subscripts often represent *tables* of values consisting of information arranged in *rows* and *columns*, where each row is the same size, and each column is the same size. To identify a particular table element, we must specify the two subscripts—by convention, the first identifies the element's row and the second identifies the element's column. Multiple-subscripted arrays can have more than two subscripts. Figure 7.13 illustrates a double-subscripted array, **a**, containing three rows and four columns (i.e., a 3-by-4 array). An array with *m* rows and *n* columns is called an *m-by-n array*.

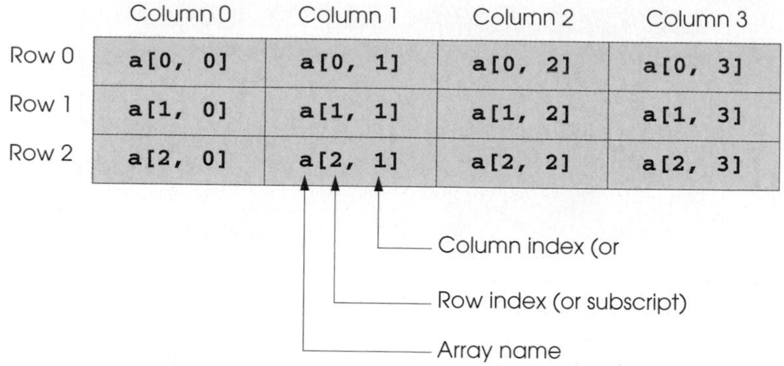

	Column 0	Column 1	Column 2	Column 3
Row 0	a[0, 0]	a[0, 1]	a[0, 2]	a[0, 3]
Row 1	a[1, 0]	a[1, 1]	a[1, 2]	a[1, 3]
Row 2	a[2, 0]	a[2, 1]	a[2, 2]	a[2, 3]

Column index (or

Row index (or subscript)

Array name

Fig. 7.13   Double-subscripted array with three rows and four columns.

Every element in array **a** is identified in Fig. 7.13 by an element name of the form **a[i , j]**, in which **a** is the name of the array, and **i** and **j** are the subscripts that uniquely identify the row and column of each element in **a**. Notice that the names of the elements in the first row all have a first subscript of **0**; the names of the elements in the fourth column all have a second subscript of **3**.

Multiple-subscripted arrays can be initialized in declarations like single-subscripted arrays. A double-subscripted array **b** with two rows and two columns could be declared and initialized with

```
int [,] b = new int [ 2, 2 ];

b[ 0, 0 ] = 1;
b[ 0, 1 ] = 2;
b[ 1, 0 ] = 3;
b[ 1, 1 ] = 4;
```

or this can be written on one line using an *initializer list* as shown below:

```
int [,] b = { { 1, 2 }, { 3, 4 } };
```

The values are grouped by row in braces. Thus, **1** and **2** initialize **b[0 , 0]** and **b[0 , 1]**, and **3** and **4** initialize **b[1 , 0]** and **b[1 , 1]**. The compiler determines the number of rows by counting the number of sub-initializer lists (represented by sets of braces) in the main initializer list. The compiler determines the number of columns in each row by counting the number of initializer values in the sub-initializer list for that row. Method **GetLength** returns the length of a particular array dimension. In the preceding example, **b.GetLength(0)** returns the length of the zeroth dimension of **b**, which is **2**.

Jagged arrays are maintained as arrays of arrays. Unlike in rectangular arrays, the arrays that compose jagged arrays can be of different lengths. The declaration

```
int [][] c = new int [ 2 ][];  // allocate rows

// allocate and initialize elements in row 0
c[ 0 ] = new int [] { 1, 2 };
```

```
                // allocate and initialize elements in row 0
                c[ 1 ] = new int[] { 3, 4, 5 };
```

creates integer array **c** with row **0** (which is an array itself) containing two elements (**1** and **2**), and row **1** containing three elements (**3**, **4** and **5**). The **Length** property of each sub-array can be used to determine the size of each column. For the jagged array **c**, the size of the **zeroth** column is **c[0].Length**, which is **2**.

The application in Fig. 7.14 demonstrates the initialization of double-subscripted arrays in declarations and the use of nested **for** loops to traverse the arrays (i.e., to manipulate each array element).

```
1    // Fig. 7.14: TwoDimensionalArrays.cs
2    // Initializing two-dimensional arrays.
3    using System;
4    using System.Drawing;
5    using System.Collections;
6    using System.ComponentModel;
7    using System.Windows.Forms;
8    using System.Data;
9
10   public class TwoDimensionalArrays : System.Windows.Forms.Form
11   {
12       private System.Windows.Forms.Button showOutputButton;
13       private System.Windows.Forms.Label outputLabel;
14
15       // Visual Studio .NET generated code
16
17       [STAThread]
18       static void Main()
19       {
20           Application.Run( new TwoDimensionalArrays() );
21       }
22
23       private void showOutputButton_Click( object sender,
24           System.EventArgs e )
25       {
26           // declaration and initialization of rectangular array
27           int[,] array1 = new int[,] { { 1, 2, 3 }, { 4, 5, 6 } };
28
29           // declaration and initialization of jagged array
30           int[][] array2 = new int[ 3 ][];
31           array2[ 0 ] = new int[] { 1, 2 };
32           array2[ 1 ] = new int[] { 3 };
33           array2[ 2 ] = new int[] { 4, 5, 6 };
34
35           outputLabel.Text = "Values in array1 by row are\n";
36
37           // output values in array1
38           for ( int i = 0; i < array1.GetLength( 0 ); i++ )
39           {
40               for ( int j = 0; j < array1.GetLength( 1 ); j++ )
41                   outputLabel.Text += array1[ i, j ] + "   ";
```

Fig. 7.14 Initializing multidimensional arrays. (Part 1 of 2.)

```
42
43                  outputLabel.Text += "\n";
44          }
45
46          outputLabel.Text += "\nValues in array2 by row are\n";
47
48          // output values in array2
49          for ( int i = 0; i < array2.Length; i++ )
50          {
51              for ( int j = 0; j < array2[ i ].Length; j++ )
52                  outputLabel.Text += array2[ i ][ j ] + "   ";
53
54              outputLabel.Text += "\n";
55          }
56
57      } // end method showOutputButton_Click
58  }
```

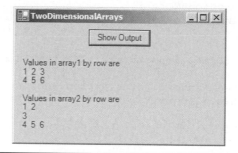

Fig. 7.14 Initializing multidimensional arrays. (Part 2 of 2.)

The declaration of **array1** (line 27) provides six initializers in two sublists. The first sublist initializes the first row of the array to the values 1, 2 and 3. The second sublist initializes the second row of the array to the values 4, 5 and 6. The declaration of **array2** (line 30) creates a jagged array of 3 arrays (specified by the 3 in the first set of square brackets). Lines 31–33 initialize each subarray so that the first subarray contains the values 1 and 2, the second contains the value 3 and the last contains the values 4, 5 and 6.

The **for** structure on lines 38–44 appends the elements of **array1** to **string output**. Note the use of a nested **for** structure to output the rows of each double-subscripted array. In the nested **for** structures for **array1**, we use method **GetLength** to determine the number of elements in each dimension of the array. Line 38 determines the number of rows in the array by invoking **array1.GetLength(0)**, and line 40 determines the number of columns in the array by invoking **array1.GetLength(1)**. Arrays with additional dimensions would require more deeply nested **for** loops to process.

The nested **for** structures on lines 49–55 output the elements of jagged array **array2**. Recall that a jagged array is essentially an array that contains additional arrays as its elements. Line 49 uses the **Length** property of **array2** to determine the number of rows in the jagged array. Line 51 determines the **Length** of each subarray with the expression **array2[i].Length**.

Many common array manipulations use **for** repetition structures. For the remainder of this section, we will focus on manipulations of jagged arrays. Imagine a jagged array **a**, which contains 3 rows, or arrays. The following **for** structure sets all the elements in the third row of array **a** to zero:

```
for ( int col = 0; col < a[ 2 ].Length; col++ )
   a[ 2 ][ col ] = 0;
```

We specified the *third* row; therefore, we know that the first subscript is always **2** (**0** is the first row and **1** is the second row). The **for** loop varies only the second subscript (i.e., the column subscript). Notice the use of **a[2].Length** in the **for** structure's conditional expression. This statement demonstrates that each row of **a** is an array in itself, and therefore the program can access a typical array's properties, such as **Length**. Assuming the length of array **a[2]** is **4**, the preceding **for** structure is equivalent to the assignment statements

```
a[ 2 ][ 0 ] = 0;
a[ 2 ][ 1 ] = 0;
a[ 2 ][ 2 ] = 0;
a[ 2 ][ 3 ] = 0;
```

The following nested **for** structure determines the total of all the elements in array **a**. We use **a.Length** in the conditional expression of the outer **for** structure to determine the number of rows in **a**, in this case, 3.

```
int total = 0;

for ( int row = 0; row < a.Length; row++ )

   for ( int col = 0; col < a[ row ].Length; col++ )
      total += a[ row ][ col ];
```

The **for** structure totals the elements of the array one row at a time. The outer **for** structure begins by setting the **row** subscript to **0**, so the elements of the first row may be totaled by the inner **for** structure. Then the outer **for** structure increments **row** to **1**, so the second row can be totaled. Finally, the outer **for** structure increments **row** to **2**, so the third row can be totaled. The result can be displayed when the nested **for** structure terminates.

The program in Fig. 7.15 performs several other array manipulations on 3-by-4 array **grades**. Each row of the array represents a student, and each column represents a grade on one of the four exams that the student took during the semester. The array manipulations are performed by four methods. Method **Minimum** (lines 64–76) determines the lowest grade of any student for the semester. Method **Maximum** (lines 79–91) determines the highest grade of any student for the semester. Method **Average** (lines 94–102) determines a particular student's semester average.

Methods **Minimum** and **Maximum** use array **grades** and the variables **students** (number of rows in the array) and **exams** (number of columns in the array). Each method loops through array **grades** by using nested **for** structures. Consider the nested **for** structure from method **Minimum** (lines 68–73). The outer **for** structure sets **i** (i.e., the row subscript) to **0** so the elements of the first row can be compared with variable **lowGrade** in the body of the inner **for** structure. The inner **for** structure loops through the four grades of a particular row and compares each grade with **lowGrade**. If a grade is less than **lowGrade**, then **lowGrade** is set to that grade. The outer **for** structure then increments the row subscript by **1**. The elements of the second row are compared with variable **lowGrade**. The outer **for** structure then increments the row subscript to **2**. The elements

```
1   // Fig. 7.15: DoubleArray.cs
2   // Manipulating a double-subscripted array.
3   using System;
4   using System.Drawing;
5   using System.Collections;
6   using System.ComponentModel;
7   using System.Windows.Forms;
8   using System.Data;
9
10  public class DoubleArray : System.Windows.Forms.Form
11  {
12     private System.Windows.Forms.Button showOutputButton;
13     private System.Windows.Forms.Label outputLabel;
14
15     int[][] grades;
16     int students, exams;
17
18     // Visual Studio .NET generated code
19
20     [STAThread]
21     static void Main()
22     {
23        Application.Run( new DoubleArray() );
24     }
25
26     private void showOutputButton_Click( object sender,
27        System.EventArgs e )
28
29     {
30        grades = new int[ 3 ][];
31        grades[ 0 ] =  new int[]{ 77, 68, 86, 73 };
32        grades[ 1 ] =  new int[]{ 96, 87, 89, 81 };
33        grades[ 2 ] =  new int[]{ 70, 90, 86, 81 };
34
35        students = grades.Length;        // number of students
36        exams = grades[ 0 ].Length;      // number of exams
37
38        // line up column headings
39        outputLabel.Text = "                     ";
40
41        // output the column headings
42        for ( int i = 0; i < exams; i++ )
43           outputLabel.Text += "[" + i + "]   ";
44
45        // output the rows
46        for ( int i = 0; i < students; i++ )
47        {
48           outputLabel.Text += "\ngrades[" + i + "]    ";
49
50           for ( int j = 0; j < exams; j++ )
51              outputLabel.Text += grades[ i ][ j ] + "    ";
52        }
```

Fig. 7.15   Example using double-subscripted arrays. (Part 1 of 3.)

```
53
54          outputLabel.Text += "\n\nLowest grade: " + Minimum() +
55             "\nHighest grade: " + Maximum() + "\n";
56
57          for ( int i = 0; i < students; i++ )
58             outputLabel.Text += "\nAverage for student " + i + " is " +
59                Average( grades[ i ] );
60
61      } // end method showOutputButton_Click
62
63      // find minimum grade in grades array
64      public int Minimum()
65      {
66         int lowGrade = 100;
67
68         for ( int i = 0; i < students; i++ )
69
70            for ( int j = 0; j < exams; j++ )
71
72               if ( grades[ i ][ j ] < lowGrade )
73                  lowGrade = grades[ i ][ j ];
74
75         return lowGrade;
76      }
77
78      // find maximum grade in grades array
79      public int Maximum()
80      {
81         int highGrade = 0;
82
83         for ( int i = 0; i < students; i++ )
84
85            for ( int j = 0; j < exams; j++ )
86
87               if ( grades[ i ][ j ] > highGrade )
88                  highGrade = grades[ i ][ j ];
89
90         return highGrade;
91      }
92
93      // determine average grade for a particular student
94      public double Average( int[] setOfGrades )
95      {
96         int total = 0;
97
98         for ( int i = 0; i < setOfGrades.Length; i++ )
99            total += setOfGrades[ i ];
100
101        return ( double ) total / setOfGrades.Length;
102     }
103
104 } // end class DoubleArray
```

Fig. 7.15 Example using double-subscripted arrays. (Part 2 of 3.)

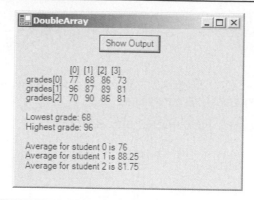

Fig. 7.15 Example using double-subscripted arrays. (Part 3 of 3.)

of the third row are compared with variable **lowGrade**. When execution of the nested structure is complete, **lowGrade** contains the smallest grade in the double-subscripted array. Method **Maximum** works similarly to method **Minimum**.

Method **Average** takes one argument—a single-subscripted array of test results for a particular student. When **Average** is called (line 59), the argument **grades[i]** specifies that a particular row of the double-subscripted array **grades** is to be passed to **Average**. For example, the argument **grades[1]** represents the four values (a single-subscripted array of grades) stored in the second row of the double-subscripted array **grades**. Remember that a jagged two-dimensional array is an array with elements that are single-subscripted arrays. Method **Average** calculates the sum of the array elements, divides the total by the number of test results and then returns the floating-point result cast as a **double** value (line 101).

7.10 `foreach` Repetition Structure

C# provides the **foreach** repetition structure for iterating through values in data structures, such as arrays. When used with one-dimensional arrays, **foreach** behaves like a **for** structure that iterates through the range of indices from **0** to the array's **Length**. Instead of a counter, **foreach** uses a variable to represent the value of each element. The program in Fig. 7.16 uses the **foreach** structure to determine the minimum value in a two-dimensional array of grades.

```
1   // Fig. 7.16: foreach.cs
2   // Demonstrating foreach structure.
3   using System;
4
5   class ForEach
6   {
7      // main entry point for the application
8      static void Main( string[] args )
9      {
```

Fig. 7.16 Using **foreach** with an array. (Part 1 of 2.)

```
10          int[,] gradeArray = { { 77, 68, 86, 73 },
11             { 98, 87, 89, 81 }, { 70, 90, 86, 81 } };
12
13          int lowGrade = 100;
14
15          foreach ( int grade in gradeArray )
16          {
17             if ( grade < lowGrade )
18                lowGrade = grade;
19          }
20
21          Console.WriteLine( "The minimum grade is: " + lowGrade );
22       }
23    }
```

```
The minimum grade is: 68
```

Fig. 7.16 Using **foreach** with an array. (Part 2 of 2.)

The header of the **foreach** structure (line 15) specifies a variable, **grade**, and an array, **gradeArray**. The **foreach** structure iterates through all elements in **grade-Array**, sequentially assigning each value to variable **grade**. Line 17 compares each value to variable **lowGrade**, which stores the lowest grade in the array.

For rectangular arrays, the repetition of the **foreach** structure begins with the element whose indices are all zero, then iterates through all possible combinations of indices, incrementing the rightmost index first. When the rightmost index reaches its upper bound, it is reset to zero, and the index to the left of it is incremented by 1. In this case, **grade** takes the values as they are ordered in the initializer list in lines 10–11. When all the grades have been processed, **lowGrade** is displayed (line 21).

Although many array calculations are handled best with a counter, **foreach** is useful when the indices of the elements are not important. The **foreach** structure is particularly useful for looping through arrays of objects, as we discuss in Chapter 10, Object-Oriented Programming: Polymorphism.

SUMMARY

- An array is a group of contiguous memory locations that all have the same name and type.
- To refer to a particular location or element in an array, specify the name of the array and the position number of the element within the array.
- The first element in every array is the zeroth element (i.e., element 0).
- The position number in square brackets is more formally called a subscript (or an index). This number must be an integer or an integer expression.
- To reference the ith element of a single-dimensional array, use i-1 as the index.
- The brackets that enclose the subscript of an array are operators that have the same level of precedence as parentheses.
- When arrays are allocated, the elements are initialized to zero for the numeric primitive-data-type variables, to **false** for **bool** variables or to **null** for reference types.
- Arrays may be declared to contain most data types.

- In an array of primitive data types, every element of the array contains one value of the declared data type of the array.

- In an array of a reference type, every element of the array is a reference to an object of the data type of the array. For example, every element of a **string** array is a reference to a **string** and that reference has the value **null** by default.

- The elements of single-dimensional and rectangular arrays can be allocated and initialized in the array declaration by following the declaration with an equal sign and a comma-separated initializer list enclosed in braces (**{** and **}**).

- A **const** variable must be declared and initialized in the same statement.

- Constants also are called named constants. They often are used to make a program more readable.

- Unlike its predecessors C and C++, .NET-compliant languages provide mechanisms to prevent accessing elements outside the bounds of the array.

- When a reference is made to a nonexistent element of an array, an **IndexOutOfRangeException** occurs.

- To pass an array argument to a method, specify the name of the array without any brackets.

- Although entire arrays are passed by reference, individual array elements of primitive data types are passed by value, as are simple variables.

- To pass an array element to a method, use the subscripted name of the array element as an argument in the method call.

- Sorting data (i.e., placing the data into a particular order, such as ascending or descending) is one of the most important computing applications.

- The chief virtue of the bubble sort is that it is easy to program. However, the bubble sort runs slowly, which becomes apparent when sorting large arrays.

- The linear search method works well for small or unsorted arrays. However, for large arrays, linear searching is inefficient.

- After each comparison, the binary search algorithm eliminates from consideration half the elements in the array being searched. The algorithm locates the middle array element and compares it to the search key. If they are equal, the search key has been found, and the subscript of that element is returned. Otherwise, the problem is reduced to searching half the array. If the search key is less than the middle array element, the first half of the array is searched; otherwise, the second half of the array is searched. The search continues until the search key is equal to the middle element of a subarray, or until the subarray consists of one element that is not equal to the search key (i.e., the search key is not found).

- The maximum number of comparisons needed for the binary search of any sorted array is the exponent of the first power of 2 that is greater than the number of elements in the array.

- There are two types of multiple-subscripted arrays—rectangular and jagged.

- In general, an array with m rows and n columns is referred to as an m-by-n array.

- Multiple-subscripted arrays can be initialized in declarations, as can single-subscripted arrays.

- The compiler determines the number of columns in each row by counting the number of initializer values in the sub-initializer list for that row.

- Jagged arrays are maintained as arrays of arrays. Unlike rectangular arrays, rows in jagged arrays can be of different lengths.

- Many common array manipulations use **for** repetition structures.

- When used with one-dimensional arrays, **foreach** behaves like a **for** structure that iterates through the range of indices from **0** to the array's **Length**.

- For rectangular arrays, the repetition of the **foreach** structure begins with the element whose indices are all zero, then iterates through all possible combinations of indices, incrementing the rightmost index first. When the rightmost index reaches its upper bound, it is reset to zero, and the index to the left of it is incremented by 1.

TERMINOLOGY

[], subscript operator
array allocated with **new**
array automatically initialized to zeros
array bounds
array declaration
array of arrays (jagged array)
bar chart
binary search algorithm
brute force
bubble sort
column
const
constant variable
declare an array
dice-rolling program
double-subscripted array
element
exception
foreach structure
graph information
histogram
ignoring element zero
initializer list
initializing double-subscripted arrays
    in declarations
innermost set of square brackets
invalid array reference
jagged array
key value
length of an array
linear search
lvalue ("left value")
m-by-*n* array

multiple-subscripted array
named constant
nested **for** loop
new operator
null
"off-by-one error"
one-dimensional array
partition
partitioning step
pass of a bubble sort
passing array element to method
passing array to method
position number
read-only variable
rectangular array
search key
searching
single-subscripted array
sinking sort
size of an array
sorting
square brackets, []
subarray
sub-initializer list
subscript
swap
table
table element
TextBox
"walk" past end of an array
zero-based counting
zeroth element

SELF-REVIEW EXERCISES

7.1   Fill in the blanks in each of the following statements:
    a) Lists and tables of values can be stored in _____.
    b) The elements of an array are related by the fact that they have the same _____ and
        _____.
    c) The number that refers to a particular element of an array is called its _____.
    d) The process of placing the elements of an array in order is called _____ the array.
    e) Determining if an array contains a certain key value is called _____ the array.
    f) Arrays that use two or more subscripts are referred to as _____ arrays.

g) _____ arrays are maintained as arrays of arrays.

h) A _____ variable must be declared and initialized in the same statement, or a syntax error will occur.

i) C# provides the _____ repetition structure for iterating through values in data structures, such as arrays.

j) When an invalid array reference is made, an _____ is generated.

7.2 State whether each of the following is *true* or *false*. If *false*, explain why.

a) An array can store many different types of values at the same time.

b) An array subscript normally should be of data type **float**.

c) An individual array element that is passed to a method and modified in that method will contain the modified value when the called method completes execution.

d) The maximum number of comparisons needed for the binary search of any sorted array is the exponent of the first power of 2 greater than the number of elements in the array.

e) There are two types of multiple-subscripted arrays—square and jagged.

f) A **const** variable must be declared and initialized in the same statement, or a syntax error will occur.

g) After each comparison, the binary search algorithm eliminates from consideration one third of the elements in the portion of the array that is being searched.

h) To determine the number of elements in an array, we can use the **NumberOfElements** property.

i) The linear search method works well for small or unsorted arrays.

j) In an *m*-by-*n* array, the *m* stands for the number of columns and the *n* stands for the number of rows.

ANSWERS TO SELF-REVIEW EXERCISES

7.1 a) arrays. b) name, type. c) subscript, index or position number. d) sorting. e) searching. f) multiple-subscripted. g.) Jagged. h) **const**. i) **foreach**. j) **IndexOutofRangeException**.

7.2 a) False. An array can store only values of the same type. b) False. An array subscript must be an integer or an integer expression. c) False. For individual primitive-data-type elements of an array, they are passed by value. If a reference to an array element is passed, then modifications to that array element are reflected in the original. An individual element of a reference type is passed to a method by reference. d) True. e) False. The two different types are called rectangular and jagged. f) True. g) False. After each comparison, the binary search algorithm eliminates from consideration half the elements in the portion of the array that is being searched. h) False. To determine the number of elements in an array, we can use the **Length** property. i) True. j) False. In an *m*-by-*n* array, the *m* stands for the number of rows and the *n* stands for the number of columns.

EXERCISES

7.3 Write statements to accomplish each of the following tasks:

a) Display the value of the seventh element of character array **f**.

b) Initialize each of the five elements of single-subscripted integer array **g** to **8**.

c) Total the elements of floating-point array **c** of 100 elements.

d) Copy 11-element array **a** into the first portion of array **b** containing 34 elements.

e) Determine the smallest and largest values contained in 99-element floating-point array **w**.

7.4 Use a single-subscripted array to solve the following problem: A company pays its salespeople on a commission basis. The salespeople receive $200 per week, plus 9% of their gross sales for that week. For example, a salesperson who grosses $5000 in sales in a week receives $200 plus 9% of $5000, or a total of $650. Write a program (using an array of counters) that determines how many of the salespeople earned salaries in each of the following ranges (assume that each salesperson's salary is truncated to an integer amount):

    a) $200–$299
    b) $300–$399
    c) $400–$499
    d) $500–$599
    e) $600–$699
    f) $700–$799
    g) $800–$899
    h) $900–$999
    i) $1000 and over

7.5   Use a single-subscripted array to solve the following problem: Read in 20 numbers, each of which is between 10 and 100, inclusive. As each number is read, print it only if it is not a duplicate of a number already read. Provide for the "worst case" (in which all 20 numbers are different). Use the smallest possible array to solve this problem.

7.6   (*Turtle Graphics*) The Logo language made famous the concept of *turtle graphics*. Imagine a mechanical turtle that walks around the room under the control of a program. The turtle holds a pen in one of two positions, up or down. While the pen is down, the turtle traces out shapes as it moves; while the pen is up, the turtle moves about without writing anything. In this problem, you will simulate the operation of the turtle and create a computerized sketchpad.

Use a 20-by-20 array **floor**, which is initialized to zeros. Read commands from an array that contains them. At all times, keep track of the current position of the turtle and whether the pen is up or down. Assume that the turtle always starts at position 0,0 of the floor with its pen up. The set of turtle commands your program must process are as follows:

Command	Meaning
1	Pen up
2	Pen down
3	Turn right
4	Turn left
5,10	Move forward 10 spaces (or a number other than 10)
6	Print the 20-by-20 array
9	End of data (sentinel)

Suppose that the turtle is somewhere near the center of the floor. The following "program" would draw and print a 12-by-12 square, leaving the pen in the up position:

```
2
5,12
3
5,12
3
5,12
3
5,12
1
6
9
```

As the turtle moves with the pen down, set the appropriate elements of array **floor** to **1**s. When the **6** command (print) is given, wherever there is a **1** in the array, display an asterisk or another character. Wherever there is a zero, display a blank. Write a program to implement the turtle graphics capabilities we have discussed. Write several turtle graphics programs to draw interesting shapes. Add commands to increase the power of your turtle graphics language.

SPECIAL SECTION: RECURSION EXERCISES

7.7   (*Palindromes*) A palindrome is a string that is spelled the same forward and backward. Some examples of palindromes are "radar," "able was i ere i saw elba" and, if blanks are ignored, "a man a plan a canal panama." Write a recursive method **TestPalindrome** that returns **true** if the string stored in the array is a palindrome and **false** otherwise. The method should ignore spaces and punctuation in the string.

7.8   (*Linear Search*) Modify Fig. 7.11 to use recursive method **LinearSearch** to perform a linear search of the array. The method should receive an integer array and the size of the array as arguments. If the search key is found, return the array subscript; otherwise, return –1.

7.9   (*Binary Search*) Modify the program in Fig. 7.12 to use a recursive method **Binary-Search** to perform the binary search of the array. The method should receive an integer array and the starting and ending subscript as arguments. If the search key is found, return the array subscript; otherwise, return –1.

7.10   (*Quicksort*) In this chapter, we discussed the sorting technique bubble sort. We now present the recursive sorting technique called Quicksort. The basic algorithm for a single-subscripted array of values is as follows:

a) *Partitioning Step*. Take the first element of the unsorted array and determine its final location in the sorted array (i.e., all values to the left of the element in the array are less than the element, and all values to the right of the element in the array are greater than the element). We now have one element in its proper location and two unsorted subarrays.

b) *Recursive Step*. Perform step 1 on each unsorted subarray.

Each time Step 1 is performed on a subarray, another element is placed in its final location of the sorted array, and two unsorted subarrays are created. When a subarray consists of one element, it must be sorted; therefore, that element is in its final location.

The basic algorithm seems simple, but how do we determine the final position of the first element of each subarray? Consider the following set of values (partitioning element in bold—it will be placed in its final location in the sorted array):

37   2   6   4   89   8   10   12   68   45

a) Starting from the rightmost element of the array, compare each element to **37** until an element less than **37** is found, then swap **37** and that element. The first element less than **37** is 12, so **37** and 12 are swapped. The new array is

12   2   6   4   89   8   10   **37**   68   45

Element 12 is italicized to indicate that it was just swapped with **37**.

b) Starting from the left of the array, but beginning with the element after 12, compare each element to **37** until an element greater than **37** is found, then swap **37** and that element. The first element greater than **37** is 89, so **37** and 89 are swapped. The new array is

12   2   6   4   **37**   8   10   *89*   68   45

    c) Starting from the right, but beginning with the element before 89, compare each element to **37** until an element less than **37** is found, then swap **37** and that element. The first element less than **37** is 10, so **37** and 10 are swapped. The new array is

         12   2   6   4   *10*   8   **37**   89   68   45

    d) Starting from the left, but beginning with the element after 10, compare each element to **37** until an element greater than **37** is found, then swap **37** and that element. There are no more elements greater than **37**, so when we compare **37** to itself, we know that **37** has been placed in its final location of the sorted array.

Once the partition has been applied to the previous array, there are two unsorted subarrays. The subarray with values less than 37 contains 12, 2, 6, 4, 10 and 8. The subarray with values greater than 37 contains 89, 68 and 45. The sort continues with both subarrays being partitioned in the same manner as the original array.

Using the preceding discussion, write recursive method **QuickSort** to sort a single-subscripted integer array. The method should receive as arguments an integer array, a starting subscript and an ending subscript. Method **Partition** should be called by **QuickSort** to perform the partitioning step.

7.11   (*Maze Traversal*) The following grid of **#**s and dots (**.**) is a double-subscripted array representation of a maze:

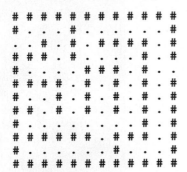

The **#**s represent the walls of the maze, and the dots represent squares in the possible paths through the maze. Moves can be made only to a location in the array that contains a dot.

There is a simple algorithm for walking through a maze that guarantees finding the exit (assuming there is an exit). If there is not an exit, you will arrive at the starting location again. Place your right hand on the wall to your right and begin walking forward. Never remove your hand from the wall. If the maze turns to the right, you follow the wall to the right. As long as you do not remove your hand from the wall, eventually you will arrive at the exit of the maze. There may be a shorter path than the one you have taken, but you are guaranteed to get out of the maze if you follow the algorithm.

Write recursive method **MazeTraverse** to walk through the maze. The method should receive as arguments a 12-by-12 character array representing the maze and the starting location of the maze. As **MazeTraverse** attempts to locate the exit from the maze, it should place the character **X** in each square in the path. The method should display the maze after each move so the user can watch as the maze is solved.

Object-Based Programming

Objectives

- To understand encapsulation and data hiding.
- To understand the concepts of data abstraction and abstract data types (ADTs).
- To be able to create, use and destroy objects.
- To be able to control access to object instance variables and methods.
- To be able to use properties to keep objects in consistent states.
- To understand the use of the **this** reference.
- To understand namespaces and assemblies.
- To be able to use the **Class View** and **Object Browser**.

My object all sublime
I shall achieve in time.
W. S. Gilbert

Is it a world to hide virtues in?
William Shakespeare, *Twelfth Night*

Your public servants serve you right.
Adlai Stevenson

Classes struggle, some classes triumph, others are eliminated.
Mao Zedong

This above all: to thine own self be true.
William Shakespeare, *Hamlet*

Outline

8.1 Introduction

In this chapter, we investigate object orientation in C#. Some readers might ask, why have we deferred this topic until now? There are several reasons. First, the objects we build in this chapter partially are composed of structured program pieces. To explain the organization of objects, we needed to establish a basis in structured programming with control structures. We also wanted to study methods in detail before introducing object orientation. Finally, we wanted to familiarize readers with arrays, which are C# objects.

In our discussions of object-oriented programs in Chapters 1–7, we introduced many basic concepts (i.c., "object think") and terminology (i.e., "object speak") that relate to C# object-oriented programming. We also discussed our program-development methodology: We analyzed typical problems that required programs to be built and determined what classes from the .NET Framework Class Library were needed to implement each program. We then selected appropriate instance variables and methods for each program and specified the manner in which an object of our class collaborated with objects from the .NET Framework classes to accomplish the program's overall goals.

Let us briefly review some key concepts and terminology of object orientation. Object orientation uses classes to *encapsulate* (i.e., wrap together) data (*attributes*) and methods (*behaviors*). Objects have the ability to hide their implementation from other objects (this principle is called *information hiding*). Although some objects can communicate with one another across well-defined *interfaces* (just like the driver's interface to a car includes a steering wheel, accelerator pedal, brake pedal and gear shift), objects are unaware of how other objects are implemented (just as the driver is unaware of how the steering, engine, brake and transmission mechanisms are implemented). Normally, implementation details are hidden within the objects themselves. Surely, it is possible to drive a car effectively without knowing the details of how engines, transmissions and exhaust systems work. Later, we will see why information hiding is so crucial to good software engineering.

In *procedural programming languages* (like C), programming tends to be *action oriented*. C# programming, however, is *object oriented*. In C, the unit of programming is the *function* (functions are called *methods* in C#). In C#, the unit of programming is the *class*. Objects eventually are *instantiated* (i.e., created) from these classes and functions are encapsulated within the "boundaries" of classes as methods.

C programmers concentrate on writing functions. They group actions that perform some task into a function and then group functions to form a program. Data are certainly important in C, but they exist primarily to support the actions that functions perform. The *verbs* in a system-requirements document describing the requirements for a new application help a C programmer determine the set of functions that will work together to implement the system.

By contrast, C# programmers concentrate on creating their own *user-defined types*, called *classes*. We also refer to classes as *programmer-defined types*. Each class contains both data and a set of methods that manipulate the data. The data components, or *data members*, of a class are called *member variables*, or *instance variables* (many C# programmers prefer the term *fields*).[1] Just as we call an instance of a built-in type—such as **int**—a *variable,* we call an instance of a user-defined type (i.e., a class) an *object*. In C#, attention is focused on classes, rather than on methods. The *nouns* in a system-requirements document help the C# programmer determine an initial set of classes with which to begin the design process. Programmers use these classes to instantiate objects that work together to implement the system.

This chapter explains how to create and use classes and objects, a subject known as *object-based programming (OBP)*. Chapters 9 and 10 introduce *inheritance* and *polymorphism*—key technologies that enable *object-oriented programming (OOP)*. Although we do not discuss inheritance in detail until Chapter 9, it is part of several class definitions in this chapter and has been used in several examples previously. For example, in the program of Section 4.13 (and several subsequent programs), we inherited a class from **System.Windows.Forms.Form** to create an application that executes in its own window.

 Software Engineering Observation 8.1

All C# objects are passed by reference.

8.2 Implementing a Time Abstract Data Type with a Class

Classes in C# facilitate the creation of *abstract data types (ADT)*, which hide their implementation from clients (or users of the class object). A problem in procedural programming

1. We sometimes use industry-standard terminology, such as data members and instance members. rather than C# terms such as fields, For a listing of C#-specific terminology, please see the C# Language Specification, which can be downloaded from **msdn.microsoft.com/vstudio/nextgen/technology/csharpdownload.asp**.

languages is that client code often is dependent on implementation details of the data used in the code. This dependency might necessitate rewriting the client code if the data implementation changes. ADTs eliminate this problem by providing implementation-independent *interfaces* to their clients. The creator of a class can change the internal implementation of that class without affecting the clients of that class.

Software Engineering Observation 8.2

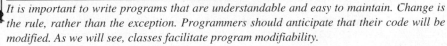

It is important to write programs that are understandable and easy to maintain. Change is the rule, rather than the exception. Programmers should anticipate that their code will be modified. As we will see, classes facilitate program modifiability.

The following example (and subsequent examples) will require multiple class definitions in the same project. To add a class to a project, select **Add Class...** from the **Project** menu. In the **Add New Item** dialog box that appears, enter the new class name in the **Name** text box and click the **Open** button. Note that the file name (ending with the **.cs** file extension) appears in the **Solution Explorer** below the project name.

Our next example consists of classes **Time1** (Fig. 8.1) and **TimeTest1** (Fig. 8.2). Class **Time1** contains the time of day in 24-hour clock format. Class **TimeTest1** contains method **Main**, which creates an instance of class **Time1** and demonstrates the features of that class.

```
1   // Fig. 8.1: Time1.cs
2   // Class Time1 maintains time in 24-hour format.
3
4   using System;
5
6   // Time1 class definition
7   public class Time1 : Object
8   {
9      private int hour;     // 0-23
10     private int minute;   // 0-59
11     private int second;   // 0-59
12
13     // Time1 constructor initializes instance variables to
14     // zero to set default time to midnight
15     public Time1()
16     {
17        SetTime( 0, 0, 0 );
18     }
19
20     // Set new time value in 24-hour format. Perform validity
21     // checks on the data. Set invalid values to zero.
22     public void SetTime(
23        int hourValue, int minuteValue, int secondValue )
24     {
25        hour = ( hourValue >= 0 && hourValue < 24 ) ?
26           hourValue : 0;
27        minute = ( minuteValue >= 0 && minuteValue < 60 ) ?
28           minuteValue : 0;
```

Fig. 8.1   **Time1** abstract data type represents the time in 24-hour format. (Part 1 of 2.)

```
29              second = ( secondValue >= 0 && secondValue < 60 ) ?
30                 secondValue : 0;
31
32          } // end method SetTime
33
34          // convert time to universal-time (24 hour) format string
35          public string ToUniversalString()
36          {
37              return String.Format(
38                 "{0:D2}:{1:D2}:{2:D2}", hour, minute, second );
39          }
40
41          // convert time to standard-time (12 hour) format string
42          public string ToStandardString()
43          {
44              return String.Format( "{0}:{1:D2}:{2:D2} {3}",
45                 ( ( hour == 12 || hour == 0 ) ? 12 : hour % 12 ),
46                 minute, second, ( hour < 12 ? "AM" : "PM" ) );
47          }
48
49      } // end class Time1
```

Fig. 8.1   **Time1** abstract data type represents the time in 24-hour format. (Part 2 of 2.)

In Fig. 8.1, line 7 begins the **Time1** class definition, indicating that class **Time1** inherits from class *Object* (namespace **System**). C# programmers use *inheritance* to create classes from existing classes. In fact, every class in C# (except **Object**) inherits from an existing class definition. On line 7, the **:** followed by class name **Object** indicates that class **Time1** inherits existing pieces of class **Object**. If a new class definition does not specify a **:** and class name to the right of the new class name, the new class implicitly inherits from class **Object**. It is not necessary to understand inheritance to learn the concepts and programs in this chapter. We explore inheritance and class **Object** in detail in Chapter 9.

The opening left brace (**{**) at line 8 and closing right brace (**}**) at line 49 delineate the *body* of class **Time1**. Any information that we place in this body is said to be encapsulated (i.e., wrapped) in the class. For example, lines 9–11 of class **Time1** declare three **int** variables—**hour**, **minute** and **second**—that represent the time of day in *universal-time* format (*24-hour clock* format). Variables declared in a class definition, but not inside a method definition, are called *instance variables*—each instance (object) of the class contains its own separate copy of the class's instance variables.

Keywords ***public*** and ***private*** are *member access modifiers*. Instance variables or methods with member access modifier **public** are accessible wherever the program has a reference to a **Time1** object. However, instance variables or methods declared with member access modifier **private** are accessible only in that class definition. A class's **public** members and **private** members can be intermixed.

Good Programming Practice 8.1

*Every instance variable or method definition should be preceded by a member access modifier. The default access modifier for class members is **private**.*

Good Programming Practice 8.2

Members in a class definition should be grouped by their member access modifiers to enhance clarity and readability.

Lines 9–11 declare each of the three **int** instance variables—**hour**, **minute** and **second**—with member access modifier **private**, indicating that these instance variables of the class are accessible only to members of the class—this is known as *data hiding*. When an object of the class encapsulates such instance variables, only methods of that object's class can access the variables. Normally, instance variables are declared **private** and methods are declared **public**. However, it is possible to have **private** methods and **public** instance variables, as we will see later. Often, **private** methods are called *utility methods*, or *helper methods*, because they can be called only by other methods of that class. The purpose of utility methods is to support the operation of a class's other methods. Using **public** data in a class is an uncommon and dangerous programming practice. Providing such access to data members is unsafe—foreign code (i.e., code in other classes) could set **public** data members to invalid values, producing potentially disastrous results.

Good Programming Practice 8.3

We prefer to list instance variables of a class first, so that, when reading the code, programmers see the name and type of each instance variable before it is used in the methods of the class.

Good Programming Practice 8.4

*Even though **private** and **public** members can be intermixed, list all the **private** members of a class first in one group, then list all the **public** members in another group.*

Software Engineering Observation 8.3

*Declare all instance variables of a class as **private**. The architecture of accessing **private** data through **public** properties which first validate the data allows the developer to ensure that an object's data remains in a consistent state.*

Software Engineering Observation 8.4

*Make a class member **private** if there is no reason for that member to be accessed outside of the class definition.*

Classes often include *access methods* that can read or display data. Another common use for access methods is to test the truth of conditions—such methods often are called *predicate methods*. For example, we could design predicate method **IsEmpty** for a *container class*—a class capable of holding many objects, such as a linked list, a stack or a queue. (These data structures are discussed in detail in Chapter 23, Data Structures.) **IsEmpty** would return **true** if the container is empty and **false** otherwise. A program might test **IsEmpty** before attempting to read another item from the container object. Similarly, a program might test another predicate method (e.g., **IsFull**) before attempting to insert an item into a container object.

Class **Time1** contains constructor **Time1** (lines 15–18) and methods **SetTime** (lines 22–32), **ToUniversalString** (lines 35–39) and **ToStandardString** (lines 42–47). These are the *public* methods (also called the *public* services or the *public* interface) of the class. *Clients* of class **Time1**, such as class **TimeTest1** (Fig. 8.2), use a **Time1**'s **public** methods to manipulate the data stored in **Time1** objects or to cause class **Time1** to perform some service.

Lines 15–18 define the *constructor* of class **Time1**. A class's constructor initializes objects of that class. When a program creates an object of class **Time1** with operator **new**, the constructor automatically is called to initialize the object. Class **Time1**'s constructor calls method **SetTime** (lines 22–32) to initialize instance variables **hour**, **minute** and **second** to **0** (representing midnight). Constructors can take arguments, but cannot return values. As we will see, a class can have overloaded constructors. An important difference between constructors and other methods is that constructors cannot specify a return type. Generally, constructors are declared **public**. Note that the constructor name must be the same as the class name.

Common Programming Error 8.1

*Attempting to **return** a value from a constructor is a syntax error.*

Method **SetTime** (lines 22–32) is a **public** method that receives three **int** parameters and uses them to set the time. A conditional expression tests each argument to determine whether the value is in a specified range. For example, the **hour** value must be greater than or equal to 0 and less than 24, because universal-time format represents hours as integers from 0 to 23. Similarly, both minute and second values must be greater than or equal to 0 and less than 60. Any values outside these ranges are invalid values and default to zero. Setting invalid values to zero ensures that a **Time1** object always contains valid data (because, in this example, zero is a valid value for **hour**, **minute** and **second**). When users supply invalid data to **SetTime**, the program might want to indicate that the time was invalid. In Chapter 11, we discuss exception handling, which can be used to indicate invalid initialization values.

Software Engineering Observation 8.5

Always define a class so that each of its instance variables always contains valid values.

Method **ToUniversalString** (lines 35–39) takes no arguments and returns a **string** in universal-time format, consisting of six digits—two for the hour, two for the minute and two for the second. For example, if the time were 1:30:07 PM, method **ToUniversalString** would return **13:30:07**. Lines 37–38 use **String** method **Format** to configure the universal time string. Line 37 passes to **Format** the *format string* **"{0:D2}:{1:D2}:{2:D2}"**, which contains several *format specifications* indicating that arguments **0**, **1** and **2** (the first three arguments after the format string argument) should each have the format **D2** (a two-digit base 10 decimal number format) for display purposes. The **D2** format specification causes single-digit values to appear as two digits with a leading **0** (e.g., **8** would be represented as **08**). The two colons that separate the curly braces **}** and **{** are the colons that separate the hour from the minute and the minute from the second in the resulting **string**.

Method **ToStandardString** (lines 42–47) takes no arguments and returns a **string** in standard-time format, consisting of the **hour**, **minute** and **second** values separated by colons and followed by an AM or a PM indicator (e.g., **1:27:06 PM**). Like method **ToUniversalString**, method **ToStandardString** uses **String** method **Format** to format the **minute** and **second** as two-digit values with leading zeros if necessary. Line 45 determines the value for **hour** in the **string**—if the **hour** is **0** or **12** (AM or PM), the **hour** appears as 12; otherwise, the **hour** appears as a value from 1–11.

After defining the class, we can use it as a type in declarations such as

```
Time1 sunset;   // reference to a Time1 object
```

The class name (**Time1**) is a type name. A class can yield many objects, just as a primitive data type, such as **int**, can yield many variables. Programmers can create class types as needed; this is one reason why C# is known as an *extensible language.*

Class **TimeTest1** (Fig. 8.2) uses an instance of class **Time1**. Method **Main** (lines 11–40) declares and initializes **Time1** instance **time** (line 13). When the object is instantiated, *operator **new*** allocates the memory in which the **Time1** object will be stored, then calls the **Time1** constructor (lines 15–18 of Fig. 8.1) to initialize the instance variables of the **Time1** object. As mentioned before, this constructor invokes method **SetTime** of class **Time1** to initialize each **private** instance variable to **0**. Operator **new** (line 13 of Fig. 8.2) then returns a reference to the newly created object; this reference is assigned to **time**.

```
1    // Fig. 8.2: TimeTest1.cs
2    // Demonstrating class Time1.
3
4    using System;
5    using System.Windows.Forms;
6
7    // TimeTest1 uses creates and uses a Time1 object
8    class TimeTest1
9    {
10       // main entry point for application
11       static void Main( string[] args )
12       {
13          Time1 time = new Time1();   // calls Time1 constructor
14          string output;
15
16          // assign string representation of time to output
17          output = "Initial universal time is: " +
18             time.ToUniversalString() +
19             "\nInitial standard time is: " +
20             time.ToStandardString();
21
22          // attempt valid time settings
23          time.SetTime( 13, 27, 6 );
24
25          // append new string representations of time to output
26          output += "\n\nUniversal time after SetTime is: " +
27             time.ToUniversalString() +
28             "\nStandard time after SetTime is: " +
29             time.ToStandardString();
30
31          // attempt invalid time settings
32          time.SetTime( 99, 99, 99 );
33
```

Fig. 8.2   Using an abstract data type. (Part 1 of 2.)

```
34              output += "\n\nAfter attempting invalid settings: " +
35                  "\nUniversal time: " + time.ToUniversalString() +
36                  "\nStandard time: " + time.ToStandardString();
37
38          MessageBox.Show( output, "Testing Class Time1" );
39
40      } // end method Main
41
42  } // end class TimeTest1
```

Fig. 8.2   Using an abstract data type. (Part 2 of 2.)

Software Engineering Observation 8.6

*Note the relationship between operator **new** and the constructor of a class. When operator **new** creates an object of a class, that class's constructor is called to initialize the object's instance variables.*

Note that the **TimeTest.cs** file does not use keyword **using** to import the namespace that contains class **Time1**. If a class is in the same namespace as the class that uses it, the **using** statement is not required. Every class in C# is part of a namespace. If a programmer does not specify a namespace for a class, the class is placed in the *default namespace*, which includes all compiled classes in the current directory that do not reside in a namespace. In Visual Studio, this current directory is the one in which the current project resides. We must specify **using** statements for classes from the .NET Framework, because they are defined outside the namespace of each new application we create. Note that **using** statements are not required if the program fully qualifies the name of each class by preceding the class name with its namespace name and a dot operator. For example, a program can invoke class **MessageBox**'s **Show** method as follows:

```
System.Windows.Forms.MessageBox.Show( "Your message here" );
```

However, such lengthy names can be cumbersome.

Line 14 declares **string** reference **output** to store the **string** containing the results, which later will be displayed in a **MessageBox**. Lines 17–20 assign to **output** the time in universal-time format (by invoking method **ToUniversalString** of the **Time1** object) and standard-time format (by invoking method **ToStandardString** of the **Time1** object). Note the syntax of the method call in each case—the reference **time** is followed by the member access operator (**.**) followed by the method name. The reference name specifies the object that will receive the method call.

Line 23 sets the time for the **Time1** object to which **time** refers by passing valid hour, minute and second arguments to **Time1** method **SetTime**. Lines 26–29 append to **output** the new time in both universal and standard formats to confirm that the time was set correctly.

To illustrate that method **SetTime** validates the values passed to it, line 32 passes invalid time arguments to method **SetTime**. Lines 34–36 append to **output** the new time in both formats. All three values passed to **SetTime** are invalid, so instance variables **hour**, **minute** and **second** are set to **0**. Line 38 displays a **MessageBox** with the results of our program. Notice in the last two lines of the output window that the time was indeed set to midnight when invalid arguments were passed to **SetTime**.

Time1 is our first example of a class that does not contain method **Main**. Thus, class **Time1** cannot be used to begin program execution. Class **TimeTest1** defines a **Main** method, so class **TimeTest1** can be used to begin program execution. A class containing method **Main** also is known as the *entry point* into the program.

Note that the program declares instance variables **hour**, **minute** and **second** as **private**. Such instance variables are not accessible outside the class in which they are defined. A class's clients should not be concerned with the data representation of that class. Clients of a class should be interested only in the services provided by that class. For example, the class could represent the time internally as the number of seconds that have elapsed since the previous midnight. Suppose the data representation changes. Clients still are able to use the same **public** methods and obtain the same results without being aware of the change in internal representation. In this sense, the implementation of a class is said to be *hidden* from its clients.

Software Engineering Observation 8.7

Information hiding promotes program modifiability and simplifies the client's perception of a class.

Software Engineering Observation 8.8

Clients of a class can (and should) use the class without knowing the internal details of how the class is implemented. If the class implementation changes (to improve performance, for example), but the class interface remains constant, the client's source code need not change. This makes it much easier to modify systems.

In this program, the **Time1** constructor initializes the instance variables to **0** (the universal time equivalent of 12 AM) to ensure that the object is created in a *consistent state*— i.e., all instance variables have valid values. The instance variables of a **Time1** object cannot store invalid values, because the constructor, which calls **SetTime**, is called to initialize the instance variables when the **Time1** object is created. Method **SetTime** scrutinizes subsequent attempts by a client to modify the instance variables.

Normally, the instance variables of a class are initialized in that class's constructor, but they also can be initialized when they are declared in the class body. If a programmer does not initialize instance variables explicitly, the compiler implicitly initializes them. When this occurs, the compiler sets primitive numeric variables to **0**, **bool** values to **false** and references to **null**.

Methods **ToUniversalString** and **ToStandardString** take no arguments, because, by default, these methods manipulate the instance variables of the particular **Time1** object on which they are invoked. This often makes method calls more concise than conventional function calls in procedural programming langauages. It also reduces the likelihood of passing the wrong arguments, the wrong types of arguments or the wrong number of arguments.

Software Engineering Observation 8.9

The use of an object-oriented programming approach often simplifies method calls by reducing the number of parameters that must be passed. This benefit of object-oriented programming derives from the fact that encapsulation of instance variables and methods within an object gives the object's methods the right to access the object's instance variables.

Classes simplify programming, because the client need be concerned only with the **public** operations encapsulated in the object. Usually, such operations are designed to be client-oriented, rather than implementation-oriented. Clients are neither aware of, nor involved in, a class's implementation. Interfaces change less frequently than do implementations. When an implementation changes, implementation-dependent code must change accordingly. By hiding the implementation, we eliminate the possibility that other program parts will become dependent on the class-implementation details.

Often, programmers do not have to create classes "from scratch." Rather, they can derive classes from other classes that provide behaviors required by the new classes. Classes also can include references to objects of other classes as members. Such *software reuse* can greatly enhance programmer productivity. Chapter 9 discusses *inheritance*—the process by which new classes are derived from existing classes. Section 8.8 discusses *composition* (or *aggregation*), in which classes include as members references to objects of other classes.

8.3 Class Scope

In Section 6.13, we discussed method scope; now, we discuss class *scope*. A class's instance variables and methods belong to that class's scope. Within a class's scope, class members are immediately accessible to all of that class's methods and can be referenced by name. Outside a class's scope, class members cannot be referenced directly by name. Those class members that are visible (such as **public** members) can be accessed only through a "handle" (i.e., members can be referenced via the format *referenceName.memberName*).

If a variable is defined in a method, only that method can access the variable (i.e., the variable is a local variable of that method). Such variables are said to have *block scope*. If a method defines a variable that has the same name as a variable with class scope (i.e., an instance variable), the method-scope variable hides the class-scope variable in that method's scope. A hidden instance variable can be accessed in a method by preceding its name with the keyword **this** and the dot operator, as in **this.hour**. We discuss keyword **this** in Section 8.9.

8.4 Controlling Access to Members

The member access modifiers **public** and **private** control access to a class's data and methods. (In Chapter 9, we introduce the additional access modifiers **protected** and **internal**.)

As previously stated, **public** methods present to the class's clients a view of the *services* that the class provides (i.e., the **public** interface of the class). Previously, we mentioned the merits of writing methods that perform only one task. If a method must execute other tasks to calculate its final result, these tasks should be performed by a helper method. A client does not need to call these helper methods, nor does it need to be concerned with how the class uses its helper methods. For these reasons, helper methods are declared as **private** members of a class.

Common Programming Error 8.2

*Attempting to access a **private** class member from outside that class is a compiler error.*

The application of Fig. 8.3 (which uses the **Time1** class from Fig. 8.1) demonstrates that **private** class members are not accessible outside the class. Lines 12–14 attempt to access the **private** instance variables **hour**, **minute** and **second** of the **Time1** object to which **time** refers. When this program is compiled, the compiler generates errors stating that the **private** members **hour**, **minute** and **second** are not accessible.

Access to **private** data should be controlled carefully by a class's methods. To allow clients to read the values of **private** data, the class can define a *property* that enables client code to access this **private** data safely. Properties, which we discuss in detail in Section 8.7, contain *accessor methods* that handle the details of modifying and returning data. A property definition can contain a **get** *accessor*, a **set** *accessor* or both. A **get** accessor enables a client to read a **private** data value; a **set** accessor enables the client to modify that value. Such modification would seem to violate the notion of **private** data. However, a **set** accessor can provide data-validation capabilities (such as range checking) to ensure that the value is set properly. A **set** accessor also can translate between the format of the data used in the interface and the format used in the underlying implementation. Similarly, a **get** accessor need not expose the data in "raw" format; rather, the **get** accessor can edit the data and limit the client's view of that data.

```
1   // Fig. 8.3: RestrictedAccess.cs
2   // Demonstrate compiler errors from attempt to access
3   // private class members.
4
5   class RestrictedAccess
6   {
7      // main entry point for application
8      static void Main( string[] args )
9      {
10        Time1 time = new Time1();
11
12        time.hour = 7;
13        time.minute = 15;
14        time.second = 30;
15     }
16
17  } // end class RestrictedAccess
```

Fig. 8.3   Accessing **private** class members from client code generates syntax errors. (Part 1 of 2.)

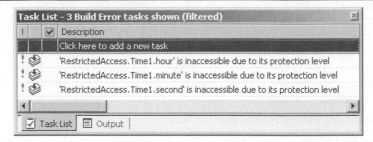

Fig. 8.3   Accessing **private** class members from client code generates syntax errors. (Part 2 of 2.)

Software Engineering Observation 8.10

*Class designers need not provide **set** or **get** accessors for each **private** data member; these capabilities should be provided only when doing so makes sense.*

Software Engineering Observation 8.11

*Declaring the instance variables of a class as **private** and the methods and properties of the class as **public** facilitates debugging, because problems with data manipulations are localized to the class methods that manipulate that data.*

8.5 Initializing Class Objects: Constructors

When a program creates an instance of a class, the program invokes the class's constructor to initialize the class's instance variables (data members). A class can contain overloaded constructors to provide multiple ways to initialize objects of that class. Instance variables can be initialized either by a constructor or when they are declared in the class body. Regardless of whether instance variables receive explicit initialization values, the instance variables always are initialized. In such cases, instance variables receive their default values (**0** for primitive numeric type variables, **false** for **bool** variable and **null** for references).

Performance Tip 8.1

Because instance variables always are initialized to default values by the runtime, avoid initializing instance variables to their default values in the constructor.

Software Engineering Observation 8.12

When appropriate, provide a constructor to ensure that every object is initialized with meaningful values.

When creating an object of a class, the programmer can provide *initializers* in parentheses to the right of the class name. These initializers are the arguments to the constructor. In general, declarations take the form:

> *ClassName objectReference* = **new** *ClassName* (*arguments*) **;**

where *objectReference* is a reference of the appropriate data type, **new** indicates that an object is being created, *ClassName* indicates the type of the new object (and the name of the constructor being called) and *arguments* specifies a comma-separated list of the values used by the constructor to initialize the object. Figure 8.4 demonstrates using initializers and overloaded constructors.

If a class does not define any constructors, the compiler provides a *default* (*no-argument*) *constructor*. This compiler-provided default constructor contains no code (i.e., the constructor has an empty body) and takes no parameters. The programmer also can provide a default constructor, as we demonstrated in class **Time1** (Fig. 8.1). Programmer-provided default constructors can have code in their bodies.

Common Programming Error 8.3

If a class has constructors, but none of the **public** *constructors is a default constructor, and a program attempts to call a no-argument constructor to initialize an object of the class, a compilation error occurs. A constructor can be called with no arguments only if there are no constructors for the class (in which case the compiler-provided default constructor is called) or if the class defines a* **public** *no-argument constructor.*

8.6 Using Overloaded Constructors

Like methods, constructors of a class can be overloaded. The **Time1** constructor in Fig. 8.1 initialized **hour**, **minute** and **second** to **0** (i.e., 12 midnight in universal time) via a call to the class **SetTime** method. However, class **Time2** (Fig. 8.4) overloads the constructor to provide a variety of ways to initialize **Time2** objects. Each constructor calls **Time2** method **SetTime**, which ensures that the object begins in a consistent state by setting out-of-range values to zero. C# invokes the appropriate constructor by matching the number, types and order of the arguments specified in the constructor call with the number, types and order of the parameters specified in each constructor definition.

```
1   // Fig. 8.4: Time2.cs
2   // Class Time2 provides overloaded constructors.
3
4   using System;
5
6   // Time2 class definition
7   public class Time2
8   {
9      private int hour;     // 0-23
10     private int minute;   // 0-59
11     private int second;   // 0-59
12
13     // Time2 constructor initializes instance variables to
14     // zero to set default time to midnight
15     public Time2()
16     {
17        SetTime( 0, 0, 0 );
18     }
19
20     // Time2 constructor: hour supplied, minute and second
21     // defaulted to 0
22     public Time2( int hour )
23     {
24        SetTime( hour, 0, 0 );
25     }
```

Fig. 8.4   Overloaded constructors provide flexible object-initialization options. (Part 1 of 2.)

```
26
27      // Time2 constructor: hour and minute supplied, second
28      // defaulted to 0
29      public Time2( int hour, int minute )
30      {
31          SetTime( hour, minute, 0 );
32      }
33
34      // Time2 constructor: hour, minute and second supplied
35      public Time2( int hour, int minute, int second )
36      {
37          SetTime( hour, minute, second );
38      }
39
40      // Time2 constructor: initialize using another Time2 object
41      public Time2( Time2 time )
42      {
43          SetTime( time.hour, time.minute, time.second );
44      }
45
46      // Set new time value in 24-hour format. Perform validity
47      // checks on the data. Set invalid values to zero.
48      public void SetTime(
49          int hourValue, int minuteValue, int secondValue )
50      {
51          hour = ( hourValue >= 0 && hourValue < 24 ) ?
52              hourValue : 0;
53          minute = ( minuteValue >= 0 && minuteValue < 60 ) ?
54              minuteValue : 0;
55          second = ( secondValue >= 0 && secondValue < 60 ) ?
56              secondValue : 0;
57      }
58
59      // convert time to universal-time (24 hour) format string
60      public string ToUniversalString()
61      {
62          return String.Format(
63              "{0:D2}:{1:D2}:{2:D2}", hour, minute, second );
64      }
65
66      // convert time to standard-time (12 hour) format string
67      public string ToStandardString()
68      {
69          return String.Format( "{0}:{1:D2}:{2:D2} {3}",
70              ( ( hour == 12 || hour == 0 ) ? 12 : hour % 12 ),
71              minute, second, ( hour < 12 ? "AM" : "PM" ) );
72      }
73
74  } // end class Time2
```

Fig. 8.4   Overloaded constructors provide flexible object-initialization options. (Part 2 of 2.)

Because most of the code in class **Time2** is identical to that in class **Time1**, this discussion concentrates only on the overloaded constructors. Lines 15–18 define the no-argument constructor that sets the time to midnight. Lines 22–25 define a **Time2** constructor that receives a single **int** argument representing the **hour** and sets the time using the specified **hour** value and zero for the **minute** and **second**. Lines 29–32 define a **Time2** constructor that receives two **int** arguments representing the **hour** and **minute** and sets the time using those values and zero for the **second**. Lines 35–38 define a **Time2** constructor that receives three **int** arguments representing the **hour**, **minute** and **second** and uses those values to set the time. Lines 41–44 define a **Time2** constructor that receives a reference to another **Time2** object. When this last constructor is called, the values from the **Time2** argument are used to initialize the **hour**, **minute** and **second** values of the new **Time2** object. Even though class **Time2** declares **hour**, **minute** and **second** as **private** (lines 9–11), the **Time2** constructor can access these values in its **Time2** argument directly using the expressions **time.hour**, **time.minute** and **time.second**.

Software Engineering Observation 8.13

*When one object of a class has a reference to another object of the same class, the first object can access all the second object's data and methods (including those that are **private**).*

Notice that the second, third and fourth constructors (lines 22, 29 and 35) have some arguments in common and that those arguments are kept in the same order. For instance, the constructor that begins on line 29 has as its two arguments an integer representing the hour and an integer representing the minute. The constructor on line 35 has these same two arguments in the same order, followed by its last argument (an integer representing the second).

Good Programming Practice 8.5

When defining overloaded constructors, keep the order of arguments as similar as possible; this makes client programming easier.

Constructors do not specify return types; doing so results in syntax errors. Also, notice that each constructor receives a different number or different types of arguments. Even though only two of the constructors receive values for the **hour**, **minute** and **second**, each constructor calls **SetTime** with values for **hour**, **minute** and **second** and uses zeros for the missing values to satisfy **SetTime**'s requirement of three arguments.

Class **TimeTest2** (Fig. 8.5) starts the application that demonstrates the use of overloaded constructors (Fig. 8.4). Lines 15–20 create six **Time2** objects that invoke various constructors of the class. Line 15 invokes the no-argument constructor by placing an empty set of parentheses after the class name. Lines 16–20 invoke the **Time2** constructors that receive arguments. To invoke the appropriate constructor, pass the proper number, types and order of arguments (specified by the constructor's definition) to that constructor. For example, line 16 invokes the constructor that is defined in lines 22–25 of Fig. 8.4. Lines 22–47 invoke methods **ToUniversalString** and **ToStandardString** for each **Time2** object to demonstrate that the constructors initialize the objects correctly.

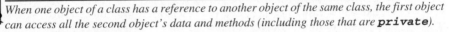

```
1   // Fig. 8.5: TimeTest2.cs
2   // Using overloaded constructors.
3
```

Fig. 8.5   Overloaded constructor demonstration. (Part 1 of 3.)

```
4   using System;
5   using System.Windows.Forms;
6
7   // TimeTest2 demonstrates constructors of class Time2
8   class TimeTest2
9   {
10     // main entry point for application
11     static void Main( string[] args )
12     {
13        Time2 time1, time2, time3, time4, time5, time6;
14
15        time1 = new Time2();                  // 00:00:00
16        time2 = new Time2( 2 );               // 02:00:00
17        time3 = new Time2( 21, 34 );          // 21:34:00
18        time4 = new Time2( 12, 25, 42 );      // 12:25:42
19        time5 = new Time2( 27, 74, 99 );      // 00:00:00
20        time6 = new Time2( time4 );           // 12:25:42
21
22        String output = "Constructed with: " +
23           "\ntime1: all arguments defaulted" +
24           "\n\t" + time1.ToUniversalString() +
25           "\n\t" + time1.ToStandardString();
26
27        output += "\ntime2: hour specified; minute and " +
28           "second defaulted" +
29           "\n\t" + time2.ToUniversalString() +
30           "\n\t" + time2.ToStandardString();
31
32        output += "\ntime3: hour and minute specified; " +
33           "second defaulted" +
34           "\n\t" + time3.ToUniversalString() +
35           "\n\t" + time3.ToStandardString();
36
37        output += "\ntime4: hour, minute, and second specified" +
38           "\n\t" + time4.ToUniversalString() +
39           "\n\t" + time4.ToStandardString();
40
41        output += "\ntime5: all invalid values specified" +
42           "\n\t" + time5.ToUniversalString() +
43           "\n\t" + time5.ToStandardString();
44
45        output += "\ntime6: Time2 object time4 specified" +
46           "\n\t" + time6.ToUniversalString() +
47           "\n\t" + time6.ToStandardString();
48
49        MessageBox.Show( output,
50           "Demonstrating Overloaded Constructors" );
51
52     } // end method Main
53
54  } // end class TimeTest2
```

Fig. 8.5   Overloaded constructor demonstration. (Part 2 of 3.)

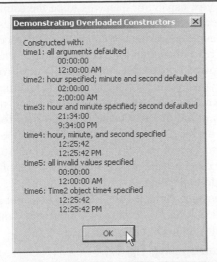

Fig. 8.5 Overloaded constructor demonstration. (Part 3 of 3.)

Each **Time2** constructor can be written to include a copy of the appropriate statements from method **SetTime**. This might be slightly more efficient, because it eliminates the extra call to **SetTime**. However, consider what would happen if the programmer were to change the representation of the time from three **int** values (requiring 12 bytes of memory) to a single **int** value representing the total number of seconds that have elapsed in the day (requiring 4 bytes of memory). Placing identical code in the **Time2** constructors and method **SetTime** makes such a change in the class definition more difficult, because every constructor's body would require modifications to manipulate the data as a single **int** rather than three **int**s. If the **Time2** constructors call **SetTime** directly, any changes to the implementation of **SetTime** must be made only once, in the body of **Set-Time**. This reduces the likelihood of introducing a programming error when altering the implementation, because we make only one change in the class, rather than changing every constructor and method **SetTime**.

Software Engineering Observation 8.14

If a method of a class provides functionality required by a constructor (or other method) of the class, call that method from the constructor (or other method). This simplifies the maintenance of the code and reduces the likelihood of introducing errors into the code.

8.7 Properties

Methods of a class can manipulate that class's **private** instance variables. A typical manipulation might be the adjustment of a customer's bank balance—a **private** instance variable of a class **BankAccount**—by a **ComputeInterest** method.

Classes often provide **public** *properties* to allow clients to *set* (i.e., assign values to) or *get* (i.e., obtain the values of) **private** instance variables. For example, in Fig. 8.6, we create three properties—**Hour**, **Minute** and **Second**—which access variables **hour**, **minute** and **second**, respectively. Each property contains a *get accessor* (to retrieve the field value) and a *set accessor* (to modify the field value).

Providing **set** and **get** capabilities appears to be the same as making the instance variables **public**. However, this is another one of C#'s subtleties that makes the language so attractive from a software-engineering standpoint. If an instance variable is **public**, the instance variable can be read or written to by any method in the program. If an instance variable is **private**, a **public get** accessor seems to allow other methods to read the data at will. However, the **get** accessor can control the formatting and display of the data. Similarly, a **public set** accessor can scrutinize attempts to modify the instance variable's value, thus ensuring that the new value is appropriate for that data member. For example, an attempt to **set** the day of the month to 37 would be rejected, and an attempt to **set** a person's weight to a negative value would be rejected. So, **set** and **get** accessors can provide access to **private** data, but the implementation of these accessors controls what the client code can do to the data.

The declaration of instance variables as **private** does not guarantee their integrity. Programmers must provide validity checking—C# provides only the framework with which programmers can design better programs.

Testing and Debugging Tip 8.1

*Methods that set the values of **private** data should verify that the intended new values are valid; if they are not, the **set** accessors should place the **private** instance variables into an appropriate consistent state.*

The **set** accessors of a property cannot return values indicating a failed attempt to assign invalid data to objects of the class. Such return values could be useful to a client of a class when handling errors. The client could take appropriate actions if the objects occupy invalid states. Chapter 11 presents exception handling—a mechanism that can be used to indicate attempts to set an object's members to invalid values.

Figure 8.6 enhances our **Time** class, now called **Time3**, to include properties for the **private** instance variables **hour**, **minute** and **second**. The **set** accessors of these properties strictly control the setting of the instance variables to valid values. An attempt to set any instance variable to an incorrect value causes the instance variable to be set to zero (thus leaving the instance variable in a consistent state). Each **get** accessor returns the appropriate instance variable's value. This application also introduces enhanced GUI event-handling techniques, as we define a GUI (Fig. 8.7) that includes several buttons the user can click to manipulate the time stored in a **Time3** object.

```
1   // Fig. 8.6: Time3.cs
2   // Class Time2 provides overloaded constructors.
3
4   using System;
5
6   // Time3 class definition
7   public class Time3
8   {
9      private int hour;     // 0-23
10     private int minute;   // 0-59
11     private int second;   // 0-59
12
```

Fig. 8.6   Properties provide controlled access to an object's data. (Part 1 of 3.)

```
13      // Time3 constructor initializes instance variables to
14      // zero to set default time to midnight
15      public Time3()
16      {
17         SetTime( 0, 0, 0 );
18      }
19
20      // Time3 constructor: hour supplied, minute and second
21      // defaulted to 0
22      public Time3( int hour )
23      {
24         SetTime( hour, 0, 0 );
25      }
26
27      // Time3 constructor: hour and minute supplied, second
28      // defaulted to 0
29      public Time3( int hour, int minute )
30      {
31         SetTime( hour, minute, 0 );
32      }
33
34      // Time3 constructor: hour, minute and second supplied
35      public Time3( int hour, int minute, int second )
36      {
37         SetTime( hour, minute, second );
38      }
39
40      // Time3 constructor: initialize using another Time3 object
41      public Time3( Time3 time )
42      {
43         SetTime( time.Hour, time.Minute, time.Second );
44      }
45
46      // Set new time value in 24-hour format. Perform validity
47      // checks on the data. Set invalid values to zero.
48      public void SetTime(
49         int hourValue, int minuteValue, int secondValue )
50      {
51         Hour = hourValue;        // invoke Hour property set
52         Minute = minuteValue;    // invoke Minute property set
53         Second = secondValue;    // invoke Second property set
54      }
55
56      // property Hour
57      public int Hour
58      {
59         get
60         {
61            return hour;
62         }
63
```

Fig. 8.6   Properties provide controlled access to an object's data. (Part 2 of 3.)

```
64            set
65            {
66                hour = ( ( value >= 0 && value < 24 ) ? value : 0 );
67            }
68
69        } // end property Hour
70
71        // property Minute
72        public int Minute
73        {
74            get
75            {
76                return minute;
77            }
78
79            set
80            {
81                minute = ( ( value >= 0 && value < 60 ) ? value : 0 );
82            }
83
84        } // end property Minute
85
86        // property Second
87        public int Second
88        {
89            get
90            {
91                return second;
92            }
93
94            set
95            {
96                second = ( ( value >= 0 && value < 60 ) ? value : 0 );
97            }
98
99        } // end property Second
100
101       // convert time to universal-time (24 hour) format string
102       public string ToUniversalString()
103       {
104           return String.Format(
105               "{0:D2}:{1:D2}:{2:D2}", Hour, Minute, Second );
106       }
107
108       // convert time to standard-time (12 hour) format string
109       public string ToStandardString()
110       {
111           return String.Format( "{0}:{1:D2}:{2:D2} {3}",
112               ( ( Hour == 12 || Hour == 0 ) ? 12 : Hour % 12 ),
113               Minute, Second, ( Hour < 12 ? "AM" : "PM" ) );
114       }
115
116   } // end class Time3
```

Fig. 8.6   Properties provide controlled access to an object's data. (Part 3 of 3.)

Lines 57–69, 72–84 and 87–99 define **Time3** properties **Hour, Minute** and **Second**, respectively. Each property begins with a declaration line that includes the property's access modifier (**public**), type (**int**) and name (**Hour, Minute** or **Second**).

The body of each property contains **get** and **set** accessors, which are declared using the reserved words **get** and **set**. The **get** accessor declarations are on lines 59–62, 74–77 and 89–92. These accessors return the **hour, minute** and **second** instance variable values that objects request. The **set** accessors are declared on lines 64–67, 79–82 and 94–97. The body of each **set** accessor performs the same conditional statement that was previously performed by method **SetTime** to set the **hour, minute** or **second**.

Method **SetTime** (lines 48–54) now uses properties **Hour, Minute** and **Second** to ensure that instance variables **hour, minute** and **second** have valid values. After we define a property, we can use it in the same way that we use a variable. We assign values to properties using the **=** (assignment) operator. When this assignment occurs, the code in the **set** accessor for that property executes. The reserved word **value** represents the argument to the **set** accessor. Similarly, methods **ToUniversalString** (102–106) and **ToStandardString** (109–114) now use properties **Hour, Minute** and **Second** to obtain the values of instance variables **hour, minute** and **second**. Referencing the property executes the **get** accessor for that property.

When we use **set** and **get** accessor methods throughout the constructors and other methods of class **Time3**, we minimize the changes that we must make to the class definition in the event that we alter the data representation from **hour, minute** and **second** to another representation (such as total elapsed seconds in the day). When such changes are made, we must provide only new **set** and **get** accessor bodies. Using this technique also enables programmers to change the implementation of a class without affecting the clients of that class (as long as all the **public** methods of the class still are called in the same way).

Software Engineering Observation 8.15

*Accessing **private** data through **set** and **get** accessors not only protects the instance variables from receiving invalid values, but also hides the internal representation of the instance variables from that class's clients. Thus, if representation of the data changes (typically, to reduce the amount of required storage or to improve performance), only the method implementations need to change—the client implementations need not change, as long as the interface provided by the methods is preserved.*

Class **TimeTest3** (Fig. 8.7) defines an application with a GUI for manipulating an object of class **Time3**. [*Note*: We do not show Visual Studio's *Windows Form Designer* generated code. Instead, line 45 provides a comment to indicate where the generated code appears in the source code file. You can view this code on the CD that accompanies this book.]

```
1   // Fig. 8.7: TimeTest3.cs
2   // Demonstrating Time3 properties Hour, Minute and Second.
3
4   using System;
5   using System.Drawing;
6   using System.Collections;
7   using System.ComponentModel;
```

Fig. 8.7   Properties demonstration for class **Time3**. (Part 1 of 5.)

```
8   using System.Windows.Forms;
9   using System.Data;
10
11  // TimeTest3 class definition
12  public class TimeTest3 : System.Windows.Forms.Form
13  {
14     private System.Windows.Forms.Label hourLabel;
15     private System.Windows.Forms.TextBox hourTextBox;
16     private System.Windows.Forms.Button hourButton;
17
18     private System.Windows.Forms.Label minuteLabel;
19     private System.Windows.Forms.TextBox minuteTextBox;
20     private System.Windows.Forms.Button minuteButton;
21
22     private System.Windows.Forms.Label secondLabel;
23     private System.Windows.Forms.TextBox secondTextBox;
24     private System.Windows.Forms.Button secondButton;
25
26     private System.Windows.Forms.Button addButton;
27
28     private System.Windows.Forms.Label displayLabel1;
29     private System.Windows.Forms.Label displayLabel2;
30
31     // required designer variable
32     private System.ComponentModel.Container components = null;
33
34     private Time3 time;
35
36     public TimeTest3()
37     {
38        // Required for Windows Form Designer support
39        InitializeComponent();
40
41        time = new Time3();
42        UpdateDisplay();
43     }
44
45     // Visual Studio .NET generated code
46
47     // main entry point for application
48     [STAThread]
49     static void Main()
50     {
51        Application.Run( new TimeTest3() );
52     }
53
54     // update display labels
55     public void UpdateDisplay()
56     {
57        displayLabel1.Text = "Hour: " + time.Hour +
58           "; Minute: " + time.Minute +
59           "; Second: " + time.Second;
```

Fig. 8.7   Properties demonstration for class **Time3**. (Part 2 of 5.)

```
60            displayLabel2.Text = "Standard time: " +
61               time.ToStandardString() + "\nUniversal time: " +
62               time.ToUniversalString();
63         }
64
65         // set Hour property when hourButton pressed
66         private void hourButton_Click(
67            object sender, System.EventArgs e )
68         {
69            time.Hour = Int32.Parse( hourTextBox.Text );
70            hourTextBox.Text = "";
71            UpdateDisplay();
72         }
73
74         // set Minute property when minuteButton pressed
75         private void minuteButton_Click(
76            object sender, System.EventArgs e )
77         {
78            time.Minute = Int32.Parse( minuteTextBox.Text );
79            minuteTextBox.Text = "";
80            UpdateDisplay();
81         }
82
83         // set Second property when secondButton pressed
84         private void secondButton_Click(
85            object sender, System.EventArgs e )
86         {
87            time.Second = Int32.Parse( secondTextBox.Text );
88            secondTextBox.Text = "";
89            UpdateDisplay();
90         }
91
92         // add one to Second when addButton pressed
93         private void addButton_Click(
94            object sender, System.EventArgs e )
95         {
96            time.Second = ( time.Second + 1 ) % 60;
97
98            if ( time.Second == 0 )
99            {
100              time.Minute = ( time.Minute + 1 ) % 60;
101
102              if ( time.Minute == 0 )
103                 time.Hour = ( time.Hour + 1 ) % 24;
104           }
105
106           UpdateDisplay();
107
108       } // end method addButton_Click
109
110 } // end class TimeTest3
```

Fig. 8.7   Properties demonstration for class **Time3**. (Part 3 of 5.)

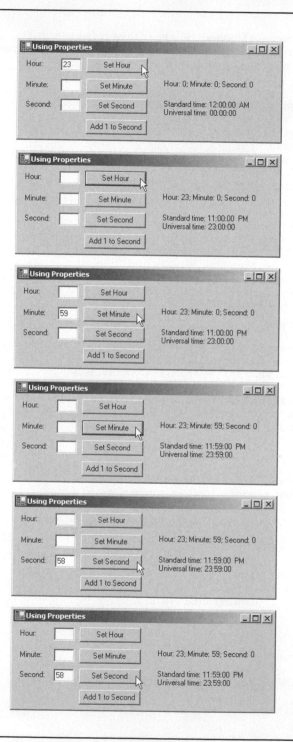

Fig. 8.7   Properties demonstration for class **Time3**. (Part 4 of 5.)

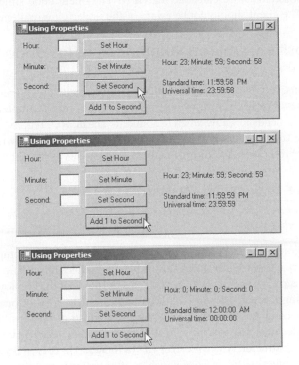

Fig. 8.7   Properties demonstration for class **Time3**. (Part 5 of 5.)

Line 34 declares **Time3** reference **time**. Line 41 in the constructor creates an object of class **Time3** and assigns it to **time**. The GUI contains three text fields in which the user can input values for the **Time3** object's **hour**, **minute** and **second** variables, respectively. Next to each text field is a button the user can click to set the value of a particular **Time3** property. Lines 66–90 declare three event-handling methods for the buttons' **Click** events. Each event handler alters the values a **Time3** property (**Hour**, **Minute** or **Second**). The GUI also contains a button that enables the user to increment the **second** value by **1**. Using the **Time3** object's properties, method **addButton_Click** (lines 93–108) determines and sets the new time. For example, **23:59:59** becomes **00:00:00** when the user presses the button. Each modification of the time results in a call to **UpdateDisplay**, which uses the **Time3** properties to display the **hour**, **minute** and **second** values, and also displays the universal- and standard-time representations.

Properties are not limited to accessing **private** data—properties also can be used to calculate values associated with an object. One example of this would be a **student** object with a property representing the student's GPA (called **GPA**). Programmers can either provide code that calculates the student's GPA in the **get** accessor for this property, or they can simply return a **private** variable containing the GPA, called **gpa**. (The value in this variable will need to be calculated in some other way, such as using a **CalculateGPA** method.) The programmer can use either technique, but we recommend using a property that calculates the GPA. Remember that client code should not be required to tell the **student** object when to calculate the GPA. The client code simply should use the GPA property. The client should not be aware of the underlying implementation.

8.8 Composition: Objects References as Instance Variables of Other Classes

In many situations, referencing existing objects is more convenient than rewriting the objects' code for new classes in new projects. Suppose we were to implement an **Alarm-Clock** object that needs to know when to sound its alarm. Referencing an existing **Time** object (like those from earlier examples in this chapter) is easier than writing a new **Time** object. The use of references to objects of preexisting classes as members of new objects is called *composition* (or *aggregation*).

Software Engineering Observation 8.16

One form of software reuse is composition, in which a class has as members references to objects of other classes.

The application of Fig. 8.8, Fig. 8.9 and Fig. 8.10 demonstrates composition. The program contains three classes. Class **Date** (Fig. 8.8) encapsulates information relating to a specific date. Class **Employee** (Fig. 8.9) encapsulates the name of the employee and two **Date** objects representing the **Employee**'s birthday and hire date. Class **CompositionTest** (Fig. 8.10) creates an object of class **Employee** to demonstrate composition.

Class **Date** declares **int** instance variables **month**, **day** and **year** (lines 9–11). Lines 16–32 define the constructor, which receives values for **month**, **day** and **year** as arguments and assigns these values to the instance variables after ensuring that the values are in a consistent state. Note that lines 25–26 print an error message if the constructor receives an invalid month value. Ordinarily, rather than printing error messages, a constructor would "throw an exception." We discuss exceptions in Chapter 11, Exception Handling. Method **ToDateString** (lines 58–61) returns the string representation of a **Date**.

```
1   // Fig. 8.8: Date.cs
2   // Date class definition encapsulates month, day and year.
3
4   using System;
5
6   // Date class definition
7   public class Date
8   {
9      private int month;   // 1-12
10     private int day;     // 1-31 based on month
11     private int year;    // any year
12
13     // constructor confirms proper value for month;
14     // call method CheckDay to confirm proper
15     // value for day
16     public Date( int theMonth, int theDay, int theYear )
17     {
```

Fig. 8.8   **Date** class encapsulates day, month and year information. (Part 1 of 2.)

```
18         // validate month
19         if ( theMonth > 0 && theMonth <= 12 )
20            month = theMonth;
21
22         else
23         {
24            month = 1;
25            Console.WriteLine(
26               "Month {0} invalid. Set to month 1.", theMonth );
27         }
28
29         year = theYear;              // could validate year
30         day = CheckDay( theDay );    // validate day
31
32      } // end Date constructor
33
34      // utility method confirms proper day value
35      // based on month and year
36      private int CheckDay( int testDay )
37      {
38         int[] daysPerMonth =
39            { 0, 31, 28, 31, 30, 31, 30, 31, 31, 30, 31, 30, 31 };
40
41         // check if day in range for month
42         if ( testDay > 0 && testDay <= daysPerMonth[ month ] )
43            return testDay;
44
45         // check for leap year
46         if ( month == 2 && testDay == 29 &&
47            ( year % 400 == 0 ||
48               ( year % 4 == 0 && year % 100 != 0 ) ) )
49            return testDay;
50
51         Console.WriteLine(
52            "Day {0} invalid. Set to day 1.", testDay );
53
54         return 1;   // leave object in consistent state
55      }
56
57      // return date string as month/day/year
58      public string ToDateString()
59      {
60         return month + "/" + day + "/" + year;
61      }
62
63   } // end class Date
```

Fig. 8.8   Date class encapsulates day, month and year information. (Part 2 of 2.)

Class **Employee** (Fig. 8.9) encapsulates information relating to an employee's birthday and hire date (lines 10–13) using instance variables **firstName**, **lastName**, **birthDate** and **hireDate**. Members' **birthDate** and **hireDate** are references to **Date** objects, each of which contains instance variables **month**, **day** and **year**. In this example, class **Employee** is *composed of* two references of type **string** and two references of class **Date**. The **Employee** constructor (lines 16–27) takes eight arguments (**first**, **last**, **birthMonth**, **birthDay**, **birthYear**, **hireMonth**, **hireDay** and **hireYear**). Line 24 passes arguments **birthMonth**, **birthDay** and **birth-Year** to the **Date** constructor to create the **birthDate** object. Similarly, line 25 passes arguments **hireMonth**, **hireDay** and **hireYear** to the **Date** constructor to create the **hireDate** object. Method **ToEmployeeString** (lines 30–35) returns a **string** containing the name of the **Employee** and the string representations of the **Employee**'s **birthDate** and **hireDate**.

Class **CompositionTest** (Fig. 8.10) runs the application with method **Main**. Lines 13–14 instantiate an **Employee** object and lines 16–17 display the string representation of the **Employee** to the user.

```
1    // Fig. 8.9: Employee.cs
2    // Employee class definition encapsulates employee's first name,
3    // last name, birth date and hire date.
4
5    using System;
6
7    // Employee class definition
8    public class Employee
9    {
10       private string firstName;
11       private string lastName;
12       private Date birthDate;    // reference to a Date object
13       private Date hireDate;     // reference to a Date object
14
15       // constructor initializes name, birth date and hire date
16       public Employee( string first, string last,
17          int birthMonth, int birthDay, int birthYear,
18          int hireMonth, int hireDay, int hireYear )
19       {
20          firstName = first;
21          lastName = last;
22
23          // create new Date objects
24          birthDate = new Date( birthMonth, birthDay, birthYear );
25          hireDate = new Date( hireMonth, hireDay, hireYear );
26
27       } // end Employee constructor
28
29       // convert Employee to String format
30       public string ToEmployeeString()
31       {
32          return lastName + ", " + firstName +
33             "  Hired: " + hireDate.ToDateString() +
34             "  Birthday: " + birthDate.ToDateString();
35       }
36
37    } // end class Employee
```

Fig. 8.9   **Employee** class encapsulates employee name, birthday and hire date.

```
1   // Fig. 8.10: CompositionTest.cs
2   // Demonstrate an object with member object reference.
3
4   using System;
5   using System.Windows.Forms;
6
7   // Composition class definition
8   class CompositionTest
9   {
10     // main entry point for application
11     static void Main( string[] args )
12     {
13        Employee e =
14           new Employee( "Bob", "Jones", 7, 24, 1949, 3, 12, 1988 );
15
16        MessageBox.Show( e.ToEmployeeString(),
17           "Testing Class Employee" );
18
19     } // end method Main
20
21  } // end class CompositionTest
```

Testing Class Employee

Jones, Bob Hired: 3/12/1988 Birthday: 7/24/1949

OK

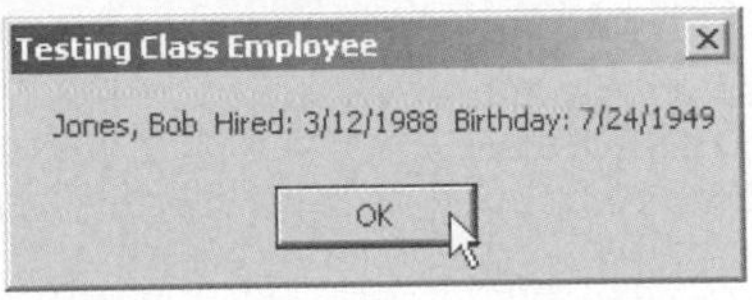

Fig. 8.10 Composition demonstration.

8.9 Using the `this` Reference

Every object can access a reference to itself, called the *this reference*. The **this** reference can refer implicitly to the instance variables, properties and methods of an object. Keyword **this** is commonly used within methods, where **this** is a reference to the object on which the method is performing operations. In the Windows application of Fig. 6.4, there are several uses of **this** in method **InitializeComponent**. The application uses the **this** keyword to reference the form that is being initialized. Every form has an **InitializeComponent** methods, so the **this** reference provides us with an easy way to access the information in the current object. Additional examples of **this** appear in Chapters 12 and 13.

We now demonstrate implicit and explicit use of the **this** reference to display the **private** data of a **Time4** object. Class **Time4** (Fig. 8.11) defines three **private** instance variables—**hour**, **minute** and **second** (lines 9–11). The constructor (lines 14–19) receives three **int** arguments to initialize a **Time4** object. Note that, for this example, we have made the parameter names for the constructor (line 14) identical to the instance variable names for the class (lines 9–11). We did this to illustrate explicit use of the **this** reference. If a method contains a local variable with the same name as an instance variable of that class, that method will refer to the local variable, rather than to the instance variable (i.e., the local variable hides the instance variable in that method's scope). However, the method can use the **this** reference to refer to the hidden instance variables explicitly (lines 16–18).

```
1   // Fig. 8.11: Time4.cs
2   // Class Time4 provides overloaded constructors.
3
4   using System;
5
6   // Time4 class definition
7   public class Time4
8   {
9      private int hour;     // 0-23
10     private int minute;   // 0-59
11     private int second;   // 0-59
12
13     // constructor
14     public Time4( int hour, int minute, int second )
15     {
16        this.hour = hour;
17        this.minute = minute;
18        this.second = second;
19     }
20
21     // create string using this and implicit references
22     public string BuildString()
23     {
24        return "this.ToStandardString(): " +
25           this.ToStandardString() +
26           "\nToStandardString(): " + ToStandardString();
27     }
28
29     // convert time to standard-time (12-hour) format string
30     public string ToStandardString()
31     {
32        return String.Format( "{0}:{1:D2}:{2:D2} {3}",
33           ( ( this.hour == 12 || this.hour == 0 ) ? 12 :
34           this.hour % 12 ), this.minute, this.second,
35           ( this.hour < 12 ? "AM" : "PM" ) );
36     }
37
38  } // end class Time4
```

Fig. 8.11   **this** reference used implicitly and explicitly to enable an object to
manipulate its own data and invoke its own methods.

Method **BuildString** (lines 22–27) returns a **string** created by a statement that
uses the **this** reference explicitly and implicitly. Line 25 uses the **this** reference explicitly to call method **ToStandardString**, whereas line 26 uses the **this** reference
implicitly to call the same method. Note that both lines perform the same task. Therefore,
programmers usually do not use the **this** reference explicitly to reference methods within
the current object.

Common Programming Error 8.4

*For a method in which a parameter (or local variable) has the same name as an instance
variable, use reference **this** if you wish to access the instance variable; otherwise, the
method parameter (or local variable) will be referenced.*

Testing and Debugging Tip 8.2

Avoid method-parameter names (or local variable names) that conflict with instance variable names to prevent subtle, hard-to-trace bugs.

Good Programming Practice 8.6

The explicit use of the **this** *reference can increase program clarity in some contexts where* **this** *is optional.*

Class **ThisTest** (Fig. 8.12) runs the application that demonstrates explicit use of the **this** reference. Line 13 instantiates an instance of class **Time4**. Lines 15–16 invoke method **BuildString** of the **Time4** object, then display the results to the user in a **MessageBox**.

The problem of parameters (or local variables) hiding instance variables can be solved by using properties. If we have a property **Hour** that accesses the **hour** instance variable, then we would not need to use **this.hour** to distinguish between a parameter (or local variable) **hour** and the instance variable **hour**—we would simply assign **hour** to **Hour**.

8.10 Garbage Collection

In previous examples, we have seen how a constructor initializes data in an object of a class after the object is created. Operator **new** allocates memory for the object, then calls that object's constructor. The constructor might acquire other system resources, such as network connections and databases or files. Objects must have a disciplined way to return memory and release resources when the program no longer uses those objects. Failure to release such resources causes *resource leaks*—potentially exhausting the pool of available resources that programs might need to continue executing.

```
1   // Fig. 8.12: ThisTest.cs
2   // Using the this reference.
3
4   using System;
5   using System.Windows.Forms;
6
7   // ThisTest class definition
8   class ThisTest
9   {
10     // main entry point for application
11     static void Main( string[] args )
12     {
13        Time4 time = new Time4( 12, 30, 19 );
14
15        MessageBox.Show( time.BuildString(),
16           "Demonstrating the \"this\" Reference" );
17     }
18  }
```

Fig. 8.12 **this** reference demonstration. (Part 1 of 2.)

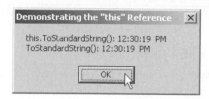

Fig. 8.12 this reference demonstration. (Part 2 of 2.)

Unlike C and C++, in which programmers must manage memory explicitly, C# performs memory management internally. The .NET Framework performs *garbage collection* of memory to return to the system memory that is no longer needed. When the *garbage collector* executes, it locates objects for which the application has no references. Such objects can be collected at that time or during a subsequent execution of the garbage collector. Therefore, the *memory leaks* that are common in such languages as C and C++, where memory is not reclaimed automatically, are rare in C#.

Allocation and deallocation of other resources, such as network connections, database connections and files, must be handled explicitly by the programmer. One technique employed to handle these resources (in conjunction with the garbage collector) is to define a *destructor* (sometimes known as a *finalizer*) that returns resources to the system. The garbage collector calls an object's destructor to perform *termination housekeeping* on that object just before the garbage collector reclaims the object's memory (called *finalization*).

Each class can contain only one destructor. The name of a destructor is formed by preceding the class name with a ~ character. For example, the destructor for class **Time** would be **~Time()**. Destructors do not receive arguments, so destructors cannot be overloaded. When the garbage collector is removing an object from memory, the garbage collector first invokes that object's destructor to clean up resources used by the class. However, we cannot determine exactly when the destructor is called, because we cannot determine exactly when garbage collection occurs. At program termination, any objects that have not been not garbage collected previously will receive destructor calls.

8.11 **static** Class Members

Each object of a class has its own copy of all the instance variables of the class. However, in certain cases, all class objects should share only one copy of a particular variable. Such variables are called **static** *variables*. A program contains only one copy of each of a class's **static** variables in memory, no matter how many objects of the class have been instantiated. A **static** variable represents *class-wide information*—all class objects share the same **static** data item.

The declaration of a **static** member begins with the keyword **static**. A **static** variable can be initialized in its declaration by following the variable name with an **=** and an initial value. In cases where a **static** variable requires more complex initialization, programmers can define a **static** *constructor* to initialize only the **static** members. Such constructors are optional and must be declared with the **static** keyword, followed by the name of the class. **static** constructors are called before any **static** members are used and before any class objects are instantiated.

We now consider a video-game example to justify the need for **static** class-wide data. Suppose that we have a video game involving **Martian**s and other space creatures. Each **Martian** tends to be brave and willing to attack other space creatures when the **Martian** is aware that there are at least four other **Martian**s present. If there are fewer than five **Martian**s present, each **Martian** becomes cowardly. For this reason, each **Martian** must know the **martianCount**. We could endow class **Martian** with **martianCount** as instance data. However, if we were to do this, then every **Martian** would have a separate copy of the instance data, and, every time we create a **Martian**, we would have to update the instance variable **martianCount** in every **Martian**. The redundant copies waste space, and updating those copies is time-consuming. Instead, we declare **martianCount** to be **static** so that **martianCount** is class-wide data. Each **Martian** can see the **martianCount** as if it were instance data of that **Martian**, but C# maintains only one copy of the **static** variable **martianCount** to save space. This technique also saves time; because there is only one copy, we do not have to increment separate copies of **martianCount** for each **Martian** object.

Performance Tip 8.2

*When a single copy of the data will suffice, use **static** variables to save storage.*

Although **static** variables might seem like *global variables* (variables that can be referenced anywhere in a program) in other programming languages, **static** variables need not be globally accessible. **static** variables have class scope.

The **public static** data members of a class can be accessed through the class name using the dot operator (e.g., **Math.PI**). The **private static** members can be accessed only through methods or properties of the class. **static** members are available as soon as the class is loaded into memory at execution time and they exist for the duration of program execution, even when no objects of that class exist. To enable a program to access a **private static** member when no objects of the class exist, the class must provide a **public static** method or property.

A **static** method cannot access instance (non-**static**) members. Unlike instance methods, a **static** method has no **this** reference, because **static** variables and **static** methods exist independently of any class objects, even when there are no objects of that class.

Common Programming Error 8.5

*Using the **this** reference in a **static** method or **static** property is a compilation error.*

Common Programming Error 8.6

*A call to an instance method or an attempt to access an instance variable from a **static** method is a compilation error.*

Class **Employee** (Fig. 8.13) demonstrates a **public static** property that enables a program to obtain the value of a **private static** variable. The **static** variable **count** (line 11) is not initialized explicitly, so it receives the value zero by default. Class variable **count** maintains a count of the number of objects of class **Employee** that have been instantiated, including those objects that have already been marked for garbage collection, but have not yet been reclaimed by the garbage collector.

```
1   // Fig. 8.13: Employee.cs
2   // Employee class contains static data and a static method.
3
4   using System;
5
6   // Employee class definition
7   public class Employee
8   {
9      private string firstName;
10     private string lastName;
11     private static int count;   // Employee objects in memory
12
13     // constructor increments static Employee count
14     public Employee( string fName, string lName )
15     {
16        firstName = fName;
17        lastName = lName;
18
19        ++count;
20
21        Console.WriteLine( "Employee object constructor: " +
22           firstName + " " + lastName + "; count = " + Count );
23     }
24
25     // destructor decrements static Employee count
26     ~Employee()
27     {
28        --count;
29
30        Console.WriteLine( "Employee object destructor: " +
31            firstName + " " + lastName + "; count = " + Count );
32     }
33
34     // FirstName property
35     public string FirstName
36     {
37        get
38        {
39           return firstName;
40        }
41     }
42
43     // LastName property
44     public string LastName
45     {
46        get
47        {
48           return lastName;
49        }
50     }
51
```

Fig. 8.13 **static** members are accessible to all objects of a class. (Part 1 of 2.)

```
52      // static Count property
53      public static int Count
54      {
55         get
56         {
57            return count;
58         }
59      }
60
61   } // end class Employee
```

Fig. 8.13 `static` members are accessible to all objects of a class. (Part 2 of 2.)

When objects of class **Employee** exist, **static** member **count** can be used in any method of an **Employee** object—in this example, the constructor (lines 14–23) increments **count**, and the destructor (lines 26–32) decrements **count**. If no objects of class **Employee** exist, the value of member **count** can be obtained through **static** property **Count** (lines 53–59); this also works when there are **Employee** objects in memory.

Class **StaticTest** (Fig. 8.14) runs the application that demonstrates the **static** members of class **Employee** (Fig. 8.13). Lines 12–13 use the **static** property **Count** of class **Employee** to obtain the current **count** value before the program creates **Employee** objects. Notice that the syntax used to access a **static** member is:

ClassName.StaticMember

On line 13, *ClassName* is **Employee** and *StaticMember* is **Count**. Recall that we used this syntax in prior examples to call the **static** methods of class **Math** (e.g., **Math.Pow**, **Math.Abs**, etc.) and other methods, such as **Int32.Parse** and **MessageBox.Show**.

Next, lines 16–17 instantiate two **Employee** objects and assign them to references **employee1** and **employee2**. Each call to the **Employee** constructor increments the **count** value by one. Lines 19–26 display the value of **Count** as well as the names of the two employees. Lines 30–31 set references **employee1** and **employee2** to **null**, so they no longer refer to the **Employee** objects. Because these were the only references in the program to the **Employee** objects, those objects can now be garbage collected.

```
1   // Fig. 8.14: StaticTest.cs
2   // Demonstrating static class members.
3
4   using System;
5
6   // StaticTest class definition
7   class StaticTest
8   {
9      // main entry point for application
10     static void Main( string[] args )
11     {
12        Console.WriteLine( "Employees before instantiation: " +
13           Employee.Count + "\n" );
14
```

Fig. 8.14 `static` member demonstration. (Part 1 of 2.)

```
15          // create two Employees
16          Employee employee1 = new Employee( "Susan", "Baker" );
17          Employee employee2 = new Employee( "Bob", "Jones" );
18
19          Console.WriteLine( "\nEmployees after instantiation: " +
20             "Employee.Count = " + Employee.Count + "\n" );
21
22          // display the Employees
23          Console.WriteLine( "Employee 1: " +
24             employee1.FirstName + " " + employee1.LastName +
25             "\nEmployee 2: " + employee2.FirstName +
26             " " + employee2.LastName + "\n" );
27
28          // remove references to objects to indicate that
29          // objects can be garbage collected
30          employee1 = null;
31          employee2 = null;
32
33          // force garbage collection
34          System.GC.Collect();
35
36          // wait until collection completes
37          System.GC.WaitForPendingFinalizers();
38
39          Console.WriteLine(
40             "\nEmployees after garbage collection: " +
41             Employee.Count );
42       }
43   }
```

```
Employees before instantiation: 0

Employee object constructor: Susan Baker; count = 1
Employee object constructor: Bob Jones; count = 2

Employees after instantiation: Employee.Count = 2

Employee 1: Susan Baker
Employee 2: Bob Jones

Employee object destructor: Bob Jones; count = 1
Employee object destructor: Susan Baker; count = 0

Employees after garbage collection: 0
```

Fig. 8.14 **static** member demonstration. (Part 2 of 2.)

The garbage collector is not invoked directly by the program. Either the garbage collector reclaims the memory for objects when the runtime determines garbage collection is appropriate, or the operating system recovers the memory when the program terminates. However, it is possible to request that the garbage collector attempt to collect available objects. Line 34 uses **public static** method *Collect* from class *GC* (namespace

System) to make this request. The garbage collector is not guaranteed to collect all objects that are currently available for collection. If the garbage collector decides to collect objects, the garbage collector first invokes the destructor of each object. It is important to understand that the garbage collector executes as an independent entity called a *thread*. (Threads are discussed in Chapter 14, Multithreading.) It is possible for multiple threads to execute in parallel on a multiprocessor system or to share a processor on a single-processor system. Thus, a program could run in parallel with garbage collection. For this reason, we call **static** method ***WaitForPendingFinalizers*** of class **GC** (line 37), which forces the program to wait until the garbage collector invokes the destructors for all objects that are ready for collection and reclaims those objects. When the program reaches lines 41, we are assured that both destructor calls completed and that the value of **count** has been decremented accordingly.

In this example, the output shows that the destructor was called for each **Employee**, which decrements the **count** value by two (once per **Employee** being collected). Lines 39–41 use property **Count** to obtain the value of **count** after invoking the garbage collector. If the objects had not been collected, the **count** would be greater than zero.

Toward the end of the output, notice that the **Employee** object for **Bob Jones** was finalized before the **Employee** object for **Susan Baker**. However, the output of this program on your system could differ. The garbage collector is not guaranteed to collect objects in a specific order.

8.12 `const` and `readonly` Members

C# allows programmers to create *constants* whose values cannot change during program execution.

Testing and Debugging Tip 8.3

If a variable should never change, make it a constant. This helps eliminate errors that might occur if the value of the variable were to change.

To create a constant data member of a class, declare that member using either the *const* or *readonly* keyword. Data members declared as **const** implicitly are **static** and must be initialized in their declaration. Data members declared as **readonly** can be initialized in their declaration or in their class's constructor. Neither **const** nor **readonly** values can be modified once they are initialized, except that **readonly** variables can be assigned values in several constructors (only one of which will be called when an object is initialized).

Common Programming Error 8.7

*Declaring a class data member as **const** but failing to initialize it in that class's declaration is a syntax error.*

Common Programming Error 8.8

*Assigning a value to a **const** variable after that variable is initialized is a compilation error.*

Common Programming Error 8.9

*The declaration of a **const** member as **static** is a syntax error, because a **const** member implicitly is **static**.*

Common Programming Error 8.10

Declaring a class data member as **readonly** *and attempting to use it before it is initialized is a logic error.*

Members that are declared as **const** must be assigned values at compile time. Therefore, **const** members can be initialized only with other constant values, such as integers, string literals, characters and other **const** members. Constant members with values that cannot be determined at compile time must be declared with keyword **readonly**. We mentioned previously that a **readonly** member can be assigned a value only once, either when it is declared or within the constructor of the class. When initializing a **static readonly** member in a constructor, a **static** constructor must be used.

Figure 8.15 demonstrates constants. The program consists of two classes—class **Constants** (lines 8–22) defines two constants, and class **UsingConstAndReadonly** (lines 25–43) demonstrates the constants in class **Constants**.

```csharp
1   // Fig. 8.15: UsingConstAndReadOnly.cs
2   // Demonstrating constant values with const and readonly.
3
4   using System;
5   using System.Windows.Forms;
6
7   // Constants class definition
8   public class Constants
9   {
10      // create constant PI
11      public const double PI = 3.14159;
12
13      // radius is a constant
14      // that is uninitialized
15      public readonly int radius;
16
17      public Constants( int radiusValue )
18      {
19         radius = radiusValue;
20      }
21
22   } // end class Constants
23
24   // UsingConstAndReadOnly class definition
25   public class UsingConstAndReadonly
26   {
27      // method Main creates Constants
28      // object and displays its values
29      static void Main( string[] args )
30      {
31         Random random = new Random();
32
33         Constants constantValues =
34            new Constants( random.Next( 1, 20 ) );
35
```

Fig. 8.15 **const** and **readonly** class member demonstration. (Part 1 of 2.)

```
36              MessageBox.Show( "Radius = " + constantValues.radius +
37                 "\nCircumference = " +
38                 2 * Constants.PI * constantValues.radius,
39                 "Circumference" );
40
41      } // end method Main
42
43  } // end class UsingConstAndReadOnly
```

Fig. 8.15   **const** and **readonly** class member demonstration. (Part 2 of 2.)

Line 11 in class **Constants** creates constant **PI** using keyword **const** and initializes **PI** with the **double** value **3.14159**—an approximation of π that the program uses to calculate the circumferences of circles. Note that we could have used the predefined constant **PI** of class **Math** (**Math.PI**) as the value, but we wanted to demonstrate how to define a **const** variable explicitly. The compiler must be able to determine a **const** variable's value at compile time; otherwise, a compilation error will occur. For example, if line 11 initialized **PI** with the expression:

```
Double.Parse( "3.14159" )
```

the compiler would generate an error. Although the expression uses **string** literal **"3.14159"** (a constant value) as an argument, the compiler cannot evaluate the method call **Double.Parse** at compile time.

Variables declared **readonly** can be initialized at execution time. Line 15 declares **readonly** variable **radius**, but does not initialize it. The **Constants** constructor (lines 17–20) receives an **int** value and assigns it to **radius** when the program creates a **Constants** object. Note that radius also can be initialized with a more complex expression, such as a method call that returns an **int**.

Class **UsingConstAndReadonly** (lines 25–43) uses the **const** and **readonly** variables of class **Constants**. Lines 33–34 use a **Random** object to generate a random **int** between **1** and **20** that corresponds to a circle's **radius**, then pass that value to the **Constants** constructor to initialize the **readonly** variable **radius**. Lines 36–39 output the radius and circumference of a circle in a **MessageBox**. Line 36 uses **Constants**'s reference **contantValues** to access **readonly** variable **radius**. Line 38 computes the circle's circumference using **const** variable **Constants.PI** and **readonly** variable **radius**. Note that we use **static** syntax to access **const** variable **PI**, because **const** variables implicitly are **static**.

8.13 Indexers

Sometimes a class encapsulates data that a program can manipulate as a list of elements. Such a class can define special properties called *indexers* that allow array-style indexed access to lists of elements. With "conventional" C# arrays, the subscript number must be an integer value. A benefit of indexers is that the programmer can define both integer subscripts and non-integer subscripts. For example, a programmer could allow client code to manipulate data using **string**s as subscripts that represent the data items' names or descriptions. When manipulating "conventional" C# array elements, the array subscript operator always returns the same data type—i.e., the type of the array. Indexers are more flexible—they can return any data type, even one that is different from the type of the data in the list of elements.

Although an indexer's subscript operator is used like an array-subscript operator, indexers are defined as properties in a class. Unlike normal properties, for which the programmer can choose an appropriate property name, indexers must be defined with keyword **this**. Indexers have the general form:

```
accessModifier returnType this[ IndexType1 name1, IndexType2 name2, ... ]
{
    get
    {
        // use name1, name2, ... here to get data
    }

    set
    {
        // use name1, name2, ... here to set data
    }
}
```

The *IndexType* parameters specified in the brackets (**[]**) are accessible to the **get** and **set** accessors. These accessors define how to use the index (or indices) to select or modify the appropriate data member. As with properties, **get** must **return** a value of type *returnType* and **set** can use the **value** keyword to reference the value that should be assigned to the data member.

Common Programming Error 8.11

Declaring indexers as **static** *is a syntax error.*

The program of Fig. 8.16 contains two classes—class **Box** (lines 14–74) represents a box with a length, a width and a height, and class **IndexerTest** (lines 77–177) demonstrates class **Box**'s indexers.

```
1   // Fig. 8.16: IndexerTest.cs
2   // Indexers provide access to an object's members via a
3   // subscript operator.
4
5   using System;
6   using System.Drawing;
7   using System.Collections;
8   using System.ComponentModel;
9   using System.Windows.Forms;
10  using System.Data;
11
```

Fig. 8.16 Indexers provide subscripted access to an object's members. (Part 1 of 6.)

```
12    // Box class definition represents a box with length,
13    // width and height dimensions
14    public class Box
15    {
16       private string[] names = { "length", "width", "height" };
17       private double[] dimensions = new double[ 3 ];
18
19       // constructor
20       public Box( double length, double width, double height )
21       {
22          dimensions[ 0 ] = length;
23          dimensions[ 1 ] = width;
24          dimensions[ 2 ] = height;
25       }
26
27       // access dimensions by integer index number
28       public double this[ int index ]
29       {
30          get
31          {
32             return ( index < 0 || index >= dimensions.Length ) ?
33                -1 : dimensions[ index ];
34          }
35
36          set
37          {
38             if ( index >= 0 && index < dimensions.Length )
39                dimensions[ index ] = value;
40          }
41
42       } // end numeric indexer
43
44       // access dimensions by their string names
45       public double this[ string name ]
46       {
47          get
48          {
49             // locate element to get
50             int i = 0;
51
52             while ( i < names.Length &&
53                name.ToLower() != names[ i ] )
54                i++;
55
56             return ( i == names.Length ) ? -1 : dimensions[ i ];
57          }
58
59          set
60          {
61             // locate element to set
62             int i = 0;
63
```

Fig. 8.16   Indexers provide subscripted access to an object's members. (Part 2 of 6.)

```
64              while ( i < names.Length &&
65                  name.ToLower() != names[ i ] )
66                  i++;
67
68              if ( i != names.Length )
69                  dimensions[ i ] = value;
70          }
71
72      } // end indexer
73
74  } // end class Box
75
76  // Class IndexerTest
77  public class IndexerTest : System.Windows.Forms.Form
78  {
79      private System.Windows.Forms.Label indexLabel;
80      private System.Windows.Forms.Label nameLabel;
81
82      private System.Windows.Forms.TextBox indexTextBox;
83      private System.Windows.Forms.TextBox valueTextBox;
84
85      private System.Windows.Forms.Button nameSetButton;
86      private System.Windows.Forms.Button nameGetButton;
87
88      private System.Windows.Forms.Button intSetButton;
89      private System.Windows.Forms.Button intGetButton;
90
91      private System.Windows.Forms.TextBox resultTextBox;
92
93      // required designer variable
94      private System.ComponentModel.Container components = null;
95
96      private Box box;
97
98      // constructor
99      public IndexerTest()
100     {
101         // required for Windows Form Designer support
102         InitializeComponent();
103
104         // create block
105         box = new Box( 0.0, 0.0, 0.0 );
106     }
107
108     // Visual Studio .NET generated code
109
110     // main entry point for application
111     [STAThread]
112     static void Main()
113     {
114         Application.Run( new IndexerTest() );
115     }
116
```

Fig. 8.16 Indexers provide subscripted access to an object's members. (Part 3 of 6.)

```
117    // display value at specified index number
118    private void ShowValueAtIndex( string prefix, int index )
119    {
120       resultTextBox.Text =
121          prefix + "box[ " + index + " ] = " + box[ index ];
122    }
123
124    // display value with specified name
125    private void ShowValueAtIndex( string prefix, string name )
126    {
127       resultTextBox.Text =
128          prefix + "box[ " + name + " ] = " + box[ name ];
129    }
130
131    // clear indexTextBox and valueTextBox
132    private void ClearTextBoxes()
133    {
134       indexTextBox.Text = "";
135       valueTextBox.Text = "";
136    }
137
138    // get value at specified index
139    private void intGetButton_Click(
140       object sender, System.EventArgs e )
141    {
142       ShowValueAtIndex(
143          "get: ", Int32.Parse( indexTextBox.Text ) );
144       ClearTextBoxes();
145    }
146
147    // set value at specified index
148    private void intSetButton_Click(
149       object sender, System.EventArgs e )
150    {
151       int index = Int32.Parse( indexTextBox.Text );
152       box[ index ] = Double.Parse( valueTextBox.Text );
153
154       ShowValueAtIndex( "set: ", index );
155       ClearTextBoxes();
156    }
157
158    // get value with specified name
159    private void nameGetButton_Click(
160       object sender, System.EventArgs e )
161    {
162       ShowValueAtIndex( "get: ", indexTextBox.Text );
163       ClearTextBoxes();
164    }
165
166    // set value with specified name
167    private void nameSetButton_Click(
168       object sender, System.EventArgs e )
169    {
```

Fig. 8.16   Indexers provide subscripted access to an object's members. (Part 4 of 6.)

```
         box[ indexTextBox.Text ] =
            Double.Parse( valueTextBox.Text );

         ShowValueAtIndex( "set: ", indexTextBox.Text );
         ClearTextBoxes();
      }

   } // end class IndexerTest
```

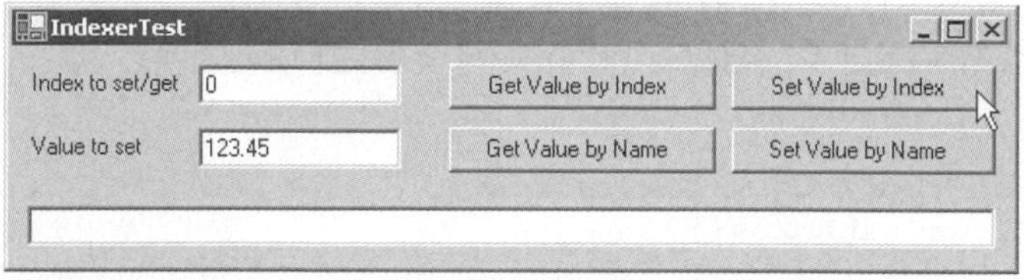

Before setting value by index number

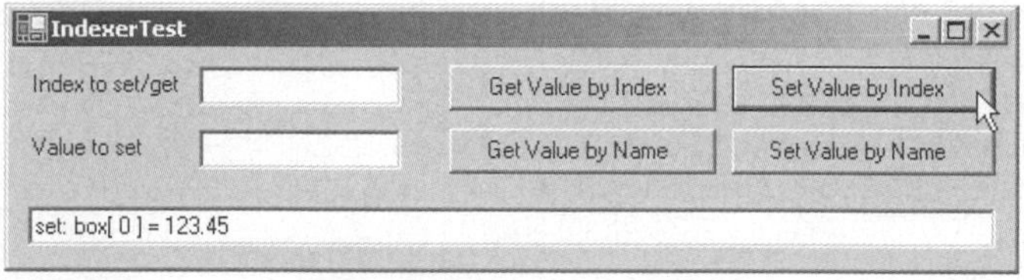

After setting value by index number

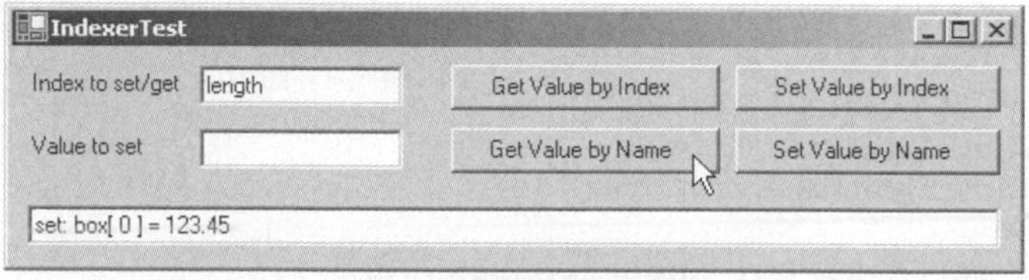

Before getting value by dimension name

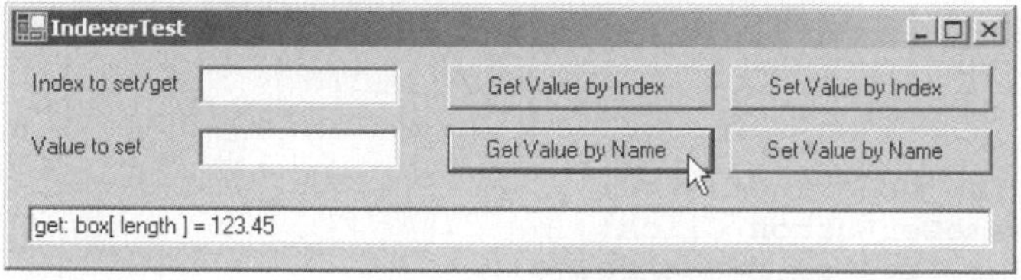

After getting value by dimension name

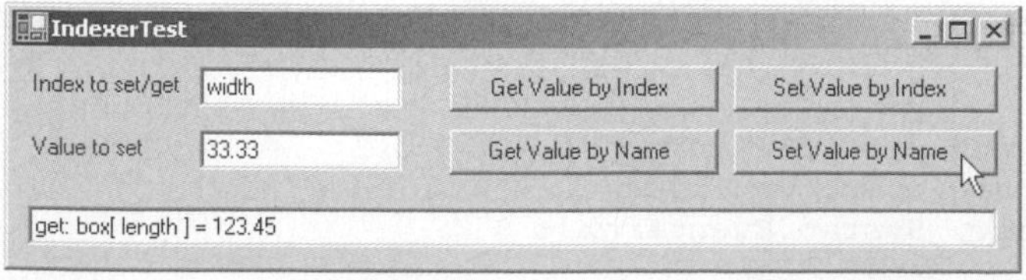

Before setting value by dimension name

Fig. 8.16 Indexers provide subscripted access to an object's members. (Part 5 of 6.)

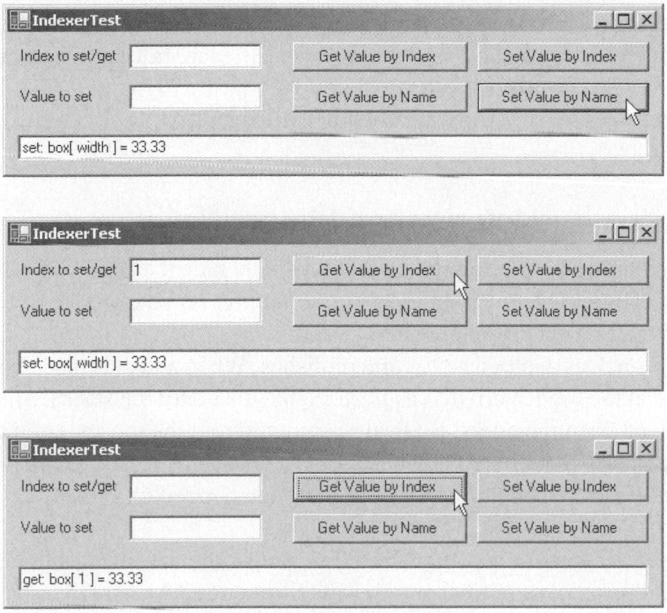

After setting value by dimension name

Before getting value by index number

After getting value by index number

Fig. 8.16 Indexers provide subscripted access to an object's members. (Part 6 of 6.)

The **private** data members of class **Box** are **string** array **names** (line 16), which contains the names (i.e., **"length"**, **"width"** and **"height"**) for the dimensions of a **Box**, and **double** array **dimensions** (line 17), which contains the size of each dimension. Each element in array **names** corresponds to an element in array **dimensions** (e.g., **dimensions[2]** contains the height of the **Box**).

Box defines two indexers (lines 28–42 and lines 45–72) that each **return** a **double** value representing the size of the dimension specified by the indexer's parameter. Indexers can be overloaded like methods. The first indexer uses an **int** subscript to manipulate an element in the **dimensions** array. The second indexer uses a **string** subscript representing the name of the dimension to manipulate an element in the **dimensions** array. Each indexer returns **-1** if its **get** accessor encounters an invalid subscript. Each indexer's **set** accessor assigns **value** to the appropriate element of **dimensions** only if the index is valid. Normally, the programmer would have an indexer throw an exception if an indexer received an invalid index. We discuss how to throw exceptions in Chapter 11, Exception Handling.

Notice that the **string** indexer uses a **while** structure to search for a matching **string** in the **names** array (lines 64–66). If a match is found, the indexer manipulates the corresponding element in array **dimensions** (line 69).

Class **IndexerTest** is a **System.Windows.Forms.Form** that manipulates the **private** data members of class **Box** through **Box**'s indexers. Instance variable **box** is declared at line 96 and initialized in the constructor at line 105 with dimensions of **0.0**. The event handler for button **Get Value by Index** (lines 139–145) invokes method **ShowValueAtIndex** (lines 118–122) to retrieve the value at the index number specified in **indexTextBox**. The event handler for button **Set Value by Index** (lines 148–156) assigns the value in **valueTextBox** to the location specified in **indexTextBox**. The event handler for button **Get Value by Name** (159–164) invokes the overloaded method **ShowValue-AtIndex** (lines 125–129) to retrieve the value with the name specified in **valueTextBox**. The event handler for button **Set Value by Name** (lines 167–175) assigns the value in **valueTextBox** to the location with the name specified in **indexTextBox**.

8.14 Data Abstraction and Information Hiding

As we pointed out at the beginning of this chapter, classes normally hide the details of their implementation from their clients. This is called *information hiding.* As an example of information hiding, let us consider a data structure called a *stack.*

Students can think of a stack as analogous to a pile of dishes. When a dish is placed on the pile, it is always placed at the top (referred to as *pushing* the dish onto the stack). Similarly, when a dish is removed from the pile, it is always removed from the top (referred to as *popping* the dish off the stack). Stacks are known as *last-in, first-out (LIFO) data structures*—the last item pushed (inserted) on the stack is the first item popped (removed) from the stack.

Stacks can be implemented with arrays and with other data structures, such as linked lists. (We discuss stacks and linked lists in Chapter 23, Data Structures.) A client of a stack class need not be concerned with the stack's implementation. The client knows only that when data items are placed in the stack, these items will be recalled in last-in, first-out order. The client cares about *what* functionality a stack offers, but not about *how* that functionality is implemented. This concept is referred to as *data abstraction.* Although programmers might know the details of a class's implementation, they should not write code that depends on these details. This enables a particular class (such as one that implements a stack and its operations, *push* and *pop*) to be replaced with another version without affecting the rest of the system. As long as the **public** services of the class do not change (i.e., every method still has the same name, return type and parameter list in the new class definition), the rest of the system is not affected.

Most programming languages emphasize actions. In these languages, data exist to support the actions that programs must take. Data are "less interesting" than actions. Data are "crude." Only a few built-in data types exist, and it is difficult for programmers to create their own data types. C# and the object-oriented style of programming elevate the importance of data. The primary activities of object-oriented programming in C# is the creation of data types (i.e., classes) and the expression of the interactions among objects of those data types. To create languages that emphasize data, the programming-languages community needed to formalize some notions about data. The formalization we consider here is the notion of *abstract data types (ADTs).* ADTs receive as much attention today as structured programming did decades earlier. ADTs, however, do not replace structured programming. Rather, they provide an additional formalization to improve the program-development process.

Consider built-in type **int**, which most people would associate with an integer in mathematics. Rather, an **int** is an abstract representation of an integer. Unlike mathematical integers, computer **int**s are fixed in size. For example, type **int** in .NET is limited approximately to the range –2 billion to +2 billion. If the result of a calculation falls outside this range, an error occurs, and the computer responds in some machine-dependent manner.

It might, for example, "quietly" produce an incorrect result. Mathematical integers do not have this problem. Therefore, the notion of a computer **int** is only an approximation of the notion of a real-world integer. The same is true of **float** and other built-in types.

We have taken the notion of **int** for granted until this point, but we now consider it from a new perspective. Types like **int**, **float**, **char** and others are all examples of abstract data types. These types are representations of real-world notions to some satisfactory level of precision within a computer system.

An ADT actually captures two notions: A *data representation* and the *operations* that can be performed on that data. For example, in C#, an **int** contains an integer value (data) and provides addition, subtraction, multiplication, division and modulus operations; however, division by zero is undefined. C# programmers use classes to implement abstract data types.

Software Engineering Observation 8.17

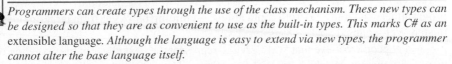

Programmers can create types through the use of the class mechanism. These new types can be designed so that they are as convenient to use as the built-in types. This marks C# as an extensible language. Although the language is easy to extend via new types, the programmer cannot alter the base language itself.

Another abstract data type we discuss is a *queue*, which is similar to a "waiting line." Computer systems use many queues internally. A queue offers well-understood behavior to its clients: Clients place items in a queue one at a time via an *enqueue* operation, then get those items back one at a time via a *dequeue* operation. A queue returns items in *first-in, first-out (FIFO)* order, which means that the first item inserted in a queue is the first item removed. Conceptually, a queue can become infinitely long, but real queues are finite.

The queue hides an internal data representation that keeps track of the items currently waiting in line, and it offers a set of operations to its clients (*enqueue* and *dequeue*). The clients are not concerned about the implementation of the queue—clients simply depend upon the queue to operate "as advertised." When a client enqueues an item, the queue should accept that item and place it in some kind of internal FIFO data structure. Similarly, when the client wants the next item from the front of the queue, the queue should remove the item from its internal representation and deliver the item in FIFO order (i.e., the item that has been in the queue the longest should be the next one returned by the next dequeue operation).

The queue ADT guarantees the integrity of its internal data structure. Clients cannot manipulate this data structure directly—only the queue ADT has access to its internal data. Clients are able to perform only allowable operations on the data representation; the ADT rejects operations that its public interface does not provide.

8.15 Software Reusability

C# programmers concentrate both on crafting new classes and on reusing classes from the Framework Class Library (FCL), which contains thousands of predefined classes. Developers construct software by combining programmer-defined classes with well-defined, carefully tested, well-documented, portable and widely available FCL classes. This kind of software reusability speeds the development of powerful, high-quality software. *Rapid applications development (RAD)* is of great interest today.

The FCL allows C# programmers to achieve software reusability across platforms that support .NET and rapid applications development. C# programmers focus on the high-level programming issues and leave the low-level implementation details to classes in the FCL. For example, a C# programmer who writes a graphics program does not need to know the details of every .NET-platform graphics capability. Instead, C# programmers concentrate on learning and using the FCL's graphics classes.

The FCL enables C# developers to build applications faster by reusing preexisting, extensively tested classes. In addition to reducing development time, FCL classes also improve programmers' abilities to debug and maintain applications, because proven software compenents are being used. For programmers to take advantage of the FCL's classes, they must familiarize themselves with the FCL's rich set of capabilities.

Software reuse is not limited to Windows-application development. The FCL also includes classes for creating *Web services*, which are applications packaged as services that clients can access via the Internet. Any C# application is a potential Web service, so C# programmers can reuse existing applications as building blocks to form larger more sophisticated Web-enabled applications.

Many people believe that Web services represent the next phase in the evolution of software development, in which the Web provides a library of functionality from which developers can build applications in a platform-independent manner. As Microsoft's premier .NET language, C# provides all the features necessary for creating scalable, robust Web services. We formally introduce Web Services in Chapter 21, ASP .NET and Web Services.

8.16 Namespaces and Assemblies

As we have seen in almost every example in the text, classes from preexisting libraries, such as the .NET Framework, must be imported into a C# program by adding a reference to the appropriate libraries (a process we demonstrated in Section 3.2). Remember that each class in the Framework Class Library belongs to a specific namespace. The preexisting code in the FCL facilitates software reuse.

Programmers should concentrate on making the software components they create reusable. However, doing so often results in *naming collisions*. For example, two classes defined by different programmers can have the same name. If a program needs both of those classes, the program must have a way to distinguish between the two classes in the code.

 Common Programming Error 8.12

Attempting to compile code that contains naming collisions will generate compilation errors.

Namespaces help minimize this problem by providing a convention for *unique class names*. No two classes in a given namespace can have the same name, but different namespaces can contain classes of the same name. With hundreds of thousands of people writing C# programs, there is a good chance the names that one programmer chooses to describe classes will conflict with the names that other programmers choose for their classes.

We begin our discussion of reusing existing class definitions in Fig. 8.17, which provides the code for class **Time3** (originally defined in Fig. 8.6). When reusing class definitions between programs, programmers create class libraries that can be imported for use in a program via a **using** statement. Only **public** classes can be reused from class libraries. Non-**public** classes can be used only by other classes in the same assembly.

The only difference between class **Time3** in this example and the version in Fig. 8.6 is that we show the **namespace**, i.e., **TimeLibrary**, in which **Time3** is defined. Each class library is defined in a **namespace** that contains all the classes in the library. We will demonstrate momentarily how to package class **Time3** into **TimeLibrary.dll**—the *dynamic link library* that we create for reuse in other programs. Programs can load dynamic link libraries at execution time to access common functionality that can be shared among many programs. A dynamic link library represents an assembly. When a project uses a class library, the project must contain a reference to the assembly that defines the class library.

```
1   // Fig. 8.17: TimeLibrary.cs
2   // Placing class Time3 in an assembly for reuse.
3
4   using System;
5
6   namespace TimeLibrary    // specifies namespace for class Time3
7   {
8      // Time3 class definition
9      public class Time3
10     {
11        private int hour;      // 0-23
12        private int minute;    // 0-59
13        private int second;    // 0-59
14
15        // Time3 constructor initializes instance variables to
16        // zero to set default time to midnight
17        public Time3()
18        {
19           SetTime( 0, 0, 0 );
20        }
21
22        // Time3 constructor: hour supplied, minute and second
23        // defaulted to 0
24        public Time3( int hour )
25        {
26           SetTime( hour, 0, 0 );
27        }
28
29        // Time3 constructor: hour and minute supplied, second
30        // defaulted to 0
31        public Time3( int hour, int minute )
32        {
33           SetTime( hour, minute, 0 );
34        }
35
36        // Time3 constructor: hour, minute and second supplied
37        public Time3( int hour, int minute, int second )
38        {
39           SetTime( hour, minute, second );
40        }
41
```

Fig. 8.17   Assembly **TimeLibrary** contains class **Time3**. (Part 1 of 3.)

```
42        // Time3 constructor: initialize using another Time3 object
43        public Time3( Time3 time )
44        {
45           SetTime( time.Hour, time.Minute, time.Second );
46        }
47
48        // Set new time value in 24-hour format. Perform validity
49        // checks on the data. Set invalid values to zero.
50        public void SetTime(
51           int hourValue, int minuteValue, int secondValue )
52        {
53           Hour = hourValue;
54           Minute = minuteValue;
55           Second = secondValue;
56        }
57
58        // property Hour
59        public int Hour
60        {
61           get
62           {
63              return hour;
64           }
65
66           set
67           {
68              hour = ( ( value >= 0 && value < 24 ) ? value : 0 );
69           }
70
71        } // end property Hour
72
73        // property Minute
74        public int Minute
75        {
76           get
77           {
78              return minute;
79           }
80
81           set
82           {
83              minute = ( ( value >= 0 && value < 60 ) ? value : 0 );
84           }
85
86        } // end property Minute
87
88        // property Second
89        public int Second
90        {
91           get
92           {
93              return second;
94           }
```

Fig. 8.17   Assembly **TimeLibrary** contains class **Time3**. (Part 2 of 3.)

```
 95
 96            set
 97            {
 98                second = ( ( value >= 0 && value < 60 ) ? value : 0 );
 99            }
100
101        } // end property Second
102
103        // convert time to universal-time (24 hour) format string
104        public string ToUniversalString()
105        {
106            return String.Format(
107                "{0:D2}:{1:D2}:{2:D2}", Hour, Minute, Second );
108        }
109
110        // convert time to standard-time (12 hour) format string
111        public string ToStandardString()
112        {
113            return String.Format( "{0}:{1:D2}:{2:D2} {3}",
114                ( ( Hour == 12 || Hour == 0 ) ? 12 : Hour % 12 ),
115                Minute, Second, ( Hour < 12 ? "AM" : "PM" ) );
116        }
117
118    } // end class Time3
119 }
```

Fig. 8.17   Assembly **TimeLibrary** contains class **Time3**. (Part 3 of 3.)

We now describe, step-by-step, how to create the class library **TimeLibrary** containing class **Time3**:

1. *Create a class library project.* From the **File** menu, choose option **New**, followed by **Project...**. In the **New Project** dialog, ensure that **C# Projects** is selected in the **Project Types** section and click **Class Library**. Name the project **TimeLibrary** and choose the directory in which you would like to store the project. A simple class library will be created, as shown in Fig. 8.18. There are two important points to note about the generated code. The first is that the class does not contain a **Main** method. This indicates that the class in the class library cannot be used to begin the execution of an application. This class is designed to be used by other programs. Also notice that **Class1** is created as a **public** class. If another project uses this library, only the library's **public** classes are accessible. We created class **Time3** as **public** for this purpose (line 9 of Fig. 8.17) by renaming the class **Class1** (created by Visual Studio as part of the project) to **Time3**. In the **Solution Explorer**, we also renamed the **Class1.cs** file as **Time3.cs**.

2. *Add the code for class* ***Time3***. Delete the code for the **Class1** constructor. Then, copy the remainder of the **Time3** code (lines 11–116) from Fig. 8.17 (you can find this file in the examples on the CD that accompanies this book) and paste the code in the body of the class definition shown in Fig. 8.18.

3. *Compile the code.* From the **Build** menu, choose option **Build Solution**. The code should compile successfully. Remember that this code cannot be executed—

there is no entry point into the program. In fact, if you try running the program by selecting the **Debug** menu and choosing **Start**, Visual Studio .NET displays an error message.

Compiling the project creates an assembly (a dynamic link library) that represents the new class library. This assembly can be found in the **bin\Debug** directory of the project. By default, the assembly name will include the namespace name. (In this case, the name will be **TimeLibrary.dll**.) The assembly file contains class **Time3**, which other projects can use. Assembly files, which have file extensions **.dll** and **.exe**, are integral to C#. The Windows operating system uses executable files (**.exe**) to run applications, whereas it uses library files (**.dll**, or *dynamic link library*) to represent code libraries that can be loaded dynamically by many applications and shared among those applications.

Next, we define a console application project containing class **AssemblyTest** (Fig. 8.19), which uses class **Time3** in assembly **TimeLibrary.dll** to create a **Time3** object and display its standard and universal string formats.

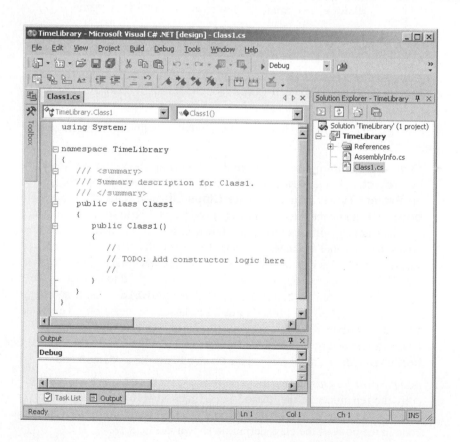

Fig. 8.18 Simple Class Library.

```
1   // Fig. 8.19: AssemblyTest.cs
2   // Using class Time3 from assembly TimeLibrary.
3
4   using System;
5   using TimeLibrary;
6
7   // AssemblyTest class definition
8   class AssemblyTest
9   {
10      // main entry point for application
11      static void Main( string[] args )
12      {
13          Time3 time = new Time3( 13, 27, 6 );
14
15          Console.WriteLine(
16              "Standard time: {0}\nUniversal time: {1}\n",
17              time.ToStandardString(), time.ToUniversalString() );
18      }
19  }
```

```
Standard time: 1:27:06 PM
Universal time: 13:27:06
```

Fig. 8.19   Assembly **TimeLibrary** used from class **AssemblyTest**.

Before class **AssemblyTest** can use class **Time3**, the project containing class **AssemblyTest** must have a reference to the **TimeLibrary** assembly. To add the reference, select **Add Reference** from the **Project** menu. Using the **Browse** button, select **TimeLibrary.dll** (located in the **bin\Debug** directory of the **TimeLibrary** project), then click **OK** to add the resource to the project. After adding the reference, use keyword **using** to inform the compiler that we will use classes from namespace **Time-Library** (line 5 in Fig. 8.19).

8.17 Class View and Object Browser

Now that we have introduced key concepts of object-based programming, we present two features that Visual Studio provides to facilitate the design of object-oriented applications—*Class View* and *Object Browser*.

The **Class View** displays the variables and methods for all classes in a project. To access this feature, select **Class View** from the **View** menu. Figure 8.20 shows the **Class View** for the **TimeTest1** project of Fig. 8.1 and Fig. 8.2 (class **Time1** and class **TimeTest1**). The view follows a hierarchical structure, positioning the project name (**TimeTest1**) as the root and including a series of nodes (e.g., classes, variables, methods etc.). If a plus sign (**+**) appears to the left of a node, that node can be expanded to show other nodes. By contrast, if a minus sign (**-**) appears to the left of a node, that node has been expanded (and can be collapsed). According to the **Class View**, project **TimeTest** contains class **Time1** and class **TimeTest1** as *children*. Class **Time1** contains methods **SetTime**, **Time1**, **ToStandardString** and **ToUniversalString** (indicated by purple boxes) and instance variables **hour**, **minute** and **second** (indicated by blue

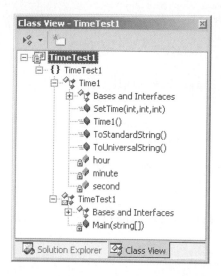

Fig. 8.20   **Class View** of class **Time1** (Fig. 8.1) and class **TimeTest** (Fig. 8.2).

boxes). The lock icons, placed to the left of the blue-box icons for the instance variables, specify that the variables are **private**. Class **TimeTest1** contains method **Main**. Note that both class **Time1** and class **TimeTest1** contain the **Bases and Interfaces** node. If you expand this node, you will see class **Object** in each case, because each class inherits from class **System.Object** (discussed in Chapter 9).

Visual Studio's **Object Browser** lists all classes included in this project. Developers use the **Object Browser** to learn about the functionality provided by a specific class. To open the **Object Browser**, right click any built-in .NET class or method in the code editor and select **Go To Definition**. Figure 8.21 depicts the **Object Browser** when the user right clicks the class name **Object** in the code editor. Note that the **Object Browser** lists all methods provided by class **Object** in the **Members of 'Object'** window—this window offers developers "instant access" to information regarding the functionality of various objects. Note also that the **Object Browser** lists in the **Objects** window all classes in the FCL. The **Object Browser** can be a quick mechanism to learn about a class or method of a class. Remember that you can view the complete description of a class or method in the online documentation available through the **Help** menu in Visual Studio.

This chapter is the first in a series of three chapters that cover the fundamentals of object-based and object-oriented programming. In this chapter, we discussed how to create proper class definitions, how to control access to class members and several features commonly used to craft valuable classes for reuse by other programmers. Chapter 9, focusses on *inheritance*. In that chapter, you will learn how to build classes that inherit data and functionality from existing class definitions. You also will learn other C# features that are specific to the inheritance relationship between classes. These features serve as the basis for the object-oriented programming concept called *polymorphism* that we present in Chapter 10.

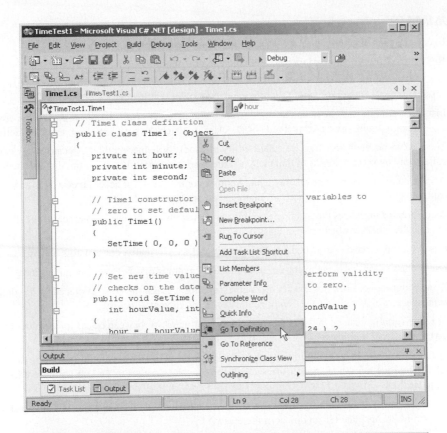

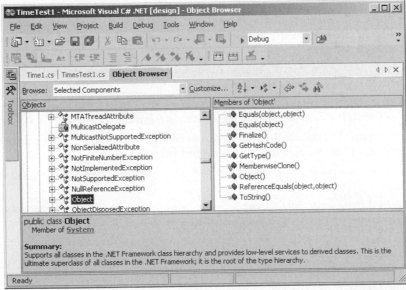

Fig. 8.21 **Object Browser** when user selects **Object** from **Time1.cs**.

SUMMARY

- Every class in C# inherits directly or indirectly from class **Object**.
- Keywords **public** and **private** are member access modifiers.
- Instance variables and methods that are declared with member access modifier **public** are accessible wherever the program has a reference to an object of that class.
- Instance variables and methods that are declared with member access modifier **private** are accessible only to non-**static** methods of the class in which the **private** members are defined.
- The **private** methods often are called utility methods, or helper methods, because they can be called only by other methods of that class and are used to support the operation of those methods.
- Access methods can read or display data. Another common use for access methods is to test the truth of conditions—such methods often are called predicate methods.
- A constructor initializes the instance variables of a class object. A class's constructor is called automatically when an object of that class is instantiated.
- It is common to have overloaded constructors for a class. Normally, constructors are **public**.
- Every class in C#, such as the classes from the .NET Framework, belongs to a namespace.
- If the programmer does not specify the namespace for a class, the class is placed in the default namespace, which includes the compiled classes in the current directory.
- Instance variables can be initialized by the class constructor, or they can be assigned values by the **set** accessor of a property.
- Instance variables that are not initialized explicitly by the programmer are initialized by the compiler (primitive numeric variables are set to **0**, **bool** values are set to **false** and references are set to **null**).
- Classes simplify programming, because the client code need only be concerned with the **public** operations encapsulated in an object of the class.
- A class's non-**static** instance variables and methods belong to that class's scope. Within a class's scope, class members are immediately accessible to all of that class's non-**static** methods and can be referenced simply by name. Outside a class's scope, class members cannot be referenced directly by name.
- Variables defined in a method are known only to that method (i.e., they are local to that method). Such variables are said to have block scope.
- If a method defines a variable that has the same name as a variable with class scope, the class-scope variable is hidden by the block-scope variable in that method.
- To allow clients to manipulate the value of **private** data, the class can provide a property definition, which will enable the user to access this **private** data in a safe way.
- A property definition contains accessor methods that handle the details of modifying and returning data.
- A property definition can contain a **set** accessor, a **get** accessor or both. A **get** accessor enables the client to read the field's value and the **set** accessor enables the client to modify the value.
- When an object is created, its members can be initialized by a constructor of that object's class.
- If no constructors are defined for a class, a default constructor will be provided by the compiler. This constructor contains no code and takes no parameters.
- Methods and constructors of a class can be overloaded. To overload a method of a class, simply provide a separate method definition with the same name for each version of the method. Remember that overloaded methods/constructors must have different parameter lists.

- Although **set** and **get** accessors can provide access to **private** data, the access is restricted by the programmer's implementation of those methods.

- One form of software reuse is composition, in which a class contains as members references to objects of other classes.

- The **this** reference is used implicitly and explicitly to refer to both the instance variables and the non-**static** methods of an object.

- The .NET Framework performs automatic garbage collection.

- Every class in C# can have a destructor that typically returns resources to the system. The destructor for an object is guaranteed to be called to perform termination housekeeping on the object just before the garbage collector reclaims the memory for the object (called finalization).

- In certain cases, all objects of a class should share only one copy of a particular variable. Programmers use **static** variables for this and other reasons.

- A **static** variable represents class-wide information—all objects of the class share the same piece of data.

- The declaration of a **static** member begins with the keyword **static**. Such variables have class scope.

- A class's **public static** members can be accessed via the class name and the dot operator (e.g., **Math.PI**).

- A class's **private static** members can be accessed only through methods or properties of the class.

- A method declared **static** cannot access non-**static** members.

- C# allows programmers to create constants whose values cannot change during program execution.

- To create a constant member of a C# class, the programmer must declare that member using either the **const** or **readonly** keyword.

- Members declared **const** must be initialized in the declaration; those declared with **readonly** can be initialized in the constructor, but must be initialized before they are used.

- Neither **const** nor **readonly** values can be modified once they are initialized.

- A class can define indexers to provide subscripted access to the data in an object of that class.

- Indexers can be defined to use any data type as the subscript.

- Each indexer can define a **get** and **set** accessor.

- Classes normally hide their implementation details from the clients of the classes. This is called information hiding.

- C# and the object-oriented style of programming elevate the importance of data. The primary activities of object-oriented programming in C# are the creation of data types (i.e., classes) and the expression of the interactions among objects of those data types.

- C# programmers concentrate on crafting new classes and reusing existing classes.

- Software reusability speeds the development of powerful, high-quality software. Rapid applications development (RAD) is of great interest today.

- Each class and interface in the .NET Framework belongs to a specific namespace (or library) that contains a group of related classes and interfaces. Namespaces provide a mechanism for software reuse.

- There is a good chance that the names you choose for classes will conflict with the names that other programmers choose for their classes. For this reason, namespaces provide a convention for unique class names.

- The Visual Studio .NET **Class View** displays the variables and methods for all classes in a project.
- The Visual Studio .NET **Object Browser** lists all classes in the C# library. Developers use the **Object Browser** to learn about the functionality provided by a specific object.

TERMINOLOGY

abstract data type (ADT)
access method
action
action-oriented
aggregation
assembly
attribute (data)
behavior (method)
block scope
body of a class definition
built-in data types
case sensitivity
class
class definition
class library
class scope
class implements abstract data type
class-scope variable hidden by
        method-scope variable
Class View
"class-wide" information
client of a class
Collect method of **GC**
compile a class
composition
consistent state
constant
constructor
create a code library
create a namespace
create a reusable class
create class from existing class definition
create data types
data abstraction
data in support of actions
data integrity
data member
data representation of an abstract data type
data structure
default constructor
destructor
division by zero is undefined
.dll
dot (**.**) operator

dynamic link library
encapsulate
enqueue operation
.exe
explicit use of **this** reference
extensible language
finalizer
first-in, first-out (FIFO) data structure
garbage collector
GC class
get accessor
GUI event handling
helper method
hide an instance variable
hide implementation details
hide internal data representation
implementation
indexer
indexer **get** accessor
indexer **set** accessor
information hiding
inheritance
initial set of classes
initialize a class object
initialize an instance variable
initialize to default values
insert an item into a container object
instance of a built-in type
instance of a user-defined type
instance variable
instantiate (or create) an object
interactions among objects
interface
internal data representation
IsEmpty
IsFull
last-in, first-out (LIFO) data structure
library
linked list
local variable of a method
member access modifier
memory leak
method overloading
namespace

new operator
no-argument constructor
non-**public** method
Object Browser
Object class
object (or instance)
object orientation
object passed by reference
"object speak"
"object think"
object-based programming (OBP)
object-oriented programming (OOP)
overloaded constructor
overloaded method
polymorphism
popping off a stack
predicate method
private keyword
private static member
procedural programming language
program-development process
programmer-defined type
public keyword
public method
public operations encapsulated in an object
public service
public static member

pushing into a stack
queue
rapid applications development (RAD)
reclaim memory
reference to a new object
resource leak
reusable software component
service of a class
set accessor of a property
signature
software reuse
stack
standard-time format
static keyword
static variable
static variables have class scope
structured programming
termination housekeeping
this keyword
universal-time format
user-defined type
utility method
validity checking
variable
WaitForPendingFinalizers method
    of class **GC**
waiting line

SELF-REVIEW EXERCISES

8.1   Fill in the blanks in each of the following statements:
  a) Client code can access a class's members via the _____ operator in conjunction
     with a reference to an object of the class.
  b) Members of a class declared _____ are accessible only to methods of the class in
     which those members are defined.
  c) A _____ initializes the instance variables of a class.
  d) A property _____ accessor is used to assign values to **private** instance variables
     of a class.
  e) Methods of a class normally are declared _____, and instance variables of a class
     normally are declared _____.
  f) A _____ accessor of a property is used to retrieve values of **private** data of a class.
  g) The keyword _____ introduces a class definition.
  h) Members of a class declared _____ are accessible anywhere that an object of the
     class is in scope.
  i) The _____ operator allocates memory dynamically for an object of a specified type
     and returns a _____ to that type.
  j) A _____ variable represents class-wide information.
  k) The keyword _____ specifies that an object or variable is not modifiable after it is
     initialized at execution time.
  l) A method declared **static** cannot access _____ class members.

8.2   State whether each of the following is *true* of *false*. If *false* explain why.
   a) All objects are passed by reference.
   b) Constructors can have return values.
   c) Properties must define **get** and **set** accessors.
   d) The **this** reference of an object is a reference to that object itself.
   e) A **static** member can be referenced when no object of that type exists.
   f) A **static** member of a class can be referenced through an instance of the class.
   g) Variables declared **const** must be initialized either in a declaration or in the class constructor.
   h) Different namespaces cannot have classes/methods with the same names.
   i) Assembly files are not required to define an entry point (**Main** method).
   j) Indexers can return any type in C#.

ANSWERS TO SELF-REVIEW EXERCISES

8.1   a) dot (**.**). b) **private**. c) constructor. d) **set**. e) **public**, **private**. f) **get**. g) **class**. h) **public**. i) **new**, reference. j) **static**. k) **readonly**. l) non-**static**.

8.2   a) True. b) False. Constructors are not permitted to return values. c) False. A property definition can specify a **set** accessor, a **get** accessor or both. d) True. e) True. f) False. A **static** member of a class can only be referenced through the class name. g) False. Variables declared **const** must be initialized when they are declared. h) False. Different namespaces can have classes/methods with the same names. i) True. j) True.

EXERCISES

8.3   Create a class called **Complex** for performing arithmetic with complex numbers. Write a driver program to test your class.

Complex numbers have the form

```
realPart + imaginaryPart * i
```

where *i* is

$$\sqrt{-1}$$

Use floating-point variables to represent the **private** data of the class. Provide a constructor that enables an object of this class to be initialized when it is declared. Provide a no-argument constructor with default values in case no initializers are provided. Provide **public** methods for each of the following:
   a) *Addition of two* **Complex** *numbers*. The real parts are added together and the imaginary parts are added together.
   b) *Subtraction of two* **Complex** *numbers*. The real part of the right operand is subtracted from the real part of the left operand and the imaginary part of the right operand is subtracted from the imaginary part of the left operand.
   c) *Printing of* **Complex** *numbers in the form* **(a, b)**, *where* **a** *is the real part and* **b** *is the imaginary part*.

8.4   Modify the **Date** class of Fig. 8.8 to perform error checking on the initializer values for instance variables **month**, **day** and **year**. Also, provide a method **NextDay** to increment the day by one. The **Date** object should always remain in a consistent state. Write a program that tests the **NextDay** method in a loop that prints the date during each iteration of the loop to illustrate that the **NextDay** method works correctly. Be sure to test the following cases:

  a) Incrementing into the next month.

  b) Incrementing into the next year.

8.5   Create a class **TicTacToe** that will enable you to write a complete program to play the game of Tic-Tac-Toe. The class contains as **private** data a 3-by-3 double array of characters. The constructor should initialize the empty board to all spaces, **' '**. Allow two players. Wherever the first player moves, place an **'X'** in the specified square; place an **'O'** wherever the second player moves. Each move must be to an empty square. After each move, determine whether the game has been won or if the game is a draw via a **GameStatus** method. [*Hint*: use an enumeration constant to return the following statuses: **WIN, DRAW, CONTINUE**.] Write Windows Application **TicTac-ToeTest** to test your class. If you feel ambitious, modify your program so that the computer makes the moves for one of the players automatically. Also, allow the player to specify whether he or she wants to go first or second. If you feel exceptionally ambitious, develop a program that will play three-dimensional Tic-Tac-Toe on a 4-by-4-by-4 board [Note: This is a challenging project that could take many weeks of effort!]

8.6   Create a **Date** class with the following capabilities:

  a) Output the date in multiple formats such as

```
MM/DD/YYYY
June 14, 2001
DDD YYYY
```

  b) Use overloaded constructors to create **Date** objects initialized with dates of the formats in part a).

8.7   Create class **SavingsAccount**. Use **static** variable **annualInterestRate** to store the interest rate for all account holders. Each object of the class contains a **private** instance variable **savingsBalance** indicating the amount the saver currently has on deposit. Provide method **CalculateMonthlyInterest** to calculate the monthly interest by multiplying the **savingsBalance** by **annualInterestRate** divided by 12; this interest should be added to **savingsBalance**. Provide a **static** method **ModifyInterestRate** that sets the **annualInterestRate** to a new value. Write a driver program to test class **SavingsAccount**. Instantiate two **savingsAccount** objects, **saver1** and **saver2**, with balances of $2000.00 and $3000.00, respectively. Set **annualInterestRate** to 4%, then calculate the monthly interest and print the new balances for each of the savers. Then set the **annualInterestRate** to 5% and calculate the next month's interest and print the new balances for each of the savers.

8.8   Write a console application that implements a **Square** shape. Class **Square** should contain an instance property **Side** that has **get** and **set** accessors for **private** data. Provide two constructors: one that takes no arguments and another that takes a **side** length as a value. Write an application class that tests class **Square**'s functionality.

Object-Oriented Programming: Inheritance

Objectives

- To understand inheritance and software reusability.
- To understand the concepts of base classes and derived classes.
- To understand member access modifier **protected** and **internal**.
- To be able to use the **base** reference to access base-class members
- To understand the use of constructors and destructors in base classes and derived classes.
- To present a case study that demonstrates the mechanics of inheritance.

Say not you know another entirely, till you have divided an inheritance with him.
Johann Kasper Lavater

This method is to define as the number of a class the class of all classes similar to the given class.
Bertrand Russell

Good as it is to inherit a library, it is better to collect one.
Augustine Birrell

Outline

9.1 Introduction

In this chapter, we begin our discussion of object-oriented programming (OOP) by introducing one of its main features—*inheritance*. Inheritance is a form of software reusability in which classes are created by absorbing an existing class's data and behaviors and embellishing them with new capabilities. Software reusability saves time during program development. It also encourages the reuse of proven and debugged high-quality software, which increases the likelihood that a system will be implemented effectively.

When creating a class, instead of writing completely new instance variables and methods, the programmer can designate that the new class should *inherit* the class variables, properties and methods of another class. The previously defined class is called the *base class*, and the new class is referred to as the *derived class.* (Other programming languages, such as Java, refer to the base class as the *superclass*, and the derived class as the *subclass*.) Once created, each derived class can become the base class for future derived classes. A derived class, to which unique class variables, properties and methods normally are added, is often larger than its base class. Therefore, a derived class is more specific than its base class and represents a more specialized group of objects. Typically, the derived class contains the behaviors of its base class and additional behaviors. The *direct base class* is the base class from which the derived class explicitly inherits. An *indirect base class* is inherited from two or more levels up the *class hierarchy*. In the case of *single inheritance,* a class is derived from one base class. C#, unlike C++, does not support *multiple inheritance* (which occurs when a class is derived from more than one direct base class). (We explain in Chapter 10 how C# can use interfaces to realize many of the benefits of multiple inheritance while avoiding the associated problems.)

Every object of a derived class is also an object of that derived class's base class. However, base-class objects are not objects of their derived classes. For example, all cars are vehicles, but not all vehicles are cars. As we continue our study of object-oriented programming in Chapters 9 and 10, we take advantage of this relationship to perform some interesting manipulations.

Experience in building software systems indicates that significant amounts of code deal with closely related special cases. When programmers are preoccupied with special cases, the details can obscure the "big picture." With object-oriented programming, programmers focus on the commonalities among objects in the system, rather than on the special cases. This process is called *abstraction*.

We distinguish between the *"is-a" relationship* and the *"has-a" relationship*. "Is-a" represents inheritance. In an "is-a" relationship, an object of a derived class also can be treated as an object of its base class. For example, a car *is a* vehicle. By contrast, "has-a" stands for composition (composition is discussed in Chapter 8). In a "has-a" relationship, a class object contains one or more object references as members. For example, a car *has a* steering wheel.

Derived-class methods might require access to their base-class instance variables, properties and methods. A derived class can access the non-**private** members of its base class. Base-class members that should not be accessible to properties or methods of a class derived from that base class via inheritance are declared **private** in the base class. A derived class can effect state changes in **private** base-class members, but only through non-**private** methods and properties provided in the base class and inherited into the derived class.

Software Engineering Observation 9.1

*Properties and methods of a derived class cannot directly access **private** members of their base class.*

Software Engineering Observation 9.2

*Hiding **private** members helps programmers test, debug and correctly modify systems. If a derived class could access its base class's **private** members, classes that inherit from that derived class could access that data as well. This would propagate access to what should be **private** data, and the benefits of information hiding would be lost.*

One problem with inheritance is that a derived class can inherit properties and methods it does not need or should not have. It is the class designer's responsibility to ensure that the capabilities provided by a class are appropriate for future derived classes. Even when a base-class property or method is appropriate for a derived class, that derived class often requires the property or method to perform its task in a manner specific to the derived class. In such cases, the base-class property or method can be *overridden* (redefined) in the derived class with an appropriate implementation.

New classes can inherit from abundant *class libraries*. Organizations develop their own class libraries and can take advantage of other libraries available worldwide. Someday, the vast majority of new software likely will be constructed from *standardized reusable components*, as most hardware is constructed today. This will facilitate the development of more powerful and abundant software.

9.2 Base Classes and Derived Classes

Often, an object of one class "is an" object of another class, as well. For example, a rectangle *is a* quadrilateral (as are squares, parallelograms and trapezoids). Thus, class **Rectangle** can be said to *inherit* from class **Quadrilateral**. In this context, class **Quadrilateral** is a base class, and class **Rectangle** is a derived class. A rectangle *is a* specific type of quadrilateral, but it is incorrect to claim that a quadrilateral *is a* rectangle—the quadrilateral could be a parallelogram or some other type of **Quadrilateral**. Figure 9.1 lists several simple examples of base classes and derived classes.

Base class	Derived classes
Student	GraduateStudent UndergraduateStudent
Shape	Circle Triangle Rectangle
Loan	CarLoan HomeImprovementLoan MortgageLoan
Employee	FacultyMember StaffMember
Account	CheckingAccount SavingsAccount

Fig. 9.1   Inheritance examples.

Every derived-class object "is an" object of its base class, and one base class can have many derived classes; therefore, the set of objects represented by a base class typically is larger than the set of objects represented by any of its derived classes. For example, the base class **Vehicle** represents all vehicles, including cars, trucks, boats, bicycles and so on. By contrast, derived-class **Car** represents only a small subset of all **Vehicle**s.

Inheritance relationships form tree-like hierarchical structures. A class exists in a hierarchical relationship with its derived classes. Although classes can exist independently, once they are employed in inheritance arrangements, they become affiliated with other classes. A class becomes either a base class, supplying data and behaviors to other classes, or a derived class, inheriting its data and behaviors from other classes.

Let us develop a simple inheritance hierarchy. A university community has thousands of members. These members consist of employees, students and alumni. Employees are either faculty members or staff members. Faculty members are either administrators (such as deans and department chairpersons) or teachers. This organizational structure yields the inheritance hierarchy, depicted in Fig. 9.2. Note that the inheritance hierarchy could contain many other classes. For example, students can be graduate or undergraduate students. Undergraduate students can be freshmen, sophomores, juniors and seniors. Each arrow in the hierarchy represents an "is-a" relationship. For example, as we follow the arrows in this class hierarchy, we can state, "an **Employee** *is a* **CommunityMember**" and "a **Teacher** *is a* **Faculty** member." **CommunityMember** is the *direct base class* of **Employee**, **Student** and **Alumnus**. In addition, **CommunityMember** is an *indirect base class* of all the other classes in the hierarchy diagram.

Starting from the bottom of the diagram, the reader can follow the arrows and apply the *is-a* relationship to the topmost base class. For example, an **Administrator** *is a* **Faculty** member, *is an* **Employee** and *is a* **CommunityMember**. In C#, an **Administrator** also *is an* **Object**, because all classes in C# have **Object** as either a direct or indirect base class. Thus, all classes in C# are connected via a hierarchical relationship in which they share the eight methods defined by class **Object**. We discuss some of these methods inherited from **Object** throughout the text.

Another inheritance hierarchy is the **Shape** hierarchy of Fig. 9.3. To specify that class **TwoDimensionalShape** is derived from (or inherits from) class **Shape**, class **TwoDimensionalShape** could be defined in C# as follows:

```
class TwoDimensionalShape : Shape
```

In Chapter 8, we briefly discussed *has-a* relationships, in which classes have as members references to objects of other classes. Such relationships create classes by *composition* of existing classes. For example, given the classes **Employee**, **BirthDate** and **TelephoneNumber**, it is improper to say that an **Employee** *is a* **BirthDate** or that an **Employee** *is a* **TelephoneNumber**. However, it is appropriate to say that an **Employee** *has a* **BirthDate** and that an **Employee** *has a* **TelephoneNumber**.

With inheritance, **private** members of a base class are not accessible directly from that class's derived classes, but these **private** base-class members are still inherited. All other base-class members retain their original member access when they become members of the derived class (e.g., **public** members of the base class become **public** members of the derived class, and, as we will soon see, **protected** members of the base class become **protected** members of the derived class). Through these inherited base-class members, the derived class can manipulate **private** members of the base class (if these inherited members provide such functionality in the base class).

It is possible to treat base-class objects and derived-class objects similarly; their commonalities are expressed in the member variables, properties and methods of the base class. Objects of all classes derived from a common base class can be treated as objects of that base class. In Chapter 10, Object-Oriented Programming: Polymorphism we consider many examples that take advantage of this relationship.

Software Engineering Observation 9.3

Constructors never are inherited—they are specific to the class in which they are defined.

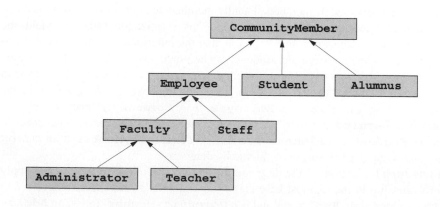

Fig. 9.2   Inheritance hierarchy for university **CommunityMember**s.

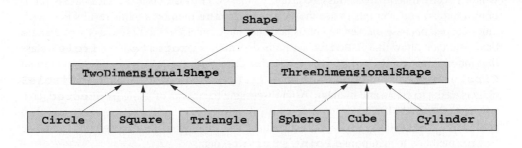

Fig. 9.3   Portion of a **Shape** class hierarchy.

9.3 `protected` and `internal` Members

Chapter 8 discussed **public** and **private** member access modifiers. A base class's **public** members are accessible anywhere that the program has a reference to an object of that base class or one of its derived classes. A base class's **private** members are accessible only within the body of that base class. In this section, we introduce two additional member access modifiers, *protected* and *internal*.

Using **protected** access offers an intermediate level of protection between **public** and **private** access. A base class's **protected** members can be accessed only in that base class or in any classes derived from that base class.

Another intermediate level of access is known as **internal** access. A base class's **internal** members can be accessed only by objects declared in the same assembly. Note that an **internal** member is accessible in any part of the assembly in which that **internal** member is declared.

Derived-class methods normally can refer to **public**, **protected** and **internal** members of the base class simply by using the member names. When a derived-class method overrides a base-class member, the base-class member can be accessed from the derived class by preceding the base-class member name with keyword *base*, followed by the dot operator (**.**). We discuss keyword **base** in Section 9.4.

9.4 Relationship between Base Classes and Derived Classes

In this section, we use a point-circle hierarchy[1] to discuss the relationship between a base class and a derived class. We divide our discussion of the point-circle relationship into several parts. First, we create class **Point**, which directly inherits from class **System.Object** and contains as **private** data an *x-y* coordinate pair. Then, we create class **Circle**, which also directly inherits from class **System.Object** and contains as **private** data an *x-y* coordinate pair (representing the location of the center of the circle) and a radius. We do not use inheritance to create class **Circle**; rather, we construct the class by writing every line of code the class requires. Next, we create a separate **Circle2** class,

---

1. The point-circle relationship may seem unnatural when we discuss it in the context of a circle "is a" point. This example teaches what is sometimes called *structural inheritance*; the example focuses on the "mechanics" of inheritance and how a base class and a derived class relate to one another. In Chapter 10, we present more natural inheritance examples.

which directly inherits from class **Point** (i.e., class **Circle2** "is a" **Point** but also contains a radius) and attempts to use the **Point private** members—this results in compilation errors, because the derived class does not have access to the base-class's **private** data. We then show that if **Point**'s data is declared as **protected**, a **Circle3** class that inherits from class **Point** can access that data. Both the inherited and non-inherited **Circle** classes contain identical functionality, but we show how the inherited **Circle3** class is easier to create and manage. After discussing the merits of using **protected** data, we set the **Point** data back to **private** (to enforce good software engineering), then show how a separate **Circle4** class (which also inherits from class **Point**) can use **Point** methods to manipulate **Point**'s **private** data.

Let us first examine the **Point** (Fig. 9.4) class definition. The **public** services of class **Point** include two **Point** constructors (lines 13–24), properties **X** and **Y** (lines 27–54) and method **ToString** (lines 57–60). The instance variables **x** and **y** of **Point** are specified as **private** (line 10), so objects of other classes cannot access **x** and **y** directly. Technically, even if **Point**'s variables **x** and **y** were made **public**, **Point** can never maintain an inconsistent state, because the *x-y* coordinate plane is infinite in both directions, so **x** and **y** can hold any **int** value. In general, however, declaring data as **private**, while providing non-**private** properties to manipulate and perform validation checking on that data, enforces good software engineering.

We mentioned in Section 9.2 that constructors are not inherited. Therefore, class **Point** does not inherit class **Object**'s constructor. However, class **Point**'s constructors (lines 13–24) call class **Object**'s constructor implicitly. In fact, the first task of any derived-class constructor is to call its direct base class's constructor, either implicitly or explicitly. (The syntax for calling a base-class constructor is discussed later in this section.) If the code does not include an explicit call to the base-class constructor, an implicit call is made to the base class's default (no-argument) constructor. The comments in lines 15 and 21 indicate where the implicit calls to the base-class **Object**'s default constructor occur.

```
1   // Fig. 9.4: Point.cs
2   // Point class represents an x-y coordinate pair.
3
4   using System;
5
6   // Point class definition implicitly inherits from Object
7   public class Point
8   {
9      // point coordinates
10     private int x, y;
11
12     // default (no-argument) constructor
13     public Point()
14     {
15        // implicit call to Object constructor occurs here
16     }
17
18     // constructor
19     public Point( int xValue, int yValue )
20     {
```

Fig. 9.4   **Point** class represents an *x-y* coordinate pair. (Part 1 of 2.)

```
21            // implicit call to Object constructor occurs here
22            X = xValue;
23            Y = yValue;
24         }
25
26         // property X
27         public int X
28         {
29            get
30            {
31               return x;
32            }
33
34            set
35            {
36               x = value; // no need for validation
37            }
38
39         } // end property X
40
41         // property Y
42         public int Y
43         {
44            get
45            {
46               return y;
47            }
48
49            set
50            {
51               y = value; // no need for validation
52            }
53
54         } // end property Y
55
56         // return string representation of Point
57         public override string ToString()
58         {
59            return "[" + x + ", " + y + "]";
60         }
61
62      } // end class Point
```

Fig. 9.4   **Point** class represents an *x-y* coordinate pair. (Part 2 of 2.)

Note that method **ToString** (lines 57–60) contains the keyword ***override*** in its declaration. Every class in C# (such as class **Point**) inherits either directly or indirectly from class **System.Object**, which is the root of the class hierarchy. As we mentioned previously, this means that every class inherits the eight methods defined by class **Object**. One of these methods is ***ToString***, which returns a **string** containing the object's type preceded by its namespace—this method obtains an object's **string** representation and sometimes is called implicitly by the program (such as when an object is concatenated to a **string**). Method **ToString** of class **Point** *overrides* the original **ToString** from class **Object**—when invoked, method **ToString** of class **Point** returns a **string** containing an ordered pair of the values **x** and **y** (line 59), instead of returning a **string** containing the object's class and namespace. To override a base-class method definition, a derived class must specify that the derived-class method overrides the base-class method with keyword **override** in the method header.

Software Engineering Observation 9.4

The C# compiler sets the base class of a derived class to **Object** *when the program does not specify a base class explicitly.*

In C#, a base-class method must be declared *virtual* if that method is to be over-ridden in a derived class. Method **ToString** of class **Object** is, in fact, declared **virtual**, which enables derived class **Point** to override this method. To view the method header for **ToString**, select **Help > Index...**, and enter **Object.ToString method** (filtered by **.Net Framework SDK**) in the search text box. The page displayed contains a description of method **ToString**, which includes the following header:

```
public virtual string ToString();
```

Keyword **virtual** allows programmers to specify those methods that a derived class can override—a method that has not been declared **virtual** cannot be overridden. We use this later in this section to enable certain methods in our base classes to be overridden.

Common Programming Error 9.1

A derived class attempting to override (using keyword **override***) a method that has not been declared* **virtual** *is a syntax error.*

Class **PointTest** (Fig. 9.5) tests class **Point**. Line 14 instantiates an object of class **Point** and assigns **72** as the *x*-coordinate value and **115** as the *y*-coordinate value. Lines 17–18 use properties **X** and **Y** to retrieve these values, then append the values to **string** **output**. Lines 20–21 change the values of properties **X** and **Y** (implicitly invoking their **set** accessors), and line 24 calls **Point**'s **ToString** method implicitly to obtain the **Point**'s **string** representation.

```
1   // Fig. 9.5: PointTest.cs
2   // Testing class Point.
3
4   using System;
5   using System.Windows.Forms;
6
7   // PointTest class definition
8   class PointTest
9   {
10     // main entry point for application
11     static void Main( string[] args )
12     {
13       // instantiate Point object
14       Point point = new Point( 72, 115 );
15
```

Fig. 9.5   PointTest class demonstrates class **Point** functionality. (Part 1 of 2.)

```
16          // display point coordinates via X and Y properties
17          string output = "X coordinate is " + point.X +
18             "\n" + "Y coordinate is " + point.Y;
19
20          point.X = 10; // set x-coordinate via X property
21          point.Y = 10; // set y-coordinate via Y property
22
23          // display new point value
24          output += "\n\nThe new location of point is " + point;
25
26          MessageBox.Show( output, "Demonstrating Class Point" );
27
28       } // end method Main
29
30    } // end class PointTest
```

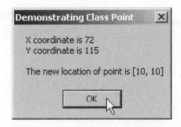

Fig. 9.5   **PointTest** class demonstrates class **Point** functionality. (Part 2 of 2.)

We now discuss the second part of our introduction to inheritance by creating and testing (a completely new) class **Circle** (Fig. 9.6), which directly inherits from class **System.Object** and represents an *x-y* coordinate pair (representing the center of the circle) and a radius. Lines 9–10 declare the instance variables **x**, **y** and **radius** as **private** data. The **public** services of class **Circle** include two **Circle** constructors (lines 13–25), properties **X**, **Y** and **Radius** (lines 28–71), methods **Diameter** (lines 74–77), **Circumference** (lines 80–83), **Area** (lines 86–89) and **ToString** (lines 92–96). These properties and methods encapsulate all necessary features (i.e., the "analytic geometry") of a circle; in the next section, we show how this encapsulation enables us to reuse and extend this class.

```
1    // Fig. 9.6: Circle.cs
2    // Circle class contains x-y coordinate pair and radius.
3
4    using System;
5
6    // Circle class definition implicitly inherits from Object
7    public class Circle
8    {
9       private int x, y;       // coordinates of Circle's center
10      private double radius; // Circle's radius
11
```

Fig. 9.6   **Circle** class contains an *x-y* coordinate and a radius. (Part 1 of 3.)

```
12       // default constructor
13       public Circle()
14       {
15          // implicit call to Object constructor occurs here
16       }
17
18       // constructor
19       public Circle( int xValue, int yValue, double radiusValue )
20       {
21          // implicit call to Object constructor occurs here
22          x = xValue;
23          y = yValue;
24          Radius = radiusValue;
25       }
26
27       // property X
28       public int X
29       {
30          get
31          {
32             return x;
33          }
34
35          set
36          {
37             x = value;   // no need for validation
38          }
39
40       } // end property X
41
42       // property Y
43       public int Y
44       {
45          get
46          {
47             return y;
48          }
49
50          set
51          {
52             y = value;   // no need for validation
53          }
54
55       } // end property Y
56
57       // property Radius
58       public double Radius
59       {
60          get
61          {
62             return radius;
63          }
64
```

Fig. 9.6   **Circle** class contains an *x-y* coordinate and a radius. (Part 2 of 3.)

```
65          set
66          {
67              if ( value >= 0 )    // validation needed
68                  radius = value;
69          }
70
71      } // end property Radius
72
73      // calculate Circle diameter
74      public double Diameter()
75      {
76          return radius * 2;
77      }
78
79      // calculate Circle circumference
80      public double Circumference()
81      {
82          return Math.PI * Diameter();
83      }
84
85      // calculate Circle area
86      public double Area()
87      {
88          return Math.PI * Math.Pow( radius, 2 );
89      }
90
91      // return string representation of Circle
92      public override string ToString()
93      {
94          return "Center = [" + x + ", " + y + "]" +
95              "; Radius = " + radius;
96      }
97
98  } // end class Circle
```

Fig. 9.6   **Circle** class contains an *x-y* coordinate and a radius. (Part 3 of 3.)

Class **CircleTest** (Fig. 9.7) tests class **Circle**. Line 14 instantiates an object of class **Circle**, assigning **37** as the *x*-coordinate value, **43** as the *y*-coordinate value and **2.5** as the radius value. Lines 17–19 use properties **X**, **Y** and **Radius** to retrieve these values, then concatenate the values to **string output**. Lines 22–24 use **Circle**'s **X**, **Y** and **Radius** properties to change the *x-y* coordinates and the radius, respectively. Property **Radius** ensures that member variable **radius** cannot be assigned a negative value. Line 28 calls **Circle**'s **ToString** method implicitly to obtain the **Circle**'s **string** representation, and lines 32–40 call **Circle**'s **Diameter**, **Circumference** and **Area** methods.

After writing all the code for class **Circle** (Fig. 9.6), we note that a major portion of the code in this class is similar, if not identical, to much of the code in class **Point**. For example, the declaration in **Circle** of **private** variables **x** and **y** and properties **X** and **Y** are identical to those of class **Point**. In addition, the class **Circle** constructors and method **ToString** are almost identical to those of class **Point**, except that they also supply **radius** information. The only other additions to class **Circle** are **private** member variable **radius**, property **Radius** and methods **Diameter**, **Circumference** and **Area**.

It appears that we literally copied code from class **Point**, pasted this code in the code from class **Circle**, then modified class **Circle** to include a radius. This "copy-and-paste" approach is often error-prone and time-consuming. Worse yet, it can result in many physical copies of the code existing throughout a system, creating a code-maintenance "nightmare." Is there a way to "absorb" the attributes and behaviors of one class in a way that makes them part of other classes without duplicating code?

```csharp
1    // Fig. 9.7: CircleTest.cs
2    // Testing class Circle.
3
4    using System;
5    using System.Windows.Forms;
6
7    // CircleTest class definition
8    class CircleTest
9    {
10       // main entry point for application.
11       static void Main( string[] args )
12       {
13          // instantiate Circle
14          Circle circle = new Circle( 37, 43, 2.5 );
15
16          // get Circle's initial x-y coordinates and radius
17          string output = "X coordinate is " + circle.X +
18             "\nY coordinate is " + circle.Y + "\nRadius is " +
19             circle.Radius;
20
21          // set Circle's x-y coordinates and radius to new values
22          circle.X = 2;
23          circle.Y = 2;
24          circle.Radius = 4.25;
25
26          // display Circle's string representation
27          output += "\n\nThe new location and radius of " +
28             "circle are \n" + circle + "\n";
29
30          // display Circle's diameter
31          output += "Diameter is " +
32             String.Format( "{0:F}", circle.Diameter() ) + "\n";
33
34          // display Circle's circumference
35          output += "Circumference is " +
36             String.Format( "{0:F}", circle.Circumference() ) + "\n";
37
38          // display Circle's area
39          output += "Area is " +
40             String.Format( "{0:F}", circle.Area() );
41
42          MessageBox.Show( output, "Demonstrating Class Circle" );
43
44       } // end method Main
```

Fig. 9.7   **CircleTest** demonstrates class **Circle** functionality. (Part 1 of 2.)

```
45
46  } // end class CircleTest
```

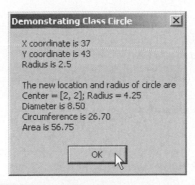

Fig. 9.7   **CircleTest** demonstrates class **Circle** functionality. (Part 2 of 2.)

In the next examples we answer that question, we use a more elegant class construction approach emphasizing the benefits of inheritance. Now, we create and test a class **Circle2** (Fig. 9.8) that inherits variables **x** and **y** and properties **X** and **Y** from class **Point** (Fig. 9.4). This class **Circle2** "is a" **Point** (because inheritance absorbs the capabilities of class **Point**), but also contains **radius** (line 9). The colon (**:**) symbol in the class declaration (line 7) indicates inheritance. As a derived class, **Circle2** inherits all the members of class **Point**, except for the constructors. Thus, the **public** services to **Circle2** include the two **Circle2** constructors (lines 12–24); the **public** methods inherited from class **Point**; property **Radius** (lines 27–40); and the **Circle2** methods **Diameter**, **Circumference**, **Area** and **ToString** (lines 43–65). We declare method **Area** as **virtual**, so that derived classes (such as class **Cylinder**, as we will see in Section 9.5) can override this method to provide a more appropriate implementation.

```
1   // Fig. 9.8: Circle2.cs
2   // Circle2 class that inherits from class Point.
3
4   using System;
5
6   // Circle2 class definition inherits from Point
7   class Circle2 : Point
8   {
9      private double radius; // Circle2's radius
10
11     // default constructor
12     public Circle2()
13     {
14        // implicit call to Point constructor occurs here
15     }
16
```

Fig. 9.8   **Circle2** class that inherits from class **Point**. (Part 1 of 3.)

```
17      // constructor
18      public Circle2( int xValue, int yValue, double radiusValue )
19      {
20         // implicit call to Point constructor occurs here
21         x = xValue;
22         y = yValue;
23         Radius = radiusValue;
24      }
25
26      // property Radius
27      public double Radius
28      {
29         get
30         {
31            return radius;
32         }
33
34         set
35         {
36            if ( value >= 0 )
37               radius = value;
38         }
39
40      } // end property Radius
41
42      // calculate Circle diameter
43      public double Diameter()
44      {
45         return radius * 2;
46      }
47
48      // calculate Circle circumference
49      public double Circumference()
50      {
51         return Math.PI * Diameter();
52      }
53
54      // calculate Circle area
55      public virtual double area()
56      {
57         return Math.PI * Math.Pow( radius, 2 );
58      }
59
60      // return string representation Circle
61      public override string ToString()
62      {
63         return "Center = [" + x + ", " + y + "]" +
64            "; Radius = " + radius;
65      }
66
67   } // end class Circle2
```

Fig. 9.8   Circle2 class that inherits from class **Point**. (Part 2 of 3.)

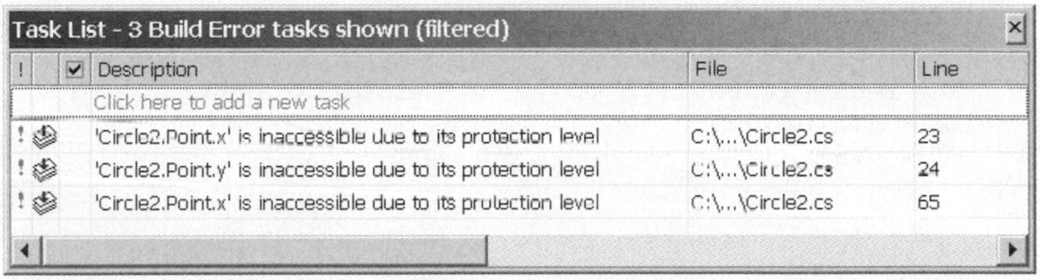

Fig. 9.8 `Circle2` class that inherits from class `Point`. (Part 3 of 3.)

Lines 14 and 20 in the `Circle2` constructors (lines 12–24) invoke the default `Point` constructor implicitly to initialize the base-class portion (variables **x** and **y**, inherited from class **Point**) of a **Circle2** object to **0**. However, because the parameterized constructor (lines 18–24) should set the *x-y* coordinate to a specific value, lines 21–22 attempt to assign argument values to **x** and **y** directly. Even though lines 21–22 attempt to set **x** and **y** values explicitly, line 20 first calls the **Point** default constructor to initialize these variables to their default values. The compiler generates syntax errors for lines 21 and 22 (and line 63, where **Circle2**'s method **ToString** attempts to use the values of **x** and **y** directly), because the derived class **Circle2** is not allowed to access the base class **Point**'s **private** members **x** and **y**. C# rigidly enforces restriction on accessing **private** data members, so that even a derived class (i.e., which is closely related to its base class) cannot access base-class **private** data.

To enable class **Circle2** to access **Point** member variables **x** and **y** directly, we can declare those variables as **protected**. As we discussed in Section 9.3, a base class's **protected** members can be accessed only in that base class or in any classes derived from that base class. Class **Point2** (Fig. 9.9) modifies class **Point** (Fig. 9.4) to declare variables **x** and **y** as **protected** (line 10) instead of **private**.

```
1   // Fig. 9.9: Point2.cs
2   // Point2 class contains an x-y coordinate pair as protected data.
3
4   using System;
5
6   // Point2 class definition implicitly inherits from Object
7   public class Point2
8   {
9      // point coordinate
10     protected int x, y;
11
12     // default constructor
13     public Point2()
14     {
15        // implicit call to Object constructor occurs here
16     }
17
```

Fig. 9.9 **Point2** class represents an *x-y* coordinate pair as **protected** data. (Part 1 of 2.)

```
18       // constructor
19       public Point2( int xValue, int yValue )
20       {
21          // implicit call to Object constructor occurs here
22          X = xValue;
23          Y = yValue;
24       }
25
26       // property X
27       public int X
28       {
29          get
30          {
31             return x;
32          }
33
34          set
35          {
36             x = value; // no need for validation
37          }
38
39       } // end property X
40
41       // property Y
42       public int Y
43       {
44          get
45          {
46             return y;
47          }
48
49          set
50          {
51             y = value; // no need for validation
52          }
53
54       } // end property Y
55
56       // return string representation of Point2
57       public override string ToString()
58       {
59          return "[" + x + ", " + y + "]";
60       }
61
62    } // end class Point2
```

Fig. 9.9   **Point2** class represents an *x-y* coordinate pair as **protected** data. (Part 2 of 2.)

Class **Circle3** (Fig. 9.10) modifies class **Circle2** (Fig. 9.8) to inherit from class **Point2** rather than inheriting from class **Point**. Because class **Circle3** is a class derived from class **Point2**, class **Circle3** can access class **Point2**'s **protected** member variables **x** and **y** directly, and the compiler does not generate errors when compiling Fig. 9.10. This shows the special privileges that a derived class is granted to access

protected base-class data members. A derived class also can access **protected** methods in any of that derived class's base classes.

```
1   // Fig. 9.10: Circle3.cs
2   // Circle2 class that inherits from class Point2.
3
4   using System;
5
6   // Circle3 class definition inherits from Point2
7   public class Circle3 : Point2
8   {
9      private double radius; // Circle's radius
10
11      // default constructor
12      public Circle3()
13      {
14         // implicit call to Point constructor occurs here
15      }
16
17      // constructor
18      public Circle3(
19         int xValue, int yValue, double radiusValue )
20      {
21         // implicit call to Point constructor occurs here
22         x = xValue;
23         y = yValue;
24         Radius = radiusValue;
25      }
26
27      // property Radius
28      public double Radius
29      {
30         get
31         {
32            return radius;
33         }
34
35         set
36         {
37            if ( value >= 0 )
38               radius = value;
39         }
40
41      } // end property Radius
42
43      // calculate Circle diameter
44      public double Diameter()
45      {
46         return radius * 2;
47      }
48
```

Fig. 9.10 **Circle3** class that inherits from class **Point2**. (Part 1 of 2.)

```
49        // calculate circumference
50        public double Circumference()
51        {
52            return Math.PI * Diameter();
53        }
54
55        // calculate Circle area
56        public virtual double Area()
57        {
58            return Math.PI * Math.Pow( radius, 2 );
59        }
60
61        // return string representation of Circle3
62        public override string ToString()
63        {
64            return "Center = [" + x + ", " + y + "]" +
65                "; Radius = " + radius;
66        }
67
68    } // end class Circle3
```

Fig. 9.10   Circle3 class that inherits from class **Point2**. (Part 2 of 2.)

Class **CircleTest3** (Fig. 9.11) performs identical tests on class **Circle3** as class **CircleTest** (Fig. 9.7) performed on class **Circle** (Fig. 9.6). Note that the outputs of the two programs are identical. We created class **Circle** without using inheritance and created class **Circle3** using inheritance; however, both classes provide the same functionality. However, observe that the code listing for class **Circle3**, which is 68 lines, is considerably shorter than the code listing for class **Circle**, which is 98 lines, because class **Circle3** absorbs part of its functionality from **Point2**, whereas class **Circle** does not. Also, there is now only one copy of the point functionality.

```
1    // Fig. 9.11: CircleTest3.cs
2    // Testing class Circle3.
3
4    using System;
5    using System.Windows.Forms;
6
7    // CircleTest3 class definition
8    class CircleTest3
9    {
10       // main entry point for application
11       static void Main( string[] args )
12       {
13           // instantiate Circle3
14           Circle3 circle = new Circle3( 37, 43, 2.5 );
15
16           // get Circle3's initial x-y coordinates and radius
17           string output = "X coordinate is " + circle.X + "\n" +
18               "Y coordinate is " + circle.Y + "\nRadius is " +
19               circle.Radius;
```

Fig. 9.11   CircleTest3 demonstrates class **Circle3** functionality. (Part 1 of 2.)

```
20
21        // set Circle3's x-y coordinates and radius to new values
22        circle.X = 2;
23        circle.Y = 2;
24        circle.Radius = 4.25;
25
26        // display Circle3's string representation
27        output += "\n\n" +
28           "The new location and radius of circle are " +
29           "\n" + circle + "\n";
30
31        // display Circle3's Diameter
32        output += "Diameter is " +
33           String.Format( "{0:F}", circle.Diameter() ) + "\n";
34
35        // display Circle3's Circumference
36        output += "Circumference is " +
37           String.Format( "{0:F}", circle.Circumference() ) + "\n";
38
39        // display Circle3's Area
40        output += "Area is " +
41           String.Format( "{0:F}", circle.Area() );
42
43        MessageBox.Show( output, "Demonstrating Class Circle3" );
44
45     } // end method Main
46
47  } // end class CircleTest3
```

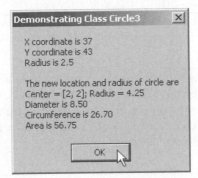

Fig. 9.11 `CircleTest3` demonstrates class `Circle3` functionality. (Part 2 of 2.)

In the previous example, we declared the base-class instance variables as **pro-tected**, so that a derived class could modify their values directly. The use of **pro-tected** variables allows for a slight increase in performance, because we avoid incurring the overhead of a method call to a property's **set** or **get** accessor. However, in most C# applications, in which user interaction comprises a large part of the execution time, the optimization offered through the use of **protected** variables is negligible.

Using **protected** instance variables creates two major problems. First, the derived-class object does not have to use a property to set the value of the base-class's **protected** data. Therefore, a derived-class object can easily assign an illegal value to the **protected** data, thus leaving the object in an inconsistent state. For example, if we were to declare **Circle3**'s variable **radius** as **protected**, a derived-class object (e.g., **Cylinder**), could then assign a negative value to **radius**. The second problem with using **protected** data is that derived-class methods are more likely to be written to depend on base-class implementation. In practice, derived classes should depend only on the base-class services (i.e., non-**private** methods and properties) and not on base-class implementation. With **protected** data in the base class, if the base-class implementation changes, we may need to modify all derived classes of that base class. For example, if for some reason we were to change the names of variables **x** and **y** to **xCoordinate** and **yCoordinate**, then we would have to do so for all occurrences in which a derived class references these base-class variables directly. In such a case, the software is said to be *fragile* or *brittle*. The programmer should be able to change the base-class implementation freely, while still providing the same services to derived classes. (Of course, if the base class services change, we must reimplement our derived classes, but good object-oriented design attempts to prevent this.)

Software Engineering Observation 9.5

*The most appropriate time to use the **protected** access modifier is when a base class should provide a service only to its derived classes (i.e., the base class should not provide the service to other clients).*

Software Engineering Observation 9.6

*Declaring base-class instance variables **private** (as opposed to declaring them **protected**) enables programmers to change base-class implementation without having to change derived-class implementation.*

Testing and Debugging Tip 9.1

*When possible, avoid including **protected** data in a base class. Rather, include non-**private** properties and methods that access **private** data, ensuring that the object maintains a consistent state.*

We reexamine our point-circle hierarchy example once more; this time, attempting to use the best software engineering. We use **Point3** (Fig. 9.12), which declares variables **x** and **y** as **private** and uses properties in method **ToString** to access these values. We show how derived class **Circle4** (Fig. 9.13) can invoke non-**private** base-class methods and properties to manipulate these variables.

```
1   // Fig. 9.12: Point3.cs
2   // Point3 class represents an x-y coordinate pair.
3
4   using System;
5
6   // Point3 class definition implicitly inherits from Object
7   public class Point3
8   {
9       // point coordinate
10      private int x, y;
11
```

Fig. 9.12   Point3 class uses properties to manipulate its **private** data. (Part 1 of 2.)

```
12      // default constructor
13      public Point3()
14      {
15          // implicit call to Object constructor occurs here
16      }
17
18      // constructor
19      public Point3( int xValue, int yValue )
20      {
21          // implicit call to Object constructor occurs here
22          X = xValue;    // use property X
23          Y = yValue;    // use property Y
24      }
25
26      // property X
27      public int X
28      {
29          get
30          {
31              return x;
32          }
33
34          set
35          {
36              x = value; // no need for validation
37          }
38
39      } // end property X
40
41      // property Y
42      public int Y
43      {
44          get
45          {
46              return y;
47          }
48
49          set
50          {
51              y = value; // no need for validation
52          }
53
54      } // end property Y
55
56      // return string representation of Point3
57      public override string ToString()
58      {
59          return "[" + X + ", " + Y + "]";
60      }
61
62  } // end class Point3
```

Fig. 9.12   **Point3** class uses properties to manipulate its **private** data. (Part 2 of 2.)

```
1   // Fig. 9.13: Circle4.cs
2   // Circle4 class that inherits from class Point3.
3
4   using System;
5
6   // Circle4 class definition inherits from Point3
7   public class Circle4 : Point3
8   {
9      private double radius;
10
11     // default constructor
12     public Circle4()
13     {
14        // implicit call to Point constructor occurs here
15     }
16
17     // constructor
18     public Circle4( int xValue, int yValue, double radiusValue )
19        : base( xValue, yValue )
20     {
21        Radius = radiusValue;
22     }
23
24     // property Radius
25     public double Radius
26     {
27        get
28        {
29           return radius;
30        }
31
32        set
33        {
34           if ( value >= 0 )    // validation needed
35              radius = value;
36        }
37
38     } // end property Radius
39
40     // calculate Circle diameter
41     public double Diameter()
42     {
43        return Radius * 2;      // use property Radius
44     }
45
46     // calculate Circle circumference
47     public double Circumference()
48     {
49        return Math.PI * Diameter();
50     }
51
```

Fig. 9.13 **Circle4** class that inherits from class **Point3**, which does not provide **protected** data. (Part 1 of 2.)

```
52        // calculate Circle area
53        public virtual double Area()
54        {
55            return Math.PI * Math.Pow( Radius, 2 );   // use property
56        }
57
58        // return string representation of Circle4
59        public override string ToString()
60        {
61            // use base reference to return Point string representation
62            return "Center= " + base.ToString() +
63                "; Radius = " + Radius;   // use property Radius
64        }
65
66   } // end class Circle4
```

Fig. 9.13   **Circle4** class that inherits from class **Point3**, which does not provide **protected** data. (Part 2 of 2.)

Software Engineering Observation 9.7

*When possible, use properties to alter and obtain the values of member variables, even if those values can be modified directly. A property's **set** accessor can prevent attempts to assign an inappropriate value to that member variable, and a property's **get** accessor can help control the presentation of the data to clients.*

Performance Tip 9.1

Using a property to access a variable's value is slightly slower than accessing the data directly. However, attempting to optimize programs by referencing data directly often is unnecessary, because the compiler optimizes the programs implicitly. [Today's so-called "optimizing compilers" are carefully designed to perform many optimizations implicitly, even if the programmer does not write what appears to be the most optimal code. A good rule is, "Do not second-guess the compiler."

For the purpose of this example, to demonstrate both explicit and implicit calls to base-class constructors, we include a second constructor that calls the base-class constructor explicitly. Lines 18–22 declare the **Circle4** constructor that invokes the second **Point3** constructor explicitly (line 19) using the *base-class constructor-call syntax* (i.e., reference **base** followed by a set of parentheses containing the arguments to the base-class constructor). In this case, **xValue** and **yValue** are passed to initialize the **private** base-class members **x** and **y**. The colon symbol (**:**) followed by the **base** keyword accesses the base-class version of that method explicitly (line 19). By making this call, we can initialize **x** and **y** in the base class to specific values, rather than to **0**.

Common Programming Error 9.2

*It is a syntax error if a derived class uses **base** to call its base-class constructor with arguments that do not match exactly the number and types of parameters specified in one of the base-class constructor definitions.*

Class **Circle4**'s **ToString** method (line 59–64) overrides class **Point3**'s **ToString** method (lines 57–60 of Fig. 9.12). As we discussed earlier, overriding this method is possible, because method **ToString** of class **System.Object** (class

Point3's base class) is declared **virtual**. Method **ToString** of class **Circle4** displays the **private** instance variables **x** and **y** of class **Point3** by calling the base class's **ToString** method (in this case, **Point3**'s **ToString** method). The call is made in line 62 via the expression **base.ToString()** and causes the values of **x** and **y** to become part of the **Circle4**'s **string** representation. Using this approach is a good software engineering practice. If an object's method performs the actions needed by another object, call that method rather than duplicating its code body. Duplicate code creates code-maintenance problems. By having **Circle4**'s **ToString** method use the formatting provided by **Point3**'s **ToString** method, we avoid duplicating code. Also, **Point3**'s **ToString** method performs part of the task of **Circle4**'s **ToString** method, so we call **Point3**'s **ToString** method from class **Circle4** with the expression **base.ToString()**.

Common Programming Error 9.3

*When a base-class method is overridden in a derived class, the derived-class version often calls the base-class version to do additional work. Failure to use the **base** reference when referencing the base class's method causes infinite recursion, because the derived-class method would then call itself.*

Common Programming Error 9.4

*The use of "chained" **base** references to refer to a member (a method, property or variable) several levels up the hierarchy (as in **base.base.mX**) is a syntax error.*

Software Engineering Observation 9.8

A redefinition in a derived class of a base-class method that uses a different signature than that of the base-class method is method overloading rather than method overriding.

Software Engineering Observation 9.9

*Although method **ToString** certainly could be overridden to perform arbitrary actions, the general understanding in the C# .NET community is that method **ToString** should be overridden to obtain an object's **string** representation.*

Class **CircleTest4** (Fig. 9.14) performs identical manipulations on class **Circle4** as did classes **CircleTest** (Fig. 9.7) and **CircleTest3** (Fig. 9.11). Note that the outputs of all three modules are identical. Therefore, although each "circle" class appears to behave identically, class **Circle4** is the most properly engineered. Using inheritance, we have efficiently and effectively constructed a well-engineered class.

```
1   // Fig. 9.14: CircleTest4.cs
2   // Testing class Circle4.
3
4   using System;
5   using System.Windows.Forms;
6
7   // CircleTest4 class definition
8   class CircleTest4
9   {
```

Fig. 9.14 **CircleTest4** demonstrates class **Circle4** functionality. (Part 1 of 2.)

```
10        // main entry point for application
11        static void Main( string[] args )
12        {
13           // instantiate Circle4
14           Circle4 circle = new Circle4( 37, 43, 2.5 );
15
16           // get Circle4's initial x-y coordinates and radius
17           string output = "X coordinate is " + circle.X + "\n" +
18              "Y coordinate is " + circle.Y + "\n" +
19              "Radius is " + circle.Radius;
20
21           // set Circle4's x-y coordinates and radius to new values
22           circle.X = 2;
23           circle.Y = 2;
24           circle.Radius = 4.25;
25
26           // display Circle4's string representation
27           output += "\n\n" +
28              "The new location and radius of circle are " +
29              "\n" + circle + "\n";
30
31           // display Circle4's Diameter
32           output += "Diameter is " +
33              String.Format( "{0:F}", circle.Diameter() ) + "\n";
34
35           // display Circle4's Circumference
36           output += "Circumference is " +
37              String.Format( "{0:F}", circle.Circumference() ) + "\n";
38
39           // display Circle4's Area
40           output += "Area is " +
41              String.Format( "{0:F}", circle.Area() );
42
43           MessageBox.Show( output, "Demonstrating Class Circle4" );
44
45        } // end method Main
46
47  } // end class CircleTest4
```

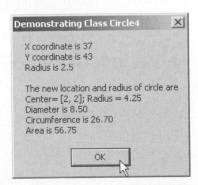

9.5 Case Study: Three-Level Inheritance Hierarchy

Let us consider a more substantial inheritance example involving a three-level point-circle-cylinder hierarchy. In Section 9.4, we developed classes **Point3** (Fig. 9.12) and **Circle4** (Fig. 9.13). Now, we present an example in which we derive class **Cylinder** from class **Circle4**.

The first class that we use in our case study is class **Point3** (Fig. 9.12). We declared **Point3**'s instance variables as **private**. Class **Point3** also contains properties **X** and **Y** for accessing **x** and **y** and method **ToString** (which **Point3** overrides from class **Object**) for obtaining a **string** representation of the *x-y* coordinate pair.

We also created class **Circle4** (Fig. 9.13), which inherits from class **Point3**. Class **Circle4** contains the **Point3** functionality, in addition to providing property **Radius**, which ensures that the **radius** member variable cannot hold a negative value, and methods **Diameter**, **Circumference**, **Area** and **ToString**. Recall that method **Area** was declared **virtual** (line 53). As we discussed in Section 9.4, this keyword enables derived classes to override a base-class method. Derived classes of class **Circle4** (such as class **Cylinder**, which we introduce momentarily) can override these methods and provide specific implementations. A circle has an area that is calculated by the formula, πr^2, in which *r* represents the circle's radius. However, a cylinder has a surface area that is calculated by the formula, $(2\pi r^2) + (2\pi rh)$, in which *r* represents the cylinder's radius and *h* represents the cylinder's height. Therefore, class **Cylinder** must override method **Area** to include this calculation, so we declared class **Circle4**'s method **Area** as **virtual**.

Figure 9.15 presents class **Cylinder**, which inherits from class **Circle4** (line 7). Class **Cylinder**'s **public** services include the inherited **Circle4** methods **Diameter**, **Circumference**, **Area** and **ToString**; the inherited **Circle4** property **Radius**; the indirectly inherited **Point3** properties **X** and **Y**; the **Cylinder** constructor, property **Height** and method **Volume**. Method **Area** (lines 41–44) overrides method **Area** of class **Circle4**. Note that, if class **Cylinder** were to attempt to override **Circle4**'s methods **Diameter** and **Circumference**, syntax errors would occur, because class **Circle4** did not declare these methods **virtual**. Method **ToString** (lines 53–56) overrides method **ToString** of class **Circle4** to obtain a **string** representation for the cylinder. Class **Cylinder** also includes method **Volume** (lines 47–50) to calculate the cylinder's volume. Because we do not declare method **Volume** as **virtual**, no derived class of class **Cylinder** can override this method.

```
1   // Fig. 9.15: Cylinder.cs
2   // Cylinder class inherits from class Circle4.
3
4   using System;
5
6   // Cylinder class definition inherits from Circle4
7   public class Cylinder : Circle4
8   {
9      private double height;
10
```

Fig. 9.15 **Cylinder** class inherits from class **Circle4** and overrides method **Area**. (Part 1 of 2.)

```
11        // default constructor
12        public Cylinder()
13        {
14            // implicit call to Circle4 constructor occurs here
15        }
16
17        // four-argument constructor
18        public Cylinder( int xValue, int yValue, double radiusValue,
19            double heightValue ) : base( xValue, yValue, radiusValue )
20        {
21            Height = heightValue; // set Cylinder height
22        }
23
24        // property Height
25        public double Height
26        {
27            get
28            {
29                return height;
30            }
31
32            set
33            {
34                if ( value >= 0 ) // validate height
35                    height = value;
36            }
37
38        } // end property Height
39
40        // override Circle4 method Area to calculate Cylinder area
41        public override double Area()
42        {
43            return 2 * base.Area() + base.Circumference() * Height;
44        }
45
46        // calculate Cylinder volume
47        public double Volume()
48        {
49            return base.Area() * Height;
50        }
51
52        // convert Cylinder to string
53        public override string ToString()
54        {
55            return base.ToString() + "; Height = " + Height;
56        }
57
58    } // end class Cylinder
```

Fig. 9.15 **Cylinder** class inherits from class **Circle4** and overrides method **Area**. (Part 2 of 2.)

Figure 9.16 is a **CylinderTest** application that tests the **Cylinder** class. Line 14 instantiates an object of class **Cylinder**. Lines 17–19 use properties **X**, **Y**, **Radius** and

Height to obtain information about the **Cylinder** object, because **CylinderTest** cannot reference the **private** data of class **Cylinder** directly. Lines 22–25 use properties **X**, **Y**, **Radius** and **Height** to reset the **Cylinder**'s *x-y* coordinates (we assume the cylinder's *x-y* coordinates specify its position on the *x-y* plane), radius and height. Class **Cylinder** can use class **Point3**'s **X** and **Y** properties, because class **Cylinder** inherits them indirectly from class **Point3**—Class **Cylinder** inherits properties **X** and **Y** directly from class **Circle4**, which inherited them directly from class **Point3**. Line 29 invokes method **ToString** implicitly to obtain the **string** representation of the **Cylinder** object. Lines 33–37 invoke methods **Diameter** and **Circumference** of the **Cylinder** object—because class **Cylinder** inherits these methods from class **Circle4** and cannot override them, these methods, exactly as listed in **Circle4**, are invoked. Lines 41–45 invoke methods **Area** and **Volume**.

Using the point-circle-cylinder example, we have shown the use and benefits of inheritance. We were able to develop classes **Circle4** and **Cylinder** using inheritance much faster than if we had developed these classes "from scratch." Inheritance avoids duplicating code and the associated code-maintenance problems.

```
1   // Fig. 9.16: CylinderTest.cs
2   // Tests class Cylinder.
3
4   using System;
5   using System.Windows.Forms;
6
7   // CylinderTest class definition
8   class CylinderTest
9   {
10     // main entry point for application
11     static void Main( string[] args )
12     {
13        // instantiate object of class Cylinder
14        Cylinder cylinder = new Cylinder(12, 23, 2.5, 5.7);
15
16        // properties get initial x-y coordinate, radius and height
17        string output = "X coordinate is " + cylinder.X + "\n" +
18           "Y coordinate is " + cylinder.Y + "\nRadius is " +
19           cylinder.Radius + "\n" + "Height is " + cylinder.Height;
20
21        // properties set new x-y coordinate, radius and height
22        cylinder.X = 2;
23        cylinder.Y = 2;
24        cylinder.Radius = 4.25;
25        cylinder.Height = 10;
26
27        // get new x-y coordinate and radius
28        output += "\n\nThe new location, radius and height of " +
29           "cylinder are\n" + cylinder + "\n\n";
30
31        // display Cylinder's Diameter
32        output += "Diameter is " +
33           String.Format( "{0:F}", cylinder.Diameter() ) + "\n";
```

Fig. 9.16 Testing class **Cylinder**. (Part 1 of 2.)

```
34
35          // display Cylinder's Circumference
36          output += "Circumference is " +
37             String.Format( "{0:F}", cylinder.Circumference() ) + "\n";
38
39          // display Cylinder's Area
40          output += "Area is " +
41             String.Format( "{0:F}", cylinder.Area() ) + "\n";
42
43          // display Cylinder's Volume
44          output += "Volume is " +
45             String.Format( "{0:F}", cylinder.Volume() );
46
47          MessageBox.Show( output, "Demonstrating Class Cylinder" );
48
49       } // end method Main
50
51    } // end class CylinderTest
```

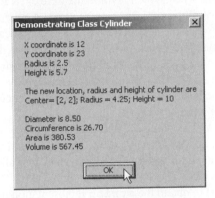

Fig. 9.16   Testing class **Cylinder**. (Part 2 of 2.)

9.6 Constructors and Destructors in Derived Classes

As we explained in the previous section, instantiating a derived-class object begins a chain of constructor calls in which the derived-class constructor, before performing its own tasks, invokes the base-class constructor either explicitly or implicitly. Similarly, if the base-class was derived from another class, the base-class constructor must invoke the constructor of the next class up in the hierarchy, and so on. The last constructor called in the chain is class **Object**'s constructor whose body actually finishes executing first—the original derived class's body finishes executing last. Each base-class constructor initializes the base-class instance variables that the derived-class object inherits. For example, consider the **Point3/Circle4** hierarchy from Fig. 9.12 and Fig. 9.13. When a program creates a **Circle4** object, one of the **Circle4** constructors is called. That constructor calls class **Point3**'s constructor, which in turn calls class **Object**'s constructor. When class **Object**'s constructor completes execution, it returns control to class **Point3**'s constructor, which initializes the *x-y* coordinates of **Circle4**. When class **Point3**'s constructor completes execution, it returns control to class **Circle4**'s constructor, which initializes the **Circle4**'s radius.

Software Engineering Observation 9.10

When a program creates a derived-class object, the derived-class constructor immediately calls the base-class constructor, the base-class constructor's body executes, then the derived-class constructor's body executes.

When the garbage collector removes a derived-class object from memory, the garbage collector calls that object's destructor. This begins a chain of destructor calls in which the derived-class destructor and the destructors of the direct and indirect base classes execute in the reverse order of the order in which the constructors executed. Executing the destructors should free all the resources the object acquired before the garbage collector reclaims the memory for that object. When the garbage collector calls a derived-class object's destructor, the destructor performs its task, then invokes the destructor of the base class. This process repeats until class **Object**'s destructor is called.

C# actually implements destructors using class **Object**'s *Finalize* method (one of the eight methods that every C# class inherits). When compiling a class definition that contains a destructor, the compiler translates a destructor definition into a **Finalize** method that performs the destructor's tasks, then invokes the base class **Finalize** method as the last statement in the derived-class **Finalize** method. As mentioned in Chapter 8, we cannot determine exactly when the destructor call will occur, because we cannot determine exactly when garbage collection occurs. However, by defining a destructor, we can specify code to execute before the garbage collector removes an object from memory.

Our next example revisits the point-circle hierarchy by defining class **Point4** (Fig. 9.17) and class **Circle5** (Fig. 9.18) that contain constructors *and* destructors, each of which prints a message when it runs.

Class **Point4** (Fig. 9.17) contains the features shown in Fig. 9.4. We modified the constructors (lines 13–17 and 20–26) to output a line of text when they are called and added a destructor (lines 29–32) that also outputs a line of text when it is called. Each output statement (lines 16, 25 and 31) adds reference **this** to the output string. This implicitly invokes the class's **ToString** method to obtain the **string** representation of **Point4**'s coordinates.

```
1   // Fig. 9.17: Point4.cs
2   // Point4 class represents an x-y coordinate pair.
3
4   using System;
5
6   // Point4 class definition
7   public class Point4
8   {
9      // point coordinate
10     private int x, y;
11
12     // default constructor
13     public Point4()
14     {
15        // implicit call to Object constructor occurs here
16        Console.WriteLine( "Point4 constructor: {0}", this );
17     }
```

Fig. 9.17 **Point4** base class contains constructors and finalizer. (Part 1 of 2.)

```
18
19        // constructor
20        public Point4( int xValue, int yValue )
21        {
22            // implicit call to Object constructor occurs here
23            X = xValue;
24            Y = yValue;
25            Console.WriteLine( "Point4 constructor: {0}", this );
26        }
27
28        // destructor
29        ~Point4()
30        {
31            Console.WriteLine( "Point4 destructor: {0}", this );
32        }
33
34        // property X
35        public int X
36        {
37            get
38            {
39                return x;
40            }
41
42            set
43            {
44                x = value; // no need for validation
45            }
46
47        } // end property X
48
49        // property Y
50        public int Y
51        {
52            get
53            {
54                return y;
55            }
56
57            set
58            {
59                y = value; // no need for validation
60            }
61
62        } // end property Y
63
64        // return string representation of Point4
65        public override string ToString()
66        {
67            return "[" + X + ", " + Y + "]";
68        }
69
70    } // end class Point4
```

Fig. 9.17   **Point4** base class contains constructors and finalizer. (Part 2 of 2.)

Class **Circle5** (Fig. 9.18) contains the features in Fig. 9.13, and we modified the two constructors (lines 12–16 and 19–24) to output a line of text when they are called. We also added a destructor (lines 27–30) that also outputs a line of text when it is called. Each output statement (lines 15, 23 and 29) adds reference **this** to the output string. This implicitly invokes the **Circle5**'s **ToString** method to obtain the **string** representation of **Circle5**'s coordinates and radius.

Class **ConstructorAndFinalizer** (Fig. 9.19) demonstrates the order in which constructors and finalizers are called for objects of classes that are part of an inheritance class hierarchy. Method **Main** (lines 11–28) begins by instantiating an object of class **Circle5**, then assigns it to reference **circle1** (line 16). This invokes the **Circle5** constructor, which invokes the **Point4** constructor immediately. Then, the **Point4** constructor invokes the **Object** constructor. When the **Object** constructor (which does not print anything) returns control to the **Point4** constructor, the **Point4** constructor initializes the *x-y* coordinates, then outputs a **string** indicating that the **Point4** constructor was called. The output statement also calls method **ToString** implicitly (using reference **this**) to obtain the **string** representation of the object being constructed. Then, control returns to the **Circle5** constructor, which initializes the radius and outputs the **Circle5**'s *x-y* coordinates and radius by calling method **ToString** implicitly.

```
1   // Fig. 9.18: Circle5.cs
2   // Circle5 class that inherits from class Point4.
3
4   using System;
5
6   // Circle5 class definition inherits from Point4
7   public class Circle5 : Point4
8   {
9      private double radius;
10
11     // default constructor
12     public Circle5()
13     {
14        // implicit call to Point3 constructor occurs here
15        Console.WriteLine( "Circle5 constructor: {0}", this );
16     }
17
18     // constructor
19     public Circle5( int xValue, int yValue, double radiusValue )
20        : base( xValue, yValue )
21     {
22        Radius = radiusValue;
23        Console.WriteLine( "Circle5 constructor: {0}", this );
24     }
25
26     // destructor overrides version in class Point4
27     ~Circle5()
28     {
29        Console.WriteLine( "Circle5 destructor: {0}", this );
30     }
```

Fig. 9.18   **Circle5** class inherits from class **Point4** and overrides a finalizer method. (Part 1 of 2.)

```
31
32      // property Radius
33      public double Radius
34      {
35         get
36         {
37            return radius;
38         }
39
40         set
41         {
42            if ( value >= 0 )
43               radius = value;
44         }
45
46      } // end property Radius
47
48      // calculate Circle5 diameter
49      public double Diameter()
50      {
51         return Radius * 2;
52      }
53
54      // calculate Circle5 circumference
55      public double Circumference()
56      {
57         return Math.PI * Diameter();
58      }
59
60      // calculate Circle5 area
61      public virtual double Area()
62      {
63         return Math.PI * Math.Pow( Radius, 2 );
64      }
65
66      // return string representation of Circle5
67                         ToString()
68      {
69         // use base reference to return Point3 string
70         return "Center = " + base.ToString() +
71            "; Radius = " + Radius;
72      }
73
74   } // end class Circle5
```

Fig. 9.18 **Circle5** class inherits from class **Point3** and overrides a finalizer method. (Part 2 of 2.)

Notice that the first two lines of the output from this program contain values for the *x*-*y* coordinates and the radius of **Circle5** object **circle1**. When constructing a **Circle5** object, the **this** reference used in the body of both the **Circle5** and **Point4** constructors refers to the **Circle5** object being constructed. When a program invokes method **ToString** on an object, the version of **ToString** that executes is always the version defined in that object's class. Because reference **this** refers to the current

Circle5 object being constructed, Circle5's ToString method executes even when ToString is invoked from the body of class Point4's constructor. [*Note*: This would not be the case if the Point4 constructor were called to initialize an object that was actually a new Point4 object.] When the Point4 constructor invokes method ToString for the Circle5 being constructed, the program displays 0 for the radius value, because the Circle5 constructor's body has not yet initialized the radius. Remember that 0 is the default value of a double variable. The second line of output shows the proper radius value (4.5), because that line is output after the radius is initialized.

```
1   // Fig. 9.19: ConstructorAndDestructor.cs
2   // Display order in which base-class and derived-class constructors
3   // and destructors are called.
4
5   using System;
6
7   // ConstructorAndDestructor class definition
8   class ConstructorAndDestructor
9   {
10      // main entry point for application.
11      static void Main( string[] args )
12      {
13         Circle5 circle1, circle2;
14
15         // instantiate objects
16         circle1 = new Circle5( 72, 29, 4.5 );
17         circle2 = new Circle5( 5, 5, 10 );
18
19         Console.WriteLine();
20
21         // mark objects for garbage collection
22         circle1 = null;
23         circle2 = null;
24
25         // inform garbage collector to execute
26         System.GC.Collect();
27
28      } // end method Main
29
30   } // end class ConstructorAndDestructor
```

```
Point4 constructor: Center = [72, 29]; Radius = 0
Circle5 constructor: Center = [72, 29]; Radius = 4.5
Point4 constructor: Center = [5, 5]; Radius = 0
Circle5 constructor: Center = [5, 5]; Radius = 10

Circle5 destructor: Center = [5, 5]; Radius = 10
Point4 destructor: Center = [5, 5]; Radius = 10
Circle5 destructor: Center = [72, 29]; Radius = 4.5
Point4 destructor: Center = [72, 29]; Radius = 4.5
```

Fig. 9.19   Order in which constructors and destructors are called.

Line 17 instantiates another object of class **Circle5**, then assigns it to reference **circle2**. Again, this begins the chain of constructor calls in which the **Circle5** constructor, the **Point4** constructor and the **Object** constructor are called. In the output, notice that the body of the **Point4** constructor executes before the body of the **Circle5** constructor. This demonstrates that objects are constructed "inside out" (i.e., the base-class constructor is called first).

Lines 22–23 set references **circle1** and **circle2** to **null**. This removes the only references to these **Circle5** objects in the program. Thus, the garbage collector can release the memory that these objects occupy. Remember that we cannot guarantee when the garbage collector will execute, nor can we guarantee that it will collect all available objects when it does execute. To demonstrate the destructor invocations for the two **Circle5** objects, line 26 invokes class **GC**'s method **Collect** to request the garbage collector to run. Notice that each **Circle5** object's destructor outputs information before calling class **Point4**'s destructor. Objects are destroyed "outside in" (i.e., the derived-class destructor completes its tasks before invoking the base-class destructor).

9.7 Software Engineering with Inheritance

In this section, we discuss the use of inheritance to customize existing software. When we use inheritance to create a new class from an existing one, the new class inherits the member variables, properties and methods of the existing class. We can customize the new class to meet our needs by including additional member variables, properties and methods, and by overriding base-class members.

Sometimes, it is difficult for students to appreciate the scope of problems faced by designers who work on large-scale software projects in industry. People experienced with such projects say that effective software reuse improves the software-development process. Object-oriented programming facilitates software reuse, thus shortening development times.

C# encourages software reuse by providing the .NET Framework Class Library (FCL), which delivers the maximum benefits of software reuse through inheritance. As interest in C# grows, interest in the FCL class libraries also increases. There is a worldwide commitment to the continued evolution of the FCL class libraries for a wide variety of applications. The FCL will grow as the .NET world grows explosively.

Software Engineering Observation 9.11

At the design stage in an object-oriented system, the designer often determines that certain classes are closely related. The designer should "factor out" common attributes and behaviors and place these in a base class. Then, use inheritance to form derived classes, endowing them with capabilities beyond those inherited from the base class.

Software Engineering Observation 9.12

The creation of a derived class does not affect its base class's source code. Inheritance preserves the integrity of a base class.

Software Engineering Observation 9.13

Just as designers of non-object-oriented systems should avoid proliferation of functions, designers of object-oriented systems should avoid proliferation of classes. Proliferation of classes creates management problems and can hinder software reusability, because it becomes difficult for a client to locate the most appropriate class of a huge class library. The alternative is to create fewer classes, in which each provides more substantial functionality, but such classes might provide too much functionality.

Performance Tip 9.2

If classes produced through inheritance are larger than they need to be (i.e., contain too much functionality), memory and processing resources might be wasted. Inherit from the class whose functionality is "closest" to what is needed.

Reading derived-class definitions can be confusing, because inherited members are not shown physically in the derived class, but nevertheless are present in the derived classes. A similar problem exists when documenting derived class members.

In this chapter, we introduced inheritance—the ability to create classes by absorbing an existing class's data members and behaviors and embellishing these with new capabilities. In Chapter 10, we build upon our discussion of inheritance by introducing *polymorphism*—an object-oriented technique that enables us to write programs that handle, in a more general manner, a wide variety of classes related by inheritance. After studying Chapter 10, you will be familiar with encapsulation, inheritance and polymorphism—the most crucial aspects of object-oriented programming.

SUMMARY

- Software reusability reduces program-development time.

- The direct base class of a derived class is the base class from which the derived class inherits [via the colon (:) symbol]. An indirect base class of a derived class is two or more levels up the class hierarchy from that derived class.

- With single inheritance, a class is derived from one base class. C# does not support multiple inheritance (i.e., deriving a class from more than one direct base class).

- Because a derived class can include its own class variables, properties and methods, a derived class is often larger than its base class.

- A derived class is more specific than its base class and represents a smaller group of objects.

- Every object of a derived class is also an object of that class's base class. However, base-class objects are not objects of that class's derived classes.

- Derived-class methods and properties can access **protected** base-class members directly.

- An "is-a" relationship represents inheritance. In an "is-a" relationship, an object of a derived class also can be treated as an object of its base class.

- A "has-a" relationship represents composition. In a "has-a" relationship, a class object has references to one or more objects of other classes as members.

- A derived class cannot access **private** members of its base class directly.

- A derived class can access the **public**, **protected** and **internal** members of its base class if the derived class is in the same assembly as the base class.

- When a base-class member is inappropriate for a derived class, that member can be overridden (redefined) in the derived class with an appropriate implementation.

- To override a base-class method definition, a derived class must specify that the derived-class method overrides the base-class method with keyword **override** in the method header.

- Inheritance relationships form tree-like hierarchical structures. A class exists in a hierarchical relationship with its derived classes.

- It is possible to treat base-class objects and derived-class objects similarly; the commonality shared between the object types is expressed in the member variables, properties and methods of the base class.

- A base class's **public** members are accessible anywhere that the program has a reference to an object of that base class or to an object of one of that base class's derived classes.

- A base class's **private** members are accessible only within the definition of that base class.

- A base class's **protected** members have an intermediate level of protection between **public** and **private** access. A base class's **protected** members can be accessed only in that base class or in any classes derived from that base class.

- A base class's **internal** members can be accessed only by objects in the same assembly.

- Unfortunately, the inclusion of **protected** instance variables often yields two major problems. First, the derived-class object does not have to use a property to set the value of the base-class's **protected** data. Second, derived class methods are more likely to be written to depend on base-class implementation.

- C# rigidly enforces restriction on accessing **private** data members, so that even derived classes (i.e,. which are closely related to their base class) cannot access base-class **private** data.

- When a derived-class method overrides a base-class method, the base-class method can be accessed from the derived class by preceding the base-class method name with the **base** reference, followed by the dot operator (**.**).

- A derived class can redefine a base-class method using the same signature; this is called *overriding* that base-class method.

- A base-class method must be declared **virtual** if that method is to be overridden in a derived class.

- When a method is overridden in a derived class and that method is called on a derived-class object, the derived-class version (not the base-class version) is called.

- When an object of a derived class is instantiated, the base class's constructor is called immediately (either explicitly or implicitly) to do any necessary initialization of the base-class instance variables in the derived-class object (before the derived classes instance variable are initialized).

- Declaring member variables **private**, while providing non-**private** properties to manipulate and perform validation checking on this data, enforces good software engineering.

- If an object's method/property performs the actions needed by another object, call that method/property rather than duplicating its code body. Duplicated code creates code-maintenance problems.

- Base-class constructors and destructors are not inherited by derived classes.

TERMINOLOGY

abstraction
base class
base-class constructor
base-class default constructor
base-class finalizer
base-class object
base-class reference
behavior
class library
colon (**:**) symbol
composition
constructor

data abstraction
default constructor
derived class
derived-class constructor
derived-class reference
direct base class
dot (**.**) operator
garbage collector
"has-a" relationship
hierarchy diagram
indirect base class
information hiding

inheritance
inheritance hierarchy
inherited instance variable
instance variable (of an object)
internal member access modifier
"is-a" relationship
member-access operator
member variable (of a class)
multiple inheritance
base reference
Object class
object of a base class
object of a derived class
object-oriented programming (OOP)
overloaded constructor
overloading

override keyword
overriding
overriding a base-class method
overriding a method
private base-class member
protected access
protected base-class member
protected member of a derived class
protected member of a base class
protected variable
public member of a derived class
reusable component
single inheritance
software reusability
software reuse
virtual keyword

SELF-REVIEW EXERCISES

9.1   Fill in the blanks in each of the following statements:

a)   _____ is a form of software reusability in which new classes absorb the data and behaviors of existing classes and embellish these classes with new capabilities.

b)   A base class's _____ members can be accessed only in the base-class definition or in derived-class definitions.

c)   In a(n) _____ relationship, an object of a derived class also can be treated as an object of its base class.

d)   In a(n) _____ relationship, a class object has one or more references to objects of other classes as members.

e)   A class exists in a(n) _____ relationship with its derived classes.

f)   A base class's _____ members are accessible anywhere that the program has a reference to that base class or to one of its derived classes.

g)   A base class's **protected** access members have a level of protection between those of **public** and _____ access.

h)   A base class's _____ members can be accessed only in the same assembly.

i)   When an object of a derived class is instantiated, the base class's _____ is called implicitly or explicitly to do any necessary initialization of the base-class instance variables in the derived-class object.

j)   Derived-class constructors can call base-class constructors via the _____ reference.

9.2   State whether each of the following is *true* or *false*. If *false*, explain why.

a)   It is possible to treat base-class objects and derived-class objects similarly.

b)   Base-class constructors are not inherited by derived classes.

c)   A "has-a" relationship is implemented via inheritance.

d)   All methods, by default, can be overridden.

e)   Method **ToString** of class **System.Object** is declared as **virtual**.

f)   When a derived class redefines a base-class method using the same signature, the derived class is said to overload that base-class method.

g)   A **Car** class has an "is a" relationship with its **SteeringWheel** and **Brakes**.

h)   Inheritance encourages the reuse of proven high-quality software.

ANSWERS TO SELF-REVIEW EXERCISES

9.1   a) Inheritance. b) **protected**. c) "is a" or inheritance. d) "has a" or composition or aggregation. e) hierarchical. f) **public**. g) **private**. h) **internal**. i) constructor. j) **base**.

9.2   a) True. b) True. c) False. A "has-a" relationship is implemented via composition. An "is-a" relationship is implemented via inheritance. d) False. Overridable methods must be declared explicitly as **virtual**. e) True. f) False. When a derived class redefines a base-class method using the same signature, the derived class overrides that base-class method. g) False. This is an example of a "has a" relationship. Class **Car** has an "is a" relationship with class **Vehicle**. h) True.

EXERCISES

9.3   Many programs written with inheritance could be written with composition instead, and vice versa. Rewrite classes **Point3**, **Circle4** and **Cylinder** to use composition, rather than inheritance. After you do this, assess the relative merits of the two approaches for both the **Point3**, **Circle4**, **Cylinder** problem, as well as for object-oriented programs in general. Which approach is more natural, why?

9.4   Some programmers prefer not to use **protected** access because it breaks the encapsulation of the base class. Discuss the relative merits of using **protected** access vs. insisting on using **private** access in base classes.

9.5   Rewrite the case study in Section 9.5 as a **Point**, **Square**, **Cube** program. Do this two ways—once via inheritance and once via composition.

9.6   Write an inheritance hierarchy for class **Quadrilateral**, **Trapezoid**, **Parallelogram**, **Rectangle** and **Square**. Use **Quadrilateral** as the base class of the hierarchy. Make the hierarchy as deep (i.e., as many levels) as possible. The **private** data of **Quadrilateral** should be the *x*-*y* coordinate pairs for the four endpoints of the **Quadrilateral**. Write a program that instantiates objects of each of the classes in your hierarchy and polymorphically outputs each object's dimensions and area.

9.7   Modify classes **Point3**, **Circle4** and **Cylinder** to contain destructors. Then, modify the program of Fig. 9.19 to demonstrate the order in which constructors and destructors are invoked in this hierarchy.

9.8   Write down all the shapes you can think of— both two-dimensional and three-dimensional— and form those shapes into a shape hierarchy. Your hierarchy should have base class **Shape** from which class **TwoDimensionalShape** and class **ThreeDimensionalShape** are derived. Once you have developed the hierarchy, define each of the classes in the hierarchy. We will use this hierarchy in the exercises of Chapter 10 to process all shapes as objects of base-class **Shape**. (This is a technique called polymorphism.)

10

Object-Oriented Programming: Polymorphism

Objectives

- To understand the concept of polymorphism.
- To understand how polymorphism makes systems extensible and maintainable.
- To understand the distinction between abstract classes and concrete classes.
- To learn how to create **sealed** classes, interfaces and delegates.

One Ring to rule them all, One Ring to find them,
One Ring to bring them all and in the darkness bind them.
John Ronald Reuel Tolkien, *The Fellowship of the Ring*

General propositions do not decide concrete cases.
Oliver Wendell Holmes

A philosopher of imposing stature doesn't think in a vacuum.
Even his most abstract ideas are, to some extent, conditioned
by what is or is not known in the time when he lives.
Alfred North Whitehead

Outline

10.1 Introduction

The previous chapter's object-oriented programming (OOP) discussion focussed on one of OOP's key component technologies, inheritance. In this chapter, we continue our study of OOP *polymorphism*. Both inheritance and polymorphism are crucial technologies in the development of complex software. Polymorphism enables us to write programs that handle a wide variety of related classes in a generic manner and facilitates adding new classes and capabilities to a system.

With polymorphism, it is possible to design and implement systems that are easily extensible. Programs can process objects of all classes in a class hierarchy generically as objects of a common base class. Furthermore, new classes can be added with little or no modification to the generic portions of the program, as long as those classes are part of the inheritance hierarchy that the program processes generically. The only parts of a program that must be altered to accommodate new classes are those program components that require direct knowledge of the new classes that the programmer adds to the hierarchy. In this chapter, we demonstrate two substantial class hierarchies and manipulate objects from those hierarchies polymorphically.

10.2 Derived-Class-Object to Base-Class-Object Conversion

Section 9.4 created a point-circle class hierarchy, in which class **Circle** inherited from class **Point**. The programs that manipulated objects of these classes always used **Point** references to refer to **Point** objects and **Circle** references to refer to **Circle** objects. In this section, we discuss the relationships between classes in a hierarchy that enable programs to assign derived-class objects to base-class references—a fundamental part of programs that process objects polymorphically. This section also discusses explicit casting between types in a class hierarchy.

An object of a derived class can be treated as an object of its base class. This enables various interesting manipulations. For example, a program can create an array of base-class references that refer to objects of many derived-class types. This is allowed despite the fact that the derived-class objects are of different data types. However, the reverse is not true—a base-class object is not an object of any of its derived classes. For example, a **Point** is not a **Circle** in the hierarchy defined in Chapter 9. If a base-class reference refers to a derived-class object, it is possible to convert the base-class reference to the object's actual data type and manipulate the object as that type.

The example in Fig. 10.1–Fig. 10.3 demonstrates assigning derived-class objects to base-class references and casting base-class references to derived-class references. Class **Point** (Fig. 10.1), which we discussed in Chapter 9, represents an *x-y* coordinate pair. Class **Circle** (Fig. 10.2), which we also discussed in Chapter 9, represents a circle and inherits from class **Point**. Each **Circle** object "is a" **Point** and also has a radius (represented via property **Radius**). We declare method **Area** as **virtual**, so that a derived class (such as class **Cylinder**) can override method **Area** to calculate the derived-class object's area. Class **PointCircleTest** (Fig. 10.3) demonstrates the assignment and cast operations.

```
1   // Fig. 10.1: Point.cs
2   // Point class represents an x-y coordinate pair.
3
4   using System;
5
6   // Point class definition implicitly inherits from Object
7   public class Point
8   {
9      // point coordinate
10     private int x, y;
11
12     // default constructor
13     public Point()
14     {
15        // implicit call to Object constructor occurs here
16     }
17
18     // constructor
19     public Point( int xValue, int yValue )
20     {
21        // implicit call to Object constructor occurs here
22        X = xValue;
23        Y = yValue;
24     }
25
26     // property X
27     public int X
28     {
29        get
30        {
31           return x;
32        }
33
```

Fig. 10.1 **Point** class represents an *x-y* coordinate pair. (Part 1 of 2.)

```
34          set
35          {
36              x = value;   // no need for validation
37          }
38
39      } // end property X
40
41      // property Y
42      public int Y
43      {
44          get
45          {
46              return y;
47          }
48
49          set
50          {
51              y = value;   // no need for validation
52          }
53
54      } // end property Y
55
56      // return string representation of Point
57      public override string ToString()
58      {
59          return "[" + X + ", " + Y + "]";
60      }
61
62  } // end class Point
```

Fig. 10.1 **Point** class represents an *x-y* coordinate pair. (Part 2 of 2.)

```
1   // Fig. 10.2: Circle.cs
2   // Circle class that inherits from class Point.
3
4   using System;
5
6   // Circle class definition inherits from Point
7   public class Circle : Point
8   {
9       private double radius; // circle's radius
10
11      // default constructor
12      public Circle()
13      {
14          // implicit call to Point constructor occurs here
15      }
16
17      // constructor
18      public Circle( int xValue, int yValue, double radiusValue )
19          : base( xValue, yValue )
20      {
```

Fig. 10.2 **Circle** class that inherits from class **Point**. (Part 1 of 2.)

```
21              Radius = radiusValue;
22           }
23
24           // property Radius
25           public double Radius
26           {
27              get
28              {
29                 return radius;
30              }
31
32              set
33              {
34                 if ( value >= 0 ) // validate radius
35                    radius = value;
36              }
37
38           } // end property Radius
39
40           // calculate Circle diameter
41           public double Diameter()
42           {
43              return Radius * 2;
44           }
45
46           // calculate Circle circumference
47           public double Circumference()
48           {
49              return Math.PI * Diameter();
50           }
51
52           // calculate Circle area
53           public virtual double Area()
54           {
55              return Math.PI * Math.Pow( Radius, 2 );
56           }
57
58           // return string representation of Circle
59           public override string ToString()
60           {
61              return "Center = " + base.ToString() +
62                 "; Radius = " + Radius;
63           }
64
65      } // end class Circle
```

Fig. 10.2 **Circle** class that inherits from class **Point**. (Part 2 of 2.)

Class **PointCircleTest** (Fig. 10.3) demonstrates assigning derived-class references to base-class references and casting base-class references to derived-class references. Lines 13–14 declare a **Point** reference (**point1**) and a **Circle** reference (**circle1**). Lines 16–17 append **string** representations of each object to **string output** to show the values used to initialize these objects. Because **point1** is reference to a **Point** object, method **ToString** of **point1** prints the object as a **Point**. Similarly, because **circle1** is reference to a **Circle** object, method **ToString** of **circle1** prints the object as a **Circle**.

```
1    // Fig. 10.3: PointCircleTest.cs
2    // Demonstrating inheritance and polymorphism.
3
4    using System;
5    using System.Windows.Forms;
6
7    // PointCircleTest class definition
8    class PointCircleTest
9    {
10       // main entry point for application.
11       static void Main( string[] args )
12       {
13          Point point1 = new Point( 30, 50 );
14          Circle circle1 = new Circle( 120, 89, 2.7 );
15
16          string output = "Point point1: " + point1.ToString() +
17             "\nCircle circle1: " + circle1.ToString();
18
19          // use 'is a' relationship to assign
20          // Circle circle1 to Point reference
21          Point point2 = circle1;
22
23          output += "\n\nCircle circle1 (via point2): " +
24             point2.ToString();
25
26          // downcast (cast base-class reference to derived-class
27          // data type) point2 to Circle circle2
28          Circle circle2 = ( Circle ) point2;
29
30          output += "\n\nCircle circle1 (via circle2): " +
31             circle2.ToString();
32
33          output += "\nArea of circle1 (via circle2): " +
34             circle2.Area().ToString( "F" );
35
36          // attempt to assign point1 object to Circle reference
37          if ( point1 is Circle )
38          {
39             circle2 = ( Circle ) point1;
40             output += "\n\ncast successful";
41          }
42          else
43          {
44             output += "\n\npoint1 does not refer to a Circle";
45          }
46
47          MessageBox.Show( output,
48             "Demonstrating the 'is a' relationship" );
```

Fig. 10.3 Assigning derived-class references to base-class references. (Part 1 of 2.)

```
49
50       } // end method Main
51
52   } // end class PointCircleTest
```

Fig. 10.3 Assigning derived-class references to base-class references. (Part 2 of 2.)

Line 21 assigns **circle1** (a reference to a derived-class object) to **point2** (a base-class reference). In C#, it is acceptable to assign a derived-class object to a base-class reference, because of the inheritance "is a" relationship. Class **Circle** inherits from class **Point**, because a **Circle** *is a* **Point** (in a structural sense, at least). However, assigning a base-class reference to a derived-class reference is potentially dangerous, as we will discuss.

Lines 23–24 invoke **point2.ToString** and append the result to **output**. When C# encounters a **virtual** method invocation (such as method **ToString**), C# determines which version of the method to call from the type of the object on which the method is called, not the type of the reference that refers to the object. In this case, **point2** refers to a **Circle** object, so C# calls **Circle** method **ToString**, rather than **Point** method **ToString** (as one might expect from the **point2** reference, which was declared as type **Point**). The decision about which method to call is an example of *polymorphism*, a concept that we discuss in detail throughout this chapter. Note that if **point2** referenced a **Point** object rather than a **Circle** object, C# would invoke **Point**'s **ToString** method.

Previous chapters used methods such as **Int32.Parse** and **Double.Parse** to convert between various built-in C# types. Now, we convert between object references of programmer-defined types. We use explicit casts to perform these conversions. If the cast is valid, our program can treat a base-class reference as a derived-class reference. If the cast is invalid, C# throws an **InvalidCastException**, which indicates that the cast operation is not allowed. Exceptions are discussed in detail in Chapter 11, Exception Handling.

Common Programming Error 10.1

Assigning a base-class object (or a base-class reference) to a derived-class reference (without an explicit cast) is a syntax error.

Software Engineering Observation 10.1

If a derived-class object has been assigned to a reference of one of its direct or indirect base classes, it is acceptable to cast that base-class reference back to a reference of the derived-class type. In fact, this must be done to send that object messages that do not appear in the base class. [Note: We sometimes use the term "messages" to represent the invocation of methods and the use of object properties.]

Line 28 casts **point2**, which currently refers to a **Circle** object (**circle1**), to a **Circle** and assigns the result to **circle2**. As we discuss momentarily, this cast would be dangerous if **point2** were referencing a **Point**. Lines 30–31 invoke method **ToString** of the **Circle** object to which **circle2** now refers (note that the fourth line of the output demonstrates that **Circle**'s **ToString** method is called). Lines 33–34 calculate and output **circle2**'s **Area**.

Line 39 explicitly casts reference **point1** to a **Circle**. This is a dangerous operation, because **point** refers to a **Point** object, and a **Point** is not a **Circle**. Objects can be cast only to their own type or to their base-class types. If this statement were to execute, C# would determine that **point1** references a **Point** object, recognize the cast to **Circle** as dangerous and indicate an improper cast with an **InvalidCastException** message. However, we prevent this statement from executing by including an **if/else** structure (lines 37–45). The condition at line 37 uses keyword **is** to determine whether the object to which **point1** refers "is a" **Circle**. Keyword **is** discovers the type of the object to which the left operand refers and compares this type to the right operand (in this case, **Circle**). In our example, **point1** does not refer to a **Circle**, so the condition fails, and line 44 appends to **output** a string that indicates the result. Note that the **is** comparison will be **true** if the left operand is a reference to an instance of the right operand or a derived class.

Common Programming Error 10.2

Attempting to cast a base-class reference to a derived-class type causes an **Invalid-CastException** *if the reference refers to a base-class object rather than an appropriate derived-class object.*

Software Engineering Observation 10.2

The **is** *keyword enables a program to determine whether a cast operation would be successful by ensuring that the reference type and target type are compatible.*

If we remove the **if** test and execute the program, C# displays a **MessageBox** that contains the message:

```
An unhandled exception of type 'System.InvalidCastException'
occurred in
```

followed by the name and path of the executing program. We discuss how to deal with such situations in Chapter 11.

Despite the fact that a derived-class object also "is a" base-class object, the derived-class and base-class objects are different. As we have discussed previously, derived-class objects can be treated as if they were base-class objects. This is a logical relationship, because the derived class contains members that correspond to all members in the base class, but the derived class can have additional members. For this reason, assigning a base-class object to a derived-class reference is not allowed without an explicit cast. Such an assignment would leave the additional derived-class members undefined.

There are four ways to mix base-class references and derived-class references with base-class objects and derived-class objects:

1. Referring to a base-class object with a base-class reference is straightforward.

2. Referring to a derived-class object with a derived-class reference is straightforward.

3. Referring to a derived-class object with a base-class reference is safe, because the derived-class object *is an* object of its base class. However, this reference can refer only to base-class members. If this code refers to derived-class-only members through the base-class reference, the compiler reports an error.

4. Referring to a base-class object with a derived-class reference generates a compiler error. To avoid this error, the derived-class reference first must be cast to a base-class reference explicitly. In this cast, the derived-class reference must reference a derived-class object, or C# generates an **InvalidCastException**.

Common Programming Error 10.3

After assigning a derived-class object to a base-class reference, attempting to reference derived-class-only members with the base-class reference is a compilation error.

Common Programming Error 10.4

Treating a base-class object as a derived-class object can cause errors.

Though it is convenient to treat derived-class objects as base-class objects by manipulating derived-class objects with base-class references, doing so can cause significant problems. For example, a payroll system, must be able to traverse an array of employees and calculate the weekly pay for each person. Intuition suggests that using base-class references would enable the program to call only the base-class payroll calculation routine (if there is such a routine in the base class). Using only base-class references, we can invoke the proper payroll calculation routine for each object, whether the object is a base-class object or a derived-class object. We learn how to create classes that exhibit this behavior as we introduce polymorphism throughout this chapter.

10.3 Type Fields and **switch** Statements

One way to determine the type of an object that is incorporated in a larger program is to use a **switch** structure. This allows us to distinguish among object types, then invoke an appropriate action for a particular object. For example, in a hierarchy of shapes in which each shape object has a **ShapeType** property, a **switch** structure could employ the object's **ShapeType** to determine which **Print** method to call.

However, using **switch** logic exposes programs to a variety of potential problems. For example, the programmer might forget to include a type test when one is warranted, or the programmer might forget to test all possible cases in a **switch** structure. When modifying a **switch**-based system by adding new types, the programmer might forget to insert the new cases in all relevant **switch** statements. Every addition or deletion of a class requires the modification of every **switch** statement in the system; tracking these statements down can be time consuming and error prone.

Software Engineering Observation 10.3

*Polymorphic programming can eliminate the need for unnecessary **switch** logic. By using C#'s polymorphism mechanism to perform the equivalent logic, programmers can avoid the kinds of errors typically associated with **switch** logic.*

Testing and Debugging Tip 10.1

An interesting consequence of using polymorphism is that programs take on a simplified appearance. They contain less branching logic and more simple, sequential code. This simplification facilitates testing, debugging and program maintenance.

10.4 Polymorphism Examples

In this section, we discuss several examples of polymorphism. If class **Rectangle** is derived from class **Quadrilateral**, then a **Rectangle** object is a more specific version of a **Quadrilateral** object. Any operation (such as calculating the perimeter or the area) that can be performed on an object of class **Quadrilateral** also can be performed on an object of class **Rectangle**. Such operations also can be performed on other kinds of **Quadrilateral**s, such as **Square**s, **Parallelogram**s and **Trapezoid**s. When a program invokes a derived-class method through a base-class (i.e., **Quadrilateral**) reference, C# polymorphically chooses the correct overriding method in the derived class from which the object was instantiated. We investigate this behavior in later examples.

Suppose that we design a video game that manipulates objects of many different types, including objects of classes **Martian**, **Venutian**, **Plutonian**, **SpaceShip** and **LaserBeam**. Also, imagine that each of these classes inherits from the common base class called **SpaceObject**, which contains method **DrawYourself**. Each derived class implements this method. A screen-manager program would maintain a container (such as a **SpaceObject** array) of references to objects of the various classes. To refresh the screen, the screen manager would periodically send each object the same message—namely, **DrawYourself**. However, each object responds in a unique way. For example, a **Martian** object would draw itself in red with the appropriate number of antennae. A **SpaceShip** object would draw itself as a bright, silver flying saucer. A **LaserBeam** object would draw itself as a bright red beam across the screen. Thus the same message sent to a variety of objects would have "many forms" of results—hence the term *polymorphism*.

A polymorphic screen manager facilitates adding new classes to a system with minimal modifications to the system's code. Suppose we want to add class **Mercurian**s to our video game. To do so, we must build a class **Mercurian** that inherits from **SpaceObject**, but provides its own definition of method **DrawYourself**. Then, when objects of class **Mercurian** appear in the container, the programmer does not need to modify the code for the screen manager. The screen manager invokes method **DrawYourself** on every object in the container, regardless of the object's type, so the new **Mercurian** objects simply "plug right in." Thus, without modifying the system (other than to build and include the classes themselves), programmers can use polymorphism to include additional types of classes that were not envisioned when the system was created.

With polymorphism, one method can cause different actions to occur, depending on the type of the object on which the method is invoked. This gives the programmer tremendous expressive capability. In the next several sections, we provide examples that demonstrate polymorphism.

Software Engineering Observation 10.4

With polymorphism, the programmer can deal in generalities and let the execution-time environment concern itself with the specifics. The programmer can command a wide variety of objects to behave in manners appropriate to those objects, even if the programmer does not know the objects' types.

Software Engineering Observation 10.5

Polymorphism promotes extensibility. Software used to invoke polymorphic behavior is written to be independent of the types of the objects to which messages (i.e., method calls) are sent. Thus, programmers can include into a system additional types of objects that respond to existing messages and can do this without modifying the base system.

10.5 Abstract Classes and Methods

When we think of a class as a type, we assume that programs will create objects of that type. However, there are cases in which it is useful to define classes for which the programmer never intends to instantiate any objects. Such classes are called *abstract classes*. Because such classes normally are used as base classes in inheritance hierarchies, we refer to such classes as *abstract base classes*. These classes cannot be used to instantiate objects, since abstract classes are incomplete. Derived classes must define the "missing pieces." Abstract classes normally contain one or more *abstract methods* or *abstract properties*, which are methods and properties that do not provide implementations. Derived classes must override inherited abstract methods and properties to enable objects of those derived classes to be instantiated. We discuss abstract classes extensively in Section 10.6 and Section 10.8.

The purpose of an abstract class is to provide an appropriate base class from which other classes may inherit. Classes from which objects can be instantiated are called *concrete classes*. Such classes provide implementations of every method and property they define. We could have an abstract base class **TwoDimensionalObject** and derive such concrete classes as **Square**, **Circle** and **Triangle**. We could also have an abstract base class **ThreeDimensionalObject** and derive such concrete classes as **Cube**, **Sphere** and **Cylinder**. Abstract base classes are too generic to define real objects; we need to be more specific before we can think of instantiating objects. For example, if someone tells you to "draw the shape," what shape would you draw? Concrete classes provide the specifics that make it reasonable to instantiate objects.

A class is made abstract by declaring it with keyword **abstract**. An inheritance hierarchy does not need to contain any abstract classes, but, as we will see, many good object-oriented systems have class hierarchies headed by abstract base classes. In some cases, abstract classes constitute the top few levels of the hierarchy. A good example of this is the shape hierarchy in Fig. 9.3. The hierarchy begins with abstract base-class **Shape**. On the next level of the hierarchy, we have two more abstract base classes, namely **TwoDimensionalShape** and **ThreeDimensionalShape**. The next level of the hierarchy would define concrete classes for two-dimensional shapes, such as **Circle** and **Square**, and for three-dimensional shapes, such as **Sphere** and **Cube**.

Software Engineering Observation 10.6

*An abstract class defines a common set of **public** methods and properties for the various members of a class hierarchy. An abstract class typically contains one or more abstract methods and properties that derived classes will override. All classes in the hierarchy can use this common set of **public** methods and properties.*

Abstract classes must specify signatures for their abstract methods and properties. C# provides keyword **abstract** to declare a method or property as abstract. Methods and properties that are **abstract** do not provide implementations—attempting to do so is a syntax error. Every concrete derived class must override all base-class **abstract** methods and properties (using keyword **override**) and provide concrete implementations of those methods or properties. Any class with an **abstract** method in it must be declared **abstract**. The difference between an **abstract** method and a **virtual** method is that a **virtual** method has an implementation and provides the derived class with the option of overriding the method; by contrast, an **abstract** method does not provide an implementation and forces the derived class to override the method (for that derived class to be concrete).

Common Programming Error 10.5

*Defining an **abstract** method in a class that has not been declared as **abstract** results is a syntax error.*

Common Programming Error 10.6

*Attempting to instantiate an object of an **abstract** class results in a compilation error.*

Common Programming Error 10.7

*Failure to override an **abstract** method in a derived class is a syntax error, unless the derived class also is an **abstract** class.*

Software Engineering Observation 10.7

*An **abstract** class can have instance data and non-**abstract** methods (including constructors), which are subject to the normal rules of inheritance by derived classes.*

Although we cannot instantiate objects of abstract base classes, we *can* use abstract base classes to declare references; these references can refer to instances of any concrete classes derived from the abstract class. Programs can use such references to manipulate instances of the derived classes polymorphically.

Let us consider another application of polymorphism. A screen manager needs to display a variety of objects, including new types of objects that the programmer will add to the system after writing the screen manager. The system might need to display various shapes, such as **Circle**, **Triangle** or **Rectangle**, which are derived from abstract class **Shape**. The screen manager uses base-class references of type **Shape** to manage the objects that are displayed. To draw any object (regardless of the level at which that object's class appears in the inheritance hierarchy), the screen manager uses a base-class reference to the object to invoke the object's **Draw** method. Method **Draw** is an **abstract** method in base class **Shape**; therefore, each derived class must implement method **Draw**. Each **Shape** object in the inheritance hierarchy knows how to draw itself. The screen manager does not have to worry about the type of each object or whether the screen manager has ever encountered objects of that type.

Polymorphism is particularly effective for implementing layered software systems. In operating systems, for example, each type of physical device could operate quite differently from the others. Even so, commands to *read* or *write* data from and to devices may have a certain uniformity. The write message sent to a device-driver object needs to be interpreted specifically in the context of that device driver and how that device driver manipulates devices of a specific type. However, the write call itself really is no different from the write to any other device in the system—place some number of bytes from memory onto that device. An object-oriented operating system might use an abstract base class to provide an interface appropriate for all device drivers. Then, through inheritance from that abstract base class, derived classes are formed that all operate similarly. The capabilities (i.e., the **public** services) offered by the device drivers are provided as abstract methods in the abstract base class. The implementations of these abstract methods are provided in the derived classes that correspond to the specific types of device drivers.

It is common in object-oriented programming to define an *iterator class* that can traverse all the objects in a container (such as an array). For example, a program can print a list of objects in a linked list by creating an iterator object, then using the iterator to obtain the next element of the list each time the iterator is called. Iterators often are used in polymorphic programming to traverse an array or a linked list of objects from various levels of a hierarchy. The references in such a list are all base-class references. (See Chapter 23, Data Structures, to learn more about linked lists.) A list of objects of base class **TwoDimensionalShape** could contain objects from classes **Square**, **Circle**, **Triangle** and so on. Using polymorphism to send a **Draw** message to each object in the list would draw each object correctly on the screen.

10.6 Case Study: Inheriting Interface and Implementation

Our next example (Fig. 10.4–Fig. 10.8) reexamines the **Point**, **Circle**, **Cylinder** hierarchy that we explored in Chapter 9. In this example, the hierarchy begins with abstract base class **Shape** (Fig. 10.4). This hierarchy mechanically demonstrates the power of polymorphism. In the exercises, we explore a more substantial shape hierarchy.

```
1   // Fig. 10.4: Shape.cs
2   // Demonstrate a shape hierarchy using an abstract base class.
3   using System;
4
5   public abstract class Shape
6   {
7      // return Shape's area
8      public virtual double Area()
9      {
10        return 0;
11     }
12
13     // return Shape's volume
14     public virtual double Volume()
15     {
16        return 0;
17     }
18
19     // return Shape's name
20     public abstract string Name
21     {
22        get;
23     }
24  }
```

Fig. 10.4 Abstract **Shape** base class.

Class **Shape** defines two concrete methods and one **abstract** property. All shapes have an area and a volume, so we include virtual methods **Area** (lines 8–11) and **Volume** (lines 14–17), which return the shape's area and volume, respectively. The volume of two-dimensional shapes is always zero, whereas three-dimensional shapes have a positive, non-zero volume. In class **Shape**, methods **Area** and **Volume** return zero, by default. Programmers can override these methods in derived classes when those classes should have different area calculations [e.g., classes **Circle2** (Fig. 10.6) and **Cylinder2** (Fig. 10.7)] and/or different volume calculations (e.g., **Cylinder2**). Read-only property **Name** (lines 20–23) is declared **abstract**, so derived classes must implement this property to become concrete classes. Note that **abstract** methods and properties are implicitly **virtual**.

Class **Point2** (Fig. 10.5) inherits from **abstract** class **Shape** and overrides the **abstract** property **Name**, which makes **Point2** a concrete class. A point's area and volume are zero, so class **Point2** does not override base-class methods **Area** and **Volume**. Lines 59–65 implement property **Name**. If we did not provide this implementation, class **Point2** would be an abstract class that would require keyword **abstract** in the first line of the class definition.

```
1   // Fig. 10.5: Point2.cs
2   // Point2 inherits from abstract class Shape and represents
3   // an x-y coordinate pair.
4   using System;
5
6   // Point2 inherits from abstract class Shape
7   public class Point2 : Shape
8   {
9      private int x, y; // Point2 coordinates
10
11     // default constructor
12     public Point2()
13     {
14        // implicit call to Object constructor occurs here
15     }
16
17     // constructor
18     public Point2( int xValue, int yValue )
19     {
20        X = xValue;
21        Y = yValue;
22     }
23
24     // property X
25     public int X
26     {
27        get
28        {
29           return x;
30        }
31
```

Fig. 10.5 **Point2** class inherits from **abstract** class **Shape**. (Part 1 of 2.)

```
32            set
33            {
34                x = value; // no validation needed
35            }
36        }
37
38        // property Y
39        public int Y
40        {
41            get
42            {
43                return y;
44            }
45
46            set
47            {
48                y = value; // no validation needed
49            }
50        }
51
52        // return string representation of Point2 object
53        public override string ToString()
54        {
55            return "[" + X + ", " + Y + "]";
56        }
57
58        // implement abstract property Name of class Shape
59        public override string Name
60        {
61            get
62            {
63                return "Point2";
64            }
65        }
66
67    } // end class Point2
```

Fig. 10.5 **Point2** class inherits from **abstract** class **Shape**. (Part 2 of 2.)

Figure 10.6 defines class **Circle2**, which inherits from class **Point2**. Class **Circle2** contains property **Radius** (lines 24–37) for accessing the circle's radius. Note that we do not declare property **Radius** as **virtual**, so classes derived from this class cannot override this property. A circle has zero volume, so we do not override base-class method **Volume**. Rather, **Circle2** inherits this method from class **Point2**, which inherited the method from **Shape**. However, a circle does have an area, so **Circle2** overrides **Shape** method **Area** (lines 52–55). Property **Name** (lines 65–71) of class **Circle2** overrides property **Name** of class **Point2**. If this class did not override property **Name**, the class would inherit the **Point2** version of property **Name**. In that case, **Circle2**'s **Name** property would erroneously return "**Point2**."

```
1   // Fig. 10.6: Circle2.cs
2   // Circle2 inherits from class Point2 and overrides key members.
3   using System;
4
5   // Circle2 inherits from class Point2
6   public class Circle2 : Point2
7   {
8      private double radius; // Circle2 radius
9
10     // default constructor
11     public Circle2()
12     {
13        // implicit call to Point2 constructor occurs here
14     }
15
16     // constructor
17     public Circle2( int xValue, int yValue, double radiusValue )
18        : base( xValue, yValue )
19     {
20        Radius = radiusValue;
21     }
22
23     // property Radius
24     public double Radius
25     {
26        get
27        {
28           return radius;
29        }
30
31        set
32        {
33           // ensure non-negative radius value
34           if ( value >= 0 )
35              radius = value;
36        }
37     }
38
39     // calculate Circle2 diameter
40     public double Diameter()
41     {
42        return Radius * 2;
43     }
44
45     // calculate Circle2 circumference
46     public double Circumference()
47     {
48        return Math.PI * Diameter();
49     }
50
51     // calculate Circle2 area
52     public override double Area()
53     {
```

Fig. 10.6 Circle2 class that inherits from class **Point2**. (Part 1 of 2.)

```
54              return Math.PI * Math.Pow( Radius, 2 );
55          }
56
57          // return string representation of Circle2 object
58          public override string ToString()
59          {
60              return "Center = " + base.ToString() +
61                  "; Radius = " + Radius;
62          }
63
64          // override property Name from class Point2
65          public override string Name
66          {
67              get
68              {
69                  return "Circle2";
70              }
71          }
72
73      } // end class Circle2
```

Fig. 10.6 `Circle2` class that inherits from class **Point2**. (Part 2 of 2.)

Figure 10.7 defines class **Cylinder2**, which inherits from class **Circle2**. Class **Cylinder2** contains property **Height** (lines 24–37) for accessing the cylinder's height. Note that we do not declare property **Height** as **virtual**, so classes derived from class **Cylinder2** cannot override this property. A cylinder has different area and volume calculations from those of a circle, so this class overrides method **Area** (lines 40–43) to calculate the cylinder's surface area (i.e., $2\pi r^2 + 2\pi rh$) and overrides method **Volume** (lines 46–49). Property **Name** (lines 58–64) overrides property **Name** of class **Circle2**. If this class did not override property **Name**, the class would inherit property **Name** of class **Circle2**, and this property would erroneously return "**Circle2**."

```
1   // Fig. 10.7: Cylinder2.cs
2   // Cylinder2 inherits from class Circle2 and overrides key members.
3   using System;
4
5   // Cylinder2 inherits from class Circle2
6   public class Cylinder2 : Circle2
7   {
8       private double height; // Cylinder2 height
9
10      // default constructor
11      public Cylinder2()
12      {
13          // implicit call to Circle2 constructor occurs here
14      }
15
```

Fig. 10.7 `Cylinder2` class inherits from class **Circle2**. (Part 1 of 2.)

```
16      // constructor
17      public Cylinder2( int xValue, int yValue, double radiusValue,
18          double heightValue ) : base( xValue, yValue, radiusValue )
19      {
20          Height = heightValue;
21      }
22
23      // property Height
24      public double Height
25      {
26          get
27          {
28              return height;
29          }
30
31          set
32          {
33              // ensure non-negative height value
34              if ( value >= 0 )
35                  height = value;
36          }
37      }
38
39      // calculate Cylinder2 area
40      public override double Area()
41      {
42          return 2 * base.Area() + base.Circumference() * Height;
43      }
44
45      // calculate Cylinder2 volume
46      public override double Volume()
47      {
48          return base.Area() * Height;
49      }
50
51      // return string representation of Circle2 object
52      public override string ToString()
53      {
54          return base.ToString() + "; Height = " + Height;
55      }
56
57      // override property Name from class Circle2
58      public override string Name
59      {
60          get
61          {
62              return "Cylinder2";
63          }
64      }
65
66  } // end class Cylinder2
```

Fig. 10.7 **Cylinder2** class inherits from class **Circle2**. (Part 2 of 2.)

Class **Test2** (Fig. 10.8), creates an object of each of the three concrete classes and manipulates those objects polymorphically using an array of **Shape** references. Lines 11–13 instantiate **Point2** object **point**, **Circle2** object **circle**, and **Cylinder2** object **cylinder**, respectively. Next, line 16 allocates array **arrayOfShapes**, which contains three **Shape** references. Line 19 assigns reference **point** to the array element **arrayOfShapes[0]**, line 22 assigns reference **circle** to the array element **arrayOfShapes[1]** and line 25 assigns reference **cylinder** to the array element **arrayOfShapes[2]**. These assignments are possible because a **Point2** is a **Shape**, a **Circle2** is a **Shape** and a **Cylinder2** is a **Shape**. Therefore, we can assign instances of derived classes **Point2**, **Circle2** and **Cylinder2** to base-class **Shape** references.

```
1   // Fig. 10.8: AbstractShapesTest.cs
2   // Demonstrates polymorphism in Point-Circle-Cylinder hierarchy.
3   using System;
4   using System.Windows.Forms;
5
6   public class AbstractShapesTest
7   {
8      public static void Main( string[] args )
9      {
10        // instantiate Point2, Circle2 and Cylinder2 objects
11        Point2 point = new Point2( 7, 11 );
12        Circle2 circle = new Circle2( 22, 8, 3.5 );
13        Cylinder2 cylinder = new Cylinder2( 10, 10, 3.3, 10 );
14
15        // create empty array of Shape base-class references
16        Shape[] arrayOfShapes = new Shape[ 3 ];
17
18        // arrayOfShapes[ 0 ] refers to Point2 object
19        arrayOfShapes[ 0 ] = point;
20
21        // arrayOfShapes[ 1 ] refers to Circle2 object
22        arrayOfShapes[ 1 ] = circle;
23
24        // arrayOfShapes[ 1 ] refers to Cylinder2 object
25        arrayOfShapes[ 2 ] = cylinder;
26
27        string output = point.Name + ": " + point + "\n" +
28           circle.Name + ": " + circle + "\n" +
29           cylinder.Name + ": " + cylinder;
30
31        // display Name, Area and Volume for each object
32        // in arrayOfShapes polymorphically
33        foreach( Shape shape in arrayOfShapes )
34        {
35           output += "\n\n" + shape.Name + ": " + shape +
36              "\nArea = " + shape.Area().ToString( "F" ) +
37              "\nVolume = " + shape.Volume().ToString( "F" );
38        }
39
```

Fig. 10.8 **AbstractShapesTest** demonstrates polymorphism in Point-Circle-Cylinder hierarchy. (Part 1 of 2.)

```
40              MessageBox.Show( output, "Demonstrating Polymorphism" );
41         }
42    }
```

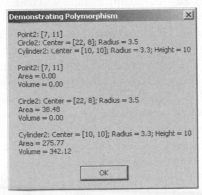

Fig. 10.8   AbstractShapesTest demonstrates polymorphism in Point-Circle-Cylinder hierarchy. (Part 2 of 2.)

Lines 27–29 access property **Name** and invoke method **ToString** (implicitly) for objects **point**, **circle** and **cylinder**. Property **Name** returns the object's class name and method **ToString** returns the object's **String** representation (i.e., *x-y* coordinate pair, radius and height, depending on each object's type). Note that lines 27–29 use derived-class references to invoke each derived-class object's methods and properties.

By contrast, the **foreach** structure (lines 33–38) uses base-class **Shape** references to invoke each derived-class object's methods and properties. The **foreach** structure calls property **Name** and methods **ToString**, **Area** and **Volume** for each **Shape** reference in **arrayOfShapes**. The property and methods are invoked on each object in **array-OfShapes**. When the compiler looks at each method/property call, the compiler determines whether each **Shape** reference (in **arrayOfShapes**) can make these calls. This is the case for property **Name** and methods **Area** and **Volume**, because they are defined in class **Shape**. However, class **Shape** does not define method **ToString**. For this method, the compiler proceeds to **Shape**'s base class (class **Object**) and determines that **Shape** inherited a no-argument **ToString** method from class **Object**.

The screen capture of Fig. 10.8 illustrates that the "appropriate" property **Name** and methods **ToString**, **Area** and **Volume** were invoked for each type of object in **array-OfShapes**. By "appropriate," we mean that C# maps each property and method call to the proper object. For example, in the **foreach** structure's first iteration, reference **arrayOfShapes[0]** (which is of type **Shape**) refers to the same object as **point** (which is of type **Point2**). Class **Point2** overrides property **Name**, and method **ToString** and inherits method **Area** and **Volume** from class **Shape**. At runtime, **arrayOfShapes[0]** accesses property **Name** and invokes methods **ToString**, **Area** and **Volume** of the **Point** object. C# determines the correct object type, then uses that type to determine the appropriate methods to invoke. Through polymorphism, the call to property **Name** returns the string **"Point2:"**; the call to method **ToString** returns the **String** representation of **point**'s *x-y* coordinate pair; and methods **Area** and **Volume** each return **0** (as shown in the second group of outputs in Fig. 10.8).

Polymorphism occurs in the next two iterations of the **foreach** structure as well. Reference **arrayOfShapes[1]** refers to the same object as **circle** (which is of type **Circle2**). Class **Circle2** provides implementations for property **Name**, method **ToString** and method **Area**, and inherits method **Volume** from class **Point2** (which, in turn, inherited method **Volume** from class **Shape**). C# associates property **Name** and methods **ToString**, **Area** and **Volume** of the **Circle2** object to reference **arrayOfShapes[1]**. As a result, property **Name** returns the string **"Circle2:"**; method **ToString** returns the **String** representation of **circle**'s *x-y* coordinate pair and radius; method **Area** returns the area (**38.48**); and method **Volume** returns **0**.

For the final iteration of the **foreach** structure, reference **arrayOfShapes[2]** refers to the same object as **cylinder** (which is of type **Cylinder2**). Class **Cylinder2** provides its own implementations for property **Name** and for methods **ToString**, **Area** and **Volume**. C# associates property **Name** and methods **ToString**, **Area** and **Volume** of the **Cylinder2** object to reference **arrayOfShapes[2]**. Property **Name** returns the string **"Cylinder2:"**; method **ToString** returns the **String** representation of **cylinder**'s *x-y* coordinate pair, radius and height; method **Area** returns the cylinder's surface area (**275.769…**); and method **Volume** returns the cylinder's volume (**342.119…**).

10.7 **sealed** Classes and Methods

In Chapter 8, Object-Based Programming, we saw that variables can be declared **const** and **readonly** to indicate that they cannot be modified after they are initialized. Variables declared with **const** must be initialized when they are declared; variables declared with **readonly** can be initialized in the constructor, but cannot be changed after they are initialized.

The keyword *sealed* is applied to methods and classes to prevent overriding and inheritance. A method that is declared **sealed** cannot be overridden in a derived class. Methods that are declared **static** and methods that are declared **private** are implicitly **sealed**.

Performance Tip 10.1

*The **sealed** keyword allows certain compiler optimizations. A **sealed** method's definition can never change, so the compiler can optimize the program by removing calls to **sealed** methods and replacing them with the expanded code of their definitions at each method call location—a technique known as inlining the code.*

Software Engineering Observation 10.8

*If a method is declared **sealed**, it cannot be overridden in derived classes. Method calls must not be sent polymorphically to objects of those derived classes. The method call still may be sent to derived classes, but they will respond identically, rather than polymorphically. Remember that a method cannot be overridden (using the keyword **override**) if it is not declared either **virtual** or **abstract**. Therefore, keyword **sealed** is not needed for these cases. Keyword **sealed** is used for methods that have been overridden, but that we do not want to be overridden in derived classes.*

Performance Tip 10.2

*The compiler can decide to inline a **sealed** method call and will do so for small, simple **sealed** methods. Inlining does not violate encapsulation or information hiding (but does improve performance, because it eliminates the overhead of making a method call).*

Performance Tip 10.3

*Pipelined processors can improve performance by executing portions of the next several instructions simultaneously, but not if those instructions follow a method call. Inlining (which the compiler can perform on a **sealed** method) can improve performance in these processors as it eliminates the out-of-line transfer of control associated with a method call.*

Software Engineering Observation 10.9

*A class that is declared **sealed** cannot be a base class (i.e., a class cannot inherit from a **sealed** class). All methods in a **sealed** class are **sealed** implicitly.*

Using the **sealed** keyword with classes allows other runtime optimizations. For example, **virtual** method calls can be transformed into non-**virtual** method calls.

A **sealed** class is the opposite of an **abstract** class in certain ways. An **abstract** class cannot be instantiated—other classes derive from the abstract base class and implement the base class's **abstract** members. A **sealed** class, on the other hand, cannot have any derived classes. This relationship is similar with regard to methods. An **abstract** method must be overridden in a derived class. A **sealed** method cannot be overridden in a derived class.

10.8 Case Study: Payroll System Using Polymorphism

Let us use **abstract** classes, **abstract** methods and polymorphism to perform payroll calculations for various types of employees. We begin by creating abstract base class **Employee**. The derived classes of **Employee** are **Boss** (paid a fixed weekly salary, regardless of the number of hours worked), **CommissionWorker** (paid a flat base salary plus a percentage of the worker's sales), **PieceWorker** (paid a flat fee per item produced) and **HourlyWorker** (paid by the hour with "time-and-a-half" for overtime).

The application must determine the weekly earnings for all types of employees, so each class derived from **Employee** requires method **Earnings**. However, each derived class uses a different calculation to determine earnings for each specific type of employee. Therefore, we declare method **Earnings** as **abstract** in **Employee** and declare **Employee** to be an **abstract** class. Each derived class overrides this method to calculate earnings for that employee type.

To calculate any employee's earnings, the program can use a base-class reference to a derived-class object and invoke method **Earnings**. A real payroll system might reference the various **Employee** objects with individual elements in an array of **Employee** references. The program would traverse the array one element at a time, using the **Employee** references to invoke the appropriate **Earnings** method of each object.

Software Engineering Observation 10.10

The ability to declare an abstract method gives the class designer considerable control over how derived classes are defined in a class hierarchy. Any class that inherits directly from a base class containing an abstract method must override the abstract method. Otherwise, the new class also would be abstract, and attempts to instantiate objects of that class would fail.

Let us consider class **Employee** (Fig. 10.9). The **public** members include a constructor (lines 11–16) that takes as arguments the employee's first and last names; properties **FirstName** (lines 19–30) and **LastName** (lines 33–44); method **ToString** (lines 47–50), which returns the first name and last name separated by a space; and **abstract** method **Earnings** (line 54). The **abstract** keyword (line 5) indicates that class **Employee** is abstract; thus, it cannot be used to instantiate **Employee** objects. Method **Earnings** is declared **abstract**, so the class does not provide a method implementation. All classes derived directly from class **Employee**—except for abstract derived classes—must implement this method. Method **Earnings** is **abstract** in **Employee**, because we cannot calculate the earnings for a generic employee. To determine earnings, we first must know of what *kind* the employee is. By declaring this method **abstract**, we indicate that we will provide an implementation in each concrete derived class, but not in the base class itself.

```
1   // Fig. 10.9: Employee.cs
2   // Abstract base class for company employees.
3   using System;
4
5   public abstract class Employee
6   {
7      private string firstName;
8      private string lastName;
9
10     // constructor
11     public Employee( string firstNameValue,
12        string lastNameValue )
13     {
14        FirstName = firstNameValue;
15        LastName = lastNameValue;
16     }
17
18     // property FirstName
19     public string FirstName
20     {
21        get
22        {
23           return firstName;
24        }
25
26        set
27        {
28           firstName = value;
29        }
30     }
31
32     // property LastName
33     public string LastName
34     {
35        get
36        {
37           return lastName;
38        }
39
```

Fig. 10.9 **abstract** class **Employee** definition. (Part 1 of 2.)

```
40            set
41            {
42                lastName = value;
43            }
44        }
45
46        // return string representation of Employee
47        public override string ToString()
48        {
49            return FirstName + " " + LastName;
50        }
51
52        // abstract method that must be implemented for each derived
53        // class of Employee to calculate specific earnings
54        public abstract decimal Earnings();
55
56    } // end class Employee
```

Fig. 10.9 **abstract** class **Employee** definition. (Part 2 of 2.)

Class **Boss** (Fig. 10.10) inherits from **Employee**. Class **Boss**'s constructor (lines 10–15) receives as arguments a first name, a last name and a salary. The constructor passes the first name and last name to the **Employee** constructor (line 12), which initializes the **FirstName** and **LastName** members of the base-class part of the derived-class object. Other **public** methods in class **Boss** include method **Earnings** (lines 34–37), which defines the calculation of a boss' earnings, and method **ToString** (lines 40–43), which returns a string that indicates the type of employee (i.e., **"Boss: "**) and the boss's name. Class **Boss** also includes property **WeeklySalary** (lines 18–31), which manipulates the value for member variable **salary**. Note that this property ensures only that **salary** cannot hold a negative value—in a real payroll system, this validation would be more extensive and carefully controlled.

```
1   // Fig. 10.10: Boss.cs
2   // Boss class derived from Employee.
3   using System;
4
5   public class Boss : Employee
6   {
7       private decimal salary; // Boss's salary
8
9       // constructor
10      public Boss( string firstNameValue, string lastNameValue,
11          decimal salaryValue)
12          : base( firstNameValue, lastNameValue )
13      {
14          WeeklySalary = salaryValue;
15      }
16
```

Fig. 10.10 **Boss** class inherits from class **Employee**. (Part 1 of 2.)

```
17      // property WeeklySalary
18      public decimal WeeklySalary
19      {
20         get
21         {
22            return salary;
23         }
24
25         set
26         {
27            // ensure positive salary value
28            if ( value > 0 )
29               salary = value;
30         }
31      }
32
33      // override base-class method to calculate Boss's earnings
34      public override decimal Earnings()
35      {
36         return WeeklySalary;
37      }
38
39      // return string representation of Boss
40      public override string ToString()
41      {
42         return "Boss: " + base.ToString();
43      }
44   }
```

Fig. 10.10 Boss class inherits from class **Employee**. (Part 2 of 2.)

Class **CommissionWorker** (Fig. 10.11) also inherits from class **Employee**. The constructor for this class (lines 12–20) receives as arguments a first name, a last name, a salary, a commission and a quantity of items sold. Line 15 passes the first name and last name to the base-class **Employee** constructor. Class **CommissionWorker** also provides properties **WeeklySalary** (lines 23–36), **Commission** (lines 39–52) and **Quantity** (lines 55–68); method **Earnings** (lines 72–75), which calculates the worker's wages; and method **ToString** (lines 78–81), which returns a string that indicates the employee type (i.e., **"CommissionWorker: "**) and the worker's name.

```
1    // Fig. 10.11: CommissionWorker.cs
2    // CommissionWorker class derived from Employee
3    using System;
4
5    public class CommissionWorker : Employee
6    {
7       private decimal salary;      // base weekly salary
8       private decimal commission;  // amount paid per item sold
9       private int quantity;        // total items sold
10
```

Fig. 10.11 CommissionWorker class inherits from class **Employee**. (Part 1 of 3.)

```
11      // constructor
12      public CommissionWorker( string firstNameValue,
13         string lastNameValue, decimal salaryValue,
14         decimal commissionValue, int quantityValue )
15         : base( firstNameValue, lastNameValue )
16      {
17         WeeklySalary = salaryValue;
18         Commission = commissionValue;
19         Quantity = quantityValue;
20      }
21
22      // property WeeklySalary
23      public decimal WeeklySalary
24      {
25         get
26         {
27            return salary;
28         }
29
30         set
31         {
32            // ensure non-negative salary value
33            if ( value > 0 )
34               salary = value;
35         }
36      }
37
38      // property Commission
39      public decimal Commission
40      {
41         get
42         {
43            return commission;
44         }
45
46         set
47         {
48            // ensure non-negative commission value
49            if ( value > 0 )
50               commission = value;
51         }
52      }
53
54      // property Quantity
55      public int Quantity
56      {
57         get
58         {
59            return quantity;
60         }
61
```

Fig. 10.11 **CommissionWorker** class inherits from class **Employee**. (Part 2 of 3.)

```
62          set
63          {
64              // ensure non-negative quantity value
65              if ( value > 0 )
66                  quantity = value;
67          }
68      }
69
70      // override base-class method to calculate
71      // CommissionWorker's earnings
72      public override decimal Earnings()
73      {
74          return WeeklySalary + Commission * Quantity;
75      }
76
77      // return string representation of CommissionWorker
78      public override string ToString()
79      {
80          return "CommissionWorker: " + base.ToString();
81      }
82
83  } // end class CommissionWorker
```

Fig. 10.11 `CommissionWorker` class inherits from class **Employee**. (Part 3 of 3.)

Class **PieceWorker** (Fig. 10.12) inherits from class **Employee**. The constructor for this class (lines 11–18) receives as arguments a first name, a last name, a wage per piece and a quantity of items produced. Line 14 then passes the first name and last name to the base-class **Employee** constructor. Class **PieceWorker** also provides properties **WagePerPiece** (lines 21–33) and **Quantity** (lines 36–48); method **Earnings** (lines 52–55), which calculates a piece worker's earnings; and method **ToString** (lines 58–61), which returns a string that indicates the type of the employee (i.e., **"PieceWorker: "**) and the piece worker's name.

```
1   // Fig. 10.12: PieceWorker.cs
2   // PieceWorker class derived from Employee.
3   using System;
4
5   public class PieceWorker : Employee
6   {
7       private decimal wagePerPiece; // wage per piece produced
8       private int quantity;         // quantity of pieces produced
9
10      // constructor
11      public PieceWorker( string firstNameValue,
12          string lastNameValue, decimal wagePerPieceValue,
13          int quantityValue )
14          : base( firstNameValue, lastNameValue )
15      {
16          WagePerPiece = wagePerPieceValue;
```

Fig. 10.12 `PieceWorker` class inherits from class **Employee**. (Part 1 of 2.)

```
17             Quantity = quantityValue;
18       }
19
20       // property WagePerPiece
21       public decimal WagePerPiece
22       {
23          get
24          {
25             return wagePerPiece;
26          }
27
28          set
29          {
30             if ( value > 0 )
31                wagePerPiece = value;
32          }
33       }
34
35       // property Quantity
36       public int Quantity
37       {
38          get
39          {
40             return quantity;
41          }
42
43          set
44          {
45             if ( value > 0 )
46                quantity = value;
47          }
48       }
49
50       // override base-class method to calculate
51       // PieceWorker's earnings
52       public override decimal Earnings()
53       {
54          return Quantity * WagePerPiece;
55       }
56
57       // return string representation of PieceWorker
58       public override string ToString()
59       {
60          return "PieceWorker: " + base.ToString();
61       }
62    }
```

Fig. 10.12 PieceWorker class inherits from class **Employee**. (Part 2 of 2.)

Class **HourlyWorker** (Fig. 10.13) inherits from class **Employee**. The constructor for this class (lines 11–17) receives as arguments a first name, a last name, a wage and the number of hours worked. Line 13 passes the first name and last name to the base-class

Employee constructor. Class **HourlyWorker** also provides properties **Wage** (lines 20–33) and **HoursWorked** (lines 36–49); method **Earnings** (lines 53–70), which calculates an hourly worker's earnings; and method **ToString** (lines 73–76), which returns a string that indicates the type of the employee (i.e., **"HourlyWorker:"**) and the hourly worker's name. Note that hourly workers are paid "time-and-a-half" for "overtime" (i.e., hours worked in excess of 40 hours).

```
1   // Fig. 10.13: HourlyWorker.cs
2   // HourlyWorker class derived from Employee.
3   using System;
4
5   public class HourlyWorker : Employee
6   {
7      private decimal wage;       // wage per hour of work
8      private double hoursWorked; // hours worked during week
9
10     // constructor
11     public HourlyWorker( string firstNameValue, string LastNameValue,
12        decimal wageValue, double hoursWorkedValue )
13        : base( firstNameValue, LastNameValue )
14     {
15        Wage = wageValue;
16        HoursWorked = hoursWorkedValue;
17     }
18
19     // property Wage
20     public decimal Wage
21     {
22        get
23        {
24           return wage;
25        }
26
27        set
28        {
29           // ensure non-negative wage value
30           if ( value > 0 )
31              wage = value;
32        }
33     }
34
35     // property HoursWorked
36     public double HoursWorked
37     {
38        get
39        {
40           return hoursWorked;
41        }
42
```

Fig. 10.13 HourlyWorker class inherits from class **Employee** (Part 1 of 2.).

```
43          set
44          {
45              // ensure non-negative hoursWorked value
46              if ( value > 0 )
47                  hoursWorked = value;
48          }
49      }
50
51      // override base-class method to calculate
52      // HourlyWorker earnings
53      public override decimal Earnings()
54      {
55          // compensate for overtime (paid "time-and-a-half")
56          if ( HoursWorked <= 40 )
57          {
58              return Wage * Convert.ToDecimal( HoursWorked );
59          }
60
61          else
62          {
63              // calculate base and overtime pay
64              decimal basePay = Wage * Convert.ToDecimal( 40 );
65              decimal overtimePay = Wage * 1.5M *
66                  Convert.ToDecimal( HoursWorked - 40 );
67
68              return basePay + overtimePay;
69          }
70      }
71
72      // return string representation of HourlyWorker
73      public override string ToString()
74      {
75          return "HourlyWorker: " + base.ToString();
76      }
77  }
```

Fig. 10.13 HourlyWorker class inherits from class **Employee** (Part 2 of 2.).

Method **Main** (lines 9–48) of class **EmployeesTest** (Fig. 10.14) declares **Employee** reference **employee** (line 22). Each employee type is handled similarly in **Main**, so we discuss only the manipulations of the **Boss** object.

Line 11 assigns to **Boss** reference **boss** a **Boss** object and passes to its constructor the boss's first name ("**John**"), last name ("**Smith**") and fixed weekly salary (**800**). Line 22 assigns the derived-class reference **boss** to the base-class **Employee** reference **employee**, so we can demonstrate the polymorphic determination of **boss**'s earnings. Line 24 passes reference **employee** as an argument to method **GetString** (lines 51–55), which polymorphically invokes methods **ToString** and **Earnings** on the **Employee** object the method receives as an argument. At this point, C# determines that the object passed to **GetString** is of type **Boss**, so lines 53–54 invoke **Boss** methods **ToString** and **Earnings**. These are classic examples of polymorphic behavior.

```
1    // Fig. 10.14: EmployeesTest.cs
2    // Demonstrates polymorphism by displaying earnings
3    // for various Employee types.
4    using System;
5    using System.Windows.Forms;
6
7    public class EmployeesTest
8    {
9       public static void Main( string[] args )
10      {
11         Boss boss = new Boss( "John", "Smith", 800 );
12
13         CommissionWorker commissionWorker =
14            new CommissionWorker( "Sue", "Jones", 400, 3, 150 );
15
16         PieceWorker pieceWorker = new PieceWorker( "Bob", "Lewis",
17            Convert.ToDecimal( 2.5 ), 200 );
18
19         HourlyWorker hourlyWorker = new HourlyWorker( "Karen",
20            "Price", Convert.ToDecimal( 13.75 ), 50 );
21
22         Employee employee = boss;
23
24         string output = GetString( employee ) + boss + " earned " +
25               boss.Earnings().ToString( "C" ) + "\n\n";
26
27         employee = commissionWorker;
28
29         output += GetString( employee ) + commissionWorker +
30            " earned " +
31            commissionWorker.Earnings().ToString( "C" ) + "\n\n";
32
33         employee = pieceWorker;
34
35         output += GetString( employee ) + pieceWorker +
36            " earned " + pieceWorker.Earnings().ToString( "C" ) +
37            "\n\n";
38
39         employee = hourlyWorker;
40
41         output += GetString( employee ) + hourlyWorker +
42            " earned " + hourlyWorker.Earnings().ToString( "C" ) +
43            "\n\n";
44
45         MessageBox.Show( output, "Demonstrating Polymorphism",
46            MessageBoxButtons.OK, MessageBoxIcon.Information );
47
48      } // end method Main
49
50      // return string that contains Employee information
51      public static string GetString( Employee worker )
52      {
```

Fig. 10.14 EmployeesTest class tests the **Employee** class hierarchy. (Part 1 of 2.)

```
53          return worker.ToString() + " earned " +
54             worker.Earnings().ToString( "C" ) + "\n";
55      }
56  }
```

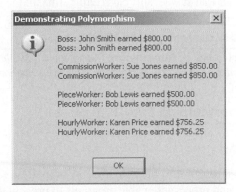

Fig. 10.14 **EmployeesTest** class tests the **Employee** class hierarchy. (Part 2 of 2.)

Method **Earnings** returns a **Decimal** object on which line 54 then calls method **ToString**. In this case, the string **"C"**, which is passed to an overloaded version of **Decimal** method **ToString**, stands for **Currency**, and **ToString** formats the string as a currency amount.

When method **GetString** returns to **Main**, lines 24–25 explicitly invoke methods **ToString** and **Earnings** through derived-class **Boss** reference **boss** to show the method invocations that do not use polymorphic processing. The output generated in lines 24–25 is identical to that generated by methods **ToString** and **Earnings** through base-class reference **employee** (i.e., the methods that use polymorphism), which verifies that the polymorphic methods invoke the appropriate methods in derived class **Boss**.

To prove that the base-class reference **employee** can invoke the proper derived-class versions of methods **ToString** and **Earnings** for the other types of employees, lines 27, 33 and 39 assign to base-class reference **employee** a different type of **Employee** object (**CommissionWorker**, **PieceWorker** and **HourlyWorker**, respectively). After each assignment, the application calls method **GetString** to return the results via the base-class reference. Then, the application calls methods **ToString** and **Earnings** of each derived-class reference to show that C# correctly associates each method call to its corresponding derived-class object.

10.9 Case Study: Creating and Using Interfaces

We now present two more examples of polymorphism using *interfaces* that specify sets of **public** services (i.e., methods and properties) that classes must implement. An interface is used when there is no default implementation to inherit (i.e., no instance variables and no default-method implementations). Whereas an abstract class is best used for providing data and services for objects in a hierarchical relationship, an interface can be used for providing services that "bring together" disparate objects that relate to one another only through that interface.

An interface definition begins with the keyword *interface* and contains a list of **public** methods and properties. To use an interface, a class must specify that it implements the interface and must provide implementations for every method and property specified in the interface definition. A class that implements an interface effectively signs a contract with the compiler that states, "this class will define all the methods and properties specified by the interface."

Common Programming Error 10.8

*When a class implements an **interface**, leaving even a single **interface** method or property undefined is an error. The class must define every method and property in the **interface**.*

Common Programming Error 10.9

*In C#, an **interface** can be declared only as **public**; the declaration of an **interface** as **private** or **protected** is an error.*

Interfaces provide uniform sets of methods and properties for objects of disparate classes. These methods and properties enable programs to process the objects of those disparate classes polymorphically. For example, consider disparate objects that represent a person, a tree, a car and a file. These objects have "nothing to do" with one another—a person has a first name and last name; a tree has a trunk, a set of branches and a bunch of leaves; a car has wheels, gears and several other mechanisms that enable the car to move; and a file contains data. Because of the lack of commonality among these classes, modeling them via an inheritance hierarchy with a common base class seems illogical. However, these objects certainly have at least one common characteristic—an age. A person's age is represented by the number of years since that person was born; a tree's age is represented by the number of rings in its trunk; a car's age is represented by its manufacture date; and file's age is represented by its creation date. We can use an interface that provides a method or property that objects of these disparate classes can implement to return each object's age.

In this example, we use interface **IAge** (Fig. 10.15) to return the age information for classes **Person** (Fig. 10.16) and **Tree** (Fig. 10.17). The definition of interface **IAge** begins at line 4 with **public interface** and ends at line 8 with a closing curly brace. Lines 6–7 specify read-only properties **Age** and **Name**, for which every class that implements interface **IAge** must provide implementations. Declaring these properties as read-only is not required—an interface can also provide methods, write-only properties and properties with both *get* and *set* accessors. By containing these property declarations, interface **IAge** provides an opportunity for an object that implements **IAge** to return its age and name, respectively. However, the classes that implement these methods are not "required" by either interface **IAge** or C# to return an age and a name. The compiler requires only that classes implementing interface **IAge** provide implementations for the interface's properties.

Line 5 of Fig. 10.16 use C#'s inheritance notation (i.e., *ClassName* **:** *InterfaceName*) to indicate that class **Person** implements interface **IAge**. In this example, class **Person** implements only one interface. A class can implement any number of interfaces in addition to inheriting from one class. To implement more than one interface, the class definition must provide a comma-separated list of interface names after the semicolon. Class **Person** has member variables **yearBorn**, **firstName** and **lastName** (lines 7–9), for which the constructor (lines 12–22) sets values. Because class **Person** implements interface **IAge**, class **Person** must implement properties **Age** and **Name**—defined on lines

25–31 and lines 34–40, respectively. Property **Age** allows the client to obtain the person's age, and property **Name** returns a **String** containing **firstName** and **lastName**. Note that property **Age** calculates the person's age by subtracting **yearBorn** from the current year (via property **Year** of property **DateTime.Now**, which returns the current date). These properties satisfy the implementation requirements defined in interface **IAge**, so class **Person** has fulfilled its "contract" with the compiler.

```
1   // Fig. 10.15: IAge.cs
2   // Interface IAge declares property for setting and getting age.
3
4   public interface IAge
5   {
6      int Age { get; }
7      string Name { get; }
8   }
```

Fig. 10.15 Interface for returning age of objects of disparate classes.

```
1   // Fig. 10.16: Person.cs
2   // Class Person has a birthday.
3   using System;
4
5   public class Person : IAge
6   {
7      private string firstName;
8      private string lastName;
9      private int yearBorn;
10
11     // constructor
12     public Person( string firstNameValue, string lastNameValue,
13        int yearBornValue )
14     {
15        firstName = firstNameValue;
16        lastName = lastNameValue;
17
18        if ( yearBornValue > 0 && yearBornValue <= DateTime.Now.Year )
19           yearBorn = yearBornValue;
20        else
21           yearBorn = DateTime.Now.Year;
22     }
23
24     // property Age implementation of interface IAge
25     public int Age
26     {
27        get
28        {
29           return DateTime.Now.Year - yearBorn;
30        }
31     }
32
```

Fig. 10.16 Person class implements **IAge** interface. (Part 1 of 2.)

```
33       // property Name implementation of interface IAge
34       public string Name
35       {
36          get
37          {
38             return firstName + " " + lastName;
39          }
40       }
41
42    } // end class Person
```

Fig. 10.16 Person class implements **IAge** interface. (Part 2 of 2.)

Class **Tree** (Fig. 10.17) also implements interface **IAge**. Class **Tree** has member variables **rings** (line 7), which represents the number of rings inside the tree's trunk—this variable corresponds directly to the tree's age. The **Tree** constructor (lines 10–14) receives as an argument an **int** that specifies in which year the tree was planted. Class **Tree** includes method **AddRing** (lines 17–20), which enables a program to increment the number of rings in the tree. Because class **Tree** implements interface **IAge**, class **Tree** must implement properties **Age** and **Name**—defined on lines 23–29 and lines 32–38, respectively. Property **Age** returns the value of **rings**, and property **Name** returns **string** "Tree."

```
1    // Fig. 10.17: Tree.cs
2    // Class Tree contains number of rings corresponding to its age.
3    using System;
4
5    public class Tree : IAge
6    {
7       private int rings; // number of rings in tree trunk
8
9       // constructor
10      public Tree( int yearPlanted )
11      {
12         // count number of rings in Tree
13         rings = DateTime.Now.Year - yearPlanted;
14      }
15
16      // increment rings
17      public void AddRing()
18      {
19         rings++;
20      }
21
22      // property Age implementation of interface IAge
23      public int Age
24      {
25         get
26         {
```

Fig. 10.17 Tree class implements **IAge** interface. (Part 1 of 2.)

```
27                 return rings;
28            }
29        }
30
31        // property Name implementation of interface IAge
32        public string Name
33        {
34            get
35            {
36                return "Tree";
37            }
38        }
39
40   } // end class Tree
```

Fig. 10.17 **Tree** class implements **IAge** interface. (Part 2 of 2.)

Class **InterfacesTest** (Fig. 10.18) demonstrates polymorphism on the objects of disparate classes **Person** and **Tree**. Line 9 instantiates object **tree** of class **Tree**, and line 10 instantiates object **person** of class **Person**. Line 13 declares **iAgeArray**—an array of two references to **IAge** objects. Line 16 and 19 assign **tree** and **person** to the first and second reference in **iAgeArray**, respectively. Lines 22–23 invoke method **ToString** on **tree**, then invoke its properties **Age** and **Name** to return age and name information for object **tree**. Lines 26–27 invoke method **ToString** on **person**, then invoke its properties **Age** and **Name** to return age and name information for object **person**. Next, we manipulate these objects polymorphically through the **iAgeArray** of references to **IAge** objects. Lines 30–34 define a **foreach** structure that uses properties **Age** and **Name** to obtain age and name information for each **IAge** object in **iAgeArray**. Note that a program also can invoke class **Object**'s **public** methods (e.g., **ToString**) using any interface reference. This is possible because every object inherits directly or indirectly from class **Object**. Therefore, every object is guaranteed to have the class **Object**'s **public** methods.

Software Engineering Observation 10.11

*In C#, an interface reference may invoke methods and properties that the interface declares and the **public** methods of class **Object**.*

Software Engineering Observation 10.12

*In C#, an interface provides only those **public** services declared in the interface, whereas an abstract class provides the **public** services defined in the abstract class and those members inherited from the abstract class's base class.*

```
1    // Fig. 10.18: InterfacesTest.cs
2    // Demonstrating polymorphism with interfaces.
3    using System.Windows.Forms;
4
5    public class InterfacesTest
6    {
```

Fig. 10.18 Demonstrate polymorphism on objects of disparate classes. (Part 1 of 2.)

```
 7      public static void Main( string[] args )
 8      {
 9         Tree tree = new Tree( 1978 );
10         Person person = new Person( "Bob", "Jones", 1971 );
11
12         // create array of IAge references
13         IAge[] iAgeArray = new IAge[ 2 ];
14
15         // iAgeArray[ 0 ] refers to Tree object polymorphically
16         iAgeArray[ 0 ] = tree;
17
18         // iAgeArray[ 1 ] refers to Person object polymorphically
19         iAgeArray[ 1 ] = person;
20
21         // display tree information
22         string output = tree + ": " + tree.Name + "\nAge is " +
23            tree.Age + "\n\n";
24
25         // display person information
26         output += person + ": " + person.Name + "\nAge is: "
27            + person.Age + "\n\n";
28
29         // display name and age for each IAge object in iAgeArray
30         foreach ( IAge ageReference in iAgeArray )
31         {
32            output += ageReference.Name + ": Age is " +
33               ageReference.Age + "\n";
34         }
35
36         MessageBox.Show( output, "Demonstrating Polymorphism" );
37
38      } // end method Main
39
40   } // end class InterfacesTest
```

Fig. 10.18 Demonstrate polymorphism on objects of disparate classes. (Part 2 of 2.)

Our next example reexamines the **Point–Circle–Cylinder** hierarchy using an interface, rather than using an abstract class, to describe the common methods and properties of the classes in the hierarchy. We now show how a class can implement an interface, then act as a base class for derived classes to inherit the implementation. We create interface **IShape** (Fig. 10.19), which specifies methods **Area** and **Volume** and property **Name** (lines 8–10). Every class that implements interface **IShape** must provide implementations for these two methods and this read-only property. Note that, even though the methods in this example interface do not receive arguments, interface methods can receive arguments (just as regular methods can).

Good Programming Practice 10.1

*By convention, begin the name of each interface with "**I**."*

Because class **Point3** (Fig. 10.20) implements interface **IShape**, class **Point3** must implement all three **IShape** members. Lines 59–62 implement method **Area**, which returns **0**, because points have an area of zero. Lines 65–68 implement method **Volume**, which also returns **0**, because points have a volume of zero. Lines 71–77 implement read-only property **Name**, which returns the class name as a **string** (**"Point3"**).

When a class implements an interface, the class enters the same kind of *is-a* relationship that inheritance establishes. In our example, class **Point3** implements interface **IShape**. Therefore, a **Point3** object *is an* **IShape**, and objects of any class that inherits from **Point3** are also **IShape**s. For example, class **Circle3** (Fig. 10.21) inherits from class **Point3**; thus, a **Circle3** *is an* **IShape**. Class **Circle3** implements interface **IShape** implicitly and inherits the **IShape** methods that class **Point** implemented. Because circles do not have volume, class **Circle3** does not override class **Point3**'s **Volume** method, which returns zero. However, we do not want to use the class **Point3** method **Area** or property **Name** for class **Circle3**. Class **Circle3** should provide its own implementation for these, because the area and name of a circle differ from those of a point. Lines 52–55 override method **Area** to return the circle's area, and lines 65–71 override property **Name** to return **String "Circle3"**.

Class **Cylinder3** (Fig. 10.22) inherits from class **Circle3**. **Cylinder3** implements interface **IShape** implicitly, because **Cylinder3** derives from **Point3**, which implements interface **IShape**. **Cylinder3** inherits method **Area** and property **Name** from **Circle3** and method **Volume** from **Point3**. However, **Cylinder3** overrides property **Name** and methods **Area** and **Volume** to perform **Cylinder3**-specific operations. Lines 40–43 override method **Area** to return the cylinder's surface area, lines 46–49 override method **Volume** to return the cylinder's volume and lines 59–65 override property **Name** to return **String "Cylinder3"**. Note that class **Point3** marks these methods/ properties as **virtual**, enabling derived classes to override them.

```
1   // Fig. 10.19: IShape.cs
2   // Interface IShape for Point, Circle, Cylinder Hierarchy.
3
4   public interface IShape
5   {
6       // classes that implement IShape must implement these methods
7       // and this property
8       double Area();
9       double Volume();
10      string Name { get; }
11  }
```

Fig. 10.19 **IShape** interface provides methods **Area** and **Volume** and property **Name**.

```
1   // Fig. 10.20: Point3.cs
2   // Point3 implements interface IShape and represents
3   // an x-y coordinate pair.
4   using System;
5
6   // Point3 implements IShape
7   public class Point3 : IShape
8   {
9      private int x, y; // Point3 coordinates
10
11     // default constructor
12     public Point3()
13     {
14        // implicit call to Object constructor occurs here
15     }
16
17     // constructor
18     public Point3( int xValue, int yValue )
19     {
20        X = xValue;
21        Y = yValue;
22     }
23
24     // property X
25     public int X
26     {
27        get
28        {
29           return x;
30        }
31
32        set
33        {
34           x = value;
35        }
36     }
37
38     // property Y
39     public int Y
40     {
41        get
42        {
43           return y;
44        }
45
46        set
47        {
48           y = value;
49        }
50     }
51
```

Fig. 10.20 Point3 class implements interface **IShape**. (Part 1 of 2.)

```
52        // return string representation of Point3 object
53        public override string ToString()
54        {
55            return "[" + X + ", " + Y + "]";
56        }
57
58        // implement interface IShape method Area
59        public virtual double Area()
60        {
61            return 0;
62        }
63
64        // implement interface IShape method Volume
65        public virtual double Volume()
66        {
67            return 0;
68        }
69
70        // implement property Name of IShape
71        public virtual string Name
72        {
73            get
74            {
75                return "Point3";
76            }
77        }
78
79  } // end class Point3
```

Fig. 10.20 Point3 class implements interface **IShape**. (Part 2 of 2.)

```
1    // Fig. 10.21: Circle3.cs
2    // Circle3 inherits from class Point3 and overrides key members.
3    using System;
4
5    // Circle3 inherits from class Point3
6    public class Circle3 : Point3
7    {
8        private double radius; // Circle3 radius
9
10       // default constructor
11       public Circle3()
12       {
13           // implicit call to Point3 constructor occurs here
14       }
15
16       // constructor
17       public Circle3( int xValue, int yValue, double radiusValue )
18           : base( xValue, yValue )
19       {
20           Radius = radiusValue;
21       }
```

Fig. 10.21 Circle3 class inherits from class **Point3**. (Part 1 of 2.)

```
22
23        // property Radius
24        public double Radius
25        {
26           get
27           {
28              return radius;
29           }
30
31           set
32           {
33              // ensure non-negative Radius value
34              if ( value >= 0 )
35                 radius = value;
36           }
37        }
38
39        // calculate Circle3 diameter
40        public double Diameter()
41        {
42           return Radius * 2;
43        }
44
45        // calculate Circle3 circumference
46        public double Circumference()
47        {
48           return Math.PI * Diameter();
49        }
50
51        // calculate Circle3 area
52        public override double Area()
53        {
54           return Math.PI * Math.Pow( Radius, 2 );
55        }
56
57        // return string representation of Circle3 object
58        public override string ToString()
59        {
60           return "Center = " + base.ToString() +
61              "; Radius = " + Radius;
62        }
63
64        // override property Name from class Point3
65        public override string Name
66        {
67           get
68           {
69              return "Circle3";
70           }
71        }
72
73     } // end class Circle3
```

Fig. 10.21 Circle3 class inherits from class **Point3**. (Part 2 of 2.)

```
1   // Fig. 10.22: Cylinder3.cs
2   // Cylinder3 inherits from class Circle2 and overrides key members.
3   using System;
4
5   // Cylinder3 inherits from class Circle3
6   public class Cylinder3 : Circle3
7   {
8      private double height; // Cylinder3 height
9
10     // default constructor
11     public Cylinder3()
12     {
13        // implicit call to Circle3 constructor occurs here
14     }
15
16     // constructor
17     public Cylinder3( int xValue, int yValue, double radiusValue,
18        double heightValue ) : base( xValue, yValue, radiusValue )
19     {
20        Height = heightValue;
21     }
22
23     // property Height
24     public double Height
25     {
26        get
27        {
28           return height;
29        }
30
31        set
32        {
33           // ensure non-negative Height value
34           if ( value >= 0 )
35              height = value;
36        }
37     }
38
39     // calculate Cylinder3 area
40     public override double Area()
41     {
42        return 2 * base.Area() + base.Circumference() * Height;
43     }
44
45     // calculate Cylinder3 volume
46     public override double Volume()
47     {
48        return base.Area() * Height;
49     }
50
51     // return string representation of Cylinder3 object
52     public override string ToString()
53     {
```

Fig. 10.22 Cylinder3 class inherits from class **Circle3**. (Part 1 of 2.)

```
54          return "Center = " + base.ToString() +
55              "; Height = " + Height;
56       }
57
58       // override property Name from class Circle3
59       public override string Name
60       {
61          get
62          {
63             return "Cylinder3";
64          }
65       }
66
67    } // end class Cylinder3
```

Fig. 10.22 Cylinder3 class inherits from class **Circle3**. (Part 2 of 2.)

Class **Interfaces2Test** (Fig. 10.23) demonstrates our point-circle-cylinder hierarchy that uses interfaces. Class **Interfaces2Test** has only two differences from the example in Fig. 10.8, which tested the class hierarchy created from the **abstract** base class **Shape**. In Fig. 10.23, line 17 declares **arrayOfShapes** as an array of **IShape** interface references, rather than **Shape** base-class references.

```
1    // Fig. 10.23: Interfaces2Test.cs
2    // Demonstrating polymorphism with interfaces in
3    // Point-Circle-Cylinder hierarchy.
4
5    using System.Windows.Forms;
6
7    public class Interfaces2Test
8    {
9       public static void Main( string[] args )
10      {
11         // instantiate Point3, Circle3 and Cylinder3 objects
12         Point3 point = new Point3( 7, 11 );
13         Circle3 circle = new Circle3( 22, 8, 3.5 );
14         Cylinder3 cylinder = new Cylinder3( 10, 10, 3.3, 10 );
15
16         // create array of IShape references
17         IShape[] arrayOfShapes = new IShape[ 3 ];
18
19         // arrayOfShapes[ 0 ] references Point3 object
20         arrayOfShapes[ 0 ] = point;
21
22         // arrayOfShapes[ 1 ] references Circle3 object
23         arrayOfShapes[ 1 ] = circle;
24
25         // arrayOfShapes[ 2 ] references Cylinder3 object
26         arrayOfShapes[ 2 ] = cylinder;
27
```

Fig. 10.23 Interfaces2Test uses interfaces to demonstrate polymorphism in Point-Circle-Cylinder hierarchy (Part 1 of 2.).

```
28        string output = point.Name + ": " + point + "\n" +
29            circle.Name + ": " + circle + "\n" +
30            cylinder.Name + ": " + cylinder;
31
32        foreach ( IShape shape in arrayOfShapes )
33        {
34            output += "\n\n" + shape.Name + ":\nArea = " +
35                shape.Area() + "\nVolume = " + shape.Volume();
36        }
37
38        MessageBox.Show( output, "Demonstrating Polymorphism" );
39    }
40 }
```

```
Demonstrating Polymorphism                              [X]

Point3: [7, 11]
Circle3: Center = [22, 8]; Radius = 3.5
Cylinder3: Center = Center = [10, 10]; Radius = 3.3; Height = 10

Point3:
Area = 0
Volume = 0

Circle3:
Area = 38.484510006475
Volume = 0

Cylinder3:
Area = 275.769003132112
Volume = 342.119439975928

                     [   OK   ]
```

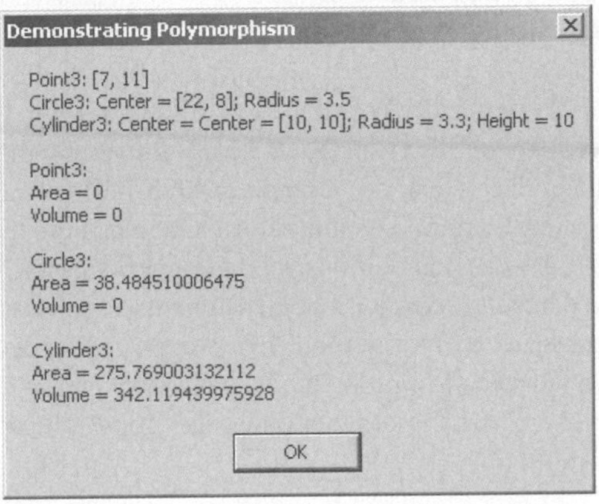

Fig. 10.23 `Interfaces2Test` uses interfaces to demonstrate polymorphism in Point-Circle-Cylinder hierarchy (Part 2 of 2.).

10.10 Delegates

In Chapter 6, we discussed how objects can pass member variables as arguments to methods. However, sometimes, it is beneficial for objects to pass methods as arguments to other methods. For example, suppose that you wish to sort a series of values in ascending and descending order. Rather than provide separate ascending and descending sorting methods (one for each type of comparison), we could provide a single method that receives as an argument a reference to the comparison method to use. To perform an ascending sort, we could pass to the sorting method the reference to the ascending-sort-comparison method; to perform a descending sort, we could pass to the sorting method the reference to the descending-sort-comparison method. The sorting method then would use this reference to sort the list—the sorting method would not need to know whether it is performing an ascending or descending sort.

C# does not allow the passing of method references directly as arguments to other methods, but does provide *delegates*, which are classes that encapsulate sets of references to methods. A delegate object that contains method references can be passed to another method. Rather than send a method reference directly, an object can send the delegate instance, which contains the reference of the method that we would like to send. The method that receives the reference to the delegate then can invoke the methods the delegate contains.

A delegate that contains a single method is known as a *singlecast delegate* and is created or derived from class **Delegate**. Delegates that contain multiple methods are *multicast delegates* and are created or derived from class **MulticastDelegate**. Both delegate classes belong to namespace **System**.

To use a delegate, we first must declare one. The delegate's declaration specifies a method header (parameters and return value). Methods whose references will be contained within a delegate object must have the same method header as that defined in the delegate declaration. We then create methods that have this signature. The second step is to create a delegate instance that contains a reference to that method. After we create the delegate instance, we can invoke the method reference that it contains. We show this process in our next example.

Class **DelegateBubbleSort** (Fig. 10.24), which is a modified version of the bubble-sort example in Chapter 7, uses delegates to sort an integer array in ascending or descending order. Lines 6–7 provide the declaration for delegate **Comparator**. To declare a delegate (line 7), we declare a signature of a method—keyword **delegate** after the member-access modifier (in this case, **public**), followed by the return type, the delegate name and parameter list. Delegate **Comparator** defines a method signature for methods that receive two **int** arguments and return a **bool**. Note that delegate **Comparator** contains no body. As we soon demonstrate, our application (Fig. 10.25) implements methods that adhere to delegate **Comparator**'s signature, then passes these methods (as arguments of type **Comparator**) to method **SortArray**. The declaration of a delegate does not define its intended role or implementation; our application uses this particular delegate when comparing two **int**s, but other applications might use it for different purposes.

```
1   // Fig. 10.24: DelegateBubbleSort.cs
2   // Demonstrating delegates for sorting numbers.
3
4   public class DelegateBubbleSort
5   {
6      public delegate bool Comparator( int element1,
7         int element2 );
8
9      // sort array using Comparator delegate
10     public static void SortArray( int[] array,
11        Comparator Compare )
12     {
13        for ( int pass = 0; pass < array.Length; pass++ )
14
15           for ( int i = 0; i < array.Length - 1; i++ )
16
17              if ( Compare( array[ i ], array [ i + 1 ] ) )
18                 Swap( ref array[ i ], ref array[ i + 1 ] );
19     }
20
21     // swap two elements
22     private static void Swap( ref int firstElement,
23        ref int secondElement )
24     {
```

Fig. 10.24 Bubble sort using delegates. (Part 1 of 2.)

```
25              int hold = firstElement;
26              firstElement = secondElement;
27              secondElement = hold;
28          }
29      }
```

Fig. 10.24 Bubble sort using delegates. (Part 2 of 2.)

Lines 10–19 define method **SortArray**, which takes an array and a reference to a **Comparator** delegate object as arguments. Method **SortArray** modifies the array by sorting its contents. Line 17 uses the delegate method to determine how to sort the array. Line 17 invokes the method enclosed within the delegate object by treating the delegate reference as the method that the delegate object contains. C# invokes the enclosed method reference directly, passing it parameters **array[i]** and **array[i + 1]**. The **Comparator** determines the sorting order for its two arguments. If the **Comparator** returns **true**, the two elements are out of order, so line 18 invokes method **Swap** (lines 22–28) to swap the elements. If the **Comparator** returns **false**, the two elements are in the correct order. To sort in ascending order, the **Comparator** returns **true** when the first element being compared is greater than the second element being compared. Similarly, to sort in descending order, the **Comparator** returns **true** when the first element being compared is less than the second element being compared.

Class **BubbleSortForm** (Fig. 10.25) displays a **Form** with two text boxes and three buttons. The first text box displays a list of unsorted numbers, and the second box displays the same list of numbers after they are sorted. The **Create Data** button creates the list of unsorted values. The **Sort Ascending** and **Sort Descending** buttons sort the array in ascending and descending order, respectively. Methods **SortAscending** (lines 42–45) and **SortDescending** (lines 60–63) each have a signature that corresponds with the signature defined by the **Comparator** delegate declaration (i.e., each receives two **int**s and returns a **bool**). As we will see, the program passes to **DelegateBubbleSort** method **SortArray** delegates containing references to methods **SortAscending** and **Sort-Descending**, which will specify class **DelegateBubbleSort**'s sorting behavior.

```
1   // Fig. 10.25: BubbleSortForm.cs
2   // Demonstrates bubble sort using delegates to determine
3   // the sort order.
4   using System;
5   using System.Drawing;
6   using System.Collections;
7   using System.ComponentModel;
8   using System.Windows.Forms;
9
10  public class BubbleSortForm : System.Windows.Forms.Form
11  {
12      private System.Windows.Forms.TextBox originalTextBox;
13      private System.Windows.Forms.TextBox sortedTextBox;
14      private System.Windows.Forms.Button createButton;
15      private System.Windows.Forms.Button ascendingButton;
```

Fig. 10.25 Bubble-sort **Form** application. (Part 1 of 3.)

```
16        private System.Windows.Forms.Button descendingButton;
17        private System.Windows.Forms.Label originalLabel;
18        private System.Windows.Forms.Label sortedLabel;
19
20        private int[] elementArray = new int[ 10 ];
21
22        // create randomly generated set of numbers to sort
23        private void createButton_Click( object sender,
24           System.EventArgs e )
25        {
26           // clear TextBoxes
27           originalTextBox.Clear();
28           sortedTextBox.Clear();
29
30           // create random-number generator
31           Random randomNumber = new Random();
32
33           // populate elementArray with random integers
34           for ( int i = 0; i < elementArray.Length; i++ )
35           {
36              elementArray[ i ] = randomNumber.Next( 100 );
37              originalTextBox.Text += elementArray[ i ] + "\r\n";
38           }
39        }
40
41        // delegate implementation for ascending sort
42        private bool SortAscending( int element1, int element2 )
43        {
44           return element1 > element2;
45        }
46
47        // sort randomly generated numbers in ascending order
48        private void ascendingButton_Click( object sender,
49           System.EventArgs e )
50        {
51           // sort array, passing delegate for SortAscending
52           DelegateBubbleSort.SortArray( elementArray,
53              new DelegateBubbleSort.Comparator(
54                 SortAscending ) );
55
56           DisplayResults();
57        }
58
59        // delegate implementation for descending sort
60        private bool SortDescending( int element1, int element2 )
61        {
62           return element1 < element2;
63        }
64
65        // sort randomly generating numbers in descending order
66        private void descendingButton_Click( object sender,
67           System.EventArgs e )
68        {
```

Fig. 10.25 Bubble-sort **Form** application. (Part 2 of 3.)

```
69          // sort array, passing delegate for SortDescending
70          DelegateBubbleSort.SortArray( elementArray,
71             new DelegateBubbleSort.Comparator(
72                SortDescending ) );
73
74          DisplayResults();
75       }
76
77       // display the sorted array in sortedTextBox
78       private void DisplayResults()
79       {
80          sortedTextBox.Clear();
81
82          foreach ( int element in elementArray )
83             sortedTextBox.Text += element + "\r\n";
84       }
85
86       // main entry point for application
87       public static void Main( string[] args )
88       {
89          Application.Run( new BubbleSortForm() );
90       }
91    }
```

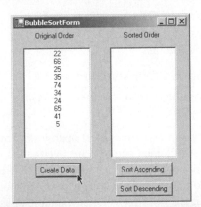

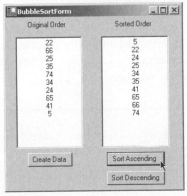
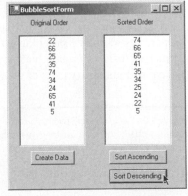

Fig. 10.25 Bubble-sort **Form** application. (Part 3 of 3.)

Methods **ascendingButton_Click** (lines 48–57) and **descending-Button_Click** (lines 66–75) are invoked when the user clicks the **Sort Ascending** and **Sort Descending** buttons, respectively. Method **ascendingButton_Click**, passes to **DelegateBubbleSort** method **SortArray** the unsorted **elementArray** (line 52) and a reference to method **SortAscending**. The syntax on lines 53–54

```
new DelegateBubbleSort.Comparator( SortAscending )
```

creates a **Comparator** delegate that contains a reference to method **SortAscending**. In method **descendingButton_Click**, lines 70–72 pass to method **SortArray** the unsorted array **elementArray** and a delegate reference to method **SortDescending**. We continue to use delegates in Chapters 12–14, when we discuss event handling and multithreading.

10.11 Operator Overloading

Manipulations on class objects are accomplished by sending messages (in the form of method calls) to the objects. This method-call notation is cumbersome for certain kinds of classes, especially mathematical classes. For these classes, it would be convenient to use C#'s rich set of built-in operators to specify object manipulations. In this section, we show how to enable C#'s operators to work with class objects—via a process called *operator overloading*.

Software Engineering Observation 10.13
Use operator overloading when it makes a program clearer than accomplishing the same operations with explicit method calls.

Software Engineering Observation 10.14
Avoid excessive or inconsistent use of operator overloading, as this can make a program cryptic and difficult to read.

C# enables the programmer to overload most operators to make them sensitive to the context in which they are used. Some operators are overloaded frequently, especially the assignment operator and various arithmetic operators, such as **+** and **-**. The job performed by overloaded operators also can be performed by explicit method calls, but operator notation often is more natural. Figure 10.27 provides an example of using operator overloading with a complex number class.

Class **ComplexNumber** (Fig. 10.26) overloads the plus (**+**), minus (**-**) and multiplication (*****) operators to enable programs to add, subtract and multiply instances of class **ComplexNumber** using common mathematical notation. Lines 7–8 declare data members for the real and imaginary parts of the complex number.

```
1   // Fig. 10.26: ComplexNumber.cs
2   // Class that overloads operators for adding, subtracting
3   // and multiplying complex numbers.
4
5   public class ComplexNumber
6   {
```

Fig. 10.26 Overloading operators for complex numbers. (Part 1 of 3.)

```
 7        private int real;
 8        private int imaginary;
 9
10        // default constructor
11        public ComplexNumber() {}
12
13        // constructor
14        public ComplexNumber( int a, int b )
15        {
16           Real = a;
17           Imaginary = b;
18        }
19
20        // return string representation of ComplexNumber
21        public override string ToString()
22        {
23           return "( " + real +
24              ( imaginary < 0 ? " - " + ( imaginary * -1 ) :
25              " + "  + imaginary ) + "i )";
26        }
27
28        // property Real
29        public int Real
30        {
31           get
32           {
33              return real;
34           }
35
36           set
37           {
38              real = value;
39           }
40
41        } // end property Real
42
43        // property Imaginary
44        public int Imaginary
45        {
46           get
47           {
48              return imaginary;
49           }
50
51           set
52           {
53              imaginary = value;
54           }
55
56        } // end property Imaginary
57
```

Fig. 10.26 Overloading operators for complex numbers. (Part 2 of 3.)

```
58          // overload the addition operator
59          public static ComplexNumber operator + (
60             ComplexNumber x, ComplexNumber y )
61          {
62             return new ComplexNumber(
63                x.Real + y.Real, x.Imaginary + y.Imaginary );
64          }
65
66          // provide alternative to overloaded + operator
67          // for addition
68          public static ComplexNumber Add( ComplexNumber x,
69             ComplexNumber y )
70          {
71             return x + y;
72          }
73
74          // overload the subtraction operator
75          public static ComplexNumber operator - (
76             ComplexNumber x, ComplexNumber y )
77          {
78             return new ComplexNumber(
79                x.Real - y.Real, x.Imaginary - y.Imaginary );
80          }
81
82          // provide alternative to overloaded - operator
83          // for subtraction
84          public static ComplexNumber Subtract( ComplexNumber x,
85             ComplexNumber y )
86          {
87             return x - y;
88          }
89
90          // overload the multiplication operator
91          public static ComplexNumber operator * (
92             ComplexNumber x, ComplexNumber y )
93          {
94             return new ComplexNumber(
95                x.Real * y.Real - x.Imaginary * y.Imaginary,
96                x.Real * y.Imaginary + y.Real * x.Imaginary );
97          }
98
99          // provide alternative to overloaded * operator
100         // for multiplication
101         public static ComplexNumber Multiply( ComplexNumber x,
102            ComplexNumber y )
103         {
104            return x * y;
105         }
106
107      } // end class ComplexNumber
```

Fig. 10.26 Overloading operators for complex numbers. (Part 3 of 3.)

Lines 59–64 overload the plus operator (+) to perform addition of **ComplexNumber**s. Keyword *operator* followed by an operator indicates that a method overloads the specified operator. Methods that overload binary operators must take two arguments. The first argument is the left operand, and the second argument is the right operand. Class **ComplexNumber**'s overloaded plus operator takes two **ComplexNumber** references as arguments and returns a **ComplexNumber** that represents the sum of the arguments. Note that this method is marked **public** and **static**, which is required for overloaded operators. The body of the method (lines 62–63) performs the addition and returns the result as a new **ComplexNumber** reference.

Software Engineering Observation 10.15

Overload operators to perform the same function or similar functions on class objects as the operators perform on objects of built-in types. Avoid non-intuitive use of operators.

Software Engineering Observation 10.16

At least one argument of an operator overload method must be a reference to an object of the class in which the operator is overloaded. This prevents programmers from changing how operators work on built-in types.

Not all .NET languages support operator overloading. Therefore, to ensure that our **ComplexNumber** class can be used in other .NET languages, we must provide an alternative method for performing addition of **ComplexNumber**s. Method **Add** (lines 68–72) provides this alternative means to add **ComplexNumber**s. Lines 75–105 provide overloaded operators and alternative methods for subtracting and multiplying **ComplexNumber**s.

Class **ComplexTest** (Fig. 10.27) provides a user interface for adding, subtracting and multiplying **ComplexNumber**s. Method **firstButton_Click** and method **secondButton_Click** each read a **ComplexNumber** from textboxes **realTextBox** and **imaginaryTextBox**. Method **addButton_Click** (lines 56–59), method **subtractButton_Click** (lines 62–66) and method **multiplyButton_Click** (lines 69–73) use overloaded operators of class **ComplexNumber** to perform addition, subtraction and multiplication.

```
1   // Fig 10.27: OperatorOverloading.cs
2   // An example that uses operator overloading
3
4   using System;
5   using System.Drawing;
6   using System.Collections;
7   using System.ComponentModel;
8   using System.Windows.Forms;
9   using System.Data;
10
11  public class ComplexTest : System.Windows.Forms.Form
12  {
13      private System.Windows.Forms.Label realLabel;
14      private System.Windows.Forms.Label imaginaryLabel;
15      private System.Windows.Forms.Label statusLabel;
16
17      private System.Windows.Forms.TextBox realTextBox;
18      private System.Windows.Forms.TextBox imaginaryTextBox;
19
```

Fig. 10.27 Using operator overloading. (Part 1 of 3.)

```
20       private System.Windows.Forms.Button firstButton;
21       private System.Windows.Forms.Button secondButton;
22       private System.Windows.Forms.Button addButton;
23       private System.Windows.Forms.Button subtractButton;
24       private System.Windows.Forms.Button multiplyButton;
25
26       private ComplexNumber x = new ComplexNumber();
27       private ComplexNumber y = new ComplexNumber();
28
29       [STAThread]
30       static void Main()
31       {
32          Application.Run( new ComplexTest() );
33       }
34
35       private void firstButton_Click(
36          object sender, System.EventArgs e )
37       {
38          x.Real = Int32.Parse( realTextBox.Text );
39          x.Imaginary = Int32.Parse( imaginaryTextBox.Text );
40          realTextBox.Clear();
41          imaginaryTextBox.Clear();
42          statusLabel.Text = "First Complex Number is: " + x;
43       }
44
45       private void secondButton_Click(
46          object sender, System.EventArgs e )
47       {
48          y.Real = Int32.Parse( realTextBox.Text );
49          y.Imaginary = Int32.Parse( imaginaryTextBox.Text );
50          realTextBox.Clear();
51          imaginaryTextBox.Clear();
52          statusLabel.Text = "Second Complex Number is: " + y;
53       }
54
55       // add complex numbers
56       private void addButton_Click( object sender, System.EventArgs e )
57       {
58          statusLabel.Text = x + " + " + y + " = " + ( x + y );
59       }
60
61       // subtract complex numbers
62       private void subtractButton_Click(
63          object sender, System.EventArgs e )
64       {
65          statusLabel.Text = x + " - " + y + " = " + ( x - y );
66       }
67
68       // multiply complex numbers
69       private void multiplyButton_Click(
70          object sender, System.EventArgs e )
71       {
```

Fig. 10.27 Using operator overloading. (Part 2 of 3.)

```
72            statusLabel.Text = x + " * " + y + " = " + ( x * y );
73        }
74
75    } // end class ComplexTest
```

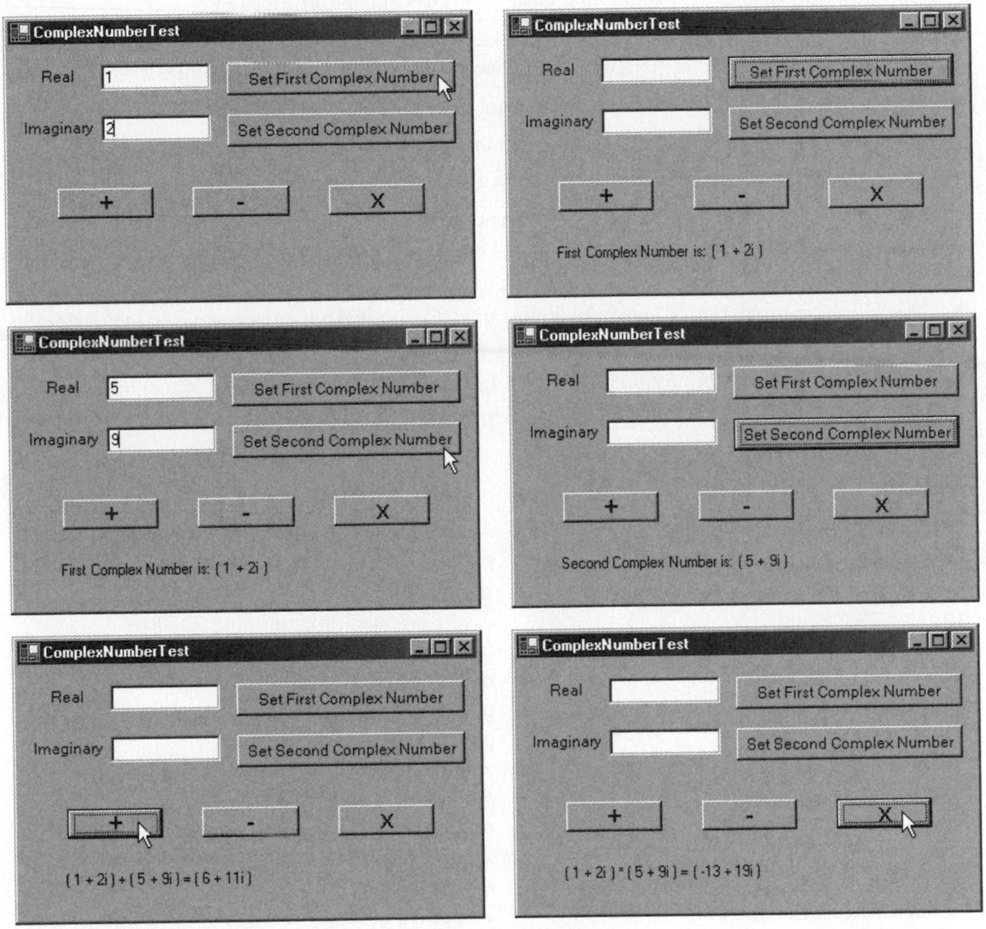

Fig. 10.27 Using operator overloading. (Part 3 of 3.)

SUMMARY

- Polymorphism enables us to write programs in a general fashion to handle a wide variety of existing and future related classes.

- One means of processing objects of many different types is to use a **switch** structure to perform an appropriate action on each object based on that object's type.

- Polymorphic programming can eliminate the need for **switch** logic.

- When we override a base class's method in a derived class, we hide the base class's implementation of that method.

- With polymorphism, new types of objects not even envisioned when a system is created may be added without modification to the system (other than the new class itself).

- Polymorphism allows one method call to perform different actions, depending on the type of the object receiving the call. The same message assumes "many forms"—hence, the term polymorphism.

- With polymorphism, the programmer can deal in generalities and let the executing program concern itself with the specifics.

- Any class with an abstract method in it must, itself, be declared **abstract**.

- A program cannot instantiate objects of **abstract** classes, but can declare references to **abstract** classes. Such references can manipulate polymorphically instances of the derived classes.

- A method that is not declared **virtual** cannot be overridden in a derived class.

- Methods that are declared **static** and or **private** are implicitly non-virtual.

- A **sealed** class cannot be a base class (i.e., a class cannot inherit from a **sealed** class).

- In C#, it is impossible to pass a method reference directly as an argument to another method. To address this problem, C# allows the creation of delegates, which are classes that encapsulate a set of references to methods.

- C# enables the programmer to overload most operators to make them sensitive to the context in which they are used.

- Methods that overload binary operators must take two arguments. The first argument is the left operand, and the second argument is the right operand.

TERMINOLOGY

abstract base class	"is-a" relationship
abstract class	method reference
abstract method	multicast delegate
abstract method	object-oriented programming (OOP)
cast	operator overloading
class declared **sealed**	**override** keyword
class hierarchy	polymorphic programming
concrete class	polymorphism
delegate	reference type
information hiding	references to abstract base class
inheritance	**sealed** class
inheritance hierarchy	singlecast delegate
interface	**switch** logic
InvalidCastException	**virtual** method

SELF-REVIEW EXERCISES

10.1 Fill in the blanks in each of the following statements:

a) Treating a base-class object as a _____ can cause errors.

b) Polymorphism helps eliminate unnecessary _____ logic.

c) If a class contains one or more **abstract** methods, it is an _____ class.

d) Classes from which objects can be instantiated are called _____ classes.

e) Classes declared with keyword _____ cannot be inherited.

f) An attempt to cast an object to one of its derived types can cause an _____.

g) Polymorphism involves using a base-class reference to manipulate _____.

h) Abstract classes are declared with the _____ keyword.

i) Class members can be overridden only with the _____ keyword.

j) _____ are classes that encapsulate references to methods.

10.2 State whether each of the following is *true* or *false*. If *false*, explain why.
   a) All methods in an abstract base class must be declared **abstract**.
   b) Referring to a derived-class object with a base-class reference is dangerous.
   c) A class with an abstract method must be declared **abstract**.
   d) Methods that are declared **abstract** still must be implemented when they are declared.
   e) Classes declared with the **sealed** keyword cannot be base classes.
   f) Polymorphism allows programmers to manipulate derived classes with references to base classes.
   g) Polymorphic programming can eliminate the need for unnecessary **switch** logic.
   h) Use keyword **abstract** to declare an abstract method.
   i) The delegate's declaration must specify its implementation.

ANSWERS TO SELF-REVIEW EXERCISES

10.1 a) derived-class   object.   b) **switch**.   c) abstract.   d) concrete.   e) **sealed**.
f) **InvalidCastException**.   g) derived-class   objects.   h) **abstract**.   i) **override**.
j) Delegates

10.2 a) False. Not all methods in an abstract class must be declared **abstract**. b) False. Referring to a base-class object with a derived-class reference is dangerous. c) True. d) False. Methods that are declared **abstract** do not need to be implemented, except in the derived, concrete class. e) True. f) True. g) True. h) False. Use keyword **abstract** to declare an abstract class. i) False. The delegate's declaration specifies only a method signature (method name, parameters and return value).

EXERCISES

10.3 How is it that polymorphism enables you to program "in the general" rather than "in the specific?" Discuss the key advantages of programming "in the general."

10.4 Discuss the problems of programming with **switch** logic. Explain why polymorphism can be an effective alternative to using **switch** logic.

10.5 Distinguish between inheriting services and inheriting implementation. How do inheritance hierarchies designed for inheriting services differ from those designed for inheriting implementation?

10.6 Modify the payroll system of Fig. 10.9–Fig. 10.14 to add **private** instance variables **birthDate** (use class **Date** from Fig 8.8) and **departmentCode** (an **int**) to class **Employee**. Assume this payroll is processed once per month. Create an array of **Employee** references to store the various employee objects. In a loop, calculate the payroll for each **Employee** (polymorphically) and add a $100.00 bonus to the person's payroll amount if this is the month in which the **Employee**'s birthday occurs.

10.7 Implement the **Shape** hierarchy shown in Fig. 9.3. Each **TwoDimensionalShape** should contain method **Area** to calculate the area of the two-dimensional shape. Each **ThreeDimensionalShape** should have methods **Area** and **Volume** to calculate the surface area and volume of the three-dimensional shape, respectively. Create a program that uses an array of **Shape** references to objects of each concrete class in the hierarchy. The program should output the **string** representation of each object in the array. Also, in the loop that processes all the shapes in the array, determine whether each shape is a **TwoDimensionalShape** or a **ThreeDimensionalShape**. If a shape is a **TwoDimensionalShape**, display its **Area**. If a shape is a **ThreeDimensionalShape**, display its **Area** and **Volume**.

10.8 Reimplement the program of Exercise 10.7 such that classes **TwoDimensionalShape** and **ThreeDimensionalShape** implement an **IShape** interface, rather than extending **abstract** class **Shape**.

11

Exception Handling

Objectives

- To understand exceptions and error handling.
- To use **try** blocks to delimit code in which exceptions may occur.
- To **throw** exceptions.
- To use **catch** blocks to specify exception handlers.
- To use the **finally** block to release resources.
- To understand the C# exception-class hierarchy.
- To create programmer-defined exceptions.

It is common sense to take a method and try it. If it fails, admit it frankly and try another. But above all, try something.
Franklin Delano Roosevelt

O! throw away the worser part of it,
And live the purer with the other half.
William Shakespeare

If they're running and they don't look where they're going
I have to come out from somewhere and catch them.
Jerome David Salinger

And oftentimes excusing of a fault
Doth make the fault the worse by the excuse.
William Shakespeare

I never forget a face, but in your case I'll make an exception.
Groucho (Julius Henry) Marx

Outline

11.1 Introduction

In this chapter, we introduce *exception handling*. An *exception* is an indication of a problem that occurs during a program's execution. The name "exception" comes from the fact that although a problem can occur, the problem occurs infrequently—if the "rule" is that a statement normally executes correctly, then the "exception to the rule" is that a problem occurs. Exception handling enables programmers to create applications that can resolve (or handle) exceptions. In many cases, handling an exception allows a program to continue executing as if no problem was encountered. A more severe problem may prevent a program from continuing normal execution, instead requiring the program to notify the user of the problem, then terminate in a controlled manner. The features presented in this chapter enable programmers to write clear, robust and more *fault-tolerant programs*.

The style and details of exception handling in C# are based in part on the work of Andrew Koenig and Bjarne Stroustrup, as presented in their paper, "Exception Handling for C++ (revised)."[1] C#'s designers implemented an exception-handling mechanism similar to that used in C++, with Koenig's and Stroustrup's work as a model.

This chapter begins with an overview of exception-handling concepts, then demonstrates basic exception-handling techniques. The chapter continues with an overview of the exception-handling class hierarchy. Programs typically request and release resources (such as files on disk) during program execution. Often, these resources are in limited supply or can be used by only one program at a time. We demonstrate a part of the exception-handling mechanism that enables a program to use a resource, then guarantees that the program releases the resource for use by other programs. The chapter continues with an example that demonstrates several properties of class `System.Exception` (the base class of all exception classes), followed by an example that shows programmers how to create and use their own exception classes. The chapter concludes with a practical application of exception handling in which a program handles exceptions generated by arithmetic calculations that result in out-of-range values for a particular data type—a condition known as *arithmetic overflow*.

---

1. Koenig, A. and B. Stroustrup, "Exception Handling for C++ (revised)," *Proceedings of the Usenix C++ Conference*, 149-176, San Francisco, April 1990.

11.2 Exception Handling Overview

The logic of the program frequently tests conditions that determine how program execution proceeds. Consider the following pseudocode:

Perform a task

If the preceding task did not execute correctly
    Perform error processing

Perform next task

If the preceding task did not execute correctly
    Perform error processing

...

In this pseudocode, we begin by performing a task. We then test whether that task executed correctly. If not, we perform error processing. Otherwise we start the entire process again and continue with the next task. Although this form of error handling logic works, intermixing the logic of the program with the error-handling logic can make the program difficult to read, modify, maintain and debug—especially in large applications. In fact, if many of the potential problems occur infrequently, intermixing program logic and error handling can degrade the performance of the program, because the program must test extra conditions to determine whether the next task can be performed.

Exception handling enables the programmer to remove error-handling code from the "main line" of the program's execution. This improves program clarity and enhances modifiability. Programmers can decide to handle whatever exceptions they choose—all types of exceptions, all exceptions of a certain type or all exceptions of a group of related types. Such flexibility reduces the likelihood that errors will be overlooked and thereby increases a program's robustness.

Testing and Debugging Tip 11.1

Exception handling helps improve a program's fault tolerance. When it is easy to write error-processing code, programmers are more likely to use it.

Software Engineering Observation 11.1

Although it is possible to do so, do not use exception for conventional flow of control. It is difficult to keep track of a larger number of exception cases and programs with a large number of exception cases are hard to read and maintain.

Exception handling is designed to process *synchronous errors*—errors that occur during the normal program flow of control. Common examples of these errors are out-of-range array subscripts, arithmetic overflow (i.e., a value outside the representable range of values), division by zero, invalid method parameters and running out of available memory. Exception handling is not designed to process *asynchronous* events, such as disk I/O completions, network message arrivals, mouse clicks, keystrokes and the like.

Good Programming Practice 11.1

Avoid using exception handling for purposes other than error handling, because this can reduce program clarity.

With programming languages that do not support exception handling, programmers often delay the writing of error-processing code and sometimes simply forget to include it. This results in less robust software products. C# enables the programmer to deal with exception handling easily from the inception of a project. Still, the programmer must put considerable effort into incorporating an exception-handling strategy into software projects.

Software Engineering Observation 11.2

Try to incorporate the exception-handling strategy into a system from the inception of the design process. Adding effective exception handling after a system has been implemented can be difficult.

Software Engineering Observation 11.3

In the past, programmers used many techniques to implement error-processing code. Exception handling provides a single, uniform technique for processing errors. This helps programmers working on large projects to understand each other's error-processing code.

The exception-handling mechanism also is useful for processing problems that occur when a program interacts with software elements, such as methods, constructors, assemblies and classes. Rather than internally handling problems that occur, such software elements often use exceptions to notify programs when problems occur. This enables programmers to implement customized error handling for each application.

Common Programming Error 11.1

Aborting a program component could leave a resource—such as file stream or I/O device—in a state in which other programs are unable to acquire the resource. This is known as a "resource leak."

Performance Tip 11.1

When no exceptions occur, exception-handling code incurs little or no performance penalties. Thus, programs that implement exception handling operate more efficiently than programs that perform error handling throughout the program logic.

Performance Tip 11.2

Exception handling should be used only for problems that occur infrequently. As a "rule of thumb," if a problem occurs at least 30% of the time when a particular statement executes, the program should test for the error inline; otherwise, the overhead of exception handling will cause the program to execute more slowly.[2]

Software Engineering Observation 11.4

*Methods with common error conditions should return **null** (or another appropriate value) rather than throwing exceptions. A program calling such a method simply can check the return value to determine success or failure of the method call.[3]*

Complex applications normally consist of predefined software components (such as those defined in the .NET Framework) and components specific to the application that use the predefined components. When a predefined component encounters a problem, that component needs a mechanism to communicate the problem to the application-specific

---

2. "Best Practices for Handling Exceptions [C#]," *.NET Framework Developer's Guide*, Visual Studio .NET Online Help.
3. "Best Practices for Handling Exceptions [C#]."

component—the predefined component cannot know in advance how each application will process a problem that occurs. Exception handling simplifies combining software components and having them work together effectively by enabling predefined components to communicate problems that occur to application-specific components, which can then process the problems in an application-specific manner.

Exception handling is geared to situations in which the method that detects an error is unable to handle it. Such a method *throws an exception*. There is no guarantee that there will be an *exception handler*—code that executes when the program detects an exception—to process that kind of exception. If there is, the exception will be *caught* and *handled*. The result of an *uncaught exception* depends on whether the program executes in debug mode or standard execution mode. In debug mode, when the program detects an uncaught exception, a dialog box appears that enables the programmer to view the problem in the debugger or continue program execution by ignoring the problem that occurred. In standard execution mode, a Windows application presents a dialog that enables the user to continue or terminate program execution, and a console application presents a dialog that enables the user to open the program in the debugger or terminate program execution.

C# uses **try** *blocks* to enable exception handling. A **try** block consists of keyword **try** followed by braces (**{}**) that define a block of code in which exceptions may occur. The **try** block encloses statements that could cause exceptions. Immediately following the **try** block are zero or more **catch** *blocks* (also called **catch** *handlers*). Each **catch** handler specifies in parentheses an exception parameter that represents the type of exception the **catch** handler can handle. If an exception parameter includes an optional parameter name, the **catch** handler can use that parameter name to interact with a caught exception object. Optionally, programmers can include a *parameterless* **catch** *handler* that catches all exception types. After the last **catch** handler, an optional **finally** *block* contains code that always executes, regardless of whether an exception occurs.

Common Programming Error 11.2

The parameterless **catch** *handler must be the last* **catch** *handler following a particular* **try** *block; otherwise a syntax error occurs.*

When a method called in a program detects an exception or when the Common Language Runtime detects a problem, the method or CLR *throws an exception*. The point in the program at which an exception occurs is called the *throw point*—an important location for debugging purposes (as we demonstrate in Section 11.6). Exceptions are objects of classes that extend class **Exception** of namespace **System**. If an exception occurs in a **try** block, the **try** block *expires* (i.e., terminates immediately) and program control transfers to the first **catch** handler (if there is one) following the **try** block. C# is said to use the *termination model of exception handling*, because the **try** block enclosing a thrown exception expires immediately when that exception occurs.[4] As with any other block of code, when a **try** block terminates, local variables defined in the block go out of scope. Next, the CLR searches for the first **catch** handler that can process the type of exception that occurred. The CLR locates the matching **catch** by comparing the thrown exception's type to each **catch**'s exception-parameter type until the CLR finds a match. A match

---

4. Some languages use the *resumption model of exception handling*, in which, after the handling of the exception, control returns to the point at which the exception was thrown and execution resumes from that point.

occurs if the types are identical or if the thrown exception's type is a derived class of the exception-parameter type. When a **catch** handler finishes processing, local variables defined within the **catch** handler (including the **catch** parameter) go out of scope. If a match occurs, code contained within the matching **catch** handler is executed. All remaining **catch** handlers that correspond to the **try** block are ignored and execution resumes at the first line of code after the **try/catch** sequence.

If no exceptions occur in a **try** block, the CLR ignores the exception handlers for that block. Program execution resumes with the next statement after the **try/catch** sequence. If an exception that occurs in a **try** block has no matching **catch** handler, or if an exception occurs in a statement that is not in a **try** block, the method containing that statement terminates immediately and the CLR attempts to locate an enclosing **try** block in a calling method. This process is called *stack unwinding* (discussed in Section 11.6).

11.3 Example: `DivideByZeroException`

Let us consider a simple example of exception handling. The application in Fig. 11.1 uses **try** and **catch** to specify a block of code that may throw exceptions and to handle those exceptions if they occur. The application displays two **TextBox**es in which the user can type integers. When the user presses the **Click To Divide** button, the program invokes method **divideButton_Click** (lines 46–84), which obtains the user's input, converts the input values to type **int** and divides the first number (**numerator**) by the second number (**denominator**). Assuming that the user provides integers as input and does not specify 0 as the denominator for the division, **divideButton_Click** displays the division result in **outputLabel**. However, if the user inputs a non-integer value or supplies 0 as the denominator, an exception occurs. This program demonstrates how to catch these exceptions.

```
1   // Fig 11.1: DivideByZeroTest.cs
2   // Basics of C# exception handling.
3
4   using System;
5   using System.Drawing;
6   using System.Collections;
7   using System.ComponentModel;
8   using System.Windows.Forms;
9   using System.Data;
10
11  // class demonstrates how to handle exceptions from
12  // division by zero in integer arithmetic and from
13  // improper numeric formatting
14  public class DivideByZeroTest : System.Windows.Forms.Form
15  {
16      private System.Windows.Forms.Label numeratorLabel;
17      private System.Windows.Forms.TextBox numeratorTextBox;
18
19      private System.Windows.Forms.Label denominatorLabel;
20      private System.Windows.Forms.TextBox denominatorTextBox;
21
22      private System.Windows.Forms.Button divideButton;
```

Fig. 11.1 Exception handlers for **FormatException** and **DivideByZeroException**. (Part 1 of 3.)

```
23        private System.Windows.Forms.Label outputLabel;
24
25        // required designer variable
26        private System.ComponentModel.Container components = null;
27
28        // default constructor
29        public DivideByZeroTest()
30        {
31           // required for Windows Form Designer support
32           InitializeComponent();
33        }
34
35        // main entry point for the application
36        [STAThread]
37        static void Main()
38        {
39           Application.Run( new DivideByZeroTest() );
40        }
41
42        // Visual Studio .NET generated code
43
44        // obtain integers input by user and divide numerator
45        // by denominator
46        private void divideButton_Click(
47           object sender, System.EventArgs e )
48        {
49           outputLabel.Text = "";
50
51           // retrieve user input and call Quotient
52           try
53           {
54              // Convert.ToInt32 generates FormatException if
55              // argument is not an integer
56              int numerator = Convert.ToInt32( numeratorTextBox.Text );
57              int denominator =
58                 Convert.ToInt32( denominatorTextBox.Text );
59
60              // division generates DivideByZeroException if
61              // denominator is 0
62              int result = numerator / denominator;
63
64              outputLabel.Text = result.ToString();
65
66           } // end try
67
68           // process invalid number format
69           catch ( FormatException )
70           {
71              MessageBox.Show( "You must enter two integers",
72                 "Invalid Number Format",
73                 MessageBoxButtons.OK, MessageBoxIcon.Error );
74           }
```

Fig. 11.1   Exception handlers for **FormatException** and
           DivideByZeroException. (Part 2 of 3.)

```
75
76          // user attempted to divide by zero
77          catch ( DivideByZeroException divideByZeroException )
78          {
79             MessageBox.Show( divideByZeroException.Message,
80                "Attempted to Divide by Zero",
81                MessageBoxButtons.OK, MessageBoxIcon.Error );
82          }
83
84       } // end method divideButton_Click
85
86    } // end class DivideByZeroTest
```

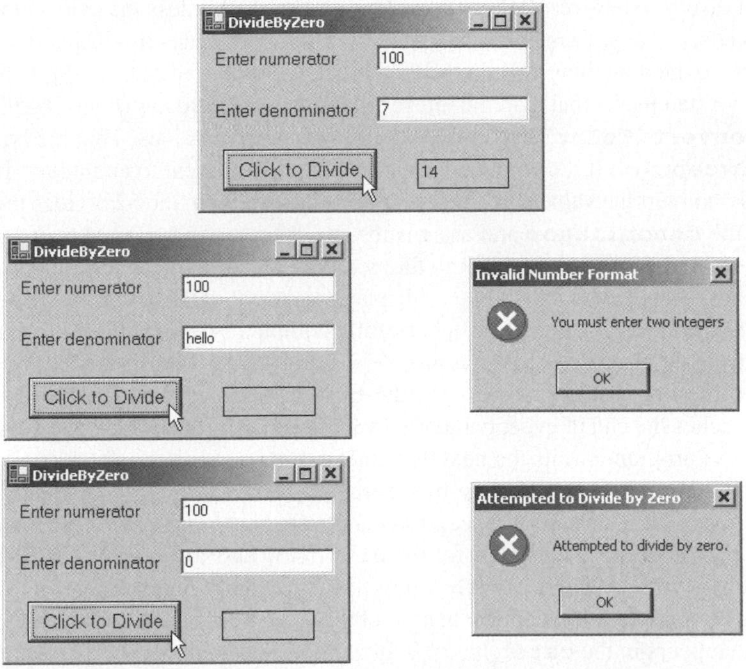

Fig. 11.1 Exception handlers for **FormatException** and
DivideByZeroException. (Part 3 of 3.)

Before we discuss the program details, consider the sample output windows in Fig. 11.1. The first window shows a successful calculation in which the user inputs the numerator **100** and the denominator **7**. Note that the result (**14**) is an integer, because integer division always yields integer results. The next two windows show the result of inputting a non-integer value—in this case, the user input **"hello"** in the second **TextBox**. When the user presses **Click To Divide**, the program attempts to convert the **string**s the user input into **int** values with method **Convert.ToInt32**. If the argument to **Convert.ToInt32** is not a valid representation of an integer (in this case a valid string representation of an integer), the method generates a *FormatException* (namespace **System**). The program detects the exception and displays an error message dialog, indicating that the user must enter two integers. The last two output windows demonstrate the result after an attempt to divide by zero. In integer arithmetic, the CLR automatically tests for division by zero and generates a *DivideByZeroException* (namespace **System**) if the denominator is zero. The program detects the exception and displays an error-message dialog, indicating an attempt to divide by zero.[5]

Let us consider the user interactions and flow of control that yield the results shown in the sample output windows. The user inputs values into the **TextBox**es that represent the numerator and denominator, then presses **ClicktoDivide**. At this point, the program invokes method **divideButton_Click** (lines 46–84). Line 49 assigns the empty **string** to **outputLabel** to clear any prior result, because the program is about to attempt a new calculation. Lines 52–66 define a **try** block that encloses the code that can throw exceptions, as well as the code that should not execute if an exception occurs. For example, the program should not display a new result in **outputLabel** (line 64) unless the calculation (line 62) completes successfully. Remember that the **try** block terminates immediately if an exception occurs, so the remaining code in the **try** block will not execute.

The two statements that read the integers from the **TextBox**es (lines 56–58) each call method **Convert.ToInt32** to convert **string**s to **int** values. This method throws a **FormatException** if it cannot convert its **string** argument to an integer. If lines 56–58 properly convert the values (i.e., no exceptions occur), then line 62 divides the **numerator** by the **denominator** and assigns the result to variable **result**. If the denominator is zero, line 62 causes the CLR to throw a **DivideByZeroException**. If line 62 does not cause an exception, then line 64 displays the result of the division. If no exceptions occur in the **try** block, the program successfully completes the **try** block by reaching line 66 by ignoring the **catch** handlers at lines 69–74 and 77–82—the program execution continues with the first statement following the **try/catch** sequence. In this example, the program reaches the end of event handler **divideButton_Click**, so the method terminates, and the program awaits the next user interaction.

Immediately following the **try** block are two **catch** handlers (also called *catch blocks*)—lines 69–74 define the exception handler for a **FormatException** and lines 77–82 define the exception handler for the **DivideByZeroException**. Each **catch** handler begins with keyword **catch** followed by an exception parameter in parentheses that specifies the type of exception handled by the **catch** handler. The exception-handling code appears in the **catch** handler. In general, when an exception occurs in a **try** block, a **catch** handler catches the exception and handles it. In Fig. 11.1, the first **catch** handler specifies that it catches the type **FormatException**s (thrown by method **Convert.ToInt32**) and the second **catch** handler specifies that it catches type **DivideByZeroException**s (thrown by the CLR). Only the matching **catch** handler executes if an exception occurs. Both the exception handlers in this example display an error-message dialog to the user. When program control reaches the end of a **catch** handler, the program considers the exception as having been handled, and pro-

---

5. The Common Language Runtime allows floating-point division by zero, which produces a positive or negative infinity result, depending on whether the numerator is positive or negative. Dividing zero by zero is a special case that results in a value called "not a number." Programs can test for these results using constants for positive infinity (*PositiveInfinity*), negative infinity (*NegativeInfinity*) and not a number (*NaN*) that are defined in structures **Double** (for **double** calculations) and **Single** (for **float** calculations).

gram control continues with the first statement after the **try/catch** sequence (the end of the method in this example).

In the second sample output, the user input **hello** as the denominator. When lines 57–58 execute, **Convert.ToInt32** cannot convert this **string** to an **int**, so **Convert.ToInt32** creates a **FormatException** object and throws it to indicate that the method was unable to convert the **string** to an **int**. When an exception occurs, the **try** block expires (terminates). Any local variables defined in the **try** block go out of scope; therefore, those variables are not available to the exception handlers. Next, the CLR attempts to locate a matching **catch** handler, starting with the **catch** at line 69. The program compares the type of the thrown exception (**FormatException**) with the type in parentheses following keyword **catch** (also **FormatException**). A match occurs, so that exception handler executes and the program ignores all other exception handlers following the corresponding **try** block. Once the **catch** handler finishes processing, local variables defined within the **catch** handler go out of scope. If a match did not occur, the program compares the type of the thrown exception with the next **catch** handler in sequence and repeats the process until a match is found.

Software Engineering Observation 11.5

*Enclose in a **try** block a significant logical section of the program in which several statements can throw exceptions, rather than using a separate **try** block for every statement that throws an exception. However, for proper exception-handling granularity, each **try** block should enclose a section of code small enough, that when an exception occurs, the specific context is known and the **catch** handlers can process the exception properly.*

Common Programming Error 11.3

*Attempting to access a **try** block's local variables in one of that **try** block's associated **catch** handlers is a syntax error. Before a corresponding **catch** handler can execute, the **try** block expires, and its local variables go out of scope.*

Common Programming Error 11.4

*Specifying a comma-separated list of exception parameters in a **catch** handler is a syntax error. Each **catch** can have only one exception parameter.*

In the third sample output, the user input **0** as the denominator. When line 62 executes, the CLR throws a **DivideByZeroException** object to indicate an attempt to divide by zero. Once again, the **try** block terminates immediately upon encountering the exception, and the program attempts to locate a matching **catch** handler, starting from the **catch** handler at line 69. The program compares the type of the thrown exception (**DivideByZeroException**) with the type in parentheses following keyword **catch** (**FormatException**). In this case, there is no match, because they are not the same exception types and because **FormatException** is not a base class of **DivideByZeroException**. So, the program proceeds to line 77 and compares the type of the thrown exception (**DivideByZeroException**) with the type in parentheses following keyword **catch** (**DivideByZeroException**). A match occurs, so that exception handler executes. Line 79 in this handler uses property ***Message*** of class **Exception** to display the error message to the user. If there were additional **catch** handlers, the program would ignore them.

11.4 .NET `Exception` Hierarchy

The exception-handling mechanism allows only objects of class **Exception** and its derived classes to be thrown and caught.[6] This section overviews several of the .NET Framework's exception classes. In addition, we discuss how to determine whether a particular method throws exceptions.

Class **Exception** of namespace **System** is the base class of the .NET Framework exception hierarchy. Two of the most important derived classes of **Exception** are ***ApplicationException*** and ***SystemException***. **ApplicationException** is a base class programmers can extend to create exception data types that are specific to their applications. We discuss creating programmer-defined exception classes in Section 11.7. Programs can recover from most **ApplicationException**s and continue execution.

The CLR can generate **SystemException**s at any point during the execution of the program. Many of these exceptions can be avoided by coding properly. These are called *runtime exceptions* and they derive from class ***SystemException***. For example, if a program attempts to access an out-of-range array subscript, the CLR throws an exception of type **IndexOutOfRangeException** (a class derived from **SystemException**). Similarly, a runtime exception occurs when a program uses an object reference to manipulate an object that does not yet exist (i.e., the reference has a **null** value). Attempting to use such a **null** reference causes a ***NullReferenceException*** (another type of **SystemException**). According to Microsoft's "Best Practices for Handling Exceptions [C#],"[7] programs typically cannot recover from most exceptions the CLR throws. Therefore, programs generally should not throw or catch **SystemException**s. [*Note:* For a complete list of derived classes of **Exception**, look up "**Exception** class" in the **Index** of the Visual Studio .NET online documentation.]

A benefit of using the exception-class hierarchy is that a **catch** handler can catch exceptions of a particular type or can use a base-class type to catch exceptions in a hierarchy of related exception types. For example, a **catch** handler that specifies an exception parameter of type **Exception** also can catch exceptions of all classes that extend **Exception**, because **Exception** is the base class of all exception classes. This allows for polymorphic processing of related exceptions. The benefit of the latter approach is that the exception handler can use the exception parameter to manipulate the caught exception. If the exception handler does not need access to the caught exception, the exception parameter may be omitted. If no exception type is specified, the catch handler will catch all exceptions.

Using inheritance with exceptions enables an exception handler to catch related exceptions with a concise notation. An exception handler certainly could catch each derived-class exception type individually, but catching the base-class exception type is more concise. However, this makes sense only if the handling behavior is the same for a base class and derived classes. otherwise, catch each derived-class exception individually.

---

6. Actually, it is possible to **catch** exceptions of types that are not derived from class **Exception** using the parameterless **catch** handler. This is useful for handling exceptions from code written in other languages that do not require all exception types to derive from class **Exception** in the .NET framework.
7. "Best Practices for Handling Exceptions [C#]," *.NET Framework Developer's Guide*, Visual Studio .NET Online Help.

At this point, we know that there are many different exception types. We also know that methods and the CLR can both throw exceptions. But, how do we determine that an exception could occur in a program? For methods in the .NET Framework classes, we can look at the detailed description of the methods in the online documentation. If a method throws an exception, its description contains a section called "Exceptions" that specifies the types of exceptions thrown by the method and briefly describes potential causes for the exceptions. For example, look up "**Convert.ToInt32** method" in the index of the Visual Studio .NET online documentation. In the document that describes the method, click the link "**public static int ToInt32(string);**." In the document that appears, the "Exceptions" section indicates that method **Convert.ToInt32** throws three exception types—**ArgumentException**, **FormatException** and **OverflowException**—and describes the reason that each exception type occurs.

Software Engineering Observation 11.6

If a method is capable of throwing exceptions, statements that invoke that method should be placed in **try** *blocks and those exceptions should be caught and handled.*

Determining when the CLR throws exceptions is more difficult. Typically, such information appears in the *C# Language Specification*, which is located in the online documentation. To access the language specification, select **Contents...** from the **Help** menu in Visual Studio. In the **Contents** window, expand **Visual Studio .NET**, **Visual Basic and Visual C#**, **Reference**, **Visual C# Language** and **C# Language Specification**.

The language specification defines the syntax of the language and specifies cases in which exceptions are thrown. For example, in Fig. 11.1, we demonstrated that the CLR throws a **DivideByZeroException** when a program attempts to divide by zero in integer arithmetic. The language specification, Section 7.7.2 discusses the division operator and its **Exception**s. In this section, you will find the details of when a **DivideByZeroException** occurs.

11.5 `finally` Block

Programs frequently request and release resources dynamically (i.e., at execution time). For example, a program that reads a file from disk first requests the opening of that file. If that request succeeds, the program reads the contents of the file. Operating systems typically prevent more than one program from manipulating a file at once. Therefore, when a program finishes processing a file, the program normally closes the file (i.e., releases the resource). This enables other programs to use the file. Closing the file helps prevent the *resource leak*, in which the file resource is unavailable to other programs because a program using the file never closed it. Programs that obtain certain types of resources (such as files) must return those resources explicitly to the system to avoid resource leaks.

In programming languages, like C and C++, in which the programmer is responsible for dynamic memory management, the most common type of resource leak is a *memory leak*. This happens when a program allocates memory (as we do with operator **new** in C#), but does not deallocate the memory when the memory is no longer needed in the program. In C#, this normally is not an issue, because the CLR performs "garbage collection" of memory no longer needed by an executing program. However, other kinds of resource leaks (such as the unclosed file mentioned previously) can occur in C#.

Testing and Debugging Tip 11.2

The CLR does not completely eliminate memory leaks. The CLR will not garbage-collect an object until the program has no more references to that object. Thus, memory leaks can occur if programmers erroneously keep references to unwanted objects.

Most resources that require explicit release have potential exceptions associated with the processing of the resource. For example, a program that processes a file might receive **IOException**s during the processing. For this reason, file-processing code normally appears in a **try** block. Regardless of whether a program successfully processes a file, the program should close the file when the file is no longer needed. Suppose a program places all resource-request and resource-release code in a **try** block. If no exceptions occur, the **try** block executes normally and releases the resources after using them. However, if an exception occurs, the **try** block may expire before the resource-release code can execute. We could duplicate all resource-release code in the **catch** handlers, but this makes the code more difficult to modify and maintain.

C#'s exception handling mechanism provides the *finally* block, which is guaranteed to execute if program control enters the corresponding **try** block. The **finally** block executes regardless of whether that **try** block executes successfully or an exception occurs. This guarantee makes the **finally** block an ideal location to place resource deallocation code for resources acquired and manipulated in the corresponding **try** block. If the **try** block executes successfully, the **finally** block executes immediately after the **try** block terminates. If an exception occurs in the **try** block, the **finally** block executes immediately after a **catch** handler completes exception handling. If the exception is not caught by a **catch** handler associated with that **try** block or if a **catch** handler associated with that **try** block throws an exception, the **finally** block executes, then the exception is processed by the next enclosing **try** block (if there is one).

Testing and Debugging Tip 11.3

A finally block typically contains code to release resources acquired in the corresponding try block; this makes the finally block an effective way to eliminate resource leaks.

Testing and Debugging Tip 11.4

The only reason a finally block will not execute if program control entered the corresponding try block is that the application terminates before finally can execute.

Performance Tip 11.3

As a rule, resources should be released as soon as it is apparent that they are no longer needed in a program, to make those resources immediately available for reuse, thus enhancing resource utilization in the program.

If one or more **catch** handlers follow a **try** block, the **finally** block is optional. If no **catch** handlers follow a **try** block, a **finally** block must appear immediately after the **try** block. If any **catch** handlers follow a **try** block, the **finally** block appears after the last **catch**. Only whitespace and comments can separate the blocks in a **try**/**catch**/**finally** sequence.

Common Programming Error 11.5

Placing the finally block before a catch handler is a syntax error.

The C# application in Fig. 11.2 demonstrates that the **finally** block always executes, even if no exception occurs in the corresponding **try** block. The program consists of method **Main** (lines 10–59) and four other **static** methods that **Main** invokes to demonstrate **finally**—**DoesNotThrowException** (lines 62–85), **ThrowExceptionWithCatch** (lines 88–114), **ThrowExceptionWithoutCatch** (lines 117–138) and **ThrowExceptionCatchRethrow** (lines 141–173). [*Note:* We use **static** methods in this example so that **Main** can invoke these methods directly without creating any objects of class **UsingExceptions**. This enables us to concentrate on the mechanics of **try/catch/finally**.]

Line 14 of **Main** invokes method **DoesNotThrowException** (lines 62–85). The **try** block (lines 65–68) begins by outputting a message (line 67). The **try** block does not throw any exceptions, so program control reaches the closing brace of the **try** block and the **catch** handler (lines 71–74) and executes the **finally** block (lines 77–81) which outputs a message. At this point, program control continues with the first statement after the **finally** block (line 83), which outputs a message indicating that the end of the method has been reached. Then, program control returns to **Main**.

Line 20 of **Main** invokes method **ThrowExceptionWithCatch** (lines 88–114), which begins in its **try** block (lines 91–97) by outputting a message. Next, the **try** block creates a new **Exception** object and uses a *throw* statement to throw the exception object (lines 95–96). The **string** passed to the constructor becomes the exception object's error message. When a **throw** statement in a **try** block executes, the **try** block expires immediately, and program control continues at the first **catch** (lines 100–103) following this **try** block. In this example, the type thrown (**Exception**) matches the type specified in the **catch**, so line 102 outputs a message indicating the exception that occurred. Then, the **finally** block (lines 106–110) executes and outputs a message. At this point, program control continues with the first statement after the **finally** block (line 112), which outputs a message indicating that the end of the method has been reached, then program control returns to **Main**. Note, that in line 102, we use the exception object's **Message** property to access the error message associated with the exception—(the message passed to the **Exception** constructor). Section 11.6 discusses several properties of class **Exception**.

Common Programming Error 11.6

*The expression of a **throw**—an exception object—must be of either class **Exception** or one of its derived classes.*

Lines 27–30 of **Main** define a **try** block in which **Main** invokes method **ThrowExceptionWithoutCatch** (lines 117–138). The **try** block enables **Main** to catch any exceptions thrown by **ThrowExceptionWithoutCatch**. The **try** block in lines 120–126 of **ThrowExceptionWithoutCatch** begins by outputting a message. Next, the **try** block throws an **Exception** (lines 124–125) and the **try** block expires immediately. Normally, program control would continue at the first **catch** following the **try** block. However, this **try** block does not have any corresponding **catch** handlers. Therefore, the exception is not caught in method **ThrowExceptionWithoutCatch**. Normal program control cannot continue until that exception is caught and processed. Thus, the CLR will terminate **ThrowExceptionWithoutCatch** and program control will return to **Main**. Before control returns to **Main**, the **finally** block (lines 129–133) executes and outputs a message. At this point, program control returns to **Main**—any statements appearing after the **finally** block would not execute. In this example, because the exception thrown at lines 127–128 is not caught: Method **ThrowExceptionWithoutCatch** always terminates after the **finally** block executes. In **Main**, the **catch** handler at lines 34–38 catches the exception and displays a message indicating that the exception was caught in **Main**.

```
1   // Fig 11.2: UsingExceptions.cs
2   // Using finally blocks.
3
4   using System;
5
6   // demonstrating that finally always executes
7   class UsingExceptions
8   {
9      // entry point for application
10     static void Main( string[] args )
11     {
12        // Case 1: No exceptions occur in called method.
13        Console.WriteLine( "Calling DoesNotThrowException" );
14        DoesNotThrowException();
15
16        // Case 2: Exception occurs and is caught
17        // in called method.
18        Console.WriteLine( "\nCalling ThrowExceptionWithCatch" );
19        ThrowExceptionWithCatch();
20
21        // Case 3: Exception occurs, but not caught
22        // in called method, because no catch handlers.
23        Console.WriteLine(
24           "\nCalling ThrowExceptionWithoutCatch" );
25
26        // call ThrowExceptionWithoutCatch
27        try
28        {
29           ThrowExceptionWithoutCatch();
30        }
31
32        // process exception returned from
33        // ThrowExceptionWithoutCatch
34        catch
35        {
36           Console.WriteLine( "Caught exception from " +
37              "ThrowExceptionWithoutCatch in Main" );
38        }
39
40        // Case 4: Exception occurs and is caught
41        // in called method, then rethrown to caller.
42        Console.WriteLine(
43           "\nCalling ThrowExceptionCatchRethrow" );
44
```

Fig. 11.2 Demonstrating that **finally** blocks always execute regardless of whether an exception occurs. (Part 1 of 4.)

```
45          // call ThrowExceptionCatchRethrow
46          try
47          {
48              ThrowExceptionCatchRethrow();
49          }
50
51          // process exception returned from
52          // ThrowExceptionCatchRethrow
53          catch
54          {
55              Console.WriteLine( "Caught exception from " +
56                  "ThrowExceptionCatchRethrow in Main" );
57          }
58
59      } // end method Main
60
61      // no exceptions thrown
62      public static void DoesNotThrowException()
63      {
64          // try block does not throw any exceptions
65          try
66          {
67              Console.WriteLine( "In DoesNotThrowException" );
68          }
69
70          // this catch never executes
71          catch
72          {
73              Console.WriteLine( "This catch never executes" );
74          }
75
76          // finally executes because corresponding try executed
77          finally
78          {
79              Console.WriteLine(
80                  "Finally executed in DoesNotThrowException" );
81          }
82
83          Console.WriteLine( "End of DoesNotThrowException" );
84
85      } // end method DoesNotThrowException
86
87      // throws exception and catches it locally
88      public static void ThrowExceptionWithCatch()
89      {
90          // try block throws exception
91          try
92          {
93              Console.WriteLine( "In ThrowExceptionWithCatch" );
94
```

Fig. 11.2 Demonstrating that **finally** blocks always execute regardless of whether or not an exception occurs. (Part 2 of 4.)

```
95              throw new Exception(
96                  "Exception in ThrowExceptionWithCatch" );
97          }
98
99          // catch exception thrown in try block
100         catch ( Exception error )
101         {
102             Console.WriteLine( "Message: " + error.Message );
103         }
104
105         // finally executes because corresponding try executed
106         finally
107         {
108             Console.WriteLine(
109                 "Finally executed in ThrowExceptionWithCatch" );
110         }
111
112         Console.WriteLine( "End of ThrowExceptionWithCatch" );
113
114     } // end method ThrowExceptionWithCatch
115
116     // throws exception and does not catch it locally
117     public static void ThrowExceptionWithoutCatch()
118     {
119         // throw exception, but do not catch it
120         try
121         {
122             Console.WriteLine( "In ThrowExceptionWithoutCatch" );
123
124             throw new Exception(
125                 "Exception in ThrowExceptionWithoutCatch" );
126         }
127
128         // finally executes because corresponding try executed
129         finally
130         {
131             Console.WriteLine( "Finally executed in " +
132                 "ThrowExceptionWithoutCatch" );
133         }
134
135         // unreachable code; would generate logic error
136         Console.WriteLine( "This will never be printed" );
137
138     } // end method ThrowExceptionWithoutCatch
139
140     // throws exception, catches it and rethrows it
141     public static void ThrowExceptionCatchRethrow()
142     {
143         // try block throws exception
144         try
145         {
146             Console.WriteLine( "In ThrowExceptionCatchRethrow" );
```

Fig. 11.2   Demonstrating that **finally** blocks always execute regardless of whether or not an exception occurs. (Part 3 of 4.)

```
147
148            throw new Exception(
149                "Exception in ThrowExceptionCatchRethrow" );
150         }
151
152      // catch any exception, place in object error
153      catch ( Exception error )
154      {
155         Console.WriteLine( "Message: " + error.Message );
156
157         // rethrow exception for further processing
158         throw error;
159
160         // unreachable code; would generate logic error
161      }
162
163      // finally executes because corresponding try executed
164      finally
165      {
166         Console.WriteLine( "Finally executed in " +
167            "ThrowExceptionCatchRethrow" );
168      }
169
170      // unreachable code; would generate logic error
171      Console.WriteLine( "This will never be printed" );
172
173   } // end method ThrowExceptionCatchRethrow
174
175 } // end class UsingExceptions
```

```
Calling DoesNotThrowException
In DoesNotThrowException
Finally executed in DoesNotThrowException
End of DoesNotThrowException

Calling ThrowExceptionWithCatch
In ThrowExceptionWithCatch
Message: Exception in ThrowExceptionWithCatch
Finally executed in ThrowExceptionWithCatch
End of ThrowExceptionWithCatch

Calling ThrowExceptionWithoutCatch
In ThrowExceptionWithoutCatch
Finally executed in ThrowExceptionWithoutCatch
Caught exception from ThrowExceptionWithoutCatch in Main

Calling ThrowExceptionCatchRethrow
In ThrowExceptionCatchRethrow
Message: Exception in ThrowExceptionCatchRethrow
Finally executed in ThrowExceptionCatchRethrow
Caught exception from ThrowExceptionCatchRethrow in Main
```

Fig. 11.2 Demonstrating that **finally** blocks always execute regardless of whether or not an exception occurs. (Part 4 of 4.)

Lines 46–49 of **Main** define a **try** block in which **Main** invokes method **Throw-ExceptionCatchRethrow** (lines 141–173). The **try** block enables **Main** to catch any exceptions thrown by **ThrowExceptionCatchRethrow**. The **try** block in lines 144–150 of **ThrowExceptionCatchRethrow** begins by outputting a message. Next, the **try** block throws an **Exception** (lines 148–149). The **try** block expires immediately, and program control continues at the first **catch** (lines 153–161) following the **try** block. In this example, the type thrown (**Exception**) matches the type specified in the **catch**, so line 155 outputs a message indicating the exception that occurred. Line 158 uses the **throw** statement to *rethrow* the exception. This indicates that the **catch** handler performed partial processing (or no processing) of the exception and is now passing the exception back to the calling method (in this case **Main**) for further processing. Note that the expression to the **throw** statement is the reference to the exception that was caught. When rethrowing the original exception, you can also use the statement

```
throw;
```

with no expression. Section 11.6 discusses the **throw** statement with an expression. Such a **throw** statement enables programmers to catch an exception, create an exception object, then throw a different type of exception from the **catch** handler. Class library designers often do this to customize the exception types thrown from methods in their class libraries or to provide additional debugging information.

Software Engineering Observation 11.7

Before throwing an exception to a calling method, the method that throws the exception should release any resources acquired within the method before the exception occurred.[8]

Software Engineering Observation 11.8

Whenever possible, a method should handle exceptions that are thrown in that method, rather than passing the exceptions to another region of the program.

The exception handling in method **ThrowExceptionCatchRethrow** did not complete, because the program cannot run code in the **catch** handler placed after the invocation of the **throw** statement (line 158). Therefore, method **ThrowException-CatchRethrow** will terminate and return control to **Main**. Once again, the **finally** block (lines 164–168) will execute and output a message before control returns to **Main**. When control returns to **Main**, the **catch** handler at lines 53–57 catches the exception and displays a message indicating that the exception was caught. Then the program terminates.

Note that the point at which program control continues after the **finally** block executes depends on the exception-handling state. If the **try** block successfully completes or if a **catch** handler catches and handles an exception, control continues with the next statement after the **finally** block. If an exception is not caught or if a **catch** handler rethrows an exception, program control continues in the next enclosing **try** block. The enclosing **try** may be in the calling method or one of its callers. Nesting a **try/catch** sequence in a **try** block is also possible, in which case the outer **try** block's catch handlers would process any exceptions that were not caught in the inner **try/catch** sequence. If a **try** block has a cor-

---

8. "Best Practices for Handling Exceptions [C#]." .NET Framework Developer's Guide, Visual Studio .NET Online Help.

responding **finally** block, the **finally** block executes even if the **try** block terminates due to a **return** statement; then the **return** occurs.

Common Programming Error 11.7

*Throwing an exception from a **finally** can be dangerous. If an uncaught exception is awaiting processing when the **finally** block executes and the **finally** block throws a new exception that is not caught in the **finally** block, the first exception is lost, and the new exception is the one passed to the next enclosing **try** block.*

Testing and Debugging Tip 11.5

*When placing code that can throw an exception in a **finally** block, always enclose that code in a **try/catch** sequence that catches the appropriate exception types. This prevents losing uncaught and rethrown exceptions that occur before the **finally** block executes.*

Software Engineering Observation 11.9

*C#'s exception-handling mechanism removes error-processing code from the main line of a program to improve program clarity. Do not place **try-catch-finally** around every statement that could throw an exception. Doing so makes programs difficult to read. Rather, place one **try** block around a significant portion of your code. Follow this **try** block with **catch** handlers that handle each of the possible exceptions and follow the **catch** handlers with a single **finally** block.*

11.6 Exception Properties

As we discussed in Section 11.4, exception data types derive from class **Exception**, which has several properties. These properties frequently are used to formulate error messages for a caught exception. Two important properties are **Message** and **StackTrace**. Property **Message** stores the error message associated with an **Exception** object. This message may be a default message associated with the exception type or a customized message passed to an exception object's constructor when the exception object is constructed. Property **StackTrace** contains a **string** that represents the *method call stack*. The runtime environment keeps a list of method calls that have been made up to a given moment. The **StackTrace string** represents this sequential list of methods that had not finished processing at the time the exception occurred. The exact location at which the exception occurs in the program is called the exception's *throw point*.

Testing and Debugging Tip 11.6

A stack trace shows the complete method call stack at the time an exception occurred. This lets the programmer view the series of method calls that led to the exception. Information in the stack trace includes names of the methods on the call stack at the time of the exception, names of the classes in which those methods are defined, names of the namespaces in which those classes are defined and line numbers. The first line number in the stack trace indicates the throw point. Subsequent line numbers indicate the locations from which each method in the stack trace was called.

Another property used frequently by class library programmers is **InnerException**. Typically, programmers use this property to "wrap" exception objects caught in their code, then throw new exception types that are specific to their libraries. For example, a programmer implementing an accounting system might have some account-number processing code in which account numbers are input as **string**s but represented with integers in the code. As you know, a program can convert **string**s to **int** values with **Convert.ToInt32**, which throws a **FormatException** when it encounters an invalid number format. When an invalid account-number format occurs, the accounting-system programmer might wish either to indicate an error message different from the default one supplied by **FormatException** or to indicate a new exception type, such as **InvalidAccountNumberFormatException**. In these cases, the programmer would provide code to catch the **FormatException**, then create an exception object in the **catch** handler, passing the original exception as one of the constructor arguments. The original exception object becomes the **InnerException** of the new exception object. When an **InvalidAccountNumberFormatException** occurs in code that uses the accounting-system library, the **catch** handler that catches the exception can view the original exception via the property **InnerException**. Thus, the exception indicates that an invalid account number was specified and that the particular problem was an invalid number format.

Our next example (Fig. 11.3) demonstrates properties **Message**, **StackTrace** and **InnerException** and method **ToString**. In addition, this example demonstrates *stack unwinding*—the process that attempts to locate an appropriate **catch** handler for an uncaught exception. As we discuss this example, we keep track of the methods on the call stack, so we can discuss property **StackTrace** and the stack-unwinding mechanism.

Program execution begins with the invocation of **Main**, which becomes the first method on the method call stack. Line 16 of the **try** block in **Main** invokes **Method1** (lines 43–46), which becomes the second method on the stack. If **Method1** throws an exception, the **catch** handler at lines 22–38 handle the exception and output information about the exception that occurred. Line 45 of **Method1** invokes **Method2** (lines 49–52), which becomes the third method on the stack. Then, line 51 of **Method2** invokes **Method3** (defined at lines 55–70) which becomes the fourth method on the stack.

Testing and Debugging Tip 11.7

When reading a stack trace, start from the top of the stack trace and read the error message first. Then, read the remainder of the stack trace, looking for the first line that indicates code that you wrote in your program. Normally, this is the location that caused the exception.

```
1   // Fig 11.3: Properties.cs
2   // Stack unwinding and Exception class properties.
3
4   using System;
5
6   // demonstrates using the Message, StackTrace and
7   // InnerException properties
8   class Properties
9   {
10     static void Main( string[] args )
11     {
12       // call Method1, any Exception it generates will be
13       // caught in the catch handler that follows
14       try
15       {
16         Method1();
17       }
```

Fig. 11.3 **Exception** properties and stack unwinding. (Part 1 of 3.)

```
18
19          // Output string representation of Exception, then
20          // output values of InnerException, Message,
21          // and StackTrace properties
22          catch ( Exception exception )
23          {
24             Console.WriteLine(
25                "exception.ToString(): \n{0}\n",
26                exception.ToString() );
27
28             Console.WriteLine( "exception.Message: \n{0}\n",
29                exception.Message );
30
31             Console.WriteLine( "exception.StackTrace: \n{0}\n",
32                exception.StackTrace );
33
34             Console.WriteLine(
35                "exception.InnerException: \n{0}",
36                exception.InnerException );
37
38          } // end catch
39
40       } // end Main
41
42       // calls Method2
43       public static void Method1()
44       {
45          Method2();
46       }
47
48       // calls Method3
49       public static void Method2()
50       {
51          Method3();
52       }
53
54       // throws an Exception containing an InnerException
55       public static void Method3()
56       {
57          // attempt to convert non-integer string to int
58          try
59          {
60             Convert.ToInt32( "Not an integer" );
61          }
62
63          // catch FormatException and wrap it in new Exception
64          catch ( FormatException error )
65          {
66             throw new Exception(
67                "Exception occurred in Method3", error );
68          }
69
70       } // end method Method3
```

Fig. 11.3 Exception properties and stack unwinding. (Part 2 of 3.)

```
71
72   } // end class UsingExceptions
```

```
exception.ToString():
System.Exception: Exception occurred in Method3 --->
   System.FormatException: Input string was not in a correct format.
   at System.Number.ParseInt32(String s, NumberStyles style,
      NumberFormatInfo info)
   at System.Convert.ToInt32(String s)
   at Properties.Method3() in
      f:\books\2001\csphtp1\csphtp1_examples\ch11\fig11_8\
         properties\properties.cs:line 60
   --- End of inner exception stack trace ---
   at Properties.Method3() in
      f:\books\2001\csphtp1\csphtp1_examples\ch11\fig11_8\
         properties\properties.cs:line 66
   at Properties.Method2() in
      f:\books\2001\csphtp1\csphtp1_examples\ch11\fig11_8\
         properties\properties.cs:line 51
   at Properties.Method1() in
      f:\books\2001\csphtp1\csphtp1_examples\ch11\fig11_8\
         properties\properties.cs:line 45
   at Properties.Main(String[] args) in
      f:\books\2001\csphtp1\csphtp1_examples\ch11\fig11_8\
         properties\properties.cs:line 16

exception.Message:
Exception occurred in Method3

exception.StackTrace:
   at Properties.Method3() in
      f:\books\2001\csphtp1\csphtp1_examples\ch11\fig11_8\
         properties\properties.cs:line 66
   at Properties.Method2() in
      f:\books\2001\csphtp1\csphtp1_examples\ch11\fig11_8\
         properties\properties.cs:line 51
   at Properties.Method1() in
      f:\books\2001\csphtp1\csphtp1_examples\ch11\fig11_8\
         properties\properties.cs:line 45
   at Properties.Main(String[] args) in
      f:\books\2001\csphtp1\csphtp1_examples\ch11\fig11_8\
         properties\properties.cs:line 16

exception.InnerException:
System.FormatException: Input string was not in a correct format.
   at System.Number.ParseInt32(String s, NumberStyles style,
      NumberFormatInfo info)
   at System.Convert.ToInt32(String s)
   at Properties.Method3() in
      f:\books\2001\csphtp1\csphtp1_examples\ch11\fig11_8\
         properties\properties.cs:line 60
```

Fig. 11.3 **Exception** properties and stack unwinding. (Part 3 of 3.)

At this point, the method call stack for the program is

```
Method3
Method2
Method1
Main
```

with the last method called (**Method3**) at the top and the first method called (**Main**) at the bottom. The **try** block (lines 58–61) in **Method3** invokes method **Convert.ToInt32** (line 60) and attempts to convert a **string** to an **int**. At this point, **Convert.ToInt32** becomes the fifth and final method on the call stack.

The argument to **Convert.ToInt32** is not in integer format, so line 60 throws a **FormatException** that is caught at line 64 in **Method3**. The exception terminates the call to **Convert.ToInt32**, so the method is removed from the method call stack. The **catch** handler creates an **Exception** object, then throws it. The first argument to the **Exception** constructor is the custom error message for our example, "**Exception occurred in Method3.**" The second argument is the **InnerException** object—the **FormatException** that was caught. Note that the **StackTrace** for this new exception object will reflect the point at which the exception was thrown (line 66). Now, **Method3** terminates, because the exception thrown in the **catch** handler is not caught in the method body. Thus, control will be returned to the statement that invoked **Method3** in the prior method in the call stack (**Method2**). This removes or *unwinds* **Method3** from the method-call stack.

Good Programming Practice 11.2

When catching and rethrowing an exception, provide additional debugging information in the rethrown exception. To do so, create an **Exception** *object with more specific debugging information and pass the original caught exception to the new exception object's constructor to initialize the* **InnerException** *property.*[9]

When control returns to line 51 in **Method2**, the CLR determines that line 51 is not in a **try** block. Therefore, the exception cannot be caught in **Method2**, and **Method2** terminates. This unwinds **Method2** from the method-call stack and returns control to line 45 in **Method1**. Here again, line 45 is not in a **try** block, so the exception cannot be caught in **Method1**. The method terminates and unwinds from the call stack, returning control to line 16 in **Main**, which is in a **try** block. The **try** block in **Main** expires, and the **catch** handler at lines (22–38) catches the exception. The **catch** handler uses method **ToString** and properties **Message**, **StackTrace** and **InnerException** to produce the output. Note that stack unwinding continues until either a **catch** handler catches the exception or the program terminates.

The first block of output (reformatted for readability) in Fig. 11.3 shows the exception's **string** representation returned from method **ToString**. This begins with the name of the exception class followed by the **Message** property value. The next eight lines show the **string** representation of the **InnerException** object. The remainder of that block of output shows the **StackTrace** for the exception thrown in **Method3**. Note that the **StackTrace** represents the state of the method-call stack at the throw

9. "Best Practices for Handling Exceptions [C#]," *.NET Framework Developer's Guide*, Visual Studio .NET Online Help.

point of the exception, not at the point where the exception eventually is caught. Each of the **StackTrace** lines that begins with "**at**" represents a method on the call stack. These lines indicate the method in which the exception occurred, the file in which that method resides and the line number in the file. Also, note that the stack trace includes the inner-exception stack trace.

Testing and Debugging Tip 11.8

*When catching and rethrowing an exception, provide additional debugging information in the rethrown exception. To do so, create an **Exception** object containing more specific debugging information and then pass the original caught exception to the new exception object's constructor to initialize the **InnerException** property.*

Method **ToString** of an exception returns a **string** containing the name of the exception, the optional character **string** supplied when the exception was constructed, the inner exception (if there is one) and a stack trace.

The next block of output (two lines) simply displays the **Message** property (**Exception occurred in Method3**) of the exception thrown in **Method3**.

The third block of output displays the **StackTrace** property of the exception thrown in **Method3**. Note that the **StackTrace** property includes the stack trace starting from line 66 in **Method3**, because that is the point at which the **Exception** object was created and thrown. The stack trace always begins from the exception's throw point.

Finally, the last block of output displays the **ToString** representation of the **InnerException** property, which includes the namespace and class names of that exception object, its **Message** property and its **StackTrace** property.

11.7 Programmer-Defined Exception Classes

In many cases, programmers can use existing exception classes from the .NET Framework to indicate exceptions that occur in their programs. However, in some cases, programmers may wish to create exception types that are more specific to the problems that occur in their programs. *Programmer-defined exception classes* should derive directly or indirectly from class **ApplicationException** of namespace **System**.

Good Programming Practice 11.3

Associating each type of malfunction with an appropriately named exception class improves program clarity.

Software Engineering Observation 11.10

Before creating programmer-defined exception classes, investigate the existing exception classes in the .NET Framework to determine whether an appropriate exception type already exists.

Software Engineering Observation 11.11

Programmers should create exception classes only if they need to catch and handle the new exceptions differently from other existing exception types.

Figure 11.4 and Fig. 11.5 demonstrate defining and using a programmer-defined exception class. Class **NegativeNumberException** (Fig. 11.4) is a programmer-defined exception class representing exceptions that occur when a program performs an illegal operation on a negative number, such as the square root of a negative number.

```
1   // Fig 11:4: NegativeNumberException.cs
2   // NegativeNumberException represents exceptions caused by illegal
3   // operations performed on negative numbers
4
5   using System;
6
7   // NegativeNumberException represents exceptions caused by
8   // illegal operations performed on negative numbers
9   class NegativeNumberException : ApplicationException
10  {
11     // default constructor
12     public NegativeNumberException()
13        : base( "Illegal operation for a negative number" )
14     {
15     }
16
17     // constructor for customizing error message
18     public NegativeNumberException( string message )
19        : base( message )
20     {
21     }
22
23     // constructor for customizing error message and
24     // specifying inner exception object
25     public NegativeNumberException(
26        string message, Exception inner )
27           : base( message, inner )
28     {
29     }
30
31  } // end class NegativeNumberException
```

Fig. 11.4 ApplicationException subclass thrown when a program performs illegal operations on negative numbers.

According to Microsoft,[10] programmer-defined exceptions should extend class **ApplicationException**, should have a class name that ends with "Exception" and should define three constructors—a default constructor, a constructor that receives a **string** argument (the error message) and a constructor that receives a **string** argument and an **Exception** argument (the error message and the inner-exception object).

NegativeNumberExceptions most likely occur during arithmetic operations, so it seems logical to derive class **NegativeNumberException** from class **ArithmeticException**. However, class **ArithmeticException** derives from class **SystemException**—the category of exceptions thrown by the CLR. **ApplicationException** specifically is the base class for exceptions thrown by a user program, not by the CLR.

Class **SquareRootTest** (Fig. 11.5) demonstrates our programmer-defined exception class. The application enables the user to input a numeric value, then invokes method **SquareRoot** (lines 42–52) to calculate the square root of that value. For this

10. "Best Practices for Handling Exceptions [C#]," *.NET Framework Developer's Guide*, Visual Studio .NET Online Help.

purpose, **SquareRoot** invokes class **Math**'s *Sqrt* method, which receives a nonnegative **double** value as its argument. If the argument is negative, method **Sqrt** normally returns constant **NaN** from class **Double**. In this program, we would like to prevent the user from calculating the square root of a negative number. If the numeric value received from the user is negative, **SquareRoot** throws a **NegativeNumberException** (lines 46–47). Otherwise, **SquareRoot** invokes class **Math**'s *Sqrt* method to compute the square root.

When the user inputs a value and clicks the **Square Root** button, the program invokes method **squareRootButton_Click** (lines 56–85). The **try** block (lines 62–68) attempts to invoke **SquareRoot** with the value input by the user. If the user input is not a valid number, a **FormatException** occurs, and the **catch** handler at lines 71–76 processes the exception. If the user inputs a negative number, method **SquareRoot** throws a **NegativeNumberException** (lines 46–47). The **catch** handler at lines 79–83 catches and handles that exception.

```
1   // Fig 11.5: SquareRootTest.cs
2   // Demonstrating a programmer-defined exception class.
3
4   using System;
5   using System.Drawing;
6   using System.Collections;
7   using System.ComponentModel;
8   using System.Windows.Forms;
9   using System.Data;
10
11  // accepts input and computes the square root of that input
12  public class SquareRootTest : System.Windows.Forms.Form
13  {
14     private System.Windows.Forms.Label inputLabel;
15     private System.Windows.Forms.TextBox inputTextBox;
16
17     private System.Windows.Forms.Button squareRootButton;
18
19     private System.Windows.Forms.Label outputLabel;
20
21     // Required designer variable.
22     private System.ComponentModel.Container components = null;
23
24     // default constructor
25     public SquareRootTest()
26     {
27        // Required for Windows Form Designer support
28        InitializeComponent();
29     }
30
31     // Visual Studio .NET generated code
32
```

Fig. 11.5   SquareRootTest class throws an exception if error occurs when calculating the square root. (Part 1 of 3.)

```
33        // main entry point for the application
34        [STAThread]
35        static void Main()
36        {
37            Application.Run( new SquareRootTest() );
38        }
39
40        // computes the square root of its parameter; throws
41        // NegativeNumberException if parameter is negative
42        public double SquareRoot( double operand )
43        {
44            // if negative operand, throw NegativeNumberException
45            if ( operand < 0 )
46                throw new NegativeNumberException(
47                    "Square root of negative number not permitted" );
48
49            // compute the square root
50            return Math.Sqrt( operand );
51
52        } // end class SquareRoot
53
54        // obtain user input, convert to double and calculate
55        // square root
56        private void squareRootButton_Click(
57            object sender, System.EventArgs e )
58        {
59            outputLabel.Text = "";
60
61            // catch any NegativeNumberExceptions thrown
62            try
63            {
64                double result =
65                    SquareRoot( Double.Parse( inputTextBox.Text ) );
66
67                outputLabel.Text = result.ToString();
68            }
69
70            // process invalid number format
71            catch ( FormatException notInteger )
72            {
73                MessageBox.Show( notInteger.Message,
74                    "Invalid Operation", MessageBoxButtons.OK,
75                    MessageBoxIcon.Error );
76            }
77
78            // display MessageBox if negative number input
79            catch ( NegativeNumberException error )
80            {
81                MessageBox.Show( error.Message, "Invalid Operation",
82                    MessageBoxButtons.OK, MessageBoxIcon.Error );
83            }
84
```

Fig. 11.5 **SquareRootTest** class throws an exception if error occurs when calculating the square root. (Part 2 of 3.)

```
85          } // end method squareRootButton_Click
86
87   } // end class SquareRootTest
```

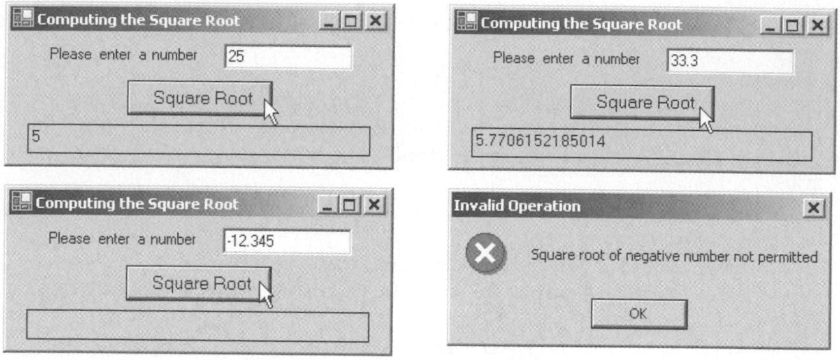

Fig. 11.5 **SquareRootTest** class throws an exception if error occurs when calculating the square root. (Part 3 of 3.)

11.8 Handling Overflows with Operators checked and unchecked

In .NET, the primitive data types are stored in fixed-size structures. For instance, the maximum value of an **int** is 2,147,483,647. In integer arithmetic, a value larger than 2,147,483,647 causes *overflow*—type **int** cannot represent such a number. Overflow also can occur with other C# primitive types. Overflows often cause programs to produce incorrect results.

C# provides operators **checked** and **unchecked** to specify whether integer arithmetic occurs in a *checked context* or *unchecked context*. In a checked context, the CLR throws an **OverflowException** (namespace **System**) if overflow occurs during evaluation of an arithmetic expression. In an unchecked context, the result is truncated if overflow occurs.

The operators **++**, **--**, *****, **/**, **+** and **-** (both unary and binary) may cause overflow when used with integral data types (such as **int** and **long**). Also, explicit conversions between integral data types can cause overflow. For example, converting the integer 1,000,000 from **int** to **short** results in overflow, because a **short** can store a maximum value of 32,767. Figure 11.6 demonstrates overflows occurring in both checked and unchecked contexts.

The program begins by defining **int** variables **number1** and **number2** (lines 11–12) and assigning each variable the maximum value for an **int**—2,147,483,647 (defined by **Int32.MaxValue**). Next, line 13 defines variable **sum** (initialized to 0) to store the **sum** of **number1** and **number2**. Then, lines 15–16 output the values of **number1** and **number2**.

Lines 19–25 define a **try** block in which line 24 adds **number1** and **number2** in a checked context. The expression to evaluate in a checked context appears in parentheses following keyword **checked**. Variables **number1** and **number2** already contain the maximum value for an **int**, so adding these values causes an **OverflowException**. The **catch** handler at lines 28–31 catches the exception and outputs its **string** representation.

Line 39 performs the same calculation in an unchecked context. The result of the calculation should be 4,294,967,294. However, this value requires more memory than an **int** can store, so operator **unchecked** truncates part of the value, resulting in **-2** in the output. As you can see, the result of the unchecked calculation is not the actual sum of the variables.

```
1   // Fig 11.6: Overflow.cs
2   // Demonstrating operators checked and unchecked.
3
4   using System;
5
6   // demonstrates using the checked and unchecked operators
7   class Overflow
8   {
9      static void Main( string[] args )
10     {
11        int number1 = Int32.MaxValue;   // 2,147,483,647
12        int number2 = Int32.MaxValue;   // 2,147,483,647
13        int sum = 0;
14
15        Console.WriteLine(
16           "number1: {0}\nnumber2: {1}", number1, number2 );
17
18        // calculate sum of number1 and number2
19        try
20        {
21           Console.WriteLine(
22              "\nSum integers in checked context:" );
23
24           sum = checked( number1 + number2 );
25        }
26
27        // catch overflow exception
28        catch ( OverflowException overflowException )
29        {
30           Console.WriteLine( overflowException.ToString() );
31        }
32
33        Console.WriteLine(
34           "\nsum after checked operation: {0}", sum );
35
36        Console.WriteLine(
37           "\nSum integers in unchecked context:" );
38
39        sum = unchecked( number1 + number2 );
40
41        Console.WriteLine(
42           "sum after unchecked operation: {0}", sum );
43
44     } // end method Main
45
46  } // end class Overflow
```

Fig. 11.6 Operators **checked** and **unchecked** and the handling of arithmetic overflow. (Part 1 of 2.)

```
number1: 2147483647
number2: 2147483647

Sum integers in checked context:
System.OverflowException: Arithmetic operation resulted in an overflow.
   at Overflow.Overflow.Main(String[] args) in
      f:\books\2001\csphtp1\csphtp1_examples\ch11\fig11_09\
         overflow\overflow.cs:line 24

sum after checked operation: 0

Sum integers in unchecked context:
sum after unchecked operation: -2
```

Fig. 11.6   Operators **checked** and **unchecked** and the handling of arithmetic overflow. (Part 2 of 2.)

By default, calculations occur in an unchecked context—a dangerous practice, unless the calculations are preformed on constant expressions (such as literal integer values). Constant expressions are evaluated in a checked context at compile time. Overflows in such expressions results in compile time errors. It is possible to specify in a project's properties that the default context for evaluating non-constant expressions should be to check for arithmetic overflow. In the properties for your project, you can set the checked context as the default. To do so, first select your project in the **Solution Explorer**. Next, in the **View** menu, select **Property Pages**. In the **Property Pages** dialog, click the **Configuration Properties** folder. Under **Code Generation**, change the value of **Check for Arithmetic Overflow/Underflow** to **true**.

Good Programming Practice 11.4

Use a checked context when performing calculations that can result in overflows. The programmer should define exception handlers that can process the overflow.

Software Engineering Observation 11.12

*Keywords **checked** and **unchecked** can evaluate blocks of statements in checked or unchecked contexts by following the appropriate keyword with a block of code in braces ({ }).*

In this chapter, we demonstrated how the exception-handling mechanism works and discussed how to make applications more robust by writing exception handlers to process potential problems. As programmers develop new applications, it is important to investigate potential exceptions thrown by the methods your program invokes or by the CLR, then implement appropriate exception-handling code to make those applications more robust.

SUMMARY

- An exception is an indication of a problem that occurs during a program's execution.
- Exception handling enables programmers to create applications that can resolve exceptions, often allowing a program to continue execution as if no problems were encountered.
- Exception handling enables programmers to write clear, robust and more fault-tolerant programs.
- Exception handling enables the programmer to remove error-handling code from the "main line" of the program's execution. This improves program clarity and enhances modifiability.

- Exception handling is designed to process synchronous errors, such as out-of-range array subscripts, arithmetic overflow, division by zero, invalid method parameters and memory exhaustion.

- Exception handling is not designed to process asynchronous events, such as disk-I/O completions, network-message arrivals, mouse clicks and keystrokes.

- When a method detects an error and is unable to handle it, the method throws an exception. There is no guarantee that there will be an exception handler to process that kind of exception. If there is, the exception will be caught and handled.

- In debug mode, when the program detects an uncaught exception, a dialog box appears that enables the programmer to view the problem in the debugger or continue program execution by ignoring the problem that occurred.

- A **try** block consists of keyword **try** followed by braces (**{}**) that delimit a block of code in which exceptions could occur.

- Immediately following the **try** block are zero or more **catch** handlers. Each **catch** specifies in parentheses an exception parameter representing the exception type the **catch** can handle.

- If an exception parameter includes an optional parameter name, the **catch** handler can use that parameter name to interact with a caught exception object.

- There can be one parameterless **catch** handler that catches all exception types.

- After the last **catch** handler, an optional **finally** block contains code that always executes, regardless of whether an exception occurs.

- When a method called in a program or the CLR detects a problem, the method or CLR throws an exception. The point in the program at which an exception occurs is called the throw point.

- Exceptions are objects of classes that inherit directly or indirectly from class **Exception**.

- C# uses the termination model of exception handling. If an exception occurs in a **try** block, the block expires and program control transfers to the first **catch** handler following the **try** block.

- The CLR searches for the first **catch** handler that can process the type of exception that occurred. The appropriate handler is the first one in which the thrown exception's type matches, or is derived from, the exception type specified by the **catch** handler's exception parameter.

- If no exceptions occur in a **try** block, the CLR ignores the exception handlers for that block.

- If no exceptions occur or if an exception is caught and handled, the program resumes execution with the next statement after the **try**/**catch**/**finally** sequence.

- If an exception occurs in a statement that is not in a **try** block, the method containing that statement terminates immediately—a process called stack unwinding.

- When a **try** block terminates, local variables defined in the block go out of scope.

- If the argument to **Convert.ToInt32** is not an integer, a **FormatException** occurs.

- In integer arithmetic, an attempt to divide by zero causes a **DivideByZeroException**.

- A **try** block encloses the code that could throw exceptions and the code that should not execute if an exception occurs.

- Each **catch** handler begins with keyword **catch** followed by an optional exception parameter that specifies the type of exception handled by the **catch** handler. The exception-handling code appears in the body of the **catch** handler.

- Only the matching **catch** handler executes if an exception occurs. When program control reaches the closing brace of a **catch** handler, the CLR considers the exception handled, and program control continues with the first statement after the **try**/**catch** sequence.

- If a **catch** handler specifies an exception type and an exception parameter name, the exception handler's body can interact with the caught exception object. The exception parameter can be omitted if the exception handler does not require access to the exception object's properties.

- The exception-handling mechanism allows only objects of class **Exception** and its derived classes to be thrown and caught. Class **Exception** of namespace **System** is the base class of the .NET Framework exception hierarchy.

- **ApplicationException** is a base class programmers can extend to create new exception data types that are specific to their applications. Programs can recover from most **ApplicationException**s and continue execution.

- The Common Language Runtime generates **SystemException**s. If a program attempts to access an out-of-range array subscript, the CLR throws an **IndexOutOfRangeException**. Attempting to manipulate an object through a **null** reference causes a **NullReferenceException**.

- Programs typically cannot recover from most exceptions thrown by the CLR. Therefore, programs generally should not throw **SystemException**s nor attempt to catch.

- A **catch** handler can catch exceptions of a particular type or can use a base-class type to catch exceptions in a hierarchy of related exception types. A **catch** handler that specifies an exception parameter of type **Exception** can catch all exceptions, because **Exception** is the base class of all exception classes.

- For methods in the .NET Framework classes, you should look at the detailed description of the method in the online documentation to determine whether that method throws exceptions.

- Information on exceptions thrown by the CLR appears in the *C# Language Specification*, which is located in the online documentation.

- Many computer operating systems prevent more than one program from manipulating a resource at the same time. Therefore, when a program no longer needs a resource, the program normally releases the resource to allow other programs to use the resource. This helps prevent resource leaks, and helps ensure that resources are available when needed.

- In C and C++, the most common resource leaks are memory leaks that occur when a program allocates memory, but does not deallocate the memory when the memory is no longer needed in the program. The Common Language Runtime performs garbage collection of memory no longer needed by an executing program, thus avoiding such memory leaks.

- A program should release a resource when the resource is no longer needed. The **finally** block is guaranteed to execute if program control enters the corresponding **try** block, regardless of whether that **try** block executes successfully or an exception occurs. This guarantee makes the **finally** block an ideal location to place resource-deallocation code for resources acquired and manipulated in the corresponding **try** block.

- If one or more **catch** handlers follow a **try** block, the **finally** block is optional. If no **catch** handlers follow a **try** block, a **finally** block must appear immediately after the **try** block. If any **catch** handlers follow a **try** block, the **finally** block appears after the last **catch**.

- Only whitespace and comments can separate the blocks in a **try/catch/finally** sequence.

- A **throw** statement throws an exception object.

- A **throw** statement can be used in a **catch** handler to rethrow an exception. This indicates that the **catch** handler performed partial processing of the exception and is now passing the exception back to a calling method for further processing.

- **Exception** property **Message** stores the error message associated with an **Exception** object. This message may be a default message associated with the exception type or a customized message passed to an exception object's constructor at the time a program creates the exception.

- **Exception** property **StackTrace** contains a string that represents the method-call stack at the throw point of the exception.

- **Exception** property **InnerException** typically is used to "wrap" a caught exception object in a new exception object, then throw the object of that new exception type.

- When an exception is uncaught in a method, the method terminates. This removes or unwinds the method from the method-call stack.

- Programmer-defined exceptions should extend class **ApplicationException**, should have a class name that ends with "Exception" and should define a default constructor, a constructor that receives a **string** argument (the error message) and a constructor that receives a **string** argument and an **Exception** argument (the error message and the inner-exception object).

- Overflow occurs in integer arithmetic when the value of an expression is greater than the maximum value that can be stored in a particular integral data type.

- C# provides operators **checked** and **unchecked** to specify whether arithmetic occurs in a checked context or an unchecked context. In a checked context, operator **checked** throws an **OverflowException** if overflow occurs when evaluating an arithmetic expression. In an unchecked context, operator **unchecked** truncates the result if overflow occurs (normally, a dangerous thing to allow).

- The operators **++**, **--**, *****, **/**, **+** and **-** (both unary and binary) can cause overflow when used with integral data types (such as **int** and **long**). Also, explicit conversions between integral data types can cause overflow.

- The expression that is to be evaluated in a checked or unchecked context appears in parentheses following keyword **checked** or **unchecked**, respectively. Also, entire blocks of code can execute in a checked or unchecked context by placing keyword checked or unchecked before the opening left brace of the block.

- By default, calculations are performed in the unchecked context.

TERMINOLOGY

ApplicationException class
arithmetic overflow
asynchronous event
C# Language Specification
call stack
catch all exception types
catch block (or handler)
checked context
checked operator
Common Language Runtime (CLR)
disk I/O completion
divide by zero
DivideByZeroException class
DivideByZeroTest.cs
Double class
eliminate resource leaks
error-processing code
exception
Exception class
exception handler
fault-tolerant program

finally block
FormatException class
handling a divide-by-zero exception
IndexOutOfRangeException class
inheritance with exceptions
InnerException property of **Exception**
integral data types
Koenig, Andrew
MaxValue constant of **Int32**
memory leak
Message
Message property of class **Exception**
Message property of **Exception**
method call stack
NaN constant of class **Double**
negative infinity
network message arrival
NullReferenceException
out-of-range array subscript
overflow
OverflowException class

polymorphic processing of related errors
positive infinity
release resource
resource leak
result of an uncaught exception
resumption model of exception handling
rethrow an exception
robust application
run-time exception
Sqrt method of **Math**
SquareRootTest.cs
stack unwinding
StackTrace property of **Exception**
Stroustrup, Bjarne

synchronous error
SystemException class
termination model of exception handling
throw an exception
throw point
throw statement
ToInt32 method of **Convert**
ToString
try block
try block expires
unchecked context
unchecked operator
programmer-defined exception classes

SELF-REVIEW EXERCISES

11.1   Fill in the blanks in each of the following statements:
a) Exception handling deals with _____ errors, but not _____ errors.
b) A method _____ an exception when that method detects that a problem occurred.
c) The _____ block associated with a **try** block always executes.
d) Exception objects are derived from class _____.
e) The statement that throws an exception is called the _____ of the exception.
f) A _____ block encloses code that could throw an exception.
g) If the catch-all exception handler is declared before another exception handler, a _____ occurs.
h) An uncaught exception in a method causes that method to _____ from the method-call stack.
i) Method **Convert.ToInt32** can throw a _____ exception if its argument is not a valid integer value.
j) Runtime exceptions derive from class _____.
k) To force an exception to occur when arithmetic overflow occurs in integer arithmetic, use operator _____.

11.2   State whether each of the following is *true* or *false*. If *false*, explain why.
a) Exceptions always are handled in the method that initially detects the exception.
b) Programmer-defined exception classes should extend class **SystemException**.
c) Accessing an out-of-bounds array subscript causes the CLR to throw an exception.
d) A **finally** block is optional after a **try** block.
e) If a **finally** block appears in a method, that **finally** block is guaranteed to execute.
f) Returning to the throw point of an exception using keyword **return** is possible.
g) Exceptions can be rethrown.
h) The **checked** operator causes a syntax error when integral arithmetic overflow occurs.
i) Property **Message** returns a **string** indicating the method from which the exception was thrown.
j) Exceptions can be thrown only by methods explicitly called in a **try** block.

ANSWERS TO SELF-REVIEW EXERCISES

11.1   a) synchronous, asynchronous. b) throws. c) **finally**. d) **Exception**. e) throw point.
f) **try**. g) syntax error. h) unwind. i) **FormatException**. j) **SystemException**. k) **checked**.

11.2   a) False. Exceptions are handled by calling methods on the method-call stack. b) False. Programmer-defined exception classes should extend class **ApplicationException**. c) True. d) False. The **finally** block is option *only* if there is at least one **catch** handler. If there are not **catch** handlers, the **finally** block is *required*. e) False. The **finally** block will execute only if program control entered the corresponding **try** block. f) False. Keyword **return** causes control to **return** to the caller. g) True. h) False. The **checked** operator causes an exception when arithmetic overflow occurs at execution time. i) False. Property **Message** returns a **string** representing the error message. j) False. Exceptions can be thrown by any method, called from a **try** block or not. Also, the CLR can throw exceptions.

EXERCISES

11.3   Use inheritance to create an exception base class and various exception-derived classes. Write a program to demonstrate that the **catch** specifying the base class catches derived-class exceptions.

11.4   Write a C# program that demonstrates how various exceptions are caught with

```
catch ( Exception exception )
```

11.5   Write a C# program that shows the importance of the order of exception handlers. Write two programs: One with the correct order of **catch** handlers, and one with an incorrect order (i.e., place the base class exception handler before the derived-class exception handlers). Show that if you attempt to catch a base-class exception type before a derived-class exception type, the derived-class exceptions are not invoked (which potentially yield logical errors in routine). Explain why these errors occur.

11.6   Exceptions can be used to indicate problems that occur when an object is being constructed. Write a C# program that shows a constructor passing information about constructor failure to an exception handler that occurs after a **try** block. The exception thrown also should contain the arguments sent to the constructor.

11.7   Write a C# program that demonstrates rethrowing an exception.

11.8   Write a C# program that shows that a method with its own **try** block does not have to **catch** every possible exception that occurs within the **try** block. Some exceptions can slip through to, and be handled in, other scopes.

12

Graphical User Interface Concepts: Part 1

Objectives

- To understand the design principles of graphical user interfaces.
- To understand, use and create events.
- To understand the namespaces containing graphical user interface components and event-handling classes and interfaces.
- To be able to create graphical user interfaces.
- To be able to create and manipulate buttons, labels, lists, textboxes and panels.
- To be able to use mouse and keyboard events.

... the wisest prophets make sure of the event first.
Horace Walpole

...The user should feel in control of the computer; not the other way around. This is achieved in applications that embody three qualities: responsiveness, permissiveness, and consistency.
Inside Macintosh, Volume 1
Apple Computer, Inc. 1985

All the better to see you with my dear.
The Big Bad Wolf to Little Red Riding Hood

Outline

12.1 Introduction

A *graphical user interface* (*GUI*) allows users to interact with a program visually. A GUI (pronounced "GOO-EE") gives a program a distinctive "look" and "feel." By providing different applications with a consistent set of intuitive user-interface components, GUIs allow users to spend less time trying to remember which keystroke sequences perform what functions and spend more time using the program in a productive manner.

Look-and-Feel Observation 12.1

Consistent user interfaces enable users to learn new applications faster.

As an example of a GUI, Fig. 12.1 contains an Internet Explorer window with some of its *GUI components* labeled. In the window, there is a *menu bar* containing *menus*, including **File**, **Edit**, **View**, **Favorites**, **Tools** and **Help**. Below the menu bar is a set of *buttons*; each has a defined task in Internet Explorer. Below the buttons is a *textbox*, in which the user can type the location of a World Wide Web site to visit. To the left of the textbox is a *label* that indicates the textbox's purpose. On the far right and bottom there are *scrollbars*. Scrollbars are used when there is more information in a window than can be displayed at once. By moving the scrollbars back and forth, the user can view different portions of the Web page. The menus, buttons, textboxes, labels and scrollbars are part of Internet Explorer's GUI. They form a user-friendly interface through which the user interacts with the Internet Explorer Web browser.

GUIs are built from GUI components (sometimes called *controls* or *widgets*—short for *window gadgets*). A GUI component is an object with which the user interacts via the mouse or keyboard. Several common GUI components are listed in Fig. 12.2. In the sections that follow, we discuss each of these GUI components in detail. In the next chapter, we discuss more advanced GUI components.

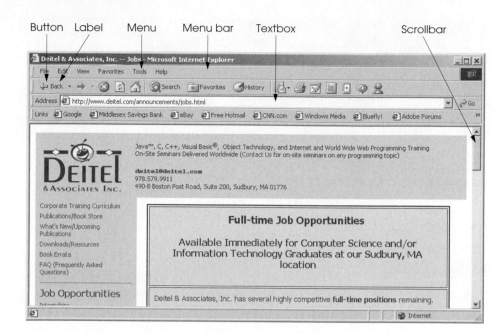

Fig. 12.1   Sample Internet Explorer window with GUI components.

Control	Description
Label	An area in which icons or uneditable text can be displayed.
TextBox	An area in which the user inputs data from the keyboard. The area also can display information.
Button	An area that triggers an event when clicked.
CheckBox	A GUI control that is either selected or not selected.
ComboBox	A drop-down list of items from which the user can make a selection, by clicking an item in the list or by typing into the box, if permitted.
ListBox	An area in which a list of items is displayed from which the user can make a selection by clicking once on any element. Multiple elements can be selected.
Panel	A container in which components can be placed.
ScrollBar	Allows the user to access a range of values that cannot normally fit in its container.

Fig. 12.2   Some basic GUI components .

12.2 Windows Forms

Windows Forms (also called *WinForms*) create GUIs for programs. A form is a graphical element that appears on the desktop. A form can be a dialog, a window or an *MDI window* (*multiple document interface window*, discussed in Chapter 13, GUI Components: Part 2). A *component* is a class that implements the ***IComponent*** *interface*, which defines the behaviors that components must implement. A *control*, such as a button or label, is a component with a graphical part. Controls are visible, whereas components, which lack graphical parts, are not.

Figure 12.3 displays the Windows Forms controls and components contained in the Visual Studio .NET **Toolbox**—the first two screens show the controls and the last screen shows the components. When the user selects a component or control, the user then can add that component or control to the form. Note that the **Pointer** (the icon at the top of the list) is not a component; rather it represents the default mouse action. Highlighting it allows the programmer to use the mouse cursor instead of adding an item. In this chapter and the next, we discuss many of these controls.

When interacting with windows, we say that the *active window* has the *focus*. The active window is the frontmost window and has a highlighted title bar. A window becomes the active window when the user clicks somewhere inside it. When a window has focus, the operating system directs user input from the keyboard and mouse to that application.

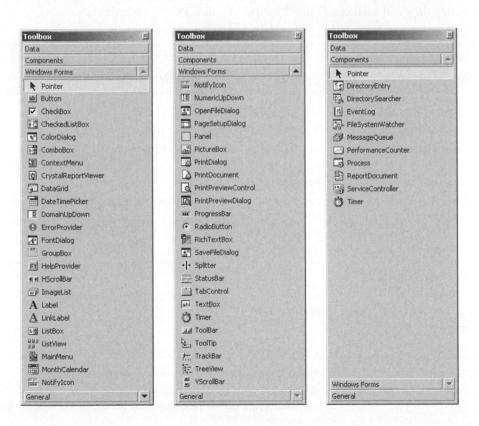

Fig. 12.3   Components and controls for Windows Forms.

The form acts as a *container* for components and controls. Controls must be added to the form using code. When we drag a control from the **Toolbox** onto the form, Visual Studio .NET generates this code for us, which instantiates the control and sets the control's basic properties. We could write the code ourselves, but it is much easier to create and modify controls using the **Toolbox** and **Properties** window, letting Visual Studio .NET handle the details. We introduced such *visual programming* earlier in the book. In the next several chapters, we build much richer GUIs through visual programming.

When the user interacts with a control by using the mouse or keyboard, events (discussed in Section 12.3) are generated, and event handlers process those events. Events typically cause something to happen in response. For example, clicking the **OK** button in a **MessageBox** generates an event. An event handler in class **MessageBox** closes the **MessageBox** in response to this event.

Each .NET Framework class (i.e., form, component and control) we present in this chapter is in the *System.Windows.Forms namespace*. Class **Form**, the basic window used by Windows applications, is fully qualified as **System.Windows.Forms.Form**. Likewise, class **Button** is actually **System.Windows.Forms.Button**.

The general design process for creating Windows applications requires creating a Windows Form, setting its properties, adding controls, setting their properties and implementing the event handlers. Figure 12.4 lists common **Form** properties and events.

Form Properties and Events	Description / Delegate and Event Arguments
Common Properties	
AcceptButton	Which button will be clicked when *Enter* is pressed.
AutoScroll	Whether scrollbars appear when needed (if data fill more than one screen).
CancelButton	Button that is clicked when the *Escape* key is pressed.
FormBorderStyle	Border of the form (e.g., **none**, **single**, **3D**, **sizable**).
Font	Font of text displayed on the form, as well as the default font of controls added to the form.
Text	Text in the form's title bar.
Common Methods	
Close	Closes form and releases all resources. A closed form cannot be reopened.
Hide	Hides form (does not release resources).
Show	Displays a hidden form.
Common Events	*(Delegate **EventHandler**, event arguments **EventArgs**)*
Load	Occurs before a form is shown. Visual Studio .NET generates a default event handler when the programmer double clicks on the form in the designer.

Fig. 12.4 Common **Form** properties and events.

Visual Studio .NET generates most GUI-related code when we create controls and event handlers. Programmers can use Visual Studio .NET to perform most of these tasks graphically, by dragging and dropping components onto the form and setting properties in the **Properties** window. In visual programming, the IDE generally maintains GUI-related code, and the programmer writes the event handlers.

12.3 Event-Handling Model

GUIs are *event driven* (i.e., they generate *events* when the program's user interacts with the GUI). Typical interactions include moving the mouse, clicking the mouse, clicking a button, typing in a textbox, selecting an item from a menu and closing a window. Event handlers are methods that process events and perform tasks. For example, consider a form that changes color when a button is clicked. When clicked, the button generates an event and passes it to the event handler, and the event-handler code changes the form's color.

Each control that can generate events has an associated delegate that defines the signature for that control's event handlers. Recall from Chapter 10 that delegates are objects that reference methods. Event delegates are *multicast* (class **MulticastDelegate**)— they contain lists of method references. Each method must have the same *signature* (i.e., the same list of parameters). In the event-handling model, delegates act as intermediaries between objects that generate events and methods that handle those events (Fig. 12.5).

Software Engineering Observation 12.1

Delegates enable classes to specify methods that will not be named or implemented until the class is instantiated. This is extremely helpful in creating event handlers. For instance, the creator of the **Form** *class does not need to name or define the method that will handle the* **Click** *event. Using delegates, the class can specify when such an event handler would be called. The programmers that create their own forms then can name and define this event handler. As long as it has been registered with the proper delegate, the method will be called at the proper time.*

Once an event is raised, every method that the delegate references is called. Every method in the delegate must have the same signature, because they are all passed the same information.

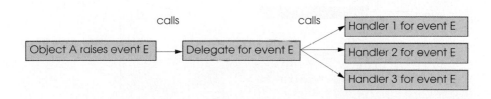

Fig. 12.5   Event-handling model using delegates.

12.3.1 Basic Event Handling

In most cases, we do not have to create our own events. Instead, we can handle the events generated by .NET controls such as buttons and text boxes. These controls already have delegates for every event they can raise. The programmer creates the event handler and registers it with the delegate—Visual Studio .NET helps with this task. In the following example, we create a form that displays a message box when clicked. Afterwards, we will analyze the event code that Visual Studio .NET generates.

First, create a new Windows application. To register and define an event handler, click the **Events** icon (the yellow lightning bolt) in the form's **Properties** window (Fig. 12.6). This window allows the programmer to access, modify and create event handlers for a control. The left panel lists the events that the object can generate. The right panel lists the registered event handlers for the corresponding event; this list is initially empty. The drop-down button indicates that multiple handlers can be registered for one event. A brief description of the event appears on the bottom of the window.

In this example, the form will take some action when clicked. Double-click the **Click** event in the **Properties** window to create an empty event handler in the program code.

```
private void FormName_Click( object sender, System.EventArgs e )
{

}
```

This is the method that will be called when the form is clicked. As a response, we will have the form display a message box. To do this, insert the statement

```
MessageBox.Show( "Form was pressed." );
```

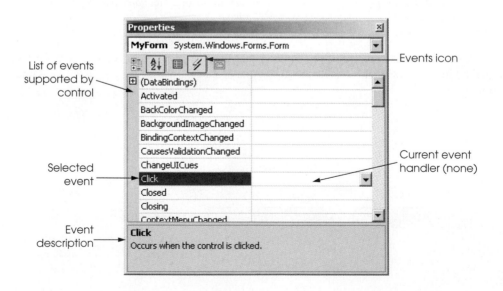

Fig. 12.6 Events section of the **Properties** window.

into the event handler to get

```
private void FormName_Click( object sender, System.EventArgs e )
{
    MessageBox.Show( "Form was pressed" );
}
```

We can now compile and execute the program, which appears in Fig. 12.7. Whenever the form is clicked, a message box appears.

We now discuss the details of the program. First, we create an event handler (lines 26–29). Every event handler must have the signature that the corresponding event delegate specifies. Event handlers are passed two object references. The first is a reference to the object that raised the event (**sender**), and the second is a reference to an event arguments object (**e**). Argument **e** is of type **EventArgs**. Class **EventArgs** is the base class for objects that contain event information.

To create the event handler, we must find the delegate's signature. When we double-click an event name in the **Properties** window, Visual Studio .NET creates a method with the proper signature. The naming convention is *ControlName_EventName*; in our case the event handler is **MyForm_Click**. If we do not use the **Properties** window, we must look up the event arguments class. Consult the documentation index under *ControlName* **class** (i.e., **Form class**) and click the **events** section (Fig. 12.8). This displays a list of all the events the class can generate. Click the name of an event to bring up its delegate, event argument type and a description (Fig. 12.9).

```
1   // Fig. 12.7: SimpleEventExample.cs
2   // Using Visual Studio .NET to create event handlers.
3
4   using System;
5   using System.Drawing;
6   using System.Collections;
7   using System.ComponentModel;
8   using System.Windows.Forms;
9   using System.Data;
10
11  // program that shows a simple event handler
12  public class MyForm : System.Windows.Forms.Form
13  {
14      private System.ComponentModel.Container components = null;
15
16      // Visual Studio .NET generated code
17
18      [STAThread]
19      static void Main()
20      {
21          Application.Run( new MyForm() );
22      }
23
```

Fig. 12.7 Simple event-handling example using visual programming. (Part 1 of 2.)

```
24        // Visual Studio .NET creates an empty handler,
25        // we write definition: show message box when form clicked
26        private void MyForm_Click( object sender, System.EventArgs e )
27        {
28            MessageBox.Show( "Form was pressed" );
29        }
30
31    } // end class MyForm
```

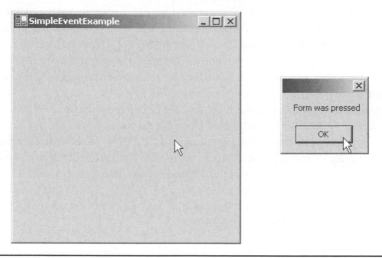

Fig. 12.7   Simple event-handling example using visual programming. (Part 2 of 2.)

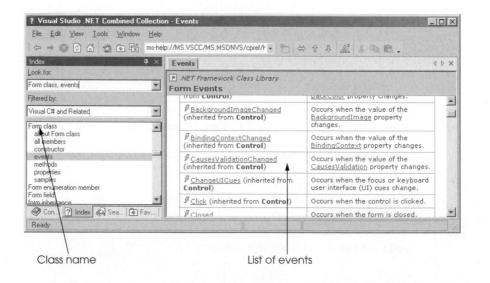

Class name   List of events

Fig. 12.8   List of **Form** events.

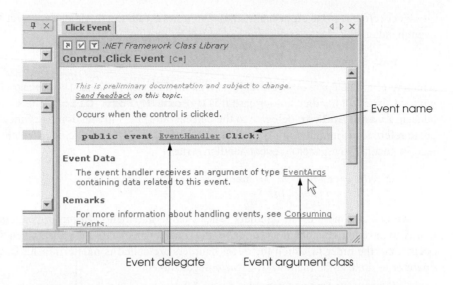

Fig. 12.9 Details of **Click** event.

The format of the event-handling method is, in general,

```
void ControlName_EventName( object sender, EventArgs e )
{
    event-handling code
}
```

where the name of the event handler is by default the name of the control, followed by an underscore (_) and the name of the event. Event handlers have return type **void** and take two arguments—an **object** (usually **sender**) and an instance of an event argument class. The differences between the various **EventArgs** classes are discussed in the following sections.

Good Programming Practice 12.1

Use the event-handler naming convention ControlName_EventName *to keep methods organized. This tells a user which event a method handles, and for which control. Visual Studio .NET uses this naming convention when creating event handlers from the **Properties** window.*

After creating the event handler, we must *register* it with the delegate object, which contains a list of event handlers to call. Registering an event handler with a delegate object involves adding the event handler to the delegate's invocation list. Controls have a *delegate reference* for each of their events—the delegate reference has the same name as the event. For example, if we are handling event *EventName* for object **myControl**, then the delegate reference is **myControl.**EventName. Visual Studio .NET registers events for us with code such as the following from method **InitializeComponent**:

```
this.Click += new System.EventHandler( this.MyForm_Click );
```

The left-hand side is the delegate reference **MyForm.Click**. (**this** refers to an object of class **MyForm**.) The delegate reference is initially empty—we must assign to it an object reference (the right-hand side). We must create a new delegate object for each event handler. We create a new delegate object by writing

new System.EventHandler(*methodName* **)**

which returns a delegate object initialized with method *methodName*. The *methodName* is the name of the event handler, in our case it is **MyForm.MyForm_Click**. The **+=** operator adds an **EventHandler** delegate to the current delegate's invocation list. Since the delegate reference is initially empty, registering the first event handler creates a delegate object. In general, to register an event handler, write

objectName.*EventName* **+= new System.EventHandler(**
MyEventHandler **);**

We can add more event handlers using similar statements. *Event multicasting* is the ability to have multiple handlers for one event. Each event handler is called when the event occurs, but the order in which the event handlers are called is indeterminate. Use the **-=** operator to remove the method from the delegate object.

Common Programming Error 12.1

Assuming that multiple event handlers registered for the same event are called in a particular order can lead to logic errors. If the order is important, register the first event handler and have it call the others in order, passing the sender and event arguments.

Software Engineering Observation 12.2

*Events for prepackaged .NET components usually have consistent naming schemes. If the event is named **EventName**, then its delegate is **EventNameEventHandler**, and the event arguments class is **EventNameEventArgs**. However, events that use class **EventArgs** use delegate **EventHandler**.*

To review: The information needed to register an event is the **EventArgs** class (a parameter for the event handler) and the **EventHandler** delegate (to register the event handler). Visual Studio .NET can create this code for us, or we can type it in ourselves. If Visual Studio .NET creates the code, the programmer does not have to deal with going through all the steps, but the programmer also does not have complete control of everything that is going on. For simple events and event handlers it is often easier to allow Visual Studio .NET to generate this code. For more complicated solutions, registering your own event handlers might be necessary. In the upcoming sections, we will indicate the **EventArgs** class and the **EventHandler** delegate for each event we cover. To find more information about a particular type of event, search the help documentation for *ClassName* **class** and refer to the **events** subcategory.

12.4 Control Properties and Layout

This section overviews properties that are common to many controls. Controls derive from class *Control* (namespace **System.Windows.Forms**). Figure 12.10 contains a list of common properties and events for class **Control**. The **Text** property specifies the text that appears on a control, which may vary depending on the context. For example, the text of a Windows Form is its title bar, and the text of a button appears on its face. The *Focus* method transfers the focus to a control. When the focus is on a control, it becomes the active control. When the *Tab* key is pressed, the **TabIndex** property determines the order in which controls are given focus. The **TabIndex** property is automatically set by Visual Studio .NET, but can be changed by the programmer. This is helpful for the user who enters information in many different locations—the user can enter information and quickly select the next control by pressing the *Tab* key. The **Enabled** property indicates whether the control can be used. Programs can set property **Enabled** to false when an option is unavailable to the user. In most cases, the control's text will appear gray (rather than black), when a control is disabled. Without having to disable a control, the control can be hidden from the user by setting the **Visible** property to **false** or by calling method **Hide**. When a control's **Visible** property is set to **false**, the control still exists, but it is not shown on the form.

Class **Control** Properties and Methods	Description
Common Properties	
BackColor	Background color of the control.
BackgroundImage	Background image of the control.
Enabled	Whether the control is enabled (i.e., if the user can interact with it). A disabled control will still be displayed, but "grayed-out"—portions of the control will become gray.
Focused	Whether a control has focus. (The control that is currently being used in some way.)
Font	**Font** used to display control's **Text**.
ForeColor	Foreground color of the control. This is usually the color used to display the control's **Text** property.
TabIndex	Tab order of the control. When the *Tab* key is pressed, the focus is moved to controls in increasing tab order. This order can be set by the programmer.
TabStop	If **true**, user can use the *Tab* key to select the control.
Text	Text associated with the control. The location and appearance varies with the type of control.
TextAlign	The alignment of the text on the control. One of three horizontal positions (left, center or right) and one of three vertical positions (top, middle or bottom).
Visible	Whether the control is visible.
Common Methods	
Focus	Transfers the focus to the control.
Hide	Hides the control (sets **Visible** to **false**).
Show	Shows the control (sets **Visible** to **true**).

Fig. 12.10 Class **Control** properties and methods.

Visual Studio .NET allows the programmer to *anchor* and *dock* controls, which help to specify the layout of controls inside a container (such as a form). Anchoring allows controls to stay a fixed distance from the sides of the container, even when the control is resized. Docking allows controls to extend themselves along the sides of their containers.

A user may want a control to appear in a certain position (top, bottom, left or right) in a form even when that form is resized. The user can specify this by *anchoring* the control to a side (top, bottom, left or right). The control then maintains a fixed distance from the side to its parent container. In most cases, the parent container is a form; however, other controls can act as a parent container.

When parent containers are resized, all controls move. Unanchored controls move relative to their original position on the form, while anchored controls move so that they will be the same distance from each side that they are anchored to. For example, in Fig. 12.11, the topmost button is anchored to the top and left sides of the parent form. When the form is resized, the anchored button moves so that it remains a constant distance from the top and left sides of the form (its parent). The unanchored button changes position as the form is resized.

Create a simple Windows application that contains two controls. Anchor one control to the right side by setting the **Anchor** property as shown in Fig. 12.12. Leave the other control unanchored. Now, resize the form by dragging the right side farther to the right. Notice that both controls move. The anchored control moves so that it is always the same distance to the right wall. The unanchored control moves so that it is in the same place on the form, relative to each side. This control will continue to be somewhat closer to whatever sides it was originally close to, but will still reposition itselft when the user resizes the application window.

Sometimes a programmer wants a control to span the entire side of the form, even when the form is resized. This is useful when we want one control to remain prevalent on the form, such as the status bar that might appear at the bottom of a program. *Docking* allows a control to spread itself along an entire side (left, right, top or bottom) of its parent container. When the parent is resized, the docked control resizes as well. In Fig. 12.13, a button is docked to the top of the form. (It lays across the top portion.) When the form is resized, the button is resized as well—the button always fills the entire top portion of the form. The `Fill` dock option effectively docks the control to all sides of its parent, which causes it to fill its entire parent. Windows Forms contain property `DockPadding`, which sets the distance from docked controls to the edge of the form. The default value is zero, causing the controls to attach to the edge of the form. The control layout properties are summarized in Fig. 12.14.

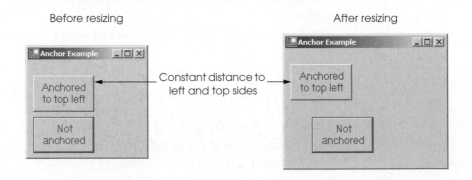

Fig. 12.11 Anchoring demonstration.

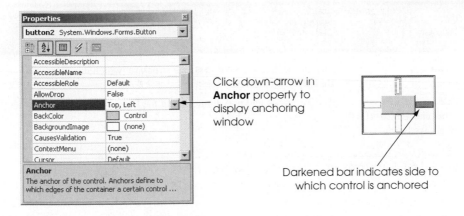

Click down-arrow in **Anchor** property to display anchoring window

Darkened bar indicates side to which control is anchored

Fig. 12.12 Manipulating the **Anchor** property of a control.

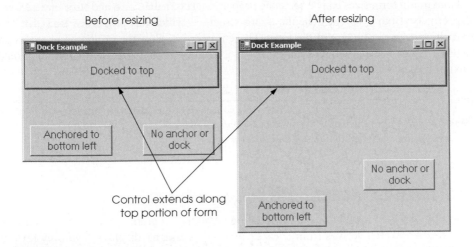

Fig. 12.13 Docking demonstration.

Common Layout Properties	Description
Common Properties	
Anchor	Side of parent container at which to anchor control—values can be combined, such as **Top, Left**.
Dock	Side of parent container to dock control—values cannot be combined.
DockPadding (for containers)	Sets the dock spacing for controls inside the container. Default is zero, so controls appear flush against the side of the container.
Location	Location of the upper left corner of the control, relative to its container.

Fig. 12.14 Class **Control** layout properties. (Part 1 of 2.)

Common Layout Properties	Description
Size	Size of the control. Takes a **Size** structure, which has properties **Height** and **Width**.
MinimumSize, **MaximumSize** (for Windows Forms)	The minimum and maximum size of the form.

Fig. 12.14 Class **Control** layout properties. (Part 2 of 2.)

The docking and anchoring options refer to the parent container, which may or may not be the form. (We learn about other parent containers later this chapter.) The minimum and maximum form sizes can be set using properties **MinimumSize** and **MaximumSize**, respectively. Both properties use the **Size** structure, which has properties **Height** and **Width**, specifying the size of the form. These properties allow the programmer to design the GUI layout for a given size range. To set a form to a fixed size, set its minimum and maximum size to the same value.

Look-and-Feel Observation 12.2

Allow Windows forms to be resized—this enables users with limited screen space or multiple applications running at once to use the application more easily. Check that the GUI layout appears consistent for all permissible form sizes.

12.5 Labels, TextBoxes and Buttons

Labels provide text instructions or information about the program. Labels are defined with class **Label**, which derives from class **Control**. A **Label** displays *read-only text*, or text that the user cannot modify. Once labels are created, programs rarely change their contents. Figure 12.15 lists common **Label** properties.

A *textbox* (class **TextBox**) is an area in which text can be either input by the user from the keyboard or displayed. A *password textbox* is a **TextBox** that hides what the user entered. As the user types in characters, the password textbox displays only a certain character (usually *****). Altering the **PasswordChar** property of a textbox makes it a password textbox and sets the appropriate character to be displayed. Deleting the value of **PasswordChar** in the **Properties** window sets the textbox back to a regular textbox. Figure 12.16 lists the common properties and events of **TextBox**es.

A *button* is a control that the user clicks to trigger a specific action. A program can use several other types of buttons, such as *checkboxes* and *radio buttons*. All the button types are derived from **ButtonBase** (namespace **System.Windows.Forms**), which defines common button features. In this section, we concentrate on the class **Button**, which is often used to initiate a command. The other button types are covered in subsequent sections. The text on the face of a **Button** is called a *button label*. Figure 12.17 lists the common properties and events of **Button**s.

Label Properties	Description / Delegate and Event Arguments
Common Properties	
Font	Thc font used by the text on the **Label**.
Text	The text to appear on the **Label**.
TextAlign	The alignment of the **Label**'s text on the control. One of three horizontal positions (**left**, **center** or **right**) and one of three vertical positions (**top**, **middle** or **bottom**).

Fig. 12.15 Label properties.

TextBox Properties and Events	Description / Delegate and Event Arguments
Common Properties	
AcceptsReturn	If **true**, pressing *Enter* creates a new line if textbox spans multiple lines. If **false**, pressing *Enter* clicks the default button of the form.
Multiline	If **true**, textbox can span multiple lines. Default is **false**.
PasswordChar	Single character to display instead of typed text, making the **TextBox** a password box. If no character is specified, **Textbox** displays the typed text.
ReadOnly	If **true**, **TextBox** has a gray background and its text cannot be edited. Default is **false**.
ScrollBars	For multiline textboxes, indicates which scrollbars appear (**none**, **horizontal**, **vertical** or **both**).
Text	The text to be displayed in the text box.
Common Events	*(Delegate **EventHandler**, event arguments **EventArgs**)*
TextChanged	Raised when text changes in **TextBox** (the user added or deleted characters). Default event when this control is double clicked in the designer.

Fig. 12.16 TextBox properties and events.

Look-and-Feel Observation 12.3

*Although **Labels**, **TextBox**es and other controls can respond to mouse-button clicks, **Button**s naturally convey this meaning. Use **Button**s (e.g., **OK**), rather than other types of controls, to initiate user actions.*

The program in Fig. 12.18 uses a **TextBox**, a **Button** and a **Label**. The user enters text into a password box and clicks the **Button**. The text then appears in the **Label**. Normally, we would not display this text—the purpose of password textboxes is to hide the text being entered by the user from anyone who may be looking over a person's shoulder.

Button properties and events	Description / Delegate and Event Arguments
Common Properties	
Text	Text displayed on the **Button** face.
Common Events	*(Delegate **EventHandler**, event arguments **EventArgs**)*
Click	Raised when user clicks the control. Default event when this control is double clicked in the designer.

Fig. 12.17 Button properties and events.

```
1   // Fig. 12.18: LabelTextBoxButtonTest.cs
2   // Using a Textbox, Label and Button to display
3   // the hidden text in a password box.
4
5   using System;
6   using System.Drawing;
7   using System.Collections;
8   using System.ComponentModel;
9   using System.Windows.Forms;
10  using System.Data;
11
12  // namespace contains our form to display hidden text
13  namespace LabelTextBoxButtonTest
14  {
15     /// <summary>
16     /// form that creates a password textbox and
17     /// a label to display textbox contents
18     /// </summary>
19     public class LabelTextBoxButtonTest :
20        System.Windows.Forms.Form
21     {
22        private System.Windows.Forms.Button displayPasswordButton;
23        private System.Windows.Forms.Label displayPasswordLabel;
24        private System.Windows.Forms.TextBox inputPasswordTextBox;
25
26        /// <summary>
27        /// Required designer variable.
28        /// </summary>
29        private System.ComponentModel.Container components = null;
30
31        // default contructor
32        public LabelTextBoxButtonTest()
33        {
34           InitializeComponent();
35        }
36
```

Fig. 12.18 Program to display hidden text in a password box. (Part 1 of 4.)

```
37          /// <summary>
38          /// Clean up any resources being used.
39          /// </summary>
40          protected override void Dispose( bool disposing )
41          {
42             if ( disposing )
43             {
44                if ( components != null )
45                {
46                   components.Dispose();
47                }
48             }
49
50             base.Dispose( disposing );
51          }
52
53          #region Windows Form Designer generated code
54          /// <summary>
55          /// Required method for Designer support - do not modify
56          /// the contents of this method with the code editor.
57          /// </summary>
58          private void InitializeComponent()
59          {
60             this.displayPasswordButton =
61                new System.Windows.Forms.Button();
62             this.inputPasswordTextBox =
63                new System.Windows.Forms.TextBox();
64             this.displayPasswordLabel =
65                new System.Windows.Forms.Label();
66             this.SuspendLayout();
67
68             //
69             // displayPasswordButton
70             //
71             this.displayPasswordButton.Location =
72                new System.Drawing.Point( 96, 96 );
73             this.displayPasswordButton.Name =
74                "displayPasswordButton";
75             this.displayPasswordButton.TabIndex = 1;
76             this.displayPasswordButton.Text = "Show Me";
77             this.displayPasswordButton.Click +=
78                new System.EventHandler(
79                this.displayPasswordButton_Click );
80
81             //
82             // inputPasswordTextBox
83             //
84             this.inputPasswordTextBox.Location =
85                new System.Drawing.Point( 16, 16 );
86             this.inputPasswordTextBox.Name =
87                "inputPasswordTextBox";
88             this.inputPasswordTextBox.PasswordChar = '*';
```

Fig. 12.18 Program to display hidden text in a password box. (Part 2 of 4.)

```
89              this.inputPasswordTextBox.Size =
90                 new System.Drawing.Size( 264, 20 );
91              this.inputPasswordTextBox.TabIndex = 0;
92              this.inputPasswordTextBox.Text = "";
93
94              //
95              // displayPasswordLabel
96              //
97              this.displayPasswordLabel.BorderStyle =
98                 System.Windows.Forms.BorderStyle.Fixed3D;
99              this.displayPasswordLabel.Location =
100                new System.Drawing.Point( 16, 48 );
101             this.displayPasswordLabel.Name =
102                "displayPasswordLabel";
103             this.displayPasswordLabel.Size =
104                new System.Drawing.Size( 264, 23 );
105             this.displayPasswordLabel.TabIndex = 2;
106
107             //
108             // LabelTextBoxButtonTest
109             //
110             this.AutoScaleBaseSize =
111                new System.Drawing.Size( 5, 13 );
112             this.ClientSize =
113                new System.Drawing.Size( 292, 133 );
114             this.Controls.AddRange(
115                new System.Windows.Forms.Control[] {
116                   this.displayPasswordLabel,
117                   this.inputPasswordTextBox,
118                   this.displayPasswordButton});
119             this.Name = "LabelTextBoxButtonTest";
120             this.Text = "LabelTextBoxButtonTest";
121             this.ResumeLayout( false );
122
123          } // end method InitializeComponent
124
125       // end collapsible region started on line 53
126       #endregion
127
128       /// <summary>
129       /// The main entry point for the application.
130       /// </summary>
131       [STAThread]
132       static void Main()
133       {
134          Application.Run( new LabelTextBoxButtonTest() );
135       }
136
137       // display user input on label
138       protected void displayPasswordButton_Click(
139          object sender, System.EventArgs e )
140       {
```

Fig. 12.18 Program to display hidden text in a password box. (Part 3 of 4.)

```
141              // text has not changed
142              displayPasswordLabel.Text =
143                  inputPasswordTextBox.Text;
144          }
145
146      } // end class LabelTextBoxButtonTest
147
148  } // end namespace LabelTextBoxButtonTest
```

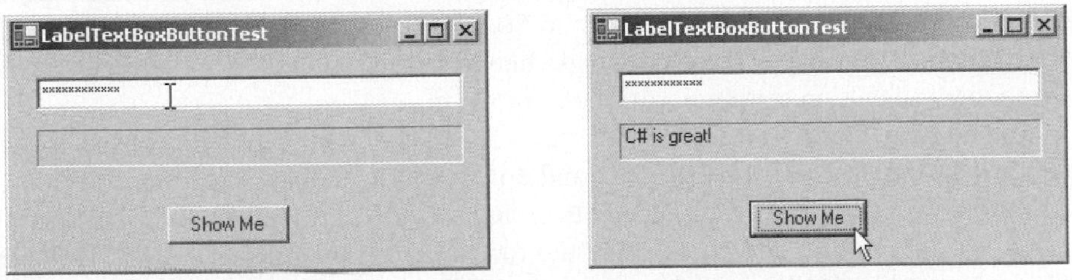

Fig. 12.18 Program to display hidden text in a password box. (Part 4 of 4.)

First, we create the GUI by dragging the components (a **Button**, a **Label** and a **TextBox**) onto the form. Once the components are positioned, we change their names in the **Properties** window (by setting the **(Name)** property) from the default values—**textBox1**, **label1**, **button1**—to the more descriptive **displayPasswordLabel**, **inputPasswordTextBox** and **displayPasswordButton**. Visual Studio .NET creates the code and places it inside method **InitializeComponent**. Now that the reader has an understanding of object-oriented programming, we can mention that the **(Name)** property is not really a property, but a means of changing the variable name of the object reference. For convenience, this value can be changed in the **Properties** window of Visual Studio .NET. This value, however, is not actually manipulated by a property.

We then set **displayPasswordLabel**'s **Text** property to "**Show Me**" and clear the **Text** of **displayPasswordLabel** and **inputPasswordTextBox** so that they are initially blank when the program runs. The **BorderStyle** property of **displayPasswordLabel** is set to **Fixed3D**, to give our **Label** a three-dimensional appearance. Notice that **TextBox**es have their **BorderStyle** property set to **Fixed3D** by default. The password character is set by assigning the asterisk character (*****) to the **PasswordChar** property. This property can take only one character.

Let us examine the code that Visual Studio .NET generates by right-clicking the design and selecting **View Code**. This is important because not every change can be made in the **Properties** window.

We have learned in previous chapters that Visual Studio .NET adds comments to our code. These comments appear throughout the code, such as on lines 15–18. In future examples we remove some of these generated comments to make programs more concise and readable (unless they illustrate a capability we have not yet covered).

Visual Studio .NET inserts declarations for the controls we add to the form (lines 22–24), namely, the **Label**, **TextBox** and **Button**. The IDE manages these declarations for us, making it easy to add and remove controls. Line 29 declares reference **components**—an array to hold the components that we add. We are not using any components in this program (only controls), and thus the reference is **null**.

The constructor for our form is created for us—it calls method **InitializeComponent**. Method **InitializeComponent** creates the components and controls in the form and sets their properties. The usual "to do" comments generated by Visual Studio .NET have been removed, because there is no more code that needs to be added to the constructor. When they existed, they would have appeared as a reminder in the **Task List** window. Method **Dispose** cleans up allocated resources, but is not called explicitly in our programs.

Lines 53–126 contain a collapsible region that encloses our **InitializeComponent** method. Recall that the **#region** and **#endregion** preprocessor directives allow the programmer to collapse code to a single line in Visual Studio .NET. This enables the programmer to focus on certain portions of a program.

Method **InitializeComponent** (lines 58–123) sets the properties of the controls added to the form (the **TextBox**, **Label** and **Button**). Lines 60–66 create new objects for the controls we add (a **Button**, a **TextBox** and a **Label**). Lines 86–88 and 92 set the **Name**, **PasswordChar** and **Text** properties for **inputPasswordTextBox**. The **TabIndex** property is initially set by Visual Studio .NET, but can be changed by the developer.

The comment on lines 54–57 advises us not to modify the contents of method **InitializeComponent**. We have altered it slightly for formatting purposes in this book, but this is not recommended. We have done this only so that the reader is able to see the important portions of the code. Visual Studio .NET examines this method to create the design view of the code. If we change this method, Visual Studio .NET may not recognize our modifications and show the design improperly. It is important to note that the design view is based on the code, and not vice versa.

Testing and Debugging Tip 12.1

*To keep the design view accurate, do not modify the code in method **InitializeComponent**. Make changes in the design window or property window.*

The **Click** event is triggered when a control is clicked. We create the handler using the procedure described in Section 12.3.1. We want to respond to the **Click** event **displayPasswordButton**, so we double click it in the **Events** window. (Alternately, we could simply have clicked on **displayPasswordButton**.) This creates an empty event handler named **displayPasswordButton_Click** (line 138). Visual Studio .NET also registers the event handler for us (line 77–79). It adds the event handler to the **Click** event, using the **EventHandler** delegate. We must then implement the event handler. Whenever **displayPasswordButton** is clicked, this method is called and displays **inputPasswordTextBox**'s text on **displayPasswordLabel**. Even though **inputPasswordTextBox** displays all asterisks, it still retains its input text in its **Text** property. To show the text, we set **displayPasswordLabel**'s **Text** to **inputPasswordTextBox**'s **Text** (line 142–143). The user must program this line manually. When **displayPasswordButton** is clicked, the **Click** event is triggered, and the event handler **displayPasswordButton_Click** runs (updating **displayPasswordLabel**).

Visual Studio .NET generated most of the code in this program. It simplifies tasks such as creating controls, setting their properties and registering event handlers. However, we should be aware of how this is done—in several programs we may set properties ourselves, using code.

12.6 GroupBoxes and Panels

GroupBoxes and *Panels* arrange components on a GUI. For example, buttons related to a particular task can be placed inside a **GroupBox** or **Panel** inside the Visual Studio .NET form designer. All these buttons move together when the **GroupBox** or **Panel** is moved.

The main difference between the two classes is that **GroupBox**es can display a caption, and **Panel**s can have scrollbars. The scrollbars allow the user to view additional controls inside the **Panel** by scrolling the visible area. **GroupBox**es have thin borders by default, but **Panel**s can be set to have borders by changing their **BorderStyle** property.

Look-and-Feel Observation 12.4
Panels and GroupBoxes can contain other Panels and GroupBoxes.

Look-and-Feel Observation 12.5
Organize the GUI by anchoring and docking controls (of similar function) inside a GroupBox or Panel. The GroupBox or Panel then can be anchored or docked inside a form. This divides controls into functional "groups" that can be arranged easily.

To create a **GroupBox**, drag it from the toolbar and place it on a form. Create new controls and place them inside the **GroupBox**, causing them to become part of this class. These controls are added to the **GroupBox**'s **Controls** property. The **GroupBox**'s **Text** property determines its caption. The following tables list the common properties of **GroupBox**es (Fig. 12.19) and **Panel**s (Fig. 12.20).

GroupBox Properties	Description
Common Properties	
Controls	The controls that the **GroupBox** contains.
Text	Text displayed on the top portion of the **GroupBox** (its caption).

Fig. 12.19 GroupBox properties.

Panel Properties	Description
Common Properties	
AutoScroll	Whether scrollbars appear when the **Panel** is too small to hold its controls. Default is **false**.
BorderStyle	Border of the **Panel** (default **None**; other options are **Fixed3D** and **FixedSingle**).
Controls	The controls that the **Panel** contains.

Fig. 12.20 Panel properties.

To create a **Panel**, drag it onto the form and add components to it. To enable the scrollbars, set the **Panel**'s **AutoScroll** property to **true**. If the **Panel** is resized and cannot hold its controls, scrollbars appear (Fig. 12.21). These scrollbars then can be used to view all the components in the **Panel** (both when running and designing the form). This allows the programmer to see the GUI exactly as it appears to the client.

Look-and-Feel Observation 12.6
*Use **Panel**s with scrollbars to avoid cluttering a GUI and to reduce the GUI's size.*

The program in Fig. 12.22 uses a **GroupBox** and a **Panel** to arrange buttons. These buttons change the text on a **Label**.

The **GroupBox** (named **mainGroupBox**) has two buttons, **hiButton** (labeled **Hi**) and **byeButton** (labeled **Bye**). The **Panel** (named **mainPanel**) has two buttons as well, **leftButton** (labeled **Far Left**) and **rightButton** (labeled **Far Right**). The **mainPanel** control also has its **AutoScroll** property set to **True**, allowing scrollbars to appear if needed (i.e., if the contents of the **Panel** take up more space than the **Panel** itself). The **Label** (named **messageLabel**) is initially blank.

The event handlers for the four buttons are located in lines 36–61. To create an empty **Click** event handler, double click the button in design mode (instead of using the **Events** window). We add a line in each handler to change the text of **messageLabel**.

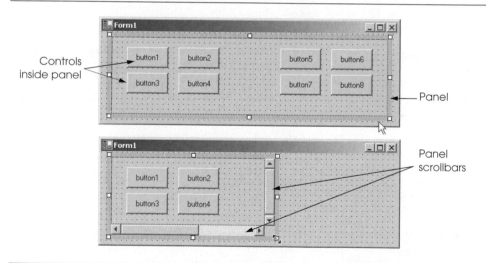

Fig. 12.21 Creating a **Panel** with scrollbars.

```
1   // Fig. 12.22: GroupBoxPanelExample.cs
2   // Using GroupBoxes and Panels to hold buttons.
3
4   using System;
5   using System.Drawing;
6   using System.Collections;
```

Fig. 12.22 Using **GroupBox**es and **Panel**s to arrange **Button**s. (Part 1 of 3.)

```
7   using System.ComponentModel;
8   using System.Windows.Forms;
9   using System.Data;
10
11  /// form to display a groupbox versus a panel
12  public class GroupBoxPanelExample : System.Windows.Forms.Form
13  {
14      private System.Windows.Forms.Button hiButton;
15      private System.Windows.Forms.Button byeButton;
16      private System.Windows.Forms.Button leftButton;
17      private System.Windows.Forms.Button rightButton;
18
19      private System.Windows.Forms.GroupBox mainGroupBox;
20      private System.Windows.Forms.Label messageLabel;
21      private System.Windows.Forms.Panel mainPanel;
22
23      private System.ComponentModel.Container components = null;
24
25      // Visual Studio .NET-generated Dispose method
26
27      [STAThread]
28      static void Main()
29      {
30          Application.Run( new GroupBoxPanelExample() );
31      }
32
33      // event handlers to change messageLabel
34
35      // event handler for hi button
36      private void hiButton_Click(
37          object sender, System.EventArgs e )
38      {
39          messageLabel.Text= "Hi pressed";
40      }
41
42      // event handler for bye button
43      private void byeButton_Click(
44          object sender, System.EventArgs e )
45      {
46          messageLabel.Text = "Bye pressed";
47      }
48
49      // event handler for far left button
50      private void leftButton_Click(
51          object sender, System.EventArgs e )
52      {
53          messageLabel.Text = "Far left pressed";
54      }
55
56      // event handler for far right button
57      private void rightButton_Click(
58          object sender, System.EventArgs e )
59      {
```

Fig. 12.22 Using **GroupBox**es and **Panel**s to arrange **Button**s. (Part 2 of 3.)

```
60            messageLabel.Text = "Far right pressed";
61      }
62
63   } // end class GroupBoxPanelExample
```

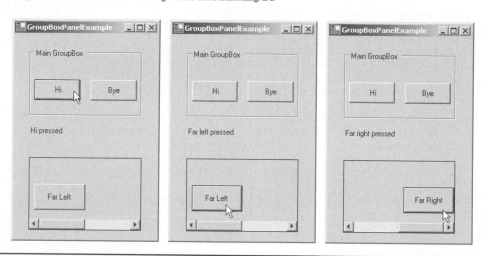

Fig. 12.22 Using **GroupBox**es and **Panel**s to arrange **Button**s. (Part 3 of 3.)

12.7 CheckBoxes and RadioButtons

Visual C# has two types of *state buttons*—***CheckBox*** and ***RadioButton***—that can be in the on/off or true/false state. Classes **CheckBox** and **RadioButton** are derived from class **ButtonBase**. A **RadioButton** is different from a **CheckBox** in that there are normally several **RadioButton**s grouped together, and only one of the **RadioButton**s in the group can be selected (true) at any time.

A checkbox is a small white square that can be blank or contain a checkmark. When a checkbox is selected, a black checkmark appears in the box. There are no restrictions on how checkboxes are used: Any number may be selected at a time. The text that appears alongside a checkbox is referred to as the *checkbox label*. A list of common properties and events of class **Checkbox** appears in Fig. 12.23.

CheckBox events and properties	Description / Delegate and Event Arguments
Common Properties	
Checked	Whether the **CheckBox** has been checked.
CheckState	Whether the **CheckBox** is checked (contains a black checkmark) or unchecked (blank). An enumeration with values **Checked**, **Unchecked** or **Indeterminate**.
Text	Text displayed to the right of the **CheckBox** (called the label).

Fig. 12.23 CheckBox properties and events. (Part 1 of 2.)

CheckBox events and properties	Description / Delegate and Event Arguments
Common Events	*(Delegate* **EventHandler***, event arguments* **EventArgs***)*
CheckedChanged	Raised every time the **CheckBox** is either checked or unchecked. Default event when this control is double clicked in the designer.
CheckState-Changed	Raised when the **CheckState** property changes.

Fig. 12.23 CheckBox properties and events. (Part 2 of 2.)

The program in Fig. 12.24 allows the user to select a **CheckBox** to change the font style of a **Label**. One **CheckBox** applies a bold style, the other an italic style. If both checkboxes are selected, the style of the font is bold and italic. When the program initially executes, neither **CheckBox** is checked.

The first **CheckBox**, named **boldCheckBox**, has its **Text** property set to **Bold**. The other **CheckBox** is named **italicCheckBox** and is labeled **Italic**. The **Label**, named **outputLabel**, is labeled **Watch the font style change**.

```
1   // Fig. 12.24: CheckBoxTest.cs
2   // Using CheckBoxes to toggle italic and bold styles.
3
4   using System;
5   using System.Drawing;
6   using System.Collections;
7   using System.ComponentModel;
8   using System.Windows.Forms;
9   using System.Data;
10
11  /// form contains checkboxes to allow
12  /// the user to modify sample text
13  public class CheckBoxTest : System.Windows.Forms.Form
14  {
15      private System.Windows.Forms.CheckBox boldCheckBox;
16      private System.Windows.Forms.CheckBox italicCheckBox;
17
18      private System.Windows.Forms.Label outputLabel;
19
20      private System.ComponentModel.Container components = null;
21
22      // Visual Studio .NET-generated Dispose method
23
24      /// The main entry point for the application.
25      [STAThread]
26      static void Main()
27      {
28          Application.Run( new CheckBoxTest() );
29      }
```

Fig. 12.24 Using **CheckBox**es to change font styles. (Part 1 of 2.)

```
30
31        // make text bold if not bold,
32        // if already bold make not bold
33        private void boldCheckBox_CheckedChanged(
34           object sender, System.EventArgs e )
35        {
36           outputLabel.Font =
37              new Font( outputLabel.Font.Name,
38              outputLabel.Font.Size,
39              outputLabel.Font.Style ^ FontStyle.Bold );
40        }
41
42        // make text italic if not italic,
43        // if already italic make not italic
44        private void italicCheckBox_CheckedChanged(
45           object sender, System.EventArgs e )
46        {
47           outputLabel.Font =
48              new Font( outputLabel.Font.Name,
49              outputLabel.Font.Size,
50              outputLabel.Font.Style ^ FontStyle.Italic );
51        }
52
53     } // end class CheckBoxTest
```

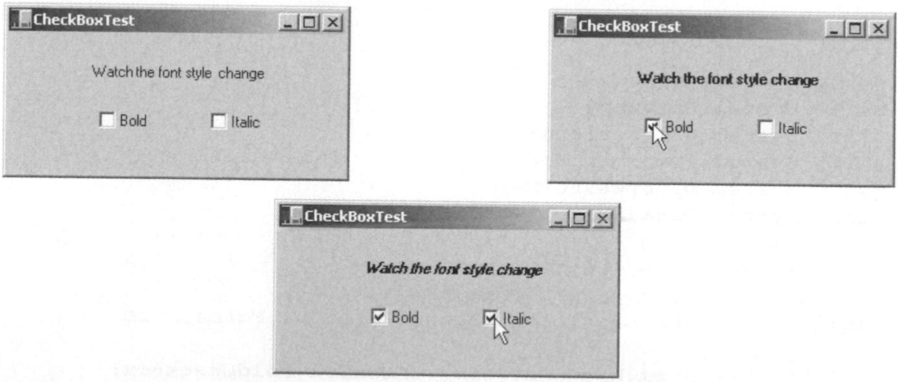

Fig. 12.24 Using **CheckBox**es to change font styles. (Part 2 of 2.)

After creating the components, we define their event handlers. Double clicking **bold-CheckBox** creates and registers an empty **CheckedChanged** event handler. To understand the code added to the event handler, we first discuss **outputLabel**'S **Font** property.

To change the font, the **Font** property must be set to a **Font** object. The **Font** constructor we use takes the font name, size and style. The first two arguments make use of **outputLabel**'s **Font** object, namely, **outputLabel.Font.Name** and **output-Label.Font.Size** (lines 37–38). The style is a member of the **FontStyle** enumeration, which contains the font styles **Regular**, **Bold**, **Italic**, **Strikeout** and **Underline**. (The **Strikeout** style displays text with a line through it, the **Under-line** style displays text with a line below it.) A **Font** object's **Style** property is set when the **Font** object is created—the **Style** property itself is read-only.

Styles can be combined using *bitwise operators*, or operators that perform manipulation on bits. Recall from Chapter 1 that all data are represented on the computer as a series of 0's and 1's. Each 0 or 1 is called a bit. Actions are taken and data are modified using these bit values. In this program, we need to set the font style so that the text will appear bold if it was not bold originally, and vice versa. Notice that on line 39 we use the bitwise XOR operator (^) to do this. Applying this operator to two bits does the following: If exactly 1 one of the corresponding bits is 1, set the result to 1. By using the ^ operator as we did on line 39, we are setting the bit values for bold in the same way. The operand on the right (**FontStyle.Bold**) always has bit values set to bold. The operand on the left, then (**outputLabel.Font.Style**) must not be bold for the resulting style to be bold. (Remember for XOR, if one value is set to 1, the other must be 0, or the result will not be 1.) If **outputLable.Font.Style** is bold, then the resulting style will not be bold. This operator also allows us to combine the styles. For instance, if the text were originally italicized, it would now be italicized and bold, rather than just bold.

We could have explicitly tested for the current style and changed it according to what we needed. For example, in the method **boldCheckBox_CheckChanged** we could have tested for the regular style, made it bold, tested for the bold style, made it regular, tested for the italic style, made it bold italic, or the italic bold style and made it italic. However, this method has a drawback—for every new style we add, we double the number of combinations. To add a checkbox for underline, we would have to test for eight possible styles. To add a checkbox for strikeout as well, we would have 16 tests in each event handler. By using the bitwise XOR operator, we save ourselves from this trouble. Each new style needs only a single statement in its event handler. In addition, styles can be removed easily, removing their handler. If we tested for every condition, we would have to remove the handler, and all the unnecessary test conditions in the other handlers.

Radio buttons (defined with class ***RadioButton***) are similar to checkboxes, because they also have two states—*selected* and *not selected* (also called *deselected*). However, radio buttons normally appear as a *group* in which only one radio button can be selected at a time. Selecting a different radio button in the group forces all other radio buttons in the group to be deselected. Radio buttons represent a set of *mutually exclusive* options (i.e., a set in which multiple options cannot be selected at the same time).

Look-and-Feel Observation 12.7

*Use **RadioButton**s when the user should choose only one option in a group.*

Look-and-Feel Observation 12.8

*Use **CheckBox**es when the user should be able to choose many options in a group.*

All radio buttons added to a form become part of the same group. To create new groups, radio buttons must be added to **GroupBox**es or **Panel**s. The common properties and events of class **RadioButton** are listed in Fig. 12.25.

Software Engineering Observation 12.3

*Forms, **GroupBox**es, and **Panel**s can act as logical groups for radio buttons. The radio buttons within each group will be mutually exclusive to each other, but not to radio buttons in different groups.*

RadioButton properties and events	Description / Delegate and Event Arguments
Common Properties	
Checked	Whether the **RadioButton** is checked.
Text	Text displayed to the right of the **RadioButton** (called the label).
Common Events	*(Delegate **EventHandler**, event arguments **EventArgs**)*
Click	Raised when user clicks the control.
CheckedChanged	Raised every time the **RadioButton** is checked or unchecked. Default event when this control is double clicked in the designer.

Fig. 12.25 **RadioButton** properties and events.

The program in Fig. 12.26 uses radio buttons to select the options for a **MessageBox**. Users select the attributes they want then press the display button, which causes the **MessageBox** to appear. A **Label** in the lower-left corner shows the result of the **MessageBox** (**Yes**, **No**, **Cancel**, etc.). The different **MessageBox** icon and button types have been displayed in tables in Chapter 5, Control Structures: Part 2.

```
1   // Fig. 12.26: RadioButtonsTest.cs
2   // Using RadioButtons to set message window options.
3
4   using System;
5   using System.Drawing;
6   using System.Collections;
7   using System.ComponentModel;
8   using System.Windows.Forms;
9   using System.Data;
10
11  /// form contains several radio buttons--user chooses one
12  /// from each group to create a custom MessageBox
13  public class RadioButtonsTest : System.Windows.Forms.Form
14  {
15      private System.Windows.Forms.Label promptLabel;
16      private System.Windows.Forms.Label displayLabel;
17      private System.Windows.Forms.Button displayButton;
18
19      private System.Windows.Forms.RadioButton questionButton;
20      private System.Windows.Forms.RadioButton informationButton;
21      private System.Windows.Forms.RadioButton exclamationButton;
22      private System.Windows.Forms.RadioButton errorButton;
23      private System.Windows.Forms.RadioButton retryCancelButton;
24      private System.Windows.Forms.RadioButton yesNoButton;
25      private System.Windows.Forms.RadioButton yesNoCancelButton;
26      private System.Windows.Forms.RadioButton okCancelButton;
27      private System.Windows.Forms.RadioButton okButton;
```

Fig. 12.26 Using **RadioButton**s to set message-window options. (Part 1 of 5.)

```
28      private System.Windows.Forms.RadioButton
29         abortRetryIgnoreButton;
30
31      private System.Windows.Forms.GroupBox groupBox2;
32      private System.Windows.Forms.GroupBox groupBox1;
33
34      private MessageBoxIcon iconType = MessageBoxIcon.Error;
35      private MessageBoxButtons buttonType =
36         MessageBoxButtons.OK;
37
38      /// The main entry point for the application.
39      [STAThread]
40      static void Main()
41      {
42         Application.Run( new RadioButtonsTest() );
43      }
44
45      // change button based on option chosen by sender
46      private void buttonType_CheckedChanged(
47         object sender, System.EventArgs e )
48      {
49         if ( sender == okButton ) // display OK button
50            buttonType = MessageBoxButtons.OK;
51
52         // display OK and Cancel buttons
53         else if ( sender == okCancelButton )
54            buttonType = MessageBoxButtons.OKCancel;
55
56         // display Abort, Retry and Ignore buttons
57         else if ( sender == abortRetryIgnoreButton )
58            buttonType = MessageBoxButtons.AbortRetryIgnore;
59
60         // display Yes, No and Cancel buttons
61         else if ( sender == yesNoCancelButton )
62            buttonType = MessageBoxButtons.YesNoCancel;
63
64         // display Yes and No buttons
65         else if ( sender == yesNoButton )
66            buttonType = MessageBoxButtons.YesNo;
67
68         // only one option left--display
69         // Retry and Cancel buttons
70         else
71            buttonType = MessageBoxButtons.RetryCancel;
72
73      } // end method buttonType_CheckedChanged
74
75      // change icon based on option chosen by sender
76      private void iconType_CheckedChanged(
77         object sender, System.EventArgs e )
78      {
79         if ( sender == errorButton ) // display error icon
80            iconType = MessageBoxIcon.Error;
```

Fig. 12.26 Using **RadioButton**s to set message-window options. (Part 2 of 5.)

```
81
82          // display exclamation point
83          else if ( sender == exclamationButton )
84             iconType = MessageBoxIcon.Exclamation;
85
86          // display information icon
87          else if ( sender == informationButton )
88             iconType = MessageBoxIcon.Information;
89
90          else // only one option left--display question mark
91             iconType = MessageBoxIcon.Question;
92
93       } // end method iconType_CheckedChanged
94
95       // display MessageBox and button user pressed
96       protected void displayButton_Click(
97          object sender, System.EventArgs e )
98       {
99          DialogResult result =
100            MessageBox.Show( "This is Your Custom MessageBox.",
101            "Custom MessageBox", buttonType, iconType, 0, 0 );
102
103         // check for dialog result and display it in label
104         switch ( result )
105         {
106            case DialogResult.OK:
107               displayLabel.Text = "OK was pressed.";
108               break;
109
110            case DialogResult.Cancel:
111               displayLabel.Text = "Cancel was pressed.";
112               break;
113
114            case DialogResult.Abort:
115               displayLabel.Text = "Abort was pressed.";
116               break;
117
118            case DialogResult.Retry:
119               displayLabel.Text = "Retry was pressed.";
120               break;
121
122            case DialogResult.Ignore:
123               displayLabel.Text = "Ignore was pressed.";
124               break;
125
126            case DialogResult.Yes:
127               displayLabel.Text = "Yes was pressed.";
128               break;
129
130            case DialogResult.No:
131               displayLabel.Text = "No was pressed.";
132               break;
133
```

Fig. 12.26 Using **RadioButton**s to set message-window options. (Part 3 of 5.)

```
134              } // end switch
135
136        } // end method displayButton_Click
137
138  } // end class RadioButtonsTest
```

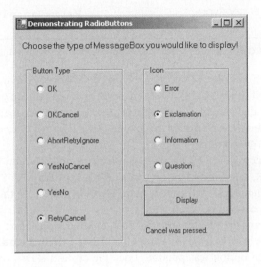

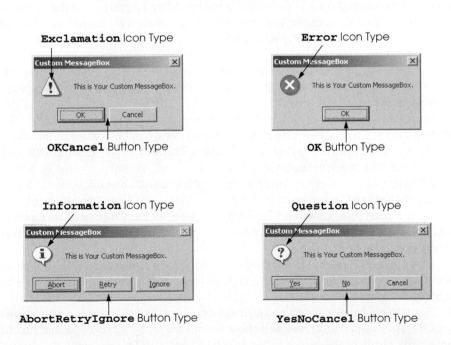

Fig. 12.26 Using **RadioButton**s to set message-window options. (Part 4 of 5.)

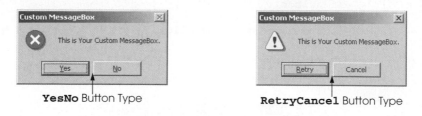

YesNo Button Type   **RetryCancel** Button Type

Fig. 12.26 Using **RadioButton**s to set message-window options. (Part 5 of 5.)

To store the user's choice of options, the objects **iconType** and **buttonType** are created and initialized (lines 34–36). Object **iconType** is a **MessageBoxIcon** enumeration that can have values **Asterisk**, **Error**, **Exclamation**, **Hand**, **Information**, **Question**, **Stop** and **Warning**. In this example we use only **Error**, **Exclamation**, **Information** and **Question**.

Object **buttonType** is a **MessageBoxButton** enumeration with values **Abort-RetryIgnore**, **OK**, **OKCancel**, **RetryCancel**, **YesNo** and **YesNoCancel**. The name indicates which buttons will appear in the **MessageBox**. In this example we use all **MessageBoxButton** enumeration values.

Two **GroupBox**es are created, one for each enumeration. Their captions are **Button Type** and **Icon**. One label is used to prompt the user (**promptLabel**), while the other is used to display which button was pressed, once the custom **MessageBox** has been displayed (**displayLabel**). There is also a button (**displayButton**) that displays the text **Display**. **RadioButton**s are created for the enumeration options, with their labels set appropriately. The radio buttons are grouped, thus only one option can be selected from each **GroupBox**.

For event handling, one event handler exists for all the radio buttons in **groupBox1**, and another for all the radio buttons in **groupBox2**. Each radio button generates a **CheckedChanged** event when clicked.

Remember, to set the event handler for an event, use the events section of the **Properties** window. Create a new **CheckedChanged** event handler for one of the radio buttons in **buttonTypeGroupBox** and rename it **buttonType_CheckedChanged**. Then set the **CheckedChanged** event handlers for all the radio buttons in **buttonTypeGroupBox** to method **buttonType_CheckedChanged**. Create a second **CheckedChanged** event handler for a radio button in **iconTypeGroupBox** and rename it **iconType_CheckedChanged**. Finally, set the **CheckedChanged** event handlers for the radio buttons in **iconTypeGroupBox** to method **iconType_CheckedChanged**.

Both handlers compare the **sender** object with every radio button to determine which button was selected. Depending on the radio button selected, either **iconType** or **buttonType** changes (lines 46–93).

The **Click** handler for **displayButton** (lines 96–136) creates a **MessageBox** (lines 99–101). Some of the **MessageBox** options are set by **iconType** and **buttonType**. The result of the message box is a **DialogResult** enumeration, with values **Abort**, **Cancel**, **Ignore**, **No**, **None**, **OK**, **Retry** or **Yes**. The **switch** statement on lines 104–134 tests for the result and sets **displayLabel.Text** appropriately.

12.8 PictureBoxes

A picture box (class **PictureBox**) displays an image. The image, set by an object of class **Image**, can be in a bitmap (**.bmp**), **.gif**, **.jpg**, icon or metafile format. (Images and multimedia are discussed in Chapter 16, Graphics and Multimedia.) *GIF (Graphics Interchange Format)* and *JPEG (Joint Photographic Expert Group)* files are widely used file formats.

The **Image** property sets the **Image** object to use, and the **SizeMode** property sets how the image is displayed (**Normal**, **StretchImage**, **AutoSize** or **CenterImage**). Figure 12.27 describes the important properties and events of class **PictureBox**.

The program in Fig. 12.28 uses **PictureBox imagePictureBox** to display one of three bitmap images—**image0**, **image1** or **image2**. They are located in the directory **images** (as usual, located in the **bin/debug** directory of our project), where the executable file is located. Whenever the **imagePictureBox** is clicked, the image changes. The **Label** (named **promptLabel**) on the top of the form includes the instructions **Click On Picture Box to View Images**.

PictureBox properties and events	Description / Delegate and Event Arguments
Common Properties	
Image	Image to display in the **PictureBox**.
SizeMode	Enumeration that controls image sizing and positioning. Values **Normal** (default), **StretchImage**, **AutoSize** and **CenterImage**. **Normal** puts image in top-left corner of **PictureBox** and **CenterImage** puts image in middle. (Both cut off image if too large.) **StretchImage** resizes image to fit in **PictureBox**. **AutoSize** resizes **PictureBox** to hold image.
Common Events	*(Delegate **EventHandler**, event arguments **EventArgs**)*
Click	Raised when user clicks the control. Default event when this control is double clicked in the designer.

Fig. 12.27 **PictureBox** properties and events.

```
1   // Fig. 12.28: PictureBoxTest.cs
2   // Using a PictureBox to display images.
3
4   using System;
5   using System.Drawing;
6   using System.Collections;
7   using System.ComponentModel;
8   using System.Windows.Forms;
9   using System.Data;
10  using System.IO;
11
```

Fig. 12.28 Using a **PictureBox** to display images. (Part 1 of 2.)

```
12   /// form to display different images when clicked
13   public class PictureBoxTest : System.Windows.Forms.Form
14   {
15      private System.Windows.Forms.PictureBox imagePictureBox;
16      private System.Windows.Forms.Label promptLabel;
17
18      private int imageNum = -1;
19
20      /// The main entry point for the application.
21      [STAThread]
22      static void Main()
23      {
24         Application.Run( new PictureBoxTest() );
25      }
26
27      // change image whenever PictureBox clicked
28      private void imagePictureBox_Click(
29         object sender, System.EventArgs e )
30      {
31         imageNum = ( imageNum + 1 ) % 3; // imageNum from 0 to 2
32
33         // create Image object from file, display on PictureBox
34         imagePictureBox.Image = Image.FromFile(
35            Directory.GetCurrentDirectory() + "\\images\\image" +
36            imageNum + ".bmp" );
37      }
38
39   } // end class PictureBoxTest
```

Fig. 12.28 Using a **PictureBox** to display images. (Part 2 of 2.)

To respond to the user's clicks, we must handle the **Click** event (lines 28–37). Inside the event handler, we use an integer (**imageNum**) to store the image we want to display. We then set the **Image** property of **imagePictureBox** to an **Image**. Class **Image** is discussed in Chapter 16, Graphics and Multimedia, but here we overview method **From-File**, which takes a **string** (the path to the image file) and creates an **Image** object.

To find the images, we use class **Directory** (namespace **System.IO**, specified on line 10) method **GetCurrentDirectory** (line 35). This returns the current directory of the executable file (usually **bin\Debug**) as a **string**. To access the **images** subdirectory, we take the current directory and append "**\\images**" followed by "****" and the file name. We use a double slash because an escape sequence is needed to print a single slash.

Alternatively, we could have used **@** to avoid the escape character (i.e., **@"\"** will print a single slash—the slash does not need to be escaped by another slash). We use **imageNum** to append the proper number, so we can load either **image0**, **image1** or **image2**. Integer **imageNum** stays between **0** and **2**, due to the modulus calculation (line 31). Finally, we append **".bmp"** to the filename. Thus, if we want to load **image0**, the string becomes "*CurrentDir***\images\image0.bmp**", where ***CurrentDir*** is the directory of the executable.

12.9 Mouse Event Handling

This section explains how to handle *mouse events,* such as *clicks*, *presses* and *moves*. Mouse events are generated when the mouse interacts with a control. They can be handled for any GUI control that derives from class **System.Windows.Forms.Control**. Mouse event information is passed using class *MouseEventArgs*, and the delegate to create the mouse event handlers is *MouseEventHandler*. Each mouse event-handling method must take an **object** and a **MouseEventArgs** object as arguments. The **Click** event, which we covered earlier, uses delegate **EventHandler** and event arguments **EventArgs**.

Class **MouseEventArgs** contains information about the mouse event, such as the *x*- and *y*-coordinates of the mouse pointer, the mouse button pressed, the number of clicks and the number of notches through which the mouse wheel turned. Note that the *x*- and *y*-coordinates of the **MouseEventArgs** object are relative to the control that raised the event. Point (0,0) is at the upper-left corner of the control. The various mouse events are described in Fig. 12.29.

Mouse Events, Delegates and Event Arguments	
*Mouse Events (Delegate **EventHandler**, event arguments **EventArgs**)*	
MouseEnter	Raised if the mouse cursor enters the area of the control.
MouseLeave	Raised if the mouse cursor leaves the area of the control.
*Mouse Events (Delegate **MouseEventHandler**, event arguments **MouseEventArgs**)*	
MouseDown	Raised if the mouse button is pressed while its cursor is over the area of the control.
MouseHover	Raised if the mouse cursor hovers over the area of the control.
MouseMove	Raised if the mouse cursor is moved while in the area of the control.
MouseUp	Raised if the mouse button is released when the cursor is over the area of the control.
*Class **MouseEventArgs** Properties*	
Button	Mouse button that was pressed (**left, right, middle** or **none**).
Clicks	The number of times the mouse button was clicked.
X	The *x*-coordinate of the event, relative to the control.
Y	The *y*-coordinate of the event, relative to the control.

Fig. 12.29 Mouse events, delegates and event arguments.

Figure 12.30 uses mouse events to draw on the form. Whenever the user drags the mouse (i.e., moves the mouse while holding down a button), a line is drawn on the form.

```
1   // Fig 12.30: Painter.cs
2   // Using the mouse to draw on a form.
3
4   using System;
5   using System.Drawing;
6   using System.Collections;
7   using System.ComponentModel;
8   using System.Windows.Forms;
9   using System.Data;
10
11  /// creates a form as a drawing surface
12  public class Painter : System.Windows.Forms.Form
13  {
14     bool shouldPaint = false; // whether to paint
15
16     /// The main entry point for the application.
17     [STAThread]
18     static void Main()
19     {
20        Application.Run( new Painter() );
21     }
22
23     // should paint after mouse button has been pressed
24     private void Painter_MouseDown(
25        object sender, System.Windows.Forms.MouseEventArgs e )
26     {
27        shouldPaint = true;
28     }
29
30     // stop painting when mouse button released
31     private void Painter_MouseUp(
32        object sender, System.Windows.Forms.MouseEventArgs e )
33     {
34        shouldPaint = false;
35     }
36
37     // draw circle whenever mouse button
38     // moves (and mouse is down)
39     protected void Painter_MouseMove(
40        object sender, System.Windows.Forms.MouseEventArgs e )
41     {
42        if ( shouldPaint )
43        {
44           Graphics graphics = CreateGraphics();
45           graphics.FillEllipse(
46              new SolidBrush( Color.BlueViolet ),
47              e.X, e.Y, 4, 4 );
48        }
49
50     } // end Painter_MouseMove
```

Fig. 12.30 Using the mouse to draw on a form. (Part 1 of 2.)

```
51
52   } // end class Painter
```

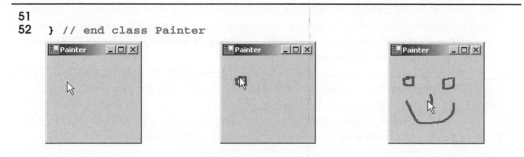

Fig. 12.30 Using the mouse to draw on a form. (Part 2 of 2.)

On line 14 the program creates variable **shouldPaint**, which determines whether we should draw on the form. We want to draw only while the mouse button is pressed down. In the event handler for event **MouseDown**, **shouldPaint** is set to true (line 27). As soon as the mouse button is released the program stops drawing: **shouldPaint** is set to false in the **MouseUp** event handler (line 34).

Whenever the mouse moves while the button is pressed down, the **MouseMove** event is generated. The event will be generated repeatedly, at a rate set by the operating system. Inside the **Painter_MouseMove** event handler (lines 39–48), the program draws only if **shouldPaint** is **true** (indicating that the mouse button is down). Line 44 creates the **Graphics** object for the form, which provides methods for drawing various shapes. Method **FillEllipse** (lines 45–47) draws a circle at every point the mouse cursor moves over (while the mouse button is pressed). The first parameter to method **FillEllipse** is a **SolidBrush** object, which determines the color of the shape drawn. We create a new **SolidBrush** object by passing the constructor a **Color** value. Structure **Color** contains numerous predefined color constants—we selected **Color.BlueViolet** (line 46). The **SolidBrush** fills an elliptical region, which lies inside a bounding rectangle. The bounding rectangle is specified by the *x*- and *y*-coordinates of its upper-left corner, its height and its width. These four parameters are the final four arguments to method **FillEllipse**. The *x*- and *y*-coordinates are the location of the mouse event: They can be taken from the mouse event arguments (**e.X** and **e.Y**). To draw a circle, we set the height and width of the bounding rectangle equal—in this case, they are each 4 pixels.

12.10 Keyboard Event Handling

This section explains how to handle *key events*. Key events are generated when keys on the keyboard are pressed and released. These events can be handled by any control that inherits from **System.Windows.Forms.Control**. There are two types of key events. The first is event **KeyPress**, which fires when a key representing an ASCII character is pressed (determined by **KeyPressEventArgs** property **KeyChar**). ASCII is a 128-character set of alphanumeric symbols. (The full listing can be found in Appendix B, ASCII Character Set.)

Using the **KeyPress** event, we cannot determine if *modifier keys* (such as *Shift*, *Alt* and *Control*) were pressed. To determine such actions, handle the **KeyUp** or **KeyDown** events, which form the second type of key event. Class **KeyEventArgs** contains information about special modifier keys. The key's **Key** *enumeration* value can be returned, giving information about a wide range of non-ASCII keys. Modifier keys are often used in conjunction with the mouse to select or highlight information. The delegates for the two classes are **KeyPressEventHandler** (event argument class **KeyPressEventArgs**) and **KeyEventHandler** (event argument class **KeyEventArgs**). Figure 12.31 lists important information about key events.

Figure 12.32 demonstrates using the key event handlers to display the key that was pressed. The program's form contains two **Label**s. It displays the key pressed on one **Label** and modifier information on the other.

The two **Label**s (named **charLabel** and **keyInfoLabel**) are initially empty. The **KeyDown** and **KeyPress** events convey different information; thus, the form (**Key-Demo**) handles them both.

Keyboard Events, Delegates and Event Arguments

*Key Events (Delegate **KeyEventHandler**, event arguments **KeyEventArgs**)*

KeyDown	Raised when key is initially pushed down.
KeyUp	Raised when key is released.

*Key Events (Delegate **KeyPressEventHandler**, event arguments **KeyPressEventArgs**)*

KeyPress	Raised when key is pressed. Occurs repeatedly while key is held down, at a rate specified by the operating system.

*Class **KeyPressEventArgs** Properties*

KeyChar	Returns the ASCII character for the key pressed.
Handled	Whether the **KeyPress** event was handled.

*Class **KeyEventArgs** Properties*

Alt	Indicates whether the *Alt* key was pressed.
Control	Indicates whether the *Control* key was pressed.
Shift	Indicates whether the *Shift* key was pressed.
Handled	Whether the event was handled.
KeyCode	Returns the key code for the key, as a **Keys** enumeration. This does not include modifier key information. Used to test for a specific key.
KeyData	Returns the key code as a **Keys** enumeration, combined with modifier information. Used to determine all information about the key pressed.
KeyValue	Returns the key code as an **int**, rather than as a **Keys** enumeration. Used to obtain a numeric representation of the key pressed.
Modifiers	Returns a **Keys** enumeration for any modifier keys pressed (*Alt*, *Control* and *Shift*). Used to determine modifier key information only.

Fig. 12.31 Keyboard events, delegates and event arguments.

```
1   // Fig. 12.32: KeyDemo.cs
2   // Displaying information about the key the user pressed.
3
4   using System;
5   using System.Drawing;
6   using System.Collections;
7   using System.ComponentModel;
8   using System.Windows.Forms;
9   using System.Data;
10
11  // form to display key press
12  // information--contains two labels
13  public class KeyDemo : System.Windows.Forms.Form
14  {
15     private System.Windows.Forms.Label charLabel;
16     private System.Windows.Forms.Label keyInfoLabel;
17
18     private System.ComponentModel.Container components = null;
19
20     /// The main entry point for the application.
21     [STAThread]
22     static void Main()
23     {
24        Application.Run( new KeyDemo() );
25     }
26
27     // display the character pressed using key char
28     protected void KeyDemo_KeyPress(
29        object sender, System.Windows.Forms.KeyPressEventArgs e )
30     {
31        charLabel.Text = "Key pressed: " + e.KeyChar;
32     }
33
34     // display modifier keys, key code, key data and key value
35     private void KeyDemo_KeyDown(
36        object sender, System.Windows.Forms.KeyEventArgs e )
37     {
38        keyInfoLabel.Text =
39           "Alt: " + ( e.Alt ? "Yes" : "No") + '\n' +
40           "Shift: " + ( e.Shift ? "Yes" : "No" ) + '\n' +
41           "Ctrl: " + ( e.Control ? "Yes" : "No" ) + '\n' +
42           "KeyCode: " + e.KeyCode + '\n' +
43           "KeyData: " + e.KeyData + '\n' +
44           "KeyValue: " + e.KeyValue;
45     }
46
47     // clear labels when key released
48     private void KeyDemo_KeyUp(
49        object sender, System.Windows.Forms.KeyEventArgs e )
50     {
51        keyInfoLabel.Text = "";
52        charLabel.Text = "";
53     }
```

Fig. 12.32 Demonstrating keyboard events (Part 1 of 2.).

```
54
55  }  // end class KeyDemo
```

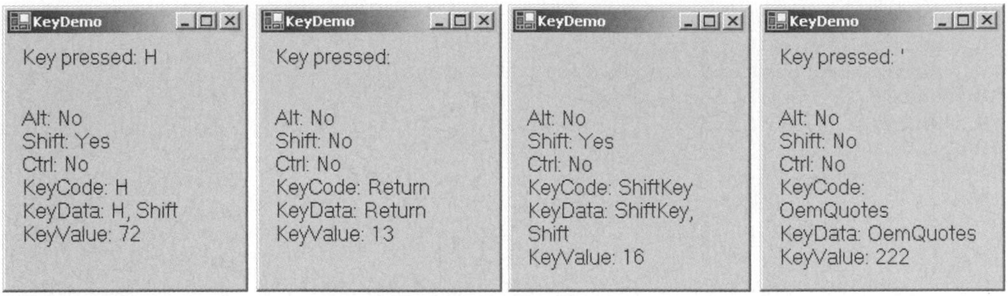

Fig. 12.32 Demonstrating keyboard events (Part 2 of 2.).

The **KeyPress** event handler (lines 28–32) accesses the **KeyChar** property of the **KeyPressEventArgs** object. This returns the key pressed as a **char** and displays in **charLabel** (line 31). If the key pressed was not an ASCII character, then the **KeyPress** event will not fire and **charLabel** remains empty. ASCII is a common encoding format for letters, numbers, punctuation marks and other characters. It does not support keys such as the *function keys* (like *F1*) or the modifier keys (*Alt*, *Control* and *Shift*).

The **KeyDown** event handler (lines 35–45) displays more information, all from its **KeyEventArgs** object. It tests for the *Alt*, *Shift* and *Control* keys (lines 39–41), using the **Alt**, **Shift** and **Control** properties, each of which returns **bool**. It then displays the **KeyCode**, **KeyData** and **KeyValue** properties.

The **KeyCode** property returns a **Keys** enumeration, which is converted to a **string** using method **ToString**. The **KeyCode** property returns the key that was pressed, but does not provide any information about modifier keys. Thus, both a capital and a lowercase "a" are represented as the *A* key.

The **KeyData** property returns a **Keys** enumeration as well, but includes data about modifier keys. Thus, if "A" is input, the **KeyData** shows that the *A* key and the *Shift* key were pressed. Lastly, **KeyValue** returns the key code for the key that was pressed as an integer. This integer is the *Windows virtual key code*, which provides an integer value for a wide range of keys and for mouse buttons. The Windows virtual key code is useful when testing for non-ASCII keys (such as *F12*).

The **KeyUp** event handler clears both labels when the key is released (lines 48–53). As we can see from the output, non-ASCII keys are not displayed in the upper **charLabel** because the **KeyPress** event was not generated. The **KeyDown** event is still raised, and **keyInfoLabel** displays information about the key. The **Keys** enumeration can be used to test for specific keys by comparing the key pressed to a specific **KeyCode**. The Visual Studio. NET documentation has a complete list of the **Keys** enumerations.

Software Engineering Observation 12.4

To cause a control to react when a certain key is pressed (such as Enter*), handle a key event and test for the key pressed. To cause a button to be clicked when the* Enter *key is pressed on a form, set the form's* **AcceptButton** *property.*

SUMMARY

- A graphical user interface (GUI) presents a pictorial interface to a program. A GUI (pronounced "GOO-EE") gives a program a distinctive "look" and "feel."

- By providing different applications with a consistent set of intuitive user interface components, GUIs allow the user to concentrate on using programs productively.

- GUIs are built from GUI components (sometimes called controls or widgets). A GUI control is a visual object with which the user interacts via the mouse or keyboard.

- Windows Forms create GUIs. A form is a graphical element that appears on the desktop. A form can be a dialog or a window.

- A component is a class that implements the **IComponent** interface.

- A control is a graphical component, such as a button. Components that are not visible usually are referred to simply as components.

- The active window has the focus. It is the frontmost window and has a highlighted title bar.

- A form acts as a container for components.

- When the user interacts with a control, an event is generated. This event can trigger methods that respond to the user's actions.

- All forms, components and controls are classes.

- The general design process for creating Windows applications involves creating a Windows Form, setting its properties, adding controls, setting their properties and configuring event handlers.

- GUIs are event driven. When a user interaction occurs, an event is generated. The event information then is passed to event handlers.

- Events are based on the notion of delegates. Delegates act as an intermediate step between the object creating (raising) the event and the method handling it.

- In many cases, the programmer will handle events generated by prepackaged controls. In this case, all the programmer needs to do is create and register the event handler.

- Use the **Events** window to create and register event handlers.

- The information we need to register an event is the **EventArgs** class (to define the event handler) and the **EventHandler** delegate (to register the event handler). Visual Studio .NET can usually register the event for us.

- Labels (class **Label**) display read-only text instructions or information on a GUI.

- A **TextBox** is a single-line area in which text can be entered. A password text box displays only a certain character (such as *****) when text is input.

- A **Button** is a control that the user clicks to trigger a specific action. Buttons typically respond to the **Click** event.

- **GroupBox**es and **Panel**s help arrange components on a GUI. The main difference between the classes is that **GroupBox**es can display text, and **Panel**s can have scrollbars.

- Visual C# has two types of state buttons—**CheckBox**es and **RadioButton**s—that have on/off or true/false values.

- A checkbox is a small white square that can be blank or contain a checkmark.

- Use the bitwise XOR operator (**^**) to combine or negate a font style.

- Radio buttons (class **RadioButton**) have two states—selected and not selected. Radio buttons appear as a group in which only one radio button can be selected at a time. To create new groups, radio buttons must be added to **GroupBox**es or **Panel**s. Each **GroupBox** or **Panel** is a group.

- Radio buttons and checkboxes use the **CheckChanged** event.

- Scrollbars are controls that allow the user to access a range of integer values. There are horizontal scrollbars and vertical scrollbars. Many container controls have an **AutoScroll** property that determines whether scrollbars will appear as needed.
- A picture box (class **PictureBox**) displays an image (set by an object of class **Image**).
- Mouse events (clicks, presses and moves) can be handled for any GUI control that derives from **System.Windows.Forms.Control**. Mouse events use class **MouseEventArgs** (**MouseEventHandler** delegate) and **EventArgs** (**EventHandler** delegate).
- Class **MouseEventArgs** contains information about the *x*- and *y*-coordinates, the button used, the number of clicks and the number of notches through which the mouse wheel turned.
- Key events are generated when keyboard's keys are pressed and released. These events can be handled by any control that inherits from **System.Windows.Forms.Control**.
- Event **KeyPress** can return a **char** for any ASCII character pressed. One cannot determine if special modifier keys (such as *Shift*, *Alt* and *Control*) were pressed.
- Events **KeyUp** and **KeyDown** test for special modifier keys (using **KeyEventArgs**). The delegates are **KeyPressEventHandler** (**KeyPressEventArgs**) and **KeyEventHandler** (**KeyEventArgs**).
- Class **KeyEventArgs** has properties **KeyCode**, **KeyData** and **KeyValue**.
- Property **KeyCode** returns the key pressed, but does not give any information about modifier keys.
- The **KeyData** property includes data about modifier keys.
- The **KeyValue** property returns the key code for the key pressed as an integer.

TERMINOLOGY

active window
Alt property
ASCII character
background color
button
Button class
button label
checkbox
CheckBox class
checkbox label
CheckedChanged event
click a button
Click event
click a mouse button
component
container
control
Control property
delegate
deselected
drag and drop
#endregion
Enter key
Enter mouse event
event

event argument
event delegate
event driven
event handler
event-handling model
event keyword
EventArgs class
Events window in Visual Studio .NET
focus
Font property
font style
form
Form class
GetCurrentDirectory method
graphical user interface (GUI)
GroupBox
GUI component
handle event
Hide property
Image property
InitializeComponent method
input data from the keyboard
key code
key data
key event

key value
keyboard
KeyDown event
KeyEventArgs class
KeyPress event
KeyPressEventArgs class
KeyUp event
label
Label class
list
menu
menu bar
mouse
mouse click
mouse event
mouse move
mouse press
MouseDown event
MouseEventArgs class
MouseEventHandler delegate
MouseHover event
MouseLeave event
MouseMove event
MouseUp event
MouseWheel event
moving the mouse
multicast
multicast event
MulticastDelegate class
mutual exclusion
Name property
NewValue property
panel
Panel class

password box
PasswordChar property
picture box
PictureBox class
radio button
radio-button group
RadioButton class
raise an event
read-only text
#region tag
register an event handler
Scroll event
scrollbar
scrollbar in panel
ScrollEventArgs class
selecting an item from a menu
Shift property
SizeMode property
System.Windows.Forms namespace
Text property
text box
TextBox class
TextChanged event
trigger an event
type in a textbox
uneditable text or icon
virtual key code
Visible property
visual programming
widget
window gadget
Windows Form
XOR

SELF-REVIEW EXERCISES

12.1   State whether each of the following is *true* or *false*. If *false*, explain why.
a)   A GUI is a pictorial interface to a program.
b)   Windows Forms commonly are used to create GUIs.
c)   A control is a nonvisible component.
d)   All forms, components and controls are classes.
e)   Events are based on properties.
f)   Class **Label** is used to provide pictorial instructions or information.
g)   Button presses raise events.
h)   Checkboxes in the same group are mutually exclusive.
i)   Scrollbars allow the user to maximize or minimize a set of data.
j)   All mouse events use the same event arguments class.
k)   Visual Studio .NET can register an event and create an empty event handler.

12.2   Fill in the blanks in each of the following statements:
   a) The active window is said to have the _____.
   b) The form acts as a _____ for the components that are added.
   c) GUIs are _____ driven.
   d) Every method that handles the same event must have the same _____.
   e) The information required when registering an event handler is the_____ class and
      the _____.
   f) A _____ textbox displays only a single character (such as an asterisk) as the user
      types.
   g) Class _____ and class _____ help arrange components on a GUI and provide
      logical group for radio buttons.
   h) Typical mouse events include _____, _____ and _____.
   i) _____ events are generated when a key on the keyboard is pressed or released.
   j) The modifier keys are _____, _____ and _____.
   k) A _____ event or delegate can call multiple methods.

ANSWERS TO SELF-REVIEW EXERCISES

12.1   a) True. b) True. c) False. A control is a visible component. d) True. e) False. Events are
based on delegates. f) False. Class **Label** is used to provide text instructions or information. g) True.
h) False. Radio buttons in the same group are mutually exclusive. i) False. Scrollbars allow the user
to view data that normally cannot fit in its container. j) False. Some mouse events use **EventArgs**,
while others use **MouseEventArgs**. k) True.

12.2   a) focus. b) container. c) event. d) signature. e) event arguments, delegate. f) password.
g) **GroupBox**, **Panel**. h) mouse clicks, mouse presses, mouse moves. i) Key. j) *Shift*, *Control*,
Alt. k) multicast.

EXERCISES

12.3   Extend the program in Fig. 12.24 to include a **CheckBox** for every font style option. [*Hint*:
Use XOR rather than testing for every bit explicitly.]

12.4   Create the GUI in Fig. 12.33. You do not have to provide any functionality.

12.5   Create the GUI in Fig. 12.34. You do not have to provide any functionality.

12.6   Extend the program of Fig. 12.30 to include options for changing the size and color of the
lines drawn. Create a GUI similar to the one in Fig. 12.35. [*Hint*: Have variables to keep track of the
currently selected size (**int**) and color (**Color** object). Set them using the event handlers for the radio buttons. For the color, use the various **Color** constants (such as **Color.Blue**). When responding to the mouse moves, simply use the size and color variables to determine the proper size and
color.]

12.7   Write a program that plays "guess the number" as follows: Your program chooses the number to be guessed by selecting an integer at random in the range 1–1000. The program then displays
the following text in a label:

```
I have a number between 1 and 1000—can you guess my number?
Please enter your first guess.
```

A **TextBox** should be used to input the guess. As each guess is input, the background color should
change to either red or blue. Red indicates that the user is getting "warmer," and blue indicates that
the user is getting "colder." A **Label** should display either "**Too High**" or "**Too Low**" to help the
user choose a number closer toward the correct answer. When the user obtains the correct answer,

"**Correct!**" should be displayed. The background should become green and the **TextBox** used for input should become uneditable. Provide a **Button** that allows the user to play the game again. When the **Button** is clicked, generate a new random number, change the background to the default color and generate the input **TextBox** to editable.

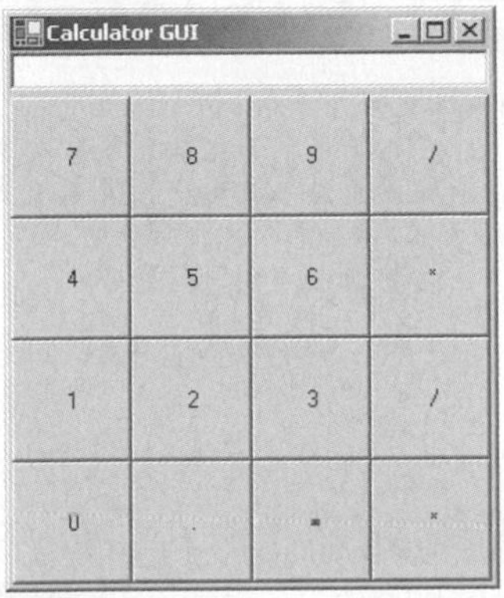

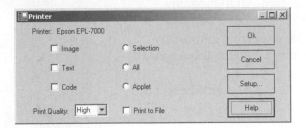

Fig. 12.33 GUI for Exercise 12.4.

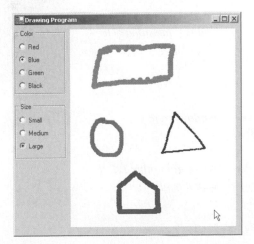

Fig. 12.34 GUI for Exercise 12.5.

Fig. 12.35 GUI for Exercise 12.6.

13

Graphical User Interface Concepts: Part 2

Objectives

- To be able to create menus, window tabs and multiple-document-interface (MDI) programs.
- To understand the use of the **ListView** and **TreeView** controls for displaying information.
- To be able to use hyperlinks with the **LinkLabel** control.
- To be able to display lists using **ListBox**es and **ComboBox**es.
- To create custom controls.

I claim not to have controlled events, but confess plainly that events have controlled me.
Abraham Lincoln

A good symbol is the best argument, and is a missionary to persuade thousands.
Ralph Waldo Emerson

Capture its reality in paint!
Paul Cézanne

But, soft! what light through yonder window breaks?
It is the east, and Juliet is the sun!
William Shakespeare

An actor entering through the door, you've got nothing. But if he enters through the window, you've got a situation.
Billy Wilder

Outline

13.1 Introduction

This chapter continues our study of GUIs. We begin our discussion of more advanced topics with a commonly used GUI component, the *menu*, which presents a user with several logically organized options. The reader will learn how to develop menus with the tools provided by Visual Studio .NET. We introduce **LinkLabel**s, powerful GUI components that enable the user to click the mouse to be taken to one of several destinations.

We consider GUI components that encapsulate smaller GUI components. We demonstrate how to manipulate a list of values via a **ListBox** and how to combine several checkboxes in a **CheckedListBox**. We also create drop-down lists using **ComboBox**es and display data hierarchically with a **TreeView** control. We present two important GUI components—tab controls and multiple-document-interface windows. These components enable developers to create real-world programs with sophisticated graphical user interfaces.

Most of the GUI components used in this book are included with Visual Studio .NET. We show how to design custom controls and add those controls to the **ToolBox**. The techniques in this chapter form the groundwork for the creation of complex GUIs and custom controls.

13.2 Menus

Menus are used to provide groups of related commands for Windows applications. Although these commands depend on the program, some—such as **Open** and **Save**—are common to many applications. Menus are an integral part of GUIs, because they make user actions possible without unnecessary "cluttering" of GUIs.

In Fig. 13.1, an expanded menu lists various commands (called *menu items*), plus *submenus* (menus within a menu). Notice that the top-level menus appear in the left portion of the figure, whereas any submenus or menu items are displayed to the right. The menu that contains a menu item is called that menu item's *parent menu*. A menu item that contains a submenu is considered to be the parent of that submenu.

All menu items can have *Alt* key shortcuts (also called *access shortcuts* or *hot keys*), which are accessed by pressing *Alt* and the underlined letter (for example, *Alt + F* retrieves the **File** menu). Menus that are not top-level menus can have shortcut keys as well (combinations of *Ctrl, Shift, Alt, F1, F2*, letter keys etc.). Some menu items display checkmarks, usually indicating that multiple options on the menu can be selected at once.

To create a menu, open the **Toolbox**, and drag a **MainMenu** control onto the form. This creates a menu bar on the top of the form and places a **MainMenu** icon underneath it. To select the **MainMenu**, click the icon. This setup is known as the Visual Studio .NET **Menu Designer**, which allows the user to create and edit menus. Menus are like other controls; they have properties, which can be accessed through the **Properties** window or the **Menu Designer** (Fig. 13.2), and events, which can be accessed through the **Class Name** and **Method Name** drop-down menus.

Look-and-Feel Observation 13.1

Buttons *also can have access shortcuts. Place the & symbol just before the character via which we wish to create a shortcut. To click the button, the user then presses* Alt *and the underlined character.*

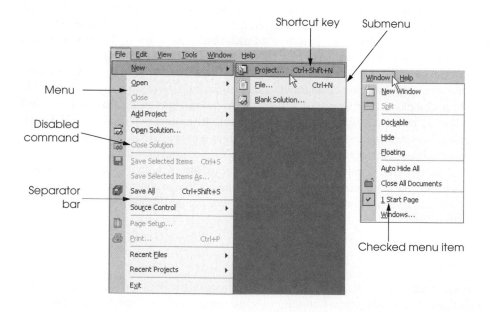

Fig. 13.1   Expanded and checked menus.

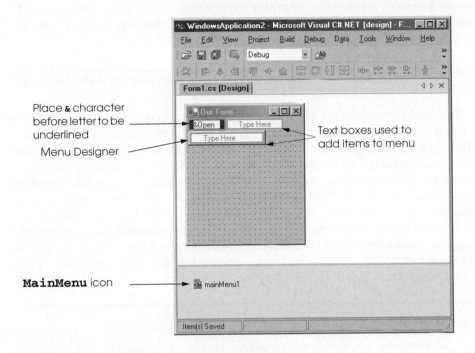

Place **&** character
before letter to be
underlined

Menu Designer

Text boxes used to
add items to menu

MainMenu icon

Fig. 13.2 Visual Studio .NET **Menu Designer**.

To add entries to the menu, click the **Type Here** textbox and type the text that should
appear in the menu. Each entry in the menu is of type **MenuItem** from the
System.Windows.Forms namespace. The menu itself is of type **MainMenu**. After the
programmer presses the *Enter* key, the menu item is added. Then, more **Type Here** textboxes appear, allowing us to add items underneath or to the side of the original menu item
(Fig. 13.2). To create an access shortcut, type an ampersand (**&**) in front of the character to
be underlined. For example, to create the **File** menu item, type **&File**. The actual ampersand character is displayed by typing **&&**. To add other shortcut keys (such as *Ctrl + F9*),
set the **Shortcut** property of the **MenuItem**.

Programmers can remove a menu item by selecting it with the mouse and pressing the
Delete key. Separator bars are inserted by right-clicking the menu and selecting **Insert
Separator** or by typing "**-**" as the menu text.

Menu items generate a **Click** event when selected. To create an empty event handler,
enter code-view mode, double click on the **MenuItem** in design view. Menus can also display the names of open windows in multiple-document-interface (MDI) forms (see
Section 13.9). Menu properties and events are summarized in Fig. 13.3.

Look-and-Feel Observation 13.2

*It is conventional to place an ellipsis (...) after a menu item that brings up a dialog (such as
Save As...). Menu items that produce an immediate action without prompting the user (such
as **Save**) should not have an ellipsis following their name.*

Class **MenuTest** (Fig. 13.4) creates a simple menu on a form. The form has a top-
level **File** menu with menu items **About** (displays a message box) and **Exit** (terminates the

program).The menu also includes a **Format** menu, which changes the text on a label. The **Format** menu has submenus **Color** and **Font**, which change the color and font of the text on a label.

Look-and-Feel Observation 13.3

Using common Windows shortcuts (such as Ctrl+F for Find operations and Ctrl+S for Save operations) decreases an application's learning curve.

We begin by dragging the **MainMenu** from the **ToolBox** onto the form. We then create our entire menu structure, using the **Menu Designer**. The **File** menu has items **About** (**aboutMenuItem**, line 21) and **Exit** (**exitMenuItem**, line 22); the **Format** menu (**formatMenu**, line 25) has two submenus. The first submenu, **Color** (**color-MenuItem**, line 28), contains menu items **Black** (**blackMenuItem**, line 29), **Blue** (**blueMenuItem**, line 30), **Red** (**redMenuItem**, line 31) and **Green** (**greenMenu-Item**, line 32). The second submenu, **Font** (**fontMenuItem**, line 40), contains menu items **Times New Roman** (**timesMenuItem**, line 35), **Courier** (**courierMenu-Item**, line 36), **Comic Sans** (**comicMenuItem**, line 37), a separator bar (**separa-torMenuItem**, line 42), **Bold** (**boldMenuItem**, line 38) and **Italic** (**italicMenuItem**, line 39).

MainMenu and MenuItem events and properties	Description / Delegate and Event Arguments
MainMenu *Properties*	
MenuItems	Lists the **MenuItem**s that are contained in the **MainMenu**.
RightToLeft	Causes text to display from right to left. Useful for languages that are read from right to left.
MenuItem *Properties*	
Checked	Indicates whether a menu item is checked (according to property **RadioCheck**). Default **False**, meaning that the menu item is not checked.
Index	Specifies an item's position in its parent menu.
MenuItems	Lists the submenu items for a particular menu item.
MergeOrder	Sets the position of a menu item when its parent menu is merged with another menu.
MergeType	Takes a value of the **MenuMerge** enumeration. Specifies how a parent menu merges with another menu. Possible values are **Add**, **MergeItems**, **Remove** and **Replace**.
RadioCheck	Indicates whether a selected menu item appears as a radio button (black circle) or displays a checkmark. **True** creates radio button, **False** displays checkmark; default **False**.
Shortcut	Specifies the shortcut key for the menu item (e.g., *Ctrl + F9* can be equivalent to clicking a specific item).

Fig. 13.3   MainMenu and **MenuItem** properties and events. (Part 1 of 2.)

MainMenu and MenuItem events and properties	Description / Delegate and Event Arguments
ShowShortcut	Indicates whether a shortcut key is shown beside menu item text. Default is **True**, which displays the shortcut key.
Text	Specifies the text to appear in the menu item. To create an *Alt* access shortcut, precede a character with **&** (e.g., **&File** for **File**).
Common Event	*(Delegate **EventHandler**, event arguments **EventArgs**)*
Click	Generated when item is clicked or shortcut key is used. Default when double-clicked in designer.

Fig. 13.3 **MainMenu** and **MenuItem** properties and events. (Part 2 of 2.)

```
1    // Fig 13.4: MenuTest.cs
2    // Using menus to change font colors and styles.
3
4    using System;
5    using System.Drawing;
6    using System.Collections;
7    using System.ComponentModel;
8    using System.Windows.Forms;
9    using System.Data;
10
11   public class MenuTest : System.Windows.Forms.Form
12   {
13       // display label
14       private System.Windows.Forms.Label displayLabel;
15
16       // main menu (contains file and format menu)
17       private System.Windows.Forms.MainMenu mainMenu;
18
19       // file menu
20       private System.Windows.Forms.MenuItem fileMenuItem;
21       private System.Windows.Forms.MenuItem aboutMenuItem;
22       private System.Windows.Forms.MenuItem exitMenuItem;
23
24       // format menu
25       private System.Windows.Forms.MenuItem formatMenuItem;
26
27       // color submenu
28       private System.Windows.Forms.MenuItem colorMenuItem;
29       private System.Windows.Forms.MenuItem blackMenuItem;
30       private System.Windows.Forms.MenuItem blueMenuItem;
31       private System.Windows.Forms.MenuItem redMenuItem;
32       private System.Windows.Forms.MenuItem greenMenuItem;
33
34       // font submenu
35       private System.Windows.Forms.MenuItem timesMenuItem;
```

Fig. 13.4 Menus for changing text font and color. (Part 1 of 5.)

```
36    private System.Windows.Forms.MenuItem courierMenuItem;
37    private System.Windows.Forms.MenuItem comicMenuItem;
38    private System.Windows.Forms.MenuItem boldMenuItem;
39    private System.Windows.Forms.MenuItem italicMenuItem;
40    private System.Windows.Forms.MenuItem fontMenuItem;
41
42    private System.Windows.Forms.MenuItem separatorMenuItem;
43
44    [STAThread]
45    static void Main()
46    {
47        Application.Run( new MenuTest() );
48    }
49
50    // display MessageBox
51    private void aboutMenuItem_Click(
52        object sender, System.EventArgs e )
53    {
54        MessageBox.Show(
55            "This is an example\nof using menus.",
56            "About", MessageBoxButtons.OK,
57            MessageBoxIcon.Information );
58    }
59
60    // exit program
61    private void exitMenuItem_Click(
62        object sender, System.EventArgs e )
63    {
64        Application.Exit();
65    }
66
67    // reset color
68    private void ClearColor()
69    {
70        // clear all checkmarks
71        blackMenuItem.Checked = false;
72        blueMenuItem.Checked = false;
73        redMenuItem.Checked = false;
74        greenMenuItem.Checked = false;
75    }
76
77    // update menu state and color display black
78    private void blackMenuItem_Click(
79        object sender, System.EventArgs e )
80    {
81        // reset checkmarks for color menu items
82        ClearColor();
83
84        // set color to black
85        displayLabel.ForeColor = Color.Black;
86        blackMenuItem.Checked = true;
87    }
88
```

Fig. 13.4   Menus for changing text font and color. (Part 2 of 5.)

```
89          // update menu state and color display blue
90          private void blueMenuItem_Click(
91             object sender, System.EventArgs e )
92          {
93             // reset checkmarks for color menu items
94             ClearColor();
95
96             // set color to blue
97             displayLabel.ForeColor = Color.Blue;
98             blueMenuItem.Checked = true;
99          }
100
101         // update menu state and color display red
102         private void redMenuItem_Click(
103            object sender, System.EventArgs e )
104         {
105            // reset checkmarks for color menu items
106            ClearColor();
107
108            // set color to red
109            displayLabel.ForeColor = Color.Red;
110            redMenuItem.Checked = true;
111         }
112
113         // update menu state and color display green
114         private void greenMenuItem_Click(
115            object sender, System.EventArgs e )
116         {
117            // reset checkmarks for color menu items
118            ClearColor();
119
120            // set color to green
121            displayLabel.ForeColor = Color.Green;
122            greenMenuItem.Checked = true;
123         }
124
125         // reset font types
126         private void ClearFont()
127         {
128            // clear all checkmarks
129            timesMenuItem.Checked = false;
130            courierMenuItem.Checked = false;
131            comicMenuItem.Checked = false;
132         }
133
134         // update menu state and set font to Times
135         private void timesMenuItem_Click(
136            object sender, System.EventArgs e )
137         {
138            // reset checkmarks for font menu items
139            ClearFont();
140
```

Fig. 13.4   Menus for changing text font and color. (Part 3 of 5.)

```
141            // set Times New Roman font
142            timesMenuItem.Checked = true;
143            displayLabel.Font = new Font(
144               "Times New Roman", 14, displayLabel.Font.Style );
145         }
146
147         // update menu state and set font to Courier
148         private void courierMenuItem_Click(
149            object sender, System.EventArgs e )
150         {
151            // reset checkmarks for font menu items
152            ClearFont();
153
154            // set Courier font
155            courierMenuItem.Checked = true;
156            displayLabel.Font = new Font(
157               "Courier New", 14, displayLabel.Font.Style );
158         }
159
160         // update menu state and set font to Comic Sans MS
161         private void comicMenuItem_Click(
162            object sender, System.EventArgs e )
163         {
164            // reset checkmarks for font menu items
165            ClearFont();
166
167            // set Comic Sans font
168            comicMenuItem.Checked = true;
169            displayLabel.Font = new Font(
170               "Comic Sans MS", 14, displayLabel.Font.Style );
171         }
172
173         // toggle checkmark and toggle bold style
174         private void boldMenuItem_Click(
175            object sender, System.EventArgs e )
176         {
177            // toggle checkmark
178            boldMenuItem.Checked = !boldMenuItem.Checked;
179
180            // use Xor to toggle bold, keep all other styles
181            displayLabel.Font = new Font(
182               displayLabel.Font.FontFamily, 14,
183               displayLabel.Font.Style ^ FontStyle.Bold );
184         }
185
186         // toggle checkmark and toggle italic style
187         private void italicMenuItem_Click(
188            object sender, System.EventArgs e)
189         {
190            // toggle checkmark
191            italicMenuItem.Checked = !italicMenuItem.Checked;
192
```

Fig. 13.4   Menus for changing text font and color. (Part 4 of 5.)

```
193          // use Xor to toggle bold, keep all other styles
194          displayLabel.Font = new Font(
195             displayLabel.Font.FontFamily, 14,
196             displayLabel.Font.Style ^ FontStyle.Italic );
197      }
198
199 } // end class MenuTest
```

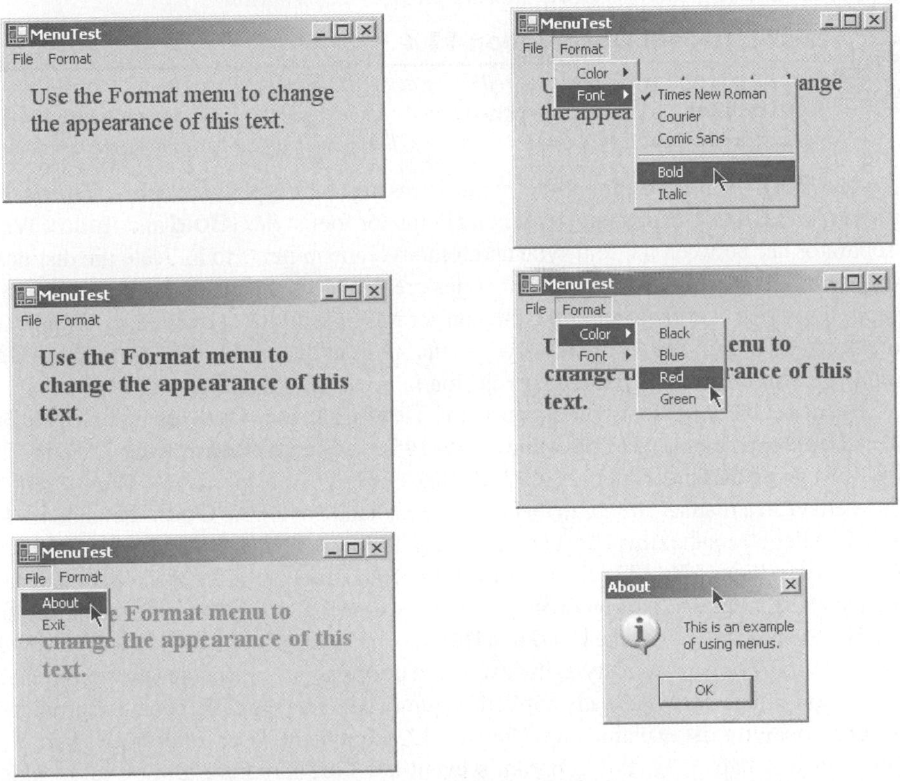

Fig. 13.4 Menus for changing text font and color. (Part 5 of 5.)

The **About** menu item in the **File** menu displays a **MessageBox** when clicked (lines 54–57). The **Exit** menu item closes the application through **static** method **Exit** of class **Application** (line 64). Class **Application** contains **static** methods used to control program execution. Method **Exit** causes our application to quit.

We made the items in the **Color** submenu (**Black**, **Blue**, **Red** and **Green**) mutually exclusive—the user can select only one at a time (we explain how we did this shortly). To indicate this behavior to the user, we set the menu item's **RadioCheck** properties to **True**. This causes a radio button to appear (instead of a checkmark) when a user selects a color-menu item.

Each **Color** menu item has its own event handler. The event handler for color **Black** is **blackMenuItem_Click** (lines 78–87). The event handlers for colors **Blue**, **Red** and **Green** are **blueMenuItem_Click** (lines 90–99), **redMenuItem_Click** (lines 102–111) and **greenMenuItem_Click** (lines 114–123), respectively. Each **Color** menu item must be mutually exclusive, so each event handler calls method **ClearColor** (lines 68–75) before setting its corresponding **Checked** property to **True**. Method **ClearColor** sets the **Checked** property of each color **MenuItem** to **False**, effectively preventing more than one menu item from being checked at a time.

Software Engineering Observation 13.1

*The mutual exclusion of menu items is not enforced by the **MainMenu**, even when the **RadioCheck** property is **True**. We must program this behavior.*

Look-and-Feel Observation 13.4

*Set the **RadioCheck** property to reflect the desired behavior of menu items. Use radio buttons (**RadioCheck** property set to **True**) to indicate mutually exclusive menu items. Use check marks (**RadioCheck** property set to **False**) for menu items that have no logical restriction.*

The **Font** menu contains three menu items for font types (**Courier**, **Times New Roman** and **Comic Sans**) and two menu items for font styles (**Bold** and **Italic**). We add a separator bar between the font-type and font-style menu items to indicate the distinction: Font types are mutually exclusive, but styles are not. This means that a **Font** object can specify only one font face at a time, but can set multiple styles at once (e.g., a font can be both bold and italic). We set the font-type menu items to display checks. As with the **Color** menu, we also must enforce mutual exclusion in our event handlers.

Event handlers for font-type menu items **TimesRoman**, **Courier** and **ComicSans** are **timesMenuItem_Click** (lines 135–145), **courierMenuItem_Click** (lines 148–158) and **comicMenuItem_Click** (lines 161–171), respectively. These event handlers behave in a manner similar to that of the event handlers for the **Color** menu items. Each event handler clears the **Checked** properties for all font-type menu items by calling method **ClearFont** (lines 126–132), then sets the **Checked** property of the menu item that generated the event to **True**. This enforces the mutual exclusion of the font-type menu items.

The event handlers for the **Bold** and **Italic** menu items (lines 174–197) use the bitwise **Xor** operator. For each font style, the exclusive or operator (^) changes the text to include the style or, if that style is already applied, to remove it. The toggling behavior provided by the **Xor** operator is explained in Chapter 12, Graphical User Interfaces: Part 1. As explained in Chapter 12, this program's event-handling structure allows us to add and remove menu entries while making minimal structural changes to the code.

13.3 LinkLabels

The **LinkLabel** control displays links to other objects, such as files or Web pages (Fig. 13.5). A **LinkLabel** appears as underlined text (colored blue by default). When the mouse moves over the link, the pointer changes to a hand; this is similar to the behavior of a hyperlink in a Web page. The link can change color to indicate whether the link is new, visited or active. When clicked, the **LinkLabel** generates a **LinkClicked** event (see Fig. 13.6). Class **LinkLabel** is derived from class **Label** and therefore inherits all of class **Label**'s functionality.

Class **LinkLabelTest** (Fig. 13.7) uses three **LinkLabel**s, to link to the **C:** drive, the Deitel Web page (**www.deitel.com**) and the Notepad application, respectively. The **Text** properties of the **LinkLabel**s **driveLinkLabel** (line 14), **deitelLinkLabel** (line 15) and **notepadLinkLabel** (line 16) are set to describe each link's purpose.

Look-and-Feel Observation 13.5

*Although other controls can perform actions similar to those of a **LinkLabel** (such as the opening of a Web page), **LinkLabel**s indicate that a link can be followed—a regular label or button does not necessarily convey that idea.*

The event handlers for the **LinkLabel** instances call static method ***Start*** of class ***Process*** (namespace **System.Diagnostics**). This method allows us to execute other programs from our application. Method **Start** can take as arguments either the file to open (a **String**) or the name of the application to run and its command-line arguments (two **String**s). Method **Start**'s arguments can be in the same form as if they were provided for input to the **Run** command in Windows. To open a file that has a file type that Windows recognizes, simply insert the file's full path name. The Windows operating system should be able to use the application associated with the given file's extension to open the file.

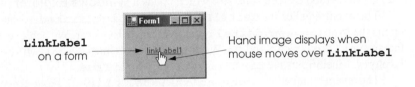

Fig. 13.5   LinkLabel control in running program.

LinkLabel properties and events	Description / Delegate and Event Arguments
Common Properties	
ActiveLinkColor	Specifies the color of the active link when clicked. Default is red.
LinkArea	Specifies which portion of text in the **LinkLabel** is treated as part of the link.
LinkBehavior	Specifies the link's behavior, such as how the link appears when the mouse is placed over it.
LinkColor	Specifies the original color of all links before they have been visited. Default is blue.
Links	Lists the **LinkLabel.Link** objects, which are the links contained in the **LinkLabel**.
LinkVisited	If **True**, link appears as if it were visited (its color is changed to that specified by property **VisitedLinkColor**). Default **False**.
Text	Specifies the text to appear on the control.
UseMnemonic	If **True**, **&** character in **Text** property acts as a shortcut (similar to the *Alt* shortcut in menus).
VisitedLinkColor	Specifies the color of visited links. Default is **Color.Purple**.

Fig. 13.6   LinkLabel properties and events. (Part 1 of 2.)

LinkLabel properties and events	Description / Delegate and Event Arguments
Common Event	*(Delegate **LinkLabelLinkClickedEventHandler**, event arguments **LinkLabelLinkClickedEventArgs**)*
LinkClicked	Generated when link is clicked. Default when control is double-clicked in designer.

Fig. 13.6   LinkLabel properties and events. (Part 2 of 2.)

The event handler for **driveLinkLabel**'s **LinkClicked** events browses the **C:** drive (lines 25–30). Line 28 sets the **LinkVisited** property to **True**, which changes the link's color from blue to purple (we can configure the **LinkVisited** colors through the **Properties** window in the Visual Studio .NET IDE). The event handler then passes **"C:\"** to method **Start** (line 29), which opens a **Windows Explorer** window.

The event handler for **deitelLinkLabel**'s **LinkClicked** events (lines 33–39) opens the Web page **www.deitel.com** in Internet Explorer. We achieve this by passing the string **"IExplore"** and the Web-page address (lines 37–38), which opens Internet Explorer. Line 36 sets the **LinkVisited** property to **True**.

The event handler for **notepadLinkLabel**'s **LinkClicked** events opens the specified Notepad application (lines 42–51). Line 46 sets the link to appear as a visited link. Line 50 passes the argument **"notepad"** to method **Start**, which calls **notepad.exe**. Note that, in line 50, the **.exe** extension is not required—Windows can determine whether the argument given to method **Start** is an executable file.

```
1   // Fig. 13.7: LinkLabelTest.cs
2   // Using LinkLabels to create hyperlinks.
3
4   using System;
5   using System.Drawing;
6   using System.Collections;
7   using System.ComponentModel;
8   using System.Windows.Forms;
9   using System.Data;
10
11  public class LinkLabelTest : System.Windows.Forms.Form
12  {
13      // linklabels to C: drive, www.deitel.com and Notepad
14      private System.Windows.Forms.LinkLabel driveLinkLabel;
15      private System.Windows.Forms.LinkLabel deitelLinkLabel;
16      private System.Windows.Forms.LinkLabel notepadLinkLabel;
17
18      [STAThread]
19      static void Main()
20      {
21          Application.Run( new LinkLabelTest() );
22      }
```

Fig. 13.7   LinkLabels used to link to a folder, a Web page and an application. (Part 1 of 3.)

```
23
24     // browse C:\ drive
25     private void driveLinkLabel_LinkClicked( object sender,
26        System.Windows.Forms.LinkLabelLinkClickedEventArgs e )
27     {
28        driveLinkLabel.LinkVisited = true;
29        System.Diagnostics.Process.Start( "C:\\" );
30     }
31
32     // load www.deitel.com in Web broswer
33     private void deitelLinkLabel_LinkClicked( object sender,
34        System.Windows.Forms.LinkLabelLinkClickedEventArgs e )
35     {
36        deitelLinkLabel.LinkVisited = true;
37        System.Diagnostics.Process.Start(
38           "IExplore", "http://www.deitel.com" );
39     }
40
41     // run application Notepad
42     private void notepadLinkLabel_LinkClicked(
43        object sender,
44        System.Windows.Forms.LinkLabelLinkClickedEventArgs e )
45     {
46        notepadLinkLabel.LinkVisited = true;
47
48        // program called as if in run
49        // menu and full path not needed
50        System.Diagnostics.Process.Start( "notepad" );
51     }
52
53  } // end class LinkLabelTest
```

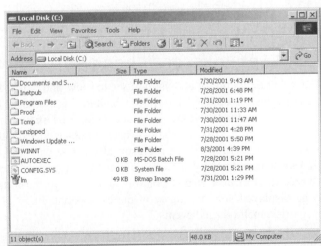

Fig. 13.7 **LinkLabel**s used to link to a folder, a Web page and an application. (Part 2 of 3.)

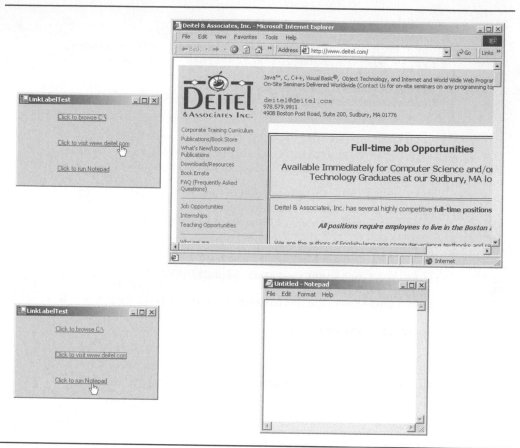

Fig. 13.7   LinkLabels used to link to a folder, a Web page and an application. (Part 3 of 3.)

13.4 ListBoxes and CheckedListBoxes

The **ListBox** control allows the user to view and select from multiple items in a list. **ListBox**es are static GUI entities, which means that users cannot enter new items in the list. The **CheckedListBox** control extends a **ListBox** by including check boxes next to each item in the list. This allows users to place checks on multiple items at once, as is possible in a **CheckBox** control (users also can select multiple items simultaneously from a **ListBox**, but not by default). Figure 13.8 displays a sample **ListBox** and a sample **CheckedListBox**. In both controls, scroll bars appear if the number of items is too large to be displayed simultaneously in the component. Figure 13.9 lists common **ListBox** properties, methods and events.

The **SelectionMode** property determines the number of items that can be selected. This property has the possible values **None**, **One**, **MultiSimple** and **MultiExtended** (from the **SelectionMode** enumeration)—the differences among these settings are explained in Fig. 13.9. The **SelectedIndexChanged** event occurs when the user selects a new item.

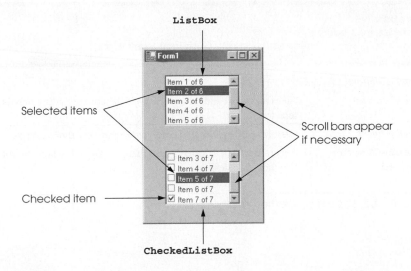

Fig. 13.8 **ListBox** and **CheckedListBox** on a form.

ListBox properties, methods and events	Description / Delegate and Event Arguments
Common Properties	
Items	Lists the collection of items within the **ListBox**.
MultiColumn	Indicates whether the **ListBox** can break a list into multiple columns. Multiple columns are used to make vertical scroll bars unnecessary.
SelectedIndex	Returns the index of the currently selected item. If the user selects multiple items, this method arbitrarily returns one of the selected indices; if no items have been selected, the method returns **-1**.
SelectedIndices	Returns a collection of the indices of all currently selected items.
SelectedItem	Returns a reference to the currently selected item (if multiple items are selected, it returns the item with the lowest index number).
SelectedItems	Returns a collection of the currently selected item(s).
SelectionMode	Determines the number of items that can be selected and the means through which multiple items can be selected. Values **None**, **One**, **MultiSimple** (multiple selection allowed) and **MultiExtended** (multiple selection allowed via a combination of arrow keys, mouse clicks and *Shift* and *Control* buttons).
Sorted	Indicates whether items appear in alphabetical order. **True** causes alphabetization; default is **False**.

Fig. 13.9 **ListBox** properties, methods and events. (Part 1 of 2.)

ListBox properties, methods and events	Description / Delegate and Event Arguments
Common Method	
GetSelected	Takes an index, and returns **True** if the corresponding item is selected.
Common Event	*(Delegate **EventHandler**, event arguments **EventArgs**)*
SelectedIndex-Changed	Generated when selected index changes. Default when control is double-clicked in designer.

Fig. 13.9   **ListBox** properties, methods and events. (Part 2 of 2.)

Both the **ListBox** and **CheckedListBox** have properties **Items**, **SelectedItem** and **SelectedIndex**. Property **Items** returns all the objects in the list as a collection. Collections are a common way of exposing lists of **Object**s in the .NET framework. Many .NET GUI components (e.g., **ListBox**es) use collections to expose lists of internal objects (e.g., items contained within a **ListBox**). We discuss collections further in Chapter 23, Data Structures and Collections. Property **SelectedItem** returns the currently selected item. If the user can select multiple items, use collection **SelectedItems** to return all the selected items as a collection. Property **SelectedIndex** returns the index of the selected item—if there could be more than one, use property **SelectedIndices**. If no items are selected, property **SelectedIndex** returns **-1**. Method **GetSelected** takes an index and returns **True** if the corresponding item is selected.

To add items to the **ListBox** or the **CheckedListBox** we must add objects to its **Items** collection. This can be accomplished by invoking method **Add** to add a **String** to the **ListBox**'s or **CheckedListBox**'s **Items** collection. For example, we could write

```
myListBox.Items.Add( "myListItem" )
```

to add **String** *myListItem* to **ListBox** *myListBox*. To add multiple objects, programmers can either use method **Add** multiple times or use method **AddRange** to add an array of objects. Classes **ListBox** and **CheckedListBox** use each submitted object's **ToString** method to determine the label for the corresponding object's entry in the list. This allows developers to add different objects to a **ListBox** or a **CheckedListBox** that later can be returned through properties **SelectedItem** and **SelectedItems**.

Alternatively, we can add items to **ListBox**es and **CheckedListBox**es visually by examining the **Items** property in the **Properties** window. Clicking the ellipsis opens the **String Collection Editor**, a text area in which we can type the items to add; each item should appear on a separate line (Fig. 13.10). Visual Studio .NET then adds these **String**s to the **Items** collection inside method **InitializeComponent**.

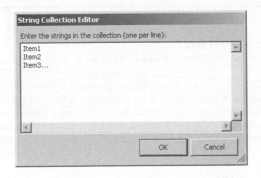

Fig. 13.10 String Collection Editor.

13.4.1 ListBoxes

Class **ListBoxTest** (Fig. 13.11) enables the user to add, remove and clear items from **ListBox displayListBox** (line 14). Class **ListBoxTest** uses **TextBox input-TextBox** (line 17) to allow the user to type in a new item. When the user clicks button **addButton** (line 20), the new item appears in **displayListBox**. Similarly, if the user selects an item and clicks **removeButton** (line 21), the item is deleted. Control **clear-Button** (line 22) deletes all entries in **displayListBox**. The user terminates the application by clicking button **exitButton** (line 23).

The **addButton_Click** event handler (lines 33–38) calls method **Add** of the **Items** collection in the **ListBox**. This method takes a **String** as the item to add to **display-ListBox**. In this case, the **String** used is the user-input text, or **inputTextBox.Text** (line 36). After the item is added, **txtInput.Text** is cleared (line 37).

The **removeButton_Click** event handler (lines 41–48) calls method **Remove** of the **Items** collection. Event handler **removeButton_Click** first uses property **SelectedIndex** to check which index is selected. Unless **SelectedIndex** is **-1** (line 45), the handler removes the item that corresponds to the selected index.

```
1    // Fig 13.11: ListBoxTest.cs
2    // Program to add, remove and clear list box items.
3
4    using System;
5    using System.Drawing;
6    using System.Collections;
7    using System.ComponentModel;
8    using System.Windows.Forms;
9    using System.Data;
10
11   public class ListBoxTest : System.Windows.Forms.Form
12   {
13       // contains user-input list of elements
14       private System.Windows.Forms.ListBox displayListBox;
15
```

Fig. 13.11 **ListBox** used in a program to add, remove and clear items. (Part 1 of 3.)

```
16        // user input textbox
17        private System.Windows.Forms.TextBox inputTextBox;
18
19        // add, remove, clear and exit command buttons
20        private System.Windows.Forms.Button addButton;
21        private System.Windows.Forms.Button removeButton;
22        private System.Windows.Forms.Button clearButton;
23        private System.Windows.Forms.Button exitButton;
24
25        [STAThread]
26        static void Main()
27        {
28           Application.Run( new ListBoxTest() );
29        }
30
31        // add new item (text from input box)
32        // and clear input box
33        private void addButton_Click(
34           object sender, System.EventArgs e )
35        {
36           displayListBox.Items.Add( inputTextBox.Text );
37           inputTextBox.Clear();
38        }
39
40        // remove item if one selected
41        private void removeButton_Click(
42           object sender, System.EventArgs e )
43        {
44           // remove only if item selected
45           if ( displayListBox.SelectedIndex != -1 )
46              displayListBox.Items.RemoveAt(
47                 displayListBox.SelectedIndex );
48        }
49
50        // clear all items
51        private void clearButton_Click(
52           object sender, System.EventArgs e )
53        {
54           displayListBox.Items.Clear();
55        }
56
57        // exit application
58        private void exitButton_Click(
59           object sender, System.EventArgs e )
60        {
61           Application.Exit();
62        }
63
64     } // end class ListBoxTest
```

Fig. 13.11 ListBox used in a program to add, remove and clear items. (Part 2 of 3.)

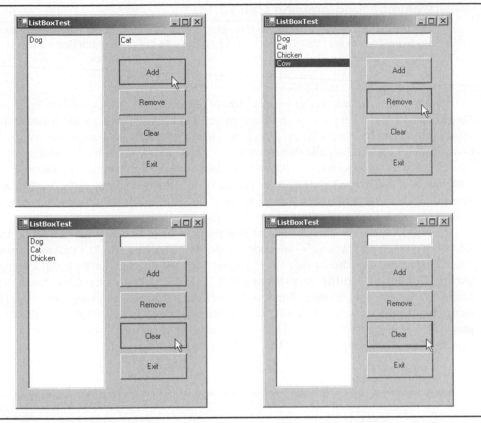

Fig. 13.11 **ListBox** used in a program to add, remove and clear items. (Part 3 of 3.)

The event handler for **clearButton_Click** (lines 51–55) calls method **Clear** of the **Items** collection (line 54). This removes all the entries in **displayListBox**. Finally, event handler **exitButton_Click** (lines 58–62) terminates the application, using method **Application.Exit** (line 61).

13.4.2 CheckedListBoxes

The **CheckedListBox** control derives from class **ListBox** and includes a checkbox next to each item in the list. As in **ListBox**es, items can be added via methods **Add** and **AddRange** or through the **String Collection Editor**. **CheckedListBox**es imply that multiple items can be selected, and the only possible values for the **SelectionMode** property are **SelectionMode.None** and **SelectionMode.One**. **Selection-Mode.One** allows multiple selection, because checkboxes imply that there are no logical restrictions on the items—the user can select as many items as required. Thus, the only choice is whether to give the user multiple selection or no selection at all. This keeps the **CheckedListBox**'s behavior consistent with that of **CheckBox**es. The programmer is unable to set the last two **SelectionMode** values, **MultiSimple** and **MultiExtended**, because the only logical selection modes are handled by **None** and **One**. Common properties and events of **CheckedListBox**es appear in Fig. 13.12.

Common Programming Error 13.1

*The IDE displays an error message if the programmer attempts to set the **Selection-Mode** property to **MultiSimple** or **MultiExtended** in the **Properties** window of a **CheckedListBox**; if this value is set by the programmer in the code, a runtime error occurs.*

Event **ItemCheck** is generated whenever a user checks or unchecks a **CheckedListBox** item. Event argument properties **CurrentValue** and **NewValue** return **CheckState** values for the current and the new state of the item, respectively. A comparison of these values allows us to determine whether the **CheckedListBox** item was checked or unchecked. The **CheckedListBox** control retains the **SelectedItems** and **SelectedIndices** properties (it inherits them from class **ListBox**). However, it also includes properties **CheckedItems** and **CheckedIndices**, which return information about the checked items and indices.

In Fig. 13.13, class **CheckedListBoxTest** uses a **CheckedListBox** and a **ListBox** to display a user's selection of books. The **CheckedListBox** named **inputCheckedListBox** (lines 14–15) allows the user to select multiple titles. In the **String Collection Editor**, items were added for some Deitel books: C++, Java, VB, Internet & WWW, Perl, Python, Wireless Internet and Advanced Java (the acronym HTP stands for "How to Program"). The **ListBox**, named **displayListBox** (line 18), displays the user's selection. In the screen shots accompanying this example, the **CheckedListBox** appears to the left, the **ListBox** to the right.

CheckedListBox properties, methods and events	Description / Delegate and Event Arguments
Common Properties	*(All the **ListBox** properties and events are inherited by **CheckedListBox**)*
CheckedItems	Lists the collection of items that are checked. This is distinct from the selected items, which are highlighted (but not necessarily checked). *Note: There can be at most one selected item at any given time.*
CheckedIndices	Returns indices for the items that are checked. Not the same as the selected indices.
SelectionMode	Determines how many items can be checked. Only possible values are **One** (allows multiple checks to be placed) or **None** (does not allow any checks to be placed).
Common Method	
GetItemChecked	Takes an index, and returns **True** if corresponding item is checked.
Common Event	*(Delegate **ItemCheckEventHandler**, event arguments **ItemCheckEventArgs**)*
ItemCheck	Generated when an item is checked or unchecked.

Fig. 13.12 CheckedListBox properties, methods and events. (Part 1 of 2.)

CheckedListBox properties, methods and events	Description / Delegate and Event Arguments

ItemCheckEventArgs Properties

CurrentValue	Indicates whether current item is checked or unchecked. Possible values are **Checked**, **Unchecked** and **Indeterminate**.
Index	Returns index of the item that changed.
NewValue	Specifies the new state of item.

Fig. 13.12 CheckedListBox properties, methods and events. (Part 2 of 2.)

```
1   // Fig. 13.13: CheckedListBoxTest.cs
2   // Using the checked list boxes to add items to a list box
3
4   using System;
5   using System.Drawing;
6   using System.Collections;
7   using System.ComponentModel;
8   using System.Windows.Forms;
9   using System.Data;
10
11  public class CheckedListBoxTest : System.Windows.Forms.Form
12  {
13     // list of available book titles
14     private System.Windows.Forms.CheckedListBox
15        inputCheckedListBox;
16
17     // user selection list
18     private System.Windows.Forms.ListBox displayListBox;
19
20     [STAThread]
21     static void Main()
22     {
23        Application.Run( new CheckedListBoxTest() );
24     }
25
26     // item about to change,
27     // add or remove from displayListBox
28     private void inputCheckedListBox_ItemCheck(
29        object sender,
30        System.Windows.Forms.ItemCheckEventArgs e )
31     {
32        // obtain reference of selected item
33        string item =
34           inputCheckedListBox.SelectedItem.ToString();
35
```

Fig. 13.13 CheckedListBox and **ListBox** used in a program to display a user selection. (Part 1 of 2.)

```
36              // if item checked add to listbox
37              // otherwise remove from listbox
38              if ( e.NewValue == CheckState.Checked )
39                 displayListBox.Items.Add( item );
40              else
41                 displayListBox.Items.Remove( item );
42
43           } // end method inputCheckedListBox_Click
44
45    } // end class CheckedListBox
```

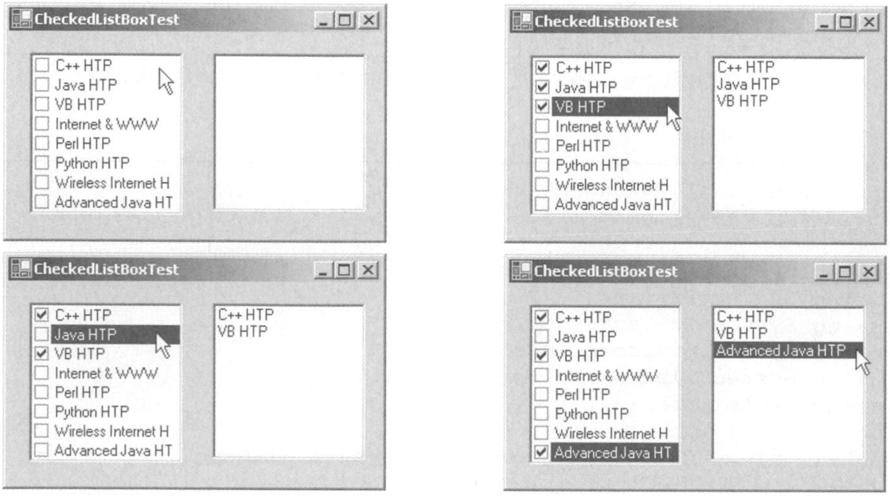

Fig. 13.13 CheckedListBox and ListBox used in a program to display a user selection. (Part 2 of 2.)

When the user checks or unchecks an item in **CheckedListBox inputCheckedListBox**, the system generates an **ItemCheck** event. Event handler **inputCheckedListBox_ItemCheck** (lines 28–43) handles the event. An **if/else** control structure (lines 38–41) determines whether the user checked or unchecked an item in the **CheckedListBox**. Line 38 uses the **NewValue** property to test for whether the item is being checked (**CheckState.Checked**). If the user checks an item, line 39 adds the checked entry to the **ListBox displayListBox**. If the user unchecks an item, line 41 removes the corresponding item from **displayListBox**.

13.5 ComboBoxes

The ***ComboBox*** control combines **TextBox** features with a *drop-down list*. A drop-down list is a GUI component that contains a list from which values can be chosen. It usually appears as a text box with a down arrow to its right. By default, the user can enter text into the text box or click the down arrow to display a list of predefined items. If a user chooses an element from this list, that element is displayed in the text box. If the list contains more elements than can be displayed in the drop-down list, a scrollbar appears. The maximum number of items that a drop-down list can display at one time is set by property ***MaxDropDownItems***. Figure 13.14 shows a sample **ComboBox** in three different states.

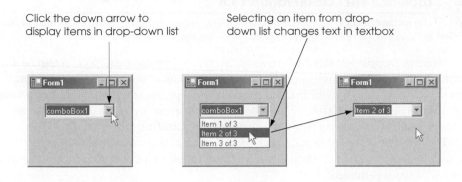

Fig. 13.14 ComboBox demonstration.

As with the **ListBox** control, the developer can add objects to collection **Items** programmatically, using methods **Add** and **AddRange**, or visually, with the **String Collection Editor**. Figure 13.15 lists common properties and events of class **ComboBox**.

ComboBox events and properties	Description / Delegate and Event Arguments
Common Properties	
DropDownStyle	Determines the type of combo box. Value **Simple** means that the text portion is editable and the list portion is always visible. Value **DropDown** (the default) means that the text portion is editable, but the user must click an arrow button to see the list portion. Value **DropDownList** means that the text portion is not editable and the user must click the arrow button to see the list portion.
Items	The collection of items in the **ComboBox** control.
MaxDropDownItems	Specifies the maximum number of items (between **1** and **100**) that can display in the drop-down list. If the number of items exceeds the maximum number of items to display, a scroll bar appears.
SelectedIndex	Returns index of currently selected item. If there is no currently selected item, **-1** is returned.
SelectedItem	Returns a reference to the currently selected item.
Sorted	Specifies whether items in a list are alphabetized. If **True**, items appear in alphabetical order. Default is **False**.
Common Event	*(Delegate **EventHandler**, event arguments **EventArgs**)*
SelectedIndex-Changed	Generated when the selected index changes (such as when a check box has been checked or unchecked). Default when control is double-clicked in designer.

Fig. 13.15 ComboBox properties and events.

Look-and-Feel Observation 13.6

*Use a **ComboBox** to save space on a GUI. The disadvantage is that, unlike with a **ListBox**, the user cannot see available items without scrolling.*

Property ***DropDownStyle*** determines the type of **ComboBox**. Style ***Simple*** does not display a drop-down arrow. Instead, a scrollbar appears next to the control, allowing the user to select a choice from the list. The user can also type in a selection. Style ***DropDown*** (the default) displays a drop-down list when the down arrow is clicked (or the down arrow key is pressed). The user can type a new item into the **ComboBox**.

The last style is ***DropDownList***, which displays a drop-down list but does not allow the user to enter a new item. Drop-down lists save room, so a **ComboBox** should be used when GUI space is limited.

The **ComboBox** control has properties **Items** (a collection), **SelectedItem** and **SelectedIndex**, which are similar to the corresponding properties in **ListBox**. There can be at most one selected item in a **ComboBox** (if zero, then **SelectedIndex** is **-1**). When the selected item changes, event **SelectedIndexChanged** is generated.

Class **ComboBoxTest** (Fig. 13.16) allows users to select a shape to draw—an empty or filled circle, ellipse, square or pie—by using a **ComboBox**. The combo box in this example is uneditable, so the user cannot input a custom item.

Look-and-Feel Observation 13.7

*Make lists (such as **ComboBox**es) editable only if the program is designed to accept user-submitted elements. Otherwise, the user might enter a custom item and then be unable to use it.*

After creating **ComboBox imageComboBox** (line 14), we make it uneditable by setting its **DropDownStyle** to **DropDownList** in the **Properties** window. Next, we add items **Circle**, **Square**, **Ellipse**, **Pie**, **Filled Circle**, **Filled Square**, **Filled Ellipse** and **Filled Pie** to the **Items** collection. We added these items using the **String Collection Editor**. Whenever the user selects an item from **imageComboBox**, the system generates a **SelectedIndexChanged** event. Event handler **imageComboBox_SelectedIndexChanged** (lines 23–77) handles these events. Lines 27–34 create a **Graphics** object, a **Pen** and a **SolidBrush**, with which the program draws on the form. The **Graphics** object (line 22) allows a pen or brush to draw on a component, using one of several **Graphics** methods. The **Pen** object is used by methods **drawEllipse**, **drawRectangle** and **drawPie** (lines 43–56) to draw the outlines of their corresponding shapes. The **SolidBrush** object is used by methods **fillEllipse**, **fillRectangle** and **fillPie** (lines 59–72) to draw their corresponding solid shapes. Line 37 colors the entire form **White**, using **Graphics** method **Clear**. These methods are discussed in greater detail in Chapter 16, Graphics and Multimedia.

```
1   // Fig. 13.16: ComboBoxTest.cs
2   // Using ComboBox to select shape to draw
3
4   using System;
5   using System.Drawing;
6   using System.Collections;
```

Fig. 13.16 ComboBox used to draw a selected shape. (Part 1 of 3.)

```
7   using System.ComponentModel;
8   using System.Windows.Forms;
9   using System.Data;
10
11  public class ComboBoxTest : System.Windows.Forms.Form
12  {
13     // contains shape list (circle, square, ellipse, pie)
14     private System.Windows.Forms.ComboBox imageComboBox;
15
16     [STAThread]
17     static void Main()
18     {
19        Application.Run( new ComboBoxTest() );
20     }
21
22     // get selected index, draw shape
23     private void imageComboBox_SelectedIndexChanged(
24        object sender, System.EventArgs e )
25     {
26        // create graphics object, pen and brush
27        Graphics myGraphics = base.CreateGraphics();
28
29        // create Pen using color DarkRed
30        Pen myPen = new Pen( Color.DarkRed );
31
32        // create SolidBrush using color DarkRed
33        SolidBrush mySolidBrush =
34           new SolidBrush( Color.DarkRed );
35
36        // clear drawing area setting it to color White
37        myGraphics.Clear( Color.White );
38
39        // find index, draw proper shape
40        switch ( imageComboBox.SelectedIndex )
41        {
42           case 0: // case circle is selected
43              myGraphics.DrawEllipse(
44                 myPen, 50, 50, 150, 150 );
45              break;
46           case 1: // case rectangle is selected
47              myGraphics.DrawRectangle(
48                 myPen, 50, 50, 150, 150 );
49              break;
50           case 2: // case ellipse is selected
51              myGraphics.DrawEllipse(
52                 myPen, 50, 85, 150, 115 );
53              break;
54           case 3: // case pie is selected
55              myGraphics.DrawPie(
56                 myPen, 50, 50, 150, 150, 0, 45 );
57              break;
```

Fig. 13.16 ComboBox used to draw a selected shape. (Part 2 of 3.)

```
58                case 4: // case filled circle is selected
59                   myGraphics.FillEllipse(
60                      mySolidBrush, 50, 50, 150, 150 );
61                   break;
62                case 5: // case filled rectangle is selected
63                   myGraphics.FillRectangle(
64                      mySolidBrush, 50, 50, 150, 150 );
65                   break;
66                case 6: // case filled ellipse is selected
67                   myGraphics.FillEllipse(
68                      mySolidBrush, 50, 85, 150, 115 );
69                   break;
70                case 7: // case filled pie is selected
71                   myGraphics.FillPie(
72                      mySolidBrush, 50, 50, 150, 150, 0, 45 );
73                   break;
74
75            } // end switch
76
77        } // end method imageComboBox_SelectedIndexChanged
78
79    } // end class ComboBoxTest
```

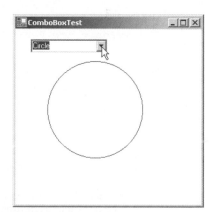

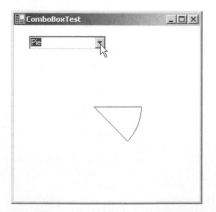

Fig. 13.16 ComboBox used to draw a selected shape. (Part 3 of 3.)

The application draws a particular shape specified by the selected item's index. The **switch** structure (lines 40–75) uses **imageComboBox.SelectedIndex** to determine which item the user selected. Class **Graphics** method *DrawEllipse* (lines 43–44) takes a **Pen**, the *x*- and *y*-coordinates of the center and the width and height of the ellipse to draw. The origin of the coordinate system is in the upper left corner of the form; the *x*-coordinate increases to the right, the *y*-coordinate increases downward. A circle is a special case of an ellipse (the height and width are equal). Lines 43–44 draw a circle. Lines 51–52 draw an ellipse that has different values for height and width.

Class **Graphics** method *DrawRectangle* (lines 47–48) takes a **Pen**, the *x*- and *y*-coordinates of the upper-left corner and the width and height of the rectangle to draw. Method *DrawPie* (line 55–56) draws a pie as a portion of an ellipse. The ellipse is bounded by a rectangle. Method **DrawPie** takes a **Pen**, the *x*- and *y*-coordinates of the upper-left corner of the rectangle, its width and height, the start angle (in degrees) and the sweep angle (in degrees) of the pie. Angles increase clockwise. The *FillEllipse* (lines 59–60 and 67–68), *FillRectange* (lines 63–64) and *FillPie* (lines 71–72) methods are similar to their unfilled counterparts, except that they take a **SolidBrush** instead of a **Pen**. Some of the drawn shapes are illustrated in the screen shots at the bottom of Fig. 13.16.

13.6 TreeViews

The *TreeView* control displays *nodes* hierarchically on a *tree*. Traditionally, nodes are objects that contain values and can refer to other nodes. A *parent node* contains *child nodes*, and the child nodes can be parents to other nodes. Two child nodes that have the same parent node are considered *sibling nodes*. A tree is a collection of nodes, usually organized in a hierarchical manner. The first parent node of a tree is the *root* node (a **TreeView** can have multiple roots). For example, the file system of a computer can be represented as a tree. The top-level directory (perhaps **C:**) would be the root, each subfolder of **C:** would be a child node and each child folder could have its own children. **TreeView** controls are useful for displaying hierarchal information, such as the file structure that we just mentioned. We cover nodes and trees in greater detail in Chapter 24, Data Structures. Figure 13.17 displays a sample **TreeView** control on a form.

A parent node can be expanded or collapsed by clicking the plus or minus box to its left. Nodes without children do not have an expand or collapse box.

The nodes displayed in a **TreeView** are instances of class **TreeNode**. Each **TreeNode** has a **Nodes** collection (type **TreeNodeCollection**), which contains a list of other **TreeNode**s—its children. The **Parent** property returns a reference to the parent node (or **null** if the node is a root node). Figure 13.18 and Fig. 13.19 list the common properties of **TreeView**s and **TreeNode**s and an event of **TreeView**s.

To add nodes to the **TreeView** visually, click the ellipsis by the **Nodes** property in the **Properties** window. This opens the **TreeNode Editor**, which displays an empty tree representing the **TreeView** (Fig. 13.20). There are buttons to create a root, to add or delete a node.

To add nodes through code, we first must create a root node. Make a new **TreeNode** object and pass it a **String** to display. Then, use method **Add** to add this new **TreeNode** to the **TreeView**'s **Nodes** collection. Thus, to add a root node to **TreeView** *myTreeView*, write *myTreeView*.**Nodes.Add(new TreeNode(** *RootLabel* **))**

where *myTreeView* is the **TreeView** to which we are adding nodes, and *RootLabel* is the text to display in *myTreeView*. To add children to a root node, add new **TreeNode**s to its **Nodes** collection. We select the appropriate root node from the **TreeView** by writing

myTreeView.**Nodes[** *myIndex* **]**

where *myIndex* is the root node's index in *myTreeView*'s **Nodes** collection. We add nodes to child nodes through the same process by which we added root nodes to *myTreeView*. To add a child to the root node at index *myIndex*, write

myTreeView.**Nodes[** *myIndex* **].Nodes.Add(new TreeNode(** *ChildLabel* **))**

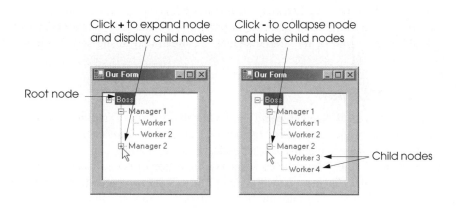

Fig. 13.17 TreeView displaying a sample tree.

TreeView properties and events	Description / Delegate and Event Arguments
Common Properties	
CheckBoxes	Indicates whether checkboxes appear next to nodes. **True** displays checkboxes. Default is **False**.
ImageList	Indicates the **ImageList** used to display icons by the nodes. An *ImageList* is a collection that contains a number of **Image** objects.
Nodes	Lists the collection of **TreeNode**s in the control. Contains methods **Add** (adds a **TreeNode** object), **Clear** (deletes the entire collection) and **Remove** (deletes a specific node). Removing a parent node deletes all its children.

Fig. 13.18 TreeView properties and events. (Part 1 of 2.)

TreeView properties and events	Description / Delegate and Event Arguments
`SelectedNode`	Currently selected node.
Common Event	*(Delegate* **TreeViewEventHandler***, event arguments* **TreeViewEventArgs***)*
`AfterSelect`	Generated after selected node changes. Default when double-clicked in designer.

Fig. 13.18 TreeView properties and events. (Part 2 of 2.)

TreeNode properties and methods	Description / Delegate and Event Arguments
Common Properties	
`Checked`	Indicates whether the **TreeNode** is checked. (**CheckBoxes** property must be set to **True** in parent **TreeView**.)
`FirstNode`	Specifies the first node in the **Nodes** collection (i.e., first child in tree).
`FullPath`	Indicates the path of the node, starting at the root of the tree.
`ImageIndex`	Specifies the index of the image to be shown when the node is deselected.
`LastNode`	Specifies the last node in the **Nodes** collection (i.e., last child in tree).
`NextNode`	Next sibling node.
`Nodes`	The collection of **TreeNode**s contained in the current node (i.e., all the children of the current node). Contains methods **Add** (adds a **TreeNode** object), **Clear** (deletes the entire collection) and **Remove** (deletes a specific node). Removing a parent node deletes all its children.
`PrevNode`	Indicates the previous sibling node.
`SelectedImageIndex`	Specifies the index of the image to use when the node is selected.
`Text`	Specifies the text to display in the **TreeView**.
Common Methods	
`Collapse`	Collapses a node.
`Expand`	Expands a node.
`ExpandAll`	Expands all the children of a node.
`GetNodeCount`	Returns the number of child nodes.

Fig. 13.19 TreeNode properties and methods.

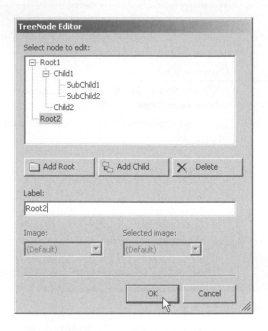

Fig. 13.20 TreeNode Editor.

Class **TreeViewDirectoryStructureTest** (Fig. 13.21) uses a **TreeView** to display the directory file structure on a computer. The root node is the **C:** drive, and each subfolder of **C:** becomes a child. This layout is similar to that used in **Windows Explorer**. Folders can be expanded or collapsed by clicking the plus or minus boxes that appear to their left.

When **TreeViewDirectoryStructureTest** loads, the system generates a **Load** event, which is handled by event handler **TreeViewDirectoryStructureTest_Load** (lines 64–72). Line 69 adds a root node (**C:**) to our **TreeView**, named **directoryTreeView**. **C:** is the root folder for the entire directory structure. Lines 70–71 call method **PopulateTreeView** (lines 25–61), which takes a directory (a **String**) and a parent node. Method **PopulateTreeView** then creates child nodes corresponding to the subdirectories of the directory that was passed to it.

```
1   // Fig. 13.21: TreeViewDirectoryStructureTest.cs
2   // Using TreeView to display directory structure
3
4   using System;
5   using System.Drawing;
6   using System.Collections;
7   using System.ComponentModel;
8   using System.Windows.Forms;
9   using System.Data;
10  using System.IO;
11
```

Fig. 13.21 TreeView used to display directories. (Part 1 of 3.)

```
12   public class TreeViewDirectoryStructureTest
13      : System.Windows.Forms.Form
14   {
15      // contains view of c: drive directory structure
16      private System.Windows.Forms.TreeView directoryTreeView;
17
18      [STAThread]
19      static void Main()
20      {
21         Application.Run(
22            new TreeViewDirectoryStructureTest() );
23      }
24
25      public void PopulateTreeView(
26         string directoryValue, TreeNode parentNode )
27      {
28         // populate current node with subdirectories
29         string[] directoryArray =
30            Directory.GetDirectories( directoryValue );
31
32         // populate current node with subdirectories
33         try
34         {
35            if ( directoryArray.Length != 0 )
36            {
37               // for every subdirectory, create new TreeNode,
38               // add as child of current node and recursively
39               // populate child nodes with subdirectories
40               foreach ( string directory in directoryArray )
41               {
42                  // create TreeNode for current directory
43                  TreeNode myNode = new TreeNode( directory );
44
45                  // add current directory node to parent node
46                  parentNode.Nodes.Add( myNode );
47
48                  // recursively populate every subdirectory
49                  PopulateTreeView( directory, myNode );
50               }
51
52            } // end if
53         }
54
55         // catch exception
56         catch ( UnauthorizedAccessException )
57         {
58            parentNode.Nodes.Add( "Access denied" );
59         }
60
61      } // end PopulateTreeView
62
```

Fig. 13.21 TreeView used to display directories. (Part 2 of 3.)

```
63        // called by system when form loads
64        private void TreeViewDirectoryStructureTest_Load(
65           object sender, System.EventArgs e)
66        {
67           // add c:\ drive to directoryTreeView and
68           // insert its subfolders
69           directoryTreeView.Nodes.Add( "C:\\" );
70           PopulateTreeView(
71              "C:\\", directoryTreeView.Nodes[ 0 ] );
72        }
73
74     } // end class TreeViewDirectoryStructure
```

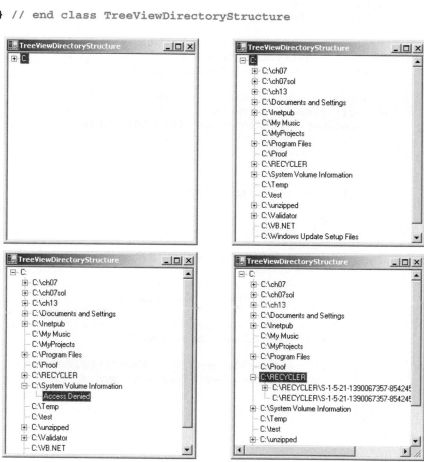

Fig. 13.21 TreeView used to display directories. (Part 3 of 3.)

Method **PopulateTreeView** (lines 25–61) obtains a list of subdirectories, using method *GetDirectories* of class **Directory** (namespace **System.IO**) on lines 29–30. Method **GetDirectories** takes a **String** (the current directory) and returns an array of **String**s (the subdirectories). If a directory is not accessible for security reasons, an **UnauthorizedAccessException** is thrown. Lines 56–59 catch this exception and add a node containing "**Access Denied**" instead of displaying the subdirectories.

If there are accessible subdirectories, each **String** in the **directoryArray** is used to create a new child node (line 43). We use method **Add** (line 46) to add each child node to the parent. Then, method **PopulateTreeView** is called recursively on every subdirectory (line 49) and eventually populates the entire directory structure. Our recursive algorithm causes our program to have an initial delay when it loads—it must create a tree for the entire **C:** drive. However, once the drive folder names are added to the appropriate **Nodes** collection, they can be expanded and collapsed without delay. In the next section, we present an alternative algorithm to solve this problem.

13.7 ListViews

The *ListView* control is similar to a **ListBox**, in that both display lists from which the user can select one or more items (to see an example of a **ListView**, look ahead to the output of Fig. 13.24). The important difference between the two classes is that a **ListView** can display icons alongside the list items in a variety of ways (controlled by its **ImageList** property). Property *MultiSelect* (a boolean) determines whether multiple items can be selected. Checkboxes can be included by setting property **CheckBoxes** (a boolean) to **True**, making the **ListView**'s appearance similar to that of a **CheckedListBox**. The **View** property specifies the layout of the **ListBox**. Property *Activation* determines the method by which the user selects a list item. The details of these properties are explained in Fig. 13.22.

ListView allows us to define the images used as icons for **ListView** items. To display images, we must use an **ImageList** component. Create one by dragging it onto a form from the **ToolBox**. Then, click the **Images** collection in the **Properties** window to display the **Image Collection Editor** (Fig. 13.23). Here, developers can browse for images that they wish to add to the **ImageList**, which contains an array of **Image**s. Once the images have been defined, set property **SmallImageList** of the **ListView** to the new **ImageList** object. Property **SmallImageList** specifies the image list for the small icons. Property **LargeImageList** sets the **ImageList** for large icons. Icons for the **ListView** items are selected by setting the item's **ImageIndex** property to the appropriate array index.

ListView events and properties	Description / Delegate and Event Arguments
Common Properties	
Activation	Determines how the user activates an item. This property takes a value in the **ItemActivation** enumeration. Possible values are **OneClick** (single-click activation), **TwoClick** (double-click activation, item changes color when selected) and **Standard** (double-click activation).
CheckBoxes	Indicates whether items appear with checkboxes. **True** displays checkboxes. Default is **False**.
LargeImageList	Indicates the **ImageList** used when displaying large icons.

Fig. 13.22 ListView properties and events. (Part 1 of 2.)

ListView events and properties	Description / Delegate and Event Arguments
Items	Returns the collection of **ListViewItem**s in the control.
MultiSelect	Determines whether multiple selection is allowed. Default is **True**, which enables multiple selection.
SelectedItems	Lists the collection of currently selected items.
SmallImageList	Specifies the **ImageList** used when displaying small icons.
View	Determines appearance of **ListViewItem**s. Values **LargeIcon** (large icon displayed, items can be in multiple columns), **SmallIcon** (small icon displayed), **List** (small icons displayed, items appear in a single column) and **Details** (like **List**, but multiple columns of information can be displayed per item).
Common Event	*(Delegate **EventHandler**, event arguments **EventArgs**)*
ItemActivate	Generated when an item in the **ListView** is activated. Does not specify which item is activated.

Fig. 13.22 **ListView** properties and events. (Part 2 of 2.)

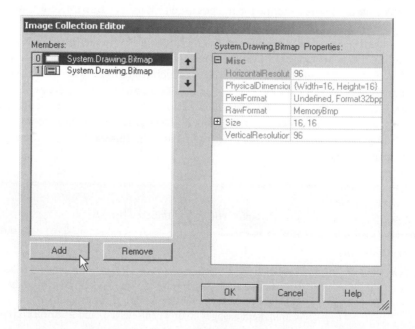

Fig. 13.23 Image Collection Editor window for an **ImageList** component.

Class **ListViewTest** (Fig. 13.24) displays files and folders in a **ListView**, along with small icons representing each file or folder. If a file or folder is inaccessible because of permission settings, a message box appears. The program scans the contents of the directory as it browses, rather than indexing the entire drive at once.

```
 1    // Fig. 13.24: ListViewTest.cs
 2    // Displaying directories and their contents in ListView.
 3
 4    using System;
 5    using System.Drawing;
 6    using System.Collections;
 7    using System.ComponentModel;
 8    using System.Windows.Forms;
 9    using System.Data;
10    using System.IO;
11
12    public class ListViewTest : System.Windows.Forms.Form
13    {
14       // display labels for current location
15       // in directory tree
16       private System.Windows.Forms.Label currentLabel;
17       private System.Windows.Forms.Label displayLabel;
18
19       // display contents of current directory
20       private System.Windows.Forms.ListView browserListView;
21
22       // specifies images for file icons and folder icons
23       private System.Windows.Forms.ImageList fileFolder;
24
25       // get current directory
26       string currentDirectory =
27          Directory.GetCurrentDirectory();
28
29       [STAThread]
30       static void Main()
31       {
32          Application.Run( new ListViewTest() );
33       }
34
35       // browse directory user clicked or go up one level
36       private void browserListView_Click(
37          object sender, System.EventArgs e )
38       {
39          // ensure item selected
40          if ( browserListView.SelectedItems.Count != 0 )
41          {
42             // if first item selected, go up one level
43             if ( browserListView.Items[ 0 ].Selected )
44             {
45                // create DirectoryInfo object for directory
46                DirectoryInfo directoryObject =
47                   new DirectoryInfo( currentDirectory );
48
49                // if directory has parent, load it
50                if ( directoryObject.Parent != null )
51                   LoadFilesInDirectory(
52                      directoryObject.Parent.FullName );
53             }
```

Fig. 13.24 ListView displaying files and folders. (Part 1 of 4.)

```
54
55          // selected directory or file
56          else
57          {
58             // directory or file chosen
59             string chosen =
60                browserListView.SelectedItems[ 0 ].Text;
61
62             // if item selected is directory
63             if ( Directory.Exists( currentDirectory +
64                "\\" + chosen ) )
65             {
66                // load subdirectory
67                // if in c:\, do not need '\',
68                // otherwise we do
69                if ( currentDirectory == "C:\\" )
70                   LoadFilesInDirectory(
71                      currentDirectory + chosen );
72                else
73                   LoadFilesInDirectory(
74                      currentDirectory + "\\" + chosen );
75             } //end if
76
77          } // end else
78
79          // update displayLabel
80          displayLabel.Text = currentDirectory;
81
82       } // end if
83
84    } // end method browserListView_Click
85
86    // display files/subdirectories of current directory
87    public void LoadFilesInDirectory(
88       string currentDirectoryValue )
89    {
90       // load directory information and display
91       try
92       {
93          // clear ListView and set first item
94          browserListView.Items.Clear();
95          browserListView.Items.Add( "Go Up One Level" );
96
97          // update current directory
98          currentDirectory = currentDirectoryValue;
99          DirectoryInfo newCurrentDirectory =
100             new DirectoryInfo( currentDirectory );
101
102          // put files and directories into arrays
103          DirectoryInfo[] directoryArray =
104             newCurrentDirectory.GetDirectories();
105
```

Fig. 13.24 ListView displaying files and folders. (Part 2 of 4.)

```
106                FileInfo[] fileArray =
107                   newCurrentDirectory.GetFiles();
108
109                // add directory names to ListView
110                foreach ( DirectoryInfo dir in directoryArray )
111                {
112                   // add directory to ListView
113                   ListViewItem newDirectoryItem =
114                      browserListView.Items.Add( dir.Name );
115
116                   // set directory image
117                   newDirectoryItem.ImageIndex = 0;
118                }
119
120                // add file names to ListView
121                foreach ( FileInfo file in fileArray )
122                {
123                   // add file to ListView
124                   ListViewItem newFileItem =
125                      browserListView.Items.Add( file.Name );
126
127                   newFileItem.ImageIndex = 1;   // set file image
128                }
129          } // end try
130
131          // access denied
132          catch ( UnauthorizedAccessException exception )
133          {
134             MessageBox.Show(
135                "Warning: Some fields may not be " +
136                "visible due to permission settings",
137                "Attention", 0, MessageBoxIcon.Warning );
138          }
139
140       } // end method LoadFilesInDirectory
141
142       // handle load event when Form displayed for first time
143       private void ListViewTest_Load(
144          object sender, System.EventArgs e )
145       {
146          // set image list
147          Image folderImage = Image.FromFile(
148             currentDirectory + "\\images\\folder.bmp" );
149
150          Image fileImage = Image.FromFile( currentDirectory +
151             "\\images\\file.bmp" );
152
153          fileFolder.Images.Add( folderImage );
154          fileFolder.Images.Add( fileImage );
155
156          // load current directory into browserListView
157          LoadFilesInDirectory( currentDirectory );
158          displayLabel.Text = currentDirectory;
```

Fig. 13.24 ListView displaying files and folders. (Part 3 of 4.)

```
159
160     }   // end method ListViewTest_Load
161
162  }  // end class ListViewTest
```

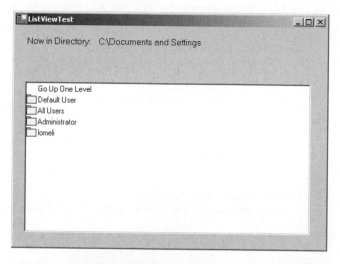

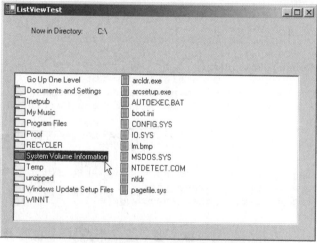

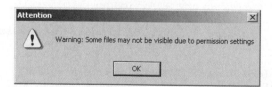

Fig. 13.24 ListView displaying files and folders. (Part 4 of 4.)

To display icons beside list items, we must create an **ImageList** for the **ListView browserListView** (line 20). First, drag and drop an **ImageList** onto the form and open the **Image Collection Editor**. Create two simple bitmap images—one for a folder (array index 0) and another for a file (array index 1). Then, set the object **browserList-View** property **SmallImageList** to the new **ImageList** in the **Properties** window. Developers can create such icons with any image software, such as Adobe® Photoshop™, Jasc® Paint Shop Pro™, or Microsoft® Paint.

Method **LoadFilesInDirectory** (lines 87–140) is used to populate **browser-ListView** with the directory passed to it (**currentDirectoryValue**). It clears **browserListView** and adds the element **"Go Up One Level"**. When the user clicks this element, the program attempts to move up one level (we see how shortly). The method then creates a **DirectoryInfo** object initialized with the string **currentDirectory** (lines 99–100). If permission is not given to browse the directory, an exception is thrown (caught on lines 132–138). Method **LoadFilesInDirectory** works differently from method **PopulateTreeView** in the previous program (Fig. 13.21). Instead of loading all the folders in the entire hard drive, method **LoadFilesInDirectory** loads only the folders in the current directory.

Class **DirectoryInfo** (namespace **System.IO**) enables us to browse or manipulate the directory structure easily. Method **GetDirectories** (lines 103–104) returns an array of **DirectoryInfo** objects containing the subdirectories of the current directory. Similarly, method **GetFiles** (lines 106–107) returns an array of class **FileInfo** objects containing the files in the current directory. Property **Name** (of both class **DirectoryInfo** and class **FileInfo**) contains only the directory or file name, such as **temp** instead of **C:\myfolder\temp**. To access the full name, use property **FullName**.

Lines 110–118 and lines 121–128 iterate through the subdirectories and files of the current directory and add them to **browserListView**. Lines 117 and 127 set the **ImageIndex** properties of the newly created items. If an item is a directory, we set its icon to a directory icon (index 0); if an item is a file, we set its icon to a file icon (index 1).

Method **browserListView_Click** (lines 36–84) responds when the user clicks control **browserListView**. Line 40 checks on whether anything is selected. If a selection has been made, line 43 determines whether the user chose the first item in **browserListView**. The first item in **browserListView** is always **Go up one level**; if it is selected, the program attempts to go up a level. Lines 46–47 create a **DirectoryInfo** object for the current directory. Line 50 tests property **Parent** to ensure that the user is not at the root of the directory tree. Property **Parent** indicates the parent directory as a **DirectoryInfo** object; if it does not exist, **Parent** returns the value **null**. If a parent directory exists, then lines 51–52 pass the full name of the parent directory to method **LoadFilesInDirectory**.

If the user did not select the first item in **browserListView**, lines 56–77 allow the user to continue navigating through the directory structure. Lines 59–60 create **String chosen**, which receives the text of the selected item (the first item in collection **SelectedItems**). Lines 63–64 test whether the user has selected a valid directory (rather than a file). The program combines variables **currentDirectory** and **chosen** (the new directory), separated by a slash (****), and passes this value to class **Directory**'s method **Exists**. Method **Exists** returns **True** if its **String** parameter is a directory. If this occurs, the program passes the **String** to method **LoadFilesInDirectory**. The **C:** directory already includes a slash, so a slash is not needed when combining **currentDirectory** and **chosen** (line 71). However, other directories must include the slash (lines 73–74). Finally, **displayLabel** is updated with the new directory (line 80).

This program loads quickly, because it indexes only the files in the current directory. This means that, rather than having a large delay in the beginning, a small delay occurs whenever a new directory is loaded. In addition, changes in the directory structure can be shown by reloading a directory. The previous program (Fig. 13.21) needs to be restarted to reflect any changes in the directory structure. This type of trade-off is typical in the software world. When designing applications that run for long periods of time, developers might choose a large initial delay to improve performance throughout the rest of the program. However, when creating applications that run for only short periods of time, developers often prefer fast initial loading times and a small delay after each action.

13.8 Tab Control

The **TabControl** control creates tabbed windows, such as those we have seen in the Visual Studio .NET IDE (Fig. 13.25). This allows the programmer to design user interfaces that fit a large number of controls or a large amount of data without using up valuable screen "real estate."

TabControls contain **TabPage** objects, which are similar to **Panel**s and **Group-Box**es in that **TabPage**s also can contain controls. The programmer first adds controls to the **TabPage** objects, then adds the **TabPage**s to the **TabControl**. Only one **TabPage** is displayed at a time. Figure 13.26 depicts a sample **TabControl**.

Programmers can add **TabControl**s visually by dragging and dropping them onto a form in design mode. To add **TabPage**s in the Visual Studio .NET designer, right-click the **TabControl**, and select **Add Tab** (Fig. 13.27). Alternatively, click the **TabPages** collection in the **Properties** window, and add tabs in the dialog that appears. To change a tab label, set the **Text** property of the **TabPage**.

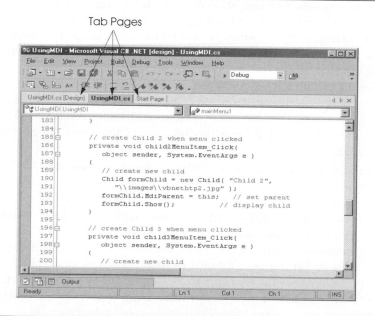

Fig. 13.25 Tabbed pages in Visual Studio .NET.

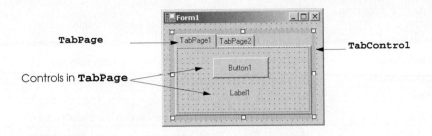

Fig. 13.26 `TabControl` with `TabPage`s example.

Note that clicking the tabs selects the `TabControl`—to select the `TabPage`, click the control area underneath the tabs. The developer can add controls to the `TabPage` by dragging and dropping items from the `ToolBox`. To view different `TabPage`s, click the appropriate tab (in either design or run mode). Common properties and events of `TabControl`s are described in Fig. 13.28.

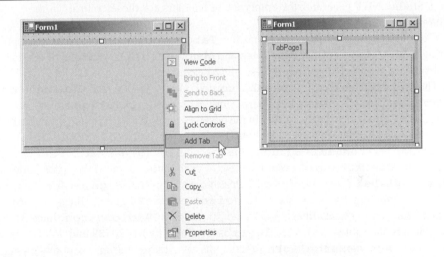

Fig. 13.27 `TabPage`s added to a `TabControl`.

`TabControl` properties and events	Description / Delegate and Event Arguments
Common Properties	
`ImageList`	Specifies images to be displayed on a tab.
`ItemSize`	Specifies tab size.
`MultiLine`	Indicates whether multiple rows of tabs can be displayed.

Fig. 13.28 `TabControl` properties and events. (Part 1 of 2.)

TabControl properties and events	Description / Delegate and Event Arguments
SelectedIndex	Indicates index of TabPage that is currently selected.
SelectedTab	Indicates the TabPage that is currently selected.
TabCount	Returns the number of tabs.
TabPages	Gets the collection of TabPages within our TabControl.
Common Event	*(Delegate EventHandler, event arguments EventArgs)*
SelectedIndexChanged	Generated when SelectedIndex changes (i.e., another TabPage is selected).

Fig. 13.28 TabControl properties and events. (Part 2 of 2.)

Each **TabPage** generates its own **Click** event when its tab is clicked. Remember, events for controls can be handled by any event handler that is registered with the control's event delegate. This also applies to controls contained in a **TabPage**. For convenience, Visual Studio .NET generates the empty event handlers for these controls in the class in which we are currently working.

Class **UsingTabs** (Fig. 13.29) uses a **TabControl** to display various options relating to the text on a label (**Color**, **Size** and **Message**). The last **TabPage** displays an **About** message, which describes the use of **TabControl**s.

The **TabControl optionsTabControl** (lines 18–19) and **TabPage**s **colorTabPage** (line 22), **sizeTabPage** (line 30), **messageTabPage** (line 39) and **aboutTabPage** (line 46) are created in the designer (as described previously). **TabPage colorTabPage** contains three radio buttons—for colors black (**blackRadioButton**, lines 26–27), red (**redRadioButton**, line 25) and green (**greenRadioButton**, lines 23–24). The **CheckChanged** event handler for each button updates the color of the text in **displayLabel** (lines 59, 66 and 73). **TabPage sizeTabPage** has three radio buttons, corresponding to font sizes 12 (**size12RadioButton**, lines 35–36), 16 (**size16RadioButton**, lines 33–34) and 20 (**size20RadioButton**, lines 31–32), which change the font size of **displayLabel**—lines 80–81, 88–89 and 96–97, respectively. **TabPage messageTabPage** contains two radio buttons—for the messages **Hello!** (**helloRadioButton**, lines 42–43) and **Goodbye!** (**goodbyeRadioButton**, lines 40–41). The two radio buttons determine the text on **displayLabel** (lines 104 and 111, respectively).

```
1   // Fig. 13.29: UsingTabs.cs
2   // Using TabControl to display various font settings.
3
4   using System;
5   using System.Drawing;
6   using System.Collections;
7   using System.ComponentModel;
8   using System.Windows.Forms;
```

Fig. 13.29 TabControl used to display various font settings. (Part 1 of 4.)

```
 9   using System.Data;
10
11   public class UsingTabs : System.Windows.Forms.Form
12   {
13      // output label reflects text changes
14      private System.Windows.Forms.Label displayLabel;
15
16      // table control containing table pages colorTabPage,
17      // sizeTabPage, messageTabPage and aboutTabPage
18      private System.Windows.Forms.TabControl
19         optionsTabControl;
20
21      // table page containing color options
22      private System.Windows.Forms.TabPage colorTabPage;
23      private System.Windows.Forms.RadioButton
24         greenRadioButton;
25      private System.Windows.Forms.RadioButton redRadioButton;
26      private System.Windows.Forms.RadioButton
27         blackRadioButton;
28
29      // table page containing font size options
30      private System.Windows.Forms.TabPage sizeTabPage;
31      private System.Windows.Forms.RadioButton
32         size20RadioButton;
33      private System.Windows.Forms.RadioButton
34         size16RadioButton;
35      private System.Windows.Forms.RadioButton
36         size12RadioButton;
37
38      // table page containing text display options
39      private System.Windows.Forms.TabPage messageTabPage;
40      private System.Windows.Forms.RadioButton
41         goodByeRadioButton;
42      private System.Windows.Forms.RadioButton
43         helloRadioButton;
44
45      // table page containing about message
46      private System.Windows.Forms.TabPage aboutTabPage;
47      private System.Windows.Forms.Label messageLabel;
48
49      [STAThread]
50      static void Main()
51      {
52         Application.Run( new UsingTabs() );
53      }
54
55      // event handler for black color radio button
56      private void blackRadioButton_CheckedChanged(
57         object sender, System.EventArgs e )
58      {
59         displayLabel.ForeColor = Color.Black;
60      }
61
```

Fig. 13.29 TabControl used to display various font settings. (Part 2 of 4.)

```
62        // event handler for red color radio button
63        private void redRadioButton_CheckedChanged(
64           object sender, System.EventArgs e )
65        {
66           displayLabel.ForeColor = Color.Red;
67        }
68
69        // event handler for green color radio button
70        private void greenRadioButton_CheckedChanged(
71           object sender, System.EventArgs e )
72        {
73           displayLabel.ForeColor = Color.Green;
74        }
75
76        // event handler for size 12 radio button
77        private void size12RadioButton_CheckedChanged(
78           object sender, System.EventArgs e )
79        {
80           displayLabel.Font =
81              new Font( displayLabel.Font.Name, 12 );
82        }
83
84        // event handler for size 16 radio button
85        private void size16RadioButton_CheckedChanged(
86           object sender, System.EventArgs e )
87        {
88           displayLabel.Font =
89              new Font( displayLabel.Font.Name, 16 );
90        }
91
92        // event handler for size 20 radio button
93        private void size20RadioButton_CheckedChanged(
94           object sender, System.EventArgs e )
95        {
96           displayLabel.Font =
97              new Font( displayLabel.Font.Name, 20 );
98        }
99
100       // event handler for message "Hello!" radio button
101       private void helloRadioButton_CheckedChanged(
102          object sender, System.EventArgs e )
103       {
104          displayLabel.Text = "Hello!";
105       }
106
107       // event handler for message "Goodbye!" radio button
108       private void goodByeRadioButton_CheckedChanged(
109          object sender, System.EventArgs e )
110       {
111          displayLabel.Text = "Goodbye!";
112       }
113
114    } // end class UsingTabs
```

Fig. 13.29 TabControl used to display various font settings. (Part 3 of 4.)

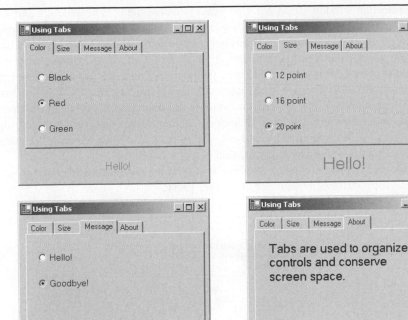

Fig. 13.29 **TabControl** used to display various font settings. (Part 4 of 4.)

Software Engineering Observation 13.2

*A **TabPage** can act as a container for a single logical group of radio buttons and enforces their mutual exclusivity. To place multiple radio-button groups inside a single **TabPage**, programmers should group radio buttons within **Panel**s or **GroupBox**es contained within the **TabPage**.*

The last **TabPage** (**aboutTabPage**, line 46) contains a **Label** (**messageLabel**, line 47) that describes the purpose of **TabControl**s.

13.9 Multiple-Document-Interface (MDI) Windows

In previous chapters, we have built only *single-document-interface (SDI)* applications. Such programs (including Notepad or Paint) support only one open window or document at a time. SDI applications usually have contracted abilities—Paint and Notepad, for example, have limited image- and text-editing features. To edit multiple documents, the user must create additional instances of the SDI application.

Multiple document interface (MDI) programs (such as PaintShop Pro and Adobe Photoshop) enable users to edit multiple documents at once. MDI programs also tend to be more complex—PaintShop Pro and Photoshop have a greater number of image-editing features than does Paint. Until now, we had not mentioned that the applications we created were SDI applications. We define this here to emphasize the distinction between the two types of programs.

The application window of an MDI program is called the *parent window*, and each window inside the application is referred to as a *child window*. Although an MDI application can have many child windows, each has only one parent window. Furthermore, a maximum of one child window can be active at once. Child windows cannot be parents themselves and cannot be moved outside their parent. Otherwise, a child window behaves like any other window (with regard to closing, minimizing, resizing etc.). A child window's functionality can be different from the functionality of other child windows of the parent. For example, one child window might edit images, another might edit text and a third might display network traffic graphically, but all could belong to the same MDI parent. Figure 13.30 depicts a sample MDI application.

To create an MDI form, create a new **Form** and set its ***IsMDIContainer*** property to **True**. The form changes appearance, as in Fig. 13.31.

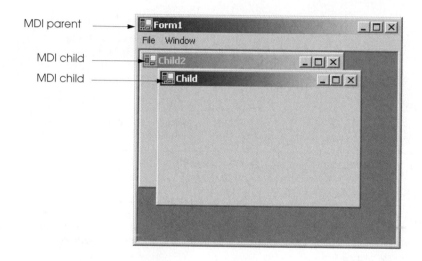

Fig. 13.30 MDI parent window and MDI child windows.

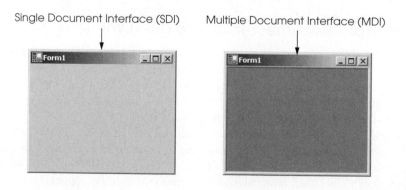

Fig. 13.31 SDI and MDI forms.

Next, create a child form class to be added to the form. To do this, right-click the project in the **Solution Explorer**, select **Add Windows Form...** and name the file. To add the child form to the parent, we must create a new child form object; set its **Mdi-Parent** property to the parent form, and call method **Show**. The code to create a child usually lies inside an event handler, which creates a new window in response to a user action. Menu selections (such as **File** followed by a submenu option of **New** followed by a submenu option of **Window**) are common methods of creating new child windows.

Form property *MdiChildren* is an array of child **Form** references. This is useful if the parent window wants to check the status of all its children (such as to ensure that all are saved before the parent closes). Property *ActiveMdiChild* returns a reference to the active child window; it returns **null** if there are no active child windows. Other features of MDI windows are described in Fig. 13.32.

Child windows can be minimized, maximized and closed independently of each other and of the parent window. Figure 13.33 shows two images, one containing two minimized child windows and a second containing a maximized child window. When the parent is minimized or closed, the child windows are minimized or closed as well. Notice that the title bar in the second image of Fig. 13.33 is **Parent Window - [Child]**. When a child window is maximized, its title bar is inserted into the parent window's title bar. When a child window is minimized or maximized, its title bar displays a restore icon, which returns the child window to its previous size (its size before it was minimized or maximized).

MDI **Form** events and properties	Description / Delegate and Event Arguments
Common MDI Child Properties	
IsMdiChild	Indicates whether the **Form** is an MDI child. If **True**, **Form** is an MDI child (read-only property).
MdiParent	Specifies the MDI parent **Form** of the child.
Common MDI Parent Properties	
ActiveMdiChild	Returns the **Form** that is the currently active MDI child (returns **null** if no children are active).
IsMdiContainer	Indicates whether a **Form** can be an MDI. If **True**, the **Form** can be an MDI parent. Default is **False**.
MdiChildren	Returns the MDI children as an array of **Form**s.
Common Method	
LayoutMdi	Determines the display of child forms on an MDI parent. Takes as a parameter an **MdiLayout** enumeration with possible values **ArrangeIcons**, **Cascade**, **TileHorizontal** and **TileVertical**. Figure 13.35 depicts the effects of these values.
Common Event	(Delegate **EventHandler**, event arguments **EventArgs**)
MdiChildActivate	Generated when an MDI child is closed or activated.

Fig. 13.32 MDI parent and MDI child events and properties.

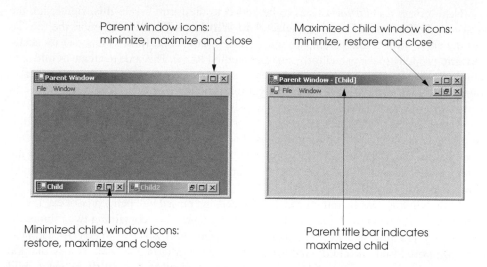

Fig. 13.33 Minimized and maximized child windows.

The parent and child forms can have different menus, which are merged whenever a child window is selected. To specify how the menus merge, programmers can set the ***MergeOrder*** and the ***MergeType*** properties for each **MenuItem** (see Fig. 13.3). **MergeOrder** determines the order in which **MenuItem**s appear when two menus are merged. **MenuItem**s with a lower **MergeOrder** value will appear first. For example, if **Menu1** has items **File**, **Edit** and **Window** (and their orders are 0, 10 and 20) and **Menu2** has items **Format** and **View** (and their orders are 7 and 15), then the merged menu contains menu items **File**, **Format**, **Edit**, **View** and **Window**, in that order.

Each **MenuItem** instance has its own **MergeOrder** property. It is likely that, at some point in an application, two **MenuItem**s with the same **MergeOrder** value will merge. Property **MergeType** resolves this conflict by following the order in which the two menus are displayed.

The **MergeType** property takes a ***MenuMerge*** enumeration value and determines which menu items will be displayed when two menus are merged. A menu item with value ***Add*** is added to its parent's menu as a new menu on the menu bar (the parent's menu items come first). If a child form's menu item has value ***Replace***, it attempts to take the place of its parent form's corresponding menu item during merging. A menu with value ***MergeItems*** combines its items with that of its parent's corresponding menu (if parent and child menus originally occupy the same space, their submenus will be brought together as one large menu). A child's menu item with value ***Remove*** disappears when the menu is merged with that of its parent.

Value **MergeItems** acts passively—if the parent's menu has a **MergeType** that is different from the child menu's **MergeType**, the child's menu setting determines the outcome of the merge. When the child window is closed, the parent's original menu is restored.

Good Programming Practice 13.1

*When creating MDI applications, include a menu item with its **MdiList** property set to **True**. This helps the user select a child window quickly, rather than having to search for it in the parent window.*

Software Engineering Observation 13.3

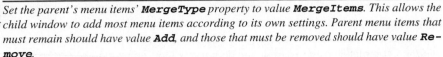

*Set the parent's menu items' **MergeType** property to value **MergeItems**. This allows the child window to add most menu items according to its own settings. Parent menu items that must remain should have value **Add**, and those that must be removed should have value **Remove**.*

C# provides a property that facilitates the tracking of which child windows are opened in an MDI container. Property ***MdiList*** (a boolean) of class **MenuItem** determines whether a **MenuItem** displays a list of open child windows. The list appears at the bottom of the menu following a separator bar (first screen in Figure 13.34). When a new child window is opened, an entry is added to the list. If nine or more child windows are open, the list includes the option **More Windows...**, which allows the user to select a window from a list, using a scrollbar. Multiple **MenuItem**s can have their **MdiList** property set; each displays a list of open child windows.

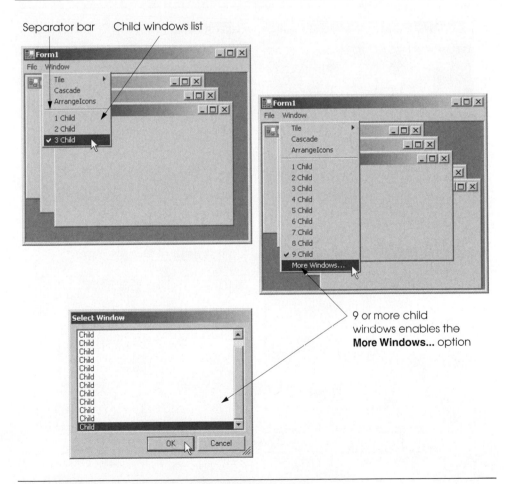

Fig. 13.34 **MenuItem** property **MdiList** example.

MDI containers allow developers to organize the placement of child windows. The child windows in an MDI application can be arranged by calling method *LayoutMdi* of the parent form. Method **LayoutMdi** takes a *MdiLayout enumeration*, which can have values *ArrangeIcons*, *Cascade*, *TileHorizontal* and *TileVertical*. *Tiled windows* completely fill the parent and do not overlap; such windows can be arranged horizontally (value **TileHorizontal**) or vertically (value **TileVertical**). *Cascaded windows* (value **Cascade**) overlap—each is the same size and displays a visible title bar, if possible. Value **ArrangeIcons** arranges the icons for any minimized child windows. If minimized windows are scattered around the parent window, value **ArrangeIcons** orders them neatly at the bottom-left corner of the parent window. Figure 13.35 illustrates the values of the **MdiLayout** enumeration.

Class **UsingMDI** (Fig. 13.36) demonstrates the use of MDI windows. Class **UsingMdi** uses three instances of class **Child** (Fig. 13.37), each of which contains a **PictureBox** and an image of a book cover. The parent MDI form contains a menu that enables users to create and arrange child forms.

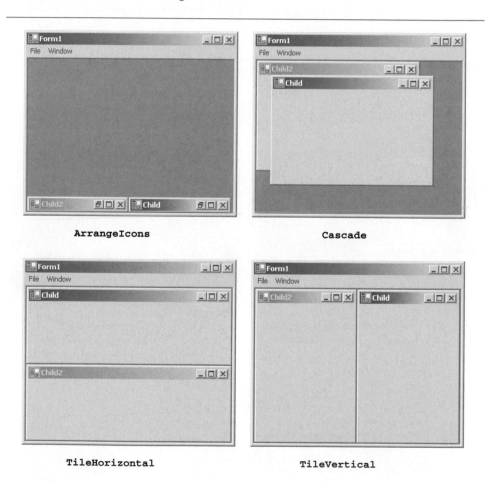

Fig. 13.35 **MdiLayout** enumeration values.

The MDI parent form (Fig. 13.36) contains two top-level menus. The first of these menus, **File** (**fileMenuItem**, line 13), contains both an **Exit** item (**exitMenuItem**, line 18) and a **New** submenu (**newMenuItem**, line 14) consisting of items for each child window. The second menu, **Format** (**formatMenuItem**, line 19), provides options for laying out the MDI children, plus a list of the active MDI children.

In the **Properties** window, we set the **Form**'s **IsMdiContainer** property to **True**, making the **Form** an MDI parent. In addition, we set **formatMenuItem** property **MdiList** to **True**. This enables **formatMenuItem** to list the active child MDI windows.

```
1   // Fig. 13.36: UsingMDI.cs
2   // Demonstrating use of MDI parent and child windows.
3   using System;
4   using System.Drawing;
5   using System.Collections;
6   using System.ComponentModel;
7   using System.Windows.Forms;
8   using System.Data;
9
10  public class UsingMDI : System.Windows.Forms.Form
11  {
12     private System.Windows.Forms.MainMenu mainMenu1;
13     private System.Windows.Forms.MenuItem fileMenuItem;
14     private System.Windows.Forms.MenuItem newMenuItem;
15     private System.Windows.Forms.MenuItem child1MenuItem;
16     private System.Windows.Forms.MenuItem child2MenuItem;
17     private System.Windows.Forms.MenuItem child3MenuItem;
18     private System.Windows.Forms.MenuItem exitMenuItem;
19     private System.Windows.Forms.MenuItem formatMenuItem;
20     private System.Windows.Forms.MenuItem cascadeMenuItem;
21     private System.Windows.Forms.MenuItem
22        tileHorizontalMenuItem;
23     private System.Windows.Forms.MenuItem
24        tileVerticalMenuItem;
25
26     [STAThread]
27     static void Main()
28     {
29        Application.Run( new UsingMDI() );
30     }
31
32     // create Child 1 when menu clicked
33     private void child1MenuItem_Click(
34        object sender, System.EventArgs e )
35     {
36        // create new child
37        Child formChild = new Child( "Child 1",
38           "\\images\\csharphtp1.jpg" );
39        formChild.MdiParent = this;   // set parent
40        formChild.Show();             // display child
41     }
42
```

Fig. 13.36 MDI parent-window class. (Part 1 of 3.)

```
43      // create Child 2 when menu clicked
44      private void child2MenuItem_Click(
45         object sender, System.EventArgs e )
46      {
47         // create new child
48         Child formChild = new Child( "Child 2",
49            "\\images\\vbnethtp2.jpg" );
50         formChild.MdiParent = this;    // set parent
51         formChild.Show();              // display child
52      }
53
54      // create Child 3 when menu clicked
55      private void child3MenuItem_Click(
56         object sender, System.EventArgs e )
57      {
58         // create new child
59         Child formChild = new Child( "Child 3",
60            "\\images\\pythonhtp1.jpg" );
61         formChild.MdiParent = this;    // set parent
62         formChild.Show();              // display child
63      }
64
65      // exit application
66      private void exitMenuItem_Click(
67         object sender, System.EventArgs e )
68      {
69         Application.Exit();
70      }
71
72      // set cascade layout
73      private void cascadeMenuItem_Click(
74         object sender, System.EventArgs e )
75      {
76         this.LayoutMdi( MdiLayout.Cascade );
77      }
78
79      // set TileHorizontal layout
80      private void tileHorizontalMenuItem_Click(
81         object sender, System.EventArgs e )
82      {
83         this.LayoutMdi( MdiLayout.TileHorizontal );
84      }
85
86      // set TileVertical layout
87      private void tileVerticalMenuItem_Click(
88         object sender, System.EventArgs e )
89      {
90         this.LayoutMdi( MdiLayout.TileVertical );
91      }
92
93   } // end class UsingMDI
```

Fig. 13.36 MDI parent-window class. (Part 2 of 3.)

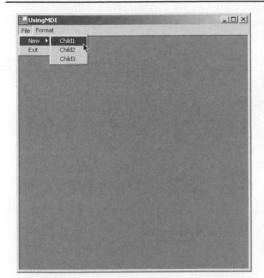 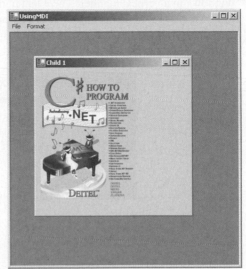

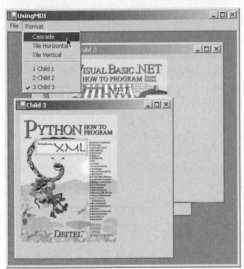 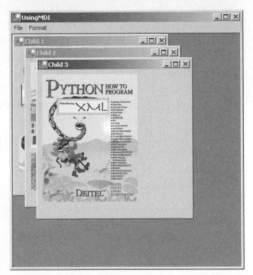

Fig. 13.36 MDI parent-window class. (Part 3 of 3.)

The **Cascade** menu item (**cascadeMenuItem**, line 20) has an event handler (**cascadeMenuItem_Click**, lines 73–77) that arranges the child windows in a cascading manner. The event handler calls method **LayoutMdi** with the argument **Cascade** from the **MdiLayout** enumeration (line 76).

The **Tile Horizontal** menu item (**tileHorizontalMenuItem**, lines 21–22) has an event handler (**mnuitmTileHorizontal_Click**, lines 80–84) that arranges the child windows in a horizontal manner. The event handler calls method **LayoutMdi** with the argument **TileHorizontal** from the **MdiLayout** enumeration (line 83).

Finally, the **Tile Vertical** menu item (**mnuitmTileVertical**, lines 23–24) has an event handler (**mnuitmTileVertical_Click**, lines 87–91) that arranges the child windows in a vertical manner. The event handler calls method **LayoutMdi** with the argument **TileVertical** from the **MdiLayout** enumeration (line 90).

To define the child class for the MDI application, right-click the project in the **Solution Explorer** and select first **Add** and then **Add Windows Form...**. Name the new class **Child** (Fig. 13.37).

Next, we add a **PictureBox** (**picDisplay**, line 11) to form **Child**. The constructor invokes method **InitializeComponent** (line 17) and initializes the form's title (line 19) and the image to display in the **PictureBox** (lines 22–23).

The parent MDI form (Fig. 13.36) creates new instances of class **Child** each time the user selects a new child window from the **File** menu. The event handlers in lines 33–63 create new child forms that contain images of Deitel and Associates, Inc. book covers. Each event handler creates a new instance of the child form, sets its **MdiParent** property to the parent form and calls method **Show** to display the child.

13.10 Visual Inheritance

In Chapter 9, Object-Oriented Programming: Inheritance, we discuss how to create classes by inheriting from other classes. In C#, we also can use inheritance to create **Form**s that display a GUI, because **Form**s are classes that derive from class **System.Windows.Forms.Form**. Visual inheritance allows us to create a new **Form** by inheriting from another **Form**. The derived **Form** class contains the functionality of its **Form** base class, including any base-class properties, methods, variables and controls. The derived class also inherits all visual aspects—such as sizing, component layout, spacing between GUI components, colors and fonts—from its base class.

Visual inheritance enables developers to achieve visual consistency across applications by reusing code. For example, a company could define a base form that contains a product's logo, a static background color, a predefined menu bar and other elements. Programmers then could use the base form throughout an application for purposes of uniformity and product branding.

```
1   // Fig. 13.37: Child.cs
2   // Child window of MDI parent.
3   using System;
4   using System.Drawing;
5   using System.Collections;
6   using System.ComponentModel;
7   using System.Windows.Forms;
8   using System.IO;
9
10  public class Child : System.Windows.Forms.Form
11  {
12     private System.Windows.Forms.PictureBox pictureBox;
13
14     public Child( string title, string fileName )
15     {
16        // Required for Windows Form Designer support
17        InitializeComponent();
```

Fig. 13.37 Child class for MDI demonstration. (Part 1 of 2.)

```
18
19          Text = title; // set title text
20
21          // set image to display in pictureBox
22          pictureBox.Image = Image.FromFile(
23              Directory.GetCurrentDirectory() + fileName );
24      }
25  }
```

Fig. 13.37 Child class for MDI demonstration. (Part 2 of 2.)

Class **VisualInheritance** (Fig. 13.38) is a form that we use as a base class for demonstrating visual inheritance. The GUI contains two labels (one with text **Bugs, Bugs, Bugs** and one with **Copyright 2002, by Bug2Bug.com.**) and one button (displaying the text **Learn More**). When a user presses the **Learn More** button, method **learnMoreButton_Click** (lines 22–29) is invoked. This method displays a message box that provides some informative text.

```
1   // Fig. 13.38: VisualInheritance.cs
2   // Base Form for use with visual inheritance
3   using System;
4   using System.Drawing;
5   using System.Collections;
6   using System.ComponentModel;
7   using System.Windows.Forms;
8   using System.Data;
9
10  public class VisualInheritance : System.Windows.Forms.Form
11  {
12      private System.Windows.Forms.Label bugsLabel;
13      private System.Windows.Forms.Button learnMoreButton;
14      private System.Windows.Forms.Label label1;
15
16      [STAThread]
17      static void Main()
18      {
19          Application.Run( new VisualInheritance() );
20      }
21
22      private void learnMoreButton_Click( object sender,
23          System.EventArgs e )
24      {
25          MessageBox.Show(
26              "Bugs, Bugs, Bugs is a product of Bug2Bug.com",
27              "Learn More", MessageBoxButtons.OK,
28              MessageBoxIcon.Information );
29      }
30  }
```

Fig. 13.38 Class **VisualInheritance**, which inherits from class **Form**, contains a button (**Learn More**). (Part 1 of 2.)

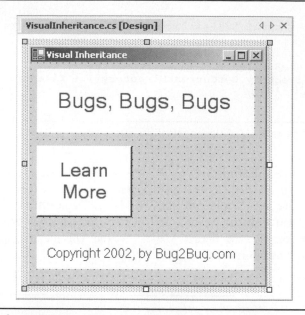

Fig. 13.38 Class **VisualInheritance**, which inherits from class **Form**, contains a
button (**Learn More**). (Part 2 of 2.)

Before deriving a form from class **VisualInheritance**, we must package class
VisualInheritance in a **.dll**. Right click on the **VisualInheritance** project
in the **Solution Explorer**, and select **Properties**. In **Common Properties > General**, change the **Output Type** to **Class Library**. Then, build the project to produce a
.dll that contains the **VisualInheritance** class.

To create the derived form through visual inheritance, create an empty project. From
the **Project** menu, select **Add Inherited Form....** This brings up the **Add New Item**
window. Select **Inherited Form** from the templates window. Clicking **Open** displays the
Inheritance Picker. The **Inheritance Picker** tool enables programmers to quickly
create a form that inherits from a specified form. Click **Browse**, and select the **.dll** file
for class **VisualInheritance**. The **.dll** file normally is located within the
bin\Debug directory of the **VisualInheritance** project directory. Click **OK**. The
Form Designer should now display the inherited form (Fig. 13.39).

Class **VisualInheritanceTest** (Fig. 13.40) derives from class **VisualInheritance**. The GUI contains those components derived from class **VisualInheritance**, plus a button with text **Learn The Program** that we added in class
VisualInheritanceTest. When a user presses this button, method
learnProgramButton_Click (lines 15–22) is invoked. This method displays a
simple message box.

Figure 13.40 demonstrates that the components, their layouts and the functionality of
the base class **VisualInheritance** (Fig. 13.38) are inherited by **VisualInheritanceTest**. If a user clicks button **Learn More**, the base-class event handler
learnMoreButton_Click displays a **MessageBox**.

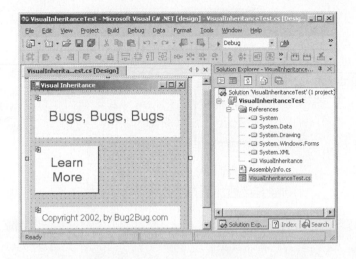

Fig. 13.39 Visual Inheritance through the Form Designer.

```
1   // Fig. 13.40: VisualInheritanceTest.cs
2   // Derived Form using visual inheritance.
3   using System;
4   using System.Collections;
5   using System.ComponentModel;
6   using System.Drawing;
7   using System.Windows.Forms;
8
9   public class VisualInheritanceTest :
10      VisualInheritance.VisualInheritance
11  {
12      private System.Windows.Forms.Button learnProgramButton;
13
14      // invoke when user clicks Learn the Program Button
15      private void learnProgramButton_Click( object sender,
16          System.EventArgs e )
17      {
18          MessageBox.Show(
19              "This program was created by Deitel & Associates",
20              "Learn the Program", MessageBoxButtons.OK,
21              MessageBoxIcon.Information );
22      }
23
24      public static void Main( string[] args )
25      {
26          Application.Run( new VisualInheritanceTest() );
27      }
28  }
```

Fig. 13.40 Class `VisualInheritanceTest`, which inherits from class `VisualInheritance.VisualInheritance`, contains an additional button. (Part 1 of 2.)

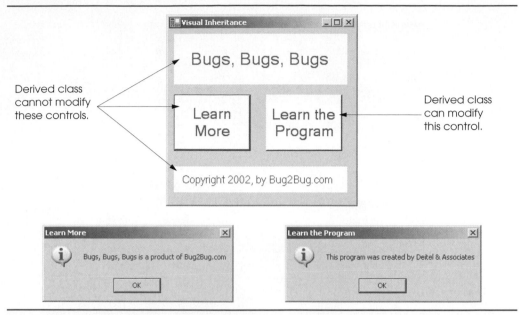

Derived class cannot modify these controls.

Derived class can modify this control.

Fig. 13.40 Class **FrmVisualTest**, which inherits from class **Visual-Form.FrmInheritance**, contains an additional button. (Part 2 of 2.)

13.11 User-Defined Controls

The .NET Framework allows programmers to create *custom controls* that inherit from a variety of classes. These custom controls appear in the user's **Toolbox** and can be added to **Form**s, **Panel**s or **GroupBox**es in the same way that we add **Button**s, **Label**s, and other predefined controls. The simplest way to create a custom control is to derive a class from an existing Windows Forms control, such as a **Label**. This is useful if the programmer wants to include functionality of an existing control, rather than having to reimplement the existing control in addition to including the desired new functionality. For example, we can create a new type of label that behaves like a normal **Label** but has a different appearance. We accomplish this by inheriting from class **Label** and overriding method **On-Paint**.

Look-and-Feel Observation 13.8

*To change the appearance of any control, override method **OnPaint**.*

All controls contain method **OnPaint**, which the system calls when a component must be redrawn (such as when the component is resized). Method **OnPaint** is passed a **PaintEventArgs** object, which contains graphics information—property **Graphics** is the graphics object used to draw, and property **ClipRectangle** defines the rectangular boundary of the control. Whenever the system generates the **Paint** event, our control's base class catches the event. Through polymorphism, our control's **OnPaint** method is called. Our base class's **OnPaint** implementation is not called, so we must call it explicitly from our **OnPaint** implementation before we execute our custom-paint code. Alternatively, if we do not wish to let our base class paint itself, we should not call our base class's **OnPaint** method implementation.

To create a new control composed of existing controls, use class ***UserControl***. Controls added to a custom control are called *constituent controls*. For example, a programmer could create a **UserControl** composed of a button, a label and a text box, each associated with some functionality (such as that the button sets the label's text to that contained in the text box). The **UserControl** acts as a container for the controls added to it. The **UserControl** contains constituent controls, so it does not determine how these constituent controls are displayed. Method **OnPaint** cannot be overridden in these custom controls—their appearance can be modified only by handling each constituent control's **Paint** event. The **Paint** event handler is passed a **PaintEventArgs** object, which can be used to draw graphics (lines, rectangles etc.) on the constituent controls.

Using another technique, a programmer can create a brand-new control by inheriting from class **Control**. This class does not define any specific behavior; that task is left to the programmer. Instead, class **Control** handles the items associated with all controls, such as events and sizing handles. Method **OnPaint** should contain a call to the base class's **OnPaint** method, which calls the **Paint** event handlers. The programmer must then add code for custom graphics inside the overridden **OnPaint** method. This technique allows for the greatest flexibility, but also requires the most planning. All three approaches are summarized in Fig. 13.41.

Custom Control Techniques and **PaintEventArgs** Properties	Description
Inherit from Windows Forms control	Add functionality to a preexisting control. If overriding method **OnPaint**, call base class **OnPaint**. Can only add to the original control appearance, not redesign it.
*Create a **UserControl***	Create a **UserControl** composed of multiple preexisting controls (and combine their functionality). Cannot override **OnPaint** methods of custom controls. Instead, add drawing code to a **Paint** event handler. Can only add to the original control appearance, not redesign it.
*Inherit from class **Control***	Define a brand-new control. Override **OnPaint** method, call base class method **OnPaint** and include methods to draw the control. Can customize control appearance and functionality.
PaintEventArgs *Properties*	*Use this object inside method **OnPaint** or **Paint** to draw on the control.*
Graphics	Indicates the graphics object of control. Used to draw on control.
ClipRectangle	Specifies the rectangle indicating boundary of control.

Fig. 13.41 Custom control creation.

We create a "clock" control in Fig. 13.42. This is a **UserControl** composed of a label and a timer—whenever the timer generates an event, the label is updated to reflect the current time.

Timers (namespace **System.Windows.Forms**) are invisible components that reside on a form and generate *Tick* events at a set interval. This interval is set by the **Timer**'s *Interval* property, which defines the number of milliseconds (thousandths of a second) between events. By default, timers are disabled.

We create a **Form** that displays our custom control, **ClockUserControl** (Fig. 13.42). Create a **UserControl** class for the project by selecting **Project > Add User Control...**. This displays a dialog from which we can select the type of control to add—user controls are already selected. We then name the file (and the class) **ClockUserControl**. This brings up our empty **ClockUserControl** as a grey rectangle.

We can treat this control like a Windows **Form**, so we can add controls (using the **ToolBox**) and set properties (using the **Properties** window). However, instead of creating an application (notice there is no **Main** method in the **Control** class), we are simply creating a new control composed of other controls. We add a **Label** (**displayLabel**, line 15) and a **Timer** (**clockTimer**, line 14) to the **UserControl**. We set the **Timer** interval to 100 milliseconds and update **displayLabel**'s text with each event (lines 18–24). Note that **clockTimer** must be enabled by setting property **Enabled** to **True** in the **Properties** window.

Structure **DateTime** (namespace **System**) contains member **Now**, which is the current time. Method **ToLongTimeString** converts **Now** to a **String** that contains the current hour, minute, and second (along with AM or PM). We use this to set **displayLabel**'s **Text** property on line 22.

Once created, our clock control appears as an item on the **ToolBox**. To use the control, we can simply drag it onto a Windows application in our project and run the Windows application. The **ClockUserControl** object has a white background to make it stand out in the form. Figure 13.42 shows the output of **ClockExample**, which is a simple form that contains our **ClockUserControl**.

```
1   // Fig. 13.42: ClockUserControl.cs
2   // User-defined control with a timer and a label.
3
4   using System;
5   using System.Collections;
6   using System.ComponentModel;
7   using System.Drawing;
8   using System.Data;
9   using System.Windows.Forms;
10
11  public class ClockUserControl
12      : System.Windows.Forms.UserControl
13  {
14     private System.Windows.Forms.Timer clockTimer;
15     private System.Windows.Forms.Label displayLabel;
16
```

Fig. 13.42 Programmer-defined control that displays the current time. (Part 1 of 2.)

```
17       // update label at every tick
18       private void clockTimer_Tick(
19          object sender, System.EventArgs e )
20       {
21          // get current time (Now), convert to string
22          displayLabel.Text = DateTime.Now.ToLongTimeString();
23
24       } // end method clockTimer_Tick
25
26    } // end class ClockUserControl
```

Fig. 13.42 Programmer-defined control that displays the current time. (Part 2 of 2.)

The above steps are useful when we need to define a custom control for the project on which we are working. Visual Studio .NET allows developers to share their custom controls with other developers. To create a **UserControl** that can be exported to other solutions, do the following:

1. Create a new **Windows Control Library** project.

2. Inside the project, add controls and functionality to the **UserControl** (Fig. 13.43).

3. Build the project. Visual Studio .NET creates a **.dll** file for the **UserControl** in the output directory. The file is not executable: **Control** classes do not have a **Main** method. Select **Project** > **Properties** to find the output directory and output file (Fig. 13.44).

4. Create a new Windows application.

5. Import the **UserControl**. In the new Windows application, right click the **ToolBox**, and select **Customize Toolbox....** In the dialog that appears, select the **.NET Framework Components** tab. Browse for the **.dll** file, which is in the output directory for the Windows control library project. Click the checkbox next to the control, and click **OK** (Fig. 13.45).

6. The **UserControl** appears on the **ToolBox** and can be added to the form as if it were any other control (Fig. 13.46).

Testing and Debugging Tip 13.1

*Control classes do not have a **Main** method—they cannot be run by themselves. To test their functionality, add them to a sample Windows application and run them there.*

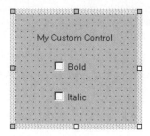

Fig. 13.43 Custom-control creation.

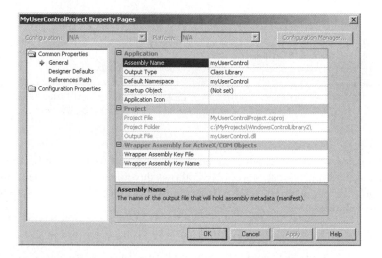

Fig. 13.44 Project properties dialog.

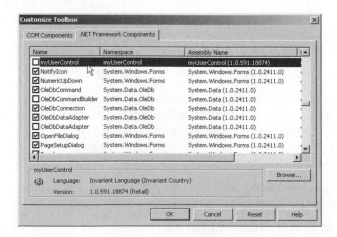

Fig. 13.45 Custom control added to the **ToolBox**.

 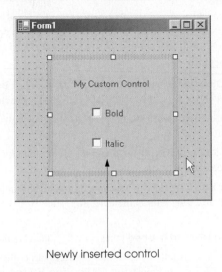

New **ToolBox** icon   Newly inserted control

Fig. 13.46 Custom control added to a **Form**.

Many of today's most successful commercial programs provide GUIs that are easy to use and manipulate. Because of this demand for user-friendly GUIs, the ability to design sophisticated GUIs is an essential programming skill. Fortunately, Visual Studio .NET provides an IDE that makes GUI development quick and easy. In the last two chapters, we have presented the basic techniques required to add various GUI components to a program. The next chapter will explore a more behind-the-scenes topic, *multithreading*. In many programming languages, the programmer can create multiple *threads*, enabling several processes to occur at once. By learning to create and manage multithreading in C#, readers will begin their study of a more robust type of software.

SUMMARY

- Menus used to provide groups of related commands for Windows applications. Menus are an integral part of GUIs, because they enable user–application interaction without unnecessarily "cluttering" the GUI.

- Window's top-level menus appear on the left of the screen—any submenus or menu items are indented. All menu items can have *Alt* key shortcuts (also called access shortcuts or hot keys).

- Non-top-level menus can have shortcut keys (combinations of *Ctrl, Shift, Alt,* function keys *F1, F2,* letter keys etc.).

- To create a menu, open the **Toolbox**, and drag a **MainMenu** control onto the form.

- To add entries to the menu, click the **Type Here** textbox, and type the text that should appear in the menu. Remove a menu item by selecting it with the mouse and pressing the *Delete* key.

- Menus generate a **Click** event when selected.

- Use the **Xor** (exclusive OR) operator to toggle single bits, such as those representing the bold and italic styles.

- The **LinkLabel** control is used to display links to other objects, such as files or Web pages. The links can change color to reflect whether each link is new, visited or active.

- When clicked, a **LinkLabel** generate a **LinkClicked** event.

- Method **Start** of class **Process** (namespace **System.Diagnostics**) can begin a new application. This method requires either the file to open (a **String**) or the application to run and the command-line arguments (two **String**s).

- The **ListBox** control allows the user to view and select multiple items from a list.

- The **CheckedListBox** control extends a **ListBox** by accompanying each item in the list with a checkbox. This allows multiple items to be selected with no logical restriction.

- The **SelectionMode** property determines how many items in a **CheckedListBox** can be selected.

- The **SelectedIndexChanged** event occurs when the user selects a new item in a **CheckedListBox**.

- **CheckBox**'s property **Items** returns all the objects in the list as a collection. Property **SelectedItem** returns the currently selected item. **SelectedIndex** returns the index of the selected item.

- Method **GetSelected** takes an index and returns **True** if the corresponding item is selected.

- Add items visually by examining the **Items** collection in the **Properties** window. Clicking the ellipsis brings up the **String Collection Editor**, in which we can type the items to add.

- **CheckedListBox**es imply that multiple items can be selected—the **SelectionMode** property can only have values **None** or **One**. **One** allows multiple selection.

- Event **ItemCheck** is generated whenever a **CheckedListBox** item is about to change.

- The **ComboBox** control combines **TextBox** features with a drop-down list. The user can either select an option from the list or type one in (if allowed by the programmer). If the number of elements exceeds the maximum that can be displayed in the drop-down list, a scrollbar appears.

- Property **DropDownStyle** determines the type of **ComboBox**.

- The **ComboBox** control has properties **Items** (a collection), **SelectedItem** and **SelectedIndex**, which are similar to the corresponding properties in **ListBox**.

- When the selected item changes, event **SelectedIndexChanged** is generated.

- A **Graphics** object allows a pen or brush to draw on a component, via one of several **Graphics** methods.

- The **TreeView** control can display nodes hierarchically on a tree.

- A node is an element that contains a value and references to other nodes.

- A parent node contains child nodes, and the child nodes can be parents themselves.

- A tree is a collection of nodes, usually organized in some manner. The first parent node of a tree is often called the root node.

- Each node has a **Nodes** collection, which contains a list of the **Node**'s children.

- To add nodes to the **TreeView** visually, click the ellipsis by the **Nodes** property in the **Properties** window. This opens the **TreeNode Editor**, where there are buttons to create a root and to add, delete and rename nodes.

- Method **GetDirectories** takes a **String** (the current directory) and returns an array of **String**s (the subdirectories).

- The **ListView** control is similar to a **ListBox**—it displays a list from which the user can select one or more items. However, a **ListView** can display icons alongside the list items in a variety of ways.

- To display images, the programmer must use an **ImageList** component. Create one by dragging it onto the form from the **ToolBox**. Click the **Images** collection in the **Properties** window to display the **Image Collection Editor**.

- Class **DirectoryInfo** (namespace **System.IO**) allows us to browse or manipulate the directory structure easily. Method **GetDirectories** returns an array of **DirectoryInfo** objects containing the subdirectories of the current directory. Method **GetFiles** returns an array of class **FileInfo** objects containing the files in the current directory.

- The **TabControl** control creates tabbed windows. This allows the programmer to provide large quantities of information while saving screen space.

- **TabControl**s contain **TabPage** objects, which can contain controls.

- To add **TabPage**s in the Visual Studio .NET designer, right-click the **TabControl**, and select **Add Tab**.

- Each **TabPage** generates its own **Click** event when its tab is clicked. Events for controls inside the **TabPage** are still handled by the form.

- Single-document-interface (SDI) applications can support only one open window or document at a time. Multiple-document-interface (MDI) programs allows users to edit multiple documents at a time.

- Each window inside an MDI application is called a child window, and the application window is called the parent window.

- To create an MDI form, set the form's **IsMDIContainer** property to **True**.

- The parent and child windows of an application can have different menus, which are merged (combined) whenever a child window is selected.

- Class **MenuItem** property **MdiList** (a boolean) allows a menu item to contain a list of open child windows.

- The child windows in an MDI application can be arranged by calling method **LayoutMdi** of the parent form.

- The .NET Framework allows the programmer to create customized controls. The most basic way to create a customized control is to derive a class from an existing Windows Forms control. If we inherit from an existing Windows Forms control, we can add to its appearance, but not redesign it. To create a new control composed of existing controls, use class **UserControl**. To create a new control from the ground up, inherit from class **Control**.

- **Timer**s are invisible components that reside on a form and generate **Tick** events at a set interval.

- We create a **UserControl** class for the project by selecting **Project**, then **Add User Control...**. We can treat this control like a Windows Form, meaning that we can add controls, using the **ToolBox**, and set properties, using the **Properties** window.

- Structure **DateTime** (namespace **System**) contains member **Now**, which is the current time.

TERMINOLOGY

& (menu access shortcut)
access shortcut
Activation property of class **ListView**
ActiveLinkColor property of class
   LinkLabel
ActiveMdiChild property of class **Form**
Add member of enumeration **MenuMerge**
Add method of **TreeNodeCollection**

Add Tab menu item
Add User Control... option in Visual Studio
Add Windows Form... option in Visual Studio
adding controls to **ToolBox**
AfterSelect event of class **TreeView**
ArrangeIcons value in **LayoutMdi**
   enumeration
boundary of a control

submenu

TabControl, adding a **TabPage**

TabControl class

TabCount property of class **TabControl**

TabPage, add to **TabControl**

TabPage class

TabPage, using radio buttons

TabPages property of class **TabControl**

Text property of class **LinkLabel**

Text property of class **MenuItem**

Text property of class **TreeNode**

Tick event of class **Timer**

TileHorizontal value in **LayoutMdi** enumeration

TileVertical value in **LayoutMdi** enumeration

ToolBox customization

tree

TreeNode class

TreeNode Editor in VS .NET

TreeView class

UseMnemonic property of class **LinkLabel**

user-defined control

UserControl class

View property of class **ListView**

VisitedLinkColor property of class **LinkLabel**

SELF-REVIEW EXERCISES

13.1 State whether each of the following is *true* or *false*. If *false*, explain why.

a) Menus provide groups of related classes.

b) Menu items can display radio buttons, checkmarks and access shortcuts.

c) The **ListBox** control allows only single selection (like a radio button), whereas the **CheckedListBox** allows multiple selection (like a check box).

d) The **ComboBox** control has a drop-down list.

e) Deleting a parent node in a **TreeView** control deletes its child nodes.

f) The user can select only one item in a **ListView** control.

g) A **TabPage** can act as a logical group for radio buttons.

h) In general, Multiple Document Interface (MDI) windows are used with simple applications.

i) An MDI child window can have MDI children.

j) MDI child windows cannot be maximized (enlarged) inside their parent.

k) There are two basic ways to create a customized control.

13.2 Fill in the blanks in each of the following statements:

a) Method _____ of class **Process** can open files and Web pages, much as can the **Run** menu in Windows.

b) If more elements appear in a **ComboBox** than can fit, a _____ appears.

c) The top-level node in a **TreeView** is the _____ node.

d) An **ImageList** is used to display icons in a _____.

e) The **MergeOrder** and **MergeType** properties determine how _____ merge.

f) The _____ property allows a menu to display a list of active child windows.

g) An important feature of the **ListView** control is the ability to display _____.

h) Class _____ allows the programmer to combine several controls into a single, custom control.

i) The _____ saves space by layering **TabPage**s on top of each other.

j) The _____ window layout option makes all windows the same size and layers them so every title bar is visible (if possible).

k) _____ are typically used to display hyperlinks to other objects, files or Web pages.

ANSWERS TO SELF-REVIEW EXERCISES

13.1 a) False. Menus provide groups of related commands. b) True. c) False. Both controls can have single or multiple selection. d) True. e) True. f) False. The user can select one or more items.

g) True. h) False. MDI windows tend to be used with complex applications. i) False. Only an MDI parent window can have MDI children. An MDI parent window cannot be an MDI child. j) False. MDI child windows cannot be moved outside their parent window. k) False. There are three methods: 1) Derive from an existing control, 2) use a **UserControl** or 3) derive from **Control** and create a control from scratch.

13.2   a) **Start**. b) scrollbar. c) root. d) **ListView**. e) menus. f) **MdiList**. g) icons. h) **User-Control**. i) **TabControl**. j) **Cascade**. k) **LinkLabel**s.

EXERCISES

13.3   Write a program that displays the names of 15 states in a **ComboBox**. When an item is selected from the **ComboBox**, remove it.

13.4   Modify your solution to Exercise 13.3 to add a **ListBox**. When the user selects an item from the **ComboBox**, remove the item from the **ComboBox**, and add it to the **ListBox**. Your program should check to ensure that the **ComboBox** contains at least one item. If it does not, print a message in a message box, and terminate program execution.

13.5   Write a program that allows the user to enter strings in a **TextBox**. Each string input is added to a **ListBox**. As each string is added to the **ListBox**, ensure that the strings are in sorted order. Any sorting method may be used.

13.6   Create a file browser (similar to Windows Explorer) based on the programs in Fig. 13.7, Fig. 13.21 and Fig. 13.24. The file browser should have a **TreeView**, which allows the user to browse directories. There should also be a **ListView**, which displays the contents (all subdirectories and files) of the directory being browsed. Double-clicking a file in the **ListView** should open it, and double-clicking a directory in either the **ListView** or the **TreeView** should browse it. If a file or directory cannot be accessed, because of its permission settings, notify the user.

13.7   Create an MDI text editor. Each child window should contain a multiline **TextBox**. The MDI parent should have a **Format** menu, with submenus to control the size, font and color of the text in the active child window. Each submenu should have at least three options. In addition, the parent should have a **File** menu with menu items **New** (create a new child), **Close** (close the active child) and **Exit** (exit the application). The parent should have a **Window** menu to display a list of the open child windows and their layout options.

13.8   Create a **UserControl** called **LoginPasswordUserControl**. The **LoginPasswordUserControl** contains a **Label** (**loginLabel**) that displays **string "Login:"**, a **TextBox** (**loginTextBox**) where the user inputs a login name, a **Label** (**passwordLabel**) that displays the **string "Password:"** and finally, a **TextBox** (**passwordTextBox**) where a user inputs a password (do not forget to set property **PasswordChar** to **"*"** in the **TextBox**'s **Properties** window). **LoginPasswordUserControl** must provide public read-only properties **Login** and **Password** that allow an application to retrieve the user input from **loginTextBox** and **passwordTextBox**. The **UserControl** must be exported to an application that displays the values input by the user in **LoginPasswordUserControl**.

14

Multithreading

Objectives

- To understand the notion of multithreading.
- To appreciate how multithreading can improve program performance.
- To understand how to create, manage and destroy threads.
- To understand the life cycle of a thread.
- To understand thread synchronization.
- To understand thread priorities and scheduling.
- To understand the role of a **ThreadPool** in efficient multithreading.

The spider's touch, how exquisitely fine!
Feels at each thread, and lives along the line.
Alexander Pope

A person with one watch knows what time it is; a person with two watches is never sure.
Proverb

Learn to labor and to wait.
Henry Wadsworth Longfellow

The most general definition of beauty...Multeity in Unity.
Samuel Taylor Coleridge

14.1 Introduction

It would be nice if we could perform one action at a time and perform it well, but that is usually difficult to do. The human body performs a great variety of operations *in parallel*— or, as we will say throughout this chapter, *concurrently*. Respiration, blood circulation and digestion, for example, can occur concurrently. All the senses—sight, touch, smell, taste and hearing—can occur at once. Computers, too, perform operations concurrently. It is common for desktop personal computers to be compiling a program, sending a file to a printer and receiving electronic mail messages over a network concurrently.

Ironically, most programming languages do not enable programmers to specify concurrent activities. Rather, programming languages generally provide only a simple set of control structures that enable programmers to perform one action at a time, proceeding to the next action after the previous one has finished. Historically, the type of concurrency that computers perform today generally has been implemented as operating system "primitives" available only to highly experienced "systems programmers."

The Ada programming language, developed by the United States Department of Defense, made concurrency primitives widely available to defense contractors building military command-and-control systems. However, Ada has not been widely used in universities and commercial industry.

The .NET Framework Class Library makes concurrency primitives available to the applications programmer. The programmer specifies that applications contain "threads of execution," each thread designating a portion of a program that may execute concurrently with other threads—this capability is called *multithreading*. Multithreading is available to all .NET programming languages, including C#, Visual Basic and Visual C++.

Software Engineering Observation 14.1

The .NET Framework Class Library includes multithreading capabilities in namespace `System.Threading`*. This encourages the use of multithreading among a larger part of the applications-programming community.*

We discuss many applications of concurrent programming. When programs download large files, such as audio clips or video clips from the World Wide Web, users do not want to wait until an entire clip downloads before starting the playback. To solve this problem, we can put multiple threads to work—one thread downloads a clip, and another plays the clip. These activities, or *tasks*, then may proceed concurrently. To avoid choppy playback, we *synchronize* the threads so that the player thread does not begin until there is a sufficient amount of the clip in memory to keep the player thread busy.

Another example of multithreading is C#'s automatic *garbage collection*. C and C++ place with the programmer the responsibility of reclaiming dynamically allocated memory. C# provides a *garbage-collector thread* that reclaims dynamically allocated memory that is no longer needed.

Performance Tip 14.1

One of the reasons for the popularity of C and C++ over the years was that their memory-management techniques were more efficient than those of languages that used garbage collectors. In fact, memory management in C# often is faster than in C or C++.[1]

Good Programming Practice 14.1

Set an object reference to **null** *when the program no longer needs that object. This enables the garbage collector to determine at the earliest possible moment that the object can be garbage collected. If such an object has other references to it, that object cannot be collected.*

Writing multithreaded programs can be tricky. Although the human mind can perform functions concurrently, people find it difficult to jump between parallel "trains of thought." To see why multithreading can be difficult to program and understand, try the following experiment: Open three books to page 1 and try reading the books concurrently. Read a few words from the first book, then read a few words from the second book, then read a few words from the third book, then loop back and read the next few words from the first book, etc. After this experiment, you will appreciate the challenges of multithreading—switching between books, reading briefly, remembering your place in each book, moving the book you are reading closer so you can see it, pushing books you are not reading aside—and amidst all this chaos, trying to comprehend the content of the books!

Performance Tip 14.2

A problem with single-threaded applications is that lengthy activities must complete before other activities can begin. In a multithreaded application, threads can share a processor (or set of processors), so that multiple tasks are performed in parallel.

14.2 Thread States: Life Cycle of a Thread

At any time, a thread is said to be in one of several *thread states* (illustrated in Fig. 14.1[2]). This section discusses these states and the transitions between states. Two classes critical for multithreaded applications are **Thread** and **Monitor** (**System.Threading** namespace). This section also discusses several methods of classes **Thread** and **Monitor** that cause state transitions.

---

1. E. Schanzer, "Performance Considerations for Run-Time Technologies in the .NET Framework," August 2001 **<http://msdn.microsoft.com/library/default.asp?url= /library/en-us/dndotnet/html/dotnetperftechs.asp>**.

2. As this book went to publication, Microsoft changed the names of the *Started* and *Blocked* thread states to *Running* and *WaitSleepJoin*, respectively.

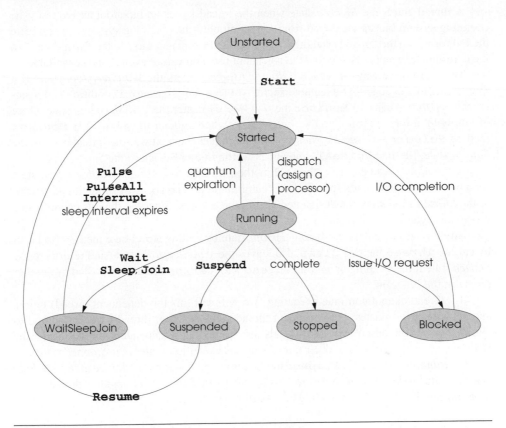

Fig. 14.1   Thread life cycle.

A new thread begins its lifecyle in the *Unstarted* state. The thread remains in the *Unstarted* state until the program calls **Thread** method **Start**, which places the thread in the *Started* state (sometimes called the *Ready* or *Runnable* state) and immediately returns control to the calling thread. Then the thread that invoked **Start**, the newly *Started* thread and any other threads in the program execute concurrently.

The highest priority *Started* thread enters the *Running* state (i.e., begins executing) when the operating system assigns a processor to the thread (Section 14.3 discusses thread priorities). When a *Started* thread receives a processor for the first time and becomes a *Running* thread, the thread executes its **ThreadStart** delegate, which specifies the actions the thread will perform during its lifecycle. When a program creates a new **Thread**, the program specifies the **Thread**'s **ThreadStart** delegate as the argument to the **Thread** constructor. The **ThreadStart** delegate must be a method that returns **void** and takes no arguments.

A *Running* thread enters the *Stopped* (or *Dead*) state when its **ThreadStart** delegate terminates. Note that a program can force a thread into the *Stopped* state by calling **Thread** method **Abort** on the appropriate **Thread** object. Method **Abort** throws a **ThreadAbortException** in the thread, normally causing the thread to terminate. When a thread is in the *Stopped* state and there are no references to the thread object, the garbage collector can remove the thread object from memory.

A thread enters the *Blocked* state when the thread issues an input/output request. The operating system blocks the thread from executing until the operating system can complete the I/O for which the thread is waiting. At that point, the thread returns to the *Started* state, so it can resume execution. A *Blocked* thread cannot use a processor even if one is available.

There are three ways in which a *Running* thread enters the *WaitSleepJoin* state. If a thread encounters code that it cannot execute yet (normally because a condition is not satisfied), the thread can call **Monitor** method **Wait** to enter the *WaitSleepJoin* state. Once in this state, a thread returns to the *Started* state when another thread invokes **Monitor** method **Pulse** or **PulseAll**. Method **Pulse** moves the next waiting thread back to the *Started* state. Method **PulseAll** moves all waiting threads back to the *Started* state.

A *Running* thread can call **Thread** method **Sleep** to enter the *WaitSleepJoin* state for a period of milliseconds specified as the argument to **Sleep**. A sleeping thread returns to the *Started* state when its designated sleep time expires. Sleeping threads cannot use a processor, even if one is available.

Any thread that enters the *WaitSleepJoin* state by calling **Monitor** method **Wait** or by calling **Thread** method **Sleep** also leaves the *WaitSleepJoin* state and returns to the *Started* state if the sleeping or waiting **Thread**'s **Interrupt** method is called by another thread in the program.

If a thread cannot continue executing (we will call this the dependent thread) unless another thread terminates, the dependent thread calls the other thread's **Join** method to "join" the two threads. When two threads are "joined," the dependent thread leaves the *WaitSleepJoin* state when the other thread finishes execution (enters the *Stopped* state).

If a *Running* **Thread**'s **Suspend** method is called, the *Running* thread enters the *Suspended* state. A *Suspended* thread returns to the *Started* state when another thread in the program invokes the Suspended thread's **Resume** method.

14.3 Thread Priorities and Thread Scheduling

Every thread has a priority in the range between **ThreadPriority.Lowest** to **ThreadPriority.Highest**. These two values come from the **ThreadPriority** enumeration (namespace **System.Threading**). The enumeration consists of the values **Lowest**, **BelowNormal**, **Normal**, **AboveNormal** and **Highest**. By default, each thread has priority **Normal**.

The Windows operating system supports a concept, called *timeslicing,* that enables threads of equal priority to share a processor. Without timeslicing, each thread in a set of equal-priority threads runs to completion (unless the thread leaves the *Running* state and enters the *WaitSleepJoin*, *Suspended* or *Blocked* state) before the thread's peers get a chance to execute. With timeslicing, each thread receives a brief burst of processor time, called a *quantum,* during which the thread can execute. At the completion of the quantum, even if the thread has not finished executing, the processor is taken away from that thread and given to the next thread of equal priority, if one is available.

The job of the thread scheduler is to keep the highest-priority thread running at all times and, if there is more than one highest-priority thread, to ensure that all such threads execute for a quantum in round-robin fashion. Figure 14.2 illustrates the multilevel priority queue for threads. In Fig. 14.2, assuming a single-processor computer, threads A and B each execute for a quantum in round-robin fashion until both threads complete execution. This means that A gets a quantum of time to run. Then B gets a quantum. Then A gets another quantum. Then

B gets another quantum. This continues until one thread completes. The processor then devotes all its power to the thread that remains (unless another thread of that priority is *Started*). Next, thread C runs to completion. Threads D, E and F each execute for a quantum in round-robin fashion until they all complete execution. This process continues until all threads run to completion. Note that, depending on the operating system, new higher-priority threads could postpone—possibly indefinitely—the execution of lower-priority threads. Such *indefinite postponement* often is referred to more colorfully as *starvation*.

A thread's priority can be adjusted with the **Priority** property, which accepts values from the **ThreadPriority** enumeration. If the argument is not one of the valid thread-priority constants, an **ArgumentException** occurs.

A thread executes until it dies, becomes *Blocked* for input/output (or some other reason), calls **Sleep**, calls **Monitor** method **Wait** or **Join**, is preempted by a thread of higher priority or has its quantum expire. A thread with a higher priority than the *Running* thread can become *Started* (and hence preempt the *Running* thread) if a sleeping thread wakes up, if I/O completes for a thread that *Blocked* for that I/O, if either **Pulse** or **PulseAll** is called on an object on which **Wait** was called, or if a thread to which the high-priority thread was **Join**ed completes.

Figure 14.3 demonstrates basic threading techniques, including the construction of a **Thread** object and using the **Thread** class's **static** method **Sleep**. The program creates three threads of execution, each with the default priority **Normal**. Each thread displays a message indicating that it is going to sleep for a random interval of from 0 to 5000 milliseconds, then goes to sleep. When each thread awakens, the thread displays its name, indicates that it is done sleeping, terminates and enters the *Stopped* state. You will see that method **Main** (i.e., the *Main thread of execution*) terminates before the application terminates. The program consists of two classes—**ThreadTester** (lines 8–41), which creates the three threads, and **MessagePrinter** (lines 44–73), which defines a **Print** method containing the actions each thread will perform.

Objects of class **MessagePrinter** (lines 44–73) control the lifecycle of each of the three threads class **ThreadTester**'s **Main** method creates. Class **MessagePrinter** consists of instance variable **sleepTime** (line 46), **static** variable **random** (line 47), a constructor (lines 50–54) and a **Print** method (lines 57–71). Variable **sleepTime** stores a random integer value chosen when a new **MessagePrinter** object's constructor is called. Each thread controlled by a **MessagePrinter** object sleeps for the amount of time specified by the corresponding **MessagePrinter** object's **sleepTime**

The **MessagePrinter** constructor (lines 50–54) initializes **sleepTime** to a random integer from 0 up to, but not including, 5001 (i.e., from 0 to 5000).

Method **Print** begins by obtaining a reference to the currently executing thread (line 60) via class **Thread**'s **static** property **CurrentThread**. The currently executing thread is the one that invokes method **Print**. Next, lines 63–64 display a message indicating the name of the currently executing thread and stating that the thread is going to sleep for a certain number of milliseconds. Note that line 64 uses the currently executing thread's **Name** property to obtain the thread's name (set in method **Main** when each thread is created). Line 66 invokes **static Thread** method **Sleep** to place the thread into the *Wait-SleepJoin* state. At this point, the thread loses the processor and the system allows another thread to execute. When the thread awakens, it reenters the *Started* state again until the system assigns a processor to the thread. When the **MessagePrinter** object enters the

Running state again, line 69 outputs the thread's name in a message that indicates the thread is done sleeping, and method **Print** terminates.

Class **ThreadTester**'s **Main** method (lines 10–39) creates three objects of class **MessagePrinter**, at lines 14, 19 and 24, respectively. Lines 15–16, 20–21 and 25–26 create and initialize three **Thread** objects. Lines 17, 22 and 27 set each **Thread**'s **Name** property, which we use for output purposes. Note that each **Thread**'s constructor receives a **ThreadStart** delegate as an argument. Remember that a **ThreadStart** delegate specifies the actions a thread performs during its lifecyle. Line 16 specifies that the delegate for **thread1** will be method **Print** of the object to which **printer1** refers. When **thread1** enters the *Running* state for the first time, **thread1** will invoke **printer1**'s **Print** method to perform the tasks specified in method **Print**'s body. Thus, **thread1** will print its name, display the amount of time for which it will go to sleep, sleep for that amount of time, wake up and display a message indicating that the thread is done sleeping. At that point method **Print** will terminate. A thread completes its task when the method specified by a **Thread**'s **ThreadStart** delegate terminates, placing the thread in the *Stopped* state. When **thread2** and **thread3** enter the *Running* state for the first time, they invoke the **Print** methods of **printer2** and **printer3**, respectively. Threads **thread2** and **thread3** perform the same tasks as **thread1** by executing the **Print** methods of the objects to which **printer2** and **printer3** refer (each of which has its own randomly chosen sleep time).

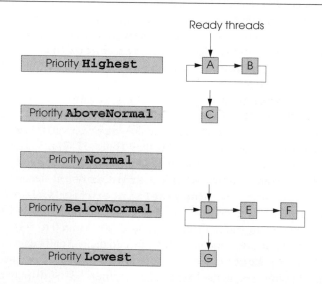

Fig. 14.2 Thread-priority scheduling.

```
1   // Fig. 14.3: ThreadTester.cs
2   // Multiple threads printing at different intervals.
3
```

Fig. 14.3 Threads sleeping and printing. (Part 1 of 3.)

```
4   using System;
5   using System.Threading;
6
7   // class ThreadTester demonstrates basic threading concepts
8   class ThreadTester
9   {
10     static void Main( string[] args )
11     {
12        // Create and name each thread. Use MessagePrinter's
13        // Print method as argument to ThreadStart delegate.
14        MessagePrinter printer1 = new MessagePrinter();
15        Thread thread1 =
16           new Thread ( new ThreadStart( printer1.Print ) );
17        thread1.Name = "thread1";
18
19        MessagePrinter printer2 = new MessagePrinter();
20        Thread thread2 =
21           new Thread ( new ThreadStart( printer2.Print ) );
22        thread2.Name = "thread2";
23
24        MessagePrinter printer3 = new MessagePrinter();
25        Thread thread3 =
26           new Thread ( new ThreadStart( printer3.Print  ) );
27        thread3.Name = "thread3";
28
29        Console.WriteLine( "Starting threads" );
30
31        // call each thread's Start method to place each
32        // thread in Started state
33        thread1.Start();
34        thread2.Start();
35        thread3.Start();
36
37        Console.WriteLine( "Threads started\n" );
38
39     } // end method Main
40
41   } // end class ThreadTester
42
43   // Print method of this class used to control threads
44   class MessagePrinter
45   {
46      private int sleepTime;
47      private static Random random = new Random();
48
49      // constructor to initialize a MessagePrinter object
50      public MessagePrinter()
51      {
52         // pick random sleep time between 0 and 5 seconds
53         sleepTime = random.Next( 5001 );
54      }
55
```

Fig. 14.3   Threads sleeping and printing. (Part 2 of 3.)

```
56      // method Print controls thread that prints messages
57      public void Print()
58      {
59          // obtain reference to currently executing thread
60          Thread current = Thread.CurrentThread;
61
62          // put thread to sleep for sleepTime amount of time
63          Console.WriteLine(
64              current.Name + " going to sleep for " + sleepTime );
65
66          Thread.Sleep ( sleepTime );
67
68          // print thread name
69          Console.WriteLine( current.Name + " done sleeping" );
70
71      } // end method Print
72
73  } // end class MessagePrinter
```

```
Starting threads
Threads started

thread1 going to sleep for 1977
thread2 going to sleep for 4513
thread3 going to sleep for 1261
thread3 done sleeping
thread1 done sleeping
thread2 done sleeping
```

```
Starting threads
Threads started

thread1 going to sleep for 1466
thread2 going to sleep for 4245
thread3 going to sleep for 1929
thread1 done sleeping
thread3 done sleeping
thread2 done sleeping
```

Fig. 14.3   Threads sleeping and printing. (Part 3 of 3.)

Testing and Debugging Tip 14.1

Naming threads helps in the debugging of a multithreaded program. Visual Studio .NET's debugger provides a **Threads** *window that displays the name of each thread and enables you to view the execution of any thread in the program.*

Lines 33–35 invoke each **Thread**'s **Start** method to place the threads in the *Started* state (sometimes called *launching a thread*). Method **Start** returns immediately from each invocation, then line 37 outputs a message indicating that the threads were started, and the **Main** thread of execution terminates. The program itself does not terminate, however, because there are still threads that are alive (i.e., the threads were *Started* and have not reached the *Stopped* state yet). The program will not terminate until its last thread dies. When the system assigns a processor to a thread, the thread enters the *Running* state and calls the method specified by the thread's **ThreadStart** delegate. In this program, each thread invokes method **Print** of the appropriate **MessagePrinter** object to perform the tasks discussed previously.

Note that the sample outputs for this program show each thread and the thread's sleep time as the thread goes to sleep. The thread with the shortest sleep time normally awakens first, then indicates that it is done sleeping and terminates. In Section 14.7, we discuss multithreading issues that could prevent the thread with the shortest sleep time from awakening first.

14.4 Thread Synchronization and Class **Monitor**

Often, multiple threads of execution manipulate shared data. If threads with access to shared data simply read that data, then there is no need to prevent the data from being accessed by more than one thread at a time. However, when multiple threads share data and that data is modified by one or more of those threads, then indeterminate results may occur. If one thread is in the process of updating the data and another thread tries to update it too, the data will reflect the update that occurs second. If the data is an array or other data structure in which the threads could update separate parts of the data concurrently, it is possible that part of the data will reflect the information from one thread while another part of the data will reflect information from a different thread. When this happens, the program has difficulty determining when the data has been updated properly.

The problem can be solved by giving one thread at a time exclusive access to code that manipulates the shared data. During that time, other threads desiring to manipulate the data should be kept waiting. When the thread with exclusive access to the data completes its manipulation of the data, one of the threads waiting to manipulate the data should be allowed to proceed. In this fashion, each thread accessing the shared data excludes all other threads from doing so simultaneously. This is called *mutual exclusion* or *thread synchronization*.

C# uses the .NET Framework's monitors[3] to perform synchronization. Class **Monitor** provides the methods for *locking objects* to implement synchronized access to shared data. Locking an object means that only one thread can access that object at a time. When a thread wishes to acquire exclusive control over an object, the thread invokes **Monitor** method *Enter* to acquire the lock on that data object. Each object has a *SyncBlock* that maintains the state of that object's lock. Methods of class **Monitor** use the data in an object's *SyncBlock* to determine the state of the lock for that object. After acquiring the lock for an object, a thread can manipulate that object's data. While the object is locked, all other threads attempting to acquire the lock on that object are blocked (i.e., they enter the *Blocked* state) from acquiring the lock. When the thread that locked the shared object no longer requires the lock, that thread invokes **Monitor** method *Exit* to release the lock. This updates the *SyncBlock* of the shared object to indicate that the lock for the object is avail-

---

3. Hoare, C. A. R., Monitors: An Operating System Structuring Concept, *Communications of the ACM*. Vol. 17, No. 10, October 1974: 549–557. *Corrigendum, Communications of the ACM*. Vol. 18, No. 2, February 1975: 95.

able again. At this point, if there is a thread that was previously blocked from acquiring the lock on the shared object, that thread acquires the lock to begin its processing of the object. If all threads with access to an object attempt to acquire the object's lock before manipulating the object, only one thread at a time will be allowed to manipulate the object. This helps ensure the integrity of the data.

Common Programming Error 14.1

Make sure that all code that updates a shared object locks the object before doing so. Otherwise a thread calling a method that does not lock the object can make the object unstable even when another thread has acquired the lock for the object.

Common Programming Error 14.2

Deadlock occurs when a waiting thread (let us call this thread1*) cannot proceed because it is waiting for another thread (let us call this* thread2*) to proceed. Similarly,* thread2 *cannot proceed because it is waiting for* thread1 *to proceed. The two threads are waiting for each other; therefore, the actions that would enable each thread to continue execution never occur.*

C# provides another means of manipulating an object's lock—keyword **lock**. Placing **lock** before a block of code (designated with braces) as in

```
lock ( objectReference )
{
    // code that requires synchronization goes here
}
```

obtains the lock on the object to which the *objectReference* in parentheses refers. The *objectReference* is the same reference that normally would be passed to **Monitor** methods **Enter**, **Exit**, **Pulse** and **PulseAll**. When a **lock** block terminates for any reason, C# releases the lock on the object to which the *objectReference* refers. We explain **lock** further in Section 14.7.

If a thread determines that it cannot perform its task on a locked object, the thread can call **Monitor** method **Wait** and pass as an argument the object on which the thread will wait until the thread can perform its task. Calling method **Monitor.Wait** from a thread releases the lock the thread has on the object **Wait** receives as an argument and places that thread into the *WaitSleepJoin* state for that object. A thread in the *WaitSleepJoin* state for an object leaves the *WaitSleepJoin* state when a separate thread invokes **Monitor** method **Pulse** or **PulseAll** with the object as an argument. Method **Pulse** transitions the object's first waiting thread from the *WaitSleepJoin* state to the *Started* state. Method **PulseAll** transitions all threads in the object's *WaitSleepJoin* state to the *Started* state. The transition to the *Started* state enables the thread (or threads) to get ready to continue executing.

There is a difference between threads waiting to acquire the lock for an object and threads waiting in an object's *WaitSleepJoin* state: The threads called **Monitor** method **Wait** with the object as an argument. Threads that are waiting to acquire the lock enter the *Blocked* state and wait there until the object's lock becomes available. Then, one of the blocked threads can acquire the object's lock.

Monitor methods **Enter**, **Exit**, **Wait**, **Pulse** and **PulseAll** all take a reference to an object—usually the keyword **this**—as their argument.

Common Programming Error 14.3

A thread in the WaitSleepJoin *state cannot reenter the* Started *state to continue execution until a separate thread invokes* **Monitor** *method* **Pulse** *or* **PulseAll** *with the appropriate object as an argument. If this does not occur, the waiting thread will wait forever and so can cause deadlock.*

Testing and Debugging Tip 14.2

When multiple threads manipulate a shared object, using monitors, ensure that, if one thread calls **Monitor** *method* **Wait** *to enter the* WaitSleepJoin *state for the shared object, a separate thread eventually will call* **Monitor** *method* **Pulse** *to transition the thread waiting on the shared object back to the* Started *state. If multiple threads may be waiting for the shared object, a separate thread can call* **Monitor** *method* **PulseAll** *as a safeguard to ensure that all waiting threads have another opportunity to perform their tasks.*

Performance Tip 14.3

Synchronization to achieve correctness in multithreaded programs can make programs run more slowly, as a result of monitor overhead and the frequent transitioning of threads among the Running, WaitSleepJoin *and* Started *states. There is not much to say, however, for highly efficient, incorrect multithreaded programs!*

14.5 Producer/Consumer Relationship without Thread Synchronization

In a *producer/consumer relationship*, the *producer* portion of an application generates data and the *consumer* portion of an application uses that data. In a multithreaded producer/consumer relationship, a *producer thread* calls a *produce method* to generate data and place it into a shared region of memory, called a *buffer*. A *consumer thread* calls a *consume method* to read that data. If the producer waiting to put the next data into the buffer determines that the consumer has not yet read the previous data from the buffer, the producer thread should call **Wait**; otherwise, the consumer never sees the previous data and that data is lost to that application. When the consumer thread reads the message, it should call **Pulse** to allow a waiting producer to proceed. If a consumer thread finds the buffer empty or finds that the previous data has already been read, the consumer should call **Wait**; otherwise, the consumer might read "garbage" from the buffer or the consumer might process a previous data item more than once—each of these possibilities results in a logic error in the application. When the producer places the next data into the buffer, the producer should call **Pulse** to allow the consumer thread to proceed.

Let us consider how logic errors can arise if we do not synchronize access among multiple threads manipulating shared data. Consider a producer/consumer relationship in which a producer thread writes a sequence of numbers (we use 1–4) into a *shared buffer*— a memory location shared between multiple threads. The consumer thread reads this data from the shared buffer then displays the data. We display in the program's output the values that the producer writes (produces) and that the consumer reads (consumes). Figure 14.4 demonstrates a producer and a consumer accessing a single shared cell (**int** variable **buffer**) of memory without any synchronization. Both the consumer and the producer threads access this single cell: The producer thread writes to the cell; the consumer thread reads from it. We would like each value the producer thread writes to the shared cell to be consumed exactly once by the consumer thread. However, the threads in this example are not synchronized. Therefore, data can be lost if the producer places new data into the slot before the consumer consumes the previous data. Also, data can be incorrectly repeated if the consumer consumes data again before the producer produces the next item. To show these possibilities, the consumer thread in the following example keeps a total of all the values it reads. The producer thread produces values from 1 to 4. If the consumer reads each value produced once and only once, the total would be 10. However, if you execute this program several times, you will see that the total is rarely, if ever, 10. Also, to emphasize our point, the producer and consumer threads in the example each sleep for random intervals of up to three seconds between performing their tasks. Thus, we do not know exactly when the producer thread will attempt to write a new value, nor do we know when the consumer thread will attempt to read a value.

The program consists of four classes—**HoldIntegerUnsynchronized** (lines 9–34), **Producer** (lines 37–70), **Consumer** (73–106) and **SharedCell** (109–144).

```
1   // Fig. 14.4: Unsynchronized.cs
2   // Showing multiple threads modifying a shared object without
3   // synchronization.
4
5   using System;
6   using System.Threading;
7
8   // this class represents a single shared int
9   public class HoldIntegerUnsynchronized
10  {
11     // buffer shared by producer and consumer threads
12     private int buffer = -1;
13
14     // property Buffer
15     public int Buffer
16     {
17        get
18        {
19           Console.WriteLine( Thread.CurrentThread.Name +
20              " reads " + buffer );
21
22           return buffer;
23        }
24
25        set
26        {
27           Console.WriteLine( Thread.CurrentThread.Name +
28              " writes " + value );
29
30           buffer = value;
31        }
32
33     } // end property Buffer
34
35  } // end class HoldIntegerUnsynchronized
```

Fig. 14.4   Producer and consumer threads accessing a shared object without synchronization. (Part 1 of 4.)

```
36
37   // class Producer's Produce method controls a thread that
38   // stores values from 1 to 4 in sharedLocation
39   class Producer
40   {
41      private HoldIntegerUnsynchronized sharedLocation;
42      private Random randomSleepTime;
43
44      // constructor
45      public Producer(
46         HoldIntegerUnsynchronized shared, Random random )
47      {
48         sharedLocation = shared;
49         randomSleepTime = random;
50      }
51
52      // store values 1-4 in object sharedLocation
53      public void Produce()
54      {
55         // sleep for random interval upto 3000 milliseconds
56         // then set sharedLocation's Buffer property
57         for ( int count = 1; count <= 4; count++ )
58         {
59            Thread.Sleep( randomSleepTime.Next( 1, 3000 ) );
60            sharedLocation.Buffer = count;
61         }
62
63         Console.WriteLine( Thread.CurrentThread.Name +
64            " done producing.\nTerminating " +
65            Thread.CurrentThread.Name + "." );
66
67      } // end method Produce
68
69   } // end class Producer
70
71   // class Consumer's Consume method controls a thread that
72   // loops four times and reads a value from sharedLocation
73   class Consumer
74   {
75      private HoldIntegerUnsynchronized sharedLocation;
76      private Random randomSleepTime;
77
78      // constructor
79      public Consumer(
80         HoldIntegerUnsynchronized shared, Random random )
81      {
82         sharedLocation = shared;
83         randomSleepTime = random;
84      }
85
```

Fig. 14.4 Producer and consumer threads accessing a shared object without synchronization. (Part 2 of 4.)

```
86          // read sharedLocation's value four times
87          public void Consume()
88          {
89             int sum = 0;
90
91             // sleep for random interval up to 3000 milliseconds
92             // then add sharedLocation's Buffer property value
93             // to sum
94             for ( int count = 1; count <= 4; count++ )
95             {
96                Thread.Sleep( randomSleepTime.Next( 1, 3000 ) );
97                sum += sharedLocation.Buffer;
98             }
99
100            Console.WriteLine( Thread.CurrentThread.Name +
101               " read values totaling: " + sum +
102               ".\nTerminating " + Thread.CurrentThread.Name + "." );
103
104         } // end method Consume
105
106    } // end class Consumer
107
108    // this class creates producer and consumer threads
109    class SharedCell
110    {
111       // create producer and consumer threads and start them
112       static void Main( string[] args )
113       {
114          // create shared object used by threads
115          HoldIntegerUnsynchronized holdInteger =
116             new HoldIntegerUnsynchronized();
117
118          // Random object used by each thread
119          Random random = new Random();
120
121          // create Producer and Consumer objects
122          Producer producer =
123             new Producer( holdInteger, random );
124
125          Consumer consumer =
126             new Consumer( holdInteger, random );
127
128          // create threads for producer and consumer and set
129          // delegates for each thread
130          Thread producerThread =
131             new Thread( new ThreadStart( producer.Produce ) );
132          producerThread.Name = "Producer";
133
134          Thread consumerThread =
135             new Thread( new ThreadStart( consumer.Consume ) );
136          consumerThread.Name = "Consumer";
137
```

Fig. 14.4   Producer and consumer threads accessing a shared object without synchronization. (Part 3 of 4.)

```
138        // start each thread
139        producerThread.Start();
140        consumerThread.Start();
141
142    } // end method Main
143
144 } // end class SharedCell
```

```
Consumer reads -1
Producer writes 1
Consumer reads 1
Consumer reads 1
Consumer reads 1
Consumer read values totaling: 2.
Terminating Consumer.
Producer writes 2
Producer writes 3
Producer writes 4
Producer done producing.
Terminating Producer.
```

```
Producer writes 1
Producer writes 2
Consumer reads 2
Producer writes 3
Consumer reads 3
Producer writes 4
Producer done producing.
Terminating Producer.
Consumer reads 4
Consumer reads 4
Consumer read values totaling: 13.
Terminating Consumer.
```

```
Producer writes 1
Consumer reads 1
Producer writes 2
Consumer reads 2
Producer writes 3
Consumer reads 3
Producer writes 4
Producer done producing.
Terminating Producer.
Consumer reads 4
Consumer read values totaling: 10.
Terminating Consumer.
```

Fig. 14.4 Producer and consumer threads accessing a shared object without
synchronization. (Part 4 of 4.)

Class **HoldIntegerUnsynchronized** (lines 9–35) consists of instance variable **buffer** (line 12) and property **Buffer** (lines 15–33), which provides **get** and **set** accessors. Property **Buffer**'s accessors do not synchronize access to instance variable **buffer**. Note that each accessor uses class **Thread**'s **static** property **Current-Thread** to obtain a reference to the currently executing thread, then uses that thread's property **Name** to obtain the thread's name.

Class **Producer** (lines 39–69) consists of instance variable **sharedLocation** (line 41), instance variable **randomSleepTime** (line 42), a constructor (lines 45–50) to initialize the instance variables and a **Produce** method (lines 53–67). The constructor initializes instance variable **sharedLocation** to refer to the **HoldInteger-Unsynchronized** object received from method **Main** as the argument **shared**. The producer thread in this program executes the tasks specified in method **Produce** of class **Producer**. Method **Produce** contains a **for** structure (lines 57–61) that loops four times. Each iteration of the loop first invokes **Thread** method **Sleep** to place producer thread into the *WaitSleepJoin* state for a random time interval between 0 and 3 seconds. When the thread awakens, line 61 assigns the value of control variable **count** to the **HoldIntegerUnsynchronized** object's **Buffer** property, which causes the **set** accessor of **HoldIntegerUnsynchronized** to modify the **buffer** instance variable of the **HoldIntegerUnsynchronized** object. When the loop completes, lines 63–65 display a line of text in the console window indicating that the thread finished producing data and that the thread is terminating, then the **Produce** method terminates and so places the producer thread in the *Stopped* state.

Class **Consumer** (73–106) consists of instance variable **sharedLocation** (line 75), instance variable **randomSleepTime** (line 76), a constructor (lines 79–84) to initialize the instance variables and a **Consume** method (lines 87–104). The constructor initializes **sharedLocation** to refer to the **HoldIntegerUnsynchronized** received from **Main** as the argument **shared**. The consumer thread in this program performs the tasks specified in class **Consumer**'s **Consume** method. The method contains a **for** structure (lines 94–98) that loops four times. Each iteration of the loop invokes **Thread** method **Sleep** to put the consumer thread into the *WaitSleepJoin* state for a random time interval between 0 and 3 seconds. Next, line 97 gets the value of the **HoldIntegerUnsynchronized** object's **Buffer** property and adds the value to the variable **sum**. When the loop completes, lines 100–102 display a line in the console window indicating the sum of all values read, then the **Consume** method terminates, which places the consumer thread in the *Stopped* state.

Note: We use method **Sleep** in this example to emphasize the fact that, in multithreaded applications, it is unclear when each thread will perform its task and for how long it will perform that task when it has the processor. Normally, these thread-scheduling issues are the job of the computer's operating system. In this program, our thread's tasks are quite simple—for the producer, loop four times and perform an assignment statement; for the consumer, loop four times and add a value to variable **sum**. Without the **Sleep** method call, and if the producer executes first, the producer would complete its task before the consumer ever gets a chance to execute. If the consumer executes first, it would consume -1 four times, then terminate before the producer can produce the first real value.

Class **SharedCell**'s **Main** method (lines 112–142) instantiates a shared **HoldIntegerUnsynchronized** object (lines 115–116) and a **Random** object (line 119) for generating random sleep times and uses them as arguments to the constructors for the objects of classes **Producer** (lines 122–123) and **Consumer** (lines 125–126). The **HoldIntegerUnsynchronized** object contains the data that will be shared between the producer and consumer threads. Lines 130–132 create and name **producerThread**. The **ThreadStart** delegate for **producerThread** specifies that the thread will execute method **Produce** of object **producer**. Lines 134–136 create and name the **consumerThread**. The **ThreadStart** delegate for the **consumerThread** specifies that the thread will execute method **Consume** of object **consumer**. Finally, lines 139–140 place the two threads in the *Started* state by invoking each thread's **Start** method, then the **Main** thread terminates.

Ideally, we would like every value produced by the **Producer** object to be consumed exactly once by the **Consumer** object. However, when we study the first output of Fig. 14.4, we see that the consumer retrieved a value (-1) before the producer ever placed a value in the shared buffer and that the value 1 was consumed three times. The consumer finished executing before the producer had an opportunity to produce the values 2, 3 and 4. Therefore, those three values were lost. In the second output, we see that the value 1 was lost, because the values 1 and 2 were produced before the consumer thread could read the value 1. Also, the value 4 was consumed twice. The last sample output demonstrates that it is possible, with some luck, to get a proper output in which each value the producer produces is consumed once and only once by the consumer. This example clearly demonstrates that access to shared data by concurrent threads must be controlled carefully; otherwise, a program may produce incorrect results.

To solve the problems of lost data and data consumer more than once in the previous example, we will (in Fig. 14.5) synchronize access of the concurrent producer and consumer threads to the code that manipulates the shared data by using **Monitor** class methods **Enter**, **Wait**, **Pulse** and **Exit**. When a thread uses synchronization to access a shared object, the object is *locked*, so no other thread can acquire the lock for that shared object at the same time.

14.6 Producer/Consumer Relationship with Thread Synchronization

Figure 14.5 demonstrates a producer and a consumer accessing a shared cell of memory with synchronization, so that the consumer consumes only after the producer produces a value and the producer produces a new value only after the consumer consumes the previous value produced. Classes **Producer** (lines 90–123), **Consumer** (lines 126–162) and **SharedCell** (lines 165–200) are identical to Fig. 14.4, except that they use the new class **HoldIntegerSynchronized** in this example. [Note: In this example, we demonstrate synchronization with class **Monitor**'s **Enter** and **Exit** methods. In the next example, we demonstrate the same concepts via a **lock** block.]

```
1   // Fig. 14.5: Synchronized.cs
2   // Showing multiple threads modifying a shared object with
3   // synchronization.
```

Fig. 14.5 Producer and consumer threads accessing a shared object with synchronization. (Part 1 of 8.)

```
4
5   using System;
6   using System.Threading;
7
8   // this class synchronizes access to an integer
9   public class HoldIntegerSynchronized
10  {
11     // buffer shared by producer and consumer threads
12     private int buffer = -1;
13
14     // occupiedBufferCount maintains count of occupied buffers
15     private int occupiedBufferCount = 0;
16
17     // property Buffer
18     public int Buffer
19     {
20        get
21        {
22           // obtain lock on this object
23           Monitor.Enter( this );
24
25           // if there is no data to read, place invoking
26           // thread in WaitSleepJoin state
27           if ( occupiedBufferCount == 0 )
28           {
29              Console.WriteLine(
30                 Thread.CurrentThread.Name + " tries to read." );
31
32              DisplayState( "Buffer empty. " +
33                 Thread.CurrentThread.Name + " waits." );
34
35              Monitor.Wait( this );
36           }
37
38           // indicate that producer can store another value
39           // because a consumer just retrieved buffer value
40           --occupiedBufferCount;
41
42           DisplayState(
43              Thread.CurrentThread.Name + " reads " + buffer );
44
45           // tell waiting thread (if there is one) to
46           // become ready to execute (Started state)
47           Monitor.Pulse( this );
48
49           // Get copy of buffer before releasing lock.
50           // It is possible that the producer could be
51           // assigned the processor immediately after the
52           // monitor is released and before the return
53           // statement executes. In this case, the producer
54           // would assign a new value to buffer before the
55           // return statement returns the value to the
```

Fig. 14.5   Producer and consumer threads accessing a shared object with synchronization. (Part 2 of 8.)

```
56                   // consumer. Thus, the consumer would receive the
57                   // new value. Making a copy of buffer and
58                   // returning the copy ensures that the
59                   // consumer receives the proper value.
60                   int bufferCopy = buffer;
61
62                   // release lock on this object
63                   Monitor.Exit( this );
64
65                   return bufferCopy;
66
67             } // end get
68
69          set
70          {
71                   // acquire lock for this object
72                   Monitor.Enter( this );
73
74                   // if there are no empty locations, place invoking
75                   // thread in WaitSleepJoin state
76                   if ( occupiedBufferCount == 1 )
77                   {
78                       Console.WriteLine(
79                           Thread.CurrentThread.Name + " tries to write." );
80
81                       DisplayState( "Buffer full. " +
82                           Thread.CurrentThread.Name + " waits." );
83
84                       Monitor.Wait( this );
85                   }
86
87                   // set new buffer value
88                   buffer = value;
89
90                   // indicate producer cannot store another value
91                   // until consumer retrieves current buffer value
92                   ++occupiedBufferCount;
93
94                   DisplayState(
95                       Thread.CurrentThread.Name + " writes " + buffer );
96
97                   // tell waiting thread (if there is one) to
98                   // become ready to execute (Started state)
99                   Monitor.Pulse( this );
100
101                  // release lock on this object
102                  Monitor.Exit( this );
103
104           } // end set
105
106     }
107
```

Fig. 14.5   Producer and consumer threads accessing a shared object with
synchronization. (Part 3 of 8.)

```
108      // display current operation and buffer state
109      public void DisplayState( string operation )
110      {
111          Console.WriteLine( "{0,-35}{1,-9}{2}\n",
112              operation, buffer, occupiedBufferCount );
113      }
114
115   } // end class HoldIntegerSynchronized
116
117   // class Producer's Produce method controls a thread that
118   // stores values from 1 to 4 in sharedLocation
119   class Producer
120   {
121      private HoldIntegerSynchronized sharedLocation;
122      private Random randomSleepTime;
123
124      // constructor
125      public Producer(
126          HoldIntegerSynchronized shared, Random random )
127      {
128          sharedLocation = shared;
129          randomSleepTime = random;
130      }
131
132      // store values 1-4 in object sharedLocation
133      public void Produce()
134      {
135          // sleep for random interval up to 3000 milliseconds
136          // then set sharedLocation's Buffer property
137          for ( int count = 1; count <= 4; count++ )
138          {
139              Thread.Sleep( randomSleepTime.Next( 1, 3000 ) );
140              sharedLocation.Buffer = count;
141          }
142
143          Console.WriteLine( Thread.CurrentThread.Name +
144              " done producing.\nTerminating " +
145              Thread.CurrentThread.Name + ".\n" );
146
147      } // end method Produce
148
149   } // end class Producer
150
151   // class Consumer's Consume method controls a thread that
152   // loops four times and reads a value from sharedLocation
153   class Consumer
154   {
155      private HoldIntegerSynchronized sharedLocation;
156      private Random randomSleepTime;
157
```

Fig. 14.5 Producer and consumer threads accessing a shared object with synchronization. (Part 4 of 8.)

```
158        // constructor
159        public Consumer(
160           HoldIntegerSynchronized shared, Random random )
161        {
162           sharedLocation = shared;
163           randomSleepTime = random;
164        }
165
166        // read sharedLocation's value four times
167        public void Consume()
168        {
169           int sum = 0;
170
171           // get current thread
172           Thread current = Thread.CurrentThread;
173
174           // sleep for random interval up to 3000 milliseconds
175           // then add sharedLocation's Buffer property value
176           // to sum
177           for ( int count = 1; count <= 4; count++ )
178           {
179              Thread.Sleep( randomSleepTime.Next( 1, 3000 ) );
180              sum += sharedLocation.Buffer;
181           }
182
183           Console.WriteLine( Thread.CurrentThread.Name +
184              " read values totaling: " + sum +
185              ".\nTerminating " + Thread.CurrentThread.Name + ".\n" );
186
187        } // end method Consume
188
189     } // end class Consumer
190
191     // this class creates producer and consumer threads
192     class SharedCell
193     {
194        // create producer and consumer threads and start them
195        static void Main( string[] args )
196        {
197           // create shared object used by threads
198           HoldIntegerSynchronized holdInteger =
199              new HoldIntegerSynchronized();
200
201           // Random object used by each thread
202           Random random = new Random();
203
204           // create Producer and Consumer objects
205           Producer producer =
206              new Producer( holdInteger, random );
207
208           Consumer consumer =
209              new Consumer( holdInteger, random );
```

Fig. 14.5 Producer and consumer threads accessing a shared object with synchronization. (Part 5 of 8.)

```
210
211          // output column heads and initial buffer state
212          Console.WriteLine( "{0,-35}{1,-9}{2}\n",
213             "Operation", "Buffer", "Occupied Count" );
214          holdInteger.DisplayState( "Initial state" );
215
216          // create threads for producer and consumer and set
217          // delegates for each thread
218          Thread producerThread =
219             new Thread( new ThreadStart( producer.Produce ) );
220          producerThread.Name = "Producer";
221
222          Thread consumerThread =
223             new Thread( new ThreadStart( consumer.Consume ) );
224          consumerThread.Name = "Consumer";
225
226          // start each thread
227          producerThread.Start();
228          consumerThread.Start();
229
230       } // end method Main
231
232  } // end class SharedCell
```

Operation	Buffer	Occupied Count
Initial state	-1	0
Producer writes 1	1	1
Consumer reads 1	1	0
Consumer tries to read. Buffer empty. Consumer waits.	1	0
Producer writes 2	2	1
Consumer reads 2	2	0
Producer writes 3	3	1
Producer tries to write. Buffer full. Producer waits.	3	1
Consumer reads 3	3	0
Producer writes 4	4	1
Producer done producing. Terminating Producer.		

continued on next page

Fig. 14.5   Producer and consumer threads accessing a shared object with synchronization. (Part 6 of 8.)

continued from previous page

Operation	Buffer	Occupied Count
Consumer reads 4	4	0
Consumer read values totaling: 10. Terminating Consumer.		

Operation	Buffer	Occupied Count
Initial state	-1	0
Consumer tries to read. Buffer empty. Consumer waits.	-1	0
Producer writes 1	1	1
Consumer reads 1	1	0
Producer writes 2	2	1
Consumer reads 2	2	0
Producer writes 3	3	1
Producer tries to write. Buffer full. Producer waits.	3	1
Consumer reads 3	3	0
Producer writes 4	4	1
Producer done producing. Terminating Producer.		
Consumer reads 4	4	0
Consumer read values totaling: 10. Terminating Consumer.		

Operation	Buffer	Occupied Count
Initial state	-1	0
Producer writes 1	1	1
Consumer reads 1	1	0
Producer writes 2	2	1

continued on next page

Fig. 14.5 Producer and consumer threads accessing a shared object with synchronization. (Part 7 of 8.)

```
                                                        continued from previous page

Consumer reads 2                    2        0

Producer writes 3                   3        1

Consumer reads 3                    3        0

Producer writes 4                   4        1

Producer done producing.
Terminating Producer.

Consumer reads 4                    4        0

Consumer read values totaling: 10.
Terminating Consumer.
```

Fig. 14.5 Producer and consumer threads accessing a shared object with synchronization. (Part 8 of 8.)

Class **HoldIntegerSynchronized** (lines 9–115) contains two instance variables—**buffer** (line 12) and **occupiedBufferCount** (line 15). Also, property **Buffer**'s **get** (lines 20–67) and **set** (lines 69–106) accessors now use methods of class **Monitor** to synchronize access to property **Buffer**. Thus, each object of class **Hold-IntegerSynchronized** has a *SyncBlock* to maintain synchronization. Instance variable **occupiedBufferCount** is known as a *condition variable*—property **Buffer**'s accessors use this **int** in conditions to determine whether it is the producer's turn to perform a task or the consumer's turn to perform a task. If **occupiedBufferCount** is **0**, property **Buffer**'s **set** accessor can place a value into variable **buffer**, because the variable currently does not contain information. However, this means that property **Buffer**'s **get** accessor currently cannot read the value of **buffer**. If **occupied-BufferCount** is **1**, the **Buffer** property's **get** accessor can read a value from variable **buffer**, because the variable currently does contain information. In this case, property **Buffer**'s **set** accessor currently cannot place a value into **buffer**.

As in Fig. 14.4, the producer thread performs the tasks specified in the **producer** object's **Produce** method. When line 140 sets the value of **HoldIntegerSynchronized** property **Buffer**, the producer thread invokes the **set** accessor at lines 69–104. Line 72 invokes **Monitor** method **Enter** to acquire the lock on the **HoldIntegerSynchronized** object. The **if** structure at lines 76–85 determines whether **occupiedBufferCount** is **1**. If this condition is **true**, lines 78–79 output a message indicating that the producer thread tries to write a value, and lines 81–82 invoke method **DisplayState** (lines 109–113) to output another message indicating that the buffer is full and that the producer thread waits. Line 84 invokes **Monitor** method **Wait** to place the calling thread (i.e., the producer) in the *WaitSleepJoin* state for the **HoldIntegerSynchronized** object and releases the lock on the object. The *WaitSleepJoin* state for an object is maintained by that object's *SyncBlock*. Now another thread can invoke an accessor method of the **HoldIntegerSynchronized** object's **Buffer** property.

The producer thread remains in the *WaitSleepJoin* state until the thread is notified that it may proceed—at which point the thread returns to the *Started* state and waits for the system to assign a processor to the thread. When the thread returns to the *Running* state, the thread implicitly reacquires the lock on the **HoldIntegerSynchronized** object and the **set** accessor continues executing with the next statement after **Wait**. Line 88 assigns **value** to **buffer**. Line 92 increments the **occupiedBufferCount** to indicate that the shared buffer now contains a value (i.e., a consumer can read the value, and a producer cannot yet put another value there). Lines 94–95 invoke method **DisplayState** to output a line to the console window indicating that the producer is writing a new value into the **buffer**. Line 99 invokes **Monitor** method **Pulse** with the **HoldInteger-Synchronized** object as an argument. If there are any waiting threads in that object's *SyncBlock*, the first waiting thread enters the *Started* state, indicating that the thread can now attempt its task again (as soon as the thread is assigned a processor). The **Pulse** method returns immediately. Line 102 invokes **Monitor** method **Exit** to release the lock on the **HoldIntegerSynchronized** object, and the **set** accessor returns to its caller.

Common Programming Error 14.4

Forgetting to release the lock on an object when that lock is no longer needed is a logic error. This will prevent the threads in your program that require the lock from acquiring the lock to proceed with their tasks. These threads will be forced to wait (unnecessarily, because the lock is no longer needed). Such waiting can lead to deadlock and indefinite postponement.

The **get** and **set** accessors are implemented similarly. As in Fig. 14.4, the consumer thread performs the tasks specified in the **consumer** object's **Consume** method. The consumer thread gets the value of the **HoldIntegerSynchronized** object's **Buffer** property (line 180) by invoking the **get** accessor at lines 20–67. Line 23 invokes **Monitor** method **Enter** to acquire the lock on the **HoldIntegerSynchronized** object.

The **if** structure at lines 27–36 determines whether **occupiedBufferCount** is **0**. If this condition is **true**, lines 29–30 output a message indicating that the consumer thread tries to read a value, and lines 32–33 invoke method **DisplayState** to output another message indicating that the buffer is empty and that the consumer thread waits. Line 35 invokes **Monitor** method **Wait** to place the calling thread (i.e., the consumer) in the *WaitSleepJoin* state for the **HoldIntegerSynchronized** object and releases the lock on the object. Now another thread can invoke an accessor method of the **HoldInteger-gerSynchronized** object's **Buffer** property.

The consumer thread object remains in the *WaitSleepJoin* state until the thread is notified that it may proceed—at which point the thread returns to the *Started* state and waits for the system to assign a processor to the thread. When the thread reenters the *Running* state, the thread implicitly reacquires the lock on the **HoldIntegerSynchronized** object, and the **get** accessor continues executing with the next statement after **Wait**. Line 40 decrements **occupiedBufferCount** to indicate that the shared buffer is now empty (i.e., a consumer cannot read the value, but a producer can place another value into the shared buffer), lines 42–43 output a line to the console window indicating the value the consumer is reading and line 47 invokes **Monitor** method **Pulse** with the **Hold-IntegerSynchronized** object as an argument. If there are any waiting threads in that object's *SyncBlock*, the first waiting thread enters the *Started* state, indicating that the thread can now attempt its task again (as soon as the thread is assigned a processor). The **Pulse** method returns immediately. Line 60 gets a copy of **buffer** before releasing lock.

It is possible that the producer could be assigned the processor immediately after the lock is released (line 63) and before the **return** statement executes (line 65). In this case, the producer would assign a new value to **buffer** before the **return** statement returns the value to the consumer. Thus, the consumer would receive the new value. Making a copy of **buffer** and returning the copy ensures that the consumer receives the proper value. Line 63 invokes **Monitor** method **Exit** to release the lock on the **HoldInteger-Synchronized** object and the **get** accessor returns **bufferCopy** to its caller.

Study the outputs in Fig. 14.5. Observe that every integer produced is consumed exactly once—no values are lost, and no values are consumed more than once. This occurs because the producer and consumer cannot perform tasks unless it is "their turn." The producer must go first; the consumer must wait if the producer has not produced, since the consumer last consumed; and the producer must wait if the consumer has not yet consumed the value the producer most recently produced. Execute this program several times to confirm that every integer produced is consumed once.

In the first and second sample outputs, notice the lines indicating when the producer and consumer must wait to perform their respective tasks. In the third sample output, notice that the producer and consumer were able to perform their tasks without waiting.

14.7 Producer/Consumer Relationship: Circular Buffer

Figure 14.5 uses thread synchronization to guarantee that two threads manipulate data in a shared buffer correctly. However, the application may not perform optimally. If the two threads operate at different speeds, one of the threads will spend more (or most) of its time waiting. For example, in Fig. 14.5 we shared a single integer between the two threads. If the producer thread produces values faster than the consumer can consume those values, then the producer thread waits for the consumer, because there are no other locations in memory to place the next value. Similarly, if the consumer consumes faster than the producer can produce values, the consumer waits until the producer places the next value into the shared location in memory. Even when we have threads that operate at the same relative speeds, over a period of time, those threads may become "out of sync," causing one of the threads to wait for the other. We cannot make assumptions about the relative speeds of asynchronous concurrent threads. There are too many interactions that occur with the operating system, the network, the user and other components, which can cause the threads to operate at different speeds. When this happens, threads wait. When threads wait, programs become less productive, user-interactive programs become less responsive and network applications suffer longer delays because the processor is not used efficiently.

To minimize the waiting for threads that share resources and operate at the same relative speeds, we can implement a *circular buffer* that provides extra buffers into which the producer can place values and from which the consumer can retrieve those values. Let us assume the buffer is implemented as an array. The producer and consumer work from the beginning of the array. When either thread reaches the end of the array, it simply returns to the first element of the array to perform its next task. If the producer temporarily produces values faster than the consumer can consume them, the producer can write additional values into the extra buffers (if cells are available). This enables the producer to perform its task even though the consumer is not ready to receive the current value being produced. Similarly, if the consumer consumes faster than the producer produces new values, the consumer can read additional values from the buffer (if there are any). This enables the consumer to perform its task even though the producer is not ready to produce additional values.

Note that the circular buffer would be inappropriate if the producer and consumer operate at different speeds. If the consumer always executes faster than the producer, then a buffer at one location is enough. Additional locations would waste memory. If the producer always executes faster, a buffer with an infinite number of locations would be required to absorb the extra production.

The key to using a circular buffer is to define it with enough extra cells to handle the anticipated "extra" production. If, over a period of time, we determine that the producer often produces as many as three more values than the consumer can consume, we can define a buffer of at least three cells to handle the extra production. We do not want the buffer to be too small, because that would cause threads to wait more. On the other hand, we do not want the buffer to be too large, because that would waste memory.

Performance Tip 14.4

Even when using a circular buffer, it is possible that a producer thread could fill the buffer, which would force the producer thread to wait until a consumer consumes a value to free an element in the buffer. Similarly, if the buffer is empty at any given time, the consumer thread must wait until the producer produces another value. The key to using a circular buffer is optimizing the buffer size to minimize the amount of thread-wait time.

Figure 14.6 demonstrates a producer and a consumer accessing a circular buffer (in this case, a shared array of two cells) with synchronization. In this version of the producer/consumer relationship, the consumer consumes a value only when the array is not empty and the producer produces a value only when the array is not full. This program is implemented as a Windows application that sends its output to a **TextBox**. Classes **Producer** (lines 174–210) and **Consumer** (lines 213–252) perform the same tasks as in Fig. 14.4 and Fig. 14.5, except that they output messages to the **TextBox** in the application window. The statements that created and started the thread objects in the **Main** methods of class **SharedCell** in Fig. 14.4 and Fig. 14.5 now appear in class **CircularBuffer** (lines 255–313), where the **Load** event handler (lines 278–311) performs the statements.

The most significant changes from Fig. 14.5 occur in class **HoldInteger-Synchronized**, which now contains six instance variables. Array **buffers** is a three-element integer array that represents the circular buffer. Variable **occupiedBuffer-Count** is the condition variable that can be used to determine whether a producer can write into the circular buffer (i.e., **occupiedBufferCount** is less than the number of elements in array **buffers**) and whether a consumer can read from the circular buffer (i.e., **occupiedBufferCount** is greater than **0**). Variable **readLocation** indicates the position from which the next value can be read by a consumer. Variable **writeLocation** indicates the next location in which a value can be placed by a producer. The program displays output in **outputTextBox** (a **TextBox** control).

```
1   // Fig. 14.6: CircularBuffer.cs
2   // Implementing the producer/consumer relationship with a
3   // circular buffer.
```

Fig. 14.6 Producer and consumer threads accessing a circular buffer. (Part 1 of 9.)

```
4
5   using System;
6   using System.Drawing;
7   using System.Collections;
8   using System.ComponentModel;
9   using System.Windows.Forms;
10  using System.Data;
11  using System.Threading;
12
13  // implement the shared integer with synchronization
14  public class HoldIntegerSynchronized
15  {
16     // each array element is a buffer
17     private int[] buffers = { -1, -1, -1 };
18
19     // occupiedBufferCount maintains count of occupied buffers
20     private int occupiedBufferCount = 0;
21
22     // variable that maintain read and write buffer locations
23     private int readLocation = 0, writeLocation = 0;
24
25     // GUI component to display output
26     private TextBox outputTextBox;
27
28     // constructor
29     public HoldIntegerSynchronized( TextBox output )
30     {
31        outputTextBox = output;
32     }
33
34     // property Buffer
35     public int Buffer
36     {
37        get
38        {
39           // lock this object while getting value
40           // from buffers array
41           lock ( this )
42           {
43              // if there is no data to read, place invoking
44              // thread in WaitSleepJoin state
45              if ( occupiedBufferCount == 0 )
46              {
47                 outputTextBox.Text += "\r\nAll buffers empty. " +
48                    Thread.CurrentThread.Name + " waits.";
49                 outputTextBox.ScrollToCaret();
50
51                 Monitor.Wait( this );
52              }
53
54              // obtain value at current readLocation, then
55              // add string indicating consumed value to output
56              int readValue = buffers[ readLocation ];
```

Fig. 14.6 Producer and consumer threads accessing a circular buffer. (Part 2 of 9.)

```
57
58              outputTextBox.Text += "\r\n" +
59                  Thread.CurrentThread.Name + " reads " +
60                  buffers[ readLocation ] + " ";
61
62              // just consumed a value, so decrement number of
63              // occupied buffers
64              --occupiedBufferCount;
65
66              // update readLocation for future read operation,
67              // then add current state to output
68              readLocation =
69                  ( readLocation + 1 ) % buffers.Length;
70              outputTextBox.Text += CreateStateOutput();
71              outputTextBox.ScrollToCaret();
72
73              // return waiting thread (if there is one)
74              // to Started state
75              Monitor.Pulse( this );
76
77              return readValue;
78
79           } // end lock
80
81        } // end accessor get
82
83        set
84        {
85           // lock this object while setting value
86           // in buffers array
87           lock ( this )
88           {
89              // if there are no empty locations, place invoking
90              // thread in WaitSleepJoin state
91              if ( occupiedBufferCount == buffers.Length )
92              {
93                 outputTextBox.Text += "\r\nAll buffers full. " +
94                     Thread.CurrentThread.Name + " waits.";
95                 outputTextBox.ScrollToCaret();
96
97                 Monitor.Wait( this );
98              }
99
100             // place value in writeLocation of buffers, then
101             // add string indicating produced value to output
102             buffers[ writeLocation ] = value;
103
104             outputTextBox.Text += "\r\n" +
105                 Thread.CurrentThread.Name + " writes " +
106                 buffers[ writeLocation ] + " ";
107
```

Fig. 14.6 Producer and consumer threads accessing a circular buffer. (Part 3 of 9.)

```
108                      // just produced a value, so increment number of
109                      // occupied buffers
110                      ++occupiedBufferCount;
111
112                      // update writeLocation for future write operation,
113                      // then add current state to output
114                      writeLocation =
115                         ( writeLocation + 1 ) % buffers.Length;
116                      outputTextBox.Text += CreateStateOutput();
117                      outputTextBox.ScrollToCaret();
118
119                      // return waiting thread (if there is one)
120                      // to Started state
121                      Monitor.Pulse( this );
122
123                   } // end lock
124
125             } // end accessor set
126
127       } // end property Buffer
128
129       // create state output
130       public string CreateStateOutput()
131       {
132          // display first line of state information
133          string output = "(buffers occupied: " +
134             occupiedBufferCount + ")\r\nbuffers: ";
135
136          for ( int i = 0; i < buffers.Length; i++ )
137             output += " " + buffers[ i ] + "   ";
138
139          output += "\r\n";
140
141          // display second line of state information
142          output += "              ";
143
144          for ( int i = 0; i < buffers.Length; i++ )
145             output += "---- ";
146
147          output += "\r\n";
148
149          // display third line of state information
150          output += "          ";
151
152          // display readLocation (R) and writeLocation (W)
153          // indicators below appropriate buffer locations
154          for ( int i = 0; i < buffers.Length; i++ )
155
156             if ( i == writeLocation &&
157                  writeLocation == readLocation )
158                output += " WR  ";
159             else if ( i == writeLocation )
160                output += " W   ";
```

Fig. 14.6   Producer and consumer threads accessing a circular buffer. (Part 4 of 9.)

```
161            else if  ( i == readLocation )
162               output += "   R   ";
163            else
164               output += "        ";
165
166       output += "\r\n";
167
168       return output;
169    }
170
171 } // end class HoldIntegerSynchronized
172
173 // produce the integers from 11 to 20 and place them in buffer
174 public class Producer
175 {
176    private HoldIntegerSynchronized sharedLocation;
177    private TextBox outputTextBox;
178    private Random randomSleepTime;
179
180    // constructor
181    public Producer( HoldIntegerSynchronized shared,
182       Random random, TextBox output )
183    {
184       sharedLocation = shared;
185       outputTextBox = output;
186       randomSleepTime = random;
187    }
188
189    // produce values from 11-20 and place them in
190    // sharedLocation's buffer
191    public void Produce()
192    {
193       // sleep for random interval up to 3000 milliseconds
194       // then set sharedLocation's Buffer property
195       for ( int count = 11; count <= 20; count++ )
196       {
197          Thread.Sleep( randomSleepTime.Next( 1, 3000 ) );
198          sharedLocation.Buffer = count;
199       }
200
201       string name = Thread.CurrentThread.Name;
202
203       outputTextBox.Text += "\r\n" + name +
204          " done producing.\r\n" + name + " terminated.\r\n";
205
206       outputTextBox.ScrollToCaret();
207
208    } // end method Produce
209
210 } // end class Producer
211
```

Fig. 14.6   Producer and consumer threads accessing a circular buffer. (Part 5 of 9.)

```
212   // consume the integers 1 to 10 from circular buffer
213   public class Consumer
214   {
215      private HoldIntegerSynchronized sharedLocation;
216      private TextBox outputTextBox;
217      private Random randomSleepTime;
218
219      // constructor
220      public Consumer( HoldIntegerSynchronized shared,
221         Random random, TextBox output )
222      {
223         sharedLocation = shared;
224         outputTextBox = output;
225         randomSleepTime = random;
226      }
227
228      // consume 10 integers from buffer
229      public void Consume()
230      {
231         int sum = 0;
232
233         // loop 10 times and sleep for random interval up to
234         // 3000 milliseconds then add sharedLocation's
235         // Buffer property value to sum
236         for ( int count = 1; count <= 10; count++ )
237         {
238            Thread.Sleep( randomSleepTime.Next( 1, 3000 ) );
239            sum += sharedLocation.Buffer;
240         }
241
242         string name = Thread.CurrentThread.Name;
243
244         outputTextBox.Text += "\r\nTotal " + name +
245            " consumed: " + sum + ".\r\n" + name +
246            " terminated.\r\n";
247
248         outputTextBox.ScrollToCaret();
249
250      } // end method Consume
251
252   } // end class Consumer
253
254   // set up the producer and consumer and start them
255   public class CircularBuffer : System.Windows.Forms.Form
256   {
257      private System.Windows.Forms.TextBox outputTextBox;
258
259      // required designer variable
260      private System.ComponentModel.Container components = null;
261
```

Fig. 14.6   Producer and consumer threads accessing a circular buffer. (Part 6 of 9.)

```
262        // no-argument constructor
263        public CircularBuffer()
264        {
265            InitializeComponent();
266        }
267
268        // Visual Studio .NET GUI code appears here in source file
269
270        // main entry point for the application
271        [STAThread]
272        static void Main()
273        {
274            Application.Run( new CircularBuffer() );
275        }
276
277        // Load event handler creates and starts threads
278        private void CircularBuffer_Load(
279            object sender, System.EventArgs e )
280        {
281            // create shared object
282            HoldIntegerSynchronized sharedLocation =
283                new HoldIntegerSynchronized( outputTextBox );
284
285            // display sharedLocation state before producer
286            // and consumer threads begin execution
287            outputTextBox.Text = sharedLocation.CreateStateOutput();
288
289            // Random object used by each thread
290            Random random = new Random();
291
292            // create Producer and Consumer objects
293            Producer producer =
294                new Producer( sharedLocation, random, outputTextBox );
295            Consumer consumer =
296                new Consumer( sharedLocation, random, outputTextBox );
297
298            // create and name threads
299            Thread producerThread =
300                new Thread( new ThreadStart( producer.Produce ) );
301            producerThread.Name = "Producer";
302
303            Thread consumerThread =
304                new Thread( new ThreadStart( consumer.Consume ) );
305            consumerThread.Name = "Consumer";
306
307            // start threads
308            producerThread.Start();
309            consumerThread.Start();
310
311        } // end CircularBuffer_Load method
312
313 } // end class CircularBuffer
```

Fig. 14.6   Producer and consumer threads accessing a circular buffer. (Part 7 of 9.)

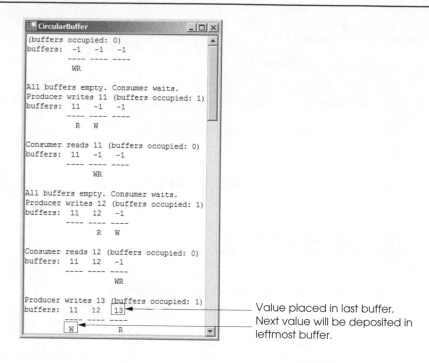

Value placed in last buffer.
Next value will be deposited in
leftmost buffer.

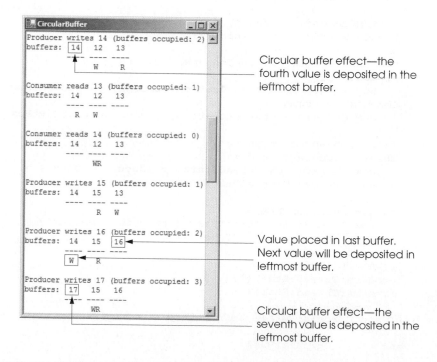

Circular buffer effect—the
fourth value is deposited in the
leftmost buffer.

Value placed in last buffer.
Next value will be deposited in
leftmost buffer.

Circular buffer effect—the
seventh value is deposited in the
leftmost buffer.

Fig. 14.6 Producer and consumer threads accessing a circular buffer. (Part 8 of 9.)

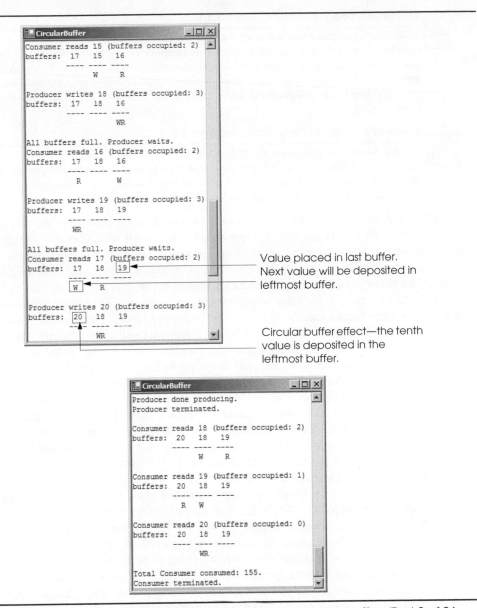

Fig. 14.6 Producer and consumer threads accessing a circular buffer. (Part 9 of 9.)

The **set** accessor (lines 83–125) of property **Buffer** performs the same tasks that it did in Fig. 14.5, with a few modifications. Rather than using **Monitor** methods **Enter** and **Exit** to acquire and release the lock on the **HoldIntegerSynchronized** object, we use a block of code preceded by keyword **lock** to lock the **HoldIntegerSynchronized** object. As program control enters the **lock** block, the currently executing thread acquires the lock (assuming the lock is currently available) on the **HoldInteger-Synchronized** object (i.e., **this**). When the **lock** block terminates, the thread releases the lock automatically.

Common Programming Error 14.5

*When using class **Monitor**'s **Enter** and **Exit** methods to manage an object's lock, **Exit** must be called explicitly to release the lock. If an exception occurs in a method before **Exit** can be called and that exception is not caught, the method could terminate without calling **Exit**. If so, the lock is not released. To avoid this error, place code that could throw exceptions in a **try** block, and place the call to **Exit** in the corresponding **finally** block to ensure that the lock is released.*

Software Engineering Observation 14.2

*Using a **lock** block to manage the lock on a synchronized object eliminates the possibility of forgetting to relinquish the lock with a call to **Monitor** method **Exit**. C# implicitly calls **Monitor** method **Exit** when a **lock** block terminates for any reason. Thus, even if an exception occurs in the block, the lock will be released.*

The **if** structure at lines 91–98 in the **set** accessor determines whether the producer must wait (i.e., all buffers are full). If the producer thread must wait, lines 93–94 append text to the **outputTextBox** indicating that the producer is waiting to perform its task and line 97 invokes **Monitor** method **Wait** to place the producer thread in the *WaitSleepJoin* state of the **HoldIntegerSynchronized** object. When execution continues at line 102 after the **if** structure, the value written by the producer is placed in the circular buffer at location **writeLocation**. Next, lines 104–106 append a message containing the value produced to the **TextBox**. Line 110 increments **occupiedBufferCount**, because there is now at least one value in the buffer that the consumer can read. Then, lines 114–115 update **writeLocation** for the next call to the **set** accessor of property **Buffer**. The output continues at line 116 by invoking method **CreateStateOutput** (lines 130–169), which outputs the number of occupied buffers, the contents of the buffers and the current **writeLocation** and **readLocation**. Finally, line 121 invokes **Monitor** method **Pulse** to indicate that a thread waiting on the **HoldIntegerSynchronized** object (if there is a waiting thread) should transition to the *Started* state. Note that reaching the closing right brace of the **lock** block at line 123 causes the thread to release the lock on the **HoldIntegerSynchronized** object.

The **get** accessor (lines 37–81) of property **Buffer** also performs the same tasks in this example that it did in Fig. 14.5, with a few minor modifications. The **if** structure at lines 45–52 in the **get** accessor determines whether the consumer must wait (i.e., all buffers are empty). If the consumer thread must wait, lines 47–48 append text to the **outputTextBox** indicating that the consumer is waiting to perform its task, and line 51 invokes **Monitor** method **Wait** to place the consumer thread in the *WaitSleepJoin* state of the **HoldIntegerSynchronized** object. Once again, we use a **lock** block to acquire and release the lock on the **HoldIntegerSynchronized** object, rather than using **Monitor** methods **Enter** and **Exit**. When execution continues at line 56 after the **if** structure, **readValue** is assigned the value at location **readLocation** in the circular buffer. Lines 58–60 appends the value consumed to the **TextBox**. Line 64 decrements the **occupiedBufferCount**, because there is at least one open position in the buffer in which the producer thread can place a value. Then, lines 68–69 update **readLocation** for the next call to the **get** accessor of **Buffer**. Line 70 invokes method **CreateStateOutput** to output the number of occupied buffers, the contents of the buffers and the current **writeLocation** and **readLocation**. Finally, line 80 invokes method **Pulse** to transition the next thread waiting for the **HoldIntegerSynchro-**

nized object into the *Started* state, and line 82 returns the consumed value to the calling method.

In Fig. 14.6, the outputs include the current **occupiedBufferCount**, the contents of the buffers and the current **writeLocation** and **readLocation**. In the output, the letters **W** and **R** represent the current **writeLocation** and **readLocation**, respectively. Notice that, after the third value is placed in the third element of the buffer, the fourth value is inserted at the beginning of the array. This provides the circular buffer effect.

SUMMARY

- Computers perform operations concurrently, such as compiling programs, printing files and receiving electronic mail messages over a network.

- Programming languages generally provide only a simple set of control structures that enable programmers to perform one action at a time and proceed to the next action after the previous one finishes.

- Historically, the concurrency that computers perform generally has been implemented as operating system "primitives" available only to highly experienced "systems programmers."

- The .NET Framework Class Library makes concurrency primitives available to the applications programmer. The programmer specifies that applications contain threads of execution, each thread designating a portion of a program that may execute concurrently with other threads—this capability is called multithreading.

- A thread that was just created is in the *Unstarted* state. A thread is initialized using the **Thread** class's constructor which receives a **ThreadStart** delegate. This delegate specifies the method that contains the tasks a thread will perform.

- A thread remains in the *Unstarted* state until the thread's **Start** method is called; this causes the thread to enter the *Started* state (also known as the *Ready* or *Runnable* state).

- A thread in the *Started* state enters the *Running* state when the system assigns a processor to the thread. The system assigns the processor to the highest-priority *Started* thread.

- A thread enters the *Stopped* (or *Dead*) state when its **ThreadStart** delegate completes or terminates. A thread is forced into the *Stopped* state when its **Abort** method is called (by itself or by another thread).

- A *Running* thread enters the *Blocked* state when the thread issues an input/output request. A *Blocked* thread becomes *Started* when the I/O it is waiting for completes. A *Blocked* thread cannot use a processor, even if one is available.

- If a thread wants to go to sleep, it calls **Thread** method **Sleep**. A thread wakes up when the designated sleep interval expires.

- If a thread cannot continue executing (we will call this the dependent thread) unless another thread terminates, the dependent thread calls the other thread's **Join** method to "join" the two threads. When two threads are "joined," the dependent thread leaves the *WaitSleepJoin* state when the other thread finishes execution (enters the *Stopped* state).

- In thread synchronization, when a thread encounters code that it cannot yet run (e.g., a producer cannot produce at the current time), the thread can call **Monitor** method **Wait** until certain actions occur that enable the thread to continue executing.

- Any thread in the *WaitSleepJoin* state can leave that state if another thread invokes **Thread** method **Interrupt** on the thread in the *WaitSleepJoin* state.

- If a thread called **Monitor** method **Wait**, a corresponding call to the **Monitor** method **Pulse** or **PulseAll** by another thread in the program will transition the original thread from the *WaitSleepJoin* state to the *Started* state.

- If **Thread** method **Suspend** is called on a thread (by the thread itself or by another thread in the program), the thread enters the *Suspended* state. A thread leaves the *Suspended* state when a separate thread invokes **Thread** method **Resume** on the suspended thread.

- Every C# thread has a priority of **ThreadPriority.Lowest**, **ThreadPriority.BelowNormal**, **ThreadPriority.Normal**, **ThreadPriority.AboveNormal** or **ThreadPriority.Highest**.

- The job of the thread scheduler is to keep the highest-priority thread running at all times and, if there is more than one highest-priority thread, to ensure that all equally high-priority threads execute for a quantum at a time in round-robin fashion.

- A thread's priority can be adjusted with the **Priority** property, which accepts an argument from the **ThreadPriority** enumeration.

- A thread that updates shared data calls **Monitor** method **Enter** to acquire the lock on that data. It updates the data and calls **Monitor** method **Exit** upon completion of the update. While that data is locked, all other threads attempting to acquire the lock on that data must wait.

- If you place the **lock** keyword before a block of code the lock is acquired on the specified object as program control enters the block; the lock is released when the block terminates for any reason.

- If a thread decides that it cannot continue execution, it can call **Wait**. This puts the thread into the *WaitSleepJoin* state. When the thread can continue execution again, **Pulse** or **PulseAll** is called to notify the thread to continue running.

- When the **lock** keyword is used, C# implicitly calls the **Exit** method whenever we leave the scope of the block.

TERMINOLOGY

Abort method of class **Thread**
AboveNormal constant (**ThreadPriority**)
accessing shared data with synchronization
acquire the lock for an object
automatic garbage collection
BelowNormal constant (**ThreadPriority**)
Blocked state
Blocked thread
built-in multithreading
circular buffer
concurrency
concurrent producer and consumer threads
concurrent programming
condition variable
consumer
Dead state
deadlock
Enter method of class **Monitor**
Exit method of class **Monitor**
garbage collection
garbage-collector thread
Highest constant in **ThreadPriority**
Hoare, C. A. R.
I/O completion
I/O request

indefinite postponement
input/output blocking
Interrupt method of class **Thread**
Join method of class **Thread**
life cycle of a thread
lock keyword
locking objects
Lowest constant in **ThreadPriority**
memory leak
Monitor class
multilevel priority queue
multithreading
Name property of class **Thread**
Normal constant in **ThreadPriority**
Priority property of class **Thread**
priority scheduling
producer
producer/consumer relationship
Pulse method of class **Monitor**
PulseAll method of class **Monitor**
quantum
quantum expiration
Ready state
release a lock
Resume method of class **Thread**

Runnable state
Running state
scheduling
shared buffer
sleep interval expires
Sleep method of class **Thread**
sleeping thread
Start method of class **Thread**
Started state
starvation
Stopped state
Suspend method of class **Thread**
SyncBlock

synchronized block of code
System.Threading namespace
task
Thread class
thread of execution
thread-priority scheduling
thread state
ThreadAbortException
ThreadPriority enumeration
ThreadStart delegate
Unstarted state
Wait method of class **Monitor**
WaitSleepJoin state

SELF-REVIEW EXERCISES

14.1 Fill in the blanks in each of the following statements:
  a) Monitor methods _____ and _____ acquire and release the lock on an object.
  b) Among a group of equal-priority threads, each thread receives a brief burst of time called a _____, during which the thread has the processor and can perform its tasks.
  c) C# provides a _____ thread that reclaims dynamically allocated memory.
  d) Four reasons a thread that is alive is not in the Started state are _____, _____, _____ and _____.
  e) A thread enters the _____ state when the method that controls the thread's lifecycle terminates.
  f) A thread's priority must be one of the **ThreadPriority** constants _____, _____, _____, _____ and _____.
  g) To wait for a designated number of milliseconds then resume execution, a thread should call the _____ method of class **Thread**.
  h) Method _____ of class **Monitor** transitions a thread in the WaitSleepJoin state to the Started state.
  i) A _____ block automatically acquires the lock on an object as the program control enters the block and releases the lock on that object when the block terminates execution.
  j) Class **Monitor** provides methods that _____ access to shared data.

14.2 State whether each of the following is true or false. If false, explain why.
  a) A thread cannot execute if it is in the Stopped state.
  b) In C#, a higher priority thread entering (or reentering) the Started state will preempt threads of lower priority.
  c) The code that a thread executes is defined in its **Main** method.
  d) A thread in the WaitSleepJoin state always returns to the Started state when **Monitor** method **Pulse** is called.
  e) Method **Sleep** of class **Thread** does not consume processor time while a thread sleeps.
  f) A blocked thread can be placed in the Started state by **Monitor** method **Pulse**.
  g) Class **Monitor**'s **Wait**, **Pulse** and **PulseAll** methods can be used in any block of code.
  h) The programmer must place a call to **Monitor** method **Exit** in a **lock** block to relinquish the lock.
  i) When **Monitor** class method **Wait** is called within a **lock**ed block, the lock for that block is released and the thread that called **Wait** is placed in the WaitSleepJoin state.

ANSWERS TO SELF-REVIEW EXERCISES

14.1   a) **Enter**, **Exit**. b) timeslice or quantum. c) garbage collector. d) waiting, sleeping, suspended, blocked for input/output. e) *Stopped.* f) **Lowest**, **BelowNormal**, **Normal**, **AboveNormal**, **Highest**. g) **Sleep**. h) **Pulse**. i) **lock**. j) synchronize.

14.2   a) True. b) True. c) False. The code that a thread executes is defined in the method specified by the thread's **ThreadStart** delegate. d) False. A thread may be in the *WaitSleepJoin* state for several reasons. Calling Pulse moves a thread from the *WaitSleepJoin* state to the *Started* state only if the thread entered the *WaitSleepJoin* state as the result of a call to **Monitor** method **Pulse**. e) True. f) False. A thread is blocked by the operating system and returns to the *Started* state when the operating system determines that the thread can continue executing (e.g., when an I/O request completes or when a lock the thread attempted to acquire becomes available). g) False. Class **Monitor** methods can be called only if the thread performing the call currently owns the lock on the object each method receives as an argument. h) False. A **lock** block implicitly relinquishes the lock when the thread completes execution of the **lock** block. i) True.

EXERCISES

14.3   The code that manipulates the circular buffer in Fig. 14.6 will work with a buffer of two or more elements. Try changing the buffer size to see how it affects the producer and consumer threads. In particular, notice that the producer waits to produce less frequently as the buffer grows in size.

14.4   Write a program to demonstrate that, as a high-priority thread executes, it will delay the execution of all lower-priority threads.

14.5   Write a program that demonstrates timeslicing among several equal-priority threads. Show that a lower-priority thread's execution is deferred by the timeslicing of the higher-priority threads.

14.6   Write a program that demonstrates a high-priority thread using **Sleep** to give lower-priority threads a chance to run.

14.7   Two problems that can occur in languages like C# that allow threads to wait are deadlock, in which one or more threads will wait forever for an event that cannot occur, and indefinite postponement, in which one or more threads will be delayed for some unpredictably long time but may eventually complete. Give an example of how each of these problems can occur in a multithreaded C# program.

14.8   (Readers and Writers) This exercise asks you to develop a C# monitor to solve a famous problem in concurrency control. This problem was first discussed and solved by P. J. Courtois, F. Heymans and D. L. Parnas in their research paper, "Concurrent Control with Readers and Writers," *Communications of the ACM*, Vol. 14, No. 10, October 1971, pp. 667–668. The interested student might also want to read C. A. R. Hoare's seminal research paper on monitors, "Monitors: An Operating System Structuring Concept," *Communications of the ACM*, Vol. 17, No. 10, October 1974, pp. 549–557. *Corrigendum, Communications of the ACM*, Vol. 18, No. 2, February 1975, p. 95. [The readers and writers problem is discussed at length in Chapter 5 of the author's book: Deitel, H. M., *Operating Systems*, Reading, MA: Addison-Wesley, 1990.]

With multithreading, many threads can access shared data; as we have seen, access to shared data needs to be synchronized to avoid corrupting the data.

Consider an airline-reservation system in which many clients are attempting to book seats on particular flights between particular cities. All the information about flights and seats is stored in a common database in memory. The database consists of many entries, each representing a seat on a particular flight for a particular day between particular cities. In a typical airline-reservation scenario, the client will probe the database looking for the "optimal" flight to meet that client's needs. A client may probe the database many times before trying to book a particular flight. A seat that was available during this probing phase could easily be booked by someone else before the client has a chance to book it after deciding on it. In that case, when the client attempts to make the reservation, the client will discover that the data has changed and the flight is no longer available.

The client probing the database is called a *reader*. The client attempting to book the flight is called a *writer*. Any number of readers can be probing shared data at once, but each writer needs exclusive access to the shared data to prevent the data from being corrupted.

Write a multithreaded C# program that launches multiple reader threads and multiple writer threads, each attempting to access a single reservation record. A writer thread has two possible transactions, **makeReservation** and **cancelReservation**. A reader has one possible transaction, **queryReservation**.

First, implement a version of your program that allows unsynchronized access to the reservation record. Show how the integrity of the database can be corrupted. Next, implement a version of your program that uses C# monitor synchronization with **Wait** and **Pulse** to enforce a disciplined protocol for readers and writers accessing the shared reservation data. In particular, your program should allow multiple readers to access the shared data simultaneously when no writer is active— but, if a writer is active, then no reader should be allowed to access the shared data.

Be careful. This problem has many subtleties. For example, what happens when there are several active readers and a writer wants to write? If we allow a steady stream of readers to arrive and share the data, they could indefinitely postpone the writer (who might become tired of waiting and take his or her business elsewhere). To solve this problem, you might decide to favor writers over readers. But here, too, there is a trap, because a steady stream of writers could then indefinitely postpone the waiting readers, and they, too, might choose to take their business elsewhere! Implement your monitor with the following methods: **startReading**, which is called by any reader who wants to begin accessing a reservation; **stopReading**, to be called by any reader who has finished reading a reservation; **startWriting**, to be called by any writer who wants to make a reservation; and **stopWriting**, to be called by any writer who has finished making a reservation.

15

Strings, Characters and Regular Expressions

Objectives

- To be able to create and manipulate immutable character string objects of class **String**.
- To be able to create and manipulate mutable character string objects of class **StringBuilder**.
- To be able to use regular expressions in conjunction with classes **Regex** and **Match**.

The chief defect of Henry King
Was chewing little bits of string.
Hilaire Belloc

Vigorous writing is concise. A sentence should contain no unnecessary words, a paragraph no unnecessary sentences.
William Strunk, Jr.

I have made this letter longer than usual, because I lack the time to make it short.
Blaise Pascal

The difference between the almost-right word & the right word is really a large matter—it's the difference between the lightning bug and the lightning.
Mark Twain

Mum's the word.
Miguel de Cervantes, *Don Quixote de la Mancha*

15.1 Introduction

In this chapter, we introduce the Framework Class Library's string and character processing capabilities and demonstrate the use of regular expressions to search for patterns in text. The techniques presented in this chapter can be employed to develop text editors, word processors, page-layout software, computerized typesetting systems and other kinds of text-processing software. Previous chapters have already presented several string-processing capabilities. In this chapter, we expand on this information by detailing the capabilities of class *String* and type *char* from the **System** namespace, class *StringBuilder* from the *System.Text* namespace and classes *Regex* and *Match* from the *System.Text.RegularExpressions* namespace.

15.2 Fundamentals of Characters and Strings

Characters are the fundamental building blocks of C# source code. Every program is composed of characters that, when grouped together meaningfully, create a sequence that the compiler interprets as a series of instructions that describe how to accomplish a task. In addition to normal characters, a program also can contain *character constants.* A character constant is a character that is represented as an integer value, called a *character code.* For example, the integer value **122** corresponds to the character constant **'z'**. The integer value **10** corresponds to the new line character **'\n'**. Character constants are established according to the *Unicode character set,* an international character set that contains many more symbols and letters than does the ASCII character set (see Appendix F, ASCII character set). To learn more about Unicode, see Appendix G, Unicode.

A string is a series of characters treated as a single unit. These characters can be uppercase letters, lowercase letters, digits and various *special characters,* such as **+, -, *, /, $** and others. A string is an object of class **String** in the **System** namespace.[1] We write *string literals,* or *string constants* (often called *literal **strings***), as sequences of characters in double quotation marks, as follows:

```
"John Q. Doe"
"9999 Main Street"
"Waltham, Massachusetts"
"(201) 555-1212"
```

A declaration can assign a **string** literal to a **string** reference. The declaration

```
string color = "blue";
```

initializes **string** reference **color** to refer to the **string** literal object **"blue"**.

Performance Tip 15.1

*If there are multiple occurrences of the same **string** literal object in an application, a single copy of the **string** literal object will be referenced from each location in the program that uses that **string** literal. It is possible to share the object in this manner, because **string** literal objects are implicitly constant. Such sharing conserves memory.*

On occasion, a **string** will contain multiple backslash characters (this often occurs in the name of a file). It is possible to exclude escape sequences and interpret all the characters in a **string** literally, using the **@** character. Backslashes within the double quotation marks are not considered escape sequences, but rather regular backslash characters. Often this simplifies programming and makes the code easier to read. For example, consider the string "**C:\MyFolder\MySubFolder\MyFile.txt**" with the following assignment:

```
string file = "C:\\MyFolder\\MySubFolder\\MyFile.txt";
```

Using the verbatim string syntax, the assignment can be altered to

```
string file = @"C:\MyFolder\MySubFolder\MyFile.txt";
```

This approach also has the advantage of allowing strings to span multiple lines by preserving all newlines, spaces and tabs.

---

1. C# provides the **string** keyword as an alias for class **String**. In this book, we use **String** to refer to the class **String** and **string** to refer to an object of class **String**.

15.3 String Constructors

Class **String** provides eight constructors for initializing **string**s in various ways. Figure 15.1 demonstrates the use of three of the constructors.

Lines 14–16 declare **string**s **output**, **originalString**, **string1**, **string2**, **string3** and **string4**. Lines 18–19 allocate the **char** array **characterArray**, which contains nine characters. Line 22 assigns literal **string "Welcome to C# programming!"** to **string** reference **originalString**. Line 23 sets **string1** to reference the same **string** literal.

Line 24 assigns to **string2** a new **string**, using the **String** constructor that takes a character array as an argument. The new **string** contains a copy of the characters in array **characterArray**.

```
1   // Fig. 15.1: StringConstructor.cs
2   // Demonstrating String class constructors.
3
4   using System;
5   using System.Windows.Forms;
6
7   // test several String class constructors
8   class StringConstructor
9   {
10      // The main entry point for the application.
11      [STAThread]
12      static void Main( string[] args )
13      {
14         string output;
15         string originalString, string1, string2,
16            string3, string4;
17
18         char[] characterArray =
19            { 'b', 'i', 'r', 't', 'h', ' ', 'd', 'a', 'y' };
20
21         // string initialization
22         originalString = "Welcome to C# programming!";
23         string1 = originalString;
24         string2 = new string( characterArray );
25         string3 = new string( characterArray, 6, 3 );
26         string4 = new string( 'C', 5 );
27
28         output = "string1 = " + "\"" + string1 + "\"\n" +
29            "string2 = " + "\"" + string2 + "\"\n" +
30            "string3 = " + "\"" + string3 + "\"\n" +
31            "string4 = " + "\"" + string4 + "\"\n";
32
33         MessageBox.Show( output, "String Class Constructors",
34            MessageBoxButtons.OK, MessageBoxIcon.Information );
35
36      } // end method Main
37
38   } // end class StringConstructor
```

Fig. 15.1   String constructors. (Part 1 of 2.)

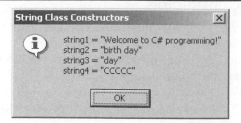

Fig. 15.1   **String** constructors. (Part 2 of 2.)

Software Engineering Observation 15.1

*In most cases, it is not necessary to make a copy of an existing **string**. All **strings** are immutable—their character contents cannot be changed after they are created. Also, if there are one or more references to a **string** (or any object for that matter), the object cannot be reclaimed by the garbage collector.*

Line 25 assigns to **string3** a new **string**, using the **String** constructor that takes a **char** array and two **int** arguments. The second argument specifies the starting index position (the *offset*) from which characters in the array are copied. The third argument specifies the number of characters (the *count*) to be copied from the specified starting position in the array. The new **string** contains a copy of the specified characters in the array. If the specified offset or count indicates that the program should access an element outside the bounds of the character array, an ***ArgumentOutOfRangeException*** is thrown.

Line 26 assigns to **string4** a new **string**, using the **String** constructor that takes as arguments a character and an **int** specifying the number of times to repeat that character in the **string**.

15.4 String Indexer, Length Property and CopyTo Method

The application in Fig. 15.2 presents the **String** indexer, which facilitates the retrieval of any character in the **string**, and the **String** property **Length**, which returns the length of the **string**. The **String** method **CopyTo** copies a specified number of characters from a **string** into a **char** array.

In this example, we create an application that determines the length of a **string**, reverses the order of the characters in the **string** and copies a series of characters from the **string** into a character array.

```
1   // Fig. 15.2: StringMethods.cs
2   // Using the indexer, property Length and method CopyTo
3   // of class String.
4
5   using System;
6   using System.Windows.Forms;
7
```

Fig. 15.2   **String** indexer, **Length** property and **CopyTo** method. (Part 1 of 2.)

```
 8    // creates string objects and displays results of using
 9    // indexer and methods Length and CopyTo
10    class StringMethods
11    {
12       // The main entry point for the application.
13       [STAThread]
14       static void Main( string[] args )
15       {
16          string string1, output;
17          char[] characterArray;
18
19          string1 = "hello there";
20          characterArray = new char[ 5 ];
21
22          // output string
23          output =
24             "string1: \"" + string1 + "\"";
25
26          // test Length property
27          output += "\nLength of string1: " + string1.Length;
28
29          // loop through character in string1 and display
30          // reversed
31          output += "\nThe string reversed is: ";
32
33          for ( int i = string1.Length - 1; i >= 0; i-- )
34             output += string1[ i ];
35
36          // copy characters from string1 into characterArray
37          string1.CopyTo( 0, characterArray, 0, 5 );
38          output += "\nThe character array is: ";
39
40          for ( int i = 0 ; i < characterArray.Length; i++ )
41             output += characterArray[ i ];
42
43          MessageBox.Show( output, "Demonstrating the string " +
44             "Indexer, Length Property and CopyTo method",
45             MessageBoxButtons.OK, MessageBoxIcon.Information );
46
47       } // end method Main
48
49    } // end class StringMethods
```

Fig. 15.2 **String** indexer, **Length** properties and **CopyTo** method. (Part 2 of 2.)

Line 27 uses **String** property **Length** to determine the number of characters in **string string1**. Like arrays, **string**s always know their own size.

Lines 33–34 append to **output** the characters of the **string string1** in reverse order. The **string** indexer returns the character at a specific position in the **string**. The **string** indexer treats a **string** as an array of **char**s. The indexer receives an integer argument as the *position number* and returns the character at that position. As with arrays, the first element of a **string** is considered to be at position 0.

Common Programming Error 15.1

*Attempting to access a character that is outside the bounds of a **string** (i.e., an index less than 0 or an index greater than or equal to the **string**'s length) results in an **Index-OutOfRangeException***.

Line 37 uses **String** method **CopyTo** to copy the characters of a **string** (**string1**) into a character array (**characterArray**). The first argument given to method **CopyTo** is the index from which the method begins copying characters in the **string**. The second argument is the character array into which the characters are copied. The third argument is the index specifying the location at which the method places the copied characters in the character array. The last argument is the number of characters that the method will copy from the **string**. Lines 40–41 append the **char** array contents to **string output** one character at a time.

15.5 Comparing **Strings**

The next two examples demonstrate the various methods that C# provides for comparing **string**s. To understand how one **string** can be "greater than" or "less than" another **string**, consider the process of alphabetizing a series of last names. The reader would, no doubt, place **"Jones"** before **"Smith"**, because the first letter of **"Jones"** comes before the first letter of **"Smith"** in the alphabet. The alphabet is more than just a set of 26 letters—it is an ordered list of characters in which each letter occurs in a specific position. For example, **z** is more than just a letter of the alphabet; **z** is specifically the twenty-sixth letter of the alphabet.

Computers can order characters alphabetically because the characters are represented internally as Unicode numeric codes. When comparing two **string**s, C# simply compares the numeric codes of the characters in the **string**s.

Class **String** provides several ways to compare **string**s. The application in Fig. 15.3 demonstrates the use of method **Equals**, method **CompareTo** and the equality operator (**==**).

The condition in the **if** structure (line 27) uses instance method **Equals** to compare **string1** and literal **string "hello"** to determine whether they are equal. Method **Equals** (inherited by **String** from class **Object**) tests any two objects for equality (i.e., checks whether the objects contain identical contents). The method returns **true** if the objects are equal and **false** otherwise. In this instance, the preceding condition returns **true**, because **string1** references **string** literal object **"hello"**. Method **Equals** uses a *lexicographical comparison*—the integer Unicode values that represent each character in each **string** are compared. Method **Equals** compares the numeric Unicode values that represent the characters in each **string**. A comparison of the **string "hello"** with the **string "HELLO"** would return **false**, because the numeric representations of lowercase letters are different from the numeric representations of corresponding uppercase letters.

The condition in the second **if** structure (line 33) uses the equality operator (**==**) to compare **string string1** with the literal **string "hello"** for equality. In C#, the equality operator also uses a lexicographical comparison to compare two **string**s. Thus, the condition in the **if** structure evaluates to **true**, because the values of **string1** and **"hello"** are equal. To compare the references of two **string**s, we must explicitly cast the **string**s to type **object** and use the equality operator (**==**).

```
1   // Fig. 15.3: StringCompare.cs
2   // Comparing strings.
3
4   using System;
5   using System.Windows.Forms;
6
7   // compare a number of strings
8   class StringCompare
9   {
10      // The main entry point for the application.
11      [STAThread]
12      static void Main( string[] args )
13      {
14         string string1 = "hello";
15         string string2 = "good bye";
16         string string3 = "Happy Birthday";
17         string string4 = "happy birthday";
18         string output;
19
20         // output values of four strings
21         output = "string1 = \"" + string1 + "\"" +
22            "\nstring2 = \"" + string2 + "\"" +
23            "\nstring3 = \"" + string3 + "\"" +
24            "\nstring4 = \"" + string4 + "\"\n\n";
25
26         // test for equality using Equals method
27         if ( string1.Equals( "hello" ) )
28            output += "string1 equals \"hello\"\n";
29         else
30            output += "string1 does not equal \"hello\"\n";
31
32         // test for equality with ==
33         if ( string1 == "hello" )
34            output += "string1 equals \"hello\"\n";
35         else
36            output += "string1 does not equal \"hello\"\n";
37
38         // test for equality comparing case
39         if ( String.Equals( string3, string4 ) )
40            output += "string3 equals string4\n";
41         else
42            output += "string3 does not equal string4\n";
43
```

Fig. 15.3 **String** test to determine equality. (Part 1 of 2.)

```
44          // test CompareTo
45          output += "\nstring1.CompareTo( string2 ) is " +
46             string1.CompareTo( string2 ) + "\n" +
47             "string2.CompareTo( string1 ) is " +
48             string2.CompareTo( string1 ) + "\n" +
49             "string1.CompareTo( string1 ) is " +
50             string1.CompareTo( string1 ) + "\n" +
51             "string3.CompareTo( string4 ) is " +
52             string3.CompareTo( string4 ) + "\n" +
53             "string4.CompareTo( string3 ) is " +
54             string4.CompareTo( string3 ) + "\n\n";
55
56          MessageBox.Show( output, "Demonstrating string " +
57             "comparisons", MessageBoxButtons.OK,
58             MessageBoxIcon.Information );
59
60       } // end method Main
61
62   } // end class StringCompare
```

Fig. 15.3 **String** test to determine equality. (Part 2 of 2.)

We present the test for **string** equality between **string3** and **string4** (line 39) to illustrate that comparisons are indeed case sensitive. Here, **static** method **Equals** (as opposed to the instance method in line 27) is used to compare the values of two **string**s. **"Happy Birthday"** does not equal **"happy birthday"**, so the condition of the **if** structure fails, and the message **"string3 does not equal string4"** is added to the output message (line 42).

Lines 46–54 use the **String** method **CompareTo** to compare **string**s. Method **CompareTo** returns **0** if the **string**s are equal, a **-1** if the **string** that invokes **CompareTo** is less than the **string** that is passed as an argument and a **1** if the **string** that invokes **CompareTo** is greater than the **string** that is passed as an argument. Method **CompareTo** uses a lexicographical comparison.

Notice that **CompareTo** considers **string3** to be larger than **string4**. The only difference between these two **string**s is that **string3** contains two uppercase letters. This example illustrates that an uppercase letter has a lower value in the Unicode character set than its corresponding lowercase letter.

The application in Fig. 15.4 shows how to test whether a **string** instance begins or ends with a given **string**. Method *StartsWith* determines whether a **string** instance starts with the **string** text passed to it as an argument. Method *EndsWith* determines whether a **string** instance ends with the **string** text passed to it as an argument. Application **StringStartEnd**'s **Main** method defines an array of **string**s (called **strings**), which contains **"started"**, **"starting"**, **"ended"** and **"ending"**. The remainder of method **Main** tests the elements of the array to determine whether they start or end with a particular set of characters.

Line 21 uses method **StartsWith**, which takes a **string** argument. The condition in the **if** structure determines whether the **string** at index **i** of the array starts with the characters **"st"**. If so, the method returns **true** and appends **strings[i]** to **string output** for display purposes.

Line 30 uses method **EndsWith**, which also takes a **string** argument. The condition in the **if** structure determines whether the **string** at index **i** of the array ends with the characters **"ed"**. If so, the method returns **true**, and **strings[i]** is appended to **string output** for display purposes.

```
1    // Fig. 15.4: StringStartEnd.cs
2    // Demonstrating StartsWith and EndsWith methods.
3
4    using System;
5    using System.Windows.Forms;
6
7    // testing StartsWith and EndsWith
8    class StringStartEnd
9    {
10       // The main entry point for the application.
11       [STAThread]
12       static void Main( string[] args )
13       {
14          string[] strings =
15                { "started", "starting", "ended", "ending" };
16          string output = "";
17
18          //test every string to see if it starts with "st"
19          for ( int i = 0; i < strings.Length; i++ )
20
21             if ( strings[ i ].StartsWith( "st" ) )
22                output += "\"" + strings[ i ] + "\"" +
23                   " starts with \"st\"\n";
24
25          output += "\n";
26
27          // test every string to see if it ends with "ed"
28          for ( int i = 0; i < strings.Length; i ++ )
29
30             if ( strings[ i ].EndsWith( "ed" ) )
31                output += "\"" + strings[ i ] + "\"" +
32                   " ends with \"ed\"\n";
33
```

Fig. 15.4 StartsWith and **EndsWith** methods. (Part 1 of 2.)

```
34                MessageBox.Show( output, "Demonstrating StartsWith and " +
35                   "EndsWith methods", MessageBoxButtons.OK,
36                   MessageBoxIcon.Information );
37
38          } // end method Main
39
40    } // end class StringStartEnd
```

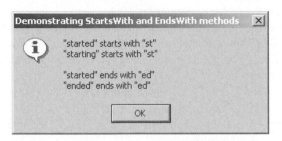

Fig. 15.4   **StartsWith** and **EndsWith** methods. (Part 2 of 2.)

15.6 String Method GetHashCode

Often, it is necessary to store **string**s and other data types in a manner that enables the information to be found quickly. One of the best ways to make information easily accessible is to store it in a hash table. A *hash table* stores an object by performing a special calculation on that object, which produces a *hash code*. The object then is stored at a location in the hash table determined by the calculated hash code. When a program needs to retrieve the information, the same calculation is performed, generating the same hash code. Any object can be stored in a hash table. Class **Object** defines method *Get-HashCode* to perform the hash-code calculation. Although all classes inherit this method from class **Object**, it is recommended that they override **Object**'s default implementation. Class **String overrides** method **GetHashCode** to provide a good hash-code distribution based on the contents of the **string**. We will discuss hashing in detail in Chapter 24, Data Structures.

The example in Fig. 15.5 demonstrates the application of the **GetHashCode** method to two **string**s (**"hello"** and **"Hello"**). Here, the hash-code value for each **string** is different. However, **string**s that are not identical can have the same hash-code value.

```
1    // Fig. 15.5: StringHashCode.cs
2    // Demonstrating method GetHashCode of class String.
3
4    using System;
5    using System.Windows.Forms;
6
```

Fig. 15.5   **GetHashCode** method demonstration. (Part 1 of 2.)

```
7   // testing the GetH-ashCode method
8   class StringHashCode
9   {
10      // The main entry point for the application.
11      [STAThread]
12      static void Main( string[] args )
13      {
14
15          string string1 = "hello";
16          string string2 = "Hello";
17          string output;
18
19          output = "The hash code for \"" + string1 +
20              "\" is " + string1.GetHashCode() + "\n";
21
22          output += "The hash code for \"" + string2 +
23              "\" is " + string2.GetHashCode() + "\n";
24
25          MessageBox.Show( output, "Demonstrating String " +
26              "method GetHashCode", MessageBoxButtons.OK,
27              MessageBoxIcon.Information );
28
29      } // end method Main
30
31  } // end class StringHashCode
```

Fig. 15.5   GetHashCode method demonstration. (Part 2 of 2.)

15.7 Locating Characters and Substrings in Strings

In many applications, it is necessary to search for a character or set of characters in a
string. For example, a programmer creating a word processor would want to provide capabilities for searching through documents. The application in Fig. 15.6 demonstrates some
of the many versions of **String** methods *IndexOf*, *IndexOfAny*, *LastIndexOf*
and *LastIndexOfAny*, which search for a specified character or substring in a **string**.
We perform all searches in this example on the **string letters** (initialized with **"ab-
cdefghijklmabcdefghijklm"**) located in method **Main** of class **StringIn-
dexMethods**.

```
1   // Fig. 15.6: StringIndexMethods.cs
2   // Using String searching methods.
3
```

Fig. 15.6   Searching for characters and substrings in **string**s. (Part 1 of 3.)

```
4   using System;
5   using System.Windows.Forms;
6
7   // testing indexing capabilities of strings
8   class StringIndexMethods
9   {
10     // The main entry point for the application.
11     [STAThread]
12     static void Main( string[] args )
13     {
14        string letters = "abcdefghijklmabcdefghijklm";
15        string output = "";
16        char[] searchLetters = { 'c', 'a', '$' };
17
18        // test IndexOf to locate a character in a string
19        output += "'c' is located at index " +
20           letters.IndexOf( 'c' );
21
22        output += "\n'a' is located at index " +
23           letters.IndexOf( 'a', 1 );
24
25        output += "\n'$' is located at index " +
26           letters.IndexOf( '$', 3, 5 );
27
28        // test LastIndexOf to find a character in a string
29        output += "\n\nLast 'c' is located at " +
30           "index " + letters.LastIndexOf( 'c' );
31
32        output += "\nLast 'a' is located at index " +
33           letters.LastIndexOf( 'a', 25 );
34
35        output += "\nLast '$' is located at index " +
36           letters.LastIndexOf( '$', 15, 5 );
37
38        // test IndexOf to locate a substring in a string
39        output += "\n\n\"def\" is located at" +
40           " index " + letters.IndexOf( "def" );
41
42        output += "\n\"def\" is located at index " +
43           letters.IndexOf( "def", 7 );
44
45        output += "\n\"hello\" is located at index " +
46           letters.IndexOf( "hello", 5, 15 );
47
48        // test LastIndexOf to find a substring in a string
49        output += "\n\nLast \"def\" is located at index " +
50           letters.LastIndexOf( "def" );
51
52        output += "\nLast \"def\" is located at " +
53           letters.LastIndexOf( "def", 25 );
54
55        output += "\nLast \"hello\" is located at index " +
56           letters.LastIndexOf( "hello", 20, 15 );
```

Fig. 15.6   Searching for characters and substrings in **string**s. (Part 2 of 3.)

```
57
58          // test IndexOfAny to find first occurrence of character
59          // in array
60          output += "\n\nFirst occurrence of 'c', 'a', '$' is " +
61             "located at " + letters.IndexOfAny( searchLetters );
62
63          output += "\nFirst occurrence of 'c, 'a' or '$' is " +
64             "located at " + letters.IndexOfAny( searchLetters, 7 );
65
66          output += "\nFirst occurrence of 'c', 'a' or '$' is " +
67            "located at " + letters.IndexOfAny( searchLetters, 20, 5 );
68
69          // test LastIndexOfAny to find last occurrence of character
70          // in array
71          output += "\n\nLast occurrence of 'c', 'a' or '$' is " +
72             "located at " + letters.LastIndexOfAny( searchLetters );
73
74          output += "\nLast occurrence of 'c', 'a' or '$' is " +
75            "located at " + letters.LastIndexOfAny( searchLetters, 1 );
76
77          output += "\nLast occurrence of 'c', 'a' or '$' is " +
78             "located at " + letters.LastIndexOfAny(
79             searchLetters, 25, 5 );
80
81          MessageBox.Show( output,
82             "Demonstrating class index methods",
83             MessageBoxButtons.OK, MessageBoxIcon.Information );
84
85      } // end method Main
86
87   } // end class StringIndexMethods
```

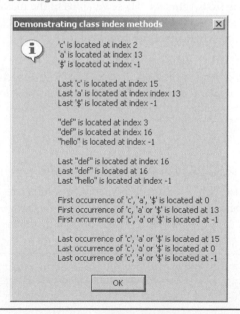

Fig. 15.6 Searching for characters and substrings in **string**s. (Part 3 of 3.)

Lines 20, 23 and 26 use method **IndexOf** to locate the first occurrence of a character or substring in a **string**. If **IndexOf** finds a character, **IndexOf** returns the index of the specified character in the **string**; otherwise, **IndexOf** returns **−1**. The expression on line 23 uses a version of method **IndexOf** that takes two arguments—the character to search for and the starting index at which the search of the **string** should begin. The method does not examine any characters that occur prior to the starting index (in this case **1**). The expression in line 26 uses another version of method **IndexOf** that takes three arguments—the character to search for, the index at which to start searching and the number of characters to search.

Lines 30, 33 and 36 use method **LastIndexOf** to locate the last occurrence of a character in a **string**. Method **LastIndexOf** performs the search from the end of the **string** toward the beginning of the **string**. If method **LastIndexOf** finds the character, **LastIndexOf** returns the index of the specified character in the **string**; otherwise, **LastIndexOf** returns **−1**. There are three versions of **LastIndexOf** that search for characters in a **string**. The expression in line 30 uses the version of method **LastIndexOf** that takes as an argument the character for which to search. The expression in line 33 uses the version of method **LastIndexOf** that takes two arguments—the character for which to search and the highest index from which to begin searching backward for the character. The expression in line 36 uses a third version of method **LastIndexOf** that takes three arguments—the character for which to search, the starting index from which to start searching backward and the number of characters (the portion of the **string**) to search.

Lines 40–56 use versions of **IndexOf** and **LastIndexOf** that take a **string** instead of a character as the first argument. These versions of the methods perform identically to those described above except that they search for sequences of characters (or substrings) that are specified by their **string** arguments.

Lines 61–79 use methods **IndexOfAny** and **LastIndexOfAny**, which take an array of characters as the first argument. These versions of the methods also perform identically to those described above except that they return the index of the first occurrence of any of the characters in the character array argument.

Common Programming Error 15.2

*In the overloaded methods **LastIndexOf** and **LastIndexOfAny** that take three parameters, the second argument must always be bigger than or equal to the third argument. This might seem counterintuitive, but remember that the search moves from the end of the string toward the start of the string.*

15.8 Extracting Substrings from **Strings**

Class **String** provides two *Substring* methods, which are used to create a new **string** by copying part of an existing **string**. Each method returns a new **string**. The application in Fig. 15.7 demonstrates the use of both methods.

```
1    // Fig. 15.7: SubString.cs
2    // Demonstrating the String Substring method.
3
```

Fig. 15.7   Substrings generated from **string**s. (Part 1 of 2.)

```
4    using System;
5    using System.Windows.Forms;
6
7    // creating substrings
8    class SubString
9    {
10      // The main entry point for the application.
11      [STAThread]
12      static void Main( string[] args )
13      {
14         string letters = "abcdefghijklmabcdefghijklm";
15         string output = "";
16
17         // invoke Substring method and pass it one parameter
18         output += "Substring from index 20 to end is \"" +
19            letters.Substring( 20 ) + "\"\n";
20
21         // invoke Substring method and pass it two parameters
22         output += "Substring from index 0 to 6 is \"" +
23            letters.Substring( 0, 6 ) + "\"";
24
25         MessageBox.Show( output,
26            "Demonstrating String method Substring",
27            MessageBoxButtons.OK, MessageBoxIcon.Information );
28
29      } // end method Main
30
31   } // end class SubString
```

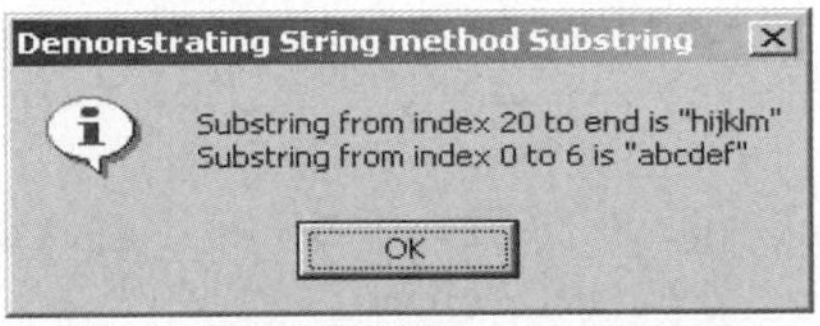

Fig. 15.7 Substrings generated from **string**s. (Part 2 of 2.)

The statement in line 19 uses the **Substring** method that takes one **int** argument. The argument specifies the starting index from which the method copies characters in the original **string**. The substring returned contains a copy of the characters from the starting index to the end of the **string**. If the index specified in the argument is outside the bounds of the **string**, the program throws an **ArgumentOutOfRangeException**.

The second version of method **Substring** (line 23) takes two **int** arguments. The first argument specifies the starting index from which the method copies characters from the original **string**. The second argument specifies the length of the substring to be copied. The substring returned contains a copy of the specified characters from the original **string**.

15.9 Concatenating Strings

The **+** operator (discussed in Chapter 3, Introduction to C# Programming) is not the only way to perform **string** concatenation. The **static** method *Concat* of class **String** (Fig. 15.8) concatenates two **string**s and returns a new **string** containing the combined characters from both original **string**s. Line 23 appends the characters from **string2** to the end of **string1**, using method **Concat**. The statement on line 23 does not modify the original **string**s.

15.10 Miscellaneous **String** Methods

Class **String** provides several methods that return modified copies of **string**s. The application in Fig. 15.9 demonstrates the use of these methods, which include **String** methods *Replace*, *ToLower*, *ToUpper*, *Trim* and *ToString*.

```
1   // Fig. 15.8: SubConcatination.cs
2   // Demonstrating String class Concat method.
3
4   using System;
5   using System.Windows.Forms;
6
7   // concatenates strings using String method Concat
8   class StringConcatenation
9   {
10      // The main entry point for the application.
11      [STAThread]
12      static void Main( string[] args )
13      {
14         string string1 = "Happy ";
15         string string2 = "Birthday";
16         string output;
17
18         output = "string1 = \"" + string1 + "\"\n" +
19            "string2 = \"" + string2 + "\"";
20
21         output +=
22            "\n\nResult of String.Concat( string1, string2 ) = " +
23            String.Concat( string1, string2 );
24
25         output += "\nstring1 after concatenation = " + string1;
26
27         MessageBox.Show( output,
28            "Demonstrating String method Concat",
29            MessageBoxButtons.OK, MessageBoxIcon.Information );
30
31      } // end method Main
32
33   } // end class StringConcatenation
```

Fig. 15.8   **Concat static** method.

Line 27 uses **String** method **Replace** to return a new **string**, replacing every occurrence in **string1** of character **'e'** with character **'E'**. Method **Replace** takes two arguments—a **string** for which to search and another **string** with which to replace all matching occurrences of the first argument. The original **string** remains unchanged. If there are no occurrences of the first argument in the **string**, the method returns the original **string**.

String method **ToUpper** generates a new **string** (line 31) that replaces any lowercase letters in **string1** with their uppercase equivalent. The method returns a new **string** containing the converted **string**; the original **string** remains unchanged. If there are no characters to convert to uppercase, the method returns the original **string**. Line 32 uses **String** method **ToLower** to return a new **string** in which any uppercase letters in **string2** are replaced by their lowercase equivalents. The original **string** is unchanged. As with **ToUpper**, if there are no characters to convert to lowercase, method **ToLower** returns the original **string**.

```csharp
1   // Fig. 15.9: StringMiscellaneous2.cs
2   // Demonstrating String methods Replace, ToLower, ToUpper, Trim
3   // and ToString.
4
5   using System;
6   using System.Windows.Forms;
7
8   // creates strings using methods Replace, ToLower, ToUpper, Trim
9   class StringMethods2
10  {
11      // The main entry point for the application.
12      [STAThread]
13      static void Main( string[] args )
14      {
15          string string1 = "cheers!";
16          string string2 = "GOOD BYE ";
17          string string3 = "   spaces   ";
18          string output;
19
20          output = "string1 = \"" + string1 + "\"\n" +
21              "string2 = \"" + string2 + "\"\n" +
22              "string3 = \"" + string3 + "\"";
23
24          // call method Replace
25          output +=
26              "\n\nReplacing \"e\" with \"E\" in string1: \"" +
27              string1.Replace( 'e', 'E' ) + "\"";
28
29          // call ToLower and ToUpper
30          output += "\n\nstring1.ToUpper() = \"" +
31              string1.ToUpper() + "\"\nstring2.ToLower() = \"" +
32              string2.ToLower() + "\"";
33
```

Fig. 15.9 **String** methods **Replace**, **ToLower**, **ToUpper**, **Trim** and **ToString**. (Part 1 of 2.)

```
34          // call Trim method
35          output += "\n\nstring3 after trim = \"" +
36             string3.Trim() + "\"";
37
38          // call ToString method
39          output += "\n\nstring1 = \"" + string1.ToString() + "\"";
40
41          MessageBox.Show( output,
42             "Demonstrating various string methods",
43             MessageBoxButtons.OK, MessageBoxIcon.Information );
44
45       } // end method Main
46
47    } // end class StringMethods2
```

Fig. 15.9   String methods **Replace, ToLower, ToUpper, Trim** and
ToString. (Part 2 of 2.)

Line 36 uses **String** method **Trim** to remove all whitespace characters that appear at the beginning and end of a **string**. Without otherwise altering the original **string**, the method returns a new **string** that contains the **string**, but omits leading or trailing whitespace characters. Another version of method **Trim** takes a character array and returns a **string** that does not contain the characters in the array argument.

Line 39 uses class **String**'s method **ToString** to show that the various other methods employed in this application have not modified **string1**. Why is the **ToString** method provided for class **String**? In C#, all objects are derived from class **Object**, which defines **virtual** method **ToString**. Thus, method **ToString** can be called to obtain a **string** representation of any object. If a class that inherits from **Object** (such as **String**) does not override method **ToString**, the class uses the default version from class **Object**, which returns a **string** consisting of the object's class name. Classes usually override method **ToString** to express the contents of an object as text. Class **String** overrides method **ToString** so that, instead of returning the class name, it simply returns the **string**.

15.11   Class **StringBuilder**

The **String** class provides many capabilities for processing **string**s. However a **string**'s contents can never change. Operations that seem to concatenate **string**s are in fact assigning **string** references to newly created **string**s (e.g., the **+=** operator creates a new **string** and assigns the initial **string** reference to the newly created **string**).

The next several sections discuss the features of class **StringBuilder** (namespace **System.Text**), used to create and manipulate dynamic string information—i.e., mutable strings. Every **StringBuilder** can store a certain number of characters that is specified by its capacity. Exceeding the capacity of a **StringBuilder** causes the capacity to expand to accommodate the additional characters. As we will see, members of class **StringBuilder**, such as methods **Append** and **AppendFormat**, can be used for concatenation like the operators **+** and **+=** for class **String**.

Software Engineering Observation 15.2

*Objects of class **String** are constant strings, whereas object of class **StringBuilder** are mutable strings. C# can perform certain optimizations involving **string**s (such as the sharing of one **string** among multiple references), because it knows these objects will not change.*

Performance Tip 15.2

*When given the choice between using a **string** to represent a string and using a **String-Builder** object to represent that string, always use a **string** if the contents of the object will not change. When appropriate, using **string**s instead of **StringBuilder** objects improves performance.*

Class **StringBuilder** provides six overloaded constructors. Class **String-BuilderConstructor** (Fig. 15.10) demonstrates the use of three of these overloaded constructors.

```
1   // Fig. 15.10: StringBuilderConstructor.cs
2   // Demonstrating StringBuilder class constructors.
3
4   using System;
5   using System.Windows.Forms;
6   using System.Text;
7
8   // creates three StringBuilder with three constructors
9   class StringBuilderConstructor
10  {
11      // The main entry point for the application.
12      [STAThread]
13      static void Main( string[] args )
14      {
15          StringBuilder buffer1, buffer2, buffer3;
16          string output;
17
18          buffer1 = new StringBuilder();
19          buffer2 = new StringBuilder( 10 );
20          buffer3 = new StringBuilder( "hello" );
21
22          output = "buffer1 = \"" + buffer1.ToString() + "\"\n";
23
24          output += "buffer2 = \"" + buffer2.ToString() + "\"\n";
25
```

Fig. 15.10 StringBuilder class constructors. (Part 1 of 2.)

```
26              output += "buffer3 = \"" + buffer3.ToString() + "\"\n";
27
28          MessageBox.Show( output,
29              "Demonstrating StringBuilder class constructors",
30              MessageBoxButtons.OK, MessageBoxIcon.Information );
31
32      } // end method Main
33
34  } // end class StringBuilderConstructor
```

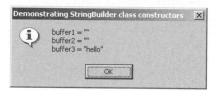

Fig. 15.10 StringBuilder class constructors. (Part 2 of 2.)

Line 18 employs the no-argument **StringBuilder** constructor to create a **StringBuilder** that contains no characters and has a default initial capacity of 16 characters. Line 19 uses the **StringBuilder** constructor that takes an **int** argument to create a **StringBuilder** that contains no characters and has the initial capacity specified in the **int** argument (i.e., **10**). Line 20 uses the **StringBuilder** constructor that takes a **string** argument to create a **StringBuilder** containing the characters of the **string** argument. The initial capacity is the smallest power of two greater than the number of characters in the **string** passed as an argument.

Lines 22–26 use **StringBuilder** method **ToString** to obtain a **string** representation of the **StringBuilder**s' contents. This method returns the **String-Builder**s' underlying string.

15.12 StringBuilder Indexer, Length and Capacity Properties, and EnsureCapacity Method

Class **StringBuilder** provides the *Length* and *Capacity* properties to return the number of characters currently in a **StringBuilder** and the number of characters that a **StringBuilder** can store without allocating more memory, respectively. These properties also can increase or decrease the length or the capacity of the **StringBuilder**.

Method *EnsureCapacity* allows programmers to guarantee that a **String-Builder** has a capacity that reduces the number of times the capacity must be increased. Method **EnsureCapacity** doubles the **StringBuilder** instance's current capacity. If this doubled value is greater than the value that the programmer wishes to ensure, it becomes the new capacity. Otherwise, **EnsureCapacity** alters the capacity to make it one more than the requested number. For example, if the current capacity is 17 and we wish to make it 40, 17 multiplied by 2 is not greater than 40, so the call will result in a new capacity of 41. If the current capacity is 23 and we wish to make it 40, 23 will be multiplied by 2 to result in a new capacity of 46. Both 41 and 46 are greater than 40, and so a capacity of 40 is indeed ensured by method **EnsureCapacity**. The program in Fig. 15.11 demonstrates the use of these methods and properties.

The program contains one **StringBuilder**, called **buffer**. Lines 15–16 of the program use the **StringBuilder** constructor that takes a **string** argument to instantiate the **StringBuilder** and initialize its value to **"Hello, how are you?"**. Lines 19–21 append to **output** the content, length and capacity of the **StringBuilder**. In the output window, notice that the capacity of the **StringBuilder** is initially 32. Remember, the **StringBuilder** constructor that takes a **string** argument creates a **StringBuilder** object with an initial capacity that is the smallest power of two greater than the number of characters in the **string** passed as an argument.

Line 24 expands the capacity of the **StringBuilder** to a minimum of 75 characters. The current capacity (**32**) multiplied by two is less than 75, so method **EnsureCapacity** increases the capacity to one greater than 75 (i.e., 76). If new characters are added to a **StringBuilder** so that its length exceeds its capacity, the capacity grows to accommodate the additional characters in the same manner as if method **EnsureCapacity** had been called.

```
1    // Fig. 15.11: StringBuilderFeatures.cs
2    // Demonstrating some features of class StringBuilder.
3
4    using System;
5    using System.Windows.Forms;
6    using System.Text;
7
8    // uses some of class StringBuilder's methods
9    class StringBuilderFeatures
10   {
11      // The main entry point for the application.
12      [STAThread]
13      static void Main( string[] args )
14      {
15         StringBuilder buffer =
16            new StringBuilder( "Hello, how are you?" );
17
18         // use Length and Capacity properties
19         string output = "buffer = " + buffer.ToString() +
20            "\nLength = " + buffer.Length +
21            "\nCapacity = " + buffer.Capacity;
22
23         // use EnsureCapacity method
24         buffer.EnsureCapacity( 75 );
25
26         output += "\n\nNew capacity = " +
27            buffer.Capacity;
28
29         // truncate StringBuilder by setting Length property
30         buffer.Length = 10;
31
32         output += "\n\nNew length = " +
33            buffer.Length + "\nbuffer = ";
34
```

Fig. 15.11 **StringBuilder** size manipulation. (Part 1 of 2.)

```
35          // use StringBuilder indexer
36          for ( int i = 0; i < buffer.Length; i++ )
37              output += buffer[ i ];
38
39          MessageBox.Show( output, "StringBuilder features",
40              MessageBoxButtons.OK, MessageBoxIcon.Information );
41
42      } // end method Main
43
44  } // end class StringBuilderFeatures
```

Fig. 15.11 StringBuilder size manipulation. (Part 2 of 2.)

Line 30 uses **Length**'s **Set** accessor to set the length of the **StringBuilder** to **10**. If the specified length is less than the current number of characters in the **String-Builder**, the contents of **StringBuilder** are truncated to the specified length (i.e., the program discards all characters in the **StringBuilder** that occur after the specified length). If the specified length is greater than the number of characters currently in the **StringBuilder**, null characters (characters with the numeric representation **0** that signal the end of a **string**) are appended to the **StringBuilder** until the total number of characters in the **StringBuilder** is equal to the specified length.

 Common Programming Error 15.3

*Assigning **null** to a **string** reference can lead to logic errors. The keyword **null** is a null reference, not a **string**. Do not confuse **null** with the empty string, **""** (the **string** that is of length 0 and contains no characters).*

15.13 StringBuilder Append and AppendFormat Methods

Class **StringBuilder** provides 19 overloaded **Append** methods that allow various data-type values to be added to the end of a **StringBuilder**. C# provides versions for each of the primitive data types and for character arrays, **String**s and **Object**s. (Remember that method **ToString** produces a **string** representation of any **Object**.) Each of the methods takes an argument, converts it to a **string** and appends it to the **StringBuilder**. Figure 15.12 demonstrates the use of several **Append** methods.

Lines 29–47 use 10 different overloaded **Append** methods to attach the objects created in lines 15–26 to the end of the **StringBuilder**. **Append** behaves similarly to the **+** operator which is used with **string**s. Just as **+** seems to append objects to a **string**, method **Append** can append data types to a **StringBuilder**'s underlying string.

Class **StringBuilder** also provides method ***AppendFormat***, which converts a **string** to a specified format and then appends it to the **StringBuilder**. The example in Fig. 15.13 demonstrates the use of this method.

```
1   // Fig. 15.12: StringBuilderAppend.cs
2   // Demonstrating StringBuilder Append methods.
3
4   using System;
5   using System.Windows.Forms;
6   using System.Text;
7
8   // testing the Append method
9   class StringBuilderAppend
10  {
11     // The main entry point for the application.
12     [STAThread]
13     static void Main( string[] args )
14     {
15        object objectValue = "hello";
16        string stringValue = "good bye";
17        char[] characterArray = { 'a', 'b', 'c', 'd',
18                                   'e', 'f' };
19
20        bool booleanValue = true;
21        char characterValue = 'Z';
22        int integerValue = 7;
23        long longValue = 1000000;
24        float floatValue = 2.5F;
25        double doubleValue = 33.333;
26        StringBuilder buffer = new StringBuilder();
27
28        // use method Append to append values to buffer
29        buffer.Append( objectValue );
30        buffer.Append( "  " );
31        buffer.Append( stringValue );
32        buffer.Append( "  " );
33        buffer.Append( characterArray );
34        buffer.Append( "  " );
35        buffer.Append( characterArray, 0, 3 );
36        buffer.Append( "  " );
37        buffer.Append( booleanValue );
38        buffer.Append( "  " );
39        buffer.Append( characterValue );
40        buffer.Append( "  " );
41        buffer.Append( integerValue );
42        buffer.Append( "  " );
43        buffer.Append( longValue );
44        buffer.Append( "  " );
45        buffer.Append( floatValue );
46        buffer.Append( "  " );
47        buffer.Append( doubleValue );
48
```

Fig. 15.12 Append methods of **StringBuilder**. (Part 1 of 2.)

```
49              MessageBox.Show( "buffer = " + buffer.ToString(),
50                 "Demonstrating StringBuilder append method",
51                 MessageBoxButtons.OK, MessageBoxIcon.Information );
52
53       } // end method Main
54
55   } // end class StringBuilderAppend
```

Fig. 15.12 Append methods of **StringBuilder**. (Part 2 of 2.)

```
1    // Fig. 15.13: StringBuilderAppendFormat.cs
2    // Demonstrating method AppendFormat.
3
4    using System;
5    using System.Windows.Forms;
6    using System.Text;
7
8    // use the AppendFormat method
9    class StringBuilderAppendFormat
10   {
11      // The main entry point for the application.
12      [STAThread]
13      static void Main( string[] args )
14      {
15         StringBuilder buffer = new StringBuilder();
16         string string1, string2;
17
18         // formatted string
19         string1 = "This {0} costs: {1:C}.\n";
20
21         // string1 argument array
22         object[] objectArray = new object[ 2 ];
23
24         objectArray[ 0 ] = "car";
25         objectArray[ 1 ] = 1234.56;
26
27         // append to buffer formatted string with argument
28         buffer.AppendFormat( string1, objectArray );
29
30         // formatted string
31         string2 = "Number:{0:d3}.\n" +
32            "Number right aligned with spaces:{0, 4}.\n" +
33            "Number left aligned with spaces:{0, -4}.";
34
```

Fig. 15.13 StringBuilder's **AppendFormat** method. (Part 1 of 2.)

```
35            // append to buffer formatted string with argument
36            buffer.AppendFormat( string2, 5 );
37
38            // display formatted strings
39            MessageBox.Show( buffer.ToString(), "Using AppendFormat",
40               MessageBoxButtons.OK, MessageBoxIcon.Information );
41
42         } // end method Main
43
44   } // end class StringBuilderAppendFormat
```

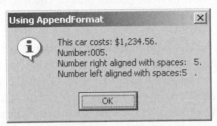

Fig. 15.13 `StringBuilder`'s `AppendFormat` method. (Part 2 of 2.)

Line 19 creates a **string** that contains formatting information. The information enclosed within the braces determines how to format a specific piece of information. Formats have the form **{X[,Y][:FormatString]}**, where **X** is the number of the argument to be formatted, counting from zero. **Y** is an optional argument, which can be positive or negative, indicating how many characters should be in the result of formatting. If the resulting **string** is less than the number **Y**, the **string** will be padded with spaces to make up for the difference. A positive integer aligns the **string** to the right; a negative integer aligns it to the left. The optional **FormatString** applies a particular format to the argument: Currency, decimal or scientific, among others. In this case, "**{0}**" means the first argument will be printed out. "**{1:C}**" specifies that the second argument will be formatted as a currency value.

Line 28 shows a version of **AppendFormat**, which takes two parameters—a **string** specifying the format and an array of objects to serve as the arguments to the format **string**. The argument referred to by "**{0}**" is in the object array at index **0**, and so on.

Lines 31–33 define another **string** used for formatting. The first format "**{0:D3}**" specifies that the first argument will be formatted as a three-digit decimal, meaning any number that has fewer than three digits will have leading zeros placed in front to make up the difference. The next format, "**{0, 4}**" specifies that the formatted **string** should have four characters and should be right aligned. The third format, "**{0, -4}**" specifies that the **string**s should be aligned to the left. For more formatting options, please refer to the documentation.

Line 36 uses a version of **AppendFormat** that takes two parameters: A **string** containing a format and an object to which the format is applied. In this case, the object is the number **5**. The output of Fig. 15.13 displays the result of applying these two version of **AppendFormat** with their respective arguments.

15.14 StringBuilder Insert, Remove and Replace Methods

Class **StringBuilder** provides 18 overloaded *Insert* methods to allow various data-type values to be inserted at any position in a **StringBuilder**. The class provides versions for each of the primitive data types and for character arrays, **String**s and **Object**s. (Remember that method **ToString** produces a **string** representation of any **Object**.) Each method takes its second argument, converts it to a **string** and inserts the **string** into the **StringBuilder** in front of the index specified by the first argument. The index specified by the first argument must be greater than or equal to **0** and less than the length of the **StringBuilder**; otherwise, the program throws an **ArgumentOutOfRange-Exception**.

Class **StringBuilder** also provides method *Remove* for deleting any portion of a **StringBuilder**. Method **Remove** takes two arguments—the index at which to begin deletion and the number of characters to delete. The sum of the starting subscript and the number of characters to be deleted must always be less than the length of the **String-Builder**; otherwise, the program throws an **ArgumentOutOfRangeException**. The **Insert** and **Remove** methods are demonstrated in Fig. 15.14.

```
1   // Fig. 15.14: StringBuilderInsertRemove.cs
2   // Demonstrating methods Insert and Remove of the
3   // StringBuilder class.
4
5   using System;
6   using System.Windows.Forms;
7   using System.Text;
8
9   // test the Insert and Remove methods
10  class StringBuilderInsertRemove
11  {
12     // The main entry point for the application.
13     [STAThread]
14     static void Main( string[] args )
15     {
16        object objectValue = "hello";
17        string stringValue = "good bye";
18        char[] characterArray = { 'a', 'b', 'c',
19                                  'd', 'e', 'f' };
20
21        bool booleanValue = true;
22        char characterValue = 'K';
23        int integerValue = 7;
24        long longValue = 10000000;
25        float floatValue = 2.5F;
26        double doubleValue = 33.333;
27        StringBuilder buffer = new StringBuilder();
28        string output;
29
30        // insert values into buffer
31        buffer.Insert(0, objectValue);
```

Fig. 15.14 StringBuilder text insertion and removal. (Part 1 of 2.)

```
32          buffer.Insert(0, "   ");
33          buffer.Insert(0, stringValue);
34          buffer.Insert(0, "   ");
35          buffer.Insert(0, characterArray);
36          buffer.Insert(0, "   ");
37          buffer.Insert(0, booleanValue);
38          buffer.Insert(0, "   ");
39          buffer.Insert(0, characterValue);
40          buffer.Insert(0, "   ");
41          buffer.Insert(0, integerValue);
42          buffer.Insert(0, "   ");
43          buffer.Insert(0, longValue);
44          buffer.Insert(0, "   ");
45          buffer.Insert(0, floatValue);
46          buffer.Insert(0, "   ");
47          buffer.Insert(0, doubleValue);
48          buffer.Insert(0, "   ");
49
50          output = "buffer after inserts: \n" +
51             buffer.ToString() + "\n\n";
52
53          buffer.Remove( 10, 1 ); // delete 2 in 2.5
54          buffer.Remove( 2, 4 );  // delete .333 in 33.333
55
56          output += "buffer after Removes:\n" +
57             buffer.ToString();
58
59          MessageBox.Show( output, "Demonstrating StringBuilder " +
60             "Insert and Remove methods", MessageBoxButtons.OK,
61             MessageBoxIcon.Information );
62
63      } // end method Main
64
65  } // end class StringBuilderInsertRemove
```

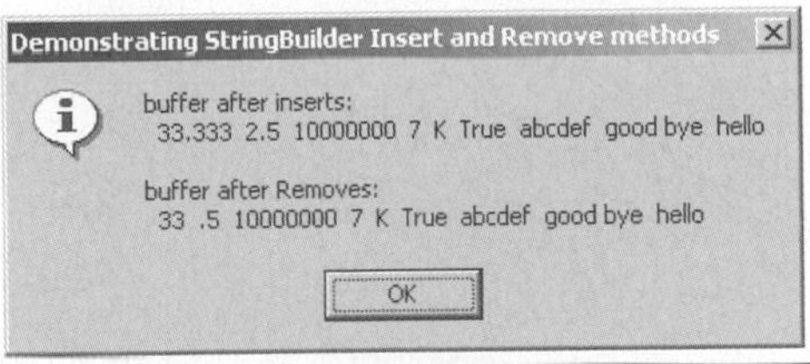

Fig. 15.14 StringBuilder text insertion and removal. (Part 2 of 2.)

Another useful method included with **StringBuilder** is **Replace**. **Replace** searches for a specified **string** or character and substitutes another **string** or character in its place. Figure 15.15 demonstrates this method.

```
1   // Fig. 15.15: StringBuilderReplace.cs
2   // Demonstrating method Replace.
3
```

Fig. 15.15 StringBuilder text replacement. (Part 1 of 2.)

```csharp
4   using System;
5   using System.Windows.Forms;
6   using System.Text;
7
8   // testing the Replace method
9   class StringBuilderReplace
10  {
11     // The main entry point for the application.
12     [STAThread]
13     static void Main( string[] args )
14     {
15        StringBuilder builder1 =
16           new StringBuilder( "Happy Birthday Jane" );
17
18        StringBuilder builder2 =
19           new StringBuilder( "good bye greg" );
20
21        string output = "Before replacements:\n" +
22           builder1.ToString() + "\n" + builder2.ToString();
23
24        builder1.Replace( "Jane", "Greg" );
25        builder2.Replace( 'g', 'G', 0, 5 );
26
27        output += "\n\nAfter replacements:\n" +
28           builder1.ToString() + "\n" + builder2.ToString();
29
30        MessageBox.Show( output,
31           "Using StringBuilder method Replace",
32           MessageBoxButtons.OK, MessageBoxIcon.Information );
33
34     } // end method Main
35
36  } // end class StringBuilderReplace
```

Fig. 15.15 StringBuilder text replacement. (Part 2 of 2.)

Line 24 uses method **Replace** to replace all instances of the **string "Jane"** with the **string "Greg"** in **builder1**. Another overload of this method takes two characters as parameters and replaces each occurrence of the first with one of the second. Line 25 uses an overload of **Replace** that takes four parameters, the first two of which are characters and the second two of which are **int**s. The method replaces all instances of the first character with the second, beginning at the index specified by the first **int** and continuing for a count specified by the second. Thus, in this case, **Replace** looks through only five characters starting with the character at index **0**. As the outputs illustrates, this version of

Replace replaces **g** with **G** in the word **"good"**, but not in **"greg"**. This is because the gs in **"greg"** do not fall in the range indicated by the **int** arguments (i.e., between indexes **0** and **4**).

15.15 Char Methods

C# provides a data type, called a *structure*, that is similar to a class. Although structures and classes are comparable in many ways, structures are a value type. Like classes, structures include methods and properties. Both use the same modifiers (such as **public**, **private** and **protected**) and access members via the member access operator (**.**). However, classes are created by using the keyword **class**, but structures are created using the keyword *struct*.

Many of the primitive data types that we have used in this book are actually aliases for different structures. For instance, an **int** is defined by structure **System.Int32**, a **Long** by **System.Int64**, and so on. These structures are derived from class *ValueType*, which in turn is derived from class **Object**. In this section, we present structure *Char*, which is the structure for characters.

Most **Char** methods are **static**, take at least one character argument and perform either a test or a manipulation on the character. We present several of these methods in the next example. Figure 15.16 demonstrates **static** methods that test characters to determine whether they are of a specific character type and **static** methods that perform case conversions on characters.

This Windows application contains a prompt, a **TextBox** into which the user can input a character, a button that the user can press after entering a character and a second **TextBox** that displays the output of our analysis. When the user clicks the **Analyze Character** button, event handler **analyzeButton_Click** (lines 32–37) is invoked. This method converts the entered data from a **string** to a **Char**, using method **Convert.ToChar** (line 35). On line 36, we call method **BuildOutput**, which is defined in lines 40–72.

Line 45 uses **Char** method *IsDigit* to determine whether character **inputCharacter** is defined as a digit. If so, the method returns **true**; otherwise, it returns **false**.

Line 48 uses **Char** method *IsLetter* to determine whether character **inputCharacter** is a letter. If so, the method returns **true**; otherwise, it returns **false**. Line 51 uses **Char** method *IsLetterOrDigit* to determine whether character **inputCharacter** is a letter or a digit. If so, the method returns **true**; otherwise, it returns **false**.

```
1   // Fig. 15.16: CharMethods.cs
2   // Demonstrates static character testing methods
3   // from Char structure
4
5   using System;
6   using System.Drawing;
7   using System.Collections;
8   using System.ComponentModel;
9   using System.Windows.Forms;
10  using System.Data;
```

Fig. 15.16 Char's **static** character-testing methods and case-conversion methods. (Part 1 of 3.)

```
11
12    // Form displays information about specific characters.
13    public class StaticCharMethods : System.Windows.Forms.Form
14    {
15       private System.Windows.Forms.Label enterLabel;
16       private System.Windows.Forms.TextBox inputTextBox;
17       private System.Windows.Forms.Button analyzeButton;
18       private System.Windows.Forms.TextBox outputTextBox;
19
20       private System.ComponentModel.Container components = null;
21
22       // The main entry point for the application.
23       [STAThread]
24       static void Main()
25       {
26          Application.Run( new StaticCharMethods() );
27       }
28
29       // Visual Studio .NET generated code
30
31       // handle analyzeButton_Click
32       private void analyzeButton_Click(
33          object sender, System.EventArgs e )
34       {
35          char character = Convert.ToChar( inputTextBox.Text );
36          BuildOutput( character );
37       }
38
39       // display character information in outputTextBox
40       private void BuildOutput( char inputCharacter )
41       {
42          string output;
43
44          output = "is digit: " +
45             Char.IsDigit( inputCharacter ) + "\r\n";
46
47          output += "is letter: " +
48             Char.IsLetter( inputCharacter ) + "\r\n";
49
50          output += "is letter or digit: " +
51             Char.IsLetterOrDigit( inputCharacter ) + "\r\n";
52
53          output += "is lower case: " +
54             Char.IsLower( inputCharacter ) + "\r\n";
55
56          output += "is upper case: " +
57             Char.IsUpper( inputCharacter ) + "\r\n";
58
59          output += "to upper case: " +
60             Char.ToUpper( inputCharacter ) + "\r\n";
61
```

Fig. 15.16 **Char**'s **static** character-testing methods and case-conversion methods. (Part 2 of 3.)

```
62                output += "to lower case: " +
63                    Char.ToLower( inputCharacter ) + "\r\n";
64
65                output += "is punctuation: " +
66                    Char.IsPunctuation( inputCharacter ) + "\r\n";
67
68                output += "is symbol: " + Char.IsSymbol( inputCharacter );
69
70                outputTextBox.Text = output;
71
72        } // end method BuildOutput
73
74    } // end class StaticCharMethods
```

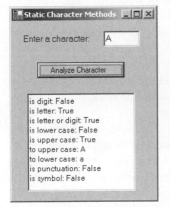 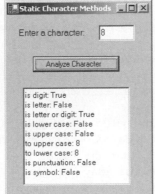 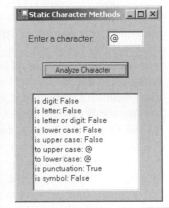

Fig. 15.16 **Char**'s **static** character-testing methods and case-conversion methods. (Part 3 of 3.)

Line 54 uses **Char** method *IsLower* to determine whether character **inputCharacter** is a lowercase letter. If so, the method returns **true**; otherwise, it returns **false**. Line 57 uses **Char** method *IsUpper* to determine whether character **inputCharacter** is an uppercase letter. If so, the method returns **true**; otherwise, it returns **false**. Line 60 uses **Char** method *ToUpper* to convert the character **inputCharacter** to its uppercase equivalent. The method returns the converted character if the character has an uppercase equivalent; otherwise, the method returns its original argument. Line 63 uses **Char** method *ToLower* to convert the character **inputCharacter** to its lowercase equivalent. The method returns the converted character if the character has a lowercase equivalent; otherwise, the method returns its original argument.

Line 66 uses **Char** method *IsPunctuation* to determine whether character **inputCharacter** is a punctuation mark. If so, the method returns **true**; otherwise, it returns **false**. Line 68 uses **Char** method *IsSymbol* to determine whether character **inputCharacter** is a symbol. If so, the method returns **true**; otherwise it returns **false**.

Structure type **Char** also contains other methods not shown in this example. Many of the **static** methods are similar; for instance, *IsWhiteSpace* is used to determine whether a certain character is a whitespace character (e.g., newline, tab or space). The structure also contains several **public** instance methods; many of these, such as methods

ToString and **Equals**, are methods that we have seen before in other classes. This group includes method ***CompareTo***, which is used to compare two character values with one another.

15.16 Card Shuffling and Dealing Simulation

In this section, we use random-number generation to develop a program that simulates the shuffling and dealing of cards. Once created, this program can be implemented in programs that imitate specific card games. We include several exercises at the end of this chapter that require card shuffling and dealing capabilities.

Class **Card** (Fig. 15.17) contains two **string** instance variables—**face** and **suit**—that store references to the face name and suit name of a specific card. The constructor for the class receives two **string**s that it uses to initialize **face** and **suit**. Method **ToString** (lines 20–24) creates a **string** consisting of the **face** of the card and the **suit** of the card.

We develop application **DeckForm** (Fig. 15.18), which creates a deck of 52 playing cards, using **Card** objects. Users can deal each card by clicking the **Deal Card** button. Each dealt card is displayed in a **Label**. Users can also shuffle the deck at any time by clicking the **Shuffle Cards** button.

Method **DeckForm_Load** (lines 35–53 of Fig. 15.18) uses the **for** structure (lines 50–51) to fill the **deck** array with **Card**s. Note that each **Card** is instantiated and initialized with two **string**s—one from the **faces** array (**string**s **"Ace"** through **"King"**) and one from the **suits** array (**"Hearts"**, **"Diamonds"**, **"Clubs"** or **"Spades"**). The calculation **i % 13** always results in a value from **0** to **12** (the thirteen subscripts of the **faces** array), and the calculation **i % 4** always results in a value from **0** to **3** (the four subscripts in the **suits** array). The initialized **deck** array contains the cards with faces ace through king for each suit.

```
1   // Fig. 15.17: Card.cs
2   // Stores suit and face information on each card.
3
4   using System;
5
6   // the representation of a card
7   public class Card
8   {
9      private string face;
10     private string suit;
11
12     public Card( string faceValue,
13        string suitValue )
14     {
15        face = faceValue;
16        suit = suitValue;
17
18     } // end constructor
19
```

Fig. 15.17 Card class. (Part 1 of 2.)

```
20      public override string ToString()
21      {
22         return face + " of " + suit;
23
24      } // end method ToString
25
26   } // end class Card
```

Fig. 15.17 Card class. (Part 2 of 2.)

```
1    // Fig. 15.18: DeckOfCards.cs
2    // Simulating card drawing and shuffling.
3
4    using System;
5    using System.Drawing;
6    using System.Collections;
7    using System.ComponentModel;
8    using System.Windows.Forms;
9    using System.Data;
10
11   // provides the functionality for the form
12   public class DeckForm : System.Windows.Forms.Form
13   {
14      private System.Windows.Forms.Button dealButton;
15      private System.Windows.Forms.Button shuffleButton;
16
17      private System.Windows.Forms.Label displayLabel;
18      private System.Windows.Forms.Label statusLabel;
19
20      private System.ComponentModel.Container components = null;
21
22      private Card[] deck = new Card[ 52 ];
23      private int currentCard;
24
25      // main entry point for application
26      [STAThread]
27      static void Main()
28      {
29         Application.Run( new deckForm() );
30      }
31
32      // Visual Studio .NET generated code
33
34      // handles form at load time
35      private void DeckForm_Load(
36         object sender, System.EventArgs e )
37      {
38         string[] faces = { "Ace", "Deuce", "Three", "Four",
39                            "Five", "Six", "Seven", "Eight",
40                            "Nine", "Ten", "Jack", "Queen",
41                            "King" };
```

Fig. 15.18 Card dealing and shuffling simulation. (Part 1 of 4.)

```
42
43        string[] suits = { "Hearts", "Diamonds", "Clubs",
44                           "Spades" };
45
46        // no cards have been drawn
47        currentCard = -1;
48
49        // initialize deck
50        for ( int i = 0; i < deck.Length; i++ )
51           deck[ i ] = new Card( faces[ i % 13 ], suits[ i % 4 ] );
52
53     } // end method deckForm_Load
54
55     // handles dealButton Click
56     private void dealButton_Click(
57        object sender, System.EventArgs e )
58     {
59        Card dealt = DealCard();
60
61        // if dealt card is null, then no cards left
62        // player must shuffle cards
63        if ( dealt != null )
64        {
65           displayLabel.Text = dealt.ToString();
66           statusLabel.Text = "Card #: " + currentCard;
67        }
68        else
69        {
70           displayLabel.Text = "NO MORE CARDS TO DEAL";
71           statusLabel.Text = "Shuffle cards to continue";
72        }
73     }
74
75     // shuffle cards
76     private void Shuffle()
77     {
78        Random randomNumber = new Random();
79        Card temporaryValue;
80
81        currentCard = -1;
82
83        // swap each card with random card
84        for ( int i = 0; i < deck.Length; i++ )
85        {
86           int j = randomNumber.Next( 52 );
87
88           // swap cards
89           temporaryValue = deck[ i ];
90           deck[ i ] = deck[ j ];
91           deck[ j ] = temporaryValue;
92        }
93
```

Fig. 15.18 Card dealing and shuffling simulation. (Part 2 of 4.)

```
94            dealButton.Enabled = true;
95
96       } // end method Shuffle
97
98       private Card DealCard()
99       {
100          // if there is a card to deal then deal it
101          // otherwise signal that cards need to be shuffled by
102          // disabling dealButton and returning null
103          if ( currentCard + 1 < deck.Length )
104          {
105             currentCard++;
106             return deck[ currentCard ];
107          }
108          else
109          {
110             dealButton.Enabled = false;
111             return null;
112          }
113
114       } // end method DealCard
115
116       // handles shuffleButton Click
117       private void shuffleButton_Click(
118          object sender, System.EventArgs e )
119       {
120          displayLabel.Text = "SHUFFLING...";
121          Shuffle();
122          displayLabel.Text = "DECK IS SHUFFLED";
123
124       } // end method shuffleButton_Click
125
126  } // end class deckForm
```

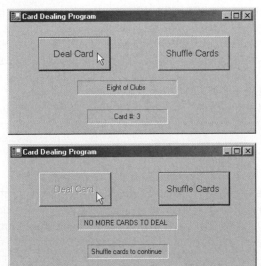

Fig. 15.18 Card dealing and shuffling simulation. (Part 3 of 4.)

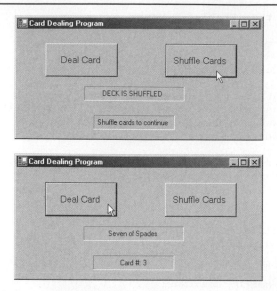

Fig. 15.18 Card dealing and shuffling simulation. (Part 4 of 4.)

When users click the **Deal Card** button, event handler **dealButton_Click** (lines 56–73) invokes method **DealCard** (defined in lines 98–114) to get the next card in the **deck** array. If the **deck** is not empty, the method returns a **Card** object reference; otherwise, it returns **null**. If the reference is not **null**, lines 65–66 display the **Card** in **displayLabel** and display the card number in the **statusLabel**.

If **DealCard** returns a **null** reference, the **string "NO MORE CARDS TO DEAL"** is displayed in **displayLabel**, and the **string "Shuffle cards to continue"** is displayed in **statusLabel**.

When users click the **Shuffle Cards** button, its event-handling method **shuffleButton_Click** (lines 117–124) invokes method **Shuffle** (defined on lines 76–96) to shuffle the cards. The method loops through all 52 cards (array subscripts **0–51**). For each card, the method randomly picks a number between **0** and **51**. Then the current **Card** object and the randomly selected **Card** object are swapped in the array. To shuffle the cards, method **Shuffle** makes a total of only 52 swaps during a single pass of the entire array. When the shuffling is complete, **displayLabel** displays the **string "DECK IS SHUFFLED"**.

15.17 Regular Expressions and Class **Regex**

Regular expressions are specially formatted **string**s used to find patterns in text and can be useful during information validation, to ensure that data is in a particular format. For example, a ZIP code must consist of five digits, and a last name must start with a capital letter. One application of regular expressions is to facilitate the construction of a compiler. Often, a large and complex regular expression is used to validate the syntax of a program. If the program code does not match the regular expression, the compiler knows that there is a syntax error within the code.

The .NET Framework provides several classes to help developers recognize and manipulate regular expressions. Class **Regex** (**System.Text.RegularExpressions** namespace) represents an immutable regular expression. It contains static methods that allow use of the **Regex** class without explicitly instantiating objects of that class. Class **Match** represents the results of a regular expression matching operation.

Class **Regex** provides method **Match**, which returns an object of class **Match** that represents a single regular expression match. **Regex** also provides method **Matches**, which finds all matches of a regular expression in an arbitrary **string** and returns a *MatchCollection* object—i.e., a set of **Match**es.

Common Programming Error 15.4

*When using regular expressions, do not confuse class **Match** with the method **Match**, which belongs to class **Regex**.*

Common Programming Error 15.5

*Visual Studio does not add **System.Text.RegularExpressions** to the list of namespaces imported in the project properties, so a programmer must import it manually with the statement **using System.Text.RegularExpressions**.*

The table in Fig. 15.19 specifies some *character classes* that can be used with regular expressions. A character class is an escape sequence that represents a group of characters.

A *word character* is any alphanumeric character or underscore. A *whitespace* character is a space, a tab, a carriage return, a newline or a form feed. A *digit* is any numeric character. Regular expressions are not limited to these character classes, however. The expressions employ various operators and other forms of notation to search for complex patterns. We discuss several of these techniques in the context of the next example.

Figure 15.20 presents a simple example that employs regular expressions. This program takes birthdays and tries to match them to a regular expression. The expression matches only birthdays that do not occur in April and that belong to people whose names begin with **"J"**.

Character	Matches	Character	Matches
\d	any digit	\D	any non-digit
\w	any word character	\W	any non-word character
\s	any whitespace	\S	any non-whitespace

Fig. 15.19 Character classes.

```
1   // Fig. 15.20: RegexMatches.cs
2   // Demonstrating Class Regex.
3
4   using System;
5   using System.Windows.Forms;
6   using System.Text.RegularExpressions;
7
```

Fig. 15.20 Regular expressions checking birthdays. (Part 1 of 2.)

```
8    // test out regular expressions
9    class RegexMatches
10   {
11       // The main entry point for the application.
12       [STAThread]
13       static void Main( string[] args )
14       {
15           string output = "";
16
17           // create regular expression
18           Regex expression =
19               new Regex( @"J.*\d[0-35-9]-\d\d-\d\d" );
20
21           string string1 = "Jane's Birthday is 05-12-75\n" +
22               "Dave's Birthday is 11-04-68\n" +
23               "John's Birthday is 04-28-73\n" +
24               "Joe's Birthday is 12-17-77";
25
26           // match regular expression to string and
27           // print out all matches
28           foreach ( Match myMatch in expression.Matches( string1 ) )
29               output += myMatch.ToString() + "\n";
30
31           MessageBox.Show( output, "Using class Regex",
32               MessageBoxButtons.OK, MessageBoxIcon.Information );
33
34       } // end method Main
35
36   } // end class RegexMatches
```

Fig. 15.20 Regular expressions checking birthdays. (Part 2 of 2.)

Line 19 creates an instance of class **Regex** and defines the regular expression pattern for which **Regex** will search. The first character in the regular expression, **"J"**, is treated as a literal character. This means that any **string** matching this regular expression is required to start with **"J"**.

In a regular expression, the dot character **"."** matches any single character except a newline character. However, when the dot character is followed by an asterisk, as in the expression **".*"**, it matches any number of unspecified characters. In general, when the operator **"*"** is applied to any expression, the expression will match zero or more occurrences of the expression. By contrast, the application of the operator **"+"** to an expression causes the expression to match one or more occurrences of that expression. For example, both **"A*"** and **"A+"** will match **"A"**, but only **"A*"** will match an empty **string**.

As indicated in Fig. 15.19, **"\d"** matches any numeric digit. To specify sets of characters other than those that have a character class, characters can be listed in square brackets, **[]**. For example, the pattern **"[aeiou]"** can be used to match any vowel. Ranges of characters can be represented by placing a dash (**-**) between two characters. In the example, **"[0-35-9]"** matches only digits in the ranges specified by the pattern. In this case, the pattern matches any digit between **0** and **3** or between **5** and **9**; therefore, it matches any digit except **4**. If the first character in the brackets is the **"^"**, the expression accepts any character other than those indicated. However, it is important to note that **"[^4]"** is not the same as **"[0-35-9]"**; the former matches any nondigit, in addition to the digits other than **4**.

Although the **"-"** character indicates a range when it is enclosed in square brackets, instances of the **"-"** character outside grouping expressions are treated as literal characters. Thus, the regular expression in line 19 searches for a **string** that starts with the letter **"J"**, followed by any number of characters, followed by a two-digit number (of which the second digit cannot be **4**), followed by a dash, another two-digit number, a dash and another two-digit number.

Lines 28–29 use a **foreach** loop to iterate through each **Match** obtained from **expression.Matches**, which used **string1** as an argument. The output in Fig. 15.20 indicates the two matches that were found in **string1**. Notice that both matches conform to the pattern specified by the regular expression.

The asterisk (*****) and plus (**+**) in the previous example are called *quantifiers*. Figure 15.21 lists various quantifiers and their uses.

We have already discussed how the asterisk (*****) and plus (**+**) work. The question mark (**?**) matches zero or one occurrences of the expression that it quantifies. A set of braces containing one number (**{n}**) matches exactly **n** occurrences of the expression it quantifies. We demonstrate this quantifier in the next example. Including a comma after the number enclosed in braces matches at least **n** occurrences of the quantified expression. The set of braces containing two numbers (**{n,m}**), matches between **n** and **m** occurrences of the expression that it qualifies. All of the quantifiers are *greedy*. This means that they will match as many occurrences as they can as long as the match is successful. However, if any of these quantifiers is followed by a question mark (**?**), the quantifier becomes *lazy*. It then will match as few occurrences as possible as long as the match is successful.

The Windows application in Fig. 15.22 presents a more involved example that validates user input via regular expressions.

When a user clicks the **OK** button, the program checks to make sure that none of the fields is empty (lines 49–52). If one or more fields are empty, the program signals the user that all fields must be filled before the program can validate the input information (lines 55–56). Line 59 calls instance method **Focus** of class **TextBox**. Method **Focus** places the cursor within the **TextBox** that made the call. The program then exits the event handler (line 61). If there are no empty fields, the user input is validated. The **Last Name** is validated first (lines 65–74). If it passes the test (i.e., if the **Success** property of the **Match** instance is **true**), control moves on to validate the **First Name** (lines 77–86). This process continues until all **TextBox**es are validated or until a test fails (**Success** is **false**) and the program sends an appropriate error message. If all fields contain valid information, success is signaled, and the program quits.

In the previous example, we searched for substrings that matched a regular expression. In this example, we want to check whether an entire **string** conforms to a regular expression. For example, we want to accept **"Smith"** as a last name, but not **"9@Smith#"**. We achieve this effect by beginning each regular expression with a **"^"** character and ending it with a **"$"** character. The **"^"** and **"$"** characters match the positions at the beginning and end of a **string**, respectively. This forces the regular expression to evaluate the entire **string** and not return a match if a substring matches successfully.

In this program, we use the **static** version of **Regex** method *Match*, which takes an additional parameter specifying the regular expression that we are trying to match. The expression in line 66 uses the square bracket and range notation to match an uppercase first letter, followed by letters of any case—**a-z** matches any lowercase letter, and **A-Z** matches any uppercase letter. The ***** quantifier signifies that the second range of characters may occur zero or more times in the **string**. Thus, this expression matches any **string** consisting of one uppercase letter, followed by zero or more additional letters.

The notation **\s** matches a single whitespace character (lines 90, 102 and 114). The expression **\d{5}**, used in the **Zip** (zip code) field, matches any five digits (line 125). In general, an expression with a positive integer **x** in the curly braces will match any **x** digits. (Notice the importance of the **"^"** and **"$"** characters to prevent zip codes with extra digits from being validated.)

Quantifier	Matches
*	Matches zero or more occurrences of the pattern.
+	Matches one or more occurrences of the pattern.
?	Matches zero or one occurrences of the pattern.
{n}	Matches exactly **n** occurrences.
{n,}	Matches at least **n** occurrences.
{n,m}	Matches between **n** and **m** (inclusive) occurrences.

Fig. 15.21 Quantifiers used in regular expressions.

```
1   // Fig. 15.22: Validate.cs
2   // Validate user information using regular expressions.
3
4   using System;
5   using System.Drawing;
6   using System.Collections;
7   using System.ComponentModel;
8   using System.Windows.Forms;
9   using System.Data;
10  using System.Text.RegularExpressions;
11
12  // use regular expressions to validate strings
13  public class ValidateForm : System.Windows.Forms.Form
14  {
15     private System.Windows.Forms.Label phoneLabel;
16     private System.Windows.Forms.Label zipLabel;
17     private System.Windows.Forms.Label stateLabel;
18     private System.Windows.Forms.Label cityLabel;
19     private System.Windows.Forms.Label addressLabel;
```

Fig. 15.22 Validating user information using regular expressions. (Part 1 of 5.)

```
20       private System.Windows.Forms.Label firstLabel;
21       private System.Windows.Forms.Label lastLabel;
22
23       private System.Windows.Forms.Button okButton;
24
25       private System.Windows.Forms.TextBox phoneTextBox;
26       private System.Windows.Forms.TextBox zipTextBox;
27       private System.Windows.Forms.TextBox stateTextBox;
28       private System.Windows.Forms.TextBox cityTextBox;
29       private System.Windows.Forms.TextBox addressTextBox;
30       private System.Windows.Forms.TextBox firstTextBox;
31       private System.Windows.Forms.TextBox lastTextBox;
32
33       private System.ComponentModel.Container components = null;
34
35       // The main entry point for the application.
36       [STAThread]
37       static void Main()
38       {
39          Application.Run( new validateForm() );
40       }
41
42       // Visual Studio .NET generated code
43
44       // handles okButton Click event
45       private void okButton_Click(
46          object sender, System.EventArgs e )
47       {
48          // ensures no textboxes are empty
49          if ( lastTextBox.Text == "" || firstTextBox.Text == "" ||
50             addressTextBox.Text == "" || cityTextBox.Text == "" ||
51             stateTextBox.Text == "" || zipTextBox.Text == "" ||
52             phoneTextBox.Text == "" )
53          {
54             // display popup box
55             MessageBox.Show( "Please fill in all fields", "Error",
56                MessageBoxButtons.OK, MessageBoxIcon.Error );
57
58             // set focus to lastTextBox
59             lastTextBox.Focus();
60
61             return;
62          }
63
64          // if last name format invalid show message
65          if ( !Regex.Match( lastTextBox.Text,
66             @"^[A-Z][a-zA-Z]*$" ).Success )
67          {
68             // last name was incorrect
69             MessageBox.Show( "Invalid Last Name", "Message",
70                MessageBoxButtons.OK, MessageBoxIcon.Error );
71             lastTextBox.Focus();
72
```

Fig. 15.22 Validating user information using regular expressions. (Part 2 of 5.)

```
73              return;
74          }
75
76          // if first name format invalid show message
77          if ( !Regex.Match( firstTextBox.Text,
78             @"^[A-Z][a-zA-Z]*$" ).Success )
79          {
80             // first name was incorrect
81             MessageBox.Show( "Invalid First Name", "Message",
82                MessageBoxButtons.OK, MessageBoxIcon.Error );
83             firstTextBox.Focus();
84
85             return;
86          }
87
88          // if address format invalid show message
89          if ( !Regex.Match( addressTextBox.Text,
90             @"^[0-9]+\s+([a-zA-Z]+|[a-zA-Z]+\s[a-zA-Z]+)$" ).Success )
91          {
92             // address was incorrect
93             MessageBox.Show( "Invalid Address", "Message",
94                MessageBoxButtons.OK, MessageBoxIcon.Error );
95             addressTextBox.Focus();
96
97             return;
98          }
99
100         // if city format invalid show message
101         if ( !Regex.Match( cityTextBox.Text,
102            @"^([a-zA-Z]+|[a-zA-Z]+\s[a-zA-Z]+)$" ).Success )
103         {
104            // city was incorrect
105            MessageBox.Show( "Invalid City", "Message",
106               MessageBoxButtons.OK, MessageBoxIcon.Error );
107            cityTextBox.Focus();
108
109            return;
110         }
111
112         // if state format invalid show message
113         if ( !Regex.Match( stateTextBox.Text,
114            @"^([a-zA-Z]+|[a-zA-Z]+\s[a-zA-Z]+)$" ).Success )
115         {
116            // state was incorrect
117            MessageBox.Show( "Invalid State", "Message",
118               MessageBoxButtons.OK, MessageBoxIcon.Error );
119            stateTextBox.Focus();
120
121            return;
122         }
123
```

Fig. 15.22 Validating user information using regular expressions. (Part 3 of 5.)

```
124          // if zip code format invalid show message
125          if ( !Regex.Match( zipTextBox.Text, @"^\d{5}$" ).Success )
126          {
127             // zip was incorrect
128             MessageBox.Show( "Invalid Zip Code", "Message",
129                MessageBoxButtons.OK, MessageBoxIcon.Error );
130             zipTextBox.Focus();
131
132             return;
133          }
134
135          // if phone number format invalid show message
136          if ( !Regex.Match( phoneTextBox.Text,
137             @"^[1-9]\d{2}-[1-9]\d{2}-\d{4}$" ).Success )
138          {
139             // phone number was incorrect
140             MessageBox.Show( "Invalid Phone Number", "Message",
141                MessageBoxButtons.OK, MessageBoxIcon.Error );
142             phoneTextBox.Focus();
143
144             return;
145          }
146
147          // information is valid, signal user and exit application
148          this.Hide();
149          MessageBox.Show( "Thank You!", "Information Correct",
150             MessageBoxButtons.OK, MessageBoxIcon.Information );
151
152          Application.Exit();
153
154       } // end method okButton_Click
155
156 } // end class ValidateForm
```

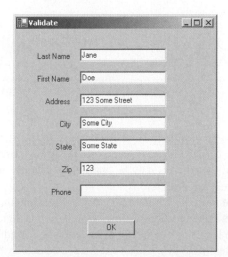

Fig. 15.22 Validating user information using regular expressions. (Part 4 of 5.)

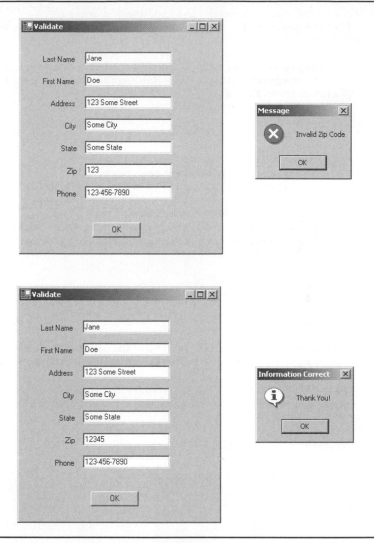

Fig. 15.22 Validating user information using regular expressions. (Part 5 of 5.)

The character "|" matches the expression to its left or to its right. For example, **Hi (John|Jane)** matches both **Hi John** and **Hi Jane**. Note the use of parentheses to group parts of the regular expression. Quantifiers may be applied to patterns enclosed in parentheses to create more complex regular expressions.

The **Last Name** and **First Name** fields both accept **string**s of any length, that begin with an uppercase letter. The **Address** field matches a number of at least one digit, followed by a space and then either one or more letters or else one or more letters followed by a space and another series of one or more letters (line 90). Therefore, **"10 Broadway"** and **"10 Main Street"** are both valid addresses. The **City** (line 102) and **State** (line 114) fields match any word of at least one character or, alternatively, any two words of at least one character if the words are separated by a single space. This means both **Waltham** and **West Newton** would match. As previously stated, the **Zip** code must be a five-digit number (line 125). The **Phone** number must be of the form **xxx-yyy-yyyy**, where the **x**s represent the area code and **y**s the number (line 137). The first **x** and the first **y** cannot be zero.

Sometimes it is useful to replace parts of a **string** with another, or split a **string** according to a regular expression. For this purpose, the **Regex** class provides **static** and instance versions of methods *Replace* and *Split*, which are demonstrated in Fig. 15.23.

```
1    // Fig. 15.23: RegexSubstitution.cs
2    // Using Regex method Replace.
3
4    using System;
5    using System.Text.RegularExpressions;
6    using System.Windows.Forms;
7
8    // Summary description for RegexSubstitution.
9    public class RegexSubstitution1
10   {
11
12       // The main entry point for the application.
13       static void Main( string[] args )
14       {
15           string testString1 =
16               "This sentence ends in 5 stars *****";
17
18           string testString2 = "1, 2, 3, 4, 5, 6, 7, 8";
19           Regex testRegex1 = new Regex( "stars" );
20           Regex testRegex2 = new Regex( @"\d" );
21           string[] results;
22           string output = "Original String 1\t\t\t" + testString1;
23
24           testString1 = Regex.Replace( testString1, @"\*", "^" );
25
26           output += "\n^ substituted for *\t\t\t" + testString1;
27
28           testString1 = testRegex1.Replace( testString1, "carets" );
29
30           output += "\n\"carets\" substituted for \"stars\"\t\t" +
31               testString1;
32
33           output += "\nEvery word replaced by \"word\"\t" +
34               Regex.Replace( testString1, @"\w+", "word" );
35
36           output += "\n\nOriginal String 2\t\t\t" + testString2;
37
38           output += "\nFirst 3 digits replaced by \"digit\"\t\t" +
39               testRegex2.Replace( testString2, "digit", 3 );
40
41           output += "\nString split at commas\t\t[";
42
43           results = Regex.Split( testString2, @",\s*" );
44
```

Fig. 15.23 **Regex** methods **Replace** and **Split**. (Part 1 of 2.)

```
45          foreach ( string resultString in results )
46          {
47             output += "\"" + resultString + "\", ";
48          }
49
50          output = output.Substring( 0, output.Length - 2 ) + "]";
51
52          MessageBox.Show( output,
53             "Substitution using regular expressions" );
54
55       } // end method Main
56
57    } // end class RegexSubstitution
```

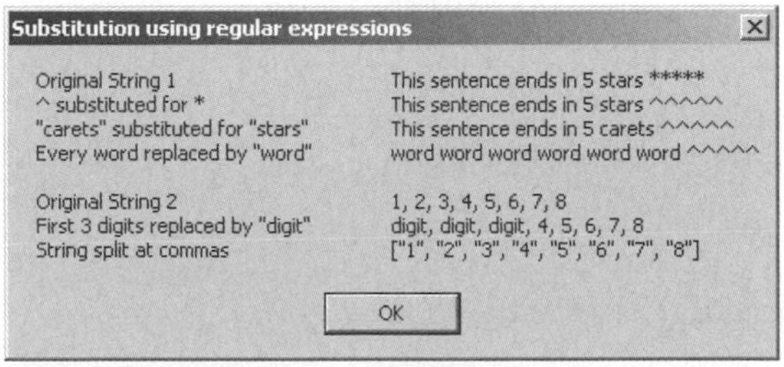

Fig. 15.23 Regex methods **Replace** and **Split**. (Part 2 of 2.)

Method **Replace** replaces text in a **string** with new text wherever the original **string** matches a regular expression. We present two versions of this method in Fig. 15.23. The first version (line 24) is **static** and takes three parameters—the **string** to modify, the **string** containing the regular expression to match and the replacement **string**. Here, **Replace** replaces every instance of **"*"** in **testString1** with **"^"**. Notice that the regular expression (**@"*"**) precedes character * with a backslash, \. Normally, * is a quantifier indicating that a regular expression should match any number of occurrences of a preceding pattern. However, in line 24, we want to find all occurrences of the literal character *; to do this, we must escape character * with character \. By escaping a special regular expression character with a \, we inform the regular-expression matching engine to find the actual character, as opposed to what it represents in a regular expression. The second version of method **Replace** (line 28) is an instance method that uses the regular expression passed to the constructor for **testRegex1** (line 19) to perform the replacement operation. In this case, every match for the regular expression **"stars"** in **testString1** is replaced with **"carets"**.

Line 20 instantiates **testRegex2** with argument **@"\d"**. The call to instance method **Replace** in line 39 takes three arguments—a **string** to modify, a **string** containing the replacement text and an **int** specifying the number of replacements to make. In other words, this version of **Replace** replaces the first three instances of a digit (**"\d"**) in **testString2** with the text **"digit"** (line 39).

Method **Split** divides a **string** into several substrings. The original **string** is broken in any location that matches a specified regular expression. Method **Split** returns an array containing the substrings between matches for the regular expression. In line 43, we use the **static** version of method **Split** to separate a **string** of comma-separated integers. The first argument is the **string** to split; the second argument is the regular expression. In this case, we use the regular expression **@",\s*"** to separate the substrings wherever a comma occurs. By matching any whitespace characters, we eliminate extra spaces from the resulting substrings.

SUMMARY

- Characters are the fundamental building blocks of C# program code. Every program is composed of a sequence of characters that is interpreted by the compiler as a series of instructions used to accomplish a task.

- A **string** is a series of characters treated as a single unit. A **string** may include letters, digits and various special characters, such as **+**, **-**, *****, **/**, **$** and others.

- All characters correspond to numeric codes. When the computer compares two **string**s, it actually compares the numeric codes of the characters in the **string**s.

- Method **Equals** uses a lexicographical comparison, meaning that if a certain **string** has a higher value than another **string**, it would be found later in a dictionary. Method **Equals** compares the integer Unicode values that represent each character in each **string**.

- Method **CompareTo** returns **0** if the **string**s are equal, a negative number if the **string** that invokes **CompareTo** is less than the **string** passed as an argument, a positive number if the **string** that invokes **CompareTo** is greater than the **string** passed as an argument. Method **CompareTo** uses a lexicographical comparison.

- A hash table stores information, using a special calculation on the object to be stored that produces a hash code. The hash code is used to choose the location in the table at which to store the object.

- Class **Object** defines method **GetHashCode** to perform the hash-code calculation. This method is inherited by all subclasses of **Object**. Method **GetHashCode** is overridden by **String** to provide a good hash-code distribution based on the contents of the **string**.

- Class **String** provides two **Substring** methods to enable a new **string** to be created by copying part of an existing **string**.

- **String** method **IndexOf** locates the first occurrence of a character or a substring in a **string**. Method **LastIndexOf** locates the last occurrence of a character or a substring in a **string**.

- **String** method **StartsWith** determines whether a **string** starts with the characters specified as an argument. **String** method **EndsWith** determines whether a **string** ends with the characters specified as an argument.

- The **static** method **Concat** of class **String** concatenates two **string**s and returns a new **string** containing the characters from both original **string**s.

- Methods **Replace**, **ToUpper**, **ToLower**, **Trim** and **Remove** are provided for more advanced **string** manipulation.

- The **String** class provides many capabilities for processing **string**s. However, once a **string** is created, its contents can never change. Class **StringBuilder** is available for creating and manipulating dynamic **string**s, i.e., **string**s that can change.

- Class **StringBuilder** provides **Length** and **Capacity** properties to return the number of characters currently in a **StringBuilder** and the number of characters that can be stored in a **StringBuilder** without allocating more memory, respectively. These properties also can be used to increase or decrease the length or the capacity of the **StringBuilder**.

- Method **EnsureCapacity** allows programmers to guarantee that a **StringBuilder** has a minimum capacity. Method **EnsureCapacity** attempts to double the capacity. If this value is greater than the value that the programmer wishes to ensure, this will be the new capacity. Otherwise, **EnsureCapacity** alters the capacity to make it one more than the requested number.

- Class **StringBuilder** provides 19 overloaded **Append** methods to allow various data-type values to be added to the end of a **StringBuilder**. Versions are provided for each of the primitive data types and for character arrays, **String**s and **Object**s.

- The braces in a format **string** specify how to format a specific piece of information. Formats have the form **{X[,Y][:FormatString]}**, where **X** is the number of the argument to be formatted, counting from zero. **Y** is an optional argument, which can be positive or negative. **Y** indicates how many characters should be in the result of formatting; if the resulting **string** is less than this number, it will be padded with spaces to make up for the difference. A positive integer means the **string** will be right aligned; a negative one means it will be left aligned. The optional **FormatString** indicates what kind of formatting should be applied to the argument: Currency, decimal, or scientific, among others.

- Class **StringBuilder** provides 19 overloaded **Insert** methods to allow various data-type values to be inserted at any position in a **StringBuilder**. Versions are provided for each of the primitive data types and for character arrays, **String**s and **Object**s.

- Class **StringBuilder** also provides method **Remove** for deleting any portion of a **StringBuilder**.

- Another useful method included with **StringBuilder** is **Replace**. **Replace** searches for a specified **string** or character and substitutes another in its place.

- C# provides **struct**s, program building blocks similar to classes.

- Structures are in many ways similar to classes, the largest difference between them being that structures encapsulate value types, whereas classes encapsulate reference types.

- Many of the primitive data types that we have been using are actually aliases for different structures. These structures are derived from class **ValueType**, which in turn is derived from class **Object**.

- **Char** is a structure that represents characters.

- Method **Char.Parse** converts data into a character.

- Method **Char.IsDigit** determines whether a character is a defined Unicode digit.

- Method **Char.IsLetter** determines whether a character is a letter.

- Method **Char.IsLetterOrDigit** determines whether a character is a letter or a digit.

- Method **Char.IsLower** determines whether a character is a lowercase letter.

- Method **Char.IsUpper** determines whether a character is an uppercase letter.

- Method **Char.ToUpper** converts a character to its uppercase equivalent.

- Method **Char.ToLower** converts a character to its lowercase equivalent.

- Method **Char.IsPunctuation** determines whether a character is a punctuation mark.

- Method **Char.IsSymbol** determines whether a character is a symbol.

- Method **Char.IsWhiteSpace** determines whether a character is a whitespace character.

- **Char** method **CompareTo** compares two character values.

- Regular expressions find patterns in text.

- The .NET Framework provides class **Regex** to aid developers in recognizing and manipulating regular expressions. **Regex** provides method **Match**, which returns an object of class **Match**. This object represents a single match in a regular expression. **Regex** also provides the method

Matches, which finds all matches of a regular expression in an arbitrary **string** and returns a **MatchCollection**—a set of **Match**es.

- Both classes **Regex** and **Match** are in namespace **System.Text.RegularExpressions**.

- In general, applying the quantifier ***** to any expression will match zero or more occurrences of that expression, and applying the quantifier **+** will match one or more occurrences of that expression.

- The pattern **"[0-35-9]"** is a regular expression that matches one in a range of characters. This **string** will match any digit **0-3** and **5-9**, so it will match any digit except **4**.

- The character "**|**" matches the expression to its left or to its right. For example, **"Hi (John|Jane)"** matches both **"Hi John"** and **"Hi Jane"**.

- Method **Replace** replaces those substrings in a **string** that match a certain regular expression with a specified **string**.

TERMINOLOGY

+ operator
+= concatenation operator
== comparison operator
alphabetizing
Append method of class **StringBuilder**
AppendFormat method of class
    StringBuilder
ArgumentOutOfRangeException
Capacity property of **StringBuilder**
char array
Char structure
Chars property of class **String**
character
character class
CompareTo method of class **String**
CompareTo method of structure **Char**
Concat method of class **String**
CopyTo method of class **String**
Enabled property of class **Control**
EndsWith method of class **String**
EnsureCapacity method of class
    StringBuilder
Equals method of class **String**
format string
garbage collector
GetHashCode
greedy quantifier
hash code
hash table
immutable **String**
IndexOf method of class **String**
IndexOfAny method of class **String**
IsDigit method of structure **Char**
IsLetter method of structure **Char**

IsLetterOrDigit method of structure **Char**
IsLower method of structure **Char**
IsPunctuation method of structure **Char**
IsSymbol method of structure **Char**
IsUpper method of structure **Char**
IsWhiteSpace method of structure **Char**
LastIndexOf method of class **String**
LastIndexOfAny method of class **String**
lazy quantifier
Length property of class **String**
Length property of class **StringBuilder**
lexicographical comparison
literal strings
Match class
MatchCollection class
page-layout software
Parse method of structure **Char**
quantifier
random-number generation
Regex class
Remove method of class **StringBuilder**
Replace method of class **Regex**
Replace method of class **String**
Replace method of class **StringBuilder**
special characters
Split method of class **Regex**
StartsWith method of class **String**
String class
string literal
string reference
StringBuilder class
struct
Substring method of class **String**
Success property of class **Match**

System namespace
System.Text namespace
System.Text.RegularExpressions
    namespace
text editor
ToLower method of class String
ToLower method of structure Char
ToString method of class String
ToString method of StringBuilder

ToUpper method of class String
ToUpper method of structure Char
trailing whitespace characters
Trim method of class String
Unicode character set
ValueType class
whitespace characters
word character

SELF-REVIEW EXERCISES

15.1   State whether each of the following is *true* or *false*. If *false*, explain why.
a) When **string**s are compared with ==, the result is *true* if the **string**s contain the same values.
b) A **string** can be modified after it is created.
c) Class **String** has no **ToString** method.
d) **StringBuilder** method **EnsureCapacity** sets the **StringBuilder** instance's capacity to the argument's value.
e) The method **Equals** and the equality operator work the same for **string**s.
f) Method **Trim** removes all whitespace at the beginning and the end of a **string**.
g) A regular expression matches a **string** to a pattern.
h) It is always better to use **string**s rather than **StringBuilder**s because **string**s containing the same value will reference the same object in memory.
i) Class **String** method **ToUpper** capitalizes just the first letter of the **string**.
j) The expression **\d** in a regular expression denotes all letters.

15.2   Fill in the blanks in each of the following statements:
a) To concatenate **string**s, use the _____ operator or class _____ method _____.
b) Method **Compare** of class **String** uses a _____ comparison of **string**s.
c) Class **Regex** is located in namespace _____.
d) **StringBuilder** method _____ first formats the specified **string**, then concatenates it to the end of the **StringBuilder**.
e) If the arguments to a **Substring** method call are out of range, an _____ exception is thrown.
f) **Regex** method _____ changes all occurrences of a pattern in a **string** to a specified **string**.
g) Method _____ is inherited by every object and calculates its hash code.
h) A **C** in a format string means to output the number as _____.
i) Regular expression quantifier _____ matches zero or more occurrences of an expression.
j) Regular expression operator _____ inside square brackets will not match any of the characters in that set of brackets.

ANSWERS TO SELF-REVIEW EXERCISES

15.1   a) True. b) False. **string**s are immutable and cannot be modified after they are created. **StringBuilder** objects can be modified after they are created. c) False. Class **String** inherits a **ToString** method from class **Object**. d) True. e) True. f) True. g) True. h) False. **StringBuilder** should be used if the **string** is to be modified. i) False. Class **String** method **ToUpper** capitalizes all letters in the **string**. j) False. The expression **\d** denotes all decimals in a regular expression.

15.2   a) **+**, **StringBuilder**, **Append**. b) lexicographical. c) **System.Text.RegularEx-pressions**. d) **AppendFormat** e) **ArgumentOutOfRangeException**. f) **Replace**. g) **GetHashCode**. h) currency. i) *****. j) **^**.

EXERCISES

15.3   Modify the program in Fig. 15.18 so that the card-dealing method deals a five-card poker hand. Then write the following additional methods:

- a) Determine if the hand contains a pair.
- b) Determine if the hand contains two pairs.
- c) Determine if the hand contains three of a kind (e.g., three jacks).
- d) Determine if the hand contains four of a kind (e.g., four aces).
- e) Determine if the hand contains a flush (i.e., all five cards of the same suit).
- f) Determine if the hand contains a straight (i.e., five cards of consecutive face values).
- g) Determine if the hand contains a full house (i.e., two cards of one face value and three cards of another face value).

15.4   Use the methods developed in Exercise 15.3 to write a program that deals two five-card poker hands, evaluates each hand and determines which is the better hand.

15.5   Write an application that uses **String** method **CompareTo** to compare two **string**s input by the user. Output whether the first **string** is less than, equal to or greater than the second.

15.6   Write an application that uses random-number generation to create sentences. Use four arrays of **string**s, called **article**, **noun**, **verb** and **preposition**. Create a sentence by selecting a word at random from each array in the following order: **article**, **noun**, **verb**, **preposition**, **article** and **noun**. As each word is picked, concatenate it to the previous words in the sentence. The words should be separated by spaces. When the final sentence is output, it should start with a capital letter and end with a period. The program should generate 20 sentences and output them to a text area.

The arrays should be filled as follows: The **article** array should contain the articles **"the"**, **"a"**, **"one"**, **"some"** and **"any"**; the **noun** array should contain the nouns **"boy"**, **"girl"**, **"dog"**, **"town"** and **"car"**; the **verb** array should contain the past-tense verbs **"drove"**, **"jumped"**, **"ran"**, **"walked"** and **"skipped"**; the **preposition** array should contain the prepositions **"to"**, **"from"**, **"over"**, **"under"** and **"on"**.

After the preceding program is written, modify the program to produce a short story consisting of several of these sentences. (How about the possibility of a random term-paper writer!)

15.7   (*Pig Latin*) Write an application that encodes English language phrases into pig Latin. Pig Latin is a form of coded language often used for amusement. Many variations exist in the methods used to form pig Latin phrases. For simplicity, use the following algorithm:

To translate each English word into a pig Latin word, place the first letter of the English word at the end of the word and add the letters "**ay**." Thus, the word "**jump**" becomes "**umpjay**," the word "**the**" becomes "**hetay**" and the word "**computer**" becomes "**omputercay**." Blanks between words remain as blanks. Assume the following: The English phrase consists of words separated by blanks, there are no punctuation marks and all words have two or more letters. Enable the user to input a sentence. Use techniques discussed in this chapter to divide the sentence into separate words. Method **GetPigLatin** should translate a single word into pig Latin. Keep a running display of all the converted sentences in a text area.

15.8   Write a program that reads a five-letter word from the user and produces all possible three-letter words that can be derived from the letters of the five-letter word. For example, the three-letter words produced from the word "bathe" include the commonly used words "ate," "bat," "bet," "tab," "hat," "the" and "tea."

16

Graphics and Multimedia

Objectives

- To understand graphics contexts and graphics objects.
- To be able to manipulate colors and fonts.
- To understand and be able to use GDI+ **Graphics** methods to draw lines, rectangles, **string**s and images.
- To be able to use class **Image** to manipulate and display images.
- To be able to draw complex shapes from simple shapes with class **GraphicsPath**.
- To be able to use Windows Media Player and Microsoft Agent in a C# application.

One picture is worth ten thousand words.
Chinese proverb

Treat nature in terms of the cylinder, the sphere, the cone, all in perspective.
Paul Cezanne

Nothing ever becomes real till it is experienced—even a proverb is no proverb to you till your life has illustrated it.
John Keats

A picture shows me at a glance what it takes dozens of pages of a book to expound.
Ivan Sergeyevich

Outline

16.1 Introduction

In this chapter, we overview C#'s tools for drawing two-dimensional shapes and for controlling colors and fonts. C# supports graphics that enable programmers to enhance their Windows applications visually. The FCL contains many sophisticated drawing capabilities as part of namespace **System.Drawing** and the other namespaces that make up the .NET resource *GDI+*. GDI+, an extension of the Graphical Device Interface, is an application programming interface (API) that provides classes for creating two-dimensional vector graphics (a way of describing graphics so that they may be easily manipulated with high-performance techniques), manipulating fonts and inserting images. GDI+ expands GDI by simplifying the programming model and introducing several new features, such as graphics paths, extended image file format support and alpha blending. Using the GDI+ API, programmers can create images without worrying about the platform-specific details of their graphics hardware.

We begin with an introduction to the .NET framework's drawing capabilities. We then present more powerful drawing capabilities, such as changing the styles of lines used to draw shapes and controlling the colors and patterns of filled shapes.

Figure 16.1 depicts a portion of the **System.Drawing** class hierarchy, which includes several of the basic graphics classes and structures covered in this chapter. The most commonly used components of GDI+ reside in the **System.Drawing** and **System.Drawing.Drawing2D** namespaces.

Class **Graphics** contains methods used for drawing **string**s, lines, rectangles and other shapes on a **Control**. The drawing methods of class **Graphics** usually require a **Pen** or **Brush** object to render a specified shape. The **Pen** draws shape outlines; the **Brush** draws solid objects.

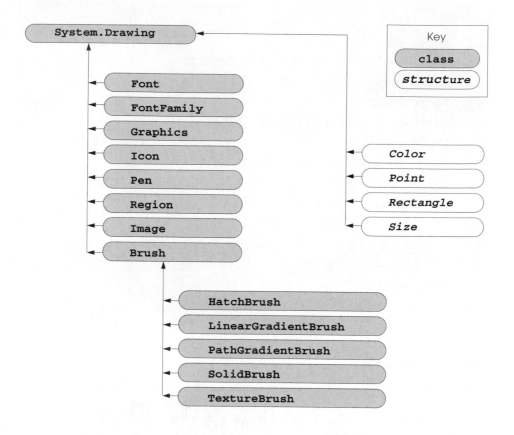

Fig. 16.1   System.Drawing namespace's classes and structures.

Structure **Color** contains numerous **static** properties, which set the colors of various graphical components, plus methods that allow users to create new colors. Class *Font* contains properties that define unique fonts. Class *FontFamily* contains methods for obtaining font information.

To begin drawing in C#, we first must understand GDI+'s *coordinate system* (Fig. 16.2), a scheme for identifying every point on the screen. By default, the upper-left corner of a GUI component (such as a **Panel** or a **Form**) has the coordinates (0, 0). A coordinate pair has both an *x-coordinate* (the *horizontal coordinate*) and a *y-coordinate* (the *vertical coordinate*). The *x*-coordinate is the horizontal distance (to the right) from the upper-left corner. The *y*-coordinate is the vertical distance (downward) from the upper-left corner. The *x-axis* defines every horizontal coordinate, and the *y-axis* defines every vertical coordinate. Programmers position text and shapes on the screen by specifying their (*x,y*) coordinates. Coordinate units are measured in *pixels* ("picture elements"), which are the smallest units of resolution on a display monitor.

The **System.Drawing** namespace provides structures **Rectangle** and **Point**. The *Rectangle structure* defines rectangular shapes and dimensions. The *Point* *structure* represents the *x-y* coordinates of a point on a two-dimensional plane.

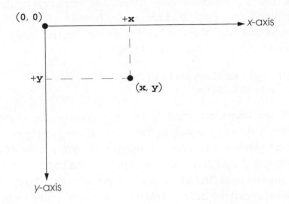

Fig. 16.2   GDI+ coordinate system. Units are measured in pixels.

Portability Tip 16.1

Different display monitors have different resolutions, so the density of pixels on such monitors will vary. This might cause the sizes of graphics to appear different on different monitors.

In the remainder of this chapter, we explore techniques for manipulating images and creating smooth animations. We also discuss class **Image**, which can store and manipulate images from various file formats. Later, we explain how to combine the graphical rendering capabilities covered in the early sections of the chapter with those for image manipulation.

16.2 Graphics Contexts and Graphics Objects

A C# *graphics context* represents a drawing surface that enables drawing on the screen. A **Graphics** object manages a graphics context by controlling how information is drawn. **Graphics** objects contain methods for drawing, font manipulation, color manipulation and other graphics-related actions. Every Windows application that derives from class **System.Windows.Forms.Form** inherits a **virtual** *OnPaint* event handler where most graphics operations are performed. The arguments to the **OnPaint** method include a **PaintEventArgs** object from which we can obtain a **Graphics** object for the control. We must obtain the **Graphics** object on each call to the method, because the properties of the graphics context that the graphics object represents could change. The **OnPaint** method triggers the **Control**'s *Paint* event.

When displaying graphical information on a **Form**'s client area, programmers can override the **OnPaint** method to retrieve a **Graphics** object from argument **PaintEventArgs** or to create a new **Graphics** object associated with the appropriate surface. We demonstrate these techniques of drawing in C# later in the chapter.

To override the inherited **OnPaint** method, use the following method definition:

```
protected override void OnPaint( PaintEventArgs e )
```

Next, extract the incoming **Graphics** object from the **PaintEventArgs** argument:

```
Graphics graphicsObject = e.Graphics;
```

Variable **graphicsObject** now is available to draw shapes and **string**s on the form.

Calling the **OnPaint** method raises the **Paint** event. Instead of overriding the **OnPaint** method, programmers can add an event handler for the **Paint** event. Visual Studio .NET generates the **Paint** event handler in this form:

```
protected void MyEventHandler_Paint(
    object sender, PaintEventArgs e )
```

Programmers seldom call the **OnPaint** method directly, because the drawing of graphics is an *event-driven process*. An event—such as the covering, uncovering or resizing of a window—calls the **OnPaint** method of that form. Similarly, when any control (such as a **TextBox** or **Label**) is displayed, the program calls that control's **Paint** method.

If programmers need to cause method **OnPaint** to run explicitly, they should not call method **OnPaint**. Rather, they can call the *Invalidate* method (inherited from **Control**). This method refreshes a control's client area and implicitly repaints all graphical components. C# contains several overloaded **Invalidate** methods that allow programmers to update portions of the client area.

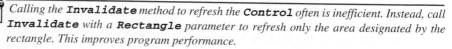

Performance Tip 16.1

*Calling the **Invalidate** method to refresh the **Control** often is inefficient. Instead, call **Invalidate** with a **Rectangle** parameter to refresh only the area designated by the rectangle. This improves program performance.*

Controls, such as **Label**s and **Button**s, do not have their own graphics contexts, but one can be created. To draw on a control, first create its graphics object by invoking the **CreateGraphics** method:

> **Graphics** *graphicsObject* = *controlName*.**CreateGraphics();**

where *graphicsObject* represents an instance of class **Graphics** and *controlName* is any control. Now, a programmer can use the methods provided in class **Graphics** to draw on the control.

16.3 Color Control

Colors can enhance a program's appearance and help convey meaning. For example, a red traffic light indicates stop, yellow indicates caution and green indicates go.

Structure **Color** defines methods and constants used to manipulate colors. Because it is a lightweight object that performs only a handful of operations and stores **static** fields, **Color** is implemented as a structure, rather than as a class.

Every color can be created from a combination of alpha, red, green and blue components. Together, these components are called *ARGB values*. All four ARGB components are **byte**s that represent integer values in the range from 0 to 255. The alpha value determines the opacity of the color. For example, the alpha value 0 results in a transparent color, the value 255 in an opaque color. Alpha values between 0 and 255 result in a weighted blending effect of the color's RGB value with that of any background color, causing a semi-transparent effect. The first number in the RGB value defines the amount of red in the color, the second defines the amount of green and the third defines the amount of blue. The larger the value, the greater the amount of that particular color. C# enables programmers to choose from almost 17 million colors. If a particular computer cannot display all these colors, it will display the color closest to the one specified. Figure 16.3 summarizes some predefined **Color** constants, and Fig. 16.4 describes several **Color** methods and properties.

The table in Fig. 16.4 describes two ***FromArgb*** method calls. One takes three **int** arguments, and one takes four **int** arguments (all argument values must be between 0 and 255). Both take **int** arguments specifying the amount of red, green and blue. The overloaded version takes four arguments and allows the user to specify alpha; the three-argument version defaults the alpha to 255. Both methods return a **Color** object representing the specified values. **Color** properties ***A***, ***R***, ***G*** and ***B*** return **byte**s that represent **int** values from 0 to 255, corresponding to the amounts of alpha, red, green and blue, respectively.

Programmers draw shapes and **string**s with **Brush**es and **Pen**s. A **Pen**, which functions similarly to an ordinary pen, is used to draw lines. Most drawing methods require a **Pen** object. The overloaded **Pen** constructors allow programmers to specify the colors and widths of the lines that they wish to draw. The **System.Drawing** namespace also provides a **Pens** collection containing predefined **Pen**s.

Constants in structure Color (all are public static)	RGB value	Constants in structure Color (all are public static)	RGB value
Orange	255, 200, 0	White	255, 255, 255
Pink	255, 175, 175	Gray	128, 128, 128
Cyan	0, 255, 255	DarkGray	64, 64, 64
Magenta	255, 0, 255	Red	255, 0, 0
Yellow	255, 255, 0	Green	0, 255, 0
Black	0, 0, 0	Blue	0, 0, 255

Fig. 16.3 Color structure **static** constants and their RGB values.

Structure Color methods and properties	Description
Common Methods	
static **FromArgb**	Creates a color based on red, green and blue values expressed as **int**s from 0 to 255. Overloaded version allows specification of alpha, red, green and blue values.
static **FromName**	Creates a color from a name, passed as a **string**.
Common Properties	
A	**byte** between 0 and 255, representing the alpha component.
R	**byte** between 0 and 255, representing the red component.

Fig. 16.4 Color structure members. (Part 1 of 2.)

Structure **Color** methods and properties	Description
G	**byte** between 0 and 255, representing the green component.
B	**byte** between 0 and 255, representing the blue component.

Fig. 16.4 **Color** structure members. (Part 2 of 2.)

All classes derived from abstract class **Brush** define objects that color the interiors of graphical shapes (for example, the **SolidBrush** constructor takes a **Color** object—the color to draw). In most **Fill** methods, **Brush**es fill a space with a color, pattern or image. Figure 16.5 summarizes various **Brush**es and their functions.

The application in Fig. 16.6 demonstrates several of the methods and properties described in Fig. 16.4. It displays two overlapping rectangles, allowing the user to experiment with color values and color names.

Class	Description
HatchBrush	Uses a rectangular brush to fill a region with a pattern. The pattern is defined by a member of the **HatchStyle** enumeration, a foreground color (with which the pattern is drawn) and a background color.
LinearGradient-Brush	Fills a region with a gradual blend of one color into another. Linear gradients are defined along a line. They can be specified by the two colors, the angle of the gradient and either the width of a rectangle or two points.
SolidBrush	Fills a region with one color. Defined by a **Color** object.
TextureBrush	Fills a region by repeating a specified **Image** across the surface.

Fig. 16.5   Classes that derive from class **Brush**.

```
1   // Fig 16.6: ShowColors.cs
2   // Using different colors in C#.
3
4   using System;
5   using System.Drawing;
6   using System.Collections;
7   using System.ComponentModel;
8   using System.Windows.Forms;
9   using System.Data;
10
```

Fig. 16.6   Color value and alpha demonstration. (Part 1 of 3.)

```csharp
11     // allows users to change colors using the name of
12     // the color or argb values
13     class ShowColors : System.Windows.Forms.Form
14     {
15         private System.ComponentModel.Container components = null;
16
17         // color for back rectangle
18         private Color behindColor = Color.Wheat;
19         private System.Windows.Forms.GroupBox nameGroup;
20         private System.Windows.Forms.GroupBox colorValueGroup;
21         private System.Windows.Forms.TextBox colorNameTextBox;
22         private System.Windows.Forms.TextBox alphaTextBox;
23         private System.Windows.Forms.TextBox redTextBox;
24         private System.Windows.Forms.TextBox greenTextBox;
25         private System.Windows.Forms.TextBox blueTextBox;
26         private System.Windows.Forms.Button colorValueButton;
27         private System.Windows.Forms.Button colorNameButton;
28
29         // color for front rectangle
30         private Color frontColor =
31             Color.FromArgb( 100, 0 , 0, 255 );
32
33         [STAThread]
34         static void Main()
35         {
36             Application.Run( new ShowColors() );
37         }
38
39         // Visual Studio .NET generated code
40
41         // override Form OnPaint method
42         protected override void OnPaint( PaintEventArgs e )
43         {
44             Graphics graphicsObject = e.Graphics; // get graphics
45
46             // create text brush
47             SolidBrush textBrush = new SolidBrush( Color.Black );
48
49             // create solid brush
50             SolidBrush brush = new SolidBrush( Color.White );
51
52             // draw white background
53             graphicsObject.FillRectangle( brush, 4, 4, 275, 180 );
54
55             // display name of behindColor
56             graphicsObject.DrawString( behindColor.Name, this.Font,
57                 textBrush, 40, 5 );
58
59             // set brush color and display back rectangle
60             brush.Color = behindColor;
61
62             graphicsObject.FillRectangle( brush, 45, 20, 150, 120 );
63
```

Fig. 16.6   Color value and alpha demonstration. (Part 2 of 3.)

```
64          // display Argb values of front color
65          graphicsObject.DrawString( "Alpha: " + frontColor.A +
66             " Red: " + frontColor.R + " Green: " + frontColor.G
67             + " Blue: " + frontColor.B, this.Font, textBrush,
68             55, 165 );
69
70          // set brush color and display front rectangle
71          brush.Color = frontColor;
72
73          graphicsObject.FillRectangle( brush, 65, 35, 170, 130 );
74
75       } // end method OnPaint
76
77       // handle colorValueButton click event
78       private void colorValueButton_Click(
79          object sender, System.EventArgs e )
80       {
81          // obtain new front color from text boxes
82          frontColor = Color.FromArgb( Convert.ToInt32(
83             alphaTextBox.Text ),
84             Convert.ToInt32( redTextBox.Text ),
85             Convert.ToInt32( greenTextBox.Text ),
86             Convert.ToInt32( blueTextBox.Text ) );
87
88          Invalidate(); // refresh Form
89       }
90
91       // handle colorNameButton click event
92       private void colorNameButton_Click(
93          object sender, System.EventArgs e )
94       {
95          // set behindColor to color specified in text box
96          behindColor = Color.FromName( colorNameTextBox.Text );
97
98          Invalidate(); // refresh Form
99       }
100
101   } // end class ShowColors
```

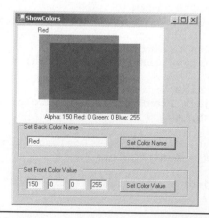

Fig. 16.6   Color value and alpha demonstration. (Part 3 of 3.)

When the application begins its execution, it calls class **ShowColors**'s **OnPaint** method to paint the window. Line 44 gets a reference to **PaintEventArgs e**'s **Graphics** object and assigns it to **Graphics** object **graphicsObject**. Lines 47–50 create a black and a white **SolidBrush** for drawing on the form. Class **SolidBrush** derives from abstract base class **Brush**; programmers can draw solid shapes with the **SolidBrush**.

Graphics method *FillRectangle* draws a solid white rectangle with the **Brush** supplied as a parameter (line 53). It takes as parameters a brush, the *x*- and *y*-coordinates of a point and the width and height of the rectangle to draw. The point represents the upper-left corner of the rectangle. Lines 56–57 display the **string Name** property of the **Brush**'s **Color** property with the **Graphics DrawString** method. The programmer has access to several overloaded **DrawString** methods; the version demonstrated in lines 56–57 takes a **string** to display, the display **Font**, a **Brush** and the *x*- and *y*-coordinates of the location for the **string**'s first character.

Lines 60–62 assign the **Color behindColor** value to the **Brush**'s **Color** property and display a rectangle. Lines 65–68 extract and display the ARGB values of **Color frontColor** and then display a filled rectangle that overlaps the first.

Button event handler **colorValueButton_Click** (lines 78–89) uses **Color** method **FromArgb** to construct a new **Color** object from the ARGB values that a user specifies via text boxes. It then assigns the newly created **Color** to **frontColor**. **Button** event handler **colorNameButton_Click** (lines 92–99) uses the **Color** method **FromName** to create a new **Color** object from the **colorName** that a user enters in a text box. This **Color** is assigned to **behindColor**.

If the user assigns an alpha value between 0 and 255 for the **frontColor**, the effects of alpha blending are apparent. In the screenshot output, the red back rectangle blends with the blue front rectangle to create purple where the two overlap.

Software Engineering Observation 16.1

*No methods in class **Color** enable programmers to change the characteristics of the current color. To use a different color, create a new **Color** object.*

The predefined GUI component *ColorDialog* is a dialog box that allows users to select from a palette of available colors. It also offers the option of creating custom colors. The program in Fig. 16.7 demonstrates the use of such a dialog. When a user selects a color and presses **OK**, the application retrieves the user's selection via the **ColorDialog**'s **Color** property.

The GUI for this application contains two **Button**s. The top one, **background-ColorButton**, allows the user to change the form and button background colors. The bottom one, **textColorButton**, allows the user to change the button text colors.

```
1   //Fig. 16.7: ShowColorsComplex.cs
2   // Change the background and text colors of a form.
3
4   using System;
5   using System.Drawing;
6   using System.Collections;
```

Fig. 16.7 **ColorDialog** used to change background and text color. (Part 1 of 3.)

```
7   using System.ComponentModel;
8   using System.Windows.Forms;
9   using System.Data;
10
11  // allows users to change colors using a ColorDialog
12  public class ShowColorsComplex : System.Windows.Forms.Form
13  {
14     private System.Windows.Forms.Button backgroundColorButton;
15     private System.Windows.Forms.Button textColorButton;
16
17     private System.ComponentModel.Container components = null;
18
19     [STAThread]
20     static void Main()
21     {
22        Application.Run( new ShowColorsComplex() );
23     }
24
25     // Visual Studio .NET generated code
26
27     // change text color
28     private void textColorButton_Click(
29        object sender, System.EventArgs e )
30     {
31        // create ColorDialog object
32        ColorDialog colorChooser = new ColorDialog();
33        DialogResult result;
34
35        // get chosen color
36        result = colorChooser.ShowDialog();
37
38        if ( result == DialogResult.Cancel )
39           return;
40
41        // assign forecolor to result of dialog
42        backgroundColorButton.ForeColor = colorChooser.Color;
43        textColorButton.ForeColor = colorChooser.Color;
44
45     } // end method textColorButton_Click
46
47     // change background color
48     private void backgroundColorButton_Click(
49        object sender, System.EventArgs e )
50     {
51        // create ColorDialog object
52        ColorDialog colorChooser = new ColorDialog();
53        DialogResult result;
54
55        // show ColorDialog and get result
56        colorChooser.FullOpen = true;
57        result = colorChooser.ShowDialog();
58
```

Fig. 16.7 **ColorDialog** used to change background and text color. (Part 2 of 3.)

```
59              if ( result == DialogResult.Cancel )
60                  return;
61
62              // set background color
63              this.BackColor = colorChooser.Color;
64
65          }  // end method backgroundColorButton_Click
66
67      }  // end class ShowColorsComplex
```

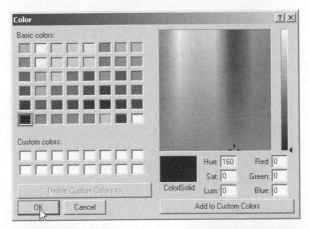

Fig. 16.7 **ColorDialog** used to change background and text color. (Part 3 of 3.)

Lines 28–45 define the event handler that is called when the user clicks **Button tex-tColorButton**. The event handler creates a new **ColorDialog** named **color-Chooser** and invokes its **ShowDialog** method, which displays the window. Property **Color** of **colorChooser** stores users' selections. Lines 42–43 set the text color of both buttons to the selected color.

Lines 48–65 define the event handler for button **backgroundColorButton**. The method modifies the background color of the form by setting **BackColor** equal to the dialog's **Color** property. The method creates a new **ColorDialog** and sets the dialog's *FullOpen* property to **true**. The dialog now displays all available colors, as shown in the screen capture in Fig. 16.7. The regular color display does not show the right-hand portion of the screen.

Users are not restricted to the **ColorDialog**'s 48 colors. To create a custom color, users can click anywhere in the **ColorDialog**'s large rectangle—this displays the various color shades. Adjust the slider, hue and other features to refine the color. When finished, click the **Add to Custom Colors** button, which adds the custom color to a square in the custom colors section of the dialog. Clicking **OK** sets the **Color** property of the

ColorDialog to that color. Selecting a color and pressing the dialog's **OK** button causes the application's background color to change.

16.4 Font Control

This section introduces methods and constants that are related to font control. Once a **Font** has been created, its properties cannot be modified. If programmers require a different **Font**, they must create a new **Font** object—there are many overloaded versions of the **Font** constructor for creating custom **Font**s. Some properties of class **Font** are summarized in Fig. 16.8.

Note that the **Size** property returns the font size as measured in design units, whereas **SizeInPoints** returns the font size as measured in points (the more common measurement). When we say that the **Size** property measures the size of the font in *design units*, we mean that the font size can be specified in a variety of ways, such as inches or millimeters. Some versions of the **Font** constructor accept a **GraphicsUnit** argument—an enumeration that allows users to specify the unit of measurement employed to describe the font size. Members of the **GraphicsUnit** enumeration include **Point** (1/72 inch), **Display** (1/75 inch), **Document** (1/300 inch), **Millimeter**, **Inch** and **Pixel**. If this argument is provided, the **Size** property contains the size of the font as measured in the specified design unit, and the **SizeInPoints** property converts the size of the font into points. For example, if we create a **Font** having size **1** and specify that **GraphicsUnit.Inch** be used to measure the font, the **Size** property will be **1**, and the **SizeInPoints** property will be **72**. If we employ a constructor that does not accept a member of the **GraphicsUnit**, the default measurement for the font size is **GraphicsUnit.Point** (thus, the **Size** and **SizeInPoints** properties will be equal).

Property	Description
Bold	Tests a font for a bold font style. Returns **true** if the font is bold.
FontFamily	Represents the **FontFamily** of the **Font** (a grouping structure to organize fonts and define their similar properties).
Height	Represents the height of the font.
Italic	Tests a font for an italic font style. Returns **true** if the font is italic.
Name	Represents the font's name as a **string**.
Size	Returns a **float** value indicating the current font size measured in design units (design units are any specified units of measurement for the font).
SizeInPoints	Returns a **float** value indicating the current font size measured in points.
Strikeout	Tests a font for a strikeout font style. Returns **true** if the font is in strikeout format.
Underline	Tests a font for a underline font style. Returns **true** if the font is underlined.

Fig. 16.8   **Font** class read-only properties.

Class **Font** has a number of constructors. Most require a *font name*, which is a **string** representing a font currently supported by the system. Common fonts include Microsoft *SansSerif* and *Serif*. Constructors also usually require the *font size* as an argument. Lastly, **Font** constructors usually require a *font style*, specified by the ***FontStyle*** enumeration: ***Bold***, ***Italic***, ***Regular***, ***Strikeout***, ***Underline***. Font styles can be combined via the '|' operator (for example, **FontStyle.Italic | FontStyle.Bold**, makes a font both italic and bold).

Graphics method ***DrawString*** sets the current drawing font—the font in which the text displays—to its **Font** argument.

Common Programming Error 16.1

Specifying a font that is not available on a system is a logic error. If this occurs, C# will substitute that system's default font.

The program in Fig. 16.9 displays text in four different fonts, each of a different size. The program uses the **Font** constructor to initialize **Font** objects (lines 32–47). Each call to the **Font** constructor passes a font name (e.g., Arial, Times New Roman, Courier New or Tahoma) as a **string**, a font size (a **float**) and a **FontStyle** object (**style**). **Graphics** method **DrawString** sets the font and draws the text at the specified location. Note that line 29 creates a **DarkBlue SolidBrush** object (**brush**), causing all **string**s drawn with that brush to appear in **DarkBlue**.

Software Engineering Observation 16.2

*There is no way to change the properties of a **Font** object—to use a different font, programmers must create a new **Font** object.*

```
1   // Fig 16.9: UsingFonts.cs
2   // Demonstrating various font settings.
3
4   using System;
5   using System.Drawing;
6   using System.Collections;
7   using System.ComponentModel;
8   using System.Windows.Forms;
9   using System.Data;
10
11  // demonstrate font constructors and properties
12  public class UsingFonts : System.Windows.Forms.Form
13  {
14     private System.ComponentModel.Container components = null;
15
16     [STAThread]
17     static void Main()
18     {
19        Application.Run( new UsingFonts() );
20     }
21
22     // Visual Studio .NET generated code
23
```

Fig. 16.9 **Font**s and **FontStyle**s. (Part 1 of 2.)

```
24       // demonstrate various font and style settings
25       protected override void OnPaint(
26          PaintEventArgs paintEvent )
27       {
28          Graphics graphicsObject = paintEvent.Graphics;
29          SolidBrush brush = new SolidBrush( Color.DarkBlue );
30
31          // arial, 12 pt bold
32          FontStyle style = FontStyle.Bold;
33          Font arial =
34             new Font( new FontFamily( "Arial" ), 12, style );
35
36          // times new roman, 12 pt regular
37          style = FontStyle.Regular;
38          Font timesNewRoman =
39             new Font( "Times New Roman", 12, style );
40
41          // courier new, 16 pt bold and italic
42          style = FontStyle.Bold | FontStyle.Italic;
43          Font courierNew = new Font( "Courier New", 16, style );
44
45          // tahoma, 18 pt strikeout
46          style = FontStyle.Strikeout;
47          Font tahoma = new Font( "Tahoma", 18, style );
48
49          graphicsObject.DrawString( arial.Name +
50             " 12 point bold.", arial, brush, 10, 10 );
51
52          graphicsObject.DrawString( timesNewRoman.Name +
53             " 12 point plain.", timesNewRoman, brush, 10, 30 );
54
55          graphicsObject.DrawString( courierNew.Name +
56             " 16 point bold and italic.", courierNew,
57             brush, 10, 54 );
58
59          graphicsObject.DrawString( tahoma.Name +
60             " 18 point strikeout.", tahoma, brush, 10, 75 );
61
62       } // end method OnPaint
63
64    } // end class UsingFonts
```

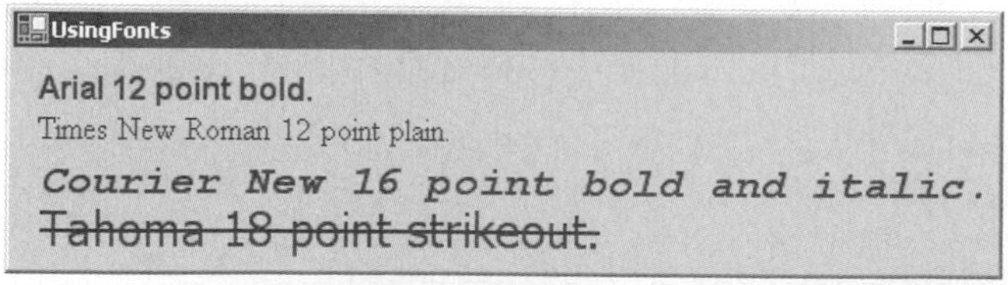

Fig. 16.9 Fonts and FontStyles. (Part 2 of 2.)

Programmers can define precise information about a font's *metrics* (or properties), such as *height*, *descent* (the amount that characters dip below the baseline), *ascent* (the amount that characters rise above the baseline) and *leading* (the difference between the ascent of one line and the decent of the previous line). Figure 16.10 illustrates these properties.

Class **FontFamily** defines characteristics common to a group of related fonts. Class **FontFamily** provides several methods used to determine the font metrics that are shared by members of a particular family. These methods are summarized in Fig. 16.11.

The program shown in Fig. 16.12 calls method **ToString** to display the metrics of two fonts. Line 32 creates **Font arial** and sets it to 12-point Arial font. Line 33 uses class **Font** property **FontFamily** to obtain object **arial**'s **FontFamily** object. Lines 38–39 call **ToString** to output the **string** representation of the font. Lines 41–55 then use methods of class **FontFamily** to return integers specifying the ascent, descent, height and leading of the font. Lines 58–77 repeat this process for font **sansSerif**, a **Font** object derived from the MS Sans Serif **FontFamily**.

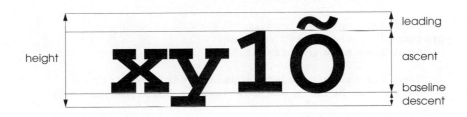

Fig. 16.10 An illustration of font metrics.

Method	Description
GetCellAscent	Returns an **int** representing the ascent of a font as measured in design units.
GetCellDescent	Returns an **int** representing the descent of a font as measured in design units.
GetEmHeight	Returns an **int** representing the height of a font as measured in design points.
GetLineSpacing	Returns an **int** representing the distance between two consecutive lines of text as measured in design units.

Fig. 16.11 **FontFamily** methods that return font-metric information.

```
1   // Fig 16.12: UsingFontMetrics.cs
2   // Displaying font metric information.
3
4   using System;
5   using System.Drawing;
6   using System.Collections;
7   using System.ComponentModel;
```

Fig. 16.12 **FontFamily** class used to obtain font-metric information. (Part 1 of 3.)

```
 8   using System.Windows.Forms;
 9   using System.Data;
10
11   // displays font information
12   public class UsingFontMetrics : System.Windows.Forms.Form
13   {
14      private System.ComponentModel.Container components = null;
15
16      [STAThread]
17      static void Main()
18      {
19         Application.Run( new UsingFontMetrics() );
20      }
21
22      // Visual Studio .NET generated code
23
24      // displays font information
25      protected override void OnPaint(
26         PaintEventArgs paintEvent )
27      {
28         Graphics graphicsObject = paintEvent.Graphics;
29         SolidBrush brush = new SolidBrush( Color.DarkBlue );
30
31         // Arial font metrics
32         Font arial = new Font( "Arial", 12 );
33         FontFamily family = arial.FontFamily;
34         Font sanSerif = new Font( "Microsoft Sans Serif",
35            14, FontStyle.Italic );
36
37         // display Arial font metrics
38         graphicsObject.DrawString( "Current Font: " +
39            arial.ToString(), arial, brush, 10, 10 );
40
41         graphicsObject.DrawString( "Ascent: " +
42            family.GetCellAscent( FontStyle.Regular ), arial,
43            brush, 10, 30 );
44
45         graphicsObject.DrawString( "Descent: " +
46            family.GetCellDescent( FontStyle.Regular ), arial,
47            brush, 10, 50 );
48
49         graphicsObject.DrawString( "Height: " +
50            family.GetEmHeight( FontStyle.Regular ), arial,
51            brush, 10, 70 );
52
53         graphicsObject.DrawString( "Leading: " +
54            family.GetLineSpacing( FontStyle.Regular ), arial,
55            brush, 10, 90 );
56
57         // display Sans Serif font metrics
58         family = sanSerif.FontFamily;
59
```

Fig. 16.12 FontFamily class used to obtain font-metric information. (Part 2 of 3.)

```
60            graphicsObject.DrawString( "Current Font: " +
61               sanSerif.ToString(), sanSerif, brush, 10, 130 );
62
63            graphicsObject.DrawString( "Ascent: " +
64               family.GetCellAscent( FontStyle.Regular ), sanSerif,
65               brush, 10, 150 );
66
67            graphicsObject.DrawString( "Descent: " +
68               family.GetCellDescent( FontStyle.Regular ), sanSerif,
69               brush, 10, 170 );
70
71            graphicsObject.DrawString( "Height: " +
72               family.GetEmHeight( FontStyle.Regular ), sanSerif,
73               brush, 10, 190 );
74
75            graphicsObject.DrawString( "Leading: " +
76               family.GetLineSpacing( FontStyle.Regular ), sanSerif,
77               brush, 10, 210 );
78
79        } // end method OnPaint
80
81    } // end class UsingFontMetrics
```

UsingFontMetrics

Current Font: [Font: Name=Arial, Size=12, Units=3, GdiCharSet=1, GdiVerticalFont=False]
Ascent: 1854
Descent: 434
Height: 2048
Leading: 2355

Current Font: [Font: Name=Microsoft Sans Serif, Size=14, Units=3, GdiCharSet=1, GdiVerticalFont=False]
Ascent: 1888
Descent: 430
Height: 2048
Leading: 2318

Fig. 16.12 FontFamily class used to obtain font-metric information. (Part 3 of 3.)

16.5 Drawing Lines, Rectangles and Ovals

This section presents a variety of **Graphics** methods for drawing lines, rectangles and ovals. Each of the drawing methods has several overloaded versions. When employing methods that draw shape outlines, we use versions that take a **Pen** and four **int**s; when employing methods that draw solid shapes, we use versions that take a **Brush** and four **int**s. In both instances, the first two **int** arguments represent the coordinates of the upper-left corner of the shape or its enclosing area, and the last two **int**s indicate the shape's width and height. Figure 16.13 summarizes the **Graphics** methods and their parameters.

The application in Fig. 16.14 draws lines, rectangles and ellipses. In this application, we also demonstrate methods that draw filled and unfilled shapes.

Methods *DrawRectangle* and *FillRectangle* (lines 33 and 42) draw rectangles on the screen. For each method, the first argument specifies the drawing object to use. The **DrawRectangle** method uses a **Pen** object, whereas the **FillRectangle** method uses a **Brush** object (in this case, an instance of **SolidBrush**—a class that derives from **Brush**). The next two arguments specify the coordinates of the upper-left corner of the *bounding rectangle*, which represents the area in which the rectangle will be drawn. The fourth and fifth arguments specify the rectangle's width and height. Method *DrawLine* (lines 36–39) takes a **Pen** and two pairs of **int**s, specifying the start and end-point of the line. The method then draws a line, using the **Pen** object passed to it.

Methods *DrawEllipse* and *FillEllipse* each provide overloaded versions that take five arguments. In both methods, the first argument specifies the drawing object to use. The next two arguments specify the upper-left coordinates of the bounding rectangle representing the area in which the ellipse will be drawn. The last two arguments specify the bounding rectangle's width and height, respectively. Figure 16.15 depicts an ellipse bounded by a rectangle. The ellipse touches the midpoint of each of the four sides of the bounding rectangle. The bounding rectangle is not displayed on the screen.

Graphics Drawing Methods and Descriptions.

Note: Many of these methods are overloaded—consult the documentation for a full listing.

DrawLine(Pen p, int x1, int y1, int x2, int y2)
Draws a line from (**x1**, **y1**) to (**x2**, **y2**). The **Pen** determines the color, style and width of the line.

DrawRectangle(Pen p, int x, int y, int width, int height)
Draws a rectangle of the specified width and height. The top-left corner of the rectangle is at point (**x**, **y**). The **Pen** determines the color, style, and border width of the rectangle.

FillRectangle(Brush b, int x, int y, int width, int height)
Draws a solid rectangle of the specified width and height. The top-left corner of the rectangle is at point (**x**, **y**). The **Brush** determines the fill pattern inside the rectangle.

DrawEllipse(Pen p, int x, int y, int width, int height)
Draws an ellipse inside a rectangle. The width and height of the rectangle are as specified, and its top-left corner is at point (**x**, **y**). The **Pen** determines the color, style and border width of the ellipse.

FillEllipse(Brush b, int x, int y, int width, int height)
Draws a filled ellipse inside a rectangle. The width and height of the rectangle are as specified, and its top-left corner is at point (**x**, **y**). The **Brush** determines the pattern inside the ellipse.

Fig. 16.13 Graphics methods that draw lines, rectangles and ovals.

```
1   // Fig. 16.14: LinesRectanglesOvals.cs
2   // Demonstrating lines, rectangles and ovals.
3
4   using System;
5   using System.Drawing;
6   using System.Collections;
7   using System.ComponentModel;
```

Fig. 16.14 Demonstration of methods that draw lines, rectangles and ellipses. (Part 1 of 3.)

```
 8   using System.Windows.Forms;
 9   using System.Data;
10
11   // draws shapes on the Form
12   public class LinesRectanglesOvals : System.Windows.Forms.Form
13   {
14      private System.ComponentModel.Container components = null;
15
16      [STAThread]
17      static void Main()
18      {
19         Application.Run( new LinesRectanglesOvals() );
20      }
21
22      // Visual Studio .NET generated code
23
24      protected override void OnPaint(
25         PaintEventArgs paintEvent )
26      {
27         // get graphics object
28         Graphics g = paintEvent.Graphics;
29         SolidBrush brush = new SolidBrush( Color.Blue );
30         Pen pen = new Pen( Color.AliceBlue );
31
32         // create filled rectangle
33         g.FillRectangle( brush, 90, 30, 150, 90 );
34
35         // draw lines to connect rectangles
36         g.DrawLine( pen, 90, 30, 110, 40 );
37         g.DrawLine( pen, 90, 120, 110, 130 );
38         g.DrawLine( pen, 240, 30, 260, 40 );
39         g.DrawLine( pen, 240, 120, 260, 130 );
40
41         // draw top rectangle
42         g.DrawRectangle( pen, 110, 40, 150, 90 );
43
44         // set brush to red
45         brush.Color = Color.Red;
46
47         // draw base Ellipse
48         g.FillEllipse( brush, 280, 75, 100, 50 );
49
50         // draw connecting lines
51         g.DrawLine( pen, 380, 55, 380, 100 );
52         g.DrawLine( pen, 280, 55, 280, 100 );
53
54         // draw Ellipse outline
55         g.DrawEllipse( pen, 280, 30, 100, 50 );
56
57      } // end method OnPaint
58
59   } // end class LinesRectanglesOvals
```

Fig. 16.14 Demonstration of methods that draw lines, rectangles and ellipses. (Part 2 of 3.)

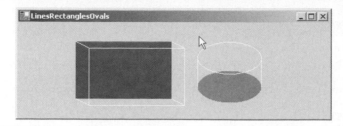

Fig. 16.14 Demonstration of methods that draw lines, rectangles and ellipses. (Part 3 of 3.)

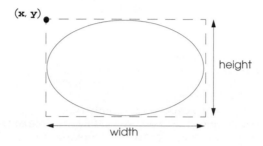

Fig. 16.15 Ellipse bounded by a rectangle.

16.6 Drawing Arcs

Arcs are portions of ellipses and are measured in degrees, beginning at a *starting angle* and continuing for a specified number of degrees called the *arc angle*. An arc is said to *sweep* (traverse) its arc angle, beginning from its starting angle. Arcs that sweep in a clockwise direction are measured in positive degrees, whereas arcs that sweep in a counterclockwise direction are measured in negative degrees. Figure 16.16 depicts two arcs. Note that the left portion of the figure sweeps downward from zero degrees to approximately 110 degrees. Similarly, the arc in the right portion of the figure sweeps upward from zero degrees to approximately –110 degrees.

Notice the dashed boxes around the arcs in Fig. 16.16. We draw each arc as part of an oval (the rest of which is not visible). When drawing an oval, we specify the oval's dimensions in the form of a bounding rectangle that encloses the oval. The boxes in Fig. 16.16 correspond to these bounding rectangles. The **Graphics** methods used to draw arcs—**DrawArc**, **DrawPie** and **FillPie**—are summarized in Fig. 16.17.

The program in Fig. 16.18 draws six images (three arcs and three filled pie slices) to demonstrate the arc methods listed in Fig. 16.17. To illustrate the bounding rectangles that determine the sizes and locations of the arcs, the arcs are displayed inside red rectangles that have the same *x*-coordinates, *y*-coordinates and width and height arguments as those that define the bounding rectangles for the arcs.

Lines 28–35 create the objects that we need to draw various arcs: **Graphics** objects, **Rectangle**s, **SolidBrush**es and **Pen**s. Lines 38–39 then draw a rectangle and an arc inside the rectangle. The arc sweeps 360 degrees, forming a circle. Line 42 changes the location of the **Rectangle** by setting its **Location** property to a new **Point**. The **Point** constructor takes the *x*- and *y*-coordinates of the new point. The **Location** property determines the upper-left corner of the **Rectangle**. After drawing the rectangle, the program draws an arc that starts at 0 degrees and sweeps 110 degrees. Because angles in C# increase in a clockwise direction, the arc sweeps downward.

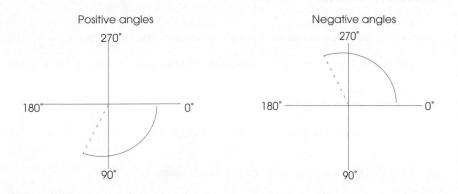

Fig. 16.16 Positive and negative arc angles.

Graphics Methods And Descriptions

Note: Many of these methods are overloaded—consult the documentation for a complete listing.

**DrawArc(Pen p, int x, int y, int width, int height,
    int startAngle, int sweepAngle)**
Draws an arc of an ellipse, beginning from angle **startAngle** (in degrees) and sweeping **sweepAngle** degrees. The ellipse is defined by a bounding rectangle of width **w**, height **h** and upper-left corner (**x,y**). The **Pen** determines the color, border width and style of the arc.

**DrawPie(Pen p, int x, int y, int width, int height,
    int startAngle, int sweepAngle)**
Draws a pie section of an ellipse, beginning from angle **startAngle** (in degrees) and sweeping **sweepAngle** degrees. The ellipse is defined by a bounding rectangle of width **w**, height **h** and upper-left corner (**x,y**). The **Pen** determines the color, border width and style of the arc.

**FillPie(Brush b, int x, int y, int width, int height,
    int startAngle, int sweepAngle)**
Functions similarly to **DrawPie**, except draws a solid arc (i.e., a sector). The **Brush** determines the fill pattern for the solid arc.

Fig. 16.17 Graphics methods for drawing arcs.

```
1   // Fig. 16.18: DrawArcs.cs
2   // Drawing various arcs on a form.
```

Fig. 16.18 Arc-method demonstration. (Part 1 of 3.)

```
3
4   using System;
5   using System.Drawing;
6   using System.Collections;
7   using System.ComponentModel;
8   using System.Windows.Forms;
9   using System.Data;
10
11  // draws various arcs
12  public class DrawArcs : System.Windows.Forms.Form
13  {
14     private System.ComponentModel.Container components = null;
15
16     [STAThread]
17     static void Main()
18     {
19        Application.Run( new DrawArcs() );
20     }
21
22     // Visual Studio .NET generated code
23
24     private void DrawArcs_Paint(
25        object sender, System.Windows.Forms.PaintEventArgs e )
26     {
27        // get graphics object
28        Graphics graphicsObject = e.Graphics;
29        Rectangle rectangle1 =
30           new Rectangle( 15, 35, 80, 80 );
31        SolidBrush brush1 =
32           new SolidBrush( Color.Firebrick );
33        Pen pen1 = new Pen( brush1, 1 );
34        SolidBrush brush2 = new SolidBrush( Color.DarkBlue );
35        Pen pen2 = new Pen( brush2, 1 );
36
37        // start at 0 and sweep 360 degrees
38        graphicsObject.DrawRectangle( pen1, rectangle1 );
39        graphicsObject.DrawArc( pen2, rectangle1, 0, 360 );
40
41        // start at 0 and sweep 110 degrees
42        rectangle1.Location = new Point( 100, 35 );
43        graphicsObject.DrawRectangle( pen1, rectangle1 );
44        graphicsObject.DrawArc( pen2, rectangle1, 0, 110 );
45
46        // start at 0 and sweep -270 degrees
47        rectangle1.Location = new Point( 185, 35 );
48        graphicsObject.DrawRectangle( pen1, rectangle1 );
49        graphicsObject.DrawArc( pen2, rectangle1, 0, -270 );
50
51        // start at 0 and sweep 360 degrees
52        rectangle1.Location = new Point( 15, 120 );
53        rectangle1.Size = new Size( 80, 40 );
54        graphicsObject.DrawRectangle( pen1, rectangle1 );
55        graphicsObject.FillPie( brush2, rectangle1, 0, 360 );
```

Fig. 16.18 Arc-method demonstration. (Part 2 of 3.)

```
56
57          // start at 270 and sweep -90 degrees
58          rectangle1.Location = new Point( 100, 120 );
59          graphicsObject.DrawRectangle( pen1, rectangle1 );
60          graphicsObject.FillPie(
61             brush2, rectangle1, 270, -90 );
62
63          // start at 0 and sweep -270 degrees
64          rectangle1.Location = new Point( 185, 120 );
65          graphicsObject.DrawRectangle( pen1, rectangle1 );
66          graphicsObject.FillPie(
67             brush2, rectangle1, 0, -270 );
68
69       } // end method DrawArcs_Paint
70
71    } // end class DrawArcs
```

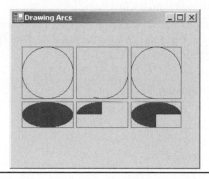

Fig. 16.18 Arc-method demonstration. (Part 3 of 3.)

Lines 47–49 perform similar functions, except that the specified arc sweeps -270 degrees. The **Size** property of a **Rectangle** determines the arc's height and width. Line 53 sets the **Size** property to a new **Size** object, which changes the size of the rectangle.

The remainder of the program is similar to the portions described above, except that a **SolidBrush** is used with method **FillPie**. The resulting arcs, which are filled, can be seen in the bottom half of the screenshot Fig. 16.18.

16.7 Drawing Polygons and Polylines

Polygons are multisided shapes. There are several **Graphics** methods used to draw polygons: **DrawLines** draws a series of connected points, **DrawPolygon** draws a closed polygon and **FillPolygon** draws a solid polygon. These methods are described in Fig. 16.19. The program in Fig. 16.20 allows users to draw polygons and connected lines via the methods listed in Fig. 16.19.

To allow the user to specify a variable number of points, line 26 declares **ArrayList points** as a container for our **Point** objects. Lines 29–31 declare the **Pen** and **Brush** used to color our shapes. The **MouseDown** event handler (lines 42–49) for **Panel drawPanel** stores mouse-click locations in the **points ArrayList**. It then calls method **Invalidate** of **drawPanel** to ensure that the panel refreshes to accommodate the new point. Method **drawPanel_Paint** (lines 51–82) handles the **Panel**'s **Paint** event. It obtains the panel's **Graphics** object (line 55) and, if the **ArrayList points** contains two or more **Point**s, displays the polygon with the method that the user selected via the GUI radio buttons (lines 58–80). In lines 61–63, we extract an **Array** from the **Array-List** via method **ToArray**. Method **ToArray** can take a single argument to determine the type of the returned array; we obtain the type from the first element in the **ArrayList**.

Method	Description
DrawLines	Draws a series of connected lines. The coordinates of each point are specified in an array of **Point**s. If the last point is different from the first point, the figure is not closed.
DrawPolygon	Draws a polygon. The coordinates of each point are specified in an array of **Point** objects. This method draws a closed polygon, even if the last point is different from the first point.
FillPolygon	Draws a solid polygon. The coordinates of each point are specified in an array of **Points**. This method draws a closed polygon, even if the last point is different from the first point.

Fig. 16.19 Graphics methods for drawing polygons.

```
1   // Fig. 16.20: DrawPolygons.cs
2   // Demonstrating polygons.
3
4   using System;
5   using System.Drawing;
6   using System.Collections;
7   using System.ComponentModel;
8   using System.Windows.Forms;
9   using System.Data;
10
11  public class PolygonForm : System.Windows.Forms.Form
12  {
13     private System.Windows.Forms.Button colorButton;
14     private System.Windows.Forms.Button clearButton;
15     private System.Windows.Forms.GroupBox typeGroup;
16     private System.Windows.Forms.RadioButton
17        filledPolygonOption;
18     private System.Windows.Forms.RadioButton lineOption;
19     private System.Windows.Forms.RadioButton polygonOption;
20     private System.Windows.Forms.Panel drawPanel;
21
22     private
23        System.ComponentModel.Container components = null;
24
25     // contains list of polygon vertices
26     private ArrayList points = new ArrayList();
27
```

Fig. 16.20 Polygon-drawing demonstration. (Part 1 of 4.)

```
28          // initialize default pen and brush
29          Pen pen = new Pen( Color.DarkBlue );
30
31          SolidBrush brush = new SolidBrush( Color.DarkBlue );
32
33          [STAThread]
34          static void Main()
35          {
36              Application.Run( new PolygonForm() );
37          }
38
39          // Visual Studio .NET generated code
40
41          // draw panel mouse down event handler
42          private void drawPanel_MouseDown(
43              object sender, System.Windows.Forms.MouseEventArgs e )
44          {
45              // add mouse position to vertex list
46              points.Add( new Point( e.X, e.Y ) );
47              drawPanel.Invalidate(); // refresh panel
48
49          } // end method drawPanel_MouseDown
50
51          private void drawPanel_Paint(
52              object sender, System.Windows.Forms.PaintEventArgs e )
53          {
54              // get graphics object for panel
55              Graphics graphicsObject = e.Graphics;
56
57              // if arraylist has 2 or more points, display shape
58              if ( points.Count > 1 )
59              {
60                  // get array for use in drawing functions
61                  Point[] pointArray =
62                      ( Point[] )points.ToArray(
63                      points[ 0 ].GetType() );
64
65                  if ( polygonOption.Checked )
66
67                      // draw polygon
68                      graphicsObject.DrawPolygon( pen, pointArray );
69
70                  else if ( lineOption.Checked )
71
72                      // draw lines
73                      graphicsObject.DrawLines( pen, pointArray );
74
75                  else if ( filledPolygonOption.Checked )
76
77                      // draw filled
78                      graphicsObject.FillPolygon(
79                          brush, pointArray );
80              }
```

Fig. 16.20 Polygon-drawing demonstration. (Part 2 of 4.)

```
81
82        } // end method drawPanel_Paint
83
84        // handle clearButton click event
85        private void clearButton_Click(
86           object sender, System.EventArgs e )
87        {
88           points = new ArrayList(); // remove points
89
90           drawPanel.Invalidate(); // refresh panel
91
92        } // end method clearButton_Click
93
94        // handle polygon radio button CheckedChanged event
95        private void polygonOption_CheckedChanged(
96           object sender, System.EventArgs e)
97        {
98           drawPanel.Invalidate(); // refresh panel
99
100       } // end method polygonOption_CheckedChanged
101
102       // handle line radio button CheckedChanged event
103       private void lineOption_CheckedChanged(
104          object sender, System.EventArgs e)
105       {
106          drawPanel.Invalidate(); // refresh panel
107
108       } // end method lineOption_CheckedChanged
109
110       // handle filled polygon radio button
111       // CheckedChanged event
112       private void filledPolygonOption_CheckedChanged(
113          object sender, System.EventArgs e)
114       {
115          drawPanel.Invalidate(); // refresh panel
116
117       } // end method filledPolygonOption_CheckedChanged
118
119       // handle colorButton click event
120       private void colorButton_Click(
121          object sender, System.EventArgs e)
122       {
123          // create new color dialog
124          ColorDialog dialogColor = new ColorDialog();
125
126          // show dialog and obtain result
127          DialogResult result = dialogColor.ShowDialog();
128
129          // return if user cancels
130          if ( result == DialogResult.Cancel )
131             return;
132
133          pen.Color = dialogColor.Color;    // set pen to color
```

Fig. 16.20 Polygon-drawing demonstration. (Part 3 of 4.)

```
134            brush.Color = dialogColor.Color; // set brush
135            drawPanel.Invalidate();          // refresh panel
136
137      } // end method colorButton_Click
138
139 } // end class PolygonForm
```

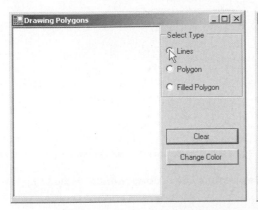
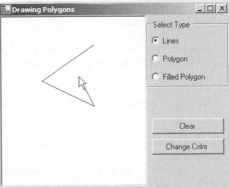
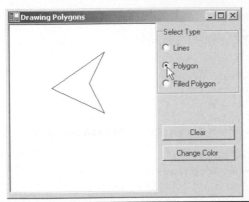
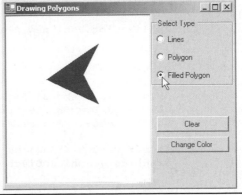

Fig. 16.20 Polygon-drawing demonstration. (Part 4 of 4.)

Method **clearButton_Click** (lines 85–92) handles the **Clear** button's click event, creates an empty **ArrayList** (causing the old list to be erased) and refreshes the display. Lines 95–117 define the event handlers for the radio buttons' **CheckedChanged** event. Each method refreshes **Panel drawPanel** to ensure that the panel display reflects the selected drawing type. Event method **colorButton_Click** (120–137) allows the user to select a new drawing color with a **ColorDialog**, using the same technique demonstrated in Fig. 16.7.

16.8 Advanced Graphics Capabilities

C# offers many additional graphics capabilities. The **Brush** hierarchy, for example, also includes *HatchBrush*, *LinearGradientBrush*, *PathGradientBrush* and *TextureBrush*.

The program in Fig. 16.21 demonstrates several graphics features, such as dashed lines, thick lines and the ability to fill shapes with patterns. These represent just a few of the additional capabilities of the **System.Drawing** namespace.

```
1    // Fig. 16.21: DrawShapes.cs
2    // Drawing various shapes on a form.
3
4    using System;
5    using System.Drawing;
6    using System.Collections;
7    using System.ComponentModel;
8    using System.Windows.Forms;
9    using System.Data;
10   using System.Drawing.Drawing2D;
11
12   // draws shapes with different brushes
13   public class DrawShapesForm : System.Windows.Forms.Form
14   {
15      private System.ComponentModel.Container components = null;
16
17      [STAThread]
18      static void Main()
19      {
20         Application.Run( new DrawShapesForm() );
21      }
22
23      // Visual Studio .NET generated code
24
25      // draw various shapes on form
26      private void DrawShapesForm_Paint(
27         object sender, System.Windows.Forms.PaintEventArgs e )
28      {
29         // references to object we will use
30         Graphics graphicsObject = e.Graphics;
31
32         // ellipse rectangle and gradient brush
33         Rectangle drawArea1 =
34            new Rectangle( 5, 35, 30, 100 );
35         LinearGradientBrush linearBrush =
36            new LinearGradientBrush( drawArea1, Color.Blue,
37            Color.Yellow, LinearGradientMode.ForwardDiagonal );
38
39         // pen and location for red outline rectangle
40         Pen thickRedPen = new Pen( Color.Red, 10 );
41         Rectangle drawArea2 = new Rectangle( 80, 30, 65, 100 );
42
43         // bitmap texture
44         Bitmap textureBitmap = new Bitmap( 10, 10 );
45
46         // get bitmap graphics
47         Graphics graphicsObject2 =
48            Graphics.FromImage( textureBitmap );
```

Fig. 16.21 Shapes drawn on a form. (Part 1 of 3.)

```
49
50      // brush and pen used throughout program
51      SolidBrush solidColorBrush =
52          new SolidBrush( Color.Red );
53      Pen coloredPen = new Pen( solidColorBrush );
54
55      // draw ellipse filled with a blue-yellow gradient
56      graphicsObject.FillEllipse(
57          linearBrush, 5, 30, 65, 100 );
58
59      // draw thick rectangle outline in red
60      graphicsObject.DrawRectangle( thickRedPen, drawArea2 );
61
62      // fill textureBitmap with yellow
63      solidColorBrush.Color = Color.Yellow;
64      graphicsObject2.FillRectangle(
65          solidColorBrush, 0, 0, 10, 10 );
66
67      // draw small black rectangle in textureBitmap
68      coloredPen.Color = Color.Black;
69      graphicsObject2.DrawRectangle(
70          coloredPen, 1, 1, 6, 6 );
71
72      // draw small blue rectangle in textureBitmpa
73      solidColorBrush.Color = Color.Blue;
74      graphicsObject2.FillRectangle(
75          solidColorBrush, 1, 1, 3, 3 );
76
77      // draw small red square in textureBitmap
78      solidColorBrush.Color = Color.Red;
79      graphicsObject2.FillRectangle(
80          solidColorBrush, 4, 4, 3, 3 );
81
82      // create textured brush and
83      // display textured rectangle
84      TextureBrush texturedBrush =
85          new TextureBrush( textureBitmap );
86      graphicsObject.FillRectangle(
87          texturedBrush, 155, 30, 75, 100 );
88
89      // draw pie-shaped arc in white
90      coloredPen.Color = Color.White;
91      coloredPen.Width = 6;
92      graphicsObject.DrawPie(
93          coloredPen, 240, 30, 75, 100, 0, 270 );
94
95      // draw lines in green and yellow
96      coloredPen.Color = Color.Green;
97      coloredPen.Width = 5;
98      graphicsObject.DrawLine(
99          coloredPen, 395, 30, 320, 150 );
100
```

Fig. 16.21 Shapes drawn on a form. (Part 2 of 3.)

```
101        // draw a rounded, dashed yellow line
102        coloredPen.Color = Color.Yellow;
103        coloredPen.DashCap = DashCap.Round;
104        coloredPen.DashStyle = DashStyle.Dash;
105        graphicsObject.DrawLine(
106            coloredPen, 320, 30, 395, 150 );
107
108    } // end method DrawShapesForm_Paint
109
110 } // end class DrawShapesForm
```

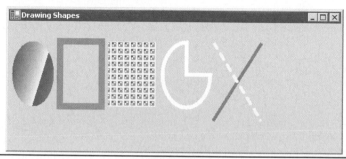

Fig. 16.21 Shapes drawn on a form. (Part 3 of 3.)

Lines 26–108 define the **Paint** event handler for our form. Lines 35–37 create **LinearGradientBrush** object **linearBrush**, which resides in namespace **System.Drawing.Drawing2D**. A **LinearGradientBrush** enables users to draw with a color gradient. The **LinearGradientBrush** used in this example takes four arguments: A **Rectangle**, two **Color**s and a member of enumeration **LinearGradientMode**. In C#, all linear gradients are defined along a line that determines the gradient endpoint. This line can be specified either by starting and ending points or by the diagonal of a rectangle. The first argument, **Rectangle drawArea1**, specifies the defining line for **LinearGradientBrush linearBrush**. This **Rectangle** argument represents the endpoints of the linear gradient—the upper-left corner is the starting point, and the bottom-right corner is the ending point. The second and third arguments specify the colors that the gradient will use. In this case, the color of the ellipse will gradually change from **Color.Blue** to **Color.Yellow**. The last argument, a type from the enumeration *LinearGradientMode*, specifies the linear gradient's direction. In our case, we use *LinearGradientMode.ForwardDiagonal*, which creates a gradient from the upper-left to the lower-right corner. We then use **Graphics** method **FillEllipse** in lines 56–57 to draw an ellipse with **linearBrush**; the color gradually changes from blue to yellow, as described above.

In line 40, we create a **Pen** object **thickRedPen**. We pass to **thickRedPen**'s constructor **Color.Red** and **int** argument **10**, indicating that we want **thickRedPen** to draw red lines that are 10 pixels wide.

Line 44 creates a new *Bitmap* image, which initially is empty. Class **Bitmap** can produce images in color and gray scale; this particular **Bitmap** is 10 pixels wide and 10 pixels tall. Method *FromImage* (line 47–48) is a **static** member of class **Graphics** and retrieves the **Graphics** object associated with an **Image**, which may be used to draw on an image. Lines 63–80 draw on the **Bitmap** a pattern consisting of black, blue, red and yellow rectangles and lines. A **TextureBrush** is a brush that fills the interior of a shape with an image, rather than a solid color. In line 86–87, **TextureBrush** object **tex-tureBrush** fills a rectangle with our **Bitmap**. The **TextureBrush** constructor version that we use takes as an argument an image that defines its texture.

Next, we draw a pie-shaped arc with a thick white line. Lines 90–91 set **col-oredPen**'s color to **White** and modify its width to be six pixels. We then draw the pic on the form by specifying the **Pen** the *x*-coordinate, *y*-coordinate, length and width of the bounding rectangle and the start angle and sweep angle.

Finally, lines 103–104 make use of **System.Drawing.Drawing2D** enumerations *DashCap* and *DashStyle* to draw a diagonal dashed line. Line 103 sets the *DashCap* property of **coloredPen** (not to be confused with the **DashCap** enumeration) to a member of the **DashCap** enumeration. The **DashCap** enumeration specifies the styles for the start and end of a dashed line. In this case, we want both ends of the dashed line to be rounded, so we use *DashCap.Round*. Line 104 sets the *DashStyle* property of **col-oredPen** (not to be confused with the **DashStyle** enumeration) to *Dash-Style.Dash*, indicating that we want our line to consist entirely of dashes.

Our next example demonstrates the use of a *general path*. A general path is a shape constructed from straight lines and complex curves. An object of class *GraphicsPath* (**System.Drawing.Drawing2D** namespace) represents a general path. The **Graph-icsPath** class provides functionality that enables the creation of complex shapes from vector-based primitive graphics objects. A **GraphicsPath** object consists of figures defined by simple shapes. The start point of each vector-graphics object (such as a line or arc) that is added to the path is connected by a straight line to the end point of the previous object. When called, the **CloseFigure** method attaches the final vector-graphic object endpoint to the initial starting point for the current figure by a straight line, then starts a new figure. Method **StartFigure** begins a new figure within the path without closing the previous figure.

The program of Fig. 16.22 draws general paths in the shape of five-pointed stars. Line 45 sets the origin of the **Graphics** object. The arguments to method **TranslateT-ransform** indicate that the origin should be translated to the coordinates (150, 150). Lines 36–39 define two **int** arrays, representing the *x*- and *y*-coordinates of the points in the star, and line 42 defines **GraphicsPath** object **star**. A **for** loop then creates lines to connect the points of the star and adds these lines to **star**. We use **GraphicsPath** method *AddLine* to append a line to the shape. The arguments of **AddLine** specify the coordinates for the line's endpoints; each new call to **AddLine** adds a line from the previous point to the current point. Line 38 uses **GraphicsPath** method *CloseFigure* to complete the shape.

```
1   // Fig. 16.22: DrawStarsForm.cs
2   // Using paths to draw stars on the form.
3
4   using System;
5   using System.Drawing;
6   using System.Collections;
7   using System.ComponentModel;
```

Fig. 16.22 Paths used to draw stars on a form. (Part 1 of 3.)

```
8   using System.Windows.Forms;
9   using System.Data;
10  using System.Drawing.Drawing2D;
11
12  // draws randomly colored stars
13  public class DrawStarsForm : System.Windows.Forms.Form
14  {
15     private
16        System.ComponentModel.Container components = null;
17
18     [STAThread]
19     static void Main()
20     {
21        Application.Run( new DrawStarsForm() );
22     }
23
24     // Visual Studio .NET generated code
25
26     // create path and draw stars along it
27     private void DrawStarsForm_Paint(
28        object sender, System.Windows.Forms.PaintEventArgs e )
29     {
30        Graphics graphicsObject = e.Graphics;
31        Random random = new Random();
32        SolidBrush brush =
33           new SolidBrush( Color.DarkMagenta );
34
35        // x and y points of the path
36        int[] xPoints =
37           { 55, 67, 109, 73, 83, 55, 27, 37, 1, 43 };
38        int[] yPoints =
39           { 0, 36, 36, 54, 96, 72, 96, 54, 36, 36 };
40
41        // create graphics path for star;
42        GraphicsPath star = new GraphicsPath();
43
44        // translate the origin to (150, 150)
45        graphicsObject.TranslateTransform( 150, 150 );
46
47        // create star from series of points
48        for ( int i = 0; i <= 8; i += 2 )
49           star.AddLine( xPoints[ i ], yPoints[ i ],
50              xPoints[ i + 1 ], yPoints[ i + 1 ] );
51
52        // close the shape
53        star.CloseFigure();
54
55        // rotate the origin and draw stars in random colors
56        for ( int i = 1; i <= 18; i++ )
57        {
58           graphicsObject.RotateTransform( 20 );
59
```

Fig. 16.22 Paths used to draw stars on a form. (Part 2 of 3.)

```
60                        brush.Color = Color.FromArgb(
61                           random.Next( 200, 255 ), random.Next( 255 ),
62                           random.Next( 255 ), random.Next( 255 ) );
63
64                        graphicsObject.FillPath( brush, star );
65                     }
66
67            } // end method DrawStarsForm_Paint
68
69    } // end class DrawStarsForm
```

Fig. 16.22 Paths used to draw stars on a form. (Part 3 of 3.)

The **for** structure in lines 56–65 draws the **star** 18 times, rotating it around the origin. Line 58 uses **Graphics** method *RotateTransform* to move to the next position on the form; the argument specifies the rotation angle in degrees. **Graphics** method **FillPath** (line 64) then draws a filled version of the **star** with the **Brush** created on lines 60–62. The application determines the **SolidBrush**'s color randomly, using **Random** method **Next**.

16.9 Introduction to Multimedia

C# offers many convenient ways to include images and animations in programs. People who entered the computing field decades ago used computers primarily to perform arithmetic calculations. As the discipline evolves, we are beginning to realize the importance of computers' data-manipulation capabilities. We are seeing a wide variety of exciting new three-dimensional applications. Multimedia programming is an entertaining and innovative field, but one that presents many challenges

Multimedia applications demand extraordinary computing power. Until recently, affordable computers with this amount of power were not available. However, today's ultrafast processors are making multimedia-based applications commonplace. As the market for multimedia explodes, users are purchasing the faster processors, larger memories and wider communications bandwidths needed to support multimedia applications. This benefits the computer and communications industries, which provide the hardware, software and services fueling the multimedia revolution.

In the remaining sections of this chapter, we introduce the use and manipulation of images and other multimedia features and capabilities. Section 16.10 discusses how to load, display and scale images; Section 16.11 demonstrates image animation; Section 16.12 presents the video capabilities of the Windows Media Player control; and Section 16.13 explores Microsoft Agent technology.

16.10 Loading, Displaying and Scaling Images

C#'s multimedia capabilities include graphics, images, animations and video. Previous sections demonstrated C#'s vector-graphics capabilities; this section concentrates on image manipulation. The Windows form that we create in Fig. 16.23 demonstrates the loading of an **Image** (**System.Drawing** namespace). The application allows users to enter a desired height and width for the **Image**, which then is displayed in the specified size.

Lines 23–24 declare **Image** reference **image**. The **static Image** method *From-File* then retrieves an image stored on disk and assigns it to **image** (line 24). Line 31 uses **Form** method *CreateGraphics* to create a **Graphics** object associated with the **Form**; we use this object to draw on the **Form**. Method **CreateGraphics** is inherited from class **Control**; all Windows controls, such as **Button**s and **Panel**s, also provide this method. When users click **Set**, the width and height parameters are validated to ensure that they are not too large. If the parameters are valid, line 59 calls **Graphics** method *Clear* to paint the entire **Form** in the current background color. Lines 62–63 call **Graphics** method *DrawImage* with the following parameters: the image to draw, the x-coordinate of the upper-left corner, the y-coordinate of the upper-left corner, the width of the image and the height of the image. If the width and height do not correspond to the image's original dimensions, the image is scaled to fit the new specifications.

```
1   // Fig. 16.23: DisplayLogoForm.cs
2   // Displaying and resizing an image.
3
4   using System;
5   using System.Drawing;
6   using System.Collections;
7   using System.ComponentModel;
8   using System.Windows.Forms;
9   using System.Data;
10
11  // displays an image and allows the user to resize it
12  public class DisplayLogoForm : System.Windows.Forms.Form
13  {
14     private System.Windows.Forms.Button setButton;
15     private System.Windows.Forms.TextBox heightTextBox;
16     private System.Windows.Forms.Label heightLabel;
```

Fig. 16.23 Image resizing. (Part 1 of 3.)

```
17      private System.Windows.Forms.TextBox widthTextBox;
18      private System.Windows.Forms.Label widthLabel;
19
20      private
21         System.ComponentModel.Container components = null;
22
23      private
24         Image image = Image.FromFile( "images/Logo.gif" );
25      private Graphics graphicsObject;
26
27      public DisplayLogoForm()
28      {
29         InitializeComponent();
30
31         graphicsObject = this.CreateGraphics();
32      }
33
34      [STAThread]
35      static void Main()
36      {
37         Application.Run( new DisplayLogoForm() );
38      }
39
40      // Visual Studio .NET generated code
41
42      private void setButton_Click(
43         object sender, System.EventArgs e )
44      {
45         // get user input
46         int width = Convert.ToInt32( widthTextBox.Text );
47         int height = Convert.ToInt32( heightTextBox.Text );
48
49         // if dimensions specified are too large
50         // display problem
51         if ( width > 375 || height > 225 )
52         {
53            MessageBox.Show( "Height or Width too large" );
54
55            return;
56         }
57
58         // clear Windows Form
59         graphicsObject.Clear( this.BackColor );
60
61         // draw image
62         graphicsObject.DrawImage(
63            image, 5, 5, width, height );
64
65      } // end method setButton_Click
66
67   } // end class DisplayLogoForm
```

Fig. 16.23 Image resizing. (Part 2 of 3.)

Fig. 16.23 Image resizing. (Part 3 of 3.)

16.11 Animating a Series of Images

The next example animates a series of images stored in an array. The application uses the same techniques to load and display **Image**s as those illustrated in Fig. 16.23. The images were created with Adobe Photoshop.

The animation in Fig. 16.24 uses a **PictureBox**, which contains the images that we animate. We use a **Timer** to cycle through the images, causing a new image to display every 50 milliseconds. Variable **count** keeps track of the current image number and increases by one every time we display a new image. The array includes 30 images (numbered 0–29); when the application reaches image 29, it returns to image 0. The 30 images were prepared in advance and placed in the **images** folder inside the **bin/Debug** directory of the project.

```
1   // Fig. 16.24: LogoAnimator.cs
2   // Program that animates a series of images.
3
```

Fig. 16.24 Animation of a series of images. (Part 1 of 3.)

```csharp
4   using System;
5   using System.Drawing;
6   using System.Collections;
7   using System.ComponentModel;
8   using System.Windows.Forms;
9   using System.Data;
10
11  // animates a series of 30 images
12  public class LogoAnimator : System.Windows.Forms.Form
13  {
14      private System.Windows.Forms.PictureBox logoPictureBox;
15      private System.Windows.Forms.Timer Timer;
16      private System.ComponentModel.IContainer components;
17
18      private ArrayList images = new ArrayList();
19      private int count = -1;
20
21      public LogoAnimator()
22      {
23          InitializeComponent();
24
25          for ( int i = 0; i < 30; i++ )
26              images.Add( Image.FromFile( "images/deitel" + i +
27                  ".gif" ) );
28
29          // load first image
30          logoPictureBox.Image = ( Image ) images[ 0 ];
31
32          // set PictureBox to be the same size as Image
33          logoPictureBox.Size = logoPictureBox.Image.Size;
34
35      } // end constructor
36
37      [STAThread]
38      static void Main()
39      {
40          Application.Run( new LogoAnimator() );
41      }
42
43      // Visual Studio .NET generated code
44
45      private void Timer_Tick(
46          object sender, System.EventArgs e )
47      {
48          // increment counter
49          count = ( count + 1 ) % 30;
50
51          // load next image
52          logoPictureBox.Image = ( Image )images[ count ];
53
54      } // end method Timer_Tick
55
56  } // end class LogoAnimator
```

Fig. 16.24 Animation of a series of images. (Part 2 of 3.)

Fig. 16.24 Animation of a series of images. (Part 3 of 3.)

Lines 25–27 load each of 30 images and place them in an **ArrayList**. **ArrayList** method **Add** allows us to add objects to the **ArrayList**; we use this method in lines 26–27 to add each **Image**. Line 30 places the first image in the **PictureBox**, using the **ArrayList** indexer. Line 33 modifies the size of the **PictureBox** so that it is equal to the size of the **Image** it is displaying. The event handler for **timer**'s **Tick** event (line 45–54) then displays the next image from the **ArrayList**.

Performance Tip 16.2

It is more efficient to load an animation's frames as one image than to load each image separately. (A painting program, such as Adobe Photoshop®, or Jasc® Paint Shop Pro™, can be used to combine the animation's frames into one image.) If the images are being loaded separately from the Web, each loaded image requires a separate connection to the site on which the images are stored; this process can result in poor performance.

Performance Tip 16.3

Loading animation frames can cause program delays, because the program waits for all frames to load before displaying them.

The following chess example demonstrates the capabilities of GDI+ as they pertain to a chess-game application. These include techniques for two-dimensional *collision detection*, the selection of single frames from a multi-frame image and *regional invalidation* (refreshing only the required parts of the screen) to increase performance. Two-dimensional collision detection is the detection of an overlap between two shapes. In the next example, we demonstrate the simplest form of collision detection, which determines whether a point (the mouse-click location) is contained within a rectangle (a chess-piece image).

Class **ChessPiece** (Fig. 16.25) is a container class for the individual chess pieces. Lines 11–19 define a public enumeration of constants that identify each chess-piece type. The constants also serve to identify the location of each piece in the chess-piece image file. **Rectangle** object **targetRectangle** (lines 25–26) identifies the image location on the chess board. The **x** and **y** properties of the rectangle are assigned in the **ChessPiece** constructor, and all chess-piece images have height and width **75**.

The **ChessPiece** constructor (lines 29–40) requires that the calling class define a chess-piece type, its **x** and **y** location and the **Bitmap** containing all chess-piece images. Rather than loading the chess-piece image within the class, we allow the calling class to pass the image. This avoids the image-loading overhead for each piece. It also increases the flexibility of the class by allowing the user to change images; for example, in this case, we use the class for both black and white chess-piece images. Lines 37–39 extract a subimage that contains only the current piece's bitmap data. Our chess-piece images are defined in a specific manner: One image contains six chess-piece images, each defined within a 75-pixel block, resulting in a total image size of 450-by-75. We obtain a single image via **Bitmap**'s **Clone** method, which allows us to specify a rectangle image location and the desired pixel format. The location is a 75-by-75 pixel block with its upper-left corner **x** equal to **75 * type** and the corresponding **y** equal to **0**. For the pixel format, we specify constant **DontCare**, causing the format to remain unchanged.

Method **Draw** (lines 43–46) causes the **ChessPiece** to draw **pieceImage** in **targetRectangle** on the passed **Graphics** object. **Method GetBounds** returns the object **targetRectangle** for use in collision detection, and **SetLocation** allows the calling class to specify a new piece location.

```
1   // Fig. 16.25 : ChessPiece.cs
2   // Storage class for chess piece attributes.
3
4   using System;
5   using System.Drawing;
6
7   // represents a chess piece
8   public class ChessPiece
9   {
10      // define chess-piece type constants
11      public enum Types
12      {
13         KING,
14         QUEEN,
15         BISHOP,
16         KNIGHT,
17         ROOK,
18         PAWN
19      }
20
21      private int currentType; // this object's type
22      private Bitmap pieceImage; // this object's image
23
24      // default display location
25      private Rectangle targetRectangle =
26         new Rectangle( 0, 0, 75, 75 );
27
28      // construct piece
29      public ChessPiece( int type, int xLocation,
30         int yLocation, Bitmap sourceImage )
31      {
32         currentType = type; // set current type
33         targetRectangle.X = xLocation; // set current x location
34         targetRectangle.Y = yLocation; // set current y location
35
36         // obtain pieceImage from section of sourceImage
37         pieceImage = sourceImage.Clone(
38            new Rectangle( type * 75, 0, 75, 75 ),
39            System.Drawing.Imaging.PixelFormat.DontCare );
40      }
```

Fig. 16.25 Container class for chess pieces. (Part 1 of 2.)

```
41
42      // draw chess piece
43      public void Draw( Graphics graphicsObject )
44      {
45          graphicsObject.DrawImage( pieceImage, targetRectangle );
46      }
47
48      // obtain this piece's location rectangle
49      public Rectangle GetBounds()
50      {
51          return targetRectangle;
52      } // end method GetBounds
53
54      // set this piece's location
55      public void SetLocation( int xLocation, int yLocation )
56      {
57          targetRectangle.X = xLocation;
58          targetRectangle.Y = yLocation;
59
60      } // end method SetLocation
61
62   } // end class ChessPiece
```

Fig. 16.25 Container class for chess pieces. (Part 2 of 2.)

Class **ChessGame** (Fig. 16.26) defines the game and graphics code for our chess game. Lines 23–33 define class-scope variables the program requires. **ArrayList chessTile** (line 23) stores the board tile images. It contains four images: Two light tiles and two dark tiles (to increase board variety). **ArrayList chessPieces** (line 26) stores all active **ChessPiece** objects and **int selectedIndex** (line 29) identifies the index in **chess-Pieces** of the currently selected piece. The **board** (line 30) is an 8-by-8, two-dimensional **int** array corresponding to the squares of a chess board. Each board element is an integer from 0 to 3 that corresponds to an index in **chessTile** and is used to specify the chess-board-square image. **const int TILESIZE** (line 33) defines the size of each tile in pixels.

The chess game GUI consists of **Form ChessGame**, the area in which we draw the tiles; **Panel pieceBox**, the window in which we draw the pieces (note that **pieceBox** background color is set to **"transparent"**); and a **Menu** that allows the user to begin a new game. Although the pieces and tiles could have been drawn on the same form, doing so would decrease performance. We would be forced to refresh the board as well as the pieces every time we refreshed the control.

The **ChessGame Load** event (lines 44–56) loads each tile image into **chessTile**. It then calls method **ResetBoard** to refresh the **Form** and begin the game. Method **Reset-Board** (lines 59–169) assigns **chessPieces** to a new **ArrayList**, loading images for both the black and the white chess-piece sets, and creates **Bitmap selected** to define the currently selected **Bitmap** set. Lines 82–167 loop through 64 positions on the chess board, setting the tile color and piece for each tile. Lines 86–87 cause the currently selected image to switch to the **blackPieces** after the fifth row. If the row counter is on the first or last row, lines 94–134 add a new piece to **chessPieces**. The type of the piece is based on the current column we are initializing. Pieces in chess are positioned in the following order, from left to right: Rook, knight, bishop, queen, king, bishop, knight and rook. Lines 137–146 add a new pawn at the current location if the current **row** is second or seventh.

A chess board is defined by alternating light and dark tiles across a row in a pattern where the color that starts each row is equal to the color of the last tile of the previous row. Lines 151–162 assign the current board-tile color as an index in the **board** array. Based on the alternating value of **bool** variable **light** and the results of the random operation on line 149, **0** and **1** are light tiles, whereas **2** and **3** are dark tiles. Line 166 inverts the value of **light** at the end of each row to maintain the staggered effect of a chess board.

```
1    // Fig. 16.26: ChessGame.cs
2    // Chess Game graphics code.
3
4    using System;
5    using System.Drawing;
6    using System.Collections;
7    using System.ComponentModel;
8    using System.Windows.Forms;
9    using System.Data;
10
11   // allows 2 players to play chess
12   public class ChessGame : System.Windows.Forms.Form
13   {
14       private System.Windows.Forms.PictureBox pieceBox;
15       private System.Windows.Forms.MainMenu GameMenu;
16       private System.Windows.Forms.MenuItem gameItem;
17       private System.Windows.Forms.MenuItem newGameItem;
18
19       private
20           System.ComponentModel.Container components = null;
21
22       // ArrayList for board tile images
23       ArrayList chessTile = new ArrayList();
24
25       // ArrayList for chess pieces
26       ArrayList chessPieces = new ArrayList();
27
28       // define index for selected piece
29       int selectedIndex = -1;
30       int[,] board = new int[ 8, 8 ]; // board array
31
32       // define chess tile size in pixels
33       private const int TILESIZE = 75;
34
35       [STAThread]
36       static void Main()
37       {
38           Application.Run( new ChessGame() );
39       }
40
41       // Visual Studio .NET generated code
42
```

Fig. 16.26 Chess-game code. (Part 1 of 8.)

```
43      // load tile bitmaps and reset game
44      private void ChessGame_Load(
45         object sender, System.EventArgs e)
46      {
47         // load chess board tiles
48         chessTile.Add( Bitmap.FromFile( "lightTile1.png" ) );
49         chessTile.Add( Bitmap.FromFile( "lightTile2.png" ) );
50         chessTile.Add( Bitmap.FromFile( "darkTile1.png" ) );
51         chessTile.Add( Bitmap.FromFile( "darkTile2.png" ) );
52
53         ResetBoard(); // initialize board
54         Invalidate(); // refresh form
55
56      } // end method ChessGame_Load
57
58      // initialize pieces to start and rebuild board
59      private void ResetBoard()
60      {
61         int current = -1;
62         ChessPiece piece;
63         Random random = new Random();
64         bool light = true;
65         int type;
66
67         // ensure empty arraylist
68         chessPieces = new ArrayList();
69
70         // load whitepieces image
71         Bitmap whitePieces =
72            ( Bitmap )Image.FromFile( "whitePieces.png" );
73
74         // load blackpieces image
75         Bitmap blackPieces =
76            ( Bitmap )Image.FromFile( "blackPieces.png" );
77
78         // set whitepieces drawn first
79         Bitmap selected = whitePieces;
80
81         // traverse board rows in outer loop
82         for ( int row = 0;
83            row <= board.GetUpperBound( 0 ); row++ )
84         {
85            // if at bottom rows, set to black pieces images
86            if ( row > 5 )
87               selected = blackPieces;
88
89            // traverse board columns in inner loop
90            for ( int column = 0;
91               column <= board.GetUpperBound( 1 ); column++ )
92            {
93               // if first or last row, organize pieces
94               if ( row == 0 || row == 7 )
95               {
```

Fig. 16.26 Chess-game code. (Part 2 of 8.)

```
96                    switch( column )
97                    {
98                        case 0:
99                        case 7: // set current piece to rook
100                          current =
101                              ( int )ChessPiece.Types.ROOK;
102                          break;
103
104                        case 1:
105                        case 6: // set current piece to knight
106                          current =
107                              ( int )ChessPiece.Types.KNIGHT;
108                          break;
109
110                        case 2:
111                        case 5: // set current piece to bishop
112                          current =
113                              ( int )ChessPiece.Types.BISHOP;
114                          break;
115
116                        case 3: // set current piece to king
117                          current =
118                              ( int )ChessPiece.Types.KING;
119                          break;
120
121                        case 4: // set current piece to queen
122                          current =
123                              ( int )ChessPiece.Types.QUEEN;
124                          break;
125                    }
126
127                    // create current piece at start position
128                    piece = new ChessPiece( current,
129                        column * TILESIZE, row * TILESIZE,
130                        selected );
131
132                    // add piece to arraylist
133                    chessPieces.Add( piece );
134                 }
135
136                 // if second or seventh row, organize pawns
137                 if ( row == 1 || row == 6 )
138                 {
139                     piece = new ChessPiece(
140                         ( int )ChessPiece.Types.PAWN,
141                         column * TILESIZE, row * TILESIZE,
142                         selected );
143
144                     // add piece to arraylist
145                     chessPieces.Add( piece );
146                 }
147
```

Fig. 16.26 Chess-game code. (Part 3 of 8.)

```
148                    // determine board piece type
149                    type = random.Next( 0, 2 );
150
151                    if ( light )
152                    {
153                       // set light tile
154                       board[ row, column ] = type;
155                       light = false;
156                    }
157                    else
158                    {
159                       // set dark tile
160                       board[ row, column ] = type + 2;
161                       light = true;
162                    }
163                 }
164
165                 // account for new row tile color switch
166                 light = !light;
167              }
168
169     } // end method ResetBoard
170
171     // display board in form OnPaint event
172     private void ChessGame_Paint(
173        object sender, System.Windows.Forms.PaintEventArgs e)
174     {
175        // obtain graphics object
176        Graphics graphicsObject = e.Graphics;
177
178        for ( int row = 0;
179           row <= board.GetUpperBound( 0 ); row++ )
180        {
181           for ( int column = 0;
182              column <= board.GetUpperBound( 1 ); column++ )
183           {
184              // draw image specified in board array
185              graphicsObject.DrawImage(
186                 (Image)chessTile[ board[ row, column ] ],
187                 new Point( TILESIZE * column,
188                 TILESIZE * row ) );
189           }
190        }
191
192     } // end method ChessGame_Paint
193
194     // return index of piece that intersects point
195     // optionally exclude a value
196     private int CheckBounds( Point point, int exclude )
197     {
198        Rectangle rectangle; // current bounding rectangle
199
```

Fig. 16.26 Chess-game code. (Part 4 of 8.)

```
200          for ( int i = 0; i < chessPieces.Count; i++ )
201          {
202             // get piece rectangle
203             rectangle = GetPiece( i ).GetBounds();
204
205             // check if rectangle contains point
206             if ( rectangle.Contains( point ) && i != exclude )
207                return i;
208          }
209
210          return -1;
211
212       } // end method CheckBounds
213
214       // handle pieceBox paint event
215       private void pieceBox_Paint(
216          object sender, System.Windows.Forms.PaintEventArgs e)
217       {
218          // draw all pieces
219          for ( int i = 0; i < chessPieces.Count; i++ )
220             GetPiece( i ).Draw( e.Graphics );
221
222       } // end method pieceBox_Paint
223
224       private void pieceBox_MouseDown(
225          object sender, System.Windows.Forms.MouseEventArgs e)
226       {
227          // determine selected piece
228          selectedIndex =
229             CheckBounds( new Point( e.X, e.Y ), -1 );
230
231       } // end method pieceBox_MouseDown
232
233       // if piece is selected, move it
234       private void pieceBox_MouseMove(
235          object sender, System.Windows.Forms.MouseEventArgs e)
236       {
237          if ( selectedIndex > -1 )
238          {
239             Rectangle region = new Rectangle(
240                e.X - TILESIZE * 2, e.Y - TILESIZE * 2,
241                TILESIZE * 4, TILESIZE * 4 );
242
243             // set piece center to mouse
244             GetPiece( selectedIndex ).SetLocation(
245                e.X - TILESIZE / 2, e.Y - TILESIZE / 2 );
246
247             // refresh immediate area
248             pieceBox.Invalidate( region );
249          }
250
251       } // end method pieceBox_MouseMove
```

Fig. 16.26 Chess-game code. (Part 5 of 8.)

```
252
253      // on mouse up deselect piece and remove taken piece
254      private void pieceBox_MouseUp(
255         object sender, System.Windows.Forms.MouseEventArgs e)
256      {
257         int remove = -1;
258
259         //if chess piece was selected
260         if ( selectedIndex > -1 )
261         {
262            Point current = new Point( e.X, e.Y );
263            Point newPoint = new Point(
264               current.X - ( current.X % TILESIZE ),
265               current.Y - ( current.Y % TILESIZE ) );
266
267            // check bounds with point, exclude selected piece
268            remove = CheckBounds( current, selectedIndex );
269
270            // snap piece into center of closest square
271            GetPiece( selectedIndex ).SetLocation( newPoint.X,
272               newPoint.Y );
273
274            // deselect piece
275            selectedIndex = -1;
276
277            // remove taken piece
278            if ( remove > -1 )
279               chessPieces.RemoveAt( remove );
280         }
281
282         // refresh pieceBox to ensure artifact removal
283         pieceBox.Invalidate();
284
285      } // end method pieceBox_MouseUp
286
287      // helper function to convert
288      // ArrayList object to ChessPiece
289      private ChessPiece GetPiece( int i )
290      {
291         return (ChessPiece)chessPieces[ i ];
292      } // end method GetPiece
293
294      // handle NewGame menu option click
295      private void newGameItem_Click(
296         object sender, System.EventArgs e)
297      {
298         ResetBoard(); // reinitialize board
299         Invalidate(); // refresh form
300
301      } // end method newGameItem_Click
302
303   } // end class ChessGame
```

Fig. 16.26 Chess-game code. (Part 6 of 8.)

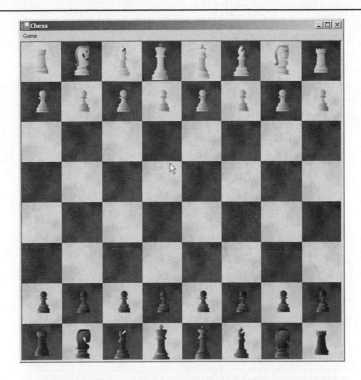

Fig. 16.26 Chess-game code. (Part 7 of 8.)

Fig. 16.26 Chess-game code. (Part 8 of 8.)

Method **ChessGame_Paint** (lines 172–192) handles this class **Form**'s **Paint** event and draws the tiles according to their values in the board array. Method **pieceBox_Paint**, which handles the **pieceBox Panel paint** event, iterates through each element of the **chessPiece ArrayList** and calls its **Draw** method.

The **MouseDown** event handler (lines 224–231) calls method **CheckBounds** with the location of the user's click to determine whether the user selected a piece. **Check-Bounds** returns an integer locating a collision from a given point.

The **MouseMove** event handler (lines 234–251) moves the currently selected piece with the mouse. Lines 244–245 set the selected piece location to the mouse-cursor position, adjusting the location by up to half a tile to center the image on the mouse. Lines 239–241 define and refresh a region of the **Panel** that spans two tiles in every direction from the mouse. As mentioned earlier in the chapter, the **Invalidate** method is slow. This means that the **MouseMove** event handler might be called again several times before the **Inval-idate** method completes. If a user working on a slow computer moves the mouse quickly, the application could leave behind *artifacts*. An artifact is any unintended visual abnormality in a graphical program. By causing the program to refresh a two-square rectangle, which should suffice in most cases, we achieve a significant performance enhancement over an entire component refresh during each **MouseMove** event.

Lines 254–285 define the **MouseUp** event handler. If a piece has been selected, lines 260–280 determine the index in **chessPieces** of any piece collision, remove the collided piece, snap (align) the current piece into a valid location and deselect the piece. We check for piece collisions to allow the chess piece to "take" other chess pieces. Line 268 checks whether any piece (excluding the currently selected piece) is beneath the current mouse location. If a collision is detected, the returned piece index is assigned to **int remove**. Lines 271–272 determine the closest valid chess tile and "snap" the selected piece to that location. If **remove** contains a positive value, line 279 removes the object at that index from the **chessPieces ArrayList**. Finally, the entire **Panel** is **Invalidate**d in line 283 to display the new piece location and remove any artifacts created during the move.

Method **CheckBounds** (lines 196–212) is a collision-detection helper method; it iterates through the **chessPieces ArrayList** and returns the index of any piece rectangle containing the point value passed to the method (the mouse location, in this example). Method **CheckBounds** optionally can exclude a single piece index (to ignore the selected index in the **MouseUp** event handler, in this example).

Lines 289–292 define helper function **GetPiece**, which simplifies the conversion from **object**s in the **ArrayList chessPieces** to **ChessPiece** types. Method **newGameItem_Click** handles the **NewGame** menu item click event, calls **RefreshBoard** to reset the game and **Invalidate**s the entire form.

16.12 Windows Media Player

The Windows Media Player control enables an application to play video and sound in many multimedia formats. These include MPEG (Motion Pictures Experts Group) audio and video, AVI (audio-video interleave) video, WAV (Windows wave-file format) audio and MIDI (Musical Instrument Digital Interface) audio. Users can find preexisting audio and video on the Internet, or they can create their own files, using available sound and graphics packages.

The application in Fig. 16.27 demonstrates the Windows Media Player control, which enables users to play multimedia files. To use the Windows Media Player control, programmers must add the control to the **Toolbox**. This is accomplished by first selecting **Customize Toolbox** from the **Tool** menu to display the **Customize Toolbox** dialog box. In the dialog box, scroll down and select the option **Windows Media Player**. Then, click the **OK** button to dismiss the dialog box. The icon for the Windows Media Player control now should appear at the bottom of the **Toolbox**.

```
1   // Fig 16.27: MediaPlayerTest.cs
2   // Demonstrates the Windows Media Player control
3
4   using System;
5   using System.Drawing;
6   using System.Collections;
7   using System.ComponentModel;
8   using System.Windows.Forms;
9   using System.Data;
10
11  // allows users to play media files using a
12  // Windows Media Player control
13  public class MediaPlayer : System.Windows.Forms.Form
14  {
15      private System.Windows.Forms.MainMenu applicationMenu;
```

Fig. 16.27 Windows Media Player demonstration. (Part 1 of 3.)

```
16        private System.Windows.Forms.MenuItem fileItem;
17        private System.Windows.Forms.MenuItem openItem;
18        private System.Windows.Forms.MenuItem exitItem;
19        private System.Windows.Forms.MenuItem aboutItem;
20        private System.Windows.Forms.MenuItem aboutMessageItem;
21        private System.Windows.Forms.OpenFileDialog
22           openMediaFileDialog;
23        private AxMediaPlayer.AxMediaPlayer player;
24
25        private
26           System.ComponentModel.Container components = null;
27
28        [STAThread]
29        static void Main()
30        {
31           Application.Run( new MediaPlayer() );
32        }
33
34        // Visual Studio .NET generated code
35
36        // open new media file in Windows Media Player
37        private void openItem_Click(
38           object sender, System.EventArgs e)
39        {
40           openMediaFileDialog.ShowDialog();
41
42           player.FileName = openMediaFileDialog.FileName;
43
44           // adjust the size of the Media Player control and
45           // the Form according to the size of the image
46           player.Size = new Size( player.ImageSourceWidth,
47              player.ImageSourceHeight );
48
49           this.Size = new Size( player.Size.Width + 20,
50              player.Size.Height + 60 );
51
52        } // end method openItem_Click
53
54        private void exitItem_Click(
55           object sender, System.EventArgs e)
56        {
57           Application.Exit();
58
59        } // end method exitItem_Click
60
61        private void aboutMessageItem_Click(
62           object sender, System.EventArgs e)
63        {
64           player.AboutBox();
65
66        } // end method aboutMessageItem_Click
67
68  } // end class MediaPlayer
```

Fig. 16.27 Windows Media Player demonstration. (Part 2 of 3.)

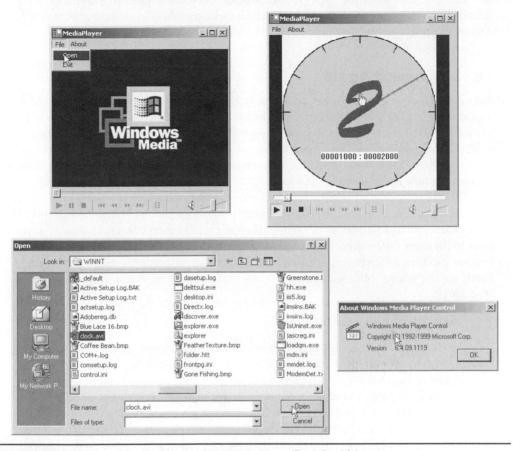

Fig. 16.27 Windows Media Player demonstration. (Part 3 of 3.)

The Windows Media Player control provides several buttons that allow the user to play the current file, pause, stop, play the previous file, rewind, forward and play the next file. The control also includes a volume control and trackbars to select a specific position in the media file.

The application provides a **MainMenu**, which includes **File** and **About** menus. The **File** menu contains the **Open** and **Exit** menu items; the **About** menu contains the **About Windows Media Player** menu item.

When a user chooses **Open** from the **File** menu, event handler **openItem_Click** (lines 37–52) executes. An **OpenFileDialog** box displays (line 40), allowing the user to select a file. The program then sets the **FileName** property of the player (the Windows Media Player control object of type **AxMediaPlayer**) to the name of the file chosen by the user. The **FileName** property specifies the file that Windows Media Player currently is using. Lines 46–50 adjust the size of **player** and the application to reflect the size of the media contained in the file.

The event handler that executes when the user selects **Exit** from the **File** menu (lines 54–59) simply calls **Application.Exit** to terminate the application. The event handler that executes when the user chooses **About Windows Media Player** from the **About** menu (lines 61–66) calls the `AboutBox` method of the player. `AboutBox` simply displays a preset message box containing information about Windows Media Player.

16.13 Microsoft Agent

Microsoft Agent is a technology used to add *interactive animated characters* to Windows applications or Web pages. Interactivity is the key function of Microsoft Agent technology: Microsoft Agent characters can speak and respond to user input via speech recognition and synthesis. Microsoft employs its Agent technology in applications such as Word, Excel and PowerPoint. Agents in these programs aid users in finding answers to questions and in understanding how the applications function.

The Microsoft Agent control provides programmers with access to four predefined characters—*Genie* (a genie), *Merlin* (a wizard), *Peedy* (a parrot) and *Robby* (a robot). Each character has a unique set of animations that programmers can use in their applications to illustrate different points and functions. For instance, the Peedy character-animation set includes different flying animations, which the programmer might use to move Peedy on the screen. Microsoft provides basic information on Agent technology at its Web site,

> `www.microsoft.com/msagent`

Microsoft Agent technology enables users to interact with applications and Web pages through speech, the most natural form of human communication. When the user speaks into a microphone, the control uses a *speech recognition engine,* an application that translates vocal sound input from a microphone into language that the computer understands. The Microsoft Agent control also uses a *text-to-speech engine*, which generates characters' spoken responses. A text-to-speech engine is an application that translates typed words into audio sound that users hear through headphones or speakers connected to a computer. Microsoft provides speech recognition and text-to-speech engines for several languages at its Web site,

> `www.microsoft.com/products/msagent/downloads.htm`

Programmers can even create their own animated characters with the help of the *Microsoft Agent Character Editor* and the *Microsoft Linguistic Sound Editing Tool*. These products are available free for download from

> `www.microsoft.com/products/msagent/devdownloads.htm`

This section introduces the basic capabilities of the Microsoft Agent control. For complete details on downloading this control, visit

> `www.microsoft.com/products/msagent/downloads.htm`

The following example, Peedy's Pizza Palace, was developed by Microsoft to illustrate the capabilities of the Microsoft Agent control. Peedy's Pizza Palace is an online pizza shop where users can place their orders via voice input. The Peedy character interacts with users by helping them choose toppings and then calculating the totals for their orders.

Readers can view this example at

agent.microsoft.com/agent2/sdk/samples/html/peedypza.htm

To run this example, students must download the Peedy character file, a text-to-speech engine and a speech-recognition engine. When the page loads, the browser prompts for these downloads. Follow the directions provided by Microsoft to complete installation.

When the window opens, Peedy introduces himself (Fig. 16.28), and the words he speaks appear in a cartoon bubble above his head. Notice that Peedy's animations correspond to the words he speaks.

Programmers can synchronize character animations with speech output to illustrate a point or to convey a character's mood. For instance, Fig. 16.29 depicts Peedy's *Pleased* animation. The Peedy character-animation set includes eighty-five different animations, each of which is unique to the Peedy character.

Look-and-Feel Observation 16.1

Agent characters remain on top of all active windows while a Microsoft Agent application is running. Their motions are not limited to within the boundaries of the browser or application window.

Peedy also responds to input from the keyboard and mouse. Figure 16.30 shows what happens when a user clicks Peedy with the mouse pointer. Peedy jumps up, ruffles his feathers and exclaims, "Hey that tickles!" or, "Be careful with that pointer!" Users can relocate Peedy on the screen by clicking and dragging him with the mouse. However, even when the user moves Peedy to a different part of the screen, he continues to perform his preset animations and location changes.

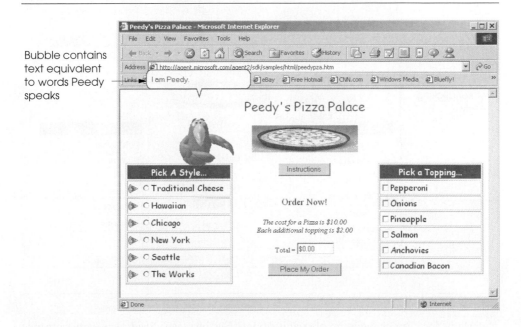

Bubble contains text equivalent to words Peedy speaks

Fig. 16.28 Peedy introducing himself when the window opens.

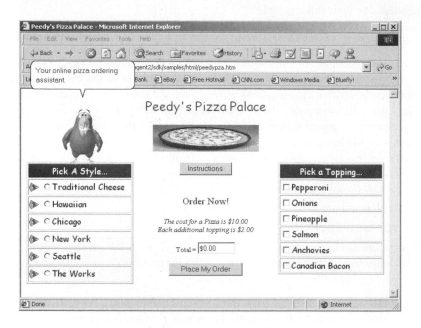

Fig. 16.29 Peedy's *Pleased* animation.

Fig. 16.30 Peedy's reaction when he is clicked.

Many location changes involve animations. For instance, Peedy can hop from one screen location to another, or he can fly (Fig. 16.31).

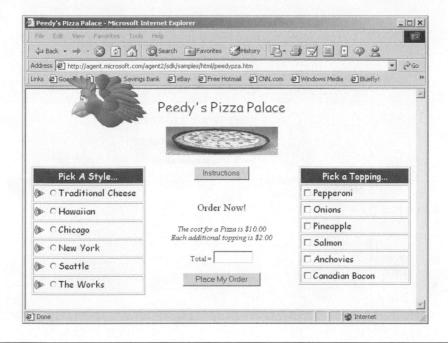

Fig. 16.31 Peedy flying animation.

Once Peedy completes the ordering instructions, a text box appears beneath him indicating that he is listening for a voice command (Fig. 16.32). A user can enter the type of pizza to order either by speaking the style name into a microphone or by clicking the radio button corresponding to their choice.

If a user chooses speech input, a box appears below Peedy displaying the words that Peedy "heard" (i.e., the words translated to the program by the speech-recognition engine). Once he recognizes the user input, Peedy gives the user a description of the selected pizza. Figure 16.33 shows what happens when the user chooses **Seattle** as the pizza style.

Peedy then asks the user to choose additional toppings. Again, the user can either speak or use the mouse to make a selection. Check boxes corresponding to toppings that come with the selected pizza style are checked for the user. Figure 16.34 shows what happens when a user chooses anchovies as an additional topping. Peedy makes a wisecrack about the user's choice.

The user can submit the order either by pressing the **Place My Order** button or by speaking "Place order" into the microphone. Peedy recounts the order while writing down the order items on his notepad (Fig. 16.35). He then calculates the figures on his calculator and reports the total to the user (Fig. 16.36).

The following example (Fig. 16.37) demonstrates how to build a simple application with the Microsoft Agent control. This application contains two drop-down lists from which the user can choose an Agent character and a character animation. When the user chooses from these lists, the chosen character appears and performs the chosen animation. The application uses speech recognition and synthesis to control the character animations and speech: Users can tell the character which animation to perform by pressing the *Scroll Lock* key and then speaking the animation name into a microphone.

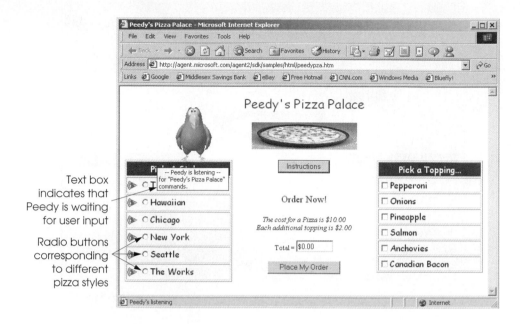

Text box
indicates that
Peedy is waiting
for user input

Radio buttons
corresponding
to different
pizza styles

Fig. 16.32 Peedy waiting for speech input.

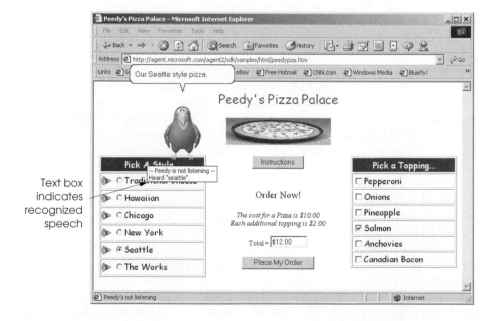

Text box
indicates
recognized
speech

Fig. 16.33 Peedy repeating the user's request for Seattle-style pizza.

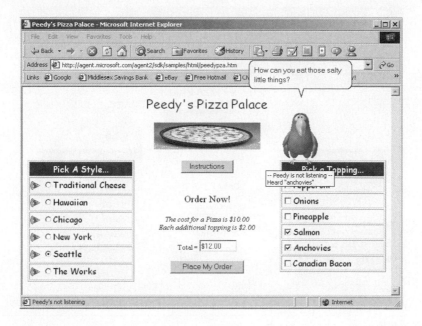

Fig. 16.34 Peedy repeating the user's request for anchovies as an additional topping.

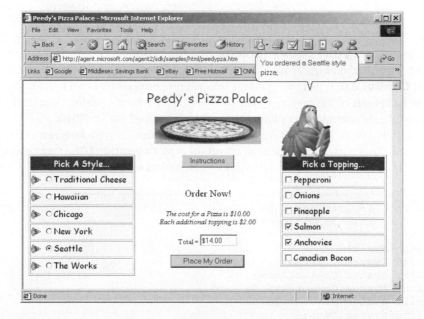

Fig. 16.35 Peedy recounting the order.

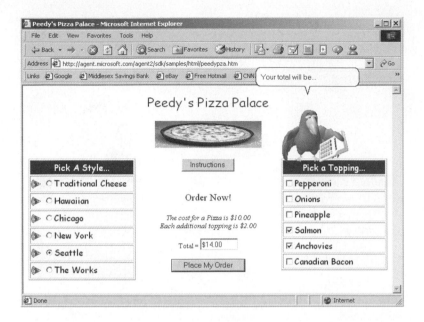

Fig. 16.36 Peedy calculating the total.

The example also allows the user to switch to a new character by speaking its name and also creates a custom command, **MoveToMouse**. In addition, the characters also speak any text that a user enters into the text box. Before running this example, readers first must download and install the control, speech-recognition engine, text-to-speech engine and character definitions from the Microsoft Agent Web site listed previously.

To use the Microsoft Agent control, the programmer first must add it to the **Toolbox**. Begin by selecting **Customize Toolbox** from the **Tools** menu to display the **Customize Toolbox** dialog. In the dialog, scroll down and select the option **Microsoft Agent Control 2.0**. When this option is selected properly, a small check mark appears in the box to the left of the option. Then, click **OK** to dismiss the dialog. The icon for the Microsoft Agent control now should appear at the bottom of the **Toolbox**.

In addition to the Microsoft Agent object **mainAgent** (of type **AxAgent**) that manages all the characters, we also need an object (of type **IAgentCtlCharacter**) to represent the current character. We create this object, named **speaker**, in line 30.

```
1   // Fig. 16.37:  Agent.cs
2   // Demonstrates microsoft agent
3
4   using System;
5   using System.Drawing;
6   using System.Collections;
7   using System.ComponentModel;
8   using System.Windows.Forms;
9   using System.Data;
```

Fig. 16.37 Microsoft Agent demonstration. (Part 1 of 7.)

```
10   using System.IO;
11
12   public class Agent : System.Windows.Forms.Form
13   {
14      // options
15      private System.Windows.Forms.ComboBox actionsCombo;
16      private System.Windows.Forms.ComboBox characterCombo;
17
18      private System.Windows.Forms.Button speakButton;
19      private System.Windows.Forms.GroupBox characterGroup;
20      private AxAgentObjects.AxAgent mainAgent;
21
22      // input
23      private System.Windows.Forms.TextBox speechTextBox;
24      private System.Windows.Forms.TextBox locationTextBox;
25
26      private
27         System.ComponentModel.Container components = null;
28
29      // current agent object
30      private AgentObjects.IAgentCtlCharacter speaker;
31
32      [STAThread]
33      static void Main()
34      {
35         Application.Run( new Agent() );
36      }
37
38      // Visual Studio .NET generated code
39
40      // KeyDown event handler for locationTextBox
41      private void locationTextBox_KeyDown(
42         object sender, System.Windows.Forms.KeyEventArgs e )
43      {
44         if ( e.KeyCode == Keys.Enter )
45         {
46            // set character location to text box value
47            string location = locationTextBox.Text;
48
49            // initialize the characters
50            try
51            {
52               // load characters into agent object
53               mainAgent.Characters.Load( "Genie",
54                  location + "Genie.acs" );
55
56               mainAgent.Characters.Load( "Merlin",
57                  location + "Merlin.acs" );
58
59               mainAgent.Characters.Load( "Peedy",
60                  location + "Peedy.acs" );
61
```

Fig. 16.37 Microsoft Agent demonstration. (Part 2 of 7.)

```
62                mainAgent.Characters.Load( "Robby",
63                    location + "Robby.acs" );
64
65                // disable TextBox for entering the location
66                // and enable other controls
67                locationTextBox.Enabled = false;
68                speechTextBox.Enabled = true;
69                speakButton.Enabled = true;
70                characterCombo.Enabled = true;
71                actionsCombo.Enabled = true;
72
73                // set current character to Genie and show him
74                speaker = mainAgent.Characters[ "Genie" ];
75
76                // obtain an animation name list
77                GetAnimationNames();
78                speaker.Show( 0 );
79            }
80            catch( FileNotFoundException )
81            {
82                MessageBox.Show( "Invalid character location",
83                    "Error", MessageBoxButtons.OK,
84                    MessageBoxIcon.Error );
85            }
86        }
87
88    } // end method locationTextBox_KeyDown
89
90    private void speakButton_Click(
91        object sender, System.EventArgs e )
92    {
93        // if textbox is empty, have the character ask
94        // user to type the words into textbox, otherwise
95        // have character say the words in textbox
96        if ( speechTextBox.Text == "" )
97            speaker.Speak(
98                "Please, type the words you want me to speak",
99                "" );
100        else
101            speaker.Speak( speechTextBox.Text, "" );
102
103    } // end method speakButton_Click
104
105    // click event for agent
106    private void mainAgent_ClickEvent( object sender,
107        AxAgentObjects._AgentEvents_ClickEvent e )
108    {
109        speaker.Play( "Confused" );
110        speaker.Speak( "Why are you poking me?", "" );
111        speaker.Play( "RestPose" );
112
113    } // end method mainAgent_ClickEvent
114
```

Fig. 16.37 Microsoft Agent demonstration. (Part 3 of 7.)

```
115      // combobox changed event, switch active agent
116      private void characterCombo_SelectedIndexChanged(
117         object sender, System.EventArgs e )
118      {
119         ChangeCharacter( characterCombo.Text );
120
121      } // end method characterCombo_SelectedIndexChanged
122
123      private void ChangeCharacter( string name )
124      {
125         speaker.Hide( 0 );
126         speaker = mainAgent.Characters[ name ];
127
128         // regenerate animation name list
129         GetAnimationNames();
130         speaker.Show( 0 );
131
132      } // end method ChangeCharacter
133
134      // get animation names and store in arraylist
135      private void GetAnimationNames()
136      {
137         // ensure thread safety
138         lock( this )
139         {
140
141            // get animation names
142            IEnumerator enumerator =
143               mainAgent.Characters[
144               speaker.Name ].AnimationNames.GetEnumerator();
145
146            string voiceString;
147
148            // clear actionsCombo
149            actionsCombo.Items.Clear();
150            speaker.Commands.RemoveAll();
151
152            // copy enumeration to ArrayList
153            while ( enumerator.MoveNext() )
154            {
155               //remove underscores in speech string
156               voiceString = ( string )enumerator.Current;
157               voiceString =
158                  voiceString.Replace( "_", "underscore" );
159
160               actionsCombo.Items.Add( enumerator.Current );
161
162               // add all animations as voice enabled commands
163               speaker.Commands.Add(
164                  ( string )enumerator.Current,
165                  enumerator.Current,
166                  voiceString, true, false );
167            }
```

Fig. 16.37 Microsoft Agent demonstration. (Part 4 of 7.)

```
168
169            // add custom command
170            speaker.Commands.Add(
171               "MoveToMouse", "MoveToMouse",
172               "MoveToMouse", true, true );
173         }
174
175      } // end method GetAnimationNames
176
177      // user selects new action
178      private void actionsCombo_SelectedIndexChanged(
179         object sender, System.EventArgs e )
180      {
181         speaker.StopAll( "Play" );
182         speaker.Play( actionsCombo.Text );
183         speaker.Play( "RestPose" );
184
185      } // end method actionsCombo_SelectedIndexChanged
186
187      // handles agent commands
188      private void mainAgent_Command( object sender,
189         AxAgentObjects._AgentEvents_CommandEvent e )
190      {
191         // get userInput property
192         AgentObjects.IAgentCtlUserInput command =
193            ( AgentObjects.IAgentCtlUserInput )e.userInput;
194
195         // change character if user speaks character name
196         if ( command.Voice == "Peedy" ||
197            command.Voice == "Robby" ||
198            command.Voice == "Merlin" ||
199            command.Voice == "Genie" )
200         {
201            ChangeCharacter( command.Voice );
202
203            return;
204         }
205
206         // send agent to mouse
207         if ( command.Voice == "MoveToMouse" )
208         {
209            speaker.MoveTo(
210               Convert.ToInt16( Cursor.Position.X - 60 ),
211               Convert.ToInt16( Cursor.Position.Y - 60 ), 5 );
212            return;
213         }
214
215         // play new animation
216         speaker.StopAll( "Play" );
217         speaker.Play( command.Name );
218
219      } // end method mainAgent_Command
220   } // end class Agent
```

Fig. 16.37 Microsoft Agent demonstration. (Part 5 of 7.)

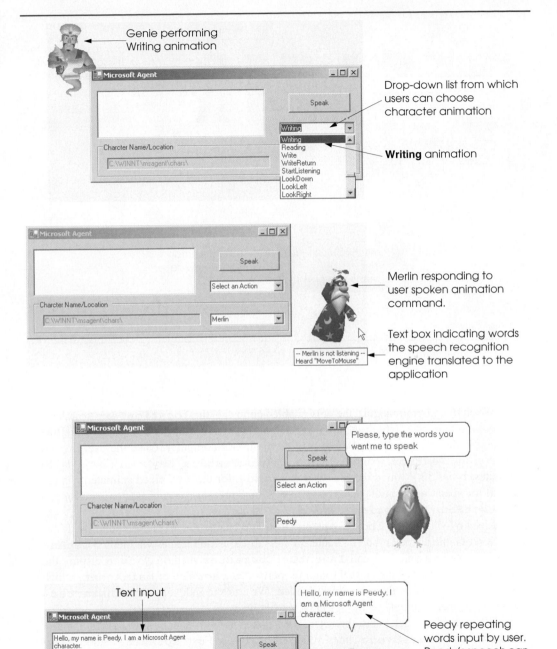

Fig. 16.37 Microsoft Agent demonstration. (Part 6 of 7.)

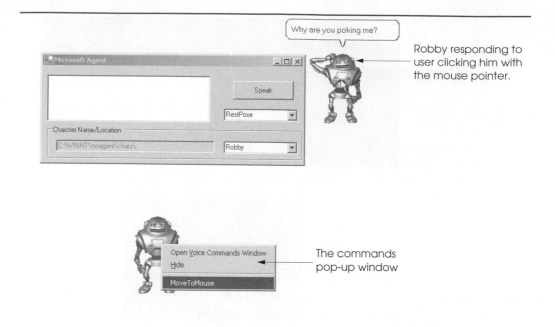

Fig. 16.37 Microsoft Agent demonstration. (Part 7 of 7.)

When the program begins, the only enabled control is the **locationTextBox**. This text box contains the default location for the character files, but the user can change this location if the files are located elsewhere on the user's computer. Once the user presses *Enter* in the **TextBox**, event handler **locationTextBox_KeyDown** (lines 41–88) executes. Lines 53–63 load the character descriptions for the predefined animated characters. If the specified location of the characters is incorrect, or if any character is missing, a **FileNotFoundException** is thrown.

Lines 67–71 disable **locationTextBox** and enable the rest of the controls. Lines 74–78 set Genie as the default character, obtain all animation names via method **GetAnimationNames** and then call **IAgentCtlCharacter** method *Show* to display the character. We access characters through property *Characters* of **mainAgent**, which contains all characters that have been loaded. We use the indexer of the **Characters** property to specify the name of the character that we wish to load (Genie).

When a user clicks the character (i.e., pokes it with the mouse), event handler **mainAgent_ClickEvent** (lines 106–113) executes. First, **speaker** method **Play** plays an animation. This method accepts as an argument a **string** representing one of the predefined animations for the character (a list of animations for each character is available at the Microsoft Agent Web site; each character provides over 70 animations). In our example, the argument to **Play** is **"Confused"**—this animation is defined for all four characters, each of which expresses this emotion in a unique way. The character then speaks, **"Why are you poking me?"** via a call to method *Speak*. Finally, the **RestPose** animation is played, which returns the character to its neutral, resting pose.

The list of valid commands for a character is contained in property **Commands** of the **IAgentCtlCharacter** object (**speaker**, in this example). The commands for an Agent character can be viewed in the **Commands** pop-up window, which displays when the user right-clicks an Agent character (the last screenshot in Fig. 16.37). Method **Add** of property **Commands** adds a new command to the command list. Method **Add** takes three **string** arguments and two **bool** arguments. The first **string** argument identifies the name of the command, which we use to identify the command programmatically. The second **string** defines the command name as it appears in the **Commands** pop-up window. The third **string** defines the voice input that triggers the command. The first **bool** specifies whether the command is active, and the second **bool** indicates whether the command is visible in the **Commands** pop-up window. A command is triggered when the user selects the command from the **Commands** pop-up window or speaks the voice input into a microphone. Command logic is handled in the **Command** event of the **AxAgent** control (**mainAgent**, in this example). In addition, Agent defines several global commands that have predefined functions (for example, speaking a character name causes that character to appear).

Method **GetAnimationNames** (lines 135–175) fills the **actionsCombo ComboBox** with the current character's animation listing and defines the valid commands that can be used with the character. The method contains a **lock** block to prevent errors resulting from rapid character changes. The method obtains the current character's animations as an enumerator (142–144), then clears the existing items in the **ComboBox** and character's **Commands** property. Lines 153–167 iterate through all items in the animation-name enumerator. For each animation, in line 156, we assign the animation name to **string voiceString**. Lines 157–158 remove any underscore characters (_) and replaces them with the **string "underscore"**; this changes the **string** so that a user can pronounce and employ it as a command activator. The **Add** method (lines 163–166) of the **Commands** property adds a new command to the current character. The **Add** method adds all animations as commands by providing the following arguments: The animation name as the new command's **name** and caption, and **voiceString** for the voice activation **string**. The method's **bool** arguments enable the command, but make it unavailable in the **Commands** pop-up window. Thus, the command can be activated only by voice input. Lines 170–172 create a new command, named **MoveToMouse**, which is visible in the **Commands** pop-up window.

After the **GetAnimationNames** method has been called, the user can select a value from the **actionsCombo ComboBox**. Event handler **actionsCombo.SelectedIndexChanged** stops any current animation and then displays the animation that the user selected from the **ComboBox**.

The user also can type text into the **TextBox** and click **Speak**. This causes event handler **speakButton_Click** (line 90–103) to call **speaker**'s method **Speak**, supplying as an argument the text in **speechTextBox**. If the user clicks **Speak** without providing text, the character speaks, **"Please, type the words you want me to speak"**.

At any point in the program, the user can choose to display a different character from the **ComboBox**. When this happens, the **SelectedIndexChanged** event handler for **characterCombo** (lines 116–121) executes. The event handler calls method **ChangeCharacter** (lines 123–132) with the text in the **characterCombo ComboBox** as an argument. Method **ChangeCharacter** calls the **Hide** method of **speaker** (line 125) to remove the current character from view. Line 126 assigns the newly selected character to **speaker**, line 129 generates the character's animation names and commands, and line 130 displays the character via a call to method **Show**.

Each time a user presses the *Scroll Lock* key and speaks into a microphone or selects a command from the **Commands** pop-up window, event handler **main-Agent_Command** is called. This method is passed an argument of type **AxAgent-Objects._AgentEvents_CommandEvent**, which contains a single property, **userInput**. The **userInput** property returns an **Object** that can be converted to type **AgentObjects.IAgentCtlUserInput**. The **userInput** object is assigned to a **IAgentCtlUserInput** object **command**, which is used to identify the command and then take appropriate action. Lines 196–204 use method **ChangeCharacter** to change the current Agent character if the user speaks a character name. Microsoft Agent always will show a character when a user speaks its name; however, by controlling the character change, we can ensure that only one Agent character is displayed at a time. Lines 207–213 move the character to the current mouse location if the user invokes the **MoveToMouse** command. The Agent method *MoveTo* takes x- and y-coordinate arguments and moves the character to the specified screen position, applying appropriate movement animations. For all other commands, we **Play** the command name as an animation on line 217.

In this chapter, we explored various graphics capabilities of GDI+, including pens, brushes and images, and some multimedia capabilities of the .NET Framework Class Library. In the next chapter, we cover the reading, writing and accessing of sequential- and random-access files. We also explore several types of streams included in Visual Studio .NET.

SUMMARY

- A coordinate system is used to identify every possible point on the screen.

- The upper-left corner of a GUI component has coordinates (0, 0). A coordinate pair is composed of an *x*-coordinate (the horizontal coordinate) and a *y*-coordinate (the vertical coordinate).

- Coordinate units are measured in pixels. A pixel is the smallest unit of resolution on a display monitor.

- A graphics context represents a drawing surface on the screen. A **Graphics** object provides access to the graphics context of a control.

- An instance of the **Pen** class is used to draw lines.

- An instance of one of the classes that derive from abstract class **Brush** is used to draw solid shapes.

- The **Point** structure can be used to represent a point in a two-dimensional plane.

- **Graphics** objects contain methods for drawing, font manipulation, color manipulation and other graphics-related actions.

- Method **OnPaint** normally is called in response to an event, such as the uncovering of a window. This method, in turn, triggers a **Paint** event.

- Structure **Color** defines constants for manipulating colors in a C# program.

- **Color** properties **R**, **G** and **B** return **int** values from 0 to 255, representing the amounts of red, green and blue, respectively, that exist in a **Color**. The larger the value, the greater the amount of that particular color.

- C# provides class **ColorDialog** to display a dialog that allows users to select colors.

- **Component** property **BackColor** (one of the many **Component** properties that can be called on most GUI components) changes the component's background color.

- Class **Font**'s constructors all take at least three arguments—the font name, the font size and the font style. The font name is any font currently supported by the system. The font style is a member of the **FontStyle** enumeration.
- Class **FontMetrics** defines several methods for obtaining font metrics.
- Class **Font** provides the **Bold**, **Italic**, **Strikeout** and **Underline** properties, which return **true** if the font is bold, italic, strikeout or underlined, respectively.
- Class **Font** provides the **Name** property, which returns a **string** representing the name of the font.
- Class **Font** provides the **Size** and **SizeInPoints** properties, which return the size of the font in design units and points, respectively.
- The **FontFamily** class provides information about such font metrics as the family's spacing and height.
- The **FontFamily** class provides the **GetCellAscent**, **GetCellDescent**, **GetEmHeight** and **GetLineSpacing** methods, which return the ascent of a font, the descent of a font, the font's height in points and the distance between two consecutive lines of text, respectively.
- Class **Graphics** provides methods **DrawLine**, **DrawRectangle**, **DrawEllipse**, **DrawArc**, **DrawLines**, **DrawPolygon** and **DrawPie**, which draw lines and shape outlines.
- Class **Graphics** provides methods **FillRectangle**, **FillEllipse**, **FillPolygon** and **FillPie**, which draw solid shapes.
- Classes **HatchBrush**, **LinearGradientBrush**, **PathGradientBrush** and **TextureBrush** all derive from class **Brush** and represent shape-filling styles.
- **Graphics** method **FromImage** retrieves the **Graphics** object associated with the image file that is its argument.
- The **DashStyle** and **DashCap** enumerations define the style of dashes and their ends, respectively.
- Class **GraphicsPath** represents a shape constructed from straight lines and curves.
- **GraphicsPath** method **AddLine** appends a line to the shape that is encapsulated by the object.
- **GraphicsPath** method **CloseFigure** completes the shape that is represented by the **GraphicsPath** object.
- Class **Image** is used to manipulate images.
- Class **Image** provides method **FromFile** to retrieve an image stored on disk and load it into an instance of class **Image**.
- **Graphics** method **Clear** paints the entire **Control** with the color that the programmer provides as an argument.
- **Graphics** method **DrawImage** draws the specified **Image** on the **Control**.
- Using Visual Studio .NET and C#, programmers can create applications that use components such as Windows Media Player and Microsoft Agent.
- The Windows Media Player allows programmers to create applications that can play multimedia files.
- Microsoft Agent is a technology that allows programmers to include interactive animated characters in their applications.

TERMINOLOGY

A property of structure **Color**
AboutBox method of **AxMediaPlayer**

Add method of class **ArrayList**
AddLine method of class **GraphicsPath**

Underline property of class **Font**
upper-left corner of a GUI component
vertical coordinate
WAV
White static property of structure **Color**
Windows Media Player
Windows wave file format (WAV)

x-axis
x-coordinate
y-axis
y-coordinate
yellow
Yellow static property of structure **Color**

SELF-REVIEW EXERCISES

16.1   State whether each of the following is *true* or *false*. If *false*, explain why.
  a) A **Font** object's size can be changed by setting its **Size** property.
  b) In the C# coordinate system, *x*-values increase from left to right.
  c) Method **FillPolygon** draws a solid polygon with a specified **Brush**.
  d) Method **DrawArc** allows negative angles.
  e) **Font** property **Size** returns the size of the current font in centimeters.
  f) Pixel coordinate (0, 0) is located at the exact center of the monitor.
  g) A **HatchBrush** is used to draw lines.
  h) A **Color** is defined by its alpha, red, green and violet content.
  i) Every **Control** has an associated **Graphics** object.
  j) Method **OnPaint** is inherited by every **Form**.

16.2   Fill in the blanks in each of the following statements:
  a) Class _____ is used to draw lines of various colors and thicknesses.
  b) Classes_____ and _____ define the fill for a shape in such a way that the fill gradually changes from one color to another.
  c) The _____ method of class **Graphics** draws a line between two points.
  d) ARGB is short for _____, _____, _____ and _____.
  e) Font sizes usually are measured in units called _____.
  f) Class_____ fills a shape using a pattern drawn in a **Bitmap**.
  g) _____ _____ _____ allows an application to play multimedia files.
  h) Class _____ defines a path consisting of lines and curves.
  i) C#'s drawing capabilities are part of the namespaces _____ and _____.
  j) Method _____ loads an image from a disk into an **Image** object.

ANSWERS TO SELF-REVIEW EXERCISES

16.1   a) False. **Size** is a read-only property. b) True. c) True. d) True. e) False. It returns the size of the current **Font** in design units. f) False. The coordinate (0,0) corresponds to the upper-left corner of a GUI component on which drawing occurs. g) False. A **Pen** is used to draw lines, a **Hatch-Brush** fills a shape with a hatch pattern. h) False. A color is defined by its alpha, red, green and blue content. i) True. j) True.

16.2   a) **Pen**. b) **LinearGradientBrush**, **PathGradientBrush**. c) **DrawLine**. d) alpha, red, green, blue. e) points. f) **TextureBrush**. g) Windows Media Player h) **GraphicsPath** i) **System.Drawing**, **System.Drawing.Drawing2D**. j) **FromFile**.

EXERCISES

16.3   Write a program that draws eight concentric circles. The circles should be separated from one another by 10 pixels. Use the **DrawArc** method.

16.4   Write a program that draws 100 lines with random lengths, positions, thicknesses and colors.

16.5　Write a program that draws a tetrahedron (a pyramid). Use class **GraphicsPath** and method **DrawPath**.

16.6　Write a program that allows the user to draw "free-hand" images with the mouse in a **PictureBox**. Allow the user to change the drawing color and width of the pen. Provide a button that allows the user to clear the **PictureBox**.

16.7　Write a program that repeatedly flashes an image on the screen. Do this by interspersing the image with a plain background-color image.

16.8　If you want to emphasize an image, you might place a row of simulated light bulbs around the image. Write a program by which an image is emphasized this way. You can let the light bulbs flash in unison or you can let them fire on and off in sequence, one after another.

16.9　(*Eight Queens*) A puzzler for chess buffs is the Eight Queens problem. Simply stated: Is it possible to place eight queens on an empty chessboard so that no queen is "attacking" any other (i.e., so that no two queens are in the same row, in the same column or along the same diagonal)?

Create a GUI that allows the user to drag-and-drop each queen on the board. Use the graphical features of Fig. 16.26. Provide eight queen images to the right of the board (Fig. 16.38), which the user can drag-and-drop onto the board. When a queen is dropped on the board, its corresponding image to the right should not be visible. If a queen is in conflict with another queen when placed on the board, display a message box and remove that queen from the board.

Fig. 16.38 GUI for Eight Queens exercise.

17

Files and Streams

Objectives

- To be able to create, read, write and update files.
- To understand the C# streams class hierarchy.
- To be able to use classes **File** and **Directory**.
- To be able to use the **FileStream** and **BinaryFormatter** classes to read objects from, and write objects to, files.
- To become familiar with sequential-access and random-access file processing.

I can only assume that a "Do Not File" document is filed in a "Do Not File" file.
Senator Frank Church
Senate Intelligence Subcommittee Hearing, 1975

Consciousness ... does not appear to itself chopped up in bits. ... A "river" or a "stream" are the metaphors by which it is most naturally described.
William James

I read part of it all the way through.
Samuel Goldwyn

17.1 Introduction

Variables and arrays offer only temporary storage of data—the data are lost when an object is garbage collected or when the program terminates. By contrast, *files* are used for long-term storage of large amounts of data and can retain data even after the program that created the data terminates. Data maintained in files often are called *persistent data*. Computers can store files on *secondary storage devices*, such as magnetic disks, optical disks and magnetic tapes. In this chapter, we explain how to create, update and process data files in C# programs. We consider both "sequential-access" files and "random-access" files, indicating the kinds of applications for which each is best suited. We have two goals in this chapter: To introduce the sequential-access and random-access file-processing paradigms and to provide the reader with sufficient stream-processing capabilities to support the networking features that we introduce in Chapter 22, Networking: Streams-Based Sockets and Datagrams.

File processing is one of a programming language's most important capabilities, because it enables a language to support commercial applications that typically process massive amounts of persistent data. This chapter discusses C#'s powerful and abundant file-processing and stream-input/output features.

17.2 Data Hierarchy

Ultimately, all data items processed by a computer are reduced to combinations of zeros and ones. This is because it is simple and economical to build electronic devices that can assume two stable states—**0** represents one state, and **1** represents the other. It is remarkable that the impressive functions performed by computers involve only the most fundamental manipulations of **0**s and **1**s.

The smallest data items that computers support are called *bits* (short for "*binary digit*"—a digit that can assume one of two values). Each data item, or bit, can assume either the value **0** or the value **1**. Computer circuitry performs various simple bit manipulations, such as examining the value of a bit, setting the value of a bit and reversing a bit (from **1** to **0** or from **0** to **1**).

Programming with data in the low-level form of bits is cumbersome. It is preferable to program with data in forms such as *decimal digits* (i.e., 0, 1, 2, 3, 4, 5, 6, 7, 8 and 9), *letters* (i.e., A through Z and a through z) and *special symbols* (i.e., $, @, %, &, *, (,), -, +, ", :, ?, / and many others). Digits, letters and special symbols are referred to as *characters.* The set of all characters used to write programs and represent data items on a particular computer is called that computer's *character set.* Because computers can process only **1**s and **0**s, every character in a computer's character set is represented as a pattern of **1**s and **0**s. *Bytes* are composed of eight bits (characters in C# are *Unicode* characters, which are composed of 2 bytes). Programmers create programs and data items with characters; computers manipulate and process these characters as patterns of bits.

In the same way that characters are composed of bits, *fields* are composed of characters. A field is a group of characters that conveys some meaning. For example, a field consisting of uppercase and lowercase letters can represent a person's name.

The various kinds of data items processed by computers form a *data hierarchy* (Fig. 17.1) in which data items become larger and more complex in structure as we progress from bits, to characters, to fields and up to larger data structures.

Typically, a *record* is composed of several fields. In a payroll system, for example, a record for a particular employee might include the following fields:

1. Employee identification number

2. Name

3. Address

4. Hourly pay rate

5. Number of exemptions claimed

6. Year-to-date earnings

7. Amount of taxes withheld

Thus, a record is a group of related fields. In the preceding example, each field is associated with the same employee. A *file* is a group of related records.[1] A company's payroll file normally contains one record for each employee. Thus, a payroll file for a small company might contain only 22 records, whereas a payroll file for a large company might contain 100,000 records. It is not unusual for a company to have many files, some containing millions, billions or even trillions of bits of information.

To facilitate the retrieval of specific records from a file, at least one field in each record is chosen as a unique *record key.* A record key identifies a record as belonging to a particular person or entity and distinguishes that record from all other records. In the payroll record described previously, the employee identification number normally would be chosen as the record key.

---

1. More generally, a file can contain arbitrary data in arbitrary formats. In some operating systems, a file is viewed as nothing more than a collection of bytes. In such an operating system, any organization of the bytes in a file (such as organizing the data into records) is a view created by the applications programmer.

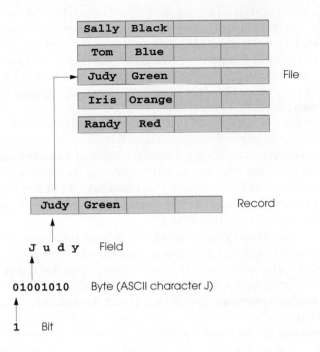

Fig. 17.1 Data hierarchy.

There are many ways of organizing records in a file. The most common type of organization is called a *sequential file*, in which records typically are stored in order by the record-key field. In a payroll file, records usually are placed in order by employee-identification numbers. The first employee record in the file contains the lowest employee-identification number, and subsequent records contain increasingly higher employee-identification numbers.

Most businesses use many different files to store data. For example, a company might have payroll files, accounts receivable files (listing money due from clients), accounts payable files (listing money due to suppliers), inventory files (listing facts about all the items handled by the business) and many other types of files. Sometimes, a group of related files is called a *database*. A collection of programs designed to create and manage databases is called a *database management system* (DBMS). We discuss databases in detail in Chapter 19, Databases, SQL and ADO.NET.

17.3 Files and Streams

C# views each file as a sequential *stream* of bytes (Fig. 17.2). Each file ends either with an *end-of-file marker* or at a specific byte number that is recorded in a system-maintained administrative data structure. When a file is *opened*, C# creates an object, then associates a stream with that object. The runtime environment creates three stream objects upon program execution, which are accessible via properties **Console.Out**, **Console.In** and **Console.Error**, respectively. These objects facilitate communication between a program and a particular file or device. Property **Console.In** returns the *standard input* *stream object*, which enables a program to input data from the keyboard. Property **Console.Out** returns the *standard output stream object*, which enables a program to output data to the screen. Property **Console.Error** returns the *standard error stream object*, which enables a program to output error messages to the screen. We have been using **Console.Out** and **Console.In** in our console applications—**Console** methods **Write** and **WriteLine** use **Console.Out** to perform output, and methods **Read** and **ReadLine** use **Console.In** to perform input.

To perform file processing in C#, namespace **System.IO** must be referenced. This namespace includes definitions for stream classes such as ***StreamReader*** (for text input from a file), ***StreamWriter*** (for text output to a file) and **FileStream** (for both input from and output to a file). Files are opened by creating objects of these stream classes, which inherit from **abstract** classes ***TextReader***, ***TextWriter*** and ***Stream***, respectively. Actually, **Console.In** and **Console.Out** are properties of class **TextReader** and **TextWriter**, respectively.

C# provides class ***BinaryFormatter***, which is used in conjunction with a **Stream** object to perform input and output of objects. *Serialization* involves converting an object into a format that can be written to a file without losing any of that object's data. *Deserialization* consists of reading this format from a file and reconstructing the original object from it. A **BinaryFormatter** can serialize objects to, and deserialize objects from, a specified **Stream**.

Class ***System.IO.Stream*** provides functionality for representing streams as bytes. This class is **abstract**, so objects of this class cannot be instantiated. Classes ***FileStream***, ***MemoryStream*** and ***BufferedStream*** (all from namespace **System.IO**) inherit from class **Stream**. Later in the chapter, we use **FileStream** to read data to, and write data from, sequential-access and random-access files. Class **MemoryStream** enables the transferal of data directly to and from memory—this type of transfer is much faster than are other types of data transfer (e.g., to and from disk). Class **BufferedStream** uses *buffering* to transfer data to or from a stream. Buffering is an I/O-performance-enhancement technique in which each output operation is directed to a region in memory called a *buffer* that is large enough to hold the data from many output operations. Then, actual transfer to the output device is performed in one large *physical output operation* each time the buffer fills. The output operations directed to the output buffer in memory often are called *logical output operations*.

C# offers many classes for performing input and output. In this chapter, we use several key stream classes to implement a variety of file-processing programs that create, manipulate and destroy sequential-access files and random-access files. In Chapter 22, Networking: Streams-Based Sockets and Datagrams, we use stream classes extensively to implement networking applications.

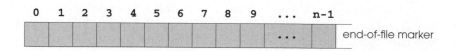

Fig. 17.2   C#'s view of an *n-byte* file.

17.4 Classes `File` and `Directory`

Information on computers is stored in files, which are organized in directories. Class ***File*** is provided for manipulating files, and class ***Directory*** is provided for manipulating directories. Class **File** cannot write to or read from files directly; we discuss methods for reading and writing files in subsequent sections.

Note that the **** *separator character* separates directories and files in a path. On UNIX systems, the separator character is **/**. C# actually processes both characters as identical in a path name. This means that, if we specified the path **c:\C_Sharp/README**, which uses one of each separator character, C# still would process the file properly.

Figure 17.3 lists some methods contained in class **File** for manipulating and determining information about particular files. Class **File** contains only **static** methods—you cannot instantiate objects of type **File**. We use several of these methods in the example of Fig. 17.5.

Class **Directory** provides capabilities for manipulating directories. Figure 17.4 lists some methods that can be used for directory manipulation. We employ several of these methods in the example of Fig. 17.5

The ***DirectoryInfo*** object returned by method **CreateDirectory** contains information about a directory. Much of the information contained in this class also can be accessed via the methods of class **Directory**.

`static` Method	Description
AppendText	Returns a **StreamWriter** that appends to an existing file or creates a file if one does not exist.
Copy	Copies a file to a new file.
Create	Creates a file and returns its associated **FileStream**.
CreateText	Creates a text file and returns its associated **StreamWriter**.
Delete	Deletes the specified file.
GetCreationTime	Returns a **DateTime** object representing the time that the file was created.
GetLastAccessTime	Returns a **DateTime** object representing the time that the file was last accessed.
GetLastWriteTime	Returns a **DateTime** object representing the time that the file was last modified.
Move	Moves the specified file to a specified location.
Open	Returns a **FileStream** associated with the specified file and equipped with the specified read/write permissions.
OpenRead	Returns a read-only **FileStream** associated with the specified file.
OpenText	Returns a **StreamReader** associated with the specified file.
OpenWrite	Returns a read/write **FileStream** associated with the specified file.

Fig. 17.3   **File** class methods (partial list).

static Method	Description
CreateDirectory	Creates a directory and returns its associated **Directory-Info**.
Delete	Deletes the specified directory.
Exists	Returns **true** if the specified directory exists; otherwise, it returns **false**.
GetLastWriteTime	Returns a **DateTime** object representing the time that the directory was last modified.
GetDirectories	Returns a **string** array representing the names of the subdirectories in the specified directory.
GetFiles	Returns a **string** array representing the names of the files in the specified directory.
GetCreationTime	Returns a **DateTime** object representing the time that the directory was created.
GetLastAccessTime	Returns a **DateTime** object representing the time that the directory was last accessed.
GetLastWriteTime	Returns a **DateTime** object representing the time that items were last written to the directory.
Move	Moves the specified directory to a specified location.

Fig. 17.4 Directory class methods (partial list).

Class **FileTestForm** (Fig. 17.5) uses methods described in Fig. 17.3 and Fig. 17.4 to access file and directory information. This class contains **TextBox inputTextBox** (line 18), which enables the user to input a file or directory name. For each key that the user presses in the text box, the program calls method **inputTextBox_KeyDown** (lines 31–93). If the user presses the *Enter* key (line 35), this method displays either file or directory contents, depending on the text the user input in the **TextBox**. (Note that, if the user does not press the *Enter* key, this method returns without displaying any content.) Line 43 uses method **Exists** of class **File** to determine whether the user-specified text is a name of an existing file. If the user specifies an existing file, line 47 invokes **private** method **GetInformation** (lines 96–115), which calls methods **GetCreationTime** (line 103), **GetLastWriteTime** (line 107) and **GetLastAccessTime** (line 111) of class **File** to access file information. When method **GetInformation** returns, line 53 instantiates a **StreamReader** for reading text from the file. The **StreamReader** constructor takes as an argument a **string** containing the name of the file to open. Line 54 calls method **ReadToEnd** of the **StreamReader** to read the file content from the file, then displays the content.

```
1   // Fig 17.5: FileTest.cs
2   // Using classes File and Directory.
3
```

Fig. 17.5   Testing classes **File** and **Directory**. (Part 1 of 4.)

```
4   using System;
5   using System.Drawing;
6   using System.Collections;
7   using System.ComponentModel;
8   using System.Windows.Forms;
9   using System.Data;
10  using System.IO;
11
12  // displays contents of files and directories
13  public class FileTestForm : System.Windows.Forms.Form
14  {
15     private System.Windows.Forms.Label directionsLabel;
16
17     private System.Windows.Forms.TextBox outputTextBox;
18     private System.Windows.Forms.TextBox inputTextBox;
19
20     private System.ComponentModel.Container components = null;
21
22     [STAThread]
23     static void Main()
24     {
25        Application.Run( new FileTestForm() );
26     }
27
28     // Visual Studio .NET generated code
29
30     // invoked when user presses key
31     private void inputTextBox_KeyDown(
32        object sender, System.Windows.Forms.KeyEventArgs e )
33     {
34        // determine whether user pressed Enter key
35        if ( e.KeyCode == Keys.Enter )
36        {
37           string fileName; // name of file or directory
38
39           // get user-specified file or directory
40           fileName = inputTextBox.Text;
41
42           // determine whether fileName is a file
43           if ( File.Exists( fileName ) )
44           {
45              // get file's creation date,
46              // modification date, etc.
47              outputTextBox.Text = GetInformation( fileName );
48
49              // display file contents through StreamReader
50              try
51              {
52                 // obtain reader and file contents
53                 StreamReader stream = new StreamReader( fileName );
54                 outputTextBox.Text += stream.ReadToEnd();
55              }
```

Fig. 17.5   Testing classes **File** and **Directory**. (Part 2 of 4.)

```
56                  // handle exception if StreamReader is unavailable
57                  catch( IOException )
58                  {
59                      MessageBox.Show( "File Error", "File Error",
60                          MessageBoxButtons.OK, MessageBoxIcon.Error );
61                  }
62              }
63
64              // determine whether fileName is a directory
65              else if ( Directory.Exists( fileName ) )
66              {
67                  // array for directories
68                  string[] directoryList;
69
70                  // get directory's creation date,
71                  // modification date, etc.
72                  outputTextBox.Text = GetInformation( fileName );
73
74                  // obtain file/directory list of specified directory
75                  directoryList = Directory.GetDirectories( fileName );
76
77                  outputTextBox.Text +=
78                      "\r\n\r\nDirectory contents:\r\n";
79
80                  // output directoryList contents
81                  for ( int i = 0; i < directoryList.Length; i++ )
82                      outputTextBox.Text += directoryList[ i ] + "\r\n";
83              }
84              else
85              {
86                  // notify user that neither file nor directory exists
87                  MessageBox.Show( inputTextBox.Text +
88                      " does not exist", "File Error",
89                      MessageBoxButtons.OK, MessageBoxIcon.Error );
90              }
91          } // end if
92
93      } // end method inputTextBox_KeyDown
94
95      // get information on file or directory
96      private string GetInformation( string fileName )
97      {
98          // output that file or directory exists
99          string information = fileName + " exists\r\n\r\n";
100
101         // output when file or directory was created
102         information += "Created: " +
103             File.GetCreationTime( fileName ) + "\r\n";
104
105         // output when file or directory was last modified
106         information += "Last modified: " +
107             File.GetLastWriteTime( fileName ) + "\r\n";
108
```

Fig. 17.5   Testing classes **File** and **Directory**. (Part 3 of 4.)

```
109           // output when file or directory was last accessed
110           information += "Last accessed: " +
111              File.GetLastAccessTime( fileName ) + "\r\n" + "\r\n";
112
113           return information;
114
115      } // end method GetInformation
116
117 } // end class FileTestForm
```

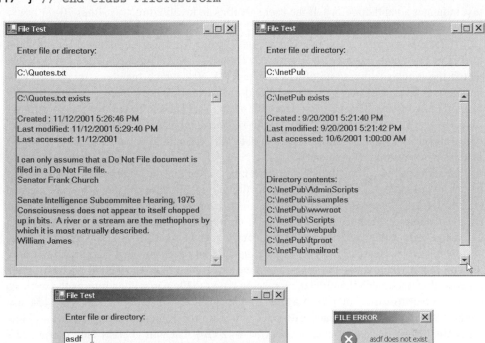

Fig. 17.5   Testing classes **File** and **Directory**. (Part 4 of 4.)

If line 43 determines that the user-specified text is not a file, line 65 determines whether it is a directory using method **Exists** of class **Directory**. If the user specified an existing directory, line 72 invokes method **GetInformation** to access the directory information. Line 75 calls method **GetDirectories** of class **Directory** to obtain a **string** array containing the names of subdirectories in the specified directory. Lines 81–82 display each element in the **string** array. Note that, if line 65 determines that the user-specified text is neither a file nor a directory, lines 87–89 notify the user (via a **MessageBox**) that the file or directory does not exist.

We now consider another example that uses C#'s file- and directory-manipulation capabilities. Class **FileSearchForm** (Fig. 17.6) uses classes **File** and **Directory** in conjunction with classes for performing regular expressions to report the number of files of each file type that exist in the specified directory path. The program also serves as a "clean-up" utility—when the program encounters a file that has the **.bak** extension (i.e., a backup file), the program displays a **MessageBox** asking whether that file should be removed, then responds appropriately to the user's input.

When the user presses the *Enter* key or clicks the **Search Directory** button, the program invokes method **searchButton_Click** (lines 52–92), which searches recursively through the directory path that the user provides. If the user inputs text in the **TextBox**, line 59 calls method **Exists** of class **Directory** to determine whether that text indicates a valid directory. If the user specifies an invalid directory, lines 70–71 notify the user of the error.

If the user specifies a valid directory, line 80 passes the directory name as an argument to **private** method **SearchDirectory** (lines 95–185). This method locates files that match the regular expression defined in lines 103–104, which matches any sequence of numbers or letters followed by a period and one or more letters. Notice the substring of format **(?<extension>***regular-expression***)** in the argument to the **Regex** constructor (line 104). All **string**s with the substring *regular-expression* are tagged with the name **extension**. In this program, we assign to the variable **extension** any **string** matching one or more characters.

Lines 115–116 call method **GetDirectories** of class **Directory** to retrieve the names of all subdirectories that belong to the current directory. Line 119 calls method **GetFiles** of class **Directory** to store in **string** array **fileArray** the names of files in the current directory. The **foreach** loop in lines 122–170 searches for all files with extension **bak**; it then calls **SearchDirectory** recursively for each subdirectory in the current directory. Lines 125–126 eliminate the directory path, so the program can test only the file name when using the regular expression. Line 129 uses method **Match** of the **Regex** object to match the regular expression with the file name, then returns the result to object **matchResult** of type **Match**. If the match is successful, lines 133–134 use method **Result** of object **matchResult** to store the extension **string** from object **matchResult** in **fileExtension** (the **string** that will contain the current file's extension). If the match is unsuccessful, line 136 sets **fileExtension** to hold a value of **"[no extension]"**.

```
1   // Fig 17.6: FileSearch.cs
2   // Using regular expressions to determine file types.
3
4   using System;
5   using System.Drawing;
6   using System.Collections;
7   using System.ComponentModel;
8   using System.Windows.Forms;
9   using System.Data;
10  using System.IO;
11  using System.Text.RegularExpressions;
12  using System.Collections.Specialized;
13
```

Fig. 17.6   Regular expression used to determine file types. (Part 1 of 5.)

```
14   public class FileSearchForm : System.Windows.Forms.Form
15   {
16       private System.Windows.Forms.Label directionsLabel;
17       private System.Windows.Forms.Label directoryLabel;
18
19       private System.Windows.Forms.Button searchButton;
20
21       private System.Windows.Forms.TextBox outputTextBox;
22       private System.Windows.Forms.TextBox inputTextBox;
23
24       private System.ComponentModel.Container components = null;
25
26       string currentDirectory = Directory.GetCurrentDirectory();
27       string[] directoryList; // subdirectories
28       string[] fileArray;
29
30       // store extensions found and number found
31       NameValueCollection found = new NameValueCollection();
32
33       [STAThread]
34       static void Main()
35       {
36          Application.Run( new FileSearchForm() );
37       }
38
39       // Visual Studio .NET generated code
40
41       // invoked when user types in text box
42       private void inputTextBox_KeyDown(
43          object sender, System.Windows.Forms.KeyEventArgs e )
44       {
45          // determine whether user pressed Enter
46          if ( e.KeyCode == Keys.Enter )
47             searchButton_Click( sender, e );
48
49       } // end method inputTextBox_KeyDown
50
51       // invoked when user clicks "Search Directory" button
52       private void searchButton_Click(
53          object sender, System.EventArgs e )
54       {
55          // check for user input; default is current directory
56          if ( inputTextBox.Text != "" )
57          {
58             // verify that user input is valid directory name
59             if ( Directory.Exists( inputTextBox.Text ) )
60             {
61                currentDirectory = inputTextBox.Text;
62
63                // reset input text box and update display
64                directoryLabel.Text = "Current Directory:" +
65                   "\r\n" + currentDirectory;
66             }
```

Fig. 17.6   Regular expression used to determine file types. (Part 2 of 5.)

```
67                else
68                {
69                    // show error if user does not specify valid directory
70                    MessageBox.Show( "Invalid Directory", "Error",
71                        MessageBoxButtons.OK, MessageBoxIcon.Error );
72                }
73            }
74
75            // clear text boxes
76            inputTextBox.Clear();
77            outputTextBox.Clear();
78
79            // search directory
80            SearchDirectory( currentDirectory );
81
82            // summarize and print results
83            foreach ( string current in found )
84            {
85                outputTextBox.Text += "* Found " +
86                    found[ current ] + " " + current + " files.\r\n";
87            }
88
89            // clear output for new search
90            found.Clear();
91
92        } // end method searchButton_Click
93
94        // search directory using regular expression
95        private void SearchDirectory( string currentDirectory )
96        {
97            // search directory
98            try
99            {
100                string fileName = "";
101
102                // regular expression for extensions matching pattern
103                Regex regularExpression = new Regex(
104                    "[a-zA-Z0-9]+\\.(?<extension>\\w+)" );
105
106                // stores regular-expression-match result
107                Match matchResult;
108
109                string fileExtension; // holds file extensions
110
111                // number of files with given extension in directory
112                int extensionCount;
113
114                // get directories
115                directoryList =
116                    Directory.GetDirectories( currentDirectory );
117
118                // get list of files in current directory
119                fileArray = Directory.GetFiles( currentDirectory );
```

Fig. 17.6   Regular expression used to determine file types. (Part 3 of 5.)

```
120
121            // iterate through list of files
122            foreach ( string myFile in fileArray )
123            {
124               // remove directory path from file name
125               fileName = myFile.Substring(
126                  myFile.LastIndexOf( "\\" ) + 1 );
127
128               // obtain result for regular-expression search
129               matchResult = regularExpression.Match( fileName );
130
131               // check for match
132                  ( matchResult.Success )
133                  fileExtension =
134                     matchResult.Result( "${extension}" );
135               else
136                  fileExtension = "[no extension]";
137
138               // store value from container
139               if ( found[ fileExtension ] == null )
140                  found.Add( fileExtension, "1" );
141               else
142               {
143                  extensionCount = Int32.Parse(
144                     found[ fileExtension ] ) + 1;
145
146                  found[ fileExtension ] = extensionCount.ToString();
147               }
148
149               // search for backup(.bak) files
150               if ( fileExtension == "bak" )
151               {
152                  // prompt user to delete (.bak) file
153                  DialogResult result =
154                     MessageBox.Show( "Found backup file " +
155                     fileName + ". Delete?", "Delete Backup",
156                     MessageBoxButtons.YesNo,
157                     MessageBoxIcon.Question );
158
159                  // delete file if user clicked 'yes'
160                  if ( result == DialogResult.Yes )
161                  {
162                     File.Delete( myFile );
163
164                     extensionCount =
165                        Int32.Parse( found[ "bak" ] ) - 1;
166
167                     found[ "bak" ] = extensionCount.ToString();
168                  }
169               }
170            }
171
```

Fig. 17.6   Regular expression used to determine file types. (Part 4 of 5.)

```
172                    // recursive call to search files in subdirectory
173                    foreach ( string myDirectory in directoryList )
174                        SearchDirectory( myDirectory );
175                 }
176
177              // handle exception if files have unauthorized access
178              catch( UnauthorizedAccessException )
179              {
180                 MessageBox.Show( "Some files may not be visible" +
181                    " due to permission settings", "Warning",
182                    MessageBoxButtons.OK, MessageBoxIcon.Information );
183              }
184
185          } // end method SearchDirectory
186
187   } // end class FileSearchForm
```

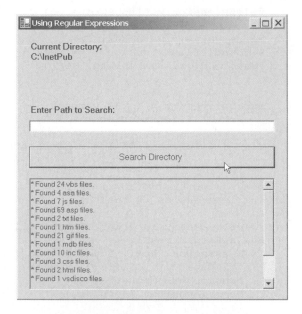

Fig. 17.6   Regular expression used to determine file types. (Part 5 of 5.)

Class **FileSearchForm** uses an instance of class *NameValueCollection* (declared in line 31) to store each file-extension type and the number of files for each type. A **NameValueCollection** contains a collection of key/value pairs, each of which is a **string**, and provides method **Add** to add a key/value pair. The indexer for this pair can index according to the order that the items were added or according to the entry key. Line

139 uses **NameValueCollection found** to determine whether this is the first occurrence of the file extension. If so, line 140 adds that extension to **found** as a key with the value **1**. If the extension is in **found** already, lines 143–144 increment the value associated with the extension in **found** to indicate another occurrence of that file extension.

Line 150 determines whether **fileExtension** equals "**bak**"—i.e., whether the file is a backup file. If so, lines 153–157 prompt the user to indicate whether the file should be removed; if the user clicks **Yes** (line 160), lines 162–167 delete the file and decrement the value for the "**bak**" file type in **found**.

Lines 173–174 call method **SearchDirectory** for each subdirectory. Using recursion, we ensure that the program performs the same logic for finding **bak** files on each subdirectory. After each subdirectory has been checked for **bak** files, method **SearchDirectory** completes, and lines 83–87 display the results.

17.5 Creating a Sequential-Access File

C# imposes no structure on files. Thus, concepts like that of a "record" do not exist in C# files. This means that the programmer must structure files to meet the requirements of applications. In this example, we use text and special characters to organize our own concept of a "record."

The following examples demonstrate file processing in a bank-account maintenance application. These programs have similar user interfaces, so we created class **BankUI-Form** (Fig. 17.7) to encapsulate a base-class GUI (see the screen capture in Fig. 17.7). Class **BankUIForm** contains four **Label**s (lines 15, 18, 21 and 24) and four **TextBox**es (lines 16, 19, 22 and 25). Methods **ClearTextBoxes** (lines 49–64), **SetTextBox-Values** (lines 67–91) and **GetTextBoxValues** (lines 94–110) clear, set the values of, and get the values of the text in the **TextBox**es, respectively.

To reuse class **BankUIForm**, we compile the GUI into a DLL library by creating a project of type **Windows Control Library** (the DLL we create is called **BankLi-brary**). This library, as well as all the code in this book, can be found on the CD accompanying the book and at our Web site, **www.deitel.com**. However, students might need to change the reference to this library, as it most likely resides in a different location on their systems.

Figure 17.8 contains class **Record** that Fig. 17.9, Fig. 17.11 and Fig. 17.12 use for reading records from, and writing records to, a file sequentially. This class also belongs to the **BankLibrary** DLL, so it is located in the same project as is class **BankUIForm**.

The *Serializable* attribute (line 6) indicates to the compiler that objects of class **Record** can be *serialized*, or represented as sets of bytes—we can read and write these bytes to our streams. Objects that we wish to write to or read from a stream must include this attribute in their class definitions.

Class **Record** contains **private** data members **account**, **firstName**, **last-Name** and **balance** (lines 9–12), which collectively represent all information necessary to store record data. The default constructor (lines 15–17) sets these members to their default (i.e., empty) values, and the overloaded constructor (lines 20–28) sets these members to specified parameter values. Class **Record** also provides properties **Account** (lines 31–43), **FirstName** (lines 46–58), **LastName** (lines 61–73) and **Balance** (lines 76–88) for accessing the account number, first name, last name and balance of each customer, respectively.

```
1    // Fig 17.7: BankUI.cs
2    // A reusable windows form for the examples in this chapter.
3
4    using System;
5    using System.Drawing;
6    using System.Collections;
7    using System.ComponentModel;
8    using System.Windows.Forms;
9    using System.Data;
10
11   public class BankUIForm : System.Windows.Forms.Form
12   {
13      private System.ComponentModel.Container components = null;
14
15      public System.Windows.Forms.Label accountLabel;
16      public System.Windows.Forms.TextBox accountTextBox;
17
18      public System.Windows.Forms.Label firstNameLabel;
19      public System.Windows.Forms.TextBox firstNameTextBox;
20
21      public System.Windows.Forms.Label lastNameLabel;
22      public System.Windows.Forms.TextBox lastNameTextBox;
23
24      public System.Windows.Forms.Label balanceLabel;
25      public System.Windows.Forms.TextBox balanceTextBox;
26
27      // number of TextBoxes on Form'
28      protected int TextBoxCount = 4;
29
30      // enumeration constants specify TextBox indices
31      public enum TextBoxIndices
32      {
33         ACCOUNT,
34         FIRST,
35         LAST,
36         BALANCE
37
38      } // end enum
39
40      [STAThread]
41      static void Main()
42      {
43         Application.Run( new BankUIForm() );
44      }
45
46      // Visual Studio .NET generated code
47
48      // clear all TextBoxes
49      public void ClearTextBoxes()
50      {
51         // iterate through every Control on form
52         for ( int i = 0; i < Controls.Count; i++ )
53         {
```

Fig. 17.7   Base class for GUIs in our file-processing applications. (Part 1 of 3.)

```
54                    Control myControl = Controls[ i ]; // get control
55
56                    // determine whether Control is TextBox
57                    if ( myControl is TextBox )
58                    {
59                        // clear Text property (set to empty strng)
60                        myControl.Text = "";
61                    }
62                }
63
64          } // end method ClearTextBoxes
65
66          // set text box values to string array values
67          public void SetTextBoxValues( string[] values )
68          {
69              // determine whether string array has correct length
70              if ( values.Length != TextBoxCount )
71              {
72                  // throw exception if not correct length
73                  throw( new ArgumentException( "There must be " +
74                      (TextBoxCount + 1) + " strings in the array" ) );
75              }
76
77              // set array values if array has correct length
78              else
79              {
80                  // set array values to text box values
81                  accountTextBox.Text =
82                      values[ ( int )TextBoxIndices.ACCOUNT ];
83                  firstNameTextBox.Text =
84                      values[ ( int )TextBoxIndices.FIRST ];
85                  lastNameTextBox.Text =
86                      values[ ( int )TextBoxIndices.LAST ];
87                  balanceTextBox.Text =
88                      values[ ( int )TextBoxIndices.BALANCE ];
89              }
90
91          } // end method SetTextBoxValues
92
93          // return text box values as string array
94          public string[] GetTextBoxValues()
95          {
96              string[] values = new string[ TextBoxCount ];
97
98              // copy text box fields to string array
99              values[ ( int )TextBoxIndices.ACCOUNT ] =
100                 accountTextBox.Text;
101             values[ ( int )TextBoxIndices.FIRST ] =
102                 firstNameTextBox.Text;
103             values[ ( int )TextBoxIndices.LAST ] =
104                 lastNameTextBox.Text;
105             values[ ( int )TextBoxIndices.BALANCE ] =
106                 balanceTextBox.Text;
```

Fig. 17.7   Base class for GUIs in our file-processing applications. (Part 2 of 3.)

```
107
108        return values;
109
110     } // end method GetTextBoxValues
111
112 } // end class BankUIForm
```

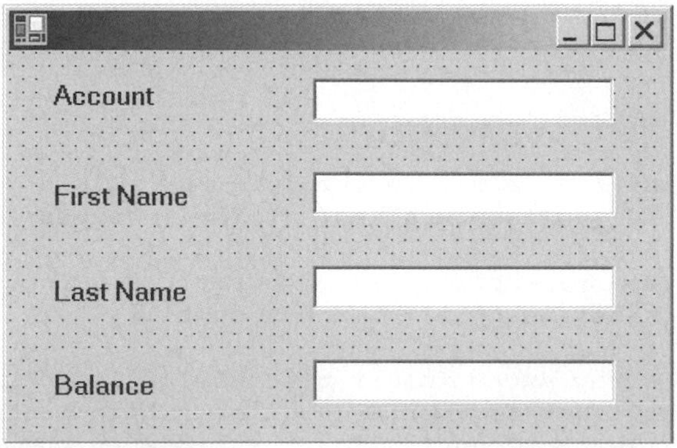

Fig. 17.7   Base class for GUIs in our file-processing applications. (Part 3 of 3.)

```
1   // Fig. 17.8: Record.cs
2   // Serializable class that represents a data record.
3
4   using System;
5
6   [Serializable]
7   public class Record
8   {
9      private int account;
10     private string firstName;
11     private string lastName;
12     private double balance;
13
14     // default constructor sets members to default values
15     public Record() : this( 0, "", "", 0.0 )
16     {
17     }
18
19     // overloaded constructor sets members to parameter values
20     public Record( int accountValue, string firstNameValue,
21        string lastNameValue, double balanceValue )
22     {
23        Account = accountValue;
24        FirstName = firstNameValue;
25        LastName = lastNameValue;
26        Balance = balanceValue;
27
28     } // end constructor
29
```

Fig. 17.8   Record for sequential-access file-processing applications. (Part 1 of 3.)

```
30       // property Account
31       public int Account
32       {
33          get
34          {
35             return account;
36          }
37
38          set
39          {
40             account = value;
41          }
42
43       } // end property Account
44
45       // property FirstName
46       public string FirstName
47       {
48          get
49          {
50             return firstName;
51          }
52
53          set
54          {
55             firstName = value;
56          }
57
58       } // end property FirstName
59
60       // property LastName
61       public string LastName
62       {
63          get
64          {
65             return lastName;
66          }
67
68          set
69          {
70             lastName = value;
71          }
72
73       } // end property LastName
74
75       // property Balance
76       public double Balance
77       {
78          get
79          {
80             return balance;
81          }
82
```

Fig. 17.8   Record for sequential-access file-processing applications. (Part 2 of 3.)

```
83            set
84            {
85                balance = value;
86            }
87
88        } // end property Balance
89
90    } // end class Record
```

Fig. 17.8   Record for sequential-access file-processing applications. (Part 3 of 3.)

Class **CreateFileForm** (Fig. 17.9) uses instances of class **Record** to create a sequential-access file that might be used in an accounts receivable system—i.e., a program that organizes data regarding money owed by a company's credit clients. For each client, the program obtains an account number and the client's first name, last name and balance (i.e., the amount of money that the client owes to the company for previously received goods or services). The data obtained for each client constitutes a record for that client. In this application, the account number represents the record key—files are created and maintained in account-number order. This program assumes that the user enters records in account-number order. However, a comprehensive accounts receivable system would provide a sorting capability. The user could enter the records in any order, and the records then could be sorted and written to the file in order. (Note that all outputs in this chapter should be read row by row, from left to right in each row.)

Figure 17.9 contains the code for class **CreateFileForm**, which either creates or opens a file (depending on whether one exists), then allows the user to write bank information to that file. Line 16 imports the **BankLibrary** namespace; this namespace contains class **BankUIForm**, from which class **CreateFileForm** inherits (line 18). Because of this inheritance relationship, the **CreateFileForm** GUI is similar to that of class **BankUIForm** (shown in the Fig. 17.9 output), except that the inherited class contains buttons **Save As**, **Enter** and **Exit**.

When the user clicks the **Save As** button, the program invokes method **saveButton_Click** (lines 41–85). Line 45 instantiates an object of class **SaveFileDialog**, which belongs to the **System.Windows.Forms** namespace. Objects of this class are used for selecting files (see the second screen in Fig. 17.9). Line 46 calls method **ShowDialog** of the **SaveFileDialog** object to display the **SaveFileDialog**. When displayed, a **SaveFileDialog** prevents the user from interacting with any other window in the program until the user closes the **SaveFileDialog** by clicking either **Save** or **Cancel**. Dialogs that behave in this fashion are called *modal dialogs*. The user selects the appropriate drive, directory and file name, then clicks **Save**. Method **ShowDialog** returns an integer specifying which button (**Save** or **Cancel**) the user clicked to close the dialog. In this example, the **Form** property **DialogResult** receives this integer. Line 53 tests whether the user clicked **Cancel** by comparing the value returned by property **DialogResult** to constant *DialogResult.Cancel*. If the values are equal, method **saveButton_Click** returns (line 54). If the values are unequal (i.e., the user clicked **Save**, instead of clicking **Cancel**), line 57 uses property *FileName* of class **SaveFileDialog** to obtain the user-selected file.

```
1    // Fig 17.9: CreateSequentialAccessFile.cs
2    // Creating a sequential-access file.
3
4    // C# namespaces
5    using System;
6    using System.Drawing;
7    using System.Collections;
8    using System.ComponentModel;
9    using System.Windows.Forms;
10   using System.Data;
11   using System.IO;
12   using System.Runtime.Serialization.Formatters.Binary;
13   using System.Runtime.Serialization;
14
15   // Deitel namespace
16   using BankLibrary;
17
18   public class CreateFileForm : BankUIForm
19   {
20       private System.Windows.Forms.Button saveButton;
21       private System.Windows.Forms.Button enterButton;
22       private System.Windows.Forms.Button exitButton;
23
24       private System.ComponentModel.Container components = null;
25
26       // serializes Record in binary format
27       private BinaryFormatter formatter = new BinaryFormatter();
28
29       // stream through which serializable data is written to file
30       private FileStream output;
31
32       [STAThread]
33       static void Main()
34       {
35           Application.Run( new CreateFileForm() );
36       }
37
38       // Visual Studio .NET generated code
39
40       // invoked when user clicks Save button
41       private void saveButton_Click(
42           object sender, System.EventArgs e )
43       {
44           // create dialog box enabling user to save file
45           SaveFileDialog fileChooser = new SaveFileDialog();
46           DialogResult result = fileChooser.ShowDialog();
47           string fileName; // name of file to save data
48
49           // allow user to create file
50           fileChooser.CheckFileExists = false;
51
```

Fig. 17.9   Create and write to a sequential-access file. (Part 1 of 5.)

```
52        // exit event handler if user clicked "Cancel"
53        if ( result == DialogResult.Cancel )
54           return;
55
56        // get specified file name
57        fileName = fileChooser.FileName;
58
59        // show error if user specified invalid file
60        if ( fileName == "" || fileName == null )
61           MessageBox.Show( "Invalid File Name", "Error",
62              MessageBoxButtons.OK, MessageBoxIcon.Error );
63        else
64        {
65           // save file via FileStream if user specified valid file
66           try
67           {
68              // open file with write access
69              output = new FileStream( fileName,
70                 FileMode.OpenOrCreate, FileAccess.Write );
71
72              // disable Save button and enable Enter button
73              saveButton.Enabled = false;
74              enterButton.Enabled = true;
75           }
76
77           // handle exception if file does not exist
78           catch ( FileNotFoundException )
79           {
80              // notify user if file does not exist
81              MessageBox.Show( "File Does Not Exist", "Error",
82                 MessageBoxButtons.OK, MessageBoxIcon.Error );
83           }
84        }
85     } // end method saveButton_Click
86
87     // invoke when user clicks Enter button
88     private void enterButton_Click(
89        object sender, System.EventArgs e )
90     {
91        // store TextBox values string array
92        string[] values = GetTextBoxValues();
93
94        // Record containing TextBox values to serialize
95        Record record = new Record();
96
97        // determine whether TextBox account field is empty
98        if ( values[ ( int )TextBoxIndices.ACCOUNT ] != "" )
99        {
100          // store TextBox values in Record and serialize Record
101          try
102          {
```

Fig. 17.9   Create and write to a sequential-access file. (Part 2 of 5.)

```
103                   // get account number value from TextBox
104                   int accountNumber = Int32.Parse(
105                      values[ ( int )TextBoxIndices.ACCOUNT ] );
106
107                   // determine whether accountNumber is valid
108                   if ( accountNumber > 0 )
109                   {
110                      // store TextBox fields in Record
111                      record.Account = accountNumber;
112                      record.FirstName =
113                         values[ ( int )TextBoxIndices.FIRST ];
114                      record.LastName =
115                         values[ ( int )TextBoxIndices.LAST ];
116                      record.Balance = Double.Parse( values[
117                         ( int )TextBoxIndices.BALANCE ] );
118
119                      // write Record to FileStream (serialize object)
120                      formatter.Serialize( output, record );
121                   }
122                   else
123                   {
124                      // notify user if invalid account number
125                      MessageBox.Show( "Invalid Account Number", "Error",
126                         MessageBoxButtons.OK, MessageBoxIcon.Error );
127                   }
128                }
129
130                // notify user if error occurs in serialization
131                catch( SerializationException )
132                {
133                   MessageBox.Show( "Error Writing to File", "Error",
134                      MessageBoxButtons.OK, MessageBoxIcon.Error );
135                }
136
137                // notify user if error occurs regarding parameter format
138                catch( FormatException )
139                {
140                   MessageBox.Show( "Invalid Format", "Error",
141                      MessageBoxButtons.OK, MessageBoxIcon.Error );
142                }
143             }
144
145          ClearTextBoxes(); // clear TextBox values
146
147       } // end method enterButton_Click
148
149       // invoked when user clicks Exit button
150       private void exitButton_Click(
151          object sender, System.EventArgs e )
152       {
153          // determine whether file exists
154          if ( output != null )
155          {
```

Fig. 17.9   Create and write to a sequential-access file. (Part 3 of 5.)

```
156            // close file
157            try
158            {
159                output.Close();
160            }
161
162            // notify user of error closing file
163            catch( IOException )
164            {
165                MessageBox.Show( "Cannot close file", "Error",
166                    MessageBoxButtons.OK, MessageBoxIcon.Error );
167            }
168        }
169
170        Application.Exit();
171
172    } // end method exitButton_Click
173
174 } // end class CreateFileForm
```

BankUI graphical
user interface

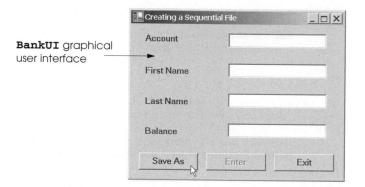

SaveFileDialog

Files and directories

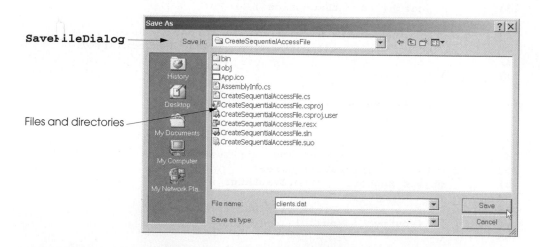

Fig. 17.9   Create and write to a sequential-access file. (Part 4 of 5.)

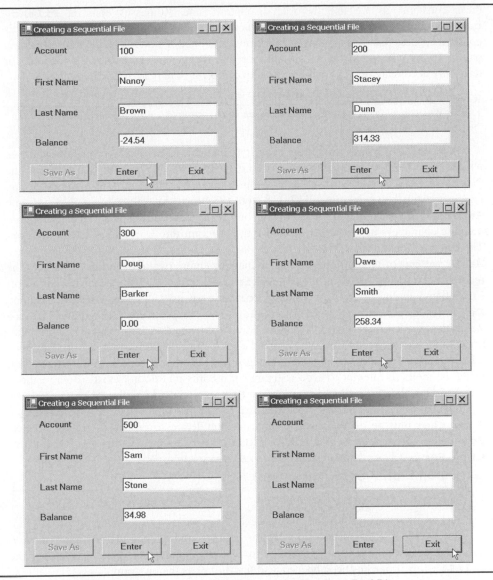

Fig. 17.9   Create and write to a sequential-access file. (Part 5 of 5.)

As we stated previously in this chapter, we can open files to perform text manipulation by creating objects of classes **FileStream**. In this example, we want the file to be opened for output, so lines 69–70 instantiate a **FileStream** object. The **FileStream** constructor that we use receives three arguments—a **string** containing the name of the file to be opened, a constant describing how to open the file and a constant describing the file permissions. Line 70 passes constant **FileMode.OpenOrCreate** to the **FileStream** constructor as the constructor's second argument. This constant indicates that the **FileStream** object should open the file if the file exists or create the file if the file does not exist. C# offers other **FileMode** constants describing how to open files; we introduce these constants as we use them in examples. Line 70 passes constant **FileAc-cess.Write** to the **FileStream** constructor as the constructor's third argument. This constant ensures that the program can perform write-only operations on the **FileStream** object. C# provides two other constants for this parameter—**FileAccess.Read** for read-only access and **FileAccess.ReadWrite** for both read and write access.

Good Programming Practice 17.1

*When opening files, use the **FileAccess** enumeration to control user access to these files.*

After the user types information in each **TextBox**, the user clicks the **Enter** button, which calls method **enterButton_Click** (lines 88–147) to save data from the **TextBox** in the user-specified file. If the user entered a valid account number (i.e., an integer greater than zero), lines 112–118 store the **TextBox** values in an object of type **Record**. If the user entered invalid data in one of the **TextBox**es (such as entering non-numeric characters in the **Balance** field), the program throws a **FormatException**. The **catch** block in lines 138–142 handles such an exception by notifying the user (via a **MessageBox**) of the improper format. If the user entered valid data, line 120 writes the record to the file by invoking method **Serialize** of the **BinaryFormatter** object (instantiated in line 27). Class **BinaryFormatter** uses methods *Serialize* and *Deserialize* to write and read objects into streams, respectively. Method **Serialize** writes the object's representation to a file. Method **Deserialize** reads this representation from a file and reconstructs the original object. Both methods throw a **Serializa-tionException** if an error occurs during serialization or deserialization (errors result when the methods attempt to access streams or records that do not exist). Both methods **Serialize** and **Deserialize** require a **Stream** object (e.g., the **FileStream**) as a parameter so that the **BinaryFormatter** can access the correct file; the **Binary-Formatter** must receive an instance of a class that derives from class **Stream**, because **Stream** is **abstract**. Class **BinaryFormatter** belongs to the *System.Run-time.Serialization.Formatters.Binary* namespace.

Common Programming Error 17.1

Failure to open a file before attempting to reference it in a program is a logic error.

When the user clicks the **Exit** button, the program invokes method **exitButton_Click** (lines 150–172) to exit the application. Line 159 closes the **FileStream** if one has been opened, and line 170 exits the program.

Performance Tip 17.1

Close each file explicitly when the program no longer needs to reference the file. This can reduce resource usage in programs that continue executing long after they finish using a specific file. The practice of explicitly closing files also improves program clarity.

Performance Tip 17.2

Releasing resources explicitly when they are no longer needed makes them immediately available for reuse by the program, thus improving resource utilization.

In the sample execution for the program in Fig. 17.9, we entered information for five accounts (Fig. 17.10). The program does not depict how the data records are rendered in

Account Number	First Name	Last Name	Balance
100	Nancy	Brown	-25.54
200	Stacey	Dunn	314.33
300	Doug	Barker	0.00
400	Dave	Smith	258.34
500	Sam	Stone	34.98

Fig. 17.10 Sample data for the program of Fig. 17.9.

the file. To verify that the file has been created successfully, in the next section, we create a program to read and display the file.

17.6 Reading Data from a Sequential-Access File

Data are stored in files so that they can be retrieved for processing when they are needed. The previous section demonstrated how to create a file for use in sequential-access applications. In this section, we discuss how to read (or retrieve) data sequentially from a file.

Class **ReadSequentialAccessFileForm** (Fig. 17.11) reads records from the file created by the program in Fig. 17.9, then displays the contents of each record. Much of the code in this example is similar to that of Fig. 17.9, so we discuss only the unique aspects of the application.

When the user clicks the **Open File** button, the program calls method **open-Button_Click** (lines 40–70). Line 44 instantiates an object of class *OpenFile-Dialog*, and line 45 calls the object's *ShowDialog* method to display the **Open** dialog (see the second screenshot in Fig. 17.11). The behavior and GUI for the two dialog types are the same (except that **Save** is replaced by **Open**). If the user inputs a valid file name, lines 63–64 create a **FileStream** object and assign it to reference **input**. We pass constant **FileMode.Open** as the second argument to the **FileStream** constructor. This constant indicates that the **FileStream** should open the file if the file exists or should throw a **FileNotFoundException** if the file does not exist. (In this example, the **FileStream** constructor will not throw a **FileNotFoundException**, because the **OpenFileDialog** requires the user to enter a name of a file that exists.) In the last example (Fig. 17.9), we wrote text to the file using a **FileStream** object with write-only access. In this example, (Fig. 17.11), we specify read-only access to the file by passing constant **FileAccess.Read** as the third argument to the **FileStream** constructor.

Testing and Debugging Tip 17.1

*Open a file with the **FileAccess.Read** file-open mode if the contents of the file should not be modified. This prevents unintentional modification of the file's contents.*

When the user clicks the **Next Record** button, the program calls method **nextButton_Click** (lines 73–113), which reads the next record from the user-specified file. (The user must click **Next Record** after opening the file to view the first record.) Lines 80–81 call method **Deserialize** of the **BinaryFormatter** object to read the next record. Method **Deserialize** reads the data and casts the result to a **Record**—this cast is necessary, because **Deserialize** returns a reference of type **Object**. Lines 84–91 then display the **Record** values in the **TextBox**es. When method **Deserialize** attempts to deserialize a record that does not exist in the file (i.e., the program has displayed all file records), the method throws a **SerializationException**. The **catch** block (lines 95–111) that handles this exception closes the **FileStream** object (line 98) and notifies the user that there are no more records (lines 109–110).

```
1    // Fig. 17.11: ReadSequentialAccessFile.cs
2    // Reading a sequential-access file.
3
4    // C# namespaces
5    using System;
6    using System.Drawing;
7    using System.Collections;
8    using System.ComponentModel;
9    using System.Windows.Forms;
10   using System.Data;
11   using System.IO;
12   using System.Runtime.Serialization.Formatters.Binary;
13   using System.Runtime.Serialization;
14
15   // Deitel namespaces
16   using BankLibrary;
17
18   public class ReadSequentialAccessFileForm : BankUIForm
19   {
20      System.Windows.Forms.Button openButton;
21      System.Windows.Forms.Button nextButton;
22
23      private System.ComponentModel.Container components = null;
24
25      // stream through which serializable data are read from file
26      private FileStream input;
27
28      // object for deserializing Record in binary format
29      private BinaryFormatter reader = new BinaryFormatter();
30
31      [STAThread]
32      static void Main()
33      {
34         Application.Run( new ReadSequentialAccessFileForm() );
35      }
36
37      // Visual Studio .NET generated code
38
39      // invoked when user clicks Open button
40      private void openButton_Click(
41         object sender, System.EventArgs e )
42      {
43         // create dialog box enabling user to open file
44         OpenFileDialog fileChooser = new OpenFileDialog();
45         DialogResult result = fileChooser.ShowDialog();
```

Fig. 17.11 Reading sequential-access files. (Part 1 of 4.)

```
46          string fileName; // name of file containing data
47
48          // exit event handler if user clicked Cancel
49          if ( result == DialogResult.Cancel )
50             return;
51
52          // get specified file name
53          fileName = fileChooser.FileName;
54          ClearTextBoxes();
55
56          // show error if user specified invalid file
57          if ( fileName == "" || fileName == null )
58             MessageBox.Show( "Invalid File Name", "Error",
59                MessageBoxButtons.OK, MessageBoxIcon.Error );
60          else
61          {
62             // create FileStream to obtain read access to file
63             input = new FileStream( fileName, FileMode.Open,
64                FileAccess.Read );
65
66             // enable next record button
67             nextButton.Enabled = true;
68          }
69
70       } // end method openButton_Click
71
72       // invoked when user clicks Next button
73       private void nextButton_Click(
74          object sender, System.EventArgs e )
75       {
76          // deserialize Record and store data in TextBoxes
77          try
78          {
79             // get next Record available in file
80             Record record =
81                ( Record )reader.Deserialize( input );
82
83             // store Record values in temporary string array
84             string[] values = new string[] {
85                record.Account.ToString(),
86                record.FirstName.ToString(),
87                record.LastName.ToString(),
88                record.Balance.ToString() };
89
90             // copy string array values to TextBox values
91             SetTextBoxValues( values );
92          }
93
94          // handle exception when no Records in file
95          catch( SerializationException )
96          {\
97             // close FileStream if no Records in file
98             input.Close();
```

Fig. 17.11 Reading sequential-access files. (Part 2 of 4.)

```
99
100             // enable Open Record button
101             openButton.Enabled = true;
102
103             // disable Next Record button
104             nextButton.Enabled = false;
105
106             ClearTextBoxes();
107
108             // notify user if no Records in file
109             MessageBox.Show( "No more records in file", "",
110                MessageBoxButtons.OK, MessageBoxIcon.Information );
111          }
112
113    } // end method nextButton_Click
114
115 } // end class ReadSequentialAccessFileForm
```

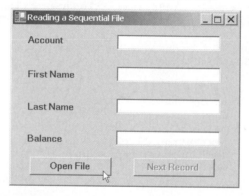

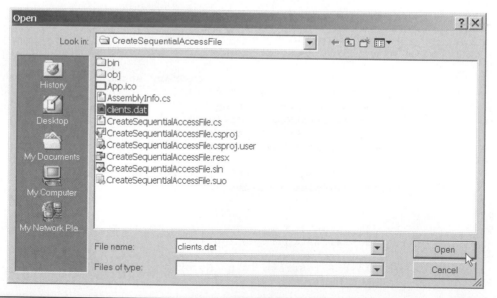

Fig. 17.11 Reading sequential-access files. (Part 3 of 4.)

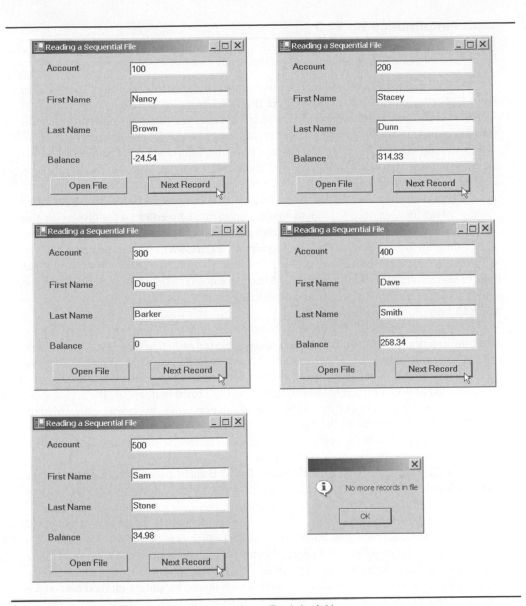

Fig. 17.11 Reading sequential-access files. (Part 4 of 4.)

To retrieve data sequentially from a file, programs normally start from the beginning of the file, reading data consecutively until the desired data are found. It sometimes is necessary to process a file sequentially several times (from the beginning of the file) during the execution of a program. A **FileStream** object can reposition its *file-position pointer* (which contains the byte number of the next byte to be read from or written to the file) to any position in the file—we show this feature when we introduce random-access file-processing applications. When a **FileStream** object is opened, its file-position pointer is set to zero (i.e., the beginning of the file)

Performance Tip 17.3

It is time-consuming to close and reopen a file for the purpose of moving the file-position pointer to the file's beginning. Doing so frequently could slow program performance.

We now present a more substantial program that builds on the concepts employed in Fig. 17.11. Class **creditInquiryForm** (Fig. 17.12) is a credit-inquiry program that enables a credit manager to display account information for those customers with credit balances (i.e., customers to whom the company owes money), zero balances (i.e., customers who do not owe the company money) and debit balances (i.e., customers who owe the company money for previously received goods and services). Note that line 21 declares a **RichTextBox** that will display the account information. **RichTextBox**es provide more functionality than do regular **TextBox**es—for example, **RichTextBox**es offer method **Find** for searching individual strings and method **LoadFile** for displaying file contents. Class **RichTextBox** does not inherit from class **TextBox**; rather, both classes inherit directly from **abstract** class *System.Windows.Forms.TextBoxBase*. We use a **RichTextBox** in this example, because a **RichTextBox** displays multiple lines of text by default, whereas a regular **TextBox** displays only one. Alternatively, we could have specified that a **TextBox** object display multiple lines of text by setting its **Multiline** property to **true**

The program in Fig. 17.12 displays buttons that enable a credit manager to obtain credit information. The **Open File** button opens a file for gathering data. The **Credit Balances** button displays a list of accounts that have credit balances, the **Debit Balances** button displays a list of accounts that have debit balances, and the **Zero Balances** button displays a list of accounts that have zero balances. The **Done** button exits the application.

When the user clicks the **Open File** button, the program calls method **openButton_Click** (lines 49–76). Line 53 instantiates an object of class *OpenFileDialog*, and line 54 calls the object's *ShowDialog* method to display the **Open** dialog, in which the user inputs the name of the file to open. .

When the user clicks **Credit Balances**, **Debit Balances** or **Zero Balances**, the program invokes method **get_Click** (lines 80–142). Line 83 casts the **sender** parameter, which is a reference to the object that sent the event, to a **Button** object. Line 86 extracts the **Button** object's text, which the program uses to determine which GUI **Button** the user clicked. Lines 96–97 create a **FileStream** object with read-only file access and assign it to reference **input**. Lines 102–125 define a **while** loop that uses **private** method **ShouldDisplay** (lines 145–170) to determine whether to display each record in the file. The **while** loop obtains each record by calling method **Deserialize** of the **FileStream** object repeatedly (line 105). When the file-position pointer reaches the end of file, method **Deserialize** throws a **SerializationException**, which the **catch** block in lines 136–140 handles: Line 139 calls the **Close** method of **FileStream** to close the file, and method **get_Click** returns.

```
1   // Fig. 17.12: CreditInquiry.cs
2   // Read a file sequentially and display contents based on
3   // account type specified by user (credit, debit or zero balances).
4
```

Fig. 17.12 Credit-inquiry program. (Part 1 of 7.)

```
5   // C# namespaces
6   using System;
7   using System.Drawing;
8   using System.Collections;
9   using System.ComponentModel;
10  using System.Windows.Forms;
11  using System.Data;
12  using System.IO;
13  using System.Runtime.Serialization.Formatters.Binary;
14  using System.Runtime.Serialization;
15
16  // Deitel namespaces
17  using BankLibrary;
18
19  public class CreditInquiryForm : System.Windows.Forms.Form
20  {
21     private System.Windows.Forms.RichTextBox displayTextBox;
22
23     private System.Windows.Forms.Button doneButton;
24     private System.Windows.Forms.Button zeroButton;
25     private System.Windows.Forms.Button debitButton;
26     private System.Windows.Forms.Button creditButton;
27     private System.Windows.Forms.Button openButton;
28
29     private System.ComponentModel.Container components = null;
30
31     // stream through which serializable data are read from file
32     private FileStream input;
33
34     // object for deserializing Record in binary format
35     BinaryFormatter reader = new BinaryFormatter();
36
37     // name of file that stores credit, debit and zero balances
38     private string fileName;
39
40     [STAThread]
41     static void Main()
42     {
43        Application.Run( new CreditInquiryForm() );
44     }
45
46     // Visual Studio .NET generated code
47
48     // invoked when user clicks Open File button
49     private void openButton_Click(
50        object sender, System.EventArgs e )
51     {
52        // create dialog box enabling user to open file
53        OpenFileDialog fileChooser = new OpenFileDialog();
54        DialogResult result = fileChooser.ShowDialog();
55
```

Fig. 17.12   Credit-inquiry program. (Part 2 of 7.)

```
56            // exit event handler if user clicked Cancel
57            if ( result == DialogResult.Cancel )
58               return;
59
60            // get name from user
61            fileName = fileChooser.FileName;
62
63            // show error if user specified invalid file
64            if ( fileName == "" || fileName == null )
65               MessageBox.Show( "Invalid File Name", "Error",
66                  MessageBoxButtons.OK, MessageBoxIcon.Error );
67            else
68            {
69               // enable all GUI buttons, except for Open file button
70               openButton.Enabled = false;
71               creditButton.Enabled = true;
72               debitButton.Enabled = true;
73               zeroButton.Enabled = true;
74            }
75
76         } // end method openButton_Click
77
78         // invoked when user clicks credit balances,
79         // debit balances or zero balances button
80         private void get_Click( object sender, System.EventArgs e )
81         {
82            // convert sender explicitly to object of type button
83            Button senderButton = ( Button )sender;
84
85            // get text from clicked Button, which stores account type
86            string accountType = senderButton.Text;
87
88            // read and display file information
89            try
90            {
91               // close file from previous operation
92               if ( input != null )
93                  input.Close();
94
95               // create FileStream to obtain read access to file
96               input = new FileStream( fileName, FileMode.Open,
97                  FileAccess.Read );
98
99               displayTextBox.Text = "The accounts are:\r\n";
100
101              // traverse file until end of file
102              while ( true )
103              {
104                 // get next Record available in file
105                 Record record = ( Record )reader.Deserialize( input );
106
107                 // store record's last field in balance
108                 Double balance = record.Balance;
```

Fig. 17.12   Credit-inquiry program. (Part 3 of 7.)

```
109
110             // determine whether to display balance
111             if ( ShouldDisplay( balance, accountType ) )
112             {
113                 // display record
114                 string output = record.Account + "\t" +
115                     record.FirstName + "\t" + record.LastName +
116                     new string( ' ', 6 ) + "\t";
117
118                 // display balance with correct monetary format
119                 output += String.Format(
120                     "{0:F}", balance ) + "\r\n";
121
122                 // copy output to screen
123                 displayTextBox.Text += output;
124             }
125         }
126     }
127
128     // handle exception when file cannot be closed
129     catch( IOException )
130     {
131         MessageBox.Show( "Cannot Close File", "Error",
132             MessageBoxButtons.OK, MessageBoxIcon.Error );
133     }
134
135     // handle exception when no more records
136     catch( SerializationException )
137     {
138         // close FileStream if no Records in file
139         input.Close();
140     }
141
142 } // end method get_Click
143
144 // determine whether to display given record
145 private bool ShouldDisplay( double balance, string accountType )
146 {
147     if ( balance > 0 )
148     {
149         // display credit balances
150         if ( accountType == "Credit Balances" )
151             return true;
152     }
153
154     else if ( balance < 0 )
155     {
156         // display debit balances
157         if ( accountType == "Debit Balances" )
158             return true;
159     }
160
```

Fig. 17.12   Credit-inquiry program. (Part 4 of 7.)

```
161            else // balance == 0
162            {
163               // display zero balances
164               if ( accountType == "Zero Balances" )
165                  return true;
166            }
167
168            return false;
169
170         } // end method ShouldDisplay
171
172         // invoked when user clicks Done button
173         private void doneButton_Click(
174            object sender, System.EventArgs e )
175         {
176            // determine whether file exists
177            if ( input != null )
178            {
179               // close file
180               try
181               {
182                  input.Close();
183               }
184
185               // handle exception if FileStream does not exist
186               catch( IOException )
187               {
188                  // notify user of error closing file
189                  MessageBox.Show( "Cannot close file", "Error",
190                     MessageBoxButtons.OK, MessageBoxIcon.Error);
191               }
192            }
193
194            Application.Exit();
195
196         } // end method doneButton_Click
197
198 } // end class CreditInquiryForm
```

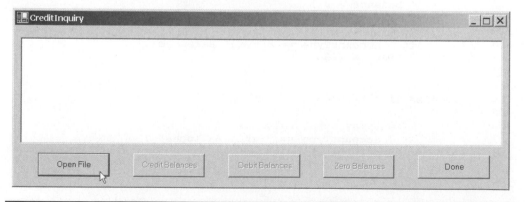

Fig. 17.12   Credit-inquiry program. (Part 5 of 7.)

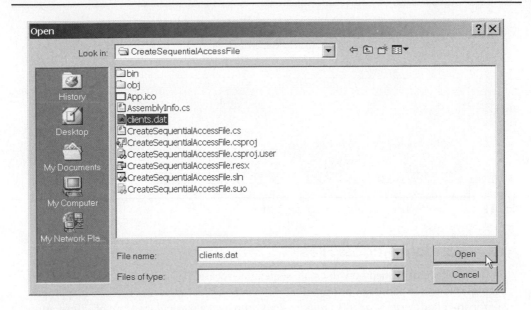

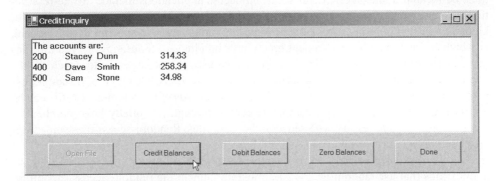

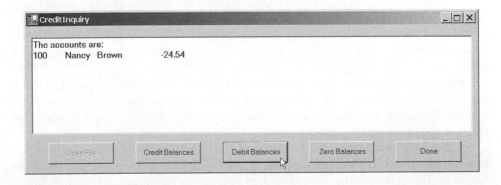

Fig. 17.12 Credit-inquiry program. (Part 6 of 7.)

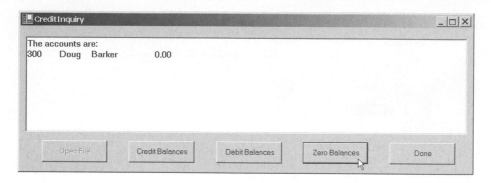

Fig. 17.12   Credit-inquiry program. (Part 7 of 7.)

17.7 Random-Access Files

So far, we have explained how to create sequential-access files and how to search through such files to locate particular information. However, sequential-access files are inappropriate for so-called *"instant-access" applications*, in which a particular record of information must be located immediately. Popular instant-access applications include airline-reservation systems, banking systems, point-of-sale systems, automated-teller machines and other kinds of *transaction-processing systems* requiring rapid access to specific data. The bank at which an individual has an account might have hundreds of thousands or even millions of other customers; however, when that individual uses an automated teller machine, the appropriate account is checked for sufficient funds in seconds. This type of instant access is made possible by *random-access files*. Individual records of a random-access file can be accessed directly (and quickly), without searching through potentially large numbers of other records, as is necessary with sequential-access files. Random-access files sometimes are called *direct-access files*.

As we discussed earlier in this chapter, C# does not impose structure on files, so applications that use random-access files must implement the random-access capability. There are a variety of techniques for creating random-access files. Perhaps the simplest involves requiring that all records in a file be of a uniform, fixed length. The use of fixed-length records enables a program to calculate (as a function of the record size and the record key) the exact location of any record in relation to the beginning of the file. We soon demonstrate how this facilitates immediate access to specific records, even in large files.

Figure 17.13 illustrates the organization of a random-access file composed of fixed-length records (each record in this figure is 100 bytes long). Students can consider a random-access file as analogous to a railroad train with many cars, some of which are empty and some of which contain contents.

Data can be inserted into a random-access file without destroying other data in the file. In addition, previously stored data can be updated or deleted without rewriting the entire file. In the following sections, we explain how to create a random-access file, write data to that file, read data both sequentially and randomly, update data and delete data that is no longer needed.

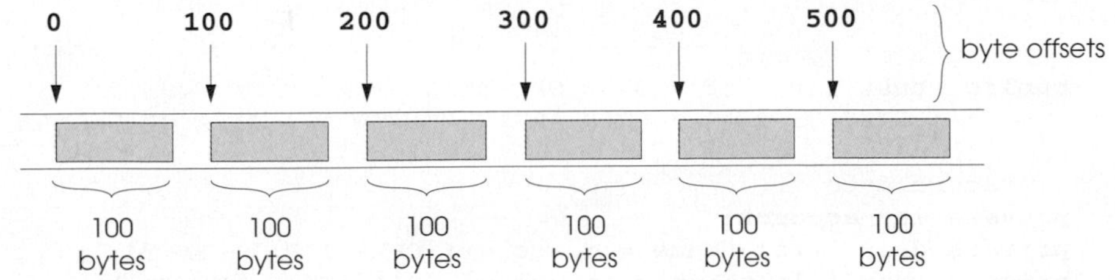

Fig. 17.13 Random-access file with fixed-length records.

Figure 17.14 contains class **RandomAccessRecord**, which is used in the random-access file-processing applications in this chapter. This class also belongs to the **Bank-Library** DLL—i.e., it is part of the project that contains classes **BankUIForm** and **Record**. (When adding class **RandomAccessRecord** to the project containing **BankUIForm** and **Record**, remember to rebuild the project.)

Like class **Record** (Fig. 17.8), class **RandomAccessRecord** contains **private** data members (lines 20–23) for storing record information, two constructors for setting these members to default and parameter-specified values, respectively, and properties for accessing these members. However, class **RandomAccessRecord** does not contain attribute **[Serializable]** before its class definition. We do not serialize this class, because C# does not provide a means to obtain an object's size at runtime. This means that, if we serialize the class, we cannot guarantee a fixed-length record size.

Instead of serializing the class, we fix the length of the **private** data members, then write those data as a byte stream to the file. To fix this length, the **set** accessors of properties **FirstName** (lines 58–91) and **LastName** (lines 94–127) ensure that members **firstName** and **lastName** are **char** arrays of exactly 15 elements. Each **set** accessor receives as an argument a **string** representing the first name and last name, respectively. If the **string** parameter contains fewer than 15 characters, the property's **set** accessor copies the **string**'s values to the **char** array, then populates the remainder with spaces. If the **string** parameter contains more than 15 characters, the **set** accessor stores only the first 15 characters of the **string** parameter into the **char** array.

```
1   // Fig. 17.14: RandomAccessRecord.cs
2   // Data-record class for random-access applications.
3
4   using System;
5
6   public class RandomAccessRecord
7   {
8       // length of firstName and lastName
9       private const int CHAR_ARRAY_LENGTH = 15;
10
11      private const int SIZE_OF_CHAR = 2;
12      private const int SIZE_OF_INT32 = 4;
13      private const int SIZE_OF_DOUBLE = 8;
```

Fig. 17.14 Record for random-access file-processing applications. (Part 1 of 4.)

```
14
15      // length of record
16      public const int SIZE = SIZE_OF_INT32 +
17         2 * ( SIZE_OF_CHAR * CHAR_ARRAY_LENGTH ) + SIZE_OF_DOUBLE;
18
19      // record data
20      private int account;
21      private char[] firstName = new char[ CHAR_ARRAY_LENGTH ];
22      private char[] lastName = new char[ CHAR_ARRAY_LENGTH ];
23      private double balance;
24
25      // default constructor sets members to default values
26      public RandomAccessRecord() : this( 0, "", "", 0.0 )
27      {
28      }
29
30      // overloaded counstructor sets members to parameter values
31      public RandomAccessRecord( int accountValue,
32         string firstNameValue, string lastNameValue,
33         double balanceValue )
34      {
35         Account = accountValue;
36         FirstName = firstNameValue;
37         LastName = lastNameValue;
38         Balance = balanceValue;
39
40      } // end constructor
41
42      // property Account
43      public int Account
44      {
45         get
46         {
47            return account;
48         }
49
50         set
51         {
52            account = value;
53         }
54
55      } // end property Account
56
57      // property FirstName
58      public string FirstName
59      {
60         get
61         {
62            return new string( firstName );
63         }
64
```

Fig. 17.14 Record for random-access file-processing applications. (Part 2 of 4.)

```
65        set
66        {
67            // determine length of string parameter
68            int stringSize = value.Length;
69
70            // firstName string representation
71            string firstNameString = value;
72
73            // append spaces to string parameter if too short
74            if ( CHAR_ARRAY_LENGTH >= stringSize )
75            {
76                firstNameString = value +
77                    new string( ' ', CHAR_ARRAY_LENGTH - stringSize );
78            }
79            else
80            {
81                // remove characters from string parameter if too long
82                firstNameString =
83                    value.Substring( 0, CHAR_ARRAY_LENGTH );
84            }
85
86            // convert string parameter to char array
87            firstName = firstNameString.ToCharArray();
88
89        } // end set
90
91    } // end property FirstName
92
93    // property LastName
94    public string LastName
95    {
96        get
97        {
98            return new string( lastName );
99        }
100
101        set
102        {
103            // determine length of string parameter
104            int stringSize = value.Length;
105
106            // lastName string representation
107            string lastNameString = value;
108
109            // append spaces to string parameter if too short
110            if ( CHAR_ARRAY_LENGTH >= stringSize )
111            {
112                lastNameString = value +
113                    new string( ' ', CHAR_ARRAY_LENGTH - stringSize );
114            }
```

Fig. 17.14 Record for random-access file-processing applications. (Part 3 of 4.)

```
115              else
116              {
117                  // remove characters from string parameter if too long
118                  lastNameString =
119                     value.Substring( 0, CHAR_ARRAY_LENGTH );
120              }
121
122              // convert string parameter to char array
123              lastName = lastNameString.ToCharArray();
124
125           } // end set
126
127       } // end property LastName
128
129       // property Balance
130       public double Balance
131       {
132          get
133          {
134             return balance;
135          }
136
137          set
138          {
139             balance = value;
140          }
141
142       } // end property Balance
143
144   } // end class RandomAccessRecord
```

Fig. 17.14 Record for random-access file-processing applications. (Part 4 of 4.)

Lines 16–17 declare **const SIZE**, which specifies the record's length. Each record contains **account** (4-byte **int**), **firstName** and **lastName** (two 15-element **char** arrays, where each **char** occupies two bytes, resulting in a total of 60 bytes) and **balance** (8-byte **double**). In this example, each record (i.e., the four **private** data members that our programs will read to and write from files) occupies 72 bytes (4 bytes + 60 bytes + 8 bytes).

17.8 Creating a Random-Access File

Consider the following problem statement for a credit-processing application:

> *Create a transaction-processing program capable of storing a maximum of 100 fixed-length records for a company that can have a maximum of 100 customers. Each record consists of an account number (which acts as the record key), a last name, a first name and a balance. The program can update an account, create an account and delete an account.*

The next several sections introduce the techniques necessary to create this credit-processing program. We now discuss the program used to create the random-access file that the programs of Fig. 17.16 and Fig. 17.17 and the transaction-processing application use to manipulate data. Class **CreateRandomAccessFile** (Fig. 17.15) creates a random-access file.

```
1   // Fig. 17.15: CreateRandomAccessFile.cs
2   // Creating a random file.
3
4   // C# namespaces
5   using System;
6   using System.IO;
7   using System.Windows.Forms;
8
9   // Deitel namespaces
10  using BankLibrary;
11
12  class CreateRandomAccessFile
13  {
14     // number of records to write to disk
15     private const int NUMBER_OF_RECORDS = 100;
16
17     [STAThread]
18     static void Main(string[] args)
19     {
20        // create random file, then save to disk
21        CreateRandomAccessFile file = new CreateRandomAccessFile();
22        file.SaveFile();
23
24     } // end method Main
25
26     // write records to disk
27     private void SaveFile()
28     {
29        // record for writing to disk
30        RandomAccessRecord blankRecord = new RandomAccessRecord();
31
32        // stream through which serializable data are written to file
33        FileStream fileOutput = null;
34
35        // stream for writing bytes to file
36        BinaryWriter binaryOutput = null;
37
38        // create dialog box enabling user to save file
39        SaveFileDialog fileChooser = new SaveFileDialog();
40        DialogResult result = fileChooser.ShowDialog();
41
42        // get file name from user
43        string fileName = fileChooser.FileName;
44
45        // exit event handler if user clicked Cancel
46        if ( result == DialogResult.Cancel )
47           return;
48
49        // show error if user specified invalid file
50        if ( fileName == "" || fileName == null )
51           MessageBox.Show("Invalid File Name", "Error",
52              MessageBoxButtons.OK, MessageBoxIcon.Error);
```

Fig. 17.15 Creating files for random-access file-processing applications. (Part 1 of 3.)

```
53           else
54           {
55              // write records to file
56              try
57              {
58                 // create FileStream to hold records
59                 fileOutput = new FileStream( fileName,
60                    FileMode.Create, FileAccess.Write );
61
62                 // set length of file
63                 fileOutput.SetLength( RandomAccessRecord.SIZE *
64                    NUMBER_OF_RECORDS );
65
66                 // create object for writing bytes to file
67                 binaryOutput = new BinaryWriter( fileOutput );
68
69                 // write empty records to file
70                 for ( int i = 0; i < NUMBER_OF_RECORDS; i++ )
71                 {
72                    // set file position pointer in file
73                    fileOutput.Position = i * RandomAccessRecord.SIZE;
74
75                    // write blank record to file
76                    binaryOutput.Write( blankRecord.Account );
77                    binaryOutput.Write( blankRecord.FirstName );
78                    binaryOutput.Write( blankRecord.LastName );
79                    binaryOutput.Write( blankRecord.Balance );
80                 }
81
82                 // notify user of success
83                 MessageBox.Show("File Created", "Success",
84                    MessageBoxButtons.OK, MessageBoxIcon.Information);
85              }
86
87              // handle exception if error occurs during writing
88              catch( IOException )
89              {
90                 // notify user of error
91                 MessageBox.Show( "Cannot write to file", "Error",
92                    MessageBoxButtons.OK, MessageBoxIcon.Error );
93              }
94           }
95
96           // close FileStream
97           if ( fileOutput == null )
98              fileOutput.Close();
99
100          // close BinaryWriter
101          if ( binaryOutput == null )
102             binaryOutput.Close();
103
104       } // end method SaveFile
105    } // end class CreateRandomAccessFile
```

Fig. 17.15 Creating files for random-access file-processing applications. (Part 2 of 3.)

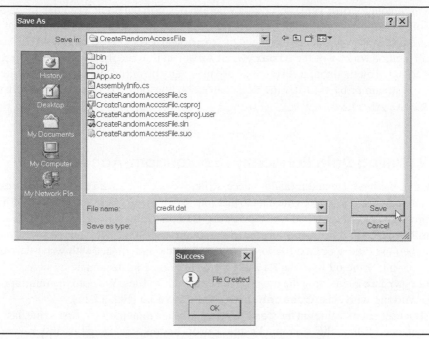

Fig. 17.15 Creating files for random-access file-processing applications. (Part 3 of 3.)

Method **Main** (lines 18–24) starts the application, which creates a random-access file by calling user-defined method **SaveFile** (lines 27–104). Method **SaveFile** populates a file with 100 copies of the default (i.e., empty) values for **private** data members **account**, **firstName**, **lastName** and **balance** of class **RandomAccessRecord**. Lines 39–40 create and display the **SaveFileDialog**, which enables a user to specify the file to which the program writes data. Using this file, lines 59–60 instantiate the **FileStream**. Note that line 60 passes constant **FileMode.Create**, which either creates the specified file, if the file does not exist, or overwrites the specified file if it does exist. Lines 63–64 sets the **FileStream**'s length, which is equal to the size of an individual **RandomAccessRecord** (obtained through constant **RandomAccess-Record.SIZE**) multiplied by the number of records we want to copy (obtained through constant **NUMBER_OF_RECORDS** in line 15, which we set to value **100**).

We now require a means to write bytes to a file. Class **BinaryWriter** of namespace **System.IO** provides methods for writing bytes to streams. The **BinaryWriter** constructor takes as an argument a reference to an instance of class **System.IO.Stream**, through which the **BinaryWriter** can write bytes. Class **FileStream** provides methods for writing streams to files and inherits from class **Stream**, so we can pass the **FileStream** object as an argument to the **BinaryWriter** constructor (line 67). Now, we can use the **BinaryWriter** to write bytes directly to the file.

Lines 70–80 populate the file with 100 copies of the empty record values (i.e., default values for **private** data members of class **RandomAccessRecord**). Line 73 changes the file-position pointer to specify the location in the file at which to write the next empty record. Now that we are working with a random-access file, we must set the file-pointer explicitly, using the **FileStream** object's **Position** property. This property receives as an argument a **long** value describing where to position the pointer relative to the beginning of the file—in this example, we set the pointer so that it advances a number of bytes that is equal to the record size (obtained by **RandomAccessRecord.SIZE**). Lines 76–79 call method **Write** of the **BinaryWriter** object to write the data. Method **Write** is an overloaded method that receives as an argument any primitive data type, then writes that type to a stream of bytes. After the **for** loop exits, lines 97–102 close the **FileStream** and **BinaryWriter** objects.

17.9 Writing Data Randomly to a Random-Access File

Now that we have created a random-access file, we use class **WriteRandomAccessFileForm** (Fig. 17.16) to write data to that file. When a user clicks the **Open File** button, the program invokes method **openButton_Click** (lines 41–84), which displays the **OpenFileDialog** for specifying the file in which to serialize data (lines 45–46); the program then uses the specified file to create a **FileStream** object with write-only access (lines 65–66). Line 69 uses the **FileStream** reference to instantiate an object of class **BinaryWriter**, enabling the program to write bytes to files. We used the same approach when working with class **CreateRandomAccessFile** (Fig. 17.15).

The user enters values in the **TextBox**es for the account number, first name, last name and balance. When the user clicks the **Enter** button, the program invokes method **enterButton_Click** (lines 87–139), which writes the data in the **TextBox**es to the file. Line 91 calls method **GetTextBoxValues** (provided by base class **BankUIForm**) to retrieve the data. Lines 104–105 determine whether the **Account Number TextBox** holds valid information (i.e., the account number is in the **1–100** range).

```
1   // Fig 17.16: WriteRandomAccessFile.cs
2   // Write data to a random-access file.
3
4   // C# namespaces
5   using System;
6   using System.Drawing;
7   using System.Collections;
8   using System.ComponentModel;
9   using System.Windows.Forms;
10  using System.Data;
11  using System.IO;
12
13  // Deitel namespaces
14  using BankLibrary;
15
16  public class WriteRandomAccessFileForm : BankUIForm
17  {
18      private System.Windows.Forms.Button openButton;
19      private System.Windows.Forms.Button enterButton;
20
21      private System.ComponentModel.Container components = null;
22
```

Fig. 17.16 Writing records to random-access files. (Part 1 of 5.)

```
23        // number of RandomAccessRecords to write to disk
24        private const int NUMBER_OF_RECORDS = 100;
25
26        // stream through which data are written to file
27        private FileStream fileOutput;
28
29        // stream for writing bytes to file
30        private BinaryWriter binaryOutput;
31
32        [STAThread]
33        static void Main()
34        {
35            Application.Run( new WriteRandomAccessFileForm() );
36        }
37
38        // Visual Studio .NET generated code
39
40        // invoked when user clicks Open button
41        private void openButton_Click(
42            object sender, System.EventArgs e )
43        {
44            // create dialog box enabling user to open file
45            OpenFileDialog fileChooser = new OpenFileDialog();
46            DialogResult result = fileChooser.ShowDialog();
47
48            // get file name from user
49            string fileName = fileChooser.FileName;
50
51            // exit event handler if user clicked Cancel
52            if ( result == DialogResult.Cancel )
53                return;
54
55            // show error if user specified invalid file
56            if ( fileName == "" || fileName == null )
57                MessageBox.Show("Invalid File Name", "Error",
58                    MessageBoxButtons.OK, MessageBoxIcon.Error);
59            else
60            {
61                // open file if file already exists
62                try
63                {
64                    // create FileStream to hold records
65                    fileOutput = new FileStream( fileName,
66                        FileMode.Open, FileAccess.Write );
67
68                    // create object for writing bytes to file
69                    binaryOutput = new BinaryWriter( fileOutput );
70
71                    // disable Open button and enable Enter button
72                    openButton.Enabled = false;
73                    enterButton.Enabled = true;
74                }
75
```

Fig. 17.16 Writing records to random-access files. (Part 2 of 5.)

```
76              // notify user if file does not exist
77              catch( IOException )
78              {
79                  MessageBox.Show("File Does Not Exits", "Error",
80                      MessageBoxButtons.OK, MessageBoxIcon.Error);
81              }
82          }
83
84      } // end method openButton_Click
85
86      // invoked when user clicks Enter button
87      private void enterButton_Click(
88          object sender, System.EventArgs e )
89      {
90          // TextBox values string array
91          string[] values = GetTextBoxValues();
92
93          // determine whether TextBox account field is empty
94          if ( values[ ( int )TextBoxIndices.ACCOUNT ] != "" )
95          {
96              // write record to file at appropriate position
97              try
98              {
99                  // get account number value from TextBox
100                 int accountNumber = Int32.Parse(
101                     values[ ( int )TextBoxIndices.ACCOUNT ] );
102
103                 // determine whether accountNumber is valid
104                 if ( accountNumber > 0 &&
105                     accountNumber <= NUMBER_OF_RECORDS )
106                 {
107                     // move file position pointer
108                     fileOutput.Seek( ( accountNumber - 1 ) *
109                         RandomAccessRecord.SIZE, SeekOrigin.Begin );
110
111                     // write data to file
112                     binaryOutput.Write( accountNumber );
113                     binaryOutput.Write(
114                         values[ ( int )TextBoxIndices.FIRST ] );
115                     binaryOutput.Write(
116                         values[ ( int )TextBoxIndices.LAST ] );
117                     binaryOutput.Write( Double.Parse( values[
118                         ( int )TextBoxIndices.BALANCE ] ) );
119                 }
120                 else
121                 {
122                     // notify user if invalid account number
123                     MessageBox.Show("Invalid Account Number", "Error",
124                         MessageBoxButtons.OK, MessageBoxIcon.Error);
125                 }
126             }
127
```

Fig. 17.16 Writing records to random-access files. (Part 3 of 5.)

```
128              // handle number-format exception
129              catch( FormatException )
130              {
131                  // notify user if error occurs when formatting numbers
132                  MessageBox.Show("Invalid Balance", "Error",
133                      MessageBoxButtons.OK, MessageBoxIcon.Error );
134              }
135          }
136
137          ClearTextBoxes(); // clear text box values
138
139      } // end method enterButton_Click
140
141  } // end class WriteRandomAccessFileForm
```

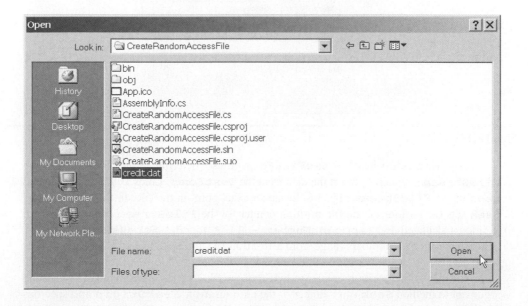

Fig. 17.16 Writing records to random-access files. (Part 4 of 5.)

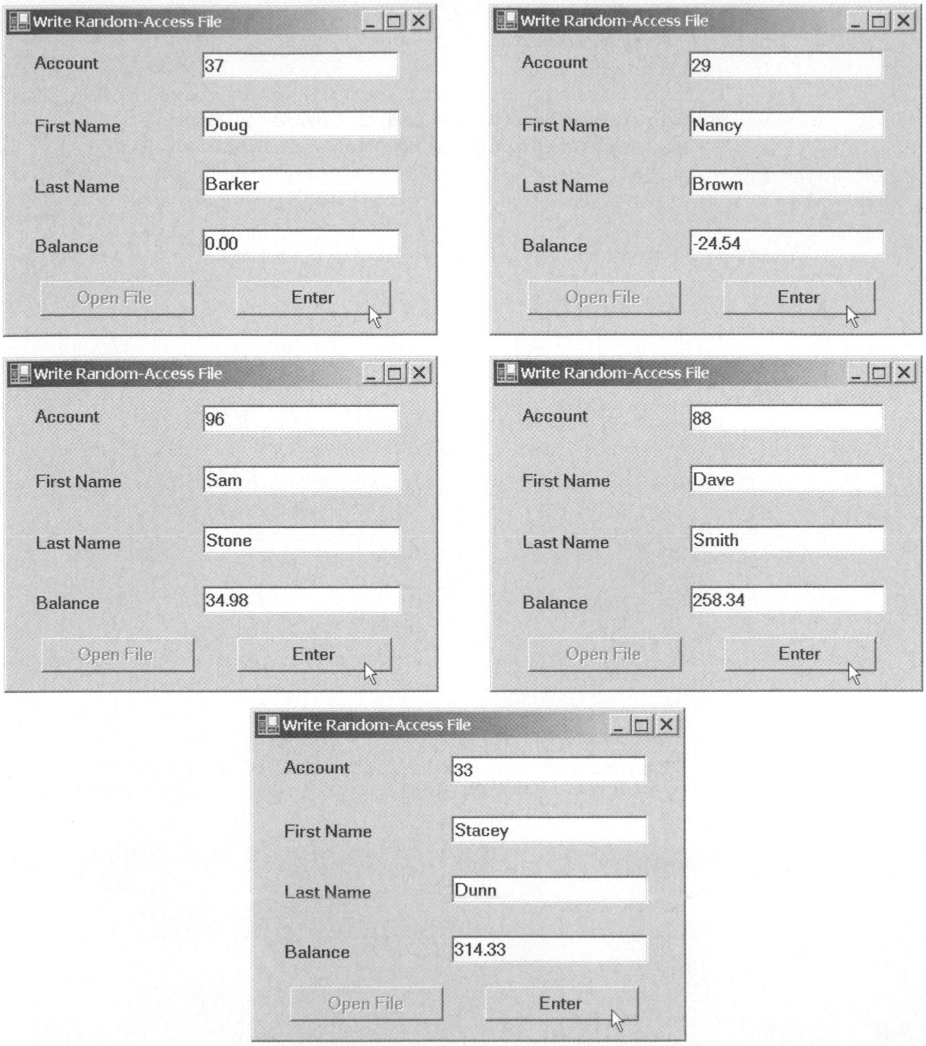

Fig. 17.16 Writing records to random-access files. (Part 5 of 5.)

Class **WriteRandomAccessFileForm** must determine the location in the **FileStream** at which to insert the data from the **TextBox**es. Lines 108–109 use method **Seek** of the **FileStream** object to locate an exact point in the file. In this case, method **Seek** sets the position of the file-position pointer for the **FileStream** object to the byte location calculated by **(accountNumber - 1) * RandomAccessRecord.SIZE**. Because the account numbers range from **1** to **100**, we subtract **1** from the account number when calculating the byte location of the record. For example, our use of method **Seek** sets the first record's file-position pointer to byte 0 of the file (the file's beginning). The second argument to method **Seek** is a member of the enumeration **SeekOrigin** and specifies the location at which the method should begin seeking. We use **const SeekOrigin.Begin**, because we want the method to seek in relation to the beginning of the file. After the program determines the file location at which to place the record, lines 112–118 write the record to the file using the **BinaryWriter** (discussed in the previous section).

17.10 Reading Data Sequentially from a Random-Access File

In the previous sections, we created a random-access file and wrote data to that file. Here, we develop a program (Fig. 17.17) that opens the file, reads records from it and displays only the records that contain data (i.e., those records in which the account number is not zero). This program also provides an additional benefit. Students should attempt to determine what it is—we will reveal it at the end of this section.

When the user clicks the **Open File** button, class **ReadRandomAccessFileForm** invokes method **openButton_Click** (lines 41–75), which displays the **OpenFile-Dialog** for specifying the file from which to read data. Lines 62–63 instantiate a **FileStream** object that opens a file with read-only access. Line 66 creates an instance of class *BinaryReader*, which reads bytes from a stream. We pass the **FileStream** object as an argument to the **BinaryReader** constructor, thus enabling the **BinaryReader** to read bytes from the file.

```
1   // Fig 17.17: ReadRandomAccessFile.cs
2   // Reads and displays random-access file contents.
3
4   // C# namespaces
5   using System;
6   using System.Drawing;
7   using System.Collections;
8   using System.ComponentModel;
9   using System.Windows.Forms;
10  using System.Data;
11  using System.IO;
12
13  // Deitel namespaces
14  using BankLibrary;
15
16  public class ReadRandomAccessFileForm : BankUIForm
17  {
18     private System.Windows.Forms.Button openButton;
19     private System.Windows.Forms.Button nextButton;
20
21     private System.ComponentModel.Container components = null;
22
23     // stream through which data are read from file
24     private FileStream fileInput;
25
26     // stream for reading bytes from file
27     private BinaryReader binaryInput;
28
29     // index of current record to be displayed
30     private int currentRecordIndex;
31
```

Fig. 17.17 Reading records from random-access files sequentially. (Part 1 of 5.)

```
32          [STAThread]
33          static void Main()
34          {
35             Application.Run( new ReadRandomAccessFileForm() );
36          }
37
38          // Visual Studio .NET generated code
39
40          // invoked when user clicks Open button
41          private void openButton_Click(
42             object sender, System.EventArgs e )
43          {
44             // create dialog box enabling user to open file
45             OpenFileDialog fileChooser = new OpenFileDialog();
46             DialogResult result = fileChooser.ShowDialog();
47
48             // get file name from user
49             string fileName = fileChooser.FileName;
50
51             // exit eventhandler if user clicked Cancel
52             if ( result == DialogResult.Cancel )
53                return;
54
55             // show error if user specified invalid file
56             if ( fileName == "" || fileName == null )
57                MessageBox.Show( "Invalid File Name", "Error",
58                   MessageBoxButtons.OK, MessageBoxIcon.Error );
59             else
60             {
61                // create FileStream to obtain read access to file
62                fileInput = new FileStream( fileName,
63                   FileMode.Open, FileAccess.Read );
64
65                // use FileStream for BinaryWriter to read bytes from file
66                binaryInput = new BinaryReader( fileInput );
67
68                openButton.Enabled = false; // disable Open button
69                nextButton.Enabled = true; // enable Next button
70
71                currentRecordIndex = 0;
72                ClearTextBoxes();
73             }
74
75          } // end method openButton_Click
76
77          // invoked when user clicks Next button
78          private void nextButton_Click(
79             object sender, System.EventArgs e )
80          {
81             // record to store file data
82             RandomAccessRecord record = new RandomAccessRecord();
83
```

Fig. 17.17 Reading records from random-access files sequentially. (Part 2 of 5.)

```
84          // read record and store data in TextBoxes
85          try
86          {
87              string[] values; // for storing TextBox values
88
89              // get next record available in file
90              while( record.Account == 0 )
91              {
92                  // set file position pointer to next record in file
93                  fileInput.Seek(
94                      currentRecordIndex * RandomAccessRecord.SIZE, 0 );
95
96                  currentRecordIndex += 1;
97
98                  // read data from record
99                  record.Account = binaryInput.ReadInt32();
100                 record.FirstName = binaryInput.ReadString();
101                 record.LastName = binaryInput.ReadString();
102                 record.Balance = binaryInput.ReadDouble();
103             }
104
105             // store record values in temporary string array
106             values = new string[] {
107                 record.Account.ToString(),
108                 record.FirstName,
109                 record.LastName,
110                 record.Balance.ToString() };
111
112             // copy string array values to TextBox values
113             SetTextBoxValues( values );
114         }
115
116         // handle exception when no records in file
117         catch( IOException )
118         {
119             // close streams if no records in file
120             fileInput.Close();
121             binaryInput.Close();
122
123             openButton.Enabled = true; // enable Open button
124             nextButton.Enabled = false; // disable Next button
125             ClearTextBoxes();
126
127             // notify user if no records in file
128             MessageBox.Show("No more records in file", "",
129                 MessageBoxButtons.OK, MessageBoxIcon.Information);
130         }
131
132     } // end method nextButton_Click
133
134 } // end class ReadRandomAccessFileForm
```

Fig. 17.17 Reading records from random-access files sequentially. (Part 3 of 5.)

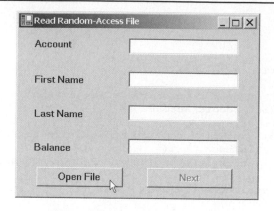

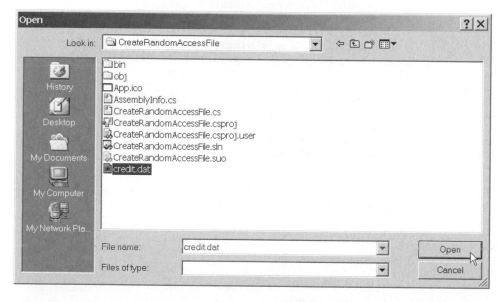

Fig. 17.17 Reading records from random-access files sequentially. (Part 4 of 5.)

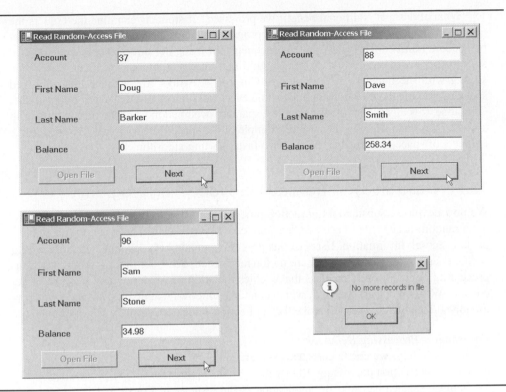

Fig. 17.17 Reading records from random-access files sequentially. (Part 5 of 5.)

When the user clicks the **Next** button, the program calls method **nextButton_Click** (lines 78–132), which reads the next record from the file. Line 82 instantiates a **RandomAccessRecord** for storing the record data from the file. Lines 90–114 define a **while** loop that reads from the file until it reaches a record that has a non-zero account number (**0** is the initial value for the account number). Lines 93–94 call method **Seek** of the **FileStream** object, which moves the file-position pointer to the appropriate place in the file where the record must be read. To accomplish this, method **Seek** uses **int currentRecordIndex**, which stores the number of records that have been read. Lines 99–102 use the **BinaryReader** object to store the file data in the **RandomAccessRecord** object. Recall that class **BinaryWriter** provides overloaded **Write** methods for writing data. However, class **BinaryReader** does not provide overloaded **Read** methods to read data. This means that we must use method **ReadInt32** to read an **int**, method **ReadString** to read a **string** and method **ReadDouble** to read a **double**. Note that the order of these method invocations must correspond to the order in which the **BinaryWriter** object wrote each data type. When the **BinaryReader** reads a valid account number (i.e., a non-zero value), the loop terminates, and lines 106–113 display the record values in the **TextBox**es. When the program has displayed all records, method **Seek** throws an **IOException** (because method **Seek** tries to position the file-position pointer to a location that is beyond the end-of-file marker). The **catch** block (lines 117–130) handles this exception by closing the **FileStream** and **BinaryReader** objects (lines 120–121) and notifying the user that no more records exist (lines 128–129).

What about that additional benefit we promised? If students examine the GUI as the program executes, they will notice that the program displays the records in ascending order by account number! This is a simple consequence of using our direct-access techniques to store these records in the file. Sorting with direct-access techniques is much faster than sorting with the bubble sort presented in Chapter 7, Arrays. We achieve this improved speed by making the file large enough to hold every possible record that a user might create. Of course, this means that the file could be sparsely occupied most of the time, resulting in a waste of storage. Here is yet another example of the space/time trade-off: By using large amounts of space, we are able to develop a faster sorting algorithm.

17.11 Case Study: A Transaction-Processing Program

We now develop a substantial transaction-processing program (Fig. 17.18–Fig. 17.23) using a random-access file to achieve "instant-access" processing. The program maintains a bank's account information. Users of this program can add new accounts, update existing accounts and delete accounts that are no longer needed. First, we discuss the transaction-processing behavior (i.e., the class that enables the addition, updating and removal of accounts). We then discuss the GUI, which contains windows that display the account information and enable the user to invoke the application's transaction-processing behavior.

Transaction-Processing Behavior

In this case study, we create class **Transaction** (Fig. 17.18), which acts as a *proxy* to handle all transaction processing. Rather than providing the transaction-processing behavior themselves, the objects in this application use an instance of **Transaction** to provide the necessary functionality. By using a proxy, we can encapsulate transaction-processing behavior in only one class, enabling various other classes in our application to reuse this behavior. Furthermore, if we decide to modify this behavior, we modify only the proxy (i.e., class **Transaction**), instead of having to modify the behavior of each class that uses the proxy.

Class **Transaction** contains methods **OpenFile**, **GetRecord** and **AddRecord**. Method **OpenFile** (lines 27–74) uses constant **FileMode.OpenOrCreate** (line 33) to create a **FileStream** object from either an existing file or one not yet created. Lines 36–39 use this **FileStream** to create **BinaryReader** and **BinaryWriter** objects for reading and writing bytes to the file, respectively. If the file is new, lines 42–64 populate the **FileStream** object with empty records. Students might recall that we used these techniques in Section 17.8.

```
1   // Fig. 17.18: Transaction.cs
2   // Handles record transactions.
3
4   // C# namespaces
5   using System;
6   using System.IO;
7   using System.Windows.Forms;
8
```

Fig. 17.18 Record-transaction class for the transaction-processor case study. (Part 1 of 4.)

```
 9      // Deitel namespaces
10      using BankLibrary;
11
12      public class Transaction
13      {
14          // number of records to write to disk
15          private const int NUMBER_OF_RECORDS = 100;
16
17          // stream through which data move to and from file
18          private FileStream file;
19
20          // stream for reading bytes from file
21          private BinaryReader binaryInput;
22
23          // stream for writing bytes to file
24          private BinaryWriter binaryOutput;
25
26          // create/open file containing empty records
27          public void OpenFile( string fileName )
28          {
29              // write empty records to file
30              try
31              {
32                  // create FileStream from new file or existing file
33                  file = new FileStream( fileName, FileMode.OpenOrCreate );
34
35                  // use FileStream for BinaryWriter to read bytes from file
36                  binaryInput = new BinaryReader( file );
37
38                  // use FileStream for BinaryWriter to write bytes to file
39                  binaryOutput = new BinaryWriter( file );
40
41                  // determine whether file has just been created
42                  if ( file.Length == 0 )
43                  {
44                      // record to be written to file
45                      RandomAccessRecord blankRecord =
46                          new RandomAccessRecord();
47
48                      // new record can hold NUMBER_OF_RECORDS records
49                      file.SetLength( RandomAccessRecord.SIZE *
50                          NUMBER_OF_RECORDS );
51
52                      // write blank records to file
53                      for ( int i = 0; i < NUMBER_OF_RECORDS; i++ )
54                      {
55                          // move file-position pointer to next position
56                          file.Position = i * RandomAccessRecord.SIZE;
57
58                          // write blank record to file
59                          binaryOutput.Write( blankRecord.Account );
60                          binaryOutput.Write( blankRecord.FirstName );
```

Fig. 17.18 Record-transaction class for the transaction-processor case study. (Part 2 of 4.)

```
61                      binaryOutput.Write( blankRecord.LastName );
62                      binaryOutput.Write( blankRecord.Balance );
63                }
64             }
65          }
66
67          // notify user of error during writing of blank records
68          catch( IOException )
69          {
70             MessageBox.Show("Cannot create file", "Error",
71                MessageBoxButtons.OK, MessageBoxIcon.Error);
72          }
73
74       } // end method OpenFile
75
76       // retrieve record depending on whether account is valid
77       public RandomAccessRecord GetRecord( string accountValue )
78       {
79          // store file data associated with account in record
80          try
81          {
82             // record to store file data
83             RandomAccessRecord record = new RandomAccessRecord();
84
85             // get value from TextBox's account field
86             int accountNumber = Int32.Parse( accountValue );
87
88             // if account is invalid, do not read data
89             if ( accountNumber < 1 ||
90                accountNumber > NUMBER_OF_RECORDS )
91             {
92                // set record's account field with account number
93                record.Account = accountNumber;
94             }
95
96             // get data from file if account is valid
97             else
98             {
99                // locate position in file where record exists
100               file.Seek( ( accountNumber - 1 ) *
101                  RandomAccessRecord.SIZE, 0 );
102
103               // read data from record
104               record.Account = binaryInput.ReadInt32();
105               record.FirstName = binaryInput.ReadString();
106               record.LastName = binaryInput.ReadString();
107               record.Balance = binaryInput.ReadDouble();
108            }
109
110            return record;
111         }
112
```

Fig. 17.18 Record-transaction class for the transaction-processor case study. (Part 3 of 4.)

```
113              // notify user of error during reading
114              catch( IOException )
115              {
116                  MessageBox.Show( "Cannot read file", "Error",
117                      MessageBoxButtons.OK, MessageBoxIcon.Error );
118              }
119
120              return null;
121
122          } // end method GetRecord;
123
124          // add record to file at position determined by accountNumber
125          public bool AddRecord(
126              RandomAccessRecord record, int accountNumber )
127          {
128              // write record to file
129              try
130              {
131                  // move file position pointer to appropriate position
132                  file.Seek( ( accountNumber - 1 ) *
133                      RandomAccessRecord.SIZE, 0 );
134
135                  // write data to file
136                  binaryOutput.Write(record.Account);
137                  binaryOutput.Write(record.FirstName);
138                  binaryOutput.Write(record.LastName);
139                  binaryOutput.Write(record.Balance);
140              }
141
142              // notify user if error occurs during writing
143              catch( IOException )
144              {
145                  MessageBox.Show( "Error Writing To File", "Error",
146                      MessageBoxButtons.OK, MessageBoxIcon.Error );
147
148                  return false; // failure
149              }
150
151              return true; // success
152
153          } // end method AddRecord
154
155      } // end class Transaction
```

Fig. 17.18 Record-transaction class for the transaction-processor case study.
(Part 4 of 4.)

Method **GetRecord** (lines 77–122) returns the record associated with the account-number parameter. Line 83 instantiates a **RandomAccessRecord** object that will store the file data. If the account parameter is valid, lines 100–101 call method **Seek** of the **FileStream** object, which uses the parameter to determine the position of the specified record in the file. Lines 104–107 then call methods **ReadInt32**, **ReadString** and **ReadDouble** of the **BinaryReader** object to store the file data in the **Random-**

AccessRecord object. Line 110 returns the **RandomAccessRecord** object. We used these techniques in Section 17.10.

Method **AddRecord** (lines 125–153) inserts a record into the file. Lines 132–133 call method **Seek** of the **FileStream** object, which uses the account-number parameter to locate the position at which to insert the record in the file. Lines 136–139 call the overloaded **Write** methods of the **BinaryWriter** object to write the **RandomAccessRecord** object's data to the file. We used these techniques in Section 17.9. Note that, if an error occurs when adding the record (i.e., either the **FileStream** or the **BinaryWriter** throws an **IOException**), lines 145–146 notify the user of the error and return **false** (failure).

Transaction-Processor GUI

The GUI for this program uses a multiple-document interface. Class **Transaction-ProcessorForm** (Fig. 17.19) is the parent window, and contains corresponding child windows **StartDialogForm** (Fig. 17.20), **NewDialogForm** (Fig. 17.22), **Update-DialogForm** (Fig. 17.21) and **DeleteDialogForm** (Fig. 17.23). **StartDialog-Form** allows the user to open a file containing account information and provides access to the **NewDialogForm**, **UpdateDialogForm** and **DeleteDialogForm** internal frames. These frames allow users to update, create and delete records, respectively.

Initially, **TransactionProcessorForm** displays the **StartDialogForm** object; this window provides the user with various options. It contains four buttons, which enable the user to create or open a file, create a record, update an existing record or delete an existing record.

```
1   // Fig. 17.19: TransactionProcessor.cs
2   // MDI parent for transaction-processor application.
3
4   using System;
5   using System.Drawing;
6   using System.Collections;
7   using System.ComponentModel;
8   using System.Windows.Forms;
9   using System.Data;
10
11  public class TransactionProcessorForm
12     : System.Windows.Forms.Form
13  {
14     private System.ComponentModel.Container components = null;
15     private System.Windows.Forms.MdiClient MdiClient1;
16
17     // reference to StartDialog
18     private StartDialogForm startDialog;
19
20     // constructor
21     public TransactionProcessorForm()
22     {
23        // required for Windows Form Designer support
24        InitializeComponent();
25
```

Fig. 17.19 **TransactionProcessorForm** class runs the transaction-processor application. (Part 1 of 2.)

```
26              startDialog = new StartDialogForm();
27              startDialog.MdiParent = this;
28              startDialog.Show();
29          }
30
31          [STAThread]
32          static void Main()
33          {
34              Application.Run( new TransactionProcessorForm() );
35          }
36
37          // Visual Studio .NET generated code
38
39      } // end class TransactionProcessorForm
```

Fig. 17.19 **TransactionProcessorForm** class runs the transaction-processor application. (Part 2 of 2.)

Before the user can modify records, the user must either create or open a file. When the user clicks the **New/Open File** button, the program calls method **open-Button_Click** (lines 42–100), which opens a file that the application uses for modifying records. Lines 46–62 display the **OpenFileDialog** for specifying the file from which to read data, then use this file to create the **FileStream** object. Note that line 52 sets property **CheckFileExists** of the **OpenFileDialog** object to **false**—this enables the user to create a file if the specified file does not exist. If this property were **true** (its default value), the dialog would notify the user that the specified file does not exist, thus preventing the user from creating a file.

```
1   // Fig. 17.20: StartDialog.cs
2   // Initial dialog box displayed to user. Provides buttons for
3   // creating/opening file and for adding, updating and removing
4   // records from file.
5
6   // C# namespaces
7   using System;
8   using System.Drawing;
9   using System.Collections;
10  using System.ComponentModel;
11  using System.Windows.Forms;
12
13  // Deitel namespaces
14  using BankLibrary;
15
16  public delegate void MyDelegate();
17
18  public class StartDialogForm : System.Windows.Forms.Form
19  {
20      private System.Windows.Forms.Button updateButton;
21      private System.Windows.Forms.Button newButton;
```

Fig. 17.20 **StartDialogForm** class enables users to access dialog boxes associated with various transactions. (Part 1 of 4.)

```
22       private System.Windows.Forms.Button deleteButton;
23       private System.Windows.Forms.Button openButton;
24
25       private System.ComponentModel.Container components = null;
26
27       // reference to dialog box for adding record
28       private NewDialogForm newDialog;
29
30       // reference to dialog box for updating record
31       private UpdateDialogForm updateDialog;
32
33       // reference to dialog box for removing record
34       private DeleteDialogForm deleteDialog;
35
36       // reference to object that handles transactions
37       private Transaction transactionProxy;
38
39       // Visual Studio .NET generated code
40
41       // invoked when user clicks New/Open File button
42       private void openButton_Click(
43          object sender, System.EventArgs e )
44       {
45          // create dialog box enabling user to create or open file
46          OpenFileDialog fileChooser = new OpenFileDialog();
47          DialogResult result;
48          string fileName;
49
50          // enable user to create file if file does not exist
51          fileChooser.Title = "Create File / Open File";
52          fileChooser.CheckFileExists = false;
53
54          // show dialog box to user
55          result = fileChooser.ShowDialog();
56
57          // exit event handler if user clicked Cancel
58          if ( result == DialogResult.Cancel )
59             return;
60
61          // get file name from user
62          fileName = fileChooser.FileName;
63
64          // show error if user specified invalid file
65          if ( fileName == "" || fileName == null )
66             MessageBox.Show( "Invalid File Name", "Error",
67                MessageBoxButtons.OK, MessageBoxIcon.Error );
68
69          // open or create file if user specified valid file
70          else
71          {
72             // create Transaction with specified file
73             transactionProxy = new Transaction();
```

Fig. 17.20 StartDialogForm class enables users to access dialog boxes associated with various transactions. (Part 2 of 4.)

```
74                  transactionProxy.OpenFile( fileName );
75
76                  // enable GUI buttons except for New/Open File button
77                  newButton.Enabled = true;
78                  updateButton.Enabled = true;
79                  deleteButton.Enabled = true;
80                  openButton.Enabled = false;
81
82                  // instantiate dialog box for creating records
83                  newDialog = new NewDialogForm( transactionProxy,
84                     new MyDelegate( ShowStartDialog ) );
85
86                  // instantiate dialog box for updating records
87                  updateDialog = new UpdateDialogForm( transactionProxy,
88                     new MyDelegate( ShowStartDialog ) );
89
90                  // instantiate dialog box for removing records
91                  deleteDialog = new DeleteDialogForm( transactionProxy,
92                     new MyDelegate( ShowStartDialog ) );
93
94                  // set StartDialog as MdiParent for dialog boxes
95                  newDialog.MdiParent = this.MdiParent;
96                  updateDialog.MdiParent = this.MdiParent;
97                  deleteDialog.MdiParent = this.MdiParent;
98               }
99
100        } // end method openButton_Click
101
102        // invoked when user clicks New Record button
103        private void newButton_Click(
104           object sender, System.EventArgs e )
105        {
106           Hide(); // hide StartDialog
107           newDialog.Show(); // show NewDialog
108
109        } // end method newButton_Click
110
111        private void updateButton_Click(
112           object sender, System.EventArgs e )
113        {
114           Hide(); // hide StartDialog
115           updateDialog.Show(); // show UpdateDialog
116
117        } // end method updateButton_Click
118
119        private void deleteButton_Click(
120           object sender, System.EventArgs e )
121        {
122           Hide(); // hide StartDialog
123           deleteDialog.Show(); // show DeleteDialog
124
125        } // end method deleteButton_Click
```

Fig. 17.20 StartDialogForm class enables users to access dialog boxes associated with various transactions. (Part 3 of 4.)

```
126
127      protected void ShowStartDialog()
128      {
129          Show();
130      }
131
132  } // end class StartDialogForm
```

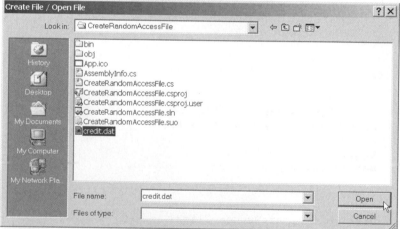

Fig. 17.20 StartDialogForm class enables users to access dialog boxes
associated with various transactions. (Part 4 of 4.)

If the user specifies a file name, line 73 instantiates an object of class **Transaction** (Fig. 17.18), which acts as the proxy for creating, reading records from and writing records to random-access files. Line 74 calls **Transaction**'s method **OpenFile**, which either creates or opens the specified file, depending on whether the file exists.

Class **StartDialogForm** also creates internal windows that enable the user to create, update and delete records. We do not use the default constructor created by Visual Studio .NET for these classes; instead, we use an overloaded constructor that takes as arguments the **Transaction** object and a delegate object that references method **ShowStartDialog** (lines 127–130). Each child window uses the second delegate parameter to display the **StartDialogForm** GUI when the user closes a child window. Lines 83–92 instantiate objects of classes **UpdateDialogForm**, **NewDialogForm** and **DeleteDialogForm**, which serve as the child windows.

When the user clicks the **New Record** button in the **Start Dialog**, the program invokes method **newButton_Click** of class **StartDialogForm** (Fig. 17.20, lines 103–109), which displays the **NewDialogForm** internal frame (Fig. 17.22). Class **NewDialogForm** enables the user to create records in the file that **StartDialogForm** opened (or created). Line 25 of Fig. 17.22 defines **MyDelegate** as a delegate to a method that does not return a value and has no parameters; method **ShowStartDialog** of class **StartDialogForm** (Fig. 17.20, lines 127–130) conforms to these requirements. Class **NewDialogForm** receives a **MyDelegate** object, which references this method as a parameter—therefore, **NewDialogForm** can invoke this method to display the start window when the user exits the **NewDialogForm**. Classes **UpdateDialogForm** and **DeleteDialogForm** also receive **MyDelegate** references as arguments, enabling them to display **StartDialogForm** after completing their tasks.

After the user enters data in the **TextBox**es and clicks the **Save Record** button, the program invokes method **saveButton_Click** (lines 51–66) to write the record to disk. Lines 54–56 call method **GetRecord** of the **Transaction** object, which should return an empty **RandomAccessRecord**. If method **GetRecord** returns a **RandomAccessRecord** that contains data, the user is attempting to overwrite that **RandomAccessRecord** with a new one. Line 60 calls **private** method **InsertRecord** (lines 69–116). If the **RandomAccessRecord** is empty, method **InsertRecord** calls method **AddRecord** of the **Transaction** object (lines 100–101), which adds the newly created **RandomAccessRecord** to the file. If the user is attempting to overwrite an existing record, lines 81–83 notify the user that the record already exists and return from the method.

When the user clicks the **Update Record** button in the **Start Dialog**, the program invokes method **updateButton_Click** of class **StartDialogForm** (Fig. 17.20, lines 111–117), which displays the **UpdateDialogForm** internal frame (Fig. 17.21). Class **UpdateDialogForm** enables the user to update existing records in the file.

To update a record, the user must enter the account number associated with that record. When the user presses *Enter*, **UpdateDialogForm** calls method **accountTextBox_KeyDown** (lines 45–84) to display the record contents. This method calls method **GetRecord** of the **Transaction** object (lines 52–54) to retrieve the specified **RandomAccessRecord**. If the record is not empty, lines 64–72 populate the **TextBox**es with the **RandomAccessRecord** values.

The **Transaction TextBox** initially contains the string **Charge or Payment**. The user should select this text, type the transaction amount (a positive value for a charge or a

negative value for a payment), then press *Enter*. The program calls method
transactionTextBox_KeyDown (lines 87–132) to add the user-specified transaction
amount to the current balance.

```
1    // Fig. 17.21: UpdateDialog.cs
2    // Enables user to update records in file.
3
4    // C# namespaces
5    using System;
6    using System.Drawing;
7    using System.Collections;
8    using System.ComponentModel;
9    using System.Windows.Forms;
10
11   // Deitel namespaces
12   using BankLibrary;
13
14   public class UpdateDialogForm : BankUIForm
15   {
16      private System.Windows.Forms.Label transactionLabel;
17      private System.Windows.Forms.TextBox transactionTextBox;
18
19      private System.Windows.Forms.Button saveButton;
20      private System.Windows.Forms.Button cancelButton;
21
22      private System.ComponentModel.Container components = null;
23
24      // reference to object that handles transactions
25      private Transaction transactionProxy;
26
27      // delegate for method that displays previous window
28      private MyDelegate showPreviousWindow;
29
30      // initialize components and set members to parameter values
31      public UpdateDialogForm(
32         Transaction transactionProxyValue,
33         MyDelegate delegateValue )
34      {
35         InitializeComponent();
36         showPreviousWindow = delegateValue;
37
38         // instantiate object that handles transactions
39         transactionProxy = transactionProxyValue;
40      }
41
42      // Visual Studio .NET generated code
43
44      // invoked when user enters text in account TextBox
45      private void accountTextBox_KeyDown(
46         object sender, System.Windows.Forms.KeyEventArgs e )
47      {
```

Fig. 17.21 **UpdateDialogForm** class enables users to update records in
transaction-processor case study. (Part 1 of 5.)

```
48              // determine whether user pressed Enter key
49              if ( e.KeyCode == Keys.Enter )
50              {
51                 // retrieve record associated with account from file
52                 RandomAccessRecord record =
53                    transactionProxy.GetRecord( GetTextBoxValues()
54                    [ ( int )TextBoxIndices.ACCOUNT ] );
55
56                 // return if record does not exist
57                 if ( record == null )
58                    return;
59
60                 // determine whether record is empty
61                 if ( record.Account != 0 )
62                 {
63                    // store record values in string array
64                    string[] values = {
65                       record.Account.ToString(),
66                       record.FirstName.ToString(),
67                       record.LastName.ToString(),
68                       record.Balance.ToString() };
69
70                    // copy string array value to TextBox values
71                    SetTextBoxValues( values );
72                    transactionTextBox.Text = "[Charge or Payment]";
73
74                 }
75                 else
76                 {
77                    // notify user if record does not exist
78                    MessageBox.Show(
79                       "Record Does Not Exist", "Error",
80                       MessageBoxButtons.OK, MessageBoxIcon.Error );
81                 }
82              }
83
84           } // end method accountTextBox_KeyDown
85
86           // invoked when user enters text in transaction TextBox
87           private void transactionTextBox_KeyDown(
88              object sender, System.Windows.Forms.KeyEventArgs e )
89           {
90              // determine whether user pressed Enter key
91              if ( e.KeyCode == Keys.Enter )
92              {
93                 // calculate balance using transaction TextBox value
94                 try
95                 {
96                    // retrieve record associated with account from file
97                    RandomAccessRecord record =
98                       transactionProxy.GetRecord( GetTextBoxValues()
99                       [ ( int )TextBoxIndices.ACCOUNT ] );
```

Fig. 17.21 UpdateDialogForm class enables users to update records in transaction-processor case study. (Part 2 of 5.)

```
100
101                    // get transaction TextBox value
102                    double transactionValue =
103                       Double.Parse( transactionTextBox.Text );
104
105                    // calculate new balance (old balance + transaction)
106                    double newBalance =
107                       record.Balance + transactionValue;
108
109                    // store record values in string array
110                    string[] values = {
111                       record.Account.ToString(),
112                       record.FirstName.ToString(),
113                       record.LastName.ToString(),
114                       newBalance.ToString() };
115
116                    // copy string array value to TextBox values
117                    SetTextBoxValues( values );
118
119                    // clear transaction TextBox
120                    transactionTextBox.Text = "";
121                 }
122
123              // notify user if error occurs in parameter mismatch
124              catch( FormatException )
125              {
126                 MessageBox.Show(
127                    "Invalid Transaction", "Error",
128                    MessageBoxButtons.OK, MessageBoxIcon.Error );
129              }
130           }
131
132     } // end method transactionTextBox_KeyDown
133
134     // invoked when user clicks Save button
135     private void saveButton_Click(
136        object sender, System.EventArgs e )
137     {
138        RandomAccessRecord record =
139           transactionProxy.GetRecord( GetTextBoxValues()
140           [ ( int )TextBoxIndices.ACCOUNT ] );
141
142        // if record exists, update in file
143        if ( record != null )
144           UpdateRecord( record );
145
146        Hide();
147        ClearTextBoxes();
148        showPreviousWindow();
149
150     } // end method saveButton_Click
151
```

Fig. 17.21 UpdateDialogForm class enables users to update records in transaction-processor case study. (Part 3 of 5.)

```
152      // invoked when user clicks Cancel button
153      private void cancelButton_Click(
154         object sender, System.EventArgs e )
155      {
156         Hide();
157         ClearTextBoxes();
158         showPreviousWindow();
159
160      } // end method cancelButton_Click
161
162      // update record in file at position specified by accountNumber
163      public void UpdateRecord( RandomAccessRecord record )
164      {
165         // store TextBox values in record and write record to file
166         try
167         {
168            int accountNumber = record.Account;
169            string[] values = GetTextBoxValues();
170
171            // store values in record
172            record.Account = accountNumber;
173            record.FirstName =
174               values[ ( int )TextBoxIndices.FIRST ];
175            record.LastName =
176               values[ ( int )TextBoxIndices.LAST ];
177            record.Balance =
178               Double.Parse(
179               values[ ( int )TextBoxIndices.BALANCE ] );
180
181            // add record to file
182            if ( transactionProxy.AddRecord(
183               record, accountNumber ) == false )
184
185               return; // if error
186         }
187
188         // notify user if error occurs in parameter mismatch
189         catch( FormatException )
190         {
191            MessageBox.Show( "Invalid Balance", "Error",
192               MessageBoxButtons.OK, MessageBoxIcon.Error );
193
194            return;
195         }
196
197         MessageBox.Show( "Record Updated", "Success",
198            MessageBoxButtons.OK,
199            MessageBoxIcon.Information );
200
201      } // end method UpdateRecord
202
203   } // end class UpdateDialogForm
```

Fig. 17.21 **UpdateDialogForm** class enables users to update records in transaction-processor case study. (Part 4 of 5.)

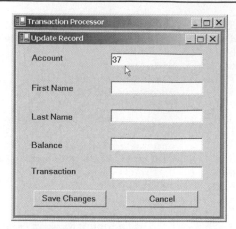

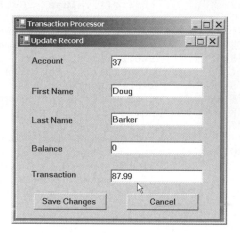

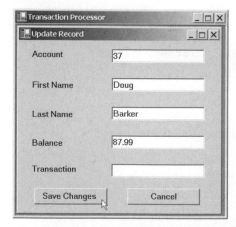

Fig. 17.21 UpdateDialogForm class enables users to update records in transaction-processor case study. (Part 5 of 5.)

The user clicks the **Save Changes** button to write the altered contents of the **Text-Box**es to the file. (Note that pressing **Save Changes** does not update the **Balance** field—the user must press *Enter* to update this field before pressing **Save Changes**.) When the user clicks **Save Changes**, the program invokes method **saveButton_Click** (lines 135–150), which calls **private** method **UpdateRecord** (lines 163–201). This method calls method **AddRecord** of the **Transaction** object (lines 182–183) to store the **TextBox** values in a **RandomAccessRecord** and overwrite the existing file record with the **RandomAccessRecord** containing the new data.

When the user clicks the **Delete Record** button of the **Start Dialog**, the program invokes method **deleteButton_Click** of class **StartDialogForm** (Fig. 17.20, lines 119–125), which displays the **DeleteDialogForm** internal frame (Fig. 17.23). Class **DeleteDialogForm** enables the user to remove existing records from the file. To remove a record, the user must enter the account number associated with that record. When the user clicks the **Delete Record** button (now, from the **DeleteDialogForm** internal frame), **DeleteDialogForm** calls method **deleteButton_Click** (lines 44–57). This method calls method **DeleteRecord** (lines 69–102), which ensures that the record to be deleted exists, then calls method **AddRecord** of the **Transaction** object (lines 87–88) to overwrite the file record with an empty one.

In this chapter, we demonstrated how to read data from files and write data to files via both sequential-access and random-access file-processing techniques. Using class **BinaryFormatter**, we serialized and deserialized objects to and from streams; we then employed **FileStream**, **BinaryWriter** and **BinaryReader** to transfer the objects' byte representation to and from files. In Chapter 18, we discuss the Extensible Markup Language (XML), a widely supported technology for describing data. Using XML, we can describe any type of data, such as mathematical formulas, music and financial reports.

```
1   // Fig. 17.22: NewDialog.cs
2   // Enables user to insert new record into file.
3
4   // C# namespaces
5   using System;
6   using System.Drawing;
7   using System.Collections;
8   using System.ComponentModel;
9   using System.Windows.Forms;
10
11  // Deitel namespaces
12  using BankLibrary;
13
14  public class NewDialogForm : BankUIForm
15  {
16      private System.Windows.Forms.Button saveButton;
17      private System.Windows.Forms.Button cancelButton;
```

Fig. 17.22 **NewDialogForm** class enables users to create records in transaction-processor case study. (Part 1 of 4.)

```
18
19        private System.ComponentModel.Container components = null;
20
21        // reference to object that handles transactions
22        private Transaction transactionProxy;
23
24        // delegate for method that displays previous window
25        public MyDelegate showPreviousWindow;
26
27        // constructor
28        public NewDialogForm( Transaction transactionProxyValue,
29           MyDelegate delegateValue )
30        {
31           InitializeComponent();
32           showPreviousWindow = delegateValue;
33
34           // instantiate object that handles transactions
35           transactionProxy = transactionProxyValue;
36        }
37
38        // Visual Studio .NET generated code
39
40        // invoked when user clicks Cancel button
41        private void cancelButton_Click(
42           object sender, System.EventArgs e )
43        {
44           Hide();
45           ClearTextBoxes();
46           showPreviousWindow();
47
48        } // end method cancelButton_Click
49
50        // invoked when user clicks Save As button
51        private void saveButton_Click(
52           object sender, System.EventArgs e )
53        {
54           RandomAccessRecord record =
55              transactionProxy.GetRecord( GetTextBoxValues()
56              [ ( int )TextBoxIndices.ACCOUNT ] );
57
58           // if record exists, add it to file
59           if ( record != null )
60              InsertRecord( record );
61
62           Hide();
63           ClearTextBoxes();
64           showPreviousWindow();
65
66        } // end method saveButton_Click
67
```

Fig. 17.22 NewDialogForm class enables users to create records in transaction-
processor case study. (Part 2 of 4.)

```
68      // insert record in file at position specified by accountNumber
69      private void InsertRecord( RandomAccessRecord record )
70      {
71         //store TextBox values in string array
72         string[] textBoxValues = GetTextBoxValues();
73
74         // store TextBox account field
75         int accountNumber = Int32.Parse(
76            textBoxValues[ ( int )TextBoxIndices.ACCOUNT ] );
77
78         // notify user and return if record account is not empty
79         if ( record.Account != 0 )
80         {
81            MessageBox.Show(
82               "Record Already Exists or Invalid Number", "Error",
83               MessageBoxButtons.OK, MessageBoxIcon.Error);
84
85            return;
86         }
87
88         // store values in record
89         record.Account = accountNumber;
90         record.FirstName =
91            textBoxValues[ ( int )TextBoxIndices.FIRST];
92         record.LastName =
93            textBoxValues[ ( int )TextBoxIndices.LAST];
94         record.Balance = Double.Parse(
95            textBoxValues[ ( int )TextBoxIndices.BALANCE ] );
96
97         // add record to file
98         try
99         {
100            if ( transactionProxy.AddRecord(
101               record, accountNumber ) == false )
102
103               return; // if error
104         }
105
106         // notify user if error occurs in parameter mismatch
107         catch( FormatException )
108         {
109            MessageBox.Show( "Invalid Balance", "Error",
110               MessageBoxButtons.OK, MessageBoxIcon.Error );
111         }
112
113         MessageBox.Show( "Record Created", "Success",
114            MessageBoxButtons.OK, MessageBoxIcon.Information );
115
116      } // end method InsertRecord
117
118 } // end class NewDialogForm
```

Fig. 17.22 NewDialogForm class enables users to create records in transaction-processor case study. (Part 3 of 4.)

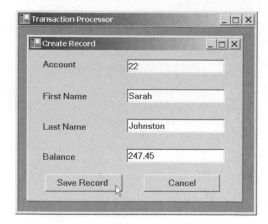

Fig. 17.22 `NewDialogForm` class enables users to create records in transaction-processor case study. (Part 4 of 4.)

```
1   // Fig. 17.23: DeleteDialog.cs
2   // Enables user to delete records in file.
3
4   // C# namespaces
5   using System;
6   using System.Drawing;
7   using System.Collections;
8   using System.ComponentModel;
9   using System.Windows.Forms;
10
11  // Deitel namespaces
12  using BankLibrary;
13
14  public class DeleteDialogForm : System.Windows.Forms.Form
15  {
16     private System.Windows.Forms.Label accountLabel;
17     private System.Windows.Forms.TextBox accountTextBox;
18
19     private System.Windows.Forms.Button deleteButton;
20     private System.Windows.Forms.Button cancelButton;
21
22     private System.ComponentModel.Container components = null;
23
24     // reference to object that handles transactions
25     private Transaction transactionProxy;
```

Fig. 17.23 `DeleteDialogForm` class enables users to remove records from files in transaction-processor case study. (Part 1 of 3.)

```
26
27       // delegate for method that displays previous window
28       private MyDelegate showPreviousWindow;
29
30       // initialize components and set members to parameter values
31       public DeleteDialogForm( Transaction transactionProxyValue,
32          MyDelegate delegateValue)
33       {
34          InitializeComponent();
35          showPreviousWindow = delegateValue;
36
37          // instantiate object that handles transactions
38          transactionProxy = transactionProxyValue;
39       }
40
41       // Visual Studio .NET generated code
42
43       // invoked when user clicks Delete Record button
44       private void deleteButton_Click(
45          object sender, System.EventArgs e)
46       {
47          RandomAccessRecord record =
48             transactionProxy.GetRecord( accountTextBox.Text );
49
50          // if record exists, delete it in file
51          if ( record != null )
52             DeleteRecord( record );
53
54          this.Hide();
55          showPreviousWindow();
56
57       } // end method deleteButton_Click
58
59       // invoked when user clicks Cancel button
60       private void cancelButton_Click(
61          object sender, System.EventArgs e)
62       {
63          this.Hide();
64          showPreviousWindow();
65
66       } // end method cancelButton_Click
67
68       // delete record in file at position specified by accountNumber
69       public void DeleteRecord( RandomAccessRecord record )
70       {
71          int accountNumber = record.Account;
72
73          // display error message if record does not exist
74          if ( record.Account == 0 )
75          {
76             MessageBox.Show( "Record Does Not Exist", "Error",
77                MessageBoxButtons.OK, MessageBoxIcon.Error );
```

Fig. 17.23 DeleteDialogForm class enables users to remove records from files in transaction-processor case study. (Part 2 of 3.)

```
78              accountTextBox.Clear();
79
80              return;
81          }
82
83          // create blank record
84          record = new RandomAccessRecord();
85
86          // write over file record with empty record
87          if ( transactionProxy.AddRecord(
88              record, accountNumber ) == true )
89
90              // notify user of successful deletion
91              MessageBox.Show( "Record Deleted", "Success",
92                  MessageBoxButtons.OK, MessageBoxIcon.Information );
93          else
94
95              // notify user of failure
96              MessageBox.Show(
97                  "Record could not be deleted", "Error",
98                  MessageBoxButtons.OK, MessageBoxIcon.Error );
99
100         accountTextBox.Clear();
101
102     } // end method DeleteRecord
103
104 } // end class DeleteDialogForm
```

Fig. 17.23 DeleteDialogForm class enables users to remove records from files in transaction-processor case study. (Part 3 of 3.)

SUMMARY

- All data items processed by a computer ultimately are reduced to combinations of zeros and ones.

- The smallest data items that computers support are called bits and can assume either the value **0** or the value **1**.

- Digits, letters and special symbols are referred to as characters. The set of all characters used to write programs and represent data items on a particular computer is called that computer's character set. Every character in a computer's character set is represented as a pattern of **1**s and **0**s (characters in C# are Unicode characters, which are composed of 2 bytes).

- At least one field in a record is chosen as a record key, which identifies that record as belonging to a particular person or entity and distinguishes that record from all other records in the file.

- A file is a group of related records.

- Files are used for long-term retention of large amounts of data and can store those data even after the program that created the data terminates.

- Data maintained in files often are called persistent data.

- Class **File** enables programs to obtain information about a file.

- Class **Directory** enables programs to obtain information about a directory.

- Class **FileStream** provides method **Seek** for repositioning the file-position pointer (the byte number of the next byte in the file to be read or written) to any position in the file.

- The most common type of file organization is the sequential file, in which records typically are stored in order by the record-key field.

- When a file is opened, an object is created, and a stream is associated with the object.

- C# imposes no structure on files. This means that concepts like that of a "record" do not exist in C#. The programmer must structure each file appropriately to meet the requirements of an application.

- A collection of programs designed to create and manage databases is called a database management system (DBMS).

- C# views each file as a sequential stream of bytes.

- Each file ends in some machine-dependent form of end-of-file marker.

- Objects of classes **OpenFileDialog** and **SaveFileDialog** are used for selecting files to open and save, respectively. Method **ShowDialog** of these classes displays that dialog.

- When displayed, both an **OpenFileDialog** and a **SaveFileDialog** prevent the user from interacting with any other program window until the dialog is closed. Dialogs that behave in this fashion are called modal dialogs.

- Streams provide communication channels between files and programs.

- To perform file processing in C#, the namespace **System.IO** must be referenced. This namespace includes definitions for stream classes such as **StreamReader**, **StreamWriter** and **FileStream**. Files are opened by instantiating objects of these classes.

- To retrieve data sequentially from a file, programs normally start from the beginning of the file, reading all data consecutively until the desired data are found.

- With a sequential-access file, each successive input/output request reads or writes the next consecutive set of data in the file.

- Instant data access is possible with random-access files. A program can access individual records of a random-access file directly (and quickly) without searching through other records. Random-access files sometimes are called direct-access files.

- With a random-access file, each successive input/output request can be directed to any part of the file, which can be any distance from the part of the file referenced in the previous request.

- Programmers can use members of the **FileAccess** enumeration to control users' access to files.

- Only classes with the **Serializable** attribute can be serialized to and deserialized from files.

- There are a variety of techniques for creating random-access files. Perhaps the simplest involves requiring that all records in a file be of the same fixed length.

- The use of fixed-length records makes it easy for a program to calculate (as a function of the record size and the record key) the exact location of any record in relation to the beginning of the file

- Data can be inserted into a random-access file without destroying other data in the file. Users can also update or delete previously stored data without rewriting the entire file.

- **BinaryFormatter** uses methods **Serialize** and **Deserialize** to write and to read objects, respectively. Method **Serialize** writes the object's representation to a stream. Method **Deserialize** reads this representation from a stream and reconstructs the original object.

- Methods **Serialize** and **Deserialize** each require a **Stream** object as a parameter, enabling the **BinaryFormatter** to access the correct file.

- Class **BinaryReader** and **BinaryWriter** provide methods for reading and writing bytes to streams, respectively. The **BinaryReader** and **BinaryWriter** constructors receive as arguments references to instances of class **System.IO.Stream**.

- Class **FileStream** inherits from class **Stream**, so we can pass the **FileStream** object as an argument to either the **BinaryReader** or **BinaryWriter** constructor to create an object that can transfer bytes directly to or from a file.

- Random-access file-processing programs rarely write a single field to a file. Normally, they write one object at a time.

- Sorting with direct-access techniques is fast. This speed is achieved by making the file large enough to hold every possible record that might be created. Of course, this means that the file could be sparsely occupied most of the time, possibly wasting memory.

TERMINOLOGY

binary digit (bit)
BinaryFormatter class
BinaryReader class
BinaryWriter class
BufferedStream class
bit manipulation
character
character set
Close method of class **StreamReader**
closing a file
Console class
Copy method of class **File**
Create method of class **File**
CreateDirectory method of class
   Directory
CreateText method of class **File**
data hierarchy
database
database management system (DBMS)
Delete method of class **Directory**
Delete method of class **File**
Deserialize method of class
   BinaryFormatter
direct-access files
Directory class

end-of-file marker
Error property of class **Console**
escape sequence
Exists method of class **Directory**
field
file
File class
file-processing programs
FileAccess enumeration
file-position pointer
FileStream class
fixed-length records
GetCreationTime method of class
   Directory
GetCreationTime method of class **File**
GetDirectories method of class
   Directory
GetFiles method of class **Directory**
GetLastAccessTime method of class
   Directory
GetLastAccessTime method of class **File**
GetLastWriteTime method of class
   Directory
GetLastWriteTime method of class **File**
In property of class **Console**

`DirectoryInfo` class

`IOException`

`MemoryStream` class

modal dialog

`Move` method of class `Directory`

`Move` method of class `File`

`Open` method of class `File`

`OpenFileDialog` class

`OpenRead` method of class `File`

`OpenText` method of class `File`

`OpenWrite` method of class `File`

`Out` property of class `Console`

pattern of `1`s and `0`s

persistent data

random-access file

`Read` method of class `Console`

`ReadDouble` method of `BinaryReader`

`ReadInt32` method of `BinaryReader`

`ReadLine` method of class `Console`

`ReadLine` method of class `StreamReader`

`ReadString` method of `BinaryReader`

record

record key

regular expression

`SaveFileDialog` class

secondary storage devices

`Seek` method of class `FileStream`

`SeekOrigin` enumeration

separation character

sequential-access file

"instant-access" application

`Serializable` attribute

`SerializationException`

`Serialize` method of class
    `BinaryFormatter`

`ShowDialog` method of class
    `OpenFileDialog`

`ShowDialog` method of class
    `SaveFileDialog`

standard error-stream object

standard input-stream object

standard output-stream object

`Stream` class

stream of bytes

stream processing

`StreamReader` class

`StreamWriter` class

`System.IO` namespace

`System.Runtime.Serialization.`
    `Formatters.Binary` namespace

`TextReader` class

`TextWriter` class

transaction-processing system

Windows Control Library project

`Write` method of class `BinaryWriter`

`Write` method of class `Console`

`Write` method of class `StreamWriter`

`WriteLine` method of class `Console`

`WriteLine` method of class `StreamWriter`

SELF-REVIEW EXERCISES

17.1 State whether each of the following is *true* or *false*. If *false*, explain why.

    a) Creating instances of classes `File` and `Directory` is impossible.

    b) Typically, a sequential file stores records in order by the record-key field.

    c) Class `StreamReader` inherits from class `Stream`.

    d) Any class can be serialized to a file.

    e) Searching a random-access file sequentially to find a specific record is unnecessary.

    f) Method `Seek` of class `FileStream` always seeks relative to the beginning of a file.

    g) C# provides class `Record` to store records for random-access file-processing applications.

    h) Banking systems, point-of-sale systems and automated-teller machines are types of transaction-processing systems.

    i) Classes `StreamReader` and `StreamWriter` are used with sequential-access files.

    j) Instantiating objects of type `Stream` is impossible.

17.2 Fill in the blanks in each of the following statements:

    a) Ultimately, all data items processed by a computer are reduced to combinations of _____ and _____.

    b) The smallest data item a computer can process is called a _____.

    c) A _____ is a group of related records.

d) Digits, letters and special symbols are collectively referred to as _____.

e) A group of related files is called a _____.

f) **StreamReader** method _____ reads a line of text from a file.

g) **StreamWriter** method _____ writes a line of text to a file.

h) Method **Serialize** of class **BinaryFormatter** takes a(n) _____ and a(n) _____ as arguments.

i) The _____ namespace contains most of C#'s file-processing classes.

j) The _____ namespace contains the **BinaryFormatter** class.

ANSWERS TO SELF-REVIEW EXERCISES

17.1 a) True. b) True. c) False. **StreamReader** inherits from **TextReader**. d) False. Only classes with the **Serializable** attribute can be serialized. e) True. f) False. It seeks relative to the **SeekOrigin** enumeration member that is passed as one of the arguments. g) False. C# imposes no structure on a file, so the concept of a "record" does not exist. h.) True. i) True. j) True.

17.2 a) **1**s, **0**s. b) bit. c) file. d) characters. e) database. f) **ReadLine**. g) **WriteLine**. h) **Stream**, **Object**. i) **System.IO**. j) **System.Runtime.Serialization.Formatters.Binary**.

EXERCISES

17.3 Create a program that stores student grades in a text file. The file should contain the name, ID number, class taken and grade of every student. Allow the user to load a grade file and display its contents in a read-only textbox. The entries should be displayed as follows:

```
LastName, FirstName:  ID#  Class  Grade
```

We list some sample data below:

```
Jones, Bob: 1 "Introduction to Computer Science" "A-"

Johnson, Sarah: 2 "Data Structures" "B+"

Smith, Sam: 3 "Data Structures" "C"
```

17.4 Modify the previous program to use objects of a class that can be serialized to and deserialized from a file. Ensure fixed-length records by fixing the lengths of the fields **LastName**, **FirstName**, **Class** and **Grade**.

17.5 Extend classes **StreamReader** and **StreamWriter**. Make the class that derives from **StreamReader** have methods **ReadInteger**, **ReadBoolean** and **ReadString**. Make the class that derives from **StreamWriter** have methods **WriteInteger**, **WriteBoolean** and **WriteString**. Think about how to design the writing methods so that the reading methods will be able to read what was written. Design **WriteInteger** and **WriteBoolean** to write **string**s of uniform size, so that **ReadInteger** and **ReadBoolean** can read those values accurately. Make sure **ReadString** and **WriteString** use the same character(s) to separate **string**s.

17.6 Create a program that combines the ideas of Fig. 17.9 and Fig. 17.11 to allow a user to write records to and read records from a file. Add an extra field of type **bool** to the record to indicate whether the account has overdraft protection.

17.7 In commercial data processing, it is common to have several files in each application system. In an accounts receivable system, for example, there is generally a master file containing detailed information about each customer, such as the customer's name, address, telephone number, outstanding balance, credit limit, discount terms, contract arrangements and possibly a condensed history of recent purchases and cash payments.

As transactions occur (i.e., sales are made and cash payments arrive in the mail), they are entered into a file. At the end of each business period (i.e., a month for some companies, a week for others and a day in some cases), the file of transactions (**trans.dat**) is applied to the master file (**oldmast.dat**), thus updating each account's record of purchases and payments. During an updating run, the master file is rewritten as a new file (**newmast.dat**), which then is used at the end of the next business period to begin the updating process again.

  File-matching programs must deal with certain problems that do not exist in single-file programs. For example, a match does not always occur. A customer on the master file might not have made any purchases or cash payments in the current business period, and, therefore, no record for this customer will appear on the transaction file. Similarly, a customer who did make some purchases or cash payments might have just moved to the community, and the company might not have had a chance to create a master record for this customer.

  When a match occurs (i.e., records with the same account number appear on both the master file and the transaction file), add the dollar amount on the transaction file to the current balance on the master file and write the **newmast.dat** record. (Assume that purchases are indicated by positive amounts on the transaction file and that payments are indicated by negative amounts.) When there is a master record for a particular account, but no corresponding transaction record, merely write the master record to **newmast.dat**. When there is a transaction record, but no corresponding master record, print the message "**Unmatched transaction record for account number...**" (fill in the account number from the transaction record).

17.8 You are the owner of a hardware store and need to keep an inventory of the different tools you sell, how many of each are currently in stock and the cost of each. Write a program that initializes the random-access file **hardware.dat** to 100 empty records, lets you input data relating to each tool, enables you to list all your tools, lets you delete a record for a tool that you no longer have and lets you update any information in the file. The tool identification number should be the record number. Use the information in Fig. 17.24 to start your file.

Record #	Tool name	Quantity	Price
3	Electric sander	18	35.99
19	Hammer	128	10.00
26	Jig saw	16	14.25
39	Lawn mower	10	79.50
56	Power saw	8	89.99
76	Screwdriver	236	4.99
81	Sledge hammer	32	19.75
88	Wrench	65	6.48

Fig. 17.24 Inventory of a hardware store.

18

Extensible Markup
Language (XML)

Objectives

- To be able to mark up data, using XML.
- To understand the concept of an XML namespace.
- To understand the relationship between DTDs,
  Schemas and XML.
- To be able to create Schemas.
- To be able to create and use simple XSLT documents.
- To be able to transform XML documents into
  XHTML, using class `XslTransform`.
- To become familiar with BizTalk™.

Knowing trees, I understand the meaning of patience.
Knowing grass, I can appreciate persistence.
Hal Borland

*Like everything metaphysical, the harmony between thought
and reality is to be found in the grammar of the language.*
Ludwig Wittgenstein

*I played with an idea and grew willful, tossed it into the air;
transformed it; let it escape and recaptured it; made it
iridescent with fancy, and winged it with paradox.*
Oscar Wilde

18.1 Introduction

The *Extensible Markup Language* (XML) was developed in 1996 by the *World Wide Web Consortium's (W3C's) XML Working Group*. XML is a portable, widely supported, *open technology* (i.e., non-proprietary technology) for describing data. XML is becoming the standard for storing data that is exchanged between applications. Using XML, document authors can describe any type of data, including mathematical formulas, software-configuration instructions, music, recipes and financial reports. XML documents are readable by both humans and machines.

The .NET Framework uses XML extensively. The Framework Class Library (FCL) provides an extensive set of XML-related classes. Much of Visual Studio's internal implementation also employs XML. In this chapter, we introduce XML, XML-related technologies and key classes for creating and manipulating XML documents.

18.2 XML Documents

In this section, we present our first XML document, which describes an article (Fig. 18.1). [*Note:* The line numbers shown are not part of the XML document.]

```
1   <?xml version = "1.0"?>
2
3   <!-- Fig. 18.1: article.xml      -->
4   <!-- Article structured with XML -->
5
6   <article>
7
8       <title>Simple XML</title>
```

Fig. 18.1   XML used to mark up an article. (Part 1 of 2.)

```
9
10     <date>December 6, 2001</date>
11
12     <author>
13        <firstName>John</firstName>
14        <lastName>Doe</lastName>
15     </author>
16
17     <summary>XML is pretty easy.</summary>
18
19     <content>In this chapter, we present a wide variety of examples
20        that use XML.
21     </content>
22
23  </article>
```

Fig. 18.1   XML used to mark up an article. (Part 2 of 2.)

This document begins with an optional *XML declaration* (line 1), which identifies the document as an XML document. The **version** *information parameter* specifies the version of XML that is used in the document. XML comments (lines 3–4), which begin with **<!--** and end with **-->**, can be placed almost anywhere in an XML document. As in a C# program, comments are used in XML for documentation purposes.

Common Programming Error 18.1

The placement of any characters, including whitespace, before the XML declaration is a syntax error.

Portability Tip 18.1

Although the XML declaration is optional, documents should include the declaration to identify the version of XML used. Otherwise, in the future, a document that lacks an XML declaration might be assumed to conform to the latest version of XML, and errors could result.

In XML, data are marked up using *tags*, which are names enclosed in *angle brackets* (**<>**). Tags are used in pairs to delimit character data (e.g., **Simple XML** in line 8). A tag that begins *markup* (i.e., XML data) is called a *start tag*, whereas a tag that terminates markup is called an *end tag*. Examples of start tags are **<article>** and **<title>** (lines 6 and 8, respectively). End tags differ from start tags in that they contain a *forward slash* (**/**) character immediately after the **<** character. Examples of end tags are **</title>** and **</article>** (lines 8 and 23, respectively). XML documents can contain any number of tags.

Common Programming Error 18.2

Failure to provide a corresponding end tag for a start tag is a syntax error.

Individual units of markup (i.e., everything included between a start tag and its corresponding end tag) are called *elements*. An XML document includes one element (called a *root element*) that contains every other element. The root element must be the first element after the XML declaration. In Fig. 18.1, **article** (line 6) is the root element. Elements are *nested* within each other to form hierarchies—with the root element at the top of the hierarchy. This allows document authors to create explicit relationships between data. For example, elements **title**, **date**, **author**, **summary** and **content** are nested within **article**. Elements **firstName** and **lastName** are nested within **author**.

Common Programming Error 18.3

Attempting to create more than one root element in an XML document is a syntax error.

Element **title** (line 8) contains the title of the article, **Simple XML**, as character data. Similarly, **date** (line 10), **summary** (line 17) and **content** (lines 19–21) contain as character data the date, summary and content, respectively. XML element names can be of any length and may contain letters, digits, underscores, hyphens and periods—they must begin with a letter or an underscore.

Common Programming Error 18.4

XML is case sensitive. The use of the wrong case for an XML element name is a syntax error.

By itself, this document is simply a text file named **article.xml**. Although it is not required, most XML documents end in the file extension **.xml**. The processing of XML documents requires a program called an *XML parser* also called *XML processors*. Parsers are responsible for checking an XML document's syntax and making the XML document's data available to applications. Often, XML parsers are built into applications such as Visual Studio or available for download over the Internet. Popular parsers include Microsoft's *msxml*, the Apache Software Foundation's *Xerces* and IBM's *XML4J*. In this chapter, we use msxml.

When the user loads **article.xml** into Internet Explorer (IE)[1], msxml parses the document and passes the parsed data to IE. IE then uses a built-in *style sheet* to format the data. Notice that the resulting format of the data (Fig. 18.2) is similar to the format of the XML document shown in Fig. 18.1. As we soon demonstrate, style sheets play an important and powerful role in the transformation of XML data into formats suitable for display.

Notice the minus (−) and plus (+) signs in Fig. 18.2. Although these are not part of the XML document, IE places them next to all *container elements* (i.e., elements that contain other elements). Container elements also are called *parent elements*. A minus sign indicates that the parent element's *child elements* (i.e., nested elements) are being displayed. When clicked, a minus sign becomes a plus sign (which collapses the container element and hides all children). Conversely, clicking a plus sign expands the container element and changes the plus sign to a minus sign. This behavior is similar to the viewing of the directory structure on a Windows system using Windows Explorer. In fact, a directory structure often is modeled as a series of tree structures, in which each drive letter (e.g., **C:**, etc.) represents the *root* of a tree. Each folder is a *node* in the tree. Parsers often place XML data into trees to facilitate efficient manipulation, as discussed in Section 18.4.

Common Programming Error 18.5

Nesting XML tags improperly is a syntax error. For example, `<x><y>hello</x></y>` is a error, because the `</y>` tag must precede the `</x>` tag.

---

1. IE 5 and higher.

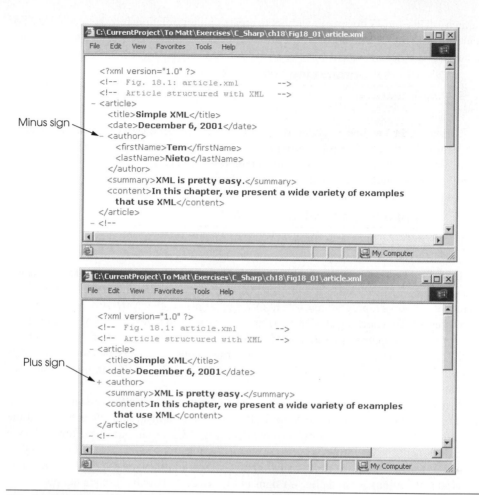

Minus sign

Plus sign

Fig. 18.2 `article.xml` displayed by Internet Explorer.

We now present a second XML document (Fig. 18.3), which marks up a business letter. This document contains significantly more data than did the previous XML document.

```
1   <?xml version = "1.0"?>
2
3   <!-- Fig. 18.3: letter.xml                    -->
4   <!-- Business letter formatted with XML -->
5
6   <letter>
7       <contact type = "from">
8           <name>Jane Doe</name>
9           <address1>Box 12345</address1>
10          <address2>15 Any Ave.</address2>
11          <city>Othertown</city>
12          <state>Otherstate</state>
```

Fig. 18.3 XML to mark up a business letter. (Part 1 of 2.)

```
13          <zip>67890</zip>
14          <phone>555-4321</phone>
15          <flag gender = "F" />
16      </contact>
17
18      <contact type = "to">
19          <name>John Doe</name>
20          <address1>123 Main St.</address1>
21          <address2></address2>
22          <city>Anytown</city>
23          <state>Anystate</state>
24          <zip>12345</zip>
25          <phone>555-1234</phone>
26          <flag gender = "M" />
27      </contact>
28
29      <salutation>Dear Sir:</salutation>
30
31          <paragraph>It is our privilege to inform you about our new
32          database managed with <technology>XML</technology>. This
33          new system allows you to reduce the load on
34          your inventory list server by having the client machine
35          perform the work of sorting and filtering the data.
36          </paragraph>
37
38          <paragraph>Please visit our Web site for availability
39          and pricing.
40          </paragraph>
41
42      <closing>Sincerely</closing>
43
44      <signature>Ms. Doe</signature>
45  </letter>
```

Fig. 18.3   XML to mark up a business letter. (Part 2 of 2.)

Root element **letter** (lines 6–45) contains the child elements **contact** (lines 7–16 and 18–27), **salutation**, **paragraph** (lines 31–36 and 38–40), **closing** and **signature**. In addition to being placed between tags, data also can be placed in *attributes*, which are name-value pairs in start tags. Elements can have any number of attributes in their start tags. The first **contact** element (lines 7–16) has attribute **type** with attribute *value* **"from"**, which indicates that this **contact** element marks up information about the letter's sender. The second **contact** element (lines 18–27) has attribute **type** with value **"to"**, which indicates that this **contact** element marks up information about the letter's recipient. Like element names, attribute names are case sensitive, can be any length; may contain letters, digits, underscores, hyphens and periods; and must begin with either a letter or underscore character. A **contact** element stores a contact's name, address and phone number. Element **salutation** (line 29) marks up the letter's salutation. Lines 31–40 mark up the letter's body with **paragraph** elements. Elements **closing** (line 42) and **signature** (line 44) mark up the closing sentence and the signature of the letter's author, respectively.

Common Programming Error 18.6

Failure to enclose attribute values in either double (" ") or single (' ') quotes is a syntax error.

Common Programming Error 18.7

Attempting to provide two attributes with the same name for an element is a syntax error.

In line 15, we introduce *empty element* **flag**, which indicates the gender of the contact. Empty elements do not contain character data (i.e., they do not contain text between the start and end tags). Such elements are closed either by placing a slash at the end of the element (as shown in line 15) or by explicitly writing a closing tag, as in

```
<flag gender = "F"></flag>
```

18.3 XML Namespaces

Object-oriented programming languages, such as C# and Visual Basic .NET, provide massive class libraries that group their features into namespaces. These namespaces prevent *naming collisions* between programmer-defined identifiers and identifiers in class libraries. For example, we might use class **Book** to represent information on one of our publications; however, a stamp collector might use class **Book** to represent a book of stamps. A naming collision would occur if we use these two classes in the same assembly, without using namespaces to differentiate them.

Like C#, XML also provides *namespaces*, which provide a means of uniquely identifying XML elements. In addition, XML-based languages—called *vocabularies*, such as XML Schema (Section 18.5), Extensible Stylesheet Language (Section 18.6) and BizTalk (Section 18.7)—often use namespaces to identify their elements.

Elements are differentiated via *namespace prefixes*, which identify the namespace to which an element belongs. For example,

```
<deitel:book>C# How to Program</deitel:book>
```

qualifies element **book** with namespace prefix **deitel**. This indicates that element **book** is part of namespace **deitel**. Document authors can use any name for a namespace prefix except the reserved namespace prefix *xml*.

Common Programming Error 18.8

Attempting to create a namespace prefix named xml in any mixture of case is a syntax error.

The mark up in Fig. 18.4 demonstrates the use of namespaces. This XML document contains two **file** elements that are differentiated using namespaces.

```
1   <?xml version = "1.0"?>
2
3   <!-- Fig. 18.4: namespace.xml -->
4   <!-- Demonstrating namespaces -->
```

Fig. 18.4   XML namespaces demonstration. (Part 1 of 2.)

```
5
6   <text:directory xmlns:text = "urn:deitel:textInfo"
7       xmlns:image = "urn:deitel:imageInfo">
8
9       <text:file filename = "book.xml">
10          <text:description>A book list</text:description>
11      </text:file>
12
13      <image:file filename = "funny.jpg">
14          <image:description>A funny picture</image:description>
15          <image:size width = "200" height = "100" />
16      </image:file>
17
18  </text:directory>
```

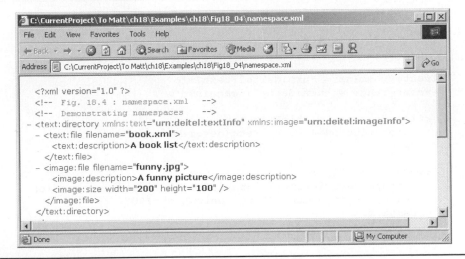

Fig. 18.4 XML namespaces demonstration. (Part 2 of 2.)

Software Engineering Observation 18.1

A programmer has the option of qualifying an attribute with a namespace prefix. However, it is not required, because attributes always are associated with elements.

Lines 6–7 use attribute **xmlns** to create two namespace prefixes: **text** and **image**. Each namespace prefix is bound to a series of characters called a *uniform resource identifier (URI)* that uniquely identifies the namespace. Document authors create their own namespace prefixes and URIs.

To ensure that namespaces are unique, document authors must provide unique URIs. Here, we use the text **urn:deitel:textInfo** and **urn:deitel:imageInfo** as URIs. A common practice is to use *Universal Resource Locators (URLs)* for URIs, because the domain names (such as, **www.deitel.com**) used in URLs are guaranteed to be unique. For example, lines 6–7 could have been written as

```
<text:directory xmlns:text =
    "http://www.deitel.com/xmlns-text"
    xmlns:image = "http://www.deitel.com/xmlns-image">
```

In this example, we use URLs related to the Deitel & Associates, Inc, domain name to iden-tify namespaces. The parser never visits these URLs—they simply represent a series of characters used to differentiate names. The URLs need not refer to actual Web pages or be formed properly.

Lines 9–11 use the namespace prefix **text** to qualify elements **file** and **description** as belonging to the namespace **"urn:deitel:textInfo"**. Notice that the namespace prefix **text** is applied to the end tags as well. Lines 13–16 apply namespace prefix **image** to elements **file**, **description** and **size**.

To eliminate the need to precede each element with a namespace prefix, document authors can specify a *default namespace*. Figure 18.5 demonstrates the creation and use of default namespaces.

```
1   <?xml version = "1.0"?>
2
3   <!-- Fig. 18.5: defaultnamespace.xml -->
4   <!-- Using default namespaces         -->
5
6   <directory xmlns = "urn:deitel:textInfo"
7      xmlns:image = "urn:deitel:imageInfo">
8
9      <file filename = "book.xml">
10        <description>A book list</description>
11     </file>
12
13     <image:file filename = "funny.jpg">
14        <image:description>A funny picture</image:description>
15        <image:size width = "200" height = "100" />
16     </image:file>
17
18  </directory>
```

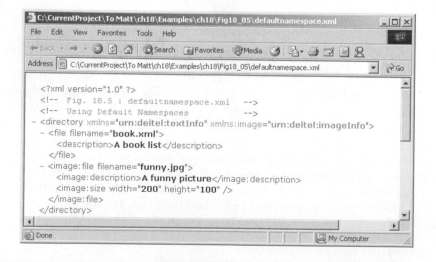

Fig. 18.5 Default namespaces demonstration.

Line 6 declares a default namespace using attribute **xmlns** with a URI as its value. Once we define this default namespace, child elements belonging to the namespace need not be qualified by a namespace prefix. Element **file** (line 9–11) is in the namespace **urn:deitel:textInfo**. Compare this to Fig. 18.4, where we prefixed **file** and **description** with **text** (lines 9–11).

The default namespace applies to the **directory** element and all elements that are not qualified with a namespace prefix. However, we can use a namespace prefix to specify a different namespace for particular elements. For example, the **file** element in line 13 is prefixed with **image** to indicate that it is in the namespace **urn:deitel:imageInfo**, rather than the default namespace.

18.4 Document Object Model (DOM)

Although XML documents are text files, retrieving data from them via sequential-file access techniques is neither practical nor efficient, especially in situations where data must be added or deleted dynamically.

Upon successful parsing of documents, some XML parsers store document data as tree structures in memory. Figure 18.6 illustrates the tree structure for the document **article.xml** discussed in Fig. 18.1. This hierarchical tree structure is called a *Document Object Model (DOM)* tree, and an XML parser that creates this type of structure is known as a *DOM parser*. The DOM tree represents each component of the XML document (e.g., **article**, **date**, **firstName**, etc.) as a node in the tree. Nodes (such as, **author**) that contain other nodes (called *child nodes*) are called *parent nodes*. Nodes that have the same parent (such as, **firstName** and **lastName**) are called *sibling nodes*. A node's *descendant nodes* include that node's children, its children's children and so on. Similarly, a node's *ancestor nodes* include that node's parent, its parent's parent and so on. Every DOM tree has a single *root node* that contains all other nodes in the document, such as comments, elements, etc.

Classes for creating, reading and manipulating XML documents are located in the C# namespace **System.Xml**. This namespace also contains additional namespaces that contain other XML-related operations.

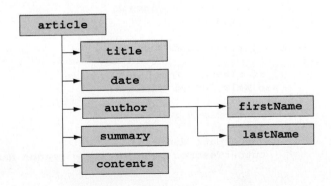

Fig. 18.6 Tree structure for Fig. 18.1.

In this section, we present several examples that use DOM trees. Our first example, the program in Fig. 18.7, loads the XML document presented in Fig. 18.1 and displays its data in a text box. This example uses class *XmlNodeReader* which is derived from *Xml-Reader*, which iterates through each node in the XML document. Class **XmlReader** is an **abstract** class that defines the interface for reading XML documents.

```
1   // Fig. 18.7: XmlReaderTest.cs
2   // Reading an XML document.
3
4   using System;
5   using System.Windows.Forms;
6   using System.Xml;
7
8   public class XmlReaderTest : System.Windows.Forms.Form
9   {
10     private System.Windows.Forms.TextBox outputTextBox;
11     private System.ComponentModel.Container components = null;
12
13     public XmlReaderTest()
14     {
15        InitializeComponent();
16
17        // reference to "XML document"
18        XmlDocument document = new XmlDocument();
19        document.Load( "..\\..\\article.xml" );
20
21        // create XmlNodeReader for document
22        XmlNodeReader reader = new XmlNodeReader( document );
23
24        // show form before outputTextBox is populated
25        this.Show();
26
27        // tree depth is -1, no indentation
28        int depth = -1;
29
30        // display each node's content
31        while ( reader.Read() )
32        {
33           switch ( reader.NodeType )
34           {
35              // if Element, display its name
36              case XmlNodeType.Element:
37
38                 // increase tab depth
39                 depth++;
40                 TabOutput( depth );
41                 outputTextBox.Text += "<" + reader.Name + ">" +
42                    "\r\n";
43
```

Fig. 18.7   **XmlNodeReader** used to iterate through an XML document. (Part 1 of 3.)

```
44                    // if empty element, decrease depth
45                    if ( reader.IsEmptyElement )
46                       depth--;
47
48                    break;
49
50                 // if Comment, display it
51                 case XmlNodeType.Comment:
52                    TabOutput( depth );
53                    outputTextBox.Text +=
54                       "<!--" + reader.Value + "-->\r\n";
55                    break;
56
57                 // if Text, display it
58                 case XmlNodeType.Text:
59                    TabOutput( depth );
60                    outputTextBox.Text += "\t" + reader.Value +
61                       "\r\n";
62                    break;
63
64                 // if XML declaration, display it
65                 case XmlNodeType.XmlDeclaration:
66                    TabOutput( depth );
67                    outputTextBox.Text += "<?" + reader.Name + " "
68                       + reader.Value + " ?>\r\n";
69                    break;
70
71                 // if EndElement, display it and decrement depth
72                 case XmlNodeType.EndElement:
73                    TabOutput( depth );
74                    outputTextBox.Text += "</" + reader.Name
75                       + ">\r\n";
76                    depth--;
77                    break;
78              } // end switch statement
79           } // end while loop
80        } // End XmlReaderTest constructor
81
82        // insert tabs
83        private void TabOutput( int number )
84        {
85           for ( int i = 0; i < number; i++ )
86              outputTextBox.Text += "\t";
87        } // end TabOutput
88
89        // Windows Form Designer generated code
90
91        [STAThread]
92        static void Main()
93        {
94           Application.Run( new XmlReaderTest() );
95        } // end Main
96  } // end XmlReaderTest
```

Fig. 18.7 XmlNodeReader used to iterate through an XML document. (Part 2 of 3.)

Fig. 18.7 `XmlNodeReader` used to iterate through an XML document. (Part 3 of 3.)

Line 6 includes the **System.Xml** namespace, which contains the XML classes used in this example. Line 18 creates a reference to an **XmlDocument** object that conceptually represents an empty XML document. The XML document **article.xml** is parsed and loaded into this **XmlDocument** object when method **Load** is invoked in line 19. Once an XML document is loaded into an **XmlDocument**, its data can be read and manipulated programmatically. In this example, we read each node in the **XmlDocument**, which is the DOM tree. In successive examples, we demonstrate how to manipulate node values.

In line 22, we create an **XmlNodeReader** and assign it to reference **reader**, which enables us to read one node at a time from the **XmlDocument**. Method **Read** of **Xml-Reader** reads one node from the DOM tree. Placing this statement in the **while** loop (lines 31–78) makes **reader Read** all the document nodes. The **switch** statement (lines 33–77) processes each node. Either the **Name** property (line 41), which contains the node's name, or the **Value** property (line 53), which contains the node's data, is formatted and concatenated to the **string** assigned to the text box **Text** property. The **NodeType** property contains the node type (specifying whether the node is an element, comment, text, etc.). Notice that each **case** specifies a node type, using **XmlNodeType** enumeration constants.

Notice that the displayed output emphasizes the structure of the XML document. Variable **depth** (line 28) sets the number of tab characters used to indent each element. The depth is incremented each time an **Element** type is encountered and is decremented each time an **EndElement** or empty element is encountered. We use a similar technique in the next example to emphasize the tree structure of the XML document in the display.

Notice that our line breaks use the character sequence **"\r\n"**, which denotes a carriage return followed by a line feed. This is the standard line break for Windows-based applications and controls.

The C# program in Fig. 18.8 demonstrates how to manipulate DOM trees programmatically. This program loads **letter.xml** (Fig. 18.3) into the DOM tree and then creates a second DOM tree that duplicates the DOM tree containing **letter.xml**'s contents. The GUI for this application contains a text box, a **TreeView** control and three buttons— **Build**, **Print** and **Reset**. When clicked, **Build** copies **letter.xml** and displays the document's tree structure in the **TreeView** control, **Print** displays the XML element values and names in a text box and **Reset** clears the **TreeView** control and text box content.

Lines 20 and 23 create references to **XmlDocument**s **source** and **copy**. Line 32 assigns a new **XmlDocument** object to reference **source**. Line 33 then invokes method **Load** to parse and load **letter.xml**. We discuss reference **copy** shortly.

Unfortunately, **XmlDocument**s do not provide any features for displaying their content graphically. In this example, we display the document's contents via a **TreeView** control. We use objects of class *TreeNode* to represent each node in the tree. Class **TreeView** and class **TreeNode** are part of the **System.Windows.Forms** namespace. **TreeNode**s are added to the **TreeView** to emphasize the structure of the XML document.

```
1    // Fig. 18.8: XmlDom.cs
2    // Demonstrates DOM tree manipulation.
3
4    using System;
5    using System.Windows.Forms;
6    using System.Xml;
7    using System.IO;
8    using System.CodeDom.Compiler;   // contains TempFileCollection
9
10   // Class XmlDom demonstrates the DOM
11   public class XmlDom : System.Windows.Forms.Form
12   {
13       private System.Windows.Forms.Button buildButton;
14       private System.Windows.Forms.Button printButton;
15       private System.Windows.Forms.TreeView xmlTreeView;
16       private System.Windows.Forms.TextBox consoleTextBox;
17       private System.Windows.Forms.Button resetButton;
18       private System.ComponentModel.Container components = null;
19
20       private XmlDocument source; // reference to "XML document"
21
22       // reference copy of source's "XML document"
23       private XmlDocument copy;
24
25       private TreeNode tree; // TreeNode reference
26
27       public XmlDom()
28       {
29           InitializeComponent();
30
31           // create XmlDocument and load letter.xml
32           source = new XmlDocument();
33           source.Load( "..\\..\\letter.xml" );
34
35           // initialize references to null
36           copy = null;
```

Fig. 18.8 DOM structure of an XML document illustrated by a class. (Part 1 of 6.)

```
37            tree = null;
38       } // end XmlDom
39
40       [STAThread]
41       static void Main()
42       {
43          Application.Run( new XmlDom() );
44       }
45
46       // event handler for buildButton click event
47       private void buildButton_Click( object sender,
48          System.EventArgs e )
49       {
50          // determine if copy has been built already
51          if ( copy != null )
52             return;  // document already exists
53
54          // instantiate XmlDocument and TreeNode
55          copy = new XmlDocument();
56          tree = new TreeNode();
57
58          // add root node name to TreeNode and add
59          // TreeNode to TreeView control
60          tree.Text = source.Name;      // assigns #root
61          xmlTreeView.Nodes.Add( tree );
62
63          // build node and tree hierarchy
64          BuildTree( source, copy, tree );
65
66          printButton.Enabled = true;
67          resetButton.Enabled = true;
68       } // end buildButton_Click
69
70       // event handler for printButton click event
71       private void printButton_Click( object sender,
72          System.EventArgs e )
73       {
74          // exit if copy does not reference an XmlDocument
75          if ( copy == null )
76             return;
77
78          // create temporary XML file
79          TempFileCollection file = new TempFileCollection();
80
81          // create file that is deleted at program termination
82          file.AddExtension( "xml", false );
83          string[] filename = new string[ 1 ];
84          file.CopyTo( filename, 0 );
85
86          // write XML data to disk
87          XmlTextWriter writer = new XmlTextWriter( filename[ 0 ],
88             System.Text.Encoding.UTF8 );
89          copy.WriteTo( writer );
```

Fig. 18.8   DOM structure of an XML document illustrated by a class. (Part 2 of 6.)

```
90          writer.Close();
91
92          // parse and load temporary XML document
93          XmlTextReader reader = new XmlTextReader( filename[ 0 ] );
94
95          // read, format and display data
96          while( reader.Read() )
97          {
98             if ( reader.NodeType == XmlNodeType.EndElement )
99                consoleTextBox.Text += "/";
100
101            if ( reader.Name != String.Empty )
102               consoleTextBox.Text += reader.Name + "\r\n";
103
104            if ( reader.Value != String.Empty )
105               consoleTextBox.Text += "\t" + reader.Value +
106                  "\r\n";
107         } // end while
108
109         reader.Close();
110      } // end printButton_Click
111
112      // handle resetButton click event
113      private void resetButton_Click( object sender,
114         System.EventArgs e )
115      {
116         // remove TreeView nodes
117         if ( tree != null )
118            xmlTreeView.Nodes.Remove( tree );
119
120         xmlTreeView.Refresh(); // force TreeView update
121
122         // delete XmlDocument and tree
123         copy = null;
124         tree = null;
125
126         consoleTextBox.Text = "";  // clear text box
127
128         printButton.Enabled = false;
129         resetButton.Enabled = false;
130
131      } // end resetButton_Click
132
133      // construct DOM tree
134      private void BuildTree( XmlNode xmlSourceNode,
135         XmlNode document, TreeNode treeNode )
136      {
137         // create XmlNodeReader to access XML document
138         XmlNodeReader nodeReader = new XmlNodeReader(
139            xmlSourceNode );
140
141         // represents current node in DOM tree
142         XmlNode currentNode = null;
```

Fig. 18.8   DOM structure of an XML document illustrated by a class. (Part 3 of 6.)

```
143
144         // treeNode to add to existing tree
145         TreeNode newNode = new TreeNode();
146
147         // references modified node type for CreateNode
148         XmlNodeType modifiedNodeType;
149
150         while ( nodeReader.Read() )
151         {
152            // get current node type
153            modifiedNodeType = nodeReader.NodeType;
154
155            // check for EndElement, store as Element
156            if ( modifiedNodeType == XmlNodeType.EndElement )
157               modifiedNodeType = XmlNodeType.Element;
158
159            // create node copy
160            currentNode = copy.CreateNode( modifiedNodeType,
161               nodeReader.Name, nodeReader.NamespaceURI );
162
163            // build tree based on node type
164            switch ( nodeReader.NodeType )
165            {
166               // if Text node, add its value to tree
167               case XmlNodeType.Text:
168                  newNode.Text = nodeReader.Value;
169                  treeNode.Nodes.Add( newNode );
170
171                  // append Text node value to currentNode data
172                  ( ( XmlText ) currentNode ).AppendData(
173                     nodeReader.Value );
174                  document.AppendChild( currentNode );
175                  break;
176
177               // if EndElement, move up tree
178               case XmlNodeType.EndElement:
179                  document = document.ParentNode;
180                  treeNode = treeNode.Parent;
181                  break;
182
183               // if new element, add name and traverse tree
184               case XmlNodeType.Element:
185
186                  // determine if element contains content
187                  if ( !nodeReader.IsEmptyElement )
188                  {
189                     // assign node text, add newNode as child
190                     newNode.Text = nodeReader.Name;
191                     treeNode.Nodes.Add( newNode );
192
193                     // set treeNode to last child
194                     treeNode = newNode;
195
```

Fig. 18.8   DOM structure of an XML document illustrated by a class. (Part 4 of 6.)

```
196                          document.AppendChild( currentNode );
197                          document = document.LastChild;
198                      }
199                      else // do not traverse empty elements
200                      {
201                          // assign NodeType string to newNode
202                          newNode.Text =
203                              nodeReader.NodeType.ToString();
204
205                          treeNode.Nodes.Add( newNode );
206                          document.AppendChild( currentNode );
207                      }
208
209                      break;
210
211                  // all other types, display node type
212                  default:
213                      newNode.Text = nodeReader.NodeType.ToString();
214                      treeNode.Nodes.Add( newNode );
215                      document.AppendChild( currentNode );
216                      break;
217              } // end switch
218
219              newNode = new TreeNode();
220          } // end while
221
222          // update the TreeView control
223          xmlTreeView.ExpandAll();
224          xmlTreeView.Refresh();
225
226      } // end BuildTree
227 } // end XmlDom
```

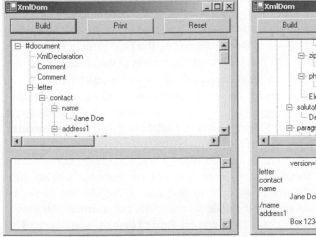
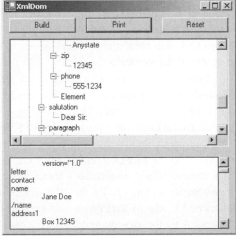

Fig. 18.8   DOM structure of an XML document illustrated by a class. (Part 5 of 6.)

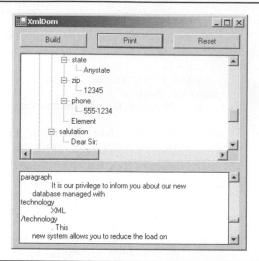

Fig. 18.8   DOM structure of an XML document illustrated by a class. (Part 6 of 6.)

When clicked, button **Build** triggers event handler **buildButton_Click** (lines 47–68), which copies **letter.xml** dynamically. The new **XmlDocument** and **TreeNode**s (i.e., the nodes used for graphical representation in the **TreeView**) are created in lines 55–56. Line 60 retrieves the **Name** of the node referenced by **source** (i.e., **#root**, which represents the document root) and assigns it to **tree**'s **Text** property. This **TreeNode** then is inserted into the **TreeView** control's node list. Method **Add** is called to add each new **TreeNode** to the **TreeView**'s **Nodes** collection. Line 64 calls method **BuildTree** to copy the **XMLDocument** referenced by **source** and to update the **TreeView**.

Method **BuildTree** (line 134–226) receives an **XmlNode** representing the source node, an empty **XmlNode** and a **treeNode** to place in the DOM tree. Parameter **treeNode** references the current location in the tree (i.e., the **TreeNode** most recently added to the **TreeView** control). Lines 138–139 instantiate a new **XmlNodeReader** for iterating through the DOM tree. Lines 142–145 declare **XmlNode** and **TreeNode** references that indicate the next nodes added to **document** (i.e., the DOM tree referenced by **copy**) and **treeNode**. Lines 150–220 iterate through each node in the tree.

Lines 153–161 create a node containing a copy of the current **nodeReader** node. Method *CreateNode* of **XmlDocument** takes a **NodeType**, a **Name** and a *NamespaceURI* as arguments. The **NodeType** cannot be an **EndElement**. If the **NodeType** is of an **EndElement** type, lines 156–157 assign **modifiedNodeType** type **Element**.

The **switch** statement in lines 164–217 determines the node type, creates and adds nodes to the **TreeView** and updates the DOM tree. When a text node is encountered, the new **TreeNode**'s **newNode**'s **Text** property is assigned the current node's value. This **TreeNode** is added to the **TreeView** control. In lines 172–174, we downcast **currentNode** to **XmlText** and append the node's value. The **currentNode** then is appended to the **document**. Lines 178–181 match an **EndElement** node type. This **case** moves up the tree, because the end of an element has been encountered. The *ParentNode* and *Parent* properties retrieve the **document**'s and **treeNode**'s parents, respectively.

Line 184 matches **Element** node types. Each nonempty **Element NodeType** (line 187) increases the depth of the tree; thus, we assign the current **nodeReader Name** to the **newNode**'s **Text** property and add the **newNode** to the **treeNode** node list. Lines 194– 197 reorder the nodes in the node list to ensure that **newNode** is the last **TreeNode** in the node list. **XmlNode currentNode** is appended to **document** as the last child, and **document** is set to its *LastChild*, which is the child we just added. If it is an empty element (line 199), we assign to the **newNode**'s **Text** property the **string** representation of the **NodeType**. Next, the **newNode** is added to the **treeNode** node list. Line 206 appends the **currentNode** to the **document**. The **default** case assigns the string representation of the node type to the **NewNode Text** property, adds the **newNode** to the **TreeNode** node list and appends the **currentNode** to the **document**.

After building the DOM trees, the **TreeNode** node list displays in the **TreeView** control. Clicking the nodes (i.e., the **+** or **–** boxes) in the **TreeView** either expands or collapses them. Clicking **Print** invokes event handler **printButton_Click** (line 71). Lines 79–84 create a temporary file for storing the XML. Line 87 creates an **XmlTextWriter** for streaming the XML data to disk. Method *WriteTo* is called to write the XML representation to the *XmlTextWriter* stream (line 89). Line 93 creates an *XmlTextReader* to read from the file. The **while** loop (line 96–107) reads each node in the DOM tree and writes tag names and character data to the text box. If it is an end element, a slash is concatenated. If the node has a **Name** or **Value**, that name or value is concatenated to the textbox text.

The **Reset** button's event handler, **resetButton_Click**, deletes both dynamically generated trees and updates the **TreeView** control's display. Reference **copy** is assigned **null** (to allow its tree to be garbage collected in line 123), and the **TreeNode** node list reference **tree** is assigned **null**.

Although **XmlReader** includes methods for reading and modifying node values, it is not the most efficient means of locating data in a DOM tree. The .NET framework provides class *XPathNavigator* in the *System.Xml.XPath* namespace for iterating through node lists that match search criteria, which are written as an *XPath expression*. XPath (XML Path Language) provides a syntax for locating specific nodes in XML documents effectively and efficiently. XPath is a string-based language of expressions used by XML and many of its related technologies (such as, XSLT, discussed in Section 18.6).

Figure 18.9 demonstrates how to navigate through an XML document with an **XPathNavigator**. Like Fig. 18.8, this program uses a **TreeView** control and **TreeNode** objects to display the XML document's structure. However, instead of displaying the entire DOM tree, the **TreeNode** node list is updated each time the **XPathNavigator** is positioned to a new node. Nodes are added to and deleted from the **TreeView** to reflect the **XPathNavigator**'s location in the DOM tree. The XML document **sports.xml** that we use in this example is presented in Figure 18.10.

This program loads XML document **sports.xml** into an *XPathDocument* object by passing the document's file name to the **XPathDocument** constructor (line 36). Method *CreateNavigator* (line 39) creates and returns an **XPathNavigator** reference to the **XPathDocument**'s tree structure.

The navigation methods of **XPathNavigator** used in Fig. 18.9 are *MoveTo-FirstChild* (line 66), *MoveToParent* (line 94), *MoveToNext* (line 122) and *MoveToPrevious* (line 151). Each method performs the action that its name implies. Method **MoveToFirstChild** moves to the first child of the node referenced by the

XPathNavigator, **MoveToParent** moves to the parent node of the node referenced by the **XPathNavigator**, **MoveToNext** moves to the next sibling of the node referenced by the **XPathNavigator** and **MoveToPrevious** moves to the previous sibling of the node referenced by the **XPathNavigator**. Each method returns a **bool** indicating whether the move was successful. In this example, we display a warning in a **MessageBox** whenever a move operation fails. Furthermore, each of these methods is called in the event handler of the button that matches its name (e.g., button **First Child** triggers **firstChildButton_Click**, which calls **MoveToFirstChild**).

Whenever we move forward via the **XPathNavigator**, as with **MoveToFirst-Child** and **MoveToNext**, nodes are added to the **TreeNode** node list. Method **DetermineType** is a **private** method (defined in lines 208–229) that determines whether to assign the **Node**'s *Name* property or *Value* property to the **TreeNode** (lines 218 and 225). Whenever **MoveToParent** is called, all children of the parent node are removed from the display. Similarly, a call to **MoveToPrevious** removes the current sibling node. Note that the nodes are removed only from the **TreeView**, not from the tree representation of the document.

The other event handler corresponds to button **Select** (line 173–174). Method **Select** (line 182) takes search criteria in the form of either an *XPathExpression* or a **string** that represents an XPath expression and returns as an **XPathNodeIterator** object any nodes that match the search criteria. The XPath expressions provided by this program's combo box are summarized in Fig. 18.11.

Method **DisplayIterator** (defined in lines 195–204) appends the node values from the given **XPathNodeIterator** to the **selectTreeViewer** text box. Note that we call the **string** method **Trim** to remove unnecessary whitespace. Method *MoveNext* (line 200) advances to the next node, which can be accessed via property *Current* (line 202).

```
1   // Fig. 18.9: PathNavigator.cs
2   // Demonstrates Class XPathNavigator.
3
4   using System;
5   using System.Windows.Forms;
6   using System.Xml.XPath; // contains XPathNavigator
7
8   public class PathNavigator : System.Windows.Forms.Form
9   {
10     private System.Windows.Forms.Button firstChildButton;
11     private System.Windows.Forms.Button parentButton;
12     private System.Windows.Forms.Button nextButton;
13     private System.Windows.Forms.Button previousButton;
14     private System.Windows.Forms.Button selectButton;
15     private System.Windows.Forms.TreeView pathTreeViewer;
16     private System.Windows.Forms.ComboBox selectComboBox;
17     private System.ComponentModel.Container components = null;
18     private System.Windows.Forms.TextBox selectTreeViewer;
19     private System.Windows.Forms.GroupBox navigateBox;
20     private System.Windows.Forms.GroupBox locateBox;
21
```

Fig. 18.9 XPathNavigator class used to navigate selected nodes. (Part 1 of 7.)

```
22      // navigator to traverse document
23      private XPathNavigator xpath;
24
25      // references document for use by XPathNavigator
26      private XPathDocument document;
27
28      // references TreeNode list used by TreeView control
29      private TreeNode tree;
30
31      public PathNavigator()
32      {
33         InitializeComponent();
34
35         // load XML document
36         document = new XPathDocument( "..\\..\\sports.xml" );
37
38         // create navigator
39         xpath = document.CreateNavigator();
40
41         // create root node for TreeNodes
42         tree = new TreeNode();
43
44         tree.Text = xpath.NodeType.ToString(); // #root
45         pathTreeViewer.Nodes.Add( tree );        // add tree
46
47         // update TreeView control
48         pathTreeViewer.ExpandAll();
49         pathTreeViewer.Refresh();
50         pathTreeViewer.SelectedNode = tree;     // highlight root
51      } // end constructor
52
53      [STAThread]
54      static void Main()
55      {
56         Application.Run( new PathNavigator() );
57      }
58
59      // traverse to first child
60      private void firstChildButton_Click( object sender,
61         System.EventArgs e )
62      {
63         TreeNode newTreeNode;
64
65         // move to first child
66         if ( xpath.MoveToFirstChild() )
67         {
68            newTreeNode = new TreeNode(); // create new node
69
70            // set node's Text property to either
71            // navigator's name or value
72            DetermineType( newTreeNode, xpath );
73
```

Fig. 18.9 **XPathNavigator** class used to navigate selected nodes. (Part 2 of 7.)

```
74              // add node to TreeNode node list
75              tree.Nodes.Add( newTreeNode );
76              tree = newTreeNode; // assign tree newTreeNode
77
78              // update TreeView control
79              pathTreeViewer.ExpandAll();
80              pathTreeViewer.Refresh();
81              pathTreeViewer.SelectedNode = tree;
82           }
83           else // node has no children
84              MessageBox.Show( "Current Node has no children.",
85                 "", MessageBoxButtons.OK,
86                 MessageBoxIcon.Information );
87        }
88
89        // traverse to node's parent on parentButton click event
90        private void parentButton_Click( object sender,
91           System.EventArgs e )
92        {
93           // move to parent
94           if ( xpath.MoveToParent() )
95           {
96              tree = tree.Parent;
97
98              // get number of child nodes, not including subtrees
99              int count = tree.GetNodeCount( false );
100
101             // remove all children
102             tree.Nodes.Clear();
103
104             // update TreeView control
105             pathTreeViewer.ExpandAll();
106             pathTreeViewer.Refresh();
107             pathTreeViewer.SelectedNode = tree;
108          }
109          else // if node has no parent (root node)
110             MessageBox.Show( "Current node has no parent.", "",
111                MessageBoxButtons.OK,
112                MessageBoxIcon.Information );
113       }
114
115       // find next sibling on nextButton click event
116       private void nextButton_Click( object sender,
117          System.EventArgs e )
118       {
119          TreeNode newTreeNode = null, newNode = null;
120
121          // move to next sibling
122          if ( xpath.MoveToNext() )
123          {
124             newTreeNode = tree.Parent; // get parent node
125
126             newNode = new TreeNode(); // create new node
```

Fig. 18.9 **XPathNavigator** class used to navigate selected nodes. (Part 3 of 7.)

```
127              DetermineType( newNode, xpath );
128              newTreeNode.Nodes.Add( newNode );
129
130              // set current position for display
131              tree = newNode;
132
133              // update TreeView control
134              pathTreeViewer.ExpandAll();
135              pathTreeViewer.Refresh();
136              pathTreeViewer.SelectedNode = tree;
137          }
138          else // node has no additional siblings
139              MessageBox.Show( "Current node is last sibling.",
140                  "", MessageBoxButtons.OK,
141                  MessageBoxIcon.Information );
142      } // end nextButton_Click
143
144      // get previous sibling on previousButton click
145      private void previousButton_Click( object sender,
146          System.EventArgs e )
147      {
148          TreeNode parentTreeNode = null;
149
150          // move to previous sibling
151          if ( xpath.MoveToPrevious() )
152          {
153              parentTreeNode = tree.Parent; // get parent node
154
155              // delete current node
156              parentTreeNode.Nodes.Remove( tree );
157
158              // move to previous node
159              tree = parentTreeNode.LastNode;
160
161              // update TreeView control
162              pathTreeViewer.ExpandAll();
163              pathTreeViewer.Refresh();
164              pathTreeViewer.SelectedNode = tree;
165          }
166          else // if current node has no previous siblings
167              MessageBox.Show( "Current node is first sibling.",
168                  "", MessageBoxButtons.OK,
169                  MessageBoxIcon.Information );
170      } // end previousButton_Click
171
172      // process selectButton click event
173      private void selectButton_Click( object sender,
174          System.EventArgs e )
175      {
176          XPathNodeIterator iterator; // enables node iteration
177
```

Fig. 18.9   XPathNavigator class used to navigate selected nodes. (Part 4 of 7.)

```
178          // get specified node from ComboBox
179          try
180          {
181             iterator = xpath.Select( selectComboBox.Text );
182             DisplayIterator( iterator ); // print selection
183          }
184
185          // catch invalid expressions
186          catch ( System.ArgumentException argumentException )
187          {
188             MessageBox.Show( argumentException.Message,
189                "Error", MessageBoxButtons.OK,
190                MessageBoxIcon.Error );
191          }
192       } // end selectButton_Click
193
194       // print values for XPathNodeIterator
195       private void DisplayIterator( XPathNodeIterator iterator )
196       {
197          selectTreeViewer.Text = "";
198
199          // prints selected node's values
200          while ( iterator.MoveNext() )
201             selectTreeViewer.Text +=
202                iterator.Current.Value.Trim()
203                + "\r\n";
204       } // end DisplayIterator
205
206       // determine if TreeNode should display current node
207       // name or value
208       private void DetermineType( TreeNode node,
209          XPathNavigator xPath )
210       {
211          // determine NodeType
212          switch ( xPath.NodeType )
213          {
214             // if Element, get its name
215             case XPathNodeType.Element:
216
217                // get current node name, and remove whitespace
218                node.Text = xPath.Name.Trim();
219                break;
220
221             // obtain node values
222             default:
223
224                // get current node value and remove whitespace
225                node.Text = xPath.Value.Trim();
226                break;
227
228          } // end switch
229       } // end DetermineType
230    } // end PathNavigator
```

Fig. 18.9 XPathNavigator class used to navigate selected nodes. (Part 5 of 7.)

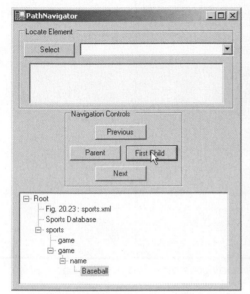

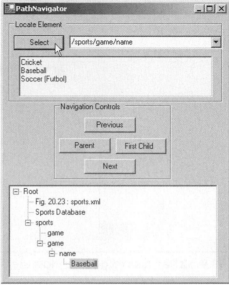

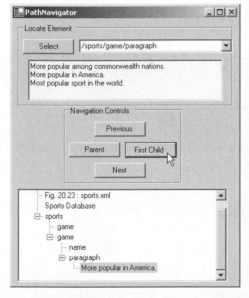

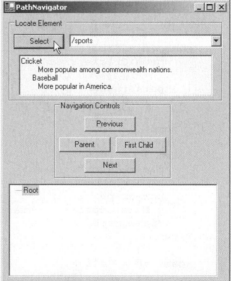

Fig. 18.9 **XPathNavigator** class used to navigate selected nodes. (Part 6 of 7.)

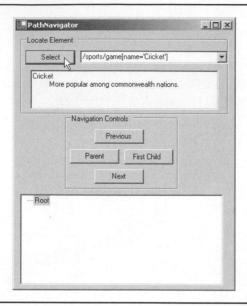

Fig. 18.9 **XPathNavigator** class used to navigate selected nodes. (Part 7 of 7.)

```
1   <?xml version = "1.0"?>
2
3   <!-- Fig. 18.10: sports.xml -->
4   <!-- Sports Database          -->
5
6   <sports>
7
8      <game id = "783">
9         <name>Cricket</name>
10
11        <paragraph>
12           More popular among commonwealth nations.
13        </paragraph>
14     </game>
15
16     <game id = "239">
17        <name>Baseball</name>
18
19        <paragraph>
20           More popular in America.
21        </paragraph>
22     </game>
23
24     <game id = "418">
25        <name>Soccer(Futbol)</name>
26        <paragraph>Most popular sport in the world</paragraph>
27     </game>
28  </sports>
```

Fig. 18.10 XML document that describes various sports.

18.5 Document Type Definitions (DTDs), Schemas and Validation

XML documents can reference optional documents that specify how the XML documents should be structured. These optional documents are called *Document Type Definitions* (*DTDs*) and *Schemas*. When a DTD or Schema document is provided, some parsers (called *validating parsers*) can read the DTD or Schema and check the XML document's structure against it. If the XML document conforms to the DTD or Schema, then the XML document is *valid*. Parsers that cannot check for document conformity against the DTD or Schema are called *non-validating parsers*. If an XML parser (validating or non-validating) is able to process an XML document (that does not reference a DTD or Schema), the XML document is considered to be *well formed* (i.e., it is syntactically correct). By definition, a valid XML document is also a well-formed XML document. If a document is not well formed, parsing halts, and the parser issues an error.

Software Engineering Observation 18.2

DTD and Schema documents are essential components for XML documents used in business-to-business (B2B) transactions and mission-critical systems. These documents help ensure that XML documents are valid.

Software Engineering Observation 18.3

Because XML document content can be structured in many different ways, an application cannot determine whether the document data it receives is complete, missing data or ordered properly. DTDs and Schemas solve this problem by providing an extensible means of describing a document's contents. An application can use a DTD or Schema document to perform a validity check on the document's contents.

Expression	Description
`/sports`	Matches the **sports** node that is child node of the document root node. This node contains the root element.
`/sports/game/name`	Matches all **name** nodes that are child nodes of **game**. The **game** node must be a child of **sports** and **sports** must be a root element node.
`/sports/game/paragraph`	Matches all **paragraph** nodes that are child nodes of **game**. The **game** node must be a child of **sports**, and **sports** must be a root element node.
`/sports/` `game[name='Cricket']`	Matches all **game** nodes that contain a child element **name** whose value is **Cricket**. The **game** node must be a child of **sports**, and **sports** must be a root element node.

Fig. 18.11 XPath expressions and descriptions.

18.5.1 Document Type Definitions

Document type definitions (DTDs) provide a means for type checking XML documents and thus verifying their *validity* (confirming that elements contain the proper attributes, elements are in the proper sequence, etc.). DTDs use *EBNF* (*Extended Backus-Naur Form*) *grammar* to describe an XML document's content. XML parsers need additional functionality to read EBNF grammar, because it is not XML syntax. Although DTDs are optional, they are recommended to ensure document conformity. The DTD in Fig. 18.12 defines the set of rules (i.e., the grammar) for structuring the business letter document contained in Fig. 18.13.

Portability Tip 18.2

DTDs can ensure consistency among XML documents generated by different programs.

Line 4 uses the ***ELEMENT*** *element type declaration* to define rules for element `letter`. In this case, `letter` contains one or more `contact` elements, one `salutation` element, one or more `paragraph` elements, one `closing` element and one `signature` element, in that sequence. The *plus sign* (**+**) *occurrence indicator* specifies that an element must occur one or more times. Other indicators include the *asterisk* (*****), which indicates an optional element that can occur any number of times, and the *question mark* (**?**), which indicates an optional element that can occur at most once. If an occurrence indicator is omitted, exactly one occurrence is expected.

The `contact` element definition (line 7) specifies that it contains the `name`, `address1`, `address2`, `city`, `state`, `zip`, `phone` and `flag` elements—in that order. Exactly one occurrence of each is expected.

```
1    <!-- Fig. 18.12: letter.dtd       -->
2    <!-- DTD document for letter.xml -->
3
4    <!ELEMENT letter ( contact+, salutation, paragraph+,
5       closing, signature )>
6
7    <!ELEMENT contact ( name, address1, address2, city, state,
8       zip, phone, flag )>
9    <!ATTLIST contact type CDATA #IMPLIED>
10
11   <!ELEMENT name ( #PCDATA )>
12   <!ELEMENT address1 ( #PCDATA )>
13   <!ELEMENT address2 ( #PCDATA )>
14   <!ELEMENT city ( #PCDATA )>
15   <!ELEMENT state ( #PCDATA )>
16   <!ELEMENT zip ( #PCDATA )>
17   <!ELEMENT phone ( #PCDATA )>
18   <!ELEMENT flag EMPTY>
19   <!ATTLIST flag gender (M | F) "M">
20
21   <!ELEMENT salutation ( #PCDATA )>
22   <!ELEMENT closing ( #PCDATA )>
23   <!ELEMENT paragraph ( #PCDATA )>
24   <!ELEMENT signature ( #PCDATA )>
```

Fig. 18.12 Document Type Definition (DTD) for a business letter.

Line 9 uses the ***ATTLIST*** *element type declaration* to define an attribute (i.e., **type**) for the **contact** element. Keyword ***#IMPLIED*** specifies that, if the parser finds a **contact** element without a **type** attribute, the application can provide a value or ignore the missing attribute. The absence of a **type** attribute cannot invalidate the document. Other types of default values include ***#REQUIRED*** and ***#FIXED***. Keyword ***#REQUIRED*** specifies that the attribute must be present in the document and the keyword ***#FIXED*** specifies that the attribute (if present) must always be assigned a specific value. For example,

```
<!ATTLIST address zip #FIXED "01757">
```

indicates that the value **01757** must be used for attribute **zip**; otherwise, the document is invalid. If the attribute is not present, then the parser, by default, uses the fixed value that is specified in the **ATTLIST** declaration. Flag ***CDATA*** specifies that attribute **type** contains a **String** that is not processed by the parser, but instead is passed to the application as is.

Software Engineering Observation 18.4

DTD syntax does not provide any mechanism for describing an element's (or attribute's) data type.

Flag ***#PCDATA*** (line 11) specifies that the element can store *parsed character data* (i.e., text). Parsed character data cannot contain markup. The characters less than (**<**) and ampersand (**&**) must be replaced by their *entities* (i.e., **<** and **&**). However, the ampersand character can be inserted when used with entities. See Appendix L (on CD) for a list of pre-defined entities.

Line 18 defines an empty element named **flag**. Keyword ***EMPTY*** specifies that the element cannot contain character data. Empty elements commonly are used for their attributes.

Common Programming Error 18.9

Any element, attribute or relationship not explicitly defined by a DTD results in an invalid document.

Many XML documents explicitly reference a DTD. Figure 18.13 is an XML document that conforms to **letter.dtd** (Fig. 18.12).

```
1   <?xml version = "1.0"?>
2
3   <!-- Fig. 18.13: letter2.xml         -->
4   <!-- Business letter formatted with XML -->
5
6   <!DOCTYPE letter SYSTEM "letter.dtd">
7
8   <letter>
9      <contact type = "from">
10        <name>Jane Doe</name>
11        <address1>Box 12345</address1>
12        <address2>15 Any Ave.</address2>
13        <city>Othertown</city>
14        <state>Otherstate</state>
15        <zip>67890</zip>
16        <phone>555-4321</phone>
```

Fig. 18.13 XML document referencing its associated DTD. (Part 1 of 2.)

```
17          <flag gender = "F" />
18      </contact>
19
20      <contact type = "to">
21          <name>John Doe</name>
22          <address1>123 Main St.</address1>
23          <address2></address2>
24          <city>Anytown</city>
25          <state>Anystate</state>
26          <zip>12345</zip>
27          <phone>555-1234</phone>
28          <flag gender = "M" />
29      </contact>
30
31      <salutation>Dear Sir:</salutation>
32
33      <paragraph>It is our privilege to inform you about our new
34          database managed with XML. This new system
35          allows you to reduce the load on your inventory list
36          server by having the client machine perform the work of
37          sorting and filtering the data.
38      </paragraph>
39
40      <paragraph>Please visit our Web site for availability
41          and pricing.
42      </paragraph>
43      <closing>Sincerely</closing>
44      <signature>Ms. Doe</signature>
45  </letter>
```

Fig. 18.13 XML document referencing its associated DTD. (Part 2 of 2.)

This XML document is similar to that in Fig. 18.3. Line 6 references a DTD file. This markup contains three pieces: The name of the root element (**letter** in line 8) to which the DTD is applied, the keyword **SYSTEM** (which in this case denotes an *external DTD*—a DTD defined in a separate file) and the DTD's name and location (i.e., **letter.dtd** in the current directory). Though almost any file extension can be used, DTD documents typically end with the **.dtd** extension.

Various tools (many of which are free) check document conformity against DTDs and Schemas (discussed momentarily). The output in Fig. 18.14 shows the results of the validation of **letter2.xml** using Microsoft's *XML Validator*. Visit **www.w3.org/XML/Schema.html** for a list of validating tools. Microsoft XML Validator is available free for download from

```
msdn.microsoft.com/downloads/samples/Internet/xml/
xml_validator/sample.asp
```

Microsoft XML Validator can validate XML documents against DTDs locally or by uploading the documents to the XML Validator Web site. Here, **letter2.xml** and **letter.dtd** are placed in folder **C:\XML**. This XML document (**letter2.xml**) is well formed and conforms to **letter.dtd**.

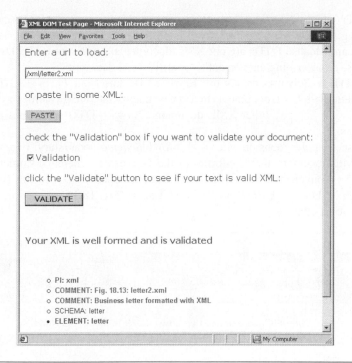

Fig. 18.14 XML Validator validates an XML document against a DTD.

XML documents that fail validation are still well-formed documents. When a document fails to conform to a DTD or Schema, Microsoft XML Validator displays an error message. For example, the DTD in Fig. 18.12 indicates that the **contacts** element must contain child element **name**. If the document omits this child element, the document is well formed, but not valid. In such a scenario, Microsoft XML Validator displays the error message shown in Fig. 18.15.

C# programs can use msxml to validate XML documents against DTDs. For information on how to accomplish this, visit:

```
msdn.microsoft.com/library/default.asp?url=/library/en-us/
cpguidnf/html/cpconvalidationagainstdtdwithxmlvalidatin-
greader.asp
```

Schemas are the preferred means of defining structures for XML documents in .NET. Although, several types of Schemas exist, the two most popular are Microsoft Schema and W3C Schema. We begin our discussion of Schemas in the next section.

18.5.2 Microsoft XML Schemas[2]

In this section, we introduce an alternative to DTDs—called Schemas—for defining an XML document's structure. Many developers in the XML community feel that DTDs are

---

2. W3C Schema, which we discuss in Section 18.5.3, is emerging as the industry standard for describing an XML document's structure. Within the next two years, we expect most developers will be using W3C Schema.

not flexible enough to meet today's programming needs. For example, DTDs cannot be manipulated (e.g., searched, programmatically modified, etc.) in the same manner that XML documents can, because DTDs are not XML documents. Furthermore, DTDs do not provide features for describing an element's (or attribute's) data type.

Unlike DTDs, Schemas do not use Extended Backus-Naur Form (EBNF) grammar. Instead, Schemas are XML documents that can be manipulated (e.g., elements can be added or removed, etc.) like any other XML document. As with DTDs, Schemas require validating parsers.

In this section, we focus on Microsoft's *XML Schema* vocabulary. Figure 18.16 presents an XML document that conforms to the Microsoft Schema document shown in Fig. 18.17. By convention, Microsoft XML Schema documents use the file extension **.xdr**, which is short for *XML-Data Reduced*. Line 6 (Fig. 18.16) references the Schema document **book.xdr**.

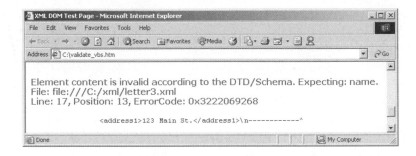

Fig. 18.15 XML Validator displaying an error message.

```
1   <?xml version = "1.0"?>
2
3   <!-- Fig. 18.16: bookxdr.xml         -->
4   <!-- XML file that marks up book data -->
5
6   <books xmlns = "x-schema:book.xdr">
7      <book>
8         <title>C# How to Program</title>
9      </book>
10
11     <book>
12        <title>Java How to Program, 4/e</title>
13     </book>
14
15     <book>
16        <title>Visual Basic .NET How to Program</title>
17     </book>
18
19     <book>
20        <title>Advanced Java 2 Platform How to Program</title>
21     </book>
```

Fig. 18.16 XML document that conforms to a Microsoft Schema document. (Part 1 of 2.)

```
22
23      <book>
24          <title>Python How to Program</title>
25      </book>
26  </books>
```

Fig. 18.16 XML document that conforms to a Microsoft Schema document. (Part 2 of 2.)

```
1   <?xml version = "1.0"?>
2
3   <!-- Fig. 18.17: book.xdr                        -->
4   <!-- Schema document to which book.xml conforms -->
5
6   <Schema xmlns = "urn:schemas-microsoft-com:xml-data">
7       <ElementType name = "title" content = "textOnly"
8           model = "closed" />
9
10      <ElementType name = "book" content = "eltOnly" model = "closed">
11          <element type = "title" minOccurs = "1" maxOccurs = "1" />
12      </ElementType>
13
14      <ElementType name = "books" content = "eltOnly" model = "closed">
15          <element type = "book" minOccurs = "0" maxOccurs = "*" />
16      </ElementType>
17  </Schema>
```

Fig. 18.17 Microsoft Schema file that contains structure to which **bookxdr.xml** conforms.

Software Engineering Observation 18.5

Schemas are XML documents that conform to DTDs, which define the structure of a Schema. These DTDs, which are bundled with the parser, are used to validate the Schemas that authors create.

Software Engineering Observation 18.6

Many organizations and individuals are creating DTDs and Schemas for a broad range of categories (e.g., financial transactions, medical prescriptions, etc.). Often, these collections—called repositories*—are available free for download from the Web.[3]*

In line 6, root element **Schema** begins the Schema markup. Microsoft Schemas use the namespace URI **"urn:schemas-microsoft-com:xml-data"**. Line 7 uses element **ElementType** to define element **title**. Attribute **content** specifies that this element contains parsed character data (i.e., text only). Element **title** is not permitted to contain child elements. Setting the **model** *attribute* to **"closed"** specifies that a conforming XML document can contain only elements defined in this Schema. Line 10 defines element **book**; this element's **content** is "elements only" (i.e., **eltOnly**). This means that the element cannot contain mixed content (i.e., text and other elements). Within the **ElementType** element named **book**, the *element* element indicates that **title** is a **child** element of **book**. Attributes *minOccurs* and *maxOccurs* are set to **"1"**, indicating that a **book** ele-

---

3. See, for example, **opengis.net/schema.htm**.

ment must contain exactly one **title** element. The asterisk (*****) in line 15 indicates that the Schema permits any number of **book** elements in element **books**. We discuss how to validate **bookxdr.xml** against **book.xdr** in Section 18.5.4.

18.5.3 W3C XML Schema[4]

In this section, we focus on *W3C XML Schema*[5]—the schema that the W3C created. XML Schema is a *Recommendation* (i.e., a stable release suitable for use in industry). Figure 18.18 shows a Schema-valid XML document named **bookxsd.xml** and Fig. 18.19 shows the W3C XML Schema document (**book.xsd**) that defines the structure for **bookxsd.xml**. Although Schema authors can use virtually any filename extension, W3C XML Schemas typically use the *.xsd* extension. We discuss how to validate **bookxsd.xml** against **book.xsd** in the next section.

```
1    <?xml version = "1.0"?>
2
3    <!-- Fig. 18.18: bookxsd.xml                    -->
4    <!-- Document that conforms to W3C XML Schema -->
5
6    <deitel:books xmlns:deitel = "http://www.deitel.com/booklist">
7       <book>
8          <title>e-Business and e-Commerce How to Program</title>
9       </book>
10      <book>
11         <title>Python How to Program</title>
12      </book>
13   </deitel:books>
```

Fig. 18.18 XML document that conforms to W3C XML Schema.

```
1    <?xml version = "1.0"?>
2
3    <!-- Fig. 18.19: book.xsd           -->
4    <!-- Simple W3C XML Schema document -->
5
6    <xsd:schema xmlns:xsd = "http://www.w3.org/2001/XMLSchema"
7       xmlns:deitel = "http://www.deitel.com/booklist"
8       targetNamespace = "http://www.deitel.com/booklist">
9
10      <xsd:element name = "books" type = "deitel:BooksType"/>
11
12      <xsd:complexType name = "BooksType">
13         <xsd:sequence>
14            <xsd:element name = "book" type = "deitel:BookType"
15            minOccurs = "1" maxOccurs = "unbounded"/>
16         </xsd:sequence>
17      </xsd:complexType>
```

Fig. 18.19 XSD Schema document to which **bookxsd.xml** conforms.   (Part 1 of 2.)

---

4. We provide a detailed treatment of W3C Schema in *XML How to Program, 2/e.*
5. For the latest on W3C XML Schema, visit **www.w3.org/XML/Schema**.

```
18
19     <xsd:complexType name = "BookType">
20        <xsd:sequence>
21           <xsd:element name = "title" type = "xsd:string"/>
22        </xsd:sequence>
23     </xsd:complexType>
24
25  </xsd:schema>
```

Fig. 18.19 XSD Schema document to which **bookxsd.xml** conforms. (Part 2 of 2.)

W3C XML Schema use the namespace URI *http://www.w3.org/2001/ XMLSchema* and often use *namespace prefix* **xsd** (line 6 in Fig. 18.19). Root element **schema** contains elements that define the XML document's structure. Line 7 binds the URI **http://www.deitel.com/booklist** to namespace prefix **deitel**. Line 8 specifies the *targetNamespace*, which is the namespace for elements and attributes that this schema defines.

In W3C XML Schema, element *element* (line 10) defines an element. Attributes *name* and *type* specify the **element**'s name and data type, respectively. In this case, the name of the element is **books** and the data type is **deitel:BooksType**. Any element (e.g., **books**) that contains attributes or child elements must define a *complex type*, which defines each attribute and child element. Type **deitel:BooksType** (lines 12–17) is an example of a complex type. We prefix **BooksType** with **deitel**, because this is a complex type that we have created, not an existing W3C XML Schema complex type.

Lines 12–17 use element *complexType* to define an element type that has a child element named **book**. Because **book** contains a child element, its type must be a complex type (e.g., **BookType**). Attribute *minOccurs* specifies that **books** must contain a minimum of one **book** element. Attribute *maxOccurs*, with value *unbounded* (line 14) specifies that **books** may have any number of **book** child elements. Element *sequence* specifies the order of elements in the complex type.

Lines 19–23 define the **complexType BookType**. Line 21 defines element **title** with *type xsd:string*. When an element has a *simple type* such as **xsd:string**, it is prohibited from containing attributes and child elements. W3C XML Schema provides a large number of data types such as *xsd:date* for dates, *xsd:int* for integers, *xsd:double* for floating-point numbers and *xsd:time* for time.

Good Programming Practice 18.1

*By convention, W3C XML Schema authors use namespace prefix **xsd** when referring to the URI **http://www.w3.org/2001/XMLSchema**.*

18.5.4 Schema Validation in C#

In this section, we present a C# application (Fig. 18.20) that uses classes from the .NET Framework Class Library to validate the XML documents presented in the last two sections against their respective Schemas. We use an instance of *XmlValidatingReader* to perform the validation.

Line 17 creates an *XmlSchemaCollection* reference named **schemas**. Line 28 calls method *Add* to add an *XmlSchema* object to the Schema collection. Method **Add** is passed a name that identifies the Schema (i.e., **"book"**) and the name of the Schema file (i.e., **"book.xdr"**). Line 29 calls method **Add** to add a W3C XML Schema. The first argument specifies the namespace URI (i.e., line 18 in Fig. 18.19) and the second argument indentifies the schema file (i.e., **"book.xsd"**). This is the Schema that is used to validate **bookxsd.xml**.

```
1   // Fig. 18.20: ValidationTest.cs
2   // Validating XML documents against Schemas.
3
4   using System;
5   using System.Windows.Forms;
6   using System.Xml;
7   using System.Xml.Schema;          // contains Schema classes
8
9   // determines XML document Schema validity
10  public class ValidationTest : System.Windows.Forms.Form
11  {
12     private System.Windows.Forms.ComboBox filesComboBox;
13     private System.Windows.Forms.Button validateButton;
14     private System.Windows.Forms.Label consoleLabel;
15     private System.ComponentModel.Container components = null;
16
17     private XmlSchemaCollection schemas;    // Schemas
18     private bool valid;                     // validation result
19
20     public ValidationTest()
21     {
22        InitializeComponent();
23
24        valid = true;   // assume document is valid
25
26        // get Schema(s) for validation
27        schemas = new XmlSchemaCollection();
28        schemas.Add( "book", "book.xdr" );
29        schemas.Add( "http://www.deitel.com/booklist", "book.xsd" );
30     } // end constructor
31
32     // Visual Studio .NET generated code
33
34     [STAThread]
35     static void Main()
36     {
37        Application.Run( new ValidationTest() );
38     } // end Main
39
40     // handle validateButton click event
41     private void validateButton_Click( object sender,
42        System.EventArgs e )
43     {
44        // get XML document
45        XmlTextReader reader =
46           new XmlTextReader( filesComboBox.Text );
47
```

Fig. 18.20 Schema-validation example. (Part 1 of 2.)

```
48          // get validator
49          XmlValidatingReader validator =
50             new XmlValidatingReader( reader );
51
52          // assign Schema(s)
53          validator.Schemas.Add( schemas );
54
55          // set validation type
56          validator.ValidationType = ValidationType.Auto;
57
58          // register event handler for validation error(s)
59          validator.ValidationEventHandler +=
60             new ValidationEventHandler( ValidationError );
61
62          // validate document node-by-node
63          while ( validator.Read() ) ; // empty body
64
65          // check validation result
66          if ( valid )
67             consoleLabel.Text = "Document is valid";
68
69          valid = true; // reset variable
70
71          // close reader stream
72          validator.Close();
73       } // end validateButton_Click
74
75       // event handler for validation error
76       private void ValidationError( object sender,
77          ValidationEventArgs arguments )
78       {
79          consoleLabel.Text = arguments.Message;
80          valid = false; // validation failed
81       } // end ValidationError
82    } // end ValidationTest
```

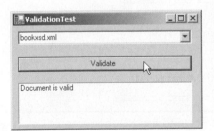
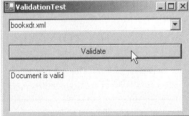

Fig. 18.20 Schema-validation example. (Part 2 of 2.)

Lines 45–46 create an **XmlReader** for the file that the user selected from **file-sComboBox**. The XML document to be validated against a Schema contained in the **XmlSchemaCollection** must be passed to the **XmlValidatingReader** constructor (lines 49–50).

Line 53 **Add**s the Schema collection referenced by **Schemas** to the *Schemas prop-erty*. This property sets the Schema used to validate the document. The *ValidationType* property (line 56) is set to the *ValidationType enumeration* constant for **Auto**matically identifying the Schema's type (i.e., XDR or XSD). Lines 59–60 register method **Valida-tionError** with *ValidationEventHandler*. Method **ValidationError** (lines 76–81) is called if the document is invalid or an error occurs, such as if the document cannot be found. Failure to register a method with **ValidationEventHandler** causes an exception to be thrown when the document is missing or invalid.

Validation is performed node-by-node by calling the method *Read* (line 63). Each call to **Read** validates the next node in the document. The loop terminates either when all nodes have been validated successfully or a node fails validation. When validated against their respective Schemas, the XML documents in Fig. 18.16 and Fig. 18.18 validate successfully.

Figure 18.21 and Fig. 18.22 list two XML documents that fail to conform to **book.xdr** and **book.xsd**, respectively. In Fig. 18.21, the extra **title** element in **book** (lines 19–22) invalidate the document. In Fig. 18.22, the extra **title** element in **book** (lines 7–10) inval-idates the document. Although both documents are invalid, they are well formed.

```
1    <?xml version = "1.0"?>
2
3    <!-- Fig. 18.22: bookxsdfail.xml                    -->
4    <!-- Document that does not conforms to W3C Schema -->
5
6    <deitel:books xmlns:deitel = "http://www.deitel.com/booklist">
7       <book>
8          <title>e-Business and e-Commerce How to Program</title>
9          <title>C# How to Program</title>
10      </book>
11      <book>
12         <title>Python How to Program</title>
13      </book>
14   </deitel:books>
```

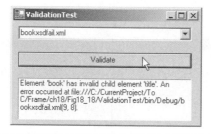

Fig. 18.21 XML document that does not conform to the XSD schema of Fig. 18.19.

```
1    <?xml version = "1.0"?>
2
3    <!-- Fig. 18.22: bookxdrfail.xml                    -->
4    <!-- XML file that does not conform to Schema book.xdr -->
5
```

Fig. 18.22 XML file that does not conform to the Schema in Fig. 18.17. (Part 1 of 2.)

```
 6   <books xmlns = "x-schema:book.xdr">
 7      <book>
 8         <title>XML How to Program</title>
 9      </book>
10
11      <book>
12         <title>Java How to Program, 4/e</title>
13      </book>
14
15      <book>
16         <title>Visual Basic .NET How to Program</title>
17      </book>
18
19      <book>
20         <title>C++ How to Program, 3/e</title>
21         <title>Python How to Program</title>
22      </book>
23
24      <book>
25         <title>C# How to Program</title>
26      </book>
27   </books>
```

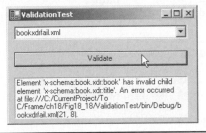

Fig. 18.22 XML file that does not conform to the Schema in Fig. 18.17. (Part 2 of 2.)

18.6 Extensible Stylesheet Language and `XslTransform`

Extensible Stylesheet Language (XSL) is an XML vocabulary for formatting XML data. In this section, we discuss the portion of XSL—called *XSL Transformations (XSLT)*—that creates formatted text-based documents from XML documents. This process is called a *transformation* and involves two tree structures: The *source tree*, which is the XML document being transformed, and the *result tree*, which is the result (i.e., any text-based format such as XHTML) of the transformation.[6] The source tree is not modified when a transformation occurs.

To perform transformations, an XSLT processor is required. Popular XSLT processors include Microsoft's msxml and the Apache Software Foundation's *Xalan*. The XML document, shown in Fig. 18.23, is transformed by msxml into an XHTML document (Fig. 18.24).

---

6. Extensible Hypertext Markup Language (XHTML) is the W3C technical recommendation that replaces HTML for marking up content for the Web. For more information on XHTML, see the XHTML Appendices K and L on the CD and visit **www.w3.org**.

```
1   <?xml version = "1.0"?>
2
3   <!-- Fig. 18.23: sorting.xml                        -->
4   <!-- XML document containing book information -->
5
6   <?xml:stylesheet type = "text/xsl" href = "sorting.xsl"?>
7
8   <book isbn = "999-99999-9-X">
9      <title>Deitel&apos;s XML Primer</title>
10
11     <author>
12        <firstName>Paul</firstName>
13        <lastName>Deitel</lastName>
14     </author>
15
16     <chapters>
17        <frontMatter>
18           <preface pages = "2" />
19           <contents pages = "5" />
20           <illustrations pages = "4" />
21        </frontMatter>
22
23        <chapter number = "3" pages = "44">
24           Advanced XML</chapter>
25
26        <chapter number = "2" pages = "35">
27           Intermediate XML</chapter>
28
29        <appendix number = "B" pages = "26">
30           Parsers and Tools</appendix>
31
32        <appendix number = "A" pages = "7">
33           Entities</appendix>
34
35        <chapter number = "1" pages = "28">
36           XML Fundamentals</chapter>
37     </chapters>
38
39     <media type = "CD" />
40  </book>
```

Fig. 18.23 XML document containing book information.

Line 6 is a *processing instruction* (*PI*), which contains application-specific information that is embedded into the XML document. In this particular case, the processing instruction is specific to IE and specifies the location of an XSLT document with which to transform the XML document. The characters **<?** and **?>** delimit a processing instruction, which consists of a *PI target* (e.g., **xml:stylesheet**) and *PI value* (e.g., **type = "text/xsl" href = "sorting.xsl"**). The portion of this particular PI value that follows **href** specifies the name and location of the style sheet to apply—in this case, **sorting.xsl**, which is located in the same directory as this XML document.

Fig. 18.24 presents the XSLT document (**sorting.xsl**) that transforms **sorting.xml** (Fig. 18.23) to XHTML.

Performance Tip 18.1

Using Internet Explorer on the client to process XSLT documents conserves server resources by using the client's processing power (instead of having the server process XSLT documents for multiple clients).

Line 1 of Fig. 18.23 contains the XML declaration. Recall that an XSL document is an XML document. Line 6 is the **xsl:stylesheet** root element. Attribute *version* specifies the version of XSLT to which this document conforms. Namespace prefix **xsl** is defined and is bound to the XSLT URI defined by the W3C. When processed, lines 11–13 write the document type declaration to the result tree. Attribute **method** is assigned **"xml"**, which indicates that XML is being output to the result tree. Attribute **omit-xml-declaration** is assigned **"no"**, which outputs an XML declaration to the result tree. Attribute **doctype-system** and **doctype-public** write the **Doctype** DTD information to the result tree.

XSLT documents contain one or more *xsl:template* elements that specify which information is output to the result tree. The template on line 16 *match*es the source tree's document root. When the document root is encountered, this template is applied, and any text marked up by this element that is not in the namespace referenced by **xsl** is output to the result tree. Line 18 calls for all the **template**s that match children of the document root to be applied. Line 23 specifies a **template** that **match**es element **book**.

```
1   <?xml version = "1.0"?>
2
3   <!-- Fig. 18.24: sorting.xsl                          -->
4   <!-- Transformation of book information into XHTML -->
5
6   <xsl:stylesheet version = "1.0"
7      xmlns:xsl = "http://www.w3.org/1999/XSL/Transform">
8
9       <!-- write XML declaration and DOCTYPE DTD information -->
10      <xsl:output method = "xml" omit-xml-declaration = "no"
11         doctype-system =
12            "http://www.w3.org/TR/xhtml11/DTD/xhtml11-strict.dtd"
13         doctype-public = "-//W3C//DTD XHTML 1.0 Strict//EN"/>
14
15      <!-- match document root -->
16      <xsl:template match = "/">
17         <html xmlns = "http://www.w3.org/1999/xhtml">
18            <xsl:apply-templates/>
19         </html>
20      </xsl:template>
21
22      <!-- match book -->
23      <xsl:template match = "book">
24         <head>
25            <title>ISBN <xsl:value-of select = "@isbn" /> -
26               <xsl:value-of select = "title" /></title>
27         </head>
```

Fig. 18.24 XSL document that transforms **sorting.xml** (Fig. 18.23) into XHTML. (Part 1 of 3.)

```
28
29          <body>
30             <h1 style = "color: blue">
31                <xsl:value-of select = "title"/></h1>
32
33             <h2 style = "color: blue">by <xsl:value-of
34                select = "author/lastName" />,
35                <xsl:value-of select = "author/firstName" /></h2>
36
37             <table style =
38                "border-style: groove; background-color: wheat">
39
40                <xsl:for-each select = "chapters/frontMatter/*">
41                   <tr>
42                      <td style = "text-align: right">
43                         <xsl:value-of select = "name()" />
44                      </td>
45
46                      <td>
47                         ( <xsl:value-of select = "@pages" /> pages )
48                      </td>
49                   </tr>
50                </xsl:for-each>
51
52                <xsl:for-each select = "chapters/chapter">
53                   <xsl:sort select = "@number" data-type = "number"
54                      order = "ascending" />
55                   <tr>
56                      <td style = "text-align: right">
57                         Chapter <xsl:value-of select = "@number" />
58                      </td>
59
60                      <td>
61                         ( <xsl:value-of select = "@pages" /> pages )
62                      </td>
63                   </tr>
64                </xsl:for-each>
65
66                <xsl:for-each select = "chapters/appendix">
67                   <xsl:sort select = "@number" data-type = "text"
68                      order = "ascending" />
69                   <tr>
70                      <td style = "text-align: right">
71                         Appendix <xsl:value-of select = "@number" />
72                      </td>
73
74                      <td>
75                         ( <xsl:value-of select = "@pages" /> pages )
76                      </td>
77                   </tr>
78                </xsl:for-each>
79             </table>
```

Fig. 18.24 XSL document that transforms **sorting.xml** (Fig. 18.23) into XHTML. (Part 2 of 3.)

```
80
81              <br /><p style = "color: blue">Pages:
82                 <xsl:variable name = "pagecount"
83                     select = "sum(chapters//*/@pages)" />
84                 <xsl:value-of select = "$pagecount" />
85              <br />Media Type:
86                 <xsl:value-of select = "media/@type" /></p>
87           </body>
88        </xsl:template>
89
90     </xsl:stylesheet>
```

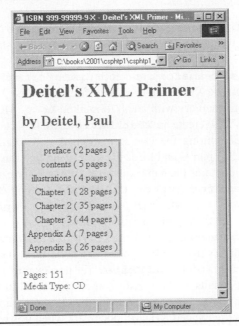

Fig. 18.24 XSL document that transforms `sorting.xml` (Fig. 18.23) into XHTML. (Part 3 of 3.)

Lines 25–26 create the title for the XHTML document. We use the ISBN of the book from attribute **isbn** and the contents of element **title** to create the title string **ISBN 999-99999-9-X - Deitel's XML Primer**. Element **xsl:value-of** selects the **book** element's **isbn** attribute.

Lines 33–35 create a header element that contains the book's author. Because the *context node* (i.e., the current node being processed) is **book**, the XPath expression **author/lastName** selects the author's last name, and the expression **author/firstName** selects the author's first name.

Line 40 selects each element (indicated by an asterisk) that is a child of element **frontMatter**. Line 43 calls *node-set function **name*** to retrieve the current node's element name (e.g., **preface**). The current node is the context node specified in the **xsl:for-each** (line 40).

Lines 53–54 sort **chapter**s by number in ascending order. Attribute **select** selects the value of context node **chapter**'s attribute **number**. Attribute *data-type* with value **"number"**, specifies a numeric sort and attribute *order* specifies **"ascending"** order. Attribute **data-type** also can, be assigned the value *"text"* (line 67) and attribute **order** also may be assigned the value *"descending"*.

Lines 82–83 use an *XSL variable* to store the value of the book's page count and output it to the result tree. Attribute **name** specifies the variable's name, and attribute **select** assigns it a value. Function *sum* totals the values for all **page** attribute values. The two slashes between **chapters** and ***** indicate that all descendent nodes of **chapters** are searched for elements that contain an attribute named **pages**.

The *System.Xml.Xsl* namespace provides classes for applying XSLT style sheets to XML documents. Specifically, an object of class *XslTransform* performs the transformation.

Figure 18.25 applies a style sheet (**sports.xsl**) to **sports.xml** (Fig. 18.10). The transformation result is written to a text box and to a file. We also show the transformation results rendered in IE.

Line 20 declares **XslTransform** reference **transformer**. An object of this type is necessary to transform the XML data to another format. In line 29, the XML document is parsed and loaded into memory with a call to method **Load**. Method **CreateNavigator** is called in line 32 to create an **XPathNavigator** object, which is used to navigate the XML document during the transformation. A call to method *Load* of class **XslTransform** (line 36) parses and loads the style sheet that this application uses. The argument that is passed contains the name and location of the style sheet.

Event handler **transformButton_Click** calls method *Transform* of class **XslTransform** to apply the style sheet (**sports.xsl**) to **sports.xml** (line 53). This method takes three arguments: An **XPathNavigator** (created from **sports.xml**'s **XmlDocument**), an instance of class *XsltArgumentList*, which is a list of **string** parameters that can be applied to a style sheet—**null**, in this case and an instance of a derived class of **TextWriter** (in this example, an instance of class **StringWriter**). The results of the transformation are stored in the **StringWriter** object referenced by **output**. Lines 59–62 write the transformation results to disk. The third screen shot depicts the created XHTML document when it is rendered in IE.

```
1   // Fig. 18.25: TransformTest.cs
2   // Applying a style sheet to an XML document.
3
4   using System;
5   using System.Windows.Forms;
6   using System.Xml;
7   using System.Xml.XPath;     // contains XPath classes
8   using System.Xml.Xsl;       // contains style sheet classes
9   using System.IO;            // contains stream classes
10
11  // transforms XML document to XHTML
12  public class TransformTest : System.Windows.Forms.Form
13  {
14     private System.Windows.Forms.TextBox consoleTextBox;
15     private System.Windows.Forms.Button transformButton;
16     private System.ComponentModel.Container components = null;
```

Fig. 18.25 XSL style sheet applied to an XML document. (Part 1 of 3.)

```
17
18        private XmlDocument document;        // Xml document root
19        private XPathNavigator navigator;    // navigate document
20        private XslTransform transformer;    // transform document
21        private StringWriter output;         // display document
22
23        public TransformTest()
24        {
25           InitializeComponent();
26
27           // load XML data
28           document = new XmlDocument();
29           document.Load( "..\\..\\sports.xml" );
30
31           // create navigator
32           navigator = document.CreateNavigator();
33
34           // load style sheet
35           transformer = new XslTransform();
36           transformer.Load( "..\\..\\sports.xsl" );
37        } // end constructor
38
39        // Windows Form Designer generated code
40
41        [STAThread]
42        static void Main()
43        {
44           Application.Run( new TransformTest() );
45        } // end Main
46
47        // transformButton click event
48        private void transformButton_Click( object sender,
49           System.EventArgs e )
50        {
51           // transform XML data
52           output = new StringWriter();
53           transformer.Transform( navigator, null, output );
54
55           // display transformation in text box
56           consoleTextBox.Text = output.ToString();
57
58           // write transformation result to disk
59           FileStream stream = new FileStream( "..\\..\\sports.html",
60              FileMode.Create );
61           StreamWriter writer = new StreamWriter( stream );
62           writer.Write( output.ToString() );
63
64           // close streams
65           writer.Close();
66           output.Close();
67        } // end transformButton_Click
68     }    // end TransformTest
```

Fig. 18.25 XSL style sheet applied to an XML document. (Part 2 of 3.)

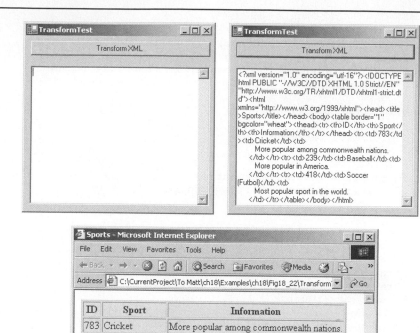

Fig. 18.25 XSL style sheet applied to an XML document. (Part 3 of 3.)

18.7 Microsoft BizTalk™

Increasingly, organizations are using the Internet to exchange critical data between business partners and their own business divisions. However, transferring data between organizations can become difficult, because companies often use different platforms, applications and data specifications that complicate data transfer. For example, consider a business that supplies raw materials to a variety of industries. If the supplier cannot receive all orders electronically because their customers use different computing platforms, an employee must input order data manually. If the supplier receives hundreds of orders a day, typing mistakes are likely, resulting in incorrect inventories or wrong order fulfillments, thereby jeorpardizing the business by losing customers.

The supplier has several options—either continue to have data entered manually, purchase the same software packages as the ones their customers use or encourage customers to adopt the applications used by the supply company. In a growing economy, a business would have to purchase and maintain disparate software packages, spend money for more employees to process data or force their business partners to standardize their own organizational software programs. To facilitate the flow of information between businesses, Microsoft developed *BizTalk* ("business talk"), an XML-based technology that helps to manage and facilitate business transactions.

　　　　BizTalk creates an environment in which data marked up as XML is used to exchange business-specific information, regardless of platform or programming applications. This section overviews BizTalk and presents a code example to illustrate the business-specific information included in the markup.

　　　　BizTalk consists of three parts: The BizTalk Server, the BizTalk Framework and the Biz-Talk Schema Library. The *BizTalk Server* (*BTS*) parses and translates all inbound and outbound messages (or documents) that are sent to and from a business, using Internet standards such as HTTP. The *BizTalk Framework* is a Schema for structuring those messages. The Framework offers a specific set of core tags. Businesses can download the Framework to use in their organizations and can submit new schemas to the BizTalk organization, at **www.biztalk.org**. Once the BizTalk organization verifies and validates the submissions, the Schemas become BizTalk Framework Schemas. The *BizTalk Schema Library* is a collection of Framework Schemas. Figure 18.26 summarizes BizTalk terminology.

　　　　Fig. 18.27 is an example BizTalk message for a product offer from a clothing company. The message Schema for this example was developed by Microsoft to facilitate online purchases by a retailer from a wholesaler. We use this Schema for a fictitious company, named ExComp.

BizTalk	Description
Framework	A specification that defines a format for messages.
Schema library	A repository of Framework XML Schemas.
Server	An application that assists vendors in converting their messages to BizTalk format. For more information, visit **www.microsoft.com/biztalkserver**
JumpStart Kit	A set of tools for developing BizTalk applications.

Fig. 18.26 BizTalk terminology.

```
1   <?xml version = "1.0"?>
2   <BizTalk xmlns =
3      "urn:schemas-biztalk-org:BizTalk/biztalk-0.81.xml">
4
5   <!-- Fig. 18.27: biztalkmarkup.xml      -->
6   <!-- Example of standard BizTalk markup -->
7
8      <Route>
9         <From locationID = "8888888" locationType = "DUNS"
10           handle = "23" />
11
12        <To locationID = "454545445" locationType = "DUNS"
13           handle = "45" />
14     </Route>
15
```

Fig. 18.27 BizTalk markup using an offer Schema. (Part 1 of 3.)

```
16        <Body>
17           <Offers xmlns =
18              "x-schema:http://schemas.biztalk.org/eshop_msn_com/
t7ntoqnq.xml">
19              <Offer>
20                 <Model>12-a-3411d</Model>
21                 <Manufacturer>ExComp, Inc.</Manufacturer>
22                 <ManufacturerModel>DCS-48403</ManufacturerModel>
23
24                 <MerchantCategory>
25                    Clothes | Sports wear
26                 </MerchantCategory>
27
28                 <MSNClassId></MSNClassId>
29
30                 <StartDate>2001-06-05 T13:12:00</StartDate>
31                 <EndDate>2001-12-05T13:12:00</EndDate>
32
33                 <RegularPrice>89.99</RegularPrice>
34                 <CurrentPrice>25.99</CurrentPrice>
35                 <DisplayPrice value = "3" />
36                 <InStock value = "15" />
37
38                 <ReferenceImageURL>
39                    http://www.Example.com/clothes/index.jpg
40                 </ReferenceImageURL>
41
42                 <OfferName>Clearance sale</OfferName>
43
44                 <OfferDescription>
45                    This is a clearance sale
46                 </OfferDescription>
47
48                 <PromotionalText>Free Shipping</PromotionalText>
49
50                 <Comments>
51                    Clothes that you would love to wear.
52                 </Comments>
53
54                 <IconType value = "BuyNow" />
55
56                 <ActionURL>
57                    http://www.example.com/action.htm
58                 </ActionURL>
59
60                 <AgeGroup1 value = "Infant" />
61                 <AgeGroup2 value = "Adult" />
62
63                 <Occasion1 value = "Birthday" />
64                 <Occasion2 value = "Anniversary" />
65                 <Occasion3 value = "Christmas" />
66
67              </Offer>
```

Fig. 18.27 BizTalk markup using an offer Schema. (Part 2 of 3.)

```
68              </Offers>
69          </Body>
70      </BizTalk>
```

Fig. 18.27 BizTalk markup using an offer Schema. (Part 3 of 3.)

All Biztalk documents have the root element **BizTalk** (line 2). Line 3 defines a default namespace for the **BizTalk** framework elements. Element **Route** (lines 8–14) contains the routing information, which is mandatory for all BizTalk documents. Element **Route** also contains elements **To** and **From** (lines 9–12), which indicate the document's destination and source, respectively. This makes it easier for the receiving application to communicate with the sender. Attribute **locationType** specifies the type of business that sends or receives the information, and attribute **locationID** specifies a business identity (the unique identifier for a business). These attributes facilitate source and destination organization. Attribute **handle** provides information to routing applications that handle the document.

Element **Body** (lines 16–69) contains the actual message, whose Schema is defined by the businesses themselves. Lines 17–18 specify the default namespace for element **Offers** (lines 17–68), which is contained in element **Body** (note that line 18 wraps—if we split this line, Internet Explorer cannot locate the namespace). Each offer is marked up using an **Offer** element (lines 19–67) that contains elements describing the offer. Note that the tags all are business-related elements, and easily understood. For additional information on BizTalk, visit **www.biztalk.com**.

In this chapter, we studied the Extensible Markup Language and several of its related technologies. In Chapter 19, we begin our discussion of databases, which are crucial to the development of multi-tier Web-based applications.

18.8 Internet and World Wide Web Resources

www.w3.org/xml
The W3C (World Wide Web Consortium) facilitates the development of common protocols to ensure interoperability on the Web. Their XML page includes information about upcoming events, publications, software and discussion groups. Visit this site to read about the latest developments in XML.

www.xml.org
xml.org is a reference for XML, DTDs, schemas and namespaces.

www.w3.org/style/XSL
This W3C page provides information on XSL, including topics such as XSL development, learning XSL, XSL-enabled tools, XSL specification, FAQs and XSL history.

www.w3.org/TR
This is the W3C technical reports and publications page. It contains links to working drafts, proposed recommendations and other resources.

www.xmlbooks.com
This site provides a list of XML books recommended by Charles Goldfarb, one of the original designers of GML (General Markup Language), from which SGML was derived.

www.xml-zone.com
The Development Exchange XML Zone is a complete resource for XML information. This site includes a FAQ, news, articles and links to other XML sites and newsgroups.

wdvl.internet.com/Authoring/Languages/XML
Web Developer's Virtual Library XML site includes tutorials, a FAQ, the latest news and extensive links to XML sites and software downloads.

www.xml.com
XML.com provides the latest news and information about XML, conference listings, links to XML Web resources organized by topic, tools and other resources.

msdn.microsoft.com/xml/default.asp
The MSDN Online XML Development Center features articles on XML, Ask the Experts chat sessions, samples and demos, newsgroups and other helpful information.

msdn.microsoft.com/downloads/samples/Internet/xml/xml_validator/sample.asp
The microsoft XML validator, which can be downloaded from this site, can validate both online and offline documents.

www.oasis-open.org/cover/xml.html
The SGML/XML Web Page is an extensive resource that includes links to several FAQs, online resources, industry initiatives, demos, conferences and tutorials.

www.gca.org/whats_xml/default.htm
The GCA site offers an XML glossary, list of books, brief descriptions of the draft standards for XML and links to online drafts.

www-106.ibm.com/developerworks/xml
The IBM XML Zone site is a great resource for developers. It provides news, tools, a library, case studies and information about events and standards.

developer.netscape.com/tech/xml/index.html
The XML and Metadata Developer Central site has demos, technical notes and news articles related to XML.

www.projectcool.com/developer/xmlz
The Project Cool Developer Zone site includes several tutorials covering introductory through advanced XML topics.

www.ucc.ie/xml
This site is a detailed XML FAQ. Developers can check out responses to some popular questions, or submit their own questions through the site.

SUMMARY

- XML is a widely supported, open technology (i.e., non-proprietary technology) for data exchange. XML is quickly becoming the standard by which applications maintain data.

- XML is highly portable. Any text editor that supports ASCII or Unicode characters can render or display XML documents. Because XML elements describe the data they contain, they are both human and machine readable.

- XML permits document authors to create custom markup for virtually any type of information. This extensibility enables document authors to create entirely new markup languages that describe specific types of data, including mathematical formulas, chemical molecular structures, music, recipes, etc.

- The processing of XML documents—which programs typically store in files whose names end with the **.xml** extension—requires a program called an XML parser. A parser is responsible for identifying components of XML documents then for storing those components in a data structure for manipulation.

- An XML document can reference another optional document that defines the XML document's structure. Two types of optional structure-defining documents are Document Type Definitions (DTDs) and Schemas.

- An XML document begins with an optional XML declaration, which identifies the document as an XML document. The **version** information parameter specifies the version of XML syntax that is used in the document.

- XML comments begin with **<!--** and end with **-->**. Data is marked up with tags whose names are enclosed in angle brackets (**<>**). Tags are used in pairs to delimit markup. A tag that begins markup is called a start tag, and a tag that terminates markup is called an end tag. End tags differ from start tags in that they contain a forward slash (**/**) character.

- Individual units of markup are called elements, which are the most fundamental XML building blocks. XML documents contain one element, called a root element, that contains every other element in the document. Elements are embedded or nested within each other to form hierarchies, with the root element at the top of the hierarchy.

- XML element names can be of any length and can contain letters, digits, underscores, hyphens and periods. However, they must begin with either a letter or an underscore.

- When a user loads an XML document into Internet Explorer (IE), msxml parses the document and passes the parsed data to IE. IE then uses a style sheet to format the data.

- IE displays minus (**–**) and plus (**+**) signs next to all container elements (i.e., elements that contain other elements). A minus sign indicates that all child elements (i.e., nested elements) are being displayed. When clicked, a minus sign becomes a plus sign (which collapses the container element and hides all children), and vice versa.

- In addition to being placed between tags, data also can be placed in attributes, which are name–value pairs in start tags. Elements can have any number of attributes.

- Because XML allows document authors to create their own tags, naming collisions (i.e., two different elements that have the same name) can occur. As in C#, XML namespaces provide a means for document authors to prevent collisions. Namespace prefixes are prepended to elements to specify the namespace to which the element belongs.

- Each namespace prefix is bound to a uniform resource identifier (URI) that uniquely identifies the namespace. A URI is a series of characters that differentiate names. Document authors create their own namespace prefixes. Virtually any name can be used as a namespace prefix except the reserved namespace prefix **xml**.

- To eliminate the need to place a namespace prefix in each element, document authors can specify a default namespace for an element and its children.

- When an XML parser successfully parses a document, the parser stores a tree structure containing the document's data in memory. This hierarchical tree structure is called a Document Object Model (DOM) tree. The DOM tree represents each component of the XML document as a node in the tree. Nodes that contain other nodes (called child nodes) are called parent nodes. Nodes that have the same parent are called sibling nodes. A node's descendant nodes include that node's children, its children's children and so on. A node's ancestor nodes include that node's parent, its parent's parent and so on. The DOM tree has a single root node that contains all other nodes in the document.

- Namespace **System.Xml**, contains classes for creating, reading and manipulating XML documents.

- **XmlReader**-derived class **XmlNodeReader** iterates through each node in the XML document.

- Class **XmlReader** is an **abstract** class that defines the interface for reading XML documents.

- An **XmlDocument** object conceptually represents an empty XML document.

- The XML documents are parsed and loaded into an **XmlDocument** object when method **Load** is invoked. Once an XML document is loaded into an **XmlDocument**, its data can be read and manipulated programmatically.

- An **XmlNodeReader** allows us to read one node at a time from an **XmlDocument**.

- Method **Read** of **XmlReader** reads one node from the DOM tree.

- The **Name** property contains the node's name, the **Value** property contains the node's data and the **NodeType** property contains the node type (i.e., element, comment, text etc.).

- Line breaks use the character sequence **"\r\n"**, which denotes a carriage return followed by a line feed. This is the standard line break for Windows-based applications and controls.

- Method **CreateNode** of **XmlDocument** takes a **NodeType**, a **Name** and a **NamespaceURI** as arguments.

- An **XmlTextWriter** streams XML data to disk. Method **WriteTo** writes an XML representation to an **XmlTextWriter** stream.

- An **XmlTextReader** reads XML data from a file.

- Class **XPathNavigator** in the **System.Xml.XPath** namespace can iterate through node lists that match search criteria, written as an XPath expression.

- XPath (XML Path Language) provides a syntax for locating specific nodes in XML documents effectively and efficiently. XPath is a string-based language of expressions used by XML and many of its related technologies.

- Navigation methods of **XPathNavigator** are **MoveToFirstChild**, **MoveToParent**, **MoveToNext** and **MoveToPrevious**. Each method performs the action that its name implies: Method **MoveToFirstChild** moves to the first child of the node referenced by the **XPathNavigator**, **MoveToParent** moves to the parent node of the node referenced by the **XPathNavigator**, **MoveToNext** moves to the next sibling of the node referenced by the **XPathNavigator** and **MoveToPrevious** moves to the previous sibling of the node referenced by the **XPathNavigator**.

- Whereas XML contains only data, XSLT is capable of converting XML into any text based document. XSLT documents typically have the extension **.xsl**.

- When transforming an XML document via XSLT, two tree structures are involved: The source tree, which is the XML document being transformed, and the result tree, which is the result (e.g., XHTML) of the transformation.

- XSLT specifies the use of element **value-of** to retrieve an attribute's value. The symbol **@** specifies an attribute node.

- The node-set function **name** retrieves the current node's element name.

- Attribute **select** selects the value of context node's attribute.

- XML documents can be transformed programmatically through C#. The **System.Xml.Xsl** namespace facilities the application of XSLT style sheets to XML documents.

- Class **XsltArgumentList** is a list of **string** parameters that can be applied to a style sheet.

- BizTalk consists of three parts: The BizTalk Server, the BizTalk Framework and the BizTalk Schema Library.

- The BizTalk Server (BTS) parses and translates all inbound and outbound messages (or documents) going to and from a business.

- The BizTalk Framework is a Schema for structuring those messages.

- The BizTalk Schema Library is a collection of different Framework Schemas. Businesses can design their own Schema or choose one from the BizTalk Schema Library.
- All Biztalk documents have the root element **BizTalk**.

TERMINOLOGY

@ character
\r\n
Add method
ancestor node
asterisk (*****) occurrence indicator
ATTLIST
attribute
attribute node
attribute value
BizTalk Framework
BizTalk Schema Library
BizTalk Server (BTS)
CDATA character data
child element
child node
container element
context node
CreateNavigator method
CreateNode method
Current property
data-type attribute
default namespace
descendant node
doctype-public attribute
doctype-system attribute
document root
Document Type Definition (DTD)
DOM (Document Object Model)
EBNF (Extended Backus-Naur Form) grammar
ELEMENT element type declaration
empty element
EMPTY keyword
end tag
Extensible Stylesheet Language (XSL)
external DTD
forward slash
#IMPLIED flag
invalid document
IsEmptyElement property
LastChild property
Load method
markup
match attribute
maxOccurs attribute
method attribute

minOccurs attribute
MoveToFirstChild property
MoveToNext property
MoveToParent property
MoveToPrevious property
MoveToRoot property
msxml parser
name attribute
name node-set function
Name property
namespace prefix
node
Nodes collection
node-set function
NodeType property
nonvalidating XML parser
occurrence indicator
omit-xml-declaration attribute
order attribute
parent node
Parent property
ParentNode property
parsed character data
parser
#PCDATA flag
PI (processing instruction)
PI target
PI value
plus-sign (**+**) occurrence indicator
processing instruction
question-mark (**?**) occurrence indicator
Read Method
recursive descent
reserved namespace prefix **xml**
result tree
root element
root node
Schema element
schema property
Schemas property
select attribute
Select method
sibling node
single-quote character (**'**)
source tree

style sheet
sum function
SYSTEM flag
System.Xml namespace
System.Xml.Schema namespace
text node
Transform method
tree-based model
type attribute
validating XML parser
ValidatingReader class
ValidationEventHandler class
ValidationType property
ValidationType.Auto constant
value property
version attribute
version information parameter
W3C XML Schema
well-formed document
.xdr extension
XML (Extensible Markup Language)
XML declaration
.xml file extension
xml namespace
XML node
XML processor
XML Schema
XML Validator

XmlDocument class
XmlNodeReader class
XmlNodeType enumeration
XmlNodeType.Comment constant
XmlNodeType.Element constant
XmlNodeType.EndElement constant
XmlNodeType.Text constant
XmlNodeType.XmlDeclaration constant
xmlns attribute
XmlPathNodeIterator class
XmlReader class
XmlSchema class
XmlSchemaCollection collection
XmlTextWriter class
XPathExpression class
XPathNavigator class
.xsl extension
XSL Transformations (XSLT)
XSL variable
xsl:apply-templates element
xsl:for-each element
xsl:output element
xsl:sort element
xsl:stylesheet element
xsl:template element
xsl:value-of element
XslTransform class
XsltTextWriter class

SELF-REVIEW EXERCISES

18.1   Which of the following are valid XML element names?
   a) **yearBorn**
   b) **year.Born**
   c) **year Born**
   d) **year-Born1**
   e) **2_year_born**
   f) **--year/born**
   g) **year*born**
   h) **.year_born**
   i) **_year_born_**
   j) **y_e-a_r-b_o-r_n**

18.2   State whether the following are *true* or *false*. If *false*, explain why.
   a) XML is a technology for creating markup languages.
   b) XML markup is delimited by forward and backward slashes (**/** and ****).
   c) All XML start tags must have corresponding end tags.
   d) Parsers check an XML document's syntax.
   e) XML does not support namespaces.
   f) When creating new XML elements, document authors must use the set of XML tags provided by the W3C.

g) The pound character (**#**), the dollar sign (**$**), ampersand (**&**), greater-than (**>**) and less-than (**<**) are examples of XML reserved characters.

18.3   Fill in the blanks for each of the following statements:

a) _____ help prevent naming collisions.

b) _____ embed application–specific information into an XML document.

c) _____ is Microsoft's XML parser.

d) XSL element _____ writes a **DOCTYPE** to the result tree.

e) Microsoft XML Schema documents have root element _____.

f) To define an element attribute in a DTD, _____ is used.

g) XSL element _____ is the root element in an XSL document.

h) XSL element _____ selects specific XML elements using repetition.

18.4   State which of the following statements are *true* and which are *false*. If *false*, explain why.

a) XML is not case sensitive.

b) C# architecture supports W3C Schema.

c) DTDs are a vocabulary of XML.

d) Schema is a technology for locating information in an XML document.

18.5   In Fig. 18.1, we subdivided the **author** element into more detailed pieces. How might you subdivide the **date** element?

18.6   Write a processing instruction that includes the stylesheet **wap.xsl** for use in Internet Explorer.

18.7   Fill in the blanks in each of the following statements:

a) Nodes that contain other nodes are called _____ nodes.

b) Nodes that are peers are called _____ nodes.

c) Class **XmlDocument** is analogous to the _____ of a tree.

d) Method _____ adds an **XmlNode** to an **XmlTree** as a child of the current node.

18.8   Write an XPath expression that locates **contact** nodes in **letter.xml** (Fig. 18.3).

18.9   Describe the **Select** method of **XPathNavigator**.

ANSWERS TO SELF-REVIEW EXERCISES

18.1   a, b, d, i, j. [Choice c is incorrect because it contains a space; Choice e is incorrect because the first character is a number; Choice f is incorrect because it contains a division symbol (**/**) and does not begin with a letter or underscore; Choice g is incorrect because it contains an asterisk (*****); Choice h is incorrect because the first character is a period (**.**) and does not begin with a letter or underscore.]

18.2   a) True. b) False. In an XML document, markup text is delimited by angle brackets (**<** and **>**), with a forward slash in the end tag. c) True. d) True. e) False. XML does support namespaces. f) False. When creating new tags, document authors can use any valid name except the reserved word **xml** (also **XML**, **Xml** etc.). g) False. XML reserved characters include the ampersand (**&**), the left-angle bracket (**<**) and the right-angle bracket (**>**), but not **#** and **$**.

18.3   a) namespaces. b) processing instructions. c) msxml. d) **xsl:output**. e) **Schema**. f) an operator (**mo**). g) **xsl:stylesheet**. h) **xsl:for-each**.

18.4   a) False. XML is case sensitive. b) True. c) False. DTDs use EBNF grammar which is not XML syntax. d) False. XPath is a technology for locating information in an XML document.

18.5
```
<date>
    <month>December</month>
    <day>6</day>
    <year>2001</year>
</date>.
```

18.6   `<?xsl:stylesheet type = "text/xsl" href = "wap.xsl"?>`

18.7   a) parent. b) sibling. c) root. d) **AppendChild**.

18.8   `/letter/contact`.

18.9   **Select** takes either an **XPathExpression** or a **string** argument containing an **XPathExpression** to select nodes referenced by the navigator.

EXERCISES

18.10   Create an XML document that marks up the nutrition facts for a package of cookies. A package of cookies has a serving size of 1 package and the following nutritional value per serving: 260 calories, 100 fat calories, 11 grams of fat, 2 grams of saturated fat, 5 milligrams of cholesterol, 210 milligrams of sodium, 36 grams of total carbohydrates, 2 grams of fiber, 15 grams of sugars and 5 grams of protein. Name this document **nutrition.xml**. Load the XML document into Internet Explorer [*Hint*: Your markup should contain elements describing the product name, serving size/amount, calories, sodium, cholesterol, proteins, etc. Mark up each nutrition fact/ingredient listed above.]

18.11   Write an XSLT style sheet for your solution to Exercise 18.10 that displays the nutritional facts in an XHTML table. Modify Fig. 18.25 (**TransformTest.cs**) to output an XHTML file, **nutrition.html**. Render **nutrition.html** in a Web browser.

18.12   Write a Microsoft Schema for Fig. 18.23.

18.13   Alter Fig. 18.20 (**ValidationTest.cs**) to include a list of Schemas in a drop-down box, along with the list of XML files. Allow the user to test for whether any XML file on the list satisfies a specific Schema. Use **books.xml**, **books.xsd**, **nutrition.xml**, **nutrition.xsd** and **fail.xml**.

18.14   Modify **XmlReaderTest** (Fig. 18.7) to display **letter.xml** (Fig. 18.3) in a **Tree-View**, instead of in a text box.

18.15   Modify Fig. 18.24 (**sorting.xsl**) to sort each section (i.e., frontmatter, chapters and appendices) by page number rather than by chapter number. Save the modified document as **sorting_byChapter.xsl**.

18.16   Modify **XmlTransform.cs** (Fig. 18.25) to take in **sorting.xml** (Fig. 18.23), **sorting.xsl** (Fig. 18.24) and **sorting_byChapter.xsl**, and print the XHTML document resulting from the transform of **sorting.xml** into two XHTML files, **sorting_byPage.html** and **sorting_byChapter.html**.

19

Database, SQL and ADO .NET

Objectives

- To understand the relational database model.
- To understand basic database queries using Structured Query Language (SQL).
- To use the classes and interfaces of namespace **System.Data** to manipulate databases.
- To understand and use ADO .NET's disconnected model.
- To use the classes and interfaces of namespace **System.Data.OleDb**.

It is a capital mistake to theorize before one has data.
Arthur Conan Doyle

Now go, write it before them in a table, and note it in a book, that it may be for the time to come for ever and ever.
The Holy Bible: The Old Testament

Let's look at the record.
Alfred Emanuel Smith

Get your facts first, and then you can distort them as much as you please.
Mark Twain

I like two kinds of men: domestic and foreign.
Mae West

19.1 Introduction

A *database* is an integrated collection of data. Many different strategies exist for organizing data in databases to facilitate easy access to and manipulation of the data. A *database management system* (*DBMS*) provides mechanisms for storing and organizing data in a manner that is consistent with the database's format. Database management systems enable programmers to access and store data without worrying about the internal representation of databases.

Today's most popular database systems are *relational databases*. Almost universally, relational databases use a language called *Structured Query Language* (*SQL*—pronounced as its individual letters or as "sequel") to perform *queries* (i.e., to request information that satisfies given criteria) and to manipulate data. [*Note*: The writing in this chapter assumes that SQL is pronounced as its individual letters. For this reason, we often precede SQL with the article "an," as in "an SQL database" or "an SQL statement."]

Some popular, enterprise-level relational database systems include Microsoft SQL Server, Oracle™, Sybase™, DB2™, Informix™ and MySQL™. This chapter presents examples using Microsoft Access—a relational database system that is packaged with Microsoft Office.

A programming language connects to, and interacts with, a relational database via an *interface*—software that facilitates communication between a database management system and a program. C# programmers communicate with databases and manipulate their data through *Microsoft ActiveX Data Objects™* (ADO), *ADO .NET*.

19.2 Relational Database Model

The *relational database model* is a logical representation of data that allows relationships among data to be considered without concern for the physical structure of the data. A relational database is composed of *tables*. Figure 19.1 illustrates an example table that might be used in a personnel system. The table name is **Employee**, and its primary purpose is to illustrate the specific attributes of various employees. A particular row of the table is called a *record* (or *row*). This table consists of six records. The **number** *field* (or *column*) of each record in the table is the *primary key* for referencing data in the table. A primary key is a field (or fields) in a table that contain(s) unique data—i.e, data that is not duplicated in other records of that table. This guarantees that each record can be identified by at least one distinct value. Examples of primary-key fields are columns that contain social security numbers, employee IDs and part numbers in an inventory system. The records of Fig. 19.1 are *ordered* by primary key. In this case, the records are listed in increasing order (they also could be listed in decreasing order).

Each column of the table represents a different field. Records normally are unique (by primary key) within a table, but particular field values might be duplicated in multiple records. For example, three different records in the **Employee** table's **Department** field contain the number 413.

number	name	department	salary	location
23603	Jones	413	1100	New Jersey
24568	Kerwin	413	2000	New Jersey
34589	Larson	642	1800	Los Angeles
35761	Myers	611	1400	Orlando
47132	Neumann	413	9000	New Jersey
78321	Stephens	611	8500	Orlando

Record/Row

Primary key   Field/Column

Fig. 19.1   Relational-database structure of an **Employee** table.

Often, different users of a database are interested in different data and different relationships among those data. Some users require only subsets of the table columns. To obtain table subsets, we use SQL statements to specify certain data we wish to *select* from a table. SQL provides a complete set of commands (including **SELECT**) that enable programmers to define complex *queries* to select data from a table. The results of a query commonly are called *result sets* (or *record sets*). For example, we might select data from the table in Fig. 19.1 to create a new result set containing only the location of each department. This result set appears in Fig. 19.2. SQL queries are discussed in detail in Section 19.4.

19.3 Relational Database Overview: Books Database

The next section provides an overview of SQL in the context of a sample **Books** database that we created for this chapter. However, before we discuss SQL, we must explain the various tables of the **Books** database. We use this database to introduce various database concepts, including the use of SQL to manipulate and obtain useful information from the database.

The database consists of four tables: **Authors**, **Publishers**, **AuthorISBN** and **Titles**. The **Authors** table (described in Fig. 19.3) consists of three fields (or columns) that maintain each author's unique ID number, first name and last name. Figure 19.4 contains the data from the **Authors** table of the **Books** database.

department	location
413	New Jersey
611	Orlando
642	Los Angeles

Fig. 19.2   Result set formed by selecting **Department** and **Location** data from the **Employee** table.

Field	Description
authorID	Author's ID number in the database. In the **Books** database, this **int** field is defined as an *auto-incremented field*. For each new record inserted in this table, the database increments the **authorID** value, ensuring that each record has a unique **authorID**. This field represents the table's primary key.
firstName	Author's first name (a **string**).
lastName	Author's last name (a **string**).

Fig. 19.3   **Authors** table from **Books**.

The **Publishers** table (described in Fig. 19.5) consists of two fields, representing each publisher's unique ID and name. Figure 19.6 contains the data from the **Publishers** table of the **Books** database.

The **AuthorISBN** table (described in Fig. 19.7) consists of two fields that maintain the authors' ID numbers and the corresponding ISBN numbers of their books. This table helps associate the names of the authors with the titles of their books. Figure 19.8 contains the data from the **AuthorISBN** table of the **Books** database. ISBN is an abbreviation for "International Standard Book Number"—a numbering scheme by which publishers worldwide assign every book a unique identification number. [*Note*: To save space, we have split the contents of this figure into two columns, each containing the **authorID** and **isbn** fields.

authorID	firstName	lastName
1	Harvey	Deitel
2	Paul	Deitel
3	Tem	Nieto
4	Kate	Steinbuhler
5	Sean	Santry
6	Ted	Lin
7	Praveen	Sadhu
8	David	McPhie
9	Cheryl	Yaeger
10	Marina	Zlatkina
11	Ben	Wiedermann
12	Jonathan	Liperi
13	Jeffrey	Listfield

Fig. 19.4 Data from the **Authors** table of **Books**.

Field	Description
publisherID	The publisher's ID number in the database. This auto-incremented **int** field is the table's primary-key field.
publisherName	The name of the publisher (a **string**).

Fig. 19.5 Publishers table from **Books**.

publisherID	publisherName
1	Prentice Hall
2	Prentice Hall PTG

Fig. 19.6   Data from the **Publishers** table of **Books**.

Field	Description
authorID	The author's ID number, which allows the database to associate each book with a specific author. The integer ID number in this field must also appear in the **Authors** table.
isbn	The ISBN number for a book (a **string**).

Fig. 19.7   **AuthorISBN** table from **Books**.

authorID	isbn	authorID	isbn
1	0130895725	2	0139163050
1	0132261197	2	013028419x
1	0130895717	2	0130161438
1	0135289106	2	0130856118
1	0139163050	2	0130125075
1	013028419x	2	0138993947
1	0130161438	2	0130852473
1	0130856118	2	0130829277
1	0130125075	2	0134569555
1	0138993947	2	0130829293
1	0130852473	2	0130284173
1	0130829277	2	0130284181
1	0134569555	2	0130895601
1	0130829293	3	013028419x
1	0130284173	3	0130161438
1	0130284181	3	0130856118
1	0130895601	3	0134569555
2	0130895725	3	0130829293
2	0132261197	3	0130284173
2	0130895717	3	0130284181
2	0135289106	4	0130895601

Fig. 19.8   Data from **AuthorISBN** table in **Books**.

The **Titles** table (described in Fig. 19.9) consists of seven fields that maintain general information about the books in the database. This information includes each book's ISBN number, title, edition number, copyright year and publisher's ID number, as well as the name of a file containing an image of the book cover and, finally, each book's price. Figure 19.10 contains the data from the **Titles** table.

Field	Description
isbn	ISBN number of the book (a **string**).
title	Title of the book (a **string**).
editionNumber	Edition number of the book (a **string**).
copyright	Copyright year of the book (an **int**).
publisherID	Publisher's ID number (an **int**). This value must correspond to an ID number in the **Publishers** table.
imageFile	Name of the file containing the book's cover image (a **string**).
price	Suggested retail price of the book (a real number). [*Note*: The prices shown in this database are for example purposes only.]

Fig. 19.9 Titles table from **Books**.

isbn	title	edition-Number	publish-erID	copy-right	imageFile	price
0130923613	Python How to Program	1	1	2002	**python.jpg**	$69.95
0130622214	C# How to Program	1	1	2002	**cshtp.jpg**	$69.95
0130341517	Java How to Program	4	1	2002	**jhtp4.jpg**	$69.95
0130649341	The Complete Java Training Course	4	2	2002	**javactc4.jpg**	$109.95
0130895601	Advanced Java 2 Platform How to Program	1	1	2002	**advjhtp1.jpg**	$69.95
0130308978	Internet and World Wide Web How to Program	2	1	2002	**iw3htp2.jpg**	$69.95
0130293636	Visual Basic .NET How to Program	2	1	2002	**vbnet.jpg**	$69.95
0130895636	The Complete C++ Training Course	3	2	2001	**cppctc3.jpg**	$109.95

Fig. 19.10 Data from the **Titles** table of **Books**. (Part 1 of 3.)

isbn	title	edition-Number	publish-erID	copy-right	imageFile	price
0130895512	The Complete e-Business & e-Commerce Programming Training Course	1	2	2001	ebecctc.jpg	$109.95
013089561X	The Complete Internet & World Wide Web Programming Training Course	2	2	2001	iw3ctc2.jpg	$109.95
0130895547	The Complete Perl Training Course	1	2	2001	perl.jpg	$109.95
0130895563	The Complete XML Programming Training Course	1	2	2001	xmlctc.jpg	$109.95
0130895725	C How to Program	3	1	2001	chtp3.jpg	$69.95
0130895717	C++ How to Program	3	1	2001	cpphtp3.jpg	$69.95
013028419X	e-Business and e-Commerce How to Program	1	1	2001	ebechtp1.jpg	$69.95
0130622265	Wireless Internet and Mobile Business How to Program	1	1	2001	wireless.jpg	$69.95
0130284181	Perl How to Program	1	1	2001	perlhtp1.jpg	$69.95
0130284173	XML How to Program	1	1	2001	xmlhtp1.jpg	$69.95
0130856118	The Complete Internet and World Wide Web Programming Training Course	1	2	2000	iw3ctc1.jpg	$109.95
0130125075	Java How to Program (Java 2)	3	1	2000	jhtp3.jpg	$69.95
0130852481	The Complete Java 2 Training Course	3	2	2000	javactc3.jpg	$109.95
0130323640	e-Business and e-Commerce for Managers	1	1	2000	ebecm.jpg	$69.95
0130161438	Internet and World Wide Web How to Program	1	1	2000	iw3htp1.jpg	$69.95

Fig. 19.10 Data from the **Titles** table of **Books**. (Part 2 of 3.)

isbn	title	edition-Number	publish-erID	copy-right	imageFile	price
0130132497	Getting Started with Visual C++ 6 with an Introduction to MFC	1	1	1999	gsvc.jpg	$49.95
0130829293	The Complete Visual Basic 6 Training Course	1	2	1999	vbctc1.jpg	$109.95
0134569555	Visual Basic 6 How to Program	1	1	1999	vbhtp1.jpg	$69.95
0132719746	Java Multimedia Cyber Classroom	1	2	1998	javactc.jpg	$109.95
0136325890	Java How to Program	1	1	1998	jhtp1.jpg	$69.95
0139163050	The Complete C++ Training Course	2	2	1998	cppctc2.jpg	$109.95
0135289106	C++ How to Program	2	1	1998	cpphtp2.jpg	$49.95
0137905696	The Complete Java Training Course	2	2	1998	javactc2.jpg	$109.95
0130829277	The Complete Java Training Course (Java 1.1)	2	2	1998	javactc2.jpg	$99.95
0138993947	Java How to Program (Java 1.1)	2	1	1998	jhtp2.jpg	$49.95
0131173340	C++ How to Program	1	1	1994	cpphtp1.jpg	$69.95
0132261197	C How to Program	2	1	1994	chtp2.jpg	$49.95
0131180436	C How to Program	1	1	1992	chtp.jpg	$69.95

Fig. 19.10 Data from the **Titles** table of **Books**. (Part 3 of 3.)

Figure 19.11 illustrates the relationships among the tables in the **Books** database. The first line in each table is the table's name. The field whose name appears in italics contains that table's primary key. A table's primary key uniquely identifies each record in the table. Every record must have a value in the primary-key field, and the value must be unique. This is known as the *Rule of Entity Integrity*. Note that the **AuthorISBN** table contains two fields whose names are italicized. This indicates that these two fields form a *compound primary key*—each record in the table must have a unique **authorID–isbn** combination. For example, several records might have an **authorID** of 2, and several records might have an **isbn** of 0130895601, but only one record can have both an **authorID** of 2 and an **isbn** of 0130895601.

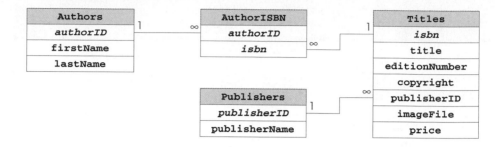

Fig. 19.11 Table relationships in **Books**.

Common Programming Error 19.1

Failure to provide a value for a primary-key field in every record breaks the Rule of Entity Integrity and causes the DBMS to report an error.

Common Programming Error 19.2

Providing duplicate values for the primary-key field of multiple records causes the DBMS to report an error.

The lines connecting the tables in Fig. 19.11 represent the *relationships* among the tables. Consider the line between the **Publishers** and **Titles** tables. On the **Publishers** end of the line, there is a **1**, and, on the **Titles** end, there is an infinity (∞) symbol. This line indicates a *one-to-many relationship*, in which every publisher in the **Publishers** table can have an arbitrarily large number of books in the **Titles** table. Note that the relationship line links the **publisherID** field in the **Publishers** table to the **publisherID** field in **Titles** table. In the **Titles** table, the **publisherID** field is a *foreign key*—a field for which every entry has a unique value in another table and where the field in the other table is the primary key for that table (e.g., **publisherID** in the **Publishers** table). Programmers specify foreign keys when creating a table. The foreign key helps maintain the *Rule of Referential Integrity*: Every foreign-key field value must appear in another table's primary-key field. Foreign keys enable information from multiple tables to be *joined* together for analysis purposes. There is a one-to-many relationship between a primary key and its corresponding foreign key. This means that a foreign-key field value can appear many times in its own table, but must appear exactly once as the primary key of another table. The line between the tables represents the link between the foreign key in one table and the primary key in another table.

Common Programming Error 19.3

Providing a foreign-key value that does not appear as a primary-key value in another table breaks the Rule of Referential Integrity and causes the DBMS to report an error.

The line between the **AuthorISBN** and **Authors** tables indicates that, for each author in the **Authors** table, the **AuthorISBN** table can contain an arbitrary number of ISBNs for books written by that author. The **authorID** field in the **AuthorISBN** table is a foreign key of the **authorID** field (the primary key) of the **Authors** table. Note, again, that the line between the tables links the foreign key in table **AuthorISBN** to the corresponding primary key in table **Authors**. The **AuthorISBN** table links information in the **Titles** and **Authors** tables.

The line between the **Titles** and **AuthorISBN** tables illustrates another one-to-many relationship; a title can be written by any number of authors. In fact, the sole purpose of the **AuthorISBN** table is to represent a many-to-many relationship between the **Authors** and **Titles** tables; an author can write any number of books, and a book can have any number of authors.

19.4 Structured Query Language (SQL)

In this section, we provide an overview of Structured Query Language (SQL) in the context of our **Books** sample database. The SQL queries discussed here form the foundation for the SQL used in the chapter examples.

Figure 19.12 lists SQL keywords and provides a description of each. In the next several subsections, we discuss these SQL keywords in the context of complete SQL queries. Other SQL keywords exist, but are beyond the scope of this text. [*Note*: To locate additional information on SQL, please refer to the bibliography at the end of this chapter.]

19.4.1 Basic SELECT Query

Let us consider several SQL queries that extract information from database **Books**. A typical SQL query "selects" information from one or more tables in a database. Such selections are performed by *SELECT queries*. The basic format for a **SELECT** query is:

    SELECT * FROM *tableName*

In this query, the asterisk (*****) indicates that all columns from the *tableName* table of the database should be selected. For example, to select the entire contents of the **Authors** table (i.e., all data depicted in Fig. 19.4), use the query:

    SELECT * FROM Authors

SQL keyword	Description
SELECT	Selects (retrieves) fields from one or more tables.
FROM	Specifies tables from which to get fields or delete records. Required in every **SELECT** and **DELETE** statement.
WHERE	Specifies criteria that determine the rows to be retrieved.
INNER JOIN	Joins records from multiple tables to produce a single set of records.
GROUP BY	Specifies criteria for grouping records.
ORDER BY	Specifies criteria for ordering records.
INSERT	Inserts data into a specified table.
UPDATE	Updates data in a specified table.
DELETE	Deletes data from a specified table.

Fig. 19.12 SQL query keywords.

To select specific fields from a table, replace the asterisk (*****) with a comma-separated list of the field names to select. For example, to select only the fields **authorID** and **lastName** for all rows in the **Authors** table, use the query:

```
SELECT authorID, lastName FROM Authors
```

This query returns only the data presented in Fig. 19.13. [*Note*: If a field name contains spaces, the entire field name must be enclosed in square brackets (**[]**) in the query. For example, if the field name is **first name**, it must appear in the query as **[first name]**.]

Common Programming Error 19.4

If a program assumes that an SQL statement using the asterisk (*) to select fields always returns those fields in the same order, the program could process the result set incorrectly. If the field order in the database table(s) changes, the order of the fields in the result set would change accordingly.

Performance Tip 19.1

If a program does not know the order of fields in a result set, the program must process the fields by name. This could require a linear search of the field names in the result set. If users specify the field names that they wish to select from a table (or several tables), the application receiving the result set knows the order of the fields in advance. When this occurs, the program can process the data more efficiently, because fields can be accessed directly by column number.

19.4.2 WHERE Clause

In most cases, users search a database for records that satisfy certain *selection criteria*. Only records that match the selection criteria are selected. SQL uses the optional ***WHERE*** clause in a **SELECT** query to specify the selection criteria for the query. The simplest format for a **SELECT** query that includes selection criteria is:

```
SELECT fieldName1, fieldName2, ... FROM tableName WHERE criteria
```

For example, to select the **title**, **editionNumber** and **copyright** fields from those rows of table **Titles** in which the **copyright** date is greater than **1999**, use the query:

authorID	lastName	authorID	lastName
1	Deitel	8	McPhie
2	Deitel	9	Yaeger
3	Nieto	10	Zlatkina
4	Steinbuhler	12	Wiedermann
5	Santry	12	Liperi
6	Lin	13	Listfield
7	Sadhu		

Fig. 19.13 **authorID** and **lastName** from the **Authors** table.

```
SELECT title, editionNumber, copyright
FROM Titles
WHERE copyright > 1999
```

Figure 19.14 shows the result set of the preceding query. [*Note*: When we construct a query for use in C#, we simply create a **string** containing the entire query. However, when we display queries in the text, we often use multiple lines and indentation to enhance readability.]

Performance Tip 19.2

Using selection criteria improves performance, because queries that involve such criteria normally select a portion of the database that is smaller than the entire database. Working with a smaller portion of the data is more efficient than working with the entire set of data stored in the database.

title	editionNumber	copyright
Internet and World Wide Web How to Program	2	2002
Java How to Program	4	2002
The Complete Java Training Course	4	2002
The Complete e-Business & e-Commerce Programming Training Course	1	2001
The Complete Internet & World Wide Web Programming Training Course	2	2001
The Complete Perl Training Course	1	2001
The Complete XML Programming Training Course	1	2001
C How to Program	3	2001
C++ How to Program	3	2001
The Complete C++ Training Course	3	2001
e-Business and e-Commerce How to Program	1	2001
Internet and World Wide Web How to Program	1	2000
The Complete Internet and World Wide Web Programming Training Course	1	2000
Java How to Program (Java 2)	3	2000
The Complete Java 2 Training Course	3	2000
XML How to Program	1	2001
Perl How to Program	1	2001
Advanced Java 2 Platform How to Program	1	2002
e-Business and e-Commerce for Managers	1	2000
Wireless Internet and Mobile Business How to Program	1	2001
C# How To Program	1	2002
Python How to Program	1	2002
Visual Basic .NET How to Program	2	2002

Fig. 19.14 Titles with copyrights after 1999 from table **Titles**.

The **WHERE** clause condition can contain operators **<**, **>**, **<=**, **>=**, **=**, **<>** and **LIKE**. Operator **LIKE** is used for *pattern matching* with wildcard characters *asterisk* (*****) and *question mark* (**?**). Pattern matching allows SQL to search for strings that "match a pattern."

A pattern that contains an asterisk (*****) searches for strings in which zero or more characters take the asterisk character's place in the pattern. For example, the following query locates the records of all authors whose last names start with the letter **D**:

```
SELECT authorID, firstName, lastName
FROM Authors
WHERE lastName LIKE 'D*'
```

The preceding query selects the two records shown in Fig. 19.15, because two of the authors in our database have last names that begin with the letter **D** (followed by zero or more characters). The ***** in the **WHERE** clause's **LIKE** pattern indicates that any number of characters can appear after the letter **D** in the **lastName** field. Notice that the pattern string is surrounded by single-quote characters.

Portability Tip 19.1

*Not all database systems support the **LIKE** operator, so be sure to read the database system's documentation carefully before employing this operator.*

Portability Tip 19.2

*Most databases use the **%** character in place of the ***** character in **LIKE** expressions.*

Portability Tip 19.3

In some databases, string data is case sensitive.

Portability Tip 19.4

In some databases, table names and field names are case sensitive.

Good Programming Practice 19.1

By convention, SQL keywords should be written entirely in uppercase letters on systems that are not case sensitive. This emphasizes the SQL keywords in an SQL statement.

A pattern string including a question mark (**?**) character searches for strings in which exactly one character takes the question mark's place in the pattern. For example, the following query locates the records of all authors whose last names start with any character (specified with **?**), followed by the letter **i**, followed by any number of additional characters (specified with *****):

authorID	firstName	lastName
1	Harvey	Deitel
2	Paul	Deitel

Fig. 19.15 Authors from the **Authors** table whose last names start with **D**.

```
SELECT authorID, firstName, lastName
FROM Authors
WHERE lastName LIKE '?i*'
```

The preceding query produces the records listed in Fig. 19.16; five authors in our database have last names in which the letter **i** is the second letter.

 Portability Tip 19.5

*Most databases use the _ character in place of the ? character in **LIKE** expressions.*

19.4.3 ORDER BY Clause

The results of a query can be arranged in ascending or descending order using the optional **ORDER BY** *clause*. The simplest forms for an **ORDER BY** clause are:

> **SELECT** *fieldName1*, *fieldName2*, ... **FROM** *tableName* **ORDER BY** *field* **ASC**
> **SELECT** *fieldName1*, *fieldName2*, ... **FROM** *tableName* **ORDER BY** *field* **DESC**

where **ASC** specifies ascending order (lowest to highest), **DESC** specifies descending order (highest to lowest) and *field* specifies the field whose values determine the sorting order.

For example, to obtain a list of authors arranged in ascending order by last name (Fig. 19.17), use the query:

```
SELECT authorID, firstName, lastName
FROM Authors
ORDER BY lastName ASC
```

Note that the default sorting order is ascending; therefore, **ASC** is optional.

authorID	firstName	lastName
3	Tem	Nieto
6	Ted	Lin
11	Ben	Wiedermann
12	Jonathan	Liperi
13	Jeffrey	Listfield

Fig. 19.16 Authors from table **Authors** whose last names contain **i** as the second letter.

authorID	firstName	lastName
2	Paul	Deitel
1	Harvey	Deitel

Fig. 19.17 Authors from table **Authors** in ascending order by **lastName**. (Part 1 of 2.)

authorID	firstName	lastName
6	Ted	Lin
12	Jonathan	Liperi
13	Jeffrey	Listfield
8	David	McPhie
3	Tem	Nieto
7	Praveen	Sadhu
5	Sean	Santry
4	Kate	Steinbuhler
11	Ben	Wiedermann
9	Cheryl	Yaeger
10	Marina	Zlatkina

Fig. 19.17 Authors from table **Authors** in ascending order by **lastName**. (Part 2 of 2.)

To obtain the same list of authors arranged in descending order by last name (Fig. 19.18), use the query:

```
SELECT authorID, firstName, lastName
FROM Authors
ORDER BY lastName DESC
```

authorID	firstName	lastName
10	Marina	Zlatkina
9	Cheryl	Yaeger
11	Ben	Wiedermann
4	Kate	Steinbuhler
5	Sean	Santry
7	Praveen	Sadhu
3	Tem	Nieto
8	David	McPhie
13	Jeffrey	Listfield
12	Jonathan	Liperi
6	Ted	Lin
2	Paul	Deitel
1	Harvey	Deitel

Fig. 19.18 Authors from table **Authors** in descending order by **lastName**.

The **ORDER BY** clause also can be used to order records by multiple fields. Such queries are written in the form:

> ORDER BY *field1 sortingOrder, field2 sortingOrder,* ...

where *sortingOrder* is either **ASC** or **DESC**. Note that the *sortingOrder* does not have to be identical for each field.

For example, the query:

```
SELECT authorID, firstName, lastName
FROM Authors
ORDER BY lastName, firstName
```

sorts all authors in ascending order by last name, then by first name. This means that, if any authors have the same last name, their records are returned sorted by first name (Fig. 19.19).

The **WHERE** and **ORDER BY** clauses can be combined in one query. For example, the query:

```
SELECT isbn, title, editionNumber, copyright, price
FROM Titles
WHERE title
LIKE '*How to Program' ORDER BY title ASC
```

returns the ISBN, title, edition number, copyright and price of each book in the **Titles** table that has a **title** ending with "**How to Program**"; it lists these records in ascending order by **title**. The results of the query are depicted in Fig. 19.20.

authorID	firstName	lastName
1	Harvey	Deitel
2	Paul	Deitel
6	Ted	Lin
12	Jonathan	Liperi
13	Jeffrey	Listfield
8	David	McPhie
3	Tem	Nieto
7	Praveen	Sadhu
5	Sean	Santry
4	Kate	Steinbuhler
11	Ben	Wiedermann
9	Cheryl	Yaeger
10	Marina	Zlatkina

Fig. 19.19 Authors from table **Authors** in ascending order by **lastName** and by **firstName**.

isbn	title	edition-Number	copy-right	price
0130895601	Advanced Java 2 Platform How to Program	1	2002	$69.95
0131180436	C How to Program	1	1992	$69.95
0130895725	C How to Program	3	2001	$69.95
0132261197	C How to Program	2	1994	$49.95
0130622214	C# How To Program	1	2002	$69.95
0135289106	C++ How to Program	2	1998	$49.95
0131173340	C++ How to Program	1	1994	$69.95
0130895717	C++ How to Program	3	2001	$69.95
013028419X	e-Business and e-Commerce How to Program	1	2001	$69.95
0130308978	Internet and World Wide Web How to Program	2	2002	$69.95
0130161438	Internet and World Wide Web How to Program	1	2000	$69.95
0130341517	Java How to Program	4	2002	$69.95
0136325890	Java How to Program	1	1998	$49.95
0130284181	Perl How to Program	1	2001	$69.95
0130923613	Python How to Program	1	2002	$69.95
0130293636	Visual Basic .NET How to Program	2	2002	$69.95
0134569555	Visual Basic 6 How to Program	1	1999	$69.95
0130622265	Wireless Internet and Mobile Business How to Program	1	2001	$69.95
0130284173	XML How to Program	1	2001	$69.95

Fig. 19.20 Books from table **Titles** whose titles end with **How to Program** in ascending order by **title**.

19.4.4 Merging Data from Multiple Tables: INNER JOIN

Database designers often split related data into separate tables to ensure that a database does not store data redundantly. For example, the **Books** database has tables **Authors** and **Titles**. We use an **AuthorISBN** table to provide "links" between authors and their corresponding titles. If we did not separate this information into individual tables, we would need to include author information with each entry in the **Titles** table. This would result in the database storing duplicate author information for authors who wrote multiple books.

Often, it is necessary for analysis purposes to merge data from multiple tables into a single set of data. Referred to as *joining* the tables, this is accomplished via an **INNER JOIN** operation in the **SELECT** query. An **INNER JOIN** merges records from two or more tables by testing for matching values in a field that is common to the tables. The simplest format for an **INNER JOIN** clause is:

```
SELECT fieldName1, fieldName2, ...
FROM table1
INNER JOIN table2
    ON table1.fieldName = table2.fieldName
```

The **ON** part of the **INNER JOIN** clause specifies the fields from each table that are compared to determine which records are joined. For example, the following query produces a list of authors accompanied by the ISBN numbers for books written by each author:

```
SELECT firstName, lastName, isbn
FROM Authors
INNER JOIN AuthorISBN
    ON Authors.authorID = AuthorISBN.authorID
ORDER BY lastName, firstName
```

The query merges the **firstName** and **lastName** fields from table **Authors** with the **isbn** field from table **AuthorISBN**, sorting the results in ascending order by **lastName** and **firstName**. Notice the use of the syntax *tableName.fieldName* in the **ON** part of the **INNER JOIN**. This syntax (called a *fully qualified name*) specifies the fields from each table that should be compared to join the tables. The "*tableName.*" syntax is required if the fields have the same name in both tables. The same syntax can be used in any query to distinguish among fields in different tables that have the same name. Fully qualified names that start with the database name can be used to perform cross-database queries.

Software Engineering Observation 19.1

*If an SQL statement includes fields from multiple tables that have the same name, the statement must precede those field names with their table names and the dot operator (e.g., **Authors.authorID**).*

Common Programming Error 19.5

In a query, failure to provide fully qualified names for fields that have the same name in two or more tables is an error.

As always, the query can contain an **ORDER BY** clause. Figure 19.21 depicts the results of the preceding query, ordered by **lastName** and **firstName**. [*Note:* To save space, we split the results of the query into two columns, each containing the **firstName**, **lastName** and **isbn** fields.]

firstName	lastName	isbn	firstName	lastName	isbn
Harvey	Deitel	0130895601	Harvey	Deitel	0130829293
Harvey	Deitel	0130284181	Harvey	Deitel	0134569555
Harvey	Deitel	0130284173	Harvey	Deitel	0130829277

Fig. 19.21 Authors from table **Authors** and ISBN numbers of the authors' books, sorted in ascending order by **lastName** and **firstName**. (Part 1 of 2.)

firstName	lastName	isbn	firstName	lastName	isbn
Harvey	Deitel	0130852473	Paul	Deitel	0130125075
Harvey	Deitel	0138993947	Paul	Deitel	0130856118
Harvey	Deitel	0130856118	Paul	Deitel	0130161438
Harvey	Deitel	0130161438	Paul	Deitel	013028419x
Harvey	Deitel	013028419x	Paul	Deitel	0139163050
Harvey	Deitel	0139163050	Paul	Deitel	0130895601
Harvey	Deitel	0135289106	Paul	Deitel	0135289106
Harvey	Deitel	0130895717	Paul	Deitel	0130895717
Harvey	Deitel	0132261197	Paul	Deitel	0132261197
Harvey	Deitel	0130895725	Paul	Deitel	0130895725
Harvey	Deitel	0130125075	Tem	Nieto	0130284181
Paul	Deitel	0130284181	Tem	Nieto	0130284173
Paul	Deitel	0130284173	Tem	Nieto	0130829293
Paul	Deitel	0130829293	Tem	Nieto	0134569555
Paul	Deitel	0134569555	Tem	Nieto	0130856118
Paul	Deitel	0130829277	Tem	Nieto	0130161438
Paul	Deitel	0130852473	Tem	Nieto	013028419x
Paul	Deitel	0138993947			

Fig. 19.21 Authors from table **Authors** and ISBN numbers of the authors' books, sorted in ascending order by **lastName** and **firstName**. (Part 2 of 2.)

19.4.5 Joining Data from Tables Authors, AuthorISBN, Titles and Publishers

The **Books** database contains one predefined query (**TitleAuthor**), which selects as its results the title, ISBN number, author's first name, author's last name, copyright year and publisher's name for each book in the database. For books that have multiple authors, the query produces a separate composite record for each author. The **TitleAuthor** query is depicted in Fig. 19.22. Figure 19.23 contains a portion of the query results.

```
1   SELECT Titles.title, Titles.isbn, Authors.firstName,
2      Authors.lastName, Titles.copyright,
3         Publishers.publisherName
4   FROM
5   ( Publishers INNER JOIN Titles
6      ON Publishers.publisherID = Titles.publisherID )
7      INNER JOIN
```

Fig. 19.22 **TitleAuthor** query of **Books** database. (Part 1 of 2.)

```
8        ( Authors INNER JOIN AuthorISBN
9          ON Authors.authorID = AuthorISBN.authorID )
10    ON Titles.isbn = AuthorISBN.isbn
11ORDER BY Titles.title
```

Fig. 19.22 **TitleAuthor** query of **Books** database. (Part 2 of 2.)

Title	isbn	first-Name	last-Name	copy-right	publisher-Name
Advanced Java 2 Platform How to Program	0130895601	Paul	Deitel	2002	Prentice Hall
Advanced Java 2 Platform How to Program	0130895601	Harvey	Deitel	2002	Prentice Hall
Advanced Java 2 Platform How to Program	0130895601	Sean	Santry	2002	Prentice Hall
C How to Program	0131180436	Harvey	Deitel	1992	Prentice Hall
C How to Program	0131180436	Paul	Deitel	1992	Prentice Hall
C How to Program	0132261197	Harvey	Deitel	1994	Prentice Hall
C How to Program	0132261197	Paul	Deitel	1994	Prentice Hall
C How to Program	0130895725	Harvey	Deitel	2001	Prentice Hall
C How to Program	0130895725	Paul	Deitel	2001	Prentice Hall
C# How To Program	0130622214	Tem	Nieto	2002	Prentice Hall
C# How To Program	0130622214	Paul	Deitel	2002	Prentice Hall
C# How To Program	0130622214	Jeffrey	Listfield	2002	Prentice Hall
C# How To Program	0130622214	Cheryl	Yaeger	2002	Prentice Hall
C# How To Program	0130622214	Marina	Zlatkina	2002	Prentice Hall
C# How To Program	0130622214	Harvey	Deitel	2002	Prentice Hall
C++ How to Program	0130895717	Paul	Deitel	2001	Prentice Hall
C++ How to Program	0130895717	Harvey	Deitel	2001	Prentice Hall
C++ How to Program	0131173340	Paul	Deitel	1994	Prentice Hall
C++ How to Program	0131173340	Harvey	Deitel	1994	Prentice Hall
C++ How to Program	0135289106	Harvey	Deitel	1998	Prentice Hall
C++ How to Program	0135289106	Paul	Deitel	1998	Prentice Hall
e-Business and e-Commerce for Managers	0130323640	Harvey	Deitel	2000	Prentice Hall
e-Business and e-Commerce for Managers	0130323640	Kate	Stein-buhler	2000	Prentice Hall

Fig. 19.23 Portion of the result set produced by the query in Fig. 19.22. (Part 1 of 2.)

Title	isbn	first-Name	last-Name	copy-right	publisher-Name
e-Business and e-Commerce for Managers	0130323640	Paul	Deitel	2000	Prentice Hall
e-Business and e-Commerce How to Program	013028419X	Harvey	Deitel	2001	Prentice Hall
e-Business and e-Commerce How to Program	013028419X	Paul	Deitel	2001	Prentice Hall
e-Business and e-Commerce How to Program	013028419X	Tem	Nieto	2001	Prentice Hall

Fig. 19.23 Portion of the result set produced by the query in Fig. 19.22. (Part 2 of 2.)

We added indentation to the query in Fig. 19.22 to make the query more readable. Let us now break down the query into its various parts. Lines 1–3 contain a comma-separated list of the fields that the query returns; the order of the fields from left to right specifies the fields' order in the returned table. This query selects fields **title** and **isbn** from table **Titles**, fields **firstName** and **lastName** from table **Authors**, field **copyright** from table **Titles** and field **publisherName** from table **Publishers**. For purposes of clarity, we fully qualified each field name with its table name (e.g., **Titles.isbn**).

Lines 5–10 specify the **INNER JOIN** operations used to combine information from the various tables. There are three **INNER JOIN** operations. It is important to note that, although an **INNER JOIN** is performed on two tables, either of those two tables can be the result of another query or another **INNER JOIN**. We use parentheses to nest the **INNER JOIN** operations; SQL evaluates the innermost set of parentheses first and then moves outward. We begin with the **INNER JOIN**:

```
( Publishers INNER JOIN Titles
    ON Publishers.publisherID = Titles.publisherID )
```

which joins the **Publishers** table and the **Titles** table **ON** the condition that the **publisherID** numbers in each table match. The resulting temporary table contains information about each book and its publisher.

The other nested set of parentheses contains the **INNER JOIN**:

```
( Authors INNER JOIN AuthorISBN ON
    Authors.AuthorID = AuthorISBN.AuthorID )
```

which joins the **Authors** table and the **AuthorISBN** table **ON** the condition that the **authorID** fields in each table match. Remember that the **AuthorISBN** table has multiple entries for **ISBN** numbers of books that have more than one author. The third **INNER JOIN**:

```
( Publishers INNER JOIN Titles
    ON Publishers.publisherID = Titles.publisherID )
INNER JOIN
( Authors INNER JOIN AuthorISBN
    ON Authors.authorID = AuthorISBN.authorID )
ON Titles.isbn = AuthorISBN.isbn
```

joins the two temporary tables produced by the two prior inner joins **ON** the condition that the **Titles.isbn** field for each record in the first temporary table matches the corresponding **AuthorISBN.isbn** field for each record in the second temporary table. The result of all these **INNER JOIN** operations is a temporary table from which the appropriate fields are selected to produce the results of the query.

Finally, line 11 of the query:

```
ORDER BY Titles.title
```

indicates that all the records should be sorted in ascending order (the default) by title.

19.4.6 INSERT Statement

The *INSERT* statement inserts a new record in a table. The simplest form for this statement is:

```
INSERT INTO tableName ( fieldName1, fieldName2, ..., fieldNameN )
    VALUES ( value1, value2, ..., valueN )
```

where *tableName* is the table in which to insert the record. The *tableName* is followed by a comma-separated list of field names in parentheses. The list of field names is followed by the SQL keyword **VALUES** and a comma-separated list of values in parentheses. The specified values in this list must match the field names listed after the table name in both order and type (for example, if *fieldName1* is specified as the **firstName** field, then *value1* should be a string in single quotes representing the first name). The **INSERT** statement:

```
INSERT INTO Authors ( firstName, lastName )
    VALUES ( 'Sue', 'Smith' )
```

inserts a record into the **Authors** table. The first comma-separated list indicates that the statement provides data for the **firstName** and **lastName** fields. The corresponding values to insert, which are contained in the second comma-separated list, are **'Sue'** and **'Smith'**. We do not specify an **authorID** in this example, because **authorID** is an auto-increment field in the database. Every new record that we add to this table is assigned a unique **authorID** value that is the next value in the auto-increment sequence (i.e., 1, 2, 3, etc.). In this case, **Sue Smith** would be assigned **authorID** number 14. Figure 19.24 shows the **Authors** table after we perform the **INSERT** operation.

authorID	firstName	lastName
1	Harvey	Deitel
2	Paul	Deitel
3	Tem	Nieto
4	Kate	Steinbuhler
5	Sean	Santry
6	Ted	Lin
7	Praveen	Sadhu

Fig. 19.24 Authors after an **INSERT** operation to add a record. (Part 1 of 2.)

authorID	firstName	lastName
8	David	McPhie
9	Cheryl	Yaeger
10	Marina	Zlatkina
11	Ben	Wiedermann
12	Jonathan	Liperi
13	Jeffrey	Listfield
14	Sue	Smith

Fig. 19.24 Authors after an **INSERT** operation to add a record. (Part 2 of 2.)

Common Programming Error 19.6

SQL statements use the single-quote (') character as a delimiter for strings. To specify a string containing a single quote (such as O'Malley) in an SQL statement, the string must include two single quotes in the position where the single-quote character should appear in the string (e.g., **'O''Malley'** *). The first of the two single-quote characters acts as an escape character for the second. Failure to escape single-quote characters in a string that is part of an SQL statement is an SQL syntax error.*

19.4.7 UPDATE Statement

An **UPDATE** statement modifies data in a table. The simplest form for an **UPDATE** statement is:

```
UPDATE tableName
    SET fieldName1 = value1, fieldName2 = value2, ..., fieldNameN = valueN
    WHERE criteria
```

where *tableName* is the table in which to update a record (or records). The *tableName* is followed by keyword **SET** and a comma-separated list of field name/value pairs written in the format, *fieldName = value*. The **WHERE** clause specifies the criteria used to determine which record(s) to update. For example, the **UPDATE** statement:

```
UPDATE Authors
    SET lastName = 'Jones'
    WHERE lastName = 'Smith' AND firstName = 'Sue'
```

updates a record in the **Authors** table. The statement indicates that **lastName** will be assigned the new value **Jones** for the record in which **lastName** currently is equal to **Smith** and **firstName** is equal to **Sue**. If we know the **authorID** in advance of the **UPDATE** operation (possibly because we searched for the record previously), the **WHERE** clause could be simplified as follows:

```
WHERE AuthorID = 14
```

Figure 19.25 depicts the **Authors** table after we perform the **UPDATE** operation.

authorID	firstName	lastName
1	Harvey	Deitel
2	Paul	Deitel
3	Tem	Nieto
4	Kate	Steinbuhler
5	Sean	Santry
6	Ted	Lin
7	Praveen	Sadhu
8	David	McPhie
9	Cheryl	Yaeger
10	Marina	Zlatkina
11	Ben	Wiedermann
12	Jonathan	Liperi
13	Jeffrey	Listfield
14	Sue	Jones

Fig. 19.25 Table **Authors** after an **UPDATE** operation to change a record.

Common Programming Error 19.7

*Failure to use a **WHERE** clause with an **UPDATE** statement could lead to logic errors.*

19.4.8 DELETE Statement

An SQL **DELETE** statement removes data from a table. The simplest form for a **DELETE** statement is:

```
DELETE FROM tableName WHERE criteria
```

where *tableName* is the table from which to delete a record (or records). The **WHERE** clause specifies the criteria used to determine which record(s) to delete. For example, the **DELETE** statement:

```
DELETE FROM Authors
    WHERE lastName = 'Jones' AND firstName = 'Sue'
```

deletes the record for **Sue Jones** from the **Authors** table.

Common Programming Error 19.8

***WHERE** clauses can match multiple records. When deleting records from a database, be sure to define a **WHERE** clause that matches only the records to be deleted.*

Figure 19.26 depicts the **Authors** table after we perform the **DELETE** operation.

authorID	firstName	lastName
1	Harvey	Deitel
2	Paul	Deitel
3	Tem	Nieto
4	Kate	Steinbuhler
5	Sean	Santry
6	Ted	Lin
7	Praveen	Sadhu
8	David	McPhie
9	Cheryl	Yaeger
10	Marina	Zlatkina
11	Ben	Wiedermann
12	Jonathan	Liperi
13	Jeffrey	Listfield

Fig. 19.26 Table **Authors** after a **DELETE** operation to remove a record.

19.5 ADO .NET Object Model

The ADO .NET object model provides an API for accessing database systems programmatically. ADO .NET was created for the .NET Framework and is the next generation of *ActiveX Data Objects™* (ADO).

Namespace ***System.Data*** is the root namespace for the ADO .NET API. The primary namespaces for ADO .NET, ***System.Data.OleDb*** and ***System.Data.SqlClient***, contain classes that enable programs to connect with and modify datasources. Namespace **System.Data.OleDb** contains classes that are designed to work with any datasource, whereas the **System.Data.SqlClient** namespace contains classes that are optimized to work with Microsoft SQL Server 2000 databases.

Instances of class ***System.Data.DataSet***, which consist of a set of **DataTable**s and relationships among those **DataTable**s, represent *caches* of data—data that a program stores temporarily in local memory. The structure of a **DataSet** mimics the structure of a relational database. An advantage of using class **DataSet** is that it is *disconnected*—the program does not need a persistent connection to the datasource to work with data in a **DataSet**. The program connects to the datasource only during the initial population of the **DataSet** and then to store any changes made in the **DataSet**. Hence, the program does not require any active, permanent connection to the datasource.

Instances of class ***OleDbConnection*** (namespace **System.Data.OleDb**) represent connections to a datasource. An instance of class ***OleDbDataAdapter*** connects to a datasource through an instance of class **OleDbConnection** and can populate a **DataSet** with data from that datasource. We discuss the details of creating and populating **DataSet**s later in this chapter. An instance of class ***OleDbCommand*** (namespace **System.Data.OleDb**) represents an arbitrary SQL command to be executed on a datasource. A program can use instances of class **OleDbCommand** to manipulate a datasource through an **OleDbConnection**. The programmer must close the active connection to the datasource explicitly once no further changes are to be made. Unlike **DataSet**s, **OleDbCommand** objects do not cache data in local memory.

19.6 Programming with ADO .NET: Extracting Information from a Database

In this section, we present two examples that introduce how to connect to a database, query the database and display the results of the query. The database used in these examples is the Microsoft Access **Books** database that we have discussed throughout this chapter. It can be found in the project directory for the application of Fig. 19.27. Each program must specify the location of this database on the computer's hard drive. When executing these examples, readers must update this location for each program. For example, before readers can run the application in Fig. 19.27 on their computers, they must change lines 234–247 so that the code specifies the correct location of the database file.

19.6.1 Connecting to and Querying an Access Data Source

The first example (Fig. 19.27) performs a simple query on the **Books** database that retrieves the entire **Authors** table and displays the data in a *DataGrid* (a **System.Windows.Forms** component class that can display a datasource in a GUI). The program illustrates the process of connecting to the database, querying the database and displaying the results in a **DataGrid**. The discussion following the example presents the key aspects of the program. [*Note*: We present all of Visual Studio's auto-generated code in Fig. 19.27 so that readers are aware of the code that Visual Studio generates for the example.]

This example uses an Access database. To register the **Books** database as a datasource, select **View > Server Explorer**. Right click the **Data Connections** node in the **Server Explorer** and then double click **Add Connection....** In the **Provider** tab of the window that appears, choose "**Microsoft Jet 4.0 OLE DB Provider**," which is the driver for Access databases. In the **Connection** tab, click the ellipses button (**...**) to the right of the textbox for the database name, which opens the **Select Access Database** window. Go to the appropriate folder, select the **Books** database and click **OK**. Now, this database is listed as a connection in the **Server Explorer**. Drag the database node onto the Windows Form. This creates an **OleDbConnection** to the source, which the Windows Form designer displays as **oleDbConnection1**.

```
1   // Fig. 19.27: TableDisplay.cs
2   // Displays data from a database table.
3
4   using System;
5   using System.Drawing;
6   using System.Collections;
7   using System.ComponentModel;
8   using System.Windows.Forms;
9   using System.Data;
```

Fig. 19.27 Accessing and displaying a database's data. (Part 1 of 7.)

```
10
11    // Summary description for TableDisplay.cs.
12    public class TableDisplay : System.Windows.Forms.Form
13    {
14        private System.Data.DataSet dataSet1;
15        private System.Data.OleDb.OleDbDataAdapter oleDbDataAdapter1;
16        private System.Windows.Forms.DataGrid dataGrid1;
17        private System.Data.OleDb.OleDbCommand oleDbSelectCommand1;
18        private System.Data.OleDb.OleDbCommand oleDbInsertCommand1;
19        private System.Data.OleDb.OleDbCommand oleDbUpdateCommand1;
20        private System.Data.OleDb.OleDbCommand oleDbDeleteCommand1;
21        private System.Data.OleDb.OleDbConnection oleDbConnection1;
22
23        private System.ComponentModel.Container components = null;
24
25        public TableDisplay()
26        {
27            InitializeComponent();
28
29            // Fill dataSet1 with data
30            oleDbDataAdapter1.Fill( dataSet1, "Authors" );
31
32            // bind data in Authors table in dataSet1 to dataGrid1
33            dataGrid1.SetDataBinding( dataSet1, "Authors" );
34        }
35
36        private void InitializeComponent()
37        {
38            this.dataSet1 = new System.Data.DataSet();
39            this.oleDbDataAdapter1 =
40                new System.Data.OleDb.OleDbDataAdapter();
41            this.dataGrid1 = new System.Windows.Forms.DataGrid();
42            this.oleDbSelectCommand1 =
43                new System.Data.OleDb.OleDbCommand();
44            this.oleDbInsertCommand1 =
45                new System.Data.OleDb.OleDbCommand();
46            this.oleDbUpdateCommand1 =
47                new System.Data.OleDb.OleDbCommand();
48            this.oleDbDeleteCommand1 =
49                new System.Data.OleDb.OleDbCommand();
50            this.oleDbConnection1 =
51                new System.Data.OleDb.OleDbConnection();
52            ((System.ComponentModel.ISupportInitialize)
53                (this.dataSet1)).BeginInit();
54            ((System.ComponentModel.ISupportInitialize)
55                (this.dataGrid1)).BeginInit();
56            this.SuspendLayout();
57            //
58            // dataSet1
59            //
60            this.dataSet1.DataSetName = "NewDataSet";
61            this.dataSet1.Locale =
62                new System.Globalization.CultureInfo("en-US");
```

Fig. 19.27 Accessing and displaying a database's data. (Part 2 of 7.)

```
63              //
64              // oleDbDataAdapter1
65              //
66              this.oleDbDataAdapter1.DeleteCommand =
67                 this.oleDbDeleteCommand1;
68              this.oleDbDataAdapter1.InsertCommand =
69                 this.oleDbInsertCommand1;
70              this.oleDbDataAdapter1.SelectCommand =
71                 this.oleDbSelectCommand1;
72              this.oleDbDataAdapter1.TableMappings.AddRange(
73                 new System.Data.Common.DataTableMapping[] {
74                    new System.Data.Common.DataTableMapping(
75                       "Table", "Authors",
76                       new System.Data.Common.DataColumnMapping[] {
77                          new System.Data.Common.DataColumnMapping(
78                             "authorID", "authorID"),
79                          new System.Data.Common.DataColumnMapping(
80                             "firstName", "firstName"),
81                          new System.Data.Common.DataColumnMapping(
82                             "lastName", "lastName")})});
83              this.oleDbDataAdapter1.UpdateCommand =
84                 this.oleDbUpdateCommand1;
85              //
86              // dataGrid1
87              //
88              this.dataGrid1.DataMember = "";
89              this.dataGrid1.HeaderForeColor =
90                 System.Drawing.SystemColors.ControlText;
91              this.dataGrid1.Location =
92                 new System.Drawing.Point(16, 16);
93              this.dataGrid1.Name = "dataGrid1";
94              this.dataGrid1.Size = new System.Drawing.Size(264, 248);
95              this.dataGrid1.TabIndex = 0;
96              //
97              // oleDbSelectCommand1
98              //
99              this.oleDbSelectCommand1.CommandText =
100                "SELECT authorID, firstName, lastName FROM Authors";
101             this.oleDbSelectCommand1.Connection =
102                this.oleDbConnection1;
103             //
104             // oleDbInsertCommand1
105             //
106             this.oleDbInsertCommand1.CommandText =
107                "INSERT INTO Authors(firstName, lastName) VALUES " +
108                "(?, ?)";
109             this.oleDbInsertCommand1.Connection =
110                this.oleDbConnection1;
111             this.oleDbInsertCommand1.Parameters.Add(
112                new System.Data.OleDb.OleDbParameter("firstName",
113                   System.Data.OleDb.OleDbType.VarWChar, 50,
114                   "firstName"));
```

Fig. 19.27 Accessing and displaying a database's data. (Part 3 of 7.)

```
115            this.oleDbInsertCommand1.Parameters.Add(
116               new System.Data.OleDb.OleDbParameter("lastName",
117                  System.Data.OleDb.OleDbType.VarWChar, 50,
118                  "lastName"));
119            //
120            // oleDbUpdateCommand1
121            //
122            this.oleDbUpdateCommand1.CommandText =
123               "UPDATE Authors SET firstName = ?, lastName = ? WHERE" +
124               " (authorID = ?) AND (firstNam" +
125               "e = ? OR ? IS NULL AND firstName IS NULL) AND " +
126               "(lastName = ? OR ? IS NULL AND las" +
127               "tName IS NULL)";
128            this.oleDbUpdateCommand1.Connection =
129               this.oleDbConnection1;
130            this.oleDbUpdateCommand1.Parameters.Add(
131               new System.Data.OleDb.OleDbParameter(
132                  "firstName",
133                  System.Data.OleDb.OleDbType.VarWChar,
134                  50, "firstName"));
135            this.oleDbUpdateCommand1.Parameters.Add(
136               new System.Data.OleDb.OleDbParameter(
137                  "lastName",
138                  System.Data.OleDb.OleDbType.VarWChar, 50,
139                  "lastName"));
140            this.oleDbUpdateCommand1.Parameters.Add(
141               new System.Data.OleDb.OleDbParameter(
142                  "Original_authorID",
143                  System.Data.OleDb.OleDbType.Integer, 0,
144                  System.Data.ParameterDirection.Input, false,
145                  ((System.Byte)(10)), ((System.Byte)(0)),
146                  "authorID", System.Data.DataRowVersion.Original,
147                  null));
148            this.oleDbUpdateCommand1.Parameters.Add(
149               new System.Data.OleDb.OleDbParameter(
150                  "Original_firstName",
151                  System.Data.OleDb.OleDbType.VarWChar, 50,
152                  System.Data.ParameterDirection.Input, false,
153                  ((System.Byte)(0)), ((System.Byte)(0)),
154                  "firstName", System.Data.DataRowVersion.Original,
155                  null));
156            this.oleDbUpdateCommand1.Parameters.Add(
157               new System.Data.OleDb.OleDbParameter(
158                  "Original_firstName1",
159                  System.Data.OleDb.OleDbType.VarWChar, 50,
160                  System.Data.ParameterDirection.Input, false,
161                  ((System.Byte)(0)), ((System.Byte)(0)),
162                  "firstName", System.Data.DataRowVersion.Original,
163                  null));
164            this.oleDbUpdateCommand1.Parameters.Add(
165               new System.Data.OleDb.OleDbParameter(
166                  "Original_lastName",
167                  System.Data.OleDb.OleDbType.VarWChar, 50,
```

Fig. 19.27 Accessing and displaying a database's data. (Part 4 of 7.)

```
168              System.Data.ParameterDirection.Input, false,
169              ((System.Byte)(0)), ((System.Byte)(0)),
170              "lastName", System.Data.DataRowVersion.Original,
171              null));
172        this.oleDbUpdateCommand1.Parameters.Add(
173           new System.Data.OleDb.OleDbParameter(
174              "Original_lastName1",
175              System.Data.OleDb.OleDbType.VarWChar, 50,
176              System.Data.ParameterDirection.Input, false,
177              ((System.Byte)(0)), ((System.Byte)(0)),
178              "lastName", System.Data.DataRowVersion.Original,
179              null));
180        //
181        // oleDbDeleteCommand1
182        //
183        this.oleDbDeleteCommand1.CommandText =
184           "DELETE FROM Authors WHERE (authorID = ?) AND " +
185           "(firstName = ? OR ? IS NULL AND firs" +
186           "tName IS NULL) AND (lastName = ? OR ? IS NULL AND " +
187           "lastName IS NULL)";
188        this.oleDbDeleteCommand1.Connection =
189           this.oleDbConnection1;
190        this.oleDbDeleteCommand1.Parameters.Add(
191           new System.Data.OleDb.OleDbParameter(
192              "Original_authorID",
193              System.Data.OleDb.OleDbType.Integer, 0,
194              System.Data.ParameterDirection.Input, false,
195              ((System.Byte)(10)), ((System.Byte)(0)),
196              "authorID", System.Data.DataRowVersion.Original,
197              null));
198        this.oleDbDeleteCommand1.Parameters.Add(
199           new System.Data.OleDb.OleDbParameter(
200              "Original_firstName",
201              System.Data.OleDb.OleDbType.VarWChar, 50,
202              System.Data.ParameterDirection.Input, false,
203              ((System.Byte)(0)), ((System.Byte)(0)),
204              "firstName", System.Data.DataRowVersion.Original,
205              null));
206        this.oleDbDeleteCommand1.Parameters.Add(
207           new System.Data.OleDb.OleDbParameter(
208              "Original_firstName1",
209              System.Data.OleDb.OleDbType.VarWChar, 50,
210              System.Data.ParameterDirection.Input, false,
211              ((System.Byte)(0)), ((System.Byte)(0)),
212              "firstName", System.Data.DataRowVersion.Original,
213              null));
214        this.oleDbDeleteCommand1.Parameters.Add(
215           new System.Data.OleDb.OleDbParameter(
216              "Original_lastName",
217              System.Data.OleDb.OleDbType.VarWChar, 50,
218              System.Data.ParameterDirection.Input, false,
219              ((System.Byte)(0)), ((System.Byte)(0)),
```

Fig. 19.27 Accessing and displaying a database's data. (Part 5 of 7.)

```
220                "lastName", System.Data.DataRowVersion.Original,
221                null));
222        this.oleDbDeleteCommand1.Parameters.Add(
223            new System.Data.OleDb.OleDbParameter(
224                "Original_lastName1",
225                System.Data.OleDb.OleDbType.VarWChar, 50,
226                System.Data.ParameterDirection.Input, false,
227                ((System.Byte)(0)), ((System.Byte)(0)),
228                "lastName", System.Data.DataRowVersion.Original,
229                null));
230        //
231        // oleDbConnection1
232        //
233        this.oleDbConnection1.ConnectionString =
234            @"Provider=Microsoft.Jet.OLEDB.4.0;Password="""";" +
235            @"User ID=Admin;Data Source=C:\Books\2001\csphtp1\" +
236            @"csphtp1_examples\ch19\Books.mdb;Mode=Share " +
237            @"Deny None;Extended Properties="""";Jet OLEDB:" +
238            @"System database="""";Jet OLEDB:Registry " +
239            @"Path="""";Jet OLEDB:Database Password="""";" +
240            @"Jet OLEDB:Engine Type=5;Jet OLEDB:Database " +
241            @"Locking Mode=1;Jet OLEDB:Global Partial Bulk " +
242            @"Ops=2;Jet OLEDB:Global Bulk Transactions=1;Jet " +
243            @"OLEDB:New Database Password="""";Jet OLEDB:" +
244            @"Create System Database=False;Jet OLEDB:Encrypt " +
245            @"Database=False;Jet OLEDB:Don't Copy Locale on " +
246            @"Compact=False;Jet OLEDB:Compact Without Replica " +
247            @"Repair=False;Jet OLEDB:SFP=False";
248        //
249        // TableDisplay
250        //
251        this.AutoScaleBaseSize = new System.Drawing.Size(5, 13);
252        this.ClientSize = new System.Drawing.Size(292, 273);
253        this.Controls.AddRange(
254            new System.Windows.Forms.Control[] {
255                this.dataGrid1});
256        this.Name = "TableDisplay";
257        this.Text = "TableDisplay";
258        ((System.ComponentModel.ISupportInitialize)
259            (this.dataSet1)).EndInit();
260        ((System.ComponentModel.ISupportInitialize)
261            (this.dataGrid1)).EndInit();
262        this.ResumeLayout(false);
263
264    }    // end of InitializeComponent
265
266    [STAThread]
267    static void Main()
268    {
269        Application.Run( new TableDisplay() );
270    }
271 }
```

Fig. 19.27 Accessing and displaying a database's data. (Part 6 of 7.)

Fig. 19.27 Accessing and displaying a database's data. (Part 7 of 7.)

Next, drag an *OleDbDataAdapter* from the **Toolbox**'s *Data* group onto the Windows Form designer. This displays the **Data Adapter Configuration Wizard** for configuring the **OleDbDataAdapter** instance with a custom query for populating a **DataSet**. Click **Next** to select a connection to use. Select the connection created in the previous step from the drop-down list and click **Next**. The resulting screen allows us to choose how the **OleDbDataAdapter** should access the database. Keep the default **Use SQL Statement** option and then click **Next**. Click the **Query Builder** button, select the **Authors** table from the **Add** menu and **Close** that menu. Place a check mark in the ***All Columns** box from the **Authors** window. Notice how that particular window lists all columns of the **Authors** table.

Next, we must create a **DataSet** to store the query results. To do so, drag **DataSet** from the **Data** group in the **Toolbox**. This displays the **Add DataSet** window. Choose the **Untyped DataSet (no schema)**, because the query with which we populate the **DataSet** dictates the **DataSet**'s *schema*, or structure.

Figure 19.27 shows all of the code generated by Visual Studio. Normally, we omit this code, because it usually only contains GUI related code. In this case, however, the code contains database functionality that we must discuss. Furthermore, we have left the default naming conventions of Visual Studio in this example to demonstrate the exact format of the auto-generated code that Visual Studio creates. Normally, we would change these names to conform to our programming conventions and style. The code generated by Visual Studio has also been formatted for presentation purposes.

Good Programming Practice 19.2

Use clear, descriptive variable names in code. This makes programs easier to understand.

Lines 233–247 initialize the **oleDbConnection** for this program. The **ConnectionString** property specifies the path to the database file on the computer's hard drive.

An instance of class **OleDbDataAdapter** populates the **DataSet** in this example with data from the **Books** database. The instance properties *DeleteCommand* (lines 66–67), *InsertCommand* (lines 68–69), *SelectCommand* (lines 70–71) and *Update-*

Command (lines 83–84) are **OleDbCommand** objects that specify how the **OleDbData-Adapter** deletes, inserts, selects and updates data in the database, respectively.

Each **OleDbCommand** object must have an **OleDbConnection** through which the **OleDbCommand** can communicate with the database. Property **Connection** is set to the **OleDbConnection** to the **Books** database. For **oleDbUpdateCommand1**, lines 128–129 set the **Connection** property, and lines 122–127 set the **CommandText**.

Although Visual Studio generates most of this program's code, we enter code in the **TableDisplay** constructor (lines 25–34) for populating **dataSet1** using an **OleDb-DataAdapter**. Line 30 calls **OleDbDataAdapter** method *Fill* to retrieve information from the database associated with the **OleDbConnection**, placing the information in the **DataSet** provided as an argument. The second argument to this method is a **string** that specifies the name of the table in the database from which to **Fill** the **DataSet**.

Line 33 invokes **DataGrid** method *SetDataBinding* to bind the **DataGrid** to a data source. The first argument is the **DataSet**—in this case, **dataSet1**—whose data the **DataGrid** should display. The second argument is a **string** representing the name of the table within the data source we want to bind to the **DataGrid**. Once this line executes, the **DataGrid** is filled with the information in the **DataSet**—the number of rows and number of columns are set from the information in **dataSet1**.

19.6.2 Querying the Books Database

The example in Fig. 19.28 demonstrates how to execute SQL **SELECT** statements on database **Books.mdb** and display the results. Although Fig. 19.28 uses only **SELECT** statements to query the data, the same program could be used to execute many different SQL statements if we made a few minor modifications.

Method **submitButton_Click** is the key part of this program. When the program invokes this event handler, lines 47–48 assign the **SELECT** query **string** to **OleDb-DataAdapter**'s **SelectCommand** property. This **string** is parsed into an SQL query and executed on the database via the **OleDbDataAdapter**'s **Fill** method (line 55). As we discussed in the previous section, method **Fill** places data from the database into **dataSet1**.

```
1   // Fig. 19.28: DisplayQueryResults.cs
2   // Displays the contents of the authors database.
3
4   using System;
5   using System.Drawing;
6   using System.Collections;
7   using System.ComponentModel;
8   using System.Windows.Forms;
9   using System.Data;
10
11  public class DisplayQueryResults : System.Windows.Forms.Form
12  {
13      private System.Data.OleDb.OleDbConnection oleDbConnection1;
14      private System.Data.DataSet dataSet1;
```

Fig. 19.28 Execute SQL statements on a database. (Part 1 of 3.)

```
15        private System.Data.OleDb.OleDbDataAdapter oleDbDataAdapter1;
16        private System.Data.OleDb.OleDbCommand oleDbSelectCommand1;
17        private System.Data.OleDb.OleDbCommand oleDbInsertCommand1;
18        private System.Data.OleDb.OleDbCommand oleDbUpdateCommand1;
19        private System.Data.OleDb.OleDbCommand oleDbDeleteCommand1;
20        private System.Windows.Forms.TextBox queryTextBox;
21        private System.Windows.Forms.Button submitButton;
22        private System.Windows.Forms.DataGrid dataGrid1;
23        private System.ComponentModel.Container components = null;
24
25        public DisplayQueryResults()
26        {
27
28            InitializeComponent();
29        }
30
31        // Visual Studio.NET generated code
32
33        [STAThread]
34        static void Main()
35        {
36            Application.Run( new DisplayQueryResults() );
37        }
38
39        // perform SQL query on data
40        private void submitButton_Click( object sender,
41            System.EventArgs e )
42        {
43            try
44            {
45                // set SQL query to what user
46                // input into queryTextBox
47                oleDbDataAdapter1.SelectCommand.CommandText =
48                    queryTextBox.Text;
49
50                // clear DataSet from previous operation
51                dataSet1.Clear();
52
53                // Fill data set with information that results
54                // from SQL query
55                oleDbDataAdapter1.Fill( dataSet1, "Authors" );
56
57                // bind DataGrid to contents of DataSet
58                dataGrid1.SetDataBinding( dataSet1, "Authors" );
59            }
60
61            catch ( System.Data.OleDb.OleDbException oleException )
62            {
63                MessageBox.Show( "Invalid query" );
64            }
65
66        } // end of submitButton_Click
67    }
```

Fig. 19.28 Execute SQL statements on a database. (Part 2 of 3.)

Fig. 19.28 Execute SQL statements on a database. (Part 3 of 3.)

Common Programming Error 19.9

*If a **DataSet** has been **Fill**ed at least once, forgetting to call a **DataSet**'s **Clear** method before calling the **Fill** method again will lead to logic errors.*

To display, or redisplay, contents in the **DataGrid**, use method **SetDataBinding**. The first argument is the datasource to be displayed in the table—a **DataSet**, in this case. The second argument is the **string** name of the datasource member to be displayed (line 58). Readers can try entering their own queries in the text box and then pressing the **Submit Query** button to execute the query.

19.7 Programming with ADO.NET: Modifying a Database

Our next example implements a simple address-book application that enables the user to insert, locate and update records in the Microsoft Access database **Addressbook**.

The **Addressbook** application (Fig. 19.29) provides a GUI enabling users to execute SQL statements on the database. Earlier in the chapter, we presented examples demonstrating the use of **SELECT** statements to query a database. Here, that same functionality is provided.

```
1   // Fig. 19.29: AddressBook.cs
2   // Using SQL statements to manipulate a database.
3
4   using System;
5   using System.Drawing;
6   using System.Collections;
7   using System.ComponentModel;
8   using System.Windows.Forms;
9   using System.Data;
10
```

Fig. 19.29 Modifying a database. (Part 1 of 8.)

```
11    public class AddressBook : System.Windows.Forms.Form
12    {
13       private System.Windows.Forms.TextBox faxTextBox;
14       private System.Windows.Forms.TextBox homeTextBox;
15       private System.Windows.Forms.TextBox firstTextBox;
16       private System.Windows.Forms.TextBox stateTextBox;
17       private System.Windows.Forms.TextBox idTextBox;
18       private System.Windows.Forms.TextBox lastTextBox;
19       private System.Windows.Forms.TextBox postalTextBox;
20       private System.Windows.Forms.TextBox addressTextBox;
21       private System.Windows.Forms.TextBox cityTextBox;
22       private System.Windows.Forms.TextBox countryTextBox;
23       private System.Windows.Forms.TextBox emailTextBox;
24       private System.Data.DataSet dataSet1;
25       private System.Data.OleDb.OleDbDataAdapter oleDbDataAdapter1;
26       private System.Data.OleDb.OleDbCommand oleDbSelectCommand1;
27       private System.Data.OleDb.OleDbCommand oleDbInsertCommand1;
28       private System.Data.OleDb.OleDbCommand oleDbUpdateCommand1;
29       private System.Data.OleDb.OleDbCommand oleDbDeleteCommand1;
30       private System.Data.OleDb.OleDbConnection oleDbConnection1;
31       private System.Windows.Forms.TextBox statusTextBox;
32       private System.Windows.Forms.Label addressLabel;
33       private System.Windows.Forms.Label cityLabel;
34       private System.Windows.Forms.Label stateLabel;
35       private System.Windows.Forms.Label idLabel;
36       private System.Windows.Forms.Label firstLabel;
37       private System.Windows.Forms.Label lastLabel;
38       private System.Windows.Forms.Label postalLabel;
39       private System.Windows.Forms.Label countryLabel;
40       private System.Windows.Forms.Label emailLabel;
41       private System.Windows.Forms.Button clearButton;
42       private System.Windows.Forms.Button helpButton;
43       private System.Windows.Forms.Button findButton;
44       private System.Windows.Forms.Button addButton;
45       private System.Windows.Forms.Button updateButton;
46       private System.Windows.Forms.Label faxLabel;
47       private System.Windows.Forms.Label homeLabel;
48       private System.ComponentModel.Container components = null;
49
50       public AddressBook()
51       {
52          InitializeComponent();
53          oleDbConnection1.Open();
54       }
55
56       // Visual Studio.NET generated code
57
58       [STAThread]
59       static void Main()
60       {
61          Application.Run( new AddressBook() );
62       }
63
```

Fig. 19.29 Modifying a database. (Part 2 of 8.)

```
64       private void findButton_Click( object sender,
65          System.EventArgs e )
66       {
67          try
68          {
69             if ( lastTextBox.Text != "" )
70             {
71                // clear DataSet from last operation
72                dataSet1.Clear();
73
74                // create SQL query to find contact with
75                // specified last name
76                oleDbDataAdapter1.SelectCommand.CommandText =
77                   "SELECT * FROM addresses WHERE lastname = '" +
78                   lastTextBox.Text + "'";
79
80                // fill dataSet1 with rows resulting from
81                // query
82                oleDbDataAdapter1.Fill( dataSet1 );
83
84                // display information
85                Display( dataSet1 );
86                statusTextBox.Text += "\r\nQuery successful\r\n";
87             }
88             else
89                lastTextBox.Text =
90                   "Enter last name here then press Find";
91          }
92
93          catch ( System.Data.OleDb.OleDbException oleException )
94          {
95             Console.WriteLine( oleException.StackTrace );
96             statusTextBox.Text += oleException.ToString();
97          }
98
99          catch ( InvalidOperationException invalidException )
100         {
101            MessageBox.Show( invalidException.Message );
102         }
103
104      }  // end of findButton_Click
105
106      private void addButton_Click( object sender, System.EventArgs e )
107      {
108         try
109         {
110            if ( lastTextBox.Text != "" && firstTextBox.Text != "" )
111            {
112               // create SQL query to insert row
113               oleDbDataAdapter1.InsertCommand.CommandText =
114                  "INSERT INTO addresses (" +
115                  "firstname, lastname, address, city, " +
116                  "stateorprovince, postalcode, country, " +
```

Fig. 19.29 Modifying a database. (Part 3 of 8.)

```
117                    "emailaddress, homephone, faxnumber" +
118                    ") VALUES ('" +
119                    firstTextBox.Text + "', '" +
120                    lastTextBox.Text + "', '" +
121                    addressTextBox.Text + "', '" +
122                    cityTextBox.Text + "', '" +
123                    stateTextBox.Text + "', '" +
124                    postalTextBox.Text + "', '" +
125                    countryTextBox.Text + "', '" +
126                    emailTextBox.Text + "', '" +
127                    homeTextBox.Text + "', '" +
128                    faxTextBox.Text + "')";
129
130                // notify user that query is being sent
131                statusTextBox.Text += "\r\nSending query: " +
132                    oleDbDataAdapter1.InsertCommand.CommandText +
133                    "\r\n" ;
134
135                // send query
136                oleDbDataAdapter1.InsertCommand.ExecuteNonQuery();
137
138                statusTextBox.Text += "\r\nQuery successful\r\n";
139             }
140             else
141                statusTextBox.Text += "\r\nEnter at least first " +
142                    "and last name then press Add\r\n";
143          }
144
145       catch ( System.Data.OleDb.OleDbException oleException )
146       {
147          Console.WriteLine( oleException.StackTrace );
148          statusTextBox.Text += oleException.ToString();
149       }
150
151    }  // end of addButton_Click
152
153    private void updateButton_Click( object sender,
154       System.EventArgs e )
155    {
156       try
157       {
158          // make sure users have found record
159          // they wish to update
160          if ( idTextBox.Text != "" )
161          {
162             // set SQL query to update all fields in
163             // table where id number matches id
164             // in idTextBox
165             oleDbDataAdapter1.UpdateCommand.CommandText =
166                "UPDATE addresses SET " +
167                "firstname ='" + firstTextBox.Text +
168                "', lastname='" + lastTextBox.Text +
169                "', address='" + addressTextBox.Text +
```

Fig. 19.29 Modifying a database. (Part 4 of 8.)

```
170                      "', city='" + cityTextBox.Text +
171                      "', stateorprovince='" + stateTextBox.Text +
172                      "', postalcode='" + postalTextBox.Text +
173                      "', country='" + countryTextBox.Text +
174                      "', emailaddress='" + emailTextBox.Text +
175                      "', homephone='" + homeTextBox.Text +
176                      "', faxnumber='" + faxTextBox.Text +
177                      "' WHERE id=" + idTextBox.Text;
178
179                  // notify user that query is being set
180                  statusTextBox.Text += "\r\nSending query: " +
181                      oleDbDataAdapter1.UpdateCommand.CommandText +
182                      "\r\n";
183
184                  // execute query
185                  oleDbDataAdapter1.UpdateCommand.ExecuteNonQuery();
186
187                  statusTextBox.Text += "\r\nQuery successful\r\n";
188              }
189              else
190                  statusTextBox.Text += "\r\nYou may only update " +
191                      "an existing record. Use Find to locate the" +
192                      "record, then modify the information and " +
193                      "press Update.\r\n";
194          }
195
196          catch ( System.Data.OleDb.OleDbException oleException )
197          {
198              Console.WriteLine( oleException.StackTrace );
199              statusTextBox.Text += oleException.ToString();
200          }
201
202      } // end of updateButton_Click
203
204      private void clearButton_Click( object sender,
205          System.EventArgs e )
206      {
207          idTextBox.Clear();
208          ClearTextBoxes();
209      }
210
211      private void helpButton_Click( object sender,
212          System.EventArgs e )
213      {
214          statusTextBox.AppendText(
215              "\r\nClick Find to locate a record\r\n" +
216              "Click Add to insert a new record.\r\n" +
217              "Click Update to update the information in a record " +
218              + "\r\nClick Clear to empty the textboxes" );
219      }
220
221      private void Display( DataSet dataSet )
222      {
```

Fig. 19.29 Modifying a database. (Part 5 of 8.)

```
223        try
224        {
225           // get first DataTable--there always will be one
226           DataTable dataTable = dataSet.Tables[ 0 ];
227
228           if ( dataTable.Rows.Count != 0 )
229           {
230              int recordNumber = ( int ) dataTable.Rows[ 0 ][ 0 ];
231
232              idTextBox.Text = recordNumber.ToString();
233              firstTextBox.Text =
234                 ( string ) dataTable.Rows[ 0 ][ 1 ];
235              lastTextBox.Text =
236                 ( string ) dataTable.Rows[ 0 ][ 2 ];
237              addressTextBox.Text =
238                 ( string ) dataTable.Rows[ 0 ][ 3 ];
239              cityTextBox.Text =
240                 ( string ) dataTable.Rows[ 0 ][ 4 ];
241              stateTextBox.Text =
242                 ( string ) dataTable.Rows[ 0 ][ 5 ];
243              postalTextBox.Text =
244                 ( string ) dataTable.Rows[ 0 ][ 6 ];
245              countryTextBox.Text =
246                 ( string ) dataTable.Rows[ 0 ][ 7 ];
247              emailTextBox.Text =
248                 ( string ) dataTable.Rows[ 0 ][ 8 ];
249              homeTextBox.Text =
250                 ( string ) dataTable.Rows[ 0 ][ 9 ];
251              faxTextBox.Text =
252                 ( string ) dataTable.Rows[ 0 ][ 10 ];
253           }
254
255           else
256              statusTextBox.Text += "\r\nNo record found\r\n";
257        }
258
259        catch( System.Data.OleDb.OleDbException oleException )
260        {
261           Console.WriteLine( oleException.StackTrace );
262           statusTextBox.Text += oleException.ToString();
263        }
264
265     } // end Display
266
267     private void ClearTextBoxes()
268     {
269        firstTextBox.Clear();
270        lastTextBox.Clear();
271        addressTextBox.Clear();
272        cityTextBox.Clear();
273        stateTextBox.Clear();
274        postalTextBox.Clear();
275        countryTextBox.Clear();
```

Fig. 19.29 Modifying a database. (Part 6 of 8.)

```
276            emailTextBox.Clear();
277            homeTextBox.Clear();
278            faxTextBox.Clear();
279      }
280  }
```

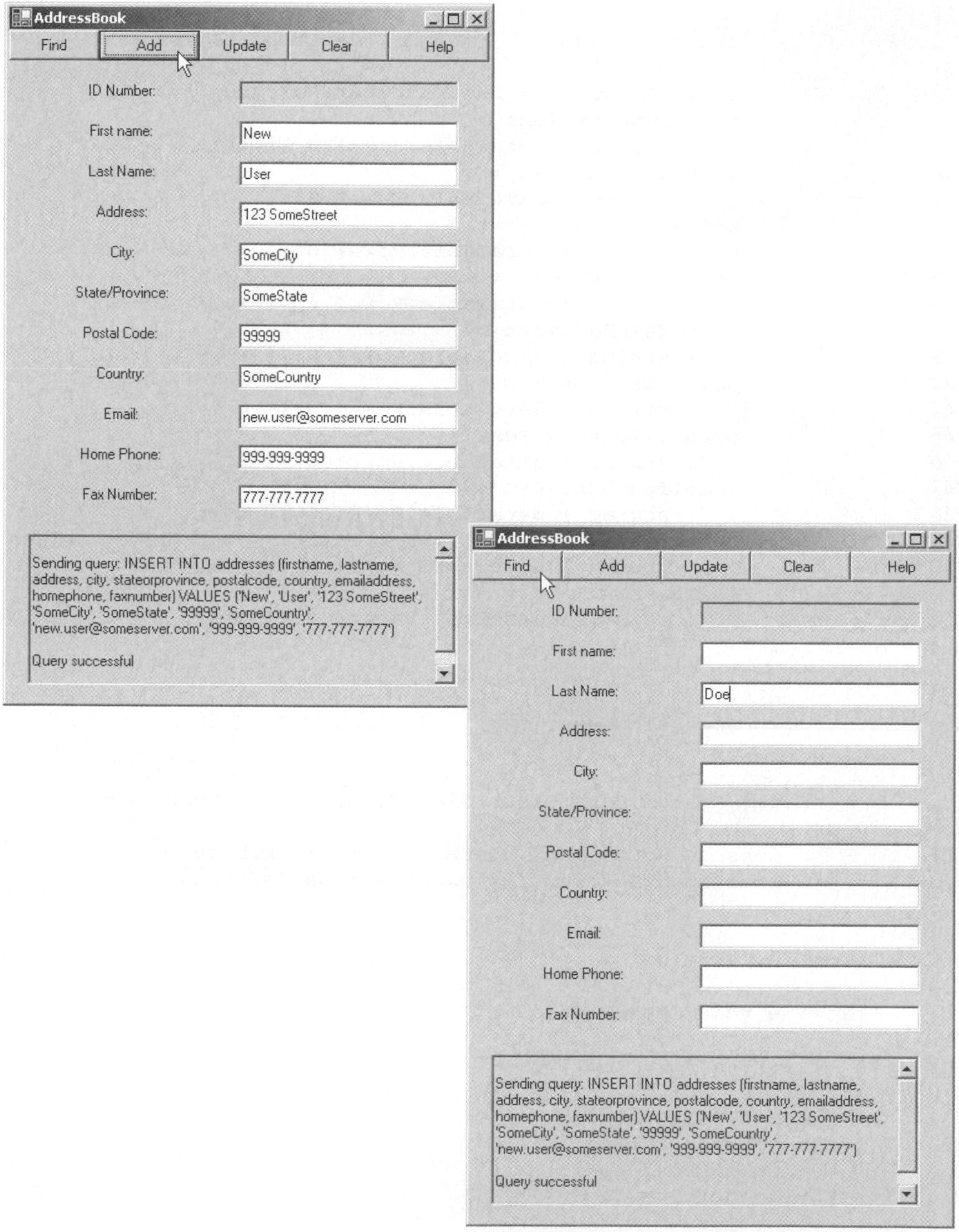

Fig. 19.29 Modifying a database. (Part 7 of 8.)

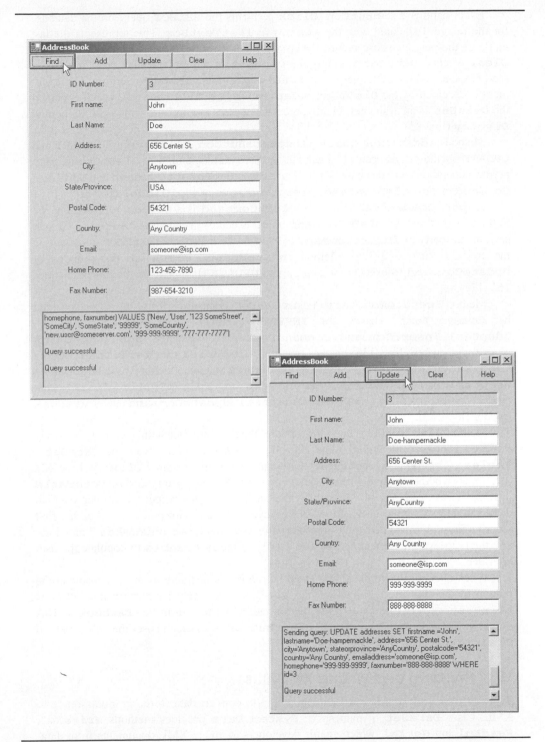

Fig. 19.29 Modifying a database. (Part 8 of 8.)

Event handler **findButton_Click** performs the **SELECT** query on the database for the record associated with the **string** in **lastTextBox**. This represents the last name of the person whose record the user wishes to retrieve. Line 72 invokes method **Clear** of class **DataSet** to empty the **DataSet** of any prior data. Lines 76–78 then modify the text of the SQL query to perform the appropriate **SELECT** operation. This statement is executed by the **OleDbDataAdapter** method **Fill** (line 82), which is passed the **DataSet** as an argument. Finally, the **TextBox**es are updated with a call to method **Display** (line 85).

Methods **addButton_Click** and **updateButton_Click** perform **INSERT** and **UPDATE** operations, respectively. Each method uses members of class **OleDbCommand** to perform operations on a database. The instance properties **InsertCommand** and **UpdateCommand** of class **OleDbDataAdapter** are instances of class **OleDbCommand**.

Property **CommandText** of class **OleDbCommand** is a **string** representing the SQL statement that the **OleDbCommand** object executes. Method **addButton_Click** sets this property of **InsertCommand** to execute the appropriate **INSERT** statement on the database (lines 113–128). Method **updateButton_Click** sets this property of **UpdateCommand** to execute the appropriate **UPDATE** statement on the database (lines 165–177).

Method *ExecuteNonQuery* of class **OleDbCommand** performs the action specified by **CommandText**. Hence, the **INSERT** statement defined by **oleDbDataAdapter1.InsertCommand.CommandText** in event handler **addButton_Click** is executed when line 136 invokes method **oleDbDataAdapter1.InsertCommand.ExecuteNonQuery**. Similarly, the **UPDATE** statement defined by **oleDbDataAdapter1.DeleteCommand.CommandText** in **updateButton_Click** event handler is executed by **oleDbDataAdapter1.UpdateCommand.ExecuteNonQuery** (line 185).

Method **Display** (lines 221–265) updates the user interface with data from the newly retrieved address-book record. Line 226 obtains a **DataTable** from the **DataSet**'s **Tables** collection. This **DataTable** contains the results of our SQL query. Line 228 determines whether the query returned any rows. The **Rows** property in class **DataTable** provides access to all records retrieved by the query. The **Rows** property is similar to a two-dimensional rectangular array. Line 230 retrieves the field with index *0, 0* (i.e., the first record's first column of data) and stores the value in variable **recordNumber**. Lines 232–252 then retrieve the remaining fields of data from the **DataTable** to populate the user interface.

When clicked, the application's **Help** button prints instructions in the console at the bottom of the application window (lines 214–218). The event handler for this button is **helpButton_Click**. The **Clear** button clears the text from the **TextBox**es. This event handler is defined in the method **clearButton_Click** and uses the utility method **ClearTextBoxes** (line 208).

19.8 Reading and Writing XML Files

A powerful feature of ADO .NET is its ability to convert data stored in a datasource to XML. Class **DataSet** of namespace **System.Data** provides methods *WriteXml*, *ReadXml* and *GetXml*, which enable developers to create XML documents from datasources and to convert data from XML into datasources. The application in Fig. 19.30 populates a **DataSet** with statistics about baseball players and then writes the data to a file as XML. The application also displays the XML in a **TextBox**.

```
1   // Fig. 19.30 XMLWriter.cs
2   // Demonstrates generating XML from an ADO .NET DataSet.
3
4   using System;
5   using System.Drawing;
6   using System.Collections;
7   using System.ComponentModel;
8   using System.Windows.Forms;
9   using System.Data;
10
11  public class DatabaseXMLWriter : System.Windows.Forms.Form
12  {
13     private System.Data.OleDb.OleDbConnection baseballConnection;
14     private System.Data.OleDb.OleDbDataAdapter playersDataAdapter;
15     private System.Data.OleDb.OleDbCommand oleDbSelectCommand1;
16     private System.Data.OleDb.OleDbCommand oleDbInsertCommand1;
17     private System.Data.OleDb.OleDbCommand oleDbUpdateCommand1;
18     private System.Data.OleDb.OleDbCommand oleDbDeleteCommand1;
19     private System.Data.DataSet playersDataSet;
20     private System.Windows.Forms.DataGrid playersDataGrid;
21     private System.Windows.Forms.Button writeButton;
22     private System.Windows.Forms.TextBox outputTextBox;
23     private System.ComponentModel.Container components = null;
24
25     public DatabaseXMLWriter()
26     {
27        //
28        // Required for Windows Form Designer support
29        //
30        InitializeComponent();
31
32        // open database connection
33        baseballConnection.Open();
34
35        // fill DataSet with data from OleDbDataAdapter
36        playersDataAdapter.Fill( playersDataSet, "Players" );
37
38        // bind DataGrid to DataSet
39        playersDataGrid.SetDataBinding( playersDataSet, "Players" );
40
41     }
42
43     // Visual Studio .NET generated code
44
45     // main entry point for application.
46     [STAThread]
47     static void Main()
48     {
49        Application.Run( new DatabaseXMLWriter() );
50     }
```

Fig. 19.30 Application that writes **DataSet** XML representation to a file. (Part 1 of 2.)

```
51
52      // write XML representation of DataSet when button is clicked
53      private void writeButton_Click(
54         object sender, System.EventArgs e)
55      {
56         // write XML representation of DataSet to file
57         playersDataSet.WriteXml( "Players.xml" );
58
59         // display XML in TextBox
60         outputTextBox.Text += "Writing the following XML:\n\n" +
61            playersDataSet.GetXml() + "\n\n";
62
63      }
64   }
```

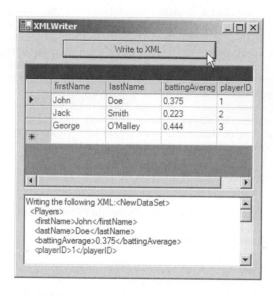

Fig. 19.30 Application that writes **DataSet** XML representation to a file. (Part 2 of 2.)

The **DatabaseXMLWriter** constructor (lines 25–41) establishes a connection to the **Baseball** database in line 33. Line 36 then calls method **Fill** of class **OleDbData-Adapter** to populate **playersDataSet** with data from the **Players** table in the **Baseball** database. Line 39 binds **playersDataGrid** to **playersDataSet** to display the information to the user.

Method **writeButton_Click** defines the event handler for the **Write to XML** button. When the user clicks this button, line 57 invokes **DataSet** method **WriteXml**, which generates an XML representation of the data contained in the **DataSet** and writes the XML to the specified file. Figure 19.31 depicts this XML representation. Each **Players** element represents a record in the **Players** table. The **firstName**, **lastName**, **batting-Average** and **playerID** elements correspond to the fields of the same names in the **Players** table. Method **GetXml** returns a **string** representing the **DataSet**'s data in XML form. Lines 60–61 append the XML **string** to **outputTextBox**.

```
1   <?xml version="1.0" standalone="yes"?>
2   <NewDataSet>
3      <Players>
4         <firstName>John</firstName>
5         <lastName>Doe</lastName>
6         <battingAverage>0.375</battingAverage>
7         <playerID>1</playerID>
8      </Players>
9
10     <Players>
11        <firstName>Jack</firstName>
12        <lastName>Smith</lastName>
13        <battingAverage>0.223</battingAverage>
14        <playerID>2</playerID>
15     </Players>
16
17     <Players>
18        <firstName>George</firstName>
19        <lastName>O'Malley</lastName>
20        <battingAverage>0.444</battingAverage>
21        <playerID>3</playerID>
22     </Players>
23  </NewDataSet>
```

Fig. 19.31 XML document generated from **DataSet** in **DatabaseXMLWriter**.

In this chapter, we discussed the fundamentals of Structured Query Language (SQL) and C#'s database capabilities. We learned that C# programmers communicate with databases and manipulate their data through *Microsoft ActiveX Data Objects™* (ADO), *ADO .NET*. In the next chapter we discuss ASP .NET Web Forms. Web Forms allow programmers to develop dynamic Web content using databases and ASP .NET features.

SUMMARY

- A database is an integrated collection of data. A database management system (DBMS) provides mechanisms for storing and organizing data.

- Today's most popular database systems are relational databases.

- A language called Structured Query Language (SQL) is used almost universally with relational-database systems to perform queries and manipulate data.

- A programming language connects to, and interacts with, relational databases via an interface— software that facilitates communications between a database management system and a program.

- C# programmers communicate with databases and manipulate their data via ADO .NET.

- A relational database is composed of tables. A row of a table is called a record.

- A primary key is a field that contains unique data, or data that is not duplicated in other records of that table.

- Each column in a table represents a different field (or attribute).

- A primary key can be composed of more than one column (or field) in the database.

- SQL provides a complete set of commands, enabling programmers to define complex queries to select data from a table. The results of a query commonly are called result sets (or record sets).

- A one-to-many relationship between tables indicates that a record in one table can have many corresponding records in a separate table.

- A foreign key is a field for which every entry in one table has a unique value in another table and where the field in the other table is the primary key for that table.

- The basic format for a **SELECT** query is:

    SELECT * FROM *tableName*

    where the asterisk (*****) indicates that all columns from *tableName* should be selected, and *tableName* specifies the table in the database from which the data will be selected.

- To select specific fields from a table, replace the asterisk (*****) with a comma-separated list of the field names to select.

- Programmers process result sets by knowing in advance the order of the fields in the result set. Specifying the field names to select guarantees that the fields are returned in the specified order, even if the actual order of the fields in the database table(s) changes.

- The optional **WHERE** clause in a **SELECT** query specifies the selection criteria for the query. The simplest format for a **SELECT** query with selection criteria is:

    SELECT *fieldName1*, *fieldName2*, ... **FROM** *tableName* **WHERE** *criteria*

- The **WHERE** clause condition can contain operators **<**, **>**, **<=**, **>=**, **=**, **<>** and **LIKE**. Operator **LIKE** is used for pattern matching with wildcard characters asterisk (*****) and question mark (**?**).

- A pattern **string** containing an asterisk character (*****) searches for strings in which zero or more characters appear in the asterisk character's location in the pattern.

- A pattern string containing a question mark (**?**) searches for strings in which exactly one character appears in the question mark's position in the pattern.

- The results of a query can be arranged in ascending or descending order via the optional **ORDER BY** clause. The simplest form of an **ORDER BY** clause is:

    SELECT *fieldName1*, *fieldName2*, ... **FROM** *tableName* **ORDER BY** *field* **ASC**
    SELECT *fieldName1*, *fieldName2*, ... **FROM** *tableName* **ORDER BY** *field* **DESC**

    where **ASC** specifies ascending order, **DESC** specifies descending order and *field* specifies the field to be sorted. The default sorting order is ascending, so **ASC** is optional.

- An **ORDER BY** clause also can sort records by multiple fields. Such queries are written in the form:

    ORDER BY *field1 sortingOrder*, *field2 sortingOrder*, ...

- The **WHERE** and **ORDER BY** clauses can be combined in one query.

- A join merges records from two or more tables by testing for matching values in a field that is common to both tables. The simplest format of a join is:

    SELECT *fieldName1*, *fieldName2*, ...
        FROM *table1* **INNER JOIN** *table2*
        ON *table1*.*fieldName* **=** *table2*.*fieldName*

    in which the **WHERE** clause specifies the fields from each table that should be compared to determine which records are joined. These fields normally represent the primary key in one table and the corresponding foreign key in another table.

- If an SQL statement uses fields that have the same name in multiple tables, the statement must fully qualify the field name by preceding it with its table name and the dot operator (**.**).

- An **INSERT** statement inserts a new record in a table. The simplest form for this statement is:

    INSERT INTO *tableName* (*fieldName1*, *fieldName2*, ..., *fieldNameN*)
        VALUES (*value1*, *value2*, ..., *valueN*)

where *tableName* is the table in which to insert the record. The *tableName* is followed by a comma-separated list of field names in parentheses. The list of field names is followed by the SQL keyword **VALUES** and a comma-separated list of values in parentheses.

- SQL statements use a single quote (**'**) as a delimiter for strings. To specify a string containing a single quote in an SQL statement, the single quote must be escaped with another single quote.

- An **UPDATE** statement modifies data in a table. The simplest form for an **UPDATE** statement is:

      UPDATE *tableName*
          SET *fieldName1* = *value1*, *fieldName2* = *value2*, ..., *fieldNameN* = *valueN*
          WHERE *criteria*

where *tableName* is the table in which to update a record (or records). The *tableName* is followed by keyword **SET** and a comma-separated list of field-name/value pairs, written in the format *fieldName = value*. The **WHERE** *criteria* determine the record(s) to update.

- A **DELETE** statement removes data from a table. The simplest form for a **DELETE** statement is:

      DELETE FROM *tableName* **WHERE** *criteria*

where *tableName* is the table from which to delete a record (or records). The **WHERE** *criteria* determine which record(s) to delete.

- **System.Data**, **System.Data.OleDb** and **System.Data.SqlClient** are the three main namespaces in ADO .NET.

- Class **DataSet** is from the **System.Data** namespace. Instances of this class represent in-memory caches of data.

- The advantage of using class **DataSet** is that it is a way to modify the contents of a datasource without having to maintain an active connection.

- One approach to ADO .NET programming uses **OleDbCommand** of the **System.Data.OleDb** namespace. In this approach, SQL statements are executed directly on the datasource.

- Use the **Add Connection** option to create a database connection in the **Data Link Properties** window.

- Use the **Data Adapter Configuration Wizard** to set up an **OleDbDataAdapter** and generate queries.

- If a **DataSet** needs to be named, use the instance property **DataSetName**.

- **OleDbCommands** commands are what the **OleDbDataAdapter** executes on the database in the form of SQL queries.

- **DataColumnMapping**s converts data from a database to a **DataSet**, and vice versa.

- Instance property **Parameters** of class **OleDbCommand** is a collection of **OleDbParameter** objects. Adding them to an **OleDbCommand** is an optional way to add parameters in a command, instead of creating a lengthy, complex command string.

- **OleDbCommand** instance property **Connection** is set to the **OleDbConnection** that the command will be executed on, and the instance property **CommandText** is set to the SQL query that will be executed on the database.

- **OleDbDataAdapter** method **Fill** retrieves information from the database associated with the **OleDbConnection** and places this information in the **DataSet** provided as an argument.

- **DataGrid** method **SetDataBinding** binds a **DataGrid** to a data source.

- Method **Clear** of class **DataSet** is called to empty the **DataSet** of any prior data.

- The instance properties **InsertCommand** and **UpdateCommand** of class **OleDbDataAdapter** are instances of class **OleDbCommand**.

- Property **CommandText** of class **OleDbCommand** is the **string** representing the SQL statement to be executed.
- Method **ExecuteNonQuery** of class **OleDbCommand** is called to perform the action specified by **CommandText** on the database.
- A powerful feature of ADO .NET is its ability to convert data stored in a datasource to XML, and vice versa.
- Method **WriteXml** of class **DataSet** writes the XML representation of the **DataSet** instance to the first argument passed to it. This method has several overloaded versions that allow programmers to specify an output source and a character encoding for the data.
- Method **ReadXml** of class **DataSet** reads the XML representation of the first argument passed to it into its own **DataSet**. This method has several overloaded versions that allow programmers to specify an input source and a character encoding for the data.

TERMINOLOGY

* SQL wildcard character
? SQL wildcard character
AcceptChanges method of **DataRow**
AcceptChanges method of **DataTable**
ADO.NET
AND
ASC (ascending order)
ascending order (ASC)
asterisk (*****)
atomic operation
authorISBN table of **books** database
authors table of **books** database
books database
books database table relationships
cache
Clear method of **DataSet**
column
column number
CommandText method of **OleDbCommand**
commit a transaction
connect to a database
data provider
database
database management system (DBMS)
database table
DataGrid class
DataSet class
default sorting order is ascending
DELETE FROM
DELETE statement
DeleteCommand property of
    OleDbAdapter
DESC
disconnected

distributed computing system
ExecuteNonQuery method of
    OleDbCommand
ExecuteReader method of **OleDbCommand**
ExecuteScalar method of **OleDbCommand**
field
Fill method of **OleDbAdapter**
foreign key
FROM
fully qualified name
GetXml method of **DataSet**
GROUP BY
infinity symbol
INNER JOIN
INSERT INTO
INSERT statement
InsertCommand property of
    OleDbAdapter
interface
joining tables
LIKE
many-to-many relationship
match the selection criteria
merge records from Tables
OLE DB data provider
OleDbCommand class
OleDbConnection class
OleDbDataAdapter class
one-to-many relationship
ORDER BY
ordered
ordering of records
pattern matching
primary key

Publishers table of books database
query
query a database
ReadXml method of DataSet
record
record set
RejectChanges method of DataRow
RejectChanges method of DataTable
relational database
relational database model
relational database table
result set
roll back a transaction
row
rows to be retrieved
Rule of Entity Integrity
Rule of Referential Integrity
SELECT
select
select all fields from a table
SelectCommand property of
   OleDbAdapter
selecting data from a table
selection criteria
SET

SetDataBinding method of DataGrid
single-quote character
SQL (Structured Query Language)
SQL keyword
SQL Server data provider
SQL statement
square brackets in a query
System.Data namespace
System.Data.OleDb namespace
System.Data.SqlClient namespace
table
table column
table in which record will be updated
table row
titles table of books database
transaction
transaction processing
UPDATE
Update method of OleDbDataAdapter
UpdateCommand property of
   OleDbAdapter
VALUES
WHERE
WriteXml method of DataSet

SELF-REVIEW EXERCISES

19.1 Fill in the blanks in each of the following statements:
  a) The most popular database query language is _____.
  b) A table in a database consists of _____ and _____.
  c) Databases can be manipulated in C# as _____ objects.
  d) Class _____ enables programmers to display data in **DataSet**s graphically.
  e) SQL keyword _____ is followed by selection criteria that specify the records to select in a query.
  f) SQL keyword _____ specifies the order in which records are sorted in a query.
  g) Selecting data from multiple database tables is called _____ the data.
  h) A(n) _____ is/are an integrated collection of data that is/are centrally controlled.
  i) A(n) _____ is/are a field(s) in a table for which every entry has/have a unique value in another table and where the field(s) in the other table is/are the primary key for that table.
  j) Namespace _____ contains special classes and interfaces for manipulating SQLServer databases in C#.
  k) C# uses _____ to transmit data between datasources.
  l) Namespace _____ is C#'s general interfacing to a database.

19.2 State which of the following are *true* or *false*. If *false*, explain why.
  a) In general, ADO .NET is a disconnected model.
  b) SQL can implicitly convert fields with the same name from two or mores tables to the appropriate field.
  c) Only the **UPDATE** SQL statement can commit changes to a database.

d) Providing a foreign-key value that does not appear as a primary-key value in another table breaks the Rule of Referential Integrity.
e) The **VALUES** keyword in an **INSERT** statement inserts multiple records in a table.
f) **SELECT** statements can merge data from multiple tables.
g) The **DELETE** statment deletes only one record in a table.
h) An **OleDbDataAdapter** can **Fill** a **DataSet**.
i) Class **DataSet** of namespace **System.Data** provides methods that enable developers to create XML documents from datasources.
j) SQLServer is an example of a managed provider.
k) Because C# uses a disconnected model, **OleDbConnection**s are optional.
l) It is always faster to assign a value to a variable than to instantiate a new **object**.

ANSWERS TO SELF-REVIEW EXERCISES

19.1   a) SQL. b) rows, columns. c) **DataSet**. d) **DataGrid**. e) **WHERE**. f) **ORDER BY**. g) joining. h) database. i) foreign key. j) **System.Data.SqlClient**. k) XML. l) **System.Data.OleDb**.

19.2   a) True. b) False. In a query, failure to provide fully qualified names for fields with the same name in two or more tables is an error. c) False. **INSERT** and **DELETE** change the database, as well. Do not confuse the SQL **Update** statement with method **OleDbDataAdapter.Update**. d) True. e) False. An **INSERT** statement inserts one record in the table. The **VALUES** keyword specifies the comma-separated list of values from which the record is formed. f) True. g) False. The **DELETE** statement deletes all records matching its **WHERE** clause. h) True. i) True. j) True. k) False. This class is required to connect to a database. l) True.

EXERCISES

19.3   Using the techniques shown in this chapter, define a complete query application for the **Authors.mdb** database. Provide a series of predefined queries with an appropriate name for each query displayed in a **System.Windows.Forms.ComboBox**. Also, allow users to supply their own queries and add them to the **ComboBox**. Provide any queries you feel are appropriate.

19.4   Using the techniques shown in this chapter, define a complete query application for the **Books.mdb** database. Provide a series of predefined queries with an appropriate name for each query displayed in a **System.Windows.Forms.ComboBox**. Also, allow users to supply their own queries and add them to the **ComboBox**. Provide the following predefined queries:
a) Select all authors from the **Authors** table.
b) Select all publishers from the **Publishers** table.
c) Select a specific author and list all books for that author. Include the title, year and ISBN number. Order the information alphabetically by title.
d) Select a specific publisher and list all books published by that publisher. Include the title, year and ISBN number. Order the information alphabetically by title.
e) Provide any other queries you feel are appropriate.

19.5   Modify Exercise 19.4 to define a complete database-manipulation application for the **Books.mdb** database. In addition to the querying capabilities, application should allow users to edit existing data and add new data to the database. Allow the user to edit the database in the following ways:
a) Add a new author.
b) Edit the existing information for an author.
c) Add a new title for an author (remember that the book must have an entry in the **AuthorISBN** table). Be sure to specify the publisher of the title.
d) Add a new publisher.
e) Edit the existing information for a publisher.

For each of the preceding database manipulations, design an appropriate GUI to allow the user to perform the data manipulation.

19.6   Modify the address-book example of Fig. 19.29 to enable each address-book entry to contain multiple addresses, phone numbers and e-mail addresses. The user should be able to view multiple addresses, phone numbers and e-mail addresses. [*Note:* This is a large exercise that requires substantial modifications to the original classes in the address-book example.]

19.7   Create an application that allows the user to modify all fields of a database using a transaction process model. The user should be able to find, modify and create entries. The GUI should include buttons **Accept Changes** and **Reject Changes**. Modifications to the datasource should be made when the user clicks **Accept Changes**, by the invoking of method `Update` of the `OleDbData-Adapter` object. The `DataSet`'s `AcceptChanges` method should be invoked *after* changes are made to the datasource.

19.8   Write a program that allows the user to modify a database graphically through an XML text editor. The GUI should be able to display the contents of the database and commit any changes in the XML text to the database.

20

ASP .NET, Web Forms and Web Controls

Objectives

- To become familiar with Web Forms in ASP .NET.
- To be able to create Web Forms.
- To be able to create an ASP .NET application that consists of multiple Web Forms.
- To be able to control user access to Web applications through forms authentication.
- To be able to use files and databases in ASP .NET applications.
- To learn how to use tracing with Web Forms.

If any man will draw up his case, and put his name at the foot of the first page, I will give him an immediate reply. Where he compels me to turn over the sheet, he must wait my leisure.
Lord Sandwich

Rule One: Our client is always right
Rule Two: If you think our client is wrong, see Rule One.
Anonymous

A fair question should be followed by a deed in silence.
Dante Alighieri

You will come here and get books that will open your eyes, and your ears, and your curiosity, and turn you inside out or outside in.
Ralph Waldo Emerson

Outline

20.1 Introduction

In previous chapters, we used Windows Forms and Windows controls to develop Windows applications. In this chapter, we introduce *Web-based application development* with Microsoft's ASP .NET technology. Web-based applications create content for Web browser clients. This Web content can include HyperText Markup Language (HTML),[1] client-side scripting, images and binary data.

We present several examples that demonstrate Web-based applications development using *Web Forms* (also known as *Web Form pages*), *Web controls* (also known as *ASP .NET server controls*) and C# programming. Web Form files have the file extension **.aspx** and contain the Web page's GUI. Programmers customize Web Forms by adding Web controls, which include labels, text boxes, images, buttons and other GUI components. The Web Form file represents what the Web page that is sent to the client browser will look like. [*Note*: From this point onward, we refer to Web Form files as *ASPX files.*]

Every ASPX file created in Visual Studio has a corresponding class written in a .NET-compliant language, such as C#. This class includes event handlers, initialization code, utility methods and other supporting code for the user interface in the ASPX file. The C# file that contains this class is called the *code-behind file* and provides the ASPX file's programmatic implementation.

---

1. Readers not familiar with HTML should read Appendices I–J before studying this chapter.

20.2 Simple HTTP Transaction

Before exploring Web-based applications development further, a basic understanding of networking and the World Wide Web is necessary. In this section, we examine the inner workings of the *HyperText Transfer Protocol (HTTP)* and discuss what occurs behind the scenes when a browser displays a Web page. HTTP is a protocol that specifies a set of *methods* and *headers* that allow clients and servers to interact and exchange information in a uniform and predictable way.

In their simplest form, Web pages are HTML documents, these are plain-text files that contains markings (*markup* or *tags*) describing the structures of the documents. For example, the HTML markup:

```
<title>My Web Page</title>
```

indicates that the text contained between the **<title>** *start tag* and the **</title>** *end tag* is the Web page's title. HTML documents also can contain *hyperlinks*, which enable users to navigate their Web browsers to other Web pages. When the user activates a hyperlink (usually by clicking it with the mouse), the requested Web page (or different part of the same Web page) is loaded into the user's browser window.

Any HTML document available on the Web has a *Uniform Resource Locator (URL)*, which indicates the location of a resource. The URL contains information that directs Web browsers to the document. Computers that run *Web server* software provide such resources. Microsoft *Internet Information Services (IIS)* is the Web server that programmers use when developing ASP .NET Web applications in Visual Studio.

Let us examine the components of the URL:

```
http://www.deitel.com/books/downloads.htm
```

The **http://** indicates that the resource is to be obtained using HTTP. The middle portion—**www.deitel.com**—is the fully qualified *hostname* of the server. The hostname is the name of the computer on which the resource resides. This computer usually is referred to as the *host*, because it houses and maintains resources. The hostname **www.deitel.com** is translated into an *IP address* (**207.60.134.230**) that identifies the server in a manner similar to that by which a telephone number uniquely defines a particular phone line. The translation of the hostname into an IP address normally is performed by a *domain name server (DNS)*—a computer that maintains a database of hostnames and their corresponding IP addresses. This translation operation is called a *DNS lookup*.

The remainder of the URL provides the name and location of the requested resource, **/books/downloads.htm** (an HTML document). This portion of the URL specifies both the name of the resource (**downloads.htm**) and its path, or location (**/books**), on the Web server. The path could specify the location of an actual directory on the Web server's file system. However, for security reasons, paths often specify the locations of a *virtual directory*. In such systems, the server translates the virtual directory into a real location on the server (or on another computer on the server's network), thus hiding the true location of the resource. Furthermore, some resources are created dynamically and do not reside anywhere on the server computer. The hostname in the URL for such a resource specifies the correct server, and the path and resource information identifies the location of the resource with which to respond to the client's request.

When given a URL, a browser performs a simple HTTP transaction to retrieve and display a Web page. Figure 20.1 illustrates this transaction in detail. The transaction consists of interaction between the Web browser (the client side) and the Web-server application (the server side).

In Fig. 20.1, the Web browser sends an HTTP request to the server. The request (in its simplest form) is

    GET /books/downloads.htm HTTP/1.1

The word **GET** is an HTTP method indicating that the client wishes to obtain a resource from the server. The remainder of the request provides the path name of the resource and the protocol's name and version number (**HTTP/1.1**).

Any server that understands HTTP (version 1.1) can translate this request and respond appropriately. Figure 20.2 depicts a Web server's response when it a successful request. The server first responds by sending a line of text that indicates the HTTP version, followed by a numeric code and phrase, both of which describe the status of the transaction. For example,

    HTTP/1.1 200 OK

indicates success, whereas

    HTTP/1.1 404 Not found

informs the client that the Web server could not locate the requested resource.

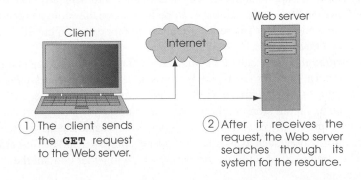

① The client sends the **GET** request to the Web server.

② After it receives the request, the Web server searches through its system for the resource.

Fig. 20.1 Web server/client interaction. Step 1: The **GET** request, **GET /books/downloads.htm HTTP/1.1**.

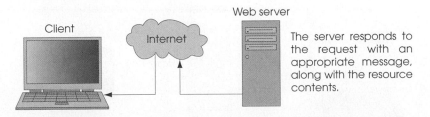

The server responds to the request with an appropriate message, along with the resource contents.

Fig. 20.2 Client interacting with Web server. Step 2: The HTTP response, **HTTP/1.1 200 OK**.

The server then sends one or more *HTTP headers,* which provide information about the data that will be sent. In this case, the server is sending an HTML text document, so the HTTP header for this example reads:

```
Content-type: text/html
```

This header specifies the *Multipurpose Internet Mail Extensions* (*MIME*) type of the content that the server is transmitting to the browser. MIME is an Internet standard used to identify various types of data so that programs can interpret those data correctly. For example, the MIME type **text/plain** indicates that the information is plain-text, which a Web browser can display directly without any special formatting. Similarly, the MIME type **image/gif** indicates that the transmitted content is a GIF image, enabling the Web browser to display the image appropriately.

The set of headers is followed by a blank line, which indicates to the client that the server is finished sending HTTP headers. The server then sends the contents of the requested HTML document (**downloads.htm**). The server terminates the connection when the transfer of the resource is complete. At this point, the client-side browser parses the HTML it has received and *renders* (or displays) the results.

20.3 System Architecture

Most Web-based applications are *multi-tier applications* (sometimes referred to as *n*-tier applications). Multi-tier applications divide functionality into separate *tiers* (i.e., logical groupings of functionality). Although tiers can be located on the same computer, the tiers of Web-based applications typically reside on separate computers. Figure 20.3 presents the basic structure of a three-tier Web-based application.

The *information tier* (also called the *data tier* or the *bottom tier*) maintains data that pertains to the application. This tier typically stores data in a *relational database management system (RDBMS)*. We discussed RDBMSs in Chapter 19, Database, SQL and ADO .NET. For example, a retail store might maintain a database for storing product information, such as descriptions, prices and quantities in stock. The same database also might contain customer information, such as user names, billing addresses and credit-card numbers. This tier can be comprised of multiple databases, which together contain the data needed for our application.

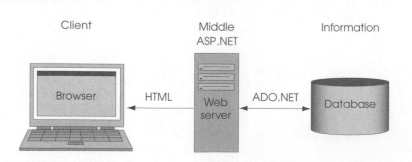

Fig. 20.3   Three-tier architecture.

The *middle tier* implements *business logic*, *controller logic* and *presentation logic* to control interactions between application clients and application data. The middle tier acts as an intermediary between data in the information tier and the application's clients. The middle-tier controller logic processes client requests (such as requests to view a product catalog) and retrieves data from the database. The middle-tier presentation logic then processes data from the information tier and presents the content to the client. Web applications typically present data to clients in the form of HTML documents.

Business logic in the middle tier enforces *business rules* and ensures that data are reliable before the server application updates the database or presents data to users. Business rules dictate how clients can and cannot access application data and how applications process data.

The *client tier*, or *top tier*, is the application's user interface, which typically is a Web browser. Users interact directly with the application through the user interface. The client tier interacts with the middle tier to make requests and to retrieve data from the information tier. The client tier then displays to the user the data retrieved by the middle tier.

20.4 Creating and Running a Simple Web Form Example

In this section, we present our first example of an ASP .NET application. When run, this program displays the text **A Simple Web Form Example**, followed by the Web server's time. As mentioned previously, the program consists of two related files—an ASPX file (Fig. 20.4) and a C# code-behind file (Fig. 20.5). We present the markup in the ASPX file, the code in the code-behind file and the output of the application first; then, we carefully guide the reader through the step-by-step process of creating this program. [*Note*: The markup in Fig. 20.4 and other ASPX file listings in this chapter has been reformatted for presentation purposes.]

```
1   <%-- Fig. 20.4: WebTime.aspx          --%>
2   <%-- A page that contains two labels. --%>
3
4   <%@ Page language="c#" Codebehind="WebTime.aspx.cs"
5       AutoEventWireup="false" Inherits="WebTime.WebTimeTest"
6       EnableSessionState="False" enableViewState="False"%>
7
8   <!DOCTYPE HTML PUBLIC "-//W3C//DTD HTML 4.0 Transitional//EN" >
9
10  <HTML>
11     <HEAD>
12        <title>WebTime</title>
13           <meta name="GENERATOR"
14              Content="Microsoft Visual Studio 7.0">
15           <meta name="CODE_LANGUAGE" Content="C#">
16           <meta name="vs_defaultClientScript"
17              content="JavaScript">
18           <meta name="vs_targetSchema"
19              content="http://schemas.microsoft.com/intellisense/ie5">
20     </HEAD>
```

Fig. 20.4 ASPX page that displays the Web server's time. (Part 1 of 2.)

```
21
22      <body MS_POSITIONING="GridLayout">
23         <form id="WebForm1" method="post" runat="server">
24            <asp:Label id="promptLabel" style="Z-INDEX: 101;
25               LEFT: 25px; POSITION: absolute; TOP: 23px"
26               runat="server" Font-Size="Medium">
27               A Simple Web Form Example
28            </asp:Label>
29
30            <asp:Label id="timeLabel" style="Z-INDEX: 102;
31               LEFT: 25px; POSITION: absolute; TOP: 55px"
32               runat="server" Font-Size="XX-Large"
33               BackColor="Black" ForeColor="LimeGreen">
34            </asp:Label>
35         </form>
36      </body>
37   </HTML>
```

Fig. 20.4   ASPX page that displays the Web server's time. (Part 2 of 2.)

Visual Studio generates the markup shown in Fig. 20.4 when the programmer drags two **Label**s onto a Web Form and sets their properties. Notice that the ASPX file contains other information, in addition to HTML.

Lines 1–2 of Fig. 20.4 are *ASP .NET comments* that indicate the figure number, the file name and the purpose of the file. ASP.NET comments begin with **<%--** and terminate with **--%>**. Lines 4–6 use a **<%@ Page...%>** *directive* to specify information needed to process this file. The *language* of the code-behind file is specified as *C#*, and the code-behind file is named **WebTime.aspx.cs**.

The **AutoEventWireup** attribute determines how event handlers are linked to a control's events. When **AutoEventWireup** is set to **true**, ASP .NET determines which methods in the class to call in response to an event generated by a user's interaction with the Web page. ASP .NET will call the proper event handlers for a Web control (based on a specific naming convention for event handlers) without using a delegate, thus eliminating the need for the programmer to add a delegate for the event handler. This elimination is particularly convenient when developers are not using Visual Studio and therefore must add all code themselves. When Visual Studio .NET generates an ASPX file, it sets **AutoEventWireup** to **false**, because Visual Studio generates the necessary event delegates for us. If we were to set **AutoEventWireup** to **true** in Visual Studio (where all the delegates are added automatically) an event handler could be called twice—once through the delegate, and once as a result of **AutoEventWireup**.

The **Inherits** attribute specifies the class in the code-behind file from which this ASP .NET document inherits—in this case, **WebTimeTest**. We say more about **Inherits** momentarily. [*Note*: We explicitly set the **EnableViewState** attribute and the **EnableSessionState** attribute to **false**. We explain the significance of these attributes later in the chapter.]

Line 8 is called the *document type declaration*, which specifies the document element name (**HTML**) and the uniform resource identifier (URI) for the DTD. Lines 10–11 contain the **<HTML>** and **<HEAD>** start tags, respectively. **HTML** documents have root element

HTML and mark up information about the document in the **HEAD** element. Line 12 sets the title for this Web page. Lines 13–19 display a series of *meta elements* that contain information about the document. Two important **meta**-element attributes are *name*, which identifies the **meta** element, and *content*, which stores the **meta** element's data. Visual Studio generates these **meta** elements when an ASPX file is created.

Line 22 contains the **<body>** start tag, which marks the beginning of the Web page's viewable content; the body contains the content that the browser displays. The **Form** that contains our controls is defined in lines 23–35. Notice the *runat* attribute in line 23, which is set to **"server"**. This attribute indicates that the server processes the **form** and generates HTML to send to the client.

Lines 24–28 and 30–34 display the markup for two **Label** Web controls. The properties that we set in the **Properties** window, such as **Font-Size** and **Text**, are attributes here. The *asp:* tag prefix in the declaration of the *Label* tag indicates that the label is an ASP .NET Web control. Each Web control maps to a corresponding HTML element.

Portability Tip 20.1

A single type of Web control can map to different HTML elements, depending on the client browser and the Web control's property settings.

In this example, the **asp:Label** control maps to the HTML *span* element. A **span** element simply contains text. This particular element is used because **span** elements facilitate the application of styles to text. Several of the property values that were applied to our labels are represented as part of the **style** attribute of the **span** element. We will see the **span** elements that are created by this control shortly.

Each Web control in our example contains the **runat="server"** attribute-value pair, because these controls must be processed on the server. If this attribute pair is not present, the **asp:Label** element is written to the client. (i.e., the control will not be converted into a **span** element, and the Web browser will not render the element properly.)

Figure 20.5 presents the code-behind file for our example. Recall that the ASPX file in Fig. 20.4 references this file in line 4. We present the complete code listing here. In the remaining examples, we omit portions of the generated code that are not relevant to our discussion. In such examples, we insert a comment to indicate where the generated code would appear.

```
1   // Fig. 20.5: WebTime.aspx.cs
2   // The code-behind file for a page
3   // that displays the Web server's time.
4
5   using System;
6   using System.Collections;
7   using System.ComponentModel;
8   using System.Data;
9   using System.Drawing;
10  using System.Web;
11  using System.Web.SessionState;
12
```

Fig. 20.5   Code-behind file for a page that displays the Web server's time. (Part 1 of 3.)

```
13    // definitions for graphical controls used in Web Forms
14    using System.Web.UI;
15    using System.Web.UI.WebControls;
16    using System.Web.UI.HtmlControls;
17
18    namespace WebTime
19    {
20       /// <summary>
21       /// display current time
22       /// </summary>
23       public class WebTimeTest : System.Web.UI.Page
24       {
25          protected System.Web.UI.WebControls.Label promptLabel;
26          protected System.Web.UI.WebControls.Label timeLabel;
27
28          // event handler for Load event
29          private void Page_Load(
30             object sender, System.EventArgs e )
31          {
32             // display current time
33             timeLabel.Text =
34                String.Format( "{0:D2}:{1:D2}:{2:D2}",
35                DateTime.Now.Hour, DateTime.Now.Minute,
36                DateTime.Now.Second );
37          }
38
39          // event handler for Init event; sets
40          // timeLabel to Web server's time
41          #region Web Form Designer generated code
42          override protected void OnInit( EventArgs e )
43          {
44             //
45             // CODEGEN: This call is required by the
46             // ASP.NET Web Form Designer.
47             //
48             InitializeComponent();
49             base.OnInit( e );
50          }
51
52          /// <summary>
53          /// Required method for Designer support - do not modify
54          /// the contents of this method with the code editor.
55          /// </summary>
56          private void InitializeComponent()
57          {
58             this.Load += new System.EventHandler(
59                this.Page_Load );
60          }
61          #endregion
62
63       } // end class WebTimeTest
64
65    } // end namespace WebTime
```

Fig. 20.5   Code-behind file for a page that displays the Web server's time. (Part 2 of 3.)

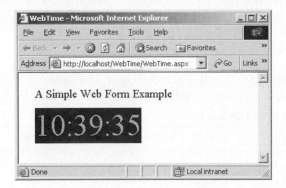

Fig. 20.5   Code-behind file for a page that displays the Web server's time. (Part 3 of 3.)

Notice the **using** statements on lines 10–16. These statements specify namespaces that contain classes for developing Web-based applications. The key namespace on which we initially focus is *System.Web*, which contains classes that manage client requests and server responses. Some of the other namespaces define the available controls and various manipulations of these controls; we discuss the other namespaces throughout the chapter as they become more relevant.

Line 23 begins the class definition for **WebTimeTest**, which inherits from class *Page*. This class defines the requested Web page and is located in the *System.Web.UI* namespace (line 14), which contains classes for the creation of Web-based applications and controls. Class **Page** also provides event handlers and objects necessary for creating Web-based applications. In addition to the **Page** class (from which all Web Forms directly or indirectly inherit), **System.Web.UI** also includes the *Control* class. This class is the base class that provides common functionality for all Web controls.

Lines 25–26 declare references to two **Label**s. These **Label**s are Web controls, defined in namespace *System.Web.UI.WebControls* (line 15). This namespace contains Web controls employed in the design of the page's user interface. Web controls in this namespace derive from class *WebControl*.

Lines 42–50 define method *OnInit*, which is called when the *Init* event is raised. This event, which is the first event raised when a client requests the Web form, indicates that the page is ready to be initialized. Method **OnInit** calls method **InitializeComponent** (defined in lines 56–60). As in Windows Forms, this method is used to set some initial properties of the application's components. The method also can be used to register events. Method **InitializeComponent** creates and attaches an event handler for the *Load* event, which is raised when the page loads (this event occurs after all the Web controls on the page have been initialized and loaded). After **InitializeComponent** executes, method **OnInit** calls the base class's (**Page**'s) **OnInit** method to perform any additional initialization that might be required (line 49).

How are the ASPX file and the code-behind file used to create the Web page that is sent to the client? First, recall that class **WebTimeTest** is the base class specified in line 5 of the ASPX file (Fig. 20.4). Class **WebTimeTest** inherits from **Page**, which defines the general functionality of a Web page. In addition to inheriting this functionality, **WebTimeTest** defines some of its own (i.e., displaying the current time). The code-behind file is the file that defines this functionality, whereas the ASPX file defines the GUI. When a client requests an ASPX file, a class is created behind the scenes that contains both the visual aspect of our page (defined in the ASPX file) and the logic of our page (defined in the code-behind file). The new class inherits from **Page**. The first time that our Web page is requested, this class is compiled, and an instance is created. This instance represents our page—it creates the HTML that is sent to the client. The assembly created from our compiled class is placed in the project's **bin** directory.

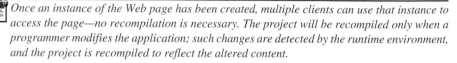

Performance Tip 20.1

Once an instance of the Web page has been created, multiple clients can use that instance to access the page—no recompilation is necessary. The project will be recompiled only when a programmer modifies the application; such changes are detected by the runtime environment, and the project is recompiled to reflect the altered content.

Let us look briefly at how the code in our Web page executes. When the Web server creates an instance of our page to serve a client request, the **Init** event occurs first, invoking method **OnInit**. This method calls **InitializeComponent**. In addition, method **OnInit** might contain code for initializing objects. After this occurs, the **Load** event is generated, which calls method **Page_Load**. This event handler executes any processing that is necessary to restore data that was used in previous requests to the page. Lines 33–36 of the **Load** event handler set **timeLabel**'s **Text** property to the Web server's time. We include this code in the **Load** event handler so that the time will be updated with every page request. After this event handler finishes executing, the page processes any events raised by the page's controls. This includes the handling of any events generated by the user, such as button clicks. When the Web Form object is ready for garbage collection, an **Unload** event is generated. Although not present in our example, event handler **Page_Unload** is inherited from class **Page**. This event handler contains code that releases resources, especially any *unmanaged resources* (i.e., resources not managed by the CLR).

Figure 20.6 depicts the HTML generated by the ASP .NET application. To view this HTML, select **View > Source** in Internet Explorer.

```
1   <!-- Fig. 20.6: WebTime.html                      -->
2   <!-- The HTML generated when WebTime is loaded. -->
3
4   <!DOCTYPE HTML PUBLIC "-//W3C//DTD HTML 4.0 Transitional//EN" >
5
6   <HTML>
7      <HEAD>
8         <title>WebTime</title>
9         <meta name="GENERATOR"
10           Content="Microsoft Visual Studio 7.0">
11        <meta name="CODE_LANGUAGE" Content="C#">
12        <meta name="vs_defaultClientScript" content="JavaScript">
13        <meta name="vs_targetSchema"
14           content="http://schemas.microsoft.com/intellisense/ie5">
15     </HEAD>
16
```

Fig. 20.6 HTML response when the browser requests **WebTime.aspx**. (Part 1 of 2.)

```
17        <body MS_POSITIONING="GridLayout">
18           <form name="WebForm1" method="post"
19              action="WebTime.aspx" id="WebForm1">
20              <input type="hidden" name="__VIEWSTATE"
21                 value="dDwtNjA2MTkwMTQ5Ozs+" />
22
23              <span id="promptLabel"
24                 style="font-size:Medium;Z-INDEX: 101; LEFT: 25px;
25                 POSITION: absolute; TOP: 23px">
26                 A Simple Web Form Example
27              </span>
28
29              <span id="timeLabel" style="color:LimeGreen;
30                 background-color:Black;font-size:XX-Large;
31                 Z-INDEX: 102; LEFT: 25px; POSITION: absolute;
32                 TOP: 55px">10:39:35
33              </span>
34           </form>
35        </body>
36     </HTML>
```

Fig. 20.6   HTML response when the browser requests **WebTime.aspx**. (Part 2 of 2.)

The contents of this page are similar to those of the ASPX file. Lines 7–15 define a document header similar to the one in Fig. 20.4. Lines 17–35 define the body of the document. Line 18 begins the form, which is a mechanism for collecting user information and sending it to the Web server. In this particular program, the user does not submit data to the Web server for processing.

HTML forms can contain visual and nonvisual components. Visual components include buttons and other GUI components with which users interact. Nonvisual components, called *hidden inputs*, store any data that the document author specifies, such as e-mail addresses entered by users of the Web page. One of these hidden inputs is defined in lines 20–21. We discuss the precise meaning of this hidden input later in the chapter. Attribute **method** of element **form** (line 18) specifies the method by which the Web browser submits the form to the server (in this example **post**). The **action** attribute in the **form** element identifies the name and location of the resource that will be requested when this form is submitted; in this case, **WebTime.aspx**. Recall that the ASPX file's **form** element contained the **runat="server"** attribute-value pair. When the **form** is processed on the server, the **name="WebForm1"** and **action="WebTime.aspx"** attribute-value pairs are added to the HTML **form** sent to the client browser.

In the ASPX file, the form's labels were Web controls. Here, we are viewing the HTML created by our application, so the **form** contains **span** elements to represent the text in our labels. In this particular case, ASP .NET maps the **Label** Web controls to HTML **span** elements. Each **span** element contains formatting information, such as size and placement of the text being displayed. Most of the information specified as properties of **timeLabel** and **promptLabel** are specified in the **style** attribute of each **span**.

Now that we have presented the ASPX file and the code-behind file, we outline the process by which we created this application:[2]

1. *Create the project.* Select **File > New > Project...** to display the **New Project** dialog (Fig. 20.7). In this dialog, select **Visual C# Projects** in the left pane and then ***ASP.NET Web Application*** in the right pane. Notice that the field for the project is grayed out. Rather than using this field, we specify the name and location of the project in the **Location** field. We want the project to be located at the Web address **http://localhost**, which is the URL for IIS's root directory (typically **C:\InetPub\wwwroot**). The name *localhost* indicates that the client and server reside on the same machine. If the Web server were located on a different machine, **localhost** would be replaced with the appropriate IP address or hostname. By default, Visual Studio assigns the project name **WebApplication1**, which we changed to **WebTime**. IIS must be running to create the project successfully. IIS can be started by executing **inetmgr.exe**, right clicking **Default Web Site** in the dialog that appears and selecting **Start**. [*Note*: Students might need to expand the node representing their computer to display the **Default Web Site**.] Below the **Location** text box, the text "**Project will be created at http://localhost/WebTime**" appears. This indicates that the project's folder is located in the Web server's root directory. When the developer clicks **OK**, the project is created; this action also produces a virtual directory, which is linked to the project folder. The ***Create New Web*** dialog is displayed next, while Visual Studio creates the Web site on the server (Fig. 20.8).

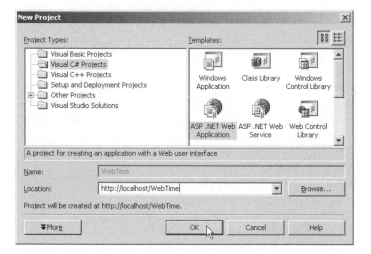

Fig. 20.7   Creating an **ASP .NET Web Application** in Visual Studio.

2. The steps provided in this chapter enable readers to create Web applications of their own. If the readers would like to run the examples included on the CD for this chapter, they must first create a virtual directory in Microsoft Internet Information Services. For instructions, visit the **Downloads/Resources** link at **www.deitel.com**. Once the virtual directory has been created and the application has been opened, students will need to set the start page for the Web application. To do this, right-click the ASPX file and select **Set as Start Page**.

Fig. 20.8 Visual Studio creating and linking a virtual directory for the **WebTime** project folder.

2. *Examine the newly created project.* The next several figures describe the new project's content; we begin with the **Solution Explorer**, shown in Fig. 20.9. As with Windows applications, Visual Studio creates several files when a new **ASP .NET Web Application** is created. **WebForm1.aspx** is the Web Form. (**WebForm1** is the default name for this file.) A code-behind file also is included as part of the project. To view the ASPX file's code-behind file, right click the ASPX file and select **View Code**. Alternatively, the programmer can click an icon to display all files, then expand the node for our ASPX page (see Fig. 20.9.). [*Note*: To see the code-behind file listed in the **Solution Explorer**, the reader might need to select the icon that displays all files.]

The next figure, Fig. 20.10, shows the **Web Forms** listed in the **Toolbox**. The left figure displays the beginning of the Web controls list, and the right figure displays the remaining Web controls. Notice that some controls are similar to the Windows controls presented earlier in the book.

Figure 20.11 shows the Web Form designer for **WebForm1.aspx**. It consists of a grid on which users drag and drop components, such as buttons and labels, from the **Toolbox**.

The Web Form designer's *HTML* mode (Fig. 20.12) allows the programmer to view the markup that represents the user interface. Clicking the **HTML** button in the lower-left corner of the Web Form designer switches the Web Form designer to HTML mode. Similarly, clicking the *Design* button (to the left of the **HTML** button) returns the Web Form designer to design mode.

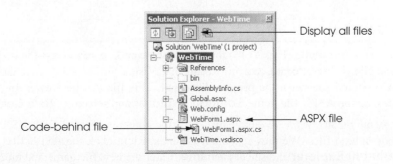

Fig. 20.9 **Solution Explorer** window for project **WebTime**.

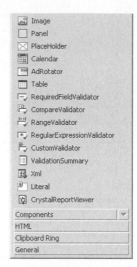

Fig. 20.10 **Web Forms** menu in the **Toolbox**.

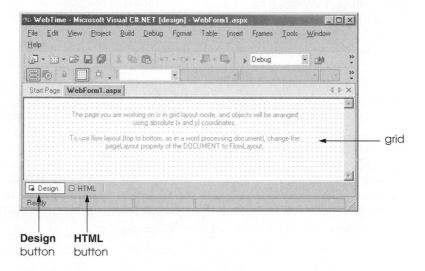

Design button   **HTML** button

Fig. 20.11 **Design** mode of Web Form designer.

The next figure (Fig. 20.13) displays **WebForm1.aspx.cs**—the code-behind file for **WebForm1.aspx**. Recall that Visual Studio .NET generates this code-behind file when the project is created. This file can be viewed by right-clicking the ASPX file in the **Solution Explorer** and selecting **View Code**.

3. *Rename the ASPX file.* We have displayed the contents of the default ASPX and code-behind files. We now rename these files. Right click the ASPX file in the **Solution Explorer** and select **Rename**. Enter the new file name and hit *Enter*. This updates the name of both the ASPX file and the code-behind file. In this example, we use the name **WebTime.aspx**.

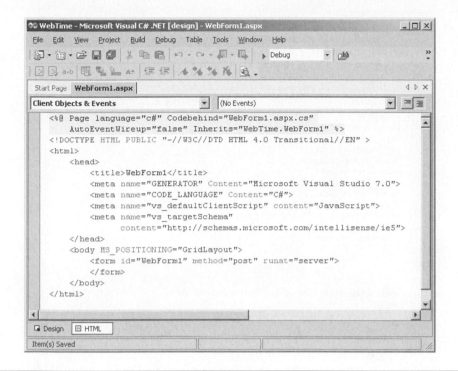

Fig. 20.12 HTML mode of Web Form designer.

4. *Design the page.* Designing a Web Form is as simple as designing a Windows Form. To add controls to the page, drag and drop them from the **Toolbox** onto the Web Form. Like the Web Form itself, each control is an object that has properties, methods and events. Developers can set these properties and events using the **Properties** window.

The ***PageLayout*** property determines how controls are arranged on the form (Fig. 20.14). By default, property **PageLayout** is set to ***GridLayout***, which specifies that all controls are located exactly where they are dropped on the Web Form. This is called *absolute positioning*. Alternatively, the developer can set the Web Form's **PageLayout** property to ***FlowLayout***, which causes controls to be placed sequentially on the Web Form. This is called *relative positioning*, because the controls' positions are relative to the Web Form's upper left corner. We use **GridLayout** for many of our examples. To view the Web Form's properties, select ***Document*** from the drop-down list in the **Properties** window; **Document** is the name used to represent the Web Form in the **Properties** window.

In this example, we use two **Label**s, which developers can place on the Web Form either by drag-and-drop or by double-clicking the **Toolbox**'s **Label** control. Name the first **Label promptLabel** and the second **timeLabel**. We delete **timeLabel**'s text, because this text is set in the code-behind file. When a **Label** does not contain text, the **Label** displays its name in square brackets in the Web Form designer (Fig. 20.15), but this name is not displayed at runtime. We set the text for **promptLabel** to **A Simple Web Form Example**.

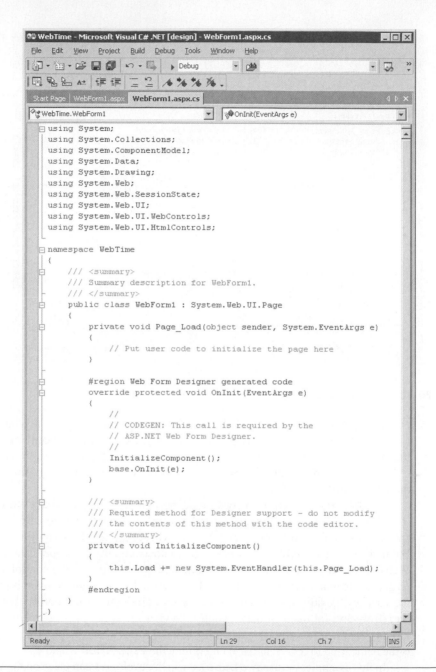

Fig. 20.13 Code-behind file for **WebForm1.aspx** generated by Visual Studio .NET.

We set **timeLabel**'s **BackColor**, **ForeColor** and **Font-Size** properties to **Black**, **LimeGreen** and **XX-Large**, respectively. To change font properties, the programmer must expand the **Font** node in the **Properties** window, then change each relevant property individually. We also set the labels' locations and sizes by dragging the controls. Finally, we set the Web Form's **_Enable-SessionState_** and **_EnableViewState_** properties to **false** (these properties are used to enable session-tracking, discussed in Section 20.6.). Once the **Label**s' properties are set in the **Properties** window, Visual Studio updates the ASPX file's contents. Figure 20.15 shows the IDE after these properties are set.

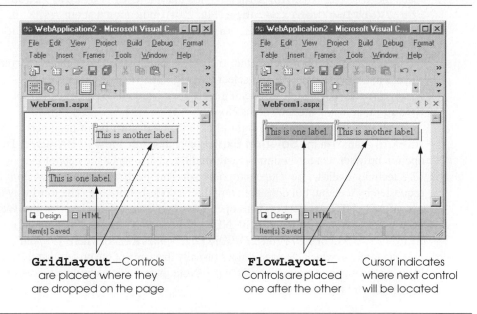

GridLayout—Controls are placed where they are dropped on the page

FlowLayout—Controls are placed one after the other

Cursor indicates where next control will be located

Fig. 20.14 GridLayout and **FlowLayout** illustration.

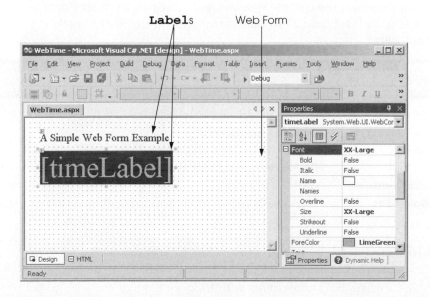

Labels   Web Form

Fig. 20.15 WebForm.aspx after adding two **Label**s and setting their properties.

5. *Add page logic.* Once the user interface has been designed, C# code must be added to the code-behind file. In this example, lines 33–36 of Fig. 20.5 are added to the code-behind file. The statement retrieves the current time and formats it so that the time is in the format *HH*:*MM*:*SS*. For example, 9 a.m. is formatted as **09:00:00**.

6. *Run the program.* Select **Debug > Start**. An Internet Explorer window opens and loads the Web page (the ASPX file). Notice that the URL is **http://localhost/WebTime/WebTime.aspx** (Fig. 20.4), indicating that our ASPX file is located within the directory **WebTime**, which is located in the Web server's root directory.

   After the Web Form is created, the programmer can view it three different ways. First, the programmer can select **Debug>Start** (as described previously), which runs the application by opening a browser window. The IDE exits **Run** or **Debug** mode when the browser is closed.

   The programmer also can right-click either the Web Form designer or the ASPX file name (in the **Solution Explorer**) and select *View In Browser*. This opens a browser window within Visual Studio and displays a preview of the page. This technique allows developers to view what the page will look like when it is requested by a client, but does not compile the code-behind file. The third way to run an ASP .NET application is to open a browser window and type in the Web page's URL. When testing an ASP .NET application on the local computer, type **http://localhost/***ProjectFolder***/***PageName***.aspx**, where *ProjectFolder* is the folder in which the page resides (usually the name of the project), and *PageName* is the name of the ASP .NET page. Note that, if this technique is used, the page must already be compiled.

20.5 Web Controls

This section introduces some of the Web controls located on the **Web Form** tab in the **Toolbox** (Fig. 20.10). Figure 20.16 summarizes some of the Web controls used in the chapter examples.[3]

Web Control	Description
Label	Displays text that the user cannot edit.
Button	Displays a button control.
TextBox	Gathers user input and displays text.
Image	Displays images (e.g., GIF and JPG).
RadioButtonList	Groups radio buttons.
DropDownList	Displays a drop-down list of choices from which the user can select one item.

Fig. 20.16 Web controls commonly used in ASP .NET applications.

3. ASP .NET also provides controls known as *HTML controls*, which represent standard HTML components. Because of the sophisticated functionality provided by the Web controls in ASP .NET, we use these types of controls in the chapter.

20.5.1 Text and Graphics Controls

The form in Fig. 20.17 gathers user input using the controls listed in Fig. 20.16. [*Note*: This example does not contain any functionality (i.e., no action occurs when the user clicks **Register**). We ask the reader to provide the functionality as an exercise. In successive examples, we demonstrate how to add functionality to many of these Web controls.]

Lines 34–37 define an *Image* control, which places an image into a Web page. The *ImageUrl* property (line 36) specifies the file location of the image to display. To specify an image, click the ellipsis button next to the **ImageUrl** property in the **Properties** window; the resulting dialog enables the programmer to browse for the desired image. The top of this dialog displays the contents of this application. If the image is not explicitly part of the project, the programmer will need to use the **Browse** button or add the image to the project. If the image is within the project directory (or any subdirectories thereof), that image can be added explicitly to the project by displaying all files in the **Solution Explorer**, right-clicking the image and selecting **Include in Project**. Once this has been done, the image will be displayed in the list of project files in the dialog that appears when the programmer selects the **ImageUrl** property. Within the dialog, the user is given the option to choose **URL TYPE**, which defines how the location of the image will be specified in the program. Developers have various options for the **URL Type**: They can specify whether they want the image to be referenced as being located on the server, on the local machine or relative to the current path. We have chosen for the location to be specified as a relative path.

Lines 49–52 define a *TextBox* control, which allows the programmer to read and display text. Lines 69–86 define a *RadioButtonList* control, which provides a series of radio buttons from which the user can select only one. Each radio button is defined using a *ListItem* element (lines 73–84). The *HyperLink* control (lines 88–92) adds a hyperlink to a Web page. The *NavigateUrl* property (line 90) of this control specifies the resource that is requested (such as **http://www.deitel.com**) when a user clicks the hyperlink. Lines 94–114 define a *DropDownList*. This control is similar to a **RadioButtonList** in that it allows the user to select exactly one option. When a user clicks the drop-down list, it expands and displays a list from which the user can make a selection. Lines 98–112 define the **ListItem**s that display when the drop-down list is expanded. Like the **Button** Windows control, the *Button* Web control (lines 137–140) represents a button; a button Web control typically maps to an **input** HTML element that has attribute **type** and value **"button"**.

```
 1    <%-- Fig. 20.17: WebControls.aspx     --%>
 2    <%-- Demonstrating some Web controls. --%>
 3
 4    <%@ Page language="c#" Codebehind="WebControls.aspx.cs"
 5        AutoEventWireup="false" Inherits="WebControls.WebForm1"
 6        EnableSessionState="False" enableViewState="False"%>
 7
 8    <!DOCTYPE HTML PUBLIC "-//W3C//DTD HTML 4.0 Transitional//EN" >
 9
10    <HTML>
11        <HEAD>
12
```

Fig. 20.17 Web controls demonstration. (Part 1 of 5.)

```
13          <title>WebForm1</title>
14          <meta name="GENERATOR"
15             Content="Microsoft Visual Studio 7.0">
16          <meta name="CODE_LANGUAGE" Content="C#">
17          <meta name="vs_defaultClientScript"
18             content="JavaScript">
19          <meta name="vs_targetSchema"
20          content="http://schemas.microsoft.com/intellisense/ie5">
21
22       </HEAD>
23
24       <body MS_POSITIONING="GridLayout">
25
26          <form id="Form1" method="post" runat="server">
27
28             <asp:Label id="welcomeLabel" style="Z-INDEX: 101;
29                LEFT: 21px; POSITION: absolute; TOP: 17px"
30                runat="server" Font-Bold="True" Font-Size="Medium">
31                This is a sample registration form.
32             </asp:Label>
33
34             <asp:Image id="operatingImage" style="Z-INDEX: 121;
35                LEFT: 21px; POSITION: absolute; TOP: 371px"
36                runat="server" ImageUrl="images\os.png">
37             </asp:Image>
38
39             <asp:Image id="publicationImage" style="Z-INDEX: 120;
40                LEFT: 21px; POSITION: absolute; TOP: 245px"
41                runat="server" ImageUrl="images\downloads.png">
42             </asp:Image>
43
44             <asp:Image id="userImage" style="Z-INDEX: 119;
45                LEFT: 21px; POSITION: absolute; TOP: 91px"
46                runat="server" ImageUrl="images\user.png">
47             </asp:Image>
48
49             <asp:TextBox id="emailTextBox" style="Z-INDEX: 118;
50                LEFT: 95px; POSITION: absolute;
51                TOP: 161px" runat="server">
52             </asp:TextBox>
53
54             <asp:TextBox id="firstTextBox" style="Z-INDEX: 117;
55                LEFT: 95px; POSITION: absolute; TOP: 127px"
56                runat="server">
57             </asp:TextBox>
58
59             <asp:TextBox id="lastTextBox" style="Z-INDEX: 116;
60                LEFT: 341px; POSITION: absolute;
61                TOP: 127px" runat="server">
62             </asp:TextBox>
63
64             <asp:TextBox id="phoneTextBox" style="Z-INDEX: 115;
65                LEFT: 341px; POSITION: absolute;
```

Fig. 20.17 Web controls demonstration. (Part 2 of 5.)

```
 66                      TOP: 161px" runat="server">
 67            </asp:TextBox>
 68
 69            <asp:RadioButtonList id="operatingRadioButtonList"
 70               style="Z-INDEX: 114; LEFT: 21px;
 71               POSITION: absolute; TOP: 409px" runat="server">
 72
 73               <asp:ListItem Value="Windows NT">Windows NT
 74               </asp:ListItem>
 75
 76               <asp:ListItem Value="Windows 2000">Windows 2000
 77               </asp:ListItem>
 78
 79               <asp:ListItem Value="Windows XP">Windows XP
 80               </asp:ListItem>
 81
 82               <asp:ListItem Value="Linux">Linux</asp:ListItem>
 83
 84               <asp:ListItem Value="Other">Other</asp:ListItem>
 85
 86            </asp:RadioButtonList>
 87
 88            <asp:HyperLink id="booksHyperLink" style="Z-INDEX: 113;
 89               LEFT: 21px; POSITION: absolute; TOP: 316px"
 90               runat="server" NavigateUrl="http://www.deitel.com">
 91               Click here to view more information about our books.
 92            </asp:HyperLink>
 93
 94            <asp:DropDownList id="booksDropDownList"
 95               style="Z-INDEX: 112; LEFT: 21px;
 96               POSITION: absolute; TOP: 282px" runat="server">
 97
 98               <asp:ListItem Value="XML How to Program 1e">
 99                  XML How to Program 1e
100               </asp:ListItem>
101
102               <asp:ListItem Value="C# How to Program 1e">
103                  C# How to Program 1e
104               </asp:ListItem>
105
106              <asp:ListItem Value="Visual Basic .NET How to Program 2e">
107                  Visual Basic .NET How to Program 2e
108               </asp:ListItem>
109
110               <asp:ListItem Value="C++ How to Program 3e">
111                  C++ How to Program 3e
112               </asp:ListItem>
113
114            </asp:DropDownList>
115
116            <asp:Image id="phoneImage" style="Z-INDEX: 111;
117               LEFT: 266px; POSITION: absolute; TOP: 161px"
118               runat="server" ImageUrl="images\phone.png">
```

Fig. 20.17 Web controls demonstration. (Part 3 of 5.)

```
119                 </asp:Image>
120
121             <asp:Image id="emailImage" style="Z-INDEX: 110;
122                 LEFT: 21px; POSITION: absolute; TOP: 161px"
123                 runat="server" ImageUrl="images\email.png">
124             </asp:Image>
125
126             <asp:Image id="lastImage" style="Z-INDEX: 109;
127                 LEFT: 266px; POSITION: absolute; TOP: 127px"
128                 runat="server" ImageUrl="images\lname.png">
129             </asp:Image>
130
131             <asp:Image id="firstImage" style="Z-INDEX: 108;
132                 LEFT: 21px; POSITION: absolute;
133                 TOP: 127px" runat="server"
134                 ImageUrl="images\fname.png">
135             </asp:Image>
136
137             <asp:Button id="registerButton" style="Z-INDEX: 107;
138                 LEFT: 21px; POSITION: absolute; TOP: 547px"
139                 runat="server" Text="Register">
140             </asp:Button>
141
142             <asp:Label id="bookLabel" style="Z-INDEX: 106;
143                 LEFT: 216px; POSITION: absolute; TOP: 245px"
144                 runat="server" ForeColor="DarkCyan">
145                 Which book would you like information about?
146             </asp:Label>
147
148             <asp:Label id="fillLabel" style="Z-INDEX: 105;
149                 LEFT: 218px; POSITION: absolute; TOP: 91px"
150                 runat="server" ForeColor="DarkCyan">
151                 Please fill out the fields below.
152             </asp:Label>
153
154             <asp:Label id="phoneLabel" style="Z-INDEX: 104;
155                 LEFT: 266px; POSITION: absolute;
156                 TOP: 198px" runat="server">
157                 Must be in the form (555)555-5555.
158             </asp:Label>
159
160             <asp:Label id="operatingLabel" style="Z-INDEX: 103;
161                 LEFT: 220px; POSITION: absolute; TOP: 371px"
162                 runat="server" Height="9px" ForeColor="DarkCyan">
163                 Which operating system are you using?
164             </asp:Label>
165
166             <asp:Label id="registerLabel" style="Z-INDEX: 102;
167                 LEFT: 21px; POSITION: absolute; TOP: 46px"
168                 runat="server" Font-Italic="True">
169                 Please fill in all fields and click Register.
170             </asp:Label>
171
```

Fig. 20.17 Web controls demonstration. (Part 4 of 5.)

```
172        </form>
173      </body>
174  </HTML>
```

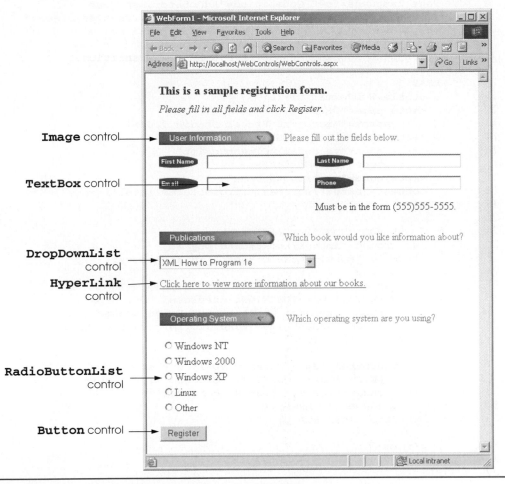

Fig. 20.17 Web controls demonstration. (Part 5 of 5.)

20.5.2 **AdRotator** Control

Web pages often contain product and service advertisements; these advertisements usually consist of images. Although Web site authors want to sell advertisements to as many sponsors as possible, Web pages can display only a limited number of advertisements at once. To address this problem, ASP .NET provides the **AdRotator** Web control for displaying advertisements. Using advertisement data located in an XML file, the **AdRotator** control randomly selects an image to display and generates a hyperlink to the Web page associated with that image. Browsers that do not support images display a text alternative, which is specified in the XML document.

Figure 20.18 demonstrates the **AdRotator** Web control. The images that we rotate in this example include the flags of eleven countries. When a user clicks the displayed flag

```
1    <%-- Fig. 20.18: AdRotator.aspx                        --%>
2    <%-- A Web Form that demonstrates class AdRotator. --%>
3
4    <%@ Page language="c#" Codebehind="AdRotator.aspx.cs"
5        AutoEventWireup="false" Inherits="AdRotatorTest.AdRotator"
6        EnableSessionState="False" enableViewState="False"%>
7
8    <!DOCTYPE HTML PUBLIC "-//W3C//DTD HTML 4.0 Transitional//EN" >
9    <HTML>
10       <HEAD>
11          <title>WebForm1</title>
12          <meta name="GENERATOR"
13             Content="Microsoft Visual Studio 7.0">
14          <meta name="CODE_LANGUAGE" Content="C#">
15          <meta name="vs_defaultClientScript"
16             content="JavaScript">
17          <meta name="vs_targetSchema"
18             content="http://schemas.microsoft.com/intellisense/ie5">
19       </HEAD>
20
21       <body MS_POSITIONING="GridLayout">
22          background="images/background.png">
23          <form id="Form1" method="post" runat="server">
24
25             <asp:AdRotator id="adRotator" style="Z-INDEX: 101;
26                LEFT: 17px; POSITION: absolute; TOP: 69px"
27                runat="server" Width="86px" Height="60px"
28                AdvertisementFile="AdRotatorInformation.xml">
29             </asp:AdRotator>
30
31             <asp:Label id="adRotatorLabel" style="Z-INDEX: 102;
32                LEFT: 17px; POSITION: absolute; TOP: 26px"
33                runat="server" Font-Size="Large">
34                AdRotator Example
35             </asp:Label> 
36
37          </form>
38       </body>
39    </HTML>
```

Fig. 20.18 AdRotator class demonstrated on a Web form.

image, the browser is redirected to a Web page containing information about the country that the flag represents. If a user clicks refresh or re-requests the page, one of the eleven flags is chosen again at random and displayed.

The ASPX file in Fig. 20.18 is similar to that of Fig. 20.4. However, instead of two **Label**s, this page contains one **Label** and one **AdRotator** control, named **adRotator**. The **background** property for our page is set to display the image **background.png**. To specify this file, click the ellipsis button provided next to the **Background** property and use the resulting dialog to browse for **background.png**.

In the **Properties** window, we set the **AdRotator** control's ***Advertisement-File*** property to **AdRotatorInformation.xml** (line 28). The Web control determines which advertisement from this file to display. We present the contents of this XML

file momentarily. As illustrated in Fig. 20.19, the programmer does not need to add any
code to the code-behind file, because the **AdRotator** control does "all the work."

The output depicts two different requests—the first time the page is requested, the
American flag is shown, and, in the second request, the Latvian flag is displayed. The last
image depicts the Web page that loads when a user clicks the Latvian flag.

```
1   // Fig. 20.19: AdRotator.aspx.cs
2   // The code-behind file for a page that
3   // demonstrates the AdRotator class.
4
5   using System;
6   using System.Collections;
7   using System.ComponentModel;
8   using System.Data;
9   using System.Drawing;
10  using System.Web;
11  using System.Web.SessionState;
12  using System.Web.UI;
13  using System.Web.UI.WebControls;
14  using System.Web.UI.HtmlControls;
15
16  namespace AdRotatorTest
17  {
18      /// page that demonstrates AdRotator
19      public class AdRotator : System.Web.UI.Page
20      {
21          protected System.Web.UI.WebControls.AdRotator adRotator;
22          protected System.Web.UI.WebControls.Label adRotatorLabel;
23
24          // Visual Studio .NET generated code
25
26      } // end class AdRotator
27
28  } // end namespace AdRotatorTest
```

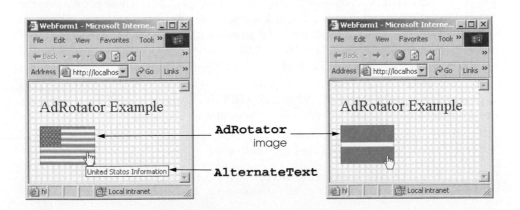

Fig. 20.19 Code-behind file for page demonstrating the **AdRotator** class. (Part 1
of 2.)

Fig. 20.19 Code-behind file for page demonstrating the **AdRotator** class. (Part 2 of 2.)

XML document **AdRotatorInformation.xml** (Fig. 20.20) contains several **Ad** elements, each of which provides information about an advertisement for the **AdRotator**. Element **ImageUrl** specifies the relative path (location) of the advertisement's image, and element **NavigateUrl** specifies the URL for the Web page that loads when a user clicks the advertisement. The **AlternateText** element contains text that displays in place of the image when the browser cannot locate or render the image (i.e., because the file is missing, or because the browser is not capable of displaying it). The **AlternateText** element's text also is a *tooltip* that the Web browser displays when a user places the mouse pointer over the image (Fig. 20.19). A tooltip is a caption that appears when the mouse hovers over a control and provides the user with information about that control. The **Impressions** element specifies how often a particular image appears, relative to the other images. An advertisement that has a higher **Impressions** value displays more frequently than an advertisement with a lower value. In our example, the advertisements display with equal probability, because each **Impressions**' value is set to **1**. Advertisers often purchase advertisements on Web sites based on the number of impressions the advertisement will receive.

```
1   <?xml version="1.0" encoding="utf-8"?>
2
3   <!-- Fig. 20.20: AdRotatorInformation.xml          -->
4   <!-- XML file containing advertisement information. -->
5
6   <Advertisements>
```

Fig. 20.20 AdvertisementFile used in **AdRotator** example. (Part 1 of 3.)

```
7        <Ad>
8            <ImageUrl>images/us.png</ImageUrl>
9            <NavigateUrl>
10             http://www.odci.gov/cia/publications/factbook/geos/us.html
11           </NavigateUrl>
12           <AlternateText>United States Information</AlternateText>
13           <Impressions>1</Impressions>
14       </Ad>
15
16       <Ad>
17         <ImageUrl>images/france.png</ImageUrl>
18         <NavigateUrl>
19             http://www.odci.gov/cia/publications/factbook/geos/fr.html
20         </NavigateUrl>
21         <AlternateText>France Information</AlternateText>
22         <Impressions>1</Impressions>
23       </Ad>
24
25       <Ad>
26         <ImageUrl>images/germany.png</ImageUrl>
27         <NavigateUrl>
28             http://www.odci.gov/cia/publications/factbook/geos/gm.html
29         </NavigateUrl>
30         <AlternateText>Germany Information</AlternateText>
31         <Impressions>1</Impressions>
32       </Ad>
33
34       <Ad>
35         <ImageUrl>images/italy.png</ImageUrl>
36         <NavigateUrl>
37             http://www.odci.gov/cia/publications/factbook/geos/it.html
38         </NavigateUrl>
39         <AlternateText>Italy Information</AlternateText>
40         <Impressions>1</Impressions>
41       </Ad>
42
43       <Ad>
44           <ImageUrl>images/spain.png</ImageUrl>
45           <NavigateUrl>
46             http://www.odci.gov/cia/publications/factbook/geos/sp.html
47           </NavigateUrl>
48           <AlternateText>Spain Information</AlternateText>
49           <Impressions>1</Impressions>
50       </Ad>
51
52       <Ad>
53           <ImageUrl>images/latvia.png</ImageUrl>
54           <NavigateUrl>
55             http://www.odci.gov/cia/publications/factbook/geos/lg.html
56           </NavigateUrl>
57           <AlternateText>Latvia Information</AlternateText>
58           <Impressions>1</Impressions>
59       </Ad>
```

Fig. 20.20 **AdvertisementFile** used in **AdRotator** example. (Part 2 of 3.)

```
60
61          <Ad>
62              <ImageUrl>images/peru.png</ImageUrl>
63              <NavigateUrl>
64                 http://www.odci.gov/cia/publications/factbook/geos/pe.html
65              </NavigateUrl>
66              <AlternateText>Peru Information</AlternateText>
67              <Impressions>1</Impressions>
68          </Ad>
69
70          <Ad>
71              <ImageUrl>images/senegal.png</ImageUrl>
72              <NavigateUrl>
73                 http://www.odci.gov/cia/publications/factbook/geos/sg.html
74              </NavigateUrl>
75              <AlternateText>Senegal Information</AlternateText>
76              <Impressions>1</Impressions>
77          </Ad>
78
79          <Ad>
80              <ImageUrl>images/sweden.png</ImageUrl>
81              <NavigateUrl>
82                 http://www.odci.gov/cia/publications/factbook/geos/sw.html
83              </NavigateUrl>
84              <AlternateText>Sweden Information</AlternateText>
85              <Impressions>1</Impressions>
86          </Ad>
87
88          <Ad>
89              <ImageUrl>images/thailand.png</ImageUrl>
90              <NavigateUrl>
91                 http://www.odci.gov/cia/publications/factbook/geos/th.html
92              </NavigateUrl>
93              <AlternateText>Thailand Information</AlternateText>
94              <Impressions>1</Impressions>
95          </Ad>
96
97          <Ad>
98              <ImageUrl>images/unitedstates.png</ImageUrl>
99              <NavigateUrl>
100                http://www.odci.gov/cia/publications/factbook/geos/us.html
101             </NavigateUrl>
102             <AlternateText>United States Information</AlternateText>
103             <Impressions>1</Impressions>
104         </Ad>
105     </Advertisements>
```

Fig. 20.20 AdvertisementFile used in **AdRotator** example. (Part 3 of 3.)

20.5.3 Validation Controls

This section introduces ASP .NET *validation controls* (or *validators*), which determine whether the data in other Web controls are in the proper format. For example, validators could determine whether a user has provided information in a required field, or whether a

ZIP-code field contains exactly five digits. Validators provide a mechanism for validating user input on the client-side. When the HTML for our page is created, the validator is converted to *ECMAScript*[4] that performs the validation. ECMAScript is a scripting language that enhances the functionality and appearance of Web pages. ECMAScript typically is executed on the client-side. However, if the client does not support scripting or scripting is disabled, validation is performed on the server.

The example in this section prompts the user to input a phone number in the form 555–4567 (i.e., three digits, followed by a hyphen and four more digits.) After the user enters a number, validators ensure that the phone-number field is filled and that the number is in the correct format before the program sends the number to the Web server for further processing. Once the phone number is submitted, the Web server responds with an HTML page containing all possible letter combinations that represent the phone number. The letters used for each digit are the letters found on a phone's key pad. For instance, the 5 button displays the letters j, k and l. For the position in the phone number where a 5 appears, we can substitute one of these three letters. Businesses often use this technique to make their phone numbers easy to remember. Figure 20.21 presents the ASPX file.

```
1   <%-- Fig. 20.21: Generator.aspx                    --%>
2   <%-- A Web Form demonstrating the use of validators. --%>
3
4   <%@ Page language="c#" Codebehind="Generator.aspx.cs"
5   AutoEventWireup="false" Inherits="WordGenerator.Generator" %>
6
7   <!DOCTYPE HTML PUBLIC "-//W3C//DTD HTML 4.0 Transitional//EN" >
8
9   <HTML>
10     <HEAD>
11       <title>WebForm1</title>
12       <meta name="GENERATOR"
13         Content="Microsoft Visual Studio 7.0">
14       <meta name="CODE_LANGUAGE" Content="C#">
15       <meta name="vs_defaultClientScript" content="JavaScript">
16       <meta name="vs_targetSchema" content=
17         "http://schemas.microsoft.com/intellisense/ie5">
18     </HEAD>
19
20     <body MS_POSITIONING="GridLayout">
21       <form id="Form1" method="post" runat="server">
22         <asp:Label id="promptLabel" style="Z-INDEX: 101;
23           LEFT: 16px; POSITION: absolute; TOP: 23px"
24           runat="server">
25           Please enter a phone number in the form 555-4567:
26         </asp:Label>
```

Fig. 20.21 Validators used in a Web Form that generates possible letter combinations from a phone number. (Part 1 of 2.)

---

4. ECMAScript (commonly known as JavaScript) is a scripting standard created by the ECMA (European Computer Manufacturer's Association). Both Netscape's JavaScript and Microsoft's JScript comply with the ECMAScript standard, but each provides additional features beyond the specification. For information on the current ECMAScript standard, visit **www.ecma.ch/ stand/ecma-262.htm**.

```
27
28              <asp:RegularExpressionValidator
29                 id="phoneNumberValidator" style="Z-INDEX: 106;
30                 LEFT: 217px; POSITION: absolute; TOP: 73px"
31                 runat="server" ErrorMessage=
32                 "The phone number must be in the form 555-4567."
33                 ControlToValidate="inputTextBox"
34                 ValidationExpression="^\d{3}-\d{4}$">
35              </asp:RegularExpressionValidator>
36
37              <asp:RequiredFieldValidator
38                 id="phoneInputValidator" style="Z-INDEX: 105;
39                 LEFT: 217px; POSITION: absolute; TOP: 47px"
40                 runat="server" ErrorMessage=
41                 "Please enter a phone number."
42                 ControlToValidate="inputTextBox">
43              </asp:RequiredFieldValidator>
44
45              <asp:TextBox id="outputTextBox" style="Z-INDEX: 104;
46                 LEFT: 16px; POSITION: absolute; TOP: 146px"
47                 runat="server" Visible="False" TextMode="MultiLine"
48                 Height="198px" Width="227px" Font-Bold="True"
49                 Font-Names="Courier New">
50              </asp:TextBox>
51
52              <asp:Button id="submitButton" style="Z-INDEX: 103;
53                 LEFT: 16px; POSITION: absolute; TOP: 86px"
54                 runat="server" Text="Submit">
55              </asp:Button>
56
57              <asp:TextBox id="inputTextBox" style="Z-INDEX: 102;
58                 LEFT: 16px; POSITION: absolute; TOP: 52px"
59                 runat="server">
60              </asp:TextBox>
61          </form>
62       </body>
63    </HTML>
```

Fig. 20.21 Validators used in a Web Form that generates possible letter combinations from a phone number. (Part 2 of 2.)

The HTML page sent to the client browser accepts a phone number in the form *555–4567* and then lists all the possible letter combinations that can be generated from both the first three digits and the last four digits. This example uses a **RegularExpression-Validator** to match another Web control's content against a regular expression. (The use of regular expressions is introduced in Chapter 15, Strings, Characters and Regular Expressions.) Lines 28–35 create a **RegularExpressionValidator** named **phoneNumberValidator**. Property **ErrorMessage**'s text (lines 31–32) is displayed on the Web Form when the validation fails. Property **ValidationExpression** specifies the regular expression with which to validate the user input (line 34). The input is valid if it matches the regular expression, **^\d{3}-\d{4}$** (i.e., the beginning of the string, followed by 3 digits, a hyphen, four additional digits and the end of the string).

Clicking property **ValidationExpression** in the **Properties** window displays a dialog containing a list of regular expressions for phone numbers, ZIP codes and other common data. However, we write our own regular expression in this example, because the phone number input should not contain an area code. Line 33 associates **inputTextBox** with **phoneNumberValidator** by setting property *ControlToValidate* to **inputTextBox**. This indicates that **phoneNumberValidator** verifies the **inputTextBox**'s contents. If the user inputs text that does not have the correct format and attempts to submit the form, the **ErrorMessage** text is displayed in red.

This example also uses a *RequiredFieldValidator*, which ensures that data has been entered in a specific control. Lines 37–43 define **RequiredFieldValidator phoneInputValidator**, which confirms that **inputTextBox**'s content is not empty. If the user does not input any data in **inputTextBox** and attempts to submit the form, validation fails, and the **ErrorMessage** for this validator is displayed in red. If validation is successful, **outputTextBox** (lines 45–50) displays the words generated from the phone number.

Figure 20.22 is the code-behind file for the ASPX file in Fig. 20.21. Note that this code-behind file does not contain any implementation related to the validators. We say more about this momentarily.

```
1   // Fig. 20.22: Generator.aspx.cs
2   // The code-behind file for a page that
3   // generates words from a phone number.
4
5   using System;
6   using System.Collections;
7   using System.ComponentModel;
8   using System.Data;
9   using System.Drawing;
10  using System.Web;
11  using System.Web.SessionState;
12  using System.Web.UI;
13  using System.Web.UI.WebControls;
14  using System.Web.UI.HtmlControls;
15
16  namespace WordGenerator
17  {
18     // page that computes all combinations of letters for first
19     // three digits and last four digits in phone number
20     public class Generator : System.Web.UI.Page
21     {
22        protected System.Web.UI.WebControls.TextBox
23           outputTextBox;
24        protected System.Web.UI.WebControls.TextBox
25           inputTextBox;
26
27        protected
28           System.Web.UI.WebControls.RegularExpressionValidator
29           phoneNumberValidator;
```

Fig. 20.22 Code-behind file for the word-generator page. (Part 1 of 5.)

```
30       protected
31          System.Web.UI.WebControls.RequiredFieldValidator
32          phoneInputValidator;
33
34       protected System.Web.UI.WebControls.Button submitButton;
35       protected System.Web.UI.WebControls.Label promptLabel;
36
37       private void Page_Load(
38          object sender, System.EventArgs e )
39       {
40          // if page loaded due to a postback
41          if ( IsPostBack )
42          {
43             outputTextBox.Text = "";
44
45             // retrieve number and remove "-"
46             string number = Request.Form[ "inputTextBox" ];
47             number = number.Remove( 3, 1 );
48
49             // generate words for first 3 digits
50             outputTextBox.Text += "Here are the words for\n";
51             outputTextBox.Text +=
52                "the first three digits:\n\n";
53             ComputeWords( number.Substring( 0, 3 ), "" );
54             outputTextBox.Text += "\n";
55
56             // generate words for last 4 digits
57             outputTextBox.Text += "Here are the words for\n";
58             outputTextBox.Text +=
59                "the first four digits:\n\n";
60             ComputeWords( number.Substring( 3 ), "" );
61
62             outputTextBox.Visible = true;
63
64          } // end if
65
66       } // end method Page_Load
67
68       // Visual Studio .NET generated code
69
70       private void ComputeWords(
71          string number, string temporaryWord )
72       {
73          if ( number == "" )
74          {
75             outputTextBox.Text += temporaryWord + "\n";
76             return;
77          }
78
79          int current =
80             Int32.Parse( number.Substring( 0, 1 ) );
81
82          number = number.Remove( 0, 1 );
```

Fig. 20.22 Code-behind file for the word-generator page. (Part 2 of 5.)

```
83
84          switch ( current )
85          {
86              // 0 can be q or z
87              case 0:
88                  ComputeWords( number, temporaryWord + "q" );
89                  ComputeWords( number, temporaryWord + "z" );
90                  break;
91
92              // 1 has no letters associated with it
93              case 1:
94                  ComputeWords( number, temporaryWord + " " );
95                  break;
96
97              // 2 can be a, b or c
98              case 2:
99                  ComputeWords( number, temporaryWord + "a" );
100                 ComputeWords( number, temporaryWord + "b" );
101                 ComputeWords( number, temporaryWord + "c" );
102                 break;
103
104             // 3 can be d, e or f
105             case 3:
106                 ComputeWords( number, temporaryWord + "d" );
107                 ComputeWords( number, temporaryWord + "e" );
108                 ComputeWords( number, temporaryWord + "f" );
109                 break;
110
111             // 4 can be g, h or i
112             case 4:
113                 ComputeWords( number, temporaryWord + "g" );
114                 ComputeWords( number, temporaryWord + "h" );
115                 ComputeWords( number, temporaryWord + "i" );
116                 break;
117
118             // 5 can be j, k or l
119             case 5:
120                 ComputeWords( number, temporaryWord + "j" );
121                 ComputeWords( number, temporaryWord + "k" );
122                 ComputeWords( number, temporaryWord + "l" );
123                 break;
124
125             // 6 can be m, n or o
126             case 6:
127                 ComputeWords( number, temporaryWord + "m" );
128                 ComputeWords( number, temporaryWord + "n" );
129                 ComputeWords( number, temporaryWord + "o" );
130                 break;
131
132             // 7 can be p, r or s
133             case 7:
134                 ComputeWords( number, temporaryWord + "p" );
135                 ComputeWords( number, temporaryWord + "r" );
```

Fig. 20.22 Code-behind file for the word-generator page. (Part 3 of 5.)

```
136                    ComputeWords( number, temporaryWord + "s" );
137                    break;
138
139                // 8 can be t, u or v
140                case 8:
141                    ComputeWords( number, temporaryWord + "t" );
142                    ComputeWords( number, temporaryWord + "u" );
143                    ComputeWords( number, temporaryWord + "v" );
144                    break;
145
146                // 9 can be w, x or y
147                case 9:
148                    ComputeWords( number, temporaryWord + "w" );
149                    ComputeWords( number, temporaryWord + "x" );
150                    ComputeWords( number, temporaryWord + "y" );
151                    break;
152
153            } // end switch
154
155        } // end method ComputeWords
156
157    } // end class Generator
158
159 } // end namespace WordGenerator
```

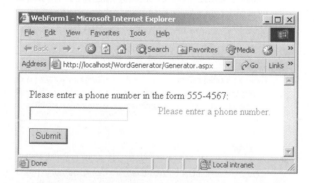

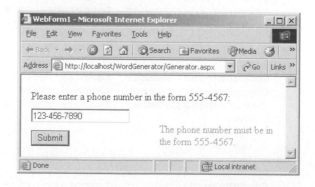

Fig. 20.22 Code-behind file for the word-generator page. (Part 4 of 5.)

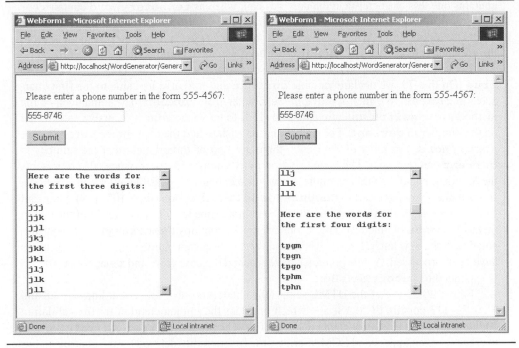

Fig. 20.22 Code-behind file for the word-generator page. (Part 5 of 5.)

   ASP .NET developers often design their Web pages such that the current page reloads when the user submits the form to process the input. This practice—known as a *postback*—groups input and processing logic, which makes the ASPX file easier to maintain. In our example, the page provides a text box where users can enter their phone numbers. Once this information has been submitted, the same page reloads, displaying the results below the original text box. One advantage of this is that the user can continue entering phone numbers without having to navigate back to an earlier page. Line 41 uses the **IsPostBack** property of class **Page** to determine whether the page is being loaded due to a postback. The first time that the Web page is requested, **IsPostBack** is **false**. When the postback occurs (due to the user clicking **Submit**), **IsPostBack** is **true**. To prepare the **outputTextBox** for display, its **Text** property is set to an empty string (**""**) in line 43. Line 46 then uses the **Request** object to retrieve **phoneTextBox**'s value from the **Form** array. When data are posted to the Web server, the HTML **form**'s data are accessible to the Web application through the **Request** object's **Form** array. Line 47 removes the hyphen from the phone number string. Method **ComputeWords** is passed a substring containing the first three numbers and an empty **string** (line 53). Line 62 sets the **outputTextBox**'s **Visible** property to **true**.

   Method **ComputeWords**, defined in lines 70–155, is a recursive method that generates a list of words from the **string** containing the digits of the phone number, minus the hyphen. The first argument—**number**—contains the digits that are being converted to letters. The first call to method **ComputeWords** (line 53) passes in the first three digits, and the second call (line 60) passes in the last four digits. The second argument, **temporaryWord**, builds up the list that the program displays. Each time this method is called, **number** contains one less character than the previous call, whereas **temporaryWord** contains one more character. Lines 73–77 define the recursion's base case, which occurs when **number** equals the empty string. When this occurs, the **temporaryWord** that has been built up from the previous calls is added to **outputTextBox**, and the method returns.

Let us discuss how **ComputeWords** works when the base case does not evaluate to **true**. On line 79, we declare variable **current** and initialize its value to the first character in **number**. We then remove this character from **number**. The remainder of the method uses a **switch** structure (lines 84–153) to make the correct recursive calls based on the number in **current**. For each digit, we wish to add the appropriate letter to **temporaryWord**. For most of the digits, there are two or three letters that the number in **current** can represent. The keypad button for the number 3, for instance, also represents the letters d, e and f. In this example, we want to exhaust all possible letter combinations, so we make a recursive call to **ComputeWords** for each option (lines 105–109). Each call passes **number** as the first argument (which contains one less digit as a result of the call to method **Remove** on line 82). The second argument contains **temporaryWord**, concatenated with the new letter. Each call adds a letter for the current number until all the numbers have been processed. At this point, we have reached the base case, and **temporaryWord** is appended to **outputTextBox**.

Figure 20.23 shows the HTML sent to the client browser. Notice that lines 25–28 and lines 72–113 contain ECMAScript, which provides the implementation for the validation controls. ASP .NET generates this ECMAScript. The programmer does not need to be able to create or even understand ECMAScript—the functionality defined for the controls in our application is converted to working ECMAScript for us.

```
1   <!-- Fig. 20.23: Generator.html                        -->
2   <!-- The HTML page that is sent to the client browser. -->
3
4   <!DOCTYPE HTML PUBLIC "-//W3C//DTD HTML 4.0 Transitional//EN" >
5   <HTML>
6      <HEAD>
7         <title>WebForm1</title>
8         <meta name="GENERATOR"
9            content="Microsoft Visual Studio 7.0">
10        <meta name="CODE_LANGUAGE" content="C#" >
11        <meta name="vs_defaultClientScript"
12           content="JavaScript">
13        <meta name="vs_targetSchema"
14           content="http://schemas.microsoft.com/intellisense/ie5">
15     </HEAD>
16
17     <body MS_POSITIONING="GridLayout">
18
19        <form name="Form1" method="post"
20           action="Generator.aspx" language="javascript"
21           onsubmit="ValidatorOnSubmit();" id="FORM1">
22           <input type="hidden" name="__VIEWSTATE"
23              value="dDwxMjgyMzM3ozs+" />
24
```

Fig. 20.23 HTML and ECMAScript sent to the client browser. (Part 1 of 3.)

```
25              <script language="javascript"
26                 src=
27         "/aspnet_client/system_web/1_0_3215_11/WebUIValidation.js">
28              </script>
29
30              <span id="phoneNumberValidator"
31                 controltovalidate="inputTextBox"
32                 errormessage=
33                    "The phone number must be in the form 555-4567."
34                 evaluationfunction=
35                    "RegularExpressionValidatorEvaluateIsValid"
36                 validationexpression="^\d{3}-\d{4}$"
37                 style="color:Red;Z-INDEX:106;LEFT:217px;
38                    POSITION:absolute;TOP:73px;visibility:hidden;">
39                    The phone number must be in the form 555-4567.
40              </span>
41
42              <input name="inputTextBox" type="text"
43                 id="inputTextBox"
44                 style="Z-INDEX: 102; LEFT: 16px;
45                 POSITION: absolute; TOP: 52px" />
46
47              <input type="submit" name="submitButton"
48                 value="Submit"
49                 onclick= "if ( " +
50                    "typeof(Page_ClientValidate) == 'function') " +
51                    "Page_ClientValidate(); " language="javascript"
52                    id="submitButton" style="Z-INDEX: 103;
53                 LEFT: 16px;
54                 POSITION: absolute;
55                 TOP: 86px" />
56
57              <span id="phoneInputValidator"
58                 controltovalidate="inputTextBox"
59                 errormessage="Please enter a phone number."
60                 evaluationfunction=
61                    "RequiredFieldValidatorEvaluateIsValid"
62                 initialvalue="" style="color:Red;Z-INDEX:105;
63                    LEFT:217px;POSITION:absolute;TOP:47px;
64                    visibility:hidden;">Please enter a phone number.
65              </span>
66
67              <span id="promptLabel" style="Z-INDEX: 101;
68                 LEFT: 16px; POSITION: absolute; TOP: 23px">
69                 Please enter a phone number in the form 555-4567:
70              </span>
71
72              <script language="javascript">
73              <!--
74                 var Page_Validators = new Array(
75                    document.all["phoneNumberValidator"],
76                    document.all["phoneInputValidator"] );
77              // -->
```

Fig. 20.23 HTML and ECMAScript sent to the client browser. (Part 2 of 3.)

```
78          </script>
79
80          <script language="javascript">
81          <!--
82              var Page_ValidationActive = false;
83
84          if (
85              typeof(clientInformation) != "undefined" &&
86              clientInformation.appName.indexOf("Explorer")
87              != -1 ) {
88
89              if ( typeof(Page_ValidationVer) == "undefined" )
90                  alert(
91                      "Unable to find script library " +
92                      "'/aspnet_client/system_web/'"+
93                      "'1_0_3215_11/WebUIValidation.js'. " +
94                      "Try placing this file manually, or " +
95                      "reinstall by running 'aspnet_regiis -c'.");
96              else if ( Page_ValidationVer != "125" )
97                  alert(
98                      "This page uses an incorrect version " +
99                      "of WebUIValidation.js. The page " +
100                     "expects version 125. " +
101                     "The script library is " +
102                     Page_ValidationVer + ".");
103             else
104                 ValidatorOnLoad();
105         }
106
107         function ValidatorOnSubmit() {
108             if (Page_ValidationActive) {
109                 ValidatorCommonOnSubmit();
110             }
111         }
112         // -->
113         </script>
114     </form>
115   </body>
116 </HTML>
```

Fig. 20.23 HTML and ECMAScript sent to the client browser. (Part 3 of 3.)

In earlier ASPX files, we explicitly set attribute **EnableViewState** to **false**. This attribute determines whether a Web control's properties persist (i.e., is retained) when a postback occurs. By default, this attribute is **true**, which indicates that control values persist. A **hidden** input in the HTML document (line 22–23) stores the properties of the controls on this page between client requests. This element always is named **__VIEWSTATE** and stores the controls' properties as encoded data.

Performance Tip 20.2

The setting of **EnabledViewState** *to* **false** *reduces the amount of data passed to the Web server.*

20.6 Session Tracking

Originally, critics accused the Internet and e-businesses of failing to provide the customized services typically experienced in brick-and-mortar stores. To address this problem, e-businesses began to establish mechanisms by which they could personalize users' browsing experiences, tailoring content to individual users while enabling them to bypass irrelevant information. Businesses achieve this level of service by tracking each customer's movement through the Internet and combining the collected data with information that the consumer provides, including billing information, personal preferences, interests and hobbies.

Personalization makes it possible for e-businesses to communicate effectively with their customers and improves users' ability to locate desired products and services. Companies that provide content of particular interest to users can establish relationships with customers and build on those relationships over time. Furthermore, by targeting consumers with personal offers, advertisements, promotions and services, e-businesses create customer loyalty. At Web sites such as **MSN.com** and **CNN.com**, sophisticated technology allows visitors to customize home pages to suit their individual needs and preferences. Similarly, online shopping sites often store personal information for customers and target them with notifications and special offers tailored to their interests. Such services can create customer bases that visit sites more frequently and make purchases from those sites more regularly.

A trade-off exists, however, between personalized e-business service and *privacy protection*. Whereas some consumers embrace the idea of tailored content, others fear the release of information that they provide to e-businesses or that is collected about them by tracking technologies will have adverse consequences on their lives. Consumers and privacy advocates ask: What if the e-businesses to which we give personal data sell or give that information to other organizations without our knowledge? What if we do not want our actions on the Internet—a supposedly anonymous medium—to be tracked and recorded by unknown parties? What if unauthorized parties gain access to sensitive private data, such as credit-card numbers or medical history? All of these are questions that must be debated and addressed by consumers, e-businesses and lawmakers alike.

To provide personalized services to consumers, e-businesses must be able to recognize specific clients when they request information from a site. As we have discussed, HTTP enables the request/response system on which the Web operates. Unfortunately, HTTP is a stateless protocol—it does not support persistent connections that would enable Web servers to maintain state information for particular clients. This means that Web servers have no capacity to determine whether a request comes from a particular client or whether the same or different clients generate a series of requests. To circumvent this problem, sites such as **MSN.com** and **CNN.com** provide mechanisms by which they identify individual clients. A *session ID* represents a unique client on the Internet. If the client leaves a site and then returns later, the client will be recognized as the same user. To help the server distinguish among clients, each client must identify itself to the server. The tracking of individual clients, known as *session tracking*, can be achieved in one of a number of ways. One popular technique uses cookies (Section 20.6.1), whereas another employs .NET's **HttpSessionState** object (Section 20.6.2). Additional session-tracking techniques include the use of hidden input form elements and URL rewriting. Using hidden form elements, the Web Form writes its session-tracking data into a **form** in the Web page that it returns to the client in response to a prior request. When the user submits the form in the new Web page, all the form data, including the hidden fields, are sent to the form handler on the Web server. When a Web site employs URL rewriting, the Web Form embeds session-tracking information directly in the URLs of hyperlinks that the user clicks to send subsequent requests to the Web server.

The reader should note that, in previous examples, we set the Web Form's **EnableSessionState** property to **false**. However, because we wish to use session tracking in the following examples, we leave this property in its default mode, which is **true**.

20.6.1 Cookies

A popular way to customize Web pages for particular users is via *cookies*. A cookie is a text file that a Web site stores on an individual's computer to enable the site to track that individual's actions and preferences. The first time a user visits the Web site, the user's computer might receive a cookie that contains a unique identifier for that user. This cookie is reactivated each subsequent time the user visits that site. The Web site uses this cookie to identify the user and to store information, such as the user's zip code or other data that might facilitate the distribution of user-specific content. The collected information is intended to be an anonymous record for personalizing the user's future visits to the site. Cookies in a shopping application might store unique identifiers for users. When a user adds items to an online shopping cart or performs another task resulting in a request to the Web server, the server receives a cookie containing the user's unique identifier. The server then uses the unique identifier to locate the user's shopping cart and perform any necessary processing.

In addition to identifying users, cookies also can indicate a client's preferences. When a Web Form receives a communication from a client, the Web Form could examine the cookie(s) it sent to the client during previous communications, identify the client's preferences and immediately display products that are of interest to the client.

Every HTTP-based interaction between a client and a server includes a header that contains information either about the request (when the communication is from the client to the server) or about the response (when the communication is from the server to the client). When a Web Form receives a request, the header includes information such as the request type (e.g., **GET**) and any cookies that the server has stored on the client machine. When the server formulates its response, the header information includes any cookies the server wants to store on the client computer, as well as information such as the MIME type of the response.

If the Web server does not set an *expiration date* for a cookie, the Web browser maintains the cookie for the duration of the browsing session (which usually ends when the user closes the Web browser). Otherwise, the Web browser maintains the cookie until the expiration date. The expiration date of a cookie can be set using the cookie's **Expires** property. When the browser requests a resource from a Web server, cookies previously sent to the client by that Web server are returned to the Web server as part of the request. Cookies are deleted when they expire.

The next Web application demonstrates the use of cookies. The example contains two pages. In the first page (Fig. 20.24 and Fig. 20.25), users select their favorite programming language from a group of radio buttons, then submit the HTML **form** to the Web server for processing. The Web server responds by creating a cookie that stores a record of the chosen language, as well as the ISBN number for a book on that topic. The server then returns an HTML document to the browser, allowing the user either to select another programming language or to view the second page in the application (Fig. 20.26 and Fig. 20.27), which lists recommended books pertaining to the programming language that the user selected previously. When the user clicks the hyperlink, the cookies previously stored on the client are read and used to form the list of book recommendations.

```
1   <%-- Fig. 20.24: OptionsPage.aspx                    --%>
2   <%-- This ASPX page allows the user to choose a language. --%>
3
4   <%@ Page language="c#" Codebehind="OptionsPage.aspx.cs"
5      AutoEventWireup="false"
6      Inherits="Cookies.OptionsPage" %>
7
8   <!DOCTYPE HTML PUBLIC "-//W3C//DTD HTML 4.0 Transitional//EN" >
9
10  <HTML>
11     <HEAD>
12        <title>RecommendationsPage</title>
13           <meta name="GENERATOR" Content=
14              "Microsoft Visual Studio 7.0">
15           <meta name="CODE_LANGUAGE" Content="C#">
16           <meta name="vs_defaultClientScript" content=
17              "JavaScript">
18           <meta name="vs_targetSchema" content=
19              "http://schemas.microsoft.com/intellisense/ie5">
20     </HEAD>
21
22     <body>
23        <form id="RecommendationsPage" method="post"
24           runat="server">
25           <P>
26              <asp:Label id="promptLabel" runat="server"
27                 Font-Bold="True">Select a programming language:
28              </asp:Label>
29
30              <asp:Label id="welcomeLabel" runat="server"
31                 Font-Bold="True" Visible="False">
32                 Welcome to Cookies! You selected
33              </asp:Label>
34           </P>
35
36           <P>
37              <asp:RadioButtonList id="languageList" runat=
38                 "server">
39              <asp:ListItem Value="C#">C#</asp:ListItem>
40
41              <asp:ListItem Value="C++">C++</asp:ListItem>
42
43              <asp:ListItem Value="C">C</asp:ListItem>
44
45              <asp:ListItem Value="Python">Python
46              </asp:ListItem>
47
48              <asp:ListItem Value="Visual Basic .NET">
49                 Visual Basic .NET
50              </asp:ListItem>
```

Fig. 20.24 ASPX file that presents a list of programming languages. (Part 1 of 2.)

```
51                </asp:RadioButtonList>
52            </P>
53
54            <P>
55                <asp:Button id="submitButton" runat="server" Text=
56                    "Submit">
57                </asp:Button>
58            </P>
59
60            <P>
61                <asp:HyperLink id="languageLink" runat="server"
62                    NavigateUrl="OptionsPage.aspx" Visible="False">
63                    Click here to choose another language.
64                </asp:HyperLink>
65            </P>
66
67            <P>
68                <asp:HyperLink id="recommendationsLink" runat=
69                    "server" NavigateUrl="RecommendationsPage.aspx"
70                Visible="False">Click here to get book recommendations.
71                </asp:HyperLink>
72            </P>
73        </form>
74    </body>
75 </HTML>
```

Fig. 20.24 ASPX file that presents a list of programming languages. (Part 2 of 2.)

The ASPX file in Fig. 20.24 contains five radio buttons (lines 39–50) with values **C#**, **C++**, **C**, **Python** and **Visual Basic .NET**. A programmer sets these values by clicking the **Items** property in the **Properties** window, then adding items via the **List Item Collection Editor**. This process is similar to that of customizing a **ListBox** in a Windows application. The user selects a programming language by clicking one of the radio buttons. The page also contains a **Submit** button, which, when clicked, creates a cookie that contains a record of the selected language. Once created, this cookie is added to the HTTP response header, and a postback occurs. Each time the user chooses a language and clicks **Submit**, a cookie is written to the client.

When the postback occurs, certain components are hidden, whereas others are displayed. Toward the bottom of the page, two hyperlinks are displayed: One that requests the current page (lines 61–64) and one that requests **Recommendations.aspx** (lines 68–71). Notice that clicking the first hyperlink (the one that requests the current page) does not cause a postback to occur. The file **OptionsPage.aspx** is specified in the **NavigateUrl** property of the hyperlink. When the hyperlink is clicked, this page is requested as a completely new request to allow the user to select a new programming language.

Figure 20.25 presents the code-behind file. Line 35 defines **books** as a **Hashtable** (namespace **System.Collections**), which is a data structure that stores *key-value pairs* (we covered **Hashtable** briefly in Chapter 15, Strings, Characters and Regular Expressions). The program uses the key to store and retrieve the associated value in the **Hashtable**. In this example, the keys are **string**s that contain the programming language names, and the values are **string**s that contain the ISBN numbers for the recommended books. Class **Hashtable** provides method ***Add***, which takes as arguments a key and a value. The value for a specific **Hashtable** entry can be obtained by indexing the hash table with that value's key. For instance,

> *HashtableName* **[** *keyName* **] ;**

returns the value from the key-value pair in which *keyName* is the key. An example of this is shown in line 92—**books[language]** returns the value that corresponds to the key contained in **language**. Class **Hashtable** is discussed in detail in Chapter 23, Data Structures.

```
1    // Fig. 20.25: OptionPage.aspx.cs
2    // A listing of program languages that the user can choose from.
3
4    using System;
5    using System.Collections;
6    using System.ComponentModel;
7    using System.Data;
8    using System.Drawing;
9    using System.Web;
10   using System.Web.SessionState;
11   using System.Web.UI;
12   using System.Web.UI.WebControls;
13   using System.Web.UI.HtmlControls;
14
15   namespace Cookies
16   {
17      // page contains language options in a RadioButtonList,
18      // will add a cookie to store their choice
19      public class OptionsPage : System.Web.UI.Page
20      {
21         protected System.Web.UI.WebControls.Label promptLabel;
22         protected System.Web.UI.WebControls.Label welcomeLabel;
23
24         protected System.Web.UI.WebControls.RadioButtonList
25            languageList;
26
27         protected System.Web.UI.WebControls.HyperLink
28            languageLink;
29         protected System.Web.UI.WebControls.HyperLink
30            recommendationsLink;
31
32         protected System.Web.UI.WebControls.Button
33            submitButton;
34
35         protected Hashtable books = new Hashtable();
36
37         // event handler for Load event
38         private void Page_Load(
39            object sender, System.EventArgs e )
40         {
```

Fig. 20.25 Code-behind file that writes cookies to the client. (Part 1 of 3.)

```
41          if ( IsPostBack )
42          {
43             // if postback has occurred, user has submitted
44             // information, so display welcome message
45             // and appropriate hyperlinks
46             welcomeLabel.Visible = true;
47             languageLink.Visible = true;
48             recommendationsLink.Visible = true;
49
50             // hide option information
51             submitButton.Visible = false;
52             promptLabel.Visible = false;
53             languageList.Visible = false;
54
55             // notify user of what they have chosen
56             if ( languageList.SelectedItem != null )
57                welcomeLabel.Text +=
58                   languageList.SelectedItem.ToString() + ".";
59             else
60                welcomeLabel.Text += "no language.";
61
62          } // end if
63
64       } // end method Page_Load
65
66       override protected void OnInit( EventArgs e )
67       {
68          // add values to Hashtable
69          books.Add( "C#", "0-13-062221-4" );
70          books.Add( "C++", "0-13-089571-7" );
71          books.Add( "C", "0-13-089572-5" );
72          books.Add( "Python", "0-13-092361-3" );
73          books.Add( "Visual Basic .NET", "0-13-456955-5" );
74
75          InitializeComponent();
76          base.OnInit( e );
77       }
78
79       // Visual Studio .NET generated code
80
81       // when user clicks Submit button
82       // create cookie to store user's choice
83       private void submitButton_Click(
84          object sender, System.EventArgs e )
85       {
86          // if choice was made by user
87          if ( languageList.SelectedItem != null )
88          {
89             string language =
90                languageList.SelectedItem.ToString();
91
92             string ISBN = books[ language ].ToString();
93
```

Fig. 20.25 Code-behind file that writes cookies to the client. (Part 2 of 3.)

```
94                  // create cookie, name-value pair is
95                  // language chosen and ISBN number from Hashtable
96                  HttpCookie cookie = new HttpCookie(
97                      language, ISBN );
98
99                  // add cookie to response,
100                 // thus placing it on user's machine
101                 Response.Cookies.Add( cookie );
102
103             } // end if
104
105         } // end method submitButton_Click
106
107     } // end class OptionsPage
108
109 } // end namespace Cookies
```

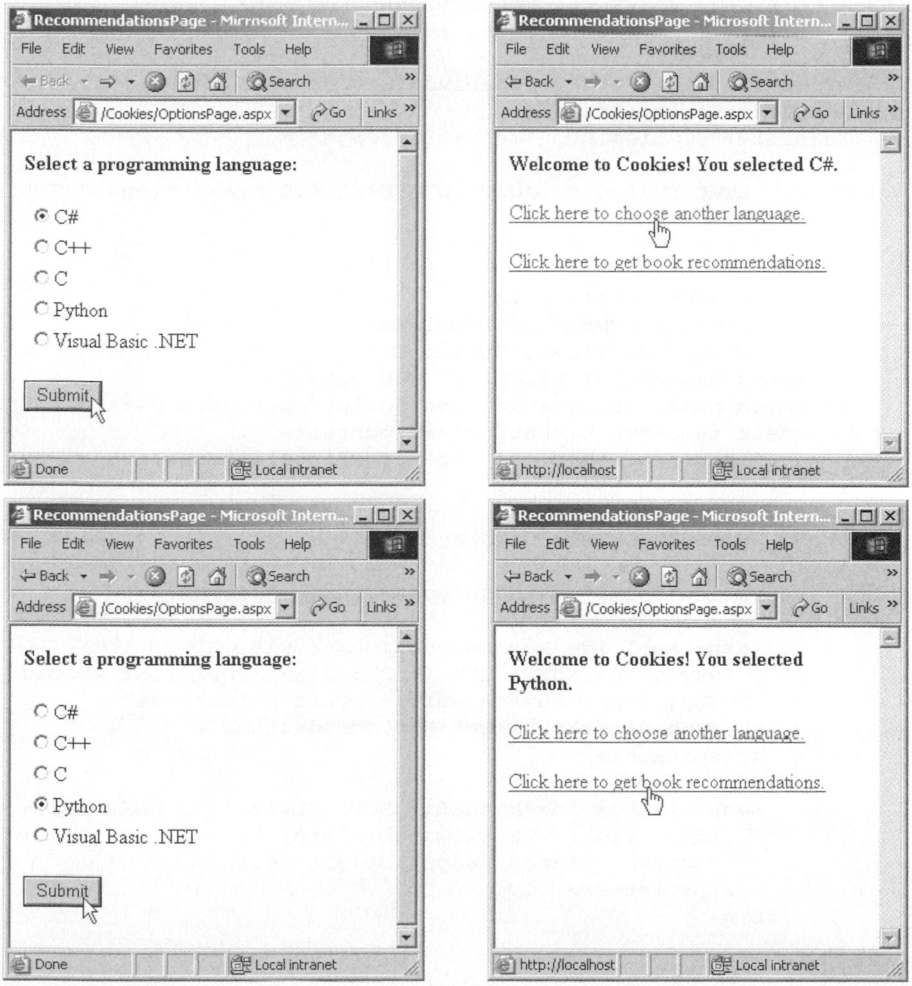

Fig. 20.25 Code-behind file that writes cookies to the client. (Part 3 of 3.)

As mentioned earlier, clicking the **Submit** button causes a postback to occur. As a result, the condition in the **if** structure of **Page_Load** (line 41) evaluates to **true**, and lines 46–60 execute. Line 56 determines whether the user selected a language. If so, that language is displayed in **welcomeLabel** (lines 57–58). Otherwise, text indicating that a language was not selected is displayed in **welcomeLabel** (line 60). The two hyperlinks are made visible in lines 47–48.

A new cookie object (of type *HttpCookie*) is created to store the **language** and its corresponding **ISBN** number (lines 96–97). This cookie then is **Add**ed to the *Cookies* collection sent as part of the HTTP response header (line 101).

```
1   <%-- Fig. 20.26: RecommendationsPage.aspx --%>
2   <%-- This page shows recommendations       --%>
3   <%-- retrieved from the Hashtable.         --%>
4
5   <%@ Page language="c#" Codebehind="RecommendationsPage.aspx.cs"
6       AutoEventWireup="false"
7       Inherits="Cookies.RecommendationsPage" %>
8
9   <!DOCTYPE HTML PUBLIC "-//W3C//DTD HTML 4.0 Transitional//EN" >
10
11  <HTML>
12     <HEAD>
13        <title>WebForm1</title>
14        <meta name="GENERATOR" Content=
15           "Microsoft Visual Studio 7.0">
16        <meta name="CODE_LANGUAGE" Content="C#">
17        <meta name="vs_defaultClientScript" content="JavaScript">
18        <meta name="vs_targetSchema" content=
19           "http://schemas.microsoft.com/intellisense/ie5">
20     </HEAD>
21
22     <body MS_POSITIONING="GridLayout">
23
24        <form id="Form1" method="post" runat="server">
25
26           <asp:Label id="recommendationsLabel"
27              style="Z-INDEX: 101; LEFT: 21px; POSITION: absolute;
28              TOP: 25px" runat="server" Font-Bold="True"
29              Font-Size="X-Large">Recommendations
30           </asp:Label>
31
32           <asp:ListBox id="booksListBox" style="Z-INDEX: 102;
33              LEFT: 21px; POSITION: absolute; TOP: 82px" runat=
34              "server" Width="383px" Height="91px">
35           </asp:ListBox>
36        </form>
37     </body>
38  </HTML>
```

Fig. 20.26 ASPX page that displays book information.

RecommendationsPage.aspx contains a label (lines 26–30) and a list box (lines 32–35). The label displays the text **Recommendations** if the user has selected one or more languages; otherwise, it displays **No Recommendations**. The list box displays the recommendations created by the code-behind file, which is shown in Fig. 20.27.

```
1   // Fig 20.27: RecommendationsPage.aspx.cs
2   // Reading cookie data from the client.
3
4   using System;
5   using System.Collections;
6   using System.ComponentModel;
7   using System.Data;
8   using System.Drawing;
9   using System.Web;
10  using System.Web.SessionState;
11  using System.Web.UI;
12  using System.Web.UI.WebControls;
13  using System.Web.UI.HtmlControls;
14
15  namespace Cookies
16  {
17     // page displays cookie information and recommendations
18     public class RecommendationsPage : System.Web.UI.Page
19     {
20        protected System.Web.UI.WebControls.ListBox booksListBox;
21        protected System.Web.UI.WebControls.Label
22           recommendationsLabel;
23
24        // Visual Studio .NET generated code
25
26        override protected void OnInit( EventArgs e )
27        {
28           InitializeComponent();
29           base.OnInit( e );
30
31           // retrieve client's cookies
32           HttpCookieCollection cookies = Request.Cookies;
33
34           // if there are cookies other than the ID cookie,
35           // list appropriate books and ISBN numbers
36           if ( cookies != null && cookies.Count != 1 )
37              for ( int i = 1; i < cookies.Count; i++ )
38                 booksListBox.Items.Add(
39                    cookies[ i ].Name +
40                    " How to Program. ISBN#: " +
41                    cookies[ i ].Value );
42
43           // if no cookies besides ID, no options were
44           // chosen, so no recommendations made
45           else
46           {
47              recommendationsLabel.Text = "No Recommendations.";
```

Fig. 20.27 Cookies being read from a client in an ASP .NET application. (Part 1 of 2.)

```
48                    booksListBox.Items.Clear();
49                    booksListBox.Visible = false;
50              }
51
52         } // end method OnInit
53
54      } // end class RecommendationsPage
55
56  } // end namespace Cookies
```

Fig. 20.27 Cookies being read from a client in an ASP .NET application. (Part 2 of 2.)

Method **OnInit** (lines 26–52) retrieves the cookies from the client using the **Request** object's *Cookies* property (line 32). This returns a collection of type *Http-CookieCollection* that contains cookies that have been written to the client previously. Cookies can be read by an application only if they were created in the domain in which that application is running—a Web server can never access cookies created outside the domain associated with that server. For example, a cookie created by a Web server in the **deitel.com** domain cannot be downloaded by a Web server in the **bug2bug.com** domain.

Line 36 determines whether at least two cookies exist. ASP .NET always adds a cookie named *ASP.NET_SessionId* to the response, so line 36 ensures that there is at least one cookie besides the **ASP.NET_SessionId** cookie. Lines 38–41 add the information in the other cookie(s) to our list box. The **for** structure iterates through all the cookies except for the first one (the **ASP.NET_SessionID** cookie). The application retrieves the name and value of each cookie by using **i**, the control variable in our **for** structure, to determine the current value in our cookie collection. The *Name* and *Value* properties of class **Http-Cookie** which contain the language and corresponding ISBN, respectively, are concatenated with **" How to Program. ISBN# "** and added to the **ListBox**. The list box displays a maximum of five books. Lines 47–49 execute if no language was selected. We summarize some commonly used **HttpCookie** properties in Fig. 20.28.

Properties	Description
Domain	Returns a **string** that contains the cookie's domain (i.e., the domain of the Web server from which the cookie was downloaded). This determines which Web servers can receive the cookie. By default, cookies are sent to the Web server that originally sent the cookie to the client.
Expires	Returns a **DateTime** object indicating when the browser can delete the cookie.
Name	Returns a **string** containing the cookie's name.
Path	Returns a **string** containing the URL prefix for the cookie. Cookies can be "targeted" to specific URLs that include directories on the Web server, enabling the programmer to specify the location of the cookie. By default, a cookie is returned to services that operates in the same directory as the service that sent the cookie or a subdirectory of that directory.
Secure	Returns a **bool**ean value indicating whether the cookie should be transmitted using a secure protocol. A value of **true** causes a secure protocol to be used.
Value	Returns a **string** containing the cookie's value.

Fig. 20.28 **HttpCookie** properties.

20.6.2 Session Tracking with **HttpSessionState**

C# provides session-tracking capabilities in the FCL's ***HttpSessionState*** class. To demonstrate basic session-tracking techniques, we modified Fig. 20.27 so that it employs ***HttpSessionState*** objects. Figure 20.29 presents the ASPX file, and Fig. 20.30 presents the code-behind file. The ASPX file is similar to that presented in Fig. 20.24.

```
1   <%-- Fig. 20.29: OptionsPage.aspx              --%>
2   <%-- Page that presents a list of language options. --%>
3
4   <%@ Page language="c#" Codebehind="OptionsPage.aspx.cs"
5      AutoEventWireup="false" Inherits=
6      "Sessions.OptionsPage" %>
7
8   <!DOCTYPE HTML PUBLIC "-//W3C//DTD HTML 4.0 Transitional//EN" >
9   <HTML>
10     <HEAD>
11       <title>RecommendationsPage</title>
12       <meta name="GENERATOR" Content=
13         "Microsoft Visual Studio 7.0">
14       <meta name="CODE_LANGUAGE" Content="C#">
15       <meta name="vs_defaultClientScript" content="JavaScript">
16       <meta name="vs_targetSchema" content=
17         "http://schemas.microsoft.com/intellisense/ie5">
18     </HEAD>
19
```

Fig. 20.29 Options supplied on an ASPX page. (Part 1 of 3.)

```
20   <body>
21      <form id="RecommendationsPage" method="post"
22         runat="server">
23         <P>
24            <asp:Label id="promptLabel" runat="server"
25               Font-Bold="True">Select a programming language:
26            </asp:Label>
27
28            <asp:Label id="welcomeLabel" runat="server"
29               Font-Bold="True" Visible="False">
30               Welcome to Cookies! You selected
31            </asp:Label>
32         </P>
33
34         <P>
35            <asp:RadioButtonList id="languageList" runat=
36               "server">
37
38               <asp:ListItem Value="C#">C#</asp:ListItem>
39
40               <asp:ListItem Value="C++">C++</asp:ListItem>
41
42               <asp:ListItem Value="C">C</asp:ListItem>
43
44               <asp:ListItem Value="Python">Python
45               </asp:ListItem>
46
47               <asp:ListItem Value="Visual Basic .NET">
48                  Visual Basic .NET
49               </asp:ListItem>
50            </asp:RadioButtonList>
51         </P>
52
53         <P>
54            <asp:Button id="submitButton" runat="server"
55               Text="Submit">
56            </asp:Button>
57         </P>
58
59         <P>
60            <asp:Label id="idLabel" runat="server">
61            </asp:Label>
62         </P>
63
64         <P>
65            <asp:Label id="timeoutLabel" runat="server">
66            </asp:Label>
67         </P>
68
69         <P>
70            <asp:Label id="newSessionLabel" runat="server">
71            </asp:Label>
72         </P>
```

Fig. 20.29 Options supplied on an ASPX page. (Part 2 of 3.)

```
73
74                <P>
75                    <asp:HyperLink id="languageLink" runat="server"
76                        NavigateUrl="OptionsPage.aspx" Visible="False">
77                        Click here to choose another language.
78                    </asp:HyperLink>
79                </P>
80
81                <P>
82                    <asp:HyperLink id="recommendationsLink" runat=
83                        "server" NavigateUrl="RecommendationsPage.aspx"
84                        Visible="False">
85                        Click here to get book recommendations.
86                    </asp:HyperLink>
87                </P>
88            </form>
89        </body>
90    </HTML>
```

Fig. 20.29 Options supplied on an ASPX page. (Part 3 of 3.)

Every Web Form includes an **HttpSessionState** object, which is accessible through property **Session** of class **Page**. Throughout this section, we use property **Session** to manipulate our page's **HttpSessionState** object. When the Web page is requested, an **HttpSessionState** object is created and assigned to the **Page**'s **Session** property. We often refer to property **Session** as the **Session** object. When the user presses **Submit**, **submitButton_Click** is invoked in the code-behind file (Fig. 20.30). Method **submitButton_Click** adds a key-value pair to our **Session** object specifying the language chosen and the ISBN number for a book on that language. Next, a postback occurs. Each time the user clicks **Submit**, **submitButton_Click** adds a new language/ISBN pair to the **HttpSessionState** object. Because much of this example is similar to the last example, we concentrate on the new features.

Software Engineering Observation 20.1

*A Web Form must not use instance variables to maintain client state information, because clients accessing that Web Form in parallel might overwrite the shared instance variables. Web Forms should maintain client state information in **HttpSessionState** objects, because such objects are specific to each client.*

```
1    // Fig. 20.30: OptionsPage.aspx.cs
2    // A listing of programming languages,
3    // choice is stored in page's Session object.
4
5    using System;
6    using System.Collections;
7    using System.ComponentModel;
8    using System.Data;
9    using System.Drawing;
```

Fig. 20.30 Sessions are created for each user in an ASP .NET Web application. (Part 1 of 4.)

```
10    using System.Web;
11    using System.Web.SessionState;
12    using System.Web.UI;
13    using System.Web.UI.WebControls;
14    using System.Web.UI.HtmlControls;
15
16    namespace Sessions
17    {
18        // page contains language options in a RadioButtonList
19        // will add cookie to store user's choice
20        public class OptionsPage : System.Web.UI.Page
21        {
22            protected System.Web.UI.WebControls.Label promptLabel;
23            protected System.Web.UI.WebControls.Label welcomeLabel;
24            protected System.Web.UI.WebControls.Label idLabel;
25            protected System.Web.UI.WebControls.Label timeoutLabel;
26
27            protected System.Web.UI.WebControls.HyperLink
28                languageLink;
29            protected System.Web.UI.WebControls.HyperLink
30                recommendationsLink;
31
32            protected System.Web.UI.WebControls.RadioButtonList
33                languageList;
34            protected System.Web.UI.WebControls.Button submitButton;
35
36            private Hashtable books = new Hashtable();
37
38            // event handler for Load event
39            private void Page_Load(
40                object sender, System.EventArgs e )
41            {
42                // if page is loaded due to postback, load session
43                // information, hide language options from user
44                if ( IsPostBack )
45                {
46                    // display components that contain session information
47                    welcomeLabel.Visible = true;
48                    languageLink.Visible = true;
49                    recommendationsLink.Visible = true;
50
51                    // hide components
52                    submitButton.Visible = false;
53                    promptLabel.Visible = false;
54                    languageList.Visible = false;
55
56                    // set labels to display Session information
57                    if ( languageList.SelectedItem != null )
58                        welcomeLabel.Text +=
59                            languageList.SelectedItem.ToString() + ".";
60                    else
61                        welcomeLabel.Text += "no language.";
```

Fig. 20.30 Sessions are created for each user in an ASP .NET Web application. (Part 2 of 4.)

```
62
63              idLabel.Text += "Your unique session ID is: " +
64                  Session.SessionID;
65
66              timeoutLabel.Text += "Timeout: " + Session.Timeout +
67                  " minutes";
68
69          } // end if
70
71      } // end method Page_Load
72
73      override protected void OnInit( EventArgs e )
74      {
75          // add values to Hashtable
76          books.Add( "C#", "0-13-062221-4" );
77          books.Add( "C++", "0-13-089571-7" );
78          books.Add( "C", "0-13-089572-5" );
79          books.Add( "Python", "0-13-092361-3" );
80          books.Add( "Visual Basic .NET", "0-13-456955-5" );
81
82          InitializeComponent();
83          base.OnInit( e );
84      }
85
86      // Visual Studio .NET generated code
87
88      // when user clicks Submit button,
89      // store user's choice in session object
90      private void submitButton_Click(
91          object sender, System.EventArgs e )
92      {
93          if ( languageList.SelectedItem != null )
94          {
95              string language =
96                  languageList.SelectedItem.ToString();
97              string ISBN = books[ language ].ToString();
98
99              // store in session object as name-value pair
100             // name is language chosen, value is
101             // ISBN number for corresponding book
102             Session.Add( language, ISBN );
103
104         } // end if
105
106     } // end method submitButton_Click
107
108   } // end class OptionsPage
109
110 } // end namespace Sessions
```

Fig. 20.30 Sessions are created for each user in an ASP .NET Web application. (Part 3 of 4.)

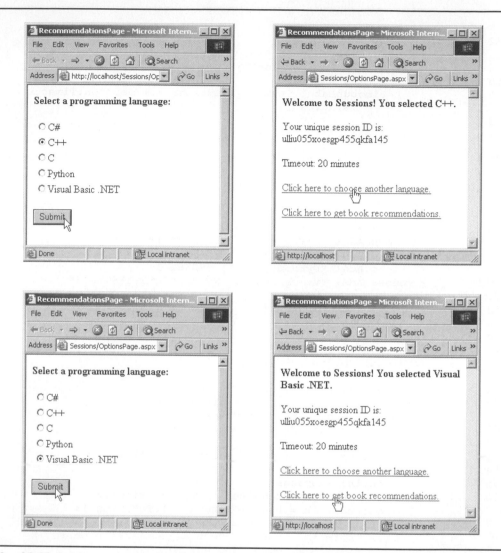

Fig. 20.30 Sessions are created for each user in an ASP .NET Web application. (Part 4 of 4.)

Like a cookie, an **HttpSessionState** object can store name—value pairs. In session terminology, these are called *session items*, and they are placed into an **HttpSession-State** object by calling method **Add**. Line 102 calls **Add** to place the language and its corresponding recommended book's ISBN number into the **HttpSessionState** object. One of the primary benefits of using **HttpSessionState** objects (rather than cookies) is that **HttpSessionState** objects can store any type of object (not just **string**s) as an attribute value. This provides C# programmers with increased flexibility in determining the type of state information they wish to maintain for their clients. If the application calls method **Add** to add an attribute that has the same name as an attribute previously stored in a session, the object associated with that attribute is replaced.

After the values are added to the **HttpSessionState** object, the application handles the postback event (lines 44–70) in method **Page_Load**. Here, we retrieve information about the current client's session from the **Session** object's properties and display this information in the Web page. The ASP .NET application contains information about the **HttpSessionState** object for the current client. Property *SessionID* (lines 63–64) contains the *session's unique ID*. The first time a client connects to the Web server, a unique session ID is created for that client. When the client makes additional requests, the client's session ID is compared with the session IDs stored in the Web server's memory. Property *Timeout* (line 66) specifies the maximum amount of time that an **HttpSessionState** object can be inactive before it is discarded. Figure 20.31 list some common **HttpSessionState** properties.

As in the cookies example, this application provides a link to **Recommendations-Page.aspx** (Fig. 20.32), which displays a list of book recommendations on the basis of the user's language selections. Lines 30–33 define a **ListBox** Web control that is used to present the recommendations to the user. Figure 20.33 presents the code-behind file for this ASPX file.

Properties	Description
Count	Specifies the number of key-value pairs in the **Session** object.
IsNewSession	Indicates whether this is a new session (i.e., whether the session was created when this page was loaded).
IsReadOnly	Indicates whether the **Session** object is read-only.
Keys	Returns a collection containing the **Session** object's keys.
SessionID	Returns the session's unique ID.
Timeout	Specifies the maximum number of minutes during which a session can be inactive (i.e., no requests are made) before the session expires. By default, this property is set to 20 minutes.

Fig. 20.31 **HttpSessionState** properties.

```
1   <%-- Fig. 20.32: RecommendationsPage.aspx --%>
2   <%-- Read the user's session data.          --%>
3
4   <%@ Page language="c#" Codebehind="RecommendationsPage.aspx.cs"
5      AutoEventWireup="false"
6      Inherits="Sessions.RecommendationsPage" %>
7
8   <!DOCTYPE HTML PUBLIC "-//W3C//DTD HTML 4.0 Transitional//EN" >
9
10  <HTML>
11     <HEAD>
12        <title>WebForm1</title>
13           <meta name="GENERATOR" Content=
14              "Microsoft Visual Studio 7.0">
```

Fig. 20.32 Session information displayed in a **ListBox**. (Part 1 of 2.)

```
15              <meta name="CODE_LANGUAGE" Content="C#">
16              <meta name="vs_defaultClientScript" content=
17                 "JavaScript">
18              <meta name="vs_targetSchema" content=
19                 "http://schemas.microsoft.com/intellisense/ie5">
20          </HEAD>
21
22      <body MS_POSITIONING="GridLayout">
23          <form id="Form1" method="post" runat="server">
24              <asp:Label id="recommendationsLabel"
25                  style="Z-INDEX: 101; LEFT: 21px; POSITION: absolute;
26                  TOP: 25px" runat="server" Font-Bold="True"
27                  Font-Size="X-Large">Recommendations
28              </asp:Label>
29
30              <asp:ListBox id="booksListBox" style="Z-INDEX: 102;
31                  LEFT: 21px; POSITION: absolute; TOP: 84px" runat=
32                  "server" Width="383px" Height="91px">
33              </asp:ListBox>
34          </form>
35      </body>
36  </HTML>
```

Fig. 20.32 Session information displayed in a **ListBox**. (Part 2 of 2.)

```
1   // Fig. 20.33: RecommendationsPage.aspx.cs
2   // Reading session data from the user.
3
4   using System;
5   using System.Collections;
6   using System.ComponentModel;
7   using System.Data;
8   using System.Drawing;
9   using System.Web;
10  using System.Web.SessionState;
11  using System.Web.UI;
12  using System.Web.UI.WebControls;
13  using System.Web.UI.HtmlControls;
14
15  namespace Sessions
16  {
17      // page displaying session information and recommendations
18      public class RecommendationsPage : System.Web.UI.Page
19      {
20          protected System.Web.UI.WebControls.ListBox booksListBox;
21
22          protected System.Web.UI.WebControls.Label
23              recommendationsLabel;
24
25          // Visual Studio .NET generated code
26
```

Fig. 20.33 Session data read by an ASP .NET Web application to provide
recommendations for the user. (Part 1 of 2.)

```
27        // event handler for Init event
28        override protected void OnInit( EventArgs e )
29        {
30           InitializeComponent();
31           base.OnInit( e );
32
33           // determine if Session contains information
34           if ( Session.Count != 0 )
35           {
36              // iterate through Session values,
37              // display in ListBox
38              for ( int i = 0; i < Session.Count; i++ )
39              {
40                 // store current key in sessionName
41                 string keyName = Session.Keys[ i ];
42
43                 // use current key to display
44                 // Session's name/value pairs
45                 booksListBox.Items.Add( keyName +
46                    " How to Program. ISBN#: " +
47                    Session[ keyName ] );
48
49              } // end for
50
51           }
52           else
53           {
54              recommendationsLabel.Text = "No Recommendations";
55              booksListBox.Visible = false;
56           }
57
58        } // end method OnInit
59
60     } // end class RecommendationsPage
61
62  } // end namespace Sessions
```

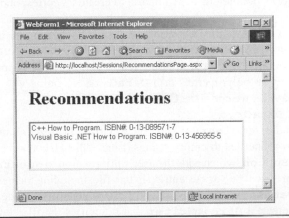

Fig. 20.33 Session data read by an ASP .NET Web application to provide recommendations for the user. (Part 2 of 2.)

Event handler **OnInit** (lines 28–58) retrieves the session information. If a user has never selected languages during any visit to this site, our **Session** object's **Count** property will be zero. This property provides the number of session items contained in a **Session** object. If **Session** object's **Count** property is zero (i.e., no language was ever selected), then we display the text **No Recommendations**.

If the user has chosen a language, the **for** structure (lines 38–49) iterates through the **Session** object. Property *Count* contains the number of key-value pairs stored in this session. The value in a key-value pair is retrieved from the **Session** object by indexing the **Session** object with the key name, using the same process by which we retrieved a value from our hash table in the last section.

We then access the *Keys* property of class **HttpSessionState** (line 41), which returns a collection that contains all the keys in the session. This line indexes our collection to retrieve the current key. Lines 45–47 concatenate **keyName**'s value to the **string " How to Program. ISBN#: "** and to the value from the session object for which **keyName** is the key. The resulting **string** is the recommendation that appears in the **ListBox**.

20.7 Case Study: Online Guest Book

Many Web sites allow users to provide feedback about the Web site in a *guest book*. Typically, users click a link on the Web site's home page to request the guest-book page. This page usually consists of an HTML **form** that contains fields for the user's name, e-mail address, and a message. Data submitted to the guest book often are stored in a database located on the Web server's machine. In this section, we create a guest-book Web Form application. The GUI is slightly more complex than the one we just described; it contains a **DataGrid**, as shown in Fig. 20.34.

The HTML **form** presented to the user consists of a user-name field, an e-mail address field and a message field. Figure 20.35 presents the ASPX file, and Fig. 20.36 presents the code-behind file for the guest book application. For the sake of simplicity, we write the guest-book information to a text file. However, in the exercises, we ask the reader to modify this example so that the application stores the guest-book information in a database.

The ASPX file generated by the GUI is shown in Fig. 20.35. After dragging the two buttons onto the form, double-click each button to create its corresponding event handler. Visual Studio adds the event handlers to the code-behind file (Fig. 20.36). A **DataGrid** named **dataGrid** displays all guest-book entries. This control can be added from the **Toolbox**. The colors for the **DataGrid** are specified using the **Auto Format...** link located near the bottom of the **Properties** window. This link will appear only when the developer is looking at the properties of a **DataGrid**. A dialog will open with several choices. In this example, we chose the **Colorful 4** option in this dialog. We discuss adding information to the **DataGrid** shortly.

The event handler for **clearButton** (lines 114–121) clears all the **TextBox**es by setting their **Text** properties to empty strings. Lines 90–111 contain the event-handling code for **submitButton**, which adds the user's information to **guestbook.txt**, a text file stored in our project. The various entries in this file, including the newest entry, will be displayed in the **DataGrid**. Let us look at how this is done in the code.

Lines 94–96 create a **StreamWriter** that references the file containing the guest-book entries. We use the **Request** object's *PhysicalApplicationPath* property to retrieve the path of the application's root directory (this will be the path of the project folder for the current application) and then concatenate to it the file name (i.e., **guest-book.txt**). The second argument (**true**) specifies that new information will be appended to the file (i.e., added to the end of the file). Lines 99–102 append the appropriate message to the guest-book file. Before the event handler exits, it calls method **FillMessageTable** (line 110).

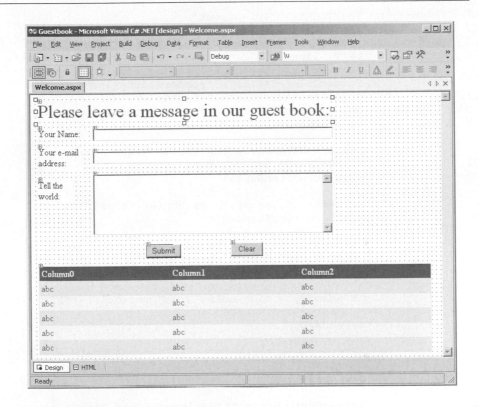

Fig. 20.34 Guest-book application GUI.

```
1    <%-- Fig. 20.35: Welcome.aspx                      --%>
2    <%-- A Web Form demonstrating a guest book. --%>
3
4    <%@ Page language="c#" Codebehind="Welcome.aspx.cs"
5        AutoEventWireup="false"
6        Inherits="Guestbook.GuestBookTest" %>
7
8    <!DOCTYPE HTML PUBLIC "-//W3C//DTD HTML 4.0 Transitional//EN" >
9
10   <HTML>
11       <HEAD>
12           <title>WebForm1</title>
```

Fig. 20.35 ASPX file for the guest book application. (Part 1 of 3.)

```
13          <meta name="GENERATOR" Content=
14              "Microsoft Visual Studio 7.0">
15          <meta name="CODE_LANGUAGE" Content="C#">
16          <meta name="vs_defaultClientScript" content="JavaScript">
17          <meta name="vs_targetSchema" content=
18              "http://schemas.microsoft.com/intellisense/ie5">
19      </HEAD>
20
21      <body MS_POSITIONING="GridLayout">
22          <form id="Form1" method="post" runat="server">
23              <asp:DataGrid id="dataGrid" style="Z-INDEX: 101;
24                  LEFT: 13px; POSITION: absolute; TOP: 301px" runat=
25                  "server" Width="698px" HorizontalAlign="Left"
26                  BorderColor="#E7E7FF" BorderWidth="1px"
27                  GridLines="Horizontal" BackColor="White"
28                  DataSource="<%# dataView %>" BorderStyle="None"
29                  CellPadding="3">
30
31                  <SelectedItemStyle Font-Bold="True" ForeColor=
32                      "#F7F7F7" BackColor="#738A9C">
33                  </SelectedItemStyle>
34
35                  <AlternatingItemStyle BackColor="#F7F7F7">
36                  </AlternatingItemStyle>
37
38                  <ItemStyle HorizontalAlign="Left" ForeColor=
39                      "#4A3C8C" BackColor="#E7E7FF">
40                  </ItemStyle>
41
42                  <HeaderStyle Font-Bold="True" ForeColor="#F7F7F7"
43                      BackColor="#4A3C8C">
44                  </HeaderStyle>
45
46                  <FooterStyle ForeColor="#4A3C8C" BackColor=
47                      "#B5C7DE">
48                  </FooterStyle>
49
50                  <PagerStyle HorizontalAlign="Right" ForeColor=
51                      "#4A3C8C" BackColor="#E7E7FF" Mode=
52                      "NumericPages">
53                  </PagerStyle>
54              </asp:DataGrid>
55
56              <asp:Button id="clearButton" style="Z-INDEX: 111;
57                  LEFT: 354px; POSITION: absolute; TOP: 262px"
58                  runat="server" Width="57px" Text="Clear">
59              </asp:Button>
60
61              <asp:Button id="submitButton" style="Z-INDEX: 110;
62                  LEFT: 205px; POSITION: absolute; TOP: 264px"
63                  runat="server" Text="Submit">
64              </asp:Button>
65
```

Fig. 20.35 ASPX file for the guest book application. (Part 2 of 3.)

```
66              <asp:TextBox id="messageTextBox" style="Z-INDEX: 109;
67                 LEFT: 111px; POSITION: absolute; TOP: 139px"
68                 runat="server" Width="427px" Height="107px"
69                 TextMode="MultiLine">
70              </asp:TextBox>
71
72              <asp:Label id="messageLabel" style="Z-INDEX: 108;
73                 LEFT: 13px; POSITION: absolute; TOP: 149px"
74                 runat="server" Width="59px" Height="9px">
75                 Tell the world:
76              </asp:Label>
77
78              <asp:Label id="emailLabel" style="Z-INDEX: 107;
79                 LEFT: 13px; POSITION: absolute; TOP: 91px"
80                 runat="server" Width="76px">E-mail address:
81              </asp:Label>
82
83              <asp:TextBox id="emailTextBox" style="Z-INDEX: 106;
84                 LEFT: 111px; POSITION: absolute; TOP: 99px"
85                 runat="server" Width="428px">
86              </asp:TextBox>
87
88              <asp:Label id="nameLabel" style="Z-INDEX: 104;
89                 LEFT: 13px; POSITION: absolute; TOP: 59px"
90                 runat="server" Width="84px">First Name:
91              </asp:Label>
92
93              <asp:TextBox id="nameTextBox" style="Z-INDEX: 105;
94                 LEFT: 111px; POSITION: absolute; TOP: 59px"
95                 runat="server" Width="428px">
96              </asp:TextBox>
97
98              <asp:Label id="promptLabel" style="Z-INDEX: 102;
99                 LEFT: 13px; POSITION: absolute; TOP: 12px"
100                runat="server" ForeColor="Blue" Font-Size="X-Large">
101                Please leave a message in our guest book:
102             </asp:Label>
103          </form>
104       </body>
105    </HTML>
```

Fig. 20.35 ASPX file for the guest book application. (Part 3 of 3.)

```
1    // Fig. 20.36: Welcome.aspx.cs
2    // The code-behind file for the guest book page.
3
4    using System;
5    using System.Collections;
6    using System.ComponentModel;
7    using System.Data;
8    using System.Drawing;
9    using System.Web;
```

Fig. 20.36 Code-behind file for the guest book application. (Part 1 of 4.)

```
10   using System.Web.SessionState;
11   using System.Web.UI;
12   using System.Web.UI.WebControls;
13   using System.Web.UI.HtmlControls;
14   using System.IO;
15
16   namespace Guestbook
17   {
18      // allows user to leave messages
19      public class GuestBookForm : System.Web.UI.Page
20      {
21         protected System.Web.UI.WebControls.Label promptLabel;
22         protected System.Web.UI.WebControls.Label nameLabel;
23         protected System.Web.UI.WebControls.Label emailLabel;
24         protected System.Web.UI.WebControls.Label messageLabel;
25
26         protected System.Web.UI.WebControls.DataGrid dataGrid;
27
28         protected System.Web.UI.WebControls.Button submitButton;
29         protected System.Web.UI.WebControls.Button clearButton;
30
31         protected System.Web.UI.WebControls.TextBox nameTextBox;
32         protected System.Web.UI.WebControls.TextBox
33            emailTextBox;
34         protected System.Web.UI.WebControls.TextBox
35            messageTextBox;
36
37         protected System.Data.DataView dataView;
38
39         // handle Page's Load event
40         private void Page_Load(
41            object sender, System.EventArgs e )
42         {
43            dataView = new DataView( new DataTable() );
44
45         } // end method Page_Load
46
47         // Visual Studio .NET generated code
48
49         // places all the messages in the guest book into a
50         // table; messages are separated by horizontal rules
51         public void FillMessageTable()
52         {
53            DataTable table = dataView.Table;
54            table.Columns.Add( "Date" );
55            table.Columns.Add( "First Name" );
56            table.Columns.Add( "e-mail" );
57            table.Columns.Add( "Message" );
58
59            // open guest book file for reading
60            StreamReader reader = new StreamReader(
61               Request.PhysicalApplicationPath +
62               "guestbook.txt" );
```

Fig. 20.36 Code-behind file for the guest book application. (Part 2 of 4.)

```
63
64              char[] separator = { '\t' };
65
66              // read in line from file
67              string message = reader.ReadLine();
68
69              while ( message != null )
70              {
71                  // split the string into its four parts
72                  string[] parts = message.Split( separator );
73
74                  // load data into table
75                  table.LoadDataRow( parts, true );
76
77                  // read in one line from file
78                  message = reader.ReadLine();
79              }
80
81              // update grid
82              dataGrid.DataSource = table;
83              dataGrid.DataBind();
84
85              reader.Close();
86
87          } // end method FillMessageTable
88
89          // add user's entry to guest book
90          private void submitButton_Click(
91              object sender, System.EventArgs e )
92          {
93              // open stream for appending to file
94              StreamWriter guestbook =
95                  new StreamWriter( Request.PhysicalApplicationPath +
96                  "guestbook.txt", true );
97
98              // write new message to file
99              guestbook.WriteLine(
100                 DateTime.Now.Date.ToString().Substring( 0, 10 ) +
101                 "\t" + nameTextBox.Text + "\t" + emailTextBox.Text
102                 + "\t" + messageTextBox.Text );
103
104             // clear textboxes and close stream
105             nameTextBox.Text = "";
106             emailTextBox.Text = "";
107             messageTextBox.Text = "";
108             guestbook.Close();
109
110             FillMessageTable();
111         } // end method submitButton_Click
112
```

Fig. 20.36 Code-behind file for the guest book application. (Part 3 of 4.)

```
113        // clear all text boxes
114        private void clearButton_Click(
115           object sender, System.EventArgs e )
116        {
117           nameTextBox.Text = "";
118           emailTextBox.Text = "";
119           messageTextBox.Text = "";
120
121        } // end method clearButton_Click
122
123     } // end class GuestBookForm
124
125  } // end namespace Guestbook
```

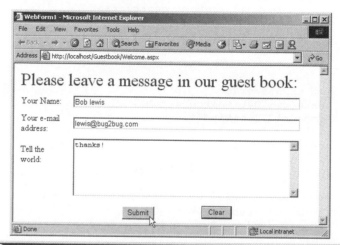

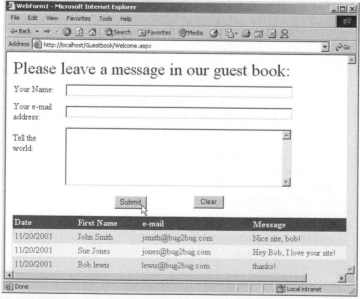

Fig. 20.36 Code-behind file for the guest book application. (Part 4 of 4.)

   Method **FillMessageTable** (lines 51–87) places the guest-book entries in
DataTable table. Lines 53–57 create a **DataTable** object from our **DataView**'s
Table property and then form the necessary columns using the **Columns** collection's
Add method. Lines 67–79 read each line in the text file. Method **Split** breaks each line
read from the file into four tokens, which are added to the **table** by calling method
LoadDataRow (line 75). The second argument to method **LoadDataRow** is **true**, indicating that any changes resulting from the addition will be accepted. The **DataTable**
places one piece of data in each column. After the **DataTable** is populated, the data are
bound to the **DataGrid**. Method **DataBind** is called to refresh the **DataView**. [*Note*:
DataView dataView was assigned to the **DataSource** property of the **DataGrid** in
the **Properties** window after it was declared in the code.]

20.8 Case Study: Connecting to a Database in ASP .NET

This case study presents a Web-based application in which a user can view a list of publications by a specified author. This program consists of two Web Forms. The first page that
a user requests is **Login.aspx** (Fig. 20.37). After accessing this page, users select their
names from the drop-down list and then enter their passwords. If their passwords are valid,
they are redirected to **Authors.aspx** (Fig. 20.40), which provides a list of authors.
When the user chooses an author and clicks the **Select** button, a postback occurs, and the
updated page displays a table that contains the titles, ISBNs and publishers of books written
by the selected author.

```
1   <%-- Fig. 20.37: Login.aspx                    --%>
2   <%-- A page that allows the user to log in. --%>
3
4   <%@ Page language="c#" Codebehind="login.aspx.cs"
5      AutoEventWireup="false" Inherits="Database.Login" %>
6   <%@ Register TagPrefix="Header" TagName="ImageHeader"
7      Src="ImageHeader.ascx" %>
8
9   <!DOCTYPE HTML PUBLIC "-//W3C//DTD HTML 4.0 Transitional//EN" >
10  <HTML>
11     <HEAD>
12        <title>WebForm1</title>
13        <meta name="GENERATOR" Content="Microsoft Visual Studio 7.0">
14        <meta name="CODE_LANGUAGE" Content="C#">
15        <meta name="vs_defaultClientScript" content="JavaScript">
16        <meta name="vs_targetSchema"
17           content="http://schemas.microsoft.com/intellisense/ie5">
18     </HEAD>
19     <body MS_POSITIONING="GridLayout" bgColor="#ffebff">
20        <form id="Form1" method="post" runat="server">
21           <asp:label id="nameLabel" style="Z-INDEX: 101;
22              LEFT: 15px; POSITION: absolute; TOP: 188px"
23              runat="server">Name
24           </asp:label>
25
```

Fig. 20.37 Log-in Web Form. (Part 1 of 2.)

```
26          <asp:label id="promptLabel" style="Z-INDEX: 108;
27             LEFT: 15px; POSITION: absolute; TOP: 145px"
28             runat="server">Please select your name and
29             enter your password to log in:
30          </asp:label>
31
32          <asp:customvalidator id="invalidPasswordValidator"
33             style="Z-INDEX: 107; LEFT: 262px; POSITION: absolute;
34             TOP: 221px" runat="server"
35             ControlToValidate="passwordTextBox" Font-Bold="True"
36             ForeColor="DarkCyan" ErrorMessage="Invalid password!">
37          </asp:customvalidator>
38
39        <asp:requiredfieldvalidator id="requiredPasswordValidator"
40             style="Z-INDEX: 106; LEFT: 262px; POSITION: absolute;
41             TOP: 221px" runat="server"
42             ControlToValidate="passwordTextBox" Font-Bold="True"
43             ForeColor="DarkCyan"
44             ErrorMessage="Please enter a password!">
45          </asp:requiredfieldvalidator>
46
47          <asp:dropdownlist id="nameList" style="Z-INDEX: 105;
48             LEFT: 92px; POSITION: absolute; TOP: 185px"
49             runat="server" Width="154px">
50          </asp:dropdownlist>
51
52          <asp:button id="submitButton" style="Z-INDEX: 104;
53             LEFT: 92px; POSITION: absolute; TOP: 263px"
54             runat="server" Text="Submit">
55          </asp:button>
56
57          <asp:textbox id="passwordTextBox" style="Z-INDEX: 103;
58             LEFT: 92px; POSITION: absolute; TOP: 221px"
59             runat="server" TextMode="Password">
60          </asp:textbox>
61
62          <asp:label id="passwordLabel" style="Z-INDEX: 102;
63             LEFT: 15px; POSITION: absolute; TOP: 220px"
64             runat="server">Password
65          </asp:label>
66
67          <Header:ImageHeader id="ImageHeader1" runat="server">
68          </Header:ImageHeader>
69       </form>
70    </body>
71 </HTML>
```

Fig. 20.37 Log-in Web Form. (Part 2 of 2.)

Much of the information provided by this Web page is accessed through databases stored in our project. **Login.aspx** retrieves valid user names for this site through **Login.mdb**, whereas all author information is retrieved from the **Books.mdb** database (also used in Chapter 19, Database, SQL and ADO .NET). The reader can view these databases by opening the **Database** directory for this chapter.

Lines 6–7 add a *Web user control* to the ASPX file. Readers might recall that we covered the definition of user controls for Windows applications in Chapter 13, Graphical User Interface Concepts: Part 2; we can define user controls for Web Forms using a similar technique. Because the ASPX files that users request do not define user controls for Web Forms, such controls do not have **HTML** or **BODY** elements. Rather, programmers specify these controls using the **<%@Register...%>** directive. For example, a programmer might want to include a *navigation bar* (i.e., a series of buttons for navigating a Web site) on every page of a site. If the site consists of a large number of pages, adding markup to create the navigation bar for each page could be time-consuming. Moreover, if the programmer subsequently modifies the navigation bar, every page on the site that uses the navigation bar must be updated. By creating a user control, the programmer can specify where on each page the navigation bar is placed using only a few lines of markup. If the navigation bar changes, the pages that use it are updated when those pages are requested in the future.

Like Web Forms, most Web user controls consist of two pages: An *ASCX file* and a code-behind file. Lines 6–7 define the user control's *tag name* (the name of this instance of the control) and tag prefix, which are **ImageHeader** and **Header**, respectively. The **ImageHeader** element is added to the file in lines 67–68. The tag definition is located in the **Src** file **HeaderImage.ascx** (Fig. 20.38). The programmer can create this file by right clicking the project name in the **Solution Explorer** and selecting **Add > Add New Item...**. From the dialog that opens, select **Web User Control**, and a new ASCX file will be added to the solution. At this point, the programmer can add controls and define any functionality in the Web user control's code-behind file. After creating the user control, the programmer can drag it from the **Solution Explorer** directly onto an open ASPX file. An instance of the control then will be created and added to the Web Form.

The form (Fig. 20.39) includes several **Label**s, a **TextBox** (**passwordTextbox**) and a **DropDownList** (**nameList**), which is populated in the code-behind file (**Login.aspx.cs**) with user names retrieved from a database. We also include two validators: A **RequiredFieldValidator** and a *CustomValidator*. A **CustomValidator** allows us to specify the conditions under which a field is valid. We define these conditions in the event handler for the *ServerValidate* event of the **CustomValidator**. The event-handling code, which is placed in the code-behind file for **Login.aspx.cs**, is discussed shortly. Both validators' **ControlToValidate** properties are set to **passwordTextbox**.

```
1   <%-- Fig. 20.38: ImageHeader.ascx          --%>
2   <%-- Listing for the header user control. --%>
3
4   <%@ Control Language="c#" AutoEventWireup="false"
5       Codebehind="ImageHeader.ascx.cs"
6       Inherits="Database.ImageHeader"
7       TargetSchema="http://schemas.microsoft.com/intellisense/ie5" %>
8
9   <asp:Image id="Image1" runat="server" ImageUrl="bug2bug.png">
10  </asp:Image>
```

Fig. 20.38 ASCX code for the header. (Part 1 of 2.)

Fig. 20.38 ASCX code for the header. (Part 2 of 2.)

```
1   // Fig. 20.39: Login.aspx.cs
2   // The code-behind file for the page that logs the user in.
3
4   using System;
5   using System.Collections;
6   using System.ComponentModel;
7   using System.Data;
8   using System.Drawing;
9   using System.Web;
10  using System.Web.SessionState;
11  using System.Web.UI;
12  using System.Web.UI.WebControls;
13  using System.Web.UI.HtmlControls;
14  using System.Web.Security;
15
16  namespace Database
17  {
18     // allows users to log in
19     public class Login : System.Web.UI.Page
20     {
21        protected System.Data.OleDb.OleDbDataAdapter
22           oleDbDataAdapter1;
23        protected System.Data.OleDb.OleDbCommand
24           oleDbSelectCommand1;
25        protected System.Data.OleDb.OleDbCommand
26           oleDbInsertCommand1;
27        protected System.Data.OleDb.OleDbCommand
28           oleDbUpdateCommand1;
29        protected System.Data.OleDb.OleDbCommand
30           oleDbDeleteCommand1;
31        protected System.Data.OleDb.OleDbConnection
32           oleDbConnection1;
```

Fig. 20.39 Code-behind file for the log-in page of authors application. (Part 1 of 4.)

```
33
34        protected System.Web.UI.WebControls.Label passwordLabel;
35        protected System.Web.UI.WebControls.Label nameLabel;
36        protected System.Web.UI.WebControls.Label promptLabel;
37
38        protected System.Web.UI.WebControls.DropDownList nameList;
39        protected System.Web.UI.WebControls.Button submitButton;
40        protected System.Web.UI.WebControls.RequiredFieldValidator
41           requiredPasswordValidator;
42        protected System.Web.UI.WebControls.CustomValidator
43           invalidPasswordValidator;
44        protected System.Web.UI.WebControls.TextBox passwordTextBox;
45
46        protected System.Data.OleDb.OleDbDataReader dataReader;
47
48        // handle Page's Load event
49        private void Page_Load( object sender, System.EventArgs e )
50        {
51           // if page loads due to postback, process information
52           // otherwise, page is loading for first time, so
53           // do nothing
54           if ( !IsPostBack )
55           {
56              // open database connection
57              oleDbConnection1.Open();
58
59              // execute query
60              dataReader =
61                 oleDbDataAdapter1.SelectCommand.ExecuteReader();
62
63              // while we can read a row from query result,
64              // add first item to drop-down list
65              while ( dataReader.Read() )
66                 nameList.Items.Add( dataReader.GetString( 0 ) );
67
68              // close database connection
69              oleDbConnection1.Close();
70           }
71        } // end Page_Load
72
73        // Visual Studio .NET generated code
74
75        // validate user name and password
76        private void invalidPasswordValidator_ServerValidate(
77           object source,
78           System.Web.UI.WebControls.ServerValidateEventArgs args )
79        {
80           // open database connection
81           oleDbConnection1.Open();
82
83           // set select command to find password of username
84           // from drop-down list
85           oleDbDataAdapter1.SelectCommand.CommandText =
```

Fig. 20.39 Code-behind file for the log-in page of authors application. (Part 2 of 4.)

```
86                "SELECT * FROM Users WHERE loginID = '" +
87                Request.Form[ "nameList" ].ToString() + "'";
88
89         dataReader =
90            oleDbDataAdapter1.SelectCommand.ExecuteReader();
91
92         dataReader.Read();
93
94         // if password is correct, create
95         // authentication ticket for this user and redirect
96         // user to Authors.aspx; otherwise set IsValid to false
97         if ( args.Value == dataReader.GetString( 1 ) )
98         {
99            FormsAuthentication.SetAuthCookie(
100               Request.Form[ "namelist" ], false );
101            Session.Add(
102               "name", Request.Form[ "nameList" ].ToString() );
103            Response.Redirect( "Authors.aspx" );
104         }
105         else
106            args.IsValid = false;
107
108         // close database connection
109         oleDbConnection1.Close();
110
111      } // end method invalidPasswordValidator_ServerValidate
112
113   } // end class Login
114
115 } // end namespace Database
```

Fig. 20.39 Code-behind file for the log-in page of authors application. (Part 3 of 4.)

Fig. 20.39 Code-behind file for the log-in page of authors application. (Part 4 of 4.)

In Fig. 20.39, the **Page_Load** event handler is defined in lines 49–71. If the page is being loaded for the first time, lines 55–70 execute. Lines 60–61 execute the SQL query that Visual Studio generates at design time—this query simply retrieves all the rows from the **Authors** table of the **Books** database. Lines 65–66 iterate through the rows, placing the item in the first column of each row (the author name) into **nameList**.

The reader might notice that we use an *OleDbDataReader*, an object that reads data from a database. We did not use an object of this type before, because the **OleDbDataReader** is not as flexible as other readers we discussed in Chapter 19. The object can read, but not update, data. We use **OleDbDataReader** in this example, because we need only to read the authors' names, and this object provides a fast and simple way to do so.

In this example, we use a **CustomValidator** to validate the user's password. We define a handler (lines 76–111) for the *ServerValidate* event of the **CustomValidator**, which executes every time the user clicks **Submit**. This event handler receives a *ServerValidateEventArgs* parameter called **args**. The object referenced by **args** has two important properties: *Value*, which contains the value of the control that the **CustomValidator** is validating, and *IsValid*, which contains a **bool**ean representing the validation result. Once the event handler completes, if **IsValid** is **true**, the HTML form is submitted to the Web server; if **IsValid** is **false**, the **CustomValidator**'s **ErrorMessage** is displayed, and the HTML **form** is not submitted to the Web server.

To create and attach an event handler for the **ServerValidate** event, double-click **CustomValidator**. The definition for this event handler (lines 76–111) tests the selected user name and the password provided by the user. If they match a valid user name and password in the database, the user is *authenticated* (i.e., the user's identity is confirmed), and the browser is redirected to **Authors.aspx** (Fig. 20.40). Lines 99–103 authenticate the user and provide access to **Authors.aspx** by calling **static** method *SetAuthCookie* of class *FormsAuthentication*. This class is in the **System.Web.Security** namespace (line 14). Method **SetAuthCookie** writes an *encrypted* cookie to the client containing information necessary to authenticate the user. Encrypted data are translated into code that only the sender and receiver can understand, thereby keeping those data private. Method **SetAuthCookie** takes two arguments: A **string** that contains the user name and a **bool**ean value that specifies whether this cookie should persist (i.e., remain on the client's computer) beyond the current session. Because we want the application to authenticate the user only for the current session, we set the **bool** value to **false**. After the user is authenticated, the user's Web browser is redirected to **Authors.aspx**. If the database query did not verify the user's identity, property *IsValid* of the **CustomValidator** is set to **false**; in this case, the application displays the *ErrorMessage*, and the user can attempt to log in again.

This example uses a technique known as *forms authentication*, which protects a page so that only authenticated users can access that page. Authentication is a crucial tool for sites that allow only members to enter the site or a portion of the site. Authentication and denial of access to unauthorized users requires several lines in *Web.config* (a file used for application configuration). This XML file is a part of every ASP .NET application created in Visual Studio. The default authentication element:

```
<authentication mode="None" />
```

disables authentication. To deny access to unauthorized users, replace this line with:

```
<authentication mode="Forms">
   <forms name="DatabaseCookie"
      loginUrl="Login.aspx" protection="Encryption" />
</authentication>
```

```
<authorization>
    <deny users="?" />
</authorization>
```

This replacement alters the value of the *mode* attribute in the **authentication** element from **"None"** to **"Forms"**, which specifies that we want to use forms authentication. The *forms* element defines the way in which users are validated. Inside the forms element, attribute **name** sets the name of the cookie that is created on the user's machine—in this case, we name it **DatabaseCookie**. Attribute *loginUrl* specifies the log-in page for our application; users that attempt to access any page in our application without logging in are redirected to this page. Attribute *protection* specifies whether the value of the cookie is encrypted. In this case, we set the value of **protection** to **"Encryption"** to encrypt the cookie's data.

Element *authorization* indicates the type of access that specific users can have. In this application, we want to allow authenticated users access to all pages on the site. We place the *deny* element inside the **authorization** element to specify users to which we wish to deny access. When we set this attribute's value to **"?"**, all anonymous (i.e., unauthenticated) users are denied access to the site.

After the user has been authenticated, they will be redirected to **Authors.aspx** (Fig. 20.40). This page provides a list of authors from which the user can choose one. After a choice has been made, a table is displayed containing information about books that author has written.

```
1   <%-- Fig. 20.40: Authors.aspx                         --%>
2   <%-- This page allows a user to chose an author and display --%>
3   <%-- that author's books.                             --%>
4
5   <%@ Page language="c#" Codebehind="Authors.aspx.cs"
6      AutoEventWireup="false" Inherits="Database.Authors" %>
7   <%@ Register TagPrefix="Header" TagName="ImageHeader"
8      Src="ImageHeader.ascx" %>
9   <!DOCTYPE HTML PUBLIC "-//W3C//DTD HTML 4.0 Transitional//EN" >
10  <HTML>
11     <HEAD>
12        <title>Authors</title>
13        <meta name="GENERATOR" Content="Microsoft Visual Studio 7.0">
14        <meta name="CODE_LANGUAGE" Content="C#">
15        <meta name="vs_defaultClientScript" content="JavaScript">
16        <meta name="vs_targetSchema"
17           content="http://schemas.microsoft.com/intellisense/ie5">
18     </HEAD>
19     <body MS_POSITIONING="GridLayout" bgColor="#ffebff">
20        <form id="Authors" method="post" runat="server">
21           <asp:DropDownList id="nameList" style="Z-INDEX: 103;
22              LEFT: 90px; POSITION: absolute; TOP: 157px"
23              runat="server" Width="158px" Height="22px">
24           </asp:DropDownList>
25
```

Fig. 20.40 ASPX file that allows a user to select an author from a drop-down list. (Part 1 of 2.)

```
26                <Header:ImageHeader id="Head1" runat="server">
27                </Header:ImageHeader>
28
29                <asp:Label id="Label2" style="Z-INDEX: 102; LEFT: 28px;
30                    POSITION: absolute; TOP: 157px" runat="server"
31                    Width="48px" Height="22px">Authors:
32                </asp:Label>
33
34              <asp:Button id="Button1" style="Z-INDEX: 104; LEFT: 29px;
35                    POSITION: absolute; TOP: 188px" runat="server"
36                    Width="78px" Text="Select">
37              </asp:Button>
38
39                <asp:Label id="Label3" style="Z-INDEX: 105; LEFT: 19px;
40                    POSITION: absolute; TOP: 127px" runat="server"
41                    Width="210px" Visible="False">You chose
42                </asp:Label>
43
44              <asp:DataGrid id="dataGrid" style="Z-INDEX: 106;
45                    LEFT: 12px; POSITION: absolute; TOP: 151px"
46                    runat="server" Height="23px" Width="700px"
47                    ForeColor="Black" AllowPaging="True"
48                    DataSource="<%# dataView1 %>" Visible="False"
49                    AllowSorting="True">
50
51                <EditItemStyle BackColor="White"></EditItemStyle>
52
53                <AlternatingItemStyle ForeColor="Black"
54                    BackColor="LightGoldenrodYellow">
55                </AlternatingItemStyle>
56
57                <ItemStyle BackColor="White"></ItemStyle>
58
59                <HeaderStyle BackColor="LightGreen"></HeaderStyle>
60
61                <PagerStyle NextPageText="Next &amp;gt; "
62                    PrevPageText="&amp;lt; Previous">
63                </PagerStyle>
64            </asp:DataGrid>
65        </form>
66    </body>
67 </HTML>
```

Fig. 20.40 ASPX file that allows a user to select an author from a drop-down list. (Part 2 of 2.)

The ASPX file (Fig. 20.40) for this page creates a number of controls: A **DropDown-List**, three **Label**s, a **Button** and a **DataGrid**. Notice that some of the controls—one of the **Label**s and the **DataGrid**—have their **Visible** properties set to **false** (line 41 and line 48). This means that the controls are not visible when the page first loads; because the user has not yet chosen an author, there is no information to display. Users select an author from the **DropDownList** and click **Submit**, causing a postback to occur.

When the postback is handled, the **DataGrid** is filled and displayed. Figure 20.41 presents the code-behind file for this ASPX file.

```
1   // Fig. 20.41: Authors.aspx.cs
2   // The code-behind file for a page that allows a user to choose an
3   // author and then view a list of that author's books.
4
5   using System;
6   using System.Collections;
7   using System.ComponentModel;
8   using System.Data;
9   using System.Drawing;
10  using System.Web;
11  using System.Web.SessionState;
12  using System.Web.UI;
13  using System.Web.UI.WebControls;
14  using System.Web.UI.HtmlControls;
15
16  namespace Database
17  {
18     // let user pick an author, then display that author's books
19     public class Authors : System.Web.UI.Page
20     {
21        protected System.Web.UI.WebControls.DropDownList nameList;
22        protected System.Web.UI.WebControls.Label choseLabel;
23        protected System.Web.UI.WebControls.Button selectButton;
24        protected System.Web.UI.WebControls.Label authorsLabel;
25        protected System.Web.UI.WebControls.DataGrid dataGrid;
26
27        protected System.Data.OleDb.OleDbDataAdapter
28           oleDbDataAdapter1;
29        protected System.Data.OleDb.OleDbConnection
30           oleDbConnection1;
31        protected System.Data.OleDb.OleDbDataReader dataReader;
32
33        protected System.Data.OleDb.OleDbCommand
34           oleDbSelectCommand1;
35        protected System.Data.OleDb.OleDbCommand
36           oleDbInsertCommand1;
37        protected System.Data.OleDb.OleDbCommand
38           oleDbUpdateCommand1;
39        protected System.Data.OleDb.OleDbCommand
40           oleDbDeleteCommand1;
41
42        protected System.Data.DataTable dataTable1 =
43           new DataTable();
44        protected System.Data.DataView dataView1;
45
46        protected static string sortString = "Title";
47
48        // on page load
49        private void Page_Load( object sender, System.EventArgs e )
50        {
```

Fig. 20.41 Database information input into a **DataGrid**. (Part 1 of 4.)

```
51          // test whether page was loaded due to postback
52          if ( !IsPostBack )
53          {
54             // open database connection
55             try
56             {
57                oleDbConnection1.Open();
58
59                // execute query
60                dataReader =
61                   oleDbDataAdapter1.SelectCommand.ExecuteReader();
62
63                // while we can read a row from result of
64                // query, add first item to dropdown list
65                while ( dataReader.Read() )
66                   nameList.Items.Add( dataReader.GetString( 0 ) +
67                      " " + dataReader.GetString( 1 ) );
68             }
69
70             // if database cannot be found
71             catch( System.Data.OleDb.OleDbException )
72             {
73                authorsLabel.Text =
74                   "Server Error: Unable to load database!";
75             }
76
77             // close database connection
78             finally
79             {
80                oleDbConnection1.Close();
81             }
82          }
83          else
84          {
85             // set some controls to be invisible
86             nameList.Visible = false;
87             selectButton.Visible = false;
88             choseLabel.Visible = false;
89
90             // set other controls to be visible
91             authorsLabel.Visible = true;
92             dataGrid.Visible = true;
93
94             // add author name to label
95             authorsLabel.Text =
96                "You Chose " + nameList.SelectedItem + ".";
97             int authorID = nameList.SelectedIndex + 1;
98
99             try
100            {
101               // open database connection
102               oleDbConnection1.Open();
103
```

Fig. 20.41 Database information input into a **DataGrid**. (Part 2 of 4.)

```
104                    // grab title, ISBN and publisher name for each book
105                    oleDbDataAdapter1.SelectCommand.CommandText =
106                       "SELECT Titles.Title, Titles.ISBN, " +
107                       "Publishers.PublisherName FROM AuthorISBN " +
108                       "INNER JOIN Titles ON AuthorISBN.ISBN = " +
109                       "Titles.ISBN, Publishers WHERE " +
110                       "(AuthorISBN.AuthorID = " + authorID + ")";
111
112                    // fill dataview with results
113                    oleDbDataAdapter1.Fill( dataTable1 );
114                    dataView1 = new DataView( dataTable1 );
115                    dataView1.Sort = sortString;
116                    dataGrid.DataBind(); // bind grid to data source
117                 }
118
119                 // if database cannot be found
120                 catch( System.Data.OleDb.OleDbException )
121                 {
122                    authorsLabel.Text =
123                       "Server Error: Unable to load database!";
124                 }
125
126                 // close database connection
127                 finally
128                 {
129                    oleDbConnection1.Close();
130                 }
131              }
132
133           } // end method Page_Load
134
135           // on new page
136           private void OnNewPage( object sender,
137              DataGridPageChangedEventArgs e )
138           {
139              // set current page to next page
140              dataGrid.CurrentPageIndex = e.NewPageIndex;
141
142              dataView1.Sort = sortString;
143              dataGrid.DataBind(); // rebind data
144
145           } // end method OnNewPage
146
147           // Visual Studio .NET generated code
148
149           // handles Sort event
150           private void dataGrid_SortCommand( object source,
151              System.Web.UI.WebControls.DataGridSortCommandEventArgs e )
152           {
153              // get table to sort
154              sortString = e.SortExpression.ToString();
155              dataView1.Sort = sortString; // sort
156              dataGrid.DataBind(); // rebind data
```

Fig. 20.41 Database information input into a **DataGrid**. (Part 3 of 4.)

```
157
158          } // end method dataGrid_SortCommand
159
160      } // end class Authors
161
162  } // end namespace Database
```

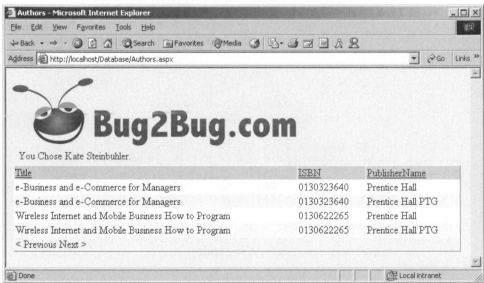

Fig. 20.41 Database information input into a **DataGrid**. (Part 4 of 4.)

Method **Page_Load** (lines 49–133) contains most of the code for this example. The
condition (line 52) determines whether the page was loaded as a result of a postback event.
Line 57 then opens the database connection, and lines 60–61 execute the database command, which retrieves all the authors' first and last names from the database. Lines 65–67
iterate through the result set and add the authors' first and last names to **nameList**.

Once the user has selected an author and submitted the form, the condition (line 52) becomes **false**, which causes lines 86–131 to execute. The initial set of controls displayed to the user (i.e., the label, drop-down list and button) are hidden in the postback. However, the label and the data grid that previously were invisible are made visible. Lines 95–96 add the selected author's name to the label control.

Lines 105–110 create a database query to retrieve the title, ISBN and publisher name for each of the author's books and assign them to the command's **CommandText** property. Method **fill** (line 113) populates its **DataTable** argument with the rows returned by our query on lines 106–110. The **DataView** class's *Sort* property sorts its data by the **string sortString** assigned it (line 115). Line 46 initially sets this **string** to **"Title"**, indicating that the rows in our table are to be sorted in ascending order by title. Ascending order is the default. If **sortString** where **"TitleDESC"**, the rows in our table would be sorted in descending order by title.

Method **OnNewPage** (lines 136–145) handles the **DataGrid**'s **PageIndex-Changed** event, which is fired when the user clicks the **Next** link at the bottom of the **DataGrid** control to display the next page of data. To enable paging, the **AllowPaging** property of the **DataGrid** is set to **true** in the Web Form designer. **DataGrid**'s **PageSize** property determines the number of entries per page, and its **PagerStyle** property customizes the display of our **DataGrid** during paging. This **DataGrid** control displays ten books per page. After the **DataGrid**'s **CurrentPageIndex** property is assigned the event argument **NewPageIndex** (line 140), we sort the data and rebind it so that the next page of data can be displayed (lines 142–143). This technique for displaying data makes the site more readable and enables pages to load more quickly (due to the fact that less data are displayed at one time).

Method **dataGrid_SortCommand** (lines 150–158) handles the **Sort** event of the **DataGrid** control. When the **AllowSorting** property in the Web Form designer is enabled, the **DataGrid** displays all table headings as *LinkButton* controls (i.e., buttons that act as hyperlinks). The **SortCommand** event is raised when the user clicks a column header name. On line 154, we use the *SortExpression* property of **e**. This property indicates the column by which the data is sorted. This value is assigned to **string sortString**, which then is assigned to our **DataView**'s **Sort** property on line 155. On line 156, we rebind the sorted data to our **DataGrid**.

20.9 Tracing

ASP .NET provides a *tracing* feature for debugging Web-based applications. Tracing is the process of placing statements throughout the code-behind file that output information during execution about the program's status.

In Windows applications, message boxes can aid in debugging; in Web Forms, a programmer might use **Response.Write** for this purpose. However, using **Response.Write** for tracing in ASP .NET has several drawbacks.

One of these drawbacks is that, once an application is executing correctly, the programmer must remove all tracing statements from the program. This is time-consuming and can introduce errors, because the programmer must differentiate between statements that are part of the program's logic and statements that are used for testing purposes. ASP .NET provides the programmer with two forms of built-in tracing: *Page tracing* and *application tracing*.

Page tracing involves the tracing of the actions of an individual page. Setting the *Trace* property of the page to **True** in the **Properties** window enables tracing for that page. Instead of calling the **Response** object's **Write** method, we call the *Trace* object's *Write* method. Object **Trace** is an instance of the *TraceContext* class and provides tracing capabilities. In addition to method **Write**, the **Trace** object includes method *Warn*, which prints warning statements in red. When tracing is disabled by setting the **Trace** property to **false**, **Trace** statements are not executed.

Figure 20.42 depicts a simple page that displays a sentence (we do not show the code for this page, as it is quite simple). The **Page_Load** event for this page includes the statement **Trace.Warn("Using warnings")**. The **Trace** property is set to **false** so **"Using warnings"** is not displayed on the page; we will see shortly when and where trace statements are displayed.

Figure 20.43 displays the same page when the **Trace** property is set to **True**. The top of the figure depicts the original page, and the tracing information generated by ASP .NET appears below. The *Request Details* section provides information about the request. The *Trace Information* section contains the information output by calling the **Write** and **Warn** methods. The second row contains the message, which displays in red.

The *Control Tree* section lists all the controls contained on the page. Several additional tables also appear in this page. The *Cookies Collection* section contains information about the program's cookies, the *Headers Collection* section catalogs the HTTP headers for the page and the *Server Variables* section provides a list of server variables (i.e., information sent by the browser with each request) and their values.

Tracing for entire projects also is available. To turn on application-level tracing, open the **Web.config** file for the project and set the *enabled* property to **true** in the *trace* element. To view the project's tracing information, navigate the browser to the *trace.axd* file in the project folder. This file does not actually exist on the hard drive; it is generated when the user requests **trace.axd**. Figure 20.44 shows the Web page that is generated when the programmer views the **trace.axd** file.

This page lists all the requests made to this application and the times when the pages were accessed. Clicking one of the **View Details** links directs the browser to a page similar to the one portrayed in Fig. 20.43.

In this chapter, we discussed ASP .NET with C# and its role in a three tier architecture. Students now should be able to create dynamic Web forms that respond to user input, track and maintain a user's session information and interact with a back-end database from a Web form. In the next chapter, we introduce ASP .NET Web services, which allow remote software to interact with methods and objects on a Web server.

Fig. 20.42 ASPX page with tracing turned off.

Page
contents —

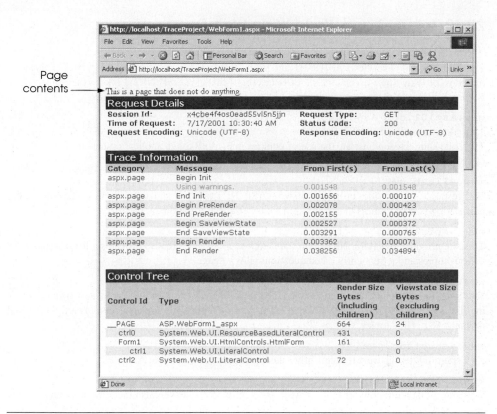

Fig. 20.43 Tracing enabled on a page.

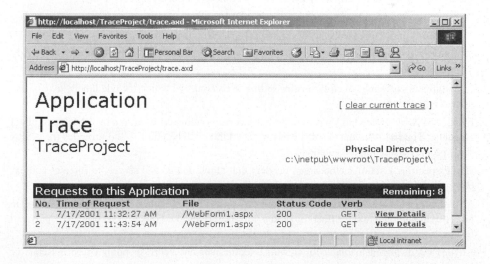

Fig. 20.44 Tracing information for a project.

20.10 Internet and World Wide Web Resources

www.asp.net

The Microsoft site overviews ASP .NET and provides a link for downloading ASP .NET. This site includes the IBuy Spy e-commerce storefront example that uses ASP .NET. Links to the Amazon and Barnes & Noble Web sites, at which the user can purchase books, also are included.

www.asp101.com/aspplus

This site overviews ASP .NET and includes articles, code examples and links to ASP .NET resources. The code samples demonstrate the use of cookies in an ASP .NET application and show how to establish a connection to a database—two key capabilities of multi-tier applications.

www.411asp.net

This resource site provides programmers with ASP .NET tutorials and code samples. The community pages allows programmers to ask questions, answer questions and post messages.

www.aspfree.com

This site provides free ASP .NET demos and source code. The site also provides a list of articles for various topics and a frequently asked questions (FAQs) page.

www.aspng.com

This site offers tutorials, links and recommendations for books on ASP .NET. Links to different mailing lists also are provided. These links are organized by topic. This site also contains articles related to many ASP .NET topics, such as "Performance Tips and Tricks."

www.aspnetfaq.com

This site provides answers to frequently asked questions (FAQs) about ASP.NET.

www.123aspx.com

This site offers a directory of links to ASP .NET resources. The site also includes daily and weekly newsletters.

SUMMARY

- Microsoft's ASP .NET technology is used for Web-based application development.
- Web-based applications create Web content for Web browser clients.
- The Web-Form file represents the Web page that is sent to the client browser.
- Web-Form files have the file extension **.aspx** and contain the GUI of the Web page currently being developed.
- Programmers customize Web Forms by adding Web controls, which include labels, text boxes, images and buttons.
- Every ASPX file created in Visual Studio has a corresponding class written in a .NET-compliant language. The file that contains this class is called the code-behind file and provides the ASPX file's programmatic implementation.
- HTTP specifies a set of methods and headers that allow clients and servers to interact and exchange information in a uniform and predictable way.
- In its simplest form, a Web page is nothing more than a HTML document. This document is a plain text file containing markings (markup or tags) that describes to a Web browser how to display and format the document's information.
- Any HTML document available for viewing over the Web has a corresponding Uniform Resource Locator (URL), which is an address indicating the location of a resource.
- Computers that run Web-server software provide resources for download over the Internet.

- The hostname is the name of the computer on which the resource resides. This computer usually is referred to as the host, because it houses and maintains resources.

- An IP address identifies a server in a manner similar to that by which a telephone number uniquely defines a particular phone line.

- MIME is an Internet standard that specifies the way in which certain data must be formatted so that programs can interpret the data correctly.

- Web-based applications are multi-tier applications, which sometimes are referred to as *n*-tier applications. Multi-tier applications divide functionality into separate tiers (i.e., logical groupings of functionality).

- The information tier maintains data pertaining to the application.

- The middle tier implements business logic, controller logic and presentation logic to control interactions between application clients and application data.

- The client tier, or top tier, is the application's user interface, which is typically a Web browser.

- Visual Studio generates the markup in our ASPX page when controls are dragged onto the Web Form.

- A **<%@ Page…%>** directive specifies information needed by the CLR to process the file.

- The **AutoEventWireup** determines how event handlers are linked to a control's events.

- The **Inherits** attribute specifies the class in the code-behind file from which this ASP. NET class inherits.

- When a control's **runat** attribute is set to **"server"**, this control is executed on a server, generating an HTML equivalent.

- The **asp:** tag prefix in the declaration of a control indicates that the control is an ASP .NET Web control.

- Each Web control maps to a corresponding HTML element.

- The same Web control can map to different HTML elements, depending on the client browser and the Web control's property settings.

- Namespace **System.Web** contains classes that manage client requests and server responses.

- Namespace **System.Web.UI** contains classes for the creation of Web-based applications and controls.

- Class **Page** defines a standard Web page, providing event handlers and objects necessary for creating Web-based applications. All code-behind classes for ASPX forms inherit from class **Page**.

- Class **Control** is the base class that provides common functionality for all Web controls.

- Namespace **System.Web.UI.WebControls** contains Web controls employed in the design of the page's user interface.

- Method **OnInit** is called when the **Init** event is raised. This event indicates that the page is ready to be initialized.

- The **Load** event is raised every time a page is requested/reloaded.

- When a client requests an ASPX file, a class is created behind the scenes that contains both the visual aspect of our page (defined in the ASPX file) and the logic of our page (defined in the code-behind file). This new class inherits from **Page**. The first time that a Web page is requested, this class is compiled, and an instance is created. This instance represents the page—it will create the HTML that is sent to the client. The assembly created from our compiled class will be placed in the project's **bin** directory.

- Changes to the Web application can be detected by the runtime, and the project is recompiled to reflect the altered content.

- The **Page_Load** event handler is usually used to execute any processing that is necessary to restore data from previous requests.

- After **Page_Load** has finished executing, the page processes any events raised by the page's controls.

- A form is a mechanism for collecting user information and sending it to the Web server.

- HTML forms can contain visual and nonvisual components. Visual components include clickable buttons and other graphical user interface components with which users interact.

- Nonvisual components in an HTML form, called hidden inputs, store any data that the document author specifies.

- The name **localhost** indicates that the client and server reside on the same machine. If the Web server were located on a different machine, **localhost** would be replaced with the appropriate IP address or hostname.

- The Web-Form designer, when in **HTML** mode, displays the markup that represents the user interface of this page. The **Design** mode allows the programmer to view the page as it will look and modify it using the drag-and-drop technique.

- The **PageLayout** property determines how controls are arranged on the form.

- By default, property **PageLayout** is set to **GridLayout**, which means that all controls remain exactly where they are dropped on the Web Form. This is known as absolute positioning.

- The developer can set the Web Form's **PageLayout** property to **FlowLayout**, which causes controls to be placed sequentially on the Web Form. This is called relative positioning, because the controls' positions are relative to the Web Form's upper-left corner.

- **Image** controls insert an image into a Web page. The **ImageUrl** property specifies the file location of the image to display.

- A **TextBox** control allows the programmer to read and display text.

- A **RadioButtonList** control provides a series of radio buttons for the user.

- A **DropDownList** control provides a list of options to the user.

- The **HyperLink** control adds a hyperlink to a Web page. The **NavigateUrl** property of this control specifies the resource that is requested when a user clicks the hyperlink.

- ASP .NET provides the **AdRotator** Web control for displaying advertisements. One advertisement is chosen at random from the advertisements stored in an XML file, specified by property **AdvertisementFile**.

- The advertisement file used for an **AdRotator** control contains **Ad** elements, each of which provides information about a different advertisement.

- Element **ImageUrl** in an advertisement file specifies the path (location) of the advertisement's image, and element **NavigateUrl** specifies the URL for the Web page that loads when a user clicks the advertisement.

- The **AlternateText** element contains text that displays in place of the image when the browser cannot locate or render the image for some reason.

- The **Impressions** element specifies how often a particular image appears, relative to the other images.

- A validation control (or validator), checks whether the data in another Web control is in the proper format.

- When the HTML for our page is created, a validator is converted into ECMAScript.

- ECMAScript is a scripting language that facilitates a disciplined approach to designing computer programs that enhance the functionality and appearance of Web pages.

- A **RegularExpressionValidator** matches a Web control's content against a regular expression. The regular expression that validates the input is assigned to property **ValidationExpression**.

- A validator's **ControlToValidate** property indicates which control will be validated.

- A **RequiredFieldValidator** is used to ensure that a control receives input from the user when the form is submitted.

- Web programmers using ASP .NET often design their Web pages so that, when submitted, the current page is requested again. This event is known as a postback.

- The **Page**'s **IsPostBack** property can be used to determine whether the page is being loaded as a result of a postback.

- The **EnableViewState** attribute determines whether a Web control's state persists (i.e., is retained) when a postback occurs.

- Personalization makes it possible for e-businesses to communicate effectively with their customers and also improves users' ability to locate desired products and services.

- To provide personalized services to consumers, e-businesses must be able to recognize clients when they request information from a site.

- The request/response system on which the Web operates is facilitated by HTTP. Unfortunately, HTTP is a stateless protocol—it does not support persistent connections that would enable Web servers to maintain state information regarding particular clients.

- A session represents a unique client on the Internet. If the client leaves a site and then returns later, the client should still be recognized as the same user. To help the server distinguish among clients, each client must identify itself to the server.

- The tracking of individual clients is known as session tracking.

- A cookie is a text file stored by a Web site on an individual's computer that allows the site to track the actions of the visitor.

- When a Web Form receives a request, the header includes such information as the request type and any cookies that have been sent previously from the server to be stored on the client machine.

- When the server formulates its response, the header information includes any cookies the server wants to store on the client computer and other information, such as the MIME type of the response.

- If the programmer of a cookie does not set an expiration date, the Web browser maintains the cookie for the duration of the browsing session.

- A cookie object is of type **HttpCookie**.

- Cookies are sent and received in the form of a collection of cookies, of type **HttpCookieCollection**.

- Cookies can be read by an application only if they were created in the domain in which the application is running—a Web server can never access cookies created outside the domain associated with that server.

- The **Name** and **Value** properties of class **HttpCookie** can be used to retrieve the key and value of the key-value pair in a cookie.

- C# provides session-tracking capabilities in the Framework Class Library's **HttpSessionState** class.

- Every Web Form includes an **HttpSessionState** object, which is accessible through property **Session** of class **Page**.

- When the Web page is requested, an **HttpSessionState** object is created and is assigned to the **Page**'s **Session** property.

- **Page** property **Session** is known as the **Session** object.

- Session object key-value pairs are often referred to as session items.

- A Web Form should not use shared instance variables to maintain client state information, because clients accessing that Web Form in parallel might overwrite the shared instance variables.

- Web Forms should maintain client state information in **HttpSessionState** objects, because such objects are specific to each client.

- Like a cookie, an **HttpSessionState** object can store name-value pairs. These session items are placed into an **HttpSessionState** object via a call to method **Add**.

- **HttpSessionState** objects can store any type of object (not just **string**s) as attribute values. This provides C# programmers with increased flexibility in determining the type of state information they wish to maintain for their clients.

- If the application calls method **Add** to add an attribute that has the same name as an attribute previously stored in a session, the object associated with that attribute is replaced.

- Property **SessionID** contains the session's unique ID. The first time a client connects to the Web server a unique session ID is created for that client. When the client makes additional requests, the client's session ID is compared with the session IDs stored in the Web server's memory.

- Property **Timeout** specifies the maximum amount of time that an **HttpSessionState** object can be inactive before it is discarded.

- **Session** object's **Count** property provides the number of session items contained in a **Session** object.

- A value in a key-value pair is retrieved from the **Session** object by indexing the **Session** object with the key name, using the same process by which a value can be retrieved from a hash table.

- The **Keys** property of class **HttpSessionState** returns a collection containing all the keys in the session.

- The colors for a **DataGrid** can be specified through the **Auto Format...** link that is located near the bottom of the **Properties** window.

- The **Request** object's **PhysicalApplicationPath** property retrieves the path of the application's root directory.

- Columns can be added to a **DataTable** object via the **Columns** collection's **Add** method.

- Information can be added to a **DataTable** via method **LoadDataRow**.

- Method **DataBind** is called to refresh the information in a **DataView**.

- Programmers can define their own Web control, known as a Web user control.

- Web user controls usually consist of two pages: An ASCX file, and a code-behind file.

- A **CustomValidator** allows us to specify the circumstances under which a field is valid. We define these circumstances in the event handler for the **ServerValidate** event of the **CustomValidator**.

- When a user's identity is confirmed, we say that the user has been authenticated.

- Method **SetAuthCookie** writes to the client an encrypted cookie containing information necessary to authenticate the user.

- Encrypted data is data translated into a code that only the sender and receiver can understand thereby keeping it private.

- A technique known as forms authentication protects a page so that only authenticated users can access it.

- Authentication and denial of access to unauthorized users involves the placement of several lines in **Web.config** (a file used for application configuration). This file is a part of every ASP .NET application created in Visual Studio.

- We can modify this file so that a user who is not authenticated will not be allowed to view any of the pages in the application. One who attempts to view a later page will be forced back to the login page.

- The **DataView** class's **Sort** property sorts its data by the **string** assigned it.

- To enable paging, the **AllowPaging** property of a **DataGrid** is set to **true**.

- When the **AllowSorting** property in the Web Form designer is enabled, a **DataGrid** displays all table headings as **LinkButton** controls (i.e., buttons that act as hyperlinks). The **Sort-Command** event is raised when the user clicks a column header name.

- The **SortExpression** property indicates the column by which the data is sorted.

- ASP .NET provides a tracing feature for the debugging of Web-based applications. Tracing is the process of placing statements throughout the code-behind file that output information during execution about the program's status.

- ASP .NET provides the programmer with two forms of built-in tracing: Page tracing and application tracing.

- Page tracing involves the tracing of the actions of an individual page. Setting the **Trace** property of the page to **true** in the **Properties** window enables tracing for that page.

- Object **Trace** is an instance of the **TraceContext** class and provides tracing capabilities.

- In addition to method **Write**, the **Trace** object includes method **Warn**, which prints warning statements in red.

- When tracing is disabled by setting the **Trace** property to **false**, **Trace** statements are not executed.

- The **Request Details** section that appears when tracing information is displayed in an ASPX page provides information about the request.

- The **Trace Information** section contains the information output by calling the **Write** and **Warn** methods.

- The **Control Tree** section lists all the controls contained on the page.

- The **Cookies Collection** section contains information about the program's cookies, the **Headers Collection** section catalogs the HTTP headers for the page and the **Server Variables** section provides a list of server variables and their values.

- Tracing for the entire project is also available. To turn on application-level tracing, open the **Web.config** file for the project. Set the **Enabled** property to **true** in the **trace** element. To view the project's tracing information, navigate the browser to the **trace.axd** file in the project folder.

TERMINOLOGY

%> tag
<% tag
Ad attribute in XML file
AdRotator class
AdRotatorInformation.xml
AdvertisementFile property of
   class **AdRotator**
AlternateText attribute in XML file
application tracing

ASCX file
ASP .NET
ASP .NET Web Application project
ASPX file
authentication element in **Web.config**
authorization element in **Web.config**
AutoEventWireup attribute of
   ASP .NET page
HTTP response

ValidationExpression property of class
   RegularExpressionValidator
validator
Value property of class
   ServerValidateEventArgs

virtual directory
Warn method of class **TraceContext**
Web Form
Web.config file

SELF-REVIEW EXERCISES

20.1   State whether each of the following is *true* or *false*. If *false*, explain why.
   a) Controls placed on a Web Form are placed using absolute positioning when the Webpage's **PageLayout** property is set to **GridLayout**.
   b) It is possible to enable tracing in an individual page or in an entire application in ASP .NET.
   c) Web Form file names typically end in **.aspx**.
   d) If no expiration data is set for a cookie, that cookie will be destroyed at the end of the session.
   e) A maximum of two validator controls can be placed on any control.
   f) The **TextBox** Web control is not the same as the **TextBox** Windows control.
   g) An **AdRotator** always displays all ads with equal frequency.
   h) The file that contains image information for an **AdRotator** can be in a format other than XML.
   i) **HttpResponse** method **Redirect** can redirect the browser only to an ASP .NET page within the same folder.
   j) Changes made to properties of controls in the **Properties** window are reflected in the **InitializeComponent** method in the code-behind file.
   k) If a Web application project is not compiled before it is requested, the page(s) will not be displayed.

20.2   Fill in the blanks in each of the following statements:
   a) The basic structure of a Web application contains three tiers: _____, _____ and _____.
   b) A control that ensures that the data in another control are in a specific format is called a _____.
   c) A _____ occurs when a page requests itself.
   d) Every ASP .NET page inherits from class _____.
   e) When a page loads, the _____ event occurs first, and the _____ event occurs afterwards.
   f) The _____ file contains the functionality for an ASP.NET page.
   g) Method _____ of the _____ object of class **Page** outputs HTML to a client.
   h) **AdRotator**'s _____ property points to the file containing information in _____ format about all the ads that will be displayed.
   i) The _____ property in the Web Form designer organizes controls either by lining them up or by placing them on a grid.
   j) Code generated by Visual Studio during the design of an ASP .NET page is placed in the _____ method.

ANSWERS TO SELF-REVIEW EXERCISES

20.1   a) True. b) True. c) True. d) True. e) False. An unlimited number of validation controls can be placed on one control. f) True. g) False. The frequency with which the **AdRotator** displays ads is specified in the **AdvertisementFile**. h) False. The **AdvertisementFile** must be an XML file. i) False. **Redirect** can redirect the user to any page. j) False. Changes to properties of controls can be seen in the ASPX file. k) True.

20.2   a) information, middle, client. b) validator. c) postback. d) **Page**. e) **Init**, **Load**. f) code-behind. g) **Write**, **Response**. h) **AdvertisementFile**, XML. i) **PageLayout**. j) **Initial-izeComponent**.

EXERCISES

20.3   Modify the **WebTime** example so that it allows a user to select a time zone from a **Drop-DownList**. The Web Form then should redirect the user to a page that displays the time in the selected zone. Update the time every thirty seconds.

20.4   Modify the Exercise 20.3 to contain drop-down lists for **Label** properties such as **Back-Color**, **ForeColor**, **Font**, etc. Allow the user to select from these lists and submit the selections; then, reload the page so that it reflects the specified changes to the properties of the **Label** displaying the time.

20.5   Create an ASP .NET page that uses a file on disk to keep track of how many hits the page has received. Display the number of hits every time the page loads.

20.6   Provide functionality for the example in Section 20.5.1. When users click **Register**, store their information in a file. On postback, thank the user for providing the information.

20.7   Using the same techniques as those covered in the guest-book case study in Section 20.7, develop an ASP .NET application for a discussion group. Allow new links to be created for new topics.

20.8   Create a set of ASP .NET pages that allows users to manipulate a database. Create a database for a book seller with the following fields: **BookName**, **Price**, **Quantity**. The main ASP .NET page should allow users to select from a drop-down list, which will contain options to enter more information into the database, view the entire database, update a row from the database and delete an item from the database. After completing an operation, the user should be able to return to the main page via a link to begin another operation.

21

ASP .NET and Web Services

Objectives

- To understand what a Web service is.
- To be able to create Web services.
- To understand the elements that comprise a Web service, such as service descriptions and discovery files.
- To be able to create a client that uses a Web service.
- To be able to use Web services with Windows and Web applications.
- To understand session tracking in Web services.
- To be able to pass user-defined data types between Web services and Web clients.

A client is to me a mere unit, a factor in a problem.
Sir Arthur Conan Doyle

...if the simplest things of nature have a message that you understand, rejoice, for your soul is alive.
Eleonora Duse

Protocol is everything.
Francoise Giuliani

They also serve who only stand and wait.
John Milton

21.1 Introduction[1]

Throughout this book, we have created dynamic link libraries (DLLs) to facilitate software reusability and modularity—the cornerstones of good object-oriented programming. However, the use of DLLs is limited by the fact that DLLs must reside on the same machine as the programs that use them. This chapter introduces the use of Web services (sometimes called *XML Web services*) to promote software reusability in distributed systems. Distributed-systems technologies allow applications to execute across multiple computers on a network. A Web service is an application that enables distributed computing by allowing one machine to call methods on other machines via common data formats and protocols, such as XML and HTTP. In .NET, these method calls are implemented using the Simple Object Access Protocol (SOAP), an XML-based protocol describing how to mark up requests and responses so that they can be transferred via protocols such as HTTP. Using SOAP, applications represent and transmit data in a standardized format—XML. The underlying implementation of the Web service is irrelevant to clients using the Web service.

Microsoft is encouraging software vendors and e-businesses to deploy Web services. As more and more people worldwide connect to the Internet via networks, applications that call methods across a network becomes more practical. Earlier in this text, we discussed the merits of object-oriented programming. Web services represents the next step in object-oriented programming: Instead of developing software from a small number of class libraries provided at one location, programmers can access countless libraries in multiple locations.

This technology also makes it easier for businesses to collaborate and grow together. By purchasing Web services that are relevant to their businesses, companies that create applications can spend less time coding and more time developing new products from existing components. In addition, e-businesses can employ Web services to provide their customers with an enhanced shopping experience. As a simple example, consider an online music store that enables users to purchase music CDs or to obtain information about artists. Now, suppose another company that sells concert tickets provides a Web service that determines the dates of upcoming concerts by various artists and allows users to buy concert

---

1. Internet Information Services (IIS) must be running to create a Web service in Visual Studio.

tickets. By licensing the concert-ticket Web service for use on its site, the online music store can sell concert tickets to its customers, which likely will result in increased traffic to its site. The company that sells concert tickets also benefits from the business relationship. In addition to selling more tickets, the company receives revenue from the online music store in exchange for the use of its Web service.

Visual Studio and the .NET Framework provide a simple way to create Web services like the one discussed in this example. In this chapter, we explore the steps involved in both the creation and accessing of Web services. For each example, we provide the code for the Web service, then give an example of an application that might use the Web service. Our initial examples are designed to offer a brief introduction to Web services and how they work in Visual Studio. In later sections, we move on to demonstrate more sophisticated Web services.

21.2 Web Services

A Web service is an application stored on one machine that can be accessed on another machine over a network. Due to the nature of this relationship, the machine on which the Web service resides commonly is referred to as a *remote machine*. The application that accesses the Web service sends a method call to the remote machine, which processes the call and sends a response to the application. This kind of distributed computing benefits various systems, including those without access to certain data and those lacking the processing power necessary to perform specific computations.

A Web service is, in its simplest form, a class. In previous chapters, when we wanted to include a class in a project, we would either define the class in our project or add a reference to the compiled DLL. This compiled DLL is placed in the **bin** directory of an application by default. As a result, all pieces of our application reside on one machine. When using Web services, the class (and its compiled DLL) we wish to include in our project are stored on a remote machine—a compiled version of this class is not placed in the current application.

Methods in a Web service are remotely invoked using a *Remote Procedure Call* (*RPC*). These methods, which are marked with the **WebMethod** attribute, often are referred to as *Web-service methods*. Declaring a method with this attribute makes the method accessible to other classes via an RPC. The declaration of a Web-service method with attribute **WebMethod** is known as *exposing* the method, or enabling it to be called remotely.

Common Programming Error 21.1

Attempting to call a remote method from a Web service if the method is not declared with the **WebMethod** *attribute is a compilation error.*

Most requests to and responses from Web services are transmitted via SOAP. This means that any client capable of generating and processing SOAP messages can use a Web service, regardless of the language in which the Web service is written.

Web services have important implications for *business-to-business* (*B2B*) *transactions*, (i.e., transactions that occur between two or more businesses). Now, instead of using proprietary applications, businesses can conduct transactions via Web services—a much simpler and more efficient means of conducting business. Because Web services and SOAP are platform-independent, companies can collaborate and use Web services without worrying about the compatibility of various technologies or programming languages. In this way, Web services are an inexpensive, readily-available solution to facilitate B2B transactions.

A Web service created in Visual Studio .NET has two parts: An *ASMX* file and a code-behind file. The ASMX file by default can be viewed in any Web browser and contains valuable information about the Web service, such as descriptions of Web-service methods and ways to test these methods. The code-behind file provides the implementation for the methods that the Web service encompasses. Figure 21.1 depicts Internet Explorer rendering an ASMX file.

The top of the page provides a link to the Web service's **Service Description**. A service description is an XML document that conforms to the *Web Service Description Language* (*WSDL*), an XML vocabulary that defines the methods that the Web service makes available and the ways in which clients can interact with those methods. The WSDL document also specifies lower-level information that clients might need, such as the required formats for requests and responses. Visual Studio .NET generates the WSDL service description. Client programs can use the service description to confirm the correctness of method calls when the client programs are compiled.

The programmer should not alter the service description, as it defines how a Web service works. When a user clicks the **Service Description** link at the top of the ASMX page, WSDL is displayed that defines the service description for this Web service (Fig. 21.2).

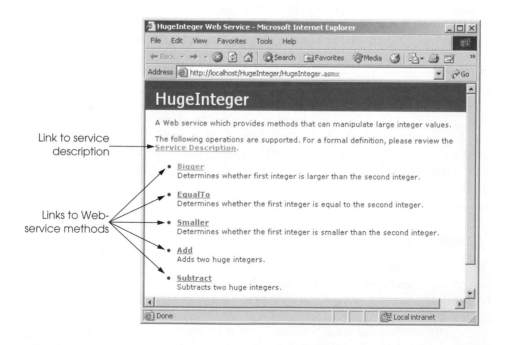

Fig. 21.1   ASMX file rendered in Internet Explorer.

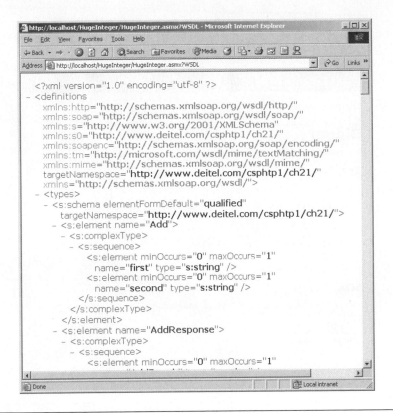

Fig. 21.2 Service description for a Web service.

Below the **Service Description** link, the Web page shown in Fig. 21.1 lists the methods that the Web service provides (i.e., all methods in the application that are declared with **WebMethod** attributes). Clicking any method name requests a test page that describes the method (Fig. 21.3). After explaining the method's arguments, the test page allows users to test the method by entering the proper parameters and clicking **Invoke**. (We discuss the process of testing a Web-service method shortly.) Below the **Invoke** button, the page displays sample request and response messages using SOAP, HTTP GET and HTTP POST. These protocols are the three options for sending and receiving messages in Web services. The protocol used to transmit request and response messages is sometimes known as the Web service's *wire protocol* or *wire format*, because the protocol specifies how information is sent "along the wire." Notice that Fig. 21.3 uses the HTTP GET protocol to test a method. Later in this chapter, when we use Web services in our C# programs, we use SOAP as the wire protocol. The advantages to using SOAP over HTTP GET and HTTP POST are discussed in the next section.

On the page depicted in Fig. 21.3, users can test a method by entering **Value**s in the **first:** and **second:** fields and then clicking **Invoke** (in this example, we tested method **Bigger**). The method executes, and a new Web browser window opens to display an XML document containing the result (Fig. 21.4). Now that we have introduced a simple example using a Web service, the next several sections explore the role of XML in Web services, as well as other aspects of Web service functionality.

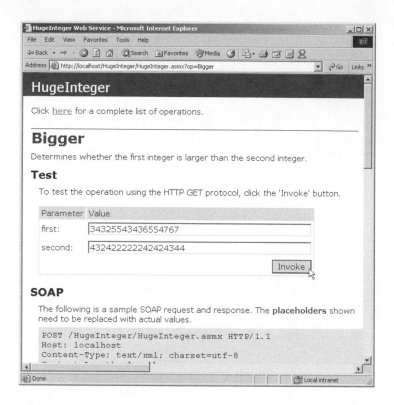

Fig. 21.3   Invoking a method of a Web service from a Web browser.

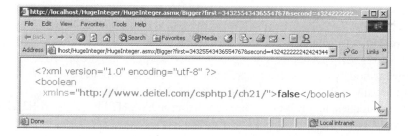

Fig. 21.4   Results of invoking a Web-service method from a Web browser.

Testing and Debugging Tip 21.1

Using the ASMX page of a Web service to test and debug methods makes that Web service more reliable and robust; it also reduces the likelihood that clients using the Web service will encounter errors.

21.3 Simple Object Access Protocol (SOAP) and Web Services

The Simple Object Access Protocol (SOAP) is a platform-independent protocol that uses XML to make remote-procedure calls over HTTP. Each request and response is packaged in a *SOAP message*—an XML message that contains all the information necessary to process its contents. SOAP messages are quite popular, because they are written in the easy-to-understand and platform-independent XML. Similarly, HTTP was chosen to transmit SOAP messages, because HTTP is a standard protocol for sending information across the Internet. The use of XML and HTTP enables different operating systems to send and receive SOAP messages. Another benefit of HTTP is that it can be used with networks that contain *firewalls*—security barriers that restrict communication among networks.

SOAP supports an extensive set of data types. Readers should note that the wire format used to transmit requests and responses must support all data types passed between the applications. Web services that use SOAP support a wider variety of data types than do Web services that employ other wire formats. The data types supported by SOAP include most basic data types, as well as **DataSet**, **DateTime**, **XmlNode** and several others. SOAP also permits the transmission of arrays of all these types. In addition, user-defined types can be used—we demonstrate how to do this in Section 21.8.

Applications send requests and responses to and from Web services via SOAP. When a program invokes a Web-service method, the request and all relevant information are packaged in a SOAP message and sent to the appropriate destination. When the Web service receives the SOAP message, it begins to process the contents (called the *SOAP envelope*), which specifies the method that the client wishes to execute and the arguments the client is passing to that method. After the Web service receives this request and parses it, the proper method is called with the specified arguments (if there are any), and the response is sent back to the client in another SOAP message. The client parses the response to retrieve the result of the method call.

The SOAP request portrayed in Fig. 21.5 was taken directly from the **Bigger** method of the **HugeInteger** Web service (Fig. 21.3). This Web service provides programmers with several methods that manipulate integers larger than those that can be stored in a **long** variable. Most programmers do not manipulate SOAP messages, allowing the Web service to handle the details of transmission.

Figure 21.5 displays a standard SOAP request that is created when a client wishes to execute the **HugeInteger** Web service's method **Bigger**. When a request to a Web service causes such a SOAP request to be created, the elements **first** and **second**'s character data (**string**s) would contain the actual values that the user entered (lines 16–17). If this envelope contained the request from Fig. 21.3, element **first** and element **second** would contain the values entered in Fig. 21.3. Placeholder **length** would contain the length of this SOAP message.

```
1   POST /HugeIntegerWebService/HugeInteger.asmx HTTP/1.1
2   Host: localhost
3   Content-Type: text/xml; charset=utf-8
4   Content-Length: length
5   SOAPAction: "http://www.deitel.com/csphtp1/ch21/Bigger"
6
7   <?xml version="1.0" encoding="utf-8"?>
8
9   <soap:Envelope
10      xmlns:xsi="http://www.w3.org/2001/XMLSchema-instance"
```

Fig. 21.5 SOAP request for the **HugeInteger** Web service. (Part 1 of 2.)

```
11          xmlns:xsd="http://www.w3.org/2001/XMLSchema"
12          xmlns:soap="http://schemas.xmlsoap.org/soap/envelope/">
13
14      <soap:Body>
15          <Bigger xmlns="http://www.deitel.com/csphtp1/ch21/">
16              <first>string</first>
17              <second>string</second>
18          </Bigger>
19      </soap:Body>
20
21      </soap:Envelope>
```

Fig. 21.5   SOAP request for the **HugeInteger** Web service. (Part 2 of 2.)

21.4 Publishing and Consuming Web Services

This section presents several examples of creating (also known as *publishing*) and using (also known as *consuming*) a Web service. An application that consumes a Web service actually consists of two parts: A *proxy* class that represents the Web service and a client application that accesses the Web service via an instance of the proxy class. The proxy class handles the transferral of the arguments for the Web-service method from the client application to the Web service, as well as the transferral of the result from the Web-service method back to the client application. Visual Studio can generate proxy classes—we demonstrate how to do this momentarily.

Figure 21.6 presents the code-behind file for the **HugeInteger** Web service (Fig. 21.1). The name of the Web service is based on the name of the class that defines it (in this case, **HugeInteger**). This Web service is designed to perform calculations with integers that contain a maximum of 100 digits. As we mentioned earlier, **long** variables cannot handle integers of this size (i.e., an overflow would occur). The Web service provides a client with methods that take two "huge integers" and determine which one is larger or smaller, whether the two numbers are equal, their sum or their difference. The reader can think of these methods as services that one application provides for the programmers of other applications (hence the term, "Web services"). Any programmer can access this Web service, use its methods and thus avoid the writing of over 200 lines of code. In the remaining examples, we hide portions of the Visual Studio generated code in the code-behind files. We do this both for brevity and for presentation purposes.

```
1    // Fig. 21.6: HugeInteger.asmx.cs
2    // HugeInteger Web Service.
3
4    using System;
5    using System.Text;
6    using System.Collections;
7    using System.ComponentModel;
8    using System.Data;
9    using System.Diagnostics;
10   using System.Web;
11   using System.Web.Services; // contains Web service related classes
```

Fig. 21.6   **HugeInteger** Web service. (Part 1 of 6.)

```
12
13   namespace HugeIntegerWebService
14   {
15       /// <summary>
16       /// performs operations on large integers
17       /// </summary>
18       [ WebService(
19          Namespace = "http://www.deitel.com/csphtp1/ch21/",
20          Description = "A Web service which provides methods that" +
21          " can manipulate large integer values." ) ]
22       public class HugeInteger : System.Web.Services.WebService
23       {
24          // default constructor
25          public HugeInteger()
26          {
27             // CODEGEN: This call is required by the ASP .NET Web
28             // Services Designer
29             InitializeComponent();
30
31             number = new int[ MAXIMUM ];
32          }
33
34          #region Component Designer generated code
35          /// <summary>
36          /// Required method for Designer support - do not modify
37          /// the contents of this method with the code editor.
38          /// </summary>
39          private void InitializeComponent()
40          {
41          }
42          #endregion
43
44          /// <summary>
45          /// Clean up any resources being used.
46          /// </summary>
47          protected override void Dispose( bool disposing )
48          {
49          }
50
51          // WEB SERVICE EXAMPLE
52          // The HelloWorld() example service returns
53          // the string Hello World
54          // To build, uncomment the following lines
55          // then save and build the project
56          // To test this web service, press F5
57
58          //    [WebMethod]
59          //    public string HelloWorld()
60          //    {
61          //       return "Hello World";
62          //    }
63
64          private const int MAXIMUM = 100;
```

Fig. 21.6 HugeInteger Web service. (Part 2 of 6.)

```
65
66          public int[] number;
67
68          // indexer that accepts an integer parameter
69          public int this[ int index ]
70          {
71             get
72             {
73                return number[ index ];
74             }
75
76             set
77             {
78                number[ index ] = value;
79             }
80
81          } // end indexer
82
83          // returns string representation of HugeInteger
84          public override string ToString()
85          {
86             StringBuilder returnString = new StringBuilder();
87
88             foreach ( int digit in number )
89                returnString.Insert( 0, digit );
90
91             return returnString.ToString();
92          }
93
94          // creates HugeInteger based on argument
95          public static HugeInteger FromString( string integer )
96          {
97             HugeInteger parsedInteger = new HugeInteger();
98
99             for ( int i = 0; i < integer.Length; i++ )
100               parsedInteger[ i ] = Int32.Parse(
101                  integer[ integer.Length - i - 1 ].ToString() );
102
103            return parsedInteger;
104         }
105
106         // WebMethod that performs integer addition
107         // represented by string arguments
108         [ WebMethod ( Description = "Adds two huge integers." ) ]
109         public string Add( string first, string second )
110         {
111            int carry = 0;
112
113            HugeInteger operand1 = HugeInteger.FromString( first );
114            HugeInteger operand2 =
115               HugeInteger.FromString( second );
116
```

Fig. 21.6 HugeInteger Web service. (Part 3 of 6.)

```
117            // store result of addition
118            HugeInteger result = new HugeInteger();
119
120            // perform addition algorithm for each digit
121            for ( int i = 0; i < MAXIMUM; i++ )
122            {
123               // add two digits in same column
124               // result is their sum, plus carry from
125               // previous operation modulus 10
126               result[ i ] =
127                  ( operand1[ i ] + operand2[ i ] ) % 10 + carry;
128
129               // store remainder of dividing
130               // sums of two digits by 10
131               carry = ( operand1[ i ] + operand2[ i ] ) / 10;
132            }
133
134            return result.ToString();
135
136         } // end method Add
137
138         // WebMethod that performs the subtraction of integers
139         // represented by string arguments
140         [ WebMethod (
141            Description = "Subtracts two huge integers." ) ]
142         public string Subtract( string first, string second )
143         {
144            HugeInteger operand1 = HugeInteger.FromString( first );
145            HugeInteger operand2 =
146               HugeInteger.FromString( second );
147            HugeInteger result = new HugeInteger();
148
149            // subtract top digit from bottom digit
150            for ( int i = 0; i < MAXIMUM; i++ )
151            {
152               // if top digit is smaller than bottom
153               // digit we need to borrow
154               if ( operand1[ i ] < operand2[ i ] )
155                  Borrow( operand1, i );
156
157               // subtract bottom from top
158               result[ i ] = operand1[ i ] - operand2[ i ];
159            }
160
161            return result.ToString();
162
163         } // end method Subtract
164
165         // borrows 1 from next digit
166         private void Borrow( HugeInteger integer, int place )
167         {
```

Fig. 21.6 HugeInteger Web service. (Part 4 of 6.)

```
168            // if no place to borrow from, signal problem
169            if ( place >= MAXIMUM - 1 )
170               throw new ArgumentException();
171
172            // otherwise if next digit is zero,
173            // borrow from digit to left
174            else if ( integer[ place + 1 ] == 0 )
175               Borrow( integer, place + 1 );
176
177            // add ten to current place because we borrowed
178            // and subtract one from previous digit -
179            // this is digit borrowed from
180            integer[ place ] += 10;
181            integer[ place + 1 ] -= 1;
182
183         } // end method Borrow
184
185         // WebMethod that returns true if first integer is
186         // bigger than second
187         [ WebMethod ( Description = "Determines whether first " +
188            "integer is larger than the second integer." ) ]
189         public bool Bigger( string first, string second )
190         {
191            char[] zeroes = { '0' };
192
193            try
194            {
195               // if elimination of all zeroes from result
196               // of subtraction is an empty string,
197               // numbers are equal, so return false,
198               // otherwise return true
199               if ( Subtract( first, second ).Trim( zeroes ) == "" )
200                  return false;
201               else
202                  return true;
203            }
204
205            // if ArgumentException occurs, first number
206            // was smaller, so return false
207            catch ( ArgumentException )
208            {
209               return false;
210            }
211
212         } // end method Bigger
213
214         // WebMethod returns true if first integer is
215         // smaller than second
216         [ WebMethod ( Description = "Determines whether the " +
217            "first integer is smaller than the second integer." ) ]
218         public bool Smaller( string first, string second )
219         {
```

Fig. 21.6   **HugeInteger** Web service. (Part 5 of 6.)

```
220            // if second is bigger than first, then first is
221            // smaller than second
222            return Bigger( second, first );
223         }
224
225      // WebMethod that returns true if two integers are equal
226      [ WebMethod ( Description = "Determines whether the " +
227         "first integer is equal to the second integer." ) ]
228      public bool EqualTo( string first, string second )
229      {
230         // if either first is bigger than second, or first is
231         // smaller than second, they are not equal
232         if ( Bigger( first, second ) ||
233            Smaller( first, second ) )
234            return false;
235         else
236            return true;
237      }
238
239   } // end class HugeInteger
240
241 } // end namespace HugeIntegerWebService
```

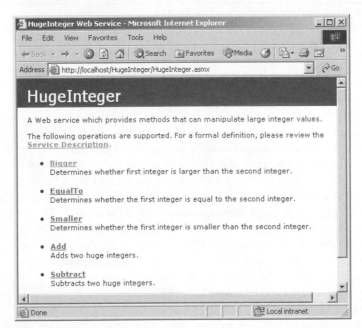

Fig. 21.6 HugeInteger Web service. (Part 6 of 6.)

Line 13 places class **HugeInteger** in namespace **HugeIntegerWebService**. Line 19 assigns the Web service namespace to **www.deitel.com/csphtp1/ch21/** to uniquely identify this Web service. The namespace is specified using the **Namespace** property of the **WebService** attribute. In lines 20–21, we use property **Description** to provide information about our Web service that appears in the ASMX file. Line 22 specifies that our class derives from *System.Web.Services.WebService*. By default, Visual Studio defines our Web service so that it inherits from the **WebService** class. Although a Web service class is not required to subclass **WebService**, class **WebService** provides members that are useful in determining information about the client and the Web service itself. Several methods in class **HugeInteger** are tagged with the *WebMethod* attribute, which *exposes* the method such that it can be called remotely. When this attribute is absent, the method is not accessible through the Web service. Notice that the **WebMethod** attribute, like the **WebService** attribute, contains a **Description** property, which provides information about the method to the ASMX page. Readers can see these descriptions in the output of Fig. 21.6.

Good Programming Practice 21.1

Specify a namespace for each Web service so that it can be uniquely identified.

Good Programming Practice 21.2

Specify descriptions for all Web services and Web-service methods so that clients can obtain additional information about the Web service and its contents.

Common Programming Error 21.2

*Web-service methods cannot be declared **static**, or a runtime error will occur when attempting to view the ASMX page. For a client to access a Web-service method, an instance of that Web service must exist.*

Lines 69–81 define an indexer for our class. This enables us to access any digit in **HugeInteger** as if we were accessing it through array **number**. Lines 108–136 and 142–163 define **WebMethod**s **Add** and **Subtract**, which perform addition and subtraction, respectively. Method **Borrow** (lines 166–183) handles the case in which the digit in the left operand is smaller than the corresponding digit in the right operand. For instance, when we subtract 19 from 32, we usually go digit by digit, starting from the right. The number 2 is smaller than 9, so we add 10 to 2 (resulting in 12), which subtracts 9, resulting in 3 for the rightmost digit in the solution. We then subtract 1 from the next digit over (3), making it 2. The corresponding digit in the right operand is now the "1" in 19. The subtraction of 1 from 2 is 1, making the corresponding digit in the result 1. The final result, when both resulting digits are combined, is 13. Method **Borrow** adds 10 to the appropriate digits and subtracts 1 from the digit to the left. Because this is a utility method that is not intended to be called remotely, it is not qualified with attribute **WebMethod**.

The screen capture in Fig. 21.6 is identical to the one in Fig. 21.1. A client application can invoke only the five methods listed in the screen shot (i.e., the methods qualified with the **WebMethod** attribute).

Now, let us demonstrate how to create this Web service. To begin, we must create a project of type **ASP.NET Web Service**. Like Web Forms, Web services are by default placed in the Web server's **wwwroot** directory on the server (**localhost**). By default, Visual Studio places the solution file (**.sln**) in the **Visual Studio Projects** folder, in a directory for the solution. (The **Visual Studio Projects** folder is usually located in the **My Documents** folder.)

Notice that, when the project is created, the code-behind file is displayed in design view by default (Fig. 21.7). If this file is not open, it can be opened by clicking

Service1.asmx. The file that will be opened, however, is **Service1.asmx.cs** (the code-behind file for our Web service). This is because, when creating Web services in Visual Studio, programmers work almost exclusively in the code-behind file. In fact, if a programmer were to open the ASMX file, it would contain only the lines:

```
<%@ WebService Language="c#" Codebehind="Service1.asmx.cs"
    Class="WebService1.Service1" %>
```

indicating the name of the code-behind file, the programming language in which the code-behind file is written and the class that defines our Web service. This is the extent of the information that this file must contain. [*Note*: By default, the code-behind file is not listed in the **Solution Explorer**. The code-behind file is displayed when the ASMX file is double clicked in the **Solution Explorer**. This file can be listed in the **Solution Explorer** by clicking the icon to show all files.]

It might seem strange that there is a design view for Web services, given that Web services do not have graphical user interfaces. A design view is provided because more sophisticated Web services contain methods that manipulate more than just strings or numbers. For example, a Web-service method could manipulate a database. Instead of typing all the code necessary to create a database connection, developers can simply drop the proper ADO .NET components into the design view and manipulate them as we would in a Windows or Web application. We show an example of this in Section 21.6.

Now that we have defined our Web service, we demonstrate how to use it. First, a client application must be created. In this first example, we create a Windows application as our client. Once this application has been created, the client must add a proxy class for accessing the Web service. A proxy class (or proxy) is a class created from the Web service's WSDL file that enables the client to call Web-service methods over the Internet. The proxy class handles all the "plumbing" required for Web-service method calls. Whenever a call is made in the client application to a Web-service method, the application actually calls a corresponding method in the proxy class. This method takes the name of the method and its arguments, then formats them so that they can be sent as a request in a SOAP message. The Web service receives this request and executes the method call, sending back the result as another SOAP message. When the client application receives the SOAP message containing the response, the proxy class decodes it and formats the results so that they are understandable to the client. This information then is returned to the client. It is important to note that the proxy class essentially is hidden from the programmer. We cannot, in fact, view it in the **Solution Explorer** unless we choose to show all the files. The purpose of the proxy class is to make it seem to clients as though they are calling the Web-service methods directly. It is rarely necessary for the client to view or manipulate the proxy class.

The next example demonstrates how to create a Web service client and its corresponding proxy class. We must begin by creating a project and adding a *Web reference* to that project. When we add a Web reference to a client application, the proxy class is created. The client then creates an instance of the proxy class, which is used to call methods included in the Web service.

To create a proxy in Visual Studio, right click the **References** folder in **Solution Explorer** and select *Add Web Reference* (Fig. 21.8). In the **Add Web Reference** dialog that appears (Fig. 21.9), enter the Web address of the Web service and press *Enter*. In this chapter, we store the Web service in the root directory of our local Web server

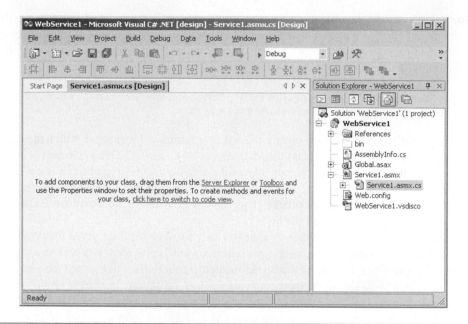

Fig. 21.7   Design view of a Web service.

(**http://localhost**, whose physical path is **C:\Inetpub\wwwroot**). We now can add a Web reference by clicking the link **Web References on Local Web Server** (Fig. 21.9). Next, we select the appropriate Web service from the list of Web services located on **localhost** (Fig. 21.10). Notice that each Web service is listed as a file with the extension **.vsdisco** that is located in the directory for the Web service project. Files with the extension **.disco** or **.vsdisco** are known as *discovery files*. We discuss discovery files, as well as the distinctions between **.disco** files and **.vsdisco** files, later in this section. Once a Web service is chosen the description of that Web service appears, and the developer can click **Add Reference** (Fig. 21.11). This adds to the **Solution Explorer** (Fig. 21.12) a **Web References** folder with a node named for the domain where the Web service is located. In this case, the name is **localhost**, because we are using the local Web server. This means that, when we reference class **HugeInteger**, we will be doing so through class **HugeInteger** in namespace **localhost**, instead of class **HugeInteger** in namespace **HugeIntegerWebService** [*Note*: The Web service class and the proxy class have the same name. Visual Studio generates a proxy for the Web service and adds it as a reference (Fig. 21.12).]

 Good Programming Practice 21.3

When creating a program that will use Web services, add the Web reference first. This will enable Visual Studio to recognize an instance of the Web service class, allowing Intellisense to help the developer use the Web service.

The steps that we described previously work well if the programmer knows the appropriate Web services reference. However, what if we are trying to locate a new Web service? There are two technologies that facilitate this process: *Universal Description, Discovery and Integration* (*UDDI*) and *Discovery files* (*DISCO*). UDDI is a project for developing a set of specifications that define how Web services should be published so that programmers searching for Web services can find them. Microsoft began this ongoing project to facilitate the locating of Web services that conform to certain specifications, allowing programmers to find different Web services using search engines. UDDI organizes and describes Web services and then places this information in a central location. Although UDDI is beyond the scope of what we are teaching, the reader can learn more about this project and view a demonstration by visiting **www.uddi.org** and **uddi.microsoft.com**. These sites contain search tools that make finding Web services fast and easy.

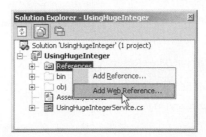

Fig. 21.8   Adding a Web service reference to a project.

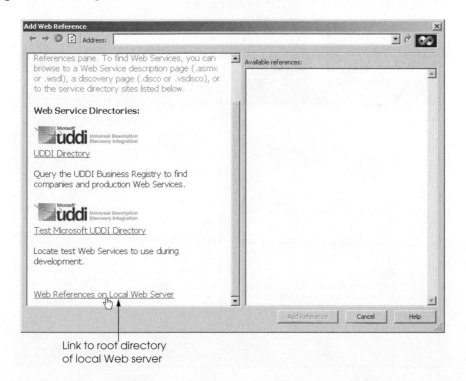

Link to root directory
of local Web server

Fig. 21.9   **Add Web Reference** dialog.

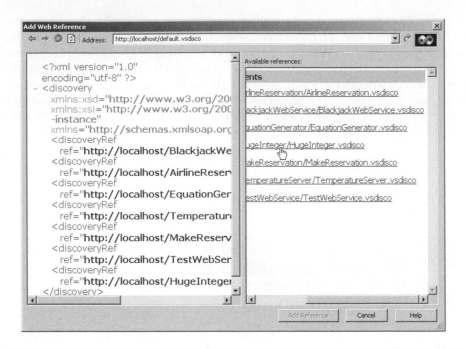

Fig. 21.10 Web services located on `localhost`.

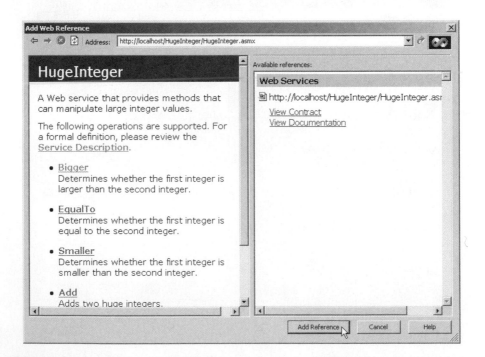

Fig. 21.11 Web reference selection and description.

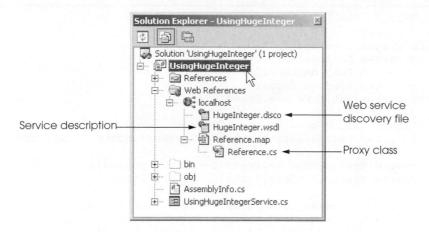

Service description

Web service
discovery file

Proxy class

Fig. 21.12 Solution Explorer after adding a Web reference to a project.

A DISCO file catalogs Web services in a particular directory. There are two types of discovery files: *Dynamic discovery* files (with a **.vsdisco** extension) and *static discovery* files (with a **.disco** extension). These files indicate both the location of the ASMX file and the service description (a WSDL file) for each Web service in the current directory, as well as any Web services in the current directory's subdirectories. When a programmer creates a Web service, Visual Studio generates a dynamic discovery file for that Web service. When a Web reference is added, the client uses the dynamic discovery file to select the desired Web service, as demonstrated in Fig. 21.10. Once the Web reference is created, a static discovery file is placed in the client's project. The static discovery file hard codes the location for the ASMX and WSDL files. (By "hard code", we mean that the location is entered directly into the file.) Dynamic discovery files, on the other hand, are created such that a list of Web services is created dynamically on the server when a client is searching for a Web service. The use of dynamic discovery enables certain extra options, such as hiding of certain Web services in subdirectories. Discovery files are a Microsoft-specific technology, whereas UDDI is not. However, the two can work together to enable a client to find a Web service. Using both technologies, the client can use a search engine to find a location with various Web services on a topic, and then use discovery files to view all the Web services in that location.

Once the Web reference is added, the client can access the Web service through our proxy. Because our proxy class is named **HugeInteger** and is located in namespace **localhost**, we must use **localhost.HugeInteger** to reference this class. The Windows Form in Fig. 21.13 uses the **HugeInteger** Web service to perform computations with positive integers up to **100** digits long. [*Note:* If using the example on this book's CD, the reader might need to regenerate the proxy.]

```
1   // Fig. 21.13: UsingHugeIntegerService.cs
2   // Using the HugeInteger Web Service.
3
```

Fig. 21.13 Using the **HugeInteger** Web service. (Part 1 of 6.)

```
4   using System;
5   using System.Drawing;
6   using System.Collections;
7   using System.ComponentModel;
8   using System.Windows.Forms;
9   using System.Web.Services.Protocols;
10
11  // allows user to perform operations on large integers
12  public class UsingHugeIntService : System.Windows.Forms.Form
13  {
14     private System.Windows.Forms.Label promptLabel;
15     private System.Windows.Forms.Label resultLabel;
16
17     private System.Windows.Forms.TextBox firstTextBox;
18     private System.Windows.Forms.TextBox secondTextBox;
19
20     private System.Windows.Forms.Button addButton;
21     private System.Windows.Forms.Button subtractButton;
22     private System.Windows.Forms.Button biggerButton;
23     private System.Windows.Forms.Button smallerButton;
24     private System.Windows.Forms.Button equalButton;
25
26     private System.ComponentModel.Container components = null;
27
28     // declare a reference Web service
29     private localhost.HugeInteger remoteInteger;
30
31     private char[] zeroes = { '0' };
32
33     // default constructor
34     public UsingHugeIntService()
35     {
36        InitializeComponent();
37
38        // instantiate remoteInteger
39        remoteInteger = new localhost.HugeInteger();
40     }
41
42     // Visual Studio .NET generated code
43
44     [STAThread]
45     static void Main()
46     {
47        Application.Run( new UsingHugeIntService() );
48
49     } // end Main
50
51     // checks whether two numbers user input are equal
52     protected void equalButton_Click(
53        object sender, System.EventArgs e )
54     {
```

Fig. 21.13 Using the **HugeInteger** Web service. (Part 2 of 6.)

```
55            // make sure HugeIntegers do not exceed 100 digits
56            if ( CheckSize( firstTextBox, secondTextBox ) )
57               return;
58
59            // call Web-service method to determine
60            // whether integers are equal
61            if ( remoteInteger.EqualTo(
62               firstTextBox.Text, secondTextBox.Text ) )
63
64               resultLabel.Text =
65                  firstTextBox.Text.TrimStart( zeroes ) +
66                  " is equal to " +
67                  secondTextBox.Text.TrimStart( zeroes );
68            else
69               resultLabel.Text =
70                  firstTextBox.Text.TrimStart( zeroes ) +
71                  " is NOT equal to " +
72                  secondTextBox.Text.TrimStart( zeroes );
73
74      } // end method equalButton_Click
75
76      // checks whether first integer input
77      // by user is smaller than second
78      protected void smallerButton_Click(
79         object sender, System.EventArgs e )
80      {
81         // make sure HugeIntegers do not exceed 100 digits
82         if ( CheckSize( firstTextBox, secondTextBox ) )
83            return;
84
85         // call Web-service method to determine whether first
86         // integer is smaller than second
87         if ( remoteInteger.Smaller(
88            firstTextBox.Text, secondTextBox.Text ) )
89
90            resultLabel.Text =
91               firstTextBox.Text.TrimStart( zeroes ) +
92               " is smaller than " +
93               secondTextBox.Text.TrimStart( zeroes );
94         else
95            resultLabel.Text =
96               firstTextBox.Text.TrimStart( zeroes ) +
97               " is NOT smaller than " +
98               secondTextBox.Text.TrimStart( zeroes );
99
100      } // end method smallerButton_Click
101
102      // checks whether first integer input
103      // by user is bigger than second
104      protected void biggerButton_Click(
105         object sender, System.EventArgs e )
106      {
```

Fig. 21.13 Using the **HugeInteger** Web service. (Part 3 of 6.)

```
107          // make sure HugeIntegers do not exceed 100 digits
108          if ( CheckSize( firstTextBox, secondTextBox ) )
109             return;
110
111          // call Web-service method to determine whether first
112          // integer is larger than the second
113          if ( remoteInteger.Bigger( firstTextBox.Text,
114             secondTextBox.Text ) )
115
116             resultLabel.Text =
117                firstTextBox.Text.TrimStart( zeroes ) +
118                " is larger than " +
119                secondTextBox.Text.TrimStart( zeroes );
120          else
121             resultLabel.Text =
122                firstTextBox.Text.TrimStart( zeroes ) +
123                " is NOT larger than " +
124                secondTextBox.Text.TrimStart( zeroes );
125
126       } // end method biggerButton_Click
127
128       // subtract second integer from first
129       protected void subtractButton_Click(
130          object sender, System.EventArgs e )
131       {
132          // make sure HugeIntegers do not exceed 100 digits
133          if ( CheckSize( firstTextBox, secondTextBox ) )
134             return;
135
136          // perform subtraction
137          try
138          {
139             string result = remoteInteger.Subtract(
140                firstTextBox.Text,
141                secondTextBox.Text ).TrimStart( zeroes );
142
143             resultLabel.Text = ( ( result == "" ) ? "0" : result );
144          }
145
146          // if WebMethod throws an exception, then first
147          // argument was smaller than second
148          catch ( SoapException )
149          {
150             MessageBox.Show(
151                "First argument was smaller than the second" );
152          }
153
154       } // end method subtractButton_Click
155
156       // adds two integers input by user
157       protected void addButton_Click(
158          object sender, System.EventArgs e )
159       {
```

Fig. 21.13 Using the **HugeInteger** Web service. (Part 4 of 6.)

```
160            // make sure HugeInteger does not exceed 100 digits
161            // and is not situation where both integers are 100
162            // digits long--result in overflow
163            if ( firstTextBox.Text.Length > 100 ||
164               secondTextBox.Text.Length > 100 ||
165               ( firstTextBox.Text.Length == 100 &&
166               secondTextBox.Text.Length == 100 ) )
167            {
168               MessageBox.Show( "HugeIntegers must not be more "
169                  + "than 100 digits\nBoth integers cannot be of"
170                  + " length 100: this causes an overflow",
171                  "Error", MessageBoxButtons.OK,
172                  MessageBoxIcon.Information );
173
174               return;
175            }
176
177            // perform addition
178            resultLabel.Text = remoteInteger.Add( firstTextBox.Text,
179               secondTextBox.Text ).TrimStart( zeroes ).ToString();
180
181         } // end method addButton_Click
182
183         // determines whether size of integers is too big
184         private bool CheckSize( TextBox first, TextBox second )
185         {
186            if ( first.Text.Length > 100 || second.Text.Length > 100 )
187            {
188               MessageBox.Show( "HugeIntegers must be less than 100"
189                  + " digits", "Error", MessageBoxButtons.OK,
190                  MessageBoxIcon.Information );
191
192               return true;
193            }
194
195            return false;
196
197         } // end method CheckSize
198
199   } // end class UsingHugeIntegerService
```

Fig. 21.13 Using the **HugeInteger** Web service. (Part 5 of 6.)

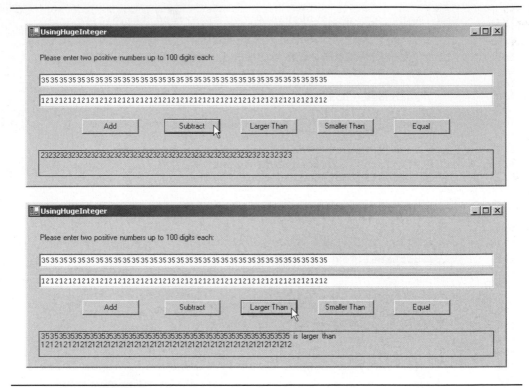

Fig. 21.13 Using the **HugeInteger** Web service. (Part 6 of 6.)

The user inputs two integers, each up to 100 digits long. The clicking of any button invokes a remote method to perform the appropriate calculation and return the result. The return value of each operation is displayed, and all leading zeroes are eliminated using **string** method **TrimStart**. Note that **UsingHugeInteger** does not have the capability to perform operations with 100-digit numbers. Instead, it creates **string** representations of these numbers and passes them as arguments to Web-service methods that handle such tasks for us.

21.5 Session Tracking in Web Services

In Chapter 20, ASP .NET, Web Forms and Web Controls, we described the importance of maintaining information about users to personalize their experiences. In the context of this discussion, we explored session tracking using cookies and sessions. In this section, we incorporate session tracking into a Web service. Sometimes, it makes sense for client applications to call several methods from the same Web service, and to call some methods several times. It would be beneficial for the Web service to maintain state information for the client. Using session tracking can be beneficial, because information that is stored as part of the session will not need to be passed back and forth between the Web service and the client. This will not only cause the client application to run faster, but it will require less effort on the part of the programmer (who likely will have to pass less information to a Web-service method).

Storing session information also can provide for a more intuitive Web service. In the following example, we create a Web service designed to assist with the computations involved in playing a game of Blackjack (Fig. 21.14). We then use this Web service to create a dealer for a game of Blackjack. This dealer handles the details for our deck of cards. The information is stored as part of the session, so that one set of cards does not get mixed up with another deck of cards being used by another client application. Our example uses casino Blackjack rules as follows:

> Two cards each are dealt to each the dealer and the player. The player's cards are dealt face up. Only one of the dealer's cards is dealt face up. Then, the player can begin taking additional cards, one at a time. These cards are dealt face up, and the player decides when to stop taking cards. If the sum of the player's cards exceeds 21, the game is over, and the player loses. When the player is satisfied with the current set of cards, the player "stays" (i.e., stops taking cards), and the dealer's hidden card is revealed. If the dealer's total is less than 17, the dealer must take another card; otherwise, the dealer must stay. The dealer must continue to take cards until the sum of the dealer's cards is greater than or equal to 17. If the dealer exceeds 21, the player wins. Otherwise, the hand with the higher point total wins. If both sets of cards have the same point total, the game is a "push" (i.e., a tie), and no one wins. Finally, if a player's first two cards total 21, the player immediately wins. This type of win is known as a "Blackjack."

The Web service that we create provides methods to deal a card and to count cards in a hand, determining a value for a specific hand. Each card is represented by a string in the form "**face suit**," where **face** is a digit that represents the face of the card, and **suit** is a digit that represents the suit of the card. After the Web service is created, we create a Windows application that uses these methods to implement a game of Blackjack.

```
1    // Fig. 21.14: BlackjackService.asmx.cs
2    // Blackjack Web Service which manipulates a deck of cards.
3
4    using System;
5    using System.Collections;
6    using System.ComponentModel;
7    using System.Data;
8    using System.Diagnostics;
9    using System.Web;
10   using System.Web.Services;
11
12   namespace BlackjackWebService
13   {
14      [ WebService(
15         Namespace = "http://www.deitel.com/csphtp1/ch21/",
16         Description = "A Web service that provides methods " +
17         "to manipulate a deck of cards." ) ]
18      public class BlackjackService : System.Web.Services.WebService
19      {
20
21         // Visual Studio .NET generated code
22
```

Fig. 21.14 Blackjack Web service. (Part 1 of 3.)

```
23          // deal new card
24          [ WebMethod( EnableSession = true,
25             Description = "Deal a new card from the deck." ) ]
26          public string DealCard()
27          {
28             string card = "2 2";
29
30             // get client's deck
31             ArrayList deck = ( ArrayList ) Session[ "deck" ];
32             card = ( string ) deck[ 0 ];
33             deck.RemoveAt( 0 );
34             return card;
35
36          } // end method DealCard
37
38          [ WebMethod( EnableSession = true,
39             Description = "Create and shuffle a deck of cards." ) ]
40          public void Shuffle()
41          {
42             Random randomObject = new Random();
43
44             ArrayList deck = new ArrayList();
45
46             // generate all possible cards
47             for ( int i = 2; i < 15; i++ ) {
48                for ( int j = 0; j < 4; j++ ) {
49                   deck.Add( i + " " + j );
50                }
51             }
52
53             // swap each card with another card randomly
54             for ( int i = 0; i < deck.Count; i++ )
55             {
56                int newIndex = randomObject.Next( deck.Count );
57                object temporary = deck[ i ];
58                deck[ i ] = deck[ newIndex ];
59                deck[ newIndex ] = temporary;
60             }
61
62             // add this deck to user's session state
63             Session[ "deck" ] = deck;
64          }
65
66          // computes value of hand
67          [ WebMethod ( Description = "Compute a " +
68             "numerical value for the current hand." ) ]
69          public int CountCards( string dealt )
70          {
71             // split string containing cards
72             char[] tab = { '\t' };
73             string[] cards = dealt.Split( tab );
74             int total = 0, face, aceCount = 0;
75
```

Fig. 21.14 Blackjack Web service. (Part 2 of 3.)

```
76              foreach ( string drawn in cards )
77              {
78                 // get face of card
79                 face =
80                    Int32.Parse( drawn.Substring(
81                       0, drawn.IndexOf( " " ) ) );
82
83                 switch ( face )
84                 {
85                    // if ace, increment number of aces in hand
86                    case 14:
87                       aceCount++;
88                       break;
89
90                    // if Jack, Queen or King, add 10 to total
91                    case 11:  case 12:  case 13:
92                       total += 10;
93                       break;
94
95                    // otherwise, add value of face
96                    default:
97                       total += face;
98                       break;
99
100                } // end switch
101
102             } // end foreach
103
104             // if any aces, calculate optimum total
105             if ( aceCount > 0 )
106             {
107                // if it is possible to count one ace as 11, and rest
108                // 1 each, do so; otherwise, count all aces as 1 each
109                if ( total + 11 + aceCount - 1 <= 21 )
110                   total += 11 + aceCount - 1;
111                else
112                   total += aceCount;
113             }
114
115             return total;
116
117          }  // end method CountCards
118
119       } // end class BlackjackService
120
121 } // end namespace BlackjackWebService
```

Fig. 21.14 Blackjack Web service. (Part 3 of 3.)

Lines 24–36 define method **DealCard** as a **WebMethod**, with property **EnableSession** set to **true**. This property needs to be set to **true** to maintain session information. This simple step provides an important advantage to our Web service. The Web service now can use an **HttpSessionState** object (called **Session**) to maintain the deck of cards for each client application that wishes to use this Web service (line 31).

We can use **Session** to store objects for a specific client between method calls. We discussed session state in detail in Chapter 20, ASP .NET, Web Forms and Web Controls.

As we discuss shortly, method **DealCard** removes a card from the deck and returns it to the client. If we were not using a session variable, the deck of cards would need to be passed back and forth with each method call. Not only does the use of session state make the method easier to call (it now requires no arguments), but we avoid the overhead that would occur from sending this information back and forth, making our Web service faster.

In our current implementation, we simply have methods that use session variables. The Web service, however, still cannot determine which session variables belong to which user. This is an important point—if the Web service cannot uniquely identify a user, it has failed to perform session-tracking properly. If the same client called method **DealCard** twice, two different decks would be manipulated (as if two different users had called **Deal-Card**). To identify various users, the Web service creates a cookie for each user. Unfortunately, the Web service has no way of determining whether or not cookies are enabled on the client's machine. If the client application wishes to use this Web service, the client must accept this cookie in a *CookieContainer* object. We discuss this in more detail shortly, when we look into the client application that uses the **Blackjack** Web service.

Method **DealCard** (lines 24–36) obtains the current user's deck as an *ArrayList* from the Web service's **Session** object (line 31). You can think of an **ArrayList** as a dynamic array (i.e., its size can change at runtime). Class **ArrayList** is discussed in greater detail in Chapter 23, Data Structures and Collections. The class's method **Add** places an **object** in the **ArrayList**. Method **DealCard** then removes the top card from the deck (line 33) and returns the card's value as a **string** (line 34).

Method **Shuffle** (lines 38–64) generates an **ArrayList** representing a card deck, shuffles it and stores the shuffled cards in the client's **Session** object. Lines 47–51 include **for** loops to generate **string**s in the form "**face suit**" to represent each possible card in a deck. Lines 54–60 shuffle the re-created deck by swapping each card with another card in the deck. Line 63 adds the **ArrayList** to the **Session** object to maintain the deck between method calls.

Method **CountCards** (lines 67–117) counts the values of the cards in a hand by trying to attain the highest score possible without going over 21. Precautions need to be taken when calculating the value of the cards, because an ace can be counted as either 1 or 11, and all face cards count as 10.

The string **dealt** is tokenized into its individual cards by calling **string** method **Split** and passing it an array that contains the tab character. The **foreach** loop (line 76–102) counts the value of each card. Lines 79–81 retrieve the first integer—the face—and use that value as input to the **switch** statement in line 83. If the card is 1 (an ace), the program increments variable **aceCount**. Because an ace can have two values, additional logic is required to process aces. If the card is a 13, 12 or 11 (King, Queen or Jack), the program adds 10 to the total. If the card is anything else, the program increases the total by that value.

In lines 105–113, the aces are counted after all the other cards. If several aces are included in a hand, only one can be counted as 11 (e.g., if two were counted as 11 we would already have a hand value of 22, which is a losing hand). We then determine if we can count an ace as 11 without exceeding 21. If this is possible, line 110 adjusts the total accordingly. Otherwise, line 112 adjusts the total by counting each ace as 1 point.

CountCards attempts to maximize the value of the current cards without exceeding 21. Imagine, for example, that the dealer has a 7 and then receives an ace. The new total could be either 8 or 18. However, **CountCards** always tries the maximize the value of the cards without going over 21, so the new total is 18.

Now, we use the **Blackjack** Web service in a Windows application called **Game** (Fig. 21.15). This program uses an instance of **BlackjackWebService** to represent the dealer, calling its **DealCard** and **CountCards** methods. The Web service keeps track of both the player's and the dealer's cards (i.e., all the cards that have been dealt).

Each player has 11 **PictureBox**es—the maximum number of cards that can be dealt without exceeding 21. These **PictureBox**es are placed in an **ArrayList**, allowing us to index the **ArrayList** to determine which **PictureBox** displays the card image.

Previously we mentioned that the client must provide a way to accept any cookies created by the Web service to identify users. Line 64 in the constructor creates a new **CookieContainer** object for the **CookieContainer** property of **dealer**. Class **CookieContainer** (defined in namespace **System.Net**) acts as a storage space for an object of the **HttpCookie** class. Creating the **CookieContainer** allows the Web service to maintain session state for the current client. This **CookieContainer** stores a **Cookie** with a unique identifier that the server can use to recognize the client when the client makes future requests. By default, the **CookieContainer** is **null**, and a new **Session** object is created by the Web Service for each client.

```
1   // Fig. 21.15: Blackjack.cs
2   // Blackjack game that uses the Blackjack Web service.
3
4   using System;
5   using System.Drawing;
6   using System.Collections;
7   using System.ComponentModel;
8   using System.Windows.Forms;
9   using System.Data;
10  using System.Net;
11
12  // game that uses Blackjack Web Service
13  public class Blackjack : System.Windows.Forms.Form
14  {
15     private System.Windows.Forms.PictureBox pictureBox1;
16     private System.Windows.Forms.PictureBox pictureBox2;
17     private System.Windows.Forms.PictureBox pictureBox3;
18     private System.Windows.Forms.PictureBox pictureBox4;
19     private System.Windows.Forms.PictureBox pictureBox5;
20     private System.Windows.Forms.PictureBox pictureBox6;
21     private System.Windows.Forms.PictureBox pictureBox7;
22     private System.Windows.Forms.PictureBox pictureBox8;
23     private System.Windows.Forms.PictureBox pictureBox9;
24     private System.Windows.Forms.PictureBox pictureBox10;
25     private System.Windows.Forms.PictureBox pictureBox11;
26     private System.Windows.Forms.PictureBox pictureBox12;
27     private System.Windows.Forms.PictureBox pictureBox13;
28     private System.Windows.Forms.PictureBox pictureBox14;
```

Fig. 21.15 Blackjack game that uses **Blackjack** Web service. (Part 1 of 8.)

```
29       private System.Windows.Forms.PictureBox pictureBox15;
30       private System.Windows.Forms.PictureBox pictureBox16;
31       private System.Windows.Forms.PictureBox pictureBox17;
32       private System.Windows.Forms.PictureBox pictureBox18;
33       private System.Windows.Forms.PictureBox pictureBox19;
34       private System.Windows.Forms.PictureBox pictureBox20;
35       private System.Windows.Forms.PictureBox pictureBox21;
36       private System.Windows.Forms.PictureBox pictureBox22;
37
38       private System.Windows.Forms.Button dealButton;
39       private System.Windows.Forms.Button hitButton;
40       private System.Windows.Forms.Button stayButton;
41
42       private System.ComponentModel.Container components = null;
43
44       private localhost.BlackjackService dealer;
45       private string dealersCards, playersCards;
46       private ArrayList cardBoxes;
47       private int playerCard, dealerCard;
48
49       // labels displaying game status, dealer and player
50       private System.Windows.Forms.Label dealerLabel;
51       private System.Windows.Forms.Label playerLabel;
52       private System.Windows.Forms.Label statusLabel;
53
54       public enum GameStatus :
55          int { PUSH, LOSE, WIN, BLACKJACK };
56
57       public Blackjack()
58       {
59          InitializeComponent();
60
61          dealer = new localhost.BlackjackService();
62
63          // allow session state
64          dealer.CookieContainer = new CookieContainer();
65
66          cardBoxes = new ArrayList();
67
68          // put PictureBoxes into cardBoxes
69          cardBoxes.Add( pictureBox1 );
70          cardBoxes.Add( pictureBox2 );
71          cardBoxes.Add( pictureBox3 );
72          cardBoxes.Add( pictureBox4 );
73          cardBoxes.Add( pictureBox5 );
74          cardBoxes.Add( pictureBox6 );
75          cardBoxes.Add( pictureBox7 );
76          cardBoxes.Add( pictureBox8 );
77          cardBoxes.Add( pictureBox9 );
78          cardBoxes.Add( pictureBox10 );
79          cardBoxes.Add( pictureBox11 );
80          cardBoxes.Add( pictureBox12 );
81          cardBoxes.Add( pictureBox13 );
```

Fig. 21.15 Blackjack game that uses **Blackjack** Web service. (Part 2 of 8.)

```
82              cardBoxes.Add( pictureBox14 );
83              cardBoxes.Add( pictureBox15 );
84              cardBoxes.Add( pictureBox16 );
85              cardBoxes.Add( pictureBox17 );
86              cardBoxes.Add( pictureBox18 );
87              cardBoxes.Add( pictureBox19 );
88              cardBoxes.Add( pictureBox20 );
89              cardBoxes.Add( pictureBox21 );
90              cardBoxes.Add( pictureBox22 );
91
92          } // end method Blackjack
93
94          // Visual Studio .NET generated code
95
96          [STAThread]
97          static void Main()
98          {
99              Application.Run( new Blackjack() );
100
101         } // end Main
102
103         // deals cards to dealer while dealer's total is
104         // less than 17, then computes value of each hand
105         // and determines winner
106         protected void stayButton_Click(
107             object sender, System.EventArgs e )
108         {
109             stayButton.Enabled = false;
110             hitButton.Enabled = false;
111             dealButton.Enabled = true;
112             DealerPlay();
113         }
114
115         // process dealers turn
116         private void DealerPlay()
117         {
118             // while value of dealer's hand is below 17,
119             // dealer must take cards
120             while ( dealer.CountCards( dealersCards ) < 17 )
121             {
122                 dealersCards += "\t" + dealer.DealCard();
123                 DisplayCard( dealerCard, "" );
124                 dealerCard++;
125                 MessageBox.Show( "Dealer takes a card" );
126             }
127
128             int dealersTotal = dealer.CountCards( dealersCards );
129             int playersTotal = dealer.CountCards( playersCards );
130
131             // if dealer busted, player wins
132             if ( dealersTotal > 21 )
133             {
134                 GameOver( GameStatus.WIN );
```

Fig. 21.15 Blackjack game that uses **Blackjack** Web service. (Part 3 of 8.)

```
135            return;
136        }
137
138        // if dealer and player have not exceeded 21,
139        // higher score wins; equal scores is a push.
140        if ( dealersTotal > playersTotal )
141           GameOver( GameStatus.LOSE );
142        else if ( playersTotal > dealersTotal )
143           GameOver( GameStatus.WIN );
144        else
145           GameOver( GameStatus.PUSH );
146
147     } // end method DealerPlay
148
149     // deal another card to player
150     protected void hitButton_Click(
151        object sender, System.EventArgs e )
152     {
153        // get player another card
154        string card = dealer.DealCard();
155        playersCards += "\t" + card;
156        DisplayCard( playerCard, card );
157        playerCard++;
158
159        int total = dealer.CountCards( playersCards );
160
161        // if player exceeds 21, house wins
162        if ( total > 21 )
163           GameOver( GameStatus.LOSE );
164
165        // if player has 21, they cannot take more cards
166        // the dealer plays
167        if ( total == 21 )
168        {
169           hitButton.Enabled = false;
170           DealerPlay();
171        }
172
173     } // end method hitButton_Click
174
175     // deal two cards each to dealer and player
176     protected void dealButton_Click(
177        object sender, System.EventArgs e )
178     {
179        string card;
180
181        // clear card images
182        foreach ( PictureBox cardImage in cardBoxes )
183           cardImage.Image = null;
184
185        // clear status from previous game
186        statusLabel.Text = "";
187
```

Fig. 21.15 Blackjack game that uses **Blackjack** Web service. (Part 4 of 8.)

```
188         // shuffle cards
189         dealer.Shuffle();
190
191         // deal two cards to player
192         playersCards = dealer.DealCard();
193         DisplayCard( 11, playersCards );
194         card = dealer.DealCard();
195         DisplayCard( 12, card );
196         playersCards += "\t" + card;
197
198         // deal two cards to dealer, only display face
199         // of first card
200         dealersCards = dealer.DealCard() ;
201         DisplayCard( 0, dealersCards );
202         card = dealer.DealCard();
203         DisplayCard( 1, "" );
204         dealersCards += "\t" + card;
205
206         stayButton.Enabled = true;
207         hitButton.Enabled = true;
208         dealButton.Enabled = false;
209
210         int dealersTotal = dealer.CountCards( dealersCards );
211         int playersTotal = dealer.CountCards( playersCards );
212
213         // if hands equal 21, it is a push
214         if ( dealersTotal == playersTotal &&
215            dealersTotal == 21 )
216            GameOver( GameStatus.PUSH );
217
218         // if player has 21 player wins with blackjack
219         else if ( playersTotal == 21 )
220            GameOver( GameStatus.BLACKJACK );
221
222         // if dealer has 21, dealer wins
223         else if ( dealersTotal == 21 )
224            GameOver( GameStatus.LOSE );
225
226         dealerCard = 2;
227         playerCard = 13;
228
229      } // end method dealButton_Click
230
231      // displays card represented by cardValue in
232      // PictureBox with number card
233      public void DisplayCard( int card, string cardValue )
234      {
235         // retrieve appropriate PictureBox from ArrayList
236         PictureBox displayBox = ( PictureBox ) cardBoxes[ card ];
237
```

Fig. 21.15 Blackjack game that uses **Blackjack** Web service. (Part 5 of 8.)

```
238        // if string representing card is empty,
239        // set displayBox to display back of card
240        if ( cardValue == "" )
241        {
242           displayBox.Image =
243              Image.FromFile( "blackjack_images\\cardback.png" );
244           return;
245        }
246
247        // retrieve face value of card from cardValue
248        int faceNumber = Int32.Parse( cardValue.Substring( 0,
249           cardValue.IndexOf( " " ) ) );
250
251        string face = faceNumber.ToString();
252
253        // retrieve the suit of the card from cardValue
254        string suit = cardValue.Substring(
255           cardValue.IndexOf( " " ) + 1 );
256
257        char suitLetter;
258
259        // determine if suit is other than clubs
260        switch ( Convert.ToInt32( suit ) )
261        {
262           // suit is clubs
263           case 0:
264              suitLetter = 'c';
265              break;
266
267           // suit is diamonds
268           case 1:
269              suitLetter = 'd';
270              break;
271
272           // suit is hearts
273           case 2:
274              suitLetter = 'h';
275              break;
276
277           // else suit is spades
278           default:
279              suitLetter = 's';
280              break;
281        }
282
283        // set displayBox to display appropriate image
284        displayBox.Image = Image.FromFile(
285           "blackjack_images\\" + face + suitLetter + ".png"  );
286
287     } // end method DisplayCard
288
289     // displays all player cards and shows
290     // appropriate game status message
```

Fig. 21.15 Blackjack game that uses **Blackjack** Web service. (Part 6 of 8.)

```
291      public void GameOver( GameStatus winner )
292      {
293         char[] tab = { '\t' };
294         string[] cards = dealersCards.Split( tab );
295
296         for ( int i = 0; i < cards.Length; i++ )
297            DisplayCard(  i, cards[ i ] );
298
299         // push
300         if ( winner == GameStatus.PUSH )
301            statusLabel.Text = "It's a tie!";
302
303         // player loses
304         else if ( winner == GameStatus.LOSE )
305            statusLabel.Text = "You Lose Try Again!";
306
307         // player wins
308         else if ( winner == GameStatus.WIN )
309            statusLabel.Text = "You Win!";
310
311         // player has won with blackjack
312         else
313            statusLabel.Text = "BlackJack!";
314
315         stayButton.Enabled = false;
316         hitButton.Enabled = false;
317         dealButton.Enabled = true;
318
319      } // end method GameOver
320
321 } // end class Blackjack
```

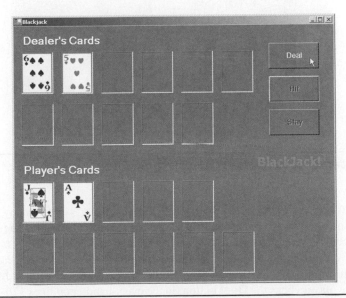

Fig. 21.15 Blackjack game that uses **Blackjack** Web service. (Part 7 of 8.)

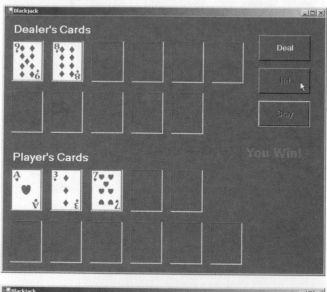

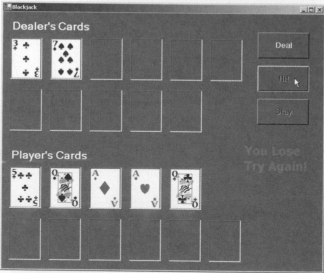

Fig. 21.15 Blackjack game that uses **Blackjack** Web service. (Part 8 of 8.)

Method **GameOver** (lines 291–319) displays all the dealer's cards (many of which are turned face down during the game) and shows the appropriate message in the status **PictureBox**. Method **GameOver** receives as an argument a member of the **GameStatus** enumeration (defined in lines 54–55). The enumeration represents whether the player tied, lost or won the game; its four members are: **PUSH**, **LOSE**, **WIN** and **BLACKJACK**.

When the player clicks the **Deal** button (in the event handler on lines 176–229), all the **PictureBox**es are cleared, the deck is shuffled and the player and dealer receive two cards each. If both obtain scores of 21, method **GameOver** is called and is passed **GameStatus.PUSH**. If the player has 21, **GameOver** is called and is passed **GameStatus.BLACKJACK**. Finally, if only the dealer has 21, method **GameOver** is called and is passed **GameStatus.LOSE**.

If **GameOver** is not called, the player can take additional cards by clicking the **Hit** button (in the event handler on lines 150–173). Each time a player clicks **Hit**, the player is dealt one card, which is displayed in the GUI. If the player exceeds 21, the game is over, and the player loses. If the player has exactly 21, the player is not allowed to take any more cards.

Players can click the **Stay** button to indicate that they do not want to risk being dealt another card. In the event handler for this event (lines 106–113), all three buttons are disabled, and method **DealerPlay** is called. This method (lines 116–147) causes the dealer to keep taking cards until the dealer's hand is worth 17 or more. If the dealer's hand exceeds 21, the player wins; otherwise, the values of the hands are compared, and **GameOver** is called with the appropriate argument.

Method **DisplayCard** (lines 233–287) retrieves the appropriate card image. It takes as arguments an integer representing the index of the **PictureBox** in the **ArrayList** that must have its image set and a **string** representing the card. An empty **string** indicates that we wish to display the back of a card; otherwise, the program extracts the face and suit from the **string** and uses this information to find the correct image. The **switch** statement (lines 260–281) converts the number representing the suit into an integer and assigns the appropriate character to **suitLetter** (**c** for Clubs, **d** for Diamonds, **h** for Hearts and **s** for Spades). The character **suitLetter** completes the image's file name.

21.6 Using Web Forms and Web Services

In the previous examples, we have accessed Web services from Windows applications. However, we can just as easily use them in Web applications. Because Web-based business is becoming more and more prevalent, it often is more practical for programmers to design Web services as part of Web applications. Figure 21.16 presents an airline-reservation Web service that receives information regarding the type of seat the customer wishes to reserve and then makes a reservation if such a seat is available.

The airline-reservation Web service has a single **WebMethod**—**Reserve** (lines 36–85)—which searches its seat database to locate a seat matching a user's request. If it finds an appropriate seat, **Reserve** updates the database, makes the reservation and returns **true**; otherwise, no reservation is made, and the method returns **false**.

Reserve takes two arguments: A **string** representing the desired type of seat (the choices are window, middle or aisle) and a **string** representing the desired class type (the choices are economy or first class). Our database contains four columns: The seat number, the seat type, the class type and a column containing either 0 or 1 to indicate whether the seat is taken. Lines 48–51 define an SQL command that retrieves the number of available seats matching the requested seat and class types. The statement in lines 52–53 executes the query. If the result of the query is not empty, the application reserves the first seat number that the query returns. The database is updated with an **UPDATE** command, and **Reserve** returns **true**, indicating that the reservation was successful. If the result of the **SELECT** query is not successful, **Reserve** returns **false**, indicating that no available seats matched the request.

```
1   // Fig. 21.16: Reservation.asmx.cs
2   // Airline reservation Web Service.
3
4   using System;
5   using System.Data;
6   using System.Diagnostics;
7   using System.Web;
8   using System.Web.Services;
9   using System.Data.OleDb;
10
11  namespace AirlineReservation
12  {
13     // performs reservation of a seat
14     [ WebService( Namespace = "http://www.deitel.com/csphtp1/ch21/",
15        Description = "Service that enables a user to " +
16        "reserve a seat on a plane." ) ]
17     public class Reservation : System.Web.Services.WebService
18     {
19        private System.Data.OleDb.OleDbCommand
20           oleDbSelectCommand1;
21        private System.Data.OleDb.OleDbCommand
22           oleDbInsertCommand1;
23        private System.Data.OleDb.OleDbCommand
24           oleDbUpdateCommand1;
25        private System.Data.OleDb.OleDbCommand
26           oleDbDeleteCommand1;
27        private System.Data.OleDb.OleDbConnection
28           oleDbConnection1;
29        private System.Data.OleDb.OleDbDataAdapter
30           oleDbDataAdapter1;
31
32        // Visual Studio .NET generated code
33
34        // checks database to determine whether
35        // matching seat is available
36        [ WebMethod ( Description = "Method to reserve seat." ) ]
37        public bool Reserve( string seatType, string classType )
38        {
39           OleDbDataReader dataReader;
40
41           // try database connection
42           try
43           {
44              // open database connection
45              oleDbConnection1.Open();
46
47              // set and execute SQL query
48              oleDbDataAdapter1.SelectCommand.CommandText =
49                 "SELECT Number FROM Seats WHERE Type = '" +
50                 seatType + "' AND Class = '" + classType +
51                 "' AND Taken = '0'" ;
52              dataReader =
53                 oleDbDataAdapter1.SelectCommand.ExecuteReader();
```

Fig. 21.16 Airline reservation Web service. (Part 1 of 2.)

```
54
55                // if there were results, seat is available
56                if ( dataReader.Read() )
57                {
58                    string seatNumber = dataReader.GetString( 0 );
59
60                    dataReader.Close();
61
62                    // update first available seat to be taken
63                    oleDbDataAdapter1.UpdateCommand.CommandText =
64                        "Update Seats Set Taken = '1' WHERE Number = '"
65                        + seatNumber + "'";
66                    oleDbDataAdapter1.UpdateCommand.ExecuteNonQuery();
67
68                    return true;
69
70                } // end if
71                dataReader.Close();
72            }
73            catch ( OleDbException ) // if connection problem
74            {
75                return false;
76            }
77            finally
78            {
79                oleDbConnection1.Close();
80            }
81
82            // no seat was reserved
83            return false;
84
85        } // end method Reserve
86
87    } // end class Reservation
88
89 } // end namespace AirlineReservation
```

Fig. 21.16 Airline reservation Web service. (Part 2 of 2.)

Earlier in the chapter, we displayed a Web service in design view (Fig. 21.7), and we explained that this design view allows the programmer to add components to a Web service. In our airline-reservation Web service (Fig. 21.16), we used various data components. Figure 21.18 shows these components in design view. Notice that it is easier to drop these components into our Web service using the **Toolbox** than to type the equivalent code.

Figure 21.18 presents the ASPX listing for the Web Form through which users can select seat types. This page allows a user to reserve a seat on the basis of its class and location in a row of seats. The page then uses the airline-reservation Web service to carry out the user's request. If the database request is not successful, the user is instructed to modify the request and try again.

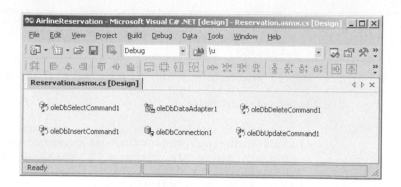

Fig. 21.17 Airline Web Service in design view.

```
1    <%-- Fig. 21.18: TicketReservation.aspx              --%>
2    <%-- A Web Form to allow users to select the kind of seat --%>
3    <%-- they wish to reserve.                           --%>
4
5    <%@ Page language="c#" Codebehind="TicketReservation.aspx.cs"
6        AutoEventWireup="false"
7        Inherits="MakeReservation.TicketReservation" %>
8
9    <!DOCTYPE HTML PUBLIC "-//W3C//DTD HTML 4.0 Transitional//EN" >
10   <HTML>
11       <HEAD>
12          <meta name="GENERATOR" Content="Microsoft Visual Studio 7.0">
13          <meta name="CODE_LANGUAGE" Content="C#">
14          <meta name="vs_defaultClientScript"
15               content="JavaScript (ECMAScript)">
16          <meta name="vs_targetSchema"
17               content="http://schemas.microsoft.com/intellisense/ie5">
18       </HEAD>
19       <body MS_POSITIONING="GridLayout">
20
21          <form id="MakeReservation" method="post" runat="server">
22
23             <asp:DropDownList id="seatList" style="Z-INDEX: 101;
24                LEFT: 16px; POSITION: absolute; TOP: 43px"
25                runat="server" Width="105px" Height="22px">
26
27                <asp:ListItem Value="Aisle">Aisle</asp:ListItem>
28                <asp:ListItem Value="Middle">Middle</asp:ListItem>
29                <asp:ListItem Value="Window">Window</asp:ListItem>
30
31             </asp:DropDownList>
32
33             <asp:DropDownList id="classList" style="Z-INDEX: 102;
34                LEFT: 145px; POSITION: absolute; TOP: 43px"
35                runat="server" Width="98px" Height="22px">
36
```

Fig. 21.18 ASPX file that takes reservation information. (Part 1 of 2.)

```
37                     <asp:ListItem Value="Economy">Economy</asp:ListItem>
38                     <asp:ListItem Value="First">First</asp:ListItem>
39
40           </asp:DropDownList>
41
42           <asp:Button id="reserveButton" style="Z-INDEX: 103;
43            LEFT: 21px; POSITION: absolute; TOP: 83px" runat="server"
44             Text="Reserve">
45           </asp:Button>
46
47           <asp:Label id="Label1" style="Z-INDEX: 104;
48             LEFT: 17px; POSITION: absolute; TOP: 13px"
49             runat="server">Please select the type of seat and
50             class you wish to reserve:
51           </asp:Label>
52
53        </form>
54     </body>
55  </HTML>
```

Fig. 21.18 ASPX file that takes reservation information. (Part 2 of 2.)

The page in Fig. 21.17 defines two **DropDownList** objects and a **Button**. One **DropDownList** displays all the seat types from which users can select. The second lists choices for the class type. Users click the **Button**, named **reserveButton**, to submit requests after making selections from the **DropDownList**s. The code-behind file (Fig. 21.19) attaches an event handler for this button.

Lines 30–31 create a **Reservation** object. When the user clicks **Reserve**, the **reserveButton_Click** event handler executes, and the page reloads. The event handler (lines 48–63) calls the Web service's **Reserve** method and passes it the selected seat and class types as arguments. If **Reserve** returns **true**, the application displays a message thanking the user for making a reservation; otherwise, the user is notified that the type of seat requested is not available, and the user is instructed to try again.

```
1   // Fig. 21.19: TicketReservation.aspx.cs
2   // Making a Reservation using a Web Service.
3
4   using System;
5   using System.Collections;
6   using System.ComponentModel;
7   using System.Data;
8   using System.Drawing;
9   using System.Web;
10  using System.Web.SessionState;
11  using System.Web.UI;
12  using System.Web.UI.WebControls;
13  using System.Web.UI.HtmlControls;
14
```

Fig. 21.19 Code-behind file for the reservation page. (Part 1 of 3.)

```
15   namespace MakeReservation
16   {
17      // allows visitors to select seat type to reserve, and
18      // then make reservation
19      public class TicketReservation : System.Web.UI.Page
20      {
21         protected System.Web.UI.WebControls.DropDownList
22            seatList;
23         protected System.Web.UI.WebControls.DropDownList
24            classList;
25
26         protected System.Web.UI.WebControls.Button
27            reserveButton;
28         protected System.Web.UI.WebControls.Label Label1;
29
30         private localhost.Reservation agent =
31            new localhost.Reservation();
32
33         private void Page_Load(
34            object sender, System.EventArgs e )
35         {
36            if ( IsPostBack )
37            {
38               seatList.Visible = false;
39               classList.Visible = false;
40               reserveButton.Visible = false;
41               Label1.Visible = false;
42            }
43         }
44
45         // Visual Studio .NET generated code
46
47         // calls Web Service to try to reserve specified seat
48         public void reserveButton_Click (
49            object sender, System.EventArgs e )
50         {
51            // if Web-service method returned true, signal success
52            if ( agent.Reserve( seatList.SelectedItem.Text,
53               classList.SelectedItem.Text ) )
54               Response.Write( "Your reservation has been made."
55                  + "  Thank you." );
56
57            // Web-service method returned false, so signal failure
58            else
59               Response.Write( "This seat is not available, " +
60                  "please hit the back button on your browser " +
61                  "and try again." );
62
63         } // end method reserveButton_Click
64
65      } // end class TicketReservation
66
67   } // end namespace MakeReservation
```

Fig. 21.19 Code-behind file for the reservation page. (Part 2 of 3.)

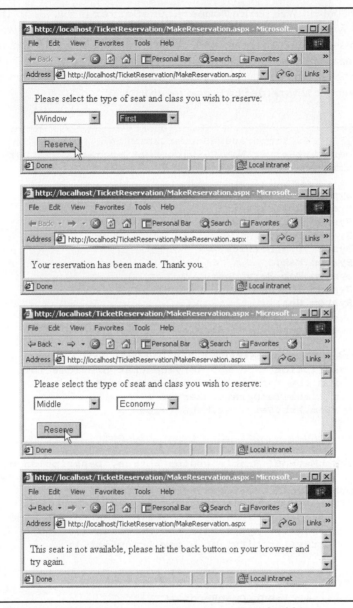

Fig. 21.19 Code-behind file for the reservation page. (Part 3 of 3.)

21.7 Case Study: Temperature Information Application

This case study discusses both a Web service that presents weather forecasts for various cities around the United States and a windows application that employs the Web service. The Web service uses networking capabilities to display the forecasts; it parses a Web page containing the required information and then extracts weather forecast data.

First, we present Web service **TemperatureServer** in Fig. 21.20. This Web service reads a Web page and collects information about the temperature and weather conditions in an assortment of American cities. [*Note*: At the time of publication, this program runs in the manner that we describe. However, if changes are made to the Web page from which the program retrieves data, the program might work differently or not at all. Please check our Web site at **www.deitel.com** for updates.]

```
1   // Fig. 21.20: TemperatureServer.asmx.cs
2   // TemperatureServer Web Service that extracts weather
3   // information from a Web page.
4
5   using System;
6   using System.Collections;
7   using System.ComponentModel;
8   using System.Data;
9   using System.Diagnostics;
10  using System.Web;
11  using System.Web.Services;
12  using System.IO;
13  using System.Net;
14
15  namespace TemperatureWebService
16  {
17     [ WebService( Namespace = "http://www.deitel.com/csphtp1/ch21/",
18        Description = "A Web service that provides information " +
19        "from the National Weather Service." ) ]
20     public class TemperatureServer :
21        System.Web.Services.WebService
22     {
23        // Visual Studio .NET generated code
24
25        [ WebMethod( EnableSession = true, Description =
26           "Method to read information from the weather service." ) ]
27        public void UpdateWeatherConditions()
28        {
29           // create WebClient to get access to Web page
30           WebClient myClient = new WebClient();
31           ArrayList cityList = new ArrayList();
32
33           // get StreamReader for response so we can read page
34           StreamReader input = new StreamReader(
35              myClient.OpenRead(
36              "http://iwin.nws.noaa.gov/iwin/us/" +
37              "traveler.html" ) );
38
39           string separator = "TAV12";
40
41           // locate first horizontal line on Web page
42           while ( !input.ReadLine().StartsWith(
43              separator ) ) ; // do nothing
44
```

Fig. 21.20 TemperatureServer Web service. (Part 1 of 3.)

```
45               // day format and night format
46               string dayFormat =
47                  "CITY             WEA       HI/LO    WEA       " +
48                  "HI/LO";
49               string nightFormat =
50                  "CITY             WEA       LO/HI    WEA       " +
51                  "LO/HI";
52               string inputLine = "";
53
54               // locate header that begins weather information
55               do
56               {
57                  inputLine = input.ReadLine();
58               } while ( !inputLine.Equals( dayFormat ) &&
59                  !inputLine.Equals( nightFormat ) );
60
61               // get first city's data
62               inputLine = input.ReadLine();
63
64               while ( inputLine.Length > 28 )
65               {
66                  // create CityWeather object for city
67                  CityWeather weather = new CityWeather(
68                     inputLine.Substring( 0, 16 ),
69                     inputLine.Substring( 16, 7 ),
70                     inputLine.Substring( 23, 7 ) );
71
72                  // add to List
73                  cityList.Add( weather );
74
75                  // get next city's data
76                  inputLine = input.ReadLine();
77               }
78
79               // close connection to NWS server
80               input.Close();
81
82               // add city list to user session
83               Session.Add( "cityList", cityList );
84
85           } // end UpdateWeatherConditions
86
87           // gets all city names
88           [ WebMethod( EnableSession = true, Description =
89              "Method to retrieve a list of cities." ) ]
90           public string[] Cities()
91           {
92              ArrayList cityList = ( ArrayList ) Session[ "cityList" ];
93              string[] cities= new string[ cityList.Count ];
94
95              // retrieve names for cities
96              for ( int i = 0; i < cityList.Count; i++ )
97              {
```

Fig. 21.20 TemperatureServer Web service. (Part 2 of 3.)

```
98              CityWeather weather = ( CityWeather ) cityList[ i ];
99
100             cities[ i ] = weather.CityName;
101          }
102
103          return cities;
104
105       } // end method Cities
106
107       // gets all city descriptions
108       [ WebMethod( EnableSession = true, Description = "Method" +
109          " to retrieve weather descriptions for a " +
110          "list of cities." )]
111       public string[] Descriptions()
112       {
113          ArrayList cityList = ( ArrayList ) Session[ "cityList" ];
114          string[] descriptions= new string[ cityList.Count ];
115
116          // retrieve weather descriptions for all cities
117          for ( int i = 0; i < cityList.Count; i++ )
118          {
119             CityWeather weather = ( CityWeather )cityList[ i ];
120
121             descriptions[ i ] = weather.Description;
122          }
123
124          return descriptions;
125
126       } // end method Descriptions
127
128       // obtains each city temperature
129       [ WebMethod( EnableSession = true, Description = "Method " +
130          "to retrieve the temperature for a list of cities." ) ]
131       public string[] Temperatures()
132       {
133          ArrayList cityList = ( ArrayList ) Session[ "cityList" ];
134          string[] temperatures= new string[ cityList.Count ];
135
136          // retrieve temperatures for all cities
137          for ( int i = 0; i < cityList.Count; i++ )
138          {
139             CityWeather weather = ( CityWeather )cityList[ i ];
140             temperatures[ i ] = weather.Temperature;
141          }
142
143          return temperatures;
144
145       } // end method Temperatures
146
147    } // end class TemperatureServer
148
149 } // end namespace TemperatureWebService
```

Fig. 21.20 TemperatureServer Web service. (Part 3 of 3.)

Method **UpdateWeatherConditions**, which gathers weather data from a Web page, is the first **WebMethod** that a client must call from the Web service. The service also provides **WebMethod**s **Cities**, **Descriptions** and **Temperatures**, which return different kinds of forecast-related information.

When **UpdateWeatherConditions** (lines 25–85) is invoked, the method connects to a Web site containing the traveler's forecasts from the National Weather Service (NWS). Line 30 creates a *WebClient* object, which we use because the **WebClient** class is designed for interaction with a source specified by a URL. In this case, the URL for the NWS page is **http://iwin.nws.noaa.gov/iwin/us/traveler.html**. Lines 34–37 call **WebClient** method *OpenRead*; the method retrieves a **Stream** from the URL containing the weather information and then uses this **Stream** to create a **StreamReader** object. Using a **StreamReader** object, the program can read the Web page's HTML markup line by line.

The section of the Web page in which we are interested starts with the **string** "**TAV12**." Therefore, lines 42–43 read the HTML markup one line at a time until this **string** is encountered. Once the string "**TAV12**" is reached, the **do/while** structure (lines 55–59) continues to read the page one line at a time until it finds the header line (i.e., the line at the beginning of the forecast table). This line starts with either **dayFormat**, indicating day format, or **nightFormat**, indicating night format. Because the line could be in either format, the structure checks for both. Line 62 reads the next line from the page, which is the first line containing temperature information.

The **while** structure (lines 64–77) creates a new **CityWeather** object to represent the current city. It parses the **string** containing the current weather data, separating the city name, the weather condition and the temperature. The **CityWeather** object is added to **cityList** (an **ArrayList** that contains a list of the cities, their descriptions and their current temperatures); then, the next line from the page is read and stored in **inputLine** for the next iteration. This process continues until the length of the **string** read from the Web page is less than or equal to **28**. This signals the end of the temperature section. Line 83 adds the **ArrayList cityList** to the **Session** object so that the values are maintained between method calls.

Method **Cities** (lines 88–105) creates an array of **string**s that can contain as many **string** elements as there are elements in **cityList**. Line 92 obtains the list of cities from the **Session** object. Lines 96–101 iterate through each **CityWeather** object in **cityList** and insert the city name into the array, which is returned in line 103. Methods **Descriptions** (lines 108–126) and **Temperatures** (lines 129–145) behave similarly, except that they return weather descriptions and temperatures, respectively.

Figure 21.21 contains the code listing for the **CityWeather** class. The constructor takes three arguments: The city's name, the weather description and the current temperature. The class provides the read-only properties **CityName**, **Temperature** and **Description** so that these values can be retrieved by the Web service.

```
1   // Fig. 21.21: CityWeather.cs
2   // Class representing the weather information for one city.
3
4   using System;
```

Fig. 21.21 Class that stores weather information about a city. (Part 1 of 2.)

```
5
6    namespace TemperatureWebService
7    {
8       public class CityWeather
9       {
10         private string cityName;
11         private string temperature;
12         private string description;
13
14         public CityWeather(
15            string city, string information, string degrees )
16         {
17            cityName = city;
18            description = information;
19            temperature = degrees;
20         }
21
22         // city name
23         public string CityName
24         {
25            get
26            {
27               return cityName;
28            }
29         }
30
31         // city temperature
32         public string Temperature
33         {
34            get
35            {
36               return temperature;
37            }
38         }
39
40         // forecast description
41         public string Description
42         {
43            get
44            {
45               return description;
46            }
47         }
48
49      } // end class CityWeather
50   } // end namespace TemperatureWebService
```

Fig. 21.21 Class that stores weather information about a city. (Part 2 of 2.)

The Windows application in Fig. 21.22 uses the **TemperatureServer** Web service to display weather information in a user-friendly format.

TemperatureClient (Fig. 21.22) is a Windows application that uses the **TemperatureServer** Web service to display weather information in a graphical and easy-to-read manner. The application consists of 36 **Label**s, which are placed in two columns. Each **Label** displays the weather information for a different city.

```
1   // Fig. 21.22: Client.cs
2   // Class that displays weather information that it receives
3   // from a Web service.
4
5   using System;
6   using System.Drawing;
7   using System.Collections;
8   using System.ComponentModel;
9   using System.Windows.Forms;
10  using System.Net;
11
12  namespace TemperatureClient
13  {
14     public class Client : System.Windows.Forms.Form
15     {
16        private System.Windows.Forms.Label label1;
17        private System.Windows.Forms.Label label2;
18        private System.Windows.Forms.Label label3;
19        private System.Windows.Forms.Label label4;
20        private System.Windows.Forms.Label label5;
21        private System.Windows.Forms.Label label6;
22        private System.Windows.Forms.Label label7;
23        private System.Windows.Forms.Label label8;
24        private System.Windows.Forms.Label label9;
25        private System.Windows.Forms.Label label10;
26        private System.Windows.Forms.Label label11;
27        private System.Windows.Forms.Label label12;
28        private System.Windows.Forms.Label label13;
29        private System.Windows.Forms.Label label14;
30        private System.Windows.Forms.Label label15;
31        private System.Windows.Forms.Label label16;
32        private System.Windows.Forms.Label label17;
33        private System.Windows.Forms.Label label18;
34        private System.Windows.Forms.Label label19;
35        private System.Windows.Forms.Label label20;
36        private System.Windows.Forms.Label label21;
37        private System.Windows.Forms.Label label22;
38        private System.Windows.Forms.Label label23;
39        private System.Windows.Forms.Label label24;
40        private System.Windows.Forms.Label label25;
41        private System.Windows.Forms.Label label26;
42        private System.Windows.Forms.Label label27;
43        private System.Windows.Forms.Label label28;
44        private System.Windows.Forms.Label label29;
45        private System.Windows.Forms.Label label30;
46        private System.Windows.Forms.Label label31;
47        private System.Windows.Forms.Label label32;
48        private System.Windows.Forms.Label label33;
49        private System.Windows.Forms.Label label34;
```

Fig. 21.22 Receiving temperature and weather data from a Web service. (Part 1 of 4.)

```
50          private System.Windows.Forms.Label label36;
51          private System.Windows.Forms.Label label35;
52
53          private System.ComponentModel.Container components =
54             null;
55
56          public Client()
57          {
58             InitializeComponent();
59
60             localhost.TemperatureServer client =
61                new localhost.TemperatureServer();
62             client.CookieContainer = new CookieContainer();
63             client.UpdateWeatherConditions();
64
65             string[] cities = client.Cities();
66             string[] descriptions = client.Descriptions();
67             string[] temperatures = client.Temperatures();
68
69             label35.BackgroundImage = new Bitmap(
70                "images/header.png" );
71             label36.BackgroundImage = new Bitmap(
72                "images/header.png" );
73
74             // create Hashtable and populate it with every label
75             Hashtable cityLabels = new Hashtable();
76             cityLabels.Add( 1, label1 );
77             cityLabels.Add( 2, label2 );
78             cityLabels.Add( 3, label3 );
79             cityLabels.Add( 4, label4 );
80             cityLabels.Add( 5, label5 );
81             cityLabels.Add( 6, label6 );
82             cityLabels.Add( 7, label7 );
83             cityLabels.Add( 8, label8 );
84             cityLabels.Add( 9, label9 );
85             cityLabels.Add( 10, label10 );
86             cityLabels.Add( 11, label11 );
87             cityLabels.Add( 12, label12 );
88             cityLabels.Add( 13, label13 );
89             cityLabels.Add( 14, label14 );
90             cityLabels.Add( 15, label15 );
91             cityLabels.Add( 16, label16 );
92             cityLabels.Add( 17, label17 );
93             cityLabels.Add( 18, label18 );
94             cityLabels.Add( 19, label19 );
95             cityLabels.Add( 20, label20 );
96             cityLabels.Add( 21, label21 );
97             cityLabels.Add( 22, label22 );
98             cityLabels.Add( 23, label23 );
99             cityLabels.Add( 24, label24 );
100            cityLabels.Add( 25, label25 );
101            cityLabels.Add( 26, label26 );
102            cityLabels.Add( 27, label27 );
```

Fig. 21.22 Receiving temperature and weather data from a Web service. (Part 2 of 4.)

```
103          cityLabels.Add( 28, label28 );
104          cityLabels.Add( 29, label29 );
105          cityLabels.Add( 30, label30 );
106          cityLabels.Add( 31, label31 );
107          cityLabels.Add( 32, label32 );
108          cityLabels.Add( 33, label33 );
109          cityLabels.Add( 34, label34 );
110
111          // create Hashtable and populate with
112          // all weather conditions
113          Hashtable weather = new Hashtable();
114          weather.Add( "SUNNY", "sunny" );
115          weather.Add( "PTCLDY", "pcloudy" );
116          weather.Add( "CLOUDY", "mcloudy" );
117          weather.Add( "MOCLDY", "mcloudy" );
118          weather.Add( "TSTRMS", "rain" );
119          weather.Add( "RAIN", "rain" );
120          weather.Add( "SNOW", "snow" );
121          weather.Add( "VRYHOT", "vryhot" );
122          weather.Add( "FAIR", "fair" );
123          weather.Add( "RNSNOW", "rnsnow" );
124          weather.Add( "SHWRS", "showers" );
125          weather.Add( "WINDY", "windy" );
126          weather.Add( "NOINFO", "noinfo" );
127          weather.Add( "MISG", "noinfo" );
128          weather.Add( "DRZL", "rain" );
129          weather.Add( "HAZE", "noinfo" );
130          weather.Add( "SMOKE", "mcloudy" );
131
132          Bitmap background = new Bitmap( "images/back.png" );
133          Font font = new Font( "Courier New", 8,
134             FontStyle.Bold );
135
136          // for every city
137          for ( int i = 0; i < cities.Length; i++ )
138          {
139             // use Hashtable cityLabels to find the next Label
140             Label currentCity = ( Label )cityLabels[ i + 1 ];
141
142             // set current Label's image to image
143             // corresponding to the city's weather condition -
144             // find correct image name in Hashtable weather
145             currentCity.Image = new Bitmap( "images/" +
146                weather[ descriptions[ i ].Trim() ] + ".png" );
147
148             // set background image, font and forecolor
149             // of Label
150             currentCity.BackgroundImage = background;
151             currentCity.Font = font;
152             currentCity.ForeColor = Color.White;
153
```

Fig. 21.22 Receiving temperature and weather data from a Web service. (Part 3 of 4.)

```
154                  // set label's text to city name
155                  currentCity.Text = "\r\n" + cities[ i ] + " " +
156                     temperatures[ i ];
157              }
158
159         } // end of constructor
160
161         // Visual Studio .NET generated code
162
163         [STAThread]
164         static void Main()
165         {
166             Application.Run( new Client() );
167         }
168
169     } // end class Client
170
171 } // end namespace TemperatureClient
```

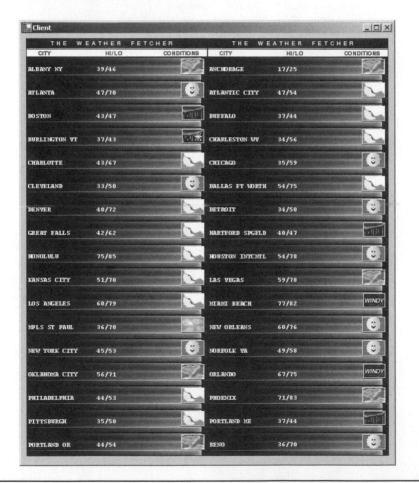

Fig. 21.22 Receiving temperature and weather data from a Web service. (Part 4 of 4.)

Lines 60–63 of the constructor instantiate a **TemperatureServer** object, create a new **CookieContainer** object and update the weather data by calling method **UpdateWeatherConditions**. Lines 65–67 call **TemperatureServer** methods **Cities**, **Descriptions** and **Temperatures** to retrieve the city's weather and description information. Because the application presents weather data for so many cities, we must establish a way to organize the information in the **Label**s and to ensure that each weather description is accompanied by an appropriate image. To address these concerns, the program uses class **Hashtable** (discussed further in Chapter 23, Data Structures and Collections) to store all the **Label**s and weather descriptions and the names of their corresponding images. A **Hashtable** stores key-value pairs, in which both the key and the value can be any type of object. Method **Add** adds key-value pairs to a **Hashtable**. The class also provides an indexer to return the key value on which the **Hashtable** is indexed. Line 75 creates a **Hashtable** object, and lines 76–109 add the **Label**s to the **Hashtable**, using the numbers **1** through **36** as keys. Then, line 113 creates a second **Hashtable** object (**weather**) to contain pairs of weather conditions and the images associated with those conditions. Note that a given weather description does not necessarily correspond to the name of the PNG file containing the correct image. For example, both "**TSTRMS**" and "**RAIN**" weather conditions use the **rain.png** file.

Lines 137–157 set each **Label** so that it contains a city name, the current temperature in the city and an image corresponding to the weather condition for that city. Line 140 uses the **Hashtable** indexer to retrieve the next **Label** by passing as an argument the current value of **i** plus **1**. We add **1** because the **Hashtable** indexer begins at 0, despite the fact that both the labels and the **Hashtable** keys are numbered from 1–36.

Lines 145–146 set the **Label**'s image to the PNG image that corresponds to the city's weather condition. The application does this by retrieving the name of the PNG image from the **weather Hashtable**. The program eliminates any spaces in the description **string** by calling **string** method **Trim**. Lines 150–156 set several **Label**s' properties to achieve the visual effect seen in the output. For each label, we specify a blue-and-black background image (line 150). Lines 155–156 set each label's text so that it displays the correct information for each city (i.e., the city's name and temperature).

21.8 User-Defined Types in Web Services

The Web service discussed in the previous section returns arrays of **string**s. It would be much more convenient if **TemperatureServer** could return an array of **CityWeather** objects, instead of an array of **string**s. Fortunately, it is possible to define and employ user-defined types (also known as custom types) in a Web service. These types can be passed into or returned from Web-service methods. Web-service clients also can use these user-defined types, because the proxy class created for the client contains these type definitions. There are, however, some subtleties to keep in mind when using user-defined types in Web services; we point these out as we encounter them in the next example.

The case study in this section presents a math-tutoring program. The Web service generates random equations of type **Equation**. The client inputs information about the kind of mathematical example that the user wants (addition, subtraction or multiplication) and the skill level of the user (1 creates equations using one-digit numbers, 2 specifies more difficult equations involving two-digit numbers and 3 specifies the most difficult equations, containing three-digit numbers). It then generates an equation consisting of random numbers that have the proper number of digits. The client receives the **Equation** and uses a Windows Form to display the sample questions to the user.

We mentioned earlier that all data types passed to and from Web services must be supported by SOAP. How, then, can SOAP support a type that is not even created yet? In Chapter 17, Files and Streams, we discussed the serializing of data types, which enables them to be written to files. Similarly, custom types that are sent to or from a Web service are serialized, enabling them to be passed in XML format. This process is referred to as *XML serialization.*

When defining objects to be returned from Web-service methods, there are several subtleties to understand. For example, any object returned by a Web-service method must have a default constructor. Although all objects can be instantiated using a default **public** constructor (even if this constructor is not defined explicitly), a class returned from a Web service must have an explicitly defined constructor, even if its body is empty.

Common Programming Error 21.3

*Failure to define explicitly a **public** constructor for a type being used in a Web service results in a run-time error.*

A few additional requirements apply to custom types in Web services. Any variables of our user-defined type that we wish to access on the client-side must be declared **public**. We also must define both the **get** and **set** accessors of any properties that we wish to access at runtime. The Web service needs to have a way both to retrieve and manipulate such properties, because objects of the user-defined type will be converted into XML (when the objects are serialized) then converted back to objects (when they are de-serialized). During serialization, the property value must be read (through the **get** accessor); during de-serialization, the property value of the new object must be set (through the **set** accessor). If only one accessor is present, the client application will not have access to the property.

Common Programming Error 21.4

*Defining only the **get** or **set** accessor of a property for a user-defined type being used in a Web service results in a property that is inaccessible to the client.*

Common Programming Error 21.5

*Clients of a Web service can access only that service's **public** members. To allow access to **private** data, the programmer should provide **public** properties.*

Figure 21.23 displays class **Equation**. The constructor that is called (lines 18–37) takes three arguments—two integers representing the left and right operands and a **string** representing the algebraic operation to carry out. We define a default constructor (line 13–15) that calls another constructor (lines 18–37) and passes some default values. The constructor sets the **left**, **right** and **operation** fields, then calculates the appropriate result. We do not use this default constructor, but it must be defined in the program.

Class **Equation** defines properties **LeftHandSide**, **RightHandSide**, **Left**, **Right**, **Operation** and **Result**. The program does not need to modify the values of some of these properties, but implementation for the **set** accessor must be provided. **LeftHandSide** returns a **string** representing everything to the left of the "=" sign, and **RightHandSide** returns a **string** representing everything to the right of the "=" sign. **Left** returns the **int** to the left of the operator (known as the left operand), and **Right** returns the **int** to the right of the operator (known as the right operand). **Result** returns

```
1   // Fig. 21.23: Equation.cs
2   // Class Equation that contains
3   // information about an equation.
4
5   using System;
6
7   public class Equation
8   {
9      private int left, right, result;
10     private string operation;
11
12     // required default constructor
13     public Equation() : this( 0, 0, "+" )
14     {
15     }
16
17     // constructor for class Equation
18     public Equation( int leftValue, int rightValue,
19        string operationType )
20     {
21        Left = leftValue;
22        Right = rightValue;
23        Operation = operationType;
24
25        switch ( operationType )
26        {
27           case "+":
28              Result = Left + Right;
29              break;
30           case "-":
31              Result = Left - Right;
32              break;
33           case "*":
34              Result = Left * Right;
35              break;
36        }
37     }
38
39     public override string ToString()
40     {
41        return Left.ToString() + " " + Operation + " " +
42           Right.ToString() + " = " + Result.ToString();
43     }
44
45     // property returning string representing
46     // left-hand side
47     public string LeftHandSide
48     {
49        get
50        {
51           return Left.ToString() + " " + Operation + " " +
52              Right.ToString();
53        }
```

Fig. 21.23 Class that stores equation information. (Part 1 of 3.)

```
54
55        set
56        {
57        }
58     }
59
60     // property returning string representing
61     // right-hand side
62     public string RightHandSide
63     {
64        get
65        {
66           return Result.ToString();
67        }
68
69        set
70        {
71        }
72     }
73
74     // left operand get and set property
75     public int Left
76     {
77        get
78        {
79           return left;
80        }
81
82        set
83        {
84           left = value;
85        }
86     }
87
88     // right operand get and set property
89     public int Right
90     {
91        get
92        {
93           return right;
94        }
95
96        set
97        {
98           right = value;
99        }
100    }
101
102    // get and set property of result of applying
103    // operation to left and right operands
104    public int Result
105    {
```

Fig. 21.23 Class that stores equation information. (Part 2 of 3.)

```
106              get
107              {
108                  return result;
109              }
110
111              set
112              {
113                  result = value;
114              }
115          }
116
117          // get and set property for operation
118          public string Operation
119          {
120              get
121              {
122                  return operation;
123              }
124
125              set
126              {
127                  operation = value;
128              }
129          }
130
131      } // end class Equation
```

Fig. 21.23 Class that stores equation information. (Part 3 of 3.)

the answer to the equation, and **Operation** returns the operator. The program does not actually need the **RightHandSide** property, but we have chosen to include it in case other clients choose to use it. Figure 21.24 presents the **Generator** Web service that creates random, customized **Equation**s.

```
1    // Fig. 21.24: Generator.asmx.cs
2    // Web Service to generate random equations based on a
3    // specified operation and difficulty level.
4
5    using System;
6    using System.Collections;
7    using System.ComponentModel;
8    using System.Data;
9    using System.Diagnostics;
10   using System.Web;
11   using System.Web.Services;
12
13   namespace EquationGenerator
14   {
15       [ WebService( Namespace = "http://www.deitel.com/csphtp1/ch21",
16           Description = "A Web service that generates questions " +
17           "based on the specified mathematical operation and " +
18           "level of difficulty chosen." ) ]
```

Fig. 21.24 Web service that generates random equations. (Part 1 of 2.)

```
19        public class Generator : System.Web.Services.WebService
20        {
21
22            // Visual Studio .NET generated code
23
24            [ WebMethod ( Description =
25                "Method that generates a random equation." ) ]
26            public Equation GenerateEquation( string operation,
27                int level )
28            {
29                // find maximum and minimum number to be used
30                int maximum = ( int ) Math.Pow( 10, level ),
31                    minimum = ( int ) Math.Pow( 10, level - 1 );
32
33                Random random = new Random();
34
35                // create equation consisting of two random numbers
36                // between minimum and maximum parameters
37                Equation equation = new Equation(
38                    random.Next( minimum, maximum ),
39                    random.Next( minimum, maximum ), operation );
40
41                return equation;
42
43            } // end method GenerateEquation
44
45        } // end class Generator
46
47    } // end namespace EquationGenerator
```

Fig. 21.24 Web service that generates random equations. (Part 2 of 2.)

Web service **Generator** contains only one method, **GenerateEquation**. This method takes as arguments a **string** representing the operation we wish to perform and an **integer** representing the desired difficulty level of the equation. Figure 21.25 demonstrates the result of executing a test call of this Web service. Notice that the return value from our Web-service method is marked up as XML. However, this example differs from previous ones in that the XML specifies the values for all **public** properties and fields of the object that is being returned. The return object has been serialized into XML. Our proxy class takes this return value and deserializes it into an object (containing the **public** data from the original object) that then is passed back to the client.

Lines 30–31 define the lower and upper bounds for the random numbers that the method generates. To set these limits, the program first calls **static** method **Pow** of class **Math**—this method raises its first argument to the power of its second argument. Integer **maximum** represents the upper bound for a randomly generated number. The program raises **10** to the power of the specified **level** argument and then passes this value as the upper bound. For instance, if **level** is **1**, **maximum** is **10**; if **level** is **2**; **maximum** is **100** and so on. Variable **minimum**'s value is determined by raising **10** to a power one less then **level**. This calculates the smallest number with **level** digits. If **level** is **2**, **minimum** is **10**; if **level** is **3**, **minimum** is **100** and so on.

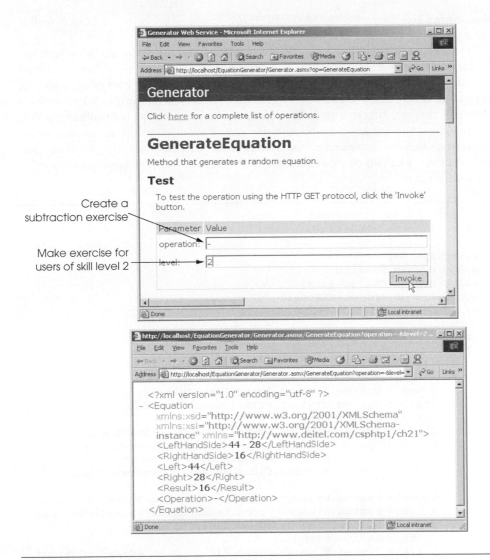

Fig. 21.25 Returning an object from a Web-service method.

Lines 37–39 create a new **Equation** object. The program calls **Random** method **Next**, which returns an integer that is greater than or equal to a specified lower bound, but less than a specified upper bound. In this example, **Random** generates a left operand value that is greater than or equal to **minimum**, but less than **maximum** (i.e., a number with **level** digits). The right operand is another random number with the same characteristics. The operation passed to the **Equation** constructor is the **string operation** that was received by **GenerateEquation**. The new **Equation** object is returned.

Figure 21.26 lists the math-tutoring application that uses the **Generator** Web service. The application calls **Generator**'s **GenerateEquation** method to create an **Equation** object. The application then displays the left-hand side of the **Equation** and waits for user input. In this example, the program accesses both class **Generator** and

class **Equation** from within the **localhost** namespace—both are placed in this
namespace when the proxy is generated.

The math-tutoring application displays a question and waits for input. The default setting for the difficulty level is **1**, but the user can change this at any time by choosing a level
from among the top row of **RadioButton**s. Clicking any of the level options invokes
levelRadioButtons_Click (lines 110–120), which sets integer **level** to the level
selected by the user. Although the default setting for the question type is **Addition**, the user
also can change this at any time by selecting one of the bottom-row **RadioButton**s.
Doing so invokes the **operationRadioButtons_Click** (lines 91–107) event handler, which sets **string operation** so that it contains the symbol corresponding to the
user's selection.

```
1    // Fig. 21.26: Tutor.cs
2    // Math tutor program.
3
4    using System;
5    using System.Drawing;
6    using System.Collections;
7    using System.ComponentModel;
8    using System.Windows.Forms;
9
10   namespace EquationGeneratorClient
11   {
12      public class Tutor : System.Windows.Forms.Form
13      {
14         private System.Windows.Forms.Panel panel1;
15         private System.Windows.Forms.Panel panel2;
16
17         private System.Windows.Forms.Label questionLabel;
18         private System.Windows.Forms.TextBox answerTextBox;
19         private System.Windows.Forms.Button okButton;
20         private System.Windows.Forms.Button generateButton;
21
22         private System.Windows.Forms.RadioButton oneRadioButton;
23         private System.Windows.Forms.RadioButton twoRadioButton;
24         private System.Windows.Forms.RadioButton
25            threeRadioButton;
26         private System.Windows.Forms.RadioButton addRadioButton;
27         private System.Windows.Forms.RadioButton
28            subtractRadioButton;
29         private System.Windows.Forms.RadioButton
30            multiplyRadioButton;
31
32         private System.ComponentModel.Container components =
33            null;
34         private int level = 1;
35
36         private localhost.Equation equation;
37         private localhost.Generator generator =
38            new localhost.Generator();
39         private string operation = "+";
```

Fig. 21.26 Math tutor application. (Part 1 of 4.)

```
40
41      // Visual Studio .NET generated code
42
43      [STAThread]
44      static void Main()
45      {
46         Application.Run( new Tutor() );
47      }
48
49      // generates new equation on click event
50      protected void generateButton_Click( object sender,
51         System.EventArgs e )
52      {
53         // generate equation using current operation
54         // and level
55         equation = generator.GenerateEquation( operation,
56            level );
57
58         // display left-hand side of equation
59         questionLabel.Text = equation.LeftHandSide;
60
61         okButton.Enabled = true;
62         answerTextBox.Enabled = true;
63
64      } // end method generateButton_Click
65
66      // check users answer
67      protected void okButton_Click( object sender,
68         System.EventArgs e )
69      {
70         // determine correct result from Equation
71         // object
72         int answer = equation.Result;
73
74         // get user's answer
75         int myAnswer = Int32.Parse( answerTextBox.Text );
76
77         // test if user's answer is correct
78         if ( answer == myAnswer )
79         {
80            questionLabel.Text = "";
81            answerTextBox.Text = "";
82            okButton.Enabled = false;
83            MessageBox.Show( "Correct! Good job!" );
84         }
85         else
86            MessageBox.Show( "Incorrect. Try again." );
87
88      } // end method okButton_Click
89
```

Fig. 21.26 Math tutor application. (Part 2 of 4.)

```
90            // set the selected operation
91            protected void operationRadioButtons_Click( object sender,
92               EventArgs e )
93            {
94               RadioButton item = ( RadioButton ) sender;
95
96               // set the operation to be the appropriate symbol
97               if ( item == addRadioButton )
98                  operation = "+";
99               else if ( item == subtractRadioButton )
100                 operation = "-";
101              else
102                 operation = "*";
103
104              generateButton.Text = "Generate " + item.Text +
105                 " Example";
106
107           } // end method operationRadioButtons_Click
108
109           // set the current level
110           protected void levelRadioButtons_Click( object sender,
111              EventArgs e )
112           {
113              if ( sender == oneRadioButton )
114                 level = 1;
115              else if ( sender == twoRadioButton )
116                 level = 2;
117              else
118                 level = 3;
119
120           } // end method levelRadioButtons_Click
121
122       } // end class Tutor
123
124   } // end namespace EquationGeneratorClient
```

Fig. 21.26 Math tutor application. (Part 3 of 4.)

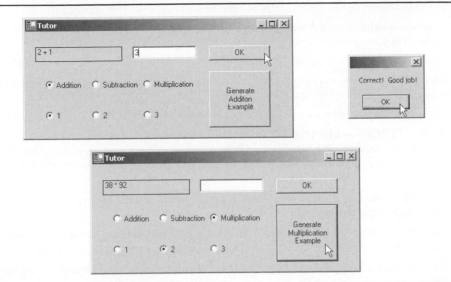

Fig. 21.26 Math tutor application. (Part 4 of 4.)

Event handler **generateButton_Click** (lines 50–64) invokes **Generator** method **GenerateEquation**. The left-hand side of the equation is displayed in **questionLabel** (line 59), and **okButton** is enabled so that the user can enter an answer. When the user clicks **OK**, **okButton_Click** (lines 67–88) checks whether the user provided the correct answer.

This chapter and the previous familiarized readers with the creation of Web applications and Web services, both of which enable users to request and receive data via the Internet. In the next chapter, we discuss the low-level details of how data are sent from one location to another (this process is called networking). Topics discussed in the next chapter include the implementation of servers and clients and the sending of data via sockets.

SUMMARY

- A Web service is an application that is stored on a remote machine and accessed through a remote procedure call.

- Distributed systems technologies enable applications to execute across multiple computers on a network.

- Web-services method calls are implemented using Simple Object Access Protocol (SOAP), an XML-based protocol describing how requests and responses are marked up so that they can be transferred via protocols such as HTTP.

- Methods are executed using a Remote Procedure Call (RPC). These methods are marked with the **WebMethod** attribute and are often referred to as Web-service methods.

- Requests to and responses from Web services are sent using SOAP by default. As long as a client can create and understand SOAP messages, the client can use Web services, regardless of the programming languages in which the Web services are written.

- A Web service in .NET has two parts: an ASMX file and a code-behind file.

- The ASMX file can be viewed in any Web browser and displays information about the Web service.

- The code-behind file contains the definition for the methods in the Web service.
- A service description is an XML document that conforms to the Web Service Description Language (WSDL).
- WSDL is an XML vocabulary that describes how Web services behave.
- The service description can be used by a client program to confirm the correctness of method calls at compile time.
- The ASMX file also provides a way for clients to execute test runs of the Web-service methods.
- SOAP, HTTP GET and HTTP POST are the three different ways of sending and receiving messages in Web services. The format used for these request and response messages is sometimes known as the wire protocol or wire format, because the format defines how information is sent "along the wire."
- The Simple Object Access Protocol (SOAP) is a platform-independent protocol that uses XML to make remote-procedure calls over HTTP.
- Requests to and responses from a Web-service method are packaged by default in a SOAP message—an XML message containing all the information necessary to process its contents.
- SOAP allows Web services to employ a variety of data types, including user-defined data types.
- When a program invokes a Web-service method, the request and all relevant information are packaged in a SOAP message and sent to the appropriate destination.
- When the Web service receives the SOAP message, it processes the message's contents, which specifies the method that the client wishes to execute and the arguments the client is passing to that method.
- When the Web service receives a request, the request is parsed, and the proper method is called with the specified arguments (if there are any). The response is sent back to the client as another SOAP message.
- An application that uses a Web service consists of two parts: a proxy class for the Web service and a client application that accesses the Web service via the proxy.
- A proxy class handles the task of transferring the arguments passed from the client into a SOAP message that is sent to the Web service. The proxy likewise handles the transferring of information in the SOAP response to the client.
- The **Namespace** property of a **WebService** attribute uniquely identifies a Web service.
- The **Description** property of a **WebService** attribute adds a description of the Web service when the Web service is displayed in a browser.
- Class **WebService** provides members that determine information about the user, the application and other topics relevant to the Web service.
- A Web service is not required to inherit from class **WebService**.
- A programmer specifies a method as a Web-service method by tagging it with the **WebMethod** attribute.
- Visual Studio provides a design view for each Web service, which allows the programmer to add components to the application.
- A proxy class is created from the Web service's WSDL file that enables the client to call Web-service methods over the Internet.
- Whenever a call is made in a client application to a Web-service method, a method in the proxy class is called. This method takes the method name and arguments passed by the client and formats them so that they can be sent as a request in a SOAP message.

- By default, the namespace of a proxy class is the name of the domain in which the Web service resides.
- UDDI is a project for developing a set of specifications that define how Web services should be discovered so that programmers searching for Web services can find them.
- A DISCO file is a file that specifies any Web services that are available in the current directory.
- There are two types of discovery files: Dynamic discovery files (**.vsdisco** extension) and static discovery files (**.disco** extension).
- Once a Web reference is created, a static discovery file is placed in the client's project. The static discovery file hard codes the locations of the ASMX and WSDL files.
- Dynamic discovery files are created so that a list of Web services is created when a client is searching for Web services.
- To store session information, the **EnableSession** property of the **WebMethod** attribute must be set to **true**.
- The use of session state in a Web service can make coding easier and reduce overhead.
- When storing session information, a Web service must have a way of identifying users between method calls. The approach is implemented using cookies, which are stored in a **CookieContainer**.
- Types can be defined by a programmer and used in a Web service. These types can be passed into or returned from Web-service methods.
- User-defined types can be sent to or returned from Web-service methods, because the types are defined in the proxy class created for the client.
- Custom types that are sent to or from a Web service are serialized as XML.
- Any object returned by a Web-service method must have a default constructor.
- Any variables of a custom type that we wish to make available to clients must be declared **public**.
- Properties of a custom type that we wish to make available to clients must have both **get** and **set** accessors defined.
- When an object is returned from a Web service, all its **public** properties and fields are marked up in XML. This information can then be transferred back into an object on the client side.

TERMINOLOGY

Add Web Reference dialog
ASMX file
ASP.NET Web Service project type
code-behind file in Web services
consuming a Web service
CookieContainer class
CookieContainer property
creating a proxy class for a Web service
Description property of a **WebMethod** attribute
Description property of a **WebService** attribute
.disco file extension
discovery (DISCO) files
distributed computing
distributed system

EnableSession property of a **WebMethod** attribute
exposing a Web-service method
firewall
Invoke button
Namespace property of a **WebService** attribute
OpenRead method of class **WebClient**
proxy class
publishing a Web service
remote machine
Remote Procedure Call (RPC)
session tracking in Web services
Simple Object Access Protocol (SOAP)
SOAP envelope
SOAP message

SOAP request
System.Net
Uniform Resource Locator (URL)
Universal Description, Discovery and
  Integration (UDDI)
.vsdisco file extension
Web service
Web Service Description Language (WSDL)

Web-service method
WebClient class
WebMethod attribute
WebService attribute
WebService class
wire format
wire protocol
XML serialization

SELF-REVIEW EXERCISES

21.1 State whether each of the following is *true* or *false*. If *false*, explain why.
   a) The purpose of a Web service is to create objects that are instantiated and used on the local machine.
   b) A Web server is required to create Web services and make them available.
   c) If a Web service is referenced by adding a Web reference to a client in Visual Studio .NET, a proxy class is not created.
   d) In .NET, a program communicating with a Web service uses HTTP GET by default to send and receive messages.
   e) A client can use only Web-service methods that are tagged with the **WebMethod** attribute.
   f) To enable session tracking in a Web-service method, the programmer sets the **EnableSession** property to **true** in the **WebMethod** attribute. No other action is required.
   g) An application can use only one Web service.
   h) Not all primitive data types can be returned from a Web service.
   i) **WebMethod**s methods cannot be declared **static**.
   j) A user-defined type used in a Web service must define both **get** and **set** accessors for any property that will be accessed in an application.

21.2 Fill in the blanks for each of the following statements:
   a) When messages are sent between an application and a Web service, each message is placed in a _____.
   b) A Web service can inherit from class _____.
   c) The class that defines a Web service usually is located in the _____ file for that Web service.
   d) The format used by a Web service to send and receive messages is usually known as the _____ or _____.
   e) A _____ file specifies any Web services that are available in the current directory.
   f) Class _____ is designed for interaction with resources identified by a URL.
   g) Web-service requests are sent over the Internet via the _____ protocol.
   h) To add a description for a Web service method in an ASMX page, the _____ property of the **WebService** attribute is used.
   i) Sending objects between a Web service and a client requires _____ of the object.
   j) A proxy class is defined in a namespace whose name is that of the _____ in which the Web service is defined.

ANSWERS TO SELF-REVIEW EXERCISES

21.1 a) False. Web services are used to execute methods on remote machines. The Web service receives the parameters it needs to execute a particular method, executes the method and then returns the result to the caller. b) True. c) True. d) False. A program communicating with a Web service uses

SOAP by default to send and receive messages. e) True. f) False. A **CookieContainer** also must be created on the client side. g) False. An application can use as many Web services as it needs. h) True. i) True. j) True.

21.2   a) SOAP message. b) **WebService**. c) code-behind. d) wire format, wire protocol. e) **.disco**. f) **WebClient**. g) HTTP. h) **Description**. i) XML serialization. j) domain.

EXERCISES

21.3   Create a Web service that stores phone-book entries in a database. Give the user the capability to enter new contacts and to find contacts by last name. Pass only primitive types as arguments to the Web service.

21.4   Modify Exercise 21.3 so that it uses a class named **PhoneBookEntry**. The client application should provide objects of type **PhoneBookEntry** to the Web service when adding contacts and should receive objects of type **PhoneBookEntry** when searching for contacts.

21.5   Modify the **Blackjack** Web service example in Section 21.5 to include a class **Card**. Have **DealCard** return an object of type **Card**. Also, have the client application keep track of what cards have been dealt, using **Card**s. Your card class should include properties to determine the face and suit of the card.

21.6   Modify the airline reservation example in Section 21.6 so that it contains two separate Web methods—one that allows users to view all available seats and another that allows users to reserve seats. Use an object of type **Ticket** to pass information to and from the Web service. This Web application should list all available seats in a **ListBox** and then allow the user to click a seat to reserve it. Your application must be able to handle cases where two users view available seats, one reserves a seat, and then the second user tries to reserve the same seat, not knowing that the database has changed since the page was loaded.

21.7   Modify the **TemperatureServer** example in Section 21.7 so that it returns an array of **CityWeather** objects that the client application uses to display the weather information.

21.8   Modify the Web service in the math-tutor example in Section 21.8 so that it includes a method that calculates how "close" the player is to the correct answer. The client application should provide the correct answer only after a user has offered numerous answers that were far from the correct one. Use your best judgment regarding what constitutes being "close" to the right answer. Remember that there should be a different formula for one-digit, two-digit and three-digit numbers. Also, give the program the capability of suggesting that users try a lower difficulty level if the users are consistently wrong.

22

Networking: Streams-Based Sockets and Datagrams

Objectives

- To be able to implement C# networking applications that use sockets and datagrams.
- To understand how to implement C# clients and servers that communicate with one another.
- To understand how to implement network-based collaborative applications.
- To construct a multithreaded server.

If the presence of electricity can be made visible in any part of a circuit, I see no reason why intelligence may not be transmitted instantaneously by electricity.
Samuel F. B. Morse

Mr. Watson, come here, I want you.
Alexander Graham Bell

What networks of railroads, highways and canals were in another age, the networks of telecommunications, information and computerization ... are today.
Bruno Kreisky, Austrian Chancellor

Science may never come up with a better office-communication system than the coffee break.
Earl Wilson

22.1 Introduction

The Internet and the World Wide Web have generated a great deal of excitement in the business and computing communities. The Internet ties the "information world" together; the Web makes the Internet easy to use while providing the flair of multimedia. Organizations see both the Internet and the Web as crucial to their information-systems strategies. C# and the .NET Framework offer a number of built-in networking capabilities that facilitate Internet-based and Web-based applications development. C# not only can specify parallelism through multithreading, but also can enable programs to search the Web for information and collaborate with programs running on other computers internationally.

In Chapters 20 and 21, we began our presentation of C#'s networking and distributed-computing capabilities. We discussed Web Forms and Web Services, two high-level networking technologies that enable programmers to develop distributed applications in C#. In this chapter, we focus on the networking technologies that support C#'s ASP.NET capabilities and can be used to build distributed applications.

Our discussion of networking focuses on both sides of a *client–server relationship*. The *client* requests that some action be performed; the *server* performs the action and responds to the client. A common implementation of this request–response model is between Web browsers and Web servers. When users select Web sites that they wish to view through a browser (the client application), the browser makes a request to the appropriate Web server (the server application). The server normally responds to the client by sending the appropriate HTML Web pages.

C#'s networking capabilities are grouped into several namespaces. The fundamental networking capabilities are defined by classes and interfaces of namespace **System.Net.Sockets**. Through this namespace, C# offers *socket-based communications*, which enable developers to view networking as if it were file I/O. This means that a program can read from a *socket* (network connection) or write to a socket as easily as it can read from or write to a file. Sockets are the fundamental way to perform network communications in the .NET Framework. The term "socket" refers to the Berkeley Sockets Interface, which was developed in 1978 for network programming with UNIX and was popularized by C and C++ programmers.

The classes and interfaces of namespace **System.Net.Sockets** also offer *packet-based communications*, through which individual *packets* of information are transmitted—

this is a common method of transmitting audio and video over the Internet. In this chapter, we show how to create and manipulate sockets and how to communicate via packets of data.

Socket-based communications in C# employ *stream sockets*. With stream sockets, a *process* (running program) establishes a *connection* to another process. While the connection is in place, data flows between the processes in continuous *streams*. For this reason, stream sockets are said to provide a *connection-oriented service*. The popular *TCP (Transmission Control Protocol)* facilitates stream-socket transmission.

By contrast, packet-based communications in C# employ *datagram sockets*, through which individual *packets* of information are transmitted. Unlike TCP, the protocol used to enable datagram sockets—*UDP*, the *User Datagram Protocol*—is a *connectionless service* and does not guarantee that packets will arrive in any particular order. In fact, packets can be lost or duplicated and can arrive out of sequence. Applications that use UDP often require significant extra programming to deal with these problems. UDP is most appropriate for network applications that do not require the error checking and reliability of TCP. For example, several online multi-player games use UDP, because speed is more important than perfect accuracy in these types of applications. Stream sockets and the TCP protocol will be the most desirable method of communication for the vast majority of C# programmers.

Performance Tip 22.1

Connectionless services generally offer better performance but less reliability than do connection-oriented services.

Portability Tip 22.1

The TCP protocol and its related set of protocols enable intercommunication among a wide variety of heterogeneous computer systems (i.e., computer systems with different processors and different operating systems).

22.2 Establishing a Simple Server (Using Stream Sockets)

Typically, with TCP and stream sockets, a server "waits" for a connection request from a client. Often, the server program contains a control structure or block of code that executes continuously until the server receives a request. On receiving a request, the server establishes a connection with the client. The server then uses this connection to handle future requests from that client and to send data to the client.

The establishment of a simple server with TCP and stream sockets in C# requires five steps. The first step is to create an object of class **TcpListener**, which belongs to namespace **System.Net.Sockets**. This class represents a TCP stream socket through which a server can listen for requests. A call to the **TcpListener** constructor, such as

```
TcpListener server = new TcpListener( port );
```

binds (assigns) the server to the specified *port number*. A port number is a numeric identifier that a process uses to identify itself at a given *network address*, also known as an *Internet Protocol Address (IP Address)*. IP addresses identify computers on the Internet. In fact, Web-site names, such as **www.deitel.com**, are aliases for IP addresses. Any process that performs networking identifies itself via an *IP address/port number pair*. Hence, no two processes can have the same port number at a given IP address. The explicit binding of a socket to a port (using method **Bind** of class **Socket**) is usually unnecessary, because class **TcpListener** and other classes discussed in this chapter hide this binding (i.e., bind sockets to ports implicitly), plus they perform other socket-initialization operations.

Software Engineering Observation 22.1

Port numbers can have values between 0 and 65535. Many operating systems reserve port numbers below 1024 for system services (such as e-mail and Web servers). Applications must be granted special privileges to use these reserved port numbers. Usually, a server-side application should not specify port numbers below 1024 as connection ports, because some operating systems might reserve these numbers.

Common Programming Error 22.1

Attempting to bind an already assigned port at a given IP address is a logic error.

To receive requests, the **TcpListener** first must listen for them. The second step in our connection process is to call **TcpListener**'s *Start* method, which causes the **TcpListener** object to begin listening for connection requests. The third step establishes the connection between the server and client. The server listens indefinitely for a request—i.e., the execution of the server-side application waits until some client attempts to connect with it. The server creates a connection to the client upon receipt of a connection request. An object of class *System.Net.Sockets.Socket* manages each connection to the client. Method *AcceptSocket* of class **TcpListener** waits for a connection request, then creates a connection when a request is received. This method returns a **Socket** object upon connection, as in the statement

```
Socket connection = server.AcceptSocket();
```

When the server receives a request, method **AcceptSocket** calls method *Accept* of the **TcpListener**'s underlying **Socket** to make the connection. This is an example of C#'s hiding of networking complexity from the programmer. The programmer can write the preceding statement into a server-side program, then allow the classes of namespace **System.Net.Sockets** to handle the details of accepting requests and establishing connections.

Step four is the processing phase, in which the server and the client communicate via methods *Receive* and *Send* of class **Socket**. Note that these methods, as well as TCP and stream sockets, can be used only when the server and client are connected. By contrast, through **Socket** methods *SendTo* and *ReceiveFrom*, UDP and datagram sockets can be used when no connection exists.

The fifth step is the connection-termination phase. When the client and server have finished communicating, the server uses method *Close* of the **Socket** object to close the connection. Most servers then return to step two (i.e., wait for another client's connection request).

One problem associated with the server scheme described in this section is that step four *blocks* other requests while processing a client's request, so that no other client can connect with the server while the code that defines the processing phase is executing. The most common technique for addressing this problem is to use multithreaded servers, which place the processing-phase code in a separate thread. When the server receives a connection request, the server *spawns*, or creates, a **Thread** to process the connection, leaving its **TcpListener** (or **Socket**) free to receive other connections.

Software Engineering Observation 22.2

Using C#'s multithreading capabilities, we can create servers that can manage simultaneous connections with multiple clients. This multithreaded-server architecture is precisely what popular UNIX and Windows network servers use.

Software Engineering Observation 22.3

*A multithreaded server can be implemented to create a thread that manages network I/O across a reference to a **Socket** object returned by method **AcceptSocket**. A multi-threaded server also can be implemented to maintain a pool of threads that manage network I/O across newly created **Socket**s.*

Performance Tip 22.2

*In high-performance systems with abundant memory, a multithreaded server can be implemented to create a pool of threads. These threads can be assigned quickly to handle network I/O across each multiple **Socket**. Thus, when a connection is received, the server does not incur the overhead of thread creation.*

22.3 Establishing a Simple Client (Using Stream Sockets)

We create TCP-stream-socket clients via a process that requires four steps. In the first step, we create an object of class **TcpClient** (which belongs to namespace **System.Net.Sockets**) to connect to the server. This connection is established through method **Connect** of class **TcpClient**. One overloaded version of this method receives two arguments—the server's IP address and the port number—as in the following:

```
TcpClient client = new TcpClient();
client.Connect( serverAddress, serverPort );
```

Here, **serverPort** is an **int** that represents the server's port number; **serverAddress** can be either an **IPAddress** instance (that encapsulates the server's IP address) or a **string** that specifies the server's hostname. Alternatively, the programmer could pass an object reference of class **IPEndPoint**, which represents an IP address/port number pair, to a different overload of method **Connect**. Method **Connect** of class **TcpClient** calls method **Connect** of class **Socket** to establish the connection. If the connection is successful, method **TcpClient.Connect** returns a positive integer; otherwise, it returns **0**.

In step two, the **TcpClient** uses its method **GetStream** to get a **NetworkStream** so that it can write to and read from the server. **NetworkStream** methods **WriteByte** and **Write** can be used to output individual bytes or sets of bytes to the server, respectively; similarly, **NetworkStream** methods **ReadByte** and **Read** can be used to input individual bytes or sets of bytes from the server, respectively.

The third step is the processing phase, in which the client and the server communicate. In this phase, the client uses methods **Read**, **ReadByte**, **Write** and **WriteByte** of class **NetworkStream** to perform the appropriate communications. Using a process similar to that used by servers, a client can employ threads to prevent blocking of communications with other servers while processing data from one connection.

After the transmission is complete, step four requires the client to close the connection by calling method **Close** of the **NetworkStream** object. This closes the underlying

Socket (if the **NetworkStream** has a reference to that **Socket**). Then, the client calls method *Close* of class **TcpClient** to terminate the TCP connection. At this point, a new connection can be established through method **Connect**, as we have described.

22.4 Client/Server Interaction with Stream-Socket Connections

The applications in Fig. 22.1 and Fig. 22.2 use the classes and techniques discussed in the previous two sections to construct a simple *client/server chat application*. The server waits for a client's request to make a connection. When a client application connects to the server, the server application sends an array of bytes to the client, indicating that the connection was successful. The client then displays a message notifying the user that a connection has been established.

Both the client and the server applications contain **TextBox**es that enable users to type messages and send them to the other application. When either the client or the server sends message "**TERMINATE**," the connection between the client and the server terminates. The server then waits for another client to request a connection. Figure 22.1 and Fig. 22.2 provide the code for classes **Server** and **Client**, respectively. Figure 22.2 also contains screen captures displaying the execution between the client and the server.

```
1   // Fig. 22.1: Server.cs
2   // Set up a Server that will receive a connection from a client,
3   // send a string to the client, and close the connection.
4
5   using System;
6   using System.Drawing;
7   using System.Collections;
8   using System.ComponentModel;
9   using System.Windows.Forms;
10  using System.Threading;
11  using System.Net.Sockets;
12  using System.IO;
13
14  // server that awaits client connections (one at a time) and
15  // allows a conversation between client and server
16  public class Server : System.Windows.Forms.Form
17  {
18      private System.Windows.Forms.TextBox inputTextBox;
19      private System.Windows.Forms.TextBox displayTextBox;
20      private Socket connection;
21      private Thread readThread;
22
23      private System.ComponentModel.Container components = null;
24      private NetworkStream socketStream;
25      private BinaryWriter writer;
26      private BinaryReader reader;
27
```

Fig. 22.1 Server portion of a client/server stream-socket connection. (Part 1 of 4.)

```
28        // default constructor
29        public Server()
30        {
31            InitializeComponent();
32
33            // create a new thread from the server
34            readThread = new Thread( new ThreadStart( RunServer ) );
35            readThread.Start();
36        }
37
38        // Visual Studio .NET generated code
39
40        [STAThread]
41        static void Main()
42        {
43            Application.Run( new Server() );
44        }
45
46        protected void Server_Closing(
47            object sender, CancelEventArgs e )
48        {
49            System.Environment.Exit( System.Environment.ExitCode );
50        }
51
52        // sends the text typed at the server to the client
53        protected void inputTextBox_KeyDown(
54            object sender, KeyEventArgs e )
55        {
56            // sends the text to the client
57            try
58            {
59                if ( e.KeyCode == Keys.Enter && connection != null )
60                {
61                    writer.Write( "SERVER>>> " + inputTextBox.Text );
62
63                    displayTextBox.Text +=
64                        "\r\nSERVER>>> " + inputTextBox.Text;
65
66                    // if the user at the server signaled termination
67                    // sever the connection to the client
68                    if ( inputTextBox.Text == "TERMINATE" )
69                        connection.Close();
70
71                    inputTextBox.Clear();
72                }
73            }
74            catch ( SocketException )
75            {
76                displayTextBox.Text += "\nError writing object";
77            }
78        } // inputTextBox_KeyDown
79
```

Fig. 22.1   Server portion of a client/server stream-socket connection. (Part 2 of 4.)

```
80          // allows a client to connect and displays the text it sends
81          public void RunServer()
82          {
83             TcpListener listener;
84             int counter = 1;
85
86             // wait for a client connection and display the text
87             // that the client sends
88             try
89             {
90                // Step 1: create TcpListener
91                listener = new TcpListener( 5000 );
92
93                // Step 2: TcpListener waits for connection request
94                listener.Start();
95
96                // Step 3: establish connection upon client request
97                while ( true )
98                {
99                   displayTextBox.Text = "Waiting for connection\r\n";
100                                                              •
101                   // accept an incoming connection
102                   connection = listener.AcceptSocket();
103
104                   // create NetworkStream object associated with socket
105                   socketStream = new NetworkStream( connection );
106
107                   // create objects for transferring data across stream
108                   writer = new BinaryWriter( socketStream );
109                   reader = new BinaryReader( socketStream );
110
111                   displayTextBox.Text += "Connection " + counter +
112                      " received.\r\n";
113
114                   // inform client that connection was successfull
115                   writer.Write( "SERVER>>> Connection successful" );
116
117                   inputTextBox.ReadOnly = false;
118                   string theReply = "";
119
120                   // Step 4: read String data sent from client
121                   do
122                   {
123                      try
124                      {
125                         // read the string sent to the server
126                         theReply = reader.ReadString();
127
128                         // display the message
129                         displayTextBox.Text += "\r\n" + theReply;
130                      }
131
```

Fig. 22.1   Server portion of a client/server stream-socket connection. (Part 3 of 4.)

```
132                 // handle exception if error reading data
133                 catch ( Exception )
134                 {
135                     break;
136                 }
137
138             } while ( theReply != "CLIENT>>> TERMINATE"  &&
139                 connection.Connected );
140
141             displayTextBox.Text +=
142                 "\r\nUser terminated connection";
143
144             // Step 5: close connection
145             inputTextBox.ReadOnly = true;
146             writer.Close();
147             reader.Close();
148             socketStream.Close();
149             connection.Close();
150
151             ++counter;
152         }
153     } // end try
154
155     catch ( Exception error )
156     {
157         MessageBox.Show( error.ToString() );
158     }
159
160   } // end method RunServer
161
162 } // end class Server
```

Fig. 22.1   Server portion of a client/server stream-socket connection. (Part 4 of 4.)

```
1   // Fig. 22.2: Client.cs
2   // Set up a Client that will read information sent from a Server
3   // and display the information.
4
5   using System;
6   using System.Drawing;
7   using System.Collections;
8   using System.ComponentModel;
9   using System.Windows.Forms;
10  using System.Threading;
11  using System.Net.Sockets;
12  using System.IO;
13
14  // connects to a chat server
15  public class Client : System.Windows.Forms.Form
16  {
17      private System.Windows.Forms.TextBox inputTextBox;
```

Fig. 22.2   Client portion of a client/server stream-socket connection. (Part 1 of 5.)

```
18      private System.Windows.Forms.TextBox displayTextBox;
19
20      private NetworkStream output;
21      private BinaryWriter writer;
22      private BinaryReader reader;
23
24      private string message = "";
25
26      private Thread readThread;
27
28      private System.ComponentModel.Container components = null;
29
30      // default constructor
31      public Client()
32      {
33         InitializeComponent();
34
35         readThread = new Thread( new ThreadStart( RunClient ) );
36         readThread.Start();
37      }
38
39      // Visual Studio .NET-generated code
40
41      [STAThread]
42      static void Main()
43      {
44         Application.Run( new Client() );
45      }
46
47      protected void Client_Closing(
48         object sender, CancelEventArgs e )
49      {
50         System.Environment.Exit( System.Environment.ExitCode );
51      }
52
53      // sends text the user typed to server
54      protected void inputTextBox_KeyDown (
55         object sender, KeyEventArgs e )
56      {
57         try
58         {
59            if ( e.KeyCode == Keys.Enter )
60            {
61               writer.Write( "CLIENT>>> " + inputTextBox.Text );
62
63               displayTextBox.Text +=
64                  "\r\nCLIENT>>> " + inputTextBox.Text;
65
66               inputTextBox.Clear();
67            }
68         }
```

Fig. 22.2   Client portion of a client/server stream-socket connection. (Part 2 of 5.)

```
69          catch ( SocketException ioe )
70          {
71              displayTextBox.Text += "\nError writing object";
72          }
73
74      } // end method inputTextBox_KeyDown
75
76      // connect to server and display server-generated text
77      public void RunClient()
78      {
79          TcpClient client;
80
81          // instantiate TcpClient for sending data to server
82          try
83          {
84              displayTextBox.Text += "Attempting connection\r\n";
85
86              // Step 1: create TcpClient and connect to server
87              client = new TcpClient();
88              client.Connect( "localhost", 5000 );
89
90              // Step 2: get NetworkStream associated with TcpClient
91              output = client.GetStream();
92
93              // create objects for writing and reading across stream
94              writer = new BinaryWriter( output );
95              reader = new BinaryReader( output );
96
97              displayTextBox.Text += "\r\nGot I/O streams\r\n";
98
99              inputTextBox.ReadOnly = false;
100
101             // loop until server signals termination
102             do
103             {
104
105                 // Step 3: processing phase
106                 try
107                 {
108                     // read message from server
109                     message = reader.ReadString();
110                     displayTextBox.Text += "\r\n" + message;
111                 }
112
113                 // handle exception if error in reading server data
114                 catch ( Exception )
115                 {
116                     System.Environment.Exit(
117                         System.Environment.ExitCode );
118                 }
119             } while( message != "SERVER>>> TERMINATE" );
120
```

Fig. 22.2   Client portion of a client/server stream-socket connection. (Part 3 of 5.)

```
121                displayTextBox.Text += "\r\nClosing connection.\r\n";
122
123            // Step 4: close connection
124            writer.Close();
125            reader.Close();
126            output.Close();
127            client.Close();
128            Application.Exit();
129        }
130
131        // handle exception if error in establishing connection
132        catch ( Exception error )
133        {
134            MessageBox.Show( error.ToString() );
135        }
136
137    } // end method RunClient
138
139 } // end class Client
```

Fig. 22.2   Client portion of a client/server stream-socket connection. (Part 4 of 5.)

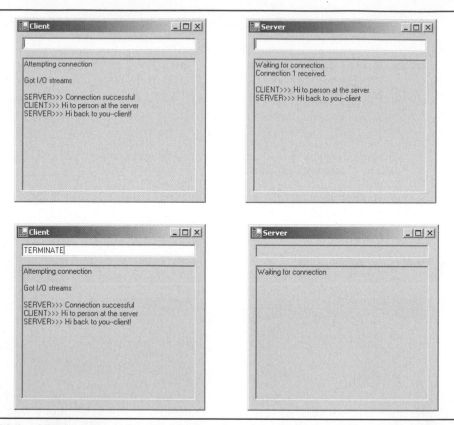

Fig. 22.2 Client portion of a client/server stream-socket connection. (Part 5 of 5.)

As we analyze this example, we begin by discussing class **Server** (Fig. 22.1). In the constructor, line 34 creates a **Thread** that will accept connections from clients. Line 35 starts the **Thread**, which invokes method **RunServer** (lines 81–160). Method **Run-Server** initializes the server to receive connection requests and process connections. Line 91 instantiates the **TcpListener** to listen for a connection request from a client at port **5000** (Step 1). Line 94 then calls method **Start** of the **TcpListener** object, which causes the **TcpListener** to begin waiting for requests (Step 2).

Lines 97–152 declare an infinite **while** loop that establishes connections requested by clients (Step 3). Line 102 calls method **AcceptSocket** of the **TcpListener** object, which returns a **Socket** upon successful connection. The thread in which method **AcceptSocket** is called stops executing until a connection is established. The **Socket** object will manage the connection. Line 105 passes this **Socket** object as an argument to the constructor of a **NetworkStream** object. Class **NetworkStream** provides access to streams across a network—in this example, the **NetworkStream** object provides access to the **Socket** connection. Lines 108–109 create instances of the ***BinaryWriter*** and ***BinaryReader*** classes for writing and reading data. We pass the **Network-Stream** object as an argument to each constructor; **BinaryWriter** can write bytes to the **NetworkStream**, and **BinaryReader** can read bytes from **NetworkStream**. Lines 111–112 append text to the **TextBox**, indicating that a connection was received.

BinaryWriter method *Write* has many overloaded versions, which enable the method to write various types to a stream. (You might remember that we used these overloaded methods in Chapter 17 to write record data to files.) Line 115 uses method **Write** to send to the client a **string** notifying the user of a successful connection. Lines 121–139 declare a **do/while** structure that executes until the server receives a message indicating connection termination (i.e., **CLIENT>>> TERMINATE**). Line 126 uses **BinaryReader** method *ReadString* to read a **string** from the stream (Step 4). (You might remember that we also used this method in Chapter 17 to read records' first-name and last-name **string**s from files.) Method **ReadString** blocks until a **string** is read. To prevent the whole server from blocking, we use a separate **Thread** to handle the transfer of information. The **while** statement loops until there is more information to read—this results in I/O blocking, which causes the program always to appear frozen. However, if we run this portion of the program in a separate **Thread**, the user can interact with the Windows **Form** and send messages while the program waits in the background for incoming messages.

When the chat is complete, lines 146–149 close the **BinaryWriter**, **BinaryReader**, **NetworkStream** and **Socket** (Step 5) by invoking their respective **Close** methods. The server then waits for another client connection request by returning to the beginning of the **while** loop (line 97).

When the user of the server application enters a **string** in the **TextBox** and presses the *Enter* key, event handler **inputTextBox_KeyDown** (lines 53–78) reads the **string** and sends it via method **Write** of class **BinaryWriter**. If a user terminates the server application, line 69 calls method **Close** of the **Socket** object to close the connection.

Lines 46–50 define the **Server_Closing** event handler for the **Closing** event. The event closes the application and uses **System.Environment.Exit** method with parameter **System.Environment.ExitCode** to terminate all threads. Method **Exit** of class **Environment** closes all threads associated with the application.

Figure 22.2 lists the code for the **Client** object. Like the **Server** object, the **Client** object creates a **Thread** (lines 35–36) in its constructor to handle all incoming messages. **Client** method **RunClient** (lines 77–137) connects to the **Server**, receives data from the **Server** and sends data to the **Server** (when the user presses *Enter*). Lines 87–88 instantiate a **TcpClient** object, then call its method **Connect** to establish a connection (Step 1). The first argument to method **Connect** is the name of the server—in our case, the server's name is *"localhost"*, meaning that the server is located on the same machine as the client. The **localhost** is also known as the *loopback IP address* and is equivalent to the IP address *127.0.0.1*. This value sends the data transmission back to the sender's IP address. [*Note*: We chose to demonstrate the client/server relationship by connecting between programs that are executing on the same computer (**localhost**). Normally, this argument would contain the Internet address of another computer.] The second argument to method **Connect** is the server port number. This number must match the port number at which the server waits for connections.

The **Client** uses a **NetworkStream** to send data to and receive data from the server. The client obtains the **NetworkStream** on line 91 through a call to **TcpClient** method **GetStream** (Step 2). The **do/while** structure in lines 102–119 loops until the client receives the connection-termination message (**SERVER>>> TERMINATE**). Line 109 uses **BinaryReader** method **ReadString** to obtain the next message from the server (Step

3). Line 110 displays the message, and lines 124–127 close the **BinaryWriter**, **BinaryReader**, **NetworkStream** and **TcpClient** objects (Step 4).

When the user of the client application enters a **string** in the **TextBox** and presses the *Enter* key, the event handler **inputTextBox_KeyDown** (lines 54–74) reads the **string** from the **TextBox** and sends it via **BinaryWriter** method **Write**. Notice that, here, the **Server** receives a connection, processes it, closes it and waits for the next one. In a real-world application, a server would likely receive a connection, set up the connection to be processed as a separate thread of execution and wait for new connections. The separate threads that process existing connections can continue to execute while the **Server** concentrates on new connection requests.

22.5 Connectionless Client/Server Interaction with Datagrams

Up to this point, we have discussed connection-oriented, streams-based transmission. Now, we consider connectionless transmission using datagrams.

Connection-oriented transmission is similar to interaction over a telephone system, in which a user dials a number and is *connected* to the telephone of the party they wish to connect. The system maintains the connection for the duration of the phone call, regardless of whether the users are speaking.

By contrast, connectionless transmission via *datagrams* more closely resembles the method by which the postal service carries and delivers mail. Connectionless transmission bundles and sends information in *packets* called datagrams, which can be thought of as similar to posted letters. If a large message will not fit in one envelope, that message is broken into separate message pieces and placed in separate, sequentially numbered envelopes. All the letters are mailed at once. The letters might arrive in order, out of order or not at all. The person at the receiving end reassembles the message pieces into sequential order before attempting to interpret the message. If the message is small enough to fit in one envelope, the sequencing problem is eliminated, but it is still possible that the message will never arrive. (Unlike with posted mail, duplicate of datagrams could reach receiving computers.) C# provides the **UdpClient** class for connectionless transmission. Like **TcpListener** and **TcpClient**, **UdpClient** uses methods from class **Socket**. The **UdpClient** methods **Send** and **Receive** are used to transmit data with **Socket**'s **SendTo** method and to read data with **Socket**'s **ReceiveFrom** method, respectively.

The programs in Fig. 22.3 and Fig. 22.4 use datagrams to send *packets* of information between a client and server applications. In the **Client** application, the user types a message into a **TextBox** and presses *Enter*. The client converts the message to a **byte** array and sends it to the server. The server receives the packet and displays the packet's information, then *echoes*, or returns, the packet back to the client. When the client receives the packet, the client displays the packet's information. In this example, the implementations of the **Client** and **Server** classes are similar.

```
1   // Fig. 22.3: Server.cs
2   // Set up a Server that will receive packets from a
3   // client and send packets to a client.
4
```

Fig. 22.3 Server-side portion of connectionless client/server computing. (Part 1 of 3.)

```
 5  using System;
 6  using System.Drawing;
 7  using System.Collections;
 8  using System.ComponentModel;
 9  using System.Windows.Forms;
10  using System.Data;
11  using System.Net;
12  using System.Net.Sockets;
13  using System.Threading;
14
15  // create the UDP server
16  public class Server : System.Windows.Forms.Form
17  {
18     private System.Windows.Forms.TextBox displayTextBox;
19     private UdpClient client;
20     private IPEndPoint receivePoint;
21     private System.ComponentModel.Container components = null;
22
23     // no-argument constructor
24     public Server()
25     {
26        InitializeComponent();
27
28        client = new UdpClient( 5000 );
29        receivePoint = new IPEndPoint( new IPAddress( 0 ), 0 );
30        Thread readThread = new Thread(
31           new ThreadStart( WaitForPackets ) );
32
33        readThread.Start();
34     }
35
36     // Visual Studio .NET generated code
37
38     [STAThread]
39     static void Main()
40     {
41        Application.Run( new Server() );
42     }
43
44     // shut down the server
45     protected void Server_Closing(
46        object sender, CancelEventArgs e )
47     {
48        System.Environment.Exit( System.Environment.ExitCode );
49     }
50
51     // wait for a packet to arrive
52     public void WaitForPackets()
53     {
54        while ( true )
55        {
56           // receive byte array from client
57           byte[] data = client.Receive( ref receivePoint );
```

Fig. 22.3 Server-side portion of connectionless client/server computing. (Part 2 of 3.)

```
58
59             // output packet data to TextBox
60             displayTextBox.Text += "\r\nPacket received:" +
61                "\r\nLength: " + data.Length + "\r\nContaining: " +
62                System.Text.Encoding.ASCII.GetString( data );
63
64             displayTextBox.Text +=
65                "\r\n\r\nEcho data back to client...";
66
67             // echo information from packet back to client
68             client.Send( data, data.Length, receivePoint );
69             displayTextBox.Text += "\r\nPacket sent\r\n";
70          }
71
72      } // end method WaitForPackets
73
74   } // end class Server
```

Fig. 22.3   Server-side portion of connectionless client/server computing. (Part 3 of 3.)

```
1   // Fig. 22.4: Client.cs
2   // Set up a Client that sends packets to a server and receives
3   // packets from a server.
4
5   using System;
6   using System.Drawing;
7   using System.Collections;
8   using System.ComponentModel;
9   using System.Windows.Forms;
10  using System.Data;
11  using System.Net;
12  using System.Net.Sockets;
13  using System.Threading;
14
```

Fig. 22.4   Client portion of connectionless client/server computing. (Part 1 of 3.)

```
15   // run the UDP client
16   public class Client : System.Windows.Forms.Form
17   {
18      private System.Windows.Forms.TextBox inputTextBox;
19      private System.Windows.Forms.TextBox displayTextBox;
20
21      private UdpClient client;
22      private IPEndPoint receivePoint;
23
24      private System.ComponentModel.Container components = null;
25
26      // no-argument constructor
27      public Client()
28      {
29         InitializeComponent();
30
31         receivePoint = new IPEndPoint( new IPAddress( 0 ), 0 );
32         client = new UdpClient( 5001 );
33         Thread thread =
34            new Thread( new ThreadStart( WaitForPackets ) );
35         thread.Start();
36      }
37
38      // Visual Studio.NET generated code
39
40      [STAThread]
41      static void Main()
42      {
43         Application.Run( new Client() );
44      }
45
46      // shut down the client
47      protected void Client_Closing(
48         object sender, CancelEventArgs e )
49      {
50         System.Environment.Exit( System.Environment.ExitCode );
51      }
52
53      // send a packet
54      protected void inputTextBox_KeyDown(
55         object sender, KeyEventArgs e )
56      {
57         if ( e.KeyCode == Keys.Enter )
58         {
59            // create packet (datagram) as string
60            string packet = inputTextBox.Text;
61            displayTextBox.Text +=
62               "\r\nSending packet containing: " + packet;
63
64            // convert packet to byte array
65            byte[] data =
66               System.Text.Encoding.ASCII.GetBytes( packet );
67
```

Fig. 22.4   Client portion of connectionless client/server computing. (Part 2 of 3.)

```
68                // send packet to server on port 5000
69                client.Send( data, data.Length, "localhost", 5000 );
70                displayTextBox.Text += "\r\nPacket sent\r\n";
71                inputTextBox.Clear();
72             }
73          } // end method inputTextBox_KeyDown
74
75          // wait for packets to arrive
76          public void WaitForPackets()
77          {
78             while ( true )
79             {
80                // receive byte array from server
81                byte[] data = client.Receive( ref receivePoint );
82
83                // output packet data to TextBox
84                displayTextBox.Text += "\r\nPacket received:" +
85                   "\r\nLength: " + data.Length + "\r\nContaining: " +
86                   System.Text.Encoding.ASCII.GetString( data ) +
87                   "\r\n";
88             }
89
90          } // end method WaitForPackets
91
92    } // end class Client
```

Client window before
sending a packet to the server

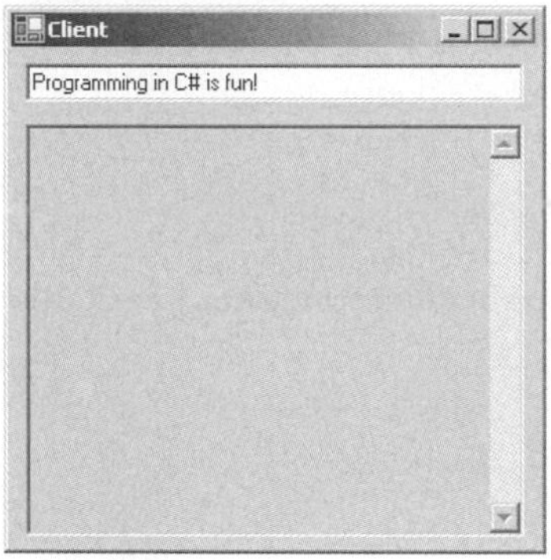

Client window after sending a packet
to the server and receiving it back

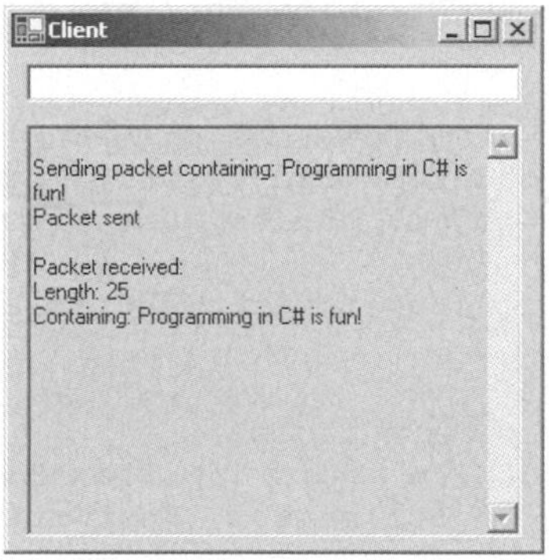

Fig. 22.4   Client portion of connectionless client/server computing. (Part 3 of 3.)

The code in Fig. 22.3 defines the **Server** for this application. Line 28 in the constructor for class **Server** creates an instance of the **UdpClient** class that receives data at port **5000**. This initializes the underlying **Socket** for communications. Line 29 creates an instance of class **IPEndPoint** to hold the IP address and port number of the client(s) that transmit to **Server**. The first argument to the constructor of **IPEndPoint** is an **IPAddress** object; the second argument to the constructor for **IPEndPoint** is the port number of the endpoint. These values are both **0**, because we need only instantiate an empty **IPEndPoint** object. The IP addresses and port numbers of clients are copied into the **IPEndPoint** when datagrams are received from clients.

Server method **WaitForPackets** (lines 52–72) executes an infinite loop while waiting for data to arrive at the **Server**. When information arrives, the **UdpClient** method **Receive** (line 57) receives a **byte** array from the client. We include **Receive** in the **IPEndPoint** object created in the constructor; this provides the method with a reference to an **IPEndPoint** into which the program copies the client's IP address and port number. This program will compile and run without an exception even if the reference to the **IPEndPoint** object is **null**, because method **Receive** initializes the **IPEndPoint** if it is **null**.

Good Programming Practice 22.1

*Initialize all references to objects (to a value other than **null**). This protects code from methods that do not check their parameters for **null** references.*

Lines 60–65 update the **Server**'s display to include the packet's information and content. Line 68 echoes the data back to the client, using **UdpClient** method **Send**. This version of **Send** takes three arguments: The byte array to send, an **int** representing the array's length and the **IPEndPoint** to which to send the data. We use array **data** returned by method **Receive** as the data, the length of array **data** as the length and the **IPEndPoint** passed to method **Receive** as the data's destination. The IP address and port number of the client that sent the data to **Server** are stored in **receivePoint**, so merely passing **receivePoint** to **Send** allows **Server** to respond to the client.

Class **Client** (Fig. 22.4) works similarly to class **Server**, except that the **Client** object sends packets only when the user types a message in a **TextBox** and presses the *Enter* key. When this occurs, the program calls event handler **inputTextBox_KeyDown** (lines 54–73). Lines 65–66 convert the **string** that the user entered in the **TextBox** to a **byte** array. Line 69 calls **UdpClient** method **Send** to send the **byte** array to the **Server** that is located on **localhost** (i.e., the same machine). We specify the port as **5000**, which we know to be **Server**'s port.

Line 32 instantiates a **UdpClient** object to receive packets at port **5001**—we choose port **5001**, because the **Server** already occupies port **5000**. Method **WaitForPackets** of class **Client** (lines 76–90) uses an infinite loop to wait for these packets. The **UdpClient** method **Receive** blocks until a packet of data is received (line 81). The blocking performed by method **Receive** does not prevent class **Client** from performing other services (e.g., handling user input), because a separate thread runs method **WaitForPackets**.

When a packet arrives, lines 84–87 display its contents in the **TextBox**. The user can type information into the **Client** window's **TextBox** and press the *Enter* key at any time, even while a packet is being received. The event handler for the **TextBox** processes the event and sends the data to the server.

22.6 Client/Server Tic-Tac-Toe Using a Multithreaded Server

In this section, we present our capstone networking example—the popular game Tic-Tac-Toe, implemented with stream sockets and client/server techniques. The program consists of a **Server** application (Fig. 22.5) and two **Client** applications (Fig. 22.6); **Server** allows the **Client**s to connect to the server and play Tic-Tac-Toe. We depict the output in Fig. 22.6. When the server receives a client connection, lines 72–83 of Fig. 22.5 create

Fig. 22.5 create an instance of class **Player** to process the client in a separate thread of execution. This enables the server to handle requests from both clients. The server assigns value **"X"** to the first client that connects (player **X** makes the first move), then assigns value **"O"** to the second client. Throughout the game, the server maintains information regarding the status of the board so that the server can validate players' requested moves. However, neither the server nor the client can establish whether a player has won the game—in this application, method **GameOver** (lines 143–147) always returns **false**. Exercise 22.7 asks the reader to implement functionality that enables the application to determine a winner. Each **Client** maintains its own GUI version of the Tic-Tac-Toe board to display the game. The clients can place marks only in empty squares on the board. Class **Square** (Fig. 22.7) is used to define squares on the Tic-Tac-Toe board.

```
1    // Fig. 22.5: Server.cs
2    // This class maintains a game of Tic-Tac-Toe for two
3    // client applications.
4
5    using System;
6    using System.Drawing;
7    using System.Collections;
8    using System.ComponentModel;
9    using System.Windows.Forms;
10   using System.Data;
11   using System.Net.Sockets;
12   using System.Threading;
13   using System.IO;
14
15   // awaits connections from two clients and allows them to
16   // play tic-tac-toe against each other
17   public class Server : System.Windows.Forms.Form
18   {
19      private System.Windows.Forms.TextBox displayTextBox;
20
21      private byte[] board;
22
23      private Player[] players;
24      private Thread[] playerThreads;
25
26      private TcpListener listener;
27      private int currentPlayer;
28      private Thread getPlayers;
29
30      private System.ComponentModel.Container components = null;
31
32      internal bool disconnected = false;
33
34      // default constructor
35      public Server()
36      {
37         InitializeComponent();
38
39         board = new byte[ 9 ];
```

Fig. 22.5   Server side of client/server Tic-Tac-Toe program. (Part 1 of 6.)

```
40
41        players = new Player[ 2 ];
42        playerThreads = new Thread[ 2 ];
43        currentPlayer = 0;
44
45        // accept connections on a different thread
46        getPlayers = new Thread( new ThreadStart( SetUp ) );
47        getPlayers.Start();
48     }
49
50  // Visual Studio .NET-generated code
51
52  [STAThread]
53  static void Main()
54  {
55     Application.Run( new Server() );
56  }
57
58  protected void Server_Closing(
59     object sender, CancelEventArgs e )
60  {
61     disconnected = true;
62  }
63
64  // accepts connections from 2 players
65  public void SetUp()
66  {
67     // set up Socket
68     listener = new TcpListener( 5000 );
69     listener.Start();
70
71     // accept first player and start a thread for him or her
72     players[ 0 ] =
73        new Player( listener.AcceptSocket(), this, 0 );
74     playerThreads[ 0 ] = new Thread(
75        new ThreadStart( players[ 0 ].Run ) );
76     playerThreads[ 0 ].Start();
77
78     // accept second player and start a thread for him or her
79     players[ 1 ] =
80        new Player( listener.AcceptSocket(), this, 1 );
81     playerThreads[ 1 ] =
82        new Thread( new ThreadStart( players[ 1 ].Run ) );
83     playerThreads[ 1 ].Start();
84
85     // let the first player know that the other player has
86     // connected
87     lock ( players[ 0 ] )
88     {
89        players[ 0 ].threadSuspended = false;
90        Monitor.Pulse( players[ 0 ] );
91     }
92  } // end method SetUp
```

Fig. 22.5 Server side of client/server Tic-Tac-Toe program. (Part 2 of 6.)

```
93
94       // appends the argument to text in displayTextBox
95       public void Display( string message )
96       {
97          displayTextBox.Text += message + "\r\n";
98       }
99
100      // determine if a move is valid
101      public bool ValidMove( int location, int player )
102      {
103         // prevent another thread from making a move
104         lock ( this )
105         {
106            // while it is not the current player's turn, wait
107            while ( player != currentPlayer )
108               Monitor.Wait( this );
109
110            // if the desired square is not occupied
111            if ( !IsOccupied( location ) )
112            {
113               // set the board to contain the current player's mark
114               board[ location ] = ( byte ) ( currentPlayer == 0 ?
115                  'X' : 'O' );
116
117               // set the currentPlayer to be the other player
118               currentPlayer = ( currentPlayer + 1 ) % 2;
119
120               // notify the other player of the move
121               players[ currentPlayer ].OtherPlayerMoved( location );
122
123               // alert the other player it's time to move
124               Monitor.Pulse( this );
125
126               return true;
127            }
128            else
129               return false;
130         }
131      } // end method ValidMove
132
133      // determines whether the specified square is occupied
134      public bool IsOccupied( int location )
135      {
136         if ( board[ location ] == 'X' || board[ location ] == 'O' )
137            return true;
138         else
139            return false;
140      }
141
142      // determines if the game is over
143      public bool GameOver()
144      {
```

Fig. 22.5   Server side of client/server Tic-Tac-Toe program. (Part 3 of 6.)

```
145          // place code here to test for a winner of the game
146          return false;
147       }
148
149  } // end class Server
150
151  public class Player
152  {
153     internal Socket connection;
154     private NetworkStream socketStream;
155     private Server server;
156     private BinaryWriter writer;
157     private BinaryReader reader;
158
159     private int number;
160     private char mark;
161     internal bool threadSuspended = true;
162
163     // constructor requiring Socket, Server and int objects
164     // as arguments
165     public Player( Socket socket, Server serverValue, int newNumber )
166     {
167        mark = ( newNumber == 0 ? 'X' : 'O' );
168
169        connection = socket;
170
171        server = serverValue;
172        number = newNumber;
173
174        // create NetworkStream object for Socket
175        socketStream = new NetworkStream( connection );
176
177        // create Streams for reading/writing bytes
178        writer = new BinaryWriter( socketStream );
179        reader = new BinaryReader( socketStream );
180
181     } // end constructor
182
183     // signal other player of move
184     public void OtherPlayerMoved( int location )
185     {
186        // signal that opponent moved
187        writer.Write( "Opponent moved" );
188        writer.Write( location ); // send location of move
189     }
190
191     // allows the players to make moves and receives moves
192     // from other player
193     public void Run()
194     {
195        bool done = false;
196
```

Fig. 22.5 Server side of client/server Tic-Tac-Toe program. (Part 4 of 6.)

```
197        // display on the server that a connection was made
198        server.Display( "Player " + ( number == 0 ? 'X' : 'O' )
199           + " connected" );
200
201        // send the current player's mark to the server
202        writer.Write( mark );
203
204        // if number equals 0 then this player is X, so send
205        writer.Write( "Player " + ( number == 0 ?
206           "X connected\r\n" : "O connected, please wait\r\n" ) );
207
208        // wait for another player to arrive
209        if ( mark == 'X' )
210        {
211           writer.Write( "Waiting for another player" );
212
213           // wait for notification from server that another
214           // player has connected
215           lock ( this )
216           {
217              while ( threadSuspended )
218                 Monitor.Wait( this );
219           }
220
221           writer.Write( "Other player connected. Your move" );
222
223        } // end if
224
225        // play game
226        while ( !done )
227        {
228           // wait for data to become available
229           while ( connection.Available == 0 )
230           {
231              Thread.Sleep( 1000 );
232
233              if ( server.disconnected )
234                 return;
235           }
236
237           // receive data
238           int location = reader.ReadInt32();
239
240           // if the move is valid, display the move on the
241           // server and signal the move is valid
242           if ( server.ValidMove( location, number ) )
243           {
244              server.Display( "loc: " + location );
245              writer.Write( "Valid move." );
246           }
247
```

Fig. 22.5   Server side of client/server Tic-Tac-Toe program. (Part 5 of 6.)

```
248                  // signal the move is invalid
249                  else
250                      writer.Write( "Invalid move, try again" );
251
252                  // if game is over, set done to true to exit while loop
253                  if ( server.GameOver() )
254                      done = true;
255
256              } // end while loop
257
258              // close the socket connection
259              writer.Close();
260              reader.Close();
261              socketStream.Close();
262              connection.Close();
263
264          } // end method Run
265
266      } // end class Player
```

Fig. 22.5   Server side of client/server Tic-Tac-Toe program. (Part 6 of 6.)

Server (Fig. 22.5) uses its constructor (lines 35–48) to create a **byte** array to store the moves the players have made (line 39). The program creates an array of two references to **Player** objects (line 41) and an array of two references to **Thread** objects (line 42). Each element in both arrays corresponds to a Tic-Tac-Toe player. Variable **current-Player** is set to **0**, which corresponds to player **"X"**. In our program, player **"X"** makes the first move (line 43). Lines 46–47 create and start **Thread getPlayers**, which the **Server** uses to accept connections so that the current **Thread** does not block while awaiting players.

Thread **getPlayers** executes method **SetUp** (lines 65–92), which creates a **TcpListener** object to listen for requests on port **5000** (lines 68–69). This object then listens for connection requests from the first and second players. Lines 72–73 and 79–80 instantiate **Player** objects representing the players, and lines 74–75 and 81–82 create two **Thread**s that execute the **Run** methods of each **Player** object.

The **Player** constructor (Fig. 22.5, lines 165–181) receives as arguments a reference to the **Socket** object (i.e., the connection to the client), a reference to the **Server** object and an **int** indicating the mark (**"X"** or **"O"**) used by that player. In this case study, **Server** calls method **Run** (lines 193–264) after instantiating a **Player** object. Lines 198–206 notify the server of a successful connection and send to the client the **char** that the client will place on the board when making a move. If **Run** is executing for **Player "X"**, lines 211–221 execute, causing **Player "X"** to wait for a second player to connect. Lines 217–218 define a **while** loop that suspends the **Player "X" Thread** until the server signals that **Player "O"** has connected. The server notifies the **Player** of the connection by setting the **Player**'s **threadSuspended** variable to **false** (line 89). When **threadSuspended** becomes **false**, **Player** exits the **while** loop of lines 217–218.

Method **Run** executes the **while** structure (lines 226–256), enabling the user to play the game. Each iteration of this structure waits for the client to send an **int** specifying where on the board to place the **"X"** or **"O"**—the **Player** then places the mark on the board, if the specified mark location is valid (e.g., that location does not already contain a mark). Note that the **while** structure continues execution only if **bool** variable **done** is **false**. This variable is set to **true** by event handler **Server_Closing** of class **Server**, which is invoked when the server closes the connection.

```
1    // Fig. 22.6: Client.cs
2    // Client for the TicTacToe program.
3
4    using System;
5    using System.Drawing;
6    using System.Collections;
7    using System.ComponentModel;
8    using System.Windows.Forms;
9    using System.Data;
10   using System.Net.Sockets;
11   using System.Threading;
12   using System.IO;
13
14   // represents a tic-tac-toe player
15   public class Client : System.Windows.Forms.Form
16   {
17      private System.Windows.Forms.Label idLabel;
18
19      private System.Windows.Forms.TextBox displayTextBox;
20
21      private System.Windows.Forms.Panel panel11;
22      private System.Windows.Forms.Panel panel12;
23      private System.Windows.Forms.Panel panel13;
24      private System.Windows.Forms.Panel panel15;
25      private System.Windows.Forms.Panel panel16;
26      private System.Windows.Forms.Panel panel14;
27      private System.Windows.Forms.Panel panel17;
28      private System.Windows.Forms.Panel panel18;
29      private System.Windows.Forms.Panel panel19;
30
31      private Square[ , ] board;
32      private Square currentSquare;
33
34      private Thread outputThread;
35
36      private TcpClient connection;
37      private NetworkStream stream;
38      private BinaryWriter writer;
39      private BinaryReader reader;
40
41      private char myMark;
42      private bool myTurn;
43
44      private SolidBrush brush;
45      private System.ComponentModel.Container components = null;
46
47      bool done = false;
```

Fig. 22.6   Client side of client/server Tic-Tac-Toe program. (Part 1 of 7.)

```
48
49      // default constructor
50      public Client()
51      {
52          InitializeComponent();
53
54          board = new Square[ 3, 3 ];
55
56          // create 9 Square objects and place them on the board
57          board[ 0, 0 ] = new Square( panel1, ' ', 0 );
58          board[ 0, 1 ] = new Square( panel2, ' ', 1 );
59          board[ 0, 2 ] = new Square( panel3, ' ', 2 );
60          board[ 1, 0 ] = new Square( panel4, ' ', 3 );
61          board[ 1, 1 ] = new Square( panel5, ' ', 4 );
62          board[ 1, 2 ] = new Square( panel6, ' ', 5 );
63          board[ 2, 0 ] = new Square( panel7, ' ', 6 );
64          board[ 2, 1 ] = new Square( panel8, ' ', 7 );
65          board[ 2, 2 ] = new Square( panel9, ' ', 8 );
66
67          // create a SolidBrush for writing on the Squares
68          brush = new SolidBrush( Color.Black );
69
70          // Make connection to sever and get the associated
71          // network stream. Start separate thread to allow this
72          // program to continually update its output in textbox.
73          connection = new TcpClient( "localhost", 5000 );
74          stream = connection.GetStream();
75
76          writer = new BinaryWriter( stream );
77          reader = new BinaryReader( stream );
78
79          // start a new thread for sending and receiving messages
80          outputThread = new Thread( new ThreadStart( Run ) );
81          outputThread.Start();
82      }  // end Client constructor
83
84      // Visual Studio .NET-generated code
85
86      [STAThread]
87      static void Main()
88      {
89          Application.Run( new Client() );
90      }
91
92      protected void Client_Paint (
93          object sender, System.Windows.Forms.PaintEventArgs e )
94      {
95          PaintSquares();
96      }
97
```

Fig. 22.6   Client side of client/server Tic-Tac-Toe program. (Part 2 of 7.)

```
98      protected void Client_Closing(
99         object sender, CancelEventArgs e )
100     {
101        done = true;
102     }
103
104     // draws the mark of each square
105     public void PaintSquares()
106     {
107        Graphics g;
108
109        // draw the appropriate mark on each panel
110        for ( int row = 0; row < 3; row++ )
111           for ( int column = 0; column < 3; column++ )
112           {
113              // get the Graphics for each Panel
114              g = board[ row, column ].SquarePanel.CreateGraphics();
115
116              // draw the appropriate letter on the panel
117              g.DrawString( board[ row, column ].Mark.ToString(),
118                 this.Font, brush, 8, 8 );
119           }
120     } // end method PaintSquares
121
122     // send location of the clicked square to server
123     protected void square_MouseUp(
124        object sender, System.Windows.Forms.MouseEventArgs e )
125     {
126        // for each square check if that square was clicked
127        for ( int row = 0; row < 3; row++ )
128           for ( int column = 0; column < 3; column++ )
129              if ( board[ row, column ].SquarePanel == sender )
130              {
131                 CurrentSquare = board[ row, column ];
132
133                 // send the move to the server
134                 SendClickedSquare( board[ row, column ].Location );
135              }
136     } // end method square_MouseUp
137
138     // control thread that allows continuous update of the
139     // textbox display
140     public void Run()
141     {
142        // first get players's mark (X or O)
143        myMark = reader.ReadChar();
144        idLabel.Text = "You are player \"" + myMark + "\"";
145        myTurn = ( myMark == 'X' ? true : false );
146
147        // process incoming messages
148        try
149        {
```

Fig. 22.6   Client side of client/server Tic-Tac-Toe program. (Part 3 of 7.)

```
150                // receive messages sent to client
151                while ( true )
152                    ProcessMessage( reader.ReadString() );
153             }
154             catch ( EndOfStreamException )
155             {
156                MessageBox.Show( "Server is down, game over", "Error",
157                    MessageBoxButtons.OK, MessageBoxIcon.Error );
158             }
159
160      } // end method Run
161
162      // process messages sent to client
163      public void ProcessMessage( string message )
164      {
165         // if the move player sent to the server is valid
166         // update the display, set that square's mark to be
167         // the mark of the current player and repaint the board
168         if ( message == "Valid move." )
169         {
170            displayTextBox.Text +=
171               "Valid move, please wait.\r\n";
172            currentSquare.Mark = myMark;
173            PaintSquares();
174         }
175
176         // if the move is invalid, display that and it is now
177         // this player's turn again
178         else if ( message == "Invalid move, try again" )
179         {
180            displayTextBox.Text += message + "\r\n";
181            myTurn = true;
182         }
183
184         // if opponent moved
185         else if ( message == "Opponent moved" )
186         {
187            // find location of their move
188            int location = reader.ReadInt32();
189
190            // set that square to have the opponents mark and
191            // repaint the board
192            board[ location / 3, location % 3 ].Mark =
193               ( myMark == 'X' ? 'O' : 'X' );
194            PaintSquares();
195
196            displayTextBox.Text +=
197               "Opponent moved.  Your turn.\r\n";
198
199            // it is now this player's turn
200            myTurn = true;
201         }
202
```

Fig. 22.6   Client side of client/server Tic-Tac-Toe program. (Part 4 of 7.)

```
203              // display the message
204              else
205                 displayTextBox.Text += message + "\r\n";
206
207        } // end method ProcessMessage
208
209        // sends the server the number of the clicked square
210        public void SendClickedSquare( int location )
211        {
212           // if it is the current player's move right now
213           if ( myTurn )
214           {
215              // send the location of the move to the server
216              writer.Write( location );
217
218              // it is now the other player's turn
219              myTurn = false;
220           }
221        }
222
223        // write-only property for the current square
224        public Square CurrentSquare
225        {
226           set
227           {
228              currentSquare = value;
229           }
230        }
231
232 } // end class Client
```

1.

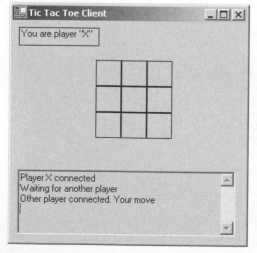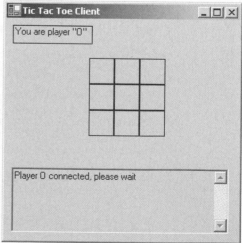

Fig. 22.6 Client side of client/server Tic-Tac-Toe program. (Part 5 of 7.)

2.
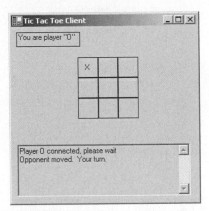

3.
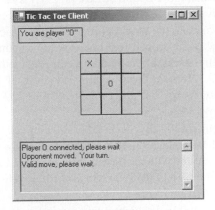
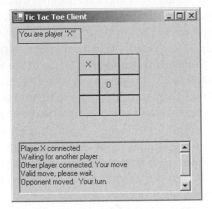

4.
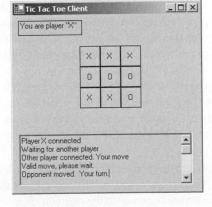
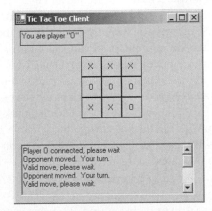

Fig. 22.6 Client side of client/server Tic-Tac-Toe program. (Part 6 of 7.)

server output after (1.)

server output after (2.)

server output after (3.)

server output after (4.)

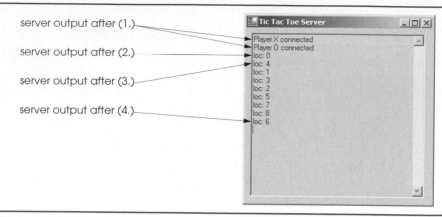

Fig. 22.6   Client side of client/server Tic-Tac-Toe program. (Part 7 of 7.)

Line 229 of Fig. 22.5 begins a **while** that loops until **Socket** property **Available** indicates that there is information to receive from the **Socket** (or until the server disconnects from the client). If there is no information, the thread goes to sleep for one second. Upon awakening, the thread uses property **Disconnected** to check for whether server variable **disconnect** is **true**. If the value is **true**, the **Thread** exits the method (thus terminating the **Thread**); otherwise, the **Thread** loops again. However, if property **Available** indicates that there is data to receive, the **while** loop of lines 229–235 terminates, enabling the information to be processed.

This information contains an **int** representing the location in which the client wants to place a mark. Line 238 calls method **ReadInt32** of the **BinaryReader** object (which reads from the **NetworkStream** created with the **Socket**) to read this **int**. Line 242 then passes the **int** to **Server** method **ValidMove**. If this method validates the move, the **Player** places the mark in the desired location.

Method **ValidMove** (lines 101–131) sends to the client a message indicating whether the move was valid. Locations on the board correspond to numbers from **0–8** (**0–2** for the first row, **3–5** for the second and **6–8** for the third). All statements in method **ValidMove** are enclosed in a **lock** statement that allows only one move to be attempted at a time. This prevents two players from modifying the game's state information simultaneously. If the **Player** attempting to validate a move is not the current player (i.e., the one allowed to make a move), that **Player** is placed in a *wait* state until it is that **Player**'s turn to move. If the user attempts to place a mark on a location that already contains a mark, method **ValidMove** returns **false**. However, if the user has selected an unoccupied location (line 111), lines 114–115 place the mark on the local representation of the board. Line 121 notifies the other **Player** that a move has been made, and line 124 invokes the **Pulse** method so that the waiting **Player** can validate a move. The method then returns **true** to indicate that the move is valid.

When a **Client** application (Fig. 22.6) executes, it creates a **TextBox** to display messages from the server and the Tic-Tac-Toe board representation. The board is created out of nine **Square** objects (Fig. 22.7) that contain **Panel**s on which the user can click, indicating the position on the board in which to place a mark. The **Client**'s constructor (line 50–82) opens a connection to the server (line 73) and obtains a reference to the connection's associated **NetworkStream** object from **TcpClient** (line 74). Lines 80–81 start a thread to read messages sent from the server to the client. The server passes messages (for example, whether each move is valid) to method **ProcessMessage** (lines 163–207). If the message indicates that a move is valid (line 168), the client sets its mark to the current square (the square that the user clicked) and repaints the board. If the message indicates that a move is invalid (line 178), the client notifies the user to click a different square. If the message indicates that the opponent made a move (line 185), line 188 reads from the server an **int** specifying where on the board the client should place the opponent's mark.

```
1    // Fig. 22.7: Square.cs
2    // A Square on the TicTacToe board.
3
4    using System.Windows.Forms;
5
6    // the representation of a square in a tic-tac-toe grid
7    public class Square
8    {
9       private Panel panel;
10      private char mark;
11      private int location;
12
13      // constructor
14      public Square( Panel newPanel, char newMark, int newLocation )
15      {
16         panel = newPanel;
17         mark = newMark;
18         location = newLocation;
19      }
20
21      // property SquarePanel; the panel which the square represents
22      public Panel SquarePanel
23      {
24         get
25         {
26            return panel;
27         }
28      } // end property SquarePanel
29
30      // property Mark; the mark of the square
31      public char Mark
32      {
33         get
34         {
35            return mark;
36         }
37
38         set
39         {
40            mark = value;
41         }
42      } // end property Mark
```

Fig. 22.7 Class **Square**. (Part 1 of 2.)

```
43
44      // property Location; the square's location on the board
45      public int Location
46      {
47         get
48         {
49            return location;
50         }
51      } // property Location
52
53   } // end class Square
```

Fig. 22.7 Class **Square**. (Part 2 of 2.)

In this chapter, we discussed how to use C#'s networking technologies by providing both connection-oriented (i.e., streams-based) transmission and connectionless (i.e., packet-based) transmission. We showed how to create a simple server and client via stream sockets, then showed how to create a multithreaded server. In Chapter 23, Data Structures and Collections, we discuss how to store data dynamically and discuss several of the key classes that belong to the C# **System.Collections** namespace.

SUMMARY

- Sockets are the fundamental way to perform network communications in the .NET Framework. The term "socket" refers to the Berkeley Sockets Interface, which was developed in 1978 to facilitate network programming with UNIX and was popularized by C and C++ programmers.

- The two most popular types of sockets are stream sockets and datagram sockets.

- Stream sockets provide a connection-oriented service, meaning that one process establishes a connection to another process, and data can flow between the processes in continuous streams.

- Datagram sockets provide a connectionless service that uses messages to transmit data.

- Connectionless services generally offer greater performance but less reliability than connection-oriented services.

- Transmission Control Protocol (TCP) is the preferred protocol for stream sockets. It is a reliable and relatively fast way to send data through a network.

- The User Datagram Protocol (UDP) is the preferred protocol for datagram sockets. UDP is unreliable. There is no guarantee that packets sent with UDP will arrive in the order in which they were sent or that they will arrive at all.

- The establishment of a simple server with TCP and stream sockets in C# requires five steps. Step 1 is to create a **TcpListener** object. This class represents a TCP stream socket that a server can use to receive connections.

- To receive connections, the **TcpListener** must be listening for them. For the **TcpListener** to listen for client connections, its **Start** method must be called (Step 2).

- **TcpListener** method **AcceptSocket** blocks indefinitely until a connection is established, at which point it returns a **Socket** (Step 3).

- Step 4 is the processing phase, in which the server and the client communicate via methods **Read** and **Write** via a **NetworkStream** object.

- When the client and server have finished communicating, the server closes the connection with the **Close** method on the **Socket** (Step 5). Most servers will then, by means of a control loop, return to the **AcceptSocket** call step to wait for another client's connection.

- A port number is a numeric ID number that a process uses to identify itself at a given network address, also known as an Internet Protocol Address (IP Address).
- An individual process running on a computer is identified by an IP address/port number pair. Hence, no two processes can have the same port number at a given IP address.
- The establishment of a simple client requires four steps. In Step 1, we create a **TcpClient** to connect to the server. This connection is established through a call to the **TcpClient** method **Connect** containing two arguments—the server's IP address and the port number
- In Step 2, the **TcpClient** uses method **GetStream** to get a **Stream** to write to and read from the server.
- Step 3 is the processing phase, in which the client and the server communicate.
- Step 4 has the client close the connection by calling the **Close** method on the **NetworkStream**.
- **NetworkStream** methods **WriteByte** and **Write** can be used to output individual bytes or sets of bytes to the server, respectively.
- **NetworkStream** methods **ReadByte** and **Read** can be used to read individual bytes or sets of bytes from the server, respectively.
- Class **UdpClient** is provided for connectionless transmission of data.
- Class **UdpClient** methods **Send** and **Receive** are used to transmit data.
- Class **IPEndPoint** represents an endpoint on a network.
- Class **IPAddress** represents an Internet Protocol address.
- Multithreaded servers can manage many simultaneous connections with multiple clients.

TERMINOLOGY

127.0.0.1
AcceptSocket method of class
   TcpListener
Berkeley Sockets Interface
BinaryReader class
BinaryWriter class
Bind method of class **Socket**
binding a server to a port
block
block until connection received
client
client/server chat
client/server model
Close method of class **Socket**
Close method of class **TcpClient**
collaborative applications
Connect method of class **TcpListener**
connection
connection attempt
connection between client and server terminates
connection port
connection to a server
connectionless service
connectionless transmission with datagrams

connection-oriented service
connection-oriented, streams-based transmission
datagram
datagram socket
duplicate of datagram
echo a packet back to a client
e-mail
Exit method of class **Environment**
ExitCode property of class **Environment**
file processing
GetStream method of class **Socket**
infinite loop
Internet Protocol Addresses (IP Address)
IP Address
IPAddress class
IPEndPoint class
LAN
Local Area Network (LAN)
localhost
loopback IP address
Loopback static member of class
   IPAddress
Microsoft Internet Explorer
Netscape Communicator

network address
networking as file I/O
NetworkStream class
OpenRead method of class **WebClient**
OpenWrite method of class **WebClient**
packet
pool of threads
port number
protocol
Read method of class **NetworkStream**
ReadByte method of **NetworkStream**
reading a file on a Web server
ReadString method of **BinaryReader**
receive a connection
receive data from a server
Receive method of class **Socket**
Receive method of class **UdpClient**
ReceiveFrom method of class **Socket**
send data to a server
Send method of class **Socket**
Send method of class **UdpClient**
SendTo method of class **Socket**
server
server Internet address

server port number
socket
socket-based communications
Socket class
spawning
Start method of class **TcpListener**
stream
stream socket
streams-based transmission
system service
System.Net namespace
System.Net.Sockets namespace
TcpClient class
TcpListener class
telephone system
Thread class
Transmission Control Protocol (TCP)
UdpClient class
User Datagram Protocol (UDP)
Web server
WebClient class
Write method of class **BinaryWriter**
Write method of class **NetworkStream**
WriteByte method of class **NetworkStream**

SELF-REVIEW EXERCISES

22.1   State whether each of the following is *true* or *false*. If *false*, explain why.
   a) UDP is a connection-oriented protocol.
   b) With stream sockets, a process establishes a connection to another process.
   c) Datagram-packet transmission over a network is reliable—packets are guaranteed to arrive in sequence.
   d) Most of the time TCP protocol is preferred over the UDP protocol.
   e) Each **TcpListener** can accept only one connection.
   f) A **TcpListener** can listen for connections at more than one port at a time.
   g) A **UdpClient** can send information only to one particular port.
   h) Packets sent via a UDP connection are sent only once.
   i) Clients need to know the port number at which the server is waiting for connections.

22.2   Fill in the blanks in each of the following statements:
   a) Many of C#'s networking classes are contained in namespaces _____ and _____.
   b) Class _____ is used for unreliable but fast datagram transmission.
   c) An object of class _____ represents an Internet Protocol (IP) address.
   d) The two types of sockets we discussed in this chapter are _____ sockets and _____ sockets.
   e) The acronym TCP stands for _____.
   f) Class _____ listens for connections from clients.
   g) Class _____ connects to servers.
   h) Class _____ provides access to stream data on a network.

ANSWERS TO SELF-REVIEW EXERCISES

22.1 a) False. UDP is a connectionless protocol, and TCP is a connection-oriented protocol. b) True. c) False. Packets can be lost, arrive out of order or even be duplicated. d) True. e) False. **TcpListener AcceptSocket** may be called as often as necessary—each call will accept a new connection. f) False. A **TcpListener** can listen for connections at only one port at a time. g) False. A **UdpClient** can send information to any port represented by an **IPEndPoint**. h) False. Packets may be sent more than once, to make it more likely that at least one copy of each packet arrives. i) True.

22.2 a) **System.Net**, **System.Net.Sockets**. b) **UdpClient**. c) **IPAddress**. d) stream, datagram. e) Transmission Control Protocol. f) **TcpListener**. g) **TcpClient**. h) **Network-Stream**.

EXERCISES

22.3 Use a socket connection to allow a client to specify a file name and have the server send the contents of the file or indicate that the file does not exist. Allow the client to modify the file contents and to send the file back to the server for storage.

22.4 Multithreaded servers are quite popular today, especially because of the increasing use of multiprocessing servers (i.e., servers with more than one processor unit). Modify the simple server application presented in Section 22.4 to be a multithreaded server. Then, use several client applications and have each of them connect to the server simultaneously.

22.5 Create a client/server application for the game of Hangman, using socket connections. The server should randomly pick a word or phrase from a file or a database. After connecting, the client should be allowed to begin guessing. If a client guesses incorrectly five times, the game is over. Display the original phrase or word on the server. Display underscores (for letters that have not been guessed yet) and the letters that have been guessed in the word or phrase on the client.

22.6 Modify the previous exercise to be a connectionless game using datagrams.

22.7 *(Modifications to the Multithreaded Tic-Tac-Toe Program)* The programs of Fig. 22.5–Fig. 22.7 implement a multithreaded, client/server version of the game Tic-Tac-Toe. Our goal in developing this game was to demonstrate a multithreaded server that could process multiple connections from clients at the same time. The server in the example is really a mediator between the two clients—it makes sure that each move is valid and that each client moves in the proper order. The server does not determine who won or lost or whether there was a draw. Also, there is no capability to allow a new game to be played or to terminate an existing game.

The following is a list of suggested modifications to the multithreaded Tic-Tac-Toe application:
   a) Modify class **Server** to test for a win, loss or draw on each move in the game. When the game is over, send a message to each client that indicates the result of the game.
   b) Modify class **Client** to display a button that, when clicked, allows the client to play another game. The button should be enabled only when a game completes. Note that both class **Client** and class **Server** must be modified to reset the board and all state information. Also, the other **Client** should be notified of a new game, so that client can reset its board and state information.
   c) Modify class **Client** to provide a button that allows a client to terminate the program at any time. When the button is clicked, the server and the other client should be notified. The server should then wait for a connection from another client so that a new game can begin.
   d) Modify class **Client** and class **Server** so that the loser of a game can choose game piece X or O for the next game. Remember that X always goes first.

22.8   *(Networked Morse Code)* Perhaps the most famous of all coding schemes is the Morse code, developed by Samuel Morse in 1832 for use with the telegraph system. The Morse code assigns a series of dots and dashes to each letter of the alphabet, each digit, and a few special characters (such as period, comma, colon and semicolon). In sound-oriented systems, the dot represents a short sound and the dash represents a long sound. Other representations of dots and dashes are used with light-oriented systems and signal-flag systems.

Separation between words is indicated by a space, or, quite simply, the absence of a dot or dash. In a sound-oriented system, a space is indicated by a short period of time during which no sound is transmitted. The international version of the Morse code appears in Fig. 22.8.

Write an application that reads an English-language phrase and encodes the phrase into Morse code. Also, write a program that reads a phrase in Morse code and converts the phrase into the English-language equivalent. Use one blank between each Morse-coded letter and three blanks between each Morse-coded word. Then, enable these two applications to send Morse Code messages to each other through a multithreaded-server application. Each application should allow the user to type normal characters into a **TextBox**. The application should then translate the characters into Morse Code and send the coded message through the server to the other client. When messages are received, they should be decoded and displayed as normal characters and as Morse Code. The application should have two **TextBox**es: One for displaying the other client's messages, and one for typing.

Character	Code	Character	Code
A	• –	T	–
B	– • • •	U	• • –
C	– • – •	V	• • • –
D	– • •	W	• – –
E	•	X	– • • –
F	• • – •	Y	– • – –
G	– – •	Z	– – • •
H	• • • •		
I	• •	Digits	
J	• – – –	1	• – – – –
K	– • –	2	• • – – –
L	• – • •	3	• • • – –
M	– –	4	• • • • –
N	– •	5	• • • • •
O	– – –	6	– • • • •
P	• – – •	7	– – • • •
Q	– – • –	8	– – – • •
R	• – •	9	– – – – •
S	• • •	0	– – – – –

Fig. 22.8   English letters of the alphabet and decimal digits as expressed in international Morse code.

23

Data Structures and Collections

Objectives

- To be able to form linked data structures using references, self-referential classes and recursion.
- To be able to create and manipulate dynamic data structures such as linked lists, queues, stacks and binary trees.
- To understand various important applications of linked data structures.
- To understand how to create reusable data structures with classes, inheritance and composition.

Much that I bound, I could not free;
Much that I freed returned to me.
Lee Wilson Dodd

'Will you walk a little faster?' said a whiting to a snail,
'There's a porpoise close behind us, and he's treading on my tail.'
Lewis Carroll

There is always room at the top.
Daniel Webster

Push on—keep moving.
Thomas Morton

I think that I shall never see
A poem lovely as a tree.
Joyce Kilmer

Outline

23.1 Introduction

The *data structures* that we have studied thus far have had fixed size, such as single- and double-subscripted arrays. This chapter introduces *dynamic data structures* that grow and shrink at execution time. *Linked lists* are collections of data items "lined up in a row"—users can make insertions and deletions anywhere in a linked list. *Stacks* are important in compilers and operating systems because insertions and deletions are made at only one end—its *top*. *Queues* represent waiting lines; insertions are made at the back (also referred to as the *tail*) of a queue, and deletions are made from the front (also referred to as the *head*) of a queue. *Binary trees* facilitate high-speed searching and sorting of data, efficient elimination of duplicate data items, representation of file system directories and compilation of expressions into machine language. These data structures have many other interesting applications as well.

We will discuss each of the major types of data structures and implement programs that create and manipulate them. We use classes, inheritance and composition to create and package these data structures for reusability and maintainability.

The chapter examples are practical programs that will be useful in more advanced courses and in industrial applications. The programs devote special attention to and focus on reference manipulation. The exercises offer a rich collection of useful applications.

23.2 Self-Referential Classes

A *self-referential class* contains a reference member that refers to an object of the same class type. For example, the class definition in Fig. 23.1 defines a type, **Node**. This type has two **private** instance variables—integer **data** and **Node** reference **next**. Member **next** references an object of type **Node**, an object of the same type as the one being declared here—hence, the term "self-referential class." Member **next** is referred to as a *link* (i.e., **next** can be used to "tie" an object of type **Node** to another object of the same type). Class **Node** also has two properties: One for variable **data** (named **Data**), and another for variable **next** (named **Next**).

Self-referential objects can be linked together to form useful data structures, such as lists, queues, stacks and trees. Figure 23.2 illustrates two self-referential objects linked together to form a list. A backslash (representing a **null** reference) is placed in the link member of the second self-referential object to indicate that the link does not refer to another object. The slash is for illustration purposes; it does not correspond to the backslash character in C#. A **null** reference normally indicates the end of a data structure.

Common Programming Error 23.1

*Not setting the link in the last node of a list (or other linear data structure) to **null** is a common logic error.*

```
1   class Node
2   {
3      private int data;
4      private Node next;
5
6      public Node( int d )
7      {
8         // constructor body
9      }
10
11     public int Data
12     {
13        get
14        {
15           // get body
16        }
17
18        set
19        {
20           // set body
21        }
22     }
23
24     public Node Next
25     {
26        get
27        {
28           // get body
29        }
30
31        set
32        {
33           // set body
34        }
35     }
36  }
```

Fig. 23.1   Sample self-referential **Node** class definition.

15 • → 10

Fig. 23.2 Two self-referential class objects linked together.

Creating and maintaining dynamic data structures requires *dynamic memory alloca-tion*—a program's ability to obtain more memory space at execution time to hold new nodes and to release space no longer needed. As we have already learned, C# programs do not explicitly release dynamically allocated memory. Rather, C# performs automatic gar-bage collection.

The limit for dynamic memory allocation can be as large as the amount of available disk space in a virtual-memory system. Often, the limits are much smaller, because the computer's available memory must be shared among many users.

Operator **new** is essential to dynamic memory allocation. Operator **new** takes as an operand the type of the object being dynamically allocated and returns a reference to a newly created object of that type. For example, the statement

```
Node nodeToAdd = new Node( 10 );
```

allocates the appropriate amount of memory to store a **Node** and stores a reference to this object in **nodeToAdd**. If no memory is available, **new** throws an **OutOfMemoryEx-ception**. The 10 is the **Node** object's data.

The following sections discuss lists, stacks, queues and trees. These data structures are created and maintained with dynamic memory allocation and self-referential classes.

Good Programming Practice 23.1

*When creating a very large number of objects, test for an **OutOfMemoryException**. Per-form appropriate error processing if the requested memory is not allocated.*

23.3 Linked Lists

A *linked list* is a linear collection (i.e., a sequence) of self-referential class objects, called *nodes,* connected by reference links—hence, the term "linked" list. A program accesses a linked list via a reference to the first node of the list. Each subsequent node is accessed via the link-reference member stored in the previous node. By convention, the link ref-erence in the last node of a list is set to **null** to mark the end of the list. Data are stored in a linked list dynamically—that is, each node is created as necessary. A node can con-tain data of any type, including objects of other classes. Stacks and queues are also linear data structures, and they are constrained versions of linked lists. Trees are nonlinear data structures.

Lists of data can be stored in arrays, but linked lists provide several advantages. A linked list is appropriate when the number of data elements to be represented in the data structure is unpredictable. Unlike a linked list, the size of a conventional C# array cannot be altered, because the array size is fixed at creation time. Conventional arrays can become full, but linked lists become full only when the system has insufficient memory to satisfy dynamic storage allocation requests.

Performance Tip 23.1

An array can be declared to contain more elements than the number of items expected, at the expense of wasting memory. Linked lists provide better memory utilization in these situations and they allow the program to adapt at run time.

Performance Tip 23.2

After locating the insertion point for a new item in a sorted linked list, inserting an element in the list is fast—only two references have to be modified. All existing nodes remain at their current locations in memory.

Programmers can maintain linked lists in sorted order simply by inserting each new element at the proper point in the list (locating the proper insertion point does take time). They do not need to move existing list elements.

Performance Tip 23.3

The elements of an array are stored contiguously in memory to allow immediate access to any array element—the address of any element can be calculated directly from its offset from the beginning of the array. Linked lists do not afford such immediate access to their elements—an element can be accessed only by traversing the list from the front.

Memory does not normally store linked list nodes contiguously. Rather, the nodes are logically contiguous. Figure 23.3 illustrates a linked list with several nodes.

Performance Tip 23.4

Using dynamic memory allocation (instead of arrays) for data structures that grow and shrink at execution time can save memory. Keep in mind, however, that references occupy space, and that dynamic memory allocation incurs the overhead of method calls.

The program of Fig. 23.4–Fig. 23.5 uses an object of class **List** to manipulate a list of miscellaneous object types. The **Main** method of class **ListTest** (Fig. 23.5) creates a list of objects, inserts objects at the beginning of the list using **List** method **InsertAtFront**, inserts objects at the end of the list using **List** method **InsertAtBack**, deletes objects from the front of the list using **List** method **RemoveFromFront** and deletes objects from the end of the list using **List** method **RemoveFromBack**. Each insertion and deletion operation invokes **List** method **Print** to display the current list contents. A detailed discussion of the program follows. If an attempt is made to remove an item from an empty list, an **EmptyListException** occurs.

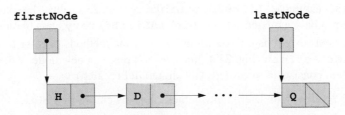

Fig. 23.3   A graphical representation of a linked list.

Performance Tip 23.5

Insertion and deletion in a sorted array can be time consuming—all the elements following the inserted or deleted element must be shifted appropriately.

The program consists of four classes—**ListNode** (Fig. 23.4, lines 9–52), **List** (Fig. 23.4, lines 55–193), **EmptyListException** (Fig. 23.4, lines 196–203) and class **ListTest** (Fig. 23.5). The classes in Fig. 23.4 create a linked-list library (defined in namespace **LinkedListLibrary**) that can be reused throughout this chapter.

Encapsulated in each **List** object is a linked list of **ListNode** objects. Class **List-Node** (Fig. 23.4, lines 9–52) consists of two member variables—**data** and **next**. Member **data** can refer to any object. Member **next** stores a reference to the next **List-Node** object in the linked list. A **List** accesses the **ListNode** member variables via the properties **Data** (lines 44–50) and **Next** (lines 30–41), respectively.

Class **List** contains **private** members **firstNode** (a reference to the first **ListNode** in a **List**) and **lastNode** (a reference to the last **ListNode** in a **List**). The constructors (lines 62–66 and 69–71) initialize both references to **null**. **InsertAt-Front** (lines 76–87), **InsertAtBack** (lines 92–104), **RemoveFromFront** (lines 107–125) and **RemoveFromBack** (lines 128–156) are the primary methods of class **List**. Each method uses a **lock** block to ensure that **List** objects are *multithread safe* when used in a multithreaded program. If one thread is modifying the contents of a **List** object, no other thread can modify the same **List** object at the same time. Method **IsEmpty** (lines 159–165) is a *predicate method* that determines whether the list is empty (i.e., the reference to the first node of the list is **null**). Predicate methods typically test a condition and do not modify the object on which they are called. If the list is empty, method **IsEmpty** returns **true**; otherwise, it returns **false**. Method **Print** (lines 168–191) displays the list's contents. Both **IsEmpty** and **Print** also use **lock** blocks so that the state of the list does not change while those methods are performing their tasks.

Class **EmptyListException** (lines 196–203) defines an exception class to handle illegal operations on an empty **List**.

Class **ListTest** (Fig. 23.5) uses the linked-list library to create and manipulate a linked list. Line 14 creates a new instance of type **List** named **list**. Lines 17–20 create data to add to the list. Lines 23–30 use **List** insertion methods to insert these objects and use **List** method **Print** to output the contents of **list** after each insertion. The code inside the **try** block (lines 36–53) removes objects via **List** deletion methods, outputs the object removed and outputs **list** after every deletion. If there is an attempt to remove an object from an empty list, this **try** block catches the **EmptyListException**. Note that class **ListTest** uses namespace **LinkedListLibrary** (Fig. 23.4); thus, the solution for class **ListTest** must have a reference to the **LinkedListLibrary** class library.

Over the next several pages, we discuss each of the methods of class **List** in detail. Method **InsertAtFront** (Fig. 23.4, lines 76–87) places a new node at the front of the list. The method consists of three steps (illustrated in Fig. 23.6):

1. Call **IsEmpty** to determine whether the list is empty (line 80).

2. If the list is empty, set both **firstNode** and **lastNode** to refer to a new **ListNode** initialized with **insertItem** (lines 81–82). The **ListNode** constructor at lines 16–19 (Fig. 23.4) calls the **ListNode** constructor at lines 23–27

(Fig. 23.4) to set instance variable **data** to refer to the **object** passed as the first argument and sets the **next** reference to **null**.

3. If the list is not empty, the new node is "threaded" (not to be confused with *multi-threading*) into the list by setting **firstNode** to refer to a new **ListNode** object initialized with **insertItem** and **firstNode** (lines 84–85). When the **ListNode** constructor (lines 23–27 of Fig. 23.4) executes, it sets instance variable **data** to refer to the **object** passed as the first argument and performs the insertion by setting the **next** reference to the **ListNode** passed as the second argument.

```
1   // Fig. 23.4: LinkedListLibrary.cs
2   // Class ListNode and class List definitions.
3
4   using System;
5
6   namespace LinkedListLibrary
7   {
8      // class to represent one node in a list
9      class ListNode
10     {
11        private object data;
12        private ListNode next;
13
14        // constructor to create ListNode that refers to dataValue
15        // and is last node in list
16        public ListNode( object dataValue )
17           : this( dataValue, null )
18        {
19        }
20
21        // constructor to create ListNode that refers to dataValue
22        // and refers to next ListNode in List
23        public ListNode( object dataValue, ListNode nextNode )
24        {
25           data = dataValue;
26           next = nextNode;
27        }
28
29        // property Next
30        public ListNode Next
31        {
32           get
33           {
34              return next;
35           }
36
37           set
38           {
39              next = value;
40           }
41        }
```

Fig. 23.4 Definitions of classes **ListNode**, **List** and **EmptyListException**. (Part 1 of 5.)

```
42
43          // property Data
44          public object Data
45          {
46             get
47             {
48                return data;
49             }
50          }
51
52       } // end class ListNode
53
54       // class List definition
55       public class List
56       {
57          private ListNode firstNode;
58          private ListNode lastNode;
59          private string name;      // string like "list" to display
60
61          // construct empty List with specified name
62          public List( string listName )
63          {
64             name = listName;
65             firstNode = lastNode = null;
66          }
67
68          // construct empty List with "list" as its name
69          public List() : this( "list" )
70          {
71          }
72
73          // Insert object at front of List. If List is empty,
74          // firstNode and lastNode will refer to same object.
75          // Otherwise, firstNode refers to new node.
76          public void InsertAtFront( object insertItem )
77          {
78             lock ( this )
79             {
80                if ( IsEmpty() )
81                   firstNode = lastNode =
82                      new ListNode( insertItem );
83                else
84                   firstNode =
85                      new ListNode( insertItem, firstNode );
86             }
87          }
88
89          // Insert object at end of List. If List is empty,
90          // firstNode and lastNode will refer to same object.
91          // Otherwise, lastNode's Next property refers to new node.
92          public void InsertAtBack( object insertItem )
93          {
```

Fig. 23.4   Definitions of classes **ListNode**, **List** and **EmptyListException**.
(Part 2 of 5.)

```
94              lock ( this )
95              {
96                  if ( IsEmpty() )
97                      firstNode = lastNode =
98                          new ListNode( insertItem );
99
100                 else
101                     lastNode = lastNode.Next =
102                         new ListNode( insertItem );
103             }
104         }
105
106         // remove first node from List
107         public object RemoveFromFront()
108         {
109             lock ( this )
110             {
111                 if ( IsEmpty() )
112                     throw new EmptyListException( name );
113
114                 object removeItem = firstNode.Data;   // retrieve data
115
116                 // reset firstNode and lastNode references
117                 if ( firstNode == lastNode )
118                     firstNode = lastNode = null;
119
120                 else
121                     firstNode = firstNode.Next;
122
123                 return removeItem;   // return removed data
124             }
125         }
126
127         // remove last node from List
128         public object RemoveFromBack()
129         {
130             lock ( this )
131             {
132                 if ( IsEmpty() )
133                     throw new EmptyListException( name );
134
135                 object removeItem = lastNode.Data;    // retrieve data
136
137                 // reset firstNode and lastNode references
138                 if ( firstNode == lastNode )
139                     firstNode = lastNode = null;
140
141                 else
142                 {
143                     ListNode current = firstNode;
144
```

Fig. 23.4 Definitions of classes **ListNode**, **List** and **EmptyListException**. (Part 3 of 5.)

```
145                   // loop while current node is not lastNode
146                   while ( current.Next != lastNode )
147                      current = current.Next;     // move to next node
148
149                   // current is new lastNode
150                   lastNode = current;
151                   current.Next = null;
152                }
153
154             return removeItem;   // return removed data
155          }
156       }
157
158       // return true if List is empty
159       public bool IsEmpty()
160       {
161          lock ( this )
162          {
163             return firstNode == null;
164          }
165       }
166
167       // output List contents
168       virtual public void Print()
169       {
170          lock ( this )
171          {
172             if ( IsEmpty() )
173             {
174                Console.WriteLine( "Empty " + name );
175                return;
176             }
177
178             Console.Write( "The " + name + " is: " );
179
180             ListNode current = firstNode;
181
182             // output current node data while not at end of list
183             while ( current != null )
184             {
185                Console.Write( current.Data + " " );
186                current = current.Next;
187             }
188
189             Console.WriteLine( "\n" );
190          }
191       }
192
193    } // end class List
194
```

Fig. 23.4 Definitions of classes **ListNode**, **List** and **EmptyListException**.
(Part 4 of 5.)

```
195     // class EmptyListException definition
196     public class EmptyListException : ApplicationException
197     {
198        public EmptyListException( string name )
199           : base( "The " + name + " is empty" )
200        {
201        }
202
203     } // end class EmptyListException
204
205  } // end namespace LinkedListLibrary
```

Fig. 23.4   Definitions of classes **ListNode**, **List** and **EmptyListException**. (Part 5 of 5.)

```
1    // Fig 23.5: ListTest.cs
2    // Testing class List.
3
4    using System;
5    using LinkedListLibrary;
6
7    namespace ListTest
8    {
9       // class to test List class functionality
10      class ListTest
11      {
12         static void Main( string[] args )
13         {
14            List list = new List();  // create List container
15
16            // create data to store in List
17            bool aBoolean = true;
18            char aCharacter = '$';
19            int anInteger =  34567;
20            string aString = "hello";
21
22            // use List insert methods
23            list.InsertAtFront( aBoolean );
24            list.Print();
25            list.InsertAtFront( aCharacter );
26            list.Print();
27            list.InsertAtBack( anInteger );
28            list.Print();
29            list.InsertAtBack( aString );
30            list.Print();
31
32            // use List remove methods
33            object removedObject;
34
```

Fig. 23.5   Demonstrating the linked list. (Part 1 of 2.)

```
35                  // remove data from list and print after each removal
36                  try
37                  {
38                      removedObject = list.RemoveFromFront();
39                      Console.WriteLine( removedObject + " removed" );
40                      list.Print();
41
42                      removedObject = list.RemoveFromFront();
43                      Console.WriteLine( removedObject + " removed" );
44                      list.Print();
45
46                      removedObject = list.RemoveFromBack();
47                      Console.WriteLine( removedObject + " removed" );
48                      list.Print();
49
50                      removedObject = list.RemoveFromBack();
51                      Console.WriteLine( removedObject + " removed" );
52                      list.Print();
53                  }
54
55                  // process exception if list empty when attempt is
56                  // made to remove item
57                  catch ( EmptyListException emptyListException )
58                  {
59                      Console.Error.WriteLine( "\n" + emptyListException );
60                  }
61
62          } // end method Main
63
64      } // end class ListTest
65  }
```

```
The list is: True

The list is: $ True

The list is: $ True 34567

The list is: $ True 34567 hello

$ removed
The list is: True 34567 hello

True removed
The list is: 34567 hello

hello removed
The list is: 34567

34567 removed
Empty list
```

Fig. 23.5   Demonstrating the linked list. (Part 2 of 2.)

Fig. 23.6 illustrates method **InsertAtFront**. Part (a) of the figure shows the list and the new node during the **InsertAtFront** operation and before the threading of the new node into the list. The dotted arrows in part (b) illustrate step 3 of the **InsertAt-Front** operation, which enables the node containing **12** to become the new list front.

Method **InsertAtBack** (Fig. 23.4, lines 92–104) places a new node at the back of the list. The method consists of three steps (illustrated in Fig. 23.7):

1. Call **IsEmpty** to determine whether the list is empty (line 96).

2. If the list is empty, set both **firstNode** and **lastNode** to refer to a new **ListNode** initialized with **insertItem** (lines 97–98). The **ListNode** constructor at lines 16–19 (Fig. 23.4) calls the **ListNode** constructor at lines 23–27 (Fig. 23.4) to set instance variable **data** to refer to the **object** passed as the first argument and sets the **next** reference to **null**.

3. If the list is not empty, thread the new node into the list by setting **lastNode** and **lastNode.next** to refer to a new **ListNode** object initialized with **insertItem** (lines 101–102). When the **ListNode** constructor (lines 16–19 of Fig. 23.4) executes, it sets instance variable **data** to refer to the **object** passed as an argument and sets the **next** reference to **null**.

Fig. 23.7 illustrates an **InsertAtBack** operation. Part a) of the figure shows the list and the new node during the **InsertAtBack** operation and before the new node has been threaded into the list. The dotted arrows in part b) illustrate the steps of method **Insert-AtBack** that enable a new node to be added to the end of a list that is not empty.

Method **RemoveFromFront** (Fig. 23.4, lines 107–127) removes the front node of the list and returns a reference to the removed data. The method throws an **EmptyList-Exception** (line 114) if the programmer tries to remove a node from an empty list. Otherwise, the method returns a reference to the removed data. The method consists of four steps (illustrated in Fig. 23.8):

1. Assign **firstNode.Data** (the data being removed from the list) to reference **removeItem** (line 116).

2. If the objects to which **firstNode** and **lastNode** refer are the same object, the list has only one element prior to the removal attempt. In this case, the method sets **firstNode** and **lastNode** to **null** (line 120) to "dethread" (remove) the node from the list (leaving the list empty).

3. If the list has more than one node prior to removal, then the method leaves reference **lastNode** as is and simply assigns **firstNode.Next** to reference **firstNode** (line 123). Thus, **firstNode** references the node that was the second node prior to the **RemoveFromFront** call.

4. Return the **removeItem** reference.

Fig. 23.8 illustrates method **RemoveFromFront**. Part a) illustrates the list before the removal operation. Part b) shows actual reference manipulations.

Method **RemoveFromBack** (Fig. 23.4, lines 130–160) removes the last node of a list and returns a reference to the removed data. The method throws an **EmptyListException** (line 137) if the program attempts to remove a node from an empty list. The method consists of several steps (illustrated in Fig. 23.9):

1. Assign **lastNode.Data** (the data being removed from the list) to reference **removeItem** (line 139).

2. If the objects to which **firstNode** and **lastNode** refer are the same object (line 142), the list has only one element prior to the removal attempt. In this case, the method sets **firstNode** and **lastNode** to **null** (line 143) to dethread (remove) that node from the list (leaving the list empty).

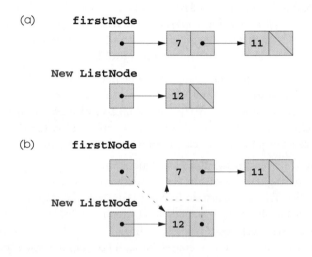

Fig. 23.6   A graphical representation of the **InsertAtFront** operation.

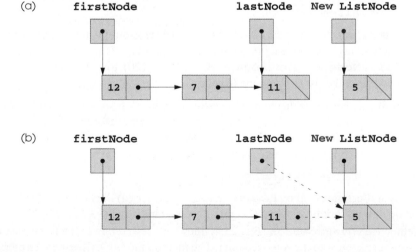

Fig. 23.7   A graphical representation of the **InsertAtBack** operation.

3. If the list has more than one node prior to removal, create the **ListNode** reference **current** and assign it **firstNode** (line 147).

4. Now "walk the list" with **current** until it references the node before the last node. The **while** loop (lines 150–151) assigns **current.Next** to reference **current** as long as **current.Next** is not equal to **lastNode**.

5. After locating the second-to-last node, assign **current** to **lastNode** (line 154) to dethread the last node from the list.

6. Set **current.Next** to **null** (line 155) in the new last node of the list to ensure proper list termination.

7. Return the **removeItem** reference (line 140).

Fig. 23.9 illustrates method **RemoveFromBack**. Part a) illustrates the list before the removal operation. Part b) shows the actual reference manipulations.

Method **Print** (Fig. 23.4, lines 172–195) first determines whether the list is empty (line 176). If so, **Print** displays a **string** consisting of the string **"Empty "** and the list's **name**, then returns control to the calling method. Otherwise, **Print** outputs the data in the list. The method prints a string consisting of the string **"The "**, the **name** and the string **" is: "**. Then, line 184 creates **ListNode** reference **current** and initializes it with **firstNode**. While **current** is not **null**, there are more items in the list. Therefore, the method prints **current.Data** (line 189), then assigns **current.Next** to **current** (line 190) to move to the next node in the list. Note that, if the link in the last node of the list is not **null**, the printing algorithm will erroneously attempt to print past the end of the list. The printing algorithm is identical for linked lists, stacks and queues.

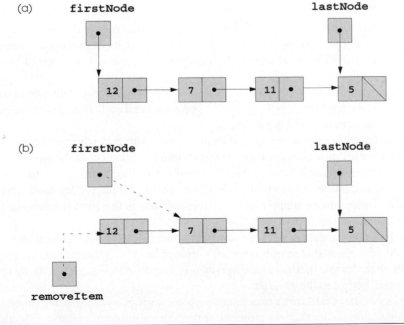

Fig. 23.8   A graphical representation of the **RemoveFromFront** operation.

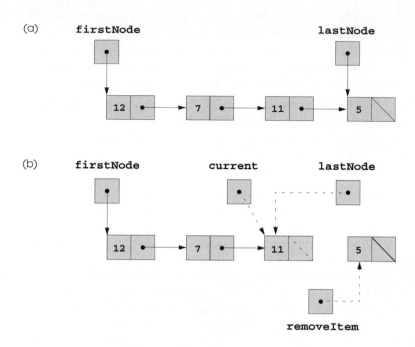

Fig. 23.9   A graphical representation of the **RemoveFromBack** operation.

23.4 Stacks

A *stack* is a constrained version of a linked list—a stack takes new nodes and releases nodes only at the top. For this reason, a stack is referred to as a *last-in, first-out* (*LIFO*) data structure. The link member in the bottom (i.e., last) node of the stack is set to **null** to indicate the bottom of the stack.

The primary operations to manipulate a stack are *push* and *pop*. Operation push adds a new node to the top of the stack. Operation pop removes a node from the top of the stack and returns the item from the popped node.

Stacks have many interesting applications. For example, when a program calls a method, the called method must know how to return to its caller, so the return address is pushed onto the *program execution stack*. If a series of method calls occurs, the successive return values are pushed onto the stack in last-in, first-out order so that each method can return to its caller. Stacks support recursive method calls in the same manner that they do conventional nonrecursive method calls.

The program-execution stack contains the space created for local variables on each invocation of a method during a program's execution. When the method returns to its caller, the space for that method's local variables is popped off the stack, and those variables are no longer known to the program.

The **System.Collections** namespace contains class **Stack** for implementing and manipulating stacks that can grow and shrink during program execution. Section 23.7 discusses class **Stack**.

We take advantage of the close relationship between lists and stacks to implement a stack class by reusing a list class. We demonstrate two different forms of reusability. First, we implement the stack class by inheriting from class **List** of Fig. 23.4. Then, we implement an identically performing stack class through composition by including a **List** object as a **private** member of a stack class. This chapter implements list, stack and queue data structures to store **object** references to encourage further reusability. Thus, any object type can be stored in a list, stack or queue.

The program of Fig. 23.10 and Fig. 23.11 creates a stack class by inheriting from class **List** of Fig. 23.4. We want the stack to have methods **Push**, **Pop**, **IsEmpty** and **Print**. Essentially, these are the methods **InsertAtFront**, **RemoveFromFront**, **IsEmpty** and **Print** of class **List**. Of course, class **List** contains other methods (such as **InsertAtBack** and **RemoveFromBack**) that we would rather not make accessible through the **public** interface of the stack. It is important to remember that all methods in the **public** interface of class **List** are also **public** methods of the derived class **StackInheritance** (Fig. 23.10).

When we implement the stack's methods, we have each **StackInheritance** method call the appropriate **List** method—method **Push** calls **InsertAtFront**, method **Pop** calls **RemoveFromFront**. Class **StackInheritance** does not define methods **IsEmpty** and **Print**, because **StackInheritance** inherits these methods from class **List** into **StackInheritance**'s **public** interface. The methods in class **StackInheritance** do not use **lock** statements. Each of the methods in this class calls a method from class **List** that uses **lock**. If two threads call **Push** on the same stack object, only one of the threads at a time will be able to call **List** method **InsertAtFront**. Note that class **StackInheritance** uses namespace **LinkedListLibrary** (Fig. 23.4); thus, the solution for the class library that defines **StackInheritance** must have a reference to the **LinkedListLibrary** class library.

StackInheritanceTest's **Main** method (Fig. 23.11) uses class **StackInheritance** to instantiate a stack of **object**s called **stack**. Lines 18–21 define four objects that will be pushed onto the stack and popped off the stack. The program pushes onto the stack (lines 24, 26, 28 and 30) a **bool** containing **true**, a **char** containing **$**, an **int** containing **34567** and a **string** containing **hello**. An infinite **while** loop (lines 36–41) pops the elements from the stack. When there are no objects left to pop, method **Pop** throws an **EmptyListException** and the program displays the exception's stack trace, which shows the program execution stack at the time the exception occurred. The program uses method **Print** (inherited from class **List**) to output the contents of the stack after each operation. Note that class **StackInheritanceTest** uses namespace **LinkedListLibrary** (Fig. 23.4) and namespace **StackInheritanceLibrary** (Fig. 23.10); thus, the solution for class **StackInheritanceTest** must have references to both class libraries.

```
1    // Fig. 23.10: StackInheritanceLibrary.cs
2    // Implementing a stack by inheriting from class List.
3
4    using System;
5    using LinkedListLibrary;
```

Fig. 23.10 **StackInheritance** extends class **List**. (Part 1 of 2.)

```
6
7    namespace StackInheritanceLibrary
8    {
9       // class StackInheritance inherits class List's capabilities
10      public class StackInheritance : List
11      {
12         // pass name "stack" to List constructor
13         public StackInheritance() : base( "stack" )
14         {
15         }
16
17         // place dataValue at top of stack by inserting
18         // dataValue at front of linked list
19         public void Push( object dataValue )
20         {
21            InsertAtFront( dataValue );
22         }
23
24         // remove item from top of stack by removing
25         // item at front of linked list
26         public object Pop()
27         {
28            return RemoveFromFront();
29         }
30
31      } // end class StackInheritance
32   }
```

Fig. 23.10 StackInheritance extends class List. (Part 2 of 2.)

Another way to implement a stack class is by reusing a list class through composition. The class in Fig. 23.12 uses a **private** object of class **List** (line 12) in the definition of class **StackComposition**. Composition enables us to hide the methods of class **List** that should not be in our stack's **public** interface by providing **public** interface methods only to the required **List** methods. This class implements each stack method by delegating its work to an appropriate **List** method. In particular, **StackComposition** calls **List** methods **InsertAtFront**, **RemoveFromFront**, **IsEmpty** and **Print**. In this example, we do not show class **StackCompositionTest**, because the only difference in this example is that we change the type of the stack from **StackInheritance** to **StackComposition**. If you execute the application from the code on the CD that accompanies this book, you will see that the output is identical.

```
1    // Fig. 23.11: StackInheritanceTest.cs
2    // Testing class StackInheritance.
3
4    using System;
5    using StackInheritanceLibrary;
6    using LinkedListLibrary;
7
```

Fig. 23.11 Using class StackInheritance. (Part 1 of 3.)

```
8   namespace StackInheritanceTest
9   {
10     // demonstrate functionality of class StackInheritance
11     class StackInheritanceTest
12     {
13        static void Main( string[] args )
14        {
15           StackInheritance stack = new StackInheritance();
16
17           // create objects to store in the stack
18           bool aBoolean = true;
19           char aCharacter = '$';
20           int anInteger = 34567;
21           string aString = "hello";
22
23           // use method Push to add items to stack
24           stack.Push( aBoolean );
25           stack.Print();
26           stack.Push( aCharacter );
27           stack.Print();
28           stack.Push( anInteger );
29           stack.Print();
30           stack.Push( aString );
31           stack.Print();
32
33           // use method Pop to remove items from stack
34           try
35           {
36              while ( true )
37              {
38                 object removedObject = stack.Pop();
39                 Console.WriteLine( removedObject + " popped" );
40                 stack.Print();
41              }
42           }
43
44           // if exception occurs, print stack trace
45           catch ( EmptyListException emptyListException )
46           {
47              Console.Error.WriteLine(
48                 emptyListException.StackTrace );
49           }
50
51        } // end method Main
52
53     } // end class StackInheritanceTest
54  }
```

```
The stack is: True

The stack is: $ True
```
                                              (continued on next page)

Fig. 23.11 Using class **StackInheritance**. (Part 2 of 3.)

```
The stack is: 34567 $ True

The stack is: hello 34567 $ True

hello popped
The stack is: 34567 $ True

34567 popped
The stack is: $ True

$ popped
The stack is: True

True popped
Empty stack
   at LinkedListLibrary.List.RemoveFromFront()
      in z:\ch23\linkedlistlibrary\linkedlistlibrary.cs:line 114
   at StackInheritanceLibrary.StackInheritance.Pop()
      in z:\ch23\stackinheritancelibrary\
      stackinheritancelibrary.cs:line 28
   at StackInheritanceTest.StackInheritanceTest.Main(String[] args
      in z:\ch23\fig23_11\stackinheritancetest.cs:line 41
```

Fig. 23.11 Using class **StackInheritance**. (Part 3 of 3.)

```
1   // Fig. 23.12: StackCompositionLibrary.cs
2   // StackComposition definition with composed List object.
3
4   using System;
5   using LinkedListLibrary;
6
7   namespace StackCompositionLibrary
8   {
9      // class StackComposition encapsulates List's capabilities
10     public class StackComposition
11     {
12        private List stack;
13
14        // construct empty stack
15        public StackComposition()
16        {
17           stack = new List( "stack" );
18        }
19
20        // add object to stack
21        public void Push( object dataValue )
22        {
23           stack.InsertAtFront( dataValue );
24        }
25
```

Fig. 23.12 StackComposition class encapsulates functionality of class **List**. (Part 1 of 2.)

```
26          // remove object from stack
27          public object Pop()
28          {
29              return stack.RemoveFromFront();
30          }
31
32          // determine whether stack is empty
33          public bool IsEmpty()
34          {
35              return stack.IsEmpty();
36          }
37
38          // output stack contents
39          public void Print()
40          {
41              stack.Print();
42          }
43
44      } // end class StackComposition
45  }
```

Fig. 23.12 **StackComposition** class encapsulates functionality of class **List**.
(Part 2 of 2.)

23.5 Queues

Another common data structure is the *queue.* A queue is similar to a checkout line in a super-market—the first person in line is served first; customers enter the line only at the end, and they wait to be served. Queue nodes are removed only from the *head* of the queue and are inserted only at the *tail* of the queue. For this reason, a queue is a *first-in, first-out* (*FIFO*) data structure. The insert and remove operations are known as *enqueue* and *dequeue*.

Queues have many applications in computer systems. Most computers have only a single processor, so they can only serve one user at a time. Entries for the other users are placed in a queue. The entry at the front of the queue receives the first available service. Each entry gradually advances to the front of the queue as users receive service.

Queues also support print spooling. A multiuser environment may have only one printer. Several users may send output to the printer. If the printer is busy, users may still generate other outputs, which are "spooled" to disk (much as thread is wound onto a spool), where they wait in a queue until the printer becomes available.

Information packets also wait in queues in computer networks. Each time a packet arrives at a network node, the routing node must route it to the next node on the network along the path to the packet's final destination. The routing node routes one packet at a time, so additional packets are enqueued until the router can route them.

A file server in a computer network handles file access requests from many clients throughout the network. Servers have a limited capacity to service requests from clients. When client requests exceed that capacity, the requests wait in queues.

The program of Fig. 23.13 and Fig. 23.14 creates a queue class through inheritance from a list class. We want the **QueueInheritance** class (Fig. 23.13) to have methods **Enqueue**, **Dequeue**, **IsEmpty** and **Print**. Note that these methods are essentially the **InsertAtBack**, **RemoveFromFront**, **IsEmpty** and **Print** methods of class **List**.

Of course, the list class contains other methods (such as **InsertAtFront** and **Remove-FromBack**) that we would rather not make accessible through the **public** interface to the queue class. Remember that all methods in the **public** interface of the **List** class are also **public** methods of the derived class **QueueInheritance**.

When we implement the queue's methods, we have each **QueueInheritance** method call the appropriate **List** method—method **Enqueue** calls **InsertAtBack**, method **Dequeue** calls **RemoveFromFront**, and **IsEmpty** and **Print** calls invoke their base-class versions. Class **QueueInheritance** does not define methods **IsEmpty** and **Print**, because **QueueInheritance** inherits these methods from class **List** into **QueueInheritance**'s **public** interface. Also, the methods in class **QueueInheritance** do not use **lock** statements. Each of the methods in this class calls a method from class **List** that uses **lock**. Note that class **QueueInheritance** uses namespace **LinkedListLibrary** (Fig. 23.4); thus, the solution for the class library that defines **QueueInheritance** must have a reference to the **LinkedListLibrary** class library.

Class **QueueInheritanceTest**'s **Main** method (Fig. 23.14) uses class **QueueInheritance** to instantiate a queue of **object**s called **queue**. Lines 18–21 define four objects that will be enqueued and dequeued. The program enqueues (lines 24, 26, 28 and 30) a **bool** containing **true**, a **char** containing **$**, an **int** containing **34567** and a **string** containing **hello**.

```
1    // Fig. 23.13: QueueInheritanceLibrary.cs
2    // Implementing a queue by inheriting from class List.
3
4    using System;
5    using LinkedListLibrary;
6
7    namespace QueueInheritanceLibrary
8    {
9       // class QueueInheritance inherits List's capabilities
10      public class QueueInheritance : List
11      {
12         // pass name "queue" to List constructor
13         public QueueInheritance() : base( "queue" )
14         {
15         }
16
17         // place dataValue at end of queue by inserting
18         // dataValue at end of linked list
19         public void Enqueue( object dataValue )
20         {
21            InsertAtBack( dataValue );
22         }
23
24         // remove item from front of queue by removing
25         // item at front of linked list
26         public object Dequeue( )
27         {
28            return RemoveFromFront();
29         }
```

Fig. 23.13 **QueueInheritance** extends class **List**. (Part 1 of 2.)

```
30
31      } // end of QueueInheritance
32  }
```

Fig. 23.13 `QueueInheritance` extends class **List**. (Part 2 of 2.)

An infinite **while** loop (lines 39–44) dequeues the elements from the queue in FIFO order. When there are no objects left to dequeue, method **Dequeue** throws an **Empty-ListException** and the program displays the exception's stack trace, which shows the program execution stack at the time the exception occurred. The program uses method **Print** (inherited from class **List**) to output the contents of the queue after each operation. Note that class **QueueInheritanceTest** uses namespace **LinkedListLibrary** (Fig. 23.4) and namespace **QueueInheritanceLibrary** (Fig. 23.13); thus, the solution for class **QueueInheritanceTest** must have references to both class libraries.

```
1   // Fig. 23.14: QueueTest.cs
2   // Testing class QueueInheritance.
3
4   using System;
5   using QueueInheritanceLibrary;
6   using LinkedListLibrary;
7
8   namespace QueueTest
9   {
10      // demonstrate functionality of class QueueInheritance
11      class QueueTest
12      {
13         static void Main( string[] args )
14         {
15            QueueInheritance queue = new QueueInheritance();
16
17            // create objects to store in the stack
18            bool aBoolean = true;
19            char aCharacter = '$';
20            int anInteger = 34567;
21            string aString = "hello";
22
23            // use method Enqueue to add items to queue
24            queue.Enqueue( aBoolean );
25            queue.Print();
26            queue.Enqueue( aCharacter );
27            queue.Print();
28            queue.Enqueue( anInteger );
29            queue.Print();
30            queue.Enqueue( aString );
31            queue.Print();
32
33            // use method Dequeue to remove items from queue
34            object removedObject = null;
35
```

Fig. 23.14 Using inheritance to create a queue. (Part 1 of 2.)

```
36              // remove items from queue
37              try
38              {
39                  while ( true )
40                  {
41                      removedObject = queue.Dequeue();
42                      Console.WriteLine( removedObject + " dequeue" );
43                      queue.Print();
44                  }
45              }
46
47              // if exception occurs, print stack trace
48              catch ( EmptyListException emptyListException )
49              {
50                  Console.Error.WriteLine(
51                      emptyListException.StackTrace );
52              }
53
54          } // end method Main
55
56      } // end class QueueTest
57  }
```

```
The queue is: True

The queue is: True $

The queue is: True $ 34567

The queue is: True $ 34567 hello

True dequeue
The queue is: $ 34567 hello

$ dequeue
The queue is: 34567 hello

34567 dequeue
The queue is: hello

hello dequeue
Empty queue
   at LinkedListLibrary.List.RemoveFromFront()
      in z:\ch23\linkedlistlibrary\linkedlistlibrary.cs:line 114
   at QueueInheritanceLibrary.QueueInheritance.Dequeue()
      in z:\ch23\queueinheritancelibrary\
      queueinheritancelibrary.cs:line 28
   at QueueTest.QueueTest.Main(String[] args)
      in z:\ch23\fig23_14\queuetest.cs:line 41
```

Fig. 23.14 Using inheritance to create a queue. (Part 2 of 2.)

23.6 Trees

Linked lists, stacks and queues are *linear data structures* (i.e., *sequences*). A *tree* is a non-linear, two-dimensional data structure with special properties. Tree nodes contain two or more links. This section discusses *binary trees* (Fig. 23.15)—trees whose nodes all contain two links (none, one or both of which may be **null**). The *root node* is the first node in a tree. Each link in the root node refers to a *child.* The *left child* is the first node in the *left subtree,* and the *right child* is the first node in the *right subtree.* The children of a specific node are called *siblings.* A node with no children is called a *leaf node.* Computer scientists normally draw trees from the root node down—exactly the opposite of the way most trees grow in nature.

Common Programming Error 23.2

*Not setting to **null** the links in leaf nodes of a tree is a common logic error.*

In our binary tree example, we create a special binary tree called a *binary search tree.* A binary search tree (with no duplicate node values) has the characteristic that the values in any left subtree are less than the value in the subtree's parent node, and the values in any right subtree are greater than the value in the subtree's parent node. Figure 23.16 illustrates a binary search tree with 12 integer values. Note that the shape of the binary search tree that corresponds to a set of data can depend on the order in which the values are inserted into the tree.

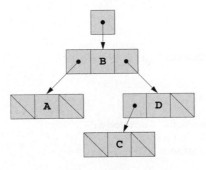

Fig. 23.15 A graphical representation of a binary tree.

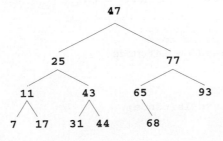

Fig. 23.16 A binary search tree containing 12 values.

23.6.1 Binary Search Tree of Integer Values

The application of Fig. 23.17 and Fig. 23.18 creates a binary search tree of integers and traverses it (i.e., walks through all its nodes) in three ways—using recursive *inorder, preorder* and *postorder traversals*. The program generates 10 random numbers and inserts each into the tree. Figure 23.17 defines class **Tree** in namespace **BinaryTreeLibrary** for reuse purposes. Figure 23.18 defines class **TreeTest** to demonstrate class **Tree**'s functionality. Method **Main** of class **TreeTest** instantiates an empty **Tree** object, then randomly generates 10 integers and inserts each value in the binary tree by calling **Tree** method **InsertNode**. The program then performs preorder, inorder and postorder traversals of the tree. We will discuss these traversals shortly.

Class **TreeNode** (lines 9–95 of Fig. 23.17) is a self-referential class containing three **private** data members—**leftNode** and **rightNode**, of type **TreeNode**, and **data**, of type **int**. Initially, every **TreeNode** is a leaf node, so the constructor (lines 16–20) initializes references **leftNode** and **rightNode** to **null**. Properties **LeftNode** (lines 23–34), **Data** (lines 37–48) and **RightNode** (lines 51–62) provide access to a **ListNode**'s **private** data members. We discuss **TreeNode** method **Insert** (lines 67–93) shortly.

```
1   // Fig. 23.17: BinaryTreeLibrary.cs
2   // Definition of class TreeNode and class Tree.
3
4   using System;
5
6   namespace BinaryTreeLibrary
7   {
8      // class TreeNode definition
9      class TreeNode
10     {
11        private TreeNode leftNode;
12        private int data;
13        private TreeNode rightNode;
14
15        // initialize data and make this a leaf node
16        public TreeNode( int nodeData )
17        {
18           data = nodeData;
19           leftNode = rightNode = null;  // node has no children
20        }
21
22        // LeftNode property
23        public TreeNode LeftNode
24        {
25           get
26           {
27              return leftNode;
28           }
29
```

Fig. 23.17 Definitions of **TreeNode** and **Tree** for a binary search tree. (Part 1 of 5.)

```
30                   set
31                   {
32                       leftNode = value;
33                   }
34               }
35
36               // Data property
37               public int Data
38               {
39                   get
40                   {
41                       return data;
42                   }
43
44                   set
45                   {
46                       data = value;
47                   }
48               }
49
50               // RightNode property
51               public TreeNode RightNode
52               {
53                   get
54                   {
55                       return rightNode;
56                   }
57
58                   set
59                   {
60                       rightNode = value;
61                   }
62               }
63
64
65               // insert TreeNode into Tree that contains nodes;
66               // ignore duplicate values
67               public void Insert( int insertValue )
68               {
69                   // insert in left subtree
70                   if ( insertValue < data )
71                   {
72                       // insert new TreeNode
73                       if ( leftNode == null )
74                           leftNode = new TreeNode( insertValue );
75
76                       // continue traversing left subtree
77                       else
78                           leftNode.Insert( insertValue );
79                   }
80
```

Fig. 23.17 Definitions of **TreeNode** and **Tree** for a binary search tree. (Part 2 of 5.)

```
81              // insert in right subtree
82              else if ( insertValue > data )
83              {
84                 // insert new TreeNode
85                 if ( rightNode == null )
86                    rightNode = new TreeNode( insertValue );
87
88                 // continue traversing right subtree
89                 else
90                    rightNode.Insert( insertValue );
91              }
92
93           }  // end method Insert
94
95        }  // end class TreeNode
96
97        // class Tree definition
98        public class Tree
99        {
100          private TreeNode root;
101
102          // construct an empty Tree of integers
103          public Tree()
104          {
105             root = null;
106          }
107
108          // Insert a new node in the binary search tree.
109          // If the root node is null, create the root node here.
110          // Otherwise, call the insert method of class TreeNode.
111          public void InsertNode( int insertValue )
112          {
113             lock ( this )
114             {
115                if ( root == null )
116                   root = new TreeNode( insertValue );
117
118                else
119                   root.Insert( insertValue );
120             }
121          }
122
123          // begin preorder traversal
124          public void PreorderTraversal()
125          {
126             lock ( this )
127             {
128                PreorderHelper( root );
129             }
130          }
131
```

Fig. 23.17 Definitions of **TreeNode** and **Tree** for a binary search tree. (Part 3 of 5.)

```
132      // recursive method to perform preorder traversal
133      private void PreorderHelper( TreeNode node )
134      {
135         if ( node == null )
136            return;
137
138         // output node data
139         Console.Write( node.Data + " " );
140
141         // traverse left subtree
142         PreorderHelper( node.LeftNode );
143
144         // traverse right subtree
145         PreorderHelper( node.RightNode );
146      }
147
148      // begin inorder traversal
149      public void InorderTraversal()
150      {
151         lock ( this )
152         {
153            InorderHelper( root );
154         }
155      }
156
157      // recursive method to perform inorder traversal
158      private void InorderHelper( TreeNode node )
159      {
160         if ( node == null )
161            return;
162
163         // traverse left subtree
164         InorderHelper( node.LeftNode );
165
166         // output node data
167         Console.Write( node.Data + " " );
168
169         // traverse right subtree
170         InorderHelper( node.RightNode );
171      }
172
173      // begin postorder traversal
174      public void PostorderTraversal()
175      {
176         lock ( this )
177         {
178            PostorderHelper( root );
179         }
180      }
181
```

Fig. 23.17 Definitions of **TreeNode** and **Tree** for a binary search tree. (Part 4 of 5.)

```
182         // recursive method to perform postorder traversal
183         private void PostorderHelper( TreeNode node )
184         {
185            if ( node == null )
186               return;
187
188            // traverse left subtree
189            PostorderHelper( node.LeftNode );
190
191            // traverse right subtree
192            PostorderHelper( node.RightNode );
193
194            // output node data
195            Console.Write( node.Data + " " );
196         }
197
198      }  // end class Tree
199   }
```

Fig. 23.17 Definitions of **TreeNode** and **Tree** for a binary search tree. (Part 5 of 5.)

```
1   // Fig. 23.18: TreeTest.cs
2   // This program tests class Tree.
3
4   using System;
5   using BinaryTreeLibrary;
6
7   namespace TreeTest
8   {
9      // class TreeTest definition
10     public class TreeTest
11     {
12        // test class Tree
13        static void Main( string[] args )
14        {
15           Tree tree = new Tree();
16           int insertValue;
17
18           Console.WriteLine( "Inserting values: " );
19           Random random = new Random();
20
21           // insert 10 random integers from 0-99 in tree
22           for ( int i = 1; i <= 10; i++ )
23           {
24              insertValue = random.Next( 100 );
25              Console.Write( insertValue + " " );
26
27              tree.InsertNode( insertValue );
28           }
29
30           // perform preorder traversal of tree
31           Console.WriteLine( "\n\nPreorder traversal" );
```

Fig. 23.18 Creating and traversing a binary tree. (Part 1 of 2.)

```
32                tree.PreorderTraversal();
33
34                // perform inorder traversal of tree
35                Console.WriteLine( "\n\nInorder traversal" );
36                tree.InorderTraversal();
37
38                // perform postorder traversal of tree
39                Console.WriteLine( "\n\nPostorder traversal" );
40                tree.PostorderTraversal();
41                Console.WriteLine();
42          }
43
44       } // end class TreeTest
45    }
```

```
Inserting values:
39 69 94 47 50 72 55 41 97 73

Preorder traversal
39 69 47 41 50 55 94 72 73 97

Inorder traversal
39 41 47 50 55 69 72 73 94 97

Postorder traversal
41 55 50 47 73 72 97 94 69 39
```

Fig. 23.18 Creating and traversing a binary tree. (Part 2 of 2.)

Class **Tree** (lines 98–198 of Fig. 23.17) manipulates objects of class **TreeNode**. Class **Tree** has as **private** data **root** (line 100)—a reference to the root node of the tree. The class contains **public** method **InsertNode** (lines 111–121) to insert a new node in the tree and **public** methods **PreorderTraversal** (lines 124–130), **InorderTraversal** (lines 149–155) and **PostorderTraversal** (lines 174–180) to begin traversals of the tree. Each of these methods calls a separate recursive utility method to perform the traversal operations on the internal representation of the tree. The **Tree** constructor (lines 103–106) initializes **root** to **null** to indicate that the tree initially is empty.

The **Tree** class's method **InsertNode** (lines 111–121) first locks the **Tree** object for thread safety, then determines whether the tree is empty. If so, line 116 allocates a new **TreeNode**, initializes the node with the integer being inserted in the tree and assigns the new node to **root**. If the tree is not empty, **InsertNode** calls **TreeNode** method **Insert** (lines 67–93), which recursively determines the location for the new node in the tree and inserts the node at that location. *A node can be inserted only as a leaf node in a binary search tree.*

The **TreeNode** method **Insert** compares the value to insert with the **data** value in the root node. If the insert value is less than the root-node data, the program determines whether the left subtree is empty (line 73). If so, line 74 allocates a new **TreeNode**, initializes it with the integer being inserted and assigns the new node to reference **leftNode**. Otherwise, line 78 recursively calls **Insert** for the left subtree to insert the value into the left subtree. If the insert value is greater than the root-node data, the program determines whether the right subtree is empty (line 85). If so, line 86 allocates a new **TreeNode**, initializes it with the integer being inserted and assigns the ncw node to reference **right-Node**. Otherwise, line 90 recursively calls **Insert** for the right subtree to insert the value in the right subtree.

Methods **InorderTraversal**, **PreorderTraversal** and **PostorderTraversal** call helper methods **InorderHelper** (lines 158–171), **PreorderHelper** (lines 133–146) and **PostorderHelper** (lines 183–196), respectively, to traverse the tree and print the node values. The purpose of the helper methods in class **Tree** is to allow the programmer to start a traversal without the need to obtain a reference to the **root** node first, then call the recursive method with that reference. Methods **InorderTraversal**, **PreorderTraversal** and **PostorderTraversal** simply take the **private** reference **root** and pass it to the appropriate helper method to initiate a traversal of the tree. For the following discussion, we use the binary search tree shown in Fig. 23.19.

Method **InorderHelper** (lines 158–171) defines the steps for an inorder traversal. Those steps are as follows:

1. If the argument is **null**, return immediately.

2. Traverse the left subtree with a call to **InorderHelper** (line 164).

3. Process the value in the node (line 167).

4. Traverse the right subtree with a call to **InorderHelper** (line 170).

The inorder traversal does not process the value in a node until the values in that node's left subtree are processed. The inorder traversal of the tree in Fig. 23.19 is

    6 13 17 27 33 42 48

Note that the inorder traversal of a binary search tree prints the node values in ascending order. The process of creating a binary search tree actually sorts the data—thus, this process is called the *binary tree sort*.

Method **PreorderHelper** (lines 133–146) defines the steps for a preorder traversal. Those steps are as follows:

1. If the argument is **null**, return immediately.

2. Process the value in the node (line 139).

3. Traverse the left subtree with a call to **PreorderHelper** (line 142).

4. Traverse the right subtree with a call to **PreorderHelper** (line 145).

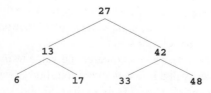

Fig. 23.19 A binary search tree.

The preorder traversal processes the value in each node as the node is visited. After processing the value in a given node, the preorder traversal processes the values in the left subtree, then the values in the right subtree. The preorder traversal of the tree in Fig. 23.19 is

27 13 6 17 42 33 48

Method **PostorderHelper** (lines 183–198) defines the steps for a postorder traversal. Those steps are as follows:

1. If the argument is **null**, return immediately.

2. Traverse the left subtree with a call to **PostorderHelper** (line 189).

3. Traverse the right subtree with a call to **PostorderHelper** (line 192).

4. Process the value in the node (line 195).

The postorder traversal processes the value in each node after the values of all that node's children are processed. The postorder traversal of the tree in Fig. 23.19 is

6 17 13 33 48 42 27

The binary search tree facilitates *duplicate elimination*. While building a tree, the insertion operation recognizes attempts to insert a duplicate value, because a duplicate follows the same "go left" or "go right" decisions on each comparison as the original value did. Thus, the insertion operation eventually compares the duplicate with a node containing the same value. At this point, the insertion operation might simply discard the duplicate value.

Searching a binary tree for a value that matches a key value is fast, especially for *tightly packed* trees. In a tightly packed tree, each level contains about twice as many elements as the previous level. Figure 23.19 is a tightly packed binary tree. A binary search tree with n elements has a minimum of $\log_2 n$ levels. Thus, at most $\log_2 n$ comparisons are required either to find a match or to determine that no match exists. Searching a (tightly packed) 1000-element binary search tree requires at most 10 comparisons, because $2^{10} > 1000$. Searching a (tightly packed) 1,000,000-element binary search tree requires at most 20 comparisons, because $2^{20} > 1,000,000$.

The chapter exercises present algorithms for other binary tree operations, such as performing a *level-order traversal of a binary tree*. The level-order traversal of a binary tree visits the nodes of the tree row by row, starting at the root-node level. On each level of the tree, a level-order traversal visits the nodes from left to right.

23.6.2 Binary Search Tree of **IComparable** Objects

The binary tree example in Section 23.6.1 works nicely when all the data is of type **int**. Suppose that you want to manipulate a binary tree of double values. You could rewrite the **TreeNode** and **Tree** classes with different names and customize the classes to manipulate double values. Similarly, for each data type you could create customized versions of classes **TreeNode** and **Tree**. This results in a proliferation of code, which can become difficult to manage and maintain. The C++ programming language provides a technology called templates that enables us to write a class definition once, then have the compiler generate new versions of the class for any data type we choose.

Ideally, we would like to define the functionality of a binary tree once and reuse that functionality for many data types. Languages like Java™ and C# provide polymorphic capabilities that enable all objects to be manipulated in a uniform manner. Using such capabilities enables us to design a more flexible data structure.

In our next example, we take advantage of C#'s polymorphic capabilities by implementing **TreeNode** and **Tree** classes that manipulate objects of any type that implements interface *IComparable* (namespace **System**). It is imperative that we be able to compare objects stored in a binary search, so we can determine the path to the insertion point of a new node. Classes that implement **IComparable** define method *CompareTo*, which compares the object that invokes the method with the object that the method receives as an argument. The method returns an **int** value less than zero if the calling object is less than the argument object, zero if the objects are equal, a positive value if the calling object is greater than the argument object. Also, both the calling and argument objects must be of the same data type; otherwise, the method throws an **ArgumentException**.

The program of Fig. 23.20 and Fig. 23.21 enhances the program from Section 23.6.1 to manipulate **IComparable** objects. One restriction on the new versions of classes **TreeNode** and **Tree** in Fig. 23.20 is that each **Tree** object can contain objects of only one data type (e.g., all **string**s or all **double**s). If a program attempts to insert multiple data types in the same **Tree** object, **ArgumentException**s will occur. We modified only six lines of code in class **TreeNode** (lines 13, 17, 38, 67, 70 and 82) and one line of code in class **Tree** (line 111) to enable processing of **IComparable** objects. With the exception of lines 70 and 82, all other changes simply replaced the type **int** with the type **IComparable**. Lines 70 and 82 previously used the **<** and **>** operators to compare the value being inserted with the value in a given node. These lines now compare **IComparable** objects via the interface's method **CompareTo**, then test the method's return value to determine whether it is less than zero (the calling object is less than the argument object) or greater than zero (the calling object is greater than the argument object), respectively.

Class **TreeTest** (Fig. 23.21) creates three **Tree** objects to store **int**, **double** and **string** values, all of which the .NET Framework defines as **IComparable** types. The program populates the trees with the values in arrays **intArray** (line 15), **doubleArray** (lines 16–17) and **stringArray** (lines 18–19), respectively.

Method **PopulateTree** (lines 38–48) receives an **Array** containing the initializer values for the **Tree**, a **Tree** into which the array elements will be placed and a **string** representing the **Tree** name as arguments, then inserts each **Array** element in the **Tree**. Method **TraverseTree** (lines 51–68) receives a **Tree** and a **string** representing the **Tree** name as arguments, then outputs the preorder, inorder and postorder traversals of the **Tree**. Note that the inorder traversal of each **Tree** outputs the data in sorted order regardless of the data type stored in the **Tree**. Our polymorphic implementation of class Tree invokes the appropriate data type's **CompareTo** method to determine the path to each value's insertion point by using the standard binary search tree insertion rules. Also, notice that the **Tree** of **string**s appears in alphabetical order.

```
1   // Fig. 23.20: BinaryTreeLibrary2.cs
2   // Definition of class TreeNode and class Tree for IComparable
3   // objects.
4
```

Fig. 23.20 Definitions of class **TreeNode** and **Tree** for manipulating **IComparable** objects. (Part 1 of 5.)

```
5   using System;
6
7   namespace BinaryTreeLibrary2
8   {
9      // class TreeNode definition
10     class TreeNode
11     {
12        private TreeNode leftNode;
13        private IComparable data;
14        private TreeNode rightNode;
15
16        // initialize data and make this a leaf node
17        public TreeNode( IComparable nodeData )
18        {
19           data = nodeData;
20           leftNode = rightNode = null;  // node has no children
21        }
22
23        // LeftNode property
24        public TreeNode LeftNode
25        {
26           get
27           {
28              return leftNode;
29           }
30
31           set
32           {
33              leftNode = value;
34           }
35        }
36
37        // Data property
38        public IComparable Data
39        {
40           get
41           {
42              return data;
43           }
44
45           set
46           {
47              data = value;
48           }
49        }
50
51        // RightNode property
52        public TreeNode RightNode
53        {
54           get
55           {
```

Fig. 23.20 Definitions of class **TreeNode** and **Tree** for manipulating **IComparable** objects. (Part 2 of 5.)

```
56               return rightNode;
57            }
58
59            set
60            {
61               rightNode = value;
62            }
63         }
64
65         // insert TreeNode into Tree that contains nodes;
66         // ignore duplicate values
67         public void Insert( IComparable insertValue )
68         {
69            // insert in left subtree
70            if ( insertValue.CompareTo( data ) < 0 )
71            {
72               // insert new TreeNode
73               if ( leftNode == null )
74                  leftNode = new TreeNode( insertValue );
75
76               // continue traversing left subtree
77               else
78                  leftNode.Insert( insertValue );
79            }
80
81            // insert in right subtree
82            else if ( insertValue.CompareTo( data ) > 0 )
83            {
84               // insert new TreeNode
85               if ( rightNode == null )
86                  rightNode = new TreeNode( insertValue );
87
88               // continue traversing right subtree
89               else
90                  rightNode.Insert( insertValue );
91            }
92
93         }  // end method Insert
94
95      }  // end class TreeNode
96
97      // class Tree definition
98      public class Tree
99      {
100         private TreeNode root;
101
102         // construct an empty Tree of integers
103         public Tree()
104         {
105            root = null;
106         }
107
```

Fig. 23.20 Definitions of class **TreeNode** and **Tree** for manipulating **IComparable** objects. (Part 3 of 5.)

```
108          // Insert a new node in the binary search tree.
109          // If the root node is null, create the root node here.
110          // Otherwise, call the insert method of class TreeNode.
111          public void InsertNode( IComparable insertValue )
112          {
113             lock ( this )
114             {
115                if ( root == null )
116                   root = new TreeNode( insertValue );
117
118                else
119                   root.Insert( insertValue );
120             }
121          }
122
123          // begin preorder traversal
124          public void PreorderTraversal()
125          {
126             lock ( this )
127             {
128                PreorderHelper( root );
129             }
130          }
131
132          // recursive method to perform preorder traversal
133          private void PreorderHelper( TreeNode node )
134          {
135             if ( node == null )
136                return;
137
138             // output node data
139             Console.Write( node.Data + " " );
140
141             // traverse left subtree
142             PreorderHelper( node.LeftNode );
143
144             // traverse right subtree
145             PreorderHelper( node.RightNode );
146          }
147
148          // begin inorder traversal
149          public void InorderTraversal()
150          {
151             lock ( this )
152             {
153                InorderHelper( root );
154             }
155          }
156
157          // recursive method to perform inorder traversal
158          private void InorderHelper( TreeNode node )
159          {
```

Fig. 23.20 Definitions of class **TreeNode** and **Tree** for manipulating **IComparable** objects. (Part 4 of 5.)

```
160              if ( node == null )
161                 return;
162
163              // traverse left subtree
164              InorderHelper( node.LeftNode );
165
166              // output node data
167              Console.Write( node.Data + " " );
168
169              // traverse right subtree
170              InorderHelper( node.RightNode );
171           }
172
173           // begin postorder traversal
174           public void PostorderTraversal()
175           {
176              lock ( this )
177              {
178                 PostorderHelper( root );
179              }
180           }
181
182           // recursive method to perform postorder traversal
183           private void PostorderHelper( TreeNode node )
184           {
185              if ( node == null )
186                 return;
187
188              // traverse left subtree
189              PostorderHelper( node.LeftNode );
190
191              // traverse right subtree
192              PostorderHelper( node.RightNode );
193
194              // output node data
195              Console.Write( node.Data + " " );
196           }
197
198        } // end class Tree
199  }
```

Fig. 23.20 Definitions of class **TreeNode** and **Tree** for manipulating **IComparable** objects. (Part 5 of 5.)

```
1    // Fig. 23.21: TreeTest.cs
2    // This program tests class Tree.
3
4    using System;
5    using BinaryTreeLibrary2;
```

Fig. 23.21 Demonstrating class Tree with **IComparable** objects. (Part 1 of 3.)

```
6
7    namespace TreeTest
8    {
9        // class TreeTest definition
10       public class TreeTest
11       {
12           // test class Tree
13           static void Main( string[] args )
14           {
15               int[] intArray = { 8, 2, 4, 3, 1, 7, 5, 6 };
16               double[] doubleArray =
17                   { 8.8, 2.2, 4.4, 3.3, 1.1, 7.7, 5.5, 6.6 };
18               string[] stringArray = { "eight", "two", "four",
19                   "three", "one", "seven", "five", "six" };
20
21               // create int Tree
22               Tree intTree = new Tree();
23               PopulateTree( intArray, intTree, "intTree" );
24               TraverseTree( intTree, "intTree" );
25
26               // create double Tree
27               Tree doubleTree = new Tree();
28               PopulateTree( doubleArray, doubleTree, "doubleTree" );
29               TraverseTree( doubleTree, "doubleTree" );
30
31               // create string Tree
32               Tree stringTree = new Tree();
33               PopulateTree( stringArray, stringTree, "stringTree" );
34               TraverseTree( stringTree, "stringTree" );
35           }
36
37           // populate Tree with array elements
38           static void populateTree(
39               Array array, Tree tree, string name )
40           {
41               Console.WriteLine( "\nInserting into " + name + ":" );
42
43               foreach ( IComparable data in array )
44               {
45                   Console.Write( data + " " );
46                   tree.InsertNode( data );
47               }
48           }
49
50           // insert perform traversals
51           static void traverseTree( Tree tree, string treeType )
52           {
53               // perform preorder traversal of tree
54               Console.WriteLine(
55                   "\n\nPreorder traversal of " + treeType );
56               tree.PreorderTraversal();
57
```

Fig. 23.21 Demonstrating class **Tree** with **IComparable** objects. (Part 2 of 3.)

```
58              // perform inorder traversal of tree
59              Console.WriteLine(
60                 "\n\nInorder traversal of " + treeType );
61              tree.InorderTraversal();
62
63              // perform postorder traversal of tree
64              Console.WriteLine(
65                 "\n\nPostorder traversal of " + treeType );
66              tree.PostorderTraversal();
67              Console.WriteLine( "\n" );
68           }
69
70        }  // end class TreeTest
71     }
```

```
Inserting into intTree:
8 2 4 3 1 7 5 6

Preorder traversal of intTree
8 2 1 4 3 7 5 6

Inorder traversal of intTree
1 2 3 4 5 6 7 8

Postorder traversal of intTree
1 3 6 5 7 4 2 8


Inserting into doubleTree:
8.8 2.2 4.4 3.3 1.1 7.7 5.5 6.6

Preorder traversal of doubleTree
8.8 2.2 1.1 4.4 3.3 7.7 5.5 6.6

Inorder traversal of doubleTree
1.1 2.2 3.3 4.4 5.5 6.6 7.7 8.8

Postorder traversal of doubleTree
1.1 3.3 6.6 5.5 7.7 4.4 2.2 8.8


Inserting into stringTree:
eight two four three one seven five six

Preorder traversal of stringTree
eight two four five three one seven six

Inorder traversal of stringTree
eight five four one seven six three two

Postorder traversal of stringTree
five six seven one three four two eight
```

Fig. 23.21 Demonstrating class **Tree** with **IComparable** objects. (Part 3 of 3.)

23.7 Collection Classes

The previous sections of this chapter discussed how to create and manipulate data structures. The discussion was "low level," in the sense that we painstakingly created each element of each data structure dynamically with **new** and modified the data structures by directly manipulating their elements and references to their elements. In this section, we consider the prepackaged data-structure classes provided by the .NET Framework. These classes are known as *collection classes*—they store collections of data. Each instance of one of these classes is known as a *collection*, which is a set of items.

With collection classes, instead of creating data structures, the programmer simply uses existing data structures, without concern for how the data structures are implemented. This methodology is a marvelous example of code reuse. Programmers can code faster and can expect excellent performance, maximizing execution speed and minimizing memory consumption.

Some examples of collections are the cards you hold in a card game, your favorite songs stored in your computer and the real-estate records in your local registry of deeds (which map book numbers and page numbers to property owners). The .NET Framework provides several collections. We demonstrate four collection classes—***Array***, ***ArrayList***, ***Stack*** and ***Hashtable***—most from namespace **System.Collections**, plus built-in array capabilities. In addition, namespace **System.Collections** provides several other data structures, including ***BitArray*** (a collection of true/false values), ***Queue*** and ***SortedList*** (a collection of key/value pairs that are sorted by key and can be accessed either by key or by index).

The .NET Framework provides ready-to-go, reusable components; you do not need to write your own collection classes. The collections are standardized so applications can share them easily, without having to be concerned with the details of their implementation. These collections are written for broad reuse. They are tuned for rapid execution and for efficient use of memory. As new data structures and algorithms are developed that fit this framework, a large base of programmers already will be familiar with the interfaces and algorithms implemented by those data structures.

23.7.1 Class **Array**

Chapter 7 presented basic array-processing capabilities, and many subsequent chapters used the techniques shown there. We discussed briefly that all arrays inherit from class **Array** (namespace **System**) which defines a **Length** property that specifies the number of elements in an array. In addition, class **Array** provides **static** methods that provide algorithms for processing arrays. Typically, class **Array** overloads these methods to provide multiple options for performing algorithms. For example, **Array** method **Reverse** can reverse the order of the elements in an entire array or can reverse the elements in a specified range of elements in an array. For a complete list of class **Array**'s **static** methods and their overloaded versions, see the online documentation for the class. Figure 23.22 demonstrates several **static** methods of class **Array**.

Line 28 uses **static** **Array** method *Sort* to sort an array of **double** values. When this method returns, the array contains its original elements sorted in ascending order.

Lines 31–32 uses **static** **Array** method *Copy* to copy elements from array **intArray** into array **intArrayCopy**. The first argument is the array to copy

(**intValues**), the second argument is the destination array (**intValuesCopy**) and the
third argument is an integer representing the number of elements to copy (in this case,
intValues.Length specifies all elements).

```
1   // Fig. 23.22: UsingArray.cs
2   // Using Array class to perform common array manipulations.
3
4   using System;
5   using System.Windows.Forms;
6   using System.Collections;
7
8   namespace UsingArray
9   {
10     // demonstrate algorithms of class Array
11     class UsingArray
12     {
13        private int[] intValues = { 1, 2, 3, 4, 5, 6 };
14        private double[] doubleValues =
15           { 8.4, 9.3, 0.2, 7.9, 3.4 };
16        private int[] intValuesCopy;
17        private string output;
18
19        // method to build and display program output
20        public void Start()
21        {
22           intValuesCopy = new int[ intValues.Length ];
23
24           output = "Initial array values:\n";
25           PrintArray();  // output initial array contents
26
27           // sort doubleValues
28           Array.Sort( doubleValues );
29
30           // copy intValues into intValuesCopy
31           Array.Copy( intValues, intValuesCopy,
32              intValues.Length );
33
34           output += "\nArray values after Sort and Copy:\n";
35           PrintArray();  // output array contents
36           output += "\n";
37
38           // search for 5 in intValues
39           int result = Array.BinarySearch( intValues, 5 );
40           output +=
41              ( result >= 0 ? "5 found at element " + result :
42                 "5 not found" ) + " in intValues\n";
43
44           // search for 8763 in intValues
45           result = Array.BinarySearch( intValues, 8763 );
46           output +=
47              ( result >= 0 ? "8763 found at element " + result :
48                 "8763 not found" ) + " in intValues";
```

Fig. 23.22 Program that demonstrates class **Array**. (Part 1 of 2.)

```
49
50              MessageBox.Show( output, "Using Class Array",
51                 MessageBoxButtons.OK, MessageBoxIcon.Information );
52           }
53
54           // append array content to output string
55           private void PrintArray()
56           {
57              output += "doubleValues: ";
58
59              foreach ( double element in doubleValues )
60                 output += element + " ";
61
62              output += "\nintValues: ";
63
64              foreach ( int element in intValues )
65                 output += element + " ";
66
67              output += "\nintValuesCopy: ";
68
69              foreach ( int element in intValuesCopy )
70                 output += element + " ";
71
72              output += "\n";
73           }
74
75           // main entry point for application
76           static void Main( string[] args )
77           {
78              UsingArray application = new UsingArray();
79
80              application.Start();
81           }
82
83      } // end class UsingArray
84  }
```

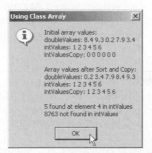

Fig. 23.22 Program that demonstrates class **Array**. (Part 2 of 2.)

Lines 39 and 45 invoke **static Array** method **BinarySearch** to perform binary searches on array **intValues**. Method **BinarySearch** receives the *sorted* array in which to search and the key for which to search. The method returns the index in the array at which it finds the key (but a negative number if the key was not found).

Other **static Array** methods include **Clear** (to set a range of elements to 0 or null), **CreateInstance** (to create a new array of a specified data type), **IndexOf** (to locate the first occurrence of an object in an array or portion of an array), **LastIndexOf** (to locate the last occurrence of an object in an array or portion of an array) and **Reverse** (to reverse the contents of an array or portion of an array).

23.7.2 Class **ArrayList**

In most programming languages, conventional arrays have a fixed size—they cannot be changed dynamically to conform to an application's execution-time memory requirements. In some applications, this fixed-size limitation presents a problem for programmers. They must choose between using fixed-size arrays that are large enough to store the maximum number of elements the program may require and using dynamic data structures that can grow and shrink the amount of memory required to store data in response to the changing requirements of a program at execution time.

The .NET Framework's class **ArrayList** collection mimics the functionality of conventional arrays and provides dynamic resizing of the collection through the class's methods. At any time an **ArrayList** contains a certain number of elements less than or equal to its *capacity*—the number of elements currently reserved for an **ArrayList**. A program can manipulate the capacity with **ArrayList** property **Capacity**. If an **ArrayList** needs to grow, it by default doubles its current **Capacity**.

Performance Tip 23.6

*As with linked lists, inserting additional elements into an **ArrayList** whose current size is less than its capacity is a fast operation.*

Performance Tip 23.7

*It is a slow operation to insert an element into an **ArrayList** that needs to grow larger to accommodate a new element.*

Performance Tip 23.8

*If storage is at a premium, use method **TrimToSize** of class **ArrayList** to trim an **ArrayList** to its exact size. This will optimize an **ArrayList**'s memory use. Be careful—if the program needs to insert additional elements, the process will be slower because the **ArrayList** must grow dynamically (trimming leaves no room for growth).*

Performance Tip 23.9

*The default capacity increment, doubling the size of the **ArrayList**, may seem to waste storage, but doubling is an efficient way for an **ArrayList** to grow quickly to "about the right size." This is a much more efficient use of time than growing the **ArrayList** by one element at a time in response to insert operations.*

ArrayLists store references to **object**s. All classes derive from class **Object**, so an **ArrayList** can contain objects of any type. Figure 23.23 lists some useful methods of class **ArrayList**.

Figure 23.24 demonstrates class **ArrayList** and several of its methods. Users can type a **string** into the user interface's **TextBox**, then press a button representing an **ArrayList** method to see that method's functionality. A **TextBox** displays messages indicating each operation's results.

Method	Description
Add	Adds an **object** to the **ArrayList**. Returns an **int** specifying the index at which the **object** was added.
Clear	Removes all the elements from the **ArrayList**.
Contains	Returns **true** if the specified **object** is in the **ArrayList**; otherwise, returns **false**.
IndexOf	Returns the index of the first occurrence of the specified **object** in the **ArrayList**.
Insert	Inserts an **object** at the specified index.
Remove	Removes the first occurrence of the specified **object**.
RemoveAt	Removes an object at the specified index.
RemoveRange	Removes a specified number of elements starting at a specified index in the **ArrayList**.
Sort	Sorts the **ArrayList**.
TrimToSize	Sets the **Capacity** of the **ArrayList** to be the number of elements the **ArrayList** currently contains.

Fig. 23.23 Some methods of class **ArrayList**.

```
1   // Fig. 23.24: ArrayListTest.cs
2   // Using class ArrayList.
3
4   using System;
5   using System.Drawing;
6   using System.Collections;
7   using System.ComponentModel;
8   using System.Windows.Forms;
9   using System.Data;
10  using System.Text;
11
12  namespace ArrayListTest
13  {
14     // demonstrating ArrayList functionality
15     public class ArrayListTest : System.Windows.Forms.Form
16     {
17        private System.Windows.Forms.Button addButton;
18        private System.Windows.Forms.TextBox inputTextBox;
19        private System.Windows.Forms.Label inputLabel;
20        private System.Windows.Forms.Button removeButton;
21        private System.Windows.Forms.Button firstButton;
22        private System.Windows.Forms.Button lastButton;
23        private System.Windows.Forms.Button isEmptyButton;
24        private System.Windows.Forms.Button containsButton;
25        private System.Windows.Forms.Button locationButton;
```

Fig. 23.24 Demonstrating the **ArrayList** class. (Part 1 of 5.)

```
26          private System.Windows.Forms.Button trimButton;
27          private System.Windows.Forms.Button statisticsButton;
28          private System.Windows.Forms.Button displayButton;
29
30          // Required designer variable.
31          private System.ComponentModel.Container components = null;
32          private System.Windows.Forms.TextBox consoleTextBox;
33
34          // ArrayList for manipulating strings
35          private ArrayList arrayList = new ArrayList( 1 );
36
37          public ArrayListTest()
38          {
39             // Required for Windows Form Designer support
40             InitializeComponent();
41          }
42
43          // Visual Studio.NET generated code
44
45          // main entry point for the application
46          [STAThread]
47          static void Main()
48          {
49             Application.Run( new ArrayListTest() );
50          }
51
52          // add item to end of arrayList
53          private void addButton_Click(
54             object sender, System.EventArgs e )
55          {
56             arrayList.Add( inputTextBox.Text );
57             consoleTextBox.Text =
58                "Added to end: " + inputTextBox.Text;
59             inputTextBox.Clear();
60          }
61
62          // remove specified item from arrayList
63          private void removeButton_Click(
64             object sender, System.EventArgs e )
65          {
66             arrayList.Remove( inputTextBox.Text );
67             consoleTextBox.Text = "Removed: " + inputTextBox.Text;
68             inputTextBox.Clear();
69          }
70
71          // display first element
72          private void firstButton_Click(
73             object sender, System.EventArgs e )
74          {
75             // get first element
76             try
77             {
```

Fig. 23.24 Demonstrating the **ArrayList** class. (Part 2 of 5.)

```
78              consoleTextBox.Text =
79                 "First element: " + arrayList[ 0 ];
80          }
81
82          // show exception if no elements in arrayList
83          catch ( ArgumentOutOfRangeException outOfRange )
84          {
85              consoleTextBox.Text = outOfRange.ToString();
86          }
87       }
88
89       // display last element
90       private void lastButton_Click(
91          object sender, System.EventArgs e )
92       {
93          // get last element
94          try
95          {
96              consoleTextBox.Text = "Last element: " +
97                 arrayList[ arrayList.Count - 1 ];
98          }
99
100         // show exception if no elements in arrrayList
101         catch ( ArgumentOutOfRangeException outOfRange )
102         {
103             consoleTextBox.Text = outOfRange.ToString();
104         }
105      }
106
107      // determine whether arrayList is empty
108      private void isEmptyButton_Click(
109         object sender, System.EventArgs e )
110      {
111         consoleTextBox.Text = ( arrayList.Count == 0 ?
112            "arrayList is empty" : "arrayList is not empty" );
113      }
114
115      // determine whether arrayList contains specified object
116      private void containsButton_Click(
117         object sender, System.EventArgs e )
118      {
119         if ( arrayList.Contains( inputTextBox.Text ) )
120            consoleTextBox.Text = "arrayList contains " +
121               inputTextBox.Text;
122         else
123            consoleTextBox.Text = inputTextBox.Text +
124               " not found";
125      }
126
127      // determine location of specified object
128      private void locationButton_Click(
129         object sender, System.EventArgs e )
130      {
```

Fig. 23.24 Demonstrating the **ArrayList** class. (Part 3 of 5.)

```
131             consoleTextBox.Text = "Element is at location " +
132                arrayList.IndexOf( inputTextBox.Text );
133          }
134
135          // trim arrayList to current size
136          private void trimButton_Click(
137             object sender, System.EventArgs e )
138          {
139             arrayList.TrimToSize();
140             consoleTextBox.Text = "Vector trimmed to size";
141          }
142
143          // show arrayList current size and capacity
144          private void statisticsButton_Click(
145             object sender, System.EventArgs e )
146          {
147             consoleTextBox.Text = "Size = " + arrayList.Count +
148                "; capacity = " + arrayList.Capacity;
149          }
150
151          // display contents of arrayList
152          private void displayButton_Click(
153             object sender, System.EventArgs e )
154          {
155             IEnumerator enumerator = arrayList.GetEnumerator();
156             StringBuilder buffer = new StringBuilder();
157
158             while ( enumerator.MoveNext() )
159                buffer.Append( enumerator.Current + "   " );
160
161             consoleTextBox.Text = buffer.ToString();
162          }
163       }
164 }
```

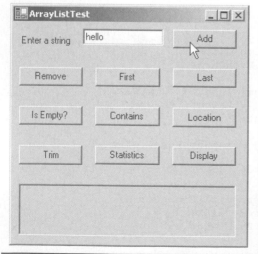
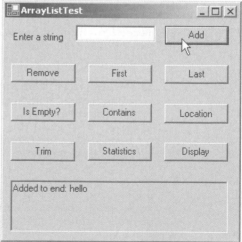

Fig. 23.24 Demonstrating the **ArrayList** class. (Part 4 of 5.)

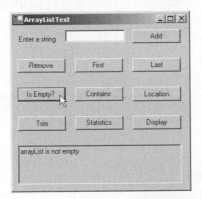

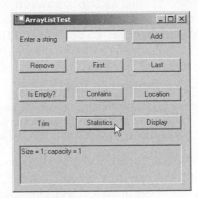

Fig. 23.24 Demonstrating the **ArrayList** class. (Part 5 of 5.)

The **ArrayList** in this example stores **string**s that users input in the **TextBox**. Line 35 creates an **ArrayList** with an initial capacity of one element. This **ArrayList** will double in size each time the user fills the array and attempts to add another element.

ArrayList method **Add** appends a new element at the end of an **ArrayList**. When the user clicks **Add**, event handler **addButton_Click** (lines 53–60) invokes method **Add** (line 56) to append the **string** in the **inputTextBox** to the **ArrayList**.

ArrayList method **Remove** deletes a specified item from an **ArrayList**. When the user clicks **Remove**, event handler **removeButton_Click** (line 63–69) invokes **Remove** (line 66) to remove the **string** specified in the **inputTextBox** from the **ArrayList**. If the object passed to **Remove** is in the **ArrayList**, the first occurrence of that object is removed, and all subsequent elements shift toward the beginning of the **ArrayList** to fill the empty position.

A program can access **ArrayList** elements like conventional array elements by following the **ArrayList** reference name with the array subscript operator (**[ ]**) and the desired index of the element. Event handlers **firstButton_Click** (lines 72–87) and **lastButton_Click** (lines 90–105) use the **ArrayList** subscript operator to retrieve the first element (line 79) and last element (line 97), respectively. An **ArgumentOutOf-RangeException** occurs if the specified index is not both greater than 0 and less than the number of elements currently stored in the **ArrayList**.

Event handler **isEmptyButton_Click** (lines 108–113) uses **ArrayList** property *Count* (line 111) to determine whether the **ArrayList** is empty. Event handler **containsButton_Click** (lines 116–125) uses **ArrayList** method **Contains** (line 119) to determine whether the the given object is currently in the **ArrayList**. If so, the method returns **true**; otherwise, it returns **false**.

Performance Tip 23.10

ArrayList method **Contains** *performs a linear search, which is a costly operation for large* **ArrayLists***. If the* **ArrayList** *is sorted, use* **ArrayList** *method* **Binary-Search** *to perform a more efficient search.*

When the user clicks **Location**, event handler **locationButton_Click** (lines 128–133) invokes **ArrayList** method *IndexOf* (line 132) to determine the index of a particular object in the **ArrayList**. **IndexOf** returns **-1** if the element is not found.

When the user clicks **Trim**, event handler **trimButton_Click** (lines 136–141) invokes method *TrimToSize* (line 139) to set the *Capacity* property to equal the **Count** property. This reduces the storage capacity of the **ArrayList** to the exact number of elements currently in the **ArrayList**.

When the user clicks **Statistics**, **statisticsButton_Click** (lines 144–149) uses the **Count** and **Capacity** properties to display the current number of elements in the **ArrayList** and the maximum number of elements that can be stored without allocating more memory to the **ArrayList**.

When users click **Display**, **displayButton_Click** (lines 152–162) outputs the contents of the **ArrayList**. This event handler uses an *IEnumerator* (sometimes called an *enumerator* or an *iterator*) to traverse the elements of an **ArrayList** one element at a time. Interface **IEnumerator** defines methods *MoveNext* and *Reset* and property *Current*. **MoveNext** moves the enumerator to the next element in the **ArrayList**. The first call to **MoveNext** positions the enumerator at the first element of the **ArrayList**. **MoveNext** returns **true** if there is at least one more element in the **ArrayList**; otherwise, the method returns **false**. Method **Reset** positions the enumerator before the first element of the **ArrayList**. Methods **MoveNext** and **Reset** throw an **InvalidOperationException** if the contents of the collection are modified in any way after the enumerator's creation. Property **Current** returns the object at the current location in the **ArrayList**.

Line 155 creates an **IEnumerator** called **enumerator** and assigns it the result of calling **ArrayList** method *GetEnumerator*. Lines 158–159 iterate while **MoveNext** returns **true**, retrieve the current item via property **Count** and append it to **buffer**. When the loop terminates, line 161 displays the contents of **buffer**.

23.7.3 Class Stack

The **Stack** class, as its name implies, implements a stack data structure. This class provides much of the functionality that we defined in our implementation in Section 23.4. Refer back to that section for a discussion of stack data structure concepts. The application in Fig. 23.25 provides a GUI that enables the user to test many **Stack** methods. Line 38 of the **Stack-Test** constructor creates a **Stack** with the default initial capacity (10 elements).

As one might expect, class **Stack** has methods **Push** and **Pop** to perform the basic stack operations. Method **Push** takes an **object** as an argument and adds it to the top of the **Stack**. If the number of items on the **Stack** (the **Count** property) is equal to the capacity at the time of the **Push** operation, the **Stack** grows to accommodate more **object**s. Event handler **pushButton_Click** (lines 51–56) uses method **Push** to add a user-specified string to the stack (line 54).

Method **Pop** takes no arguments. This method removes and returns the object currently on top of the **Stack**. Event handler **popButton_Click** (lines 59–73) calls method **Pop** (line 57) to remove an object from the **Stack**. An **InvalidOperation-Exception** occurs if the **Stack** is empty when the program calls **Pop**.

```csharp
1   // Fig. 23.25: StackTest.cs
2   // Demonstrates class Stack of namespace System.Collections.
3
4   using System;
5   using System.Drawing;
6   using System.Collections;
7   using System.ComponentModel;
8   using System.Windows.Forms;
9   using System.Data;
10  using System.Text;
11
12  namespace StackTest
13  {
14      // demonstrate Stack collection
15      public class StackTest : System.Windows.Forms.Form
16      {
17          private System.Windows.Forms.Label inputLabel;
18          private System.Windows.Forms.TextBox inputTextBox;
19          private System.Windows.Forms.Button pushButton;
20          private System.Windows.Forms.Button popButton;
21          private System.Windows.Forms.Button peekButton;
22          private System.Windows.Forms.Button isEmptyButton;
23          private System.Windows.Forms.Button searchButton;
24          private System.Windows.Forms.Button displayButton;
25          private System.Windows.Forms.Label statusLabel;
26
27          // Required designer variable.
28          private System.ComponentModel.Container components = null;
29
30          private Stack stack;
31
32          public StackTest()
33          {
34              // Required for Windows Form Designer support
35              InitializeComponent();
36
37              // create Stack
38              stack = new Stack();
39          }
40
41          // Visual Studio.NET generated code
42
```

Fig. 23.25 Using the **Stack** class. (Part 1 of 4.)

```
43          // main entry point for the application
44          [STAThread]
45          static void Main()
46          {
47              Application.Run( new StackTest() );
48          }
49
50          // push element onto stack
51          private void pushButton_Click(
52              object sender, System.EventArgs e )
53          {
54              stack.Push( inputTextBox.Text );
55              statusLabel.Text = "Pushed: " + inputTextBox.Text;
56          }
57
58          // pop element from stack
59          private void popButton_Click(
60              object sender, System.EventArgs e )
61          {
62              // pop element
63              try
64              {
65                  statusLabel.Text = "Popped: " + stack.Pop();
66              }
67
68              // print message if stack is empty
69              catch ( InvalidOperationException invalidOperation )
70              {
71                  statusLabel.Text = invalidOperation.ToString();
72              }
73          }
74
75          // peek at top element of stack
76          private void peekButton_Click(
77              object sender, System.EventArgs e )
78          {
79              // view top element
80              try
81              {
82                  statusLabel.Text = "Top: " + stack.Peek();
83              }
84
85              // print message if stack is empty
86              catch ( InvalidOperationException invalidOperation )
87              {
88                  statusLabel.Text = invalidOperation.ToString();
89              }
90          }
91
92          // determine whether stack is empty
93          private void isEmptyButton_Click(
94              object sender, System.EventArgs e )
95          {
```

Fig. 23.25 Using the **Stack** class. (Part 2 of 4.)

```
96              statusLabel.Text = ( stack.Count == 0 ?
97                 "Stack is empty" : "Stack is not empty" );
98          }
99
100         // determine whether specified element is on stack
101         private void searchButton_Click(
102            object sender, System.EventArgs e )
103         {
104            string result = stack.Contains( inputTextBox.Text ) ?
105               " found" : " not found";
106
107            statusLabel.Text = inputTextBox.Text + result;
108         }
109
110         // display stack contents
111         private void displayButton_Click(
112            object sender, System.EventArgs e )
113         {
114            IEnumerator enumerator = stack.GetEnumerator();
115            StringBuilder buffer = new StringBuilder();
116
117            // while the enumerator can move on to the next element
118            // print that element out.
119            while ( enumerator.MoveNext() )
120               buffer.Append( enumerator.Current + " " );
121
122            statusLabel.Text = buffer.ToString();
123         }
124      }
125 }
```

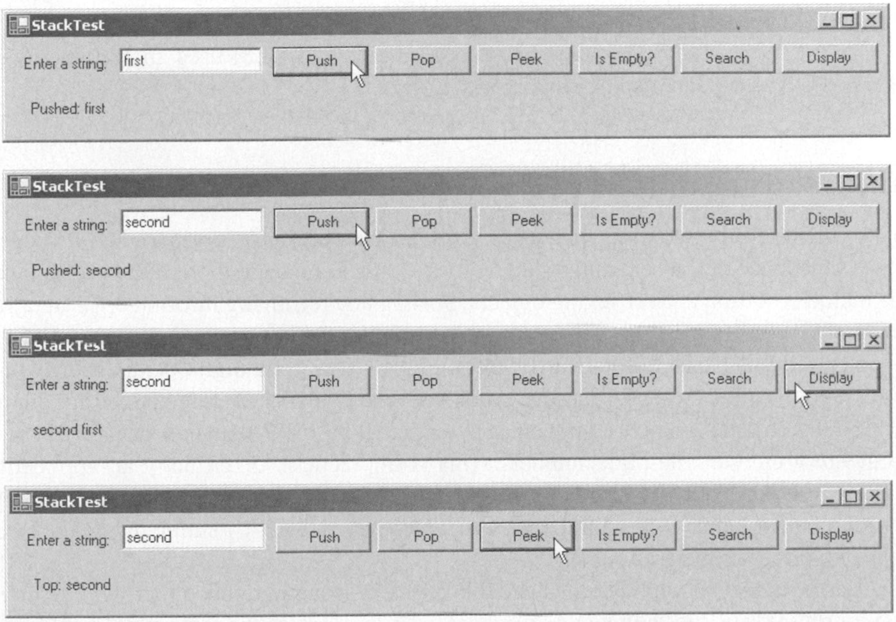

Fig. 23.25 Using the **Stack** class. (Part 3 of 4.)

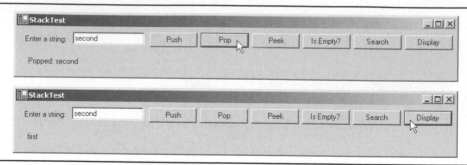

Fig. 23.25 Using the **Stack** class. (Part 4 of 4.)

Method **Peek** returns the value of the top stack element, but does not remove the element from the **Stack**. We demonstrate **Peek** at line 82 in event handler **peekButton_Click** (lines 76–90) to view the object on top of the **Stack**. As with **Pop**, an **InvalidOperationException** occurs if the **Stack** is empty when the program calls **Peek**.

Common Programming Error 23.3

*Attempting to **Peek** or **Pop** an empty **Stack** (a **Stack** whose **Count** property equals 0) causes an **InvalidOperationException**.*

Event handler **isEmptyButton_Click** (lines 93–98) determines whether the **Stack** is empty by comparing the **Stack**'s **Count** property to 0. If it is 0, the **Stack** is empty; otherwise, it is not. Event handler **searchButton_Click** (lines 101–108) uses **Stack** method **Contains** (lines 104–105) to determine whether the **Stack** contains the object specified as its argument. **Contains** returns **true** if the **Stack** contains the specified object, **false** otherwise.

Event handler **isEmptyButton_Click** (lines 111–123) uses an IEnumerator to traverse the **Stack** and display its contents.

23.7.4 Class **Hashtable**

Object-oriented programming languages facilitate creating new types. When a program creates objects of new or existing types, it then needs to manage those objects efficiently. This includes sorting and retrieving objects. Sorting and retrieving information with arrays is efficient if some aspect of your data directly matches the key value and if those keys are unique and tightly packed. If you have 100 employees with nine-digit Social Security numbers and you want to store and retrieve employee data by using the Social Security number as a key, it would nominally require an array with 999,999,999 elements, because there are 999,999,999 unique nine-digit numbers. This is impractical for virtually all applications that key on Social Security numbers. If you could have an array that large, you could get very high performance storing and retrieving employee records by simply using the Social Security number as the array index.

A large variety of applications have this problem—namely, that either the keys are of the wrong type (i.e., not nonnegative integers), or they are of the right type, but they are sparsely spread over a large range.

What is needed is a high-speed scheme for converting keys such as Social Security numbers and inventory part numbers into unique array subscripts. Then, when an application needs to store something, the scheme could convert the application key rapidly into a subscript and the record of information could be stored at that location in the array. Retrieval occurs the same way— once the application has a key for which it wants to retrieve the data record, the application simply applies the conversion to the key, which produces the array subscript where the data resides in the array and retrieves the data.

The scheme we describe here is the basis of a technique called *hashing*. Why the name? Because, when we convert a key into an array subscript, we literally scramble the bits, forming a kind of "mishmash" number. The number actually has no real significance beyond its usefulness in storing and retrieving this particular data record.

A glitch in the scheme occurs when *collisions* occur [i.e., two different keys "hash into" the same cell (or element) in the array]. Since we cannot sort two different data records into the same space, we need to find an alternative home for all records beyond the first that hash to a particular array subscript. Many schemes exist for doing this. One is to "hash again" (i.e., to reapply the hashing transformation to the key to provide a next candidate cell in the array). The hashing process is designed to be quite random, so the assumption is that with just a few hashes, an available cell will be found.

Another scheme uses one hash to locate the first candidate cell. If the cell is occupied, successive cells are searched linearly until an available cell is found. Retrieval works the same way—the key is hashed once, the resulting cell is checked to determine whether it contains the desired data. If it does, the search is complete. If it does not, successive cells are searched linearly until the desired data is found.

The most popular solution to hash-table collisions is to have each cell of the table be a hash "bucket," typically a linked list of all the key/value pairs that hash to that cell. This is the solution that the .NET Framework's **Hashtable** class implements.

The *load factor* is one factor that affects the performance of hashing schemes. The load factor is the ratio of the number of occupied cells in the hash table to the size of the hash table. The closer the ratio gets to 1.0, the greater the chance of collisions.

Performance Tip 23.11

The load factor in a hash table is a classic example of a space/time trade-off: By increasing the load factor, we get better memory utilization, but the program runs slower due to increased hashing collisions. By decreasing the load factor, we get better program speed because of reduced hashing collisions, but we get poorer memory utilization because a larger portion of the hash table remains empty.

Programming hash tables properly is too complex for most casual programmers. Computer science students study hashing schemes thoroughly in courses called "Data Structures" and "Algorithms." Recognizing the value of hashing, C# provides class **Hashtable** and some related features to enable programmers to take advantage of hashing without the complex details.

The preceding sentence is profoundly important in our study of object-oriented programming. Classes encapsulate and hide complexity (i.e., implementation details) and offer user-friendly interfaces. Crafting classes to do this properly is one of the most valued skills in the field of object-oriented programming.

A *hash function* performs a calculation that determines where to place data in the hashtable. The hash function is applied to the key in a key/value pair of objects. Class **Hash-**

table can accept any object as a key. For this reason, class **Object** defines method **GetHashCode**, which all objects in C# inherit. Most classes that are candidates to be used as keys in a hash table override this method to provide one that performs efficient hashcode calculations for a specific data type. For example, a **string** has a hashcode calculation that is based on the contents of the **string**. Figure 23.26 demonstrates several methods of class **Hashtable**.

```
1   // Fig. 23.26: HashtableTest.cs
2   // Demonstrate class Hashtable of namespace System.Collections.
3
4   using System;
5   using System.Drawing;
6   using System.Collections;
7   using System.ComponentModel;
8   using System.Windows.Forms;
9   using System.Data;
10  using System.Text;
11
12  namespace HashTableTest
13  {
14     // demonstrate Hashtable functionality
15     public class HashTableTest : System.Windows.Forms.Form
16     {
17        private System.Windows.Forms.Label firstNameLabel;
18        private System.Windows.Forms.Label lastNameLabel;
19        private System.Windows.Forms.Button addButton;
20        private System.Windows.Forms.TextBox lastNameTextBox;
21        private System.Windows.Forms.TextBox consoleTextBox;
22        private System.Windows.Forms.TextBox firstNameTextBox;
23        private System.Windows.Forms.Button getButton;
24        private System.Windows.Forms.Button removeButton;
25        private System.Windows.Forms.Button emptyButton;
26        private System.Windows.Forms.Button containsKeyButton;
27        private System.Windows.Forms.Button clearTableButton;
28        private System.Windows.Forms.Button listObjectsButton;
29        private System.Windows.Forms.Button listKeysButton;
30        private System.Windows.Forms.Label statusLabel;
31
32        // Required designer variable.
33        private System.ComponentModel.Container components = null;
34
35        // Hashtable to demonstrate functionality
36        private Hashtable table;
37
38        public HashTableTest()
39        {
40           // Required for Windows Form Designer support
41           InitializeComponent();
42
43           // create Hashtable object
44           table = new Hashtable();
45        }
```

Fig. 23.26 Using the **Hashtable** class. (Part 1 of 5.)

```
46
47       // Visual Studio.NET generated code
48
49       // main entry point for the application
50       [STAThread]
51       static void Main()
52       {
53          Application.Run( new HashTableTest() );
54       }
55
56       // add last name and Employee object to table
57       private void addButton_Click(
58          object sender, System.EventArgs e )
59       {
60          Employee employee = new Employee( firstNameTextBox.Text,
61             lastNameTextBox.Text );
62
63          // add new key/value pair
64          try
65          {
66             table.Add( lastNameTextBox.Text, employee );
67             statusLabel.Text = "Put: " + employee.ToString();
68          }
69
70          // if key is null or already in table, output message
71          catch ( ArgumentException argumentException )
72          {
73             statusLabel.Text = argumentException.ToString();
74          }
75       }
76
77       // get object for given key
78       private void getButton_Click(
79          object sender, System.EventArgs e )
80       {
81          object result = table[ lastNameTextBox.Text ];
82
83          if ( result != null )
84             statusLabel.Text = "Get: " + result.ToString();
85          else
86             statusLabel.Text = "Get: " + lastNameTextBox.Text +
87                " not in table";
88       }
89
90       // remove key/value pair from table
91       private void removeButton_Click(
92          object sender, System.EventArgs e )
93       {
94          table.Remove( lastNameTextBox.Text );
95          statusLabel.Text = "Object Removed";
96       }
97
```

Fig. 23.26 Using the **Hashtable** class. (Part 2 of 5.)

```
98          // determine whether table is empty
99          private void emptyButton_Click(
100            object sender, System.EventArgs e )
101         {
102            statusLabel.Text = "Table is " + (
103               table.Count == 0 ? "empty" : "not empty" );
104         }
105
106         // determine whether table contains specified key
107         private void containsKeyButton_Click(
108            object sender, System.EventArgs e )
109         {
110            statusLabel.Text = "Contains key: " +
111               table.ContainsKey( lastNameTextBox.Text );
112         }
113
114         // discard all table contents
115         private void clearTableButton_Click(
116            object sender, System.EventArgs e )
117         {
118            table.Clear();
119            statusLabel.Text = "Clear: Table is now empty";
120         }
121
122         // display list of objects in table
123         private void listObjectsButton_Click(
124            object sender, System.EventArgs e )
125         {
126            IDictionaryEnumerator enumerator =
127               table.GetEnumerator();
128            StringBuilder buffer = new StringBuilder();
129
130            while ( enumerator.MoveNext() )
131               buffer.Append( enumerator.Value + "\r\n" );
132
133            consoleTextBox.Text = buffer.ToString();
134         }
135
136         // display list of keys in table
137         private void listKeysButton_Click(
138            object sender, System.EventArgs e )
139         {
140            IDictionaryEnumerator enumerator =
141               table.GetEnumerator();
142            StringBuilder buffer = new StringBuilder();
143
144            while ( enumerator.MoveNext() )
145               buffer.Append( enumerator.Key + "\r\n" );
146
147            consoleTextBox.Text = buffer.ToString();
148         }
149
150      } // end class HashtableTest
```

Fig. 23.26 Using the **Hashtable** class. (Part 3 of 5.)

```
151
152     // class Employee for use with HashtableTest
153     class Employee
154     {
155        private string first, last;
156
157        // constructor
158        public Employee( string fName, string lName )
159        {
160           first = fName;
161           last = lName;
162        }
163
164        // return Employee first and last names as string
165        public override string ToString()
166        {
167           return first + " " + last;
168        }
169
170     } // end class Employee
171  }
```

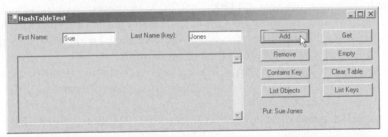

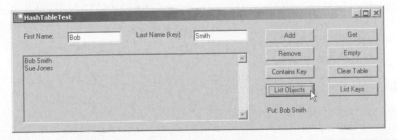

Fig. 23.26 Using the **Hashtable** class. (Part 4 of 5.)

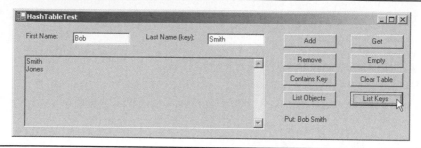

Fig. 23.26 Using the **Hashtable** class. (Part 5 of 5.)

Event handler **addButton_Click** (lines 57–75) reads the first name and last name of an employee from the user interface, creates an object of class Employee (defined at lines 153–170) and adds that **Employee** to the **Hashtable** with method **Add** (line 66). This method receives two arguments—a key object, and a value object. In this example, the key is the last name of the **Employee** (a **string**), and the value is the corresponding **Employee** object. An **ArgumentException** occurs if the **Hashtable** already contains the key or if the key is **null**.

Event handler **getButton_Click** (lines 78–88) retrieves the object associated with a specific key, using the **Hashtable**'s subscript operator as shown on line 81. The expression in square brackets is the key for which the **Hashtable** should return the corresponding object. If the key is not found, the result is **null**.

Event handler **removeButton_Click** (lines 91–96) invokes **Hashtable** method **Remove** to delete a key and its associated object from the **Hashtable**. If the key does not exist in the table, nothing happens.

Event handler **emptyButton_Click** (lines 99–104) uses **Hashtable** property **Count** to determine whether the **Hashtable** is empty (i.e., **Count** is 0).

Event handler **containsKeyButton_Click** (lines 107–112) invokes **Hashtable** method **ContainsKey** to determine whether the **Hashtable** contains the specified key. If so, the method returns **true**; otherwise, it returns **false**.

Event handler **clearTableButton_Click** (lines 115–120) invokes **Hashtable** method **Clear** to delete all **Hashtable** entries.

Class **Hashtable** provides method **GetEnumerator** that returns an enumerator of type **IDictionaryEnumerator**, which derives from **IEnumerator**. Such enumerators provide properties **Key** and **Value** to access the information for a key/value pair. The event handler at lines 123–134 (**listObjectsButton_click**) uses the **Value** property of the enumerator to output the objects in the **Hashtable**. The event handler at lines 123–134 (**listKeysButton_click**) uses the **Key** property of the enumerator to output the keys in the **Hashtable**.

SUMMARY

- Dynamic data structures can grow and shrink at execution time.
- Creating and maintaining dynamic data structures requires dynamic memory allocation—the ability for a program to obtain more memory at execution time (to hold new nodes) and to release memory no longer needed.

- The limit for dynamic memory allocation can be as large as the available physical memory in the computer or the amount of available disk space in a virtual-memory system.

- Operator **new** takes as an operand the type of the object being dynamically allocated and returns a reference to a newly created object of that type. If no memory is available, **new** throws an **OutOfMemoryException**.

- A self-referential class contains a data member that refers to an object of the same class type. Self-referential objects can be linked to form useful data structures such as lists, queues, stacks and trees.

- A linked list is a linear collection (i.e., a sequence) of self-referential class objects called nodes, connected by reference links.

- A node can contain data of any type, including objects of other classes.

- A linked list is accessed via a reference to the first node of the list. Each subsequent node is accessed via the link-reference member stored in the previous node.

- By convention, the link reference in the last node of a list is set to **null** to mark the end of the list.

- Stacks are important in compilers and operating systems.

- A stack is a constrained version of a linked list—new nodes can be added to a stack and removed from a stack only at the top. A stack is referred to as a last-in, first-out (LIFO) data structure.

- The primary stack operations are push and pop. Operation push adds a new node to the top of the stack. Operation pop removes a node from the top of the stack and returns the data object from the popped node.

- Queues represent waiting lines. Insertions occur at the back (also referred to as the tail) of a queue and deletions occur from the front (also referred to as the head) of a queue.

- A queue is similar to a checkout line in a supermarket: The first person in line is served first; other customers enter the line only at the end and wait to be served.

- Queue nodes are removed only from the head of the queue and are inserted only at the tail of the queue. For this reason, a queue is referred to as a first-in, first-out (FIFO) data structure.

- The insert and remove operations for a queue are known as enqueue and dequeue.

- Binary trees facilitate high-speed searching and sorting of data.

- Tree nodes contain two or more links.

- A binary tree is a tree whose nodes all contain two links. The root node is the first node in a tree.

- Each link in the root node refers to a child. The left child is the first node in the left subtree and the right child is the first node in the right subtree.

- The children of a node are called siblings. A node with no children is called a leaf node.

- A binary search tree (with no duplicate node values) has the characteristic that the values in any left subtree are less than the values that subtree's parent node and the values in any right subtree are greater than the values in that subtree's parent node.

- A node can be inserted only as a leaf node in a binary search tree.

- An inorder traversal of a binary search tree processes the node values in ascending order.

- The process of creating a binary search tree actually sorts the data—hence, the term "binary tree sort."

- In a preorder traversal, the value in each node is processed as the node is visited. After the value in a given node is processed, the values in the left subtree are processed, then the values in the right subtree are processed.

- In a postorder traversal, the value in each node is processed after the node's left and right subtrees are processed.

- The binary search tree facilitates duplicate elimination. As the tree is created, attempts to insert a duplicate value are recognized because a duplicate follows the same "go left" or "go right" decisions on each comparison as the original value did. Thus, the duplicate eventually is compared with a node containing the same value. The duplicate value may simply be discarded at this point.

- Class **ArrayList** can be used as a dynamically growing array.

- **ArrayList** method **Add** adds an **object** to the **ArrayList**.

- **ArrayList** method **Remove** removes the first occurrence of the specified **object** from the **ArrayList**.

- The **ArrayList** subscript operator accesses elements of an **ArrayList** as if it were an array.

- Class **Stack** is provided in the **System.Collections** namespace.

- **Stack** method **Push** performs the push operation on the **Stack**.

- **Stack** method **Pop** performs the pop operation on the **Stack**.

- Class **Hashtable** is provided in the **System.Collections** namespace.

- **Hashtable** method **Add** adds a key/value pair to the **Hashtable**.

- Any class that implements the **IEnumerator** interface must define methods **MoveNext** and **Reset** and the **Current** property.

- Method **MoveNext** must be called before the **Current** property is accessed for the first time.

- Methods **MoveNext** and **Reset** throw an **InvalidOperationException** if the contents of the collection were modified in any way after the enumerator's creation.

TERMINOLOGY

Add method of **ArrayList**
ArgumentException
ArrayList class
binary tree
BinarySearch method of **ArrayList**
Capacity property of **ArrayList**
Clear method of **ArrayList**
Clear method of **Hashtable**
collection
Contains method of **ArrayList**
Contains method of **Stack**
ContainsKey method of **Hashtable**
Count property of **ArrayList**
Count property of **Stack**
Current property of **IEnumerator**
data structures
dynamic data structures
enumerator
GetEnumerator method of **IEnumerable**
GetHashCode method of **Object**
Hashtable class
head
IDictionaryEnumerator interface

IEnumerator interface
IndexOf method of **ArrayList**
InvalidOperationException
linked list
MoveNext method of **IEnumerator**
Peek method of **Stack**
Pop method of **Stack**
Push method of **Stack**
queue
Remove method of **ArrayList**
Remove method of **Hashtable**
RemoveAt method of **ArrayList**
RemoveRange method of **ArrayList**
Reset method of **IEnumerator**
searching
self-referential class
Sort method of **ArrayList**
sorting
stack
Stack class
System.Collections namespace
TrimToSize method of **ArrayList**
waiting line

SELF-REVIEW EXERCISES

23.1   State whether each of the following is *true* or *false*. If *false*, explain why.
   a) In a queue, the first item to be added, is the last item to be removed.
   b) Trees can have no more than two child nodes per node.
   c) A tree node with no children is called a leaf node.
   d) Class **Stack** is in the **System.Collections** namespace.
   e) A class implementing interface **IEnumerator** must define only methods **MoveNext** and **Reset**.
   f) A hashtable stores key/value pairs.
   g) Linked list nodes are stored contiguously in memory.
   h) The primary operations of the stack data structure are enqueue and dequeue.
   i) Lists, stacks and queues are linear data structures.

23.2   Fill in the blanks in each of the following statements:
   a) A _____ class is used to define nodes that form dynamic data structures, which can grow and shrink at execution time.
   b) Operator _____ allocates memory dynamically; this operator returns a reference to the allocated memory.
   c) A _____ is a constrained version of a linked list in which nodes can be inserted and deleted only from the start of the list; this data structure returns node values in last-in, first-out order.
   d) A queue is a _____ data structure, because the first nodes inserted are the first nodes removed.
   e) A _____ is a constrained version of a linked list in which nodes can be inserted only at the end of the list and deleted only from the start of the list.
   f) A _____ is a nonlinear, two-dimensional data structure that contains nodes with two or more links.
   g) The nodes of a _____ tree contain two link members.
   h) **IEnumerator** method _____ advances the enumerator to the next item.
   i) The tree-traversal algorithm that processes the node and then processes all the nodes to its left followed by all the nodes to its right is called _____.
   j) If the collection it references was altered after the enumerator's creation, calling method **Reset** will cause an _____.

ANSWERS TO SELF-REVIEW EXERCISES

23.1   a) False. A queue is a first-in, first-out data structure—the first item added is the first item removed. b) False. In general, trees may have as many child nodes per node as is necessary. Only binary trees are restricted to no more than two child nodes per node. c) True. d) True. e) False. The class must also implement property **Current**. f) True. g) False. Linked-list nodes are logically contiguous, but they need not be stored in a physically contiguous memory space. h) False. Those are the primary operations of a queue. The primary operations of a stack are push and pop. i) True.

23.2   a) self-referential. b) **new**. c) stack. d) first-in, first-out (FIFO). e) queue. f) tree. g) binary. h) **MoveNext**. i) preorder. j) **InvalidOperationException**.

EXERCISES

23.3   Write a program that merges two ordered list objects of integers into a single ordered list object of integers. Method **Merge** of class **ListMerge** should receive references to each of the list objects to be merged and should return a reference to the merged list object.

23.4   Write a program that inputs a line of text and uses a stack object to print the line reversed.

23.5   Write a program that uses a stack to determine whether a string is a palindrome (i.e., the string is spelled identically backward and forward). The program should ignore spaces and punctuation.

23.6   Stacks are used by compilers to help in the process of evaluating expressions and in generating machine language code. In this and the next exercise, we investigate how compilers evaluate arithmetic expressions consisting only of constants, operators and parentheses.

Humans generally write expressions like **3 + 4** and **7 / 9**, in which the operator (**+** or **/** here) is written between its operands—this is called *infix notation.* Computers "prefer" *postfix notation*, in which the operator is written to the right of its two operands. The preceding infix expressions would appear in postfix notation as **3 4 +** and **7 9 /**, respectively.

To evaluate a complex infix expression, a compiler would first convert the expression to postfix notation, then evaluate the postfix version of the expression. Each of these algorithms requires only a single left-to-right pass of the expression. Each algorithm uses a stack object in support of its operation, and in each algorithm the stack is used for a different purpose.

In this exercise, you will write a C# version of the infix-to-postfix conversion algorithm. In the next exercise, you will write a C# version of the postfix expression evaluation algorithm. In a later exercise, you will discover that code you write in this exercise can help you implement a complete working compiler.

Write class **InfixToPostfixConverter** to convert an ordinary infix arithmetic expression (assume a valid expression is entered), with single-digit integers, such as

> **(6 + 2) * 5 - 8 / 4**

to a postfix expression. The postfix version of the preceding infix expression (note that no parentheses are needed) is

> **6 2 + 5 * 8 4 / -**

The program should read the expression into **StringBuilder infix**, then use class **Stack-Composition** (implemented in Fig. 23.12) to help create the postfix expression in **String-Builder postfix**. The algorithm for creating a postfix expression is as follows:

a) Push a left parenthesis **'('** on the stack.
b) Append a right parenthesis **')'** to the end of **infix**.
c) While the stack is not empty, read **infix** from left to right and do the following:
   If the current character in **infix** is a digit, append it to **postfix**.
   If the current character in **infix** is a left parenthesis, push it onto the stack.
   If the current character in **infix** is an operator:
      Pop operators (if there are any) at the top of the stack while they have equal or higher precedence than the current operator, and append the popped operators to **postfix**.
      Push the current character in **infix** onto the stack.
   If the current character in **infix** is a right parenthesis:
      Pop operators from the top of the stack and append them to **postfix** until a left parenthesis is at the top of the stack.
      Pop (and discard) the left parenthesis from the stack.

The following arithmetic operations are allowed in an expression:

+   addition
–   subtraction
*   multiplication
/   division
^   exponentiation
%   modulus

Some of the methods you may want to provide in your program follow:
   a) Method **ConvertToPostfix**, which converts the infix expression to postfix notation.
   b) Method **IsOperator**, which determines whether **c** is an operator.
   c) Method **Precedence**, which determines whether the precedence of **operator1** (from the infix expression) is less than, equal to or greater than the precedence of **operator2** (from the stack). The method returns **true** if **operator1** has lower precedence than **operator2**. Otherwise, **false** is returned.
   d) Add this method to the class definition for class **StackComposition**.

23.7   Write class **PostfixEvaluator**, which evaluates a postfix expression (assume it is valid) such as

       6 2 + 5 * 8 4 / -

The program should read a postfix expression consisting of digits and operators into a **String-Builder**. Using class **StackComposition** from Exercise 23.6, the program should scan the expression and evaluate it. The algorithm is as follows:
   a) Append a right parenthesis (**')'**) to the end of the postfix expression. When the right-parenthesis character is encountered, no further processing is necessary.
   b) When the right-parenthesis character has not been encountered, read the expression from left to right.
           If the current character is a digit do the following:
                   Push its integer value on the stack (the integer value of a digit character is its value in the computer's character set minus the value of **'0'** in Unicode).
           Otherwise, if the current character is an *operator*:
                   Pop the two top elements of the stack into variables **x** and **y**.
                   Calculate **y** *operator* **x**.
                   Push the result of the calculation onto the stack.
   c) When the right parenthesis is encountered in the expression, pop the top value of the stack. This is the result of the postfix expression.

[*Note*: In b) above (based on the sample expression at the beginning of this exercises), if the operator is **'/'**, the top of the stack is **2** and the next element in the stack is **8**, then pop **2** into **x**, pop **8** into **y**, evaluate **8 / 2** and push the result, **4**, back on the stack. This note also applies to operator **'-'**.] The arithmetic operations allowed in an expression are:
   +   addition
   -   subtraction
   *   multiplication
   /   division
   ^   exponentiation
   %   modulus

You may want to provide the following methods:
   a) Method **EvaluatePostfixExpression**, which evaluates the postfix expression.
   b) Method **Calculate**, which evaluates the expression **op1** *operator* **op2**.

23.8   (*Binary Tree Delete*) In this exercise, we discuss deleting items from binary search trees. The deletion algorithm is not as straightforward as the insertion algorithm. There are three cases that are encountered when deleting an item—the item is contained in a leaf node (i.e., it has no children), the item is contained in a node that has one child or the item is contained in a node that has two children.

   If the item to be deleted is contained in a leaf node, the node is deleted and the reference in the parent node is set to null.

   If the item to be deleted is contained in a node with one child, the reference in the parent node is set to reference the child node and the node containing the data item is deleted. This causes the child node to take the place of the deleted node in the tree.

The last case is the most difficult. When a node with two children is deleted, another node in the tree must take its place. However, the reference in the parent node simply cannot be assigned to reference one of the children of the node to be deleted. In most cases, the resulting binary search tree would not adhere to the following characteristic of binary search trees (with no duplicate values): *The values in any left subtree are less than the value in the parent node, and the values in any right subtree are greater than the value in the parent node.*

Which node is used as a *replacement node* to maintain this characteristic—either the node containing the largest value in the tree less than the value in the node being deleted, or the node containing the smallest value in the tree greater than the value in the node being deleted. Let us consider the node with the smaller value. In a binary search tree, the largest value less than a parent's value is located in the left subtree of the parent node and is guaranteed to be contained in the rightmost node of the subtree. This node is located by walking down the left subtree to the right until the reference to the right child of the current node is null. We are now referencing the replacement node which is either a leaf node or a node with one child to its left. If the replacement node is a leaf node, the steps to perform the deletion are as follows:

   a) Store the reference to the node to be deleted in a temporary reference variable.
   b) Set the reference in the parent of the node being deleted to reference the replacement node.
   c) Set the reference in the parent of the replacement node to null.
   d) Set the reference to the right subtree in the replacement node to reference the right subtree of the node to be deleted.
   e) Set the reference to the left subtree in the replacement node to reference the left subtree of the node to be deleted.

The deletion steps for a replacement node with a left child are similar to those for a replacement node with no children, but the algorithm also must move the child into the replacement node's position in the tree. If the replacement node is a node with a left child, the steps to perform the deletion are as follows:

   a) Store the reference to the node to be deleted in a temporary reference variable.
   b) Set the reference in the parent of the node being deleted to reference the replacement node.
   c) Set the reference in the parent of the replacement node reference to the left child of the replacement node.
   d) Set the reference to the right subtree in the replacement node reference to the right subtree of the node to be deleted.
   e) Set the reference to the left subtree in the replacement node to reference the left subtree of the node to be deleted.

Write method **DeleteNode**, which takes as its argument the value to be deleted. Method **DeleteNode** should locate in the tree the node containing the value to be deleted and use the algorithms discussed here to delete the node. If the value is not found in the tree, the method should print a message that indicates whether the value is deleted. Modify the program of Fig. 23.18 to use this method. After deleting an item, call the methods **InorderTraversal**, **PreorderTraversal** and **PostorderTraversal** to confirm that the delete operation was performed correctly.

23.9   (*Level-Order Binary Tree Traversal*) The program of Fig. 23.18 illustrated three recursive methods of traversing a binary tree—inorder, preorder, and postorder traversals. This exercise presents the *level-order traversal* of a binary tree, in which the node values are printed level by level, starting at the root-node level. The nodes on each level are printed from left to right. The level-order traversal is not a recursive algorithm. It uses a queue object to control the output of the nodes. The algorithm is as follows:

a) Insert the root node in the queue.
b) While there are nodes left in the queue, do the following:
    Get the next node in the queue.
    Print the node's value.
    If the reference to the left child of the node is not null:
        Insert the left child node in the queue.
    If the reference to the right child of the node is not null:
        Insert the right child node in the queue.

Write method **LevelOrder** to perform a level-order traversal of a binary tree object. Modify the program of Fig. 23.18 to use this method. [*Note*: You also will need to use the queue-processing methods of Fig. 23.13 in this program.]

24

Accessibility

Objectives

- To introduce the World Wide Web Consortium's Web Content Accessibility Guidelines 1.0 (WCAG 1.0).
- To understand how to use the **alt** attribute of the HTML **<img>** tag to describe images to people with visual impairments, mobile-Web-device users and others unable to view images.
- To understand how to make tables more accessible to page readers.
- To understand how to verify that XHTML tags are used properly and to ensure that Web pages can be viewed on any type of display or reader.
- To understand how VoiceXML™ and CallXML™ are changing the way in which people with disabilities access information on the Web.
- To introduce the various accessibility aids offered in Windows 2000.

'Tis the good reader that makes the good book...
Ralph Waldo Emerson

I once was lost, but now am found,
Was blind, but now I see.
John Newton

Outline

24.1 Introduction

Throughout this book, we discuss the creation of C# applications. Later chapters also introduce the development of Web-based content using Web Forms, ASP .NET, XHTML and XML. In this chapter, we explore the topic of *accessibility*, which refers to the level of usability that an application or Web site provides to people with various disabilities. Disabilities that might affect an individual's computer or Internet usage are common; they include visual impairments, hearing impairments, other physical injuries (such as the inability to use a keyboard or a mouse) and learning disabilities. In today's computing environment, such impediments prevent many users from taking full advantage of applications and Web content.

The design of applications and sites to meet the needs of individuals with disabilities should be a priority for all software companies and e-businesses. People affected by disabilities represent a significant portion of the population, and legal ramifications could exist for companies that discriminate by failing to provide adequate and universal access to their resources. In this chapter, we explore the World Wide Web Consortium's *Web Accessibility Initiative* and its guidelines and review various laws regarding the availability of computing and Internet resources to people with disabilities. We also highlight companies that have developed systems, products and services that meet the needs of this demographic. As students use C# and its related technologies to design applications and Web sites, they should keep in mind the accessibility requirements and recommendations that we discuss in this chapter.

24.2 Regulations and Resources

Over the past several years, the United States has taken legislative steps to ensure that people with disabilities are given the tools they need to use computers and access the Web. A wide variety of legislation, including the *Americans With Disabilities Act* (ADA) of 1990, governs the provision of computer and Web accessibility (Fig. 24.1). These laws have inspired significant legal action. For example, according to the ADA, companies are required to offer equal access to individuals with visual problems. The National Federation for the Blind (NFB) cited this law in a 1999 suit against AOL, responding to the company's failure to make its services available to individuals with disabilities.

There are 54 million Americans with disabilities, and these individuals represent an estimated $1 trillion in annual purchasing power. In addition to legislation, many organizations and resources focus on assisting individuals with disabilities to access computers and the Internet. **WeMedia.com**™ (Fig. 24.2) is a Web site that provides news, information, products and services to the millions of people with disabilities and to their families, friends and caregivers.

Act	Purpose
Americans with Disabilities Act	The ADA prohibits discrimination on the basis of disability in employment, state and local government, public accommodations, commercial facilities, transportation and telecommunications.
Telecommunications Act of 1996	The Telecommunications Act of 1996 contains two amendments to Section 255 and Section 251(a)(2) of the Communications Act of 1934. These amendments require that communication devices, such as cell phones, telephones and pagers, be accessible to individuals with disabilities.

Fig. 24.1 Acts designed to improve Internet and computer accessibility for people with disabilities. (Part 1 of 2.)

Act	Purpose
Individuals with Disabilities Education Act of 1997	The Individuals with Disabilities Education Act stipulates that education materials in schools must be made accessible to children with disabilities.
Rehabilitation Act	Section 504 of the Rehabilitation Act states that college sponsored activities receiving federal funding cannot discriminate against individuals with disabilities. Section 508 mandates that all government institutions receiving federal funding must design their Web sites so that they are accessible to individuals with disabilities. Businesses that sell services to the government also must abide by this act.

Fig. 24.1 Acts designed to improve Internet and computer accessibility for people with disabilities. (Part 2 of 2.)

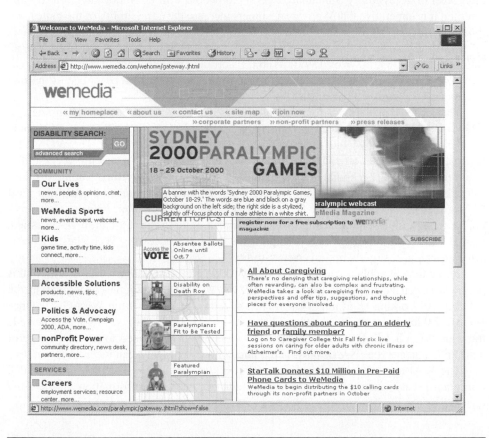

Fig. 24.2 We Media's home page. (Courtesy of WeMedia, Inc.)

As these laws and resources exemplify, computer and Internet accessibility for individuals with disabilities is quickly becoming a reality. Such accessibility enables individuals with disabilities to work in a vast array of new fields. This is partly because the Internet provides a medium through which disabled people can telecommute to jobs and interact easily with others without traveling. Such technologies as voice activation, visual enhancers and auditory aids create additional employment opportunities. For example, people with visual impairments can use computer monitors with enlarged text, and people with physical impairments can use head pointers with on-screen keyboards. In the remaining sections of this chapter, we explore various organizations, techniques, products and services that help provide computer and Internet access to people with disabilities.

24.3 Web Accessibility Initiative

Currently, most Web sites are considered to be either partially or totally inaccessible to people with visual, learning or mobility impairments. Total accessibility is difficult to achieve, because of the variety of disabilities that must be accommodated and because of problems resulting from language barriers and hardware and software inconsistencies. However, a high level of accessibility is attainable. As more people with disabilities begin to use the Internet, it is imperative that Web-site designers increase the accessibility of their sites. Although computer and Web accessibility is the focus of some recent legislation, standards organizations also see the need for industry recommendations. In an attempt to address issues of accessibility, the World Wide Web Consortium (W3C) launched the *Web Accessibility Initiative* (WAI™) in April 1997. To learn more about the WAI or to read its mission statement, visit **www.w3.org/WAI**.

This chapter explains various techniques used to develop accessible Web sites. In 1999, the WAI published the *Web Content Accessibility Guidelines* (*WCAG*) *1.0* to help businesses determine whether their Web sites are universally accessible. The WCAG 1.0 (available at **www.w3.org/TR/WCAG10**) uses checkpoints to list specific accessibility requirements. Each checkpoint is accompanied by a corresponding priority rating that indicates the requirement's level of importance. *Priority-one checkpoints* are goals that must be met to ensure accessibility; we focus on these points in this chapter. *Priority-two checkpoints*, though not essential, are highly recommended. If these checkpoints are not satisfied, people with certain disabilities will experience difficulty accessing Web sites. *Priority-three checkpoints* slightly improve accessibility.

At the time of publication, the WAI was working on *WCAG 2.0*; a working draft of this publication can be found at **www.w3.org/TR/WCAG20**. A single checkpoint in the WCAG 2.0 Working Draft might encompass several checkpoints from WCAG 1.0. Once WCAG 2.0 has been reviewed and published by the W3C, its checkpoints will supersede those of WCAG 1.0. Furthermore, the new version can be applied to a wider range of markup languages (i.e., XML, WML, etc.) and content types than can its predecessor.

The WAI also presents a supplemental checklist of *quick tips*, which reinforce ten important points relating to accessible Web–site design. More information on the WAI Quick Tips can be found at **www.w3.org/WAI/References/Quicktips**.

24.4 Providing Alternatives for Images

One important WAI requirement specifies that every image on a Web page should be accompanied by a textual description that clearly defines the purpose of the image. To accomplish this task, Web developers can use the **alt** attribute of the **img** and **input** tags to include a textual equivalent for every image or graphic included on a site.

Web developers who do not use the **alt** attribute to provide text equivalents increase the difficulties that people with visual impairments experience in navigating the Web. Specialized *user agent*s (or *accessibility aids*), such as *screen readers* (programs that allow users to hear all text that is displayed on their screens) and *braille displays* (devices that receive data from screen-reading software and then output the data as braille), enable people with visual impairments to access text-based information that normally is displayed on the screen. A user agent visually interprets Web-page source code and translates it into a format that is accessible to people with various disabilities. Web browsers, such as Microsoft Internet Explorer and Netscape Communicator, and the screen readers mentioned throughout this chapter are examples of user agents.

Similarly, Web pages that do not provide text equivalents for video and audio clips are difficult for people with visual and hearing impairments to access. Screen readers cannot interpret images, movies and most other non-XHTML content from these Web pages. However, by providing multimedia-based information in a variety of ways (e.g., using the **alt** attribute or providing in-line descriptions of images), Web designers can help maximize the accessibility of their sites' content.

Web designers should provide useful and appropriate text equivalents in the **alt** attribute for use by nonvisual user agents. For example, if the **alt** attribute describes a sales-growth chart, it should provide a brief summary of the data, but should not describe the data in the chart. Instead, a complete description of the chart's data should be included in the *longdesc* (long description) *attribute*, which is intended to augment the **alt** attribute's description. The **longdesc** attribute contains a link to a Web page describing the image or multimedia content. Currently, most Web browsers do not support the **longdesc** attribute. An alternative to the **longdesc** attribute is *D-link*, which provides descriptive text about graphs and charts. More information on D-links can be obtained at the *CORDA Technologies* Web site (**www.corda.com**).

The use of a screen reader to facilitate Web-site navigation can be time-consuming and frustrating, because screen readers cannot interpret pictures and other graphical content. The inclusion of a link at the top of each Web page providing direct access to the page's content could allow disabled users to bypass long lists of navigation links and other irrelevant or inaccessible content. This jump can save time and eliminate frustration for individuals with visual impairments.

Emacspeak (**www.cs.cornell.edu/home/raman/emacspeak/emacspeak.html**) is a screen interface that improves the quality of Internet access for individuals with visual disabilities by translating text to voice data. The open-source product also implements auditory icons that play various sounds. Emacspeak can be customized with Linux operating systems and provides support for the IBM *ViaVoice* speech engine.

In March 2001, We Media introduced another user agent, the *WeMedia Browser*, which allows people with vision impairments and cognitive disabilities (such as dyslexia) to use the Internet more conveniently. The WeMedia Browser enhances traditional browser capabilities by providing oversized buttons and keystroke commands that assist in navigation. The browser "reads" text that the user selects, allowing the user to control the speed and volume at which the browser reads the contents of the Web page. The WeMedia Browser free download is available at **www.wemedia.com**

IBM Home Page Reader (HPR) is another browser that "reads" text selected by the user. The HPR uses IBM ViaVoice technology to synthesize an audible voice. A trial version of HPR is available at **www-3.ibm.com/able/hpr.html**.

24.5 Maximizing Readability by Focusing on Structure

Many Web sites use XHTML tags for aesthetic purposes, ignoring the tags' intended functions. For example, the **<h1>** heading tag often is used erroneously to make text large and bold, rather than to indicate a major section head for content. This practice might create a desired visual effect, but it causes problems for screen readers. When the screen-reader software encounters the **<h1>** tag, it might verbally inform the user that a new section has been reached. If this is not in fact the case, the **<h1>** tag might confuse users. Therefore, developers should use the **h1** only in accordance with its XHTML specifications (e.g., to mark up a heading that introduces an important section of a document). Instead of using **h1** to make text large and bold, developers can use CSS (Cascading Style Sheets) or XSL (Extensible Stylesheet Language) to format and style the text. For further examples of this nature, refer to the WCAG 1.0 Web site at **www.w3.org/TR/WCAG10**. [*Note:* The **<strong>** tag also can be used to make text bold; however, screen readers emphasize bold text, which affects the inflection of what is spoken.]

Another accessibility issue is *readability*. When creating a Web page intended for the general public, it is important to consider the reading level (i.e., level of difficulty to read and understand) at which content is written. Web-site designers can make their sites easier to read by using shorter words. Furthermore, slang terms and other nontraditional language could be problematic for users from other countries, so developers should limit the use of such words.

WCAG 1.0 suggests using a paragraph's first sentence to convey its subject. When a Web site states the point of a paragraph in this paragraph's first sentence, it is easier for individuals with disabilities both to find crucial information and to bypass unwanted material.

The *Gunning Fog Index*, a formula that produces a readability grade when applied to a text sample, can evaluate a Web site's readability. To obtain more information about the Gunning Fog Index, visit **www.trainingpost.org/3-2-inst.htm**.

24.6 Accessibility in Visual Studio .NET

In the previous sections, we have outlined various accessibility guidelines presented in the W3C's Web Accessibility initiative. However, Visual Studio .NET provides its own guidelines for designing accessible software within its programming environment. For instance, one guideline recommends reserving the use of color for the enhancement or emphasis of information, instead of for aesthetic purposes. A second guideline recommends providing information about objects (e.g., desktop icons and open windows) to the accessibility aids (specialized software that renders applications to individuals with disabilities). Such information might include the name, location and size of a window. A third guideline recommends designing user interfaces so that they can accommodate user preferences. For example, people with visual disabilities should be able to modify the font size of a user interface. A fourth guideline recommends allowing users to adjust the time setting for applications that have time constraints. For example, users with mobility or speech disabilities might experience difficulty when using applications that require users to enter input within a predetermined period of time (such as 10 seconds). However, if such applications provide adjustable time settings, users can modify the settings to suit their needs.

In addition to suggesting guidelines the help developers create accessible applications, Visual Studio .NET also offers features that enable disabled individuals to use the development environment itself. For example, users can enlarge icons and text, customize the toolbox and keyboard and rearrange windows. The next subsections illustrate these capabilities.

24.6.1 Enlarging Toolbar Icons

To enlarge icons in Visual Studio, select **Customize** from the **Tools** menu. In the **Customize** window's **Options** tab, select the **Large Icons** check box (Fig. 24.3), and select **Close**. Figure 24.4 depicts the enlarged icons on the Visual Studio development window.

Fig. 24.3   Enlarging icons using the **Customize** feature.

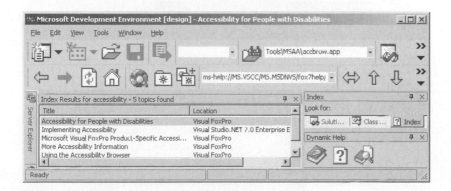

Fig. 24.4   Enlarged icons in the development window.

24.6.2 Enlarging the Text

Visual Studio uses the default operating-system font settings when displaying text. However, some individuals cannot read these default font settings, causing the applications to be inaccessible to them. To remedy this, Visual Studio allows users to modify the font size. Select **Options** from the **Tools** menu. In the **Options** window, open the **Environment** directory and choose **Fonts and Colors**. In the **Show settings for** drop-down box, select **Text Editor**. In the **Font** drop-down box, select a different style of font and, in the **Size** drop-down box, select a different font size. Figure 24.5 depicts the **Text Editor** before we modified the font size, Fig. 24.6 shows the **Options** window with new font settings and Fig. 24.7 displays the **Text Editor** after the changes have been applied.

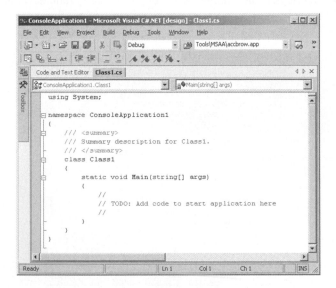

Fig. 24.5   Text Editor before modifying the font size.

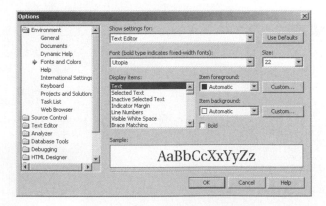

Fig. 24.6   Enlarging text in the **Options** window.

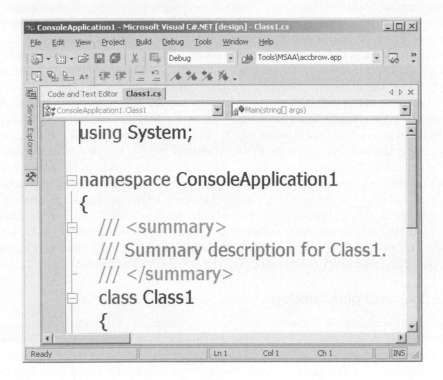

Fig. 24.7   Text Editor after the font size is modified.

24.6.3 Modifying the Toolbox

The **Toolbox** feature of Visual Studio contains numerous design elements that facilitate the creation Web applications; however, some developers might use only a few of these design elements. To accommodate the needs of individual developers, Visual Studio allows programmers to customize the toolbox by creating new tabs and then inserting design elements into the tabs. This eliminates the need for users with disabilities to navigate among multiple tabs or scroll through long lists in search of design elements. To create a new tab, right-click any existing tab and select **Add Tab** from the context menu. In the text box, type an identifier for the tab (such as "Frequently Used") and click *Enter*. By default, the **Pointer** element is placed in all tabs (Fig. 24.8). The **Pointer** element simply allows the cursor to function normally.

To insert elements into the newly created tab, select **Customize Toolbox** from the **Tools** menu. In the **.NET Framework Components** tab, select the elements to include in the new tab and click **OK**. The selected elements now will appear in the tab.

24.6.4 Modifying the Keyboard

Another accessibility feature in Visual Studio .NET allows individuals with disabilities to customize their keyboards by creating *shortcut keys* (i.e., combinations of keyboard keys that, when pressed together, perform frequent tasks; for example, *Ctrl* + *V* causes text to be pasted from the clipboard). To create a shortcut key, begin by selecting **Options** from the **Tools** menu. In the **Options** window, select the **Keyboard** item from the **Environment** directory. From the **Keyboard mapping scheme** drop-down list, select a scheme and click the **Save As** button. Then, assign a name to the scheme in the **Save Scheme** dialog box and click **OK**. Enter the task of the shortcut key in the **Show commands containing** text box. For example, if we were creating a shortcut key for the paste function, we would enter **Paste** in the text box, or we would select the proper task from the selection list directly below the text box. Then, in the **Use new shortcut** drop-down list, select the applications that will use the shortcut key. If the shortcut key will be used in all applications, select **Global**. Finally, in the **Press shortcut key(s)** text box, assign a shortcut key to the task in the form *non-text key + text key*. Valid non-text keys include *Ctrl*, *Shift* and *Alt*; valid text keys include A–Z, inclusive. [*Note*: To enter a non-text key, select the key itself—do not type the word *Ctrl*, *Shift* or *Alt*. It is possible to include more than one non-text key as part of a shortcut key. Do not enter the + symbol.] Thus, a valid shortcut key might be *Ctrl+Alt+D*. After assigning a shortcut key, select **Assign** and then **OK**. Figure 24.9 illustrates the process of creating a shortcut key for the `NewBreakpoint` function. The shortcut key (*Ctrl+Alt+D*) is valid only in the **Text Editor**.

24.6.5 Rearranging Windows

Some screen readers have difficulty interpreting user interfaces that include multiple tabs; this is because most screen readers can read information on only one screen. To accommodate such screen readers, Visual Studio allows developers to customize their user interfaces so that only the console window appears. To remove tabs, select **Options** from the **Tools** menu. Then, in the **Options** window, select the **General** item from the **Environment** directory. In the **Settings** section, select the **MDI environment** radio button and click **OK**. Figure 24.10 depicts the **Options** window, and Fig. 24.11 illustrates a console window with and without tabs.

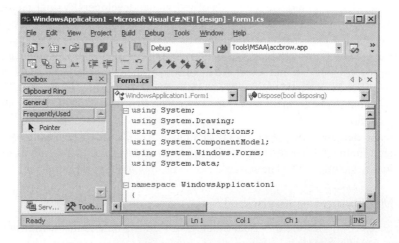

Fig. 24.8   Adding tabs to the **Toolbox**.

operation selection   application to apply shortcuts   mapping scheme   key designation

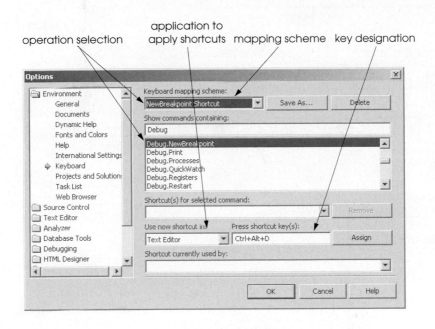

Fig. 24.9   Shortcut key creation.

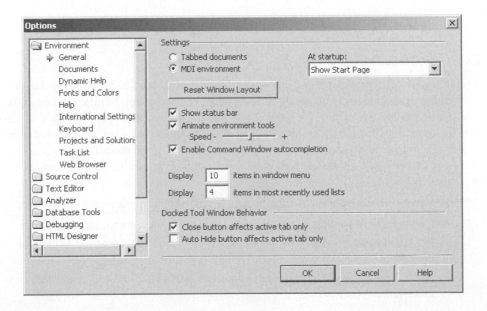

Fig. 24.10 Removing tabs from Visual Studio environment.

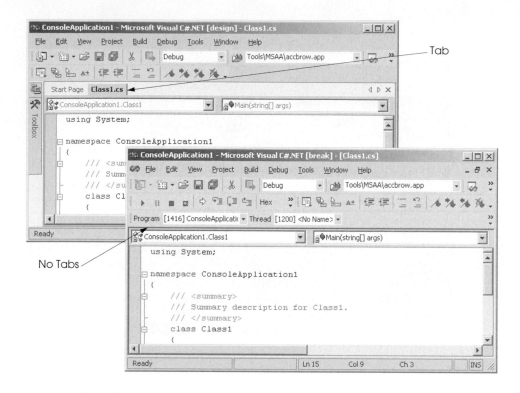

Fig. 24.11 Console windows with tabs and without tabs.

24.7 Accessibility in C#

Visual Studio .NET provides extensive accessibility features and also presents guidelines for creating accessible applications in its development environment. Similar recommendations guide the development of C# applications that are accessible to people with disabilities. It is important that C# programmers gear applications toward as many potential users as possible, rather then toward only the average user. WIth some modifications, most applications can be made accessible to a wide variety of individuals. General guidelines for designing accessible applications are:

1. Use larger-sized fonts—this helps people with visual impairments see the text.

2. Create flexible applications that provide keyboard shortcuts for all features within the application—this allows people to use the application without employing a mouse.

3. Allow information to be conveyed to the user both in a visual and in an audio context.

4. Use graphics and images whenever helpful—visual cues can increase accessibility for people who have trouble reading text on the screen.

5. Never signal information with sound only—someone accessing the information might not have speakers or might have hearing impairments.[1]

6. Test the application without using either a mouse or a keyboard. Access to an application's functionality should not be limited to one input device.

For more information on these and other design guidelines for accessible applications, please refer to the Visual Studio .NET documentation under the **overview** subsection of the index topic **accessibility**. This section provides links to discussions of how to design more accessible Windows and ASP.NET applications.

One specific way that programmers can make their applications more accessible is to use a *text-to-speech* control in their programs. A text-to-speech control can convert text into speech—a computerized voice speaks the words provided as text to the control. Text-to-speech controls facilitate access for people who cannot see the screen.

Another way to make applications more accessible is to use *tab stops*. A tab stop occurs when the user presses the *Tab* key, causing the focus to transfer to another control. The order in which the controls gain focus is called the *tab order*, which is determined by the **TabIndex** value of the controls (controls gain focus in ascending order). Each control also has a **TabStop** property—if this property is **true**, the control is included in the tab order; otherwise, it is not. Using the **TabIndex** and **TabStop** properties makes it simple to create more easily navigable applications. If these properties are set incorrectly, the logical ordering of the application might not be maintained. Consider an application that has **TextBox**es in which a user inputs a first name, a last name and an address. The logical tab order would take the user from the **TextBox** for the first name to the one for the last name and then to the one for the address.

A third and important way in which programmers can increase the accessibility of their applications is to use specific classes provided by .NET. Class **Control**, for example, has many properties designed for conveying information to users. These applications can then, in turn, find the required information stored as properties. Figure 24.12 lists some properties of class **Control** that are designed to provide information to users.

Property	Purpose
AccessibleDescription	Describes the control to an accessibility client application. For example, a **CheckBox** that says **"New User"** would not require more description, but a **CheckBox** with an image of a cat would have its **AccessibleDescription** property set to something like, **"A CheckBox with an image of a cat on it"**.
AccessibleName	Contains a short name or identifier for the control.

Fig. 24.12 Properties of class **Control** related to accessibility. (Part 1 of 2.)

---

1. "Basic Principles of Accessible Design," *.NET Framework Developer's Guide*, Visual Studio .NET Online Help

Property	Purpose
AccessibleRole	Member of the **AccessibleRole** enumeration. Represents the role of this control in the application—this information might help the accessibility client application determine what actions it should take.
IsAccessible	Contains a **bool** value specifying whether the control is visible to accessibility client applications.

Fig. 24.12 Properties of class **Control** related to accessibility. (Part 2 of 2.)

The application in Fig. 24.13 uses a text-to-speech control, tab stops and class **Control**'s accessibility-related properties. It consists of a form with three **Label**s, three **TextBox**es and a **Button**, enabling a user to submit the information. Submitting the information simply terminates the application—the application is intended only to demonstrate the use of the text-to-speech control.

The accessibility features in this program work as follows: When the mouse is over a **Label**, the text-to-speech control prompts the user to enter the appropriate information in the **TextBox** located to the right of the **Label**. If the mouse is over a **TextBox**, the contents of the **TextBox** are spoken. Lastly, if the mouse is over **Button Submit**, the user is told that the button should be clicked to submit the information. The tab order is the following: The **TextBox**es where the user inputs the name, phone number and password, then the **Button**. The **Label**s and text-to-speech control are not included in the tab order, because the user cannot interact with them, and their inclusion would serve no purpose. The accessibility properties are set so that accessibility client applications will obtain appropriate information about the controls. Please note that only the relevant code generated by Visual Studio .NET is included in Fig. 24.13. To use the text-to-speech control, first add it to the **Toolbox**. This is accomplished by selecting **Customize Toolbox** from the **Tools** menu. The **Customize Toolbox** dialog pops up—check the box next to the **TextToSpeech Class** option. Click **OK** to dismiss the dialog box. The **VText** control now is in the **ToolBox** and can be dragged onto a form int he same way that any other control.

The application has three **Label**s that prompts for the user's name, phone number and password. Three corresponding **TextBox**es accept the user's input and, a **Button** allows the user to submit the form. Line 25 declares a text-to-speech control named **speaker**. We want the user to hear audio descriptions of controls when the mouse is located over those controls. Lines 112–139 define the **controls_MouseHover** event handler—we attach this method to the three **TextBox**es and the **Button** as the event handler for the **MouseHover** event.

```
1   // Fig. 24.13: TextToSpeech.cs
2   // Providing audio for people with visual impairments.
3
4   using System;
5   using System.Drawing;
```

Fig. 24.13 Application with accessibility features. (Part 1 of 4.)

```
 6    using System.Collections;
 7    using System.ComponentModel;
 8    using System.Windows.Forms;
 9    using System.Data;
10
11    // helps users navigate form with aid of audio cues
12    public class TextToSpeech : System.Windows.Forms.Form
13    {
14        private System.Windows.Forms.Label nameLabel;
15        private System.Windows.Forms.Label phoneLabel;
16
17        private System.Windows.Forms.TextBox nameTextBox;
18        private System.Windows.Forms.TextBox phoneTextBox;
19        private System.Windows.Forms.TextBox passwordTextBox;
20
21        private System.Windows.Forms.Button submitButton;
22
23        private System.Windows.Forms.Label passwordLabel;
24
25        private AxHTTSLib.AxTextToSpeech speaker;
26
27        private System.ComponentModel.Container components = null;
28
29        // default constructor
30        public TextToSpeech()
31        {
32            InitializeComponent();
33
34            // set Form to be visible to accessibility applications
35            this.IsAccessible = true;
36
37            // let all controls be visible to accessibility applications
38            foreach ( Control current in this.Controls )
39                current.IsAccessible = true;
40        }
41
42        private void InitializeComponent()
43        {
44            this.nameLabel.AccessibleDescription = "User Name";
45            this.nameLabel.AccessibleName = "User Name";
46            this.nameLabel.TabIndex = 5;
47            this.nameLabel.MouseHover +=
48                new System.EventHandler( this.controls_MouseHover );
49
50            this.phoneLabel.AccessibleDescription =
51                "Phone Number Label";
52            this.phoneLabel.AccessibleName = "Phone Number Label";
53            this.phoneLabel.TabIndex = 6;
54            this.phoneLabel.MouseHover +=
55                new System.EventHandler( this.controls_MouseHover );
56
57            this.nameTextBox.AccessibleDescription =
58                "Enter User Name";
```

Fig. 24.13 Application with accessibility features. (Part 2 of 4.)

```
59            this.nameTextBox.AccessibleName = "User Name TextBox";
60            this.nameTextBox.TabIndex = 1;
61            this.nameTextBox.MouseHover +=
62               new System.EventHandler( this.controls_MouseHover );
63
64            this.phoneTextBox.AccessibleDescription =
65               "Enter Phone Number";
66            this.phoneTextBox.AccessibleName = "Phone Number TextBox";
67            this.phoneTextBox.TabIndex = 2;
68            this.phoneTextBox.MouseHover +=
69               new System.EventHandler( this.controls_MouseHover );
70
71            this.passwordTextBox.AccessibleDescription =
72               "Enter Password";
73            this.passwordTextBox.AccessibleName = "Password TextBox";
74            this.passwordTextBox.TabIndex = 3;
75            this.passwordTextBox.MouseHover +=
76               new System.EventHandler( this.controls_MouseHover );
77
78            this.submitButton.AccessibleDescription =
79               "Submit the Information";
80            this.submitButton.AccessibleName = "Submit Information";
81            this.submitButton.TabIndex = 4;
82            this.submitButton.Text = "&Submit";
83            this.submitButton.Click +=
84               new System.EventHandler( this.submitButton_Click );
85            this.submitButton.MouseHover +=
86               new System.EventHandler( this.controls_MouseHover );
87
88            this.passwordLabel.AccessibleDescription =
89               "Password Label";
90            this.passwordLabel.AccessibleName = "Password Label";
91            this.passwordLabel.TabIndex = 7;
92            this.passwordLabel.MouseHover +=
93               new System.EventHandler( this.controls_MouseHover );
94
95            this.speaker.AccessibleDescription =
96               "Give Information about Form";
97            this.speaker.AccessibleName = "Speaker";
98            this.speaker.TabIndex = 8;
99            this.speaker.TabStop = false;
100
101           this.AccessibleDescription = "Registration Form";
102           this.AccessibleName = "Registration Form";
103        }
104
105        [STAThread]
106        static void Main()
107        {
108           Application.Run( new TextToSpeech() );
109        }
110
```

Fig. 24.13 Application with accessibility features. (Part 3 of 4.)

```
111    // tell user over which control mouse is
112    private void controls_MouseHover(
113       object sender, System.EventArgs e )
114    {
115       // if mouse is over Label, tell user to enter information
116       if ( sender.GetType() == nameLabel.GetType() )
117       {
118          Label temporary = ( Label) sender;
119          speaker.Speak( "Please enter your " + temporary.Text +
120             " in the textbox to the right" );
121       }
122
123       // if mouse is over TextBox, tell user what
124       // information was entered
125       else if ( sender.GetType() == nameTextBox.GetType() )
126       {
127          TextBox temporary = ( TextBox ) sender;
128          speaker.Speak( "You have entered " +
129             ( temporary.Text == "" ? "nothing" :
130             temporary.Text ) + " in the " + temporary.Name );
131       }
132
133       // otherwise, user is over Button, so tell user to click
134       // it to submit information
135       else
136          speaker.Speak(
137             "Click on this button to submit your information" );
138
139    } // end method controls_MouseHover
140
141    // thank user for information submission
142    private void submitButton_Click(
143       object sender, System.EventArgs e )
144    {
145       speaker.Speak(
146          "Thank you, your information has been submitted." );
147
148       Application.Exit();
149    }
150
151 } // end class TextToSpeech
```

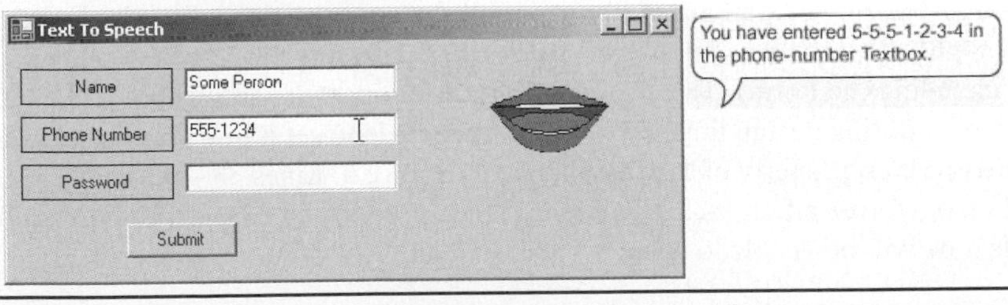

Fig. 24.13 Application with accessibility features. (Part 4 of 4.)

Method **controls_MouseHover** determines which type of control the mouse is hovering over and generates the appropriate audio. Line 116 determines whether the type of the control calling the method is the same as that of **nameLabel**. Here, we use method **GetType** of class **Type**, which returns an instance of class **Type**; this class represents information about a particular class. We call method **GetType** on object **sender**. Event-handler argument **sender** is a reference to the control that triggered the event. When the condition at line 116 evaluates to **true** (i.e., the control that triggered the event is **name-Label**), lines 118–120 execute. Line 118 casts **sender** to a **Label** (now that we know it is one) and assigns it to **Label temporary**. Lines 119–120 call **speaker**'s method **Speak**, which provides the **string** that should be converted to speech.

A similar process is performed to determine whether the mouse is over a **TextBox** (line 125) and to generate the appropriate audio (lines 127–130). Lastly, if the control over which the mouse is hovering is neither a **Label** nor a **TextBox**, it must be the **Button**; lines 136–137 tell the user to click the button to submit information. Method **submitButton_Click** (lines 142–149) executes when the user clicks the **Button**. This event handler calls **speaker**'s method **Speak**, providing as an argument a thank-you message, and then exits the application.

Line 82 sets the **Text** property of **submitButton** to **"&Submit"**. This is an example of providing keyboard access to the functionality of the application. Recall that, in Chapter 13, we assigned shortcut keys by placing **"&"** in front of the letter that would become the shortcut key. Here, we do the same for **submitButton**—pressing **Alt+S** on the keyboard is equivalent to clicking the **submitButton**.

We establish the tab order in this application by setting the **TabIndex** and **TabStop** properties. The **TabIndex** properties of the controls are assigned in lines 46, 60, 67, 74, 81, 91 and 98. The **TextBox**es are assigned the tab indices 1–3, in order of their appearance (vertically) on the form. The **Button** is assigned tab index 4, and the rest of the controls are given tab indices 5–8. We want the tab order to include only the **TextBox**es and the **Button**. The default setting for the **TabStop** property of **Label**s is **false**—thus, we do not need to change it; the labels will not be included in the tab order. The **TabStop** property of **TextBox**es and **Button**s is **true**, which means that we do not need to change the values for those controls either. The **TabStop** property of **speaker**, however, is **true** by default. We set it to **false**, indicating that we do not want **speaker** included in the tab order. In general, those controls with which the user cannot directly interact should have their **TabStop** properties set to **false**.

The last accessibility feature in this application involves setting the accessibility properties of the controls so that client accessibility applications can access and process the controls properly. Lines 44, 50–51, 57–58, 64–65, 71–72, 78–79, 88–89 and 95–96 set the **AccessibleDescription** properties of all the controls (including the Form). Lines 45, 52, 59, 66, 73, 80, 90 and 97 set the **AccessibleName** properties of all the controls (again including the Form). The **IsAccessible** property is not visible in the **Properties** window during design time, so we must write code to set it to **true**. Line 35 sets the **IsAccessible** property of **TextToSpeech** to **true**. Lines 38–39 loop through each control on the form and set each **IsAccessible** property to **true**. The Form and all its controls now will be visible to client accessibility applications.

24.8 Accessibility in XHTML Tables

Complex Web pages often contain tables that format content and present data. However, many screen readers are incapable of translating tables correctly unless developers design the tables with screen-reader requirements in mind. For example, the *CAST eReader*, a screen reader developed by the Center for Applied Special Technology (**www.cast.org**), starts at the top-left-hand cell and reads columns from left to right, top to bottom. This technique of reading data from a table is referred to as *linearized*. Figure 24.14 creates a simple table listing the costs of various fruits; later, we provide this table to the CAST eReader to demonstrate its linear reading of the table. The CAST eReader reads the table in Fig. 24.14 as follows:

> *Price of Fruit Fruit Price Apple $0.25 Orange $0.50 Banana $1.00 Pineapple $2.00*

This reading does not present the content of the table adequately: The reading neither specifies caption and header information nor links data contained in cells to the column headers that describe them. WCAG 1.0 recommends using Cascading Style Sheets (CSS) instead of tables, unless a table's content linearizes in an understandable manner.

```
1   <?xml version = "1.0"?>
2   <!DOCTYPE html PUBLIC "-//W3C//DTD XHTML 1.0 Strict//EN"
3       "http://www.w3.org/TR/xhtml1/DTD/xhtml1-strict.dtd">
4
5   <!-- Fig. 24.14: withoutheaders.html -->
6   <!-- Table without headers            -->
7
8   <html xmlns = "http://www.w3.org/1999/xhtml">
9       <head>
10          <title>XHTML Table Without Headers</title>
11
12          <style type = "text/css">
13             body { background-color: #ccffaa;
14                    text-align: center }
15          </style>
16      </head>
17
18      <body>
19
20          <p>Price of Fruit</p>
21
22          <table border = "1" width = "50%">
23
24              <tr>
25                  <td>Fruit</td>
26                  <td>Price</td>
27              </tr>
28
29              <tr>
30                  <td>Apple</td>
31                  <td>$0.25</td>
32              </tr>
33
```

Fig. 24.14 XHTML table without accessibility modifications. (Part 1 of 2.)

```
34              <tr>
35                  <td>Orange</td>
36                  <td>$0.50</td>
37              </tr>
38
39              <tr>
40                  <td>Banana</td>
41                  <td>$1.00</td>
42              </tr>
43
44              <tr>
45                  <td>Pineapple</td>
46                  <td>$2.00</td>
47              </tr>
48
49          </table>
50
51      </body>
52  </html>
```

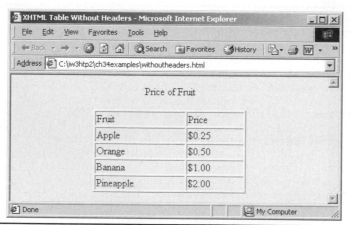

Fig. 24.14 XHTML table without accessibility modifications. (Part 2 of 2.)

If the table in Fig. 24.14 were large, the screen reader's linearized reading would be even more confusing to users. However, modifying the **<td>** tag with the **headers** attribute and modifying *header cells* (cells specified by the **<th>** tag) with the **id** attribute causes the table to be read as intended. Figure 24.15 demonstrates how these modifications change the way in which a screen reader interprets the table.

```
1   <?xml version = "1.0"?>
2   <!DOCTYPE html PUBLIC "-//W3C//DTD XHTML 1.0 Strict//EN"
3       "http://www.w3.org/TR/xhtml1/DTD/xhtml1-strict.dtd">
4
5   <!-- Fig. 24.15: withheaders.html  -->
6   <!-- Table with headers            -->
7
```

Fig. 24.15 Table optimized for screen reading, using attribute **headers**. (Part 1 of 3.)

```
8   <html xmlns = "http://www.w3.org/1999/xhtml">
9      <head>
10        <title>XHTML Table With Headers</title>
11
12        <style type = "text/css">
13           body { background-color: #ccffaa;
14                  text-align: center }
15        </style>
16     </head>
17
18     <body>
19
20     <!-- This table uses the id and headers attributes to   -->
21     <!-- ensure readability by text-based browsers. It also  -->
22     <!-- uses a summary attribute, used by screen readers to  -->
23     <!-- describe the table.                                   -->
24
25        <table width = "50%" border = "1"
26           summary = "This table uses th elements and id and
27           headers attributes to make the table readable
28           by screen readers">
29
30           <caption><strong>Price of Fruit</strong></caption>
31
32           <tr>
33              <th id = "fruit">Fruit</th>
34              <th id = "price">Price</th>
35           </tr>
36
37           <tr>
38              <td headers = "fruit">Apple</td>
39              <td headers = "price">$0.25</td>
40           </tr>
41
42           <tr>
43              <td headers = "fruit">Orange</td>
44              <td headers = "price">$0.50</td>
45           </tr>
46
47           <tr>
48              <td headers = "fruit">Banana</td>
49              <td headers = "price">$1.00</td>
50           </tr>
51
52           <tr>
53              <td headers = "fruit">Pineapple</td>
54              <td headers = "price">$2.00</td>
55           </tr>
56
57        </table>
58
59     </body>
60  </html>
```

Fig. 24.15 Table optimized for screen reading, using attribute **headers**. (Part 2 of 3.)

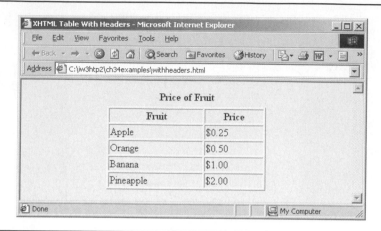

Fig. 24.15 Table optimized for screen reading, using attribute **headers**. (Part 3 of 3.)

This table does not appear to be different from the standard XHTML table shown in Fig. 24.14. However, the formatting of this table allows a screen reader to read the contained data more intelligently. A screen reader vocalizes the data from the table in Fig. 24.15 as follows:

```
Caption: Price of Fruit
Summary: This table uses th elements and id and headers
attributes to make the table readable by screen readers
Fruit: Apple, Price: $0.25
Fruit: Orange, Price: $0.50
Fruit: Banana, Price: $1.00
Fruit: Pineapple, Price: $2.00
```

Every cell in the table is preceded by its corresponding header when read by the screen reader. This format helps the listener understand the table. The *headers* *attribute* is intended specifically for use in tables that hold large amounts of data. Most small tables linearize fairly well, as long as the **<th>** tag is used properly. We also suggest using the **summary** attribute and **caption** element to enhance clarity. To view additional examples that demonstrate how to make tables accessible, visit **www.w3.org/TR/WCAG**.

24.9 Accessibility in XHTML Frames

Web designers often use frames to display more than one XHTML file in a single browser window. Frames are a convenient way to ensure that certain content always displays on the screen. Unfortunately, frames often lack proper descriptions, and this prevents users with text-based browsers and users listening via speech synthesizers from navigating the Web site.

A site that uses frames must provide a meaningful description of each frame in the frame's **<title>** tag. Examples of good titles include "*Navigation Frame*" and "*Main Content Frame.*" Users navigating via text-based browsers, such as Lynx, must choose which frame they want to open; descriptive titles make this choice simpler. However, the assignment of titles to frames does not solve all the navigation problems associated with frames. Web designers also should use the **<noframes>** tag, which provides alternative content for browsers that do not support frames.

Look-and-Feel Observation 24.1

Always provide titles for frames to ensure that user agents that do not support frames have alternatives.

Look-and-Feel Observation 24.2

*Include a title for each frame's contents with the **frame** element; if possible, provide links to the individual pages within the frameset, so that users still can navigate through the Web pages. To provide alternative content to browsers that do not support frames, use the **<noframes>** tag. This also improves access for browsers that offer limited support for frames.*

WCAG 1.0 suggests using Cascading Style Sheets (CSS) as an alternative to frames, because CSS can provide similar functionality and is highly customizible. Unfortunately, the ability to display multiple XHTML documents in a single browser window requires the complete support of HTML 4, which is not widespread. However, the second generation of Cascading Style Sheets (CSS2) can display a single document as if it were several documents. CSS2 is not yet fully supported by many user agents.

24.10 Accessibility in XML

XML gives developers the freedom to create new markup languages. Although this feature provides many advantages, the new languages might not incorporate accessibility features. To prevent the proliferation of inaccessible languages, the WAI is developing guidelines—the *XML Guidelines (XML GL)*—to facilitate the creation of accessible XML documents. The XML Guidelines recommend including a text description, similar to XHTML's **<alt>** tag, for each non-text object on a page. To enhance accessibility further, element types should allow grouping and classification and should identify important content. Without an accessible user interface, other efforts to implement accessibility are less effective. Therefore, it is essential to create stylesheets that can produce multiple outputs, including document outlines.

Many XML languages, including Synchronized Multimedia Integration Language (SMIL) and Scalable Vector Graphics (SVG), have implemented several of the WAI guidelines. The WAI XML Accessibility Guidelines can be found at **www.w3.org/WAI/PF/xmlgl.htm**.

24.11 Using Voice Synthesis and Recognition with VoiceXML™

A joint effort by AT&T®, IBM®, Lucent™ and Motorola® has created an XML vocabulary that marks up information for use by *speech synthesizers*, or tools that enable computers to speak to users. This technology, called *VoiceXML*, can provide tremendous benefits to people with visual impairments and to people who are illitcrate. VoiceXML-enabled applications read Web pages to the user and then employ *speech recognition* technology to understand words spoken into a microphone. An example of a speech-recognition tool is IBM's *ViaVoice* (**www-4.ibm.com/software/speech**). To learn more about speech recognition and synthesis, consult Chapter 16, Graphics and Multimedia.

The VoiceXML interpreter and the VoiceXML browser process VoiceXML. In the future, Web browsers might incorporate these interpreters. VoiceXML is derived from XML, so VoiceXML is platform–independent. When a VoiceXML document is loaded, a *voice server* sends a message to the VoiceXML browser and begins a verbal conversation between the user and the computer.

The IBM *WebSphere Voice Server SDK 1.5* is a VoiceXML interpreter that can be used to test VoiceXML documents on the desktop. To download the VoiceServer SDK, visit **www.alphaworks.ibm.com/tech/voiceserversdk**. [*Note*: To run the VoiceXML program in Fig. 24.16, download *Java 2 Platform Standard Edition* (Java SDK) 1.3 from **www.java.sun.com/j2se/1.3**. Installation instructions for both the VoiceServerSDK and the Java SDK are located on the Deitel & Associates, Inc., Web site at **www.deitel.com**.]

Figure 24.16 and Fig. 24.17 depict examples of VoiceXML that could be included on a Web site. The computer speaks a document's text to the user, and the text embedded in the VoiceXML tags enables verbal interaction between the user and the browser. The output included in Fig. 24.17 demonstrates a conversation that might take place between a user and a computer after this document is loaded.

```
1    <?xml version = "1.0"?>
2    <vxml version = "1.0">
3
4    <!-- Fig. 24.16: main.vxml -->
5    <!-- Voice page            -->
6
7    <link next = "#home">
8       <grammar>home</grammar>
9    </link>
10
11   <link next = "#end">
12      <grammar>exit</grammar>
13   </link>
14
15   <var name = "currentOption" expr = "'home'"/>
16
17   <form>
18      <block>
19         <emp>Welcome</emp> to the voice page of Deitel and
20         Associates. To exit any time say exit.
21         To go to the home page any time say home.
22      </block>
23
24      <subdialog src = "#home"/>
25   </form>
26
27   <menu id = "home">
28      <prompt count = "1" timeout = "10s">
29         You have just entered the Deitel home page.
30         Please make a selection by speaking one of the
31         following options:
32         <break msecs = "1000" />
33         <enumerate/>
34      </prompt>
35
36      <prompt count = "2">
37         Please say one of the following.
38         <break msecs = "1000" />
```

Fig. 24.16 Home page written in VoiceXML. (Part 1 of 3.)

```
39              <enumerate/>
40          </prompt>
41
42          <choice next = "#about">About us</choice>
43          <choice next = "#directions">Driving directions</choice>
44          <choice next = "publications.vxml">Publications</choice>
45      </menu>
46
47      <form id = "about">
48          <block>
49              About Deitel and Associates, Inc.
50              Deitel and Associates, Inc. is an internationally
51              recognized corporate training and publishing
52              organization, specializing in programming languages,
53              Internet and World Wide Web technology and object
54              technology education. Deitel and Associates, Inc. is a
55              member of the World Wide Web Consortium. The company
56              provides courses on Java, C++, Visual Basic, C, Internet
57              and World Wide Web programming and Object Technology.
58              <assign name = "currentOption" expr = "'about'"/>
59              <goto next = "#repeat"/>
60          </block>
61      </form>
62
63      <form id = "directions">
64          <block>
65              Directions to Deitel and Associates, Inc.
66              We are located on Route 20 in Sudbury,
67              Massachusetts, equidistant from route
68              <sayas class = "digits">128</sayas> and route
69              <sayas class = "digits">495</sayas>.
70              <assign name = "currentOption" expr = "'directions'"/>
71              <goto next = "#repeat"/>
72          </block>
73      </form>
74
75      <form id = "repeat">
76          <field name = "confirm" type = "boolean">
77              <prompt>
78                  To repeat say yes. To go back to home, say no.
79              </prompt>
80
81              <filled>
82                  <if cond = "confirm == true">
83                      <goto expr = "'#' + currentOption"/>
84                  <else/>
85                      <goto next = "#home"/>
86                  </if>
87              </filled>
88
89          </field>
90      </form>
91
```

Fig. 24.16 Home page written in VoiceXML. (Part 2 of 3.)

```
92   <form id = "end">
93      <block>
94         Thank you for visiting Deitel and Associates voice page.
95         Have a nice day.
96         <exit/>
97      </block>
98   </form>
99
100  </vxml>
```

Fig. 24.16 Home page written in VoiceXML. (Part 3 of 3.)

```
101  <?xml version = "1.0"?>
102  <vxml version = "1.0">
103
104  <!-- Fig. 24.17: publications.vxml       -->
105  <!-- Voice page for various publications -->
106
107  <link next = "main.vxml#home">
108     <grammar>home</grammar>
109  </link>
110
111  <link next = "main.vxml#end">
112     <grammar>exit</grammar>
113  </link>
114
115  <link next = "#publication">
116     <grammar>menu</grammar>
117  </link>
118
119  <var name = "currentOption" expr = "'home'"/>
120
121  <menu id = "publication">
122
123     <prompt count = "1" timeout = "12s">
124        Following are some of our publications. For more
125        information visit our web page at www.deitel.com.
126        To repeat the following menu, say menu at any time.
127        Please select by saying one of the following books:
128        <break msecs = "1000" />
129        <enumerate/>
130     </prompt>
131
132     <prompt count = "2">
133        Please select from the following books.
134        <break msecs = "1000" />
135        <enumerate/>
136     </prompt>
137
138     <choice next = "#java">Java.</choice>
139     <choice next = "#c">C.</choice>
```

Fig. 24.17 Publication page of Deitel and Associates' VoiceXML page. (Part 1 of 4.)

```
140        <choice next = "#cplus">C plus plus.</choice>
141   </menu>
142
143   <form id = "java">
144      <block>
145          Java How to program, third edition.
146          The complete, authoritative introduction to Java.
147          Java is revolutionizing software development with
148          multimedia-intensive, platform-independent,
149          object-oriented code for conventional, Internet,
150          Intranet and Extranet-based applets and applications.
151          This Third Edition of the world's most widely used
152          university-level Java textbook carefully explains
153          Java's extraordinary capabilities.
154          <assign name = "currentOption" expr = "'java'"/>
155          <goto next = "#repeat"/>
156      </block>
157   </form>
158
159   <form id = "c">
160      <block>
161          C How to Program, third edition.
162          This is the long-awaited, thorough revision to the
163          world's best-selling introductory C book! The book's
164          powerful "teach by example" approach is based on
165          more than 10,000 lines of live code, thoroughly
166          explained and illustrated with screen captures showing
167          detailed output.World-renowned corporate trainers and
168          best-selling authors Harvey and Paul Deitel offer the
169          most comprehensive, practical introduction to C ever
170          published with hundreds of hands-on exercises, more
171          than 250 complete programs written and documented for
172          easy learning, and exceptional insight into good
173          programming practices, maximizing performance, avoiding
174          errors, debugging, and testing. New features include
175          thorough introductions to C++, Java, and object-oriented
176          programming that build directly on the C skills taught
177          in this book; coverage of graphical user interface
178          development and C library functions; and many new,
179          substantial hands-on projects.For anyone who wants to
180          learn C, improve their existing C skills, and understand
181          how C serves as the foundation for C++, Java, and
182          object-oriented development.
183          <assign name = "currentOption" expr = "'c'"/>
184          <goto next = "#repeat"/>
185      </block>
186   </form>
187
188   <form id = "cplus">
189      <block>
190          The C++ how to program, second edition.
191          With nearly 250,000 sold, Harvey and Paul Deitel's C++
192          How to Program is the world's best-selling introduction
```

Fig. 24.17 Publication page of Deitel and Associates' VoiceXML page. (Part 2 of 4.)

```
193        to C++ programming. Now, this classic has been thoroughly
194        updated! The new, full-color Third Edition has been
195        completely revised to reflect the ANSI C++ standard, add
196        powerful new coverage of object analysis and design with
197        UML, and give beginning C++ developers even better live
198        code examples and real-world projects. The Deitels' C++
199        How to Program is the most comprehensive, practical
200        introduction to C++ ever published with hundreds of
201        hands-on exercises, roughly 250 complete programs written
202        and documented for easy learning, and exceptional insight
203        into good programming practices, maximizing performance,
204        avoiding errors, debugging, and testing. This new Third
205        Edition covers every key concept and technique ANSI C++
206        developers need to master: control structures, functions,
207        arrays, pointers and strings, classes and data
208        abstraction, operator overloading, inheritance, virtual
209        functions, polymorphism, I/O, templates, exception
210        handling, file processing, data structures, and more. It
211        also includes a detailed introduction to Standard
212        Template Library containers, container adapters,
213        algorithms, and iterators.
214        <assign name = "currentOption" expr = "'cplus'"/>
215        <goto next = "#repeat"/>
216     </block>
217 </form>
218
219 <form id = "repeat">
220    <field name = "confirm" type = "boolean">
221
222        <prompt>
223            To repeat say yes. Say no, to go back to home.
224        </prompt>
225
226        <filled>
227            <if cond = "confirm == true">
228                <goto expr = "'#' + currentOption"/>
229            <else/>
230                <goto next = "#publication"/>
231            </if>
232        </filled>
233     </field>
234 </form>
235 </vxml>
```

Computer speaks:
**Welcome to the voice page of Deitel and Associates. To exit any time
say exit. To go to the home page any time say home.**

User speaks:
Home

(continued on next page)

Fig. 24.17 Publication page of Deitel and Associates' VoiceXML page. (Part 3 of 4.)

(continued from previous page)

Computer speaks:
You have just entered the Deitel home page. Please make a selection by
speaking one of the following options: About us, Driving directions,
Publications.

User speaks:
Driving directions

Computer speaks:
Directions to Deitel and Associates, Inc.
We are located on Route 20 in Sudbury,
Massachusetts, equidistant from route 128
and route 495.
To repeat say yes. To go back to home, say no.

Fig. 24.17 Publication page of Deitel and Associates' VoiceXML page. (Part 4 of 4.)

A VoiceXML document contains a series of dialogs and subdialogs, resulting in spoken interaction between the user and the computer. The **<form>** and **<menu>** tags implement the dialogs. A *form* element both presents information to the user and gathers data from the user. A *menu* element provides the user with list options and then transfers control to another dialog in response to the user's selection.

Lines 7–9 (of Fig. 24.16) use element *link* to create an active link to the home page. Attribute *next* specifies the URL to which the browser is directed when a user selects the link. Element *grammar* marks up the text that the user must speak to select the link. In the **link** element, we navigate to the element containing **id home** when a user speaks the word **home**. Lines 11–13 use element **link** to create a link to **id end** when a user speaks the word **exit**.

Lines 17–25 create a form dialog using element **form**, which collects information from the user. Lines 18–22 present introductory text. Element **block**, which can exist only within a **form** element, groups together elements that perform an action or an event. Element **emp** indicates that a section of text should be spoken with emphasis. If the level of emphasis is not specified, then the default level—*moderate*—is used. Our example uses the default level. [*Note*: To specify an emphasis level, use the **level** attribute. This attribute accepts the following values: *strong*, *moderate*, *none* and *reduced*.]

The **menu** element in line 27 enables users to select the page to which they would like to link. The *choice* element, which always is part of either a **menu** or a **form**, presents the options. The **next** attribute indicates the page that is loaded when a user makes a selection. The user selects a **choice** element by speaking the text marked up between the tags into a microphone. In this example, the first and second **choice** elements in lines 42–43 transfer control to a *local dialog* (i.e., a location within the same document) when they are selected. The third **choice** element transfers the user to the document **publications.vxml**. Lines 28–34 use element *prompt* to instruct the user to make a selection. Attribute *count* maintains a record of the number of times that a prompt is spoken (i.e., each time the computer reads a prompt, **count** increments by one). The **count** attribute transfers control to another prompt once a certain limit has been reached. Attribute **time-**

out specifies how long the program should wait after outputting the prompt for users to respond. In the event that the user does not respond before the timeout period expires, lines 36–40 provide a second, shorter prompt that reminds the user to make a selection.

When the user chooses the **publications** option, **publications.vxml** (Fig. 24.17) loads into the browser. Lines 107–113 define **link** elements that provide links to **main.vxml**. Lines 115–117 provide links to the **menu** element (lines 121–141), which asks users to select one of the following publications: Java, C or C++. The **form** elements in lines 143–217 describe books that correspond to these topics. Once the browser speaks the description, control transfers to the **form** element with an **id** attribute whose value equals **repeat** (lines 219–234).

Figure 24.18 provides a brief description of each VoiceXML tag that we used in the previous example (Fig. 24.17).

VoiceXML Tag	Description
<assign>	Assigns a value to a variable.
<block>	Presents information to users without any interaction between the user and the computer (i.e., the computer does not expect any input from the user).
<break>	Instructs the computer to pause its speech output for a specified period of time.
<choice>	Specifies an option in a **menu** element.
<enumerate>	Lists all the available options to the user.
<exit>	Exits the program.
<filled>	Contains elements that execute when the computer receives input for a **form** element from the user.
<form>	Gathers information from the user for a set of variables.
<goto>	Transfers control from one dialog to another.
<grammar>	Specifies grammar for the expected input from the user.
<if>, <else>, <elseif>	Indicates a control statement used for making logic decisions.
<link>	Performs a transfer of control similar to the **goto** statement, but a **link** can be executed at any time during the program's execution.
<menu>	Provides user options and then transfers control to other dialogs on the basis of the selected option.
<prompt>	Specifies text to be read to users when they must make a selection.
<subdialog>	Calls another dialog. After executing the subdialog, the calling dialog resumes control.
<var>	Declares a variable.
<vxml>	Top-level tag that specifies that the document should be processed by a VoiceXML interpreter.

Fig. 24.18 VoiceXML tags.

24.12 CallXML™

Another advancement benefiting people with visual impairments is *CallXML*, a voice technology created and supported by *Voxeo* (**www.voxeo.com**). CallXML creates phone-to-Web applications that control incoming and outgoing telephone calls. Examples of CallXML applications include voice mail, interactive voice-response systems and Internet call waiting. VoiceXML allows computers to read Web pages to users with visual impairments; CallXML reads Web content to users via a telephone. CallXML has important implications for individuals who do not have a computer, but do have a telephone.

When users access CallXML applications, a *text-to-speech (TTS)* engine converts text to an automated voice. The TTS engine then reads information contained within CallXML elements to the users. CallXML applications are tailored to respond to input from callers. [*Note*: Users must have a touch-tone phone to access CallXML applications.]

Typically, CallXML applications play prerecorded audio clips or text as output, requesting responses as input. An audio clip might contain a greeting that introduces callers to the application, or it might recite a menu of options, requesting that callers make a touch-tone entry. Certain applications, such as voice mail, might require both verbal and touch-tone input. Once the application receives the necessary input, it responds by invoking CallXML elements (such as **text**) that contain the information a TTS engine reads to users. If the application does not receive input within a designated time frame, it prompts the user to enter valid input.

When a user accesses a CallXML application, the incoming telephone call is referred to as a *session*. A CallXML application can support multiple sessions, which means that the application can process multiple telephone calls at once. Each session is independent of the others and is assigned a unique *sessionID* for identification. A session terminates either when the user hangs up the telephone or when the CallXML application invokes the **hangup** element.

Our first CallXML application demonstrates the classic "Hello World" example (Fig. 24.19). Line 1 contains the optional *XML declaration*. Value **version** indicates the XML version to which the document conforms. The current XML recommendation is version **1.0**. Value **encoding** indicates the type of *Unicode* encoding that the application uses. For this example, we empty UTF-8, which requires eight bits to transfer and receive data. More information on Unicode can be found in Appendix G, Unicode®.

The **<callxml>** tag in line 6 declares that the content is a CallXML document. Line 7 contains the **Hello World text**. All text that is to be spoken by a text-to-speech (TTS) engine must be placed within **<text>** tags.

```
1   <?xml version = "1.0" encoding = "UTF-8"?>
2
3   <!-- Fig. 24.19: hello.xml          -->
4   <!-- The classic Hello World example -->
5
6   <callxml>
7      <text>Hello World.</text>
8   </callxml>
```

Fig. 24.19 Hello World CallXML example. (Part 1 of 2.) (Courtesy of Voxeo, © Voxeo Corporation 2000–2001.)

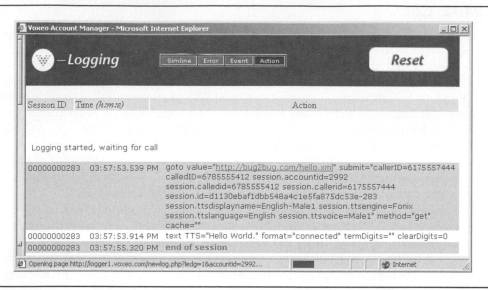

Fig. 24.19 Hello World CallXML example. (Part 2 of 2.) (Courtesy of Voxeo, © Voxeo Corporation 2000–2001.)

To deploy a CallXML application, register with the *Voxeo* Community (**commu-nity.voxeo.com**), a Web resource that facilitates the creation, debugging and deployment of phone applications. For the most part, Voxeo resources are free, but the company does charge fees when CallXML applications are deployed commercially. The Voxeo Community assigns a unique telephone number to each CallXML application so that external users can access and interact with the application. [*Note*: Voxeo assigns telephone numbers only to applications that reside on the Internet. If you have access to a Web server (such as IIS, PWS or Apache), use it to post your CallXML application. Otherwise, open an Internet account through one of the many Internet-service companies (such as **www.geocities.com**, **www.angelfire.com**, **www.stormpages.com**, **www.freewebsites.com**, or **www.brinkster.com**). These companies allow individuals to post documents on the Internet using their Web servers.]

Figure 24.19 also demonstrates the *logging* feature of the **Voxeo Account Manager**, which is accessible to registered members. The logging feature records and displays the "conversation" between the user and the application. The first row of the logging feature lists the URL of the CallXML application and the *global variables* associated with that session. When a session begins, the application creates and assigns values to global variables that the entire application can access and modify. The subsequent row(s) display the "conversation." This example demonstrates a one-way conversation (i.e., the application does not accept any input from the user) in which the TTS engine says **Hello World**. The last row displays the **end of session** message, which states that the phone call has terminated. The logging feature assists developers in the debugging of their applications. By observing a CallXML "conversation," a developer can determine the point at which the application terminates. If the application terminates abruptly ("crashes"), the logging feature displays information regarding the type and location of the error, pointing the developer toward the section of the application that is causing the problem.

The next example (Fig. 24.20) depicts a CallXML application that reads the ISBN numbers of three Deitel textbooks—*Internet and World Wide Web How to Program: Second Edition*, *XML How to Program* and *Java How to Program: Fourth Edition*—on the basis of a user's touch-tone input. [*Note*: The code has been formatted for presentation purposes.]

```
1   <?xml version = "1.0" encoding = "UTF-8"?>
2
3   <!-- Fig. 24.20: isbn.xml                          -->
4   <!-- Reads the ISBN value of three Deitel books -->
5
6   <callxml>
7      <block>
8         <text>
9            Welcome. To obtain the ISBN of the Internet and World
10           Wide Web How to Program: Second Edition, please enter 1.
11           To obtain the ISBN of the XML How to Program,
12           please enter 2. To obtain the ISBN of the Java How
13           to Program: Fourth Edition, please enter 3. To exit the
14           application, please enter 4.
15        </text>
16
17        <!-- Obtains the numeric value entered by the user and -->
18        <!-- stores it in the variable ISBN. The user has 60   -->
19        <!-- seconds to enter one numeric value               -->
20        <getDigits var = "ISBN"
21           maxDigits = "1"
22           termDigits = "1234"
23           maxTime = "60s" />
24
25        <!-- Requests that the user enter a valid numeric -->
26        <!-- value after the elapsed time of 60 seconds   -->
27        <onMaxSilence>
28           <text>
29              Please enter either 1, 2, 3 or 4.
30           </text>
31
32           <getDigits var = "ISBN"
33              termDigits = "1234"
34              maxDigits = "1"
35              maxTime = "60s" />
36
37        </onMaxSilence>
38
39        <onTermDigit value = "1">
40           <text>
41              The ISBN for the Internet book is 0130308978.
42              Thank you for calling our CallXML application.
43              Good-bye.
44           </text>
45        </onTermDigit>
46
```

Fig. 24.20 CallXML example that reads three ISBN values. (Part 1 of 2.) (Courtesy of Voxeo, © Voxeo Corporation 2000–2001.)

```
47          <onTermDigit value = "2">
48             <text>
49                 The ISBN for the XML book is 0130284173.
50                 Thank you for calling our CallXML application.
51                 Good-bye.
52             </text>
53          </onTermDigit>
54
55          <onTermDigit value = "3">
56             <text>
57                 The ISBN for the Java book is 0130341517.
58                 Thank you for calling our CallXML application.
59                 Good-bye.
60             </text>
61          </onTermDigit>
62
63          <onTermDigit value = "4">
64             <text>
65                 Thank you for calling our CallXML application.
66                 Good-bye.
67             </text>
68          </onTermDigit>
69       </block>
70
71       <!-- Event handler that terminates the call -->
72       <onHangup />
73    </callxml>
```

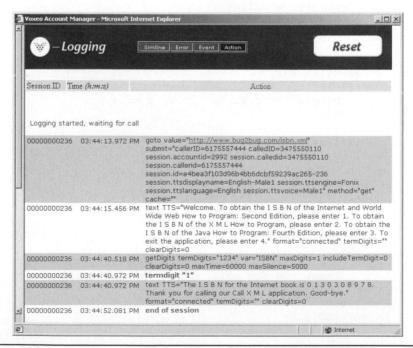

Fig. 24.20 CallXML example that reads three ISBN values. (Part 2 of 2.) (Courtesy of Voxeo, © Voxeo Corporation 2000–2001.)

The **<block>** tag (line 7) encapsulates other CallXML tags. Usually, sets of CallXML tags that perform similar tasks are enclosed within **<block>**...**</block>**. The **block** element in this example encapsulates the **<text>**, **<getDigits>**, **<onMaxSilence>** and **<onTermDigit>** tags. A **block** element also can be nested in other **block** elements.

Lines 20–23 contain some attributes of the **<getDigits>** tag. The **getDigits** element obtains the user's touch-tone response and stores it in the variable declared by the **var** attribute (i.e., **ISBN**). The **maxDigits** attribute (line 21) indicates the maximum number of digits that the application can accept. This application accepts only one character. If no maximum is stated, then the application uses the default value, *nolimit*.

The **termDigits** attribute (line 22) contains the list of characters that terminate user input. When a user inputs a character from this list, the application is notified that it has received the last acceptable input; any character entered after this point is invalid. These characters do not terminate the call; they simply notify the application to proceed to the next instruction, because the necessary input has been received. In our example, the values for **termDigits** are **1**, **2**, **3** and **4**. The default value for **termDigits** is the null value (**""**).

The **maxTime** attribute (line 23) indicates the maximum amount of time that the application will wait for a user response. If the user fails to enter input within the given time frame, then the CallXML application invokes the event handler **onMaxSilence**. The default value for this attribute is 30 seconds.

The **onMaxSilence** element (lines 27–37) is an event handler that is invoked when attribute **maxTime** (or **maxSilence**) expires. The event handler notifies the application of the appropriate action to perform when a user fails to respond. In this case, the application asks the user to enter a value, because the **maxTime** has expired. After receiving input, **getDigits** (line 32) stores the entered value in the **ISBN** variable.

The **onTermDigit** element (lines 39–68) is an event handler that notifies the application of the appropriate action to perform when a user selects one of the **termDigits** characters. At least one **<onTermDigit>** tag must be associated with (i.e., must appear after) the **getDigits** element, even if the default value (**""**) is used. We provide four actions that the application can perform in response to the specific **termDigits** value entered by the user. For example, if the user enters **1**, the application reads the ISBN value for the *Internet and World Wide Web How to Program: Second Edition* textbook.

Line 72 contains the **<onHangup/>** event handler, which terminates the telephone call when the user hangs up the telephone. Our **<onHangup>** event handler is an empty tag (i.e., no action is performed when this tag is invoked).

The logging feature (Fig. 24.20) displays the "conversation" between the application and the user. As in the previous example, the first row specifies the URL of the application and the global variables of the session. The subsequent rows display the "conversation": The application asks the caller which ISBN value to read; the caller enters **1** (*Internet and World Wide Web How to Program: Second Edition*), and the application reads the corresponding ISBN. The **end of session** message states that the application has terminated.

We provide brief descriptions of various logic and action CallXML elements in Fig. 24.21. *Logic elements* assign values to, and clear values from, the session variables; *action elements* perform specified tasks, such as answering and terminating a telephone call during the current session. A complete list of CallXML elements is available at:

www.oasis-open.org/cover/callxmlv2.html

24.13 JAWS® for Windows

JAWS (Job Access with Sound) is one of the leading screen readers currently on the market. Henter-Joyce, a division of Freedom Scientific™, created this application to help people with visual impairments interact with technology.

To download a demonstration version of JAWS, visit **www.freedomscientific.com**. The JAWS demo is fully functional and includes an extensive, highly customized help system. Users can select the voice that "reads" Web content and the rate at which text is spoken. Users also can create keyboard shortcuts. Although the demo is in English, the full version of JAWS allows the user to choose one of several supported languages.

JAWS also includes special key commands for popular programs, such as Microsoft Internet Explorer and Microsoft Word. For example, when browsing in Internet Explorer, JAWS' capabilities extend beyond the reading of content on the screen. If JAWS is enabled, pressing *Insert + F7* in Internet Explorer opens a **Links List** dialog, which displays all the links available on a Web page. For more information about JAWS and the other products offered by Henter-Joyce, visit **www.freedomscientific.com**.

Elements	Description
assign	Assigns a **value** to a variable, **var**.
clear	Clears the contents of the **var** attribute.
clearDigits	Clears all digits that the user has entered.
goto	Navigates to another section of the current CallXML application or to a different CallXML application. The **value** attribute specifies the URL of the invoked application. The **submit** attribute lists the variables that are passed to the invoked application. The **method** attribute states whether to use the HTTP *get* or *post* request type when sending and retrieving information. A *get* request retrieves data from a Web server without modifying the contents, whereas the *post* request receives modified data.
run	Starts a new CallXML session for each call. The **value** attribute specifies the CallXML application to retrieve. The **submit** attribute lists the variables that are passed to the invoked application. The **method** attribute states whether to use the HTTP *get* or *post* request type. The **var** attribute stores the identification number of the session.
sendEvent	Allows multiple sessions to exchange messages. The **value** attribute stores the message, and the **session** attribute specifies the identification number of the session that receives the message.
answer	Answers an incoming telephone call.
call	Calls the URL specified by the **value** attribute. The **callerID** attribute contains the phone number that is displayed on a CallerID device. The **maxTime** attribute specifies the length of time to wait for the call to be answered before disconnecting.

Fig. 24.21 CallXML elements. (Part 1 of 2.)

Elements	Description
conference	Connects multiple sessions so that individuals can participate in a conference call. The **targetSessions** attribute specifies the identification numbers of the sessions, and the **termDigits** attribute indicates the touch-tone keys that terminate the call.
wait	Waits for user input. The **value** attribute specifies how long to wait. The **termDigits** attribute indicates the touch-tone keys that terminate the **wait** element.
play	Plays an audio file or pronounces a value that is stored as a number, date or amount of money and is indicated by the **format** attribute. The **value** attribute contains the information (location of the audio file, number, date or amount of money) that corresponds to the **format** attribute. The **clearDigits** attribute specifies whether or not to delete the previously entered input. The **termDigits** attribute indicates the touch-tone keys that terminate the audio file, etc.
recordAudio	Records an audio file and stores it at the URL specified by **value**. The **format** attribute indicates the file extension of the audio clip. Other attributes include **termDigits**, **clearDigits**, **maxTime** and **maxSilence**.

Fig. 24.21 CallXML elements. (Part 2 of 2.)

24.14 Other Accessibility Tools

Many accessibility products are available to assist people with disabilities. One such technology, Microsoft's *Active Accessibility*®, establishes a protocol by which an accessibility aid can retrieve information about an application's user interface in a consistent manner. Accessibility aids require information such as the name, location and layout of particular GUI elements within an application, so that the accessibility aid can render the information properly to the intended audience. Active Accessibility also enables software developers and accessibility-aid developers to design programs and products that are compatible with each other. Moreover, Active Accessibility is packaged in two components, enabling both programmers and individuals who use accessibility aids to employ the software. The *Software Development Kit (SDK)* component is intended for programmers: It includes testing tools, programmatic libraries and header files. The *Redistribution Kit (RDK)* component is intended for those who use accessibility aids: It installs a runtime component into the Microsoft operating system. Accessibility aids use the Active Accessibility runtime component to interact with and obtain information from any application software. For more information on Active Accessibility, visit:

> **www.microsoft.com/enable/msaa**

Another important accessibility tool for individuals with visual impairments is the *braille keyboard*. In addition to providing keys labeled with the letters they represent, a braille keyboard also has the equivalent braille symbol printed on each key. Most often, braille keyboards are combined with a speech synthesizer or a braille display, enabling users to interact with the computer to verify that their typing is correct.

Speech synthesis also provides benefits to people with disabilities. *Speech synthesizers* have been used for many years to aid people who are unable to communicate verbally. However, the growing popularity of the Web has prompted a surge of interest in the fields of speech synthesis and speech recognition. Now, these technologies are allowing individuals with disabilities to use computers more than ever before. The development of speech synthesizers also is enabling the improvement of other technologies, such as VoiceXML and *AuralCSS* (**www.w3.org/TR/REC-CSS2/aural.html**). These tools allow people with visual impairments and illiterate people to access Web sites.

Despite the existence of adaptive software and hardware for people with visual impairments, the accessibility of computers and the Internet is still hampered by the high costs, rapid obsolescence and unnecessary complexity of current technology. Moreover, almost all software currently available requires installation by a person who can see. *Ocularis* is a project launched in the open-source community that aims to address these problems. (Open-source software for people with visual impairments already exists; although it is often superior to its proprietary, closed-source counterparts, it has not yet reached its full potential.) Ocularis ensures that the blind can access and use all aspects of the Linux operating system. Products that integrate with Ocularis include word processors, calculators, basic finance applications, Internet browsers and e-mail clients. In addition, a screen reader is included for use with programs that have a command-line interface. The official Ocularis Web site is located at

ocularis.sourceforge.net.

People with visual impairments are not the only beneficiaries of efforts to improve markup languages. People with hearing impairments also have a number of tools to help them interpret auditory information delivered over the Web. One of these tools, *Synchronized Multimedia Integration Language* (SMIL™), is designed to add extra *tracks (*layers of content found within a single audio or video file) to multimedia content. The additional tracks can contain closed captioning.

Technologies are being designed to help people with severe disabilities, such as quadriplegia, a form of paralysis that affects the body from the neck down. One such technology, *EagleEyes*, developed by researchers at Boston College (**www.bc.edu/ eagleeyes**), is a system that translates eye movements into mouse movements. A user moves the mouse cursor by moving his or her eyes or head and is thereby able to control the computer.

GW Micro, Henter-Joyce and Adobe Systems, Inc., also are working on software that assists people with disabilities. Adobe Acrobat 5.0 complies with Microsoft's application programming interface (API) to allow businesses to provide information to a wider audience. JetForm Corp is also accommodating the needs of people with disabilities by developing server-based XML software. The new software allows users to download information in a format that best meets their needs.

There are many services on the Web that assist e-businesses in designing Web sites so that they are accessible to individuals with disabilities. For additional information, the U.S. Department of Justice (**www.usdoj.gov**) provides extensive resources detailing legal and technical issues related to people with disabilities.

24.15 Accessibility in Microsoft® Windows® 2000

Because of the prominence of the Windows operating system, it is crucial that this operating system provide proper accessibility to individuals with disabilities. Beginning with Microsoft *Windows 95*, Microsoft has included accessibility features in its operating systems and many of its applications, including *Office 97*, *Office 2000* and *Netmeeting*. In Microsoft *Windows 2000*, Microsoft significantly enhanced the operating system's accessibility features. All the accessibility options provided by Windows 2000 are available through the **Accessibility Wizard**, which guides users through Windows 2000 accessibility features and then configures users' computers in accordance with the chosen specifications. This section uses the **Accessibility Wizard** to guide users through the configuration of their Windows 2000 accessibility options.

To access the **Accessibility Wizard**, users' computers must be equipped with Microsoft Windows 2000. Click the **Start** button and select **Programs**, followed by **Accessories**, **Accessibility** and **Accessibility Wizard**. When the wizard starts, the **Welcome** screen displays. Click **Next**. The next dialog (Fig. 24.22) asks the user to select a font size. Modify the font size if necessary and then click **Next**.

Figure 24.22 depicts the **Display Settings** dialog. This dialog allows the user to activate the font-size settings chosen in the previous window, change the screen resolution, enable the *Microsoft Magnifier* (a program that displays an enlarged section of the screen in a separate window) and disable personalized menus. Personalized menus hide rarely used programs from the start menu and can be a hindrance to users with disabilities. Make appropriate selections and click **Next**.

The **Set Wizard Options** dialog (Fig. 24.23) asks questions about the user's disabilities; the answers to these questions allow the **Accessibility Wizard** to customize Windows to better suit the user's needs. For demonstration purposes, we selected every type of disability included in the dialogue. Click **Next** to continue.

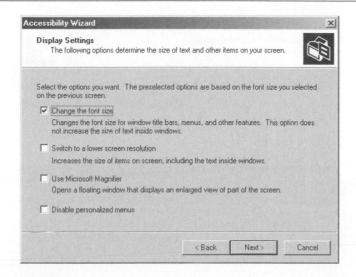

Fig. 24.22 Display Settings dialog.

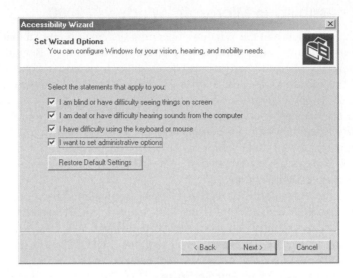

Fig. 24.23 Accessibility Wizard initialization options.

24.15.1 Tools for People with Visual Impairments

When we check all the options in Fig. 24.23, the wizard begins to configure Windows so that it is accessible to people with visual impairments. The dialog box shown in Fig. 24.24 allows the user to resize the scroll bars and window borders to increase their visibility. Click **Next** to proceed to the next dialog.

Figure 24.25 contains a dialog that allows the user to resize icons. Users with poor vision and users who are illiterate or have trouble reading benefit from large icons.

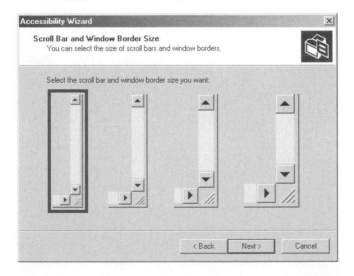

Fig. 24.24 Scroll Bar and Window Border Size dialog.

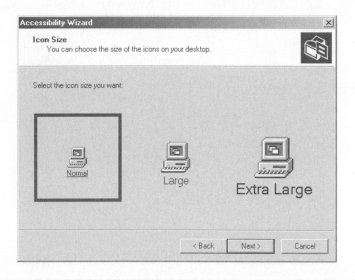

Fig. 24.25 Adjusting window-element sizes.

Clicking **Next** displays the **Display Color Settings** dialog (Fig. 24.26). These settings enable the user to change the Windows color scheme and resize various screen elements.

Click **Next** to view the dialog (Fig. 24.27) that enables customization of the mouse cursor. Anyone who has ever used a laptop computer knows how difficult it can be to see the mouse cursor. This is even more problematic for people with visual impairments. To address this problem, the wizard offers users the options of larger cursors, black cursors and cursors that invert the colors of objects underneath them. Click **Next**.

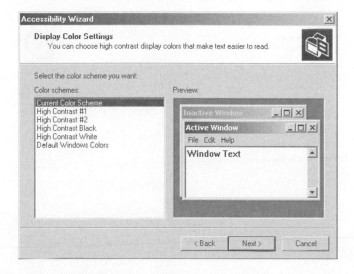

Fig. 24.26 **Display Color Settings** options.

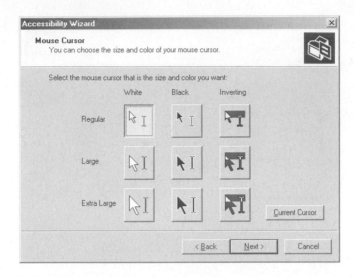

Fig. 24.27   **Accessibility Wizard** mouse cursor adjustment tool.

24.15.2 Tools for People with Hearing Impairments

This section, which focuses on accessibility for people with hearing impairments, begins with the ***SoundSentry*** window (Fig. 24.28). **SoundSentry** is a tool that creates visual signals to notify users of system events. For example, people with hearing impairments are unable to hear the beeps that normally indicate warnings, so **SoundSentry** flashes the screen when a beep occurs. To continue on to the next dialog, click **Next**.

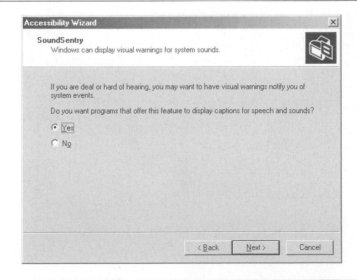

Fig. 24.28 SoundSentry dialog.

The next window is the ***ShowSounds*** window (Fig. 24.29). **ShowSounds** adds captions to spoken text and other sounds produced by today's multimedia-rich software. Note that, for **ShowSounds** to work in a specific application, developers must provide the captions and spoken text specifically within their software. Make selections and click **Next**.

24.15.3 Tools for Users Who Have Difficulty Using the Keyboard

The next dialog describes **StickyKeys** (Fig. 24.30). ***StickyKeys*** is a program that helps users who have difficulty pressing multiple keys at the same time. Many important computer commands can be invoked only by pressing specific key combinations. For example, the reboot command requires the user to press *Ctrl+Alt+Delete* simultaneously. **Sticky-Keys** enables the user to press key combinations in sequence, rather than at the same time. Click **Next** to continue to the **BounceKeys** dialog (Fig. 24.31).

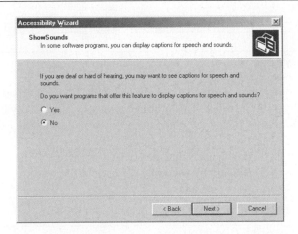

Fig. 24.29 ShowSounds dialog.

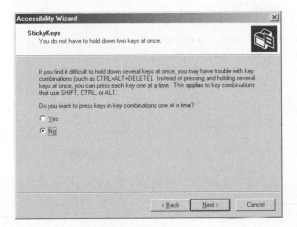

Fig. 24.30 StickyKeys window.

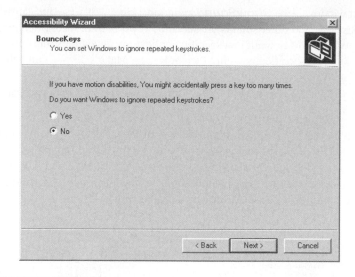

Fig. 24.31 BounceKeys dialog.

Another common problem that affects certain users with disabilities is the accidental pressing of the same key multiple times. This problem typically is caused by holding a key down too long. ***BounceKeys*** forces the computer to ignore repeated keystrokes. Click **Next**.

ToggleKeys (Fig. 24.32) alerts users that they have pressed one of the lock keys (i.e., *Caps Lock*, *Num Lock* or *Scroll Lock*) by sounding an audible beep. Make selections and click **Next**.

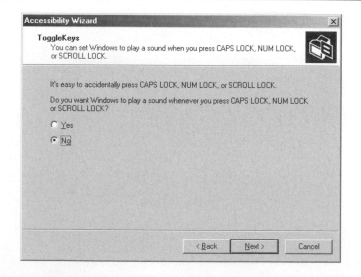

Fig. 24.32 ToggleKeys window.

Next, the **Extra Keyboard Help** dialog (Fig. 24.33) is displayed. This dialog can activate a tool that displays information such as keyboard shortcuts and tool tips when such information is available. Like **ShowSounds**, this tool requires that software developers provide the content to be displayed.

Clicking **Next** will load the **MouseKeys** (Fig. 24.34) customization window. *MouseKeys* is a tool that uses the keyboard to imitate mouse movements. The arrow keys direct the mouse, and the 5 key indicates a single click. To double click, the user must press the + key; to simulate the holding down of the mouse button, the user must press the *Ins* (Insert) key. To release the mouse button, the user must press the *Del* (Delete) key. Choose whether to enable **MouseKeys** and then click **Next.**

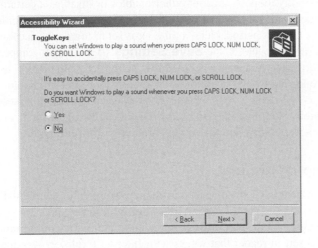

Fig. 24.33 Extra Keyboard Help dialog.

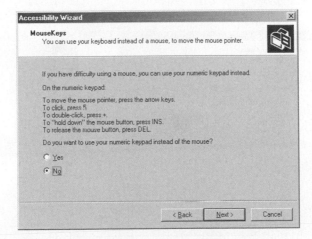

Fig. 24.34 MouseKeys window.

Today's computer tools, including most mice, are designed almost exclusively for right-handed users. Microsoft recognized this problem and added the ***Mouse Button* Settings** window (Fig. 24.35) to the **Accessibility Wizard**. This tool allows the user to create a virtual left-handed mouse by swapping the button functions. Click **Next**.

Users can adjust mouse speed through the **MouseSpeed** (Fig. 24.36) section of the **Accessibility Wizard**. Dragging the scroll bar changes the speed. Clicking the **Next** button sets the speed and displays the wizard's **Set Automatic Timeouts** window (Fig. 24.37). Although accessibility tools are important to users with disabilities, they can be a hindrance to users who do not need them. In situations where varying accessibility needs exist, it is important that the user be able to turn the accessibility tools on and off as necessary. The ***Set Automatic Timeouts*** window specifies a *timeout* period for enabling or disabling accessibility tools. A timeout either enables or disables a certain action after the computer has idled for a specified amount of time. A screen saver is a common example of a program with a timeout period. Here, a timeout is set to toggle the accessibility tools.

After the user clicks **Next**, the **Save Settings to File** dialog appears (Fig. 24.38). This dialog determines whether the accessibility settings should be used as the *default settings*, which are loaded when the computer is rebooted or after a timeout. Set the accessibility settings as the default if the majority of users needs them. Users also can save multiple accessibility settings. The user can create an **.acw** file, which, when chosen, activates the saved accessibility settings on any Windows 2000 computer.

24.15.4 Microsoft Narrator

Microsoft Narrator is a text-to-speech program designed for people with visual impairments. It reads text, describes the current desktop environment and alerts the user when certain Windows events occur. **Narrator** is intended to aid in the configuration of Microsoft Windows. It is a screen reader that works with Internet Explorer, Wordpad, Notepad and most programs in the **Control Panel**. Although its capabilities are limited outside these applications, **Narrator** is excellent at navigating the Windows environment.

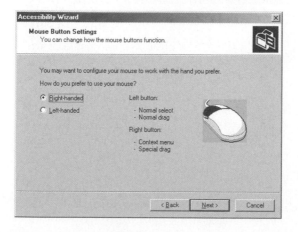

Fig. 24.35 Mouse Button Settings window.

To explore **Narrator**'s functionality, we explain how to use the program in conjunction with several Windows applications. Click the **Start** button and select **Programs**, followed by **Accessories**, **Accessibility** and **Narrator**. Once **Narrator** is open, it describes the current foreground window. It then reads the text inside the window aloud to the user. When the user clicks **OK**, the dialog in Fig. 24.39 displays.

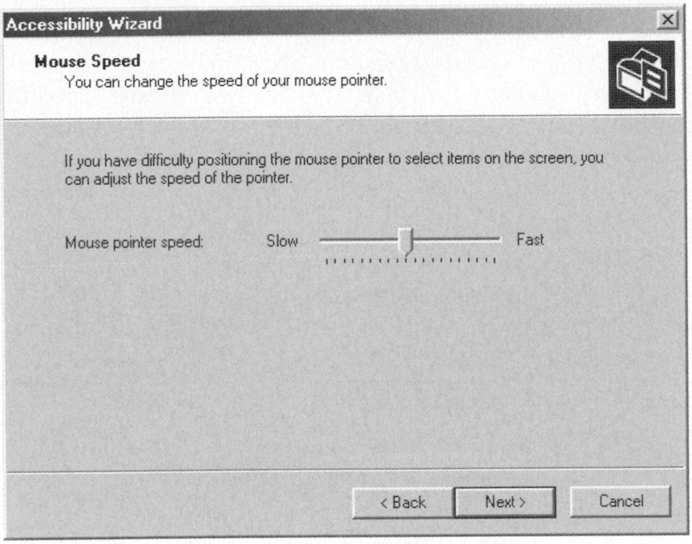

Fig. 24.36 Mouse Speed dialog.

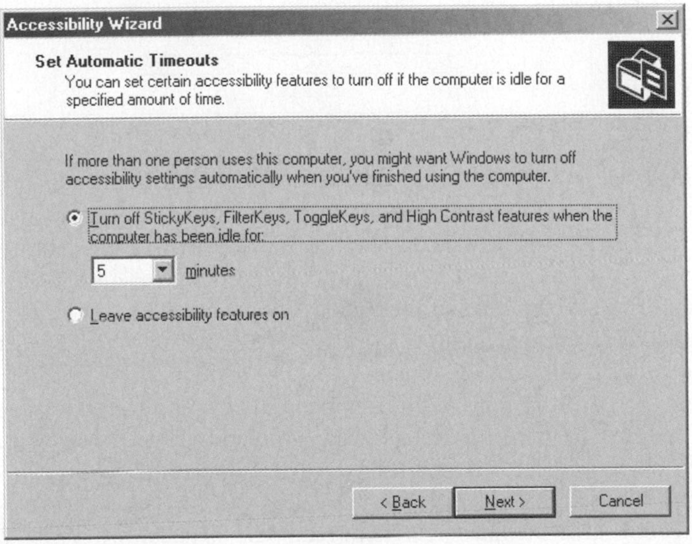

Fig. 24.37 Set Automatic Timeouts dialog.

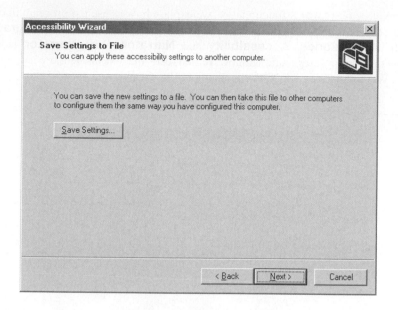

Fig. 24.38 Saving new accessibility settings.

Fig. 24.39 Narrator window.

Checking the first option instructs **Narrator** to describe menus and new windows when they are opened. The second option instructs **Narrator** to speak the characters that users type as they type them. The third option moves the mouse cursor to the region currently being read by **Narrator**. Clicking the **Voice...** button enables the user to change the pitch, volume and speed of the narrator voice (Fig. 24.40).

Now, we demonstrate **Narrator** in various applications. When **Narrator** is running, open **Notepad** and click the **File** menu. **Narrator** announces the opening of the program and begins to describe the items in the **File** menu. As a user scrolls down the list, **Narrator** reads the item to which the mouse currently is pointing. Type some text and press *Ctrl-Shift-Enter* to hear **Narrator** read it (Fig. 24.41). If the **Read typed characters** option is checked, **Narrator** reads each character as it is typed. Users also can employ the keyboard's direction arrows to make **Narrator** read. The up and down arrows cause **Narrator** to speak the lines adjacent to the current mouse position, and the left and right arrows cause **Narrator** to speak the characters adjacent to the current mouse position.

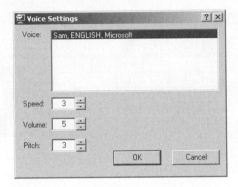

Fig. 24.40 Voice-settings window.

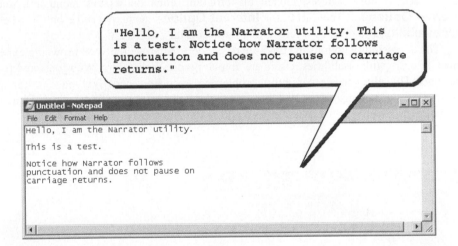

Fig. 24.41 Narrator reading **Notepad** text.

24.15.5 Microsoft On-Screen Keyboard

Some computer users lack the ability to use a keyboard, but are able to use a pointing device, such as a mouse. For these users, the ***On-Screen Keyboard*** is helpful. To access the On-Screen Keyboard, click the **Start** button and select **Programs**, followed by **Accessories**, **Accessibility** and **On-Screen Keyboard**. Figure 24.42 depicts the layout of the Microsoft On-Screen Keyboard.

Users who have difficulty using the On-Screen Keyboard can purchase more sophisticated products, such as *Clicker 4*[TM] by *Inclusive Technology*. Clicker 4 is an aid designed for people who cannot use a keyboard effectively. Its best feature is that it can be customized. Keys can have letters, numbers, entire words or even pictures on them. For more information regarding Clicker 4, visit **www.inclusive.co.uk/catalog/clicker.htm**.

Fig. 24.42 Microsoft **On-Screen Keyboard**.

24.15.6 Accessibility Features in Microsoft Internet Explorer 5.5

Internet Explorer 5.5 offers a variety of options that can improve usability. To access IE5.5's accessibility features, launch the program, click the **Tools** menu and select **Internet Options....** Then, from the **Internet Options** menu, press the button labeled **Accessibility...** to open the accessibility options (Fig. 24.43).

The accessibility options in IE5.5 are designed to improve the Web browsing experiences of users with disabilities. Users are able to ignore Web colors, Web fonts and font-size tags. This eliminates accessibility problems arising from poor Web-page design and allows users to customize their Web browsing. Users can even specify a *style sheet*, which formats every Web site that users visit according to their personal preferences.

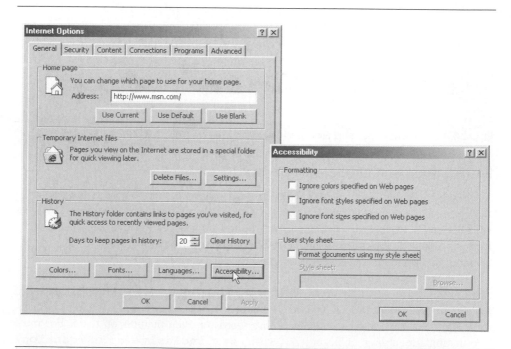

Fig. 24.43 Microsoft Internet Explorer 5.5's accessibility options.

In the **Internet Options** dialog, click the **Advanced** tab. This opens the dialog depicted in Fig. 24.44. The first available option is labeled **Always expand ALT text for images**. By default, IE5.5 hides some of the `<alt>` text if the size of the text exceeds that of the image it describes. This option forces IE5.5 to show all the text. The second option reads: **Move system caret with focus/selection changes**. This option is intended to make screen reading more effective. Some screen readers use the *system caret* (the blinking vertical bar associated with editing text) to determine what to read. If this option is not activated, screen readers might not read Web pages correctly.

Web designers often forget to take accessibility into account when creating Web sites, and, in attempts to provide large amounts of content, they use fonts that are too small. Many user agents have addressed this problem by allowing the user to adjust the text size. Click the **View** menu and select **Text Size** to change the font size in pages rendered by IE5.5. By default, the text size is set to **Medium**.

In this chapter, we presented a wide variety of technologies that help people with various disabilities use computers and the Internet. We hope that all our readers will join us in emphasizing the importance of these capabilities in their schools and workplaces.

Well, that's it for now. We sincerely hope that you have enjoyed learning with *C# How To Program*. As this book went to the presses, we were already at work on *Advanced C# How To Program*, a book appropriate for professional developers writing enterprise applications and for students enrolled in advanced software-development courses.

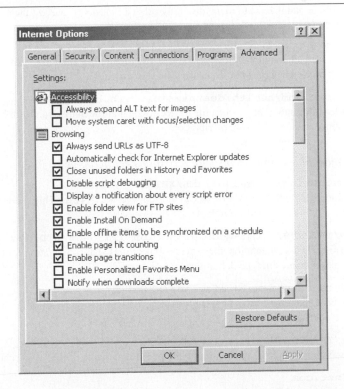

Fig. 24.44 Advanced accessibility settings in Microsoft Internet Explorer 5.5.

24.16 Internet and World Wide Web Resources

There are many accessibility resources available on the Internet and World Wide Web; this section lists a variety of these resources.

General Information, Guidelines and Definitions

www.w3.org/WAI
The World Wide Web Consortium's *Web Accessibility Initiative (WAI)* site promotes the design of universally accessible Web sites. This site contains the current guidelines and forthcoming standards for Web accessibility.

www.w3.org/TR/xhtml1
The *XHTML 1.0 Recommendation* contains XHTML 1.0 general information, compatibility issues, document type definition information, definitions, terminology and much more.

www.abledata.com/text2/icg_hear.htm
This page contains a consumer guide that discusses technologies designed for people with hearing impairments.

www.washington.edu/doit
The University of Washington's DO-IT (Disabilities, Opportunities, Internetworking and Technology) site provides information and Web-development resources for the creation of universally accessible Web sites.

www.webable.com
The *WebABLE* site contains links to many disability-related Internet resources; the site is geared towards those developing technologies for people with disabilities.

www.webaim.org
The *WebAIM* site provides a number of tutorials, articles, simulations and other useful resources that demonstrate how to design accessible Web sites. The site provides a screen-reader simulation.

deafness.about.com/health/deafness/msubvib.htm
This site provides information on vibrotactile devices, which allow individuals with hearing impairments to experience audio in the form of vibrations.

Developing Accessible Applications with Existing Technologies

wdvl.com/Authoring/Languages/XML/XHTML
The Web Developers Virtual Library provides an introduction to XHTML. This site also contains articles, examples and links to other technologies.

www.w3.org/TR/1999/xhtml-modularization-19990406/DTD/doc
The XHTML 1.0 DTD documentation site provides links to DTD documentation for the strict, transitional and frameset document type definitions.

www.webreference.com/xml/reference/xhtml.html
This Web page contains a list of the frequently used XHTML tags, such as header tags, table tags, frame tags and form tags. It also provides a description of each tag.

www.w3.org/TR/REC-CSS2/aural.html
This site discusses Aural Style Sheets, outlining the purpose and uses of this new technology.

www.islandnet.com
Lynxit is a development tool that allows users to view any Web site as if they were using a text-only browser. The site's form allows you to enter a URL and returns the Web site in text-only format.

www.trill-home.com/lynx/public_lynx.html
This site allows users to browse the Web with a Lynx browser. Users can view how Web pages appear to users who are not using the most current technologies.

java.sun.com/products/java-media/speech/forDevelopers/JSML
This site outlines the specifications for JSML, Sun Microsystem's Java Speech Markup Language. This language, like VoiceXML, helps improve accessibility for people with visual impairments.

ocfo.ed.gov/coninfo/clibrary/software.htm
This is the U.S. Department of Education's Web site that outlines software accessibility requirements. The site helps developers produce accessible products.

www.speech.cs.cmu.edu/comp.speech/SpeechLinks.html
The *Speech Technology Hyperlinks* page has over 500 links to sites related to computer-based speech and speech-recognition tools.

www.islandnet.com/accessibility.html
This page provides a list of tips for creating accessible Web pages.

www.chantinc.com/technology
This page is the *Chant* Web site, which discusses speech technology and how it works. Chant also provides speech–synthesis and speech-recognition software.

searchmiddleware.techtarget.com/sdefinition/
0,,sid26_gci518993,00.html
This site provides definitions and information about several topics, including CallXML. Its thorough definition of CallXML differentiates CallXML from VoiceXML, another technology developed by Voxeo. The site also contains links to other published articles that discuss CallXML.

www.oasis-open.org/cover/callxmlv2.html
This site provides a comprehensive list of the CallXML tags, complete with a description of each tag. The site also provides short examples on how to apply the tags in various applications.

web.ukonline.co.uk/ddmc/software.html
This site provides links to software designed for people with disabilities.

www.freedomscientific.com
Henter-Joyce is a division of Freedom Scientific that provides software for people with visual impairments. It is the homepage of JAWS (Job Access with Sound).

www-3.ibm.com/able/
This is the homepage of IBM's accessibility site. It provides information on IBM products and their accessibility and discusses hardware, software and Web accessibility.

www.w3.org/TR/voice-tts-reqs
This page explains the speech-synthesis markup requirements for voice markup languages.

www.cast.org
CAST (Center for Applied Special Technology) offers software, including a valuable accessibility checker, that can help individuals with disabilities use computers. The accessibility checker is a Web-based program that validates the accessibility of Web sites.

Information on Disabilities

deafness.about.com/health/deafness/msubmenu6.htm
This is the home page of **deafness.about.com**. It provides a wealth of information on the history of hearing loss, the current state of medical developments and other resources related to these topics.

www.trainingpost.org/3-2-inst.htm
This site presents a tutorial on the Gunning Fog Index. The Gunning Fog Index is a method of grading text according to its readability.

laurence.canlearn.ca/English/learn/accessibility2001/neads/index.shtml
INDIE stands for "Integrated Network of Disability Information and Education." This site is home to a search engine that helps users find information on disabilities.

www.wgbh.org/wgbh/pages/ncam/accesslinks.html
This page provides links to other accessibility pages across the Web.

SUMMARY

- Enabling a Web site to meet the needs of individuals with disabilities is an important issue.

- Enabling a Web site to meet the needs of individuals with disabilities is an issue relevant to all business owners.

- Technologies such as voice activation, visual enhancers and auditory aids enable individuals with disabilities to have access to the web and software applications.

- In 1997, the World Wide Web Consortium (W3C) launched the Web Accessibility Initiative (WAI). The WAI is an attempt to make the Web more accessible; its mission is described at **www.w3.org/WAI**.

- Accessibility refers to the level of usability of an application or Web site for people with disabilities. Total accessibility is difficult to achieve because there are many different disabilities, language barriers, and hardware and software inconsistencies.

- The majority of Web sites are considered to be either partially or totally inaccessible to people with visual, learning or mobility impairments.

- The WAI published the Web Content Accessibility Guidelines 1.0, which assign accessibility priorities to a three-tier structure of checkpoints. The WAI currently is working on a draft of the Web Content Accessibility Guidelines 2.0.

- One important WAI requirement is to ensure that every image, movie and sound on a Web site is accompanied by a description that clearly defines the item's purpose; the description is called an **<alt>** tag.

- Specialized user agents, such as screen readers (programs that allow users to hear what is being displayed on their screen) and braille displays (devices that receive data from screen-reading software and output the data as braille), allow people with visual impairments to access text-based information that normally is displayed on the screen.

- Using a screen reader to navigate a Web site can be time consuming and frustrating, because screen readers are unable to interpret pictures and other graphical content that do not have alternative text.

- Including links at the top of each Web page provides easy access to the page's main content.

- Web pages with large amounts of multimedia content are difficult for user agents to interpret unless they are designed properly. Images, movies and most non-XHTML objects cannot be read by screen readers.

- Misused heading tags (**<h1>**) also present challenges to some Web users—particularly those who cannot use a mouse.

- Web designers should avoid misuse of the **alt** attribute; it is intended to provide a short description of an XHTML object that might not load properly on all user agents.

- The value of the **longdesc** attribute is a text-based URL, linked to a Web page, that describes the image associated with the attribute.

- When creating a Web page for the general public, it is important to consider the reading level at which it is written. Web site designers can make their sites more readable through the use of shorter words; some users may have difficulty understanding slang and other nontraditional language.

- Web designers often use frames to display more than one XHTML file at a time. Unfortunately, frames often lack proper descriptions, which prevents users with text-based browsers and users with visual impairments from navigating the Web site.

- The **<noframes>** tag allows the designer to offer alternative content to users whose browsers do not support frames.

- VoiceXML has tremendous implications for people with visual impairments and for illiterate people. VoiceXML, a speech recognition and synthesis technology, reads Web pages to users and understands words spoken into a microphone.

- A VoiceXML document is composed of a series of dialogs and subdialogs, which result in spoken interaction between the user and the computer. VoiceXML is a voice-recognition technology.

- CallXML, a language created and supported by Voxeo, creates phone-to-Web applications. These applications tailor themselves to the user's input.

- When a user accesses a CallXML application, the incoming telephone call is referred to as a session. A CallXML application can support multiple sessions that enable the application to receive multiple telephone calls at any given time.

- A session terminates either when the user hangs up the telephone or when the CallXML application invokes the **hangup** element.

- The contents of a CallXML application are inserted within the **<callxml>** tag.

- CallXML tags that perform similar tasks should be enclosed between the **<block>** and **</block>** tags.

- To deploy a CallXML application, register with the Voxeo Community, which assigns a telephone number to the application so that other users may access it.

- Voxeo's logging feature enables developers to debug their telephone application by observing the "conversation" between the user and the application.

- Braille keyboards are similar to standard keyboards, except that in addition to having each key labeled with the letter it represents, braille keyboards have the equivalent braille symbol printed on the key. Most often, braille keyboards are combined with a speech synthesizer or a braille display, so users are able to interact with the computer to verify that their typing is correct.

- People with visual impairments are not the only beneficiaries of the effort being made to improve markup languages. Individuals with hearing impairments also have a great number of tools to help them interpret auditory information delivered over the Web.

- Speech synthesis is another area in which research is being done to help people with disabilities.

- Open-source software for people with visual impairments already exists and is often superior to most of its proprietary, closed-source counterparts. However, it still does not use the Linux OS to its fullest extent.

- People with hearing impairments will soon benefit from what is called Synchronized Multimedia Integration Language (SMIL). This markup language is designed to add extra tracks—layers of content found within a single audio or video file. The additional tracks can contain such data as closed captioning.

- EagleEyes, developed by researchers at Boston College (**www.bc.edu/eagleeyes**), is a system that translates eye movements into mouse movements. Users move the mouse cursor by moving their eyes or head and are thereby able to control the computer.

- All of the accessibility options provided by Windows 2000 are available through the **Accessibility Wizard**. The **Accessibility Wizard** takes a user step by step through all of the Windows accessibility features and configures his or her computer according to the chosen specifications.

- Microsoft Magnifier enlarges the section of your screen surrounding the mouse cursor.

- To solve problems seeing the mouse cursor, Microsoft offers the ability to use larger cursors, black cursors and cursors that invert objects underneath them.

- **SoundSentry** is a tool that creates visual signals when system events occur.

- **ShowSounds** adds captions to spoken text and other sounds produced by today's multimedia-rich software.

- **StickyKeys** is a program that helps users who have difficulty pressing multiple keys at the same time.

- **BounceKeys** forces the computer to ignore repeated keystrokes, solving the problem of accidentally pressing the same key more than once.

- **ToggleKeys** causes an audible beep to alert users that they have pressed one of the lock keys (i.e., *Caps Lock*, *Num Lock*, or *Scroll Lock*).

- **MouseKeys** is a tool that uses the keyboard to emulate mouse movements.

- The **Mouse Button Settings** tool allows you to create a virtual left-handed mouse by swapping the button functions.

- A timeout either enables or disables a certain action after the computer has idled for a specified amount of time. A common use of a timeout is in a screen saver.

- Default settings are loaded when the computer is rebooted.

- You can create an **.acw** file, which, when chosen, will automatically activate the saved accessibility settings on any Windows 2000 computer.

- Microsoft **Narrator** is a text-to-speech program for people with visual impairments. It reads text, describes the current desktop environment and alerts the user when certain Windows events occur.

TERMINOLOGY

<alt> tag
accessibility
accessibility aids in Visual Studio .NET
Accessibility Wizard
Accessibility Wizard initialization option
Accessibility Wizard mouse-cursor
   adjustment tool
AccessibilityDescription property
   of class **Control**
AccessibilityName property of class
   Control
AccessibleDescription property of
   Control
AccessibleName property of **Control**
AccessibleRole enumeration
AccessibleRole property of **Control**

action element
Active Accessibility
Acts designed to ensure Internet access for
   people with disabilities
.acw
ADA (Americans with Disabilities Act)
advanced accessibility settings in Microsoft
   Internet Explorer 5.5
alt attribute
Americans with Disabilities Act (ADA)
answer element
assign element
<assign> tag (**<assign>...</assign>**)
Aural Style Sheet
AuralCSS
block element

SELF-REVIEW EXERCISES

24.1 Expand the following acronyms:
    a) W3C.
    b) WAI.
    c) JAWS.
    d) SMIL.
    e) CSS.

24.2 Fill in the blanks in each of the following statements.

a) The highest priority of the Web Accessibility Initiative is to ensure that _____, _____ and _____ are accompanied by descriptions that clearly define their purposes.

b) Technologies such as _____, _____ and _____ enable individuals with disabilities to work in a large number of positions.

c) Although they are a great layout tool for presenting data, _____ are difficult for screen readers to interpret and convey clearly to a user.

d) To make a frame accessible to individuals with disabilities, it is important to include _____ tags on the page.

e) Blind people using computers often are assisted by _____ and _____.

f) CallXML is used to create _____ applications that allow individuals to receive and send telephone calls.

g) A _____ tag must be associated with the **<getDigits>** tag.

24.3 State whether each of the following is *true* or *false*. If *false*, explain why.

a) Screen readers have no problem reading and translating images.

b) When writing Web pages for the general public, it is important to consider the reading level of the context.

c) The **<alt>** tag helps screen readers describe the images on a Web page.

d) Blind people have been helped by the improvements made in speech-recognition technology more than any other group of people.

e) VoiceXML lets users interact with Web content using speech recognition and speech synthesis technologies.

f) Elements such as **onMaxSilence**, **onTermDigit** and **onMaxTime** are event handlers because they perform specified tasks when invoked.

g) The debugging feature of the **Voxeo Account Manager** assists developers in debugging their CallXML applications.

ANSWERS TO SELF-REVIEW EXERCISES

24.1 a) World Wide Web Consortium. b) Web Accessibility Initiative. c) Job Access with Sound. d) Synchronized Multimedia Integration Language. e) Cascading Style Sheets.

24.2 a) image, movie, sound. b) voice activation, visual enhancers and auditory aids. c) tables. d) **<noframes>**. e) braille displays, braille keyboards. f) phone-to-Web. g) **<onTermDigit>**.

24.3 a) False. Screen readers cannot directly interpret images. If the programmer includes an **alt** attribute inside the **<img>** tag, the screen reader reads this description to the user. b) True. c) True. d) False. Although speech-recognition technology has had a large impact on blind people, speech-recognition technology has had also a large impact on people who have trouble typing. e) True. f) True. g) False. The logging feature assists developers in debugging their CallXML application.

EXERCISES

24.4 Insert XHTML markup into each segment to make the segment accessible to someone with disabilities. The contents of images and frames should be apparent from the context and filenames.

```
a) <img src = "dogs.jpg" width = "300" height = "250" />
b) <table width = "75%">
       <tr><th>Language</th><th>Version</th></tr>
       <tr><td>XHTML</td><td>1.0</td></tr>
```

```
        <tr><td>Perl</td><td>5.6.0</td></tr>
        <tr><td>Java</td><td>1.3</td></tr>
     </table>
c) <map name = "links">
        <area href = "index.html" shape = "rect"
           coords = "50, 120, 80, 150" />
        <area href = "catalog.html" shape = "circle"
           coords = "220, 30" />
     </map>
     <img src = "antlinks.gif" width = "300" height = "200"
        usemap = "#links" />
```

24.5   Define the following terms:
a) Action element.
b) Gunning Fog Index.
c) Screen reader.
d) Session.
e) Web Accessibility Initiative (WAI).

24.6   Describe the three-tier structure of checkpoints (priority-one, priority-two and priority-three) set forth by the WAI.

24.7   Why do misused **<h1>** heading tags create problems for screen readers?

24.8   Use CallXML to create a voice-mail system that plays a voice-mail greeting and records a message. Have friends and classmates call your application and leave a message.

Operator Precedence Chart

Operators are shown in decreasing order of precedence from top to bottom with each level of precedence separated by a horizontal line.[1]

Operator	Type	Associativity
.	member access	left-to-right
( )	parenthesized expression	
[]	element access	
++	post increment	
--	post decrement	
new	object creation	
typeof	typeof	
checked	checked	
unchecked	unchecked	
+	unary plus	left-to-right
-	unary minus	
!	unary	
~	unary	
++	pre-increment	
--	pre-decrement	

Fig. A.1   Operator precedence chart. (Part 1 of 2.)

1. This operator-precedence chart is based on Section 7.2.1, *Operator precedence and associativity*, of the C# Language Specification (for more information, visit **msdn.microsoft.com/library/default.asp?url=/library/en-us/csspec/html/CSharpSpec-Start.asp**).

Operator	Type	Associativity
* / %	multiplication division modulus	left-to-right
+ -	addition subtraction	left-to-right
<< >>	shift left shift right	left-to-right
< > <= >= is	relational less than relational greater than relational less than or equal to relational greater than or equal to type comparison	left-to-right
== !=	relational is equal to relational is not equal to	left-to-right
&	logical AND	left-to-right
^	logical exclusive OR	left-to-right
|	logical inclusive OR	left-to-right
&&	conditional AND	left-to-right
||	conditional OR	left-to-right
?:	conditional	right-to-left
= *= /= += -= <<= >>= &= ^= |=	assignment multiplication assignment division assignment addition assignment subtraction assignment shift left assignment shift right assignment logical AND assignment logical exclusive OR assignment logical inclusive OR assignment	right-to-left

Fig. A.1   Operator precedence chart. (Part 2 of 2.)

Number Systems
(on CD)

Objectives

- To understand basic number system concepts such as base, positional value and symbol value.
- To understand how to work with numbers represented in the binary, octal and hexadecimal number systems
- To be able to abbreviate binary numbers as octal numbers or hexadecimal numbers.
- To be able to convert octal numbers and hexadecimal numbers to binary numbers.
- To be able to covert back and forth between decimal numbers and their binary, octal and hexadecimal equivalents.
- To understand binary arithmetic and how negative binary numbers are represented using two's complement notation.

Appendix B is included on the CD that accompanies this book in printable Adobe® Acrobat® PDF format. The appendix includes pages 1276–1289.

Career Opportunities (on CD)

Objectives

- To explore the various online career services.
- To examine the advantages and disadvantages of posting and finding jobs online.
- To review the major online career services Web sites available to job seekers.
- To explore the various online services available to employers seeking to build their workforces.

Appendix C is included on the CD that accompanies this book in printable Adobe® Acrobat® PDF format. The appendix includes pages 1290–1311.

Visual Studio .NET Debugger

Objectives

- To understand syntax and logic errors.
- To become familiar with the Visual Studio .NET debugging tools.
- To understand the use of breakpoints to suspend program execution.
- To be able to examine data using expressions in the debugging windows.
- To be able to debug methods and objects.

And often times excusing of a fault
Doth make the fault the worse by the excuse.
William Shakespeare

To err is human, to forgive divine.
Alexander Pope, *An Essay on Criticism*

D.1 Introduction

Two types of errors occur during software development: syntax errors and logic errors. Syntax errors (or compilation errors) occur when program statements violate the grammatical rules of a programming language, such as failure to end a statement with a semicolon. When a compiler detects syntax errors, the compiler terminates without building the application. By contrast, logic errors do not prevent programs from compiling or executing, but rather prevent programs from operating as expected.

Syntax errors are easier to fix than are logic errors. Upon detecting a syntax error, the compiler gives the description and line number in the *Task List* window (Fig. D.1). This information gives the programmer a "clue" as to how to eliminate the error, so the compiler can create the program. However, logic errors often are more subtle and usually do not inform the user exactly where in the program the error occurred. This appendix overviews both types of errors and details Visual Studio .NET's capabilities for detecting and correcting the these logic errors.

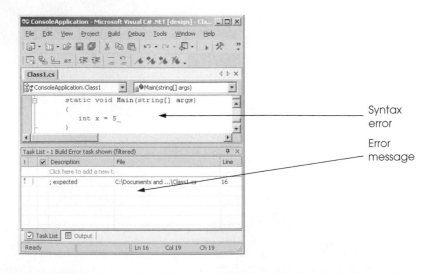

Fig. D.1   Syntax error.

Testing and Debugging Tip D.1

After fixing one error, you may observe that the number of overall errors perceived by the compiler is significantly reduced.

Testing and Debugging Tip D.2

When the compiler reports a syntax error on a particular line, check that line for the syntax error. If the error is not on that line, check the preceding few lines of code for the cause of the syntax error.

Debugging is the process of finding and correcting *logic errors* in applications. Logic errors are more subtle than syntax errors because a program that includes a logic error compiles successfully but does not run as expected. Logic errors often are difficult to debug, because the programmer cannot see the code as it executes. One strategy that novice programmers often use to debug programs is to display program data directly, using message boxes or **Console.WriteLine** statements. For example, the programmer might print the value of a variable when its value changes to determine whether the variable is assigned the correct value. This approach is cumbersome, because programmers must insert a line of code wherever they suspect there might be a problem. Furthermore, once the program has been debugged, the programmer then must remove the extraneous statements, which often can be difficult to distinguish from the original program code.

A *debugger* is software that allows a programmer to analyze program data and trace the flow of program execution while the application runs. A debugger provides capabilities that allow the programmer to suspend program execution, examine and modify variables, call methods without changing the program code and more. In this appendix, we introduce the Visual Studio .NET debugger and several of its debugging tools. [*Note*: A program must successfully compile before it can be used in the debugger.]

D.2 Breakpoints

Breakpoints are a simple but effective debugging tool. A breakpoint is a marker that a programmer places in a code listing. When a program reaches a breakpoint, execution pauses—this allows the programmer to examine the state of the program and ensure that it is working as expected. Figure D.2 is a program that outputs the value of ten factorial (10!),[1] but contains two logic errors—the first iteration of the loop multiplies **x** by **10** instead of multiplying **x** by **9**, and the result of the factorial calculation is multiplied by **0** (so the result is always **0**). We use this program to demonstrate Visual Studio .NET's debugging abilities—using its breakpoint capabilities as our first example.

```
1   // Fig. D.2: DebugExample.cs
2   // Sample program to debug.
3
4   using System;
5
```

Fig. D.2   Debug sample program. (Part 1 of 2.)

---

1. The factorial of **x** (**x**!) is defined as the product of all digits less than or equal to **x** but greater than zero. For example, 10! = 10 * 9 * 8 * 7 * 6 * 5 * 4 * 3 * 2 * 1.

```
6   namespace Debug
7   {
8      class DebugExample
9      {
10        static void Main( string[] args )
11        {
12           int x = 10;
13
14           Console.Write( "The value of " + x + " factorial is: " );
15
16           // loop to determine x factorial, contains logic error
17           for ( int i = x; i >= 0; i-- )
18              x *= i;
19
20           Console.Write( x );
21
22           Console.ReadLine(); // delay program exit
23
24        } // end main
25
26     } // end class DebugExample
27
28  } // end namespace Debug
```

```
The value of 10 factorial is: 0
```

Fig. D.2   Debug sample program. (Part 2 of 2.)

To set breakpoints in Visual Studio, click the gray area to the left of any line of code or right-click a line of code and select **Insert Breakpoint**. A solid red circle appears, indicating that the breakpoint has been set (Fig. D.3). The program execution is suspended when it reaches the line containing the breakpoint.

To enable breakpoints and other debugging features, we must compile the program using the debug configuration (Fig. D.4). Select **Debug** from the configuration toolbar if it is not already selected. Alternatively, select **Build > Configuration Manager** and change the **Active Solution Configuration** to **Debug**.

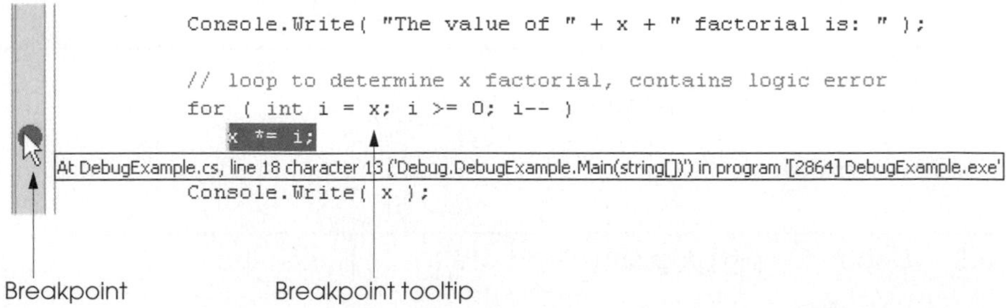

```
                    Console.Write( "The value of " + x + " factorial is: " );

                    // loop to determine x factorial, contains logic error
                    for ( int i = x; i >= 0; i-- )
                       x *= i;
     At DebugExample.cs, line 18 character 13 ('Debug.DebugExample.Main(string[])') in program '[2864] DebugExample.exe'
                    Console.Write( x );
```

Breakpoint   Breakpoint tooltip

Fig. D.3   Setting a breakpoint.

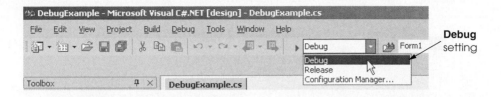

Fig. D.4   Debug configuration setting.

Selecting **Debug > Start** compiles the program and begins debugging. When debugging a console application, the console window appears (Fig. D.5), allowing program interaction (input and output). When the debugger reaches the breakpoint (line 18) program execution is suspended, and the IDE becomes the active window. Programmers may need to switch between the IDE and the console window while debugging programs.

Figure D.6 shows the IDE with program execution suspended at the breakpoint. The *yellow arrow* to the left of the statement

```
x *= i;
```

indicates the line at which execution is suspended and that the line contains the next statement to execute. Note that the title bar of the IDE displays **[break]**—this indicates that the IDE is in *break mode* (i.e., the debugger is running). Once the program reaches the breakpoint, a programmer can "hover" with the mouse on a variable (in this case **x** or **i**) in the source code to view the value of that variable in a tooltip as shown in Fig. D.6.

Testing and Debugging Tip D.3

Placing a breakpoint after a loop in a program allows the loop to complete without stopping before the breakpoint is reached.

D.3 Examining Data

Visual Studio .NET includes several debugging windows that allow programmers to examine variables and expressions. All the windows are accessible from the **Debug > Windows** submenu. Some windows are listed only when the IDE is in break mode (also called *debug mode*). The ***Watch*** window, which is available only in break mode (Fig. D.7), allows programmers to examine the values of related groups of variables and expressions. Visual Studio .NET provides a total of four **Watch** windows.

Fig. D.5   Console application suspended for debugging.

Title bar displays **[break]**

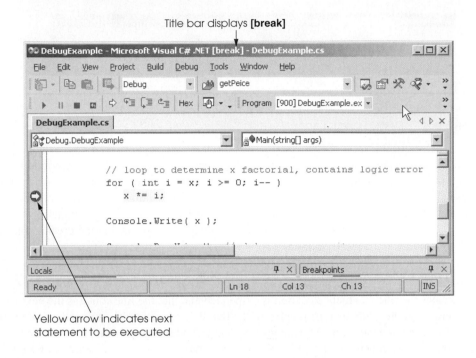

Yellow arrow indicates next
statement to be executed

Fig. D.6   Execution suspended at a breakpoint.

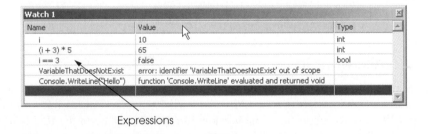

Expressions

Fig. D.7   **Watch** window.

Upon first opening, the **Watch** window will not contain any expressions to evaluate. To examine data, type an expression into the **Name** field. Most valid C# expressions can be entered in the **Name** field, including expressions that contain method calls. Consult the documentation under "**debugger, expressions**" for a full description of valid expressions.

Once an expression is entered, its type and value appear in the **Value** and **Type** fields. The first expression entered is the variable **i**, which has a value of **10** (line 12 assigns the value of **10** to variable **x**, and line 17 assigns the value of **x** to **i**). The **Watch** window also can evaluate more complex arithmetic expressions (e.g., **(i + 3) * 5**). Thus, the **Watch** window provides a convenient way to display various types of program data without modifying code.

By entering the variables and expressions that are relevant to a program's logic error, programmers can trace incorrect values to the source of the error and eliminate it. For example, to debug the program in Fig. D.2, we might enter the expression **i * x** in the **Watch** window. When we reach the breakpoint for the first time, the expression has a value **100** instead of **90**, which indicates a logic error in our program. This occurs because the loop at lines 17–18 started multiplying **x** by **10** as opposed to multiplying by **9**. We subtract **1** from the initial value that the **for** loop assigns to **i** (i.e., change **10** to **9**) to correct the error.

If a **Name** field in the **Watch** window contains a variable name, the variable's value can be modified for debugging purposes. To modify a variable's value, click its value in the **Value** field and enter a new value. Any modified value appears in red.

If an expression is invalid, an error appears in the **Value** field. For example, **Variable-ThatDoesNotExist** is not an identifier used in the program (fourth line in Fig. D.7). Therefore, Visual Studio .NET issues an error message in the **Value** field. To remove an expression, select it and press *Delete*.

Visual Studio also provides the ***Locals***, ***Autos*** and ***This*** windows (Fig. D.8), which are similar to the **Watch** window, except the programmer does not specify their contents. The **Locals** window displays the name and current value for all the variables that have block scope in the method containing the current statement (indicated by the yellow arrow in Fig. D.6). The **Autos** window displays the variables and values of the current statement and the previous statement. Variables can be changed in either window by clicking the appropriate **Value** field and entering a new value. The **This** window displays data that has class scope for an object. If the program is inside a **static** method (such as method **Main** in a console application), the **This** window is empty.

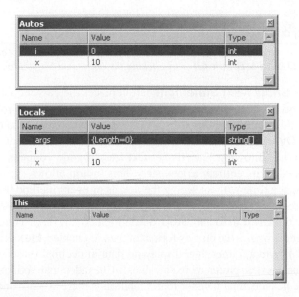

Fig. D.8   **Autos**, **Locals** and **This** windows.

A programmer can evaluate expressions line-by-line in the **Immediate** window (Fig. D.9). To evaluate an expression, a programmer types this expression into the window and presses *Enter*. For example, when a programmer enters `Console.WriteLine(i)` and presses *Enter*, the value of **i** is output to the console window. A developer also can use the assignment operator (**=**) to perform assignments in the **Immediate** window. Notice that the values for **i** and **x** in the **Locals** window contain these updated values.

Testing and Debugging Tip D.4

*Use the **Immediate** window to call a method one time. Placing a method call inside the **Watch** window calls that method every time the program breaks.*

D.4 Program Control

The Visual Studio .NET Debugger give programmers considerable control over the execution of a program. Using breakpoints and program-control commands provided by the debugger, programmers conveniently can analyze the execution of code at any point in a program. This is useful when a program contains multiple calls to methods that are known to execute properly. The **Debug** toolbar contains buttons that provide convenient access for controlling the debugging process (Fig. D.10). To display the **Debug** toolbar, select **View > Toolbars > Debug**.

The debug toolbar in Fig. D.10 controls debugger execution. The **Restart** button executes the program from the beginning, pausing at the beginning of the program to allow the programmer to set breakpoints before the program executes again. The **Continue** button resumes execution of a suspended program. The **Stop Debugging** button ends the debugging session, and the **Break All** button allows the programmer to suspend an executing program directly (i.e., without explicitly setting breakpoints). After execution suspends, the yellow arrow appears indicating the next statement to be executed.

Testing and Debugging Tip D.5

*When a program is executing, problems such as infinite loops usually can be interrupted by selecting **Debug > Break All** or by clicking the corresponding button on the toolbar.*

Clicking the **Show Next Statement** button places the cursor on the same line as the yellow arrow. This command is useful when a programmer needs to return to the current execution point after setting breakpoints in a program that contains many lines of code.

The **Step Over** button executes the next executable statement and advances the yellow arrow to the following line. If the next line of code contains a method call, the method is executed in its entirety as one step. This button allows the user to execute the program one line at a time without seeing the details of every method that is called. This is useful when a program contains multiple calls to methods that are known to execute properly. We discuss the **Step Into** and **Step Out** buttons in the next section.

The **Hex** button toggles the display format of data. If enabled, **Hex** displays data in hexadecimal (base 16) format, rather than displaying data in decimal (base 10) format. Experienced programmers often prefer to read values in hexadecimal format—especially large numbers because hexadecimal number representation is more concise and can be converted easily to binary (base 2) form. For more information about the hexadecimal and decimal number formats, see Appendix B, Number Systems.

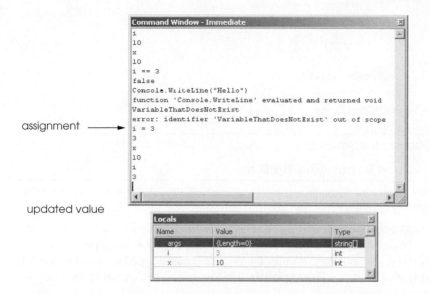

assignment ——→

updated value ——→

Fig. D.9   Immediate window.

The **Breakpoints** window displays all the breakpoints set for the program (Fig. D.11). A checkbox appears next to each breakpoint, indicating whether the breakpoint is *active* (checked) or *disabled* (unchecked). Lines with disabled breakpoints contain an unfilled red circle rather than a solid one (Fig. D.12). The debugger does not pause execution at disabled breakpoints.

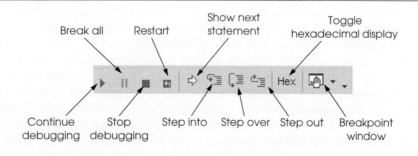

Fig. D.10   Debug toolbar icons.

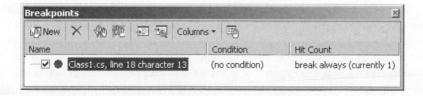

Fig. D.11   Breakpoints window.

```
// loop to determine x factorial, contains logic error
for ( int i = x; i >= 0; i-- )
    x *= i;

Console.Write( x );
```

Disabled breakpoint

Fig. D.12 Disabled breakpoint.

Testing and Debugging Tip D.6

Disabled breakpoints allow the programmer to maintain breakpoints in key locations in the program so they can be reactivated when needed. Disabled breakpoints are always visible.

In the **Breakpoints** window (Fig. D.11), the *Condition* field displays the condition that must be satisfied to suspend program execution at that breakpoint. The *Hit Count* field displays the number of times the debugger has stopped at each breakpoint. Double-clicking an item in the **Breakpoints** window moves the cursor to the line containing that breakpoint.

A programmer can add breakpoints to a program by clicking the *New* button in the **Breakpoints** window. This causes a **New Breakpoint** dialog to display (Fig. D.13). The **Function**, **File**, **Address** and **Data** tabs allow the programmer to suspend execution at either a method, a line in a particular file, an instruction in memory or when the value of a variable changes. The **Hit Count...** button (Fig. D.14) can be used to specify when the breakpoint should suspend the program (the default is to **always break**). A breakpoint can be set to suspend the program when the hit count reaches a specific number, when the hit count is a multiple of a number or is greater than or equal to a specific number.

The Visual Studio debugger also allows execution to suspend at a breakpoint depending on the value of an expression. Clicking the **Condition...** button opens the *Breakpoint Condition* dialog (Fig. D.15). The **Condition** checkbox indicates whether breakpoint conditions are enabled. The radio buttons determine how the expression in the text box is evaluated. The **is true** radio button pauses execution at the breakpoint whenever the expression is true. The **has changed** radio button causes program execution to suspend when it first encounters the breakpoint and again each time the expression differs from its previous value when the breakpoint is encountered. When the **New Breakpoint** dialog has been closed, the **Breakpoints** window displays the condition and hit count options for the new break point.

Suppose we set **x * i != 0** as the condition for the breakpoint in our loop, with the **has changed** option enabled. (We might choose to do this because the program produces an incorrect output of **0**). Program execution suspends when it first reaches the breakpoint and records that the expression has a value of **true**, because **x * i** is **100** (or **10** if we fixed the earlier logic error). We continue, and the loop decrements **i**. While **i** is between **10** and **1**, the condition's value never changes, and execution is not suspended at that breakpoint. When **i** is **0**, the expression **x * i != 0** is **false**, and execution is suspended. At this point, the programmer identifies the second logic error in our program—the final iteration of the **for** loop multiplies the result by **0**. To return the IDE to design mode, click the **Stop Debugging** button on the **Debug** toolbar.

Function tab   File tab   Address tab   Data tab

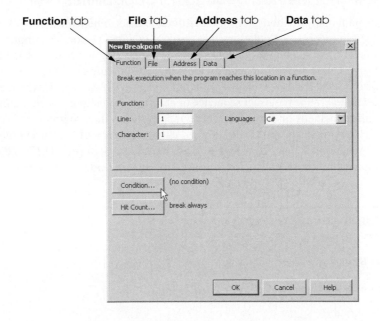

Fig. D.13   New Breakpoint dialog.

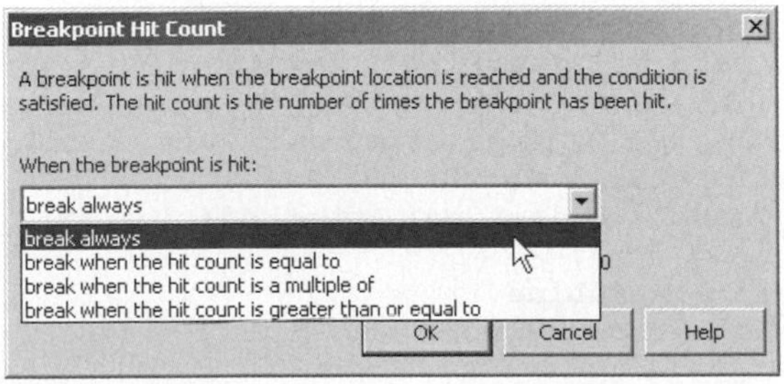

Fig. D.14   Breakpoint Hit Count dialog.

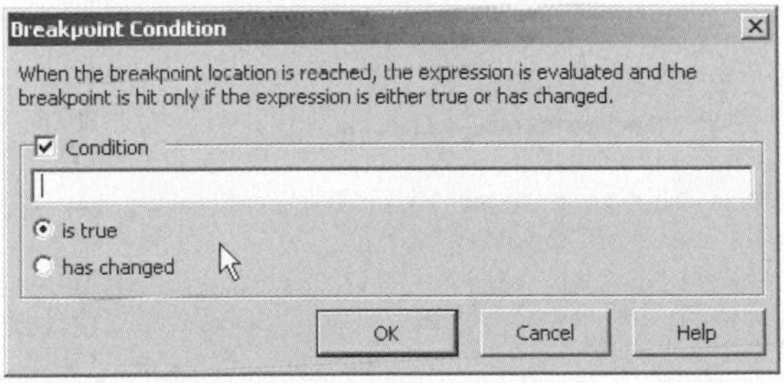

Fig. D.15   Breakpoint Condition dialog.

D.5 Additional Method Debugging Capabilities

In programs with many methods, it is often difficult to determine which methods may have been involved in incorrect calculations that resulted in a logic error. To simplify this process, the Visual Studio debugger includes tools for analyzing methods and method calls. We demonstrate some method-debugging tools in the following example (Fig. D.16).

The **Call Stack** window contains the program's *method call stack*, which allows the programmer to determine the exact sequence of calls that lead to the current method and to examine calling methods on the stack. This window allows the programmer to determine the flow of control in the program that resulted in the execution of the current method. For example, a breakpoint is inserted in **MyMethod**, the call stack in (Fig. D.17) indicates that the program called method **Main** first, followed by **MyMethod**.

```
1   // Fig. D.16: MethodDebugExample.cs
2   // Demonstrates debugging methods.
3
4   using System;
5
6   namespace Debug
7   {
8
9      // provides methods on which to demonstrate
10     // Visual Studio's debug tools
11     class MethodDebug
12     {
13        // entry point for application
14        static void Main( string[] args )
15        {
16           // display MyMethod return values
17           for ( int i = 0; i < 10; i++ )
18              Console.WriteLine( MyMethod( i ) );
19
20           Console.ReadLine();
21        } // end method main
22
23        // perform calculation
24        static int MyMethod( int x )
25        {
26           return ( x * x ) - ( 3 * x ) + 7;
27        } // end method MyMethod
28
29        // method with logic error
30        static int BadMethod( int x )
31        {
32           return 1 / ( x - x );
33        } // end method BadMethod
34
35     } // end class MethodDebug
36
37  } // end namespace Debug
```

Fig. D.16 Debugging methods.

Most recently called method

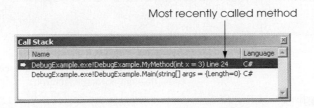

Fig. D.17 **Call Stack** window.

Double-clicking any line in the **Call Stack** window displays the next line to be executed in that method. This allows the programmer to determine how the result of each method will affect the calling method's execution. Visual Studio .NET highlights the line in green and displays the tooltip shown in Fig. D.18.

Visual Studio .NET also provides additional program-control buttons for debugging methods. The **Step Over** button executes one statement in a method, then pauses program execution at the following line. Using **Step Over**, if an evaluated statement invokes a method, the method is invoked, and execution stops at the next statement. Using *Step Into*, if a statement invokes a method, control transfers to the method for line-by-line. The *Step Out* button finishes executing the current method and returns control to the line that called the method.

Testing and Debugging Tip D.7

*Use **Step Out** to finish a method that was stepped into accidentally.*

Figure D.19 lists each program-control debug feature, its shortcut key and a description. Experienced programmers often prefer using these shortcut keys to access menu commands.

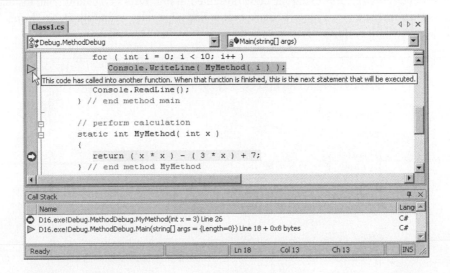

Fig. D.18 IDE displaying a method's calling point.

Control Button	Shortcut Key	Description
Continue	*F5*	Continues program execution. Execution continues until either a breakpoint is encountered or the program ends (through normal execution).
Stop Debugging	*Shift + F5*	Stops debugging and returns to Visual Studio design mode.
Step Over	*F10*	Advances to next statement, does not step into method calls.
Step Into	*F11*	Executes next statement. If the statement contains a method call, control transfers to the method for line-by-line debugging. If the statement does not contain a method call, **Step Into** behaves like **Step Over**.
Step Out	*Shift + F11*	Finishes executing the current method and suspends program execution in the calling method.

Fig. D.19 Debug program control features.

Programmers can use the **Immediate** window, discussed in Section D.3 for testing method arguments passed to a method (Fig. D.20). Testing the arguments helps determine if a method is functioning properly.

D.6 Additional Class Debugging Capabilities

In most sophisticated C# programs, a large portion of program data is contained in objects. For these purposes, Visual Studio includes class debugging features, which allow programmers to determine the current state of objects used in a program. We demonstrate some class debugging features using the code presented in Fig. D.21. To examine an instance of class **DebugEntry**, we place a breakpoint at line 43, as shown in Fig. D.22. [*Note*: A C# file may contain multiple classes, as is the case with this example.]

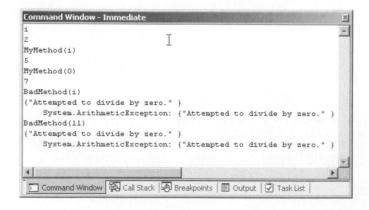

Fig. D.20 Using the **Immediate** window to debug methods.

```
1   // Fig. D.21: DebugClass.cs
2   // Console application to demonstrate object debugging.
3
4   using System;
5
6   namespace ClassDebug
7   {
8
9      // creates array containing three different classes
10     public class DebugEntry
11     {
12        public int someInteger = 123;
13        private int[] integerArray = { 74, 101, 102, 102 };
14        private DebugClass debugClass;
15        private Random randomObject;
16        private object[] list = new object[ 3 ];
17
18         // constructor
19         public DebugEntry()
20         {
21            randomObject = new Random();
22            debugClass = new DebugClass( "Hello World",
23              new object() );
24
25            list[ 0 ] = integerArray;
26            list[ 1 ] = debugClass;
27            list[ 2 ] = randomObject;
28         }
29
30         // display values retrieved from three objects
31         public void DisplayValues()
32         {
33           Console.WriteLine( randomObject.Next() );
34           Console.WriteLine( debugClass.SomeString );
35           Console.WriteLine( integerArray[ 0 ] );
36         }
37
38        // main entry point for application
39        [STAThread]
40        public static void Main()
41        {
42            DebugEntry entry = new DebugEntry();
43            entry.DisplayValues();
44        }
45     } // end class DebugEntry
46
47     // demonstrates class debugging
48     public class DebugClass
49     {
50        // private variables
51        private string someString;
52        private object privateObject;
53
```

Fig. D.21 Object debugging example. (Part 1 of 2.)

```
54          // constructor
55          public DebugClass( string stringData,
56             object objectData )
57          {
58             someString = stringData;
59             privateObject = objectData;
60          }
61
62          // accessor property for someString
63          public string SomeString
64          {
65             get
66             {
67                return someString;
68             }
69
70             set
71             {
72                someString = value;
73             }
74          } // end property SomeString
75
76       } // end class DebugClass
77
78    } // end namespace ClassDebug
```

Fig. D.21   Object debugging example. (Part 2 of 2.)

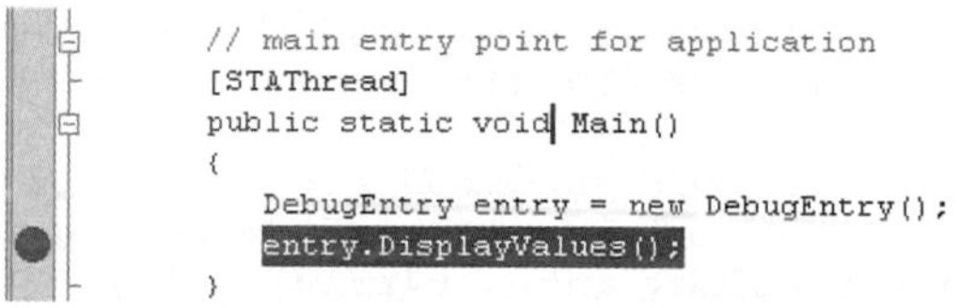

```
// main entry point for application
[STAThread]
public static void Main()
{
    DebugEntry entry = new DebugEntry();
    entry.DisplayValues();
}
```

Fig. D.22   Breakpoint location for class debugging.

To assist class debugging, Visual Studio .NET allows the programmer to expand and view all data members and properties of a class, including **private** members. In any of the three windows (i.e., **Watch**, **Locals**, **Autos** and **This**), a class that has data members is displayed with a plus (+) (Fig. D.23). When a programmer clicks the plus box, all the object's data members and their values display. If a member references an object, the object's data members also can be listed by clicking the object's plus box.

Many logic errors are the result of incorrect array calculations. To simplify the identification of such errors, the debugger includes the ability to display all the values in an array. Figure D.24 displays the contents of the **list** array. The object at index **0** is and **int** array, which is expanded to show its contents. Index **1** contains a **DebugClass** object—expanded to show the object's **private** data members, as well as a **public** property. Index **2** contains a **Random** object, defined in the Framework Class Library (FCL).

The Visual Studio debugger contains several other debugging windows, including **Threads**, **Modules**, **Memory**, **Disassembly** and **Registers**. These windows are used by experienced programmers to debug large, complex projects—consult the Visual Studio .NET documentation for more details on these features.

In this appendix we demonstrated several techniques for debugging programs, methods and classes. The Visual Studio .NET debugger is a powerful tool, which allows programmers to build more robust, fault-tolerant programs.

SUMMARY

- Debugging is the process of finding logic errors in applications.

- Syntax errors (or compilation errors) occur when program statements violate the grammatical rules of a programming language. These errors are caught by the compiler.

- Logic errors are more subtle than syntax errors. They occur when a program compiles successfully, but does not run as expected.

- Debuggers can suspend a program at any point, which allows programmers to examine and set variables and call methods.

- A breakpoint is a marker set at a line of code. When a program reaches a breakpoint, execution is suspended. The programmer then can examine the state of the program and ensure that the program is working properly.

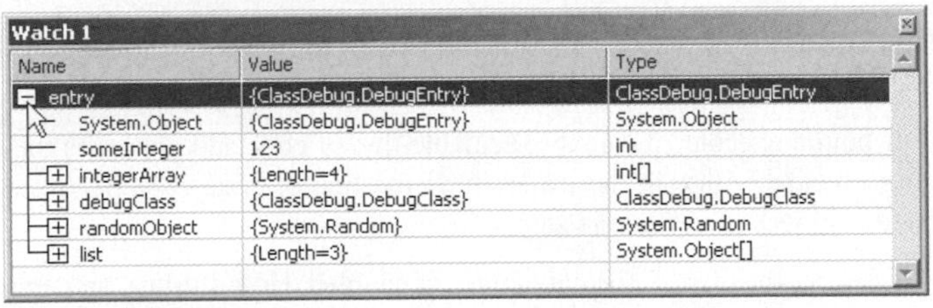

Fig. D.23   Expanded class in **Watch** window.

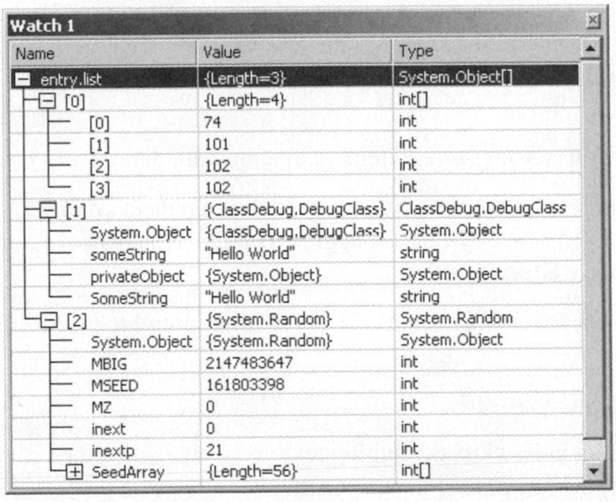

Fig. D.24   Expanded array in **Watch** window.

- To enable the debugging features, the program must be compiled using the debug configuration.

- To set breakpoints, click the gray area to the left of any line of code. Alternatively, right-click a line of code and select **Insert Breakpoint**.

- The **Watch** window allows the programmer to examine variable values and expressions. To examine data, type a valid Visual Basic expression, such as a variable name, into the **Name** field. Once the expression has been entered, its type and value appear in the **Type** and **Value** fields.

- Variables in the **Watch** window can be modified by the user for testing purposes. To modify a variable's value, click the **Value** field and enter a new value.

- The **Locals** window displays the name and current value for all the local variables or objects in the current scope.

- The **Autos** window displays the variables and objects used in the previous statement and the current statement (indicated by the yellow arrow).

- To evaluate an expression in the **Immediate** window, simply type the expression into the window and press *Enter*.

- The **Continue** button resumes execution of a suspended program.

- The **Stop Debugging** button ends the debugging session.

- The **Break All** button allows the programmer to place an executing program in break mode.

- The **Show Next Statement** button places the cursor on the same line as the yellow arrow that indicates the next statement to execute.

- The **Step Over** button executes the next executable line of code and advances the yellow arrow to the following executable line in the program. If the line of code contains a method call, the method is executed in its entirety as one step.

- The **Hex** button toggles the display format of data. If enabled, **Hex** displays data in a hexadecimal (base 16) form, rather than decimal (base 10) form.

- The **Breakpoints** window displays all the breakpoints currently set for a program.

- Disabled breakpoints allow the programmer to maintain breakpoints in key locations in the program so they can be used again when needed.

- The **Call Stack** window contains the program's method call stack, which allows the programmer to determine the exact sequence of calls that led to the current method and to examine calling methods on the stack.

- The **Step Over** button executes one statement in a method, then pauses program execution.

- The **Step Into** button executes next statement. If the statement contains a method call, control transfers to the method for line-by-line debugging. If the statement does not contain a method call, **Step Into** behaves like **Step Over**.

- The **Step Out** finishes executing the method and returns control to the line that called the method.

- The **Immediate** window is useful for testing arguments passed to a method. This helps determine if a method is functioning properly.

- Visual Studio .NET includes class debugging features which allow the programmer to determine the current state of any objects used in a program.

- To assist class debugging, Visual Studio .NET allows the programmer to expand and view all data members variables and properties of an object, including those declared `private`.

Generating Documentation in Visual Studio (on CD)

Objectives

- To introduce Visual Studio .NET's documentation generation tool.
- To introduce XML documentation comments.
- To understand XML documentation tags and their use.
- To be able to generate HTML and XML documentation files.

Appendix E is included on the CD that accompanies this book in printable Adobe® Acrobat® PDF format. The appendix includes pages 1330–1348.

ASCII Character Set

	0	1	2	3	4	5	6	7	8	9
0	nul	soh	stx	etx	eot	enq	ack	bel	bs	ht
1	nl	vt	ff	cr	so	si	dle	dc1	dc2	dc3
2	dc4	nak	syn	etb	can	em	sub	esc	fs	gs
3	rs	us	sp	!	"	#	$	%	&	`
4	(	)	*	+	,	-	.	/	0	1
5	2	3	4	5	6	7	8	9	:	;
6	<	=	>	?	@	A	B	C	D	E
7	F	G	H	I	J	K	L	M	N	O
8	P	Q	R	S	T	U	V	W	X	Y
9	Z	[	\	]	^	_	'	a	b	c
10	d	e	f	g	h	i	j	k	l	m
11	n	o	p	q	r	s	t	u	v	w
12	x	y	z	{	|	}	~	del		

Fig. F.1   ASCII character set.

The digits at the left of the table are the left digits of the decimal equivalent (0–127) of the character code, and the digits at the top of the table are the right digits of the character code. For example, the character code for "F" is 70, and the character code for "&" is 38.

Most users of this book are interested in the ASCII character set used to represent English characters on many computers. The ASCII character set is a subset of the Unicode character set used by C# to represent characters from most of the world's languages. For more information on the Unicode character set, see Appendix G.

G

Unicode® (on CD)

Objectives

- To become familiar with Unicode.
- To discuss the mission of the Unicode Consortium.
- To discuss the design basis of Unicode.
- To understand the three Unicode encoding forms: UTF-8, UTF-16 and UTF-32.
- To introduce characters and glyphs.
- To discuss the advantages and disadvantages of using Unicode.
- To provide a brief tour of the Unicode Consortium's Web site.

Appendix G is included on the CD that accompanies this book in printable Adobe® Acrobat® PDF format. The appendix includes pages 1350–1362.

COM Integration
(on CD)

Appendix H is included on the CD that accompanies this book in printable Adobe® Acrobat® PDF format. The appendix includes pages 1363–1374.

Introduction to HyperText Markup Language 4: Part 1

Objectives

- To understand the key components of an HTML document.
- To be able to use basic HTML elements to create World Wide Web pages.
- To be able to add images to your Web pages.
- To understand how to create and use hyperlinks to traverse Web pages.
- To be able to create lists of information.

Appendix I is included on the CD that accompanies this book in printable Adobe® Acrobat® PDF format. The appendix includes pages 1375–1397.

Introduction to HyperText Markup Language 4: Part 2

Objectives

- To be able to create tables with rows and columns of data.
- To be able to control the display and formatting of tables.
- To be able to create and use forms.
- To be able to create and use image maps to aid hyperlinking.
- To be able to make Web pages accessible to search engines.
- To be able to use the **frameset** element to create more interesting Web pages.

Appendix J is included on the CD that accompanies this book in printable Adobe® Acrobat® PDF format. The appendix includes pages 1398–1430.

Introduction to XHTML: Part 1

Objectives

- To understand important components of XHTML documents.
- To use XHTML to create World Wide Web pages.
- To be able to add images to Web pages.
- To understand how to create and use hyperlinks to navigate Web pages.
- To be able to mark up lists of information.

Appendix K is included on the CD that accompanies this book in printable Adobe® Acrobat® PDF format. The appendix includes pages 1431–1456.

Introduction to XHTML:
Part 2

Objectives

- To be able to create tables with rows and columns of data.
- To be able to control table formatting.
- To be able to create and use forms.
- To be able to create and use image maps to aid in Web-page navigation.
- To be able to make Web pages accessible to search engines through **<meta>** tags.
- To be able to use the **frameset** element to display multiple Web pages in a single browser window.

Appendix L is included on the CD that accompanies this book in printable Adobe® Acrobat® PDF format. The appendix includes pages 1457–1491.

HTML/XHTML Special Characters

The table of Fig. M.1 shows many commonly used HTML/XHTML special characters—called *character entity references* by the World Wide Web Consortium. For a complete list of character entity references, see the site

`www.w3.org/TR/REC-html40/sgml/entities.html`

Character	HTML/XHTML encoding	Character	HTML/XHTML encoding
non-breaking space	` `	ê	`&#234;`
§	`&#167;`	ì	`&#236;`
©	`&#169;`	í	`&#237;`
®	`&#174;`	î	`&#238;`
π	`&#188;`	ñ	`&#241;`
∫	`&#189;`	ò	`&#242;`
Ω	`&#190;`	ó	`&#243;`
à	`&#224;`	ô	`&#244;`
á	`&#225;`	õ	`&#245;`
â	`&#226;`	÷	`&#247;`
ã	`&#227;`	ù	`&#249;`
å	`&#229;`	ú	`&#250;`
ç	`&#231;`	û	`&#251;`
è	`&#232;`	•	`&#8226;`
é	`&#233;`	™	`&#8482;`

Fig. M.1 XHTML special characters.

HTML/XHTML Colors

Colors may be specified by using a standard name (such as **aqua**) or a hexadecimal RGB value (such as **#00FFFF** for **aqua**). Of the six hexadecimal digits in an RGB value, the first two represent the amount of red in the color, the middle two represent the amount of green in the color, and the last two represent the amount of blue in the color. For example, **black** is the absence of color and is defined by **#000000**, whereas **white** is the maximum amount of red, green and blue and is defined by **#FFFFFF**. Pure **red** is **#FF0000**, pure green (which is called **lime**) is **#00FF00** and pure **blue** is **#0000FF**. Note that **green** in the standard is defined as **#008000**. Figure N.1 contains the HTML/XHTML standard color set. Figure N.2 contains the HTML/XHTML extended color set.

Color name	Value	Color name	Value
aqua	#00FFFF	navy	#000080
black	#000000	olive	#808000
blue	#0000FF	purple	#800080
fuchsia	#FF00FF	red	#FF0000
gray	#808080	silver	#C0C0C0
green	#008000	teal	#008080
lime	#00FF00	yellow	#FFFF00
maroon	#800000	white	#FFFFFF

Fig. N.1   HTML/XHTML standard colors and hexadecimal RGB values.

Color name	Value	Color name	Value
aliceblue	#F0F8FF	deeppink	#FF1493
antiquewhite	#FAEBD7	deepskyblue	#00BFFF
aquamarine	#7FFFD4	dimgray	#696969
azure	#F0FFFF	dodgerblue	#1E90FF
beige	#F5F5DC	firebrick	#B22222
bisque	#FFE4C4	floralwhite	#FFFAF0
blanchedalmond	#FFEBCD	forestgreen	#228B22
blueviolet	#8A2BE2	gainsboro	#DCDCDC
brown	#A52A2A	ghostwhite	#F8F8FF
burlywood	#DEB887	gold	#FFD700
cadetblue	#5F9EA0	goldenrod	#DAA520
chartreuse	#7FFF00	greenyellow	#ADFF2F
chocolate	#D2691E	honeydew	#F0FFF0
coral	#FF7F50	hotpink	#FF69B4
cornflowerblue	#6495ED	indianred	#CD5C5C
cornsilk	#FFF8DC	indigo	#4B0082
crimson	#DC1436	ivory	#FFFFF0
cyan	#00FFFF	khaki	#F0E68C
darkblue	#00008B	lavender	#E6E6FA
darkcyan	#008B8B	lavenderblush	#FFF0F5
darkgoldenrod	#B8860B	lawngreen	#7CFC00
darkgray	#A9A9A9	lemonchiffon	#FFFACD
darkgreen	#006400	lightblue	#ADD8E6
darkkhaki	#BDB76B	lightcoral	#F08080
darkmagenta	#8B008B	lightcyan	#E0FFFF
darkolivegreen	#556B2F	lightgoldenrodyellow	#FAFAD2
darkorange	#FF8C00	lightgreen	#90EE90
darkorchid	#9932CC	lightgrey	#D3D3D3
darkred	#8B0000	lightpink	#FFB6C1
darksalmon	#E9967A	lightsalmon	#FFA07A
darkseagreen	#8FBC8F	lightseagreen	#20B2AA
darkslateblue	#483D8B	lightskyblue	#87CEFA
darkslategray	#2F4F4F	lightslategray	#778899
darkturquoise	#00CED1	lightsteelblue	#B0C4DE
darkviolet	#9400D3	lightyellow	#FFFFE0

Fig. N.2   XHTML extended colors and hexadecimal RGB values. (part 1 of 2)

Color name	Value	Color name	Value
limegreen	#32CD32	peru	#CD853F
mediumaquamarine	#66CDAA	pink	#FFC0CB
mediumblue	#0000CD	plum	#DDA0DD
mediumorchid	#BA55D3	powderblue	#B0E0E6
mediumpurple	#9370DB	rosybrown	#BC8F8F
mediumseagreen	#3CB371	royalblue	#4169E1
mediumslateblue	#7B68EE	saddlebrown	#8B4513
mediumspringgreen	#00FA9A	salmon	#FA8072
mediumturquoise	#48D1CC	sandybrown	#F4A460
mediumvioletred	#C71585	seagreen	#2E8B57
midnightblue	#191970	seashell	#FFF5EE
mintcream	#F5FFFA	sienna	#A0522D
mistyrose	#FFE4E1	skyblue	#87CEEB
moccasin	#FFE4B5	slateblue	#6A5ACD
navajowhite	#FFDEAD	slategray	#708090
oldlace	#FDF5E6	snow	#FFFAFA
olivedrab	#6B8E23	springgreen	#00FF7F
orange	#FFA500	steelblue	#4682B4
orangered	#FF4500	tan	#D2B48C
orchid	#DA70D6	thistle	#D8BFD8
palegoldenrod	#EEE8AA	tomato	#FF6347
palegreen	#98FB98	turquoise	#40E0D0
paleturquoise	#AFEEEE	violet	#EE82EE
palevioletred	#DB7093	wheat	#F5DEB3
papayawhip	#FFEFD5	whitesmoke	#F5F5F5
peachpuff	#FFDAB9	yellowgreen	#9ACD32

Fig. N.2   XHTML extended colors and hexadecimal RGB values. (part 2 of 2)

Bit Manipulation
(on CD)

Objectives

- To understand the concept of bit manipulation.
- To be able to use bitwise operators.
- To be able to use class **BitArray** to perform bit manipulation.

Appendix O is included on the CD that accompanies this book in printable Adobe® Acrobat® PDF format. The appendix includes pages 1498–1513.

Crystal Reports® for Visual Studio .NET

P.1 Introduction

All industries collect and maintain data relevant to their businesses. For example, manufacturing companies maintain information about inventories and production, retail shops record sales, health care organizations maintain patient records and publishers track book sales and inventories. However, just storing data is not enough: Managers must use these data to make informed business decisions. Information must be properly organized, easily accessible and shared among various individuals, departments and affiliates. This facilitates data analysis that can reveal business-critical information, such as sales trends or potential inventory shortages. To make this possible, developers have created reporting software—a key tool enabling the presentation of stored data sources.

Crystal Reports® was first released in 1992 as a Windows-based report writer, and Microsoft adopted the reporting software as the standard for Visual Basic in 1993.[1] Visual Studio .NET now integrates a special edition of Crystal Reports, further tying Crystal Reports to all .NET programming languages, including C#, and to Windows and Web development. This appendix presents the resources that *Crystal Decisions*, the company that produces Crystal Reports, offers on its Web site, and overviews Crystal Report's unique functionality and features in Visual Studio .NET.

P.2 Crystal Reports Web Site Resources

Crystal Decisions offers resources to developers working in Visual Studio .NET at their Web site, **www.crystaldecisions.com/net**. The site updates the changes in Visual Studio .NET versions in English, Simplified Chinese, Traditional Chinese, French, German, Italian, Japanese, Korean and Spanish. Crystal Decisions also provides e-mail-based technical support for Crystal Reports C# developers. The site offers walkthroughs, an on-

---

1. "Company History," **<www.crystaldecisions.com/about/ourcompany/ history.asp>**.

line newsletter, a multimedia product demo, discussion groups, a developer's zone and an overview of Crystal Reports in Visual Studio .NET.

P.3 Crystal Reports and Visual Studio .NET

Developers working in Visual Studio .NET's integrated development environment (IDE) can create and integrate reports in their applications using Crystal Reports software. The Visual Studio .NET edition of the software provides powerful capabilities to developers. Features in the Visual Studio .NET Crystal Reports include an API (application programming interface) that allows developers to control how reports are cached on servers—setting timeouts, restrictions, etc. Developers can create reports in multiple languages, because Crystal Reports now fully supports Unicode data types. The reports that are created can be viewed in many file formats. A user can convert a report to Microsoft Word, Adobe's Portable Document Format (PDF), HyperText Markup Language (HTML) and others so that report information can be distributed easily and used in a wide variety of documentation. Any Crystal Report created in Visual Studio .NET can become an embedded resource for use in Windows and Web applications and Web services. This section overviews the initial stages of creating reports as well as some more advanced capabilities.

To aid Visual Studio .NET developers design reports, Crystal Reports provides a *Report Expert*. Experts are similar to "templates" and "wizards"—they guide users through the creation of a variety of reports while handling the details of how the report is created, so the user need not be concerned with them. The available Experts create several types of reports, including standard, form-letter, form, cross-tab, subreport, mail label and drill-down reports (Fig. P.1). Figure P.2 illustrates the **Standard Report Expert** interface.

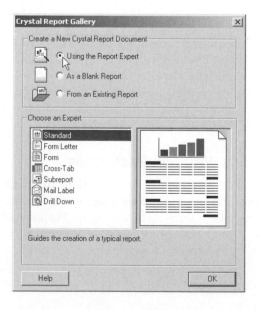

Fig. P.1   Report expert choices. (Courtesy Crystal Decisions.)

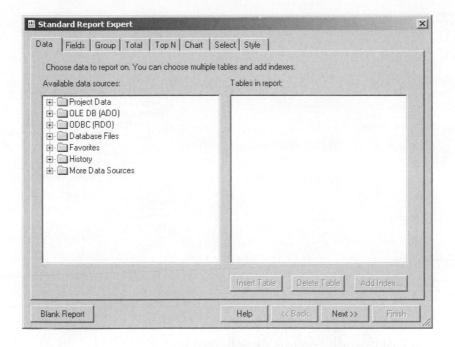

Fig. P.2   Expert formatting menu choices. (Courtesy of Crystal Decisions.)

The Crystal Reports software for Visual Studio .NET is comprised of several components. Once a report is set up, either manually or by using an Expert, developers use the Crystal Reports Designer in Visual Studio .NET to modify, add and format objects and fields, as well as to format the report layout and manipulate the report design (Fig. P.3). The Designer then generates RPT files (`.rpt` is the file extension for a Crystal Report). These RPT files are processed by the Crystal Reports engine, which delivers the report output to one of two Crystal Report viewers—a Windows Forms viewer control or a Web Forms viewer control, depending on the type of application the developer specifies. The viewers then present the formatted information to the user.

Walkthroughs illustrating the new functionality are available on the Crystal Decisions Web site at **www.crystaldecisions.com/x-jump/scr_net/default.asp**. The walkthroughs include integrating and viewing Web reports through Windows applications, creating interactive reports in Web applications, exposing Crystal Reports through Web services and reporting from ActiveX Data Objects (ADO) .NET data.[2] (For a detailed discussion of ADO .NET and other database tools, see Chapter 19, Databases, SQL and ADO .NET.) This section overviews the functionality of some of the Web applications and Web services walkthroughs.

---

2. The walkthroughs on the Crystal Decisions Web site were tested using C# in Visual Studio .NET, but a developer should be able to use the walkthroughs with any language supported by Visual Studio .NET.

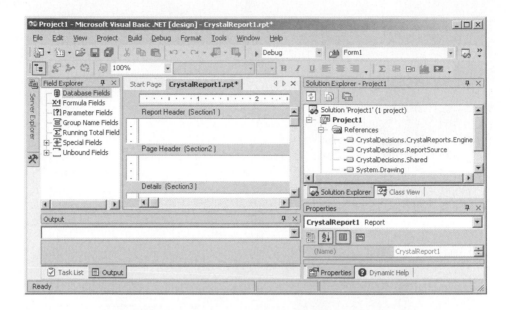

Fig. P.3   Crystal Reports designer interface. (Courtesy of Crystal Decisions.)

P.3.1 Crystal Reports in Web Applications

Using Visual Studio .NET, a developer can integrate a Crystal Report in a static Web page, or can use a variety of technologies available in Visual Studio .NET to create interactive and dynamic reports in Web applications. ASP .NET technology integrated into Visual Studio .NET enables interactivity by producing cross-platform, dynamic Web applications. We discuss these technologies in detail in Chapter 20, ASP .NET, Web Forms and Web Controls.

Web Forms consist of HTML files with embedded Web Controls and code-behind files that contain event-handling logic. Crystal Reports provides a Web Forms Report Viewer, which is a Web Form that hosts the report. When a client accesses such a Web form, the event handler can update and format information in a Crystal Report and send the updated report to the user.[3]

A walkthrough on the Crystal Decision's Web site instructs a programmer how to enable Web page interactivity and how to use ASP .NET and its controls. In the walkthrough, the user accesses information about countries by first entering a country name in the text box. When the user submits the information, the country name is passed to the Web forms viewer control and the report is updated—the Web forms page updates the report in HTML and sends it to the client browser.

P.3.2 Crystal Reports and Web Services

Any Crystal Report created in C# can be published as a part of a Web application or a Web service. A Web service provides methods that are accessible over the Internet to any appli-

---

3. "Interactivity and Reports in Web Applications," *Crystal Reports for Visual Studio .NET.*
   <www.crystaldecisions.com>.

cation, independent of programming language or platform. A report Web service would be an excellent vehicle with which business partners could access specific report information. Crystal Decisions provides a walkthrough to overview the steps to familiarize the user with implementing a report as a Web service. (We discuss Web services in detail in Chapter 21, ASP .NET and Web Services.)

When a Crystal report is published as a Web service, Visual Studio .NET generates a DLL file that contains the report, and an XML file. Both files are published to a Web server so that a client can access the report. The XML-based Simple Object Access Protocol (SOAP) message passes the data to and from the Web service.

When a developer uses Visual Studio .NET to create and publish the Web service, the developer can bind the service either to a Windows or to a Web application to display the data returned from the Web service. The walkthrough details how to create and generate the Web service, bind the service to either a Windows or Web viewer and how to build the client application that will view the service.[4]

---

4. "Exposing Reports as Web Services," *Crystal Reports for Visual Studio .NET.* **<www.crystal-decidecisions.com>**.

Bibliography

Albahari, B., P. Drayton and B. Merrill. *C# Essentials*. Cambridge, MA: O'Reilly & Associates, 2001.

Anderson, R., A. Homer, R. Howard and D. Sussman. *A Preview of Active Server Pages+*. Birmingham, UK: Wrox Press, 2001.

Anderson, R., B. Francis, A. Homer, R. Howard, D. Sussman and K. Watson. *ASP .NET*. Chicago, IL: Wrox Press, Inc., 2001.

Archer, T. *Inside C#*. Redmond, WA: Microsoft Press, 2001.

Blaha, M. R., W. J. Premerlani and J. E. Rumbaugh. "Relational Database Design Using an Object-Oriented Methodology." *Communications of the ACM*. Vol. 31, No. 4, April 1988, 414–427.

Carr, D. F. "Dave Winer: The President of Userland and SOAP Co-Creator Surveys the Changing Scene." *Internet World*. March 2001, 53–58.

Carr, D. "Hitting a High Note." *Internet World*. March 2001, 71.

Carr, D. "Slippery SOAP." *Internet World*. March 2001, 72–74.

Chappel, D. "A Standard for Web Services: SOAP vs. ebXML." *Application Development Trends*, February 2001, 17.

Chappel, D. "Coming Soon: The Biggest Platform Ever." *Application Development Trends Magazine*, May 2001, 15.

Codd, E. F. "A Relational Model of Data for Large Shared Data Banks." *Communications of the ACM*, June 1970.

Codd, E. F. "Fatal Flaws in SQL." *Datamation*, Vol. 34, No. 16, August 15, 1988, 45–48.

Codd, E. F. "Further Normalization of the Data Base Relational Model." *Courant Computer Science Symposia*, Vol. 6, *Data Base Systems*. Upper Saddle River, N.J.: Prentice Hall, 1972.

Conard, J., P. Dengler, B. Francis, J. Glynn, B. Harvey, B. Hollis, R. Ramachandran, J. Schenken, S. Short and C. Ullman. *Introducing .NET*. Birmingham, UK: Wrox Press, 2000.

Correia, E. J. "Visual Studio .NET to Speak in Tongues." *Software Development Times*, April 2001, 12.

Cornell, G. and J. Morrison. *Moving to VB .NET: Strategies, Concepts, and Code*. Berkeley, CA: Apress Publishing, 2001.

Date, C. J. *An Introduction to Database Systems, Seventh Edition*. Reading, MA: Addison-Wesley Publishing, 2000.

Davydov, M. "The Road to the Future of Web Services." *Intelligent Enterprise*. May 2001, 50–52.

Deitel, H. M. *Operating Systems, Second Edition*. Reading, MA: Addison Wesley Publishing, 1990.

Deitel, H. M. and Deitel, P. J. *Java How To Program, Fourth Edition*. Upper Saddle River, NJ: Prentice Hall, 2001

Deitel, H. M., Deitel, P. J. and T. R. Nieto. *Visual Basic 6 How To Program*. Upper Saddle River, NJ: Prentice Hall, 1999.

Deitel, H. M., P. J. Deitel, T. R. Nieto, T. M. Lin and P. Sadhu. *XML How To Program*. Upper Saddle River, NJ: Prentice Hall, 2001

Dejong, J. "Microsoft's Clout Drives Web Services." *Software Development Times*, March 2001, 29, 31.

Dejong, J. "One-Stop Shopping: A Favored Method." *Software Development Times*, February 2001, 20.

Dejong, J. "Raising the Bar." *Software Development Times*, March 2001, 29–30.

Erlanger. L. "Dissecting .NET." *Internet World*, March 2001, 30–36.

Erlanger. L. ".NET Services." *Internet World*, March 2001, 47.

Esposito, D. "Data Grid In-Place Editing." *MSDN Magazine*, June 2001, 37–45.

Esposito, D. "Server-Side ASP .NET Data Binding: Part 2: Customizing the Data Grid Control." *MSDN Magazine*, April 2001, 33–45.

Finlay, D. "GoXML Native Database Clusters Data, Reduces Seek Time." *Software Development Times*, March 2001, 5.

Finlay, D. "New York Prepares for .NET Conference." *Software Development Times*, June 2001, 23.

Finlay, D. "UDDI Works on Classification, Taxonomy Issues." *Software Development Times*, March 2001, 3.

Fontana, J. "What You Get in .NET." *Network World*, April 2001, 75.

Galli, P. and R. Holland. ".NET Taking Shape, But Developers Still Wary." *eWeek*, June 2001, pages 9, 13.

Gillen, A. "Sun's Answer to .NET." *EntMag*, March 2001, 38.

Gillen, A. "What a Year It's Been." *EntMag*, December 2000, 54.

Gladwin, L. C. "Microsoft, eBay Strike Web Services Deal." *Computer World*, March 2001, 22.

Grimes, R. "Make COM Programming a Breeze with New Feature in Visual Studio .NET." *MSDN Magazine*, April 2001, 48–62.

Gunnerson, E. *A Programmer's Introduction to C#: Second Edition*. New York, NY: Apress, 2001.

Harvey, B., S. Robinson, J. Templeman and K. Watson. *C# Programming With the Public Beta*. Birmingham, UK: Wrox Press, 2000.

Holland, R. "Microsoft Scales Back VB Changes." *eWeek*, April 2001, 16.

Holland, R. "Tools Case Transition to .NET Platform." *eWeek*, March 2001, 21.

Hulme, G, V. "XML Specification May Ease PKI Integration." *Information Week*, December 2000, 38.

Hutchinson, J. "Can't Fit Another Byte." *Network Computing*, March 2001, 14.

Jepson, B. "Applying .NET to Web Services." *Web Techniques*, May 2001, 49–54.

Jones, B. *Sams Teach Yourself C# in 21 Days*. Indianapolis, IN: Sams Publishing, 2002.

Karney. J. ".NET Devices." *Internet World*, March 2001, 49–50.

Kiely, D. "Doing .NET In Internet Time." *Information Week*, December 2000, 137–138, 142–144, 148.

Kirtland, M. "The Programmable Web: Web Services Provides Building Blocks for the Microsoft .NET Framework." *MSDN Magazine*, September 2000 **<msdn.microsoft.com/msdnmag/issues/0900/WebPlatform/WebPlatform.asp>**.

Levitt, J. "Plug-And-Play Redefined." *Information Week*, April 2001, 63–68.

McCright, J. S. and D. Callaghan. "Lotus Pushes Domino Services." *eWeek*, June 2001, 14.

Michaelis, M. and P. Spokas. *C# Developer's Headstart*. New York, NY: Osbourne/McGraw-Hill, 2001.

"Microsoft Chimes in with New C Sharp Programming Language." Xephon Web site. June 30, 2000 **<www.xephon.com/news/00063019.html>**.

Microsoft Corporation, *Microsoft C# Language Specifications*. Redmond, VA: Microsoft Press, 2001.

Microsoft Developer Network Documentation. Visual Studio .NET CD-ROM, 2001.

Microsoft Developer Network Library. .NET Framework SDK. Microsoft Web site **<msdn.microsoft.com/library/default.asp>**.

Moran, B. "Questions, Answers, and Tips." *SQL Server Magazine*, April 2001, 19–20.

MySQL Manual. MySQL Web site **<www.mysql.com/doc/>**.

Oracle Technology Network Documentation. Oracle Web site. **<otn.oracle.com/docs/content.html>**.

Otey, M. "Me Too .NET." *SQL Server Magazine*. April 2001, 7.

Papa, J. "Revisiting the Ad-Hoc Data Display Web Application." *MSDN Magazine*, June 2001, 27–33.

Powell, R. and R. Weeks. *C# and the .NET Framework: The C# Perspective*. Indianapolis, IN: Sams Publishing, 2002.

Pratschner, S. "Simplifying Deployment and Solving DLL Hell with the .NET Framework." *MSDN Library*, September 2000 **<msdn.microsoft.com/library/techart/dplywithnet.htm>**.

Prosise, J. "Wicked Code." *MSDN Magazine*, April 2001, 121–127.

Relational Technology, *INGRES Overview*. Alameda, CA: Relational Technology, 1988.

Ricadela, A. "IBM Readies XML Middleware." *Information Week*, December 2000, 155.

Ricadela, A. and P. McDougall. "eBay Deal Helps Microsoft Sell .NET Strategy." *Information Week*, March 2001, 33.

Richter, J. "An Introduction to Delegates." *MSDN Magazine*, April 2001, 107–111.

Richter, J. "Delegates, Part 2." *MSDN Magazine*, June 2001, 133–139.

Rizzo, T. "Let's Talk Web Services." *Internet World*, April 2001, 4–5.

Rizzo, T. "Moving to Square One." *Internet World*, March 2001, 4–5.

Robinson, S., O. Cornes, J. Glynn, B. Harvey, C. McQueen, J. Moemeka, C. Nagel, M. Skinner and K. Watson. *Professional C#*. Birmingham, UK: Wrox Press, 2001.

Rollman, R. "XML Q & A." *SQL Server Magazine*, April 2001, 57–58.

Rubinstein, D. "Suit Settled, Acrimony Remains." *Software Development Times*, February 2001, 1, 8.

Rubinstein, D. "Play It Again, XML." *Software Development Times*, March 2001, 12.

Scott, G. "Adjusting to Adversity." *EntMag*, March 2001, 38.

Scott, G. "Putting on the Breaks." *EntMag*, December 2000, 54.

Sells, C. "Managed Extensions Bring .NET CLR Support to C++." *MSDN Magazine*. July 2001, 115–122.

Seltzer, L. "Standards and .NET." *Internet World*, March 2001, 75–76.

Shohoud, Y. "Tracing, Logging, and Threading Made Easy with .NET." *MSDN Magazine*, July 2001, 60–72.

Sliwa, C. "Microsoft Backs Off Changes to VB .NET." *Computer World*, April 2001, 14.

Songini, Marc. "Despite Tough Times, Novell Users Remain Upbeat." *Computer World*, March 2001, 22.

Spencer, K. "Cleaning House." *SQL Server Magazine*, April 2001, 61–62.

Spencer, K. "Windows Forms in Visual Basic .NET." *MSDN Magazine*, April 2001, 25–45.

Stonebraker, M. "Operating System Support for Database Management." *Communications of the ACM*, Vol. 24, No. 7, July 1981, 412–418.

Surveyor. J. ".NET Framework." *Internet World*, March 2001, 43–44.

Tapang, C. C. "New Definition Languages Expose Your COM Objects to SOAP Clients." *MSDN Magazine*, April 2001, 85–89.

Thai, T. and H. Q. Lam. *.NET Framework*. Cambridge, MA: O'Reilly & Associates, Inc., 2001.

Troelsen, A. *C# and the .NET Platform*. New York, NY: Apress, 2001.

Utley, C. *A Programmer's Introduction to Visual Basic .NET*. Indianapolis, IN: Sams Publishing, 2001.

Visual Studio .NET ADO .NET Overview. Microsoft Developers Network Web site **<msdn.microsoft.com/vstudio/nextgen/technology/adoplusdefault.asp>**.

Ward, K. "Microsoft Attempts to Demystify .NET." *EntMag*, December 2000, 1.

Waymire, R. "Answers from Microsoft." *SQL Server Magazine*, April 2001, 71–72.

Whitney, R. "XML for Analysis." *SQL Server Magazine*, April 2001, 63–66.

Wille, C. *Presenting C#*. Indianapolis, IN: Sams Publishing, 2000.

Winston, A. "A Distributed Database Primer." *UNIX World*, April 1988, 54–63.

Zeichick, A. "Microsoft Serious About Web Services." *Software Development Times*, March 2001, 3.

Index

Symbols

! (logical NOT) 160, 163

!= is not equal to 81, 160

" (double quotation) 64, 67

"" 844

% (modulus operator) 76, 77, 78

%= (modulus assignment operator) 121

& (bitwise AND) 1496, 1497, 1500

& (boolean logical AND) 160, 166

& (menu access shortcut) 522, 523

&& (logical AND) 160, 162

&= (bitwise AND assignment operator) 1507

& 1387

© 1387

¼ 1446

< 1445, 1446

(GCD) greatest common divisor 235

(GUI) graphical user interface 23, 37, 69, 475

* SQL wildcard character 881, 908

*/ end a multiline comment 61

*= (multiplication assignment operator) 121

+ operator 78, 647

++, preincrement/postincrement 121

+= (addition assignment operator) 120

--, predecrement/postdecrement 121, 122

. (dot operator) 181

.disco file extension 1057

.vsdisco file extension 1057

// single-line comment 61

/= (division assignment operator) 121

; (empty statement) 70, 104

; (statement terminator) 64

< is-less-than operator 81

<%@Page…%> directive 954

<%@Register…%> directive 1015

<< (left-shift operator) 1496, 1497, 1498, 1504

<<= (left-shift assignment operator) 1508

<= less than or equal 81, 160

<> angle brackets 840

<? and **?>** delimiters 878

= (assignment operator) 74, 120

-= (subtraction assignment operator) 121

== comparison operator 81, 638

> is-greater-than operator 81

>= is-greater-than-or-equal-to operator 81

>> (right-shift operator) 1496, 1497, 1504

>>= (right-shift assignment operator) 1508

? regular expression metacharacter 766

? SQL wildcard character 908

?: (ternary conditional operator) 101, 123

[] (brackets) 238, 239, 249

**** separator character 761

\' escape sequence 68

**** escape sequence 68

\n escape sequence 67, 68

\r escape sequence 68

\t escape sequence 68

\u*yyyy* unicode format 1356

^ (bitwise exclusive OR) 1496, 1497, 1500, 1508

^ (boolean logical exclusive OR) 160

^= (bitwise exclusive OR assignment operator) 1507

_ (underscore) 62

{ (left brace) 63, 104

| (bitwise inclusive OR) 1496, 1497, 1500, 1508

| (boolean logical inclusive OR) 160

|= (bitwise inclusive OR assignment operator) 1507

|| (logical OR) 160, 161

} (right brace) 63, 104

~ (bitwise complement operator) 1496, 1497, 1500

, (comma) 149

Creating DLL 331 (handwritten)

Prentice Hall License Agreement and Limited Warranty

SOFTWARE shall result in the immediate termination of this Agreement.

6.   TERMINATION: This license is effective until terminated. This license will terminate automatically without notice from the Company and become null and void if you fail to comply with any provisions or limitations of this license. Upon termination, you shall destroy the Documentation and all copies of the SOFTWARE. All provisions of this Agreement as to warranties, limitation of liability, remedies or damages, and our ownership rights shall survive termination.

7.   MISCELLANEOUS: This Agreement shall be construed in accordance with the laws of the United States of America and the State of New York and shall benefit the Company, its affiliates, and assignees.

8.   LIMITED WARRANTY AND DISCLAIMER OF WARRANTY: The Company warrants that the SOFTWARE, when properly used in accordance with the Documentation, will operate in substantial conformity with the description of the SOFTWARE set forth in the Documentation. The Company does not warrant that the SOFTWARE will meet your requirements or that the operation of the SOFTWARE will be uninterrupted or error-free. The Company warrants that the media on which the SOFTWARE is delivered shall be free from defects in materials and workmanship under normal use for a period of thirty (30) days from the date of your purchase. Your only remedy and the Company's only obligation under these limited warranties is, at the Company's option, return of the warranted item for a refund of any amounts paid by you or replacement of the item. Any replacement of SOFTWARE or media under the warranties shall not extend the original warranty period. The limited warranty set forth above shall not apply to any SOFTWARE which the Company determines in good faith has been subject to misuse, neglect, improper installation, repair, alteration, or damage by you. EXCEPT FOR THE EXPRESSED WARRANTIES SET FORTH ABOVE, THE COMPANY DISCLAIMS ALL WARRANTIES, EXPRESS OR IMPLIED, INCLUDING WITHOUT LIMITATION, THE IMPLIED WARRANTIES OF MERCHANTABILITY AND FITNESS FOR A PARTICULAR PURPOSE. EXCEPT FOR THE EXPRESS WARRANTY SET FORTH ABOVE, THE COMPANY DOES NOT WARRANT, GUARANTEE, OR MAKE ANY REPRESENTATION REGARDING THE USE OR THE RESULTS OF THE USE OF THE SOFTWARE IN TERMS OF ITS CORRECTNESS, ACCURACY, RELIABILITY, CURRENTNESS, OR OTHERWISE.

IN NO EVENT, SHALL THE COMPANY OR ITS EMPLOYEES, AGENTS, SUPPLIERS, OR CONTRACTORS BE LIABLE FOR ANY INCIDENTAL, INDIRECT, SPECIAL, OR CONSEQUENTIAL DAMAGES ARISING OUT OF OR IN CONNECTION WITH THE LICENSE GRANTED UNDER THIS AGREEMENT, OR FOR LOSS OF USE, LOSS OF DATA, LOSS OF INCOME OR PROFIT, OR OTHER LOSSES, SUSTAINED AS A RESULT OF INJURY TO ANY PERSON, OR LOSS OF OR DAMAGE TO PROPERTY, OR CLAIMS OF THIRD PARTIES, EVEN IF THE COMPANY OR AN AUTHORIZED REPRESENTATIVE OF THE COMPANY HAS BEEN ADVISED OF THE POSSIBILITY OF SUCH DAMAGES. IN NO EVENT SHALL LIABILITY OF THE COMPANY FOR DAMAGES WITH RESPECT TO THE SOFTWARE EXCEED THE AMOUNTS ACTUALLY PAID BY YOU, IF ANY, FOR THE SOFTWARE.

SOME JURISDICTIONS DO NOT ALLOW THE LIMITATION OF IMPLIED WARRANTIES OR LIABILITY FOR INCIDENTAL, INDIRECT, SPECIAL, OR CONSEQUENTIAL DAMAGES, SO THE ABOVE LIMITATIONS MAY NOT ALWAYS APPLY. THE WARRANTIES IN THIS AGREEMENT GIVE YOU SPECIFIC LEGAL RIGHTS AND YOU MAY ALSO HAVE OTHER RIGHTS WHICH VARY IN ACCORDANCE WITH LOCAL LAW.

ACKNOWLEDGMENT

YOU ACKNOWLEDGE THAT YOU HAVE READ THIS AGREEMENT, UNDERSTAND IT, AND AGREE TO BE BOUND BY ITS TERMS AND CONDITIONS. YOU ALSO AGREE THAT THIS AGREEMENT IS THE COMPLETE AND EXCLUSIVE STATEMENT OF THE AGREEMENT BETWEEN YOU AND THE COMPANY AND SUPERSEDES ALL PROPOSALS OR PRIOR AGREEMENTS, ORAL, OR WRITTEN, AND ANY OTHER COMMUNICATIONS BETWEEN YOU AND THE COMPANY OR ANY REPRESENTATIVE OF THE COMPANY RELATING TO THE SUBJECT MATTER OF THIS AGREEMENT.

Should you have any questions concerning this Agreement or if you wish to contact the Company for any reason, please contact in writing at the address below.

Robin Short
Prentice Hall PTR
One Lake Street
Upper Saddle River, New Jersey 07458

The DEITEL & DEITEL Suite of Products...

C# How to Program

© 2002, 1400 pp., paper
(0-13-062221-4)

An exciting new addition to the *How to Program* series, *C# How to Program* provides a comprehensive introduction to Microsoft's new object-oriented language. C# builds on the skills already mastered by countless C++ and Java programmers, enabling them to create powerful Web applications and components—ranging from XML-based Web services on Microsoft's .NET platform to middle-tier business objects and system-level applications. *C# How to Program* begins with a strong foundation in the introductory and intermediate programming principles students will need in industry. It then explores such essential topics as object-oriented programming and exception handling. Graphical user interfaces are extensively covered, giving readers the tools to build compelling and fully interactive programs. Internet technologies such as XML, ADO .NET and Web services are also covered as well as topics including regular expressions, multithreading, networking, databases, files and data structures.

Visual Basic .NET How to Program
Second Edition

© 2002, 1400 pp., paper
(0-13-029363-6)

Teach Visual Basic .NET programming from the ground up! This introduction of Microsoft's .NET Framework marks the beginning of major revisions to all of Microsoft's programming languages. This book provides a comprehensive introduction to the next version of Visual Basic—Visual Basic .NET—featuring extensive updates and increased functionality. *Visual Basic .NET How to Program, Second Edition* covers introductory programming techniques as well as more advanced topics, featuring enhanced treatment of developing Web-based applications. Other topics discussed include an extensive treatment of XML and wireless applications, databases, SQL and ADO .NET, Web forms, Web services and ASP .NET.

Also coming soon in the Deitels' *.NET Series:*
• *Visual C++ .NET How to Program*

C How to Program
Third Edition

© 2001, 1253 pp., paper
(0-13-089572-5)

Highly practical in approach, the Third Edition of the world's best-selling C text introduces the fundamentals of structured programming and software engineering and gets up to speed quickly. This comprehensive book not only covers the full C language, but also reviews library functions and introduces object-based and object-oriented programming in C++ and Java. The Third Edition includes a new 346-page introduction to Java 2 and the basics of GUIs, and the 298-page introduction to C++ has been updated to be consistent with the most current ANSI/ISO C++ standards. Plus, icons throughout the book point out valuable programming tips such as Common Programming Errors, Portability Tips and Testing and Debugging Tips.

C++ How to Program
Third Edition

© 2001, 1168 pp., paper
(0-13-089571-7)

The world's best-selling C++ text teaches programming by emphasizing object-oriented programming, software reuse and component-oriented software construction. This comprehensive book uses the Deitels' signature LIVE-CODE™ Approach, presenting every concept in the context of a complete, working C++ program followed by a screen capture showing the program's output. It also includes a rich collection of exercises and valuable insights in its set of Common Programming Errors, Software Engineering Observations, Portability Tips and Testing and Debugging Tips. The Third Edition features an extensive treatment of the Standard Template Library and includes a new case study that focuses on object-oriented design with the UML, illustrating the entire process of object-oriented design from conception to implementation. In addition, it adheres to the latest ANSI/ISO C++ standards. The accompanying CD-ROM contains Microsoft® Visual C++™ 6.0 Introductory Edition software, source code for all examples in the text and hyperlinks to C++ demos and Internet resources.

Getting Started with Microsoft® Visual C++™ 6 with an Introduction to MFC

©2000, 163 pp., paper (0-13-016147-0)

Internet & World Wide Web How to Program, Second Edition

BOOK / CD-ROM

©2002, 1428 pp., paper
(0-13-030897-8)

The revision of this groundbreaking book in the Deitels' *How to Program* series offers a thorough treatment of programming concepts that yield visible or audible results in Web pages and Web-based applications. This book discusses effective Web-based design, server- and client-side scripting, multitier Web-based applications development, ActiveX® controls and electronic commerce essentials. This book offers an alternative to traditional programming courses using markup languages (such as XHTML, Dynamic HTML and XML) and scripting languages (such as JavaScript, VBScript, Perl/CGI, Python and PHP) to teach the fundamentals of programming "wrapped in the metaphor of the Web." Updated material on **www.deitel.com** and **www.prenhall.com/deitel** provides additional resources for instructors who want to cover Microsoft® or non-Microsoft technologies. The Web site includes an extensive treatment of Netscape® 6 and alternate versions of the code from the Dynamic HTML chapters that will work with non-Microsoft environments as well.

Python How to Program

BOOK / CD-ROM

©2002, 1400 pp., paper
(0-13-092361-3)

This exciting new book provides a comprehensive introduction to Python—a powerful object-oriented programming language with clear syntax and the ability to bring together various technologies quickly and easily. This book covers introductory-programming techniques and more advanced topics such as graphical user interfaces, databases, wireless Internet programming, networking, security, process management, multithreading, XHTML, CSS, PSP and multimedia. Readers will learn principles that are applicable to both systems development and Web programming. The book features the consistent and applied pedagogy that the *How to Program* series is known for, including the Deitels' signature LIVE-CODE™ Approach, with thousands of lines of code in hundreds of working programs; hundreds of valuable programming tips identified with icons throughout the text; an extensive set of exercises, projects and case studies; two-color four-way syntax coloring and much more.

Wireless Internet & Mobile Business How to Program

©2002, 1327 pp., paper
(0-13-062226-5)

While the rapid expansion of wireless technologies, such as cell phones, pagers and personal digital assistants (PDAs), offers many new opportunities for businesses and programmers, it also presents numerous challenges related to issues such as security and standardization. This book offers a thorough treatment of both the management and technical aspects of this growing area, including coverage of current practices and future trends. The first half explores the business issues surrounding wireless technology and mobile business, including an overview of existing and developing communication technologies and the application of business principles to wireless devices. It also discusses location-based services and location-identifying technologies, a topic that is revisited throughout the book. Wireless payment, security, legal and social issues, international communications and more are also discussed. The book then turns to programming for the wireless Internet, exploring topics such as WAP (including 2.0), WML, WMLScript, XML, XHTML™, wireless Java programming (J2ME), Web Clipping and more. Other topics covered include career resources, wireless marketing, accessibility, Palm™, PocketPC, Windows CE, i-mode, Bluetooth, MIDP, MIDlets, ASP, Microsoft .NET Mobile Framework, BREW™, multimedia, Flash and VBScript.

e-Business & e-Commerce for Managers

©2001, 794 pp., cloth
(0-13-032364-0)

This comprehensive overview of building and managing e-businesses explores topics such as the decision to bring a business online, choosing a business model, accepting payments, marketing strategies and security, as well as many other important issues (such as career resources). The book features Web resources and online demonstrations that supplement the text and direct readers to additional materials. The book also includes an appendix that develops a complete Web-based shopping-cart application using HTML, JavaScript, VBScript, Active Server Pages, ADO, SQL, HTTP, XML and XSL. Plus, company-specific sections provide "real-world" examples of the concepts presented in the book.

XML How to Program

BOOK / CD-ROM

© 2001, 934 pp., paper (0-13-028417-3)

This book is a comprehensive guide to programming in XML. It teaches how to use XML to create customized tags and includes chapters that address standard custom-markup languages for science and technology, multimedia, commerce and many other fields. Concise introductions to Java, JavaServer Pages, VBScript, Active Server Pages and Perl/CGI provide readers with the essentials of these programming languages and server-side development technologies to enable them to work effectively with XML. The book also covers cutting-edge topics such as XSL, DOM™ and SAX, plus a real-world e-commerce case study and a complete chapter on Web accessibility that addresses Voice XML. It includes tips such as Common Programming Errors, Software Engineering Observations, Portability Tips and Debugging Hints. Other topics covered include XHTML, CSS, DTD, schema, parsers, XPath, XLink, namespaces, XBase, XInclude, XPointer, XSLT, XSL Formatting Objects, JavaServer Pages, XForms, topic maps, X3D, MathML, OpenMath, CML, BML, CDF, RDF, SVG, Cocoon, WML, XBRL, and BizTalk™ and SOAP™ Web resources.

Perl How to Program

BOOK / CD-ROM

© 2001, 1057 pp., paper (0-13-028418-1)

This comprehensive guide to Perl programming emphasizes the use of the Common Gateway Interface (CGI) with Perl to create powerful, dynamic multi-tier Web-based client/server applications. The book begins with a clear and careful introduction to programming concepts at a level suitable for beginners, and proceeds through advanced topics such as references and complex data structures. Key Perl topics such as regular expressions and string manipulation are covered in detail. The authors address important and topical issues such as object-oriented programming, the Perl database interface (DBI), graphics and security. Also included is a treatment of XML, a bonus chapter introducing the Python programming language, supplemental material on career resources and a complete chapter on Web accessibility. The text includes tips such as Common Programming Errors, Software Engineering Observations, Portability Tips and Debugging Hints.

e-Business & e-Commerce How to Program

BOOK / CD-ROM

© 2001, 1254 pp., paper (0-13-028419-X)

This innovative book explores programming technologies for developing Web-based e-business and e-commerce solutions, and covers e-business and e-commerce models and business issues. Readers learn a full range of options, from "build-your-own" to turnkey solutions. The book examines scores of the top e-businesses (examples include Amazon, eBay, Priceline, Travelocity, etc.), explaining the technical details of building successful e-business and e-commerce sites and their underlying business premises. Learn how to implement the dominant e-commerce models—shopping carts, auctions, name-your-own-price, comparison shopping and bots/ intelligent agents—by using markup languages (HTML, Dynamic HTML and XML), scripting languages (JavaScript, VBScript and Perl), server-side technologies (Active Server Pages and Perl/CGI) and database (SQL and ADO), security and online payment technologies. Updates are regularly posted to **www.deitel.com** and the book includes a CD-ROM with software tools, source code and live links.

ORDER INFORMATION

SINGLE COPY SALES:
Visa, Master Card, American Express, Checks, or Money Orders only
Toll-Free: 800-643-5506; Fax: 800-835-5327

GOVERNMENT AGENCIES:
Prentice Hall Customer Service
(#GS-02F-8023A)
Phone: 201-767-5994; Fax: 800-445-6991

COLLEGE PROFESSORS:
For desk or review copies, please visit us on the World Wide Web at www.prenhall.com

CORPORATE ACCOUNTS:
Quantity, Bulk Orders totaling 10 or more books. Purchase orders only — No credit cards.
Tel: 201-236-7156; Fax: 201-236-7141
Toll-Free: 800-382-3419

CANADA:
Pearson Education Canada
26 Prince Andrew Place
Don Mills, ON M3C 2T8 Canada
Tel: 416 447 5101; Fax: 416 443 0948
E-mail: phcinfo.pubcanada@pearsoned.com

UK/IRELAND:
Pearson Education
Edinburgh Gate
Harlow, Essex CM20 2JE UK
Tel: 01279 623928; Fax: 01279 414130
E-mail: enq.orders@pearsoned-ema.com

EUROPE, MIDDLE EAST & AFRICA:
Pearson Education
P.O. Box 75598
1070 AN Amsterdam, The Netherlands
Tel: 31 20 5755 800; Fax: 31 20 664 5334
E-mail: amsterdam@pearsoned-ema.com

ASIA:
Pearson Education Asia
317 Alexandra Road #04-01
IKEA Building
Singapore 159965
Tel: 65 476 4688; Fax: 65 378 0370

JAPAN:
Pearson Education
Nishi-Shinjuku, KF Building 101
8-14-24 Nishi-Shinjuku, Shinjuku-ku
Tokyo, Japan 160-0023
Tel: 81 3 3365 9001; Fax: 81 3 3365 9009

INDIA:
Pearson Education Indian Liaison Office
90 New Raidhani Enclave, Ground Floor
Delhi 110 092, India
Tel: 91 11 2059850 & 2059851
Fax: 91 11 2059852

AUSTRALIA:
Pearson Education Australia
Unit 4, Level 2
14 Aquatic Drive
Frenchs Forest, NSW 2086, Australia
Tel: 61 2 9454 2200; Fax: 61 2 9453 0089
E-mail: marketing@pearsoned.com.au

NEW ZEALAND/FIJI:
Pearson Education
46 Hillside Road
Auckland 10, New Zealand
Tel: 649 444 4968; Fax: 649 444 4957
E-mail: sales@pearsoned.co.nz

SOUTH AFRICA:
Pearson Education
P.O. Box 12122
Mill Street
Cape Town 8010 South Africa
Tel: 27 21 686 6356; Fax: 27 21 686 4590

LATIN AMERICA:
Pearson Education Latinoamerica
815 NW 57th Street Suite 484
Miami, FL 33158
Tel: 305 264 8344; Fax: 305 264 7933

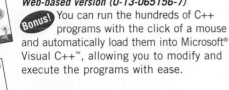

www.InformIT.com/deitel

Deitel & Associates, Inc. is partnering with Prentice Hall's parent company, Pearson PLC, and its information technology Web site, InformIT (www.informit.com) to launch the Deitel InformIT site at www.InformIT.com/deitel. The Deitel InformIT kiosk will be up and running in Q1 2002 with information on the continuum of Deitel products, including:

 • **Free informational articles**

 • **Deitel e-Matter**
• **Books and new e-Books**

• **Instructor-led training**
• **Web-based training**
• *Complete Training Courses/Cyber Classrooms*

Deitel will contribute to a weekly column in the popular InformIT newsletter, currently subscribed to by more than 800,000 IT professionals worldwide (for opt-in registration, see www.informit.com). This column will provide information on topics including:

• Deitel publications and products including the complete Deitel Catalog for product ordering information and updates
• Resources and articles on leading-edge technologies and IT issues

• WBT and e-learning updates
• Instructor-led training information
• Programming tips and methods
• Progress reports on forthcoming publications
• Deitel research and development activities

Web-Based Tutorials

Deitel is committed to continuous research and development in e-learning and is enhancing its series of self-paced CD-ROM and Web-based tutorials using content from the Deitel *How to Program Series* textbooks. The tutorials are appropriate for distance education and on-campus courses. Our instructional designers are currently developing features that include:

• Interactive Macromedia® Flash™ animations demonstrating key programming concepts.
• Interactive Questions (with answers) relating to specific lines of code.
• Dynamic Glossary linking designated keywords or phrases to small windows containing definitions.
• More abundant audio, including some examples with animated, interactive code walk-throughs highlighting each section of code as it is mentioned.

A Sneak Peek at the Interactive Animation in the *Java Multimedia Cyber Classroom 4/e*

1. When the animation starts a ball is dropped into a bucket signifying that the flow through the flowchart has begun. The ball continues through the flowchart stopping three times along the way.

2. First, the loop-continuation condition is checked; next, a line is drawn in a simulated output window...

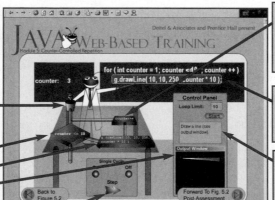

3. ...then the value of the conditional variable is incremented.

4. At each step, the appropriate code is highlighted...

5. ...and a short description of that step is given on the control panel.

If the user misses something in the animation, it can be repeated as needed. The animation may also be switched to "single-cycle" mode, allowing the student to step through the code manually one action at a time.

Future Publications

Here are some new titles we are considering for 2002/2003 release:

Computer Science Series: *Theory and Principles of Operating Systems: a Simulation Approach, Data Structures in C++, Data Structures in Java, Theory and Principles of Database Systems.*

Database Series: *Oracle How to Program, SQL Server How to Program, MySQL How to Program.*

Internet and Web Programming Series: *Open Source Software Development: Apache, Linux, MySQL and PHP How to Program, Perl 6 How to Program 2/e.*

Programming Series: *Flash™ How to Program, Multimedia How to Program.*

.NET Programming Series: *Advanced C# .NET How to Program, Advanced Visual Basic .NET How to Program, Visual C++ .NET How to Program, Advanced Visual C++ .NET How to Program, ASP .NET How to Program.*

Object Technology Series: *OOAD with the UML, Design Patterns, Java™ and XML.*

Advanced Java™ Series: *JDBC How to Program, Enterprise JavaBeans How to Program, Java Media Framework (JMF) How to Program, Java Security and Java Cryptography (JCE) How to Program, Java Servlets How to Program, Java2D and Java3D How to Program, JavaServer Pages (JSP) How to Program, JINI How to Program, Java 2 Micro Edition (J2ME) How to Program.*

Deitel Newsletter

Deitel and Associates, Inc. is launching a free, opt-in newsletter that will include:

• Updates and commentary on industry trends and developments

• Resources and links to articles from our published books and upcoming publications.

• Information on the Deitel publishing plans, including future publications and product-release schedules

To sign up for the Deitel Newsletter, visit `www.deitel.com`.

E-Books

We are committed to providing our content in traditional print formats and in emerging electronic formats, such as e-books, to fulfill our customers' needs. We are currently exploring several solutions. Visit `www.deitel.com` for periodic updates.

E-Learning

(Cyber Classrooms, Web-Based Training and Course Management Systems)

Deitel is committed to continuous research and development in e-Learning. On the page to the left, we provide a sneak peek at our plans for Web-based training, including a five-way Macromedia® Flash™ animation of a **for** loop in Java™. We are pleased to announce that we have incorporated this example into the *Java 2 Multimedia Cyber Classroom, 4/e* (which is included in *The Complete Java 2 Training Course, 4/e*). Our instructional designers and Flash animation team are developing additional simulations that demonstrate key programming concepts. We are enhancing the *Multimedia Cyber Classroom* products to include more audio, pre- and post-assessment questions and Web-based labs with solutions for the benefit of professors and students alike. In addition, our *Multimedia Cyber Classroom* products, available in both CD and Web-based formats, are being ported to Pearson's CourseCompass course-management system—a powerful e-platform for teaching and learning.

Turn the page to find out more about Deitel & Associates!

ANNOUNCING THE NEW DEITEL™ DEVELOPER SERIES

We are pleased to announce the launch of the DEITEL™ Developer Series—a new Deitel book series for practicing professionals and upper-level courses in colleges and universities. This series offers focused treatments of emerging technologies.

Deitel & Associates is internationally recognized for its best-selling *How to Program* texts for the academic market and its signature LIVE-CODE™ Approach to teaching and programming. The DEITEL™ Developer Series books contain the same LIVE-CODE™ Approach teaching methods, but do not include any of the pedagogic features found in the *How to Program* series (e.g., exercises, programming tips, chapter summaries, etc.).

The first three titles are described in the next two pages. If you have any questions regarding the DEITEL™ Developer Series, its features, future titles and more, please e-mail us at **deitel@deitel.com**.

Web Services: A Technical Introduction

Harvey M. Deitel, Paul J. Deitel and Lauren Trees, all from Deitel & Associates, Inc.

© 2003, 400 pp., paper (0-13-046135-0)

Web Services: A Technical Introduction familiarizes programmers, technical managers and project managers with key concepts surrounding Web services, including what Web services are and why they are revolutionary. The book covers the business case for Web services—the underlying technologies, ways in which Web services can provide competitive advantages and opportunities for Web services-related businesses. Readers learn the latest Web-services standards, including SOAP, WSDL, UDDI and ebXML; acquire knowledge of Web services implementations in .NET and Java™; benefit from an extensive comparison of Web services products and vendors; and learn about Web services security options. Although this is not a programming book, the text shows .NET and Java™ code examples to demonstrate the structure of Web services applications and documents. In addition, the book includes numerous case studies describing ways in which organizations are implementing Web services to increase efficiency, simplify business processes, create new revenue streams and better interact with partners and customers.

Ordering
Visual Studio .NET

Visual Studio.NET can be ordered directly from Microsoft.

Please go to the following link for more details and to order:

`http://msdn.microsoft.com/vstudio/default.asp`

If you are a member of the Microsoft Developer Network then please use the following link:

`http://msdn.microsoft.com/default.asp`